CADOGAN
*guides*

Dana Facaros

# GREEK ISLANDS

D1280145

**Cadogan Books plc**
London House, Parkgate Road, London SW11 4NQ, UK

Distributed in North America by
**The Globe Pequot Press**
6 Business Park Road, PO Box 833, Old Saybrook,
Connecticut 06475–0833

Copyright © Dana Facaros 1979, 1981, 1986, 1988, 1993, 1995
Updated by Stephanie Ferguson
Illustrations © Suzan Kentli 1995

Book and cover design by Animage
Cover illustrations by Povl Webb
Maps © Cadogan Guides, drawn by Map Creation Ltd

Series Editors: Rachel Fielding and Vicki Ingle

Project Manager: Linda McQueen
Editing: Linda McQueen and Toby Bourne
Proofreading: Stephanie Ferguson and Toby Bourne
Indexing: Dorothy Frame
DTP assistance: Jacqueline Lewin
Production: Rupert Wheeler Book Production Services

First published as *Greek Island Hopping* in 1979, revised 1981.
Third revised edition published as a Cadogan Guide in 1986.
Fourth revised edition 1988. Fifth revised edition 1993.
This fully revised and updated edition published 1995.

A catalogue record for this book is available from the British Library
ISBN 1–86–0110–10X

Printed and bound in Finland
by Werner Söderström Oy

*The author and publishers have made
every effort to ensure the accuracy of
the information in the book at the
time of going to press. However, they
cannot accept any responsibility for
any loss, injury or inconvenience
resulting from the use of information
contained in this guide.*

We have done our best to ensure that the information in this guide is correct at the time of going to press. But
places and facilities are constantly changing, and standards and prices fluctuate. We would be delighted to
receive any comments concerning existing entries or omissions. Significant contributions will be acknowledged
in the next edition, and authors of the best letters will receive a copy of a Cadogan Guide of their choice.

## About the Author

Dana Facaros lives in France with her husband, writer Michael Pauls, and children Jackson and Lily. Her Greek father comes from Ikaría and her golfing mother once shot three holes-in-one in a single year.

## Acknowledgements

I would like to thank the many members of the National Tourist Organization of Greece for their kind assistance in writing this guide, plus the following people: the ever-faithful Michael Davidson and Brian Walsh for their help with Athens, Piraeus and the Saronic islands; Bill Alexander, Linda, Nikos and Tanya Theodorou, Helen Morgan, Mark Stanley, Greg Christoforides, Frida Hristofski, Perry Rusken, Anna, Hans, Martyn and Jeroem Bloemska, Vassilis Dikeoulias, Stella, Dimitris, George and Natasha Katagas, Evanthia Protopsaltis, Mary Vogia, Veta Panayiotopoulou, Evangelos Kladidis; also Alexis on Sámos, Hillary Whitton Paipeti, Mayor George Kritikos of Ikaría, Machis on Skópelos, Olga in Chaniá, Michelis and Despina in Sitía, Lily and Big Bob Johnstone. In this sixth editon, special thanks go to my better half, Michael, who added the interesting bits, to my aunt and uncle, Toula and Kosta Cavaligos, and to Stephanie for her well-informed updating; plus a round of applause for Linda at Cadogan, who made it all come together.

## About the Updater

Freelance journalist and travel writer Stephanie Ferguson has hopped around nearly fifty islands and believes the joy of travelling in Greece lies not so much in arriving but in what happens on the way. A specialist on the Dodecanese, she has contributed to two guide books, updated two, and written Greek travel features for *The Independent* and other UK publications.

## Updater's Acknowledgements

Thanks to everyone for support, moral and physical, especially: Stella Karavokyros and staff at the NTOG in Rhodes; Jonathan Abery of the *Rodos News*, Dr Yannis and Tanya Chiotis; Alex and Denise Zikas on Kos (for giving me their daughter's nursery when there was no room at the inn); Chris and Christina Kokkonis at DRM Travel, Léros; Kate Murdoch and the Laskarina Holidays team; Manos Holidays and Premier Travel on Kálymnos; Jenny May of Direct Holidays for Líndos; Specialist Vacations and Lynne at Sunnyland Travel on Sými; Kostas Stefanakis on Tílos; Petros Kavalkris at the Venetiko, Sýros; Poppy Vichou and Carmel on Mílos; Shirley Durant in Athens. Lastly, special thanks to my mother, Rosemary Lucas, for holding the fort, and Damian Hallam for holding the reins.

# Contents

*Contents*　　v

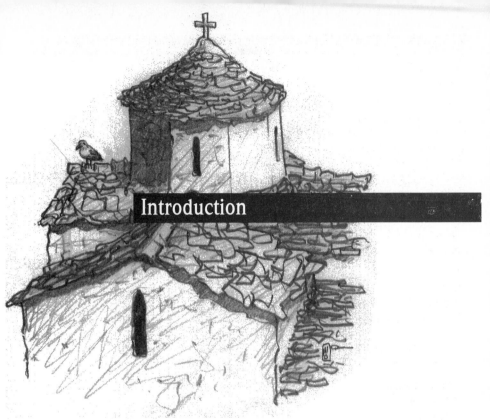

# Introduction

*What weighs the bosom of Abraham and the immaterial spectres of Christian paradise against this Greek eternity made of water, rock and cooling winds?*

—Níkós Kazantzákis

There's nothing like the Greek islands to make the rest of the world seem blurred, hesitant and grey. Their frontiers are clearly defined by a sea that varies from emerald and turquoise to indigo blue, with none of the sloppiness of a changing tide; the clear sky and dry air cut their mountainous contours into sharp outline; the whiteness and simplicity of their architecture is both abstract and organic. Even the smells, be they fragrant (lemon blossoms, incense, wild thyme, grilling fish) or stinks (donkey flops, caique diesel engines, plastic melted cheese sandwiches) are pure and unforgettable. In such an environment, the islanders themselves have developed strong, open and often quirky characters; they have bright eyes and are quick to laugh or cry or scream in fury, or shamelessly inquire into the intimate details of your personal life ('Just how much do you weigh?') or offer unsolicited lectures on politics, how to brush your teeth or find a good husband. 'Greece,' as the country's perenniel president, Karamanlís once said, 'reminds me of an enormous madhouse.'

Since the 1970s this clarity and bright madness have been magnets to the blurred, hesitant, grey world beyond. After shipping, tourism is Greece's most important source of income, to the extent that swallows from the north have become a regular fixture in the seasonal calendar: first comes Lent and Greek Easter, then the tourists, followed by the grape harvest, and, in December, the olives. From June to September, ferries and flights are packed with holiday-makers, both Greek and foreign. Popular sites and beaches are crowded by day, and often by night as well, by people unable to find a room, anywhere—they've been booked for months in advance. Yet, as each island has its own strong character, each has responded to the tourism cash cow in a different way. On some islands, resort hotels have toadstooled up willy-nilly in search of the fast package-tour buck, sacrificing beauty, environmental health and even sanity itself in their desire to please all-comers. And then there are other islands and villages, more self-reliant, clinging stubbornly to their traditions and doing all they can to keep outside interests from exploiting their coasts. Others still, including some of the most visited islands, are enjoying a renaissance of traditional arts and customs, often led by the young who are pained to see their centuries-old heritage eroding into Euro-blandness. A few islands have developed co-operatives and settlement schemes to offer visitors a taste of rural life; others have gone swanky, with sparkling new tennis courts, yacht marinas and cocktail bars.

Gentle reader, may this book help you find the island or islands you seek, whether you want all the mod-cons of home, sports facilities and dancing until dawn, or an island rich in ancient sites, Byzantine frescoes, landscapes and beautiful villages, or just an escape to a secluded shore, where there's the luxury of doing nothing at all. Or perhaps you want a bit of each. For, in spite of all the rush to join the 20th century, the Greek islands have retained the enchantment that inspired Homer and Byron—the 'wine-dark sea', the scent of jasmine at twilight and nights alive with shooting stars. The ancient Greeks dedicated the islands to the gods, and they have yet to surrender them entirely to us mortals. They have kept something pure and true and alive. Or, as the poet Palamás wrote, 'Here reigns nakedness. Here shadow is a dream.'

## A Note on Pronunciation

There is no general agreement within Greece on a standard method of transliterating the Greek alphabet into Roman letters. This means that you will constantly come across many variations in the spellings of place names and words, on maps, in books and on road signs. To help you, this book includes island names and those of major towns in the Greek alphabet. When transcribing, we have used D for the Greek *delta* (Δ), which you may see elsewhere as DH or TH, CH for *chi* (Χ), which is pronounced like the 'ch' in 'loch' and which you may see written as H, e.g. in Chaniá or Chóra; F for *fi* (Φ), which you may see elsewhere as PH; and G for the Greek *gamma* (Γ), which sounds more like a guttural GH verging on a Y, e.g. with *agios* (saint), pronounced more like 'ayios'. Exceptions to this are made where there is a very common ancient name or modern English spelling such as Phaistos or Rhodes.

Stressing the right syllable is vital to the correct pronunciation of Greek; in this book the stressed letter of each word or name is accented with an acute (´) accent.

*See* also **Language** pp.579–88.

The 3000 islands of Greece (of which a mere 170 or so are inhabited) are divided into seven major groupings: the Cyclades in the Aegean, surrounding the holy island of Délos; the Dodecanese, lying off the southwest coast of Asia Minor; the Northeastern Aegean islands, stretching from Thássos to Ikaría; the Ionian islands, sprinkled between Greece and Italy; the Saronic islands, in the Saronic Gulf; the Sporades, spread off the coast of Thessaly and Évia; and Crete, the largest island in Greece.

Picking an island is as personal as choosing a flavour in an ice-cream parlour. You may want to head for a lively cosmopolitan place, followed by a few days of peace and quiet (say, Mýkonos

# The Islands at a Glance

and then Amorgós). Or you may decide to follow the Greeks to Évia and Tínos. The following thumbnail sketches start with the most touristy and end with the least.

**Mýkonos**, as jet-setty as you can get, still retains an air of class, despite the hordes that it attracts. It has great beaches and the best nightlife (both gay and straight) is only a short boat ride from holy Délos, now an outdoor archaeological museum. Cosmopolitan **Skiáthos**, lusher, greener, with some of the best beaches in the Mediterranean, matches Mýkonos in prices, if not in spirit. In **Íos** you'll feel old at 25; the emphasis here is definitely on pubbing and beachlife. The lovely islands of **Kos** and **Zákynthos** have lost much of their original character under the strain of mass package tourism, but there's plenty going on to keep you amused, as in **Páros**, which paradoxically has retained its island charm, despite being one of the top destinations for backpackers of all ages. Volcanic, dramatically beautiful **Santoríni** is the number one spot for backpackers from both hemispheres, visiting cruise ships and practically every first-timer to Greece. If you tire of the breathtaking views and chi-chi bars in Fíra, the main town, you can escape to smaller villages. The two queens of Greek tourism, **Corfu** and **Rhodes**, are both large enough to absorb huge numbers of tourists, but both suffer from pockets of mass package tourism of the least attractive type. Stay clear of those spots and there's plenty left. Both have stunning capitals and charming mountain villages.

**Crete** has everything for everyone: the glories of Minoan civilization, the dubious delight of overexposed Ag. Nikólaos, the mighty mountain ranges

and the Gorge of Samariá, the Venetian charm of Chaniá, the laid-back ex-hippie colony of Mátala or trendy Ag. Galíni.

Arguably the best type of island holiday can be found on islands where there are enough tourists to ensure more than basic facilities—places with watersports, a choice of decent tavernas, a bar or two for an evening drink and, most of all, a place to sit out and watch life idle by. **Sérifos, Sífnos, Kálymnos, Kefaloniá, Léfkas, Náxos, Spétses, Skópelos, Skýros, Ándros** and **Sýros** fall happily into this category; all have a mixture of rugged island scenery, typical villages, good restaurants and swimming. There are special gems like sophisticated **Pátmos**, with its famous medieval monastery; **Tínos** of the white dovecotes, mecca for pilgrims and popular with Greeks and families; olive-covered **Paxí**, with its sheltered bays, harbours and coves, a haven for sailors; **Kárpathos**, with dramatic scenery and strong folklore tradition. The islands of **Kéa** and **Kýthnos**, while close to Athens, are seldom visited except for passing yachtsmen and Greek tourists. **Hýdra**, even closer, aspires to be Greece's St Tropez, although, like **Aegina**, with its superb temple of Aphaia and green, friendly **Póros**, its proximity to Athens has made it an easy target for daytrippers and big weekend crowds. Off in the Northeastern Aegean, the large, lush and lovely islands of **Sámos, Chíos, Lésbos** and **Thássos** provide everything required for the perfect island holiday, as well as plenty of places to explore. Greek tourists have always preferred them to the barren Cyclades.

There remain a few islands that come under the heading of 'almost away from it all'—not quite your desert island in that they have several places to stay, eat, swim and explore, but beyond that not a lot to do after a couple of days, unless you are resourceful—**Folégandros, Mílos, Astypálaia, Amorgós, Alónissos, Límnos, Samothráki, Ikaría, Léros, Níssyros, Chálki, Kastellórizo, Kýthera, Tílos, Lipsí, Ithaca** and **Sými**, although the latter is becoming somewhat trendy. If, however, you genuinely want to get away from it all and don't mind eating in the same little taverna every night, then head for the cluster of 'Back' islands east and south of Náxos: **Koufoníssi, Kéros, Schinoússa** and **Heráklia**, or even more remote, **Antikýthera, Psará, Inoússes, Kímolos, Ag. Efstrátios,** and **Meganísi** or the islands north of Corfu: **Othoní, Eríkousa** and **Mathráki**. On any of these islands you can treat yourself to some serious introspection, read big fat novels and brush up on your modern Greek with the locals.

Lastly, **Évia** and **Salamína** hardly feel like islands at all, but this can be part of their charm. The former has stunning scenery and an endless number of beaches, with a high percentage of Greek tourists to ensure you are experiencing the Real Thing. Salamína is little more than an Athenian suburb—as unglamorous as you can possibly get but very Greek in every way, from its nondescript houses to its excellent, cheap little tavernas.

Timing is important. From mid-July to 20 August the footloose independent traveller can expect nothing but frustration trying to find an unbooked room on the more popular islands or on the smaller ones with a limited number of beds. Also, don't assume that the more isolated the island, the cheaper the rooms. You could well pay more in Folégandros than in Corfu town, where accomodation is far more plentiful. Out of season you can pick and choose; islands with a high percentage of Greek tourists (Kýthnos, Kéa and Évia) who tend to go in the height of summer can be especially good value. Most hotels close in November and reopen in April; Rhodes and Crete open the earliest and are the last to shut.

## Travel

*By Air*

## Charter Flights

'The air and sky are free,' Daedalus told son Ikaros as he planned his escape from Crete on those ill-fated wings. They aren't any more, but you can fly for less if you look around.

Charter flights to Athens and the islands are frequent in the summer from European and North American capitals. Check the travel sections in the weekend newspapers, or get advice from travel agencies. In the **UK** 'bucket shops' specialise in spare charter tickets, or try the consolidators, firms like Avro who offer flight-only deals, often at the last minute and very cheap. They all advertise widely: browse through *Time Out*, the *Evening Standard* or the Sunday papers. **Americans** and **Canadians** with more time than money may well find their cheapest way of getting to Greece is to take a trans-Atlantic economy flight to London and from there to buy a bucket shop ticket to Greece, although this may be difficult in July or August. Trans-Atlantic bargains can still be found, but bear in mind that the peak season runs from late May to mid-September. Most UK charters run from May to mid-October but some firms feature early specials in March and April depending on when Greek Easter falls, usually from Gatwick and Manchester.

Charter flight tickets have fixed outward and return dates and are governed by several rules as the Greek Civil Aviation Authority sees them as concessions, like rail saver tickets, and imposes similar restrictions. Tickets are valid for a minimum of 3 days and a maximum of 6 weeks and must be accompanied by an accommodation voucher stating the name and address of the hotel, villa or campsite, even if it's mythical or a dormitory in downtown Athens. Although a formality, every so often there is a crackdown aimed at what the Greeks consider undesirables flouting the law. Because they subsidise airline landing fees they want to prevent charter flights being used as a cheap way to get to other countries, especially Turkey. Visitors to Greece using a charter flight may visit Turkey or any neighbouring country for the day, but must not stay overnight. To be on the safe side, make sure you don't get a Turkish stamp in your passport; Turkish officials will happily stamp a removable piece of paper. If you deliberately stay in Turkey and have your passport stamped you will forfeit your return ticket home. Travellers with stamps from previous holidays in Turkey will not be barred entry, but if you have Turkish Cypriot stamps check with the Passport Office before you go.

**Student/youth charters** are exempt from the voucher system and can also be sold as one-way tickets. If you're under 26 or a full-time student under 32 with an **International Student Identity Card** to prove it, you can stay longer. If you're not a student but under 26, STA Travel offers a **Go 25** card, a subsitute for the ISIC. Even if you intend to stay longer than 4 weeks or travel to other countries, using just half a charter ticket may be cheaper than a scheduled flight, so shop around. Sometimes last-minute package deals, especially in spring and autumn, can be even cheaper than flights if you are prepared to drop everything and jet off. If you are going it alone and travelling light some companies sell courier seats cheap. Your stay is restricted to 10–14 days and you can only take 10kg of hand baggage.The new Greek departure tax is added on to all ticket prices. The good news is that you can now fly 'open jaws' into one Greek airport and out of another. Not all tour operators offer this option so check before you buy your ticket.

Flights to Greece from **Ireland** are generally more expensive. British Airways fly from Belfast, and there are also charters from Belfast to Corfu, Crete, Rhodes and Zákynthos.

## Scheduled Flights

Scheduled flights direct to Athens operate daily from London and New York and less frequently from Toronto and Montreal. There are also direct flights from London to Thessaloníki. While the basic carriers from the United States are **Olympic Airways** and **TWA**, from London **Olympic**, **British Airways** and **Virgin Atlantic** are the main carriers. East European airlines like the Czech **CSA**, **Balkan** and **Malev** also fly to Athens and can work out substantially cheaper, but you may have to wait for connections in Prague, Sofia or Budapest. Delays are likely and in-flight service is utilitarian. There's a vast and ever-changing number of airlines serving Athens—**Air UK** and **Britannia** also do scheduled flights, so again it's advisable to shop around and see which offers the best deal.

Superpex flights offer substantially reduced fares, with flights from London to Athens ranging from £190 low season to £280 high season. They must, however, be paid for instantly and are not refundable or flexible. Olympic has a Superpex Saver from Heathrow to Athens and Thessaloníki which must be booked by the end of June, valid for a month from the end of March until the end of October. Rates range from £212 return midweek in low season to £298 weekends in high. American economy fares range from $900 New York–Athens in low season to $1300 high season.

| | |
|---|---|
| **Olympic Airways:** | London ✆ (0171) 409 3400/493 3965. |
| | New York ✆ (212) 838 3600. |
| | Athens ✆ (01) 966 6666. |
| **British Airways:** | London ✆ (0181) 897 4000. |
| **Virgin Atlantic:** | London ✆ (01293) 747747; rec. info. ✆ (01293) 511581. |
| **Delta:** | New York ✆ (800) 241 4141/(800) 221 1212. |
| **KLM:** | Montreal ✆ (514) 933 1314. |
| **TWA:** | New York ✆ (800) 892 4141; ✆ (212) 290 2141. |
| | London ✆ (0171) 439 0707. |

Bona-fide students under 26 are sometimes eligible for discounts, especially with Olympic Airways who currently offer 25% discount to ISIC card holders on all connecting flights from Athens to the islands, even when booked from London: **Trailfinders**, 42–50 Earls Court Road W8 6FT, ✆ (0171) 937 5400; **STA Travel**, 86 Old Brompton Road, London SW7 or 117 Euston Road NW1, ✆ (0171) 937 9962; and **Campus Travel**, 52 Grosvenor Gardens SW1, ✆ (0171) 730 8111, can get you some of the best current deals. Returning from Greece, it is advisable to confirm your return flight a few days prior to departure.

### *discounts and special deals*

**Avro plc**, ✆ (0181) 715 1999/1910; (0161) 489 2989; (01293) 567916; (0141) 303 0303. Flights to Athens and major islands from Gatwick, Manchester, Glasgow, Luton, Cardiff, Newcastle and Birmingham.

**Owners Abroad Travel Ltd**, ✆ (01293) 554400; (0161) 742 2277; (0121) 666 6688. Flights from Gatwick, Manchester, Birmingham.

**Delta Travel,** ✆ (0161) 272 8455; (0151) 708 7955; (0121) 471 2282. Manchester-based Cyprus specialists now featuring Greece. Agents for Olympic scheduled flights from Heathrow to Athens; Swissair and KLM from Manchester and Birmingham for Athens and Thessaloniki; wide range of island charters.

**Meridian Travel,** ✆ (0171) 493 4312/0641. Athens charters from Gatwick and Manchester.

**Aleco's Tours,** ✆ (0171) 267 2092. Olympic Airways consolidator.

**Island Wandering,** ✆ (01580) 860733. Reasonable schedules to Athens, Olympic island packages and open jaws routes. Use Olympic Airways flights.

**Joe Walsh Tours,** ✆ (01) 678 9555. Budget fares from Dublin.

**Campus Travel,** London, ✆ (0171) 730 3402, Leeds, ✆ (0113) 246 1155; Bradford, ✆ (01274) 383261; Bristol, ✆ (0117) 929 2494; Manchester, ✆ (0161) 274 3105; Edinburgh, ✆ (0131) 668 3303; Oxford, ✆ (01865) 242067; Cambridge, ✆ (01223) 324283. Runs own student/youth charters to Athens in summer.

**STA Travel,** London, ✆ (0171) 937 9921, Bristol, ✆ (0117) 929 4399; Leeds, ✆ (0113) 244 9212; Manchester, ✆ (0161) 834 0668; Oxford, ✆ (01865) 792800; Cambridge, ✆ (01223) 66966. Has special youth/student deals and open jaws tickets.

**USIT,** Branches include: Dublin, ✆ (01) 677 8117; Cork, ✆ (021) 270 900; Belfast, ✆ (01232) 324 073. Student/youth fares from Eire and Northern Ireland.

### children and pregnancy

Free child places on package holidays and discount air fares for tiny travellers vary from company to company. So if you are travelling with babies or toddlers it pays to get a good travel agent, trawl through the brochures and read all the small print. The big package operators geared to family holidays like Thomson offer a wide range of child discounts and seasonal savers with in-resort amusements, kiddie clubs and baby-sitting for the very young as well as deals for children under twelve in hotels and teenagers up to seventeen in self-catering accommodation. **Laskarina Holidays** (✆ (01629) 824881) offer a free place to under-twelves with parties of three or more adults and a set price for infants under two including child insurance, use of cots and bed-linen service. On some UK charter flights infants under two travel free on a full fare-paying adult's lap, while on others you may be charged £15–£20 for the baby, usually 10% of the adult fare. Children from two to twelve cost between 25%–65%, and over twelve you'll have to fork out full fare. On Olympic scheduled flights you'll have to pay 67% of adult fare for children aged two to twelve, 10% for infants under two. Children go for half the full fare on all Greek domestic flights. By law children aged two and over travelling on British registered airlines must occupy a seat and have a full baggage allowance. Babies under six months must travel on your lap with a lap strap, as must infants up to two unless there's a vacant seat. They don't have a baggage allowance but you can take a pushchair free. Otherwise infants can travel in a car seat with a safety harness as long as it can be secured facing forward in the aircraft seat. You have to supply your own seat—approved models include Mothercare and Britax Two Way, Two Stage and Recliner—and give the manufacturer's instructions to the cabin crew. Most package companies will charge you a percentage of normal child fare or child holiday price, whichever is cheaper, and you get full baggage allowance. Watch out for birthdays; if your toddler has crossed the magic two-year-old age barrier by the return journey you'll have to pay for another seat. As most airlines won't let single mothers travel with two infants, it may be the answer to have one on the lap and the other in the car seat if you are travelling alone. Explain the position to the airline when you book in case they are adamant on the one child per adult rule or turn you away at the check-in. Some airlines have in-flight carry-cots for babies, and most have free play packs. **Britannia Airways** is especially child-friendly, offering free colouring book and crayons, video cartoons, junior radio show, special children's meals and drinks and nappy-changing facilities.

If you're pregnant, think before you fly. Greek hospitals and maternity services are basic to say the least so make sure your insurance covers repatriation. Most airlines will carry women up to 34 weeks of pregnancy—Olympic even later—but you will have to provide a doctor's certificate after 28 weeks to prove you are fit and well enough to fly. Again check when you book.

## Getting to and from Ellinikon Airport, Athens

Ellinikon Airport is divided into two terminals: East Terminal (for charters and international airlines) and West Terminal (for Olympic Airlines, both international and domestic flights) usually known as Olympiki. Blue and yellow double-decker express buses leave for either terminal (but not both, so be sure you are getting on the right one: East Terminal is number 091, West Terminal 090) from Amalías Avenue, at the bottom of Sýntagma Square, outside McDonald's every 20 minutes between 6am and 11.30pm and at night at 12.40am, 1.59am, 2.50am, 4am and 5am. These buses also pick up travellers from Omónia Square (Stadíou at Aeólou Street), and 091 also stops at Diákou Street near the Olympic Hotel. The fare is 160dr from 6am to midnight, 200dr otherwise. From Piraeus, express bus no.19 goes to both the East and West terminals (160dr). Bus information (in Greek only) ✆ 185. In English there's a general information number, ✆ 322 2545.

### by taxi

Compared to other Western cities, Athenian taxis are cheap. A taxi between Athens and the airport should cost you about 1100dr (more at night). Piraeus is particularly prone to cowboys preying on unsuspecting tourists heading from and to the ferries. Travellers should make sure they take proper yellow taxis with meters and official licence numbers. The tricksters hassle you (especially at Piraeus, less so at the airport) and charge 2–3000dr for the journey; it should be around half that. If there's no meter, watch out. Prices are double from 1–6am and on holidays such as Easter. You will have to pay surcharges on luggage, 50dr a piece, plus a 100dr supplement for an airport or Piraeus run. In Athens cabs are difficult to find during the rush hour, when the drivers are knocking off for lunch, and when everyone is going back to work in the evenings. Hailing a cab is not for the faint-hearted. You almost have to hurl yourself in front of it and yell out your destination. Sharing is common and you all pay the full fare. Just check the meter reading when you get in so you don't get overcharged. Sharing (at full price) is also common on the islands.

### by metro

The **metro** is an important means of getting across Athens, especially from Piraeus. It runs to Kifissiá, stopping at Thissío, Monastiráki, Omónia and Plateía Viktorías. Trolley buses run throughout the city centre from the Laríssis station to Omónia and Sýntagma and out to Koukáki, or linking Sýntagma and Omónia with Patissíon and the National Archaeological Museum. The network is currently being extended with major excavations throughout the city to provide several new stops including Sýntagma Square.

**Airlines in Athens (℗ 01–)**

**Aeroflot:** 14 Xenofóndos; ℗ 322 0986.

**Air Canada:** 10 Óthonos; ℗ 322 3206.

**Air France:** 4 Karageórgi Servias; ℗ 323 8507. Airport ℗ 969 9334.

**Air Zimbabwe:** 39 Panepistimíou; ℗ 323 9101.

**Alitalia:** 10 Níkis; ℗ 322 9414; airport ℗ 961 3512.

**Austrian Airlines:** 8 Óthonos; ℗ 323 0844; airport ℗ 961 0335.

**British Airways:** 10 Óthonos; ℗ 325 0601; airport ℗ 961 0402.

**Canadian Pacific:** 4 Karageórgi Servias; ℗ 323 0344.

**Cyprus Airways:** 10 Filellínon; ℗ 324 6965; airport ℗ 961 0325.

**Iberia:** 8 Xenofóndos; ℗ 323 4523; airport ℗ 969 9813.

**Japan Airlines:** 4 Amalías; ℗ 324 8211; airport ℗ 961 3615.

**KLM:** 22 Voúlis; ℗ 988 0177; airport ℗ 969 9733.

**Lufthansa:** 11 Vass. Sofías; ℗ 771 6002; airport ℗ 961 3628.

**Olympic:** 6 Óthonos or 96 Syngroú, among many branches; ℗ 966 6666.

**Qantas:** 11 Vass. Sofías; ℗ 360 9411.

**Sabena:** 8 Óthonos; ℗ 323 6821; airport ℗ 961 3903.

**SAS:** 6 Sina & Vissariónos; ℗ 363 4444; airport ℗ 961 4201.

**South African Airways:** 11 Vass. Sofías; ℗ 361 6305.

**Swissair:** 4 Óthonos; ℗ 323 1871; airport ℗ 961 0203.

**TWA:** 8 Xenofóndos; ℗ 322 6451; airport ℗ 961 0012.

## Flights from Athens to the Islands

Flights from Athens to the islands can be booked in advance through Olympic Airways, 11 Conduit Street, London W1R 0LS, ℗ (0171) 493 3965. Americans who do not have an Olympic Airways office in their town can call toll-free ℗ (800) 223 1226 for information. There's a special price deal but to be assured of a seat, especially in the summer, you should book your ticket as far in advance as possible. Children go half-price on all domestic flights. Otherwise, you'll have to pay 67% of adult fare for children aged two to twelve, 10% for infants up to 2 years old.

In the past few years Olympic Airways have been offering **island-to-island flights** in season, a pleasant innovation that precludes the need to go to Athens. Although these have a habit of changing from year to year, routes between Crete and Rhodes, Crete and Santoríni, Crete and Mýkonos, Rhodes and Kos, Rhodes and Santoríni, and Rhodes and Mýkonos seem fairly well-established. It's now possible to get a schedule 'open-jaws' ticket to Athens and on to any permutation of islands, but you have to return home from Athens. As the recently privatized Olympic Airways no longer has a monopoly on inter-island flights, recently formed Greek airlines such as SEEA to Corfu are beginning to set up in competition or try out new routes.

At the time of writing the **prices** of one-way flights from Athens to airports on the islands range between 11,000 and 16,000dr, except for Léros, Kárpathos, Rhodes and Thessaloníki, which are between 18,000 and 24,000dr.

**Olympic Airways (Athens)**
6 Óthonos, ✆ 926 9111 (Int. and Dom.)
96 Leofóros Syngroú, ✆ 926 7251/4
East Airport, ✆ 969 9703 (Int.)
West Airport, ✆ 936 9111 (Int. and Dom.)

## By Train

There are 3 daily trains from London to Athens, the *Athenai Express*, the *Acropolis Express* and the *Hellas Express*, all of which take about 3 days. And a hot, crowded, stuffy 3 days too. Given the current situation in the former Yugoslavia it is advisable to double-check on trains from Britain to Greece with British Rail International, ✆ (0171) 834 2345. The alternative and pleasant though slightly costlier route is to go through Italy, either to Ancona or further south to Brindisi, and take the ferry over to Corfu and Pátras. British people under age 26 can travel on **Interail** passes, good for a month's rail travel in Europe—which gets you there and back, at a reasonable price. Interail passes are also available to British residents over 26 for either 15 days or a month.

Americans and Canadians can buy 2-month **Eurail** and **Youth Eurail** passes before leaving home. However, the Eurail Pass is a bad bargain if you're only going to Greece, which has a limited rail service. For men over 65 and women over 60, the **Rail Europ** senior card saves up to 50% on rail fares in Greece and several other European countries, 30% in Germany, and 30% on most sea crossings. It costs £5 and can be purchased at any British Rail Travel Centre by holders of a British Rail card.

Hardy souls who deny themselves even one night in a couchette or cabin are advised to bring with them 3 days' provisions, including water, and some toilet paper. Those who intend to sleep in a prone position, beneath seats and feet, should also bring something to lie on. Wear the oldest and most comfortable clothes you own (and save yourself the trouble of washing them before you go).

### Domestic Train Routes

| | | |
|---|---|---|
| Athens–Thessaloníki | (for NE Aegean Is.) | 10 a day |
| Athens–Alexandroúpolis | (for Samothráki) | 2 a day |
| Thessaloníki–Alexandroúpolis | | 2 a day |
| Athens–Chalkí | (Évia) | 17 a day |
| Athens–Pátras | (for Ionian Is.) | 7 a day |
| Athens–Kalamáta | (for Kýthera) | 8 a day |
| Athens–Vólos | (for Sporades) | 7 a day |

Groups of more than 10 people can obtain a 30% discount on domestic fares; foreign students receive no special reductions.

In Athens, the railway station for northern Greece is Laríssa Station, Deligiánni Street, ✆ 524 0601. The station for the Peloponnese is across the tracks, ✆ 513 1601. In Piraeus, the station for the Peloponnese is near the Piraeus–Athens metro on Aktí Kalimassióti. The station for northern Greece lies further down the road on Aktí Kondíli. For further information telephone the OSE (Hellenic Railways Organization), ✆ 522 2491 or 323 6747.

## London to Athens

Taking a bus from London to Athens is always a possible alternative for those who decide that a train trip is too expensive or too easy a route to travel. It isn't usually much cheaper than a standby flight. But with 2½ days (or more) on the road and Adriatic ferry, adventures are practically included in the ticket price. **Eurolines**, 52 Grosvenor Gardens, Victoria, London SW1W 0AU, ✆ (0171) 730 8235, offers 3-day journeys from London to Athens which cost around £218 return if you're over 26; there's a £12 saving if you're under 26. Departures from London are on Friday mornings in July, August and September only. **Olympic Bus Ltd**, 70 Brunswick Centre, London WC1 1AE, ✆ (0171) 837 9141 offers 2½-day journeys from London to Athens via Brussels and Italy for a mere £50 one-way, or £100 return, departing London on Friday evenings. In Greece, you'll find agencies selling bus tickets on the most obscure islands, as well as in Athens; **Filellínon Street** near Sýntagma Square is Athens' budget travellers' boulevard, so check there for other possibilities.

## Domestic Buses

The domestic bus service in Greece is efficient and regular, if not always a bargain. Each bus is decorated at the whim of its driver, with pin-ups, saints, wallpaper, tinsel, tassels, and plastic hands which wave violently when the bus falls into a pothole. Bus services from Athens relevant to this book are as follows:

| Athens to | No. daily | Terminal | ✆ | Duration |
|---|---|---|---|---|
| Chalkí (Évia) | 33 | Liossíon | 831 7153 | 1.30hrs |
| Loutrá/Edipsoú (Évia) | 3–4 | Liossíon | 831 7253 | 3.15hrs |
| Gýthion | 4 | Kifissoú | 512 4913 | 5.30hrs |
| Igoumenítsa (for Corfu) | 4 | Kifissoú | 512 5954 | 8.30hrs |
| Kefaloniá | 4 | Kifissoú | 512 9498 | 8hrs |
| Kérkyra (Corfu) | 4 | Kifissoú | 512 9443 | 11hrs |
| Lefkás | 4 | Kifissoú | 513 3583 | 5.30hrs |
| Pátras (for Ionian Is.) | 16 | Kifissoú | 513 6185 | 3hrs |
| Rafína (for Cyclades & Évia) | 18 | Mavromatéon | 821 0872 | 1.30hr |
| Thessaloníki (for NE Aegean Is.) | 10 | Kifissou | 514 8856 | 7.30hrs |
| Vólos (for Sporades) | 10 | Liossíon | 831 7186 | 5.15hrs |
| Zákynthos | 3 | Kifissoú | 512 9432 | 7hrs |

To get to the terminal at 100 Kifissoú Street, take bus no.051 from Omónia Square (Zinonos and Menandroú Sts). For the terminal at 260 Liossíon Street take bus no.24 from Leofóros Amalias, by the National Garden (tell the driver you want the terminal; the bus doesn't go in it). Take a tram 5 or 9 towards Areos Park on 28th Octovríou Street for the Mavromatéon terminal.

During the summer it is advisable to reserve seats in advance on the long-distance buses. Tickets for these journeys must normally be purchased before boarding the bus. Note that two islands, Léfkas and Évia, are joined to the mainland by bridge, which is good to remember if no ferries are running to the islands owing to either strikes or bad weather.

There are never enough buses on the islands in the summer, nor is it customary to queue. However, you will not be left behind if it is humanly possible for you to squeeze on. If you can wake up in time, you will find that buses are rarely crowded early in the morning.

Within the Athens area the bus fare is 75dr. Purchase tickets before boarding and stamp them on the bus to validate them—if you can fight your way to the machine, that is.

---

### By Sea

The most common sea route to Greece is from Italy, with daily ferry services from Ancona, Bari, Brindisi, Otranto and Venice. The most popular of these is the daily service from Brindisi, which leaves at 10pm (connecting with the train from Rome) and arrives in Corfu the next morning. Passengers are allowed a free infinite stopover in Corfu if that island is not their ultimate destination, before continuing to Igoumenítsa or Pátras, but make sure it is noted on your ticket. If you plan to sail in the summer, it's advisable to make reservations in advance, especially if you bring a car (most travel agents can do this for you). Students and young people can get a discount of up to 20%. Discounts of up to 20% are also offered when buying a return ticket. The quality of service among the different lines varies; some ships are spanking clean and are plushly furnished—one at least even has a laser disco—while others have been in service so long that they creak. However, the sullen demeanour of the crews seems to be uniform.

New **catamaran** and **hydrofoil** services now link Brindisi with Corfu and the other Ionian Island in under 4 hours but neither take cars. Contact Ilio Lines, 4 Spyromiliou Arcade, Sýntagma, Athens, ✆ 322 5139.

## Ferries

| Ports | Frequency | Company |
|---|---|---|
| Ancona–Corfu–Pátras | 6 times a week | Strinzis Lines<br>26 Aktí Possidónos<br>Piraeus, ✆ 412 9815 |
| Ancona–Corfu–Igoumenítsa–<br>Pátras–Trieste | 2/4 times a week | ANEK Lines<br>54 Amalías Avenue<br>Athens, ✆ 323 3481 |
| Ancona–Igoumenítsa–Corfu–Pátras | 5 times a week | Minoan Lines<br>2 Vass. Konstantinoú<br>Athens, ✆ 751 2356 |
| Ancona–Igoumenítsa–Pátras | 2 times a week | Marlines<br>38 Aktí Possidónos<br>Piraeus, ✆ 411 0777 and<br>422 4950 |
| Brindisi–Corfu–Igoumenítsa–Pátras | 3 times a week | Hellenic Mediterranean Lines<br>28 Amalías Avenue<br>Athens, ✆ 323 6333 |

| | | |
|---|---|---|
| Bari–Corfu–Kefaloniá–Igoumenítsa –Pátras | Daily | Ventouris Ferries 26 Amalías Avenue Athens, ✆ 324 0276 |
| Bari–Igoumenítsa | Daily | Arkadia Lines 215 Kifissiás Avenue Athens ✆ 612 3402 |
| Brindisi–Corfu–Igoumenítsa–Pátras | Daily | Fragline 5a Réthymnou Street Athens, ✆ 822 1285 |
| | Daily | Adriatica 85 Aktí Miaoúli 18538 Piraeus ✆ 429 1397 |
| | Daily | Hellenic Mediterranean Lines (see above) |
| Brindisi–Pátras | Daily | Vergina Ferries 274 Alkiviádou Street Piraeus, ✆ 453 1882 |
| | 4 times a week | European Seaways 86 Fílonos Street 18536 Piraeus ✆ 429 3903 |
| Brindisi–Kefaloniá–Pátras | Daily in summer | Hellenic Mediterranean Lines (see above) |
| Brindisi–Corfu | Daily in summer | Marlines (see above) |
| Venice–Bari–Piraeus–Herákleon– Alexandria | Once a week March–Jan | Adriatica (see above) |
| Ancona–Corfu–Kefaloniá–Piraeus– Páros–Sámos–Kuşadasi | Daily in summer (see above) | Minoan Lines |

## Boats to the Islands

The daily newspaper *I Nay Temporíki* lists all the activities of the port at Piraeus and publishes weekly ship schedules. The National Tourist Office also publishes a monthly list of ship departures, both abroad and to the islands.

A little travelling through the islands will soon show you that each boat is an individual. The many new ones are clean and comfortable and often air-conditioned. The older boats may lack some modern refinements but nevertheless they can be pleasant if you remain out on deck. The drinking water is never very good on the boats, but all sell beer, Coca Cola and lemon or orange soda. Biscuits and cigarettes complete the fare on the smaller boats, while the larger ones offer sandwiches, cheese pies or even full meals.

All the boats are privately owned and although the Greek government controls the prices some will charge more for the same journey, depending on the facilities offered, speed, etc. If caiques relay you from shore to ship, you will pay more. In most cases children under the age of 4 travel free, and between 4 and 10 for half-fare. Over 10 they are charged the full fare. In the summer it is wise to buy tickets in advance, to guarantee a place and because they often cost 20% more when bought on board. Refunds are rarely given unless the boat itself never arrives, stuck in Piraeus for tax delinquencies. Boats will arrive late or divert their course for innumerable reasons, so if you have to catch a flight home allow for the eccentricities of the system and leave a day early to be safe.

When purchasing a ticket, either in Piraeus or on the islands, it's always best to do so from your ship's central agency. Other agencies may tell you that the boat is full, when in truth they've merely sold all the tickets allotted them by the central agency. On many islands, agents moonlight as bartenders or grocers and may only have a handwritten sign next to the door advertising their ship's departures.To get unbiased, non-partisan answers to sailing schedule questions, telephone the island's port authority (they don't often speak English, however, so you may have to get a Greek to help).

Because Piraeus is so busy, there's a trend to use smaller mainland ports, especially Rafína and Lávrion. Neither of these is far from Athens, and bus connections are frequent. They are a bit of a bother for most tourists, though, which means that islands mainly served by these outlying ports are often quieter, if you take the trouble to go.

Most inter-island ferries have three or four classes: the first class, with an airconditioned lounge and cabins (and often as expensive as flying); the second class, often with its own lounge as well, but smaller cabins; tourist class, for which you can reserve a cabin, segregated by sex, and deck class, which usually gives you access to the typically large, stuffy rooms full of 'airline seats' and the snack bar area. As a rule the Greeks go inside and the tourists stay out— on summer nights in particular this is perhaps the most pleasant alternative if you have a sleeping bag.

You'd do well to always keep your ticket with you on a Greek ship, at least until the crew enacts its 'ticket control', a comedy routine necessitated by the fact that Greeks don't always check tickets when passengers board. Instead, after one or two pleas on the ship's loudspeaker system for passengers without tickets to purchase them forthwith, you suddenly find all the doors on the boat locked or guarded by a bored but obdurate sailor, while bands of officers rove about the boat checking tickets. Invariably mix-ups occur: children are separated from their parents, others have gone to the WC, someone has left a ticket with someone on the other side of the immovable sailor, crowds pile up at the doors, and stowaways are marched to the purser's office. In the worst cases, this goes on for an hour; on smaller ships it's usually over in 15 minutes.

**Prices,** though no longer cheap, are still reasonable for passengers, but rather dear for cars.

On the following pages is a list of some of the more popular scheduled mainland and inter-island connections. Duration of each boat trip and approximate 1995 prices are given in drachmas but are subject to change without notice.

| Piraeus to | 2nd Class (dr) | Tourist Class (dr) | 3rd Class (dr) | hours |
|---|---|---|---|---|
| Ag. Kýrikos, Ikaria | 6380 | 4640 | 3650 | 10 |
| Ag. Nikólaos, Crete | 11120 | 8560 | 6610 | 13 |
| Amorgós | 5080 | 4020 | 3870 | 11 |
| Anáfi | 9000 | 7050 | 5600 | 18 |
| Astypálaia | 8470 | 6510 | 5010 | 13 |
| Chaniá, Crete | 8300 | 6500 | 5000 | 11 |
| Chíos | 7400 | 5400 | 4200 | 9 |
| Donoússa | 5070 | 4010 | 3860 | 10 |
| Évdilos, Ikaría | 6380 | —— | 3650 | 10 |
| Folégrandros | 7310 | 5740 | 4380 | 12 |
| Chálki | 13640 | 10232 | 7794 | 17 |
| Heráklia | 5078 | 4013 | 3863 | 15 |
| Herákleon, Crete | 8900 | 6700 | 5400 | 11 |
| Ios | 6695 | 5190 | 4006 | 10 |
| Kálymnos | 8473 | 6507 | 5012 | 13 |
| Karlóvassi, Samos | 7624 | —— | 4053 | 12 |
| Kárpathos | 11270 | 7918 | 6218 | 18 |
| Kássos | 11290 | 7920 | 6220 | 18 |
| Kastellórizo | 12,400 | 9500 | 8600 | 23 |
| Kímolos | —— | 4300 | 3640 | 8 |
| Kos | 10360 | 7940 | 6210 | 15 |
| Koufoníssia, Shínoussa | 5075 | 4020 | 3860 | 14 |
| Kýthnos | 4010 | 3100 | 2530 | 4 |
| Léros | 8470 | 6510 | 5010 | 11 |
| Límnos | 8470 | —— | 5670 | 18 |
| Mílos | 5560 | 4300 | 3640 | 8 |
| Mýkonos | 5240 | 4160 | 3520 | 6 |
| Lésbos, Mytilíni | 8250 | 6243 | 4910 | 15 |
| Náxos | 5560 | 4240 | 3970 | 8 |
| Níssyros | 10370 | 7940 | 6210 | 22 |
| Páros | 4690 | 3752 | 3230 | 6 |
| Pátmos | 8470 | 6510 | 5010 | 10 |
| Rhodes | 11,300 | 8800 | 7800 | 18 |
| Santoríni | 6680 | 5190 | 4380 | 10 |
| Sírifos | 4470 | 3470 | 2800 | 5 |
| Sífnos | 4850 | 38620 | 3350 | 6 |
| Síkinos | 8570 | 6670 | 5070 | 10 |
| Sitía, Crete | 12360 | 9440 | 7290 | 13 |
| Sými | 10370 | 7940 | 6210 | 22 |

| | | | | |
|---|---|---|---|---|
| Sýros | 4470 | 3640 | 3220 | 5 |
| Tílos | 10360 | 7940 | 6210 | 24 |
| Tínos | — | 4000 | 3520 | 5 |

Not included in the above prices are port taxes (minimal) and VAT (currently 8%).

## Argo-Saronic Islands (© 411 5801/451 1311)

| Piraeus to | Tourist Class (dr.) | Flying Dolphin (dr.) | Ferry Duration (hours) |
|---|---|---|---|
| Aegina | 950 | 1700 | 2.00 |
| Hýdra | 1900 | 4000 | 4.00 |
| Póros | 1600 | 3000 | 3.30 |
| Spétses | 2300 | 4400 | 5.00 |

## Sporades Line (© 417 8084/2415)

| Ag. Konstantínos to | Tourist Class (dr.) | Duration (hours) |
|---|---|---|
| Alónissos | 4000–7500 | 5.30 |
| Glóssa | 3600–6800 | 4.25 |
| Skiáthos | 3200–6000 | 3.15 |
| Skópelos | 3800–7000 | 5.30 |
| **Kými, Évia to** | | |
| Skýros | 2200 | 2.00 |
| **Vólos to** | | |
| Alónissos | 3300 | 5.00 |
| Glóssa | 2800 | 3.45 |
| Skiáthos | 2400 | 3.00 |
| Skópelos | 3100 | 4.30 |

## Évia and Cyclades Line (© 0294 26166)

| Rafína to | | |
|---|---|---|
| Amorgós | 4000 | 8.00 |
| Ándros | 2500 | 2.30 |
| Kárystos, Évia | 2000 | 4.00 |
| Marmári, Évia | 1300 | 2.00 |
| Mýkonos | 3300 | 5.00 |
| Náxos | 3200 | 6.30 |
| Páros | 3100 | 5.00 |
| Tínos | 2900 | 4.00 |

## Kéa–Kýthnos Line © (0292) 25249

| Lávrion to | | |
|---|---|---|
| Kéa | 1700 | 2.30 |
| Kýthnos | 2200 | 4.00 |

# Hydrofoils

There are several fleets of hydrofoils thumping over the Greek seas, and new lines are added every year. The Flyink (sic) Dolphins and a new catamaran leave Piraeus Zéa Marína for three of the Saronic islands—Póros, Hýdra and Spétses, and link them with neighbouring mainland ports at Pórto Chéli and Náfplion; one goes as far as Kýthera. For Aegina, hydrofoils leave from the main harbour in Piraeus. Two services ply the Dodecanese, from Rhodes all the way north to Sámos, calling at Kálymnos, Kos, Léros and Pátmos in between. Others connect the Northeastern Aegean Islands, another the Ionian Islands, another the most popular Cyclades, another the Sporades; a catarmaran runs between Herákleon and Santoríni. Most hydrofoils run throughout the year but are considerably less frequent in winter. Hydrofoils as a rule travel twice as fast as ships and are twice as expensive (in some cases as much as a plane). In the peak season they are often fully booked, so buy tickets as early as you can. In a choppy sea a trip may leave you saddle-sore, and if the weather is very bad, they don't leave port.

# Tourist Excursion Boats

These are generally slick and clean, and have become quite numerous in recent years. They are more expensive than the regular ferries or steamers, but often have schedules that allow visitors to make day excursions to nearby islands (though you can also take them one way), and are very convenient, having largely taken the place of the little caique operators, many of whom now specialize in excursions to remote beaches instead of island-hopping on request. They may well be the only transport available to the most remote islands, but do inquire about scheduled ferries. Friendly yachtsmen may give you a lift—it never hurts to ask.

# Boats to Turkey

Whatever axes are currently being ground between Greece and Turkey, a kind of *pax tourista* has fallen over the mutually profitable exchange of visitors from the Greek islands to the Turkish mainland. Connections run daily year-round between Rhodes and Marmaris (3½ hrs); between Kos and Bodrum daily in summer, less frequently in winter (1½ hrs); from Chíos to Çeşme daily from spring to autumn (1 hr); from Sámos to Kuşadasi (near Ephesus) at least twice a day, April–October (1½ hrs); and from Lésbos to Ayvalik daily in summer (2 hrs). While there isn't much difference in crossing times, prices can vary enormously according to when you go and whose boat you take (both Greek and Turkish boats make the crossings). There is a mysterious array of taxes, everywhere different (sometimes less if you only make a day excursion); generally speaking, the return fare is 16,000dr—i.e. £45 or $60. On the whole, Turkish shops around the ports will take drachmae, but the Greeks will not take Turkish lira—and the exchange rate between the two is pretty dreadful. Also, beware the charter restriction: with things as they are, if you have spent a night in Turkey the Greek airport authorities might invoke the law and refuse you passage home on your flight.

For the most recent information on Greek sea connections, get a copy of the monthly *Greek Travel Pages* or *Key Travel Guide*, which is updated every week. Travel agents in Great Britain often have a copy, and it is easy to find in Greece itself.

---

## By Car

Driving from London to Athens (and taking the ferry from Italy to Greece) at a normal pace takes around 3½ days. Don't even consider driving down unless you are planning to spend a few weeks on one or two islands, and if that's the case the smaller the better, both for squeezing it on to the ferry, and for negotiating the sometimes very narrow village roads. Alternatively, there are countless rent-a-car companies on the mainland and the islands; many are family run, and many are ripe rip offs: read the small print with care, and if it's off season, don't be shy about negotiating. Arriving at a car hire agent's with a handful of brochures from the competition has been known to strengthen one's bargaining position.

An **International Driving Licence** is not required by British, Austrian, Belgian or German citizens. Other nationals can obtain an international licence at home, or at one of the Automobile Club offices in Greece (ELPA), by presenting a national driving licence, passport and photograph. The minimum age is 18 years.

**The Motor Insurance Bureau** at 10 Xenofóntos Street, Athens, ✆ (01) 323 6733, can tell you which Greek insurance company represents your own, or provide you with additional cover for Greece.

The **Greek Automobile Club** (ELPA) operates a breakdown service within 60km (40 miles) of Athens, Thessaloníki, Laríssa, Pátras and Herakleon: dial 104

### Greek Automobile Club (ELPA) Addresses

**Athens:** 68 Hérakles Avenue, ✆ (01) 779 1615.

**Chaniá** (Crete): 1 Apokorónou and Skoúla, ✆ (0821) 96611 and 97177.

**Corfu:** New Port Pier, ✆ (0661) 39504.

**Herákleon** (Crete): Knossós Avenue and G. Papandréou, ✆ (0181) 288180.

**Kavála:** 8 Cristostómou Smýrnis, ✆ (051) 226 638 and 226 645.

**Laríssa:** At the 3rd km on the national road Athens/Laríssa, ✆ (041) 660 641.

**Pátras:** Astíngos and 127 Korínthou, ✆ (061) 425411 and 425141.

**Rhodes:** 34 Karpáthou Street, ✆ (0241) 25066.

**Thessaloníki:** 230 Vass. Ólgas and Egeoú, ✆ (031) 426319 and 426320.

**Tripolis:** 47 Náfplio, ✆ (0171) 224101.

**Vólos:** 89 Iólkou, ✆ (0421) 25001.

**Customs** formalities are very easy and usually take very little time. You are allowed a year of free use of the car in Greece, and after that can apply for a 4-month extension. North Americans and Australians are allowed 2 years. If you leave Greece without your car, you must have it withdrawn from circulation by a customs authority. ELPA has a list of lawyers who can offer free legal advice on car problems. They also have a 24-hour number of information useful to foreign motorists; call ✆ 174, and speak English.

**Parking** in the centre of Athens, or the Green Zone, is forbidden outside designated parking areas. The following streets form the Green Zone borders: Sékeri, Botássi, Stoúrnara, Marni, Menándrou, Pireás, Likourgoú, Athinás, Mitropóleos, Filellínon, Amalías and Vassilíssis Soffas.

While driving in the centre of Athens may be a hair-raising experience, the rest of Greece is easy and pleasant. There are few cars on most roads, even in summer, and all signs have their Latin equivalents. Traffic regulations and signalling comply with standard practice on the European Continent (i.e. driving on the right). Crossroads and low visibility in the mountains are probably the greatest hazards. Where there are no right-of-way signs at a crossroads, give priority to traffic coming from the right, and always beep your horn on blind corners. Take special care when approaching an unguarded railway level crossing. If you're exploring, you may want to take a spare container of petrol along, as petrol stations can be scarce on the ground and only open shop hours. There is a speed limit of 50km per hour (30mph) in inhabited areas: other speed limits are indicated by signposts in kilometres. Horn-blowing is prohibited in Athens and other big cities, though you'd never guess it from the cacophony that starts when the red light changes to green.

### By Motorbike or Moped

Motorbikes and even more popular mopeds are ideal for the islands in the summer. It almost never rains, and what could be more pleasant than a gentle thyme-scented breeze freshening your journey over the mountains? Motorbikes (the Greeks call them *papákia*, 'little ducks', supposedly for the noise they make) are both more economical and more practical than cars. They can fit into almost any boat and travel paths where cars fear to tread. Many islands have rentals which are not expensive, and include third party coverage in most cases. For larger motorbikes you may be asked to show a driver's licence. The down-sides: not a few hospital beds in Greece are occupied every summer by tourists who have been careless about safety rules, and the noise in the villages drives everyone (at least everyone not astride one) buggy. Many islands have laws about operating them after midnight and in the wee hours of the morning. By law, helmets are required at all times; in practice, the only ones you'll see are worn about the elbow, which judging by the daredevil way they pilot their machines is where many young Greeks keep their brains.

### By Bicycle

Cycling has not caught on in mountainous Greece, either as a sport or as a means of transport, though you can usually hire an old bike in most major resorts. Trains and planes carry bicycles for a small fee, and Greek boats generally take them along, for nothing. Crete and Évia are the best islands for cycling enthusiasts, Crete being the more rugged by far. On both islands you will find fresh water, places to camp, and a warm and surprised welcome in the villages.

### Hitch-hiking

With the rarest of exceptions, hitch-hiking, or 'autostop' as it is known in Greece, is perfectly safe. However, the lack of cars makes it a not particularly speedy mode of transport. The Greek double standard produces the following percentages for hopeful hitch-hikers:

Single woman: 99% of cars will stop. You hardly have to stick out your thumb.
Two women: 75% of cars will find room for you.
Woman and man: 50%; more if the woman is pretty.
Single man: 25% if you are well dressed with little luggage; less otherwise.
Two men: start walking.

The best time for soliciting a ride is when you disembark from a ship. Ask your fellow passengers, or better still write your destination on a piece of paper (in Greek if possible) and pin it to your shirt with a naïve, friendly smile. What you lose in dignity you will generally gain in a lift.

## Specialist Holidays

A list of tour operators including specialist ones is available from the **National Tourist Organization of Greece**, ℗ (0171) 734 5997 (London), (212) 421 5777 (New York), (312) 782 1084 (Chicago), (213) 626696 (Los Angeles).

**Specialist Vacations**, 63 Cambridge Grove Road, Kingston-upon-Thames, Surrey KT1 3HB, ✆ (0181) 974 8373. Painting with Muriel Owen, vice president of the Society of Women Artists, in Kastellórizo, Níssyros, Pátmos, Sámos, Sými.

**British Museum Tours**, 46 Bloomsbury Street, London WC1B 3QQ, ✆ (0171) 323 8895. Archaeological guided tours, such as the 'Palaces and Tombs of the Mycenaean Kings'.

**Filoxenia**, Sourdock Hill, Barkisland, Halifax HX4 0AG, ✆ (01422) 371796. Guided archaeological tours in Western Crete; spring naturewatch tour and walking in ancient Crete; painting groups in Kýthira, and various holidays in Évia.

**Candili Centre for Creative Holidays**, details from **Elysia Holidays**, 4 Sutherland Gardens, London SW14 8DB, ✆ (0181) 878 4778. Courses in everything from pottery to Aegean cookery.

**Greco-File**, ✆ (01422) 375999. Expert advice on where to go, flights and 'couture' holidays to unusual islands for the discerning traveller.

**Laskarina Holidays**, St Mary's Gate, Wirksworth, Derbyshire DE4 4DQ, ✆ (01629) 8248. Painting in Sými.

**Simply Crete**, Chiswick Gate, 598–608 Chiswick High Road, London W4 5RT, ✆ (0181) 994 4462. Painting in Crete.

**Artscape**, Suite 4, Hamlet Court Business Centre, 18 Hamlet Court Road, Westcliff on Sea, Essex SS0 7LX, ✆ (01702) 435990. Painting courses in Western Crete appealing to golden girls and more mature professional women.

**Cox & Kings Travel Ltd**, 4th Floor, Gordon House, 10 Greencoat Lane, London SW1P 1PH, ✆ (0171) 834 7472. Botanic and natural history holidays.

**Exodus**, 9 Weir Road, London, SW12 0LT, ✆ (0181) 675 5550. Trekking holidays.

**Pure Crete**, 979 George Street, Croydon, Surrey CR0 1LP, ✆ (0181) 760 0879. Wildflower and painting holidays.

**Swan Hellenic Ltd**, 77 New Oxford Street, London WC1A 1PP, ✆ (0171) 800 2200. Cultural, archaeological and art history tours and cruises.

**Island Holidays**, Drummond Street, Comrie, Perthshire PH6 2DS, ✆ (01764) 670107. Island trips including natural history and painting holidays.

**Skyros Institute**, 92 Prince of Wales Road, London NW5 3NE, ✆ (0171) 284 3065. The holiday centre on the island of Skýros runs creative writing courses led by leading authors and poets ranging from Sue Townsend, Andrew Davis, Nell Dunn and Wendy Cope. Also personal and spiritual development courses, artists' workshops, holistic bodywork workshops in Alexander technique, dance and massage. Alternatively a whole range of activities are on offer at the secluded holistic holiday centre of Ataista.

**Candili Mountain Pottery**, 340–4 Prokópi, Évia, Greece, ✆ (00 30) 227 41298, ✉ 41204. Scottish potter Alan Bain and wife Schoniad run a wide range of pottery courses for all abilities from raku to ceramic sculpture on the idyllic Ahmetaga Estate of the Noel-Baker family in Western Évia. Ethnic accommodation, swimming pool, beach trips and good home cooking. Dutch weaving expert Anneke van Eyk also runs weaving and handicraft courses for women. ✆ (00 30) 227 41381 or Amsterdam 020 671 2287.

**Inter-Church Travel**, The Saga Building, Middleburg Square, Folkestone, Kent CT20 1AZ, ✆ (01303) 711535. Holiday pilgrimage to the islands to follow the footsteps of St Paul.

**Greek Islands Sailing Club**, 66 High Street, Walton-on-Thames, Surrey KT12 1BU, ✆ (01932) 220416. Painting, sailing and windsurfing holidays, plus sometimes birdwatching and photography.

**Waymark Holidays**, 44 Windsor Road, Slough SL1 2EJ, ✆ (01753) 516477. Guided hiking groups on Mílos, Chíos, Crete and Sámos, spring and autumn breaks.

**Peregrine Holidays**, 40–41 South Parade, Summertown, Oxford OX2 7JP, ✆ (01865) 511642. Wildlife and walking tours in Crete and other islands.

**Norfolk and Suffolk Wildlife Holidays**, Dudwick House, Buxton, Norwich NR10 5HX, ✆ (01603) 278296. Join members of the Norfolk and Suffolk Wildlife Trust on botany and birdwatching trips to Crete, Rhodes, Lesbos and Corfu.

**Ramblers Holidays**, Box 43, Welwyn Garden City, Hertfordshire AL8 6PQ, ✆ (01707) 331133. Walking tours in Crete, Kefaloniá and Ithaca with emphasis on archaeology and wildflowers.

**Bike and Sun Tours**, 42 Whitby Avenue, Guisborough, Cleveland TS14 7AN, ✆ (01287) 639739. Leathers on, tour Greece by motorbike.

### USA

**Central Holiday Tours, Inc.**, 206 Central Avenue, Jersey City, NJ 07307, ✆ (201) 798 5777, toll free (800) 935 5000, ✆ 963 0966. Tours in ancient history and archaeology, 'In the Steps of St Paul', mythology and theatre.

**Classic Adventures**, PO Box 153, Hamlin, NY 14464, ✆ (716) 964 8488, ✆ 964 7297. Bicycling and walking holidays in Sámos and Chíos.

**Cloud Tours**, 645 5th Avenue, New York, NY 10022, ✆ (212) 753 6104, toll free (800) 223 7880, ✆ 980 6941. Scuba diving, biking, honeymoon tours, religious history tours and many others.

**Experts in Greece**, 121 East 5th Street, Austin, TX 78701, ✆ (512) 479 8997, ✆ 479 6858.

**Homeric Tours, Inc.**, 55 East 59th Street, 17th Floor, New York, NY 10022, ✆ (212) 753 1100, toll free (800) 223 5570, ✆ 753 0319.

**IST Cultural Tours**, 225 West 34th Street, Suite 913, New York, NY 10122, ✆ (212) 563 1202, toll free (800) 833 2111, ✆ 594 6953. Customised tours including yacht cruises with lectures on archaeology.

**Olympia Tours, Inc.**, 20335 Biscayne Blvd., Suite 10, N. Miami Beach, FL 33180, ✆ (305) 935 4555, toll free (800) 367 6718, ✆ 937 4025.

**Metro Tours**, 484 Lowell Street, Peabody, MA 01960, ✆ (508) 535 4000, toll free (800) 221 2810, ✆ 535 8830. Art tours, 'In the Steps of St Paul' religious tours, senior citizens' tours.

**The Greek Island Connection**, 418 E. 14th Street, Suite 3, New York, NY 10009, ✆ (212) 674 4072, toll free (800) 241 2417, ✆ 674 4582.

**Zeus Tours Network**, 566 7th Avenue, New York, NY 10018, (212) 221 0006, toll free (800) 447 5667, ✆ 764 7912.

## Flotilla and Sailing Holidays

If you want to float among the islands on the wine-dark sea, but don't own your own yacht, or lack the experience to charter one, a flotilla holiday may be just the answer. A growing number of English-based flotilla companies offer one- or two-week sailing holidays, some of which will take on instructing even the most inexperienced sailors (usually beginning with a week based on land). High season prices for a fortnight's holiday range from £550 per person to £1000 per person, depending on the number of people per yacht. The yachts have 4–8 berths (there are shared boats available for couples and singles) and sail in flotillas, usually from six to a dozen yachts, supervised by a lead boat, with experienced skipper, engineer and social hostess. Plenty of free time and free days are built in.

**Sovereign Sailing**, ✆ (01273) 626284, 120 St George's Road, Brighton, E. Sussex, BN2 1EA.

**Odysseus Yachting Holidays**, 33 Grand Parade, Brighton BN2 2QA, ✆ (01273) 695094.

**Women on Watch**, West Cottage, Westcliff,Whitstable, Kent CT5 1DJ. Sailing holidays for women of all abilities from pedalo to Maiden standards. Skipper Gina Seller based on Póros offers tuitional sailing in the Saronic Islands, Peloponnese and Cyclades from April to October. No keel-hauling, plenty of time for tavernas, sight-seeing, shopping. Learn to helm, navigate and become more focused on yourself on the all-women's boat *Geba Ferez*. Experienced sailors interested in becoming skippers welcome.

**Womanship**, Learn to Sail Cruises For and By Women, ✆ (800) 324 9295. North American company specialising in women-only flotilla holidays in the Greek islands.

Also for dinghies, flotillas, tuitional sailing and watersports:

**Sunsail**, The Port House, Port Solent, Portsmouth PO6 4TH, ✆ (01705) 210345.

**Explore Worldwide**, 1 Frederick Street, Aldershot, Hants GUII ILQ, ✆ (01252) 344161. Island sailing and rambles in western Crete.

## Lotus Eaters and Party Animals

Nudism, singles, clubs and cruises:

**Peng Travel**, 86 Station Road, Gidea Park, Romford, Essex RM2 6DB, ✆ (01708) 471832, naturist holidays in Crete.

**Solos Holidays Ltd**, 41 Watford Way, London NW4 3JH, ✆ (0181) 202 0855. Singles holidays in four-star hotels in Kos, Rhodes, Corfu and Crete for independent people in the 30–49 and 50–69 age brackets. Also spring and autumn rambling breaks in Corfu, Rhodes, Crete.

**Sovereign Small World**, Astral Tower, Betts Way, Crawley, West Sussex RH10 2GX, ✆ (01293) 599966. Villa parties for single travellers in traditional houses on Symi and Kálymnos. Also Caique Cruising for singles afloat. Like a villa party on the ocean wave with excellent food and drink and a chance to meet people and see the islands. One week's cruise can also be combined with a week on dry land.

**Travel Companions**, 110 High Mount, Station Road, London NW4 3ST, ✆ (0181) 202 8478. Vera Coppard can match you up with a kindred spirit , for a £40 fee, if you don't want to travel alone.

**Club Mediterranée**, 106 Brompton Road, London SW3 1JJ, ✆ (0171) 581 1161. All-inclusive luxury beach holidays for the sporty and gregarious on Corfu and Kos.

**Amethyst,** Skiáthos, Sporades, ✆ (00 30) 427 22520. Therapy centre on Skiáthos dealing with a wide range of disorders from drugs, alcohol, sex abuse, to stress and emotional problems.

## Women's Agro-Tourist Cooperatives

Two islands, Mytilíni and Chíos, have women's Agro-Tourist Cooperatives that offer accommodation and a taste of Greek rural life. Bookings are made directly with the cooperatives; someone will speak English. If you have difficulty the Greek National Tourist Organisation can help, and has booking forms and leaflets (for addresses *see* p.16). Alternatively, contact **Zoe Holidays**, 34 Thornhill Road, Surbiton KT6 7TL, ✆ (0181) 390 7623, which organizes rural holidays in conjunction with the women's cooperative. Information and reservations:

**Women's Agricultural Cooperative of Pétra,** Mytilíni, ✆ 0253 41238 (*see* p.478).

**Women's Agricultural Cooperative of Chíos,** Pyrgí, 82102, Chíos, ✆ 0271 72496 (*see* p.459).

## Entry Formalities

All **European Union** members can stay indefinitely from 1995 on. The only reason you would need special permission to stay would be for working or if complicated banking procedures were involved requiring proof of residence; contact the Aliens Bureau: 173 Leof. Alexandrás, 115 22 Athens, ✆ 790 57211. The formalities for **non-EU tourists** entering Greece are very simple. American, Australian, and Canadian citizens can stay for up to 3 months in Greece on presentation of a valid passport. South Africans are permitted 2 months.

## Yachting

One of the great thrills of sailing the Greek waters is the variety of places to visit in a relatively short time, with the bonus that nowhere in Greece is far from safe shelter or harbours with good facilities for yachtsmen. There is little shallow water, except close to the shoreline, few currents and no tides or fog. The 100,000 miles of coastline, and a collection of islands and islets numbering three thousand, provide a virtually inexhaustible supply of secluded coves and empty beaches, even at the height of the tourist season. Equally, there are berthing facilities in the most popular of international hotspots—it's all there beneath the blue skies and bright sunshine. The Greek National Tourist Organization has initiated a programme of rapid expansion in the face of mounting competition from Turkey and Spain; facilities are being improved and new marinas are being constructed throughout the country.

Individual island maps show main yacht supply stations and ports of entry and exit. The colour map on the inside front cover shows weather forecast areas in Greece and the islands.

Greek weather guarantees near-perfect sailing conditions. The only real problem you'll encounter are the strong winds in parts of the country at certain times of the year, notably April to October, when most yachtsmen are at sea.

The Ionian Sea and the west coast of the Peloponnese are affected by the *maistros*, a light-to-moderate northwest wind which presents itself in the afternoon only. Less frequently there are westerly winds, from moderate to strong, to the west and south of the Peloponnese. To the south of Attica, and east of the Peloponnese, the sea is to a great extent sheltered by land masses and it is not until summer that the menacing *meltémi* blows. The Aegean Sea is affected by a northwest wind in the south, and a northeasterly in the north, and when the *meltémi* blows in August and September, it can reach force eight, testing all your skills at the helm. The Turkish coast has light, variable breezes, which are rudely interrupted by the forceful *meltémi*.

## Average wind speeds (in knots) during the months April to October

| Area | Apr | May | Jun | Jul | Aug | Sep | Oct |
|---|---|---|---|---|---|---|---|
| N.E. Aegean | NE | NE | NE | NE | NE | NE | NE |
| (Límnos) | 10.2 | 8.2 | 8.2 | 10.2 | 10.2 | 10.2 | 11.4 |
| Thrakiko | NE | NE | NE | NE | NE | NE | NE |
| (Thássos) | 1.4 | 1.4 | 1.4 | 1.4 | 1.4 | 1.6 | 2.3 |
| Kos–Rhodes | WNW | WNW | NW | NW | NW | NW | WNW |
| (Kos) | 13.6 | 13.0 | 13.0 | 13.6 | 13.6 | 13.0 | 11.4 |
| S.W. Aegean | N | SW | N | N | N | N | N |
| (Mílos) | 9.0 | 6.6 | 6.6 | 8.6 | 8.6 | 8.6 | 9.8 |
| W. Cretan | SW | NNW | NWN | NNW | N | N | N |
| (Chaniá) | 5.0 | 4.4 | 4.4 | 4.4 | 4.1 | 4.1 | 3.8 |
| E. Cretan | NW | NW | NW | NW | NW | NW | NW |
| (Herákleon) | 6.6 | 4.4 | 6.2 | 8.2 | 7.4 | 6.6 | 5.8 |
| E. Cretan | NW | NW | NW | NW | NW | NW | NW |
| (Sitía) | 6.6 | 5.0 | 7.0 | 8.6 | 8.2 | 6.6 | 5.0 |
| Kýthera | NE | W | W | NE | NE | NE | NE |
| (Kýthera) | 9.8 | 8.2 | 7.8 | 7.4 | 8.2 | 9.0 | 10.6 |
| Sámos Sea | NW | NW | NW | NW | NW | NW | NW |
| (Sámos) | 9.4 | 7.8 | 9.4 | 11.0 | 10.2 | 8.6 | 7.0 |
| W. Karpathion | W | W | W | W | W | W | W |
| (Kárpathos) | 6.6 | 6.2 | 8.6 | 10.6 | 9.4 | 8.2 | 6.2 |
| N. Ionian | SE | WSE | W | NWW | NW | SE | SE |
| (Corfu) | 2.9 | 2.6 | 2.9 | 2.6 | 2.6 | 2.3 | 2.6 |
| N.Ionian | NW | NW | NW | NW | NW | NWN | NWNE |
| (Argostóli) | 5.8 | 5.0 | 5.4 | 5.8 | 5.4 | 4.4 | 5.0 |
| S. Ionian | N | NEN | NE | N | NNE | N | NE |
| (Zákynthos) | 9.8 | 9.4 | 9.8 | 10.2 | 9.8 | 9.0 | 10.2 |
| S.Ionian | W | W | W | W | W | W | NE |
| (Methóni) | 11.8 | 11.0 | 11.4 | 11.8 | 11.0 | 10.2 | 9.8 |

If you wish to skipper a yacht anywhere within the Greek seas, you must consult the *Compile Index Chart of Greek Seas*, otherwise known as *XEE*, published by the Hellenic Navy Hydrographic Service. Basically it is a map of Greece divided into red squares, each with an index number, from which you can select the appropriate charts and order them accordingly

For non-Greeks, you can buy what is known as *XEE 64*, a booklet of abbreviations explaining the signs on the charts, with texts in English and Greek.

You also need one of the Pilot series books, which cost 2500dr each and cover the following areas in great detail:

*Pilot A*: South Albania to Kýthera; Ionian Sea, Corinthian Gulf and North Peloponnese shores.

*Pilot B*: Southeastern Greek shores; Crete, Eastern Peloponnese, Saronic Gulf and Cyclades.

*Pilot C*: Northeastern Greek shores; Evoikos, Pagassitikos, Sporades, Thermaikos, Chalkidikí.

*Pilot D*: North and Eastern Aegean shores; Eastern Macedonia, Thrace, Límnos, Lésbos, Chíos, Sámos, the Dodecanese and Asia Minor.

These describe geographical data, possible dangers, and the present state of transportation and communication. All ports and marinas are mentioned, including where to obtain fresh water and fuel, and there are descriptions of visible inland features. The Hydrographic Service constantly updates the books and sends additional booklets to authorized sellers and to all port authorities, where you may consult them. The nautical charts are updated using the latest most sophisticated methods, and follow standardized dimensions. They are on a 1:100,000 scale for bigger areas and 1:750,000 for ports. Heights and depths are given in metres with functional conversion tables for feet and fathoms.

Further information is provided in booklets called *Notes to Mariners*, published monthly and available for consultation at port authorities. These give information on any alterations to naval charts you have purchased for your voyage. Besides all this there is the Navtex service. A special department of the Hydrographic Service keeps you informed about the weather or any special warnings for the day, through telex, or Navtex. The text is in Greek and English, and there are four re-transmission coastal stations covering the Greek seas. Weather forecasts for yachtsmen are broadcast at intervals throughout the day on VHF Channel 16 (in Greek and English); security warnings are also broadcast on this channel, e.g. dangerous wrecks, lights not in operation, etc.

The following is a list of **bunkering ports and supply stations** where fuelling facilities and other provisions may be obtained:

Adámas (Mílos)*, Aegina, Ag. Nikólaos (Kéa), Ag. Nikólaos (Crete)*, Alexandroúpolis*, Álimos Marína, Argostóli (Kefaloniá)*, Chíos*, Corfu Port*, Ermoúpolis (Sýros)*, Flísvos Marína, Goúvia Marína*, Gýthion*, Chalkís*, Chaniá (Crete)*, Hýdra, Itéa*, Kalamáta*, Kálymnos, Kamáres (Sífnos), Kapsáli (Kýthera), Kastellórizo, Kástro (Ándros), Katákolo*, Katápola (Amorgós), Kavála*, Kými (Évia), Korínthos*, Kos*, Lákki (Léros), Lávrion*, Lefkás, Liméni (Máni), Linariá (Skýros), Mýrina (Límnos)*, Mytilíni*, Monemvásia, Mýkonos*, Náfpaktos, Náfplion*, Náxos, Néa Róda, Paléa Epidávros, Paleokastrítsa, Párga, Parikía (Páros), Pigádia (Kárpathos), Pílos*, Póros, Pórto Koufó, Pórto Ráfti, Préveza*, Rhodes (Mandráki)*, Skála (Pátmos)*, Skiáthos*, Skópelos, Spétses, Thessaloníki Marína*, Thessaloníki Port*, Tínos, Váthi (Ithaca)*, Vólos*, Vouliagméni Marína, Zákynthos*, Zéa Marína.

* indicates official ports of entry and exit, where there are port, customs and health authorities, as well as immigration and currency control services. Others are: Égion, Gerakini (Chalkidikí), Glyfáda, Igoumenítsa, Herákleon, Kimássi (Évia), Pátras, Pérama, Pithagórion and Vathí (Samos), Dáfni (Agion Óros), Elefsína, Fíra (Santoríni), Ivira (Agion Óros), Kalí Liménes (Crete), Drépanon (Achaía) and Stilí (Lamia).

**Main port authority telephone numbers**

| | |
|---|---|
| **Piraeus:** | ✆ (01) 451 1311 |
| **Elefsína:** | ✆ (01) 554 3504 |
| **Thessaloníki:** | ✆ (031) 531505 |
| **Corfu:** | ✆ (0661) 326555 |
| **Herákleon:** | ✆ (0181) 244956 |
| **Chíos:** | ✆ (0271) 22837 and 44433 |
| **Lefkáda:** | ✆ (0645) 22322 |
| **Kavála:** | ✆ (051) 223716 |
| **Pátras:** | ✆ (061) 341002 |
| **Rhodes:** | ✆ (0241) 28888 |
| **Vólos:** | ✆ (0421) 38888 |

Yachts entering Greek waters must fly the code flag 'Q' until cleared by entry port authorities. Upon arrival the port authority (*Limenarkíon*) issues all yachts with a transit log, which entitles the yacht and crew to unlimited travel in Greek waters. It also allows crew members to buy fuel, alcohol and cigarettes duty free. It must be kept on board and produced when required, and returned to the customs authorities on leaving Greece at one of the exit ports. Permission is normally given for a stay of 6 months, but this can be extended. Small motor, sail or rowing boats do not require a '*carnet de passage*', and are allowed into Greece duty free for 4 months. They are entered in your passport and deleted on exit. For more information, apply to the Greek National Tourist Organisation, 4 Conduit Street, London W1R 0DJ, ✆ (0171) 734 5997, who produce a useful leaflet *Sailing the Greek Seas*.

Anyone taking a yacht by road is strongly advised to obtain boat registration documentation from the DVLA, Swansea SA99 1BX, ✆ (0792) 783355. The Royal Yachting Association, R.Y.A. House, Romsey Road, Eastleigh, Hampshire SO5 4YA, ✆ (0703) 629962, is a useful source of yachting information.

A brief guide to **monthly mooring rates:**

| *In Álimos Marína (Athens)* | *summer* | *winter* |
|---|---|---|
| Up to 7m 3 | 3000dr per m | 2800dr per m |
| 8–17m | 3600dr " " | 2900dr " " |
| 18m and above | 3700dr " " | 3000dr " " |
| *In Gouviá Marína (Corfu)* | | |
| Up to 7m | 2000dr " " | 1700dr " " |
| 8–17m | 2200dr " " | 1800dr " " |
| 18m and above | 2400dr " " | 1900dr " " |

## Yacht Charter

Chartering yachts is very popular these days, and, as the promotional literature says, can be cheaper than staying in a hotel (if you have enough friends or family to share expenses). Between the various firms there are over a thousand vessels currently available in all sizes, with or without a crew (though without a crew—bareboat charter—both the charterer and another member of the party must show proof of seamanship: a sailing certificate or letter of recommendation from a recognized yacht or sailing club). There are various options: motor yachts (without sails), motor sailors (primarily powered by motor, auxiliary sail power) and sailing yachts (with auxiliary motor power). Charters can be arranged through licensed firms of yacht brokers, or by contacting yacht owners directly. The Greek National Tourist Organisation has a list of Greek charter firms; the **Yacht Charter Association**, 60 Silverdale, New Milton, Hampshire BH25 7DE, ✆ (01425) 619004, supplies a list of its recognized yacht charter operators and offers advice on chartering overseas. For more information on chartering in Greece, write to **The Hellenic Professional Yacht Owners Association**, Zéa Marína A818 536, Piraeus, ✆ 452 6335, ✆ 452 6335 and 428 0465, and **Greek Yacht Brokers and Consultants Association**, 7 Filellínon Street, 105 57 Athens, ✆ 323 0330. One of the largest and most reputable firms is **Valef**, located at 22 Aktí Themistokléous, Piraeus, ✆ 428 1920, ✆ 428 1926 (in the USA: 7254 Fir Rd,. PO Box 391, Ambler, Pa 19002). They have more than 300 craft, accommodating 4–50 people in comfort.

The Plum Pudding Club, at Zéa Marína, in Piraeus, is said to be the place to look for work aboard yachts, although it looked a bit sleepy on a recent visit.

See also p.19 for flotilla holidays which include sailing tuition for the less experienced.

### Yacht Charter Operators Based in England

Bareboat yacht charter prices start from around £350–£400 per week for a 31ft boat in low season and £2500 for a 48ft boat in high season. Prices peak during July and August and are lower during the spring and autumn months.

**BUOYS Cruising Club**, 8 Chase Side, Enfield, Middlesex EN2 6NF, ✆ (0181) 367 8462. Offers charters from Athens.

**The Moorings**, 188 Northdown Road, Cliftonville, Kent CT9 2QN, ✆ (01843) 227140. Offers charters from Corfu, Rhodes, Kos and Athens.

**McCulloch Marine**, 32 Fairfield Road, London E3 2QB, ✆ (0181) 983 1487. Offers charters from Athens.

**Tenrag Yacht Charters**, Bramling House, Bramling, Canterbury, Kent CT3 1NB, ✆ (01227) 721874. Offers charters from Poros and Skiathos.

**World Expeditions Ltd**, 7 North Road, Maidenhead, Berkshire SL6 1TL, ✆ (01628) 74174. Embarkation points are from Athens and a number of Greek islands.

# Practical A–Z

Greece enjoys hot, dry, clear and bright Mediterranean summers, cooled by winds, of which the *meltémi* from the northeast is the most notorious and most likely to upset Aegean sailing schedules. Winters are mild, and in general the wet season begins at the end of October–beginning of November when it can rain 'tables and chairs' as the Greeks say. It begins to feel springlike in February, specially in Crete and Rhodes, when the first wildflowers appear.

## Average Daily Temperatures

| | Athens | | Crete | | Cyclades | | Dodecs | | Ionian | | N.E.Aeg | | Saronic | | Spor'des | |
|------|------|------|------|------|------|------|------|------|------|------|------|------|------|------|------|------|
| | | | (HERAK'N) | | (MYKONOS) | | (RHODES) | | (CORFU) | | (MYTILINI) | | (HYDRA) | | (SKYROS) | |
| | F° | C° | F° | C° | F° | C° | F° | C° | F° | C° | F° | C° | F° | C° | F° | C° |
| Jan | 48 | 11 | 54 | 12 | 54 | 12 | 54 | 12 | 50 | 10 | 50 | 10 | 53 | 12 | 51 | 10 |
| Feb | 49 | 11 | 54 | 12 | 54 | 12 | 54 | 13 | 51 | 10 | 48 | 10 | 53 | 12 | 51 | 10 |
| Mar | 54 | 12 | 58 | 14 | 56 | 13 | 58 | 14 | 52 | 12 | 52 | 12 | 56 | 13 | 52 | 11 |
| Apr | 60 | 16 | 62 | 17 | 60 | 17 | 60 | 17 | 60 | 15 | 60 | 16 | 61 | 16 | 58 | 15 |
| May | 68 | 20 | 68 | 20 | 68 | 20 | 66 | 20 | 66 | 19 | 68 | 20 | 68 | 20 | 66 | 19 |
| Jun | 76 | 25 | 74 | 24 | 74 | 23 | 73 | 21 | 71 | 21 | 74 | 24 | 76 | 25 | 74 | 23 |
| Jul | 82 | 28 | 78 | 26 | 76 | 25 | 78 | 27 | 78 | 27 | 80 | 27 | 82 | 28 | 77 | 25 |
| Aug | 82 | 28 | 78 | 26 | 76 | 25 | 79 | 27 | 78 | 26 | 80 | 27 | 81 | 28 | 78 | 25 |
| Sep | 76 | 25 | 76 | 24 | 74 | 23 | 78 | 25 | 74 | 23 | 74 | 23 | 76 | 25 | 71 | 22 |
| Oct | 66 | 19 | 70 | 21 | 68 | 20 | 72 | 21 | 66 | 19 | 66 | 19 | 71 | 21 | 65 | 19 |
| Nov | 58 | 15 | 64 | 18 | 62 | 17 | 66 | 17 | 58 | 15 | 58 | 15 | 62 | 17 | 58 | 15 |
| Dec | 52 | 12 | 58 | 14 | 58 | 14 | 58 | 14 | 54 | 12 | 52 | 12 | 58 | 15 | 51 | 12 |

Two Greek **measurements** you may come across are the *strémma*, a Greek land measurement (1 *strémma* = ¼ acre), and the *oká*, an old-fashioned weight standard, divided into 400 drams (1 *oká* = 3lb; 35 drams = ¼lb, 140 drams = 1lb).

The **electric current** in Greece is mainly 220 volts, 50Hz; plugs are continental two-pin.

**Greek time** is Eastern European, or two hours ahead of Greenwich Mean Time, seven hours ahead of Eastern Standard Time in North America.

## Embassies and Consulates

**Australia:** 37 D. Soútsou Street, 115 21 Athens, ✆ 644 7303, ✉ 644 3633.

**Austria:** 26 Leof. Alexándras, 106 83 Athens, ✆ 821 1036, ✉ 821 9823.

**Canada:** 4 I. Gennadíou Street, 115 21 Athens, ✆ 725 4011, ✉ 725 3994.

**France:** 7 Vass. Sofías, 106 71 Athens, ✆ 361 1663/5, ✉ 360 2256.

**Germany:** 10 Vass. Sofías, 151 24 Athens, ✆ 369 4111, ✉ 725 1205.

**Ireland:** 7 Vass. Konstantínou, 106 74 Athens, ✆ 723 2771, ✉ 724 0217.

**Japan:** Athens Twr., 2–4 Messogíou Street, 115 27 Athens, ✆ 775 8101, ✆ 770 5964.

**New Zealand:** 9 Semitélou Street, 115 28 Athens ✆ 771 0112.

**South Africa:** 60 Kifissías & Iatrídou, 151 25 Maroússi ✆ 689 5330, ✆ 689 5320.

**United Kingdom:** 1 Ploutárchou Street, 106 75 Athens, ✆ 723 6211, ✆ 724 1872.

**US:** 91 Vass. Soffas, 115 21 Athens, ✆ 721 2951, ✆ 645 6282.

**United Nations:** 36 Amalías Avenue, Athens, ✆ 322 9624.

## Events and Cultural Attractions

From folk-dancing to wine-tasting, ballet to drama, there are all kinds of festivals going on throughout Athens and the islands. Here are some of the main attractions:

### April

**Páros Amateur Creation Week.** Music, theatre and film evenings on the island. Ticket information, ✆ 0284 21222.

**Ándros Amateur Creation Week.** Cinema, music and drama plus a television programme of local interest. ✆ 0281 23411.

### June–September

**Athens Festival.** International culture. modern and ancient theatre, jazz, classical music and dance, often with visiting British companies, in the stunning setting of the Herodus Atticus Odeon beneath the Acropolis. Also a wide range of performances at the Lycabettus Theatre, Likavitós Hill, including the **International Jazz and Blues Festival** in late June.

**Epídávros Festival** in the Peloponnese. Ancient Greek drama under the stars in the authentic setting of the amphitheatre at weekends. Special buses from Athens. Ancient stone seats so take a cushion or something to sit on. Festivals Box Office 4 Stadíou Street, Athens, in the arcade, ✆ 322 1459 or 322 3111, ext 240.

**Cultural July** at Elefsína (Eleusis), Attica, just outside Athens. A new slant on the Mysteries with theatre, folk music and dance, arts and crafts in the old soap factory on the beach.

### June

**Klidónas Day, Chaniá, Crete.** Traditional feast celebrating the old custom of water-divining for a husband, with amusing songs and ethnic dances. Also celebrated as Koukkoumas on Sými in May.

**Tomato Day.** Age-old Cretan festival in the village of Plátanos near Kíssamos.

### June–August

**Lefkáda Literature and Art Festival.** Theatre, dance, lectures. The event culminates in the presentation of the Peace Medal to individuals or organisations for outstanding contributions to world peace.

## July

**Ithaca Music Contest.** Modern Greek composers show off their work.

**Ikaría Elefthería.** Literature and art festival to celebrate the Aegean islands' liberation from the Turks.

**Kéa Simonida Festival** celebrating the work of the island's famous son, lyric poet Simonídes, 556–468 BC, with theatre, lectures, exhibitions and dance.

**Lato Festival**, Crete. Artistic events in Ag. Nikólaos and the ancient city of Lato.

**Kyrvia Festival**, Crete. Festivities in Ierápetra celebrating one of the town's ancient names. Ticket information, ✆ (0842) 22246.

**Kritsá Festival.** More culture in the village of Krítsá near Agios Nikólaos, Crete.

**Kornaria Festival**, Sitía. Wide range of cultural events in the birthplace of 15th century Cretan poet Kornáros.

**Crete International Festival**, Chaniá. Greek and foreign dance troupes, exhibitions and local celebrations.

**Homage to Cretans Abroad.** Evenings of traditional Cretan music and song, athletics games and folk art exhibitions at Kastélli-Kíssamou.

**Dáphní Wine Festival** near Athens.

## August

**Dionýsia Festival, Náxos.** Modern version of Dionysian revels honouring the god of wine with twenty days of fun including art exhibitions, theatre, sea sports races, free food and wine in the main square, folk dancing in local costumes and a fair on the beach. Also the **Irákleio Festival**, Herákleon, and **Réthimno Wine Festival and Renaissance Fair**, Réthymnon, Crete, ✆ (0831) 22522.

**Sultanina Grape Festival.** Knees-up in Sitía, Crete, ✆ (0843) 28204.

## August–September

**Santoríni Music Festival**, Thíra.

**Kefaloniá International Choir Festival**, Lixoúri. Gathering of Greek and foreign choirs, symphony orchestras and folk dance groups, ✆ (0671) 23535.

## August–October

**Rhodes Festival** with a wide programme of arts activities but the cork has been pulled on the wine tastings in Rodíni Park.

## September

**Gavalchori Folk Festival** with festivities organised by the local Folk Art Museum in the Cretan village.

**Aeschylia Festival**, Elefsína (now a workaday suburb of Athens). Festivities in honour of the founder of Greek tragedy, Aeschylus, born in Eleusis, 525–456 BC.

**Itháki Theatre Competition**, young writers present their plays on Ithaca.

**Chestnut Festival**, Crete. Merry-making and old songs in the village of Élos near Kíssamos where sweets made from chestnuts are offered to visitors.

## November

**Tsikoudiá Festival**. More action in the Kíssamos region, Crete, this time in the village of Voukoliés where you can taste the local *tsikoudiá* liqueur, slightly less powerful than rocket fuel.

## Food and Drink

*Life's fundamental principle is the satisfaction of the needs and wants of the stomach. All important and trivial matters depend on this principle and cannot be differentiated from it.*

Epicurus

The ancient Greeks knew how to let their hair down at their Dionysian revels and these days their descendants share the same philosophy of eat, drink and be merry, for tomorrow...who knows? Food is still important to the Greeks. They eat with relish and zest for life Zorba-style, usually surrounded by family and friends. Greek meals aren't about scaling gastronomic heights—although Epicurus, the classical answer to Egon Ronay, knew a thing or two when it came to food and wine and has given his name to gourmets ever since. Traditional food and cookery reminds the Greeks of who they are and what their country has to offer—fish from the seas, lamb from the mountains, wild herbs and vegetables, *chórta* from the fields, olives from the groves. Food plays a major part in the national identity and varies with the seasons, the Greek Orthodox calendar, festivals and family milestones. Like the people themselves, it has been influenced by the Turks and the Italians and has a Middle Eastern feel.

For all that, Greece has acquired an unjustly poor reputation for food. Most people's idea of taverna fare is the ubiquitous village salad, sad reheated moussaká, kebabs, taramosaláta and more kebabs. Even more insidious are the big resorts where too many tourists spoil the broth and restaurant-owners are pandering to international tastes churning out strange hybrid dishes to appeal to Germans, Brits, Scandinavians who want food from back home. Instead of being welcomed into the kitchens to choose your meal—for many people one of the joys of a Greek holiday—garish photo-boards are springing up outside tavernas to show off what's on the menu McDonald's-style. *Wiener Schnitzel*, fish and chips, pizza, *smorgasbord*, English breakfast are all on offer along with that other delicacy, 'amboorgass', otherwise known as hamburgers. Greek food is being reduced to shrivelled-up *souvlákia*, moussaká in cute earthernware dishes, mass-produced starters like Russian salad and livid pink taramosalata that tastes like polystyrene. Add cold tough chops, barbecued chicken, a few stuffed vine leaves and expensive fish and those out to make a fast buck have compounded the misguided view that all Greek food is unimaginative, largely inedible and best fed to the cats.

It's a vicious circle. Some restaurant owners serve up Euro-nosh because they think it's what we foreigners want. Some, like the hotel owner in Páxos who dished out tinned sprouts with everything because his guests were English—next stop Yorkshire pudding?—try hard but get it all wrong. Tourists eat this junk because by and large they think's there's nothing else. But there is, and it's not too difficult to find. Just follow the Greek families and your nose into the back streets away from the posh white tablecloths, fancy wine glasses and touting waiters of the obvious tourist traps and you can find a treasury of ethnic dishes.

For every taverna that's sold out you can find the real thing if you are prepared to look. Vegetables like butter beans, green beans and okra in rich tomato and olive oil sauces; veal in egg and lemon; *briáms* of aubergines and courgettes; spicy sausages; beetroot with hot garlic *skordaliá* dip; *pastítsio* pasta pie with deep bechamel topping, and island specialities like stuffed, lightly battered courgette flowers, prawns in filo parcels, octopus *stifádo*, beef stew with baby onions, ragout of snails, and whitebait so fresh they're almost wriggling.

Recipes are handed down from mother to daughter, usually over a hot stove, and always make the best of what's in season. Through poverty and resourcefulness Greek cooks have always gathered food for free—fresh young greens from the hills, wild asparagus, sea urchins, snails, fish, fruit and nuts. Bread was baked daily, they made their own cheese, and meals reflected the church calendar, customs and traditions from May Day picnics to Easter feasts. These days the microwave has brought some liberation in the kitchen. But in many places women still cook for their families on tiny gas rings or wood-burning ovens outside the house and rely on the local baker to roast their meat or bake their big trays of biscuits.

One criticism levelled at Greek food by tourists is that it's stone-cold. It usually is, and that's because Greek eating habits differ from ours. They think tepid food is better for the digestion than hot. The climate calls for cool food, too, although in winter you can find plenty of hot stews and casseroles. The pace of life is different. There's no rush. They like to linger over meals with lunches stretching long into the afternoon and dinners into the small hours. While we tend to shovel down TV dinners then rush off, Greeks eat to enjoy, to relax, to share and to celebrate life often bursting into song or dance as the mood takes them. A night out eating with friends is their idea of entertainment and one of the joys of visiting Greece is getting caught up in it all and swept along by the atmosphere.

Greek cuisine often gets slagged off because 'it's swimming in grease'. Food without olive oil is unthinkable to Greeks. They think it aids digestion—it certainly has laxative qualities—and think we're crazy boiling our vegetables until sodden, destroying all the vitamins. They hate water-logged food. Many recipes call for the rich, oily tomato sauce which is a staple for ragouts and vegetable dishes known as *latherá* so it's difficult to avoid. If you don't like oil you can ask for things *chorís láthi*, without oil, or stick to grills and roasts from the barbecue or rotisserie. Look for grills to order, *tis óras*, delicious free-range chickens, lamb or fish scattered with local herbs. People who carp on about Greek food have probably never eaten anything from a real Greek kitchen. Their opinions tend to be based on what they have had in restaurants in the UK which are largely Cypriot, usually serving anglicised versions of the *mezéthes* from home like fried cheese *saganáki* and *chaloúmi* bacon with pitta bread which you won't find on many Greek island menus.

Eating habits are changing, though, as modern, Western ways get a grip. Fast food is becoming popular in the cities, especially with young people, and it's all the rage in Athens to queue up for a Wendy burger or go out for an Italian-style ice-cream, cappuccino or Nescafé frappé with sticky cakes at a gelataria. McDonald's has even sprouted up in Sýntagma Square, a rival attraction to the changing of the guard. While we nibble the traditional Greek takeaways, cheese pies, *tyrópitta*, and *gýro* kebabs, Athenian youth craves Chicken McNuggets and Big Macs. They don't want the greasy spoon tavernas and *kafeneíons* of their grandparents' day, the very places we tourists find enchanting and authentic. While we try to escape the rat race to find sleepy villages and a taste of real Greece, they want junk food, burger joints, cocktail bars and cafeterias, to go with their 501s, Swatches and designer labels. But if your kids have got withdrawal symptoms you know where to send them.

## vegetarians

Of all the people in the EU, the Greeks eat the most meat per capita, but they also eat more cheese per head than anybody, even the French. Basically they just eat a lot, which means there are plenty of dishes for vegetarians, a wide range of pulses and fresh vegetables from artichokes to aubergines as well as okra, beetroot leaves, spinach-style greens with lemon and in some places *cápari*, pickled caper plant which looks like prunings from a rose bush but tastes delicious. There are delicate cheese and spinach pies in flaky filo pastry; stuffed peppers and tomatoes; deep fried courgettes; *dolmádes*, sometimes using cabbage leaves instead of vines; and in Crete *oftés patátes*, potatoes roasted in their jackets. If you're a vegetarian or used to buying pre-packed, sanitised meat, it's worth pointing out that in many parts of Greece, especially the remoter islands, food comes on the hoof, on the wing or in the net. It's not uncommon to see a kid or sheep despatched near a taverna by day and then turn up on the menu at night. Bunnies hopping round the village also hop into the pot, the family pig turns into sausages, free-range chickens end up being barbecued and after a while the washing line of drying octopus becomes part of the scenery.

---

## Eating Out

So how can you find a good place to eat when you're on your travels? In Britain they say the best Chinese restaurants are those packed with Chinese customers and the same applies here. Greek families, workmen, fishermen aren't going to throw away hard-earned cash on tourist food. The back-street taverna may look grotty with plastic tablecloths held down by elastic, hard wooden chairs, and plates and cutlery that don't match, but you can bet that the cooks know what's what and you'll have a meal to remember for a fraction of tourist-trap prices. When you wander round wondering where to eat, use the Old Greek Salad Test. The price of a standard village salad, *choriátiki*, varies enormously—as does the interpretation of the salad—so if it's expensive you can bet the rest will be overpriced too: walk swiftly past. It pays to shop around and go exploring. If you take an interest in food and compliment the chefs, more often than not the wife, Mum and daughters, you could well end up with the recipes, free bottles of wine and invitations to eat with the family. Like everything else in Greece, it's the luck of the draw.

Greek eating places are divided into five categories by the police, who fix the prices. **Tavernas** and **estiatória** or restaurants are found everywhere and the differences between them tend to get a bit blurred. But you'll generally find the *estiatório* has a wider menu, is a bit more upmarket and serves the kind of food you'll find in Greek homes. Tavernas are like family-run bistros and can range from shacks on the beach to barn-like affairs providing music and entertainment in the evening. There may not be a menu as such. The waiter will reel off what's on or you can go and have a look for yourself. Mine host may have some special fish, a lobster or even a 'dish of the day'. In some places there might not be much food at all. One front-room taverna on Kárpathos had only eggs and potatoes on offer which the enterprising owner served up as chip omelettes.

There'll usually be a range of starters from *taramosaláta* to *tzatzíki* or *saganáki* (fried cheese with lemon), maybe a few oven dishes like *pastítsio*, moussaká or stuffed vegetables. Tavernas also feature meat grilled while you wait, *tis óras*, and you can usually choose from chops (*brizóles*) lamb cutlets (*paidhákia*), maybe meatballs like *keftédes* or *tsousoukákia* or sausages, *loukanika*. The menu often includes big trays of different filo pastry pies; maybe green beans, okra or butter beans in sauce or fried courgettes and aubergines. At the seaside you'll find the fish tavernas, *psarotavérnes*, specialising in all kinds of seafood from freshly fried calamari, shrimps, giant prawns, to red mullet, swordfish, bream and sardines. Fish is very expensive in Greece, which seems crazy, but you can get some cheapies like huge dishes of fresh whitebait (*marídes*), cuttlefish stew (*soupiá*), small shrimps (*garídes*), sometimes cooked in feta cheese; and fish soups like *psarósoupa* or spicy *kakavia*, a meal in themselves with hunks of fresh bread and a bottle of wine. When eating fish soup it's customary to remove the fish, put it on a plate, drink the broth then tuck into the fish. Note that each type of fish has its own price, and portions are priced by weight.

If you're a red-blooded **meat eater** then head for the nearest *hasapotavérna*, which is a grill room attached to a local butcher's shop. Not that common, they offer fresh meat of all kinds, kebabs, home-made sausages and sometimes delicious stews. The *psistariá* is another version of the theme specialising in chicken, lamb, pork or *kokorétsi*, a kind of lamb's offal doner kebab, spit-roast over charcoal. Some have electric rotisseries, others hand-cranked *soúvla*.

The *estiatório* is generally open all day and is particularly busy at lunchtime with a wide range of dishes simmering away in the kitchen. As well as all the vegetable dishes in oil, *lathera*, in giant pots there will be fricassees and ragouts like *stifádo* and *kokinistó*, maybe veal *youvétsi* with tear-drop pasta, lamb roast in paper bags, fish with special sauces, liver, as well as the usual pies and starters. Wherever you eat, a typical meal will be bread, a selection of communal starters, salads and main courses, although a recent trend is meals that consist entirely of **mezédes**—a wide variety of well prepared starters, salads or small portions, served with a basket of bread. Only touristy places serve sweets, although you may be able to get yogurt with honey or fresh fruit like watermelon or apple sprinkled with cinnamon. In Crete the **mayerikó** is a cousin of the *estiatório*, a cooking stall where you take your food from the stove by the plateful, *miá merítha*, rather than pick and mix from different pots.

Finding your way round a **Greek menu**, *katálogos*, can be a trial for foreigners with its two-tier prices—with and without tax; you pay the highest. Prices are fixed according to category and there can be seasonal fluctuations like at Easter. If you suspect you're being ripped off, the system makes it easier to complain. Menus usually come in Greek and English, or German, sometimes Italian or Scandinavian languages in big international resorts. The English is often hand-scrawled and full of howlers like Fresh Crap and Lamp Chops (*see* **Topics**, p.68).

And so to Greek **table manners**, which are among the least formal on this planet. It's quite acceptable to pitch into someone else's plate with your fork or offer choice morsels to your neighbour, although what's OK at the local taverna might raise a few eyebrows in top Athenian hotels and international restaurants. Greeks eat fish heads with gusto, pick up chicken, gnaw at bones. Men enjoy feeding women guests tit-bits like baby birds, so if you're eating out with a group of friends including local people don't be surprised if you suddenly get a prawn or a chunk of watermelon thrust at you while your table mates keep pinching your chips. Communal eating with forks and fingers is the norm, usually with dishes arriving at once, and starters are shared. Stagger your orders if you don't want to be overwhelmed.

In the more touristy areas there's been a move to introduce courses, Euro-style, and some restaurants even serve sweets and coffee, something unheard of in the past, when you moved on to the *kafeneío*, cafeteria or *zacharoplasteío* for coffee and a gooey cake or pudding. Side-plates are rare in many tavernas and you just plonk your chunk of bread on a paper napkin. You pour wine for each other—always guests first—and drink constant toasts, glasses chinking—*steen yámass*, good health to us, *steen yássoo* or *yássas*, good health to you or, in Crete, *Avíva* or *Áspro Páto*—bottoms up. By all means clink glasses with someone else, but on no account bring your glass down on another person's (unless your intentions for the evening are entirely dishonourable). If a man does it to your glass, it's best to say 'Cheers' and act dumb, unless you want to take him up on it.

Greeks find the sight of a person eating alone—especially a female—a piteous spectacle, so you may well be asked to join a table. They're naturally hospitable and for many it's still a question of honour to make *xenoí*—the name for guests and strangers are one and the same—feel welcome. For many visitors to Greece, this casual communal spirit is part of the appeal. Most tavernas cram people in, joining up tables, adding chairs to Last Supper proportions, so you won't feel lonely for long. Unless you expressly want to be on your own, or have a romantic table for two, sharing is common and it's easy to get chatting to fellow travellers and holidaymakers if you need some company. Sociability is all if you eat with Greeks and there's no Western nit-picking over who's had what. You share the food, drink, company and the bill, *to logariasmó*, although hosts will seldom let foreign guests part with a drachma. Unless you've agreed to go Dutch or are determined to stand your corner, the idea of women paying is anathema to them.

This welcome is extended to kids of all ages. Some more clued-up places have high chairs, and it's common for Greek families to take the pram and rock baby during the meal, while toddlers crawl under the table and the older children get up to goodness knows what. As Greek children sleep in the afternoons, they always stay up late.

Eating out in Greece has always been something of a movable feast with national rituals. Because of the intense heat in summer, Greek families tend to eat late lunch at home, followed by their siesta or *mesiméri*. Housewives will spend all morning cooking but in the evening everyone will head out to the local taverna, especially at weekends. After the evening *vólta* or stroll to see and be seen—once, and in some remote islands still, the marriage market—you browse around and decide where to go. Greeks eat late, rarely before 10pm, and meals can go on into the small hours. Dinner is often boisterous, punctuated with fiery discussions, maybe bursts of song or dance. It's all to do with the spirit of bonhomie, or *kéfi*, and the more company they have round the table the merrier, and the more likely your meal to turn into a spontaneous cabaret that no tour operator's organized 'Greek Night' can match. You may even get your table whipped away from under you in the jaws of a dancing waiter. *Kalí órexi.* Enjoy. *Bon appetit!*

### prices

An average taverna meal—if you don't order a major fish—usually runs at around 2000–2500dr a head with house wine, which comes by the litre. Prices at restaurants or blatantly touristy places tend to be a bit higher, and places on remote islands can be just as costly because of extra transport prices. In the 'Eating Out' sections of this book, any price given is per person with house wine.

### cafés

Cafés or **kafeneíons** (in small villages these are frequented almost exclusively by men, who discuss the latest news, and play cards or backgammon) serve Greek coffee (*café hellinikó*), which is the same stuff as Turkish coffee. There are 40 different ways to make this, although *glykó* (sweet), *métrio* (medium) and *skéto* (no sugar) are the basic orders. It is always served with a glass of water. Nescafé with condensed Dutch milk has by popular tourist demand become available everywhere, though Greeks prefer it iced (*frappé*) with or without sugar and milk. Soft drinks and ouzo round out the average café fare. Ouzo is a clear anise-flavoured aperitif which many dilute (and cloud) with water. As the Greeks look askance at drunkenness (as they did in ancient times, when they diluted their wine with water and honey), ouzo is traditionally served with a little plate of snacks called *mezédes* which can range from grilled octopus through nuts to cheese and tomatoes, though these days you must request *mezédes* especially in tourist areas. Brandy, or Metaxá (the Greeks know it by the most popular brand name), is usually a late-night treat. The more stars on the label (from three to seven) the higher the price, and in theory at least, the better the quality. In tourist haunts, attempts at milk-shakes, fruit juices, cocktails and even cappuccino are available; in the backwaters you can usually get at least ice cream and good Greek yoghurt (cow, sheep or goat's milk) and honey.

### bars

In the last few years the influx of tourists has resulted in the growth of trendy bars, usually playing the latest hit records and serving fancy cocktails as well as standard drinks. These establishments come to life later in the evening, when everyone has spent the day on the beach and the earlier part of the evening in a taverna. Bars used to close at 3 or 4am or later, although amid protest, the Greek Government in 1994 made this 2am, claiming that the nation is nodding off at work after a night on the tiles. In general they're not cheap, sometimes outrageously dear by Greek standards, and it can be disconcerting to realize that you have paid the same for your Harvey Wallbanger as you paid for your entire meal half an hour before in the taverna next door. Cocktails have now risen to beyond the 1000dr mark in many bars, but before you complain remember that the measures are triples by British standards. If in doubt stick to beer, ouzo, wine and Metaxá (Metaxá and Coke, if you can stomach it, is generally about half the price of the better-known Bacardi and Coke). You may have difficulty in finding beer, as the profit margin is so small that many bars stop serving it in the peak season, thus obliging you to plump for the higher-priced drinks. Another unfortunate practice on the islands is the doctoring of bottles, whereby some bar owners buy cheaper versions of spirits and use them to refill brand-name bottles. The only way to be sure is to see the new bottle being opened in front of you.

## Wine

The best-known wine of Greece, **retsina**, has a very distinctive taste of pine resin, dating from the time when Greeks stored their wine in untreated pine casks. It is an acquired taste, and many people can be put off by the pungent odour and sharp taste of some bottled varieties. Modern retsínas show increasingly restrained use of resin; all retsinas are best appreciated well-chilled. Draught retsína (*retsína varelísio*) can be found only on some islands, but in Athens it is the accepted, delicious accompaniment to the meal. Any taverna worth its salt will serve it, and if it's not available you're in the wrong place, unless you've chosen a foreign or fairly exclusive Greek restaurant. In cases of desperation, where no barrelled retsina is on offer, the wine house Kourtáki produces a very acceptable bottled version at a low price. Retsína is admirably suited to Greek food, and after a while a visitor may find non-resinated wines a rather bland alternative. Traditionally it is served in small tumblers, and etiquette requires that they are never filled to the brim or drained empty; you keep topping up your colleagues' glasses, as best you can.

Ordinary red and white **house wines** are often locally produced bargains—*krasí varelísio* or *krasi cheéma, krasí* meaning wine, *varelísio* from the barrel; *cheéma*, 'loose'. The customary way of serving these is in small, copper-anodized jugs, in various metric measures (500ml and 250ml being the most common; a standard wine bottle holds 750cl). These wines are generally fine, though you may be unlucky and get one that's a stinker.

Greece has an ample selection of medium-priced red and white wines, often highly regionalized with each island and village offering their own unique wines. There are many indigenous Greek grape varieties which avoid the tyranny of Cabernet Sauvignon and Chardonnay. All the principal wine companies—Boutari, Achaia-Clauss, Carras, Tsantali, Kourtaki—produce acceptable table wines at very affordable prices. These large Greek wine producers have been investing heavily in new equipment and foreign expertise over the last decade, and it shows; even that humblest of bottles (and Greece's best-seller) **Deméstika** has become very acceptable of late, and bears little resemblance to the rough stuff that earned it some unflattering sound-alike nicknames. Look out for the nobler labels; Boutari Náoussa is an old-style, slightly astringent red, while Boutari's Grande Réserve is their best red; Lac des Roches is their most popular white on the islands. Peloponnesiakos from Achaia-Clauss is an easy-drinking, light white wine which is faddishly popular at the moment anywhere within exportable distance of the Peloponnese. From Carras, Château Carras is a Bordeaux-style red wine made from the Cabernet Sauvignon and Merlot grapes; if you're lucky you might find Carras Limnio, one of Greece's most distinct red wines. Boutari's Santoríni is their finest island white, while in Rhodes CAIR supplies Greece with its sparkling *méthode traditionelle* white, Caïr. Emery produces some good whites including Villare.

In recent years small wine producers have become very fashionable with the wine-drinking elite of Greece. Some of these island wine-makers are superb; others deserve obscurity. But for the most part you are unlikely to come across them in the average taverna. If you're a wine buff, it's worth seeking them out from local recommendations in off-licences and high-class restaurants; or better still, consult Maggie McNie of the Greek Wine Bureau in London © (0171) 823 3799, who is a Master of Wine and probably the best-qualified expert on Greek wines; she can tell you what to try, or what to bring back with you.

Sámos produces an excellent dessert Muscat. There are various local spirits too; on Níssyros, *soumáda* liqueur is made from almonds.

## Health

In theory there is at least one doctor (*iatrós*) on every island, whose office is open from 9 to 1 and from 5 to 7. On many islands too there are hospitals which are open all day, and usually have an outpatient clinic, open in the mornings. British travellers are often urged to carry a Form E111, available from DSS offices (apply well in advance on a form CM1 from post offices), which admit them to the most basic IKA (Greek NHS) hospitals for treatment; but this doesn't cover medicines or nursing care, which still have to be paid for. In any case, the E111 seems to be looked on with total disregard outside Athens. As private doctors and hospital stays can be very expensive, you should take out a travel insurance policy, then claim your money back on return. Greek general practitioners' fees are, however, usually reasonable.

If you have a serious injury or illness, consider leaving Greece for treatment back home if you are well enough to travel, because even the best hospitals (in Athens) lag many years behind northern Europe or the USA in their methods of care and treatment. It's quite common for families to bring food in for the patient. Make sure your holiday insurance has adequate repatriation cover. Most doctors pride themselves on their English, as do the pharmacists (found in the *farmakeío*), whose advice on minor ailments is good, although their medicine is not particularly cheap. If you forgot to bring your own condoms and are caught short, they are widely available from *farmakeío* and even kiosks, with lusty brand names such as 'Squirrel' or 'Rabbit'. If you can't see them on display, the word *kapótes* (condom) gets results. You can also get the Pill (*chápi antisiliptikó*) morning-after Pill and HRT over the pharmacy counter without a prescription. Be sure to take your old packet to show them the brand you use.

A few hints: Coca Cola or retsina reduces the impact of the oil in Greek foods. Fresh parsley can also help stomach upsets. If anything else goes wrong, old islanders suggest peeing on it.

## Money

The word for **bank** in Greek is *trápeza*, derived from the word *trapézi*, or table, used back in the days of money-changers. On all the islands with more than goats and a few shepherds there is some sort of banking establishment. If there's no bank on the island you're on, the shipping agent will change money, and the post office will change Eurocheques. If you plan to spend time on one of the more remote islands, however, such as Kastellórizo, it is safest to bring enough drachma with you. On the other hand, the small but popular islands often have only one bank, where exchanging money can take a long time. Waiting can be avoided if you go at 8am, when the banks open (normal banking hours are 8–2, 8–1 on Fri). Most island banks are closed on Saturdays and Sundays. Better still, **post offices** will exchange cash, travellers's cheques and Eurocheques; they also charge less commission than banks, and the queues are usually shorter. The numbers of 24-hour **automatic cash-tellers** are growing in Athens and large resorts.

**Credit cards** can be used to withdraw cash at banks; put your account into credit before going abroad, and this will often be the cheapest way to transfer money. The Commercial Bank of Greece will allow you to withdraw money by Visa, and the National Bank of Greece will exchange on Access (MasterCard). Money can also be withdrawn from some automatic tellers (24 hours daily).

**Bank cards**—there are increasing numbers of cash dispensers for Eurocheque cards, Cirrus and Plus cards in Athens and the big tourist resorts.

**Eurocheques** are accepted in banks and post offices.

**Traveller's cheques** are always useful even though commission rates are less for cash. The major brands of traveller's cheques (Thomas Cook and American Express) are accepted in all banks and post offices; take your passport as ID, and shop around for commission rates.

**Running out?** Athens and Piraeus, with offices of many British and American banks, are the easiest places to have money sent by cash transfer from someone at home if you run out—though it may take a few days.

**The Greek drachma** is circulated in coins of 100, 50, 20, 10, 5, 2 and 1 drachma and in notes of 100, 500, 1000 and 5000 drachma. Shops will always round up (or down) to the nearest 5dr.

## Museums

All significant archaeological sites and museums have regular admission hours. Nearly all are closed on Mondays, and open other weekdays from 8 or 9 to around 2, though outdoor sites tend to stay open later, until 4 or 5pm. As a rule, plan to visit cultural sites in the mornings to avoid disappointment, or unless the local tourist office can provide you with current opening times. Hours tend to be shorter in the winter. Students with a valid identification card get a discount on admission fees; on Sundays admission is generally free for EC nationals.

If you're currently studying archaeology, the history of art or the classics and intend to visit many museums and sites in Greece, it may be worth your while to obtain a free pass by writing several weeks in advance of your trip to the Museum Section, Ministry of Science and Culture, Aristídou 14, Athens, enclosing verification of your studies from your college or university. Entrance fees for sites or museums are not listed in this book. Count on 400–800dr in most cases; exceptions are Knossós and the Herákleon Archaeology Museum and the Acropolis and National Archaeology Museum in Athens, plus any others listed in this book as *adm exp.*

## Music and Dancing

Greek music is either city music or village music. The music of the city includes the popular tunes, *rembétika* (derived from the hashish dens of Asia Minor) and most bouzoúki music, whereas village music means traditional tunes played on the Greek bagpipes (*tsamboúna*), the clarinet (*klaríno*), the violin and sometimes the hammer dulcimer (*sandoúri*). Cretan music specializes in the *lýra*, similar to a lap-held fiddle, and is in a category of its own.

On the islands you can hear both city and village music, the former at the *bouzoúkia*, or Greek nightclubs, which feature popular singers. Many play records or washed-out muzak until midnight as the customers slowly arrive. You generally buy a bottle of white wine and fruit and dance until four in the morning, though expect to pay a pretty drachma for the privilege. Smaller, rougher night clubs are called *boites* or *skilákia*—'dog' shops. To hear traditional music, you must go into the villages, to the festivals or weddings; in some places Sunday evening is an occasion for song and dance. Authentic village music is generally unamplified and unpretentious, while city music is the domain of the professional singers, although any bold member of the audience with a good voice can get up to sing a few songs. After a few hours of drinking, a particular favourite or a good dancer is liable to make the enthusiasts

forget the law against *spásimo*, or plate breaking, and supporters may end up paying for missing place settings. If the mood really heats up, men will dance with wine glasses or bottles on their heads, or even sink their teeth into a fully set table and dance without spilling a drop. When the matrons begin to belly-dance on the table, you know it's time to leave.

A phenomenon in recent years on popular islands is packaged 'Greek Nights', in country tavernas where tourists are brought in by coach and entertained by singing and dancing waiters Athens is awash with such tourist shows and discotheques during the summer but starts pulsating to all kinds of Greek music in November, when Pláka is returned to the Athenians. Most musicians on the islands go to Athens in the winter.

The lyrics to most Greek songs deal with the ups and downs of love; *s'agapó*, which you hear in nearly every song, means 'I love you'. Serious composers (Mikis Theodorakis is the best known) often put poetry to music, providing splendid renderings of the lyrics of George Seferis, Odysseas Elytis and Yánnis Rítsos. The guerrillas (*partizánis*) and the Communists have a monopoly on the best political songs, many by Theodorakis. Cretan songs are often very patriotic (for Crete) and many are drawn from the 17th-century epic poem, the *Erotókritos*, written in the Cretan dialect by Vitzéntzios Kornáros.

Every island in Greece has its special dance, although today it is often only the young people's folkdance societies that keep them alive, along with the island's traditional costumes. The best time to find them dancing is on each island's Day of Liberation from the Turks or any other anniversary of local significance. One of the best-known professional folkdance companies, based in Athens, is **Dora Stratou Greek Folk Dances**, Dóra Strátou Theatre, Philopáppou Hill, ✆ 324 4395 or ✆ 921 4650. From beginning of May to end of September, shows begin at 10pm every day, with an additional show at 8pm on Wednesdays and Sundays. Tickets average 1500dr; 8–900dr for students.

Although these shows are beautiful and interesting, there's nothing like getting up to dance yourself—a splendid way to work off the big dinner just consumed at a *panegýri* (festival). For a brief overview of the most popular dances, *see* p.64.

Note that most businesses and shops close down for the afternoon before and the morning after a religious holiday. If a national holiday falls on a Sunday, the following Monday is observed. The Orthodox Easter is generally a week or so after the Roman Easter.

| | | |
|---|---|---|
| **1 January** | New Year's Day | *Protochroniá*; also *Ag. Vassílios* (Greek Father Christmas) |
| **6 January** | Epiphany | *Ta Fórce/ Epifánia* |
| **February–March** | 'Clean Monday' (precedes Shrove Tuesday, and follows a three-week carnival) | *Katharí Deftéra* |
| **25 March** | Greek Independence Day | *Evangelismós* |
| **late March–April** | Good Friday | *Megáli Paraskeví* |
| | Easter Sunday | *Páscha* |
| | Easter Monday | *Theftéra tou Páscha* |
| **May** | Labour Day | *Protomayá* |
| **15 August** | Assumption of the Virgin | *Koímisis tis Theotókou* |
| **28 October** | 'Ochí' Day (in celebration of Metaxás' 'no' to Mussolini) | |
| **25 December** | Christmas | *Christoúyena* |
| **26 December** | Gathering of the Virgin | *Sináxi Theotókou* |

In Greece, Easter is the big national holiday, the equivalent of Christmas and New Year in northern climes and the time of year when far-flung relatives return to Greece to see their families back home; it's a good time of year to visit for atmosphere, with fireworks and feasting. On Kálymnos and Sými they even throw dynamite. After the priest has intoned: '*O Christós Anésti!*'—Christ has risen!—families return home with lighted candles, mark the sign of the cross on the doorpost, and tuck into a special meal of *magirítsa* (lamb innards) soup. On Easter Sunday the Paschal lamb is spit-roasted and music and dancing goes on day and night. After Easter and May 1, spring (*ánixi*—the opening) has offically come, and the tourist season begins. Festival dates for saints' days vary over a period of several given days, or even weeks, due to the Greek liturgical calendar's calculations for Easter; check these locally. It is also important to remember that the main partying for many saintly feasts happens the night *before* the saint's day.

## Packing

Even in the height of summer, evenings can be chilly in Greece, especially when the *meltémi* wind is blowing. Always bring at least one warm sweater and a pair of long trousers. Those who venture off the beaten track into the thorns and rocks should bring sturdy and comfortable shoes—trainers (sneakers) are good. Cover the ankles if you really like wilderness, where scorpions and harmful snakes can be a problem. Plastic swimming shoes are recommended for rocky beaches, where there are often sea urchins; you can easily buy them near any beach if you don't want to carry them around with you.

Summer travellers following whim rather than a predetermined programme should bring a sleeping bag, as lodgings of any sort are often full to capacity. Serious sleeping-baggers should also bring a Karrimat or similar insulating layer to cushion them from the gravelly Greek ground. Torches are very handy for moonless nights, caves and rural villages.

On the pharmaceutical side, seasickness pills, insect bite remedies, tablets for stomach upsets and aspirin will deal with most difficulties encountered. Women's sanitary towels and sometimes Tampax are sold from general stores, but on remote islands you'll need to seek out the *farmakeío*; if there's no pharmacy, you've had it. Soap, washing powder, a clothes line and especially a towel are necessary for those staying in class C hotels or lower. Most important of all, buy a universal-fitting sink plug if you like sinks full of water; Greek sinks rarely have working ones. A knife is a good idea for picnics and *panegýria*, where you are often given a slab of goat meat with only a spoon or fork to eat it with. A photo of the family and home is always appreciated by new Greek friends.

On all the Greek islands except for the most remote of the remote you can buy whatever you forgot to bring. Toilet paper and mosquito coils are the two most popular purchases on arrival. However, special needs such as artificial sweeteners, contact lens products and so on can generally be found in Athens and the more popular islands.

Let common sense and the maxim 'bring as little as possible and never more than you can carry' dictate your packing; work on the theory that however much money and clothing you think you need, halve the clothing and double the money.

## Photography

Greece lends herself freely to beautiful photography, but a fee is charged at archaeological sites and museums. For a movie camera of any kind, including camcorders, you are encouraged to buy a ticket for the camera; with a tripod you pay per photograph at sites, but cameras (especially tripod-mounted ones) are not allowed in museums, for no particular reason other than the museum maintaining a monopoly on its own (usually very dull) picture stock. 35mm film, both print and slide, can be found in many island shops, though it tends to be expensive and the range of film speeds limited (100 ASA and 64 ASA are easily available though if you take slides). Disposable and underwater cameras are on sale in larger holiday resorts. Large islands even have 1-hour developing services, though again this costs more than at home.

The light in the summer is often stronger than it seems and is the most common cause of ruined photographs; opting for slow film (100 ASA or less) will help. Greeks usually love to have their pictures taken, and although it's more polite to ask first, you should just go ahead and take the photo if you don't want them to rush off to beautify themselves and strike a pose. You should avoid taking pictures (well, who would want to anyway?) of the aircraft, military installations and barracks, communications systems on mountain tops, and Army look-out posts. The 'Photography Forbidden' sign shows a camera with a cross through it and speaks for itself.

If you bring an expensive camera to Greece, it never hurts to insure it. Above all, never leave it alone 'for just a few minutes'. Although Greeks themselves very rarely steal anything, other tourists are not so honest.

## Post Offices

Signs for post offices (*tachidromío*) as well as postboxes (*grammatokivótio*) are bright yellow and easy to find. Many post office employees speak English. Stamps can also be bought at kiosks and in some tourist shops, although they charge a small commission. Stamps are *grammatósima*. Postcards can take up to three weeks to arrive at their destinations, or only a week if you're lucky; letters sent abroad are faster, taking just over a week, depending on the route. If you're really in a hurry you can send letters express for extra cost.

If you do not have an address, mail can be sent to you poste restante to any post office in Greece, and can be picked up with proof of identity. After one month all unretrieved letters are returned to sender. If someone has sent you a parcel, you will receive a notice of its arrival, and you must go to the post office to collect it. You will have to pay a handling fee of 650dr, and customs charges and duties should the parcel contain dutiable articles. 'Fragile' stickers attract scant attention. In small villages, particularly on the islands, mail is not delivered to the house but to the village centre, either a café or bakery. Its arrival coincides with that of a ship from Athens.

If you want to mail a package, any shop selling paper items will wrap it for a small fee.

## Sports

### watersports

Naturally these predominate in the islands. All popular beaches these days hire out pedal boats and windsurf boards; some have paragliding and jet skis. Waterskiing prevails on most islands and large hotel complexes. Several islands offer sailing and windsurfing instruction. For more details contact: **Greek Windsurfing Association**, 7 Filellínon Street, Athens ✆ 323 3696.

**Nudism** is forbidden by law in Greece, except in designated areas, such as the more remote beaches of Mýkonos. In practice, however, many people shed all in isolated coves, at the far ends of beaches, or ideally on beaches accessible only by private boat; Rhodes has a particularly high nudity quotient. On the other hand, topless sunbathing is now legal on the majority of popular beaches away from settlements, but do exercise discretion. It isn't worth wounding local sensibilities, no matter how prudish other people's attitudes may seem. You could be arrested on the spot and end up with three days in jail or a stiff fine. Canoodling on public beaches in broad daylight can also offend.

**Underwater activities** with any kind of breathing apparatus are strictly forbidden to keep divers from snatching any antiquities and to protect marine life. However, snorkelling is fine, and Rhodes and Corfu have a diving school. Even if you already know how to dive, you have to go out with their boats.

## Average Sea Temperatures

| Jan | Feb | Mar | Apr | May | Jun | Jul | Aug | Sep | Oct | Nov | Dec |
|-----|-----|-----|-----|-----|-----|-----|-----|-----|-----|-----|-----|
| 59°F | 59°F | 59°F | 61°F | 64°F | 72°F | 75°F | 77°F | 75°F | 72°F | 64°F | 63°F |
| 15°C | 15°C | 15°C | 16°C | 18°C | 22°C | 24°C | 25°C | 24°C | 22°C | 18°C | 17°C |

**Tennis** is very popular in Athens with numerous clubs from Glyfáda to Kifissiá. Otherwise there are courts at all major resort hotels, where, if you are not a resident, you may be allowed to play in the off season.

Greece's arid climate and mountainous terrain make **golf** a rare sport. There are courses on Rhodes and Corfu that admit non-members.

The **Afandou Golf Club**, 19km (12 miles) from Rhodes town, ✆ (0241) 51 255, has 18 holes, par 70. The club has equipment hire and shop, lounges, changing rooms, and a restaurant. Fees are from 3000dr per round, or 16,000dr for seven rounds in one week, lessons 4000dr per half-hour. The Corfu Golf Club, Rópa Valley, P.O. Box 71, ✆ (0663) 94 220, has 18 holes, par 72, practice range, equipment hire and shop, changing rooms and restaurant. Green fees are 7000dr daily in May, Sept and Oct, and less in other months.

Many small riding stables offer horse riding on the islands. In Athens, call the **Riding Club of Greece**, Parádissos, ✆ 682 6128 and Riding Club of Athens, Gerakos, ✆ 661 1088.

## Telephones

The Organismós Telefikoinonía Elládos, or OTE, has offices in the larger towns and at least one on every island that has a telephone service; these are the best place to make international calls. You can call both direct and collect (reverse charges), although the latter usually takes at least half an hour to put through. On the larger islands you may dial abroad direct (for Great Britain dial 0044 and for the USA 001 before the area code). A 3-minute call to the UK will cost about 750dr, to the US 1600dr. You should also use OTE for calling other places in Greece. Telegrams can be sent from OTE or the post office.

Payphones don't exist as such; the few that there were have been replaced with cardphones. Calls can be made from kiosks (more expensive), *kafeneíons*, some travel agents and shops (always ask first). Phonecards are sold at *periptera* for 1000dr for 100 units or *monádes*. It is often impossible to call Athens from the islands in mid-morning; chances improve in the evening. To defeat the beeps, whirrs, and buzzes you often get instead of a connection, wait for the series of six clicks after the area code is dialled before proceeding.

## Toilets

Greek plumbing has improved in the past few years, and in the newer hotels you can flush everything away as merrily as you do at home, at least as often as your conscience lets you on arid islands strapped for water. Tavernas, *kafeneíons* and sweet shops almost always have facilities (it's good manners to buy something before you excuse yourself); there are often public pay toilets in strategic area of the towns.

In older pensions and tavernas, the plumbing often makes up in inventiveness for what it lacks in efficiency. Do not tempt fate by disobeying the little notices 'the papers they please to throw in the basket'—or it's bound to lead to trouble. Also, a second flush in immediate succession will gurgle and burp instead of swallow. Many places in Greece have only a ceramic hole. Women who confront this for the first time should take care not to wet their feet: squat about halfway and lean back as far as you can. Always have paper of some sort handy.

If you stay in a private room or pension you may have to have the electric water heater turned on for about 20 minutes before you take a shower, so if you were promised hot water but it fails to appear, ask. In most smaller pensions, water is heated by a solar panel on the roof, so the best time to take a shower is in the late afternoon, or the early evening (before other residents use up the finite supply of hot water). In larger hotels there is often hot water in the mornings and evenings, but not in the afternoons. Actually 'cold' showers in the summer aren't all that bad, because the tap water itself is generally lukewarm, especially after noon. A good many showers are of the hand-held variety; sinks in Greece rarely have plugs.

Greek tap water is perfectly safe to drink, but on some islands like Chálki and Kálymnos it's very salty and tastes terrible. Big plastic bottles of spring water are widely available, even on ships, and taste better than tap water. On dry islands, remember to ask what time the water is turned off.

## Tourist Information

If the National Tourist Organization of Greece (in Greek the initials are **EOT**) can't answer your questions about Greece, at least they can refer you to someone who can.

**Athens**

> **EOT Information Desk:** National Bank of Greece, Sýntagma Square, 2 Karageórgi Servías Street, ✆ (01) 322 2545, 323 4130.
>
> **EOT, East Airport:** ✆ (01) 969 9500.
>
> Head Office: 2 Amerikís Street, Athens 10564, ✆ (01) 322 3111; ✉ 322 2841.

**Australia**

> 51–57 Pitt Street, Sydney, NSW 2000, ✆ 241 1663/4; ✉ 235 2174.

**Canada**

> 1300 Bay Street, Toronto, Ontario, ✆ (416) 968 2220, ✉ 968 6533.
>
> 1233 De La Montagne, Montreal, Quebec, ✆ (514) 871 1535, ✉ 871 1498

**Great Britain**

> 4 Conduit Street, London W1R 0DJ, ✆ (0171) 734 5997, ✉ 287 1369.

**USA**

> Head Office: Olympic Tower, 645 Fifth Avenue, 5th Floor, New York, NY 10022, ✆ (212) 421 5777; ✉ 826 6940.
>
> 168 N. Michigan Avenue, Chicago, Illinois. 60601, ✆ (312) 782 1084; ✉ 782 1091.
>
> 611 West Sixth Street, Suite 2198, LA, Calif. 90017, ✆ (213) 626 6696; ✉ 489 9744.

Islands without a branch of the EOT often have some form of local tourist office; if not, most have tourist police (often located in an office in the town's police station). You can always tell a tourist policeman from other cops by the little flags he wears on his pocket, showing which languages he speaks. They have information about the island, and can often help you find a room. In Athens there are four tourist police stations, and a magic telephone number—**171**. The voice on 171 not only speaks good English, but can tell you everything from ship departures to where to spend the night.

**Tourist Police in Athens**

Dimitrakopoúlou 77, Veïkoú (the new home of agent 171), open 24 hours

Larissa Train Station, ☎ 821 3574

West Airport, Olympic Airways, ☎ 981 4093

East Airport, ☎ 969 9523

At Piraeus the Tourist Police are on Aktí Miaoúli, ☎ 429 0664, open 8am–11pm only.

## Travelling with Children

Greece is one of the best Mediterranean countries to bring a child, as children are not barely tolerated as they are in more 'sophisticated' holiday resorts, but generally enjoyed and encouraged. Depending on their age, they go free or receive discounts on ships and buses. You can also save on hotel bills by bringing sleeping bags for the children. However, if they're babies, don't count on island pharmacies stocking your baby's brand of milk powder or baby foods—they may have some, but it's safest to bring your own supply. Disposable nappies, especially Pampers, are widely available, even on the smaller islands.

Travelling with a baby is like having a special passport. Greeks adore them, so don't be too surprised if your infant is passed round like a parcel. Greek children usually have an afternoon nap (as do their parents) so it's quite normal for Greeks to eat *en famille* until the small hours. The attitude to children is very different to the British one of being seen but not heard—Greek children are spoiled rotten. Finding a babysitter is never a problem.

Superstitions are still given more credit than you might expect; even in the most cosmopolitan of households, you'll see babies with amulets pinned to their clothes or wearing blue beads to ward off the evil eye before their baptism. Beware of commenting on a Greek child's intelligence, beauty or whatever, as this may call down the jealous interest of the old gods. The response in the old days was to spit in the admired child's face, but these days, superstitious grannies will say the ritual 'phtew-phtew-phtew', as if spitting, to protect the child from harm.

## Where to Stay

### Hotels

All hotels in Greece are divided into six categories: Luxury, A, B, C, D and E. This grading system bears little relationship to the quality of service; it's more to do with how the building is constructed, size of bedrooms, etc. If the hotel has a marble-clad bathroom it gets a higher rating. For this reason, some D and C class hotels can be better than Bs. You may come across government-run hotels, *xenias*, many of which look like barracks. Some of these are better than others. Pensions, some without restaurants, are a confusing subdivision in Greek hotel classifications, especially as many call themselves hotels. They are family-run and more modest (an A class pension is roughly equivalent to a C or D class hotel and is priced accordingly).

### prices

Prices are set and strictly controlled by the tourist police. Off season you can generally get a discount, sometimes as much as 40%. In the summer season prices can be increased by up to 20%. Other charges include an 8% government tax, a 4.5% community bed tax, a 12% stamp tax, an optional 10% surcharge for stays of only one or two days, an air-conditioning surcharge, as well as a 20% surcharge for an extra bed. All these prices are listed on the door of every room and authorized and checked at regular intervals. If your hotelier fails to abide by the posted prices, or if you have any other reason to believe all is not on the level, take your complaint to the tourist police.

---

**1995 hotel rates (drachma) for mid–high season** (1 May–30 Sept)

|  | L | A | B | C | D |
|---|---|---|---|---|---|
| Single room with bath | 9000–30,000 | 6700–15,000 | 6700–10,000 | 4500–8000 | 2700–5000 |
| Double room with bath | 13,100–35,000 | 9900–17,000 | 5700–14,000 | 4600–10,000 | 4000–6000 |

Prices for E hotels are about 20% less than D rates.

---

During the summer, hotels with restaurants may require guests to take their meals in the hotel, either full pension or half pension, and there is no refund for an uneaten dinner. Twelve noon is the official check-out time, although on the islands it is usually geared to the arrival of the next boat. Most Luxury and class A, if not B, hotels situated far from the town or port supply buses or cars to pick up guests. Hotels down to class B all have private bathrooms. In C most do. In D you will usually find a hot shower down the hall, and in E forget it. In these hotels neither towel nor soap is supplied, although the bedding is clean.

The importance of reserving a room in advance, especially during July and August, cannot be over-emphasized. Reservations can be made through the individual hotel or through the Hellenic Chamber of Hotels, 24 Stadíou St, 105 61 Athens, ✆ (01) 323 5485 (from Athens: between 8 and 2); ✉ (01) 322 5449.

In the 'Where to Stay' sections of this book, accommodation is listed according to the following price categories:

| | |
|---|---|
| *luxury* | 28,000 to astronomical |
| *expensive* | 12,000–28,000 |
| *moderate* | 6000–12,000 |
| *inexpensive* | 4000–6000 |

Please note that prices quoted are for double rooms and are approximate.

---

### Rooms (domátia) in Private Homes

These are for the most part cheaper than hotels and are sometimes more pleasant. On the whole, Greek houses aren't much in comparison to other European homes mainly because the Greeks spend so little time inside them; but they are clean, and the owner will often go out of his or her way to assure maximum comfort for the guest. Staying in someone's house can also offer rare insights into Greek domestic taste, which ranges from a near-Japanese simplicity to a clutter of bulging plastic cat pictures that squeak when you touch them; lamps shaped like ships, made entirely of macaroni; tapestries of dogs shooting pool; and flocked sofas covered in heavy plastic that only the Patriarch of the Orthodox Church is allowed to sit on. Increasingly, however, rooms to rent to tourists are built in a separate annexe and tend to be rather characterless concrete barracks, yet some of the newer ones are nicer than hotels.

While room prices are generally fixed in the summer (the going rate in high season is now 4000dr) out of season they are always negotiable with a little finesse, even in June.

Prices depend a lot on the island; fashionable ones like Mýkonos or Santoríni are very expensive. Speaking some Greek is the biggest asset in bargaining, although not strictly necessary. Claiming to be a poor student is generally effective. Always remember, however, that you are staying in someone's home, and do not waste more water or electricity than you need. The owner will generally give you a bowl to wash your clothes in, and there is always a clothes line.

The tourist police on each island have all the information on rooms and will be able to find you one, if you do not meet a chorus of Greeks chanting 'Rooms? Rooms?' as you leave the boat. Many houses also have signs.

### Youth Hostels

Some of these are official and require a membership card from the Association of Youth Hostels, or alternatively an International Membership Card (about 2600dr) from the Greek Association of Youth Hostels, 4 Dragatsaníou Street, Athens, ✆ 323 4107; other hostels are informal, have no irksome regulations, and admit anyone. Most charge extra for a shower, sometimes for sheets. Expect to pay 1200–2000dr a night, depending on the quality of facilities and services offered. The official ones have a curfew around midnight.

### Camping Out

The climate of summertime Greece is perfect for sleeping out of doors. Unauthorized camping is illegal in Greece, although each village on each island enforces the ban as it sees fit. Some couldn't care less if you put up a tent at the edge of their beach; in others the police may pull up your tent pegs and fine you. All you can do is ask around to see what other tourists or friendly locals advise. In July and August you only need a sleeping bag to spend a pleasant night on a remote beach, cooled by the sea breezes that also keep the mosquito menace at bay. Naturally, the more remote the beach, the less likely you are to be disturbed. If a policeman does come by and asks you to move, though, you had best do so; be diplomatic. Many islands have privately operated camping grounds—each seems to have at least one. These are reasonably priced, though some have only minimal facilities. The National Tourist Office controls other, 'official' campsites which are rather plush and costly.

There are three main reasons behind the camping law: one is that the beaches have no sanitation facilities for crowds of campers; secondly, forest fires are a real hazard in summer; and thirdly, the law was enacted to displace gypsy camps, and is still used for this purpose. If the police are in some places lackadaisical about enforcing the camping regulations, they come down hard on anyone lighting any kind of fire in a forest, and may very well put you in jail for two months; every year forest fires damage huge swathes of land.

Camping prices are not fixed by law but these are the approximate guidelines.

### National Tourist Office of Greece (EOT) camping rates (per day during high season)

| | |
|---|---|
| Adult | 800–900dr |
| Child (4–12) | 400–500dr |
| Caravan | 1000dr |

| Small tent | 650dr |
|------------|-------|
| Large tent | 900dr |
| Car | 500dr |
| Electricity | 500dr |

## Renting a House or Villa

On most islands it is possible to rent houses or villas, generally for a month or more at a time. Villas can often be reserved from abroad: contact a travel agent or the National Tourist Organisation (EOT) for names and addresses of rental agents, or see the list below. In the off season villas may be found on the spot with a little enquiry; with luck you can find a house sleeping 2–3 people, and depending on the facilities it can work out quite reasonably per person. Quite a few islands now have sophisticated villa rentals (i.e. with a large number of purpose-built properties with all the amenities, handled by agents in Athens, Great Britain and North America). Facilities normally include a refrigerator, hot water, plates and utensils, etc. Generally, the longer you stay the more economical it becomes. Things to check for are leaking roofs, creeping damp, water supply (the house may have a well) and a supply of lamps if there is no electricity.

## self-catering holidays

More than a hundred British tour operators run package holidays to Greece from the big high street names offering the usual sun, sea, sand and whatever else take your fancy at the main-stream resorts to the small independent companies featuring the more remote or unspoiled islands. Packages vary with accommodation in luxury hotel complexes to basic village rooms, converted windmills, fisherman's cottages to beautifully restored mansions. Rooms over tavernas, family-run pensions, traditional ethnic settlements and purpose-built villas are all there for the taking depending on what you want from your Greek odyssey. Packages include flights, transfers by coach, ferry, hydrofoil or domestic planes, and accommodation. If you prefer to have everything arranged for you but don't want to be herded, many of the operators listed here offer 'loosely packaged' holidays that will appeal to free spirits and independently-minded travellers.

By and large you won't find the specialist brochures at your travel agent as many are small operations belonging to the **Association of Independent Tour Operators** who tend to advertise in the quality Sunday papers or depend on word-of-mouth recommendations from clients. So if you're looking for something completely different get a copy of the tour operators' list from your Greek National Tourist Organisation (for telephone numbers, *see* p.16) or 4 Conduit Street, London W1R 0DJ, ✆ 0171 734 5997.

The specialist companies listed below offer packages on a wide range of islands with hand-picked accommodation ranging from villas and small hotels to restored village houses and unusual ethnic gems, designed for visitors who want to avoid the concrete jungles of mass tourism and enjoy the true spirit of Greece.

**Kosmar Villa Holidays Plc**, 358 Bowes Road, Arnos Grove, London N11 1AN, ✆ (0181) 368 6833. Self-catering villas, studios and apartments from Crete to Corfu, Rhodes, Sými, Kos and the Argo-Saronics. Two-centre holidays, flights from Glasgow and Newcastle and family savers.

**Laskarina Holidays**, St Mary's Gate, Wirksworth, Derbyshire, ✆ 01629 822203/4 and 824881/4. Named after the heroine of Spétses, Laskarina has the largest independent programme in Greece and now embraces the late lamented **Timsway**. Specialising in the Sporades, the lesser known islands of the Dodecanese and Spétses, with restored traditional accommodation stringently selected by directors Kate and Ian Murdoch. There is a knowledgeable information team with a green approach. The Murdochs were made citizens of Sými for services rendered and Kate Murdoch shares honorary citizenship of Chálki, the former UNESCO island of Peace and Friendship, with Baroness Thatcher. Two-centre holidays, out of season long stays available.

**Greek Sun Holidays**, 1 Bank Street, Sevenoaks, Kent TN13 1UW, ✆ (01732) 740317. Helpful, family-run Greek specialists offering Athens and wide range of unusual islands like Síkinos, Mílos and Límnos. Tailor-made holidays, tours and two-centre breaks.

**Greek Islands Club**, 66 High Street, Walton-on-Thames KT12 1BU, ✆ (01932) 220477. Ionian Islands specialists including Kýthera, plus sailing and activity holidays.

**Filoxenia Ltd**, Sourdock Hill, Barkisland, Halifax, West Yorkshire HX4 0AG, ✆ (01422) 371796. Not so much tailor-made as haute couture holidays to Athens and a select range of islands from tiny Elafónissos and unknown Amoliani to arty Hýdra, Chíos and quiet parts of Corfu. Suzi Stembridge and family have scoured Greece for unusual holiday places and pass on their favourites to fellow Grecophiles. Houses, villas, tavernas, pensions, fly-drive and special interest tours. Also **Opus 23** for travellers with disabilities.

**Manos Holidays**, 168–172 Old Street, London EC1V 9BP, ✆ (0171) 216 8000. Good value holidays to the major resorts and lesser-known islands, island-hopping and two-centres. Friendly approach, ideal for children, low season specials and singles deals.

**Direct Greece**, Halliburton House, 5 Putney Bridge Approach, London SW6 3JD, ✆ (0171) 371 9595. Particularly good for Líndos on Rhodes with a wealth of traditional Lindian houses. Jenny May is uncrowned queen of Líndos and an expert on the area. Also villas and apartments on Andros, Lésbos, Chálki, Lefkáda and Zákynthos plus low season specials.

**Corfu à la Carte**, 8 Deanwood House, Stockross, Newbury, Berks RG16 8JP, ✆ (01635) 30621. Select range of beach and rural cottages on Skiáthos, Corfu and Páxos.

**Specialist Vacations**, 63 Cambridge Grove Road, Kingston-upon-Thames, Surrey KT1 3HB, ✆ (0181) 974 8373. Focus on the lesser-known Dodecanese islands like Chálki, Léros and Kálymnos, plus Sámos. Aim to fill the gap left by former Twelve Islands Holidays and Timsway with villas, apartments and select small hotels. Infants travel free, courtesy hampers and bar packs await to mix with your duty frees.

**Simply Simon Holidays Ltd**, 1/45 Nevern Square, London SW5 9PF, ✆ (0171) 373 1933. Cyclades specialists for Mýkonos, Kýthnos and Kéa.

**Pure Crete**, 90–92 Southbridge Road, Croydon, Surrey CRO 1AF, ✆ (0181) 760 0879. Houses and farms on Crete.

**Skiathos Holidays**, 4 Holmedale Road, Kew Gardens, Richmond, Surrey GU13 8AA, ✆ (0181) 940 5157. Packages to Skiáthos and other Sporades islands.

**Ilios Island Holidays**, 18 Market Square, Horsham, West Sussex RH12 1EU, ✆ (01403) 259788 Holidays to the Ionians and Sporades, Tínos and Náxos and the chance to rent the island of Argirónissos oppisite Évia.

**Catherine Secker (Crete)**, 102A Burnt Ash Lane, Bromley, Kent BR1 4DD, ✆ (0181) 460 8022. Home-run business with the personal touch featuring luxury villas with swimming pools on the Akrotíri Peninsula near Chaniá. Catherine Secker offers all mod cons in quiet beachside villages with everything from hairdryers to highchairs and toyboxes. Removal of noisy dogs and cockerels guaranteed.

**CV Travel**, 43 Cadogan Street, London SW3 2PR, ✆ (0171) 581 0851. Upmarket villas on Corfu and Páxos.

**Island Wandering**, 51A London Road, Hurst Green, Sussex TN19 7QP, ✆ (01580) 860733, 📠 (01580) 860282. Island-hopping without tears. Perm any 40 isles in the Cyclades, Dodecanese, Northeast Aegean pre-booked before you go or with a wandering voucher system. Also Open Jaws Argosy, fly/drive on Crete. Charters from most UK airports plus scheduled Athens flights.

**Sunseekers**, Revenue Chambers, St Peter's Street, Huddersfield, West Yorks HD1 1DL, ✆ (01484) 511224. Good for northern travellers with flights from Leeds/Bradford and Manchester including Lésbos, Kálymnos, Sámos, Santoríni, plus the only direct UK flight to Kárpathos.

**Cycladic Environments**, PO Box 382622, Cambridge, MA 02238-2622, ✆ (800) 719 5260, 📠 (617) 492 5881. This USA-based conservation group has a range of traditional properties to let in the village of Oía on Santoríni, furnished with local embroideries and handcarved furniture. All houses are located on the volcanic cliffside, with private terraces overlooking the caldera. Special rates available for students on fellowships and academic researchers.

### *art centres of the School of Fine Arts*

Four of the five annexes of the Athenian School of Fine Arts are located on the islands, at Rhodes, Lésbos, Hýdra and Mýkonos. These provide inexpensive accommodation for foreign artists (for up to 20 days in the summer and 30 in the winter) as well as studios, etc. One requirement is a recommendation from the Greek embassy in the artist's home country. Contact its Press and Information Office for further information.

## Women Travellers

Greece is fine for women travellers but foreign women travelling alone can be viewed as an oddity. Be prepared for a fusillade of questions. Greeks tend to do everything in groups or pairs and can't understand people who want to go solo. That said, Greece is a choice destination for women travelling on their own. Out of respect, Greeks on the whole refrain from annoying women as other Mediterranean men are known to do, while remaining friendly and easy to meet; all Greek men from sixteen to sixty like to chat up foreign women, but extreme coercion and violence such as rape is rare. While some Greek men can't fathom what sexual equality might possibly mean—they are usually the same who hold the fantasy that for a woman a night without company is unbearable mortification of the flesh—they are ever courteous and will rarely allow even the most liberated female (or male) guest to pay for anything.

In the major resorts like Rhodes and Corfu tourist women are considered fair game, fish to be speared in more ways than one by the local lads throughout the season. A *kamáki* is a harpoon in Greek, and it's what the Greeks call those Romeos who roar about on motorbikes, hang out in the bars and cafés, and hunt in pairs or packs. Their aim is to collect as many women as possible, notching up points for different nationalities. There are highly professional *kamákis* in the big resorts, gigolos who live off women tourists, gathering as many foreign hearts plus gold chains and parting gifts as they can; they overwinter all over the world with members of their harem. Other Greeks look down on them, and consider them dishonourable and no good.

Many young Greek women are beginning to travel alone—that leggy blonde with the rucksack could just as well be Greek as Swedish nowadays—but this is no indication that traditional values are disappearing. Although many women in the larger towns now have jobs, old marriage customs still exert a strong influence, even in Athens. Weddings are sometimes less a union of love than the closing of a lengthily negotiated business deal. In the evenings, especially at weekends, you'll see many girls of marriageable age join the family for a seaside promenade, or *vólta*, sometimes called 'the bride market'. A young man, generally in his late twenties or early thirties, will spot a likely girl on the promenade or will hear about her through the grapevine. He will then approach the father to discover the girl's dowry—low wages and high housing costs demand that it contains some sort of living quarters from the woman's father, often added on top of the family house. The suitor must have a steady job. If both parties are satisfied, the young man is officially introduced to the daughter, who can be as young as 16 in the villages. If they get along well together, the marriage date is set. The woman who never marries and has no children is sincerely pitied in Greece. The inordinate number of Greek widows (and not all wear the traditional black) is due to the average 10- to 20-year age difference between husband and wife.

Because foreign men don't observe the Greek customs, their interest in a Greek woman will often be regarded with suspicion by her family.

## Working

If you run out of money in Greece, it usually isn't too difficult to find a temporary job on the islands, ranging from polishing cucumbers to laying cement or working in a bar or restaurant in a resort (although with the influx of impecunious Albanians these are becoming harder to find). The local *kafeneíon* is a good place to enquire. Work on yachts can sometimes be found by asking around at the Athenian marinas, especially at Zéa Marína. The theatre agents, for work as extras in films, are off Academiás Ave, by Kánigos Square. Teachers may apply to one of the seven English/American schools in Athens, or apply as an English teacher to a *frontistírion* or private school. These usually demand a university degree or TEFL (teaching English as a foreign language) certificate. EU citizens can often find jobs as greeters/co-ordinators with island travel offices that deal with package tour companies. The *Athens News*, the country's English daily, and *The Athenian*, a monthly publication, often have classified advertisements for domestic, tutorial, and secretarial jobs.

# Modern History, Art and Architecture

*Greece has been undergoing a political crisis for the past 3000 years.*

–politician during a recent election campaign

Aristotle declared man to be a political animal, and to this day no animal is as political as a Greek. If there are two *kafenéions* in a village, one inevitably will be the haunt of the Socialists, the other the Conservatives. Even barber shops have their political affiliations. On the average, over 50 parties crowd the ballot in the national elections, among them five different flavours of Communists and exotica like the the Self-respect party, the Fatalist party (this one is quite popular) and the Party of Parents of Many Children. If you visit during an election, all means of transport to the islands will be swamped with Athenians returning to their native villages to vote. To understand current Greek views and attitudes, a bit of recent history under your belt is essential; ancient and Byzantine history, which touches Greece less closely today, is dealt with under Athens and the individual islands.

## The Spirit of Independence

From the days of Alexander the Great, Greeks have lived not only within the boundaries of modern-day Greece but throughout Asia Minor and the Middle East. Although founded as a new Rome by Constantine, Constantinople was their Christian capital, *The City* of the Greeks; in the Middle Ages Athens was a backwater. Not even during the 400-year Turkish occupation did the Greeks stop considering themselves Greeks—and the Turks, for the most part, were content to let them be Greek as long as they paid their taxes.

The revolutionary spirit that swept through Europe at the end of the 18th and beginning of the 19th centuries did not fail to catch hold in Greece, by now more than weary of the lethargic inactivity and sporadic cruelties of the Ottomans. The Greek War of Independence began in the Peloponnese in 1821, and continued for more than six years in a series of bloody atrocities and political intrigues and divisions. In the end the Great Powers, namely Britain, Russia and France, came to assist the Greek cause, especially in the decisive battle of Navarino (20 October 1827) which in effect gave the new Greek government the Peloponnese and the peninsula up to a line between the cities of Arta and Volos. Count John Capodístria of Corfu, ex-secretary to the Tsar of Russia, became the first President of Greece. While a king was sought for the new state, Capodístria's independent policies offended the pro-British and pro-French factions in Greece—and also the powerful Mavromikális, family who assassinated him in 1831. Before the subsequent anarchy spread too far, the Great Powers found a king of the Greeks in Otho, a high-handed son of Ludwig I of Bavaria, who immediately offended Greek sensibilities by giving Germans all the official posts.

## The Birth of The Great Idea

The fledgling Greek state was born with what was known as the *Megáli Idéa* or 'Great Idea' of liberating and uniting all the Greeks into a kind of Byzantium Revisited, although Athens lacked the muscle to do anything about it. Otho's arrogant inadequacies led to revolts and his dethronement in 1862, but the Great Powers found a replacement in William George, son of the King of Denmark. The National Assembly drew up a constitution in 1864 which made the nation officially a democracy under a king, a system that began to work practically under Prime Minister Kharílaos Trikoúpis in 1875. In the long reign of George I, Greece began to develop, with an economy based on shipping.

In 1910 the great statesman from Crete, Elefthérios Venizélos, became Prime Minister of Greece for the first time. Under his direction, a chance to further the Great Idea came in the form of the two Balkan Wars of 1912–13; as a result Crete, the Northeastern Aegean islands, Macedonia and southern Epirus were annexed to Greece. In the meantime King George was assassinated by a madman, and Constantine I ascended to the throne. Constantine had married Kaiser Wilhelm's sister, and, when the First World War broke out, so did an internal dispute in Greece. Venizélos supported the Allies and Constantine the Central Powers, although officially he remained neutral until the Allies forced him to mobilize the Greek army. Meanwhile, in the north of Greece, Venizélos had set up his own government with volunteers in support of the Allies.

The war to end all wars hardly extinguished the Great Idea. Venizélos took advantage of the anarchy in Turkey to claim Smyrna at Versailles. Believing they had the backing of the Great Powers, especially Britain's Lloyd George, Venizélos' successors ordered Greek forces to occupy Smyrna and advance on Ankara. It was, as the Greeks call it, a catastrophe. The Turks, under nationalist leader Mustapha Kemal (later Atatürk) had grown far more formidable after their defeats in the Balkans and elsewhere than the Greeks had imagined, and in August 1922 the Greek army was forced back and routed at Smyrna, with enough atrocities commited on both sides to embitter relations for decades. Constantine immediately abdicated in favour of his son George II; the government fell and Colonel Plastiras with his officers took over, ignobly executing the ministers who had ordered the invasion. Tragically, massive population exchanges were seen to be the only solution to the crisis; nationalistic ethnic cleansing was invented and Greece, then with a population of 4,800,000, was confronted with the difficulties of finding housing and work for over a million Anatolian refugees.

In 1929 a republic was proclaimed which lasted for ten shaky years. Trade unions and the Greek communist party, or KKE, were formed and gained strength. Venizélos was re-elected President and set the present borders of Greece (except for the Dodecanese Islands, which belonged to Italy until 1945). His term saw the first uprising by Greek Cypriots, four-fifths of the population of what was then a British Crown Colony, who desired union with Greece.

## World War–Civil War

The republic, beset with economic difficulties, collapsed in 1935, and King George II returned to Greece, with General Metaxás as his Prime Minister. Metaxás assumed dictatorial control under the regime of 4 August, which crushed the trade unions and all leftist activities, installed rigorous censorship and exiled the opposition. Although a sympathizer with Fascist forms of government, Metaxás prepared the Greek army in advance against occupation, and on 28 October 1940, as the story goes, responded with a laconic '*Óchi!*' (No!) to Mussolini's demands that his troops massed on the Albanian border be allowed passage through Greece. Greece was the first Allied country voluntarily to join Britain against the Axis, and not only stopped the Italians, but pushed them back into Albania.

But by May 1941, after the Battle of Crete, all Greece was in the hands of the Nazis, and George II was in exile in Egypt. The miseries of Occupation (an estimated 500,000 people starved to death) were compounded by political strife, fired by the uncertain constitutionality of a monarch who had been acting for so many years without parliamentary support. The Communist-organized EAM, the National Liberation Front, and its army, ELAS, led the resistance and had vast popular support, but its politics were hardly palatable to Churchill, who was keen on restoring the monarchy. Neither side would compromise and Civil War broke out three short months after the liberation of Greece, beginning in Athens with fighting between British troops and ELAS and followed by drawn-out guerrilla campaigns in the mountains. At the end of the Second World War, Britain's Stop-the-Reds policy was taken over by the Truman Doctrine and American economic support and advisors poured into Greece. The Civil War dragged on until 1949; leftists who were not shot or imprisoned went into exile.

## Recovery and Cyprus

Recovery was very slow, even if orchestrated by America, and the Greek diaspora that began at the beginning of the 20th century became so great that entire villages, especially on the islands, were abandoned. With the Korean War in 1951 Greece and Turkey became full members of NATO, an uncomfortable arrangement from the start because of the unresolved issue of Cyprus, still ruled by Britain. General Papagos of the American-backed Greek Rally party won the elections of 1952. In 1954, the Greek Cypriots, led by Archbishop Makários, clamoured and rioted for union with Greece. Either for military reasons or to prevent a new conflict between Greece and Turkey, the Americans and British turned a deaf ear. Meanwhile Papagos died, and the more liberal Konstantínos Karamanlís replaced him as Prime Minister for the next eight years, inaugurating an era of stability and prosperity as agriculture and tourism began to make their contributions to the economy. The opposition to Karamanlís criticized him for his pro-Western policy and inability to solve the worsening situation in Cyprus. Because of the island's one-fifth Turkish population, Turkey would not agree on union for Cyprus—the independence or partitioning of the island was as far as Ankara would go. In 1960, a British-brokered compromise was reached, although it had little appeal for the Greeks: Cyprus became an independent republic and elected Makários its first President. Britain took care to retain sovereignity over its military bases.

To add to the unhappiness over Cyprus, unemployment reached new heights. The royal family, especially the neo-Fascist Queen Frederíka, were unpopular, there were strikes and strong anti-American feelings. In 1963 came the assassination of left-wing Deputy Lambrákis (see Costa Gravas' film *Z*) for which police officers were tried and convicted. Karamnlís resigned and lost the next elections in 1965 to George Papandréou of the centre-left opposition. At the same time, King Paul, son of George II, died and was succeeded by his son, the 23-year-old strongly conservative Constantine II. The combination did not bode well; a quarrel with the King over reforming the equally strongly conservative military led to Papandréou's resignation in 1966. Constantine was meant to call for new elections but, fearing Papandréou's re-election, he tried instead to organize a coalition (around future Néa Demokratikí leader, Konstantínos Misotákis). Massive discontent finally forced Constantine to call for elections in May; on 21 April 1967, a coup by an obscure group of colonels established a military dictatorship and imprisoned George Papandréou and his son Andréas (an economics professor at Harvard and Adlai Stevenson's campaign manager), charging the latter with treason. Colonel George Papadópoulos became dictator of the junta. Constantine II attempted a ridiculous counter-coup and then fled to Rome.

## Greece's Moral Cleansing

The proclaimed aim of the colonels' junta—propped up by the CIA—was a moral cleansing of 'Orthodox Christian Greece'. Human rights were suppressed, strict and often absurd censorship undermined the nation's cultural life, and the secret police imprisoned and tortured thousands of dissidents—or their children. The internal situation went from bad to worse, and on 17 November 1973 students of the Polytechnic school in Athens went on strike. Tanks were brought in and many students were killed. After this incident, popular feeling rose to such a pitch that Papadópoulos was arrested, only to be replaced by his arrester, the head of the secret military police, Ioannídes. Greece was in turmoil. Attempting to save the situation by rallying the national Great Idea, Ioannídes tried to launch a coup in Cyprus, to assassinate Makários and replace him with a president who would declare the long-desired union of Cyprus with Greece. It was a fiasco. Makários fled, and the Turkish army invaded Cyprus, occupying 40% of the island. The Greek military rebelled, the dictatorship resigned and Karamanlís hurriedly returned from his exile in Paris to form a new government, release the political prisoners, order a ceasefire in Cyprus and legalize the Communist party.

## A New Greek Alphabet: ND, EEC, PASOK

Karamanlís and his conservative Néa Dimokratikí (ND) easily won the November 1974 elections; the monarchy did less well in the subsequent plebiscite and Greece became a republic and member of the European Economic Community (EEC). Karamanlís brought stability but neglected the economic and social reforms Greece needed so badly; these, along with a desire for national integrity and an independent foreign policy, were to be the ticket to populist Andréas Papandréou's victories beginning in 1981. His party, PASOK (the Pan-Hellenic Socialist Movement, with a rising green sun symbol) promised much, beginning with withdrawal from NATO and the EEC, and the removal of US air bases; understandably, Papandréou's anti-US and Europe rhetoric was music to Greek ears. PASOK's sun shone over some long-awaited reforms, especially women's rights, and a heady and hedonistic liberalization swept the land, leading PASOK to triumph in the 1985 elections, in spite of Papandréou's failure actually to deliver Greece from the snares of NATO, the US or the EEC or to keep his promises on the economic front. Inflation soared, and after the election Greece had to be bailed out by a huge EEC loan and an unpopular belt-tightening austerity programme. In the end, however, it was scandals and corruption that brought PASOK down; the elderly Papandréou's open affair with a much younger woman—Dímitri (Mimi) Liáni, now his wife—and the Bank of Crete corruption scandal didn't go down well in an essentially conservative country.

In 1990 the PASOK sun was eclipsed as Misotákis and the Néa Demokratikí (ND) conservatives took a slim majority in the elections to grapple with Greece's economic problems. ND immediately launched a wave of austerity measures which proved even more unpopular than Papandréou—a crackdown on tax evasion, which is rife in Greece; a wage freeze for civil servants; privatization of most state-run companies, including Olympic Airways; and steep increases in charges for public services. This sparked off a wave of strikes in 1991 and 1992. By late 1992 Mitsotákis was also involved in political scandals, and in 1993 a splinter party formed, Political Spring, led by Antónis Samarás. The principal effect of this was to split the votes and topple ND when a general election was held in October 1993.

Voters decided that PASOK, led by gritty old Andréas Papandréou, was the lesser of two evils. Papandréou started off his term by forming a cosy political dynasty, appointing his young wife as chief of staff, his son the deputy foreign minister, and his own doctor the minister of health. But the increasingly senile Papandréou's own health is poor, and most Greeks doubt his ability to administer the medicine Greece needs. Economic problems and the rising foreign debt haunt the country, as even the pop songs sing the wonders of the 'Delors Package' which has brought the country new roads, schools, sewers, and agricultural subsidies, courtesy of European Union taxpayers. Greece's relations with its Balkan neighbours continue to range from uneasy to nasty: continuing conflict with Turkey over Cyprus and Aegean borders, the influx of impoverished Albanian refugees and troubles over ethnic Greeks in Albania, and the suspect intentions of an independent Macedonia and Bulgaria on the northern frontier. Sometimes a Greek will suddenly ask you, 'Why doesn't anybody like us?'. The new disease among teenagers and young adults, in spite of all the designer clothes and electronic gear lavished on them by the new breed of Greek parents, is melancholia.

## A Brief Outline of Greek Art and Architecture

The oldest known settlements on the Greek islands date back to approximately 6000 BC—Knossós and Phaistós on **Crete**, obsidian-exporting Fylokopí on **Mílos**, sophisticated Paleóchnoe on **Límnos** and Ag. Iríni on **Kéa**. Artistic finds are typical of the era elsewhere—dark burnished pottery, decorated with spirals and wavy lines and statuettes of the fertility goddess in stone or terracotta.

### Bronze Age: Cycladic and Minoan styles (3000–1100 BC)

Contacts with Anatolia and the Near East brought Crete and the Cyclades to the cutting edge of not only Greek, but European civilization. Around 2600 BC Cycladic dead were buried with extraordinary white marble figurines rubbed smoothly into shape with emery that border on the modern abstract (in the museums in **Náxos** and **Athens**). In the same period the first Minoans in Crete were demonstrating a precocious artistic talent in their polychrome pottery, elegant stone vases and gold jewellery. By the Middle Minoan period (2000–1700 BC) when Crete ruled the Aegean with its mighty fleet the Minoan priest-kings were secure enough from external and internal threats to build themselves unfortified palaces and cities, inevitably centred around a large rectangular courtyard. They installed a complex system of canals and drains, and, judging by the translations of the writing they left

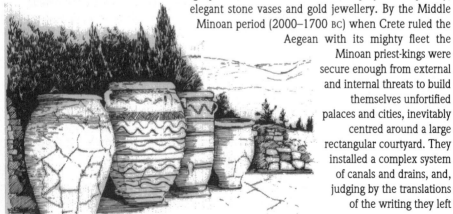

behind, Linear A and Linear B, they were great bureaucrats who kept careful accounts of the magazines of oil, honey, wine and grain stored in huge *pithoi* which characterize Minoan palaces and villas. The civilization reached its apogee between 1700–1450 BC. The Minoans had colonies across the Aegean and their elegant ambassadors figured in the tomb paintings of the Pharaohs; their own palaces at **Knossós, Phaistós, Zákros, Mália** and at their outpost of Akrotíri on the island of **Santoríni** were adorned with elegant frescoes of flowers, animals, human figures and bull dancers and other treasures now in the archaeology museums of **Herákleon** and **Athens**.

Built mostly of wood and unbaked brick, the Minoan palaces collapsed like card castles in the earthquakes and dramatic fires that marked the end of their civilization. The Achaeans of Mycenae rushed in to fill the vacuum of power and trade in the Aegean, taking over the Minoan colonies, adopting Linear B script and Minoan artistic techniques, especially in gold-work and ceramics. Little of this ever reached the islands, although many have vestiges of the Achaeans' impressive stone walls, known as **cyclopean** after their gigantic blocks. Impressive as they are, they failed to keep out the northern invaders known as the Dorians, who destroyed what remained of Aegean unity in the confusing aftermath of the Trojan War and ushered in one of history's perennial Dark Ages.

## Geometric (1000–700 BC) and Archaic (700–500 BC)

The break-up of the Minoan and Mycenaean world saw a return to agriculture and the evolution of the *pólis*, or city-state. In art the Geometric period refers to the simple, abstract decoration of the pottery; traces of Geometric temples of brick and wood are much rarer. The temple of Apollo at Dréros on Crete and the first Temple of Hera on **Sámos** were built around the 8th century, although the discovery in 1981 of the huge sanctuary at **Lefkándi** on Évia, believed to date from *c.* 900 BC, has called previous chronological assumptions into question. The most complete Geometric town discovered so far is Zagorá on **Ándros**.

The Archaic Period is marked by the change to stone, especially limestone, for the building of temples and a return to representational art in decoration. The first known stone temple—and a prototype of the Classical temple with its columns, pediments and metopes—was **Corfu**'s stout-columned Doric Temple of Artemis (580 BC), its pediment decorated with a formidable 3½m relief of Medusa (now in Corfu's museum). The beautiful Doric Temple of Aphaia on **Aegina** was begun in the same period and decorated with a magnificent 6th-century pediment sculpted with scenes from the Trojan war (now in Munich). The

DORIC

IONIC

CORINTHIAN

excavations at Embório, on **Chíos**, are among the best extant records we have of an Archaic town; the 6th-century Efplinion tunnel at Pythagório, **Sámos** was the engineering feat of the age.

This era also saw the beginning of life-size—and larger—figure sculpture, inspired by the Egyptians; poses are stiff, formal, and rigid, one foot carefully placed before the other. Unlike Egyptian models, however, Greek statues are marked by their easy, confident Archaic smiles, as if life were all really a secret joke. The favourite masculine figure was the *kouros*, or young man (see the giants of **Sámos** and **Náxos**); the favourite feminine figure was the *kore*, or maiden, dressed in graceful drapery. The 7th century also saw the development of regional schools of pottery, influenced by the black-figured techniques of Corinth: **Rhodes** and the Cycladic islands produced some of the best.

## Classic (500–380 BC)

As Athens became the dominant power in the Aegean, it attracted much of the artistic talent of the Greek world and concentrated its most refined skills on its showpiece Acropolis, culminating with the extraordinary mathematical precision and perfect proportions of the Parthenon, the greatest of all Doric temples, yet built without a single straight line in the entire building. Nothing on the islands approaches it, although there are a few Classical era sites to visit: Liménas on **Thássos** and Erétria on **Évia**, Líndos, Kámiros and Iálysos on **Rhodes**. In ceramics, there was a change over to more naturalistic red-figured black vases around 500 BC; again, the best collection is in the National Archaeology Museum, Athens.

ACROPOLIS, ATHENS

## Hellenistic (380–30 BC)

This era brought new stylistic influences from the eastern lands, conquered and Hellenized by Alexander the Great and his lieutenants. Compared to the cool, aloof perfection of the Classical era, Hellenistic sculpture is characterized by a more emotional, Baroque approach, of windswept drapery, violence and passion. Much of what remains of **Samothráki**'s Sanctuary of the Great Gods, and the Louvre's dramatic *Victory of Samothrace* and *Venus de Milo*, are from the Hellenistic period. Ancient Rhodes was at the height of its powers, and produced its long-gone Colossus, as well as the writhing *Laocoön* (now in the Vatican museum) and Aphrodite statues in the **Rhodes** museum. Houses became decidedly more plush, many decorated with mosaics and frescoes as in the commercial town of **Délos** and in the suburbs of **Kos**.

# Roman (30 BC–AD 529)

The Pax Romana not only ended the rivalries between the Greek city-states but pretty much dried up the sources of their inspiration, although sculptors, architects, and other talents found a ready market for their skills in Rome, cranking out copies of Classic and Hellenistic master-pieces. The Romans themselves built little in Greece: the stoa and theatre of Herodes Atticus (AD 160) were the last large monuments erected in ancient Athens. On the islands, the largest site is Górtyna, the Roman capital of **Crete**.

# Byzantine (527–1460)

The art and architecture of the Byzantine Empire began to show its stylistic distinction under the reign of Justinian (527–565), and the immediate post-Justinian period saw a first golden age in the splendour of Ag. Sofia in Istanbul and the churches of Ravenna, Italy. On the islands you'll find only the remains of simple three-naved basilicas—with two important exceptions: the 6th-century Ekatontapylianí of **Páros** and 7th-century Ag. Títos at Górtyna, **Crete**.

After the austere art purge of the Iconoclasm (726–843) the Macedonian style (named after the Macedonian emperors) slowly infiltrated the Greek provinces. The old Roman basilica plan was jettisoned in favour of what became the classic Byzantine style: a central Greek-cross plan crowned by a dome, elongated in front by a vestibule (narthex) and outer porch (exonarthex) and at the back by a choir and three apses. **Dafní** just outside Athens and Néa Moní on **Chíos**, with its massive cupola, are superb examples; both are decorated with extraordinary mosaics from the second golden age of Byzantine art, under the dynasty of the Comnenes (12th–14th centuries). As in Italy, this period marked a renewed interest in antique models: the stiff, elon-gated hieratic figures with staring eyes are given more naturalistic proportions in graceful, rhythmic compositions. The age of the Comnenes also produced some fine painting: the 12th-century frescoes and manuscripts at the Monastery of St John on **Pátmos**, and the beautifully frescoed early 13th-century Kerá Panagía at Kritsá, near Ag. Nikólaos on **Crete**. Crete's occu-pation by Venice after 1204 marked the beginning of an artistic cross-fertilization that developed into the highly-esteemed Cretan school of painting, as seen in the Byzantine museums in **Herákleon** and **Athens**.

What never changed was the intent of Byzantine art, which is worth a small digression because the 15th-century Western sacred art went off in an entirely different direction—so much so that everything before is disparagingly labelled 'primitive' in most art books. One of the most obvious differences is the strict iconography in Byzantine painting: if you know the code you can instantly identify each saint by the cut of beard, the key or pen in their hand, or other attributes. Their appeal to the viewer, even in the 11th century when the figures were given more naturalistic proportions, is equally purely symbolic; a Byzantine Christ on the Cross, the Virgin *Panagía*, the 'all-holy', angels, saints and martyrs never make a play for the heartstrings, but reside on a purely spiritual and intellectual plane, miles away from Western art invented in the Renaissance 'based on horror, physical charm, infant-worship and easy weeping' as Patrick Leigh Fermor put it. Icons and Byzantine frescoes never ask the viewer to relive vicariously the passion of Christ or coo over Baby Jesus; Byzantine angels never lift their draperies to reveal a little leg; the remote, wide-eyed *Panagía* has none of the luscious charms of the Madonna. They never stray from their remote otherworldliness.

And yet, in the last gasp of Byzantine art under the Paleologos emperors (14th–early 15th centuries), humanist and naturalistic influences combined to produce the Byzantine equivalent of the late Gothic/early Renaissance painting in Italy, in Mistras in the Peloponnese. It is the great might-have-been of Byzantine art: after the Turkish conquest the best painters took refuge on Mount Áthos, or on Zákynthos and Corfu, but none of their work radiates the same charm or confidence in the temporal world.

## Turkish Occupation to the Present

The Turks left few important monuments in Greece, and much of what they did build was wrecked or neglected to death by the Greeks after independence. **Rhodes** town has the best surviving mosques, hammams, houses and public buildings, not only because the Turks loved it well, but because it only became Greek in 1945. **Crete** and **Corfu** remained Venetian longer than most places and have some fine architectural souvenirs: impressive fortifications and gates, fountains, public buildings and town houses. Elsewhere, islands with their own fleets, especially **Hýdra**, **Spétses** and **Sými**, have impressive captain's mansions, while other islands continued traditional architectural styles: the whitewashed asymmetry of the Cyclades, the patterned sgraffito in the mastic villages of Chíos, the Macedonian wooden upper floors and balconies of the northernmost islands.

In the 19th century, nearly all the erected public buildings in both Athens and **Sýros** (briefly Greece's chief port) are neoclassical, restrained and elegantly simple. A host of grandiose neo-Byzantine churches went up, while many older ones were unfortunately tarted up with tired bastard painting, Byzantine in iconography but most of it no better than the contents of a third-rate provincial museum in Italy.

On the whole, the less said about 20th century architecture on the islands, the better: the Fascist architecture left by the Italians on the Dodecanese islands has a sense of style, which is more than can be said of the cheap concrete slabs that have gone up elsewhere. Prosperity in the 1980s has brought an increased interest in local architecture and historic preservation: following the lead of the National Tourist Organization's traditional settlement programme, private individuals have begun to restore old monasteries, abandoned villages, and captains' mansions; most of the newest resort developments make an effort to harmonize with traditional local styles. One individual who won't be restoring any of his Palaces is ex-King Constantine of Greece, whose property was expropriated by the Papandréou Government in 1994.

# Topics

*...there too is Knossos, a mighty city, where Minos was king for nine years, a familiar of mighty Zeus.*

—*Odyssey, book XIX*

The so-called 'Toreador Fresco', found in the palace at Knossós, has become one of the most compelling icons of the lost world of ancient Crete. The slender, sensual bare-breasted maidens who seem to be controlling the action are painted in white, the moon's colour, as in all Cretan frescoes, while the athlete vaulting through the bull's horns appears like all males in red, the colour of the sun. Mythology and archaeology begin to agree, and the roots of the story of Theseus, Ariadne and the Minotaur seem tantalizingly close at hand.

When you see this fresco in Herákleon's Archaeology Museum, take time to look at the decorative border—four striped bands and a row of multicoloured lunettes. Neither Arthur Evans nor any archaeologist since noticed anything unusual about it. A professor of English in Maine named Charles F. Herberger (*The Thread of Ariadne*, Philosophical Library, New York, 1972) was the first to discover that this border is in fact a complex ritual calendar, the key to the myth of Theseus in the Labyrinth and to much else. The pairs of stripes on the tracks, alternately dark and light, for day and night, count on average 29 through each cycle of the five-coloured lunettes, representing the phases of the moon—this is the number of days in a lunar month. By counting all the stripes on the four tracks, Herberger found that each track gives roughly the number of days in a year; the whole, when doubled, totals exactly the number of days in an eight-year cycle of 99 lunar months, a period in which the solar and lunar years coincide—the marriage of the sun and moon.

To decipher the calendar, you can't simply count in circuits around the border; there are regular diagonal jumps to a new row, giving the course of the eight-year cycle the form of a rectangle with an 'x' in it. The box with the 'x' is intriguing, a motif in the art of the Cretans and other ancient peoples as far afield as the Urartians of eastern Anatolia. A Cretan seal shows a bull apparently diving into a crossed rectangle of this sort, while a human figure vaults through his horns. Similar in form is the most common and most enigmatic of all Cretan symbols, the double axe or *labrys*. The form is echoed further in a number of Cretan signet-rings that show the x-shaped cross between the horns of a bull, or between what appear to be a pair of crescent moons.

The home of the *labrys*, the axe that cuts two ways, is the labyrinth. Arthur Evans believed the enormous, rambling palace of Knossós itself to be the labyrinth, a pile so confusing that even a Greek hero would have needed Ariadne's golden thread to find his way through it. In the childhood of archaeology, men could read myths so literally as to think there was a tangible labyrinth, and perhaps

*The 'Toreador Fresco', Knossos*

even a Minotaur. Now, it seems more likely that the labyrinth was the calendar itself, the twisting path that a Minos, a generic name for Cretan priest-kings, representing the sun, followed in his eight-year reign before his inevitable rendezvous with the great goddess. This meeting may originally have meant his death (in a bull mask perhaps) and replacement by another Theseus. Later it would have been simply a ceremony of re-marriage to the priestess that stood in the transcendent goddess' place, celebrated by the bull-vaulting ritual. It has been claimed that the occasion was also accompanied by popular dancing, following the shape of the labyrinth, where the dancers proceeded in a line holding a cord—Ariadne's thread. Homer said 'nine years', and other sources give nine years as the period after which the Athenians had to send their captives to Crete to be devoured by the Minotaur—it's a common ancient confusion, really meaning 'until the ninth', in the way the French still call the interval of a week *huit jours*. Whatever this climax of the Cretan cycle was, it occurred with astronomical precision according to the calendar, and followed a rich, many-layered symbolism difficult for us scoffing moderns ever to comprehend.

That the Cretans had such a complex calendar should be no surprise—for a people that managed modern plumbing and three-storey apartment blocks, and still found time to rule the seas of the eastern Mediterranean. The real attraction lies not simply in the intricacies of the calendar (the nasty Mesopotamians and many other peoples had equally interesting calendars) but more particularly in the scene in the middle, where the diagonals cross and where the ancient science translates into celebration, into dance. Cretan art speaks to everyone, with a colour, beauty and immediacy never before seen in art, and all too lacking in our own time. No other art of antiquity displays such an irresistible grace and joy, qualities which must have come from a profound appreciation of the beauties and rhythms of nature—the rhythms captured and framed in the ancient calendar.

## Endangered Animals and Some Plain Old Pests

For years Greek environmentalists have pushed for legislation to protect rare species of wildlife in the Aegean and Ionian Seas. National parks, wildlife sanctuaries and hunting laws are well regulated on the mainland, but it is the fragile ecologies of the dying seas that cry out most desperately for protection. Laws limiting industrial fishing are constantly flouted—demand for fish has drained the Aegean's key resource by nearly 60% in recent years, making what used to be the cheapest staple food in Greece the most expensive. In the early 1980s, efforts to save the Mediterranean green loggerhead turtle centred on their nesting grounds, which just happened to be the most popular beaches on Zákynthos.

Another bright spot is the designation of the crystalline seas around the northern Sporades as the country's first National Marine Park. It encompasses some of the most beautiful and untouched islands and a diversity of marine life, including the most endangered species in Europe, the monk seal. Biologists believe the seal to be our closest relative in the sea, and use the animal as a yardstick to measure the sea's health, habitability and biological balance. It doesn't bode well; only 300 monk seals remain in Greek waters, and a mere 500 in the entire world. A research station and rehabilitation centre established on Alónissos run by the Hellenic Society for the Study and Protection of Monk Seals (HSSPMS) has managed to rehabilitate 5 orphaned seals in the past three years—a 20% increase in the park's population of 30. Tourists have helped by observing the park laws, such as not entering caves where seals are born and suckled, and not disturbing islands known to be inhabited by seals. Another endangered species in the park is Eleanora's falcon, a small migratory falcon which nests almost exclusively in the Sporades in spring and summer.

Many other birds use the islands as a stepping stone on their spring migratory paths—swallows, storks, pelicans, herons and egrets all pass at one time of the year or another, and there are a wide variety of indiginous birds to keep them company. Eagles and vultures float over the mountains and cliffs, including the massive Griffon vulture and rare lammergeier, with wingspans nearly 10 feet across. Closer to ground, Greece's extraordinary variety of wild-flowers–some 6000 native species–draws an equally colourful array of butterflies.

As for creatures unfortunately *not* on the endangered list, the wily mosquito tops the list for pure incivility. Most shops stock the usual defences: lotions, sprays and insect coils; or pick up one of those inexpensive electric mosquito repellents that fit right in the wall plug and don't stink as badly as the smouldering coils. Even then you may have the misfortune to share your room with some newly evolved genetically invincible high-pitched whining blood-suckers that only surrender to a rolled-up newspaper. Public insect enemy Number Two is the wasp, either taking bites out of that honey-oozing baklava you've just ordered, or spoiling your picnic on the beach (a special hazard on the lush Ionian islands). Dangers lurk in the sea as well: harmless pale brown jellyfish (*méduses*) may drift in anywhere depending on winds and currents, but the oval transparent model (*tsoúchtres*) are stinging devils that can leave scars on tender parts of your anatomy if you brush against them. Pincushiony sea urchins live by rocky beaches, and if you're too cool to wear rubber swimming shoes and step on one, it hurts like hell. The spines may break and embed themselves even deeper if you try to force them out; the Greeks recommend olive oil and a lot of patience to get the spine to slip out.

Much less common are Greece's shy scorpions, who hide out in between the rocks in rural areas; unless you're especially sensitive, their sting is no more or less painful than a bee's. Always avoid the back legs of mules, unless you've been properly introduced. The really lethal creatures are rare: there are several species of small viper that lives in the nooks and crannies of stone walls, where it is well camouflaged, which only comes out occasionally to sun itself. Since the time of Homer, mountain sheepdogs have been a more immediate danger in outer rural areas; by stooping as if to pick up a stone to throw, you might keep a dog at bay.

## On *Kéfi* and Dancing

In the homogenized European Union of the 1990s, only the Spaniards and Greeks still dance to their own music with any kind of spontaneity, and it's no coincidence that both have untranslatable words to describe the 'spirit' or 'mood' that separates going through the motions and true dancing. In Spain, the word is *duende*, which, with the hard driving rhythms of flamenco, has an ecstatic quality; in Greek, the word is *kéfi*, which comes closer to 'soul'. For a Greek to give his all, he must have *kéfi*; to dance without it could be considered dishonest. The smart young men in black trousers and red sashes who dance for you at a 'Greek Night' taverna excursion don't have it; two craggy old fishermen, in a smoky café in Crete, who crank up an old gramophone and dance for their own pleasure, do. You can feel the *kéfi* at Easter when the village elders join hands and dance an elegant *kalamatianó*, or when a group of children celebrate the local saint's day in North Kárpathos.

Every island has its own dances or slight variations, many of which are extremely difficult and ideally seen at village weddings or *panegýria*, saint's day feasts when the villagers of all ages join in. Cretan dances are among the most vigorous and ancient, demanding furious, machine-gunfire steps and hops that go on until your adrenalin has pumped its last. But toss back another *rakí*, and before you know it you'll be up dancing another *pedektó*, a general term for a dance that requires energtic jumping and stamping. Another broad heading of Greek dance is the *syrtó*, with slow and somewhat shuffling pace throughout. For many people, the *kalamatianó*, a 12-step *sýrto*, is *the* national dance; everyone joins in, holding hands at shoulder level,

*Musicians from the Tomb of the Leopards 480–470 BC Fresco*

while the leader improvises. Nearly as common is the dignified *tsamikó*, where the leader and the next dancer in line hold the ends of a handkerchief. If danced by an especially acrobatic leader, the handkerchief begins to look like the only thing that keeps him from flying away altogether. Women are the centre of attention in the *tsíphte téli*, a free-spirited, sensuous belly dance from Asia Minor for the loose-limbed, swivel-hipped and well-oiled, but just as often men (usually old and fat) steal the show.

Other dances are normally but not exclusively performed by men. The *zeybékiko* is a serious, deliberate, highly charged solo (or sometimes duo) dance with outstretched arms, evoking the swooping flight of the eagle; a companion will go down on one knee to encourage the dancer, hiss like a snake and clap out the rhythm. As it's an introspective dance from the soul, the performer keeps his eyes lowered, almost in a hypnotic state; because it's private, you must never applaud. Another intense dance, the *hasápiko*, or butchers' dance, is perhaps better known as the Zorba dance in the West. The *syrtáki* is more exuberant, traditionally performed by two men or three men, often to the *rembétika* tune; the leader signals the steps and it will require some practice but is well worth learning—like Alan Bates, who finally began to fathom *kéfi* from Anthony Quinn at the end of the film *Zorba the Greek.*

## Orthodoxy

With the exception of a handful of Catholics in the Cyclades, nearly all Greeks belong to the Orthodox, or Eastern church; indeed, being Orthodox and speaking Greek are the two most important criteria in defining a Greek, whether born in Athens, Alexandria or Australia. Orthodoxy is so fundamental that even the greatest sceptics can hardly conceive of marrying outside the church, or neglecting to have their children baptized, even though Papandréou's government legalized civil marriages in the early 1980s.

One reason for this deep national feeling is that, unlike everything else in Greece, Orthodoxy has scarcely changed since the founding of the church by Constantine in the 4th century. As Constantinople took the place of Rome as the political and religious capital, the Greeks believe their church to be the only true successor to the original church of Rome. Therefore, a true Greek is called a *Romiós* or Roman, and the Greek language of today is called *Roméika*. It is considered perfect and eternal and beyond all worldly change; if it weren't, its adherents could not expect to be saved. One advantage is that the Greeks have been spared the changes that have rocked the West, from Vatican II to discussions over women in the clergy to political questions of abortion, birth control and so on—matters on which Orthodoxy has always remained aloof. Much emphasis is put on ceremony and ritual, the spiritual and aesthetic, with very little appeal to the emotions.

This explains the violence of Iconoclasm, the one time someone tried to change the rules. Back in the early 8th century, Byzantine Emperor Leo III the Isaurian, shamed by what his Muslim neighbours labelled idolatry, deemed the images of divine beings to be sacrilegious. Iconoclasm began the rift with Rome, which worsened in 800 when the Pope crowned Charlemagne as emperor, usurping the position of the Emperor of Constantinople. Further divisions arose over the celibacy of the clergy (Orthodox priests may marry before they are ordained) and the use of the phrase *filioque*, 'and the son', in the Holy Creed, the issue which caused the final, fatal schism in 1054 when the Papal legate Cardinal Humbert excommunicated the Patriarch of Constantinople and the Patriarch excommunicated the Pope. Ever since then the Orthodox heirarchy have kept a patriarchal throne vacant, ready for the day when the Pope comes back to his senses.

After the fall of the Byzantine Empire (that 'thousand-year-long mass for the dead' as one recent Greek writer put it), the Turks not only tolerated the Orthodox church, but had the political astuteness to impart considerable powers to the patriarch. The church was thus able to preserve many Greek traditions and Greek education through the dark age of Ottoman rule; on the other hand it often abused this power against its own flock, especially on a local scale. According to an old saying, priests, headmen and Turks were the three curses of Greece and the poor priests (who in truth are usually quite amiable fellows) have not yet exonerated themselves from the list they now share with the king and the cuckold.

The extraordinary quantity of churches and chapels on some islands has little to do with the priests, however. Nearly all were built by families or individuals, especially by sailors, seeking the protection of a patron saint, to keep a promise, or in simple thanksgiving. Architecturally they come in an endless variety of styles depending on the region, period and terrain, as well as the wealth and whim of the builder. All but the tiniest have an *iconóstasis*, or altar screen, made of wood or stone to separate the *heirón* or sanctuary, where only the ordained are allowed, from the rest of the church. Most of the chapels are locked up thanks to light-fingered tourists; if you track down the caretaker, leave a few drachmae for upkeep.

Almost all these chapels have only one service a year, on the name day of the patron saint (name days are celebrated in Greece rather than birthdays: 'Many years!' (*Chrónia pollá!*) is the proper way to greet someone on their name day). This annual celebration is called a *yiortí* or more frequently *panegýri*, and is the cause for feasts and dancing before or after the church service. If feasible, *panegýria* take place directly in the churchyard; if not, in neighbouring wooded areas, tavernas, and specially built party centres. The food is more often than not basic but plentiful; for a set price you receive more than your share of stewed goat. *Panegýria* (festivals) are also the best places to hear traditional island music and learn the dances, and it's sad that they're only a fond memory in most major tourist centres. Apart from Easter, the Assumption of the Virgin, 15 August, is the largest *panegýri* in Greece. The faithful sail to Tínos, the Lourdes of Greece, and to a dozen centres connected with Mary, making mid-August a very uncomfortable time to island-hop, especially in the Cyclades. Not only are the ships packed to the brim, but the *meltémi* wind also blows with vigour, and Greek matrons, the most ardent pilgrims of all, are the worst of all sailors.

Orthodox weddings are another lovely if long-winded ritual. The bride and groom stand solemnly before the chanting priest, while family and friends in attendance seem to do everything but follow the proceedings. White crowns, bound together by a white ribbon, are placed on the heads of bride and groom, and the *koumbáros*, or best man, exchanges them back and forth. The newlyweds are then led around the altar three times, while the guests bombard the happy couple with fertility-bringing rice and flower petals. After congratulating the bride and groom, guests are given a small *boboniéra* of candied almonds. This is followed by the marriage feast and dancing, which in the past could last up to five days. If you are in the vicinity of a village wedding you may be offered a sweet cake; you may even be invited to come along to the feasting as a special guest.

Baptisms are cause for similar celebration. The priest completely immerses the baby in the Holy Water three times (unlike Achilles, there are no vulnerable spots on modern Greeks) and almost always gives the little one the name of a grandparent. For extra protection from the forces of evil, babies often wear a *filaktó*, or amulet, the omnipresent blue glass eye bead. If you visit a baby at home you may well be sprinkled first with Holy Water, and chances are there's a bit of beneficial garlic squeezed somewhere under the cradle. Compliments to the little one's parents should be kept to a minimum: the gods do get jealous.

Funerals in Greece, for reasons of climate, are carried out as soon as possible, and are announced by the tolling of the village church bells. The dead are buried for three to five years (longer if the family can pay) after which time the bones are exhumed and placed in the family box to make room for the next resident. *Aforismós*, or Orthodox excommunication, is believed to prevent the body decaying after death—the main source of Greek vampire stories. Memorials for the dead take place three, nine and forty days after death, and on the first anniversary. They are sometimes repeated annually. Sweet buns and sugared wheat and raisin *koúliva* are given out after the ceremony. But for all the trappings of Christianity, the spirit of Charos, the ferryman of death and personification of inexorable nature, is never far away, as beautifully expressed in perhaps the most famous of myrologies, or dirges:

> *Why are the mountains dark and why so woe-begone?*
> *Is the wind at war there, or does the rain storm scourge them?*
> *It is not the wind at war there, it is not the rain that scourges,*
> *It is only Charos passing across them with the dead;*
> *He drives the youths before him, the old folk drags behind,*
> *And he bears the tender little ones in a line at his saddle-bow.*
> *The old men beg a grace, the young kneel to impore him,*
> *'Good Charos, halt in the village, or halt by some cool fountain,*
> *That the old men may drink water, the young men play at the stone-throwing,*
> *And that the little children may go and gather flowers.'*
> *'In never a village will I halt, nor yet by a cool fountain,*
> *The mothers would come for water, and recognize their children,*
> *The married folk would know each other, and I should never part them.'*

## The *Períptero* and the Plane Tree

In Greece you'll see it everywhere, the greatest of modern Greek inventions, the indispensable *períptero*. It is the best-equipped kiosk in the world, where people gather to chat, make local or international calls, or grab a few minutes' shade under the little projecting roof. The *períptero* is a substitute bar, selling everything from water to ice-cream to ice-cold beer; an emergency pharmacy stocked with aspirin, mosquito killers, condoms and Band Aids; a convenient newsagent for Greek and international publications, from *Ta Néa* to *Die Zeit*; a tourist shop offering maps, guides, postcards and stamps; a toy shop for balloons and plastic swords; a general store for shoelaces, cigarettes, batteries and rolls of film; recently one in Póros produced breakfast. In Athens they're at most traffic lights. On the islands they are a more common sight than a donkey. You'll wonder how you ever survived before *perípteros* and the treasures they contain.

The other great meeting centre of Greek life is the mighty plane tree, or *plátanos*, for centuries the focal point of village life, where politics and philosophy have been argued since time immemorial. Since Hippocrates the Greeks have believed that plane shade is wholesome and beneficial (unlike the enervating shadow cast by the fig) and one of the most extraordinary sights in the islands is 'Hippocrates' plane tree' on Kos, propped up on scaffolding and as protected as any national monument would be. In Greek the expression *cheréte mou ton plátano* loosely translates as 'go tell it to the marines', presumably because the tree has heard all that nonsense before. For a Greek the *plátanos* represents the village's identity; the tree is a source of life, for it only grows near abundant fresh water, its deep roots a symbol of stability, continuity and protection—a huge majestic umbrella, as even the rain cannot penetrate its sturdy leaves. Sit under its spreading branches and sip a coffee as the morning unfolds before you; the temptation to linger there for the day is irresistible.

## Lamp Chops and Sweat Coffee

For a country cursed with a rusty, outmoded, and mindlessly pedantic system of public education, where rote memorization is the only key to academic success, the Greeks speak astonishingly good English. The Greek dislike of, not to mention their thorough incompetence at dubbing the likes of *Miami Vice* and *Santa Monica* may have something to do with it, as well as the dogged efforts of thousands of *frontistérion* (private school) teachers, whose task is to get their pupils through their proficiency exams in spite of Greek public education.

All of the above is enough to make the devoted observer of Greek ways suspect that the English mistakes on taverna menus are no accident, but rather part of some calculated plot worthy of the crafty Odysseus to keep tourists out of the locals' own secret haunts by making taverna menus such compelling reading that by the time you've spotted the Lamp Chops, Eye Eggs (ie. sunnyside up), or Sandwitches the waiter has conned you into sitting down for lunch. Will you have the Rabeet Soupee, Brawn Beans, Stuffed Vine Lives, String Deans, Sours Various, You Court with Gurig and Gogumbers, Eggfish, Chief's Salad or Beet Poots to start? For main course, the Harmbougger sounds distinctly threatening; perhaps it's best to stick with dishes you know the Greeks do well: Staffed Tomatoes, Reformed Schnitzel, Sguids in Spies, See Food Various, Chicken Pain, Souvlaki Privates, Stake, Veal Gogglets and Shrimp Shave. There's munch more! Vegetable dishes such as Zucchini Bulls, Gorgettes, or perhaps Grass Hill (it turned out to be a small mound of boiled greens). On Skópelos, you can smack your lips over a Rude Sausage or Rude Meat Pie; on Páros, you can ponder where your parents went wrong over a Freud Juice or Freud Salad; in Mytilíni, either sex can enjoy a delicious (and perfectly correct) Fish in Lesbian Sauce. Then it's off to the Snake Bar for a Sweat Coffee, Kaputsino, or perhaps a Ouisgi before driving off in your Fully Incurable Rent-a-Care from the Vague Travel Agency of Piraeus.

If the Greek islands were the cutting edge of European culture from 2000–500 BC, the past thousand years or so have shoved them into such an out-of-the-way corner that they have been goldmines of old beliefs and traditions, some going back to deepest antiquity. Crete, Skýros, Lésbos (where they still sacrifice bulls) Límnos, Ándros, Kéa and Kárpathos have proved especially rich sources for ethnologists—but won't be much longer as community life is undermined by rural depopulation, mass tourism and television. Nevertheless, if you were to spend a year in an island village, you would find that St Basil, the Greek Santa Claus, still comes on New Year's Day with gifts, and coins are still baked in pies called *vassilopíta* that bring good luck to the finder; since ancient times **January** has been closely associated with the Fates. In Crete, water is brought in from a spring, where the Fates have bathed; a pomegranate is broken on the threshold to bring richness, a stone is cast to give the household health and 'hard heads' against headaches. On Epiphany, 6 January, houses are sprinkled with holy water, and ashes from the hearth kept ablaze since Christmas, to ward off werewolves and goblins (the *kallikántzaroi*), are scattered for good luck. Vineyards and trees are pruned and everyone huddles around the pot bellied stove in the *kafeneíon*.

**February** has a reputation for lameness and wetness; on of its names, Flevarius, suggests opening of veins (*fleva*) of water; a dry February means drought. The first finches are a harbinger of spring. Olive groves are ploughed in **March**, a very variable month with strange nicknames—the Five-Minded, the Grumbler, the Flayer and *Paloukokáftis*, 'the Burning Pale'. Little bracelets of red and white thread called a *Mertoátano* are tied on children's wrists to protect them from the sun; on Kárpathos they say they tie up 'fatness, beauty, whims and the March sun.' The first swallows come back on Annunciation Day.

On Rhodes, **April** used to be called the Goggler; food supplies put up in the autumn would run out, leaving everyone 'goggle eyed'—hungry; in the Cyclades they call it 'the basket thrower' for the same reason. Wildflowers are gathered to decorate each church's Good Friday *Epitáphios*, or bier of Christ; the flowers or candles used in the service are in great demand for their special power against the evil eye. Easter eggs are dyed red, doors are painted with blood from the Easter lamb, and just after midnight the Resurrection (*Christós Anésti!*) is announced with bells, fireworks, candles, kissing and general pandemonium; on Corfu women throw old crockery off the balconies. Afterwards, everyone eats *magirítsa*, a soup made of minced lamb's tripe that soothes the stomach after the long Lenten fast. On Easter day everyone dresses up for the service of Divine Love, then feasts on spit-roast lamb with all the trimmings, and drinks, sings and dances into the night; in many places effigies of Judas are burned, and special Easter swings are raised for the girls on Anáfi and Lésbos.

**May** is the month of flowers,when the olive trees bloom, and sheep and goats are sheared. In ancient times temples and statues would be purified then, and to this day it's a month for mischief and sorcery. On 1 May it's important to get up early and eat garlic before the first donkey brays or first cuckoo sings to avoid being 'stuffed'—losing the appetite, or being made somehow asinine. Everyone, even the urbane Athenians, goes to the countryside to 'fetch the May' and make wreaths to bring spring's blessing to the house. On Ándros a pig's tongue is cooked to ward off backbiting, and everywhere it's bad luck to lend anything or be married— unless you're a king or a donkey. Ascension Day is traditionally time for the first swim of the year, to 'go to the 40 waves', and if you find a stone with 'sea fluff' on it to take home and put under your bed, all the better. In **June** wheat and barley are harvested (often a corner of the field is left 'because the hare must eat, too'), cherries, apricots and peaches are picked and the first tomatoes, aubergines, beans and pulses are ripe. Bonfires are lit for St John's Eve and the young people take turns leaping over the flames. As the year changes with the summer solstice, so does luck. A widespread custom is the *kledónas*; after the bonfire has gone out, water is silently drawn from a well to fill a pot, where everyone dips in a personal item. The water is left open to the stars and the next day a little girl announces each destiny as she pulls the items out of the *kledónas*; unmarried girls look in the water to see their future husband.

Hot **July** is the month for threshing and gathering herbs; the first melons, watermelons, figs and grapes are ripe. On 17 July, songs summon Ag. Marína to cure the bites and stings of snakes, scorpions and insects; on 20 July it's the turn of Prophet Elijah, the saint of mountaintop chapels who inherited Zeus' meteorological tasks, controlling the rain, winds and sun. Cretans say anyone who sees a headless shadow at noon will not survive the year. **August** is known as the Vintner, for the grape harvests begin, or the fig-gatherer or the table-bearer for the abundant fruits that are ripe. It's also the best month to eat mackerel. However, the first six days, the *Drymes*, are unlucky, associated with nymphs, who make hair fall out if it's washed or combed. The pious fast two weeks before the Assumption of the Virgin on 15 August, celebrated everywhere in Greece but especially on Tínos, at Agiássos, Lésbos, on Astypália, Sámos, and Markópoulo on Kefaloniá where little snakes mysteriously appear and disappear. **September** is the month of wine-making. In Byzantine times 1 September was New Year's Day (and still is in the Orthodox ecclesiastical calendar), the day when Archangel Michael gets out his book and notes all the souls he will take during the coming year. On Kos children make New Year's garlands of garlic, grapes, pomegranates and a leaf from Hippocrates' plane tree; on Crete some people put a walnut on their roof at midnight and judge their chances for survival for the next year by the wholeness of the kernel. Sowing begins after 14 September, but take care not to cross a woman en route to the fields.

**October** usually has the first rains but generally fine weather; Greek Indian summer is the 'little summer of Ag. Dimítros'. Cranes fly south to Africa, chrysanthemums adorn the tables, priests bless and open the first wine barrel. **November**, 'the showery', signals the beginning of the olive harvests. Flocks are brought down from the mountain pastures, and in some places icons are placed around the newly sown fields. Pancakes are made on 30 November for St Andrew, who is mysteriously known as *Trypanoteganitís*, the 'frying pan piercer'; a good housewife will use all her frying pans that day to keep them from getting holes. **December** is called 'good morning, good evening' for its short days. Eating sweet things on 4 December, St Barbara's Day, was believed to ward off smallpox, and women hide their brooms and refrain from cooking beans. Her holiday generally elides with that of St Nikólaos on the 6th, the protector of sailors, when boats are decorated and icons paraded around the shore. Christmas Eve marks the beginning of the twelve-day holiday period when the demonic *kallikántzaroi* and werewolves are afoot but can be kept at bay by not letting the hearth fire go out, so everyone chooses the fattest 'Christ log' they can. Pigs are slaughtered, and in the villages pork is the traditional Christmas meal. Among the many cakes are sweets made with flaky filo pastry to represent Christ's swaddling clothes. On Kímolos the oxen can magically speak at midnight but, like people, all they do is complain about their fodder.

## Athens and Piraeus

ACROPOLIS, ATHENS

*Love for Athens, a city once famous, wrote these words, a love that plays with shadows, that gives a little comfort to burning desire... Though I live in Athens I see Athens nowhere: only sad, empty, and blessed dust.*

Michael Akominátos, 12th century

Many travellers to the Greek islands eventually find themselves in Athens and Piraeus, but it's rarely love at first sight; Athens, with its ramshackle architecture and dusty exterior, wins no beauty prizes. Look closely, however, and you may be won over by this urban crazy quilt of villages—small oases of green parks hidden amidst the hustle and bustle; tiny family-run tavernas tucked away in the most unexpected places; the feverish pace of its nightlife and summer festivals devoted to wine and song; and best of all, the Athenians themselves, whose friendliness belies the reputation of most inhabitants of capital cities.

## A Brief Historical Outline

Inhabited by pre-Hellenic tribes in the Neolithic Age (*c.* 3500 BC), Athens made its proper debut on history's stage in the second millennium, when Ionians from Asia Minor invaded Attica and established several small city-states. Their main centre was Kekropia, named for the serpent god Kekrops (later to be identified with King Erechtheus, the official original founder of Athens and himself a snake from the waist down). The owl was sacred to Kekropia—as it was to the goddess Athena, whose worship and name gradually came to preside in the city.

In the 14th century BC Athens, as part of the Mycenaean empire of the Achaeans, invaded Crete, fought Thebes, and conquered Troy, but managed to escape the subsequent Dorian invasion which brought chaos to the Mycenaean world. Two hundred years later, however, it was Attica's turn to meet the uncouth Dorians, who brought with them Greece's first Dark Age. This endured until the 8th century BC, far too long for the sophisticated Ionians, who went back to their homelands in Asia Minor and settled many of the Aegean islands.

Some time during the 8th century BC all the towns of Attica were peaceably united, an accomplishment attributed to the mythical King Theseus (1300 BC). Athens at the time was ruled by a king (the chief priest), a polemarch (or general), and an archon (or civil authority), positions that were annually elective by the 6th century. It was the conflict between the landed aristocracy and rising commercial classes that gradually brought about the momentous invention of democratic government, beginning under the reforms of Solon. Yet under every stone there lurked a would-be tyrant; Solon was still warm in the grave when Pisistratos, leader of the popular party, made himself boss (545 BC) and began the naval build-up that for the first time made Athens a threat to the other independent city-states of Greece.

Pisistratos' son was followed by another reformer, Kleisthenes, who discarded Athens' ancient but unsatisfactory political classifications by dividing the population into ten tribes. Each selected by lot 50 members of the people's assembly, from which a further lot was drawn to select ten archons, one from each tribe. The head archon gave his name to the Athenian year.

Meanwhile, as Persian strength grew in the east, Ionian intellectuals and artists took refuge in Athens, bringing with them philosophy, science and the roots of Attic tragedy. They encouraged Athens to aid Ionia against the Persians, an unsuccessful adventure that landed the city in the soup when the vengeful Darius, Persian King of Kings, turned to subdue Greece, and in particular Athens. In 490 BC Darius' vast army landed at Marathon only to be defeated by a much smaller Athenian force under Miltiades. Powerful Sparta and the other Greek states then recognized the eastern threat, but continued to leave 'national' defence primarily to Athens and in particular the Athenian fleet, which grew ever mightier under Themistocles. However, it failed to keep the Persians from having another go at Greece, and in 480 BC the new King of Kings, Xerxes, showed up with the greatest fleet and army the ancient world had ever seen. Athens was destroyed, but the Persian navy was neatly outmanoeuvred by the Athenian ships at Salamis and the invasion was finally repelled by the Athenians and Spartans at the battle of Plateía.

Having proved her naval might, Athens set about creating a maritime empire, not only to increase her power but also to stabilize her combustible internal politics. She ruled the confederacy at Delos, demanding contributions from the islands in return for protection from the Persians. Sea trade became necessary to support the city's growing population, while the founding of new colonies around the Mediterranean ensured a continual food supply for Athens. Athenian democracy became truly imperialistic under Pericles, who brought the treasure of Delos to Athens to 'protect it'—and to skim off funds to rebuild and beautify the city and build the Parthenon. It was the golden age of Athens, the age of the sculptures of Phidias, the histories of Herodotus, the plays of Sophocles and Aristophanes, the philosophy of Socrates.

The main cause of the Peloponnesian War (431–404 BC) was Athenian expansion in the west. Back and forth the struggle went, Sparta and its allies with superiority on land, Athens on the seas, until both city-states were near exhaustion. Finally Lysander captured Athens, razed the walls, and set up the brief rule of the Thirty Tyrants.

Although democracy and imperialism made quick recoveries in Athens (by 378 the city had set up its second Maritime League), the Peloponnesian War had struck a blow from which Athens could not totally recover. The population grew dissatisfied with public life, and refused to tolerate innovators and critics to the extent that Socrates was put to death. Economically, Athens had trouble maintaining the trade she so desperately needed. Yet her intellectual tradition held true in the 4th century BC, bringing forth the likes of Demosthenes, Praxiteles, Menander, Plato and Aristotle.

Philip II of Macedon took advantage of the general discontent and turmoil to bully the city-states into joining Macedon for an expedition against Greece's eternal rival Persia. Athenian patriotism and independence were kept alive by the orator Demosthenes until Philip subdued the city (338 BC). He was assassinated shortly before beginning the Persian campaign, leaving his son Alexander to conquer the East. When Alexander died, Athens had to defend herself against his striving generals, beginning with Dimitrios Poliorketes (the Besieger) who captured the city in 294 BC. Alexandria, Rhodes and Pergamon became Athens' intellectual rivals, although Athens continued to be honoured by them.

In 168 BC Rome captured Athens, but again granted her many privileges including the island of Delos. Eighty years later Athens betrayed Roman favour by siding with Mithridates of Pontus, and to punish her Sulla destroyed Piraeus and the walls of the city. But Rome always remembered her cultural debt; leading Romans attended Athens' schools and gave the city gifts, and, Romans being Romans, many Greek treasures ended up in Rome. St Paul started the Athenians on the road to Christianity in AD 44. In the 3rd century Goths and barbarians sacked Athens, and when they were driven away the city joined the growing Byzantine Empire.

Justinian closed the philosophy schools in 529 and converted the temples to churches and the Parthenon into a cathedral. It was a largely symbolic act; by then Athens had lost almost all of her former importance. She next enters history as the plaything of the Franks after they pillaged Constantinople in 1204. St Louis appointed Guy de la Roche as Duke of Athens, a dukedom which passed through many outstretched hands: the Catalans, Neapolitans and Venetians all controlled it at various times. In 1456 it was the turn of the Ottomans, who made the Parthenon into a mosque and the Erechtheion into a harem. The Venetians made several attempts to wrench it away; in the siege of 1687 Morosini and the Venetians blew up part of the Parthenon, where the Turks had stored their gunpowder. In 1800 Lord Elgin began the large-scale removal of monuments from Athens to the British and other museums.

In 1834, after the War of Independence, Athens—at the time a few hundred war-scarred houses deteriorating under the Acropolis—was declared the capital of the new Greek state. Otho of Bavaria, the first King of the Greeks, brought his own architects with him and laid out a new city, based on the lines of Stadíou and El. Venezélou Streets, which still boast most of Otho's neoclassical public buildings. Much of the rest of the city's architecture was abandoned to unimaginative, quickly erected concrete blocks, spared monotony only by the hilly Attic terrain. More and more of these hills are being pounded into villas and flats by the ubiquitous cement mixer; Greater Athens squeezes in over three million lively, opinionated inhabitants— a full third of the entire Greek population—who thanks to native ingenuity and EU member-ship (popular songs sing the praises of the '*pakéta* Delors') are now more prosperous than they have been since the age of Pericles. Unfortunately this means a million cars now crawl the ancient streets, creating the worst smog problem east of Mexico City and one that threatens to choke this unique city. The word for smog is *néfos*, and if you happened to arrive on a brown day you'll soon know too much about it. The first lines of an underground transit network are under construction in the centre, making things worse before they get better—in 1997.

Modern Athens has a touchy new, and potentially nefarious problem with ethnic tensions. The gipsies have traditionally been looked on as the underclass in Greece, blamed for every petty crime and theft. But since thousands of impoverished refugees poured into northern Greece from Albania in 1990, the Albanians have taken their place as the new whipping boys, especially those who are not ethnically Greek. Albanians are blamed for an increase in unem-ployment, street crime, burglaries and violence, previously very rare in Athens and its suburbs (and still rare, compared to other major capitals). With each flare-up in volatile Greco-Albanian relations the Albanians are rounded up and taken to the border. Most of them filter back, often to take up under-the-table jobs from the very politicians who just booted them out; nothing balances a municipal budget easier than an underpaid Albanian road crew.

---

### Athens and Piraeus Basics

EOT publishes a free booklet *The Week in Athens* with listings of important phone numbers, museums, island ferries (and prices) bus information etc that is updated weekly. Ask at the central Syntagma information 'office'. Alternatively, pick up a copy of *Athenórama* or *Athenscope*, weekly publications (350dr) with what's on in Athens, listings of restaurants, bars etc. For more in-depth news in English about what's happening in the city, get the monthly *The Athenian*, which also has a good restaurant guide and other listings.

**Left luggage:** Bellair Travel & Tourism, 15 Níkis (just down from Sýntagma Square), ✆ 323 9261, offers left luggage service at 200dr a piece per day (daily 9–5, Sat 9–2, closed Sunday). Useful for people with time to kill before taking a plane/boat out who want to visit Acropolis/Pláka etc. There's a new left luggage facility in the international airport, down at the far end beyond the charters hall. In Piraeus, the left luggage store next to the HML ticket agency opens at 7am and stays open until midnight, 300dr an hour, or 500dr for the whole day.

**Dirty clothes:** There's a laundry at 710 Angélou Gerondá, Plateía Filomoúson, in the Plaka. Two-hour service wash and dry for 1500dr.

**Good bookshop:** Compendium, for new and secondhand books, 28 Níkis (Sýntagma), ✆ 322 1248.

## Orientation

**Sýntagma** (ΣΨΝΤΑΓΜΑ) (or **Constitution**) **Square** is to all intents and purposes the centre of the the city, and it's here that the **Parliament Building** is to be found, backing on to the **National Gardens** and **Záppeion Park**, a haven of green and shade to escape the summer heat, with ducks to feed and a hundred benches useful for grabbing a few winks. Sýntagma Square itself is a something of a glorified roundabout with traffic whizzing past, but this doesn't deter people from sitting a few feet away at the outdoor tables of the overpriced cafés and the great big McDonald's. The McPresence may be a golden arch blasphemy for old Athens hands, but it's packed just the same, and mostly with Greeks who don't give a hang about culture pollution. At the time of writing Sýntagma Square is further convulsed with the construction of the new $2.8 billion Metro; a Roman bathhouse was found under all the traffic jams, and it and other archaeological finds from the subway digs will be displayed in a smart underground concourse. The National Tourist Organization (EOT)'s main, central, one and only **tourist information** office is in Sýntagma as well, in a dirty window by the National Bank. It's easy to spot: just look for long snaking queue of hot and bothered tourists in danger of sunstroke waiting to shout into a microphone at one hapless beleaguered woman, only to discover that she ran out of maps of Athens and Greece several months ago. Perhaps EOT should hire a few Albanians to lend a hand.

From Sýntagma Square it's a short walk down to the far more interesting **Pláka** (ΠΛΑΚΑ), the medieval centre at the foot of the Acropolis, where many of the older houses have been converted into intimate tavernas or bars, each tinkling away with its own bouzouki. This is also a good place to look for mid-priced accommodation, and a fun part of the city to wander around in day or evening, where street musicians and the occasional escaped piglet (the mascot of one of the gift shops) add to the excitement.

During the day meander through Athens' nearby flea market district, to the west of **Monastiraki** (ΜΟΝΑΣΤΙΡΑΚΙ) **Square** (and the metro station), where bulging shops sell everything from good quality woollen goods and fake Caterpillar boots to furniture and second-hand fridges. To reach the flea market, you'll find several streets en route that all claim to be the flea market, but are nothing more than tourist trap alleys peddling fake icons, fake Greek vases and lots of T-shirts with 'Hellas' printed on them.

A 10-minute walk from Syntagma will take you to **Kolonáki Square**, Athens' Knightsbridge in miniature, complete with fancypants shops and restaurants (all of course expensive) and plenty of well-heeled 'Kolonáki Greeks'—Athenian Sloane Rangers—to patronize them. Up from the square (it's a long haul on foot, but there's a funicular) is the hill of **Lycavitós** (ΛΥΚΑΒΕΤΟΣ), illuminated like a fairytale tower at night. On the top sits the chapel of **St George**, a restaurant/bar, and a cannon that is fired on national holidays. It offers the best panoramic views of Athens, including a sweeping vista down to the sea at Piraeus, *néfos* permitting.

In complete contrast to upmarket Kolonáki, **Exárchia**, the area behind the National Archaeological Museum and Strefi Hill, attracts alternative types, students and the literati. Plateía Exárchia teems with lively cafés, bars and tavernas where trendies, intellectuals and anarchists mingle under the shade of the trees. Off the tourist trail it's one of the city's liveliest and most happening nightl;ife centres, with traditional *ouzeries* and *boîtes* where you're likely to find rave and new music alongside bluesy, smoke-filled rembetika clubs, now enjoying a renaissance. To the establishment and oldies Exárchia has become synonymous with Anarchia, and home to druggies, disaffected youth nd graffiti-sprayers. But it's tame by London or New York standards. There are some good eateries for those on a budget, and the atmosphere everywhere is generally laid-back and relaxed. Single women travellers are less likely to get hassled here than other parts of the city.

Two other areas off the tourist trail and pleasant places to stay are residential **Veikoú** and **Koukáki**, reached from the southern slopes of the Acroplois or Filopáppou Hill, both on the nos.1, 5 and 9 trolley-bus routes. Proper Greek neighbourhoods, the local shops, tavernas and *ouzeries* have few concessions to tourism and excellent, authentic food. Good places to go for a leisurely lunch or to round off an evening.

A 20-minute walk from Sýntagma, along Vass. Soffas, brings you to the Hilton Hotel, a useful landmark. Behind it are the essential Athenian neighbourhoods of **Ilíssia** and **Pangráti**, the best place to get a feel for everyday life in the city. Lose yourself in their back streets and you may find your own little taverna (of which there are plenty), rather than restrict yourself to the tourist haunts in the centre. Across Konstantínos Avenue from Záppeion Park and behind the Olympic Stadium you'll find **Mets**, a neighbourhood popular with artists and media folk with some fine old houses and small pensions. If you don't mind the walk into the centre of Athens, it's a good place to stay, and some authentic tavernas and *kafenéions* as well as trendy discos.

From Záppeion Park buses run frequently down to the coast and suburbs of **Glyfáda**, **Voúla** and **Vouliagménis**. Glyfada, close to the airport, is a green and pleasant suburb that has grown into a busy resort and rival Kolonáki with its glossy shopping malls. Many smart city dwellers shop at the ritzy boutiques, and berth their gin palaces in the swish marina, ready for weekend jaunts over to Kéa and other nearby islands. At the other end of the scale it's the hub of British package holidays to the so-called Apollo Coast, and the bars tend to get packed with personnel from the local US bases and foreign tourists. Here and further down the coast at Voúla are pay beaches run by EOT, usually jammed with well-heeled Athenians escaping from their apartments. There are all kinds of facilities and the sea is cleaner at some than others—watch out for that sewage outfall—but nothing like the crystal waters of the more remote islands. There's also good swimming beyond Voúla in the rocky coves at Vouliagménis, a smart place for a fish lunch and haven for Greek yachties. En route, **Kavoúri** has excellent fish restaurants, ideal for a romantic dinner overlooking the sea. Beyond Vouliagménis, the road continues along the coast to **Várkiza**, another beach playground, and winds to stunning **Cape Soúnion** and its **Temple of Poseidon** (440 BC), famous for its magnificent position and sunsets and where there's always at least one tourist searching for the column where Byron carved his name.

## Museums and Sites in Athens

### Agora Museum (the Theseum and Ancient Agora)

*Open 8.30–2.45, closed Mon; adm.*

The Agora was not only the market but the centre of Athenian civic and social life. This is where citizens spent much of their day and where Socrates buttonholed passers-by to question their basic assumptions about life and law. After the Persians destroyed all the buildings of the Agora in 480 BC, it was rebuilt in a much grander style; since then many landmarks have suffered from the wrath of the Romans or fires set by the barbarians, and from Athenians in need of cheap building stone. Only the foundations remain of the council house or **Bouleuterion** and the neighbouring Temple of the Mother of the Gods, the **Metroön**, built by the Athenians as reparation for slaying of a priest from her cult. The round **Tholos** or administration centre is where the administrators or prytanes worked, and as some had to be on call day and night, kitchens and sleeping quarters were included. Its final reconstruction took place after Sulla's rampage in 88 BC. To the right of the Tholos is the **horos**, or boundary stone; a path from here leads to the foundations of the prison where Socrates spent his last days and drank the fatal hemlock. Opposite the Metroön, only a wall remains of the **Sanctuary of the Eponymous Heroes of Athens**, the ten who gave their names to Kleisthenes' ten tribes. The **altar of Zeus Agoraios** received the oaths of the new archons, a practice initiated by Solon.

The 4th-century **Temple of Apollo** was dedicated to the mythical father of the Ionians, who believed themselves descended from Ion, son of Apollo. It held the huge cult statue of Apollo now in the Agora museum. Almost nothing remains of the **Stoa Basileios**, or of Zeus Eleutherios, which played a major role in Athenian history as the court of the annual archon, where trials concerning the security of the state took place. By the Stoa of Zeus stood the **Altar of the Twelve Gods**, from which all distances in Attica were measured. Alongside it ran the sacred **Panathenaic Way**; some signs of its Roman rebuilding may be seen by the Church of the Holy Apostles. After crossing the Agora, this ceremonial path ascended to the Acropolis, where devotees celebrated the union of Attica. South of the Altar of Twelve Gods is the site of the Doric **Temple to Ares** (5th century BC). The **Three Giants** nearby were originally part of the **Odeon of Agrippa** (15 BC); parts of the orchestra remain intact after the roof collapsed in 190 AD. Confusingly, the site and the giants were reused in the façade of a 5th-century AD gymnasium, that for a century served as the site of the University of Athens until Justinian closed it down. Near the **Middle Stoa** (2nd century BC) are ruins of a **Roman temple** and the ancient shops and booths. On the other side of the Middle Stoa is the people's court, or **Heliaia**, organized by Solon in the 6th century BC to hear political questions; it remained active well into Roman times.

Between the **South and East Stoas** (2nd century BC) is the 11th-century **Church of the Holy Apostles** (Ag. Apóstoli), built on the site where St Paul addressed the Athenians and restored, along with its fine paintings, in 1952. Across the Panathenaic Way run the remains of **Valerian's Wall** thrown up in 257 AD against the barbarian, its stone cannibalized from Agora buildings wrecked by the Romans. Between Valerian's Wall and the Stoa of Attalos are higgledy-piggledy ruins of the **Library of Pantainos**, built by Flavius Pantainos in AD 100 and destroyed 167 years later. Finds from the entire Agora are in the museum in the **Stoa of Attalos**, the 2nd-century BC portico built by King Attalos II of Pergamon, reconstructed by John D. Rockefeller.

The same ticket gets you into the mid 5th-century BC **Theseum**, nothing less than the best-preserved Greek temple in existence. Doric in order and dedicated to Hephaistos, the god of metals and smiths, it may well have been designed by the architect of the temple at Sounion. It is constructed almost entirely of Pentelic marble and decorated with metopes depicting the lives of Heracles and Theseus (for whom the temple was named). Converted into a church in the 5th century, it was the burial place for English Protestants until 1834, when the government declared it a national monument.

## The Acropolis

*Open summer Mon–Fri 8–6.45, Sat and Sun 8.30–3; winter Mon–Fri 8–5, Sat and Sun 8.30–3; adm.*

The naturally fortified **Acropolis** was inhabited from the end of the Neolithic Age. The Mycenaeans added a Cyclopean wall and the palace of their king. This was later replaced by a temple of Poseidon and Athena. In mythology, these two divinities took part in a contest to decide who would be the patron of the new city. With his trident Poseidon struck the spring Klepsydra out of the rock of the Acropolis, while Athena invented the olive tree, which the Athenians judged the better trick.

The tyrant Pisistratos ordered a great gate constructed in the wall, but Delphi cursed it and the Athenians dismantled it. In 480 BC the temple's cult statue of Athena was hurriedly bundled off to Salamis, just before the Persians burnt the Acropolis. Themistocles built a new rampart out of the old Parthenon, and under Pericles the present plan of the Acropolis buildings was established.

The path to the Acropolis follows the Panathenaic Way, laid out at the consecration of the Panathenaic Festival in 566 BC. The Acropolis entrance is defended by the **Beulé Gate** (named after Ernest Beulé, the archaeologist who found it); the monumental stairways were built by the Romans and the two lions are from Venice. The reconstructed Panathenaic ramp leads to the equally reconstructed **Propylaia**, the massive gateway built by Pericles' architect Mnesikles to replace Pisistratos' cursed gate. The ancient Greeks considered the Propylaia the architectural equal of the Parthenon itself, although it was never completed because of the Peloponnesian War. On either side of the Propylaia's entrance are two wings; the north held a picture gallery (Pinakothéke) while the smaller one to the south consisted of only one room of an unusual shape, because the priests of the neighbouring Nike temple didn't want the wing in their precinct. The original entrance had five doors, the central one pierced by the Panathenaic Way.

## Temple of Athena Nike

The Ionic Temple of Athena Nike, or *Wingless Victory*, was built by the architect Kallikrates in 478 BC of Pentelic marble. It housed the cult statue of Athena, a copy of a much older wooden statue. Its lack of wings, unlike later victory statues, gave it its second name. In 1687 the Turks destroyed the temple to build a tower. It was rebuilt in 1835 and again in 1936, when the bastion beneath it threatened to crumble away. Cement casts replace the north and western friezes taken to England by Lord Elgin. From the temple of Athena Nike the whole Saronic Gulf could be seen in the pre-smog days, and it was here that King Aegeus watched for the return of his son Theseus from his Cretan adventure with the Minotaur. Theseus was to have signalled his victory with a white sail but forgot; at the sight of the black sail of death, Aegeus threw himself off the precipice in despair.

## The Parthenon

The Parthenon, the glory of the Acropolis and probably the most famous building in the world, is a Doric temple constructed between 447 and 432 BC under the direction of Phidias, the greatest artist and sculptor of the Periclean age. Originally called the Great Temple, brightly painted and shimmering with gold, it took the name Parthenon (Chamber of Virgins) a hundred years after its completion. Constructed entirely of Pentelic marble, it originally held Phidias' famous chryselephantine (ivory and gold) statue of Athena Parthenos, who stood over 36ft high. The builders of the Parthenon wrote the book on mathematical perfection, subtlety, grace and *entasis*, the art of curving a form to create the visual illusion of straight lines. Look closely, and you'll see that the foundation is curved slightly to prevent an illusion of drooping caused by straight horizontals. The columns bend a few centimetres inward, and those on the corners are wider to complete the illusion of perfect form.

The outer colonnade consists of 46 columns and above them are the remnants of the Doric frieze left behind by the beaverish Lord Elgin: the east side portrayed the battle of giants and gods, the south the Lapiths and Centaurs (mostly in the British Museum today), on the west the Greeks and the Amazons, and on the north the battle of Troy. Little remains of the pediment sculptures of the gods. Above the interior colonnade, the masterful Ionic frieze designed by Phidias himself shows the quadrennial Panathenaic Procession in which Athena was brought a golden crown and a new sacred garment, or *peplos*.

The Parthenon was intact until 1687, when a Venetian bomb hit the Turks' powder stores and blew the roof off; an earthquake in 1894 was another serious blow. Entrance within the Parthenon has been forbidden, to save on wear and tear. Preserving the building, and undoing the damage of previous restorations, has been the subject of intense study over the past 15 years, when the alarming effects of the *néfos* on the marble could no longer be ignored: while discovering how to use hot, pressurized carbon dioxide to re-harden stone surfaces, Greek scientists have learned about ancient building techniques, and after all these years are picking up the pieces to reconstruct as much of the temple as possible, stringing column drums on new non-rusting titanium rods.

## The Erechtheion

The last great monument on the Acropolis is the Erechtheion, a peculiar Ionic temple that owes its idiosyncrasies to the various cult items and the much older sanctuary it was built to encompass. Beneath the temple stood the Mycenaean House of Erechtheus, mentioned by

Homer, and the primitive cult sanctuary of Athena; on one side of this grew the Sacred Olive Tree created by Athena, while under the north porch was the mark left by Poseidon's trident when he brought forth the divine spring. The tomb of the snake man Kekrops, the legendary founder of Athens, is in the Porch of the Maidens or Caryatids, where Erechtheus died at the hand of either Zeus or Poseidon. Within the temple stood the ancient primitive cult statue of Athena Polias, endowed with the biggest juju of them all, solemnly dressed in the sacred *peplos* and crown. After the Persian fires, the sanctuary was quickly restored, but the marble temple planned by Pericles was not begun until 421 BC. Converted into a church in the 7th century, the Turks made it a harem and used the sacred place of the trident marks as a toilet.

Basically the Erechtheion is a rectangular building with three porches. Inside were two cellas, or chambers: the East Cella dedicated to Athena Polias, the smaller to Poseidon-Erechtheus. Six tall Ionic columns mark the north porch where the floor and roof were cut away to reveal Poseidon's trident marks, as it was sacrilegious to hide such divine work from the view of the gods. The famous maidens or caryatids gracefully supporting the roof on their heads are another Ionian motif. Lord Elgin nicked parts of this temple as well, including one of the six caryatids (now in the British Museum); the *néfos* has forced the other girls to come indoors and be replaced by casts.

## The Acropolis Museum

*Open Tues–Fri 8–6.45, Mon 11–6.45, Sat and Sun 8.30–2.30.*

The museum houses sculptures and reliefs from the temples, in particular the Erechtheion's maidens, or Kores. Anti-*néfos* filters have been installed to show the British parliament that Greece is ready to properly care for the Elgin marbles, when and if they should ever vote to return them. Below the Acropolis is the **Areópagos**, or hill of the war god Ares. There sat the High Council, who figured so predominantly in Aeschylus' play *The Eumenides* where mercy defeated vengeance for the first time in history during the trial of the matricide Orestes. Although Pericles removed much of the original power of the High Council, under the control of the ex-archons it continued to advise on the Athenian constitution for hundreds of years.

## The Ancient Theatres

On the south side of the Acropolis two theatres are tucked into the hill. The older, the **Theatre of Dionysos,** was used from the 6th century BC when Thespis created the first true drama, and was continually modified up to the time of Nero. In this theatre the annual Greater Dionysia was held, in honour of the god of wine and patron divinity of the theatre, Dionysos, dramatic competitions that led to the premières of some of the world's greatest tragedies. The stage that remains is from the 4th century BC, while the area before the stage, or *proskenion*, is decorated with 1st century AD scenes based on the life of Dionysos. Beside the theatre stood two temples to Dionysos Eleutherios.

Above the theatre is an **Asklepeion**, a sanctuary to the god of healing. The stoa is from the second rebuilding, while the first and oldest sanctuary to the west first belonged to a water goddess, but very little of it remains. Both the old and new Asklepeions were connected with the parent cult at Epidauros.

The **Theatre of Herodes Atticus** (161 AD) was originally partly covered when it was built by the Rockefeller of his day, Herodes Atticus (whose life reads like something out of the *Arabian Nights*; his extraordinary wealth began when he found a vast golden treasure outside Rome). The theatre hosts the annual mid-May and September **Festival of Athens**, where modern

European and ancient Greek cultures mix and meet in theatre, ballet, and classical music concerts performed by companies from all over the world.

## Other Museums

**Benáki Museum**: On the corner of Vassilís Soffas and Koumbári Street, *open 8.30–3, daily. (Closed for renovations throughout 1995, but the shop is open)*.

This museum holds the collection of Antónios Benáki, who spent 35 years amassing Byzantine and Islamic objects from Europe and Asia. The Byzantine artworks (6th–14th centuries) are fascinating examples of early Christian art: icons, jewellery, ceramics, silver and embroidery; while the post-Byzantine exhibits (15th–17th century) show the influences of Islamic and Italian art. There are two icons by the Cretan-born El Greco, painted before his departure to Venice and Spain—the *Adoration of the Magi* (1560–65) and the *Evangelist Luke* (1560). The section on folk art, dating from the Ottoman occupation, contains a superb collection of costumes and artefacts from the Ionian islands to Cyprus.

**National Archaeology Museum**: Patissíon and Tossítsa Streets, *open 8–5, Sat and Sun 8.30–3, Mon 11–5; adm free Sun* (✆ 821 7719).

This is the big one, and deserves much more space than permitted here. It contains some of the most spectacular and beautiful works of ancient Greek world—the Minoan frescoes from Santorini, gold from Mycenae (including the famous mask of Agamemnon), statues, reliefs, tomb stelae, and ceramics and vases from every period. The Cycladic collection includes one of the first known musicians of the Greek world, the sculpture of the little harpist that has become the virtual symbol of the Cyclades. The star of the sculpture rooms is a virile bronze of Poseidon (5th century BC) about to launch his trident, found off the coast of Evia in 1928; around him are some outstanding archaic Kouros statues and the Stele of Hegeso, an Athenian beauty, enveloped by the delicate folds of her robe, seated on a throne. Don't miss the so-called Antikýthera Mechanism, the world's first computer, made on Rhodes *c.* 70 BC (*see* 'Antikýthera', p.422). The museum has a shop on the lower level, with reproductions of exhibits by expert craftsmen, so accurate that each piece is issued with a certificate declaring it an authentic fake so you can take it out of the country.

**National Gallery**: 50 Vass. Konstantínou, across from the Athens Hilton, *open 9–3, Sun and holidays 10–2, closed Mon* (✆ 721 1010).

Also known as the Alexander Soústou Museum, the National Gallery concentrates on art by modern Greek artists. Works by the leading contemporary painter, Níkos Hadzikyriákos-Ghíkas, are permanently displayed on the ground floor, while the lower level is used for rotating exhibitions. The museum shop has posters, cards, catalogues and jewellery, and there's a pleasant outdoor café, for when you've done the rounds.

**Historical and Ethnological Museum**: At the Paleá Voulí (Old Parliament), Stadiou Street, *open 9–1, Sat and Sun 9–12.30, closed Mon* (✆ 323 7617).

This imposing neoclassical edifice is the guardian of Greek history, from the fall of Constantinople to the present day. The bronze warrior on horseback is Theodóros Kolokotrónis, hero of the War of Independence, while exhibits within trace the history of modern Greece in paintings, sculptures, armaments (including Byron's sword and helmet), maps, folk costumes, jewellery and more covering every period, from Ottoman rule to resistance against the Nazis in 1940.

**Museum of Greek Folk Art**, 17 Kydathinaíon Street, *open 10–2, closed Mon; adm* (℗ 321 3018).

The museum has a collection of Greek folk art, both religious and secular, along with paintings by naïve artists.

**The Pnyx**: On the hill west of the Acropolis.

The Pnyx once hosted the General Assembly of Athens and the great speeches of Pericles and Demosthenes. On assembly days citizens were literally rounded up to fill the minimum attendance quota of 5000, but they were paid for their services to the state. Later the assembly was transferred to the theatre of Dionysos. On the summit of the nearby Hill of the Muses is the **Philopáppos Monument**, the tomb of Caius Julius Antiochos Philopappos, a Syrian Prince and citizen of Athens. The monument was built for him by the Athenians in 114 AD in gratitude for his beneficence to the city.

**Roman Agora:** Located between the Agora and the Acropolis, *open 8.30–3pm, closed Mon; adm exp* (℗ 324 5220).

Dating from the end of the Hellenistic age, the Roman Agora contains the celebrated **Tower of the Winds**, or Clock of Andronikos, built in the 1st century BC. Run by a hydraulic mechanism, it stayed open day and night so that the citizens could know the time. Its name comes from the frieze of the eight winds that decorate its eight sides, although it has lost its ancient bronze Triton weathervane. The Roman Agora also contains the **Gate of Athena Archegetis**, built by money sent over from Julius and Augustus Caesar; there is also a court and the ruins of stoae. Beside the Agora is the Fehiye Camii, the Victory or Corn Market Mosque.

**Byzantine Museum**: 22 Vassilís Soffas, *open 8.30–3, closed Mon* (℗ 723 1570).

This monumental collection of religious treasures and paintings dates from the Early Byzantine period to the 19th century—not only icons but marble sculptures, mosaics, woodcarvings, frescoes, manuscripts and ecclesiastical robes. There are three rooms on the ground floor arranged as chapels, one Early Christian, another Middle Byzantine, and the third post-Byzantine.

**Museum of Cycladic Art**: 4 Neofóros Doúka Street (between Byzantine and Benáki museums), *open 10–4, Sat 10–2.30, closed Tues and Sun* (℗ 724 9706).

This museum houses a vast collection of Cycladic figurines and objects dating back to 3200–2000 BC, illustrating everyday life. The female figurines with folded arms are unique. The newest addition is the 'Treasure of Keros', a small island near Náxos where excavations in the 1950s and 60s unearthed a wealth of figurines.

**Keramikós and Museum**: 148 Ermoú Street, *open 8.30–3, closed Mon* (℗ 346 3552).

The ancient cemetery or Keramikós was used for burials from the 12th century BC into Roman times, but the most impressive and beautiful finds are in the rich private tombs built by the Athenians in the 4th century BC. Large stone vases mark the graves of the unmarried dead, while others are in the form of miniature temples and stelae; the best are in the National Museum.

**Temple of Olympian Zeus:** Ólgas and Amalías Avenues, *open 8.30–3, closed Mon* (℗ 922 6330).

Fifteen columns recall what Livy called 'the only temple on earth of a size adequate to the greatness of the god'. The foundations were laid by the tyrant Pisistratos, but work ground to a halt with the fall of his dynasty, only to be continued in 175 BC by a Roman architect, Cossutius. It was half finished when Cossutius' patron, Antiochos IV of Syria, kicked the bucket, leaving the Emperor Hadrian to complete it in 131 AD. Nearby are the ruins of ancient houses and a bath and at the far end stands **Hadrian's Arch**, neatly dividing the city of Theseus from the city of Hadrian. The Athenians traditionally come here to celebrate the Easter Resurrection.

**Museum of the City of Athens**: Plateía Klafthmónos, *open Mon, Wed, Fri, Sat 9–1.30; adm, free Wed.*

Located in the re-sited neoclassical palace of King Otho, this new museum contains photos, memorabilia and a model of Athens as it was soon after it became the capital of modern Greece.

## Byzantine Churches and Monasteries in Athens

**Agii Theódori:** This 11th-century church in Klafthmónos Square at the end of Dragatsaníou St is most notable for its beautiful door; the bell tower and some of the decorations inside are more recent additions.

**Kapnikaréa:** A few blocks from Agii Theódori, on Ermoú Street. Tiny Kapnikaréa (the chapel of the University of Athens) was built in the late 11th century in the shape of a Greek cross, its central cupola sustained by four columns with Roman capitals.

**Panagía Gorgoepikoos** (or Ag. Elefthérios): Situated in Mitropóleos Square and known as the little Metropolitan to distinguish it from the nearby cathedral, this is the loveliest church in Athens. It was built in the 12th century almost entirely of ancient marbles: note the ancient calendar of state festivals embedded over the door. The **Cathedral** (just to the north) was built in 1840–55 with the same collage technique, using bits and pieces from 72 destroyed churches.

**Moní Pendéli:** Buses from Mouseío to Paliá Pendéli. Founded in 1578, in a lovely setting with plenty of shady trees, this is a popular weekend refuge from the *néfos*. Greek families come out for lunch under the gargantuan plane tree at the excellent taverna **O Telis**, ✆ 804 0484.

**Dafní and its Wine Festival:** 10km from Athens; take bus 282 from Elefthérios Square. The name Dafní derives from the temple of Apollo Dafneíos (of the laurel), built near the Sacred Way. The site became a walled monastery in the 6th century and in 1080 a new church was built, decorated with the best Byzantine mosaics in southern Greece. These are dominated in the vault of the dome by the tremendous figure of Christ Pantokrátor 'the all powerful', his eyes spellbinding and tragic, 'as though He were in flight from an appalling doom' according to Patrick Leigh Fermor. From mid-August until September, every evening from 7.45pm–12.30am, the monastery park holds a festival with over 60 different Greek wines (free once you've paid the 300dr admission at the gate) accompanied by poor and overpriced food, singing and dancing, an event well-attended by Athenians and visitors alike.

*Athens ✆ (01–)*

### Where to Stay in Athens

Athens is a big noisy city, especially so at night when you want to sleep—unless you do as the Greeks do and take a long afternoon siesta. Piraeus (*see* below) may be a better bet, no less noisy but much more convenient for catching those up-at-the-crack-of-dawn ships to the islands, although women on their own may find too many sailors and working girls about to feel at ease. All accommodation fills up quickly in the summer and if you don't have a reservation, or erratic boat schedules have mangled your booking, it's best to head straight for the end of the queue at the EOT office on Sýntagma Square (in the National Bank building) and use their hotel-finding service.

### *luxury*

The **Grande Bretagne**, ✆ 323 0251, ✉ 322 8034 (*lux*) was originally built in 1862 to house members of the Greek royal family who couldn't squeeze into the main palace (the current Parliament building) up the square. The Grande Bretagne is the only 'grand' hotel in Greece worthy of the description, with a vast marble lobby, elegant rooms (now air-conditioned and appointed with such modern conveniences as direct dial phones and colour TV), a formal dining room, and an appearance of grandeur and style that the newer hotels, with all their plushness, may never achieve. Having said that, on our most recent stay there we found the service to be positively complacent, which is disappointing at the prices they charge. Even if you're not going to stay there, you may want to poke your head in (there's a pleasant bar) to see where the crowned heads of Europe lodge in Athens—and where the Nazis set up their headquarters during the Second World War. Winston Churchill spent Christmas 1944 at the Grande Bretagne and was lucky to escape a bomb meant for him, planted in the hotel's complex sewer system. Down from the Grande Bretagne on Sýntagma Square the **Meridian Athens**, 2 Vass Geórgiou, ✆ 325 5301, ✉ 323 5856 (*lux*) is a modern favourite, and all rooms are soundproofed, an important consideration if you want a lie-in instead of an Athens morning traffic sonar disturbance; it also has a very respectable restaurant.

On a less exalted level, but with a far more fetching view, is the **Royal Olympic Hotel** at 28 Diákou, ✆ 922 6411, ✉ 923 3317 (*lux*), facing the Temple of Olympian Zeus and Mount Lykavitós. Rooms here are American in spirit, with a number of family-sized suites, and if you have the misfortune to get a room without a view, there's a wonderful panorama from the rooftop bar. The **Amalia**, ✆ 323 7301 (*A*) has an excellent location on Amalía St opposite the National Gardens. **St George Lycabettus**, 2 Kleoménous, up in Kolonáki, ✆ 729 0711, ✉ 729 0439 (*lux*), has an intimate, family-run atmosphere and wonderful views up to Lykavitós or out to the sea, and a pool, too. The Grand Balcon dining room has views that take in most of Athens. New luxury chain hotels are mushrooming up everywhere just outside the city centre—among them, the **Ledra Marriott** at 113–115 Syngroú, ✆ 934 7711, ✉ 935 8603 (*lux*), featuring a Chinese-Japanese restaurant, and a hydrotherapy pool you can soak in with a view of the Parthenon. Out in the swish northern suburb of Kifissiá, the gorgeous old **Pentelikon**, 66 Diligiánni Street, Kefalári, ✆ 808 0311, ✉ 801 0314 (*lux*) has a lovely garden and pool.

### *expensive*

The **Electra Palace** at 18 Nikodímou Street, ✆ 324 1401, ✉ 324 1875 (*A*) has views of the Acropolis and a wonderful rooftop swimming pool in a garden setting—something you don't find every day in Athens. Rooms are air-conditioned and there's a garage adjacent to the hotel. The hotel is quite close to the good tavernas of Pláka. More reasonable, and centrally located just off Sýntagma Square, the **Astor**, 16 Karagiórgi Servías, ✆ 325 5555 (*A*), also has fully air-conditioned rooms and a rooftop garden restaurant. The **Parthenon,** 6 Makrí Street, ✆ 923 4594, 🖷 921 5569 (*A*) is not far from Hadrian's Gate and the Acropolis, and has a pretty outdoor breakfast area.

### *moderate*

**Adams Hotel,** Herefóntos and Thálou, ✆ 322 5381 (*B pension*) is in a quiet but central location on the edge of the Pláka, 3 minutes from Hadrian's Arch; rooms are traditional, comfortable, and good value. The **Hotel Museum,** 16 Bouboulínas Street, ✆ 360 5611 (*C*), right at the back of the Archaeology Museum, has rooms are about the same, but the prices are a bit higher. **Hotel Tempi,** 29 Eólou Street, ✆ 321 3175 (*D*), near Monastiráki, is more downgrade, but is cheaper and has washing facilities. **Art Gallery** at Eréchthiou 5, Veíkoú, ✆ 923 8376 (*C pension*) is a pleasant place at the lower end of this price category, though it is out of the centre; Pláka is a 20-minute walk, more if you're fumbling with a map. **Hotel Hermes,** 19 Apollónos, ✆ 323 5514, near Sýntagma (*C*) is comfortable and friendly, with a small bar and roof garden with Acropolis views. The **Athenian Inn,** 22 Cháritos Street, Kolonáki, ✆ 723 8097, 🖷 721 8756 (*D*) is good value for this swanky part of town, and apparently was the favourite of Lawrence Durrell; rates near the top of this category. **Hotel Hera,** 9 Falírou at Veikoú, ✆ 923 6683 (*C*) is modern but tasteful with a garden on the ground and roof. Out in Kifissiá, **Hotel Katerina,** 3 Mykónou, ✆ 801 9826 (*C*) is one of the least expensive and friendliest places up in posh Kifissiá. In Chalándri, a bit closer to Athens, the **Akropol,** 71 Pentélis Ave, ✆ 682 6650, 🖷 684 5057 (*C*) is very nice with a garden, popular with business people, American tourists and anyone who wants to stay above the *néfos* line.

### *inexpensive*

Most of the inexpensive hotels are around Pláka. For better or worse, the government has shut down many of the old dormitory houses that grew up in the 1960s to contain the vanguard of mass tourism in Greece—every hippy in Europe, or at least so it seemed to the amazed Greeks. Survivors of the government purge have upgraded themselves but are still a bargain—and many still let you sleep on the roof for a thousand drachmas (not an unpleasant option in the thick heat of August). Best bets in the cheaper category include:

**Pension Adonis,** 3 Kódrou, ✆ 324 9737, is a gem, clean and well run by the Greek who managed the Annapolis Hilton. Lovely breakfast roof garden and bar with views (rates include breakfast, and can sometimes tip into the moderate category). Ditto for the **Akropolis House,** 6–8 Kodroú, ✆ 322 3244, 🖷 324 4143, which has modernized rooms but in a traditional style, with antique furnishings. **Hotel Phaedra,** 16 Herefóndos St, ✆ 323 8461, just off Filellínon St, has free hot showers, an unreconstructed pre-war interior, and pleasant staff. **John's Place,** 5 Patróou St, ✆ 322 9719 (near Metropóleos St) is simple and cheap, with bathrooms down the hall. **Kouros,** 11 Kódrou St (just off Kidathinéou St), ✆ 322 7431, is in a quietish backwater, in an old house near the Greek Folk Art Museum in the Plaka, just opposite the small park area on Kidathinaíon. **Byron,** Víronos 19, ✆ 325 3554, is a small and pleasant pension. **Villa Olympia,** 16 Karatzá, Koukáki, ✆ 923 7650, is British-run, cheap, small and friendly and does a full English breakfast to get you going in the morning. **Marble House,** 35 A. Zínni, Koukáki, ✆ 923 4058, is a comfortable Greek-French-run pension that offers good value. **Leto,** 15 Missaralioútou, Veíkou, ✆ 923 1768, is basic but adequate. **Student Inn**, 16 Kidathinéon, ✆ 324 4808, very conveniently placed in the Pláka, is ideal for the rowdy younger crowd (1.30am curfew, though).

The **Student's Hostel** at 75 Damaréos St, Pangráti, ✆ 751 9530, is central and not a member of YHA, but the nearest **campsites** to Athens are at Dafní Monastery, and down on the coast at Voúla. When your make you way through the metro station at Piraeus, you're likely to have fliers thrust in your hand for other rock-bottom options.

### hotels near the airport

If you have an early or delayed flight, or just one day to spend in Athens, there are quite a few hotels handy for the airport. Note that they tend to be desperately noisy— some are practically on the runway. The **Emmantina**, 33 Vass. Georgíou, Glyfáda, ✆ 898 0683, ✆ 894 8110 (*A; exp*) is one of the better ones, with a pool on the roof and shuttle bus to and from the airport. Convenient, moderate-priced C-class choices in Glyfáda include: the **Blue Sky**, 26 Eleftherías, ✆ 894 3445; **Avra**, 5 Gr. Lambraki, ✆ 894 7185 and **Beau Rivage**, 87 Vass. Geórgiou, ✆ 894 9292. **Kreoli**, 17 Vass. Georgíou, ✆ 894 4301, ✆ 894 8986 (*B; mod*) is basic, but friendly and family run, with a pool and breakfast room. Front room and ear plugs essential, air-conditioning extra. A bit further out, in Fáliro, try the **Best Western Coral**, 35 Possidónos, ✆ 981 6441, ✆ 983 1207 (*B; mod*).

---

### Eating Out in Athens

Athenians rarely dine out before 10 or 11pm, and they want to be entertained afterwards. If it's warm, chances are they'll drive out to the suburbs or the sea shore. Glyfáda, near the airport, is a popular destination and on a summer evening the cool sea breeze can be a life-saver after the oppressive heat of Athens. The obvious meal to choose is something from the sea, and most of the tavernas specialize in fish (especially red mullet, or *barboúnia*), lobster, squid and shrimp, although, remember as everywhere in Greece, it's the most expensive food on the menu. Remember that prices marked for fish usually indicate how much per kilo, not per portion.

## Glyfáda

Leading off the main square in Glyfáda is a street almost entirely devoted to excellent restaurants and friendly, inexpensive bars. At reasonably priced **George's**, the steak will be cooked according to your specifications and the meatballs (*keftédes*) are a speciality. To feed the large foreign community in Glyfáda, a plethora of fast-food joints has mushroomed up, and now expensive Arab and Lebanese restaurants (complete with imported Middle Eastern singers and belly dancers) have made an appearance on the scene, especially along the stretch of coast between Piraeus and the airport.

## Central Athens

The legendary **Gerofinikas**, 10 Pindárou, Kolonáki, ✆ 362 2719, still has the ancient palm tree that gave it its name, growing right out of the middle of the restaurant; the food is famous, expensive, and the whole meal an experience. **Costayiannis**, 37 Zaími (✆ 821 2496), near the National Archaeology Museum, with a succulent display of food in the glass cabinets near the entrance preparing you for a memorable culinary evening. Apart from the superb seafood, the 'ready food' is unbeatable—roast pork in wine and herb sauce or the rabbit *stifádo*, accompanied by barrelled retsina, if you've developed a taste for it. Prices here are very reasonable—3500dr for a full evening meal. To enjoy the after-theatre ambience, don't get there too early. (*Closed lunchtimes and Sundays*). As near to a traditional taverna as you'll find, the **Taverna Karavitis** ✆ 721 3155 is a few streets up from the old Olympic stadium, on the corner of Arkitinoú and Pafsaníou and housed in a long, low white building, with barrels lining the walls. Athenians come here for a good time: the food is better than average, wine is served from the barrel, and it's open till late (*3000dr*). Just off Mikalakopoúlou St, and not far from the Hilton Hotel, is **John's Village** (**To Chorio tou Yianni**), ✆ 779 4479, a cut above the ordinary taverna and warmly decorated with hand-woven rugs and island pottery. The accompanying music, played by a strolling minstrel, makes this a favourite spot to spend an evening without breaking the bank. There's a good variety of well-prepared dishes and a meal will cost about 4000dr. Behind the Hilton, the Cypriot restaurant **Othello's** at 45 Mikalakopoúlou, ✆ 729 1481, serves delicious, authentic cuisine at around 4500dr for a meal. **Syntrivani tou Syntagmatos**, 5 Filellínon Street, is named for the small fountain in its courtyard; good and inexpensive. At the end of the little arcade off the same street, **Calypso**, ✆ 322 5796, is just next door to the USIT office, a cute little *ouzerie* and beer garden, with a shady courtyard surprisingly tucked away, and two indoor eating levels. It's great for a *mezédes* lunch, and popular with the press and politicians. **Kioupi**, 4 Kolonáki Square, in the basement opposite the British Council, ✆ 361 4033, is a great place for cheap eats in Kolonáki, with cheap and cheerful dishes, including good *laderá*; it does takeaways and half-portions so you can try several dishes—until 5 in the morning.

## The Pláka

Pláka is the place to head for pleasant restaurants and al fresco dining in the evening— the tinkling glasses, music, chatter and laughter richochet off the medieval walls. There are scores of places catering for the passing tourist trade, and they are all very competent, though few serve the true, vernacular food that you'll find on the islands (if you make the effort to look for it). Despite this, the Pláka is still the perennial favourite with both Greeks and tourists, and although it's not a tourist trap, you should be selective where you eat. A few places may entice you with Greek dancers whirling and leaping on stages the size of postage stamps, but their menu prices are adjusted accordingly, and the food rarely rises above the mediocre. A typical charming Pláka taverna is the rooftop **Thespes** , 18 Thespídou, ✆ 323 8243, where a selection of starters, such as tzatziki, taramasalata and fried aubergine followed by lamb chops and plenty of wine, won't cost you much more than 3000dr. One other outstanding exception is **Platanos**, 4 Diogénis, ✆ 322 0666, the oldest taverna in the Plaka, near the Tower of the Four Winds. The food here is good and wholesome, but forget about perusing the menu—it's definitely an 'in the kitchen and point' joint, and inexpensive at 2000–3000dr. for a meal. In the heart of Pláka, in Filomousón Square, where every visitor lands up sooner or later, you can eat well at **Byzantino** (formerly O Kostis), 18 Kidathinéon, ✆ 322 7368, which serves big portions (the fish soup and lamb fricassee are excellent) at its tables under the trees (*3000dr*). It's also one of the few decent places open for Sunday lunch. Just around the corner is the famous **Xynou Taverna**, 4 Angeloú Gerontá Street, ✆ 322 1065, which serves excellent Greek and international food in a garden setting or inside, where the walls are painted with naive murals of Pláka characters. Strolling guitarists play traditional Greek music. (*Reservations are a must; closed on Sat and Sun, and all July; 3500–4000dr*). Off touristy Adrianoú Street, with all its souvenirs, try the family-run taverna **Tsegouras**, ✆ 323 3710, with consistently good food (*stifádo*, veal and snails) charmingly served in an indoor courtyard. Over the road, **To Yenari** (or **Ouzerie Kouklis**), 14 Tripódon, is a popular split-level taverna in an old house with a summer terrace. Dine on *mezédes* and sausages cooked at the table while perusing the naughty turn-of-the-century photos on the walls. For non-meat-eaters, Athens' only vegetarian restaurant is **Eden**, 12 Lissíou and Mnissikléous, ✆ 324 8858, with vegetarian quiches and moussakas, although they sometimes go off a bit in the summer. If you come out of season (*Oct–Apr*), try the famous **To Ipogio** (The Cellar), 30 Kidathinaíon, with superb Greek fare and atmosphere, evenings only. For a quiet coffee or drink, **Paradokiako Kafeneion** on Hadzimicháli is surprisingly quiet place to linger under a vine-covered terrace.

While walking around Pláka, you're likely to pass **Brettos**, a small but colourfully lit shop selling own-label *mastiká* and liqueurs. Try some; it beats bringing back a bottle of ouzo with you on the aeroplane.

### Around the Pláka

On the edge of the Pláka, towards the Temple of Olympian Zeus, **Daphne's**, 4 Lysikrátous, ✆ 322 7971, has an elegant dining room and beautiful garden—a rarity in Athens—with a menu of well-prepared traditional Greek and international dishes at around 6000dr a head, still a bargain for what you get. Just outside the Pláka, two blocks south of Hadrian's Arch at 5 Lembéssi Street, **O Kouvelos**, ✆ 922 1183, is another typical, reliable Athenian taverna, serving excellent *mezé* and barrelled retsina. They'll save you the bother of ordering the *mezé* by planting it on the table in front of you; don't be shy to change it if you want something different (*3000dr*). In the same area (cross Makriyiánni Street), you could try **Socrates Prison**, ✆ 922 3434, 20 Mitséon, a real favourite with locals and ex pats, serving Greek food with flair in attractive surroundings, although the service can be variable (*3000–4000dr; evenings only, closed Sun*). You can dine in affordable luxury within a stone's throw of the Acropolis at **Diogenes**, an Athenian landmark. The comfortable surroundings and live violin music is matched by superior Greek cuisine which is well priced (*4000dr, but more if you opt for their fine wines*).

A few blocks west of here, at 7 Gariváldi St, the **Greek House** has dining on a rooftop terrace with a most beautiful view of the Acropolis. Don't be put off by the name; this restaurant serves superb and reasonably priced specialities—try the 'Virginia', slices of *filet mignon* with mushrooms, or the shrimp salad. They also make wonderful spinach and cheese pies (*2500 dr*). Near the Monastiráki Elektrikó station, search out **Taverna Sigalas**, a bustling place where you can soak up the least pretentious side of Athenian life; usual Greek food served at unpredictable temperatures, and Greek folk music to make you feel you never want to go home (*2500dr*). Two minutes' walk from Sýntagma Square, **Galleria del Brazilian**, 2 Voukourestioú, ✆ 325 1350 (keep your eyes open for the courtyard set back from the street) is a cut above the average and is popular with local business people, not all of whom are on expense accounts. Don't let the name confuse—it's decidedly Greek cuisine.

## Around Omónia Square

Sleazy Omónia Square is a great place to try Greek street food. You can buy bags of nuts, coconut sweets, savoury pies (*tyrópitta*—cheese, and *spanakópitta*—spinach), late-night *souvláki*, and sandwiches, and it's all very cheap. The restaurants near Omónia Square displaying cuts of roast lamb, pork and the occasional grinning sheep's head. They're really worth a try if you are watching your drachmae but feel like a 'proper' meal—a portion of chicken with rubber fried spuds and a small bottle of retsina will set you back about 1000dr. Of the half-a-dozen or so places, try **Taygetos** on Satombriándou; it's the most popular and traditional and won't require an Alka-seltzer chaser (*1500–2000dr*). Inevitably most of the international burger joints have invaded, but if you're in a hurry or on a budget, resist the temptation: head instead for the **Neon Cafeteria** (one of a very small Athenian chain) in a restored neoclassical building on the square, with a choice of quick wholesome meals and good coffee.

## Exárchia and Koukáki

**I Gardenia**, 29 Zínni, Koukáki, has a cool setting, with cheap casserole food and barrelled wine. *Lunch only in the summer.* **O Yeros tou Morea**, 4 Arváli, Koukáki, is the haunt of bachelors having oven food for lunch, tasty *mezédes* and wine from the barrel. **To Meltemi**, Zínni 26, is an *ouzerie* with seafood. **Psistaria To Sokaki** (The Alley) is a bit smarter, with outdoor tables and good grilled chicken and *mezédes*. In studenty Exárchia, the **Attikon Taverna**, Plateía Exárchia, is a friendly place for lunch, with reasonable prices. **Vangelis** on Sachini off Liossíon is one of the friendliest and most traditional tavernas around. **O Leftheris**, Ioulanoú 84, has a walled garden and good casseroles.

### ethnic cuisine

Athens is well supplied with ethnic eating places—French, Italian, Spanish, Chinese, Japanese, Mexican, American and restaurants of other nationalities are scattered around the capital, but your bill will be two to three times that of the average taverna. Of particular note for lovers of German food is the **Ritterburg**, at 11 Formiónos in Pangráti, ✆ 723 8421, where the boiled and grilled sausages and pork with sauerkraut are tops. North German dishes are on the menu in the small, intimate and aptly named **Delicious** in the Status center building Vouliagméni, near Glyfáda (Athinás and Aéros 2a, ✆ 896 4618)—marinated fish, *bratkartoffeln*, lovely goulasch and home-made black bread (*4500dr*). Asian restaurants are all relatively expensive. The Chinese-Malaysian **Rasa Sayang**, ✆ 962 3629, in the seaside suburb of Glyfáda, on Paleá Leofóros Vouliagménis and 2 Kíou, serves great Peking duck and beef with mango slices, among many other items (*5000dr*). A little further down the coast at Voúla, **Loon Fung Tien**, 143 Alkyonídon, ✆ 895 8083, does fixed-price dim sum (buffet) lunchtimes on Sunday. *Closed Mondays.* Between the airport and Piraeus, on the coast road, the **Singing Bamboo**, 22 Posidónos, ✆ 982 8343, is another good Chinese eatery, and has an all-you-can-eat Sunday buffet for 4000dr. Italian restaurants are established in every major European city, and Athens is no exception. In Kolonáki the trendy **Pane e Vino/Solserino**, 8 Spefsípou, is popular for its *antipasti* (aubergine and gorgonzola rolls) and pasta (*tagliolini* with smoked salmon), together with main dishes such as sole with mussels or scaloppine with prosciutto (*4–5000dr; closed Sun*). A collection of top-class, expensive French restaurants have graced the Athens culinary scene for years. In Kolonáki **Je Reviens**, 49 Xenokrátous, is an old favourite, with live music and outdoor seating (*5000dr*). Near the American Embassy **Balthazar**, 27 Tsóha and Vournázou, ✆ 644 1215; is a renovated mansion with an attractive bar and a comprehensive selection of international dishes, but it's best to book; (*3500dr*). For the adventurous, a bus or trolley ride north of the National Archaeology museum (along Patissíon) will take you to Koliátsou Square and the restaurant **Axum**, with exotic Ethiopian specialities (✆ 201 1774). One block up from Leof. Alexándras (at the Ambelókipi, or eastern end) the **Bohemia**, 5 Dímou Tséliou, ✆ 642 6341, has authentic Czech dishes and is very reasonably priced. Finally, unashamed carnivores are made very welcome at **El Gaucho** in Ano Glyfáda, 185 Gounari, ✆ 963 4780, where you can eat your fill of Argentinian beef and *ebanados*, whatever they are. Live music.

### hotel restaurants

Some of the luxury hotels in Athens have some swish theme restaurants (with swish prices, of course). The **Ledra Marriott**, 115 Syngroú, ✆ 934 7717, has the 'Polynesian' **Kona Kai** in an exotic tropical setting, with the delicacies from that other island paradise; a few blocks down, the **Athenaeum Intercontinental** also has Asian cuisine in its **Kublai Khan** restaurant, ✆ 902 3666. The Hilton, opposite the National Gallery, has set-price buffet dinners (Thursday—Italian, Friday—seafood) for 7000dr without wine, and is well worth the treat.

### Entertainment and Nightlife

Pláka has masses of tavernas with bouzouki shows, but they can be expensive. **Yeros tou Morea**, 27 Misikléos is open-air and you can have a go at Greek dancing. For *rembétika*, try **Alexandriani**, 3 Lamáchou, off Filellínon, with a 1950s style band and real bouzouki. In a neoclassical building **Taksimi**, 29 Isavron, in Exárhia is similar, and can get crowded (closed July and Aug). In summer, the most happening bars and clubs are out in Glyfáda: **Mercedes B 52**, **La Playa**, **Bouzias** and **Amazon**. In adjacent Voúla, the **Aerodromio Club** at 25 Pergámou is an upmarket disco complete with a plane hanging from the ceiling, and stays open until 4am (it can be ideal if you have a 6am flight to catch). Other bars include **Rock In** behind the Hilton, **Memphis**, **Café de Paris** near the University, **Quartier Latin** near the law school on Panepistimíou. In Pláka, there's **Skolaxeio** on Tripodes and **To Kafeneio**. **Loft** is the place in Kifissiá.

## Piraeus

The port of Athens, Piraeus (ΠΕΙΡΑΙΑΣ)—pronounced pi-ray-A or the old way, Pirevs—was the greatest port of the ancient world and remains today one of the busiest in the Mediterranean. In Greece, a country that derives most of its livelihood from the sea in one way or another, Piraeus is the true capital, while Athens is merely a sprawling suburb where the bureaucrats live. Still, it takes a special visitor to find much charm in the tall grey buildings and dusty hurly-burly in the streets, although Marína Zéa and Mikrolimáni with their yachts, brightly lit tavernas and bars are a handsome sight, as are the neon signs flashing kinetically as you sail to or from Piraeus in the evening.

## A Historical Outline

Themistocles founded the port of Piraeus in the 5th century BC when Pháliron, Athens' ancient port, could no longer meet the growing needs of the city. From the beginning Piraeus was cosmopolitan and up-to-date: the Miletian geometrician Hippodamos laid it out in a

Communications

A  Subway Station
B  Railway Station for Peloponnese
C  Railway Station for Northern Greece (Larissis)
D  Departure point for the Aegean Islands–Dodecanese–Crete
E  Departure point for the Saronic Gulf Islands
F  Departure point of Hydrofoil for Aegina
G  Departure point of Hydrofoil for the other islands of the Saronic Gulf
H  Departure point for abroad
I  Bus Terminal (Athens–Omonia)
J  Bus Terminal (Athens–Syntagma)

Piraeus

straight grid of streets that have changed little today. The centre of action was always the huge agora in the middle of the city. Under its stoae the world's first commercial fairs and trade expositions were held, some on an international scale. All religions were tolerated, and women were allowed for the first time to work outside the home.

As Piraeus was so crucial to Athens' power, the conquering Spartan Lysander destroyed the famous Long Walls that linked city and port in 404, at the end of the Peloponnesian War. Piraeus made a brief come-back under Konon and Lykurgos, who rebuilt its arsenals. After the 100-year Macedonian occupation and a period of peace, Sulla decimated the city to prevent any anti-Roman resistance, and for 1900 years Piraeus dwindled away into an insignificant village with a population as low as 20, even losing its name to become Porto Leone (after an ancient lion statue, carved in 1040 with runes by future king of Norway Harald Hadraada and his Vikings and carted off by Morosini to embellish Venice's Arsenal). Since the selection of Athens as the capital of independent Greece, Piraeus has regained its former glory as the reigning port of a seagoing nation.

### Getting Around

In Piraeus this usually means getting out of town as quickly as possible. **Ships** are grouped according to their destination and almost anyone you ask will be able to tell you the precise location of any vessel. The cluster of ticket agents around the port is very noisy and competitive, but prices to the islands are fixed, so the only reason to shop around is to see if there is an earlier or faster ship to the island of your choice. Beware that ticket agents often don't know or won't tell you information on lines other than the ones they carry. Only the tourist police on Aktí Miaoúli have complete information on boat schedules.

The **Elektrikó** or **Metro**, now being extended, is the quickest way into central Athens, with stations at the Theseíon, the flea market (Monastírion) or Omónia Square. It runs from 5am to 12.15am.

**Buses** to Athens run day and night, the main 'Green' line (no.040) taking you directly to Sýntagma Square. The express line no.19 bus service to East and West Airport leaves from Karaiskáki Square.

### Tourist Police

Aktí Miaoúli, ✆ (01) 452 3670.

Iroón Politechníou, ✆ (01) 412 0325.

## The Sights

If you find yourself in Piraeus with time to kill on a Sunday morning, take a prowl through the flea market parallel to the underground (Elektrikó) line, where you may well happen across some oddity brought back by a Greek Sinbad. If culture beckons, there's an **Archaeology Museum** at 31 Har. Trikoúpi Street, with an above average collection of antiquities (*open 8.30–3, closed Mon*), or perhaps the **Maritime Museum** on Akti Themistoclés by Freatídos Street, with intriguing plans of Greece's greatest naval battles, ship models and mementoes from the War of Independence (*open 8.30–1.30, closed Sun and Mon*). The **Hellenistic Theatre** at Zéa occasionally has performances in the summer.

**Beaches** are not far away, although the sea isn't exactly sparkling. Kastélla is the closest, followed by New Pháliron. Buses go to Ag. Kósmos by the airport, where you can play tennis or volleyball; at Glyfáda, further down the road, there's more wholesome swimming and a golf course for duffers.

Zéa, Glyfáda and Vouliagméni are the three **marinas** organized by the National Tourist Organization. Piraeus is also the place to charter yachts or sail boats, from 12ft dinghies to deluxe twin-screw yachts, if you've missed your island connection (*see* 'Yachting', p.20). Zéa, a ten-minute walk from the main port in Piraeus, is the best for idle people- and yacht-watching.

---

### Where to Stay in Piraeus

Hotel accommodation in Piraeus is geared towards businessmen, and unfortunately less so towards people who have arrived on a late-night ship or plan to depart on an early morning one. There are plenty of sleazy hotels within a 10-minute walk of the Elektrikó station. Brave souls sleep out in the squares, particularly in Karaiskáki.

#### expensive

If you're with the kids, try the quiet and very clean **Hotel Anemoni**, at Karaóli Demetríou and Evripídou 65–67, ✆ 411 1768 (*C*); since it's not directly on the port you miss the sailors and some of the racket. All rooms are air-conditioned, and there's a free transfer service to the port. **Castella**, 75 Vass. Pávlou, ✆ 411 4735 (*B*), is a nice place on the waterfront beyond Mikrolimáni, with a roof garden. Even more swish is the **Cavo d'Oro**, 19 Vass. Pávlou, ✆ 411 3744 (*B*), with a restaurant and disco, and the most expensive of all, **Mistral**, Vass. Pávlou 105, ✆ 412 1425 (*B*) comes with a pool, restaurant and air-conditioning.

#### moderate

If you want to be within walking distance of the docks, the **Hotel Triton**, ✆ 417 3457 (*B*) is one of the best of the many in the area; its B-class doubles start at 5500dr, but go shooting up in high summer. All rooms have private bath and breakfast is available. **Hotel Park**, on Kolokotróni, ✆ 452 4611 (*B*). The **Lilia**, 131 Zéas, Passalimáni, ✆ 417 9108, ✉ 411 4311 (*C*), is pleasant and offers free transport to the port. The **Ideal**, 142 Notará Street, ✆ 451 1727 (*C*), 50m from the customs house, offers air-conditioning and private bath, but should be renamed the Mediocre.

#### inexpensive

Known to seasoned travellers as the One Onion, **The Ionian**, 10 Kapodistríou, ✆ 417 0992 (*C*) is basic but very convenient for an early ferry or if you've just fallen off one. On the lower end of the scale there are many small C and D class hotels, some of which are not as appetizing as they might be, but their rates range from 3000dr to around 5000dr. Typical of these are **Achillion**, 63 Notará Street, ✆ 412 4029 (*D*), **Aenos**, near the main harbour, ✆ 417 4879 (*C*), **Santorini**, ✆ 452 2147 (*C*), and **Acropole**, ✆ 417 3313 (*C*), all used to backpackers.

---

### Eating Out in Piraeus

Around the port the fare is generally fast food and giro spinners, while the tavernas are so greasy it's a wonder they don't slide off the street. For seafood, the bijou little harbour of Mikrolímano (or Turkolímano) is the traditional place to go, although too many tourists with too much money have inflated the price to a nasty pitch. However, if someone else is picking up the tab, aim for **Zorba's**. A far better idea is to forgo fish and eat up at the excellent **Kaliva**, 60 Vass. Pávlou, Kastélla, with a splendid view down over the harbour (excellent meat dinners for 2500dr) followed by a stroll through Mikrolímano for a coffee and Metaxa on the harbour front.

Just down from the Kaliva, away from Mikrolímano, the **Chorio** is a rustic old taverna with all the old favourites. **Folia**, 30 Kalimasióti, near Aktí Poseidónas, is a handy place to grab a good cheap meal by the ferries, a working men's lunchtime taverna with excellent home cooking and *laderá*. For a real experience, try **Vassilenas**, Etólikou 72, ✆ 461 2457, a former grocer's with a grocery décor, but famous for its lack of a written menu, giant helpings, *mezé*, and fish specialities served on a rooftop garden. The Greek Royal family used to dine there, and certainly wish they could once more. Bookings essential; expensive. For great music, **Cafe Aman**, 109 Koundouriótou, ✆ 422 04359, is a friendly unpretentious taverna with special music from Smyrna on Tuesdays; authentic *rembétika* at other times, but never on Sunday.

On Piraeus' highest hill by the Bowling Club (take a taxi), **Rigas** is an excellent family taverna with a huge choice of delicious starters to choose from a heaving tray, and some unusual main courses to go along with the old favourites from the grill, oven or stew pot (*around 3500dr*). Top it off with a coffee and brandy on the terrace of the **Bowling Club** opposite, with a superb view over Piraeus.

But if it's fish you must have, head over to Fratídas, around from the Zéa Marína yacht harbour, where several moderately priced places offer fresh fish and sea views, or better yet, continue along the coast to the Kalípoli bulge (bus 904 or 905 from Elektrikó Square) where a number of *ouzeries* and fish tavernas line the road. **Samaras** is easily the most reasonably priced *ouzerie*, specializing in *mezédes*: a plate of meatballs or squid or salad to go with your drink. **Diasimos** is one of the big favourites in this area; Athenians drive down on Sundays to enjoy the sea views and seafood. For something less pricey but memorable, locate the Naval School near here: the favourite for excellent fish, salad and wine is the **Margaro**, at the school gate. If it's packed (which it often is) walk up the road away from the Naval School, pass the traffic lights and keep your eyes peeled for two fish tavernas. There's absolutely no view at all, but the variety, freshness and price of the seafood is its own reward; buses 904 and 905 go right past.

Further along the coast at Kalamáki, the **Apaggio**, 8 Megístis Street, ✆ 983 9093, specializes in dishes from different Greek regions. The menu changes daily, but often includes rarely seen delicacies such as lamb with prunes and almonds and onion pie. It's one of the in places for Greek foodies, but not expensive. *Bookings are essential; closed Mon.*

TRIADA MONASTERY

# Crete (Kríti)

*Column of the Levant,*
*My Crete, beautiful island,*
*Your soil is made of gold,*
*Your each stone a diamond.*

traditional Cretan *mantináda*

Crete, on the map an odd, horned, wasp-waisted creature that seems to scoot along the 35th parallel, is Greece's largest island (roughly 260 by 50km), and in a hundred ways its most extraordinary. Endowed by a generous nature with every earthly delight, Crete nurtured the very first civilization on European soil, the Minoan, which, at least according to its discoverer, Arthur Evans, was so advanced, graceful, peaceful, inventive and politically correct that Europe has yet to see the like. Birthplace of Zeus, the father of the gods, Crete gave Greece its most ancient myths, and in its remote mountain villages customs survive that have been long abandoned elsewhere.

These days you're far less likely to be prematurely punctured than suffocated by the worst excesses of mass tourism. The lovely beaches along the north coast have been raped by toadstool strips of jerry-built hotels, shops, restaurants, and discos, veritable Euro-tourist compounds often run by Athenians or foreigners, where bars advertize daily video showings of 'The Beverly Hillbillies' (or the Dutch, or German, or Finnish equivalents), the latest football scores, baked beans and permanent happy hours. Crete's hot climate makes it a major package holiday destination from early spring until the end of October; each year it becomes more difficult to visit even fairly remote corners such as the Minoan palace of Zákro or the Diktean cave without a dozen coachloads of tourists and rubber-tonsilled guides on your back. If you have mytho-poetic fantasies of tripping through the labyrinth of Knossós on your own, book your flight for December or January; after the Acropolis, it receives more visitors than any site in Greece.

As on Corfu, as on Rhodes, Crete's crushing popularity is a tribute to its extraordinary charms. Four mountain ranges lend the island a dramatic grandeur entirely disproportionate to its size; the White Mountains in the west are vast enough to hold the Gorge of Samariá, the longest in Europe. Some 1500 kinds of wild flowers, including a few hundred species unique to Crete, brighten the landscape in the spring with all the intensity of 1950s Technicolor. No island can approach Crete's agricultural importance or diversity. Vineyards, olive and citrus groves cover the coastal plains and hillside terraces; cereals, potatoes, pears, apples, walnuts and chestnuts come from the well-watered mountain plains, especially up around Lassíthi; acres of plastic greenhouses blanket the south coast—only 320km from Egypt—providing no advantage to the landscape but bushels of winter vegetables and fruit for the rest of Greece, including bananas and now avocados. Cretan art and architecture afford an equally rich feast: the fabled Minoan sites and artefacts in Herákleon's superb archaeology museum,

Byzantine churches and monasteries adorned with frescoes and icons by the Cretan School, the Venetian and Turkish quarters of Chaniá and Réthymnon, small mountain villages that do credit to the native Greek sense of design.

Of all the islands, Crete has the sharpest sense of a separate identity and the most ferocious love of liberty, manifest in its own culture, dialect, music and dances, and in the works of its most famous sons, El Greco, Elefthérios Venizélos, Níkos Kazantzákis, and Míkis Theodorákis. This culture is even more predominately masculine than that of other islands: in the mountain villages, older women still wrap themselves in drab scarves and rarely join in *kafeneíon* society, while their men cut a dash in their baggy breeches, high boots and black-fringed headbands and pour disdain on 'the long-trousered men' who have exploited the coast. Young women, however, are increasingly joining the men taking up the *lyra*, a three-stringed fiddle made of ivy or black mulberry wood, held upright on the lap, which plays the quarter-tone lead in Cretan melodies, accompanied by a large mandolin called the *lauto*, traditionally picked with an eagle quill. On feast days in the country, people sing *mantinádes*, improvised couplets, or *rizítika*, 'songs from the roots', with themes of Cretan patriotism. And such patriotism is, despite first appearances, far from dead. In the face of creeping homogenized Euro-crud, many young Cretans (especially returned immigrants) are taking an active role in preserving their traditions, even moving back up to their ancestral mountain villages, where EU subsidies assure them a decent living from their grandfather's olives. Paradoxes are rife, but after all, the island can take some credit for inventing paradox as an art form, when the Cretan philospher Epimenides declared: 'All Cretans are liars.'

## When to Go

The ideal time to visit Crete is towards the end of April, when you'll avoid the worst crowds; the Libyan Sea is usually warm enough for bathing, the flowers are glorious and the higher mountains are still capped with snow. Note that the Gorge of Samariá doesn't open until 1 May, when its torrent recedes sufficiently for safe passage. October is another good month, with many perfect days and a lingering warm sea.

## Note

The mountain ranges of Crete neatly divide the island into four sections. These have become modern Crete's political divisions and are used for reference in this book. West of the White Mountains is the *nomós* (county) of Chaniá; between the White Mountains and Psilorítis (Mount Ida) is the *nomós* of Réthymnon; between Psilorítis and the Lassíthi Mountains lies the *nomós* of Herákleon; and east of the Lassíthi Mountains is the *nomós* of Lassíthi, of which Ag. Nikólaos is the capital.

# Mythology

As Cronos (the Latin Saturn), the ruler of the world, had been warned that he would be usurped by his own child, he swallowed every baby his wife Rhea, daughter of the Earth, presented to him. After this had happened five times, Rhea determined on a different fate for her sixth child, Zeus.

When he was born she smuggled him to Crete and gave Cronos a stone instead, which the old fellow duly swallowed. Mother Earth hid the baby in the Diktean cave and set young Cretan warriors called the Kouretes to guard him; they were ordered to shout and dance and beat their shields to drown out the baby's cries.

Zeus grew up and indeed dethroned his father by castrating him with a sickle; the lost member fell into the sea off Cyprus and gave birth to Aphrodite, e goddess of love. She was scarcely born when a Phoenician girl, Europa, caught Zeus' fancy. Zeus disguised himself as a beautiful bull and carried Europa off to Crete, where she bore him three sons: Minos, Rhadamanthys and Sarpedon, and gave her name to an entire continent. When Minos became the King of Crete at Knossós, he was asked to prove that his claim to the throne had divine sanction. Minos remembered the form his father had taken and asked Poseidon to send him a bull from the sea to sacrifice to the gods. However, the bull was so magnificent that Minos didn't kill it, but sent it to service his herds.

The kingdom of Minos prospered, ruling the seas and exacting tributes from across the Mediterranean. But Poseidon, weary of waiting for the promised sacrifice, caused Minos' wife Pasiphaë to fall in love with the bull. The unfortunate Pasiphaë confided her problem to the inventor Daedalus, who constructed a hollow wooden cow covered with hide for her to enter and mate with the bull. This union resulted in the Minotaur, born with the head of a bull and the body of a man. Minos hid the monster in another invention of Daedalus, the Labyrinth, an impossible maze of corridors under his palace, and fed it with the blood of his enemies. Among these were seven maidens and seven youths from Athens, sent to Crete every nine years, the tribute extorted by Minos when his son was slain in an Athenian game.

Two tributes had been paid when Theseus, the son of Aegeus, King of Athens, demanded to be sent as one of the victims to do what he could to end the humiliating tribute. Conveniently, Minos' daughter Ariadne fell in love with him as he stepped off the ship. She asked Daedalus to help her save his life, and the inventor gave her a ball of thread. Unwinding the thread as he went, Theseus made his way into the labyrinth, slew the Minotaur with his bare hands, retraced his way out with the ball of thread and escaped, taking the Cretan princess and the other Athenians along with him.

Minos was furious when he discovered the part Daedalus had played in the business and threw the inventor and his young son Icarus into the Labyrinth. Although they managed to find their way out, escape from Crete was impossible, as Minos controlled the seas. But Daedalus, never at a loss, decided that what they couldn't accomplish by sea they would do by air. He fashioned wings of feathers and wax for himself and Icarus, and on the first fine day they flew towards Asia Minor. All went well until an exhilarated Icarus disobeyed his father's command not to fly too close to the sun. The wax in his wings melted, and he plunged and drowned off the island that took his name, Ikaria.

Minos heard of Daedalus' escape and pursued him all over the Mediterranean, hoping to trap the wily inventor by offering a great reward to whoever could pass a thread through a nautilus shell. Finally, in Sicily, Minos met a king who took the shell away and brought it back threaded—Daedalus was indeed there, and had performed the task by tying the thread to an ant. At once Minos demanded that the king turn Daedalus over to him. The king hedged, and instead invited Minos to stay at his palace. While

Minos was in his bath, Daedalus put a pipe through the ceiling and poured boiling water through it, scalding him to death. Zeus then sent him down to Hades to judge the dead, a task he shared with his brother Rhadamanthys and his enemy Aeacus.

## History

The first Cretans were Neolithic sailors who arrived on the island around 8000 BC, and probably came from Asia Minor. They built small houses in Knossós and other future Minoan sites, with small rooms clustered around a central open area, presaging the floor-plans of the famous palaces. They worshipped fertility goddesses in the depths of caves, especially in caves on top of mountains—the future peak sanctuaries of the **Minoans**.

As the first civilization on European soil, Minoan Crete exerts a special fascination. Poetically, we know it first from Homer:

> *One of the great islands of the world in midsea, in the winedark sea, is Krete: spacious and rich and populous, with ninety cities and a mingling of tongues. Akhaians there are found, along with Kretan hillmen of the old stock, and Kydonians, Dorians in three blood-lines, Pelasgians—and one among their ninety towns is Knossós. Here lived King Minos whem great Zeus received every ninth year in private council.*

(translated by Robert Fitzgerald)

Archaeologically, we know the Minoans only from 1900, when Arthur Evans began excavating Knossós, searching for hieroglyphic seals and finding instead a whole new Copper and Bronze Age culture that he labelled 'Minoan'. Since then, discoveries in Crete have continued apace, including some remarkable finds that have altered Evans' vision of the Minoans as a non-violent society of artsy flower children. Current opinion fairly agrees with the following, although if the data read by the newest techniques is to be believed, you must add another few centuries to all the dates; i.e. Santoríni is now believed to have erupted around 1750 BC.

Trade contacts established and expanded in Egypt, the Cyclades, and Middle East at the end of the Neolithic era introduced bronze to Crete and brought about the changes that distinguish the first Minoan period, the **Pre-Palatial** (2600–1900 BC), according to Professor Níkos Pláton's widely accepted revision of Evans' chronology. Characteristic of the Pre-Palatial era are the first monumental *tholos* tombs (as at Archánes), the building of sanctuaries at the highest points of settlements, and the apparent beginning of a ruling or priestly (or priestessly) class, who dwelt in large palaces (or temples) with red-plastered walls. The Minoan taste for refinement shines through at the end of the period, in exquisite work in gold, semi-precious stones and miniature sealstones, some bearing the first signs of writing in ideograms.

Pláton's **Old Palace period** (Evans' Middle Minoan; 1900–1700 BC) saw a hitherto unheard of concentration of wealth in Crete. Power, too, seems to have been concentrated in a few areas, in the 'palaces' of Knossós, Mália, Phaistós, and Zákros (although some argue they are really temples, or even the shrines of a cult of the dead). These were kitted out with the first known plumbing and lavishly decorated with frescoes and stylized sacred 'horns of consecration'. Bulls played an important role in religion, which was dominated by the goddess, pictured in Minoan imagery in three aspects: as the mistress of the wild animals and earth; as the snake goddess, mistress of the underworld; and as the dove goddess, mistress of the sky.

Towns and palaces were unfortified, suggesting political unity on the island and giving substance to the thalassocracy, or sea reign, of myth: no walls were needed thanks to the

Minoans' powerful fleet. Their ships, laden with olive oil, honey, wine and art, traded extensively with Cyprus, Egypt and the Greek islands; Minoan colonies have been found at Kéa, Mílos and Kýthera. The palaces/temples all had important stores, acting either as warehouses or distribution points for the surrounding territory. There was a system of writing in ideograms, most famously on the Phaistós disc in the Herákleon museum. Roads paved with flagstones linked the island, and the first large irrigation projects were dug. Art reached new heights, in sealstone making and in pottery, especially decorated Kamáres-ware. In 1700 BC a huge earthquake ripped across the Eastern Mediterranean and devastated the buildings.

Forced to start afresh, the Minoans rebuilt better than ever in the **New Palace period** (1700–1450 BC). The palace complexes were rebuilt in the same style, a warren of rooms illuminated by light wells, overlooking a central and western court, where religious ceremonies and the famous bull leaping took place. To build the new palaces more 'give' in case of earthquakes, wooden beams and columns (the distinctive reversed cedar trunks, thin at the bottom and wide at top) were combined with stone. Workshops and vast store-rooms were clustered around the palaces, the contents of the latter recorded on clay tablets in a writing system known as Linear A. Fancy villas were built outside the palaces, most famously at Ag. Triáda, and scattered throughout the countryside were centralized farms, with pottery kilns, wine presses, and looms. Densely populated towns have been excavated at Gourniá, Móchlos, Palaíkastro, Zákros and Pseíra island. Burials were more elaborate, more monumental, more various; many were in painted clay sarcophagi, or *larnaxes*. Impressive port facilities were built, especially along the north and east coasts, and new trade counters were established on Santoríni, Rhodes, Skópelos, and on the mainlands of Greece and Asia Minor. Shields, daggers, swords and helmets have been found, although land defences are still non-existent.

The Herákleon museum is jammed full of testimonials to the extraordinary, exuberant art of the period. The Minoans delighted in natural forms and designs, especially floral and marine motifs. They portrayed themselves with wasp waists and long black curls, the men clad in codpieces and loincloths, the women with eyes blackened with kohl and lips painted red, clad in their famous bodices that exposed the breast, flounced skirts decorated with complex patterns, and exotic hats. All move with a natural, sensuous grace, completely unlike the stiffly stylized hieratical figures in Egyptian and the Near Eastern art. The strong feminine quality of the art suggests that Minoan society was matriarchal, and that women were the equals of men, participating in the same sports, hunts and ceremonies. Vases and rhytons (libation vessels) made of basalt, marble and porphyry are unsurpassed in beauty and technique. Culturally their influence spread north to mainland Greece, recently invaded by northerners known as Achaeans or Mycenaeans; the Minoan Linear A script was adopted by Mycenean merchants, but in their own language (Linear B)—a very early version of Greek.

But some time around 1450 BC disaster struck again. A tremendous volcanic eruption from Santoríni, and subsequent tidal waves and earthquakes left Crete in ruins; in some places along the north coast a 20cm layer of tefra (volcanic ash) has been found—under structures belonging to the Late Minoan or **Post-Palace period** (1450–1100 BC). The old theory that Mycenaeans from the mainland invaded Crete, taking advantage of its disarray, has lost favour before the idea that their infiltration was much more gradual, and that for a long period the Mycenaeans co-existed peacefully side by side with the Minoans. Of the great palaces, only Knossós was rebuilt, only to burn once and for all in c. 1380 BC; in other places, such as Ag. Triáda, typical Mycenaean palaces, or *megarons*, have been found. Linear B becomes the dominant script, and the free natural decoration of pottery of the New Palace period becomes ever more conventional and stylized. Clay figurines of the goddess lose not only their sex appeal but any pretensions to realism; they resemble bells with upraised arms, primitive faces and bee-sting breasts. The island maintained its great fleet (if often for piratical ends), and was able to contribute 90 ships to the Trojan War.

## After the Minoans

By 1100 BC, Minoan-Mycenaean civilization ground to a halt; trade disintegrated as the Dorians, armed with latest technology—iron weapons—invaded Greece, and then Crete. Their coming brought confusion and a cultural dark age (the **Proto-Geometric period**, 1100–900 BC). The last Minoans took to the hills, especially south of Sitía, surviving in memory as the Eteocretans, or true Cretans. Their art grew weird and misshapen as they declined; in Praisós they left mysterious inscriptions in the Greek alphabet still waiting to be translated. Other Cretans were treated according to the amount of resistance they had offered the Dorians; those who fought the most were divided among the conquerors as slaves.

MINOAN BELL GODDESS

By the **Geometric period** (900–650 BC) Crete was politically divided, like the Greek mainland, into autonomous city-states: a hundred, according to ancient writers. The Minoan goddess became identified with the patriarchal Greek pantheon—Atana became Athena, Britomartis became Artemis, her son and consort Welchanos became Zeus, father of the gods. Art from the period shows Eastern influences; works in bronze are especially fine. Towards the end of the period the first bronze statuettes by Daedalos (not to be confused with the inventor of myth) and his school appear, with their charactistic wide eyes, thick hair, and parted legs.

The style reached its peak in the **Archaic period** (650–550 BC), when Doric Crete was one of the art centres of Greece. It declined, not only because of the Dorians' innate austerity, but before the expansion of Ionian commercial and cultural influence in the Mediterranean that created Greece's **Classical Age**. During this period Crete sat out on the margins of history. By the 2nd century BC such anarchy prevailed that the coasts became little more than pirates' bases. When these pirates sufficiently niggled Rome by kidnapping the families of Roman nobles at Ostia, the Senate sent Quintus Metellus Creticus to conquer Crete (69–67 BC).

## Roman and Byzantine Crete

With the Romans, the centre of power on the island moved south to Górtyn on the fertile Mesará plain, especially after the Romans made it capital of the province of Crete and Cyrene (Libya) in West Africa. With peace, the population on Crete soared to some 300,000. Christianity came to the island early when St Paul appointed one of his Greek disciples, Titus, to found the first church at Górtyn in 58 AD. Christian Crete especially prospered after the founding of Constantinople in 300, when rich basilicas were constructed across the island, most importantly at Knossós, Cheroínissos, Górtyn, Lissós, Sýia, Itanos and Kainoúrios.

In 823 Saracen Arabs conquered the island, plunging much of it in misery and decimating Górtyn. One lasting feature of their stay was the building of the first castle at Herákleon, called Kandak ('deep moat'), or Candia, a name which grew to mean all of Crete in the Middle Ages (and eventually became synonymous with the sweet honey and nuts it exported, hence 'candy'). In 961 Byzantine general and future Emperor Nikephóros Phokás reconquered Crete and sent the fabulous treasure of the Arabs back to Constantinople. The victorious Greek soldiers were among the first new colonists given tracts of land, in an attempt to repopulate the land; Emperor Aléxis Comnenús later sent his own son and other young Byzantine aristocrats to Crete to give the island a ruling class, one that continued to dominate Cretan life for centuries.

## Venetian and Ottoman Crete

With the conquest of Constantinople in the Fourth Crusade in 1204 and the division of the empire's spoils among its conquerors, Crete was awarded to Boniface of Montferrat. He soon sold the island to the Venetians, who after a brief tussle with arch-rival Genoa occupied the island from 1210 to 1669. The first two centuries of rule by the Most Serene Republic were neither serene nor republican; the Venetians high-handedly imposed the feudal system and their model of government, to the extent that the island was even divided into the same six *sestieri* as Venice itself, ruled by its own doge, or Duca, out of Herákleon. Laws attempted to diminish the influence of the Orthodox church and replaced the Orthodox hierarchy with a Catholic one. Uprisings lasting several years occurred, often led by the *árchons*, or old Byzantine nobles. Nearly each time they won important concessions from the Venetians, until, by the 15th century, the Greek Orthodox majority and Venetian Catholics (some 10,000) lived in reasonable harmony, all reasonably happy—except of course for the majority, the *villani,* or serfs, who in addition to working long hours for their lords were compelled to build the immense walls around the cities, even though they were not allowed to live inside them.

Cretan-Venetian relations were cemented with the fall of Constantinople in 1453, when the Venetians were keen to keep the Greeks on their side. In Greece's age-old tradition of absorbing the invader, many Venetians were hellenized, spoke Greek better than Italian and converted to Orthodoxy. As a refuge for scholars and painters from Constantinople and mainland Greece, Crete became the key point of contact between the East and the Italian Renaissance in the 15th and 16th centuries and in art produced, most famously, Doméniko Theotokópoulos, who moved to Venice and Spain, where he became known as El Greco. Cretan-Venetian schools and academies, architecture, theatre, literature, song and romantic epic poetry blossomed, culminating in the dialect epic poem *Erotókritos* by Vicénzo Kornáros.

Although several raids, especially by such dire nasties as Barbarossa and Dragout, had taken place ever since the fall of Constantinople, the Ottomans finally caught Crete by surprise. In 1645, Sultan Ibrahim declared war on the Knights of Malta after the knights captured his wife and son as they sailed to Mecca, and sent a fleet of 1440 ships after them. They stopped in Kýthera for coffee and sugar, and the Venetian commander there sent word to his counterpart in Chaniá to allow the fleet safe passage; on 12 June, as the sultan's ships began to sail past, they turned their guns on the city. Herákleon resisted until 1669, a 21-year siege that was one of the longest in history.

Under the Ottoman Empire, Crete descended into a new spiritual and economic dark age. Turkish reprisals for Crete's long resistance were horrific, in human and material terms. The most fertile lands were given to Turkish colonists and, although the Orthodox religion was tolerated, many Cretans became crypto-Christians, publicly converted to Islam to avoid the punishing head and property taxes that turned most Christian farmers into serfs. Those who could emigrated to the Venetian-held Ionian islands; those who couldn't rose up against the Turks more than 400 times, in a great crescendo of revolts throughout the 19th century.

In 1898, Greece declared war on Turkey, and asked the Great Powers for aid. Britain did little, in spite of searing articles of atrocities sent home by Arthur Evans, until the Turks made the fatal mistake of killing the British consul and 14 British soldiers in Herákleon. As British, French, Russian and Italian troops subdued sections of the island, Prince George was appointed High Commissioner of an independent Crete. Prince George's high-handed ways and imposition of a foreign administration led in 1905 to the Revolution of Therisso, led by Elefthérios Venizélos of Chaniá. In 1909 Venizélos was appointed Prime Minister of Greece, a position that enabled him to secure Crete's union to Greece after the Balkan War of 1913.

## The Battle of Crete

As the Germans overran Greece, the government in Athens took refuge on Crete (23 April 1943), the last bit of Greek territory, defended by 30,000 British, New Zealand and Australian troops hastily transferred from the mainland. Crete's battalions were trapped near the Albanian frontier; the only Greek soldiers on the island were cadets and untrained recruits. But then again, no one suspected what Goering and General Student, his second-in-command of the Luftwaffe, had in store. After a week of bomb raids, Nazi paratroopers launched the world's first successful invasion by air on Crete (20 May 1941). The Allied and Greek forces, along with hundreds of poorly armed men, women and children, put up a such a stubborn resistance for ten days that the Germans were forced to expend the cream of their forces to subdue the island in ten days—at the cost of 170 aircraft, 4000 specially trained paratroopers killed, and the decimation of their 7th airborne division. As Churchill wrote, 'In Crete Goering won a Pyrrhic victory, because with the forces he wasted there he could easily have conquered Cyprus, Syria, Iraq or even Persia...'

In spite of brutal German reprisals, resistance to the occupation, aided by British agents in the mountains and based in Egypt, was legendary, especially Major Patrick Leigh Fermor and Captain Billy Moss's daring abduction of General Kreipe, the German commander of Crete, from Herákleon in 1943. As a massive manhunt combed the island, the British and Cretan Resistance transported Kreipe across the mountains and away to Egypt from Rodákino on the southwest coast, earning a final, grudging comment from the General: 'I am beginning to wonder who is occupying the island—us or the English.'

## Food and Wine

Although not readily apparent from the run-of-the-mill taverna menu, Crete has a number of distinctive dishes based on the dizzying variety and richness of its agriculture. Nearly every kind of fruit, from apples to bananas to oranges, grow on the big island, and the plastic farms along the south coast provide many of Greece's winter vegetables. A wander through the large markets at Herákleon or Chaniá will reveal counters of herbs grown on the island (many prettily packaged to make inexpensive gifts, although be aware that what looks at first like an incredibly good deal in saffron is merely a decent buy in turmeric). Cretan mountain honey and its cheeses have had a high reputation since antiquity: fresh white *anthótiro* or dried *anthótiro xeró*; *myzíthra*, a white soft cheese sold in bags similar to fresh ricotta, *ladótiro*, a cheese cured in olive oil; *stáka*, a rich white cheese, often baked in a cheese

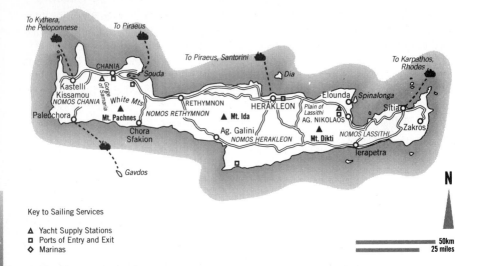

Key to Sailing Services

▲ Yacht Supply Stations
□ Ports of Entry and Exit
◇ Marinas

50km
25 miles

pie or served fried as a creamy starter; and yellow *graviéra* (gruyère). The Cretans do delicious things with lamb, as in *boksádes* (baked in pastry with cheese, or baked in a yogurt and egg and lemon sauce), and kid (stewed, for instance, in fruit juice or served with a rice pilaf); and they eat more snails (*saligária*) than most Greeks, served as a *mezé*, or cooked with rice, tomatoes, garlic and cinnamon. A *xerotígana* is a delicious traditional sweet pancake, filled with honey and nuts (although in most resort areas the only pancakes you'll find are in the new international creperies); *amygadalópitta* is a delicious almond pie; *kaltzouni* are sugary tarts. At Christmas, look for biscuits called *melomakárona*. The best wines from Crete are labelled *Kritikós Topikós Oénos,* the Greek equivalent of a *vin de pays*: look for the fresh white wine of Péza, made from a unique variety of grape called vilana, and the spicy red wines from Archanes, made of *kotsífali* and tannin-rich *mandelári* grapes, the latter one of Greece's most ancient varieties. *Rakí* (or *tsikoudiá*), an *eau-de-vie* distilled in a hundred illegal mountain stills, is Crete's firewater, its moonshine, its pure hot-blooded soul, minus the anise flavouring of ouzo.

## Getting There

**By air**: Herákleon, and to a lesser extent Chaniá, are linked by direct charter flights with London, Manchester etc. and other European cities. Olympic runs 5 to 6 flights daily from Athens to Herákleon, and 3 daily to Chaniá, as well as 3 flights a week between Herákleon and Thessaloníki, 1 a week between Thessaloníki and Chaniá, and 4 a week between Herákleon and Rhodes. Kríti Air runs additional flights between Athens and Chaniá and Herákleon, as does another new independent airline, Air Greece. Crete's third airport, at Sitía, offers a weekly Olympic flight to Kárpathos and Kássos.

**By sea**: the people of Crete own the large clean and comfortable ships—among the finest in Greece—that link Herákleon and Chaniá to Piraeus daily. The 12-hour journey through the night, in a cabin, or on a warm night out on deck, can be quite pleasant and the restaurant prices on board are astonishingly low. Ferries from Alexandria, Haifa, Turkey, Cyprus, Ancona and Venice call at Herákleon once or twice a week. There are daily ships in the summer to Santoríni, and frequent connections to Mýkonos, Náxos, Páros, Tínos, Sýros, Rhodes and Thessaloníki. In summer there is a new fast catamaran service to Santoríni for day trippers.

Other inter-island connections are now made via Crete's smaller ports. From Kastélli you can sail twice a week to Kýthera, as well as to Gýthion, Neápolis and Monemvassía in the Peloponnese. Ag. Nikólaos has a twice-weekly connection with Kássos, Kárpathos, Rhodes, Mílos and Piraeus, and at least once-weekly with Santoríni, Síkinos, Folégandros, Sífnos, Sými and Chálki. From Sitía there are boats 3 times a week to Piraeus, twice a week to Kássos, Kárpathos, Rhodes and Mílos, and once a week to Folégandros, Santoríni, Chálki, Sífnos and Síkinos.

**By bus**: a daily bus runs from Thessaloníki to Piraeus/Athens, then boards the ferry to Crete, and takes you directly to Chaniá or Réthymnon. And vice versa. In Chaniá, call ✆ (0821) 23 052; in Thessaloniki, ✆ (031) 512 122.

## Tourist Information

Crete has an information number with English-speaking operators, ✆ 131.

# Chaniá (XANIA)

Unless you have only a few days on Crete and want to concentrate on the high shrines of Minoan culture around Herákleon, consider easing yourself into this complex island by starting with Crete's urbane second city, **Chaniá**, the most elegant of the four provincial capitals that punctuate the island's north coast. With the ghostly forms of the White Mountains, the snow-capped Lefká Ori, hovering just over the rooftops, Chaniá (ancient Kydonia, Venetian La Canea) adroitly combines handsome relics of its Venetian and Turkish past with the needs of a busy Greek town, sprinkled throughout with stately neoclassical buildings left over from the days when Chaniá became Crete's capital, from 1850 until the island's annexation to Greece.

## Getting Around

Chaniá's **airport** is in Soúda, ✆ (0821) 63 264 or 63 219. Olympic Airways office is at Stratigoú Tzanakáki 88, ✆ (0821) 58 005; buses run from here to coincide with Olympic flights. **Ferry** tickets from Soúda to Piraeus are available from ANEK (daily at 8pm), on Venizélou, in the market square ✆ 23 636 or 25 656, and from Minoan (3 times a week, at 7.45pm), also in the market square, ✆ 45 911 or 45 912. The nightly Piraeus-Chaniá ferry is met by early-bird local buses to Chaniá. **Port authority**, ✆ (0821) 43 052. The **bus** station is at Kidonías, just west of central Plateía 1866, information ✆ 23 306. Buses travel at least once a day to all the larger villages of the *nomós* and there are departures at least once an hour to Herákleon and Réthymnon.

## Tourist Information

**NTOG**: 18 Kriári Street, ✆ 26 426 or 42 624. **Municipal tourist office**: Sifákia 22, ✆ (0821) 59 990. Note that the latter address may change in mid-1995.

**Tourist police:** 44 Karaiskáki Street, ✆ (0821) 24 477 or 51 111.

### Festivals

Chaniá commemorates the anniversary of the battle of Crete during the Chaniá Festival, which runs from the **middle to the end of May;** for information, call ✆ (0821) 87 098. On **15 August** Chaniá hosts the Pan Cretan Festival.

## Venetian Chaniá

The vortex of daily life in Chaniá is its cruciform **covered market,** or Agora (1911), in the centre of the city, where locals come to shop for food and wonder about the sanity of all those Germans videoing slabs of meat and cheese. The back stairs of the market and a left turn will take you down Odós Skrídlof, a narrow lane jam-packed with shops selling leather goods, long a traditional craft in Chaniá. This gives on to Odós Chalídon, Chaniá's main tourist and jewellery-shop-lined funnel down to the outer **port,** lined with handsome Venetian buildings.

Topanás, the neighbourhood on the west side of the port, is a national landmark, where façades may not be altered but interiors are rapidly being restored and converted to pensions, restaurants and jazz clubs. The newly restored **Fírkas tower** at the far west end of the port saw the official raising of the Greek flag over Crete in November 1913 in the presence of King Constantine and his Prime Minister Venizélos, a native of Chaniá, and the erection of a marble plaque that reads 'Turkish Rule in Crete 1669–1913. 267 years, 7 months and 7 days of Tribulation.' The tower now contains a summer theatre, with frequent tourist performances of Cretan dances, as well as ships' models from ancient and modern times and paintings in the **Naval Museum of Crete** (*open 10–4, closed Sun*). Wandering through the nearby maze of tiny streets, look for the ruined synagogue and the Venetian church of **San Salvatore,** used by the Turks as a mosque. On Theofánou Street (off Zambéliou) a gate bears the Renieri coat-of-arms, dated 1608; Theotokopoúlou Street, in the same vicinity, is Chaniá's most picturesque.

## Kastélli and Splántza Quarters

The east end of the harbour has Chaniá's two most photographed landmarks: a graceful light-house in golden stone restored under the Egyptians and the **Mosque of the Janissaries** (1645), crowned with its distinctive ostrich and chicken egg domes. Here the Christian-born troops of the Ottoman Empire worshipped. Beyond the mosque lies the Kastélli quarter, spread acoss a low hill at the east end of the harbour. This was the acropolis of Chaniá's prede-cessor, ancient Kydonia, one of the Minoans' most westerly outposts on Crete. Whatever traces remain lie buried under the modern city, although in 1984 a new site was opened up along Kanevárou Street in Kastélli, where bits of ancient walls can still be seen.

The name Kastélli derives from the fortress built here in 1252 by the Venetians, which shel-tered the handsome palazzi of their nobles. In the late 15th century, just after Barbarossa left his usual calling card of death and desolation in Réthymnon, the Venetians created an **Outer Wall** around the entire town and surrounded it with a moat more than 45m wide and 9m deep; you can see the date, 1590, on the Koum Kapissi Gate on Mínos Street. As it turned out, these precautions did little to keep out the Turks in 1645, when they captured Chaniá in only two months and installed pashas and beys at Kastélli.

Although Kastélli took the brunt of the Luftwaffe bombs during the parachute landings of the Battle of Crete, you can still pick out the odd Venetian architectural detail, especially along

Kanevárou and Lythínon streets. By the inner fishing harbour, a ruined loggia faces the port and the vaults (1600) of the **Venetian Arsenal**. The harbourside streets to the east fill up at night with locals, who shun the more cosmopolitan tourist temptations around the Venetian port.

Just east of Kastélli is Splántza, or the Turkish quarter of Chaniá. Some interesting churches are concentrated here, such as the curious underground **Ag. Iríni**, dating from the 15th century, in Kallergón Street; south in Vourdouba Street, near an enormous plane tree, Venetian-built **Ag. Nikólaos** (note the coffered ceiling) was converted by the Turks into an Imperial mosque to shelter a magical healing sword.

## The Archaeology Museum

On Chalídon Street, opposite the cathedral, the 14th-century Venetian church of San Francesco may not look like much from the outside, but within it has been beautifully restored after bomb damage to house Chaniá's **Archaeology Museum** (*open Tues–Fri 8.30–3; adm*), a sumptuous collection of treasures found in Western Crete from the Neolithic era to Roman times. Especially intriguing are the finds from Chaniá's Minoan incarnation as Kydonia—the only town in Western Crete so far where inscriptions in both Linear A and B have been discovered, along with a fine selection of polychrome clay sarcophagi, or *larnax*. Amongst the seals (which always merit a close look for their inventiveness and skilled artistry on a tiny scale, as much as for their clues into the Minoan religious mind) is a celebrated if minute Late Minoan (*c.* 1450 BC) clay sealing in high relief that shows the commanding figure of a young Minoan proudly holding a staff, standing high over the sea that breaks against the gates of a city—Kydonia itself, perhaps—the roofs crowned with stylized bulls' horns. Believed to show the chief Minoan male deity, Poteidan (Poseidon), master of the sea, earth, bulls, and earthquakes, it has been suggested that the curious sea rock under the god is really a tidal wave or *tsunami*, perhaps the very one that is believed to have clobbered Crete when Santoríni flipped its lid around 1450 BC. Other cases contain Minoan jewels, vases, ceramics imported from Cyprus by the ancient Kydonians, statues and ex-votos from the shrine of Diktean Artemis, a fine 4th century BC clay 'Tanagraia' head, and, from a 3rd century AD Roman house excavated in Chaniá, a series of mosaic floors based on the stories of Dionysos.

## The Newer Quarters

From the market, Tzanakáki Street leads southeast into the **Chalepa** quarter with its many 19th-century mansions, and the house and statue of statesman Elefthérios Venizélos. Opposite Venizélos' house stands a Russian Orthodox church donated by the mother of a former governor. In a villa near the cool shade of the Public Gardens (with a small zoo and outdoor cinema, often showing films in English), the **Historical Archives of Crete** (*open weekdays 9–1, closed weekends*), 20 Sfakianáki Street, houses Greece's second largest collection of historical material, dating back from the Venetian occupation to the liberation of Crete in 1944, although most of it will be lost on you if you don't read Greek. The town beach, **Néo Chorá**, is a 15-minute walk west from the harbour. Although sandy, shallow and safe for children, it's not especially attractive. The beaches improve the further west you go; the municipal buses go as far as Kalamáki and **Oasis beach**, a popular place with good swimming and windsurfing, cafés and tavernas.

---

*Chaniá ℂ (0821–)*                                   ***Where to Stay***

Chaniá's hotels have more character than any others in Crete, although be aware that some of the most picturesque places installed around the Venetian port can be noisy at night. The Association Rent Rooms & Apartments, 12 Isódion Street, ✆ 43 601, ✉ 46 277 has a list of inexpensive quality lodgings, complete with a map.

### expensive

**Chalepa**, 164 El. Venizélou, ✆ 53 544, ✉ 43 335, (*B*), offers 45 fully air-conditioned rooms in a 19th-century mansion, with a quiet garden. **Pandora**, 29 Lythínon, ✆ 43 589, ✉ 55 213, has comfortable, traditionally furnished apartments available by the day. **Bozzali Studios**, Gavaládon (a quiet lane off Sífaka), ✆ 50 824 offers 15 A-class rooms in a lovingly restored house. *Open Mar–Nov*. The **Contessa**, Theofánous 15, ✆ 98 566 (*A*) has the intimate air of an old-fashioned guesthouse, furnished in traditional Cretan style. The owners speak little English, but make up for it by being extremely helpful; reserve well in advance. A similar warning prevails for the desirable **Palazzo**, Theotokopoúlou Street, ✆ 43 255 (*A*), with 11 traditional rooms, most with balcony, and for the nearby **El Greco**, Theotokopoúlou 49, ✆ 90 432, ✉ 95 566 (*B*), a pretty place draped in creeper. **Casa Delfino**, Theofánous 9, ✆ 93 098, ✉ 96 500, (*B*), has very comfortable air conditioned rooms in overlooking an inner courtyard, with mini-bars and satellite TV. If you want to be alone, the **Xenia**, Theotokopoúlou, ✆ 91 238, ✉ 72 238 (*B*) has 80 modern rooms overlooking the sea around the corner from the Fírkas tower.

### moderate

There are a number of small hotels located in refurbished Venetian houses, among them **Nostos**, Zambelíou 46, ✆ 54 833 (*B*), on a quiet flowery lane, many of whose rooms have views, or **Pension Thereza**, 8 Ángelou, ✆ 40 118, has been lovingly restored and has magnificent views from the rooftop terrace and rooms. **Vranas Suites**, 23–25 Ag. Déka, ✆ 58 618 or 43 788, have been recently done up in an attractive, traditional style on a quiet side street near the old port. **Pension Kastélli**, 39 Kanevárou Street, ✆ 57 057, on the quieter east end of the harbour, has rooms with kitchen facilities priced near the bottom of this category.

### inexpensive

Chaniá is blessed with a vast selection of pleasant pensions and inexpensive rooms, most located within a few blocks of the Venetian or inner harbour. Some of the nicer rooms are: **Esta**, in a charming pink house (no phone) and **Konaki**, ✆ 52 240 both on Kondiláki Street; **Meltemi**, Angelou 2, ✆ 40 192 and **Maria**, Angelou 4, ✆ 51 052, both near the Naval Musem; **Venus**, 42 Sarpáki, a quiet street in the Turkish quarter, in a lovingly restored house.

Chaniá's **youth hostel**, at 33 Drakonianoú, ✆ 53 565, is decent and exceptionally quiet because it's almost out of the city limits. To get there, take the Ag. Ioánnes bus, leaving every 15 minutes from in front of the market (no card necessary). There are two campsites near Chaniá, though again you'll need a bus to reach them: **Camping Ag. Marína**, ✆ 48 555, is 8km west of the town and open throughout the season (buses leave from the main bus station), and the more basic **Camping Chania** at Ag. Apóstoli, 5km west of town, ✆ 31 686 (city bus from Platéia 1866). Both are within easy walking distance of fine beaches.

It's hard not to find a restaurant in Chaniá—the harbour is one great crescent of tavernas and pizzerias. Around the corner from the mosque at the end of the waterfront you'll find a number of fish restaurants straggling along the water's edge, any of which you can safely choose for an excellent seafood dinner in a lovely setting; **Dino's**, overlooking the inner port on Aktí Enóseos, is a long-time, reliable favourite at 4–5000dr. **Monastiri**, on the inner port behind the Mosque of the Janisseries, serves fresh fish, traditional Cretan dishes and barrelled wine in the same price range; if you need a change, try the Thai and Korean food at the **Golden Wok** next door. Note that restaurants without good views try harder in the kitchen, like those along Pórtou Street (along the Venetian Wall, in the Venetian quarter of Topanás). One of the smallest tavernas here, **El Greco**, has solid, inexpensive Cretan food, while its neighbour, **Les Vagabonds**, 48 Pórtou ☎ 91 089, makes a valiant effort to recreate a taste of France, serving *salade Niçoise* and *boeuf Bourguignon* for about 3000dr, accompanied by jazz or classical music. Middle Eastern and Anatolian specialities, sometimes accompanied by live Arabic music, happen at **The Well of the Turk**, in Rougiá Square, ☎ 54 547 (*3500dr*). At the **Taverna Apovrado**, Isódon Street, ☎ 58 151, you can try a number of Chaniot specialities, including the local wine and country sausages. **Taverna Alana**, on Zambelíou, features well-prepared, moderately priced Greek dishes and live Greek music. The **Emerald Bistro**, a friendly Irish restaurant just off the harbour front at 17 Kondiláki, serves all the comfort foods you may have developed a longing for—steaks, prawn cocktails, baked potatoes and, naturally, Irish coffee (*2000dr*).

## Entertainment and Nightlife

Of the many bars on the Venetian port, **Remezzo**, at the mosque end, commands the best place to sit and watch the activity flow by. The hole-in-the-wall **Lyraki**, at Kallergón 22 (just in from the fishing harbour) is something of a local institution, where from 9pm on you can enjoy some of Crete's finest traditional music for the price of an inexpensive after-dinner *raki*, accompanied by *mezé* and more often than not by impromptu dancing. **Skala**, nearby at 12 Kallergón, ☎ 53 995, often features live *rembétika*—Greek blues. **Café Avekoloto**, in the old harbour, frequently offers blues and other live music; similar fare happens at **Fedra**, Isóderon 7, ☎ 40 789. **I Mouraria tou Pouni Mourgali**, 20 Sífaka, offers over 80 kinds of beer.

# Nomós Chaniá

Crete's westernmost province, or *nomós* of Chaniá, is the land of the stunning White Mountains, which hit the sky at 2453m at Mount Pachnés and are sliced down the middle by one of Crete's five-star attractions, the Gorge of Samariá. Beach resorts in the province, because they developed later, are innocent of the worst mass-touristy features that blight those in the east, although the seaside Babylon just west of Chaniá is quickly approaching saturation point. Inland, landscapes are delightfully rural; the *nomós* produces excellent oranges, honey, olive oil, and chestnuts, and Kastélli and Kíssamos wines are known throughout Greece.

# Nomós Chaniá

20km
10 miles

N

NOMOS RETHYMNON

RETHYMNON

DRAPANON

AKROTIRI

Gouvernetou Monastery
Ag. Triada
Proffis Ilias
CHANIA
Stavros
Kourakies
Aroni
Souda
Nea Souda
Ag. Theodoro
Platanias
Ag. Marina
Galatas
Maleme
Mournies
Malaxa
Neo Chorio
Fre
Aptera
Kalyves
Almirida
Kokkino Chora
Kefalas
Yamos
Vryssis
Alikampos
Georgioupolis
Lake Kournas
Askyfou
Asigonia
Asfendos
Rodakino
Frangokastello

Kolimbari
Moni Gonias Monastery
Menias (Diktyna)
Ag. Ioannis Gionas
SPADA
RODOPOU
Afrata
Rodopos
Tavronitis
Kastelli
Kissamou
Platanos
Polyrenia
Sfinari
Kambos
Kouneni
Elos
Topolia
Kakodiki
Kandanos
Temenia
Elyros
Lissos
Sougia
Paleochora
Chrysoskalitissa Monastery

Agriagramvousa
Gramvousa
Phalassarna
Elafonisi

Fournes
Meskla
Therisso
Souvra
Lakki
Alikianos
Prassa
Omalos
Ag. Roumeli
Gorge of Samaria
White Mountains
Mt. Pachnes
(2451m / 8045ft)
Ag. Ioannis
Anopolis
Chora
Stakion
Loutro

Libyan Sea

To Piraeus
To Gavdos

110

Not a single one of the countless beach hotels along this sandy stretch of coast and fertile plain existed when the strange rain of white parachutes fell on 20 May 1941. Few signs of the battle remain, although 2km west of Chaniá stands the monument of the diving eagle, known locally as the **Kakó Poulí**, or 'Bad Bird', the German memorial to the 2nd Parachute Regiment.

### Getting Around

**By road**: there are **buses** every 15 minutes from Chaniá bus station to all the coastal resorts as far as the Maleme Beach hotel; roughly every hour they continue to Kastélli-Kíssamou. There are also early morning connections from all the resorts to Omalós for the Gorge of Samariá.

### Festivals

Ag. Marína, **17 July**. Kolybári, **15 August** and **29 August** pilgrimage to the chapel of St John the Hermit. Tavronítis, **14 September**.

## Beach Sprawl and the Spáda Peninsula

The first town beyond the reach of Chaniá's city bus lines is **Ag. Marína**, with a smattering of old Venetian and Turkish houses, and a long, partially shaded beach and lots of hotels, tavernas and watersports facilities. It looks out to the inaccessible islet of **Ag. Theódori**, a refuge for the wild Cretan goat, the *kri kri*. The vast gaping mouth of its cave originally belonged to a sea monster, bearing down on Ag. Marína with an appetite as big as all Crete before Zeus spotted the threat and petrified the monster with a thunderbolt. Just west of Ag. Marína, **Plataniás** is another built up resort town, with a sandy beach and a cane forest, planted to protect the orange groves from the wind. Further west, the Battle of Crete began at **Máleme**, where Chaniá airport was at the time. There's a large German war cemetery as a grim reminder and, near by, a recently excavated Post-Palatial Minoan tomb. Beyond, the resort village of **Tavronítis** marks the crossroads for Paleochóra.

At the foot of the rugged Spáda peninsula, **Kolimvári** (ΚΟΛΥΜΒΑΡΙ) has a pebbly beach, and is a lovely spot for a swim and a meal. A bust in the village centre is of Timoléon Vássos, commander of 1500 Greek volunteers, who in 1897 landed in Kolimvári and declared (again prematurely) Crete's union with Greece. A kilometre north of the village is the **Moní Gonías**, or Odigítrias, founded in 1618 and whose patriotic monks were often besieged by the Turks; a cannon ball shot in 1866 is still embedded in the walls. The monastery is home of an Orthodox academy and has a small museum of 17th- and 18th-century icons (note especially the *Genesis* (1662) and a *Crucifixion* of 1637). At **Afráta**, the last village on Spáda accessible by car, you can visit the cave **Ellenóspilios**, its 90m-long corridors lined with stalactites and stalagmites. Out of Afráta you can pick your way down to rocky coves for a swim in crystal-clear water or follow the difficult track (here and there still using the old Roman road) to **Meniás**. The charming cove here is rocky as well, but the sea is transparent, and seaside caves offer shelter from the sun. Only a few meagre ruins here recall that Menías was the port of ancient **Diktyna**, once a celebrated shrine to Artemis perhaps dating back to the Minoans.

Just 2km south of Kolimbári, **Spiliá**'s 12th-century church of the Virgin has some 14th-century wall paintings; others are further south in **Drakóna**, in 9th-century Ag. Stéfanos. But most interesting of all is the **Rotunda** in **Episkopí**, the only church in Crete with a concentric beehive dome. It wasn't the first church on this spot; nearby are bits of mosaic floor left over from the Byzantine original. The nearest sandy beaches are at **Plakálona**, just west of the Spáda peninsula, where some of the densest olive groves in Crete provide a silvery green backdrop.

*© (0821–)* **Where to Stay and Eating Out**

### Káto Galatás

**Panorama**, *©* 31 700, *@* 31 708 (*A; lux*). Built in the modern Mediterranean style; all rooms have air-conditioning and balconies with sea views. There are 2 swimming pools, for those who find the 50m walk to the sea too strenuous.

### Ag. Marína

**Santa Marina**, on the beach, *©* 68 460, *@* 99 221 (*B; mod*). Set in a lovely garden with a pool, and often comes up with a room when the season is in full swing. Near the beach **Alexia**, *©* 68 110 (*B pension; mod*) is small and attractive, with a pool and fridges in every room. **Angelika**, *©* 68 642, has rooms with kitchens; **Villa Margarita**, *©* 68 581, doesn't and costs even less (*both inexpensive*).

### Plataniás

**Geraniotis**, by the beach, *©* 68 681 (*B; exp*) is one of the more attractive of Plataniás' many hotels, set in lush green lawns. *Open April–Oct.* **Kronos Apartments**, *©* 68 630 (*C; mod*) is a well-kept, moderate size complex of 53 units, with a pool near the sea. If you hanker after a traditional Greek taverna, try **O Platanos**, by the main road. (*2500dr*).

### Máleme

The **Maleme Beach**, *©* 62 221, *@* 62 406 (*A; lux*). Shaped like a giant trident to give each of its 767 rooms a sea view, this former member of the luxurious Chandrís chain is still one of the most comfortable and classiest hotels along the coast, albeit in need of a lick of paint. *Open April–Oct.* The fancy pants **Creta Paradise**, in nearby Geráni, *©* 61 315, *@* 61 134 (*A; lux*) opened in 1992 and is even slicker and glossier.

## The Far West

West of the Spáda peninsula lies the ancient province of Kissamos, one of the least visited parts of Crete, and the unruly west coast offers not only some of Crete's loveliest beaches, but a chance to find a strand of your very own. The chief town and port here is Kastélli (ΚΑΣΤΕΛΛΙ) or officially, Kastélli-Kíssamou, a dusty, workaday wine town rather charmingly devoid of any tourist attraction whatsoever.

*Getting Around*

Kastélli's port (2km from the centre—take a taxi) is linked by Míras **ferries** to ports in the Peloponnese: 3 times a week to Kalamáta, once to Gýthion, twice to Monemvassía and Neápolis; there are 2 weekly sailings to Piraeus and 3 to Kythira and Antikythira, tickets from Horeftákis Tours in Kastélli, *©* (0822) 23 888 or Omalós Tours, Plateía 1866, Chaniá, *©* (0821) 97 119. **Buses** from Kastélli: 2 a day to Phalassarná, 5 to Chóra Sfakíon, 6 to Paliochóra, 2 to Omalós and 1 bus to Topólia, Chrisoskalítissa and Elafonísi. The Elafonísi Boat (𝒫 (0823) 41 755 connects the islet of Elafonísi to Paliochóra every afternoon in summer.

### Festivals

Kastélli: **30 May**, wine festival in **early August**, and **29 August** (Ag. Ioannes). Phalassarná: **26 July**. Monastery Chrysoskalítissa: a huge festival every **14–15 August**. Elos: Chestnut festival, first Sunday after **20 October**.

## Kastélli-Kíssamou

Kastélli sits between a long pebble beach in at the bottom of a deep gulf and a beautiful plain densely planted with olives and vineyards surrounded by knobbly hills. Its double-barrelled name, which hasn't really caught on among the Cretans, recalls its ancient predecessor Kissamos, the port of ancient Polyrenia. Excavations of the ancient city behind the modern health centre have unearthed a lovely mosaic floor. The town **archaeology museum**, with finds from ancient Kissamos, is currently being rearranged in the Venetian commandery.

Ancient Kissamos' temple and theatre were dismantled by the Venetians in 1550 and refashioned as a castle—hence Kastélli. This castle has a melodramatic history: when the Cretan Kaptános Kantanoléo captured it from the Venetians, the Venetians pretended to recognize Kantanoléo's authority and offered a highborn Venetian girl as his son's bride. At the wedding the Cretans were given drugged wine, the Venetians slit their throats, and recaptured the fort.

**Polyrenia**, a scenic 8km south of Kastélli, was founded by the Achaeans and Dorians. Polyrenia ('many flocks') supported a large population, supplied by a still visible aqueduct. Ancient walls, roads and houses remain, added to by the Romans and perhaps the Turks. The church of the 99 Holy Fathers was built from the stone of an ancient temple.

## The West Coast: Phalassarná to Elafonísi

Crete's west coast is wild and dramatic where the mountains plunge sheer into the sea. Of the beaches, **Phalassarná** (ΦΑΛΑΣΑΡΝΑ), 15km from Kastélli, is the easiest to reach, vast and sandy, and one of the finest in Crete, dotted with a handful of tavernas and an increasing number of rooms to rent. If it's too crowded for your taste, walk in either direction to find others. A mysterious stone throne and a few walls by Koutrí pinpoint the site of the Hellenistic Phalassarná among a sea of plastic tunnels for tomatoes.

From its new port you can hire a caique to sail to the top of wild Cape Voúxa and the islet of **Agria,** where the Venetian fortress of **Gramvoúsa** was occupied during the War of Independence by Greek refugees, especially from the devastated islands of Psará and Kássos. Forced to make a living in troubled times, these refugees took to pirating so successfully that Greece's first Prime Minister, Capodístria, had to personally intervene to prevent a diplomatic row, and turn Gramvoúsa over to the Turks.

South of Phalassarná, the coastal road provides some spectacular scenery down through **Plátanos** (where a proto-Geometric tomb was unearthed during the road construction) to **Sfinári**, which has a pebble beach nearby, some tavernas and simple places to stay.

The rough road winds south to the Libyan Sea and to the windswept **convent of Chrysoskalítissa**, 'Our Lady of the Golden Stair' (although only those without sin, or, according to some, non-liars can see which of the 90 steps is made of gold). The main lure of this remote corner of Crete is 5km southwest, the islet **Elafonísi** (ΕΛΑΦΟΝΗΣΙ) where the tours end up. The water is a glorious blue, and the pinkish sand of its numerous beaches gives Elafonísi a tropical aura; the water is only 2ft deep so you can walk there the coast.

## Inland: Chestnut Villages

Rather than backtrack along the coast, a popular way to return from Chrysoskalitíssa to Kastélli is through Crete's chestnut country, an area of dramatic, mountainous beauty reminiscent of Corsica. Nine villages in the area live off the chestnut; in July they have some of the best weddings in Crete. One, **Kefáli**, has a frescoed church, the **Metamórphosis tou Sotírou** (1320). From **Elos**, the road descends leisurely to Koutsomatádos and enters the 1500m **Topólia ravine**; high above the entrance the pretty stalactite cave of **Ag. Sofía** was a holy place since Neolithic and Minoan times and still shelters a little troglodyte church. **Topólia**, at the end of the ravine, is a handsome village and a mere 8km from the main road.

---

✆ (0822–)    *Where to Stay and Eating Out*

### Kastélli

**Playies**, 800m from the beach, ✆ 23 404 (*A; exp*), is the most lavish hotel in town, each room endowed with a large balcony overlooking the bay. **Holiday Bay**, by the sea, ✆ 23 488 (*B pension; mod*) is modern and comfortable. **Castle Hotel**, Plateía Kastélliou, ✆ 22 140 (*C; mod*) a decent fairly modern place, and rooms have private bath. **Gallini Beach**, ✆ 23 288 (*inexp*) has quiet rooms at the far end of the beach. Of the several seaside tavernas, try **Alatopiperi**, 'Salt and Pepper', a pleasant little place with fresh fish. There's also a restaurant up at Polyrenía—the village is so small you can't miss it. The food is average, but the view is wonderful.

### Phalassarná

**Aqua Marine**, ✆ 41 414 and **Stathis**, ✆ 41 480 have inexpensive rooms to rent near the beach, or else camp out—that's about it. There are a couple of tavernas on the beach (expect to pay a bit more because of transport costs).

## The Southwest: Paleochóra and the Sélino

The white mountains only permit a few north–south roads to breach their rocky fastness. Those to the southwest run into the Eparchy of Selino, where the still very attractive resort town of Paleochóra is the centre attraction, along with a score of decorated medieval churches that escaped the ravages of time, especially around the martyr village of Kándanos.

---

*Getting Around*

Paleochóra is served by 5 **buses** a day from Chaniá; a 6am bus goes to Omalós for the Gorge of Samariá. Every Tuesday and Thursday, small **boats** leave Paleochóra for Gávdos; on Friday and Sunday a larger boat sails from Paleochóra to Soúgia, Ag. Roúmeli, and Gávdos. Other boats leave Paliochóra for Chóra Sfakíon, Loutró, Soúgia, Pahiá Ammos beach, and the island of Elafónisos ✆ (0823) 41 755. Two buses run daily between

Chaniá and Soúgia; Soúgia also is linked daily by boat to Ag. Roúmeli when the Gorge of Samariá is open.

Paleochóra: Musical August, **1–10 August**. Soúgia: **8 September**.

## Along the Main Road from Chaniá

Of the three roads from the north that wriggle down the western reaches of the White Mountains to the Sélino, the main one from Tavronítis gets the most takers, allowing you to stop over in **Kándanos**. Although inhabited at least since Roman times, nothing in Kándanos is over 50 years old; the men, women, and children, armed with whatever weapons they could find, resisted the Nazi advance with such stubborn ferocity (23 May 1941) that 25 Germans were killed. The rest were forced to retreat and return with reinforcements the next day, shooting everyone they could find and burning the village to the ground. Excavations have recently revealed a building believed to be a Roman *praetorium*.

From Kándanos, take the left turn on the Soúgia road for **Anisaráki**. There are five Byzantine churches to see in the next three or four kilometres. **Taxiárchos Michaíl**, near Koufalotó, was frescoed in 1327 by one of the best artists of the age, Ioánnis Pageménos. In Anisaráki itself you'll find three 14th-century churches: the Venetian-Byzantine **Panagía**, with well-preserved paintings, **Ag. Ioánnes**, and **Ag. Paraskeví**, the latter with more frescoes. The paintings and iconostasis in a fourth church in Anisaráki, **Ag. Anna**, date from the 1460s. Just south of Kándanos, in Plemanianá, **Ag. Geórgios** has frescoes from 1410. **Kakodíki** to the southwest has a hundred springs with soft mineral waters known for curing kidney stones; here two small churches house frescoes, **Taxiárchos Michaíl** (1387) and **Ag. Isódoros** (1420). Further south, a sign points out the road to **Kádros**, site of a late 14th-century church of the **Panagía**, with more frescoes.

## Paleochóra and Europe at its Southernmost

The Venetians called it Castello Selino, the Bride of the Libyan Sea. The Greeks call it simply the Old Town, or **Paleochóra** (ΠΑΛΑΙΟΧΩΡΑ). If no longer nuptially fresh, Paleochóra still attracts thousands of suitors, an incongruous but jovial mixture of charter flight tourists and hippies. It also has the rare advantage of straddling two beaches—one wide, sandy, and lined with tamarisks, the other stony—never subject to the winds at the same time.

On the tip of the peninsula, the Venetians built Paleochóra's **Castello Selino** in 1279, more to police the ornery Greeks than protect their new territory. When tested in 1539 by Khair Eddin Barbarossa, Castel Selino failed to measure up, and was captured and demolished by the pillaging Turks, leaving only the walls to defend the poppies that fill it every April.

Over frequently rough seas, 30km to the south, the triangular barren islet of **Gávdos** (ancient Clauda, pop. 115—down from 20,000), is, at 35°10, the southernmost point in Europe. It also puts in a fairly limp claim to have been the home of the fair Calypso, although Gávdos' very lack of tourist amenities can be seductive for anyone seeking the Greek island of decades ago. There are good beaches, a Venetian castle, shepherds and plenty of fish, which is just as well, for there's little choice in the way of food, save what's imported from Crete.

From Paleochóra it is an hour's caique trip to **Soúgia**, ancient Syia, the port of Doric Elyros, endowed with a long, pebbly beach that never gets too crowded. The ruins that stand are a modest blast from Syia's Roman past: walls, vaulted tombs, an aqueduct and baths. Prettiest of all, however, is the 6th-century mosaic floor, reused in the foundations of the modern church. From Soúgia, you can walk in about an hour and a half to Doric-Roman-Byzantine **Lissós**, a tiny port set in a pretty green landscape. The population of Lissós these days is exactly one: the caretaker, who watches over the ancient theatre, baths, houses and an Asklepeion or healing sanctuary, dating from the 3rd century BC, when Lissós was the port of ancient Yrtakina.

The new road to Soúgia passes by Rodováni, a modern village just west of ancient **Elyros**, one of the largest Doric settlements on Crete. According to legend, two sons of Apollo, Philakides and Philandros, founded the pugnacious town, which exported bows, arrows and bronze and had risen to the level of a bishopric when the Saracens destroyed it in the 9th century. Walls and the acropolis are scattered on the hill. The road west continues to modern **Teménia,** a muscat-producing village with a photogenic old stone church of the Sotír, or Saviour.

---

✆ *(0823–)*                                    ***Where to Stay and Eating Out***

### Paleochóra

**Elman**, at the end of the sandy beach, ✆ 41 412 (*B; exp*) is the biggest and most modern choice, with rooms and apartments, but for something really classy reserve a beautifully furnished studio or apartment from English-speaking **Efthisis Sfinarolakis**, ✆ 41 594 or 41 596 (*exp*). **Polydoros**, on the main street between the beaches, ✆ 41 068 (*C; mod*) is an old favourite and serves good breakfasts. By the sandy beach, **Pension Ari**, ✆ 41 502 (*B; mod*) is a good bet. *Open all year.* Little **Pension Lissos**, near the bus station ✆ 41 266 (*C; mod*), is nice and often has a place if everything else is full.

Paleochóra has a fair selection of pensions and rooms in the 4000dr range, among them **Ostria**, in the middle of the sandy beach, ✆ 41 055 and **Oassis**, ✆ 41 328. For a bit more, **Kalypso**, in the centre, ✆ 41 429 offers rooms with kitchens in an old stone house. There's a campsite with shade by the pebble beach, ✆ 41 120.

Near the pebble beach, **Portofino** is for a serious Italian splurge, serving pasta dishes such as tagliatelle with smoked salmon (*around 5000dr for a full meal, much less for pizza*). **Kyma**, nearby, has a wide choice of fish and typical taverna food (*2500dr*). **Pizzeria Niki**, in the centre, makes good, fresh and cheap pies with some seating outside. A few steps from the sandy beach, vegetarians can forgo their usual Greek salad and cheese pie at **The Third Eye**, ✆ 41 055 for spicy Asian and Mexican specialities; carnivores can also chose from barbecued meats. **Elite**, right on the sandy beach, serves up tasty Greek food in the 3–4000dr range and has Cretan music and dancing every Saturday night.

### Soúgia

**Pikilassos**, ✆ 51 1242 (*B; mod*) has the 9 fanciest beds in the village, but there is a fair choice of inexpensive rooms, such as **Lissos**, ✆ 51 244, **Koumakakis**, ✆ 51 298, and even cheaper, **Maria Marinaki**, ✆ 51 338 and **George Ellinakis**, ✆ 51 339.

In Paleochóra, the open-air **Cine Attikon** features a different, subtitled film every day on the week in the summer. The **Music Pub**, up by the castle, offers lovely views to go with its drinks and snacks, or linger by the beach at the **Jetée Cocktail Bar**, just beyond the Elman hotel.

## South of Chaniá to Omalós and the Gorge of Samariá

The single most spectacular stretch of Cretan scenery is squeezed into the 18km **Gorge of Samariá**, the longest in Europe and the last refuge of many species of the island's unique flora and fauna. Once considered a rather adventurous excursion, the walk is now firmly inscribed on the programme of every tour operator on the island; the Gorge has been spruced up as a National Park and in short you may as well forget any private communion with Mother Nature before you even start out. The walk takes most people between five and eight hours going down from Omalós at the top of the gorge south to Ag. Roúmeli on the Libyan Sea, and twice as long if you're Arnold Schwarzenegger or just plain crazy and insist on walking up.

*Getting Around*

The bus ride from Chaniá to Omalós itself is quite an adventure on the steep slopes of the White Mountains. Buses leave Chaniá at 6.15, 7.30, 8.30 and at 1.30; from Kastélli-Kíssamou at 5, 6, and 7; Réthymnon at 6.15 and 7; others leave early from Plataniás, Ag. Marína, Tavronítis, Chandrís, Kolimvári, and Georgioúpoli. Organized tour buses leave almost as early (you can, however, get a slight jump on the crowds by staying overnight at Omalós). Once through to Ag. Roúmeli, boats run all afternoon to Chóra Sfakíon, Soúgia and Paleochóra, where you can pick up a late afternoon bus back to the north coast. Consider paying the bit extra for a tour bus, especially in the summer, to make sure you have a seat on the return journey; your tired dogs could turn rabid if you make them stand up for two hours on a bus after doing Samariá.

## On the road to Omalós: Citrus Villages

If you're planning only a peek down into Samariá from the Omalós tourist pavilion, you can spend a pleasant morning exploring the Keríti valley along the route. The best oranges in Crete grow here and, as the locals will tell you, Cretan oranges are the best in the world; the entire valley has an estimated million trees. At **Alikianós**, just off the main Chaniá–Omalós road, the infamous wedding massacre of Kantanoléo's Cretans took place, at the ruined Venetian tower of Da Molino; next to it, the little church of Ag. Geórgios (1243) has exceptional frescoes, painted in 1430 by Pávlos Provatás. In nearby **Kouphós**, the early Byzantine church of Ag. Kyr-Yánnis is decorated with more superb frescoes, added throughout the centuries.

**Fournés,** on the Chaniá road, alone claims more than 120,000 shimmering orange trees. If you're not in a hurry, take the 5km detour southeast of Fournés for **Mesklá**, a lovely little village set in lush green countryside, where one glossy orange grove succeeds another. The little church of the Panagía (next to the big modern church) has traces of mosaics from a temple of Aphrodite, left by the ancient city of Rizinia; another church, Sotiros, has frescoes from 1303 by Theódoros and Michaíl Véneris. Above Mesklá, a rough 4-wheel-drive road leads up to **Zoúrva**, a whitewashed village with amazing views, then circles around into the dramatic 18km **Thérisson gorge** (do note, however, that the gorge is pierced by a much easier road, directly south of Chaniá).

After Fournés the road begins to rise rapidly to **Lákki**, another picturesque village immersed in greenery. The road continues to rise, reaching 1200m at the pass before descending to Omalós Plateau, itself no shorty at 1080m. In the village of **Omalós**, the chief monument is the house and tomb of the 19th-century rebel leader, Chadjimicháli Yánnaris.

## The Gorge of Samariá

*The gorge is open officially from 1 May–31 Oct from 6am–4pm, when the water is low enough to ensure safe fording of the streams, and when the staff of the National Forest Service patrols the area (it's for their services that you're asked to pay admission). Although last admission to the gorge is at 3pm, almost everyone starts much earlier, to avoid the midday heat, and to make the excursion a single day's round-trip outing. It is absolutely **essential** to wear good walking shoes and socks; a hat and a bite to eat are only slightly less vital, and binoculars a decided bonus. The fresh streams along the gorge provide good drinking water at regular intervals. Beware, however, that early in the year the stream that runs through the centre of Samariá can be high and quite dangerous—drownings (and heart attacks) have happened.*

Some of the most spectacular views are the first, from the tourist pavilion (where you can have breakfast) hanging over the edge of the gorge, overlooking the sheer face of mighty 2083m Mount Gýnglio. A well-maintained zigzag path with a wooden railing, known as the **Xylóskalo**, waits to lead you gently down into the gorge, with scenic lookouts along the way. The name Samariá derives from Ossa Maria, a chapel (1379) and abandoned village halfway down the gorge. There are several other abandoned chapels along the way, traditional stone *mitáto* huts (used by shepherds as shelter or for cheese making), and, near the end, the famous **Sideróportes** ('the iron gates'), the oft-photographed section of the gorge where the sheer rock walls rise almost 300m on either side of a passage only 3m wide. Not a few people return from Samariá having only seen their own feet and the back of the person in front; the path down is that rough. Planning to stay in Ag. Roúmeli may be the answer; it will allow you more leisure to enjoy the unique beauty of the gorge and rare cliff-hanging flowers and herbs that infuse Samariá with an intoxicating fragrance in the summer. Although the gorge is in the White Mountains National Park, the last refuge of the *kri kri*, the long-horned Cretan chamois, no one ever sees them any more; rare birds of prey, however, are less shy, and often circle high overhead. If you haven't the energy to make the whole trek, you can at least sample Samariá by descending only a mile or so into the gorge down the big wooden stair (the rub is you have to walk back up again). A less strenuous (and less rewarding) alternative, proposed by tourist agencies as 'the lazy way', is walking an hour or so up from Ag. Roúmeli to the Sideróportes.

**Ag. Roúmeli**, at the southern mouth of the gorge, was built on the site of ancient Tarra and its sanctuary of Tarranean Apollo. In Roman times Tarra was famed for its fine glassware. The Venetians built a frescoed church, **Panagías**, on the foundation of a temple to Artemis. Since it has no roads, Ag. Roúmeli was all but abandoned until the 1960s, when people began to come in through the gorge. Now it has numerous places to stay and eat, along with a pebble beach for a well-deserved swim. From Ag. Roúmeli the caiques take 1½ hours either to Paleochóra or to Chóra Sfakíon (*see* p.122); less to Soúgia which is less tourist-orientated but also less frequently served by bus.

**Omalós** ✆ (0821–)

> **Neos Omalos**, ✆ 67 269, 🖂 67 190 (*C; mod*). Recently built, with 18 centrally heated rooms, bar and restaurant. **To Exari**, ✆ 67 180, (*C; mod*) is a bit larger and almost as nice. There's a mountain shelter up at **Kallergis** (1657m) reached by road from just in front of the Xylóskalo.

**Ag. Roúmeli** ✆ (0825–)

> Ag. Roúmeli has plenty of rooms, but thanks to the popularity of the gorge and transport costs, prices are over the odds. There are several restaurant-pension combos, such as **Aghia Roumeli**, ✆ 91 241, 🖂 91 232 (*B; exp*). *Open Mar–Oct.* For something inexpensive, try **Tara** rooms, ✆ 91 231 or **Lefka Ori**, ✆ 91 219. None of the tavernas especially stands out.

## Between Chaniá and Réthymnon

**Akrotíri**, the most bulbous of the three headlands that thrust out of Crete's northwest coast, shelters Chaniá's port of Soúda from the winds. Its strategic position has assured it of plenty of history, and the fine views of Chaniá from the **Profítis Ilías** church (4.5km east of Chaniá by way of Eleftheríou Venizélou Street and the airport road) so charmed Elefthérios Venizélos (1864–1936) that he asked to be buried here. He had a patriotic reason as well: in 1897, in the midst of a bombardment by international navies who had come to help the Turks put down a revolt, the Cretans raised the Greek flag. The admirals were so impressed by the sheer audacity of the Cretans that they stopped fighting and applauded. Later in the day, a Russian shell destroyed the church, but it is said that Prophet Elijah got his revenge by blowing up part of the Russian ship the next day. If it's Easter Day afternoon, the place to be is the nearby convent at **Kourakiés**, where the bishop of Chaniá reads the 'Vespers of Love' in a score of languages to the crowd in the flower-bedecked courtyard.

Akrotíri has Chaniá's airport, a fact that hasn't stopped the wealthier Chaniots from dotting the headland with new villas, a conurbation that has begun to encroach on the **monastery of Ag. Triáda**, north of Kambáni. Founded at the beginning of the 17th century by Jeremiah Zangarola, a Venetian who became an Orthodox monk, it has a lovely cruciform Renaissance church with an austere Venetian façade and tangerine trees all around. The second monastery, the fortified **Moní Gouvernétou**, 5km above Ag. Triáda, stands on a remote plateau. It is dedicated to the 7th-century saint, John the Hermit (or the Stranger) who lived, died and is buried in a narrow stalagmite cave, half an hour's walk down by the sea by way of steps carved in the rock. One of Crete's most important pilgrimages happens here on 6–7 October, when the faithful file in to dip their hands in the Holy Water that collects near the entrance. But this place has long been holy: along the path you can visit another cave, **Arkoudiótissa** ('Bear' cave), where an altar to the Virgin keeps cosy company with her predecessor—a stalactite once revered as the goddess Artemis turned into a bear. Near St John's cave stand ruins of the original monastery, or Katholikón. There's a rocky, often deserted place to swim below the cave, or head west to **Stavrós**, with a lovely circular bay providing good swimming and shallow water safe for the youngest child, as well as a couple of tavernas for lunch.

The sprawl of Chaniá stretches all along the road to **Soúda** (ΣΟΥΔΑ), the main port for Western Crete, tucked at the magnificent sheltered bay formed by Akrotíri. Soúda will never win a beauty contest, but it is the departure point for a number of excursions that more or less require private transport. A pretty road 2km southwest of Soúda leads to the 16th-century walled convent, **Moní Chryssopigí** (*open 8–12 and 3–6*), confiscated by the Germans in 1941, but since 1977 repopulated and restored. The nuns restore old icons and books and operate on Crete's most prestigious icon painting workshops (*open by appointment only*), based on Byzantine tradition. From here (or Aptera, *see* below) you can pick up the road to **Maláxa**, an ancient mining centre. The most spectacular sight is the ravine to the south, 400m deep, riddled with caves.

East of Soúda, along the north coast highway, stretches the recently abandoned NATO base, for years the source of a hundred local gripes (not least of which was the behaviour of the soldiers in Chaniá's bars), and the long yellow walls of an active Greek base. But NATO was hardly the first to appreciate the superb harbour of Soúda Bay, one of the finest in the Mediterranean. The Venetians fortified the bay's islet, **Néa Soúda**, and when they and the Greeks who took refuge there surrendered at last in 1715 (50 years after the Turkish conquest of the rest of Crete) it was only by way of a treaty, in spite of frequent attacks and the 5000 Christian heads that the Turks piled gruesomely around the walls. The Turks had an excellent if rather frustrating view of defiant Néa Soúda and the entire Bay of Soúda from an expropriated Venetian fortress on the south end of the bay, still known by its Turkish name, **Idzeddin.** Now Chaniá's prison, Idzeddin was built of stone cannibalized from ancient **Aptera**, high up a twisting narrow road 8.5km east of Soúda, beyond the modern village of Megála Choráphia (signposted to the south of the Chaniá-Réthymnon highway). Dedicated to Artemis, Aptera was founded in the 8th century BC and remained important into the Christian era. Its curious name (*aptera* or 'featherless') came from a singing contest held between the Muses and the Sirens. The Sirens were sore losers, and tore out their feathers and plunged into the sea, where they turned into offshore rocks. The most impressive ancient remains are Aptera's 3rd century BC walls, which once stretched for 4km, a classical temple, a Roman basilica, a theatre, and, behind the Monastery of St John, two impressive vaulted cisterns built by the Romans.

South from Aptera, **Stílos** saw the Anzac forces' last stand in the battle of Crete, and if they were cut down by the overwhelming German war machine, a special relationship survives to this day with New Zealand, where many Chaniots emigrated after the war. From Stílos it's 5km up to the village of **Samonás**, where archaeologists are unearthing a Late Minoan settlement and the Byzantine church of Ag. Nikólaos contains frescoes. Three kilometres further south, **Néo Chorió** has vast citrus orchards and a few remains of ancient habitations. **Vrýses** (ΒΡΥΣΕΣ), further south (at the crossroads for Chóra Sfakíon, *see* below) is a pleasant village of shady trees. Locals come here to picnic and swim in its creek.

After Aptera, the highway (with most of the buses) dives inland to avoid rugged Cape Drápanon, missing much of the area's finest scenery. A pair of small resort towns dot the somewhat exposed north coast of Drápanon: **Kalýves** has a long beach near the Apokoróna fortress, but **Almirída** is perhaps more attractive with a sheltered bay and pleasant beach with good windsurfing. East of Almirída, the road continues to the picturesque villages of **Pláka** and **Kókkino Chóra**, the latter used in the film *Zorba the Greek*. In the summer it seems too bright to fit the bill; come back in the winter for the brooding, overcast atmosphere. There are a few small beaches in the area, and the road south of Kókkino Chóra towards Georgioúpolis passes several other pretty villages, especially **Kefalás**.

**Georgioúpolis** (ΓΕΩΡΓΙΟΥΠΟΛΗ), where the Cape Drápanon road meets the main highway, was named in honour of Prince George and has a long sandy (if sometimes rough and windy) beach. Although a favourite area for hotel builders, it hasn't been completely swamped in cement and you can still find cheap rooms to rent around the village.

South of the higway are a few spots that might tempt a detour. At **Mathés**, the church of Ag. Antónios has a carob tree for its roof. Crete's only lake, **Kournás**, is near here as well, deep and eerie and full of eels. If you're looking for a place to stay, there's a taverna with a few rooms on the lake shore, which is a better bet than staying in the nearby village of Mourí.

---

### Where to Stay and Eating Out

**Stavrós** ✆ (0821–)

**Rea**, 800 yards from the sea, ✆ 39 001, 🖷 39 541 (*B; exp*). Built in 1992, this air-conditioned complex offers a wide range of activities, from a basketball court, tennis, swimming pool, and babysitting. **Zorba's Studio Flats**, by the beach, ✆ 39 010, 🖷 42 616 (*mod/exp*), are perfect for a family holiday, with tennis, garden, and a playground. **Kavos Beach**, ✆ 68 623 (*inexp*) are among the nicest rooms to rent.

**Vrýsses** ✆ (0825–)

There's little hotel **Orfeas**, ✆ 61 218 (*C; mod*), while the **Two Brothers,** on the main street, is a reasonably priced taverna-pizzeria.

**Georgioúpolis** ✆ (0825–)

**Mare Monte**, ✆/🖷 61 390 (*A; lux*) stands out as one of the west coast's most luxurious hotels. **Pilot Beach**, ✆ 22 313 (*A; exp*) is a stylish complex with a pool, a good family bet spread out in a number of different buildings, smack on the beach in a garden setting. **Mina**, at Kávros (the next beach east), ✆ 61 257 (*C; mod*) is a pleasant, medium-sized hotel. **Almyros**, ✆ 61 349 (*E; inexp*) is 100m from the sea *Open all year*. **Villa Mouria**, ✆ 61 342 and **Voula**, ✆ 61 259 have even cheaper rooms; **Siggerlakis** (no phone) cheaper still.

## South to Sfakiá

Sfakiá, long isolated under the White Mountains in the southeast corner of the *nomós* of Chaniá, was the cradle of the island's most daring and most mustachioed desperados, who clobbered each other in blood feuds but in times of need became Crete's bravest freedom fighters. Now connected to civilization on the north coast by a good (and dramatically beautiful) road, the Sfakióts prey no more than any other Cretan on invading foreigners. Although most tourists see the chief town, Chóra Sfakíon, only as the place where they catch the bus after the boat ride after the Gorge of Samariá, you may want to linger on this sun-bleached coast. There's even a remote gorge to walk through, if the Gorge of Samariá is too busy for your taste.

Chóra Sfakíon is linked by **bus** to Chaniá 4 times a day, and once to Kastélli-Kíssamou, Kolimvári, Tavronítis, Chandrís, Plataniás, Stalos, Stavrós, Omalós, Georgioúpolis, Réthymnon, and Plakiás, and there is 1 bus a day from Chaniá to Anópolis, Frangokástello and Skalotí. The **boat** service between Chóra Sfakíon, Loutró and Ag. Roúmeli, at the mouth of the Gorge of Samariá, is frequent, with 1 or 2 boats a day continuing west of Ag. Roúmeli to Soúgia and Paleochóra. Morning excursion boats link Chóra Sfakíon to Sweetwater beach; 2 boats a week sail south to the island of Gávdos.

**Last Sunday in May**, Chóra Sfakíon; **15 August**, Alíkampos; **23 August** at the church of Ag. Geórgios, Asigoniá; **15 September**, Frangokástello.

## Vrýssis to Chóra Sfakíon

The twisting mountain road to Sfakiá begins at Vrýssis (*see* above), mid-way between Chaniá and Réthymnon. After 5km, a left turn leads up (1.5km) to the village of **Alíkampos**, with the church of the Panagía frescoed in 1315 by Ioánnis Pagoménos. The main road then ascends the Krapí valley to the edge of the **Langos tou Katre**, the narrow 2km ravine known as the Thermopylae of Sfakiá that spelt doom to the 400 Turkish soldiers fleeing Frangokástello in 1821 (*see* below). The road and ravine give on to the striking mountain plateau of **Askýfou**, where the grey ruins of the fortress of Koulés drape a long shadow over fields of wheat and potatoes, and where a monument on the edge of the village commemorates Sfakía's uprising in 1770 (*see* below). Further south, another by-road to the left leads to **Asfendos**, a seldom-visited mountain village built along a roaring brook; not far beyond the Asfendos crossroads, the blue Libyan sea comes into view below as the road windsdown the steep, wooded **Imbros gorge**, before zigzagging down the last barren mountain crusts to Chóra Sfakíon.

Legendary in Crete for its ferocity, **Chóra Sfakíon** (ΧΩΡΑ ΣΦΑΚΙΩΝ) today is hardly distinguishable from the island's other coastal villages, with its seaside tavernas, hotels, souvenir shops and pebble beach. At one time, however, this village was the capital of its own province, one that often turned to smuggling and piracy to support itself. In an attempt to police the locals after the revolt of 1570, the Venetians constructed a castle on the pine-clad hill over Chóra after the revolt of 1570, to supplement their 1317 fortress of Ag. Nikítas at Frangokástello. At one time Chóra Sfakíon was said to have a hundred churches, enabling the townfolk to gather at seemingly harmless *panegýria* every two or three days to plot the next moves of a revolt. The tradition of resistance was continued after the Battle of Crete, when the locals helped the rearguard New Zealand and Australian soldiers to flee to North Africa.

## The Ghosts of Frangokástello

The oldest Venetian fortress in Sfakía is austere, crenellated Ag. Nikítas, or **Frangokástello** (ΦΡΑΓΚΟΚΑΣΤΕΛΛΟ), 14km east of Chóra Sfakíon, once splendidly isolated on its long sandy beach but now joined by a straggle of concrete buildings. It was built in 1317, to keep the wild Sfakiots under control. During the War of Independence, an Epirot insurgent, Khatzimichális Daliánis, held Frangokástello with 650 Cretans until 8000 Turkish troops arrived to force them out. The Turks took the fort, and all of the Greeks inside were slain, including Daliánis. The Turks' victory was short-lived: bands of Cretans who had remained outside the fort quickly recaptured Frangokástello, while other Cretan chieftains captured the mountain passes and caused havoc when the remainder of the Turkish army turned to the north, seizing guns and much-needed supplies.

The Massacre of Frangokástello has given rise to the one of the most authenticated of the million or so Greek ghost stories that exist. On 17 May, the anniversary of the massacre, the phantoms of the Cretan dead rise up at dawn, fully armed, and march silently towards the fortress, then disappear into the sea. These are the famous Drosoulités, the 'dew shades', still ready to fight the enemy Turk. So many people have seen them that scientific explanations have been attempted, although as yet none has proved satisfactory. On other days of the year, Frangokástello is a rather sleepy seaside resort with a long, beach of fine sand that offers some of the best swimming waters in Crete.

## Anópolis and Loutró

If the Gorge of Samariá is too crowded, catch the bus from Chaniá or Chóra Sfakíon up to **Anópolis**, a pleasant village on a plateau with a handful of inns and restaurants. The statue in the centre is of the Sfakiót hero Daskaloyánnis ('Yiannis the Teacher'), the first Cretan to organise a revolt against the Turks (1770).

Because of Sfakiá's rugged terrain, the Turks were content to leave the territory alone in exchange for the payment of a heavy poll tax. Daskaloyánnis, a well-educated ship owner, was the representative of Sfakía. In his travels he met emissaries of Catherine the Great who convinced him that Russia would come to his aid if he rebelled against the Turks, and, after two years of planning, he and 2000 well-armed Sfakiots drove out the Ottoman tax collector and began to terrorize the Turks living in the villages north of the mountains. When the expected Russian fleet failed to materialize, the Turkish response was swift; 15,000 men were sent down to Sfakiá. Women and children had already been sent off to Kýthera, leaving Daskaloyánnis and his troops holed up in mountain strongholds, to watch in despair as the Turks systematically destroyed Sfakiá's villages. In March 1771, Daskaloyánnis gave himself up, hoping to spare Sfakiá from worst; the pasha ordered him to be flailed alive.

From Anópolis, follow the road 4km west to Arádena, a ghost village, where a track descends into the beautiful **Gorge of Arádena**, recently fitted with a suspension bridge. On the opposite side is the abandoned Byzantine monastery of **Ag. Ioánnis**. The path brings you back to Loutró. The coast around **Loutró** has many quiet beaches, including, an hour's walk away, the isolated strand of Glyká Neró, or **Sweetwater Beach**, cut off on one side by sheer cliffs and on the other by deep blue sea. True to its name, small springs provide fresh drinking water, and there's a taverna in season when you need something more substantial. A few vestiges remain of the autonomous ancient city, Aradin, some of which were cannibalized for the church of Archistrátigos Michaíl (Archangel Michael in his role as heaven's *generalissimo*). The environs are pitted with caves. **Drakoláki cave** is noteworthy—an underground labyrinth with a bottomless lake that requires both a torch and Ariadne's ball of string to explore.

### Chóra Sfakíon

**Vritomartis**, on the road north of the village, © 91 222 (*B; exp*). A new, self-contained holiday complex on a ledge overlooking the sea, the Vritomartis has a pool complex, tennis courts, and frequent minibus service to Chóra Sfakíon. **Livikon**, on the quay, © 91 211 is new, stylish, and comfortable, near the **Xenia**, © 91 202 (*B pension; mod*), one of the oldest hotels in the village. There are also plenty of rooms. The port tavernas offer a wide selection of ready food, or **Limani**, by the port, offers a fish fry or mixed grill and salad for 3500dr. If you're looking for a snack, try one of Sfakiá's famous *myzithrópittes* (cheese pies).

### Frangokástello

Inexpensive rooms here include **Castello**, © 92 068, **Flisvos**, © 92 069 and **Pollakis**, © 92 088.

### Loutró

**Porto Loutro**, © 91 091 (*B; exp*), is new and very comfortable, and has a number of water sports facilities. *Open April–Oct.*

## Réthymnon (ΡΕΘΥΜΝΟ)

Réthymnon, Crete's third city, has long bemoaned its lack of a proper harbour. The Venetians dug a cute, nearly perfectly round one, but even now it keeps silting up. In several ways this has proved a blessing, for Réthymnon has escaped much of what passes for progress. Like Chaniá, its Venetian and Turkish architecture has earned it national historical landmark status, but Réthymnon suffered far less from Nazi bombing. Two minarets lend the skyline an exotic touch; wooden balconies left over from the Turkish occupation project overhead, darkening the already piquant narrow streets. Its relative isolation attracted scholars who fled Constantinople, making Réthymnon something of an intellectual centre, a reputation it maintains to this day as the new seat of the University of Crete. Until recently Réthymnon retained its traditional crafts and old shops in the centre, but the relentless economics of tourism is quickly converting the old carpenters' and cobblers' shops into more profitable souvenir stalls.

### Getting There

Olympic airways buses link Réthymnon to Chaniá airport twice a day; contact the Olympic Office at Koumoundoúrou 5, © 27 353. Réthymnon is linked by a **ferry** to Piraeus 4 times a week on Réthymnon Lines, 250 Arkadíou, © 25 876/29 221. The short- and long-distance **bus** stations (© 22 785) occupy the crossroads of Dimokratías and Moátsou where confusions and traffic jams are the speciality.

### Tourist Information

**NTOG**, along the town beach at E. Venizélou, © (0831) 24 143. **Tourist police**: Plateía Heróon, © (0831) 28 156. The **post office** is on Moátsou, in the new town; the **OTE telephones** are on Gerakári.

## Festivals

On **Wednesdays** Réthymnon hosts a big market fair. Look out for **Carnival** and **Midsummer's Day**, with bonfires. The Cretan Wine Festival and Handicrafts Exhibition is on the **last 10 days of July**; there's also the Renaissance Festival for **20 days in August**, with concerts and theatre performing in the Venetian fortress.

## The Old Town

All that remains of Réthymnon's Venetian walls is the picturesque **Guóra**, the grand gate that leads into the old city from the Plateía of the Four Martyrs, a square named after four young men beheaded by the Turks. Just below the gate is the picturesque 17th-century lion-headed **Rimondi Fountain**, built by the Venetians in 1629 at the junction of several streets, now jam-packed with bars. Réthymnon's finest Venetian building, the **Loggia** (1600), nearby on Arkadíou Street, where Venice's soldiers would gather, is now Réthymnon's library. If it's re-opened, climb the minaret of the 18th-century **Neradzes Mosque** (a former Venetian church) on Manoúli Vernádou for a good view over Réthymnon.

Réthymnon's waterfront has inevitably been given over to the tourist trade. Seafood restaurants solidly line the bijou little **Venetian harbour**, patrolled by a fleet of black and white swans and a blatantly corny pirate ship, waiting to take you out to catch your own dinner. From here it's a short walk to the entrance of the massive **Fortezza** (*open 8am–8pm*), built over the acropolis of ancient Rithymna. Réthymnon was put to the sack by Barbarossa in 1538, and in 1562 and 1571 Uluch Ali repeated his performance. At that the Venetians decided enough was enough. They walled in the entire city and built the Fortezza, using the forced labour of the peasants. It is one of the best-preserved Venetian castles in Greece, and one of the largest. In 1645 after a bitter two-month siege, the defending garrison was forced to surrender it to the Turks. The church, converted into a mosque—a strikingly austere cube with a spherical dome—is fairly well preserved, and the rest has been left in dishevelled, poetic abandon; trees grow out of the old ramparts, from where there are fine views.

The former Turkish prison at the entrance to the Fortezza is now the **Archaeology Museum** (*open 8.30–3, closed Mon*) and houses a modest collection of finds from the *nomós*: Egyptian art (the only foreign works that the Minoans imported in any quantity), Neolithic finds, Minoan larnaxes and pottery and a very late goddess from Pagalchori, discs and mirrors from the Idean cave, Graeco-Roman marble and bronze statues.

Nearby, at 28 Mesolongíou, the **Historical and Folk Art Museum** (*open 9–1, closed Sun*), offers a delicious collection of traditional costumes, embroidery, photos, farming implements, and pottery from a bygone age; nearby, on Chimáras, the new **Municipal Centre of Contemporary Art** (*open 10–2 and 5–8, closed Mon*) features changing and quite often excellent exhibitions.

Just outside the Guóra Gate, an old Turkish cemetery was converted in the 1920s into the **Municipal Garden**; its cool melancholy paths seem haunted by discreet slippered ghosts—except during Réthymnon's July wine festival, when it overflows with jovial imbibers reviving Crete's ancient Dionysian rites.

# Where to Stay
## luxury

**Grecotel Creta Palace**, 4km east of Réthymnon, ✆ 55 181, ✉ 54 085, a hotel and bungalow complex built on the beach in 1989, with an indoor heated pool and two outdoor ones, illuminated tennis courts and lots of sports, especially for children. *Open Mar–Nov.* Grecotel also owns the nearly as plush **Rithymna Beach Hotel and Bungalows** in Ádele (7km) ✆ 29 491, ✉ 71 002 (A). On a lovely beach with similar facilities, it's very popular (especially with American families), filling up early in the spring and staying that way, so book early.

## expensive

**Mythos Suites Hotel**, 12 Plateía Karaóli, ✆ 53 917 (*B*) has 10 suites furnished in a traditional style, sleeping 2–5 people in a 16th-century manor house; all are air-conditioned and there's a pool in the sunny central patio. **Palazzo Rimondi**, Xarthoúdou, ✆ 51 289 (*A*) is similar, containing 25 suites in a renovated mansion, built around a courtyard with a small pool. **Hotel Fortezza** is just under the castle walls at Melissínou 16, ✆ 21 551, ✉ 20 073 (*B*); all rooms have balconies, and there's a garden courtyard and swimming pool. Less expensive, **Garden House**, 82 N. Fokás (near the Fortezza), ✆ 28 586, is a small but delightful historical residence, with a fountain and beautiful rooms (but book well in advance). **Liberty**, near the bus station, ✆ 21 851 (*B*) is new, green and comfortable, and only a minute from the town beach. Another good choice, **Hotel Ideon**, ✆ 28 667, (*B*) is well placed by the ferry dock, and also has a small pool; reserve.

## moderate

**Leo**, Váfe 2, ✆ 29 851, is a charming bed and breakfast inn, done up in traditional Cretan style. **Hotel Brascos**, at Ch. Daskaláki and Th. Moátsou, ✆ 23 721 (*B*) is slick and clean, and open all year. For peace and quiet, **Zorba** at the east end of the beach, ✆ 28 540, is reasonably priced; rooms come with private shower and WC. Before trekking out there, give them a ring to see if there's a vacancy.

## inexpensive

The **youth hostel**, Tombázi 41, ✆ 23 943, is exceptionally nice and convenient, only a few blocks from the tourist office. You don't need a card to stay there; breakfast and cooking facilities are available. **Zania**, Pávlou Vlasátou (a block from the sea) ✆ 28 169, has a handful of pleasant rooms, although in season the price is at the top of this range. **Hotel Achillion**, at 151 Arkadíou, ✆ 22 581 (*E*) is less expensive, and offers a hint of former elegance and a view of the harbour from the balcony—and lots of noise at night. **Rent Rooms Eliza**, at Plastíra 12, ✆ 22 581 is adequate enough and near the Venetian harbour. A few kilometres east of Réthymnon there are two neighbouring campsites, **Elizabeth**, ✆ 28 694 and **Arkadia Camping**, ✆ 22 361.

# Eating Out

The trendy place to eat, with its tiny fish restaurants, is the Venetian harbour, but expect to pay at least 4000dr for the privilege (although the quality and variety are excellent; nearly every place has a special menu, some offering lobster lunches for two for 8000dr). All by itself, on the west side of the Fortezza, is the Heliovasilemata, better known as the **Sunset Taverna**, with good solid Greek food and an extensive wine list (*about 4000dr for fish, 2000dr for pizza*). For something different, try **Famagusta** on Nikálou Plastirá, a moderately priced eatery specializing in Cypriot dishes. Near Plateía Petiháki, in a row of popular tavernas, **Agrimio**, serves all the old favourites, including pizza. **Taverna Alana** in Salamínos Street (just south of the Fortezza) is a nice enough place to bring your parents, and serves a good fish-based menu for 6000dr for two. But, as is so often the case, to find the genuine article you have to head out of town, in this case 5km in the direction of Chaniá, to **Faros**, an enormous restaurant serving up excellent grilled food, good barrelled wine and live Cretan music. A further 12km on there's **Kaklis**, which is equally popular, with a more limited but still excellent menu, wonderful local wine and live music.

### Entertainment and Nightlife

**T. N. Gounaki** on Koronaíou Street (near the church of the Mikrí Panagías) is a simple place summed up by its own sign: 'Every day folk Cretan music with Gounakis Sons and their father gratis/free/for nothing and Cretan meal/dish/food/dinner thank you'—expect to pay around 3000dr. The slicker **Odysseus Club**, by the port at Ioul. Peticháki, specializes in bouzouki and Cretan music, again more for tourists than locals; for the real McCoy, try the aforementioned Faros and Kaklis. The **Cinema Dancing Bar** in Salamínos Street offers some of the campest entertainment on Crete, from male strippers to Greeks doing Michael Jackson imitations. For a quiet drink in a cosy pub atmosphere, try the **Punch Bowl Bar** in main Theod. Armbatzólogou.

## Nomós Réthymnon

The *nomós* of Réthymnon is the most mountainous on Crete, dominated in the east by Mount Ida, or Psilorítis (2452m); several paths lead to its summit and to its sacred cave. Two of Crete's most famous fortress-monasteries, Préveli and Arkadí, are in the *nomós*, and in the south you can still find undeveloped beaches, as well as the popular resort of Ag. Galíni.

### Getting Around

Three **buses** daily link Chaniá and Réthymnon to Arkadí. Plakiás has connections every 2 hours with Chaniá and Réthymnon, as well as 1 bus a day west along the south coast as far as Chóra Sfakíon, via Frangokástello. Ag. Galíni has 8 buses a day from Réthymnon, as well as connections to Herákleon, Phaistós, and Mátala via Mýres. Every half-hour, the Chaniá–Réthymnon–Herákleon buses ply the coast. **Port authority**, ✆ (0831) 28 971.

### Festivals

Plakiás: **23 April** and the **Friday after Easter**. Préveli: **8 May**. Spíli: **27 May** and **29 June**. Arkadí: **8–9 November**.

## Arkadí

**Arkadí Monastery** (*open daily 8am–8pm*), something of a holy shrine in Crete, is 25km from Réthymnon, and a favourite destination for a day out. Prettily set on the lonesome flanks of Psilorítis, the monastery was founded in the 11th century; the present building dates from the 17th century and the lovely, sun-ripened stone façade, an essay in Venetian mannerism, is from 1587. Even so, Arkadí resembles a small fort, which is one reason why Koroneos, at the head of the Revolutionary Committee of 1866, chose it as a base and a store for his powder magazine. When the Turks demanded that the abbot, Gabriel Marinákis, hand over the rebels, he refused; in response, a Turkish expeditionary force marched on Arkadí and in terror people from the surrounding villages took refuge inside the thick monastery walls. On 7 November 1866, the Turks under Mustafa Kyrtil Pasha attacked Arkadí, and after a 2-day siege they breached the walls. Rather than surrender, Abbot Gabriel set fire to the powder magazines, blowing up 829 Greeks and Turks. The event caused a furore in Europe, as Swinburne and Victor Hugo took up the cause of Cretan independence. At the monastery you can visit the Gunpowder Room, where the blast left a gaping hole in the roof, and three rooms of relics.

## To the Libyan Coast

The road directly south of Réthymnon leads to **Arméni**, a village named for the Armenian soldiers granted land here by Byzantine general Nikephóros Phokás after the conquest of Crete from the Arabs in 961. Recently an unusually large, scarcely plundered Late Minoan cemetery of rock-cut tombs was discovered near the crossroads with Somatás (signposted from the main road; the guardian lives in Arméni and can show you around); it suggests that there was an important Minoan town in the vicinity, but so far no one has found it. The crossroads for **Préveli Monastery** (*open 8–1 and 3–7*) is at Koxaré; from here the road cuts through the dramatically wild and barren Kourtaliótiko ravine to the monastery, beautifully situated on the coast. Although founded in the 17th-century, the buildings are fairly recent; Préveli is best known as a resistance centre during the Turkish and German occupations. In 1941 it sheltered Allied troops from the Nazis until they could be picked up by submarine from 'Palm Beach' below and taken to Egypt; in gratitude the British gave Préveli two silver candlesticks and a marble plaque, now lovingly cared for by two remaining monks.

Just before Préveli, the road branches west for the village and resort of **Plakiás** (ΠΛΑΚΙΑΣ) near a good beach, with more accommodation of every type added each year. It's a great centre for long walks and serious swimming on some splendid sandy coves with a taverna or two under the tamarisks, especially 2km away at **Damnóni**; quieter beaches are only attainable on foot. Late in the afternoon, head up to Mírthios, where the taverna terrace offers a superb sunset view of the coves below. To the west is tiny mountain village of **Rodákino** ('the peach'), with another lovely beach of soft sand and caves.

---

*Plakiás ✆ (0832–)*                    ***Where to Stay and Eating Out***

**Calypso Cretan Village**, ✆ 31 296 (*A; exp*) is the big new fancy pants hotel on this coast, with all the trimmings. **Livikon**, next to Plakiás bus station, ✆ 31 216 (*C*) and **Lamon**, ✆ 31 318 (*B*); both have good rates for private rooms with bath. There is a **youth hostel** in Plakiás, ✆ 31 306, which doesn't even demand a card; if it's full,

# Nomós Réthymnon

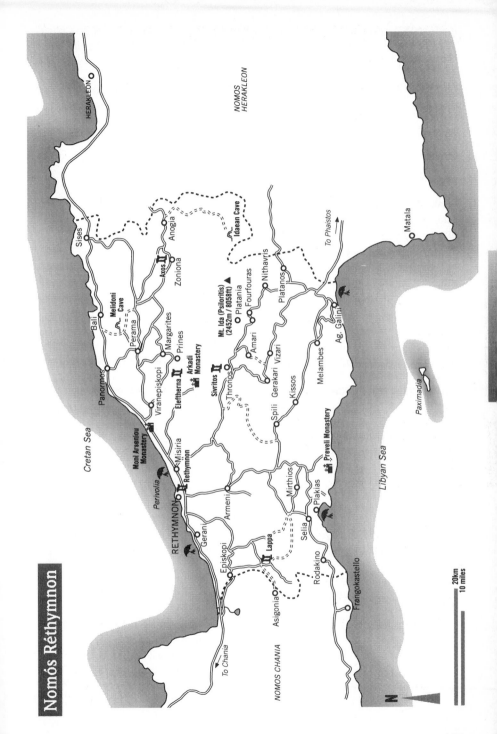

there's another, and rather nicer one up at Mírthios (✆ 31 202). Plump for a sword-fish steak on the terrace at **Kolamios** or the excellent spread at **Gorgons** before resorting to the local nightspots.

## Amári: The Western Slopes of Mount Ida

On these western slopes of snow-capped Mount Ida, the ancient province of Amári is well known for its fighting spirit and resistance in the last war, for fruit and olive trees, and a fine collection of frescoed Byzantine churches. The main approach on the to Ag. Galíni road is by way of **Spíli** (ΣΠΗΛΙ), a charming village immersed in greenery. The village centrepiece is a long fountain, where water splashes from a row of 17 Venetian lion-heads.

The little villages of the Amári itself are more pleasantly bucolic than spectacular. East of Spíli, **Gerakári** has many houses from the Middle Ages, along with a tower. **Amári**, one-time capital of the province, is a tranquil village with enchanting views and the church Ag. Anna with the oldest dated frescoes in Crete, from 1225.

North of Amári, the sleepy village of **Thrónos** stands over the walls of ancient Sívritos, destroyed by the Saracens in the 9th century. In the centre of the village, the ruins of a basilica with a mosaic floor lie near the frescoed church of the Panagía (14th century). From **Fourfourás** a shale path leads up to one of the peaks of Mount Ida, a 5-hour trek in good walking shoes. There is a little chapel on top, as well as an unforgettable view of Crete.

## Ag. Galíni

The roads to the south end up at **Ag. Galíni** (ΑΓΙΑ ΓΑΛΗΝΗ), the trendiest and most photogenic resort on the south coast. Once a fishing village, it now does most of its fishing for the tourists; the beach is small and not all that good, but some of the best cooks in Crete work in the numerous restaurants here. Boat excursions go out to Préveli Monastery and its pretty beaches, to Mátala and Ag. Geórgios (a beach with three tavernas, 15 minutes from Ag. Galíni), Ag. Pávlos (50 minutes away, a remote sandy beach with no facilities) and to the pebble-beached islets to the southwest, called **Paximáthia** for their resemblance to the crunchy twice-baked bread sold in Greek bakeries.

---

✆ (0832–)                                              *Where to Stay and Eating Out*

**Spíli**

Green Hotel, ✆ 22 225 (*C; mod*), bedecked with flowers and plants, is a delightful refuge when the coasts are unbearably hot and crowded. You can also find rooms to rent, as well as good food, at the **Yparxo** taverna on the main road.

**Ag. Galíni**

Although stacked with all sorts of accommodation, don't arrive in Ag. Galíni without a reservation in the summer, when package companies block book nearly every hotel. **Galini Mare**, ✆ 91 358 (*C; mod*) has good views and facilities; **Areti**, at the top of town, ✆ 91 240 (*D; mod*) is your best chance if everything else is full up. **Hotel Minos** (*D; mod*), ✆ 91 218, has a good view. **Aktaeon**, Kountouriótou, ✆ 91 208 (*E; inexp*), with private baths and good views over the town offers good value.

Other inexpensive places not on any package company's list are **Argiro's Studios and Rooms,** ✆ 91 470; there's also **Rent Rooms Acropol** (*inexp*)—the rooms aren't up to much but the situation, on the top of the cliff, is superb. Near the bus station, **Manos,** ✆ 91 394, has among the cheapest rooms in town, some with private bath.

The restaurants of Ag. Galíni loom over the waterfront: **Madame Ordanz**, up on the second floor and lined with photographs of old Ag. Galíni, serves well-prepared French and Greek dishes with a glamorous touch (*around 4000dr*). The popular **Ariston taverna** serves good *stifádo*, moussaka, and an excellent aubergine salad—3000dr for a full meal; **El Greco** next door is just as good. One of Ag. Galíni's favourites is **Onar**, where excellent Cretan food, cooked by Mother, can be enjoyed while gazing out over the deep blue sea. **La Strada** in the centre has a real pizza oven, and serves it up to jazz music. **Stelios,** a bar on the main street, serves warm fragrant *loukoumádes* (fritters in honey and cinnamon sauce) every Wednesday and Saturday evening.

# Réthymnon to Herákleon: the Coastal Route

Between Réthymnon and Herákleon you have a choice of routes: the scenic, fast, coast-skirting E75 highway, with a few small resorts for stopovers, or the old, winding, leisurely routes through a score of villages over the northern slopes of Mount Ida. If you're sticking to the coast, **Viranepiskopí,** a popular camping area on the north coast, possesses two churches of interest: a 10th-century basilica near a sanctuary of Artemis, and a 16th-century Venetian church. Further east, **Pánormos** has a small sandy beach at the mouth of the Milópotamos river, guarded by a fortress built by the Genoese in 1206, but taken by their arch-rivals, the Venetians, only six years later. Pánormos also has the ruins of a 5th-century basilica. Further east along the coastal expressway, **Balí** (ΜΠΑΛΙ), in part thanks to the exotic cachet of its name, has been transformed from a quiet steep-stepped fishing village overlooking a pair of cute coves to a jam-packed resort in summer. However, if you're passing, the delicious cove behind its port is well worth a swim and lunch. Near Balí and 4km northeast of Pérama, **Melidóni cave** (bring sturdy non-slip shoes and a torch) is vast and full of stalactites and stalagmites. The Minoans worshipped here, and just to the right of the entrance is an inscription to Hermes Talaios from the 3rd century BC, who shared offerings here with Zeus Talaios and Talos.

Talos was a mechanical bronze giant made by the smithy god Hephaistos and given by Zeus to Minos to guard the coasts of Crete. Talos' job was to run around the island three times each day, flinging boulders at foreign ships; if an enemy happened to land, Talos would hop into a fire until he was red-hot, then seize the invader and burn him alive in his fiery metal embrace, laughing like thunder. It was also his task to visit all the towns of Crete with bronze tablets bearing Minos' laws. When the *Argo* appeared on the horizon, Talos bombarded it with boulders until Medea hypnotized him from afar, and removed the pin from his heel, draining away his ichor, or immortal blood.

Melidóni was to see much worse in 1824, when 324 women and children and 30 revolutionaries took refuge here during the War of Independence. When the Turks discovered their hideaway, they refused to surrender; the Turks built a fire at the entrance and suffocated them all. Altars along the walls commemorate the victims.

Continuing east, **Fódele** lies 3km south of the highway through nearly solid orange groves. According to tradition this pleasant village was the birthplace of Doménikus Theotokópoulos, better known as El Greco, although there isn't much to see beyond a plaque erected in his honour by the University of Toledo and a pretty Byzantine church of the Panagía (1383). The highway continues to the junction for the attractive, up-market resort of **Ag. Pelagía**, where large hotels gaze down over the quiet coves and protected beaches. Five kilometres east of the junction, keep your eyes peeled for the striking seaside Venetian fort of **Palaiókastro**.

---

*Ag. Pelagía ☎ (081–)*                                 **Where to Stay and Eating Out**

**Capsis Beach Resort**, ☎ 811 212, ✆ 811 076 (*A; lux*) has just about every luxury you can imagine, plus three beaches, several swimming pools, a watersports school and an ultra-modern conference centre. **Panorama**, ☎ 811 002, ✆ 811 273 (*B; exp*) is a comfortable, large resort hotel with a pool, water sports and tennis. **Amazon**, ☎ 811 169 (*D; mod*) is one of the nicer, less expensive choices near the sea.

---

## Réthymnon to Herákleon: the Inland Route

From Réthymnon, the easiest route inland is to follow the coastal hotel sprawl east as far as Stavroménos, where you can pick up the road for Pérama. A possible detour, just before Pérama, is to seldom-visited **Margarítes**, 7km south, home of a thriving pottery industry and the **Maranthospílios cave**. High and precipitous, **Axós**, 30km east along the mountain road, was believed to have been founded in 1100 BC by Minoans seeking refuge from the Dorian invaders, Axós was the only town on the island still to have a king into the 7th century BC, and it continued to thrive well into the Byzantine period, when it counted 46 churches. A sign in the village points the way up to the ancient site, scattered on terraces under its 8th-century BC acropolis walls and ruins of an Archaic sanctuary. Just west of Axós, near the hamlet of Zonianá, you can visit the **cave of Sedóni**, beautifully set on a spur of Mount Ida and containing one of Crete's most striking collections of stalactites, cave draperies and petrified waves. The formations were discovered by a little girl, who according to the locals was lured away by the fairies, or nereids; after an eight-day search she was found dead at the far end of the cave with a beatific smile on her face.

Axós is 9km from **Anógia** (ΑΝΩΓΕΙΑ), a stalwart resistance centre, burned by both the Turks and the Germans, the latter in reprisal for the daring kidnapping of General Kreipe, who was hidden in the village by the Resistance. Today rebuilt in the original style (albeit in concrete instead of stone) it produces some of Crete's finest woven cloth, with 700 traditional patterns in all, and also Crete's best *rakí* (or *tsikoútha*, oúzo's stronger cousin). Recently Anógia has taken advantage of its weaving traditions to become a 'typical' village for tour groups; brace yourself for a mugging by a score of little old ladies touting their wares.

Just east of Anógia begins the mostly paved 26km road ascending 1540m to the **Idaean cave** (IΔAIO ANTPO), which as far back as Archaic times took over the Diktean cave's thunder, so to speak, in claiming to be the birthplace of Zeus. Ancient even to the ancients, the Idaean cave cult preserved remnants of Minoan religion into Classical times, presided over by Idaean Dactyls or 'finger men'. According to his ancient biographer, Pythagoras was initiated by the Idaean Dactyls into the Orphic mysteries of midnight Zagreus (i.e. Zeus fused with the mystic role of Dionysos), a cult that was believed to be the origins of his mystical theories on numbers and vegetarianism; in the Herákleon museum Minoan seals bear the five-pointed star symbol he would adopt as his own. A clue to what they got up to in the cave is preserved in a fragment of Euripides' lost play, *The Cretans,* in the confession of Cretan mystics:

*My days have run, the servant I,*
*Initiate, of Idaean Jove;*
*Where midnight Zagreus roves, I rove;*
*I have endured his thunder-cry;*
*fulfilled his red and bleeding feasts;*
*Held the Great Mother's mountain flame;*
*I am Set Free and named by name*
*A Bacchus of the Mailed Priests.*

Since 1982 Yánnis Sakellarákis' exavations have produced a vast number of votive offerings dating from Neolithic times to the 5th century AD; at the time of writing, the cave is still off limits although it may reopen soon—ask before you set out. A ski resort has opened near by, and there's a marked track from the cave to the summit of **Psilorítis**, Crete's highest peak (2456m), about 7 hours' round trip if you're a reasonably experienced hiker.

The road from Anógia continues east to **Goniés**, a village set in an amphitheatre under Mount Ida at the entrance to the Malevízi, the grape-growing region that gave its name to Malmsey, a favourite red wine in medieval Venice and England. From Goniés the road continues in a valley to **Sklavokámbos**, where a Minoan megaron went up in flames so intense that its limestone walks were baked as if in a kiln. Much more remains to be seen further east in the pretty village of **Týlisos**, swathed in olives and vineyards, where three large Minoan villas with similar plans were unearthed in 1902–13 (*open Tues–Sun, 8.45–3*). Built in the New Palace period and destroyed *c.* 1450 BC, they stood two or three storeys high and contained small apartments and extensive storage facilities; you can get a fair notion of their plans from the surviving stairs, pavements, walls, and pillars. Water was pumped in from 2km away by aqueduct; the north villa, rebuilt in the Post Palace period, has sophisticated plumbing and a reservoir.

# Herákleon (ΗΡΑΚΛΕΙΟ)

Herákleon (also Iraklion among other spelling variations) is Crete's capital and Greece's fifth largest city, with a population nearing 120,000. It holds little charm for most visitors, and the centre overflows with all the noisy hustle and bustle that most people come to the Greek islands to escape. However, nearly everyone visiting Crete ends up here at least once, for not only is Herákleon the transport hub of Crete, but it has the world's greatest collection of Minoan artefacts and the grand palace of Knossós in its suburbs. The Venetians have also left their mark in Herákleon, endowing it with some of Crete's finest public buildings and churches.

Herákleon began modestly enough as one of Knossós' two ports, and as such survived until the Dark Ages. The Saracens built a new town over its ruins, and called it Kandak ('moat') for the trench they dug around its walls. Used as a base for piracy, Kandak also became the leading slave market in the Mediterranean. Candia, as it later became known, remained the capital of Crete under the Turks until 1850 when they transferred it to Chaniá. After independence the Greeks revived the city's ancient name, Herákleon, and it was made the island's administrative capital when Crete was united with Greece.

### Getting There and Around

**By air**: Herákleon's airport, 4km east of the city in Amnisós, ✆ 245 644, is linked to the city by public bus (no.1), beginning at Pórta Chaníon and passing through the centre of town; Olympic bus connects to all Olympic flights from Plateía Eleftherías.

# Herákleon

*(map labels)* MAKARIOU · MAKARIOU · DAMVERGIDON · SKORDILON · KISAMOU · SAVATHIANON · MIRIONOU · VOURDOUBADON · NEA ODOS NTENTIDAKI · Plateía Kóraka · KALOKERINOU · PORTA CHANION · C · A · MONIS KARDIOTISIS · PLASTIRA · TOBAZI · SPINALOGAS · KOMENO BENTENI

For Olympic information, call ✆ 223 400 or 229 191. If you're flying to or from Athens, look into Air Greece flights, which tend to be cheaper than Olympic.

**By sea**: travel and shipping agents line Odós 25 Avgoústou, the main street down at the Venetian harbour. Herákleon also has connections by ferry every night to Piraeus on Minoan Lines (✆ 244 603) and ANEK (✆ 289 545); also to Sitía, Kássos and Kárpathos (1 a week). **Port authority**, ✆ (0812) 44 912.

**By road**: Herákleon has a medley of **bus stations**. For destinations east of Herákleon (including Ierápetra and the Lassíthi Plateau) depart from the port station outside the walls, just east of the Venetian port; on the busy Herákleon–Ag. Nikólaos route you may get a ride on KTEL's new double deckers. The

station for points west—Réthymnon and Chaniá—is adjacent. From just outside the Pórta Chaníon on the west side of the city, buses head southwest to Ag. Galíni, Górtyn, Phaestós, Mátala, Tílossos, Anógia and Milapótamo. From outside the Evans Gate (Plateía Kírpou) buses head to Ano Viános, Mýrtos and Thrapsanó. Buses for Archánes depart from central Plateía Venizélou. City buses for the nearest beaches to the west (Amoudári) depart from the Astoria hotel in Plateía Eleftherías (no.6); for Amnisós to the east take bus no.7, just opposite.

### Tourist Information

**NTOG**: 1 Xanthoudídou Street, across from the archaeology museum, ✆ (081) 22 24 87; open Mon–Fri 8–2.30. **Tourist police**: Dikeosínis Street, ✆ (081) 28 31 90. **Post office**: Plateía Daskaloyiánnis. **OTE telephones**: El Greco Park, open 24 hours a day.

### Festivals

Herákleon flower festival **2–6 June**; grape festival **11–19 September**; and a huge *panegýri* for the patron saint Ag. Minás on **11 November**.

## Venetian Herákleon

When Crete won its autonomy in 1900, Arthur Evans (*see* p.142), already popular on the island for his news reports in Britain on Turkish atrocities, was instrumental in persuading the Cretans to safeguard their Venetian walls and monuments. Herákleon's old front door, the **Venetian Harbour,** although now a couple of hundred yards west of the modern ferry docks and main bus station, still gives the best introduction to this busy city. Two monuments evoke the Venetians' ability to supply Herákleon during the 21-year siege by the vastly superior Turkish forces: out on the harbour mole, the recently restored 16th-century fortress **Rocco al Mare**, guarded by a fierce Lion of St Mark (*open 8–3*), and the **Venetian Arsenali**, or shipyards, its looming arches partially obscured the street. Here Daskaloyánnis, one of Crete's most revered revolutionaries, was publicly flayed alive by the Turks in 1774 (*see* p.123).

The main thoroughfare ascending from the Venetian Harbour, 25 Avgoustou, has always been lined with the sort of businesses it supports today; shipping agents, car rental shops, and banks. Halfway up, handsomely set back in its own square, the Byzantine church of **Ag. Títos** owes its stately cubic form to the Turks, who used it as a mosque and reconstructed it after various earthquakes. The Cretans use the chapel to the left of the narthex to house the island's most precious relic, the head of St Titus, a favourite disciple of St Paul, who converted the island to Christianity and died in Górtyn *c.* 96 AD. When forced to give up Crete, the Venetians made off with Titus' skull and only returned it when the Pope forced them to, in 1966.

Near the top of 25 Avgoustou Street, Herákleon's City Hall occupies the lovely **Venetian Loggia** (1620s), built as a meeting place for the Venetian and Cretan nobility and completely reconstructed after taking a direct hit in the Battle of Crete. The inner exedra is decorated all over with fine Renaissance reliefs of weapons and frowning bookworm lions (the damaged originals are in the Historical Museum). Further up 25 Avgoustou is **San Marco** (Ag. Márkos), the first church built by the Venetians on Crete (1239), twice rebuilt after earthquakes, converted into a mosque, and since restored for use as a concert hall and exhibition centre. Across from San Marco, at the head of flagstoned Plateía Venizélou, water dribbles (usually) from the mouths of the lions of the **Morosini Fountain**, commissioned in 1626 by the then Venetian governor.

South of Platĕía Venizélou, the city's busy **outdoor market** runs along Odós 1866. Several stalls sell dried Cretan wedding cakes—golden wreaths decorated with scrolls and rosettes. Similar forays into the Baroque may be seen at the south end of the market in Platĕía Kornárou, in the carvings adorning the **Bembo Fountain** (1588) which was put together by the Venetians from ancient fragments, including a headless Roman statue brought in from Ierápetra; the Turks added the charming kiosk-fountain the **Koúbes**, now converted into a café, and the Cretans added the modern sculptures of Erotókritos and Arethoúsa, the hero and heroine of their romantic national epic poem.

## The Archaeology Museum

*To avoid the endless tour groups, arrive early—the doors open at 8am in the summer and at 8.30 from Nov–May, and close at 7pm (also closed Mon morning); adm exp.*

A few blocks east of Platĕía Venizélou or Platĕía Kornárou is Herákion's largest square, the great hemicycle of **Platĕía Eleftherías**, dotted with monuments to great Cretans with equally great moustaches. Just north of Platĕía Eleftherías on Xanthoudídou is Herákleon's **Archaeology Museum**, an ungainly, somewhat airless coffer that holds nearly all the treasures of Minoan civilization. By law every important antiquity found on Crete belongs to the museum; the result is dazzling, delightful and too much to digest in one visit.

Arranged in chronological order, **Room I** holds finds from the Neolithic (from 5000 BC) and Pre-Palatial periods (from 2600–2000 BC). The fine craftsmanship that would characterize Minoan civilization proper is already apparent in the delicate golden leaf pendants, the polished stone ritual vessels, the boldly shaped red and black Vasiliki pottery and carved sealstones (note especially the unique 16-sided hieroglyphic seal found in Archánes, in Case 11). The future Minoan obsession with bulls is revealed in three tiny noodly clay men clinging to the head of a bull; early Cycladic idols and Egyptian seals discovered in the tombs of Messara point to a precocious trade network. **Rooms II and III** are devoted to the Old Palace period (2000–1700 BC), when the Minoans made their first polychromatic Kamares ware, vases that follow the rules of Art Nouveau: each work individually crafted, marrying form and decoration, using stylized motifs from the natural world. The virtuosity of Minoan potters 3500 years ago is especially expressed in their 'eggshell ware' cups, named for their delicate thin walls. One case displays the Knossós Town Mosaic: faïence plaques, each shaped and painted like a miniature Minoan house. Phaistós in particular flourished in the Old Palace period. The mysterious clay **Phaistós Disc** (1700 BC), displayed in the centre of Room III, is believed to be the world's first example of moveable type: 45 different symbols are stamped on both sides in a spiral. The theory that the disc is a forgery has been disproved by other items discovered to have similar pictures and/or phonetic ideograms, which may well be in the primordial Minoan tongue.

The vast majority of finds date from the 'Minoans' Golden Age', the New Palace period (1700–1450 BC), divided more or less geographically in **Rooms IV–IX**. Potters turned to even freer, more naturalistic designs, divided into the floral and marine styles. Stone carving became ever more rarefied as the Minoans sought the hardest and rarest marbles, porphyrys and semi-precious stones to carve into vases and rhytons (ritual pouring vessels), magnificently cut and polished to bring out their swirling grains. **Room IV** contains one of their masterpieces: a magnificent naturalistic bull's head rhyton carved in black steatite, with eyes of rock crystal and jasper, found in the Little Palace at Knossós. Other unique works found in Knossós are here as well: the famous bare-breasted snake goddess statuettes, the draughts board in ivory, rock crystal and blue glass paste and gold and silver leaf, complete with four gaming pieces, and the ivory bull leaper, the first known statue of a freely moving human figure. Note the carefully carved muscles and tendons, especially in the hand. Fragments of two other ivory figures were found, suggesting that the bull leaper was part of a composition, not unlike the one shown in the famous bull leaping fresco.

**Room V** also contains more finds from Knossós, in particular those just pre-dating its destruction in 1450 BC, when the Linear A and Linear B clay tablets in Case 69 were accidently baked in the general conflagration. Note the model of a Minoan palace c. 1600 BC. **Room VI** contains finds from the cemeteries at Knossós, Archánes and Phaistós (New Palace and Post-Palace periods, 1450–1300 BC). Miniature sculptures offer clues about Minoan funerary practices, banquets and dances; an ivory *pyxis* (jewellery box) shows a band of men hunting a bull. The Mycenaeans influenced a number of works in this room (note the ivory plaques, decorated with warriors' heads) and are generally made to answer for the weapons that suddenly make an appearance—the boar tusk and bronze helmets and 'gold-nailed swords' as described by Homer. Goldwork reached its height in this period, especially the elipitical rings and especially the Isopata ring, showing four ladies ecstatically dancing, and another in a similar style, believed to show tree-worship.

Items found in the *megara*, or luxurious country villas, of central Crete fill **Room VII**. The show-stoppers here are the gold jewels, especially the exquisite pendant of two bees depositing a drop of honey in a comb (found near Mália), and the three black steatite vessels from Ag. Triáda, decorated in beautifully executed low reliefs that offer insights into Minoan life.

The New Palace period contents of **Room VIII** come from Zákros, the only large palace yet discovered that escaped the notice of ancient plunderers. The floral and marine pottery is especially good, and the stone vases superb, most notably a little rock crystal amphora with a curved handle of crystal beads and a green stone rhyton showing a scene of a Minoan peak sanctuary, with wild goats springing all around and birds presumably appearing as an epiphany of the goddess. In **Room IX**, items from ordinary Minoan houses of the New Palace Period are displayed. The collection of lovely and mysterious seals is exceptional; no two are alike, although many repeat the same motifs, in general natural or religious scenes. The Minoans probably used the seals to secure private property and correspondence, and their engravers achieved an astounding technique; suspicions that they had to use lenses to execute such tiny work was confirmed when one made of rock crystal was found in Knossós.

After the Golden Age, the Post-Palace period artefacts in **Room X** (1450–1100 BC) show a gradual decline in inspiration, a coarsening, and ever heavier Mycenaean artistic influences. Pottery decoration becomes increasingly limited to strict bands of ordered patterns. Figures lose their typical Minoan grace and *joie de vivre*; the clay statuettes of the goddess are stiff and stylized, their flouncy skirts reduced to smooth bells, their breasts reduced to nubs, their arms invariably lifted, as if imploring the fickle heavens. One goddess has poppies sprouting from her hat; some historians believe many of the Minoans' myths and religious cults and artistic imagination owed a good deal to the extensive use of opium and alcohol. This may also explain their apparent lack of aggression and bossy overlords typical of other 'cradles of civilization'.

The Dorian invasion, generally seen as an ancient Dark Age, is evident in the Sub-Minoan and Early Geometric periods of **Room XI** (1100–900 BC); the quality of the work is poor all around, generally limited to simple, abstract linear decoration, whether made by tenacious pockets of unconquered Minoans or by the invaders; note especially votive offerings from the cave of Inatos, dedicated to Eileithyia, the protectress of childbirth, and a rhyton in the form of an ox-drawn chariot. The pieces in **Room XII** demonstrate an improvement in life and art on Crete in the Mature Geometric and Orientalizing periods (900–650 BC). Familiar Greek gods make an appearance: Zeus holding an eagle and three thunderbolts on a pot lid, Hermes with sheep and goats on a bronze votive plaque. Huge Geometric vases are decorated with polychromatic patterns; Orientalizing pottery, as the name suggests, show the strong eastern influences that dominated Greek civilization in the 8th–7th centuries. Griffons, sphinxes and lions are favourite motifs. One vase, in Case 163, shows a unique pair of lovers, naturally presumed to be Theseus and Ariadne. Bronze offerings found in the Idaean cave are especially interesting, one a boat showing a couple travelling. Some fine gold work has survived, as well as a curious terracotta model of a tree covered with doves.

At the foot of the stairs, **Room XIII** contains Minoan larnaxes, or terracotta sarcophagi. Minoans were laid out in a foetal position, so they are quite small; in the Old Palace days they were made of wood, and the changeover to clay suggests the Minoans were over-exploiting their forests. The belief that living Minoans used their larnaxes for bathtubs before they died seems completely ridiculous but common, perhaps because it supports Evans' designation of the Queen's bathroom at Knossós.

Yet another art the Minoans excelled at was fresco, displayed upstairs in **Rooms XIV–XVI**. Almost as fascinating as the paintings themselves is the amount of work (and, some would say, imagination) that went into their reconstruction by the Gillierons, the Swiss father-and-son team hired by Evans. In painting the Cretans followed Egyptian conventions in colour: women are white, men are red, monkeys are blue. The first room contains the larger frescoes from the palace of Knossós, such as the nearly completely intact *Cup-Bearer* from the *Procession* fresco, which originally lined the Corridor of the Procession and great Propylaeum and is believed to have had 350 figures altogether. Here too are *The Dolphins*, *The Prince of the Lilies*, *The Shields*, and *The Bull Leapers* (or Toreadors), where the decorative border is actu-ally a ritual Minoan calendar (*see* **Topics**, pp.62–3); also the charming *Partridges* found in the 'Caravanserai', near Knossós, and the *Lilies* from Amnisós. At the end of the room is an intri-cate wooden model of the palace of Knossós.

Occupying pride of place in the centre is the famous Ag. Triáda sarcophagus, the only one in stone ever found on Crete, covered with a layer of plaster painted so elaborately that chances are the sarcophagus originally held the remains of a VIP before it was stolen and re-used in an insignificant tomb in Ag. Triáda. The subject is a Minoan burial ceremony: on one side a bull is sacrificed, and its blood pouring from its neck runs into a vase. A woman makes an offering on an altar, next to a sacred tree with a bird in its branches, the epiphany of the goddess. A man plays a flute as three other women enter in a procession. On the other long side of the sarcoph-agus, two women on the left are bearing buckets, perhaps of bull's blood, which are emptied into a larger pot between pillars topped by birds and double axes. They are accompanied by a man in female dress, playing a lyre. On the right three men are bearing animals and a model boat, which they appear to be offering to an armless, legless man, presumed to be a dead man, partially wrapped up like a mummy. One the narrow sides of the sarcophagus, pairs of women ride in chariots pulled by griffons and a horse.

The 'miniature frescoes' in the other two rooms include the celebrated *Parisienne*, as she was dubbed by her founders in 1903, with her eye paint, lipstick and 'sacral knot' jauntily tied at the back; others, full of tiny figures, show a ceremonial dance and a tripartite shrine ritual. *The Saffron Gatherer*, one of the oldest frescoes, originally restored as a boy, has been reconstructed as a monkey picking crocuses after a similar subject was found on Santoríni. The adjacent Giamalakis collection in **Room XVII** contains some unique items from all the previous periods, from a finely worked Neolithic goddess, unusually seated in the lotus position, to a model of a round shrine from the Proto-Geometric era. Two figures on the roof peer down through a light-well at the Goddess (with uplifted arms), revealed through a detachable door.

Downstairs, products of ancient Crete's last great breath of artistic inspiration, the bold, severe and powerfully moulded 'Daedalic style' from the Archaic period (700–650 BC) are contained in **Rooms XVIII and XIX**. Amongst the terracotta votives from Górtyn, note the figure of Athena, with a face like an African mask and a fish hook helmet. There is a striking frieze of warriors from a temple at Rizenia (modern Priniás) and lavish votive bronze shields and cymbals, discovered in the Idaean Cave, one showing Zeus holding a lion over his head while the Curetes bang their shields. The bronze figures of Apollo, Artemis and Leto from the Temple of Apollo at Dreros are other key works in the 'Daedalic style'; the bronze goddesses, mother and daughter, here are reduced to anthropomorphic pillars, their once graceful dancing arms now glued to their sides, their once outlandish hats, jewellery and flounced topless skirts reduced to something approaching a nun's habit. They could be a salt and pepper set. Yet the real anticlimax is reserved for **Room XX**, the Classical Greek and Graeco-Roman periods (5th century BC–4th century AD), when Crete, one of the cradles of the 'Greek miracle', was reduced to an insignificant backwater.

## Historical and Byzantine Museums

On the northwest side of Herákleon, at 7 Kalokairinoú (near the Xenia Hotel and the ruined Venetian church of St Peter, currently being excavated), you'll find the **Historical Museum of Crete** (*open Mon–Fri, 9.30–4.30, Sat 9.30–2.30, closed Sun and holidays; adm*). Housed in the neoclassical mansion of its founder, Andréas Kalokairinós, this excellent collection picks up the thread where the archaeology museum leaves off, with artefacts from Early Christian times. In the basement you'll find some delightful 18th-century Turkish frescoes of imaginary towns are pretty odds and ends salvaged from Venetian churches, a 12th-century marble well carved with hunting scenes, Venetian and Turkish tombs, coats-of arms, the original carvings from the Loggia, and a delightful Venetian wall fountain consisting of tiny ships' prows. The ground floor offers a post-Byzantine Almanack of 1690, ships' figureheads, sultans' firmans, the 1912 'Freedom or Death' flag, and portraits of Cretan revolutionary leaders, a large coin collection, icons and religious items, and excellent 14th-century wall paintings in a chapel setting, from Kardoulianó Pediádos, showing the influences of the naturalistic Macedonian school. Next door, in a little room all to itself, hangs the *Imaginary View of Mount Sinai and the Monastery of St Catherine* by Doménikos Theotokópoulos (El Greco), his only known painting on Crete, dating around 1576. One of his few landscapes—in 16th-century Italy and Spain, where he spent the rest of his life, landscapes weren't very marketable—it is still very post-Byzantine and iconographic in style, although the mountains in particular foreshadow a bit of the magic of his famous *View of Toledo*. On the first floor are photographs of Cretan *kapetános*, each bristling with bigger moustaches and more weapons in his bandolier than the last, a handful of photographs from the Battle of Crete, and the reconstructed libraries of Emmanuél Tsouderós, one-time prime minister of Greece, and of modern Herákleon's most famous son, Níkos Kazantzákis, who spent his later life in Antibes.

West of Plateía Venizélou, and just south of Kalokerinoú, the elephantine 19th-century cathedral dedicated to Herákleon's patron saint **Ag. Minás** is fairly ghastly, especially next to its smaller predecessor: the sun-bleached **Ag. Ekaterína** (1555), in the same square was in its day an important school linked to the Monastery of St Catherine in the Sinai. One subject taught here was icon-painting (El Greco may have studied there before leaving for Venice) and today the church, appropriately, holds a noteworthy **Museum of Byzantine Icons** (*open Mon–Sat 9.30–1; also Tues, Thurs and Fri, 5–7; adm*). The pride of the museum are six icons by Mikális Damaskinós, the 16th-century contemporary of El Greco who also went to Venice but returned to Crete to adorn his motherland with Renaissance-inspired icons.

## The Walls

Michele Sammicheli, the greatest military architect of the 16th century, designed Candia's walls so well that it took the Turks 21 years, from 1648 to 1669, to breach them. From the beginning the Venetians tried to rally Europe to Candia's cause, but only got the occasional, ineffectual aid from the French. Nevertheless, stalemate characterized the first 18 years, so frustrating to the Sultan that he banned the mention of Candia in his presence. In 1667, both sides, keen to put an end to the siege, appointed their most brilliant generals, the Venetian Francesco Morosini (uncle of the Francesco Morosini who blew the top off the Parthenon) and the Turk Köprülü. The arrival of the latter outside the walls of Herákleon with 40,000 fresh troops finally pushed the Europeans and the Holy Roman Emperor to action, but they arrived only to quarrel, and their fresh troops and supplies were all too little, too late. Seeing that his men could only hold out a few more days, Morosini carefully negotiated the city's surrender on 5 September, and with 20 days of safe conduct sailed away with nearly all the Christian inhabitants (many ended up on the Ionian Islands) and the city's archives, a result bought with the lives of 30,000 Christians and 137,000 Turks.

Brilliantly restored, Sammicheli's massive walls surrounding the historic centre are nearly as vexing to get on top of today as they were for the besieging Turks—4000m in their total length, in places 14m thick, with 12 fort-like bastions. Tunnels have been pierced through the old gates, although the **Chaniá Gate** at the end of Kalokairinoú preserves much of its original appearance. From Plastirá Street, a side street is rumoured to lead up to the Martinengo Bastion; if you can't find it either, the only way to get to the top of the walls is by way of the Bastion of Sant'Antonio, and from there stroll along to Martinengo to see the simple **tomb of Níkos Kazantzákis**. Herákleon's great writer, who died in 1957, chose his own epitaph: 'I believe in nothing, I hope for nothing, I am free.'

## Knossós

*Every 10 minutes a city bus (no.2) departs from Herákleon's harbour or east bus station for Knossós with a stop in Plateía Venizélou. The site is open daily except for important holidays, 8–7 (8–5 in winter); adm exp. To avoid the crowds, or at least to be at the head of the stampede, arrive as the gate opens. At the time of writing, four paths of varying length are being laid out in the labyrinth, to lessen the wear on the soft gypsum and sandstone floors.*

The weird dream image has come down through the ages: Knossós (ΚΝΩΣΟΣ), the House of the Double Axe, the deadly Labyrinth of King Minos, and its unsolved secrets and mysteries evoke a deep and irresistible mythopoeic resonance that few places in Europe can equal.

Thanks in good part to Arthur Evans' imaginative if controversial reconstructions, brightly painted in primary colours and rising up two storeys against the hill girded plain, Knossós has become the second most visited place in Greece after the Acropolis, with nearly a million admissions a year. These days Evans' reconstructions are themselves historical monuments, so that not a little of the work you may see on the site is on the reconstructions of reconstructions.

The word labyrinth seems to derive from the ancient word *labrys*, or 'Double Axe'. The double axe, a symbol etched in the pillars and walls throughout Knossós, would kill both the victim and slayer; among other things, the Labyrinth was the descent into the underworld, ruled by the Snake Goddess Ariadne, from which only an exceptional hero (like Theseus) could emerge alive, 'reborn' (as in the myth, *see* pp.97–9).

## History

The first Neolithic houses on the hill next to the river Kairatos, a stream navigable until Classical times, date from the 7th millennium BC, or perhaps earlier; few Neolithic sites in Europe lay so deeply embedded in the earth. In the 3rd millennium, an important Early Minoan or Pre-Palace settlement was built over the Neolithic houses, and *c.* 1950 BC the first palace (or temple, as many students of the Minoans now believe) was erected on top. It collapsed in the earthquake of 1700. Construction of a new palace followed, even grander and more splendid than the first, and it is the remains of this that dominate the site today. For the next three centuries or so new buildings went up all over the outskirts of Knossós; vast cemeteries, stretching all the way to Herákleon's modern cemetery of Ag. Konstantínos, attest to a considerable population. In 1450 BC (give or take a century or two) Knossós was again destroyed by a cataclysmic fire, believed to have been caused by the eruption of Santoríni. Unlike the other Minoan palaces, Knossós was repaired once more, probably by Mycenaeans, and survived at least until 1380 BC. After a final destruction, the site of the labyrinth was never built on again; it was considered evil, cursed in some way. Evans noted at the beginnings of his excavations that the guardians he hired to watch the site heard ghosts moaning in the night.

In the Geometric era, a community near Knossós adopted its name. By the 3rd century BC this Knossós became one of the leading cities of Crete, although following a war with Lyttos it lost its supremacy to Górtyn. The Romans built a large city in the area that survived until the early Byzantine period, when the annals of the church refer to a bishop of Knossós. Afterwards Knossós slowly accumulated a thin layer of dirt that covered the walls, although they were not forgotten; unlike Troy and Mycenae, the site was always known. Cretans would go there to gather what they called *galopetres*—'milkstones'—Minoan sealstones, in fact, which nursing mothers prized as amulets to increase their milk.

Interest in the rediscovery and excavation of Knossós had to wait until Heinrich Schliemann electrified the world with his excavations of Troy and Mycenae; Schliemann himself made serious negotations for the purchase of the Knossós site, but the Turkish owner asked for a price Schliemann was unwilling to pay, especially as all the finds had by law to remain on Crete. In 1878 a merchant from Herákleon, appropriately named Mínos Kalokairinós, dug the first trenches into the palace of his namesake, at once striking the enormous *pithoi* in the palace store rooms and uncovering the first Linear B tablet, which he showed to Sir Arthur Evans in 1894. Evans, curator of the Ashmolean Museum in Oxford, was a keen student of early forms of writing, and was already particularly fascinated by the mysterious signs on Cretan seal stones, on which he recognized two scripts, one linear, one pictorial or heiroglyphic. He purchased the property and with the permission of High Commissioner Prince George began excavations in concert with the British School in 23 March 1900. Of the workmen hired, Evans insisted that half be Greek and half Turk as a symbol of cooperation for the newly independent Crete. Within three weeks the throne room had been excavated, along with fresco fragments and the first Linear A tablets. Rather than find more engraved seals to translate, the 48-year-old Evans had found a project to occupy a lifetime. When his father died, he used his considerable inheritance to reconstruct part of what he labelled Minos' palace. In recent years archaeologists have disputed the accuracy of these reconstructions, sniffing at them as if they were an archaeological Disneyland; they disagree perhaps even more on the purposes and names Evans assigned the different rooms of the palace, along with his entire interpretation of the Minoans as peaceful flower-loving sophisticates. Evans' queen's bathroom, for instance, is another man's basin where dead bodies were pickled in precious oils before mummification. At the end of the day, no single conjecture sufficiently covers all the physical evidence, all the myths; the true meaning and use of Knossós may only lie in an epiphany of the imagination. The Cretans of 4000 years ago saw a different world through different eyes.

## The Site

Despite all the controversy, Evans' reconstructions result from guesses as good as anyone else's and succeed in his goal of making Knossós come alive for the casual visitor, evoking the grandeur of a Middle Minoan palace *c.* 1700 BC that none of the unreconstructed sites can match; a visit here first will make Phaistós and Mália easier to understand. Detailed guides and plans are on sale at the excavations; the guided tours go through so frequently that it's easy to tag along or overhear the explanations as you follow the maze.

Unlike most of their ancient contemporaries, the Minoans built their palaces facing west, not east, and the modern entrance is still by the west court of the palace. Before going in, directly to the left, you'll find the oldest paved road in Europe, the **Royal Road**. At the head of it stands the **Theatre** (it looks more like a large stairway) where 500 people could sit, to view religious processions or dances, as pictured in the frescoes and perhaps Homer's 'dancing floor like that which Daedalus once fashioned in spacious Knossós for Ariadne of the lovely hair'. As you enter the west court, note the three holes, of mysterious use (sacrificial pits, silos?); a porch on the right leads to the **Corridor of the Procession**, named for the fresco now in the Herákleon museum, and the partially restored **Propylaeum**, or south entrance, with reproductions of the original frescoes on the wall.

A staircase from the Propylaeum leads to an upper floor, which Evans, inspired by Venetian palaces, called the '**Piano Nobile**'. Of all his reconstructions, this is considered the most fanciful, although the **Tripartite Shrine**, with its three columns, is a typical feature of Minoan palaces, and may have been used to worship the Goddess in her three aspects of mistress of heaven, earth and the underworld. A narrower staircase descends to **Central Court**. Originally this was closed in on all four sides by tall buildings, which may have provided, among other things, safe seats to view the bull leaping that took place in the Court. This was a sporting form of human sacrifice, with little chance of the bull leapers surviving to perform an encore, according to the Spanish matadors questioned by historians. The monumental sacral horns that decorate the cornices and altars are the most universal Minoan religious and decorative symbol. It probably had multiple levels of meaning; in one Minoan picture, there's a bull with a double axe between its horns.

From here, enter the West Wing of the palace, site of the surprisingly tiny **Throne Room**, where Evans uncovered a scallop-edged stone throne in the same place as it stood 3800 years ago. Unfortunately, wear and tear by so many visitors has made it necessary to rope off the throne so that you can no longer sit where Minos—or a Minoan priestess, or dead Minoan in state, propped and swaddled up as on the Ag. Triáda sarcophagus—supposedly sat (although if you're elected judge of the Court of International Justice in The Hague you may sit on its reproduction). On either side are gypsum benches and frescoes of griffons, the heraldic escorts of the goddess. The **Lustral Basin** in the Throne Room, like others throughout Knossós, may have held water used in rituals, or merely served to reflect light that descended in light wells into the rather poky rooms, or perhaps both. Evans found evidence here of what appeared to be a last-ditch effort to placate the gods as disaster swept through Knossós.

The stair south of the antechamber of the Throne Room ascends to an upper floor, used in part for storage, as in the **Room of the Tall Pithos** and the **Temple Repositories,** where the famous Snake Goddess statuette was found. Note the pillars that thicken near the top, unique to Minoan architecture but distinctly similar to the trunk of the 'horizontal' cypress native to the Gorge of Samariá. The Minoans may have hoped the form would make the palace more earthquake-resistant. Returning to the Central Court, note the high relief fresco copy of the **'Prince of the Lilies'** to the south, at the end of the Corridor of the Procession.

Evans, who grew up taking monarchies for granted, had no doubt that the more elaborate **East Wing** of the palace contained the 'Royal Apartments'. Here the unreconstructed **Grand Stairway** and **Central Light Well** are an architectural *tour de force*, but when you actually descend into the two lower floors (which were found intact) it is hard to imagine that any royal family would choose to have their living quarters buried so deep in the palace, with little in the way of light and air, in spite of all the Minoans' clever architectural devices; the near proximity of the 'Royal Workshops' would have made them awfully noisy as well. The rooms did have something that modern royals couldn't live without: plumbing. The excellent water and sewer system that supplied Knossós is visible under the floor in the **Queen's Megaron** and its bathroom, complete with a fill-up bucket and flush toilet—an amenity that Versailles could scarcely manage. The queen's bathtub, however, looks suspiciously like a Minoan sarcophagus. The King's Megaron, also known as **Hall of the Double Axes,** is decorated with a copy of the fresco of the large, cowhide figure-of-eight shields. North of the royal apartments are the impressive **Magazines of Giant Pithoi** and the long **Corridor of the Draught-board,** where the superb game-board in the Herákleon Museum was found and where you can see the clay pipes used to bring in water from the 5-mile-long Mount Juktas aqueduct. As you leave through the north, there's a relief copy of the bull fresco, and near this the so-called **Customs House,** supported by eight pillars. This stands at the end of the Amnisós harbour road, and may have been used for processing imports and exports.

Some highly intriguing Minoan buildings have been and continue to be excavated outside the palace, such as the unique **Royal Temple Tomb,** but they remain off limits without special authorization. One especially controversial find was Peter Warren's 1980 unearthing of the **House of the Sacrificed Children,** a typical Minoan house that was found to contain a large cache of children's bones bearing the marks of knives, as if they had been carved up for supper. The Minoans, just having been found guilty of human sacrifice in the Anemospilia shrine at Archánes (*see* p.147), now had cannibalism to answer for. Many historians now believe that the children had already died, and their bodies were in the process of being stripped of any last flesh before re-burial.

Bus no.1 from Plateía Eleftherías crawls through Herákleon's suburbs of Póros and Néa Alikárnassos (populated by refugees from Asia Minor) to the popular if not exceptionally attractive city beach of **Kraterós** (7km). In the next kilometre, overlooking the islet of Día (another sanctuary for Crete's wild goats) is **Amnisós** (ΑΜΝΙΣΟΣ), the first of the long string of resorts east of Herákleon, although the sand is on the grubby side, and charter flights swoop overhead with alarming frequency. But Amnisós has been a busy place since Neolithic times. A port of Knossós (along with Herákleon and Katsámbas) it was from here that tradition has Idomeneus and his 90 ships sailing for Troy. In the 1930s, while excavating Amnisós' Minoan 'Harbour Master's Office' Limenarcheion, Spyridon Marinátos discovered a layer of pumice, the physical evidence he needed to support his theory that Minoan civilization had been devastated in its prime by ash flung from Santoríni's volcano. The Minoan town was spread around the hill topped by the ruins of a Venetian village; on the east end you can see the fenced off villa of 1600 BC that yielded the lovely lily frescoes in the Herákleon museum. An Archaic sanctuary of Zeus Thenatas occupies the northwest side of hill. A kilometre up from Amnisós up the road to Elia is the atmospheric **Cave of Eileithyia**, goddess of fertility and childbirth, daughter of Zeus and Hera and mother of Eros. Few ancient divinities enjoyed Eileithyia's incredible staying power; her cave, mentioned by Homer, attracted women far and wide from the Neolithic era to the 5th century AD. Stalagmites, resembling a mother and her children (the latter are rather hard to make out) were the main focus of worship; pregnant women would rub their bellies against a third one, resembling a pregnant belly complete with a naval.

---

*Herákleon ☎ (081–)*                                     ***Where to Stay***

Do book well ahead in the summer. If you haven't and can't find a place to stay in Herákleon try the **Hotel Managers' Union**, Idomenous and Malikoúti, ☎ 223 967, or the Association of Room Renters, 1 Yamaláki, ☎ 224 260.

***expensive***

**Atlantis Hotel**, near the museum at Mirabélou and Ighías, ☎ 229 103, ✆ 226 265, is an imposing A class hotel with a pool, satellite TV, roof garden and nearly everything else you could want (including a garage). The **Galaxy**, just outside the walls to the southeast at Demokratías 67, ☎ 238 812, ✆ 211 211 (*A*) offers contemporary serenity and full air-conditioning; ask for a room overlooking the pool and sun terrace. **Atrion**, K. Paleológou 9, ☎ 229 225, ✆ 223 292, (*B*) is relatively new, moderate-sized and air-conditioned, with a garden, patio, and a two-storey underground garage. Then there are plush resort hotels on the beaches on either side of the city. To the east in Amnisós, the **Minoa Palace**, ☎ 227 802, ✆ 227 868 (*A*) is a big fancy beachside complex with a pool, floodlit tennis court, and a score of activities and sports for all ages. *Open April–Oct.* To the west in Amoudári, the **Agapi Beach**, ☎ 250 502, ✆ 25 731 (*A*) has similar resort facilities in a garden setting. If you have a car, **Arolithos Hotel**, Servilí Týlissou, P.O. Box 2032, Herákleon 71002, ☎ 821 050, ✆ 821 051 (*A*) is a quiet place built of stone and wood in the traditional Cretan manner.

***moderate***

**Pension Ilaria**, on Epimenídou, ☎ 227 103 (*B*) is conveniently located on a fairly quiet street near the port, and has a roof garden; **Hotel Lato**, on the same street,

✆ 228 103 (*C*) has modern rooms short on character, although all have balconies and some have sea views. **Hotel Daedalos**, Daedálou Street ✆ 22 43 91, (*C*) is convenient for the archaeological museum and other sights in the central city, yet located on the pedestrian-only street. Paintings by local artists are in the lobby, but otherwise it's plain and modern. **Atlas Pension**, Kandaoléontos 6, ✆ 288 989 (*C*) offers a touch of streamlined Art Deco on a pedestrian-only street, a few steps from the centre, although the rooms don't all live up to the promise of the exterior. *Open April–Oct.*

### inexpensive

**Hotel Rea**, Kalimeráki 1, ✆ 223 638, (*D*) is one of the most pleasant cheap choices, near the sea and quiet. The **youth hostel** at Víronos 5, ✆ 286 281 is well run and convenient, with usually a dorm bed to spare. **Yours Hostel**, Chandáka 24, ✆ 280 858, in the old youth hostel building, has all sorts of accommodation available at low prices. **Lena**, ✆ 223 280 (*E*) has clean rooms on a quiet street. **Hotel Hellas**, Kandanoléontos 11, ✆ 225 121 is pleasant, friendly and has a courtyard. **Idaeon Andron**, behind the Venetian Loggia, on Perdikári 1, ✆ 281 795, has pleasant small rooms and a tiny courtyard. **Camping Herákleon**, 5km west of town on Ammoudári beach, ✆ 25 09 86 is a large A class campsite with all modern facilities; take bus no.6 from Plateía Eleftherías.

---

*Herákleon ✆ (081–)*                                                    **Eating Out**

The youngish trendies in Herákleon have created a quiet, car-free haven for themselves in the narrow streets between Daedálou and Ag. Títou; buildings have been cleaned up and restored, and the city's most charming little restaurants, pizzerias, and bars appeared on cue to fill them up. Prices are a bit over the odds, but the food is better too in places like **Loukoulous**, on Koráli, an elegant Italian restaurant with a real pizza oven (*around 4000dr, less for pizza*). If you've brought a friend, **Giovanni** in the same street offers a variety of fixed-price menus for two fish, traditional Greek or vegetarian with wine (*between 5000–5500dr*); the **New Chinese Restaurant** is here as well (around 5000dr). Not far, the **Curry House** near Daedálou Street off Perdikári Street features several curry specialities daily at around 3000dr a meal.

The ten or so tavernas jammed along the narrow confines of Fotíou ('Dirty') Lane between Odós 1866 (the market street) and Evans Street are a favourite place to dine, all offering basic Greek cuisine and grilled meats at moderate prices (*2500–3500dr for a dinner*). The attractive restaurants around the Morosini fountain are a tourist rip off, where the waiters compete aggressively for the custom of passers-by; for a reasonable 3000dr you'll do better in the brasher, bigger environs of Plateía Eleftherías, with a wide range of fast and slow food tavernas, and tolerable pizzerias. If you've a hankering for fish, the long established **Ta Psaria** at the foot of 25 Avgoustou Street has the day's catch at reasonable prices (depending of course on what you order) and there's seating outside, overlooking the Venetian harbour.

---

### Entertainment and Nightlife

When the Herákleoniots want to spend a night on the town, they usually leave it; the clubs and discos west of the city are especially popular with young boppers. If you'd rather stay in town, keep a look out for posters. Big name events are often held in the football stadium; in the summer concerts and the occasional theatrical performance happen in the **Rocco al Mare** citadel on the Venetian Harbour, itself a favourite place for an evening *vólta*, or stroll. There's often live *rembétika* music at the **Taverna I Palia Argli** at the end of Theríssou, ✆ 252 600, or quiet backgammon and drinks at the **Ideion Andron**, one of several late night bars in the aforementioned trendy zone. The discotheque behind Ag. Titos seems to change its name every year, but remains perenially popular among the Cretans who love to dance.

# Nomós Herákleon

The *nomós* of Herákleon has plenty to see: not only most of Crete's Minoan sites, but also its ancient Roman capital Górtyn and once notorious Mátala Beach, on the south coast. Most of the villages are on one of the bus routes from the city (*see* 'Getting There and Around' to find the right station) although check on return times before setting out.

---

*Festivals*

Krousónas: Ag. Charálambos' Day, **10 February**. Ag. Mýronas: **8 August**.

## South of Knossós: Archánes and Vathýpetro

'All Cretans are liars,' said the Cretan philosopher Epimenides, and one of the ancient proofs of his paradox was the fact that Zeus the immortal was born on Crete, and buried there as well, the profile of his face visible in the lines of the Mount Júktas ridge, and visible from the ancient village of **Archánes** (ΑΡΧΑΝΕΣ). Since antiquity, this has been Crete's major producer of wine and table grapes (*rozáki*); the first left after the village leads through the vineyards to the Byzantine church of the **Asómatos** (the Bodiless one: an Orthodox attribute for St Michael) with good frescoes of 1315, stylistically similar to those in Ag. Triáda and showing the founder of the church and his wife as well as religious scenes. But what makes Archánes especially interesting are the rich Minoan remains scattered across its periphery. The most important sites—the large necropolis at Phourní, the temple at Anemopiliá, and the villa at Vathýpetro—are closed because of ongoing excavations, although the Herákleon tourist office can refer you to the caretaker who can let you in. Excavated since 1966, the **necropolis of Phourní** (dramatically set atop a ridge, 1.5km southwest of Archánes) has proved to be the most important prehistoric cemetery in the Aegean, in use for 1250 years (2500–1250 BC) and yielding three tholos tombs, an unplundered royal lady's tomb (Tholos A), filled with 140 pieces of gold and ivory jewellery and the remains of a sacrificed horse and bull, and a Mycenaean grave circle with six shaft tombs—the only one discovered outside of Mycenae.

Above Archánes's town dump, on a windswept promontory of **Anemopiliá** (5km southwest of Archánes) a Minoan shrine was discovered by Giánnis and Efi Sakellarákis in 1979. It contained four skeletons, of people buried in the sanctuary as the great earthquake struck *c.* 1700 BC. One of the skeletons, of a 17-year-old boy, was found bound on a sacrificial block, next to a dagger; the coroner's account from the skeleton shows that the blood had been drained from his upper body, and that he had probably had his throat cut. The other three skeletons are surmised to be the priest, priestess, and a servant of indeterminate sex, caught in the act of carrying a rhyton full of the boy's blood to the main altar, in an attempt to appease the furious god, probably Poseidon, the Earth-shaker.

Two kilometres south of Archánes, the Minoan complex of **Vathýpetro** is spectactularly set high on a spur of Mount Júktas. In plan it resembles a two-storey baby Knossós: it has a small west court and larger central court, a tripartite shrine, and three-columned portico, with a small courtyard to the east of the portico, closed off by a fancy structure found nowhere else, recessed in the centre and supported by symmetrical square plinths. First built *c.* 1580 BC, Vathýpetro was shattered, probably by an earthquake, *c.* 1550. It seems to have been rebuilt as a rural craft centre; clay loom weights and potters' wheels were found, along with the oldest wine press in Greece. The adjacent cool cellar rooms suggest that the Minoans were already sophisticated winemakers 3500 years ago.

From Vathýpetro a dirt road climbs over Mount Júktas and turns south for **Kanlí Kastélli**, or the Bloody Fortress, believed to have been built by the future emperor Niképhoros Phókas when he liberated Crete from the Saracens in 961. It later sheltered a harried Duke of Crete when the Duke of Náxos, Marco Sanudo, captured towns in Crete in defiance of Venice. Alternatively, you could circle back to Herákleon through Choudétsi, and **Myrtiá**, where the **Kazantzákis Museum** (*open 9–1, and Wed, Sat and Sun 4–8, closed Thurs, but ☎ (081) 741 689 to check*) is set in the birthplace of the father of Crete's greatest novelist, with dioramas of his theatrical pieces and an audio-visual programme in English about Kazantzákis and his work.

## Southwest of Herákleon

The road southwest of Herákleon to Górtyn, Phaistós and Mátala passes through dense vine-yards that produce some of Crete's finest wine (especially around Dáfnes). If you have your own set of wheels two seldom-visited ancient sites await along the alternative road south, by way of **Ag. Mýronas**, a large village with a 13th-century Venetian church; the scanty ruins of ancient **Rafkos** are just north. South, near **Káto Asítes**, you can spend the night on the slopes of Mount Ida, in the Hellenic Alpine Club's Prinos shelter. Further south, in the afternoon shadow of Mount Ida, **Priniás** has a pair of cave tombs and lies 3.5km east of **Ryzenía** (fl. 1600 BC–200 BC). High on a hill known as the Patella tou Priniá, Ryzanía controlled the main road between Knossós and Górtyn. On the acropolis are two ruined Archaic temples and a Hellenistic fort; a Geometric era cemetery has recently been found below.

Both routes converge upon straggling **Ag. Varvára**, approximately at the geographical centre of the big island; a chapel dedicated to Profítis Ilías sits atop a large rock known as the '*omphalos*', or navel of Crete. A pretty if windy road west of Ag. Varvára skirts the olive groves and rich orchards on the south flanks of Psilorítis for **Zarós** (17km), near two fine churches: **Moní Vrondisíou**, which, although burned by the Turks for its revolutionary activities, conserves some 14th-century frescoes and a charming 15th-century Venetian fountain; and, even better, off a rough track 5km further west is the **Moní Valsamonérou** (just below the road, or by path from **Vorízia**, where you can pick up the key from the guardian). Originally one of the most important monasteries in the area, it is now reduced to one little but enchanting assymetrical church with two naves, and a third added like an afterthought around the corner, painted in part by 14th-century master Konstantínos Ríkos (the portrait of Christ and Divine Liturgy). The road continues to **Kamáres** (with tavernas and rooms), the base for the 3–4 hour walk up to the **Kamáres cave** on the flank of Mount Ida which gave its name to the fine, colourful Minoan pottery first discovered here. Experienced walkers only should attempt the difficult 6-hour path up to the summit of Psilorítis from the cave.

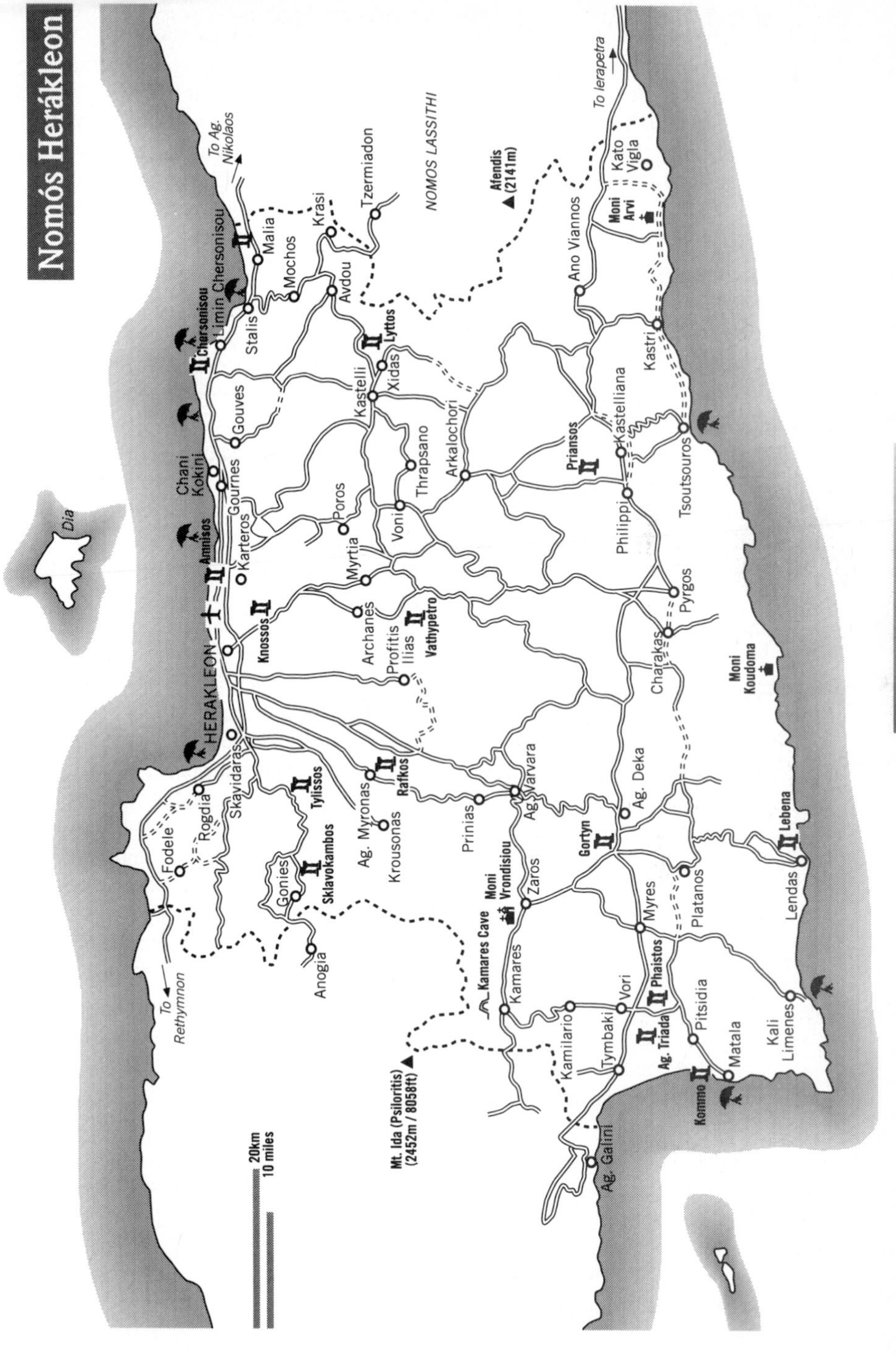

To Ag. Nikolaos

Tzermiadon

*NOMOS LASSITHI*

Afendis ▲ (2141m)

To Ierapetra

Kato Vigla

Moni Arvi

Ano Viannos

Kastri

Malia
Krasi
Mochos
Avdou
Stalis
Limin Chersonisou
Chersonisou
Gouves
Kastelli
Xidas  Lyttos
Thrapsano
Arkalochori
Kastelliana
Priansos
Philippi
Tsoutsouros

Chani Kokini
Karteros
Gournes
Poros
Myrtia
Voni
Pyrgos

Dia

Amnisos
HERAKLEON
Knossos
Archanes
Profitis Ilias
Vathypetro
Charakas
Moni Koudoma

Skavidaras
Tylissos
Rafkos
Ag. Myronas
Krousonas
Prinias
Ag. Varvara
Ag. Deka
Gortyn
Lebena
Lendas

Rogdia
Fodele
Gonies
Sklavokambos
Angia

Kamares Cave
Moni Vrondisiou
Zaros
Myres
Platanos
Kamares
Kamilario
Vori
Phaistos
Pitsidia
Kali Limenes
Matala
Ag. Triada
Kommo
Tymbaki
Ag. Galini

To Rethymnon

Mt. Ida (Psiloritis)
(2452m / 8058ft) ▲

20km
10 miles

Tucked under the southern foothills of Mount Ida, the Mesará is the breadbasket of Crete and has been one of its most densely populated areas since time began. After the Dorian invasion **Górtyn** (or Gortys, ΓΟΡΤΥΣ), the big town on the plain, supplanted Knossós as one of the ruling cities of Crete, with ports at Mátala and Lebena. In 189 BC Hannibal passed through Górtyn; the Romans made it the capital not only of their provinces of Crete, but of Cyrenaica (Libya). Although the *Iliad* describes Górtyn, 'the second city of Crete', as walled, the walls you see today are Hellenistic, begun by Ptolemy Philopator. In 828 the Saracens destroyed the city.

In its prime, Górtyn had a population of 300,000 and its ruins are scattered over a mile or so (*open daily 8–7, adm*); a small museum on the site will help orientate you. Near the entrance stands the apse of the great 6th-century **Basilica of Ag. Títos**, bearing traces of early frescoes; Titus was one of St Paul's favourite disciples, sent to convert Górtyn and become its first bishop. Beyond, built into the walls of the elegant **Roman Odeon** (reconstructed by Trajan in 100 AD), is Górtyn's prize, the **Law Code of Gortyn**.

The first block of engraved limestone, accidentally discovered in a mill stream in 1857, was purchased by the Louvre. It attracted a good deal of attention. At the time no one had ever seen a Greek inscription so ancient and unfathomable, and it wasn't until 1878 that this first bit, dealing with adoption, was translated, using the writing on ancient coins as a study guide. No one suspected that there was any more to it until one summer day in 1884 when Halbherr, the Italian who would later excavate Phaistós, noticed a submerged building—the Odeon—while cooling his feet in the same millstream, which was shallower than usual because of a drought. The rest of the inscription, covering over 600 lines, divided on 12 blocks, was found soon after in a farmer's field; only the tops of blocks X and XII and a piece of block IX are missing. The code, written in *boustrophedon*, 'as the ox ploughs' from left to right, then right to left, is in the Dorian dialect of *c.* 500 BC. It is the longest such inscription to survive from antiquity, and because of it the civil laws of Crete on the verge of the Classical era are better known in their precise specific detail than Roman law. Significantly, the code was made for public display; also significantly, in spite of the built-in inequalities of the ancient Greek class system, the Górtyn Code allows women property rights they've lacked in more recent laws (the Code Napoléon, for one); slaves had recourse against cruel masters; and there was a presumption of innocence until proven guilty long before it became the core of Anglo-American law.

Górtyn's theatre is under its **acropolis**, topped with an 8th-century BC temple and long sacrificial altar. Other well preserved buildings include the 2nd-century AD residence of the Roman governor, or **Praetorium**, the oft-rebuilt Archaic **Temple of Pythian Apollo**, and a small **Temple of Isis and Serapis**, the Egyptian gods who became popular in the late Empire. To the south is the massive brick **Roman Great Gate**, and ruins of an amphitheatre and stadium.

More bits and bobs of Górtyn lie scattered about the surrounding olive groves, and in its much more modest but pleasant successor, **Ag. Déka**, named for ten saints martyred here in the 3rd century, and whose tombs in the crypt of the new church are the subject of much Cretan devotion. There are a handful of tavernas and rooms to rent. **Mýres** (ΜΟΙΡΕΣ), 9km to the west, is now the Mesará's chief town and the centre of the local bus network, where you may have to change for Phaistós and Mátala.

*The Palace of Phaistós is open Mon–Fri 8–7; Sat, Sun and holidays 8.30–3; adm exp. Try to arrive early or late to avoid the crowds. A tourist pavilion on the site has a café and food.*

Superbly situated halfway up a high hill overlooking the lush Mesará plain and Idaean mountains, **Phaistós** (ΦΑΙΣΤΟΣ) was one of the oldest cities in Crete, in Minoan times second only to Knossós in importance. According to myth, Phaistós was the fief of Rhadamanthys, and it was the birthplace of Epimenides, one of the Seven Sages of ancient Greece. Its first palace was constructed in the Old Palace period, around 2000 BC, and destroyed in an earthquake in 1700 BC; the second palace was built on top of the first and destroyed in 1400 BC. Below the palace, 50,000 people lived and worked; ruins of Minoan villages are scattered across the Mesará. During Archaic, Classical and Hellenistic times Phaistós remained an independent little city state, warring with Górtyn, until finally crushed by its rival in the 3rd century BC. Excavations by the Italians, led by Frederico Halbherr, began in 1900.

Archaeological purists dismayed by Evans' reconstructions at Knossós will breathe a sigh of relief at Phaistós, where only your imagination will reconstruct the original three-storey palace from the low, complicated walls and foundations. Visits begin in the northwest, in the paved **Upper Court** with its raised **Processional Way**. This carries down the steps into the **West Court**, passing the **theatre** (eight straight tiers of seats) and branching off to two circular stone-lined cisterns or granaries, which may originally have been domed. When the Palace was rebuilt in 1700, it was set 20ft further back from the West Court. The **Grand Stairway** was carved with special care; note how the steps are slightly convex, to let rainwater run off quickly.

At the top of the Grand Stairway, the **Propylon** or main entrance to the West Wing stands just before a light-well with three columns. Another stair descends to the **Antechamber of the Storerooms**, where Halbherr found a huge cache of sealstones. A corridor from here passes between the impressive storage rooms; one room, covered with a roof, still contains its giant *pithoi*, and has a built-in vessel in the floor to collect wine or oil. West of the antechamber is the **Central Court**, dating from the first palace—the only part the architects re-used after the earthquake, when the lines of the palace were otherwise completely re-orientated. Before crossing it, turn right, where an important corridor separated the storage areas from the main **shrine**, lined with stone benches.

The **East Wing** of Phaistós has partially collapsed, but its small chambers, a bathroom, and gypsum-paved lustral basin with stairs has suggested a prince's apartment to some. A horseshoe-shaped **forge**, used for smelting metals, is at the end of the corridor north of the apartments. North of the Central Court, another corridor leads to yet more 'royal apartments' paved with alabaster, the **Queen's Megaron**, furnished with alabaster benches and the **King's Megaron**, decorated with frescoes. The Phaistós Disc (*see* p.137) was found to the east of here, in a series of rooms from the Old Palace.

## Ag. Triáda

Only 3km east of Phaistós, a paved road runs to the smaller Minoan palace of Ag. Triáda (ΑΓ. ΤΡΙΑΔΑ) (*open daily 8.30–3; adm*), named after a small Venetian church near the site. No one knows what its original name might have been, or why such a lavish little estate was built so close to Phaistós. Guesses are that it may have been a royal summer villa or perhaps a wealthy Minoan simply fell in love with the splendid setting. Ag. Triáda was inhabited ever since Neolithic times; tholos tombs and dwellings were discovered under the 'palace', built around 1600 BC. This burned in the great island-wide destruction of 1450 BC; the Minoans reoccupied it, and the Mycenaeans built a megaron over the top. The site, excavated by the Italians off and on since 1902, yielded some of the Minoans' finest art, especially the famous sarcophagus, or larnax of Ag. Triáda, now in Herákleon's museum.

## Mátala and the Coast

This corner offers more than the fossils of long-lost civilizations. Just to the north of Phaistós, the old village of **Vóri** on the road to Ag. Galíni (*see* p.130) hopes to waylay you with its **Museum of Ethnology** (*open 10–6; adm*), illustrating traditional country life in Crete with exhibitions of pottery, musical instruments, furniture, tools and costumes.

This is a rocky and wild coast, that only here and there permits tortuous roads to descend to the sea. One south of Phaistós leads to **Mátala** (ΜΑΤΑΛΑ), the lovely and very popular beach enclosed by sandstone cliffs. The cliffs are riddled with tombs from the 1st and 2nd centuries AD, which over the years Cretans have enlarged into cosy little rooms. In the early 1960s, young Americans bumming around Europe on one dollar a day found that the caves made a perfect (and free) place to crash in the winter, and before long these pioneers were joined by a sizeable international hippy colony. In the killjoy 1990s, the impecunious hippies have been banished (although you can poke around the caves during the day) for the hard currency of package tourism, but something of their spirit lingers on in Mátala's laid-back atmosphere. If the town beach is a massive body jam, a path over the rocks will take you in about 20 minutes to Mátala's second beach, Kókino Ámmos, the 'red sand'; excursion boats sail south to other small beaches at Ag. Farago and Vathí. It's also important to avoid walking on the beach on summer nights, when sea turtles make their nests (see the turtle information booth near the newsagents'). On the road between Mátala and Pitsídia a track leads to **Kommó**, where Canadian archaeologists in the last few years have uncovered substantial remains of Minoan Phaistós' port and an important sanctuary with four altars from the Classical period—all currently off limits to visitors.

To continue east to Górtyn's other ports, you have to delve inland by way of Mýres. There are deserted beaches set amid the cliffs at **Kalí Liménes**, the 'fair havens' where St Paul is thought to have landed while being taken to Rome, and there are (albeit scant) Roman ruins and Minoan tholos tombs as proof of its antique authenticity just east at Lasaia. Yet another of Górtyn's harbours, **Levín** (or Lebena) was near the rather ramshackle fishing village of **Léndas** (take the slow rough road east of Kalí Liménes, or the new road south of Górtyn and Miamoú, which even sees a few buses daily from Herákleon). The natural hot springs here (now pumped elsewhere) led to the construction in the 4th-century BC of an Asklepeion, a sanctuary of the god of healing, east of the village. Nearly all the wallowing in Léndas these days happens 3km west at **Yerókambos**, a magnificent sandy beach with a pair of bars and tavernas.

*Mátala ℂ (0892–)*  **Where to Stay and Eating Out**

Although Mátala closes shop at the end of October (to the extent that no one would care if you discreetly moved into a cave), by Easter it's nearly impossible to find a room in or around Mátala, as many Greeks flock down for their first official swim of the year. The **Valley Village,**

☎ 42 776 (*B; exp*), on the edge of the village (and out of earshot of most the bars) has a swimming pool, Greek dancing shows and barbecue nights. *Open April–Oct.* The **Zafira Hotel**, ☎ 42 112 (*D; mod*), is the first thing you see, handy for town and beach, and reasonably priced, although completely booked by operators in season. *Open all year.* The **Coral** pension, just outside Mátala, ☎ 42 375 (*E; inexp*), has an area for children to play. **Pension Sofia**, ☎ 42 134 (*E; inexp*) and **Pension Nikos**, ☎ 42 375 (*inexp*) with a little garden, are among the pleasant choices on a whole lane of rooms to rent. The police are tough cookies if you disobey the notices about no sleeping in the caves or on the beach, but **Matala Camping** just behind the beach is a good cool place to stay with low prices. There are also cheap beds in the neighbouring villages of Kalamáki and Pitsidiá.

In Mátala people tend to drink more than eat; **Giorgio's Bar**, at the far end of the little bay, offers cocktails to go with Mátala's famous sunsets. **Syrtaki** has the centre spot in the row of seaside tavernas and serves all the Greek favourites (with barrelled wine) at reasonable prices. Right on the beach, **Zeus Beach Taverna** offers moussaka, stuffed tomatoes and other ready food made by mama, and you can feed your extra bread to the white ducks (*around 2500dr*).

## East of Górtyn

The region along the main road east of Górtyn towards Ierápetra has no major attractions, no picture postcard beaches, no Minoan palaces, and next to no tourists. Inhabited since early Minoan times, **Áno Viánnos**, an important mountain village built in the southwest flanks of Mount Díkti, set up a colony on the Rhône, along the chief route to the tin mines of the British Isles, which still bears its Cretan name: Vienne. In more recent times the village was a citadel of resistance against the Turks (who in reprisals flattened it twice, in 1822 and 1866) and the Germans, who executed 820 people in the area. On the ancient acropolis of Áno Viánnos are the ruins of a Venetian castle and Turkish tower; in the Pláka area are little white Ag. Pelagía (1360) and 14th-century Ag. Geórgios, both with frescoes. Don't miss the incredible plane tree by one of the *kafeneíons*, believed to be the oldest and largest in Greece after the grand-daddy of them all on Kos. On the coast, there is a castle near **Kastrí**, and an excellently preserved Venetian fort called **Vigla of Keratókambos**, watching over the beach where the Saracens first invaded Crete in 823. A rough road east along the coast (alternatively, continue east from Áno Viánnos and turn right at Amíras) is **Arvi**, with a pretty beach at the head of valley of banana plantations.

## West of Herákleon to Mália

West of Herákleon and Amnisós (*see* p.145), Europa, once raped on the island by Cretan Zeus in the form of a bull, gets her revenge on Crete. Here greedy developers—the 'long-trousered men' as the mountaineers call them—raped the lovely coastline, building most flagrantly and myopically. Even if a cup of REAL ENGLIHS (*sic*) TEA isn't yours, you may find a reason or two to put on the brakes in this holiday la-la land, beginning at Vathianó Kambó to see **Nírou Cháni** (adjacent to the hotel Demetra), a well-preserved Minoan villa known as the House of the High Priest, where a trove of 40 tripods and enormous double axes was found. Square-shaped, it has two paved courts and stone benches, perhaps used in ceremonies. In **Goúves** signs point the way to the enormous **cave of Skotinó**, set in a hollow on a plateau. It has several chambers, the first a stunning 50m-high ballroom lit by sun pouring through the mouth of the cave, with a stalagmite mass in the centre. A huge amount of Minoan cult activity took place in the smaller, dimmer, low-ceilinged chambers at the back, around curious rock formations (one looks like the bearded head of Zeus) and natural rock altars.

Further east, past the turn-off at Lagada for the Plain of Lassíthi (*see* below), **Chersónisos** (ΧΕΡΣΟΝΗΣΟΣ) or more properly Limén Chersonísou, is a synthetic tourist ghetto from end to end, complete with a synthetic Cretan village on one end (near the water slides) for a safe, pre-chewed dose of local culture when the charms of the Hard Rock Café and a score of clones begin to pale. What can you say about a town that has its own Finnish doctor? In more innocent times, Chersónisos was the port of ancient Lyttos and had a famous temple to Britomartis Artemis. Little remains of this: a reconstructed Roman fountain by the beach, bits of harbour installations, and a Roman aqueduct (inland at Xerokámares, along the road to Lassíthi); on the west side of town, overlooking the harbour, are the ruins of a 5th-century basilica with three aisles, believed to be the seat of one of Crete's first bishoprics; a second basilica, from the next century, can be seen on the east end of town near the church of Ag. Nikólaos.

## Inland from Chersónisos

Some interesting real Cretan villages high in the western foothills of Mount Díkti may be reached by a good road south of Chersónisos. **Kastélli** (29km) is the largest village of the region, topped by a ruined Venetian castle. A short detour just to the west in **Sklaverochóri** has its reward in the 15th-century church **Eisódia tis Theotókou** (Presentation of the Virgin) decorated with excellent frescoes. Ancient **Lyttos** (modern Xidás), 4km east of Kastélli, was after the Doric invasion a fierce rival of Knossós. It remained sufficiently powerful and wealthy to mint its own coins until 220 BC, when Knossós, allied with Górtyn, captured and demolished it; in spite of aid sent from Sparta, Lyttos never really recovered. As the Minoans hog the funds and fascination on Crete, Lyttos has never been excavated, but you can see Hellenistic walls and remains of other buildings, including an early Christian basilica. **Arkalochóri**, 15km further south in the middle of the island, is the scene every Saturday of large produce and animal fair. In 1932 Marinátos and Pláton excavated the village's sacred cave and brought forth some exceptionally meaty Minoan ritual weapons: gold axes, the longest prehisitoric Greek bronze sword ever found, bronze axes, one engraved in Linear A, the other with symbols similar to those on the Phaistós Disc—which put paid to notions that the disc was a forgery.

## Mália

East of Chersónisos, in the centre of a wide sand-edged bay, modern Mália (ΜΑΛΙΑ) is another busy tentacle of the same beach sprawl. Stay put on the bus for another 3km for the **Minoan Palace of Mália** (*open 8.30–3, closed Mon; adm*), where Minos' brother Sarpedon held sway. Its history follows the same palace pattern: inhabited from the Neolithic era, the first palace was built on the site in 1900 BC. When it was devastated by the earthquake 200 years later, another palace was built over the first, then ruined in the mysterious catastrophe traditionally dated at 1450 BC and never rebuilt. Unlike Knossós and Phaistós, Mália was built from local stone, and apparently had no frescoes.

The entrance to the palace is by way of the **West Court**, crossed by the usual raised Processional Walkway. Eight large round 'silos', originally covered with vaulted domes, are on the south end of this, and are believed to have stored grain. The design of the **Central Court** is similar to Phaistós, with porticoed galleries on the north and east ends. In the middle the supports of an altar were discovered, lending weight to the argument that the palaces were really temples. The Grand Stairway led up into the important **West Wing**, where a number of rooms obviously had some kind of ritual role; in the **Pillar Crypt**, a variety of potent symbols (double axes, stars and tridents) are carved in the pillars. Another little room further north is set at an oblique angle to the others, and might have been used for moon study or worship. A suite of 'Royal Apartments,' with a lustral basin are in the northwest corner. To the east of the Central Court, narrow storerooms are full of gargantuan *pithoi.*

If Mália seems somewhat poor next to Knossós and Phaistós, the large Minoan estates found in the outskirts have been especially sumptuous, especially the one to the northeast of the palace. In the cemetery by the sea, the **Chrysolakkos tomb** is believed by many to have been the last resting place of Mália's royal family; although looted over the centuries (significantly, its name means 'Gold pit'), the French found the magnificent bee pendant inside.

---

℗ *(0897–)*                                     **Where to Stay and Eating Out**

### Chersónisos

Don't expect to find cheap rooms here, or anything in a hotel without booking in advance. **Creta Maris Hotel and Bungalow complex**, ℗ 22 115 (*lux*) is the most luxurious. There are two campsites.

### Mália

**Ikaros Village**, ℗ 31 267 (*A; exp*) is a large hotel complex, designed as a traditional Cretan village (most of the big hotels lack any design whatsoever); pool, tennis, and sea sports are among the offerings. *Open April–Oct.* **Malia Park**, ℗ 31 460, (*A; exp*) has air-conditioned bungalows, watersports and a mountain bike centre. **Alexander Beach**, ℗ 32 124, ✆ 31 038 (*B; exp*) is a recently built complex a stone's throw from the beach, and a heated pool if the water's a mite chilly, a well as tennis and other sports. In Mália proper, there are a large number of small, cheaper hotels: **Elen**, ℗ 31 545, a kilometre from the beach, is typical (*C; mod*) and favoured by British tour operators) while **Ermioni**, ℗ 31 093 (*E; inexp*) is one of the cheapest hotels in town. The **youth hostel** just east of town, ℗ 31 555, is new, very nice but fills up fast. The best place to eat in Mália is in the old village, south of the main road, where tavernas serve barrelled wine and good food at fair prices.

## Nomós Lassíthi

East of Herákleon, Lassíthi (ΛΑΣΙΘΙ; the name comes from a corruption of the Venetian La Sitía) is the most varied county in Crete: its famous mountain plain covered with windmills is too cold for olives, but produces apples and wheat, while down at the eastern end there is Vái, a luxuriant palm-lined tropical beach. Lassíthians claim to be the best lovers on the island, although this is not by any means unanimously conceded; other Cretans mention only Lassíthi's superlative potatoes and pigs. The hot southeast coast is endowed with beaches, especially on either side of Ierápetra. Gourniá and Zákros are the chief Minoan sites, Sitía one of Crete's most pleasant small cities, and a church near Ag. Nikólaos, Panagía Kéra, has the island's best frescoes.

Ag. Geórgios: **23 April**. Psychró: 3 day long *panegýri* **29–31 August**.

## The Plateau of Lassíthi and the Birthplace of Zeus

Buses from Mália, Herákleon and Ag. Nikólaos wind their way up to the spectacular high Plateau of Lassíthi; a trail of tour buses make the ascent too, and you may want to spend a night or two to get a feel for the place. For it is unique: a green carpet hemmed in on all sides by the Lassíthi Mountains, irrigated by white-sailed windmills designed by Venetian engineers in 1464, to re-establish the orchards that had been destroyed to punish rebellious locals.

The road up from the east is the easier approach, and passes a series of frescoed Byzantine churches: the 14th-century Panagía at **Potamiés**; and 14th-century Ag. Antónios at **Avdoú**, a pretty village dotted with several small Byzantine churches. **Krási**, further up, boasts one of the largest plane trees on Crete, some 80ft in circumference. Near the hilltop village of **Kerá** the **Monastery Kardiótissa** owes its unusual form to four different building stages, beginning in the 12th century. It has more 14th-century frescoes, but its pride and joy is the miraculous icon, known as the 'Virgin Chained'; the story goes that it was twice carried off to Constantinople but made its way back to the monastery on its own, the second time in spite of being chained to a column; the uprooted column may still be seen in the courtyard.

**Tzermiádon** (pop. 1500) is the largest of the 18 villages encircling the plateau. Its Trápeza Cave was inhabited since 5000 BC (a path leads up to the entrance, although it's no longer open to the public). If you've got your walking shoes on, a path from Tzermiádon leads up in an hour to the ancient fortified city of **Karphí** ('the nail'), excavated by John Pendlebury from 1937 to 1939. Originally the loftiest of all Minoan peak sanctuaries at 1158m, Karphí was inhabited by Minoan refugees (the Eteo-Cretans) during the Doric invasion in 1100 BC, but its difficult situation caused it soon to be abandoned. A 200-year-old farmhouse in **Ag. Geórgios** is the site of a **Folk Museum**, complete with everything a Cretan mountain family needed to get by, including a wine-press that doubled as a bed.

**Psychró** (ΨΥΧΡΟ), on the west end of the plain, is the base for visiting the plateau's chief attraction, the **Diktean cave**, the birthplace of Zeus (*open 8–5, adm*). From the car park it's a one-kilometre ascent up a rocky, stepped path; sure-footed donkeys are available at the site, along with local guides who have lanterns in case you haven't brought a torch of your own. Rubber-soled shoes are equally important; the descent into the gaping maw of the deep and often-slippery cave is difficult (tour group leaders naughtily fail to warn their elderly clients, creating massive single-file jam-ups at the entrance). The cave is a haunting, other-worldly place worthy of myth. It was only rediscovered in the 1880s and found to contain cult items from Middle Minoan up to Archaic times; its role as the birthplace and hiding place of Zeus predates the Idaean cave's claims and is confirmed by the *Hymn of the Kouretes*, found engaved in a stone in Palaiókastro. Down in its shadowy bowels the guides point out formations that vaguely resemble the baby god, his cradle, his mantle, the chamber of his birth and the place where his nannygoat Amaltheia nursed him; Rhea, his mother, spurted her own breast milk into the heavens, creating the Milky Way. Other stories claim that Europa conceived Minos in the cave, and that when he became king he returned there every nine years for paternal advice from Zeus.

# Nomós Lassíthi

## Tzermiádon

**Kourites**, © 22 194 (*B; mod*) is the smartest place to stay on the plateau, its 13 comfortable rooms. *Open all year.* **Lassithi**, © 22 194 (*E; inexp*) is just as small and has a restaurant open all year. **Kronias** does good food as well; try the plateau's famous potatoes if they're in season. Two kilometres south of Tzermiádon, the **Kristallénia Monastery**, built in 1541, has an inexpensive hostel for men.

## Psychró

In Psychró, where many people stay, there are quite a few rooms to supplement the **Zeus**, © 31 284 (*D; inexp*) and the **Dikteon Andron**, © 31 504 (*E; inexp*). *Both open all year.* The tourist restaurant above the souvenir shop in the Diktean cave car park has good pizzas and ready food (*around 2000dr*). In Ag. Geórgios, try the **Rhea Hotel**, © 31 209 (*E, inexp*).

## Between Mália and Ag. Nikólaos

Leaving the main highway at Mália to follow the coast, you'll find two more sandy beaches with two more resorts, **Sísi** and **Paralía Milátos**, the beach of Milátos proper. Myth has it that the three brothers Minos, Rhadamanthys and Sarpedon competed for the affections of a beautiful boy. When Sarpedon won, there was so much ill will that he left Crete for Asia Minor, taking with him not only the boy but the inhabitants of Milátos, where they founded the great city of Miletus. 'When Minos was in his prime, his very name terrified great nations: but now he was weak and very much afraid of Miletus, the son of Deione and Apollo, for the latter was young and strong,' Ovid wrote in the *Metamophoses*, summing up the decline of Crete and rise of Ionia in the 8th and 7th century BC.

In 1823, during the War of Independence, the large stalactite **Cave of Milátos** (on the edge of a vertiginous ravine, 3km from the centre, then a 20-minute walk) served as a refuge for two weeks for 3600 people. The Turks led by General Hasan besieged them, and after two battles the refugees surrendered; the Turks had promised them safe conduct, but instead massacred all the men and children, and enslaved the women. One large chamber has a chapel, or Heroön, containing all the bones found scattered in the cave.

A road south of Milátos leads to **Latsída**, just north of the main highway, where the churches of Ag. Paraskeví and the Panagía both have 14th- and 15th-century frescoes. Prosperous **Neápolis** (ΝΕΑΠΟΛΙΣ) is the largest village on the Herákleon–Ag. Nikólaos road; in its former incarnation as a village named Karés, it witnessed the birth of Pétros Fílagros in 1340. Raised by Catholics, he became a professor of theology and was elected Pope Alexander V in 1409, one of several popes-for-a-year during the Great Schism. Karés predeceased him, however, when the Venetians destroyed it in 1347 after a revolt. The rebuilt town became the 'new town', Neápolis. It has a small museum with items from Eloúnda and Dreros.

Up a winding mountain road north of Neápolis, set in a saddle between two hills (each topped with an acropolis) was ancient **Dreros**, discovered at the beginning of this century. In between the twin acropoli, walls, a cistern, an Archaic agora and a 7th-century BC Geometric temple to Apollo Delphinios were found; the latter yielded the oldest hammered bronze statues ever found in Greece (now in the Herákleon museum). South of Neápolis, the tiny mountain village of **Zénia** tells the following tale: during the Turkish occupation a lovely young girl in Zénia who had hair down to her knees caught the eye of a Turkish captain, who threatened to destroy her village if she would not marry him. On those terms, she reluctantly agreed. During the wedding feast she poured him more wine than he could hold, and during the night she decapitated him. Running to the church, she cut off her famous hair and took the clothes of a soldier and the name of Captain Manólis, performing many heroic deeds before she was killed. Her hair and the murder weapon are still on display in the church.

## Ag. Nikólaos

When Ag. Nikólaos (ΑΓ. ΝΙΚΟΛΑΟΣ) was selected capital of *nomós* Lassíthi in 1905 only 95 people lived in the little village, built as an amphitheatre overlooking a little round lake, the sea, and breathtaking Mirabélo Bay. It didn't even have a proper port; ships called off Pachiá Ámmos. A newly built port in 1965 attracted the first yachties and jet setters, charmed by 'Agios' as the locals call it. What has happened since is not exactly hard to guess, although if this is your first visit, exaggerate, perhaps mathematically cube, what you imagine mass tourism has wrought on this town named after Santa Claus. The resident population has multiplied by 100. The British contingency who swarm there haved dubbed it Agnik, a name with all the charm of an industrial by-product.

### Getting Around

**By sea:** Ag. Nikólaos port (✆ 22 312) has three ferries a week to Piraeus and Sitía, and one ferry a week to Kássos, Kárpathos and Rhodes; also Santoríni, Síkinos, Folégrandros and Mílos. Daily boat excursions from the port run to Spinalónga. **Port authority,** ✆ (0841) 22 312.

**By road:** the **bus** station (✆ 22 234) is near a rocky beach of Ámmos at the end of Sof. Venizélou. Beaches within easy bus range are Eloúnda (*see* below) and Kaló Chorió (on the road to Sitía). Other buses go to Herákleon, the Diktean cave and villages of the Lassíthi plateau; Kristá, Sitía, Ierápetra, and other points in the *nomós*.

### Tourist Information

**Tourist office:** Between the lake and the sea, 20 Aktí Koundoúrou, ✆ (0841) 22 357. **Tourist police:** in town, ✆ (0841) 26 900. The post office is on 28 Oktovríou, near the lake; **OTE telephones** are on 25 Martíou.

### Festivals

**New Year** and **Easter** festivities. **29 May**, Ag. Triáda. Nautical week **27 June–3 July**, with a firework display on the last day. **6 December**, Ag. Nikólaos.

## Around Town

In ancient times, Ag. Nikólaos was the port of Lato, and the town still concentrates much of its rather mercenary soul around the port, overlooking the islet of **Ag. Pándes**, a refuge for the *kri kri*. The chapel of the same name draws pilgrims on 20 June, but at other times you need special permission to escape from it all with the goats. The other tourist vortex is round duck-filled **Lake Voulisméni**; although its Greek name means 'bottomless', it has been measured at 210ft/64m. Believed to be the mouth of an underground river, Voulisméni tended to be stagnant, and in 1867 it was connected to the sea by the pasha of Crete. Behind the tourist office, there's a small **Ethnographic Museum** (*open 8–2 and 6–8*). Aktí Koundoúrou follows the sea shore, past rocky places where you can swim. There is a beach at the very end and the little church that gave the town its name, **Ag. Nikólaos**, with 9th- and 14th-century frescoes (ask at the police station for the key). A second church, the 12th-century **Panagía**, is off Plateía Venizélou.

The excellent **Archaeology Museum** up the hill at 68 Kon. Palaiológou (*open 8.30–3, closed Mon*) displays artefacts discovered in Eastern Crete: among the highlights are Middle Minoan vases from a shipwreck near Pseíra islet, a unique Neolithic phallus-shaped idol from Zákros, and the peculiar Early Minoan 'Goddess of Myrtos'. There is gold jewellery from Móchlos, a clay staff from Mália, imprinted with Linear A writing on four sides, and a Late Minoan infant burial discovered in a baby tholos tomb. Daedalic figurines from the 7th century share space with a handsome Archaic head. In the last room, a 1st century AD skull still has a gold burial wreath clinging to its brow.

Many tourists are surprised to discover that Agnik was asleep when God was handing out beaches: there's little shingly **Kitroplateía** south of the Marina, named for the cypress wood once exported from here. The little sand beach of **Ammoúdi** is at the end of Aktí Koudoúrou; the municipal beach has a bit of sand south of the other side of the stadium; from there, a walking path leads in one kilometre to the bamboo-curtained naturalist beach **Almyrós**.

## Eloúnda and Spinalónga

View after view across the sublime Bay of Mirabélo unfold along the 12 kilometres from Ag. Nikólaos north to Eloúnda; below the rocky coastline is interspersed with pocket-sized coves, draped with Crete's most glamorous hotels. Just before Eloúnda, a little bridge crosses an artificial channel dug by Napoleon's soldiers, separating the promontory of Spinalónga ('Long Thorn') from mainland Crete. Not far from the windmill/coffee-house is ancient **Olous**, the unexcavated port of Dreros and goal of the much advertized 'sunken city' from Ag. Nikólaos (the walls of the port are in the channel). The moon goddess Artemis Britomartis, inventor of the fishing net, was worshipped here, and was represented by a wooden cult statue with a fishtail made by Daedalos; one story has her turning into a fish to wiggle away from the embrace of King Minos. Fish mosaics also figure on the floor of an Early Byzantine basilica excavated to the northwest.

**Eloúnda** (ΕΛΟΥΝΤΑ) is just to the north. The central square overlooking the sea is a particularly pleasant place to sit and relax. Every here and there are pocket-sized shingle or sandy beaches, and if you've brought your snorkelling gear, so much the better. The tiny island of **Spinalónga** (ΣΠΙΝΑΛΟΓΚΑ, not to be confused with the promontory) is a half-hour

FISHERMAN

caique trip from Eloúnda, or longer excursion boat from Ag. Nikólaos. Venetian engineers detached it from the promontory in 1579 when they dug a canal to defend their huge fortress, built on the ruins of the ancient fort of Olous. During the Turkish occupation, it held out like the other small island forts of Nea Soúda and Gramboúsa as a shelter for Cretan refugees and base to harry the Turks; in 1715, the Venetians gave up all hope of ever re-conquering Crete and handed the forts over to the Ottomans. The Turks settled the island with soldiers and civilians. When they were evacuated in 1904, Spinalónga became a leper colony—the last in Europe—that survived until 1957, when word filtered through to Crete that leprosy wasn't contagious. Today the poignant little streets, houses and the lepers' church are abandoned and forlorn. **Pláka**, opposite the islet, was the supply centre for the lepers and now has a tiny laid-back colony of its own, dedicated to rest and relaxation by the little pebble beach.

---

## Ag. Nikólaos ✆ (0841–)          *Where to Stay*

Sometimes it seems as if all Europe has descended on Ag. Nikólaos, and if you come between June and the end of September without booking ahead, sleeping on the beach is a wretched alternative.

### *luxury*

Ag. Nikólaos' reputation as a posy tourist hotspot owes much to the posh hotels in the area, such as the **Elounda Mare,** in Eloúnda, ✆ 41 512 (reservations) or 41 102, ✉ 41 307, a member of the prestigious Relais et Chateaux complex with 50 hotel rooms and 40 bungalows—and 35 private swimming pools on the seafront. **Minos Beach**, on the secluded garden-covered promontory of Ammoúdi, ✆ 22 345, ✉ 22 548, has 132 sumptuous bungalows. Although built back practically in the Minoan era by Agnik standards (1962) it is still one of the best. The complex includes a good restaurant and three bars, but the beach is nondescript. **Elounda Beach**, ✆ 41 412, ✉ 41 373, incorporates traditional Cretan architectural features in its central hotel and bungalows, and has a sandy beach as well as its own cinema, deep-sea diving expeditions, fitness centre, heated pool and other luxuries. **St Nicolas Bay**, spread over a narrow peninsula 2km from Ag. Nikólaos, ✆ 25 041, ✉ 24 556, is a 130 bungalow complex which has a private sandy beach, three adult pools, and every other comfort, including an art gallery. *Open Mar–Nov.*

### *expensive*

**Candia Park Village**, between Ag. Nikólaos and Eloúnda, ✆ 26811, ✉ 22 367 (*A*) is recent and perfect for families, with a wide range of sporting activities from the *de rigueur* large pool to basketball, windsurfing, waterskiing and a small aqua park; all rooms are air-conditioned with kitchen facilities. *Open April–Oct.* **Villa Olga**, 3 Pitarokili, ✆ 23 382, ✉ 24 655 offers furnished apartments or studios near the centre of Agnik, with a small pool. **Moskonas**, by Almyrós Beach, ✆ 22 605, has apartments sleeping up to 5 people; **Melas**, 26 Aktí Koundoúrou, ✆ 28 734, also has stylish apartments, sleeping 2–5; book in the winter through Ioánna Melás, 47 Amarilládos Street, 15452 Athens, ✆ (1) 647 0133. **Korfos Beach**, ✆ 41 591 (*B*) is the pick of the hotels in Eloúnda, complete with a private beach.

### *moderate*

**Panorama** on Aktí Koundoúrou, ✆ 28 890 (*C*) has a good view over the harbour, and all rooms come with bath. **Hotel New York**, near the bus station at

21 Kontogiáni Street, © 28 577 (*C*) and **Possidonas**, in the same vicintiy © 24 086 (*C*) are known for having rooms when the other hotels are all booked up with package tours, and are open all year.

*inexpensive*

The tourist office lists over 1000 rooms in Ag. Nikólaos but just try to find one—and when you do, expect to pay more than anywhere else on Crete for what you get. The **Green House**, 15 Modátsou, © 22 025, has little wooden rooms leading out to a small courtyard, filled to overflowing with shrubs and trees, and patrolled by a small army of cats. Shared facilities and friendly owners. **Loukas**, in central Plateía Eleftherías, offers good value rooms with bathrooms and kitchen facilities, although summer prices verge on the moderate range. A row of inexpensive guesthouses— **Adonis**, **Perla**, **Salaminos**, and **Linda**—lurk just off the centre of Aktí Koundoúrou.

---

*Ag. Nikólaos © (0841–)* **Eating Out**

Restaurants and tavernas across the spectrum compete for your dinner drachma. **Pelagos**, on Strateokóraka (just inland from Aktí Koundoúrou) is a trendy Greek seafood restaurant, with a long list of tasty *mezés* to start with (*4–5000dr*). In the same area and price range, **Il Capriccio**, 31 Aktí Koundoúrou serves authentic Itlaian pizzas and pasta dishes. Near the tourist office on Kondyláki street, **The Embassy** does a wide variety of reasonably priced vegetarian, Indian, and even Weight Watcher's dishes, as well as a traditional English Sunday lunch. Its neightbour, the **New Dragon**, offers a better than average 4000dr Chinese menu.

On Kitroplateía beach, there's a whole row of tavernas, including the romantic **Myrto** which has lovely views across the water. Excellent grilled food, especially chicken (*3000dr*). The last taverna on the stretch, the **Oriental**, serves delicious Egyptian specialities (*3000dr*). At Ammoúdi beach the **Dolphin**, has good food served by jovial twin waiters (*2500dr*). If you're on a tight budget, down by the bus station are a clutch of greasy spoons where you can fill up on *souvláki*, *gyros*, or hamburgers with chips, and salad for around 1000dr, while savouring murals of Canadian mountains.

---

# Above Ag. Nikólaos: Kritsá and Kroústas

In 1956, Jules Dassin chose the lovely untouched village of **Kritsá** (ΚΡΙΤΣΑ) just west of Ag. Nikólaos as the set for his film *He Who Must Die* starring Melina Mercouri, and ever since the tourist boom in Ag. Nikólaos its role has been as something of a film set, as the traditional Cretan village swamped by tourists from the capital, who are in turn swamped by villagers selling them tablecloths. Some of the finest Cretan weddings take place around here, and although there are far too many foreigners around now for anyone to hope for a casual invite as in the past, in August weddings are re-enacted with food, drink and dancing for fee-paying 'guests'. Kritsá has a couple of other trumps up its sleeve: the 13th-century church of **Kíra Panagía** (*open 9–2; adm*), a kilometre before the village, its entire wall surface covered with the finest Byzantine fresco cycle in Crete. The paintings are in two distinct styles, the 13th-century 'archaicizing linear style' (*The Nativity*, *Last Supper*, and *Paradise*, where the patriarchs sit in a garden, clutching to their bosoms platters holding the souls of the Just) and the more naturalistic 14th-century Palaeologan style (the *Birth of the Virgin* and the *Second*

*Coming,* covering the whole north aisle). A very scenic 4km walk or drive north of Kritsá leads up to the extensive remains of Archaic **Lato**, splendidly situated in a depression between two hills that formed twin acropolises. Although built in the 7th century BC, Minoan influences have been noted in the architecture of its agora, with its sanctuary and well, and the stairway, leading up to the agora from the double gateway.

A few buses from Kritsá continue up to **Kroústas** (ΚΡΟΥΣΤΑΣ), which is just as pretty but has been spared the tourist hordes. It has some Byzantine frescoed churches and a huge festival on 25 June, the feast of St John, celebrated with bonfires and dances. A rough road continues to flower-bedecked **Prína**, affording magnificent views and the chance to circle back to Ag. Nikólaos by way of Kaló Chorió (*see* below).

## East of Ag. Nikólaos to Sitía: the Gulf of Mirabélo and Gourniá

The stunningly beautiful coastline that lends Ag. Nikólaos its panache got its name from the Genoese fortress of Mirabélo, demolished by the Turks. Where sheer precipices aren't crowding the sea, the land around Mirabélo is immensely fertile, and has been densely populated for some 5000 years; archaeological zoning of the area has kept Agnikish development here to a minimum, although frequent buses run between the capital and the popular sandy beach of **Kaló Chório** (ΚΑΛΟ ΧΩΡΙΟ, 12km from Ag. Nikólaos). From Kaló Chorió a path leads to **Vrókastro**, a Late Minoan peak sanctuary used as a refuge settlement during the Doric invasion. A Geometric-era fort stands on the hill.

The main road continues 4km east of Kaló Chorió to the turn-off for the 12th-century monastery of **Faneroménis**, high on the hill and the site of many resistance activities during the Turkish occupation. The road then passes directly below striking hillside site of **Gourniá** (*open Tues–Sun, 8.30–3*), the best-preserved Minoan town on Crete. Excavated between 1901 and 1904 by American Harriet Boyd (a Minoan pioneer archaeologist and the first woman to lead a major dig), Gourniá reached its peak in the Late Minoan period, around 1550 BC, and was never rebuilt after a massive fire *c.* 1225 BC. Narrow, stone-paved lanes meander up and down the town, densely packed with workshops, storerooms, houses and, at the highest point, a small 'palace' built around the obligatory rectangular court. The fact that Boyd found no Linear A tablets (the script used for formal religious offerings) here has led to the suspicion that Gourniá had only limited local authority. From Gourniá, it's a short drive or easy walk down to **Pachiá Ámmos**, a rather woebegone-looking resort village along a sandy beach. It stands at the beginning of the Ierápetra road bisecting the Cretan isthmus, a mere 12km of land separating the Aegean from the Libyan sea. There are plans to build Ag. Nikólaos an international airport of its very own here—a move guaranteed to encourage its worst Agnikiness—by **Vasilikí**, 5km south, near a 'Cretan paper mill Visitors Welcome' sign. Here a Pre-Palace Minoan settlement (2600–2000 BC) discovered in 1906 yielded the first known specimens of what has since been known as 'Vasilikí ware', the Minoans' first distinctive pottery style, boldly mottled in red and black (produced by uneven firing).

## Pachiá Ámmos to Sitía: the Cretan Riviera

Pachiá Ámmos (ΠΑΧΕΙΑ ΑΜΜΟΣ) is also the crossroads for Sitía, some 47km east down a new corniche road that rates among the most scenic on all Crete, slithering along the jagged and often precipitous coast of the Gulf of Mirabélo, with the bright lights of Ag. Nikólaos twinkling far below. **Kavoúsi**, 6km east of Pachiá Ammos, is just below two small Late Minoan sites: a settlement and cemetery at **Vrondá**, high on a plateau in the Thriptís mountains, and even further up, 700m above sea level, **Kástro**, located near a fresh spring, with the whole Gulf of Mirabélo spread out below. Both have received a good deal of attention lately from American archaeologists, who believe Vrondá was settled by refugees from Gourniá; when the Dorians invaded, they moved to Kástro and stayed there until the 7th century BC.

The earliest Minoan site along the gulf is **Móchlos**, a budding resort with the only accessible beach along the coast, down, down, down from the main road. Minoan Móchlos occupied an islet, barely a stone's throw from the mainland (you can easily swim there), giving it the advantage of two harbours, one facing east and the other west. Abandoned after the disaster of 1470 BC, its cemetery in particular has helped scholars understand the trade and industry of a proto-urban Minoan town of 300 souls; Móchlos apparently specialized in pots with lid handles shaped like reclining dogs. Recently, seven intact chamber tombs with their clay larnaxes were discovered cut into the cliffs facing the islet. One Late Minoan building on Móchlos is known as 'the House of the Theran Refugees' for its architectural similarities to the top-floor timbered houses at Akrotíri, on Santoríni; pot shards from Akrotíri littered the floor *on top of* a 20cm layer of volcanic ash. Obviously life went on after the Big Bang. Yet another Minoan settlement existed from 3000 BC—and likewise continued to exist after the eruption—on **Pseíra**, 2km offshore, where the inhabitants used the pumice that floated ashore to build up the floor of their shrine. Pseíra's House of the Pillar Partitions, with a bathroom equipped with a sunken tub, plughole and drains, is one of the most elegant in eastern Crete.

A few panoramic cafés and restaurants have sprung up along the corniche road at **Plátanos** and **Myrsíni**, the latter a Venetian village with important Minoan tombs in the vicinity. Visitors are welcome to Myrsíni's pottery and weaving workshops. Two beehive tombs in **Mésa Moulianá** date from the end of the Bronze Age; and in **Éxo Moulianá**, famous for its red wine, Ag. Geórgios has frescoes (1426). **Chamézi**, high above Sitía, has an oval, prehistoric house or sanctuary, as well as a charming local folklore museum, open by request (ask for Yianni).

---

### *Where to Stay and Eating Out*

**Kaló Chorió** ✆ (0841–)

**Istron Bay**, ✆ 61 303, 📠 61 383 (*lux*). Fancy white and built into the hillside under the road, with everything a lazy holiday requires, from a special children's pool and game rooms to seawater pool, jewellery shop, and private beach and beach bar. *Open April–Oct.* **Elpida**, ✆ 61 403 (*C; mod*), is on the west side of the beach, 500 yards from the sea, but with a restaurant and pool. *Open April–Oct.*

**Móchlos** ✆ (0834–)

**Aldiana,** ✆ 94 322 (*B; exp*) precludes the need to go anywhere else, with a restaurant, sports, a pool, and nightclub. *Open April–Oct.* **Sofia**, ✆ 94 240 (*D; mod*) is pleasant and small. *Open Mar–Oct.* **Mochlos**, ✆ 94 205 (*E; inexp*) is 20 yards from the sea. *Open all year.* There are also a few cheaper rooms, and a few pricey tavernas.

## Sitía

An antidote to the tourist mills of Ag. Nikólaos, sunny **Sitía** (ΣΗΤΕΙΑ) has kept its Greek soul and natural courtesy to a greater extent than any other town on the north coast, perhaps because it has a livelihood of its own, devoted to sultanas and wine. It is more pleasant than stunningly beautiful, set in an amphitheatre and endowed with a long, sandy beach that flies the blue flag of environmental righteousness. Sitía was once ringed by Byzantine, Genoese and Venetian walls, before earthquakes and the bombardment of Barbarossa toppled them, leaving only a Venetian fortress to close off the western end of the port.

### Getting There and Around

Sitía's little airport is linked by regular weekly **flights** to Kárpathos and Kássos, and to Athens twice a week. **Ferries** run twice a week to Kárpathos and Kássos, Ag. Nikólaos and Pireaus; and once a week to Chálki, Sými and Rhodes. Summer excursion boats run to Koufónisi (*see* Ierápetra). **Port authority**, ✆ (0843) 22 310.

### Festivals

**24 June**, large local festival, Piskokéfalo; **mid-August**, a 3-day wine festival, Sitía.

## Around the Town

Sitía has a couple of museums to top off the lazy charms of its beach, its pelican, and portside waterholes (there's an especially nice group of bars by the sea, just west of the dock). The **Archaeology Museum**, incongruously set among the garages, near the triangular square at the top of Itanos Street (*open 8.45–3, Sun 9.30–2, closed Mon; adm*) has a small but interesting collection of finds from the *nomós*: Minoan larnaxes, a wine press from Zákros, and votives from the 7th century in the Daedalic stayle. There's also a small **Folklore Museum** near the very top of town on G. Arkadíon Street with colourful examples of local arts and crafts, especially weavings and embroideries. But what Sitía is best known for is Vincénzo Kornáros, the 17th-century Creto-Venetian author of the *Erotókritos*, the Cretan national epic poem.

A 10,000-line romance, inspired by Ariosto and written in the Cretan dialect, the *Erotókritos* is still memorized and sung today to the *lýra* and *láuto*; some shepherds can rattle off thousands of verses off the top of their heads. The story is set in Byzantine times and tells of the love between Erotokritos, son of a poor commoner, and Aretousa, daughter of King Heracles of Athens. After serenading the princess Aretousa incognito, Erotokritos is forced to flee Athens after slaying two of the guards the king sent to ambush him. Although Erotokritos boldly returns to win a knightly tournament, the king still refuses his marriage petition because of his humble birth, exiles him, then cuts off his daughter's long hair and throws her in prison for loving Erotokritos and refusing to marry the prince of Byzantium. Three years later, the kingdom of Athens is invaded by the Vlachs, and all seems lost until Erotokritos reappears on the scene to pummel them, unrecognized by all thanks to a magic potion that turned his skin black. The Vlachs' greatest warrior, a giant, challenges him to single combat, and, when Erotokritos slays him, their army withdraws. Aretousa eventually recognizes her lover in spite of his new skin colour, although he drinks another magic potion to change it back before they are happily married and he accedes to the throne of Athens. Interspersed with all the action, Kornáros included enough philosophy to make the *Erotókritos* a rich source for *mantinade* singers or others in search of the *mot juste* for any occasion; for example, the favourite overleaf:

*Clouds and mists in*
*Time disperse;*
*Great blessings in time*
*Become a curse.*

## Around Sitía

The region around Sitía has a plethora of minor archaeological sites, especially Minoan country villas, built *c.* 1550 when Crete apparently experienced a population boom. One such villa is at **Zou**, south of Sitía (take the road in front of the archaeology museum), and another is in **Achládia**, 5km west of **Piskokéfalo**, where a tholos tomb of 1300 BC may be seen as well. **Maronía**, south of Piskoképhalo, is a charming white village set amid emerald terraces. Néa Praisós, 15km south of Sitía, is just below ancient **Praisós**, the chief stronghold of the Eteocretans—the 'true Cretans' or Minoans—who took refuge here before the Dorian invasion and survived into the 3rd century BC, worshipping Diktean Zeus and other ancient cults on their three acropoli. The most intriguing finds at Praisós are Eteocretan inscriptions in Greek letters; if they could ever be deciphered, it could lead to the translation of the Minoan words of Linear A. Praisós was destroyed by its arch enemy Ierápetra in 146 BC; houses, tholos tombs, and the foundations of a temple have survived. To the south, off the main road, the village **Etiá** was one of the major towns in the Byzantine and Venetian periods, noted for its lovely setting. The region was ruled by the De Mezzo family, who in the 15th century built themselves a fortified *palazzo*, the most beautiful Venetian building on Crete—three storeys high, with vaulted ceilings and intricate sculptural decorations. Destruction began when a band of Turks were besieged here, and a later fire and earthquake finished the job. Now partially restored, it has inscriptions in the many outlying buildings, the wall, gate and fountain house. **Lithínes**, back on the main road, is a charming village with the remains of a Venetian tower; the Libyan sea can just be seen below.

*Sitía ✆ (0843–)*

### Where to Stay

#### moderate

**Denis**, 60 El. Venizélou, ✆ 28 356 (*B*) is in the centre of the action, above Zorba's restaurant. **Hotel Itanos,** Plateía Venizélou, ✆ 22 146 (*C*) a stylish hotel class near the park. **Alice**, 34 Papanastassíou, ✆ 28 450 (*C*) is good value, modern and offers Cretan evenings once a week. **Crystal**, 17 Kapetán Sífi, ✆ 22 284 (*C*) 50m from the water, has modern, comfortable rooms.

#### inexpensive

**Hotel Star**, 37 M. Kolyváki, ✆ 22 917 (*D*) offers some peace and quiet, and convenience for ferry boats. **Flisvos**, by the bus station at K. Karamalí 4, ✆ 22 422 (*D*) is simple, comfortable enough and has sea views. **Archontiko**, ✆ 28 172 (*D*) is a nice quiet little hotel on the west edge of town, by the whitewashed steps. The **youth hostel**, 4 Theríssou Street, ✆ 22 693, is just east of town and again, quite pleasant and friendly, with kitchen facilities and a garden.

*Sitía ✆ (0843–)*

### Eating Out

If you're going to eat fish in Crete, Sitía is the place to do it: **Zorba's** has a wonderful location on the water, and although the ready food can look a bit tired, the seafood and grilled meats are fresh and delicious (*3500dr*). **O Mixos Taverna Ouzeri**, two streets in from the port, serves lamb baked or on the spit with barrelled wine (*3000dr*). Two kilometres out on the road to Ierápetra, look out for **Klimateria**, a country taverna serving wonderful *mezé* and grilled foods. Two kilometres out in the other direction **Karavopetka** is next to the sea and also serves good *mezé*; try their sausages *omaties*, a local speciality.

## East of Sitía: the Monastery of Toploú

This, one of Crete's wealthiest monasteries, is really named Panagía Akroterianí, but Toploú ('cannon' in Turkish) is more aptly evokes this fortress of the faith, isolated on a plateau, 3.5km from the Sitía–Palaíkastro road. The first building here is believed to have been a chapel dating from Nikephóros Phokás' liberation of Crete, dedicated to Ag. Isidóro (hence Cape Sideros). The monastery itself was founded in the 15th century by the Kornáros family, and rebuilt first after its destruction by the buccaneering Knights of Malta, and then the earthquake of 1612. Square 30ft walls defend Toploú; the gate, which once moved on a wheel, is directly under a hole named the *foniás* ('killer'), through which the besieged monks used to pour stones and boiling oil on their attackers. Much of Toploú's building stone came from the ancient Itanos: note the inscription from the 2nd century BC embedded in the façade, recording the arbitration of Magnesia in a dispute between Itanos and Ierapytna.

Toploú has a venerable history as a place of refuge, revolution and resistance, and more than once the monks have paid for their activities. At the beginning of the War of Independence in 1821, the Turks captured it and hanged twelve monks over the gate as a warning to other rebels, although as usual it only made the Cretans mad as hell, and by the end of the war Toploú was theirs again. During the Second World War, the abbot was shot by the Germans for operating a radio transmitter for the Resistance. Among the monastery's icons is one of the masterpieces of Cretan art: the beautiful *Great is the Lord*, by Ioánnis Kornáros (1770), with 61 lively scenes illustrating the Orthodox prayer of Megálos Agiasmós.

## Palaíkastro, Vái and Itanos

Palaíkastro (ΠΑΛΑΙΚΑΣΤΡΟ) is a pleasant village, overlooking a fine beach a kilometre away, lined with restaurants and tavernas. The first edition of Palaíkastro was down here, at **Roussolakos**: a late Minoan settlement with streets and houses by the sea, that had no palace and may have been under the jurisdiction of Zákros. A rough track south of here leads to **Petsofás**, where a Minoan peak sanctuary dedicated to the goddess yielded a trove of votive offerings. From Geometric to Hellenistic times, the inhabitants moved up the hill to **Kastrí**, where in the ruins of a Classical temple to Diktean Zeus an important 4th-century BC hymn to Zeus was found engraved on a stone. Two kilometres north of the village, a narrow, sign-posted road leads down to **Koureménos beach**.

Palaíkastro is the last bus stop before **Vái** (ΒΑΙ, from the Cretan *váyies*, or palm), Crete's most stunningly beautiful beach, where silver sands are lined with Europe's only wild palm trees, a species unique to Crete called *Phoenix theophrastii*. As you approach, signs among the 5000 palms direct you to a banana plantation to complete the Caribbean ambience. There are plans to make Vái a National Park, and camping is strictly forbidden. The only way to avoid sharing this tropical paradise with thousands of body bakers is to get there at the crack of dawn or star in the next Bounty Bar ad filmed on the beach. There's a mediocre overpriced taverna overlooking the beach—and if you wonder why people are hopping about in the water, it's because the fish sometimes bite. A number of small beaches around Vái act as crowd overflow tanks and free campsites. The path north from Vái leads in 25 minutes up Cape Sideros to ancient **Itanos**, also accessible by road. Although inhabited from Early Minoan times, the small remains you see of Itanos today date from the Geometric to Hellenistic periods, when Ptolemy used the port as a naval station, and the city exported dyes and glass. Pirates forced its abandonment in Early Christian times, and also spoiled a 15th-century attempt at re-settlement.

## Zákros

From Palaíkastro, the road south runs through a string of olive groves and sleepy hamlets to **Zákros** (ΖΑΚΡΟΣ), where a rich Minoan villa was excavated by the English archaeologist Hogarth in 1901, complete with wall paintings, sewers, wine presses and cellars. The villa is a short walk from the head of the dramatic gorge, the stark, rocky, inhospitable 'Valley of Death', named for the rock-cut Minoan tombs from 2600 BC found along the way. On foot it's an 8km walk down the ravine to Káto Zákros (the bus will leave you at the top of it) but softies can take the road; buses make the descent as well. For decades local farmers found seals and other Minoan relics in the curious purple soil of Káto Zákros, but the Minoan **palace of Zákros** (*open 8.30–3, closed Mon*), the fourth largest on Crete, was only found in 1961 by Níkos Pláton; because the east coast of Crete is sinking, part of the ancient harbour is submerged. Built in the New Palace period (*c.* 1700 BC), the town that surrounded the palace was probably the Minoans' chief port for Egypt, the base of the 'Keftiu' (as the Minoans may have called themselves) who appear in hieroglyphs on the pyramids. The palace collapsed in the general catastrophe of 1450 BC, followed by fire, and was never rebuilt, never plundered; Pláton found over 10,000 items here, including large quantities of ivory, which may have been a local speciality. The finest pieces have a room to their own in the Herákleon museum, but few are of precious metals, suggesting that the residents had time to grab their treasures before disaster overwhelmed them. Like other Minoan palaces, Zákros has a long Central Court, and a well for sacrificial offerings; at the bottom Pláton found a bowl of perfectly preserved Minoan olives, although they quickly shrivelled up on contact with the air. The West Wing of the palace apparently held sanctuaries and ritual chambers, and perhaps workshops. The East Wing, with a lustral basin, is interpreted as either the royal apartments or a shrine. On the north end, a kitchen and banquet hall have fragments of original decoration.

As a protected archaeological area, the little fishing hamlet of **Káto Zákros** has no new buildings or big hotels. Its pebbly beach is fine for a swim or a snorkel, but if it's remote soft sands you have a yen for, make your way down the tortuous coastal road to **Xerókambos**.

© *(0843–)*                                                **Where to Stay and Eating Out**

### Palaíkastro

Palaíkastro is a convenient, relaxing place to stay for the beaches and sights on the far east end of Crete. **Hotel Hellas**, near the central square, © 61 240 (*B; exp*), is the most comfortable. *Open all year.* **Marina Village**, below the village, 500m from the sea © 61 284 (*C; mod*) is a little resort complex with its own restaurant, pool and tennis courts. **Hotel Thalia**, © 61 448 (*D*) is a nice little place on a side street, smothered in bougainvillaea. *Open April–Oct.* Many people rent rooms; a little municipal tourist office on the main street can help you out.

### Zákros

**Hotel Zakros,** *⊘* 93 379 (*C; mod*) is small, a bit frayed at the edges, and open all year. In the summer there are a few rooms to let along the road to Káto Zákros, and about 30 beds scattered in the various rent-rooms along the shore. Three small tavernas compete for the tour groups who show up; **Maria's** (*mod*), serving fresh fish under the tamarisks, is the best, but not by much.

## Ierápetra and Southeast Crete

By all rights, **Ierápetra** (ΙΕΡΑΠΕΤΡΑ, pop. 7000), as the southernmost town in Europe—a mere 370km from Africa—and main market centre for Crete's banana, pineapple and winter veg crops, should be a fascinating place instead of an irritatingly dull dodoburg with a long grey sand beach and a plastic-wrapped hinterland. The myths say it was founded by the mysterious, mist-making Telchines who named it Kamiros, the same name they gave to the city they had founded on Rhodes. When the Telchines began to foul up Crete's weather, Zeus sent them packing, and the Dorians, to keep things straight, renamed the town Ierapytna. Ierapytna did so well in Hellenistic times that it became the most powerful city in eastern Crete, strong enough to hold out against the Romans after they had conquered all the rest of the island. Piqued, the Romans flattened it, then to show there was no hard feelings rebuilt it in such grand style that Ierápetra soon recovered. The Byzantines made it a bishopric, but it was sacked by the Saracens and toppled by an earthquake in 1508. The only building to survive was the 13th-century Venetian **Kastélli**, a small fort later rebuilt by Sammicheli (*open 9am–9pm, although there's precious little to see inside*) standing on the south mole of the ancient harbour, now a port bobbing with fishing and pleasure craft. Nearby, in a warren of narrow streets, is a house where Napoleon supposedly spent the night of 26 June 1798, before sailing off to campaign in Egypt. There's a neglected (as usual) little mosque and minaret further on, and, to the west, a few Roman remains including a theatre. The most beautiful things in Ierápetra are the Late Minoan painted clay larnax found in Episkopí and the Roman statue of Demeter in its **museum**, Plateía Dimarchéiou (*⊘ 28 165 for opening hours*).

All in all, the best thing to do in Ierápetra is leave—take one of several excursions out to the golden sands of **Chrisí**, an uninhabited islet 8 miles off in the Libyan sea, where one of Crete's last natural cedar forests survives intact. The sea is immaculate and deposits seashells by the millions on Chrisí's shores; in season tavernas by the beach ward off any chance of starvation. In high summer you can also find excursion boats to **Koufonísi**, a remote island to the east, where the seashells were mostly of the murex variety, used to dye cloth royal purple. This resource made it a prize, and Ierápetra and Itanos fought over it endlessly; a theatre and settlement have been recently been excavated, and the water is crystal-clear for snorkelling.

### Along the South Coast near Ierápetra

West of Ierápetra **Ammoudáres** and **Mýrtos** are both small resorts with beaches; in the latter, in 1968 the British School excavated an Early Minoan town that had been a weaving centre, dating from 2500 to 2100 BC. Some of the finds are in the local schoolhouse, while the more important ones (including the famous goddess of Mýrtos) are in the Ag. Nikólaos museum. If you fancy a day's trek, you can follow the riverbed down from **Máles** to Mýrtos, after taking in Máles' frescoed church, Panagía Messochorítissa (1431).

Every year new developments sprout up along the coast east of Ierápetra. Old houses at the abandoned village of **Koutsounári** have been restored to rent out to visitors; **Férma** and **Ag. Fotiá** and **Makrigialós** (with an excellent sandy beach and remains of a Late Minoan villa) are all small resorts. From Makrigialós the main highway heads north to Sitía; if you continue along the coast, you'll see the striking white walls of **Moní Kápsa** built into the austere cliff, draped with cascades of prickly pears.

---

© (0842–)                              ***Where to Stay***

### luxury

Modern **Petra Mare**, on the edge of Ierápetra's beach, © 23 341 is the closest to town. **Lyktos Beach Hotel**, © 61 480, 📠 61 318 (*A*) is the queen of the resort hotels on the coast near Ierápetra. Seven kilometres from town, it sits on a lovely beach, and offers 7 floodlit tennis courts, watersports, gymnasium, sauna, jacuzzi, basketball and volleyball courts, children's pool, 3 restaurants, nightclub and piano bar. 'Let yourself be pampered' is their slogan. All rooms are air-conditioned and have their own balcony or terrace. **Sunwing** at Makrigialós, © (0843) 51 621 (*A*) is in a similar vein.

### expensive

Try **Traditional Cottages**, 8km east at Koutsounári, © 61 291 (*A*), each decorated in Cretan style, and with full cooking facilities. The beach is an 800m walk. In Ierápetra itself, the brand new, pristine **Astron**, 56 M. Kothrí, © 25 114 (*C*), is pleasant, and all rooms are air-conditioned, with sea-view balconies.

### moderate

**Hotel Iris**, 36 M. Kothrí, © 23 136 (*D*) by the water, with 12 pleasant rooms, is typical for price and comfort, as is **El Greco**, 42 M. Kothrí, © 28 471 (*C*), open all year round. If you don't fancy staying in town, go west along the coast to Mýrtos and the **Myrtos Hotel**, © 51 226 (*C*), with a good restaurant. *Open all year.*

### inexpensive

The **Ierapytna**, Plateía Ag. Ioánnou Kale, © 28 530 (*D*) offers good value in this range. **Coral**, Emm. Nikikatsanváki 12, © 22 743 (*D*) is a simple place in a quiet neighbourhood, not far from the castle, with balconies; if it's full, try the nearby **Gorgona**, 16 Manóli Triadaphillídi, a pretty blue and white pension. **Rooms Leon**, a few steps from the beach on Grannákou (near the Astron hotel) is another good bet.

---

© (0842–)                                      ***Eating Out***

The great favourite is **Napoleon**, on the waterfront, with authentic Greek and Cretan food. Fresh fish (the owner has his own caique) and varieties of snails are specialities (*around 4000dr for fish*). Near the town beach, **Siciliana** has a real pizza oven that produces a good honest pie (*around 2000dr*). The local favourite is a small no-name restaurant grill in the little square by the mosque (*2500dr for a full meal*).

## The Cyclades

OIA, SANTORINI

Say 'Greek island', and many people picture one of the Cyclades (the 'circling' islands, surrounding sacred Délos): barren rocks rising from a crystal blue sea, where the hills spill over with little villages of asymmetrical white houses and narrow labyrinthine streets, a pocket-sized church squeezed in at every corner. Few places are so irresistibly stark and clear, so visually pure and honest, so sharply defined in light and shadow; none of the islands is very large, and you can always see several floating dreamily on the horizon, beckoning, framing a sunset or a rosy-fingered dawn.

The Cyclades are understandably among the top tourist attractions in Greece. But even Mýkonos, the busiest, manages to retain an air of class in spite of the hordes it attracts. This is as jet-setty as you can get, with great beaches and the best nightlife, only a short boat ride from holy Délos, now an outdoor archaeological museum. In Íos you'll feel old at 25; the emphasis here is definitely on pubbing and beachlife. Lovely Páros and Náxos get swamped by mass package tourism, but Páros has paradoxically retained its island charm. Spectacular, volcanic Santoríni has a lot to live up to as almost everyone's favourite. Lesser known Sérifos, Sífnos and Sýros offer a seductive mixture of rugged island scenery, typical villages, good restaurants and swimming. Then there are special gems like Tínos, mecca for pilgrims and popular with Greeks. Stand-offish Ándros is still largely tourist-free (Batsí excepted). The islands of Kéa and Kýthnos, while close to Athens, are seldom visited except by passing yachtsmen and Greek tourists. A few islands even come under the heading of 'almost away from it all': Folégandros, Mílos and Amorgós, or the tiny islands east and south of Naxos: Koufoníssi, Schinoússa and Heráklia.

The climate of the Cyclades, more than anywhere else in Greece, is influenced by the winds. Winter is plagued by the *voreas,* the north wind that turns ship schedules into a fictional romance. After March the *sirocco* blows from the south, warming islands still green from the winter rains. By July many of the Cyclades look brown and parched, except where there are sources of underground water. From July to September the notorious *meltémi* from the Russian steppes huffs and puffs like the big bad wolf, quadrupling sales of dramamine in the ports. If you're really a landlubber you can fly: Páros, Mýkonos, Mílos, Santoríni, Náxos and Sýros have airports. Another high summer consideration is the sheer number of visitors; without a reservation you can expect only frustration on the more popular islands, or the smaller ones with a limited number of beds. Don't assume that the more isolated the island the cheaper the accommodation, as supply and demand dictate the prices. You could well pay more for a room in Folégandros, for example, than on Páros, where rooms are far more plentiful. Out of season you can pick and choose, and places with a high percentage of Greek tourists (Kýthnos, Kéa), who tend to go for a 6-week burst in the height of summer, are a bargain.

Water continues to be a problem on some islands, and it may be turned off for part of the day. However, since these islands are so popular with visitors (and

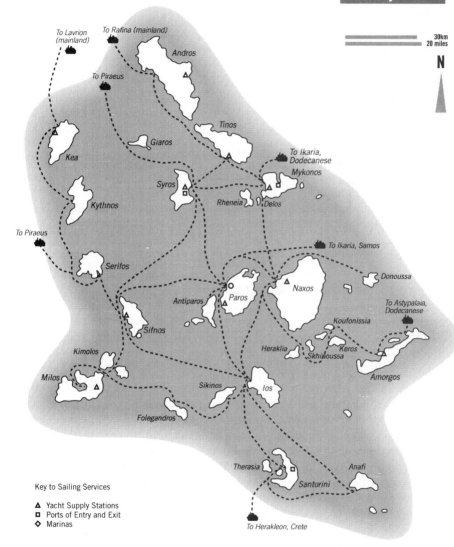

The Cyclades

To Lavrion (mainland)

To Rafina (mainland)

Andros

To Piraeus

Tinos

30km
20 miles

N

Giaros

Kea

To Ikaria, Dodecanese

Mykonos

Syros

Kythnos

Rheneia

Delos

To Piraeus

To Ikaria, Samos

Serifos

Donoussa

Antiparos

Paros

Naxos

To Astypalaia, Dodecanese

Sifnos

Koufonissia

Kimolos

Heraklia

Keros

Skhinoussa

Milos

Sikinos

Ios

Amorgos

Folegandros

Therasia

Anafi

Santorini

Key to Sailing Services

△ Yacht Supply Stations
□ Ports of Entry and Exit
◇ Marinas

To Herakleon, Crete

thus important to the national economy), efforts have been made to ensure they and their new hotels have ample water supplies, even in August. Before the advent of tourism, the population of the Cyclades dropped to an all time low; it was simply too hard to make a living from the dry, rocky soil. Even now, the winter months can be lonely as many islanders retreat to flats in Athens.

## History

Archaeological evidence suggests that the Cyclades have been inhabited since at least 6000 BC, the first settlers arriving from what is now Karia in Asia Minor and speaking a non-Greek language. At the beginning of the Bronze Age (3000–2000 BC) the islanders developed a culture known as Early Cycladic, which if nothing else had a staggeringly modern sense of design in their elegant, almost abstract pure white marble figurines, not carved but patiently sanded into shape with emery.

In myth, King Minos of Crete conquered the Aegean Islands in order to rid himself of his overly just brother Rhadamanthys, whom he sent to administer the new Cretan colonies, most famously Akrotíri on Santoríni. This corresponds to the Minoan influence that marks the prosperous Middle Cycladic period, when artists adopted a more natural style. The Late Cycladic period coincides with the fall of Crete and the rise of the Mycenaeans. When the Mycenaeans in turn were overrun by the uncouth Dorians, the islands dropped out of history for hundreds of years. The luckier islands fell under the sway of the Ionians, and at the end of the 8th century BC, were part of the Ionian cultural rebirth in the Archaic period.

The rise of the Persians forced the Ionians to flee westwards to Attica, leaving the islands in Persian hands; several sided with the Persians at Marathon and Salamis, and were subsequently punished by Athens. To prevent future breakaways, Athens obliged the islands to enter into the new maritime league at Délos in 478 BC, replacing an older Ionian council, or Amphictyony. But what began as a league of allies gradually turned into vassals paying tribute to the Athenians, whose fleet was the only one capable of protecting the islands from the Persian menace. Cycladic resentment often flared into open revolt, and the Athenians had to work ever harder to extort the islands' annual contribution of money and ships.

During the Peloponnesian War the islands tended to side with the front-runner at any given time, and many jumped at the chance to support Sparta against their Athenian oppressors. But when Athens recovered from the war in 378 BC, it was only to form a second Delian league, again subjugating the Cyclades. Most of the islands turned to Philip of Macedon as a saviour from the Athenian bullies, only to be fought over a generation later by the generals of Alexander the Great. Only the 2nd-century BC Roman conquest brought the Cyclades peace, except for the islands given to Rhodes, a less kindly ruler than distant Rome. The fall of Rome spelt centuries of hardship; although the Cyclades remained part of the Byzantine Empire, Constantinople could not protect them from marauders, and the islanders were left to fend for themselves, building villages in the most inaccessible places possible.

When Constantinople fell in 1204, the Frankish conquerors allotted the Aegean to the Venetians, and the Archipelago, as the Byzantines called it, became the prey of grasping young noblemen and pirates (often one and the same). The Cyclades became the special territory of Marco Sanudo, nephew of Doge Enrico Dandolo, the mastermind of the Fourth

Crusade. Marco Sanudo declared himself Duke of Náxos and personally ruled that island and Páros, and gave his faithful thugs the smaller Cyclades as fiefs. The Sanudos gave way to the Crispi dynasty in 1383, but, threatened by pirates and the growing Ottoman Empire, Venice herself stepped in to police the Cyclades at the end of the 15th century. There was little even Venice could do against the fierce renegade admiral Khair-ed-din-Barbarossa, who systematically decimated the islands in the name of the Sultan. By the mid 16th century they were under Turkish domination, ruled by a puppet Duke of Náxos.

Venetian priests had converted many of the Greeks on the Cyclades to Catholicism, in particular on Sýros, Tínos, Santoríni and Náxos, and despite the Ottoman occupation both Orthodox and Catholic monasteries thrived. Turkish rule in the Archipelago was harsh only in economic terms and most of the islands were spared the cruelties inflicted on Crete. From 1771–74, one of the more outlandish episodes in Greek history brought a brief interlude from the Ottomans: Russia and Turkey were at each other's throats over Poland, so Catherine the Great decided to open a second front in the war by capitalizing on Greek discontent. Her fleet in the Aegean led an insurrection against the Sultan and occupied some of the Cyclades. By the time the Russians gave it up and went home, they had made themselves unpopular with all concerned.

When the Greek War of Independence broke out, the Cyclades offered naval support and provided a safe harbour for refugees; the islands with large Catholic populations were brought under the protection of the French and remained neutral in the conflict. Nevertheless, the Cyclades were soon incorporated in the new Greek state, and Sýros became the country's leading port until Piraeus took over with the advent of the steamship. Today Sýros' capital, Ermoúpolis, is still the largest town and administrative centre of the Cyclades.

# Amorgós (ΑΜΟΡΓΟΣ)

Easternmost of the Cyclades, Amorgós is also one of the most dramatically rugged islands. On the south coast cliffs plunge vertically into the sea, and trying to cross the island from north to south by road is so rocky a journey that most people prefer to get about by caique. Long and narrow, like Kárpathos in the Dodecanese, it's virtually two islands, with the main port of Katápola in the southwest almost a stranger to Aegiáli in the northeast. For years an island of political exile, Amorgós gradually became a destination for the adventurous, then whoosh!— suddenly travellers arrived en masse seeking the quiet Cycladic life of their dreams, swooping off the ferries until there were people camping out in the streets. There still aren't enough rooms to accommodate everyone in high season, so if you come in August without a reservation be prepared to sleep under the stars.

## History

Both Amorgós and its neighbouring islet Kéros were inhabited as far back as 3300 BC. In 1885 the German archaeologist Dummler uncovered 11 ancient cemeteries, producing many fine ceramics and marbles now to be seen in the museums of Oxford and Copenhagen; artefacts pointed to early trade with Mílos and Egypt. Three ancient independent cities occupied Amorgós, each minting its own coins and worshipping Dionysos and Athena: Kástri (modern Arkesíni) was settled by Naxians, Minoa by Samians, and Aegiáli by Milians.

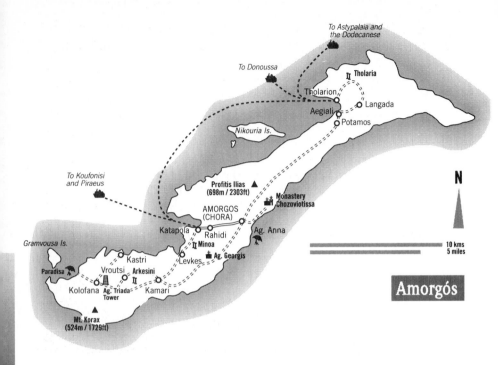

After Alexander the Great, Amorgós came under the rule of his general, Ptolemy of Egypt, who made it a centre of worship of the Alexandrian gods Serapis and Isis. The Romans were the first to use the island as a place of exile, beginning a downhill trend which continued as Goths, Vandals and Slavs savaged and ravaged it during the Byzantine period. One bright moment in this dark history came during the War of the Iconoclasts, when a miraculous icon sailed to Amorgós, set adrift, according to tradition, by a pious lady from Constantinople. As the icon showed a distinct preference for staying by the cliffs on Amorgós' south coast, Emperor Alexis Comnenus founded the Chozoviótissa monastery there in 1088. In 1209 the Duke of Náxos, Marco Sanudo, seized the island, and gave it to the Gizzi, who built the town castle. In spite of the Turkish occupation, Amorgós prospered in the 17th century, mostly from the export of exquisite embroideries made by the women, some of which are now in the Victoria and Albert Museum in London. Between the 17th and 19th centuries so many of these extraordinary pieces were sold that a hero of the War of Independence, General Makriyiánnis, threatened to declare war on Amorgós should the island send any more abroad. Rather than do battle with Makriyiánnis, the island simply ran out of embroideries, and no one today remembers how to make them. Political prisoners were exiled on the island during the sixties under the colonels' junta. The highlight of more recent history was the filming of Luc Besson's cult 1988 movie *The Big Blue*, attracting trendy tourists, especially the French, keen to see the wreck of the *Olympia* to the west of the island which figured largely in the film.

## Getting There and Around

**By sea:** most **ferries** call at both Katápola and Aegiáli but check. Daily links in summer with Náxos, Koufoníssi, Schinoússa and Heráklia; 5 times a week to Donoússa, and to Piraeus via Náxos, Páros, Sýros; 6 times with Tínos; 8 with Mýkonos; twice a week with Píso Livádi on Páros; links with Astypálaia in the Dodecanese, Santoríni, Mílos and Náfplion, plus Rafína via Ándros. **Hydrofoils:** *Ilío* service once a week to Koufoníssi, Schinoússa, Heráklia, Santoríni, Íos, Náxos, Páros, Mýkonos, Tínos and Sýros. **Port authority,** © 71 259.

**By road:** roads are being improved and there is a frequent **bus service** from Katápola to the Chóra (Amorgós town). There are also buses in July and August to Aegiáli via Chóra as well as to the Choziovíotissa Monastery, Ag. Ánna and Paradísi beaches, and to Langáda from Aegiáli. There is also an ancient **taxi** in Katápola; call © 71 255.

## Tourist Information

Information office on the quay in Katápola, © (0285) 71 278; also regular police, © 71 210.

## Festivals

The good people of Amorgós have yet to become bored by tourism, and they go out of their way to invite guests to their celebrations: **26 July**, Ag. Paraskeví at Arkesíni; **15 August** at Langáda and **21 November** at the Chozovíotissa Monastery.

## Katápola and Amorgós Capital

Because of the condition of the road linking the two halves of Amorgós, ships call at both island ports, **Katápola** (ΚΑΤΑΠΟΛΑ) in the south and Aegiáli in the north. Katápola has a pretty horseshoe bay with fishing boats, a handful of authentic tavernas, an open-air disco bar near the beach, which is a bit grotty but beloved of the local ducks, and a great view up to the dazzling white Chóra, above which a line of windmills stand sentinel.

The harbour links three villages—**Xýlokeratídi** at the northern end and Rachídi on the hillside with Katápola in the middle, a bustling, workaday and very Greek port with smallholders selling produce from their trucks and villagers sending parcels via the bus to families in the Chóra. The waterfront is lined with cafés and the hub of life is the ticket agency-cum-*kafeneíon Navtikón Praktoreíon*, where everyone waits for the ferries, old men play with their worry beads and waiters clamber over rucksacks. Katápola is lively in the evenings but Xýlokeratídi a little more laid-back. From Katápola you can walk up the hill to the ancient city of **Minoa** where walls, part of the acropolis, a gymnasium and a few remains of a temple to Apollo can still be seen. The name Minoa comes from Minos, the King of the Mountain, or Minos, the King of Crete, although the great city states of Amorgós, geographically closer to Asia Minor than the other Cyclades, were closely linked to the Ionians. At **Rahídi**, a 45-minute walk east of Katápola, the church of **Ag. Geórgios Balsamíte** (St George the Comforter), is built on the site of an ancient oracle with a sacred spring believed to cure lepers. The islet of **Nikouriá** opposite was once a leper colony. Amorgós has yielded up many Cycladic treasures: the largest figurine in the National Archaeological Museum in Athens was unearthed near Katápola.

The capital, **Amorgós Town**, or **Chóra**, is a typical white Cycladic town, perched more than 400m above sea level. Its dazzling houses spill out beneath a neat column of decapitated windmills—each family had its own—which once laboured with the winds that rose up the dizzying precipices from the sea. With its plane-shaded *plateía* and tasteful gift shops Chóra is a trendy little place, famous for its shadow puppets made for the traditional Karaghiózis theatre; you can see all the characters in the puppet-makers shop on the square. There's also a small **archaeological museum**, but it's rarely open. In the middle of town, steps lead up the rocky mount to the well-preserved Venetian fortress built by Geremia Gizzi in 1290. The locals call it **Apáno Kástro**, and it affords a panoramic view of the island. Chóra also boasts the smallest church in Greece, the chapel of **Ag. Fanoúrios**, with room for just three faithful.

## The Monastery of Chozoviótissa

A road has been built to the island's main sight, the spectacular **Monastery of Chozoviótissa**, and cars have replaced mules as the easiest form of transport. Most people, however, prefer to make the 20-minute walk along the dramatic, serpentine path from the bus stop. Above the dirt track, spilling out stark white from the 180m orange cliffs, the monastery is a huge fortress, resembling one great wall built into the living rock (*open 8–2 and 5–8; donation; modest dress only*). Within are some 50 rooms, two churches and exactly three monks. The miraculous icon of the Madonna, also believed to have been put in the sea by monks from Hozova in the Middle East—hence its name—is still in place, and the library contains 98 hand-written manuscripts. For many years a mysterious spear was stuck in the cliff above the monastery, and, although it finally fell, there are still many stories about it. Keen walkers can also take another route. A steep, rubbly *kalderími* path runs from the helipad in Chóra and is signposted through a gate. It zig-zags down the magnificient natural amphitheatre to the monastery and pebble beaches at **Ag. Ánna**. The series of coves lead to a larger bay, popular with nudists, a trifle sacriligious given the neighbours.

## Arkesíni

The other ancient city in the southern half of Amorgós is **Arkesíni**, which has extensive tombs, walls and houses on the cape of Kástri, near **Vroútsi**, accessible on foot. The easiest way to get there is to take the bus to modern Arkesíni, get off at **Kamári**—there's a taverna—and head north. Another path begins at Minoa near Rahídi and passes through Vroútsi to the well-preserved Hellenistic tower at **Ag. Triás**, known locally as the **Pírgos**, near modern Arkesíni. There are several quiet beaches. **Paradísa** on the west coast is delightful and you can also walk from Kamári to **Notína**, **Moúros** and **Poulopódi**, all clean and calm. Most people who stay in Chóra swim at **Ag. Ánna**, where the water is deep blue and crystal-clear.

## Aegiáli

Although it's easiest to reach the north side of Amorgós by boat, a rough track braves the wild terrain, guarded on either side by an occasional tower (the walk takes about 5 hours). Small and charming **Aegiáli** (ΑΙΓΙΑΛΗ), also known confusingly as **Ormós Aegiáli**, is Amorgós' northern port and main resort, boasting the island's one genuine sandy beach. The tone is young, with many back-packers, and the pace is slow, but that's not what the powers that be want and there are plans in the pipeline to turn the harbour into a yacht marina, fix the roads and run a regular bus service to Katápola. There's a handful of eating places, the island's poshest hotel, and a beachside disco with a chapel in the grounds. Donkeys as well as motorbikes are for hire and there are several excursions available. In some shops here, and in Chóra, you can find embroidered scarves made locally, but they are nothing like the original work that made Amorgós briefly famous. The main beach is sandy but you can follow the path over the headlands to a series of isolated bays from sand to shingle, bathing costumes optional.

From Aegiáli you can take in the scant remains of ancient Aegiáli or the hill villages of **Tholária**, named for its vaulted tholos tombs from the Roman period, and **Langáda**, one of the island's prettiest villages, where the stepped street is painted with daisies and lovehearts. Both villages have rooms, tavernas and a bus service from Aegiáli. But there's also a circular walk along the herb-scented hill ridge linking them and the port; the walk from Langáda's church of the Panagía to Tholária poignantly passes through 'the valley of the old, useless, doomed donkeys' and takes about and hour and a half.

---

*Amorgós ⓒ (0285–)*　　　　　　　　　　　*Where to Stay and Eating Out*

## Katápola

There's the comfortable, upmarket **Hotel Minoa**, ⓒ 71 480 (*C; mod*), set back from the square. **Voula Beach Rooms**, ⓒ 71 221 (*inexp*) near the port police, are simple and set around a garden full of geraniums. The basic but friendly **Pension Amorgos**, ⓒ 71 214 (*mod–inexp*), is handy for the ferry; **Pension Anna**, ⓒ 71 218 (*inexp*) has a rose-covered trellis. **Pension Tasia**, ⓒ 71 313 (*inexp*) offers garden rooms with shared bathroom. Along the beach at Xýlokeratídi, **Kaliope Prekas** ⓒ 71 294 (*inexp*) also has rooms, while in Rahídi **Dimitri's Place**, ⓒ 71 309 (*inexp*), has basic rooms set in a lovely orchard. **Camping Amorgos**, ⓒ 71 257, is signposted from the beach at Katápola, left as you disembark. Grim toilet facilities, pleasant café. *Open July–mid-Sept, reception hours daily 9am–12noon, 6–9pm.* Ag. Ánna beach is also OK for unofficial camping on the south half of the island. The deservedly most popular, but expensive, seafront taverna is **Vitzentos**, where arriving late could mean missing the day's speciality. Try the kid and potato casserole (*patatáto*, the island's speciality), or stuffed aubergines with tomatoes, mushroom, parsley and onion. **Taverna Minos**, at the quieter south end of the waterfront, is an old-fashioned place with good home-cooking; try the tuna *souvláki*. **Psarotoura** is an amiable *psarotavérna* where you choose your fish from wooden trays before it's hurled on to the barbecue. Tourists flock to **Mourayio** but the locals hang out at **O Kamari**, further along the quay. Ferry-hoppers gather over ouzo and *mezédes* at the **Navtikon Praktoreíon**.

## Chóra

There are numerous rooms here but no hotels, although a new rooms complex was on the cards in 1994 and may be ready when you arrive. Just outside the village, **Pension Chora**, ⓒ 71 110 (*mod*) is comfortable with a minibus pick-up service; **Pension To Panorama** at the beginning of the village is small and OK, no phone, while the **Loudaros** family's rooms, ⓒ 71 216/541 (*mod*) are in a pretty house with a walled courtyard. **Klimataria** and **Kastanis** are both good, inexpensive and very Greek tavernas. Chóra also boasts the **Vegera Café Bar**, the trendiest on the island, serving the likes of carrot cake and milkshakes. **Taverna Dimitri** is good for cheap grilled fish and traditional Greek food, and **Café Doza** is an authentic *ouzerie*. **To Steki** in the upper square is always popular with the café crowd late afternoons.

## Aegiáli

Nicest place here is the **Lakki Pension**, ✆ 73 253, ✉ 73 244 (*B; mod*), set back from the beach in a lovely gardens with a tree house for kids. Cycladic-style, immaculate self-contained rooms, excellent food served outdoors from their own taverna. The **Aegialis Hotel**, under the same management, ✆ 73 393, ✉ 73 244 (*B; exp–mod*), is a smart hotel complex with pool and taverna, and a great sea view from the veranda. There's also a minibus service. **The Guest House**, book via Athens ✆ (01) 970 7315 (*inexp*), is an excellent budget option, while the **Mike Hotel**, ✆ 71 252 (*C; mod*) was the port's first hotel and a bit past its sell-by date. *Open only in the summer.* There's a new **campsite** ✆ 73 333 in a field off the Tholaria road, near Pension Lakki, with decent facilities and a café. Those who can't find rooms or don't care to can sleep out on the beach without too many hassles. The favourite grazing ground is **To Limani**, known to all as **Katerina's**, packed out for its great food, wine from the barrel and mellow sounds; the **Korali Restaurant** has tasty fish and the best sunset views.

Up in Langáda, **Taverna Nikos**, ✆ 73 310 (*inexp*) has clean, comfortable rooms and bougainvillaea casacading over the terrace; it specializes in roast kid and baked aubergines and has a German influence; **Yianni's Taverna** is also a good bet. In Tholária, **Vigia Rooms**, ✆ 73 288 (*mod*) are recommended. There are also rooms over the friendly and excellent fish taverna **Adelfi Vekri**, ✆ 73 345/254 (*mod–inexp*). The **Panorama** has wonderful views; **Taverna Tholaria** fills up fast thanks to its good food and an exuberant atmosphere.

---

### Entertainment and Nightlife

Nightlife on Amorgós mainly consists of hanging out at the waterside tavernas and bars or gathering in the Chóra. Along the front at **Xýlokeratídi** the cocktail bar **Le Grand Bleu** is stylish and popular for aperitifs and nightcaps with nightly screenings of the eponymous Luc Besson film. The **Moon Bar** gets packed after dinner but it's a pleasant place to linger over a pricey beer or cocktail and listen to anything from REM to The Doors. In the Chóra, **Kastanis Taverna** sometimes has live Greek music. At Aegiáli there's **Katerina's** and the **Seline Bar** as well as the beach-side **disco**.

## Between Amorgós and Náxos: the Back Islands

Between Amorgós and Náxos lie a bevy of tiny islands, known as the Back Islands because they're in the back of beyond—Schinoússa, Koufoníssi, Donoússa and Heráklia (or Iráklia). The islands all have rooms to rent, Koufoníssi has an hotel, and they all now have a post office and OTE, but phones are erratic. Take plenty of money with you, as there's no bank, and exchanging cash can be a problem. The islands are quiet in low season, with sandy beaches and wonderful walking country. Although Koufoníssi and Heráklia are gearing up for an increase in guests, Donoússa can't cope with the seasonal invasion and fresh produce is scarce. If you plan to stay any length of time, take some food along, and be prepared to be sparing with the water.

**By sea**: the islands are served by the daily **boat** *Skopelitis*, which rolls and buckets its way between Náxos and Amorgós, and the occasional **ferry** from Piraeus. There are two ferries a week via Sýros, Páros and Náxos and via Sýros, Tínos and Mýkonos. There is also a **catamaran** in July and August from the Trocadero marina, 8km east of Piraeus at Flísvos, to Donoússa, Amorgós, Koufoníssi, Schinoússa and Heráklia. The **hydrofoil** from Amorgós also calls in at the islands apart from Donoússa.

## Koufoníssi (ΚΟΥΦΟΝΗΣΙ)

Koufoníssi is actually two islands, **Páno** and **Káto**, upper and lower Koufoníssi, but only Páno is inhabited; Káto is home to goats and goatherds. Páno Koufoníssi, the least primitive of the Back Islands, is tiny—you can walk around it in about three hours—and it has a thriving fishing fleet so doesn't depend on tourism. Once a hideaway discovered by intrepid independent travellers, it now gets jammed in July and August with trendy Athenians and Italians mainly into spear-fishing and perfecting their tans. The *meltémi* rages at exactly the same time, and has been known to blast tents into space from the free but unsheltered campsite by **Fínikas Beach**. The village, on a low hill above the quay, has its back to the sea. Life centres on the cobbled main street; in summer it turns into a big party and fashion parade with batik-clad island-hoppers carousing at the tables outside every taverna and *ouzerie*. Koufoníssi has gorgeous beaches tucked under golden rocks. The first, **Fínikas**, east of the village, is lined with sleeping bags in high season. Topless is in, nudism out, and there are two tavernas. Over a rocky spit there are two more lovely beaches, **Charakópou** and **Porí**. There are daily excursions in season on the caique *Prásinos* to **Káto Koufoníssi** for swimming and you may also be able to take a trip to the island of **Kéros**, ancient Karos, which has the ruins of a Neolithic settlement at **Daskálio** on the west coast, and an abandoned medieval settlement in the north.

### Tourist Information

**Port police**: ✆ (0285) 71 375; the **travel agency** or *praktoreíon*, on the main village street next door to post office, ✆ 71 438, changes money; the owner sells ferry tickets on the quay and runs excursions.

✆ *(0285–)*                                   *Where to Stay*

If room-owners don't meet you at the ferries, try the crop of *domátia* to rent at the beginning of the village. There's a free campsite to the east of the port behind Fínikas beach, with two areas each fronted by tavernas. The **Hotel Finikas**, ✆ 71 368 (*C; mod*) has self-contained double rooms in a cluster of white buildings near Fínikas beach. The owner meets ferries with his minibus. There are also inexpensive rooms to let over the main taverna **Afroessa** and the newer **Soroccos**. Behind the port, **O Lefteris Restaurant**, ✆ 71 458 (*mod*) has reasonable rooms plus a bar and children's playground. **Katerina's Rooms**, ✆ 71 455 (*mod*), with ebullient landlady, are just up the hill from the port.

Taverna Melissa on the main street is great value, with Greek favourites served on the terrace; **Afroessa** is also popular, as is **O Lefteris** on the front. In the village the **Ouzerie** serves octopus, *kalamári* and shrimps from an outside brazier, and there's also a **gyro** place. *Evenings only.* At night the snazzy **Kalamia Bar** plays loud rock and **The Mill**, an old windmill atop the village converted into a bar which is a great place to watch the sun set.

## Schinoússa (ΣΧΟΙΝΟΥΣΣΑ)

**Schinoússa**, scenically less attractive than the other small islands, is also getting popular although it's still very Greek and very charming. There are only 85 inhabitants in winter, in summer around 200, most of them farmers trying to make ends meet. Ferries dock at the tiny port of **Myrsíni** with a good taverna and rooms to let, but the main settlement is the **Chóra**, also known as **Schinoússa**, less than a mile up the hill. You can take the old cobbled mule track for a short-cut. Chóra has rooms to rent and village life goes on regardless of tourists. From there a steep track runs down to the grey sand beach at **Tsigoúra**, fringed by tamarisk trees, with a rather expensive taverna and disco and plans for a bar and gelateria. There are about seventeen beaches on the island, many bleak and littered by the wind, but **Psilí Ámmos** is worth the 45-minute walk from Chóra across the island via the hamlet of **Messariá**. A rough cobbled track takes you to the duny sands with crystalline turquoise waters; in summer it's a favourite unofficial camping spot. Schinoússa is blessed with fresh springs, and a species of mastic bush grows on its relatively flat terrain.

### Tourist Information

No **tourist police**. There is a **tourist centre** agency in Chóra, ℗ (0285) 71 175, ✆ 71 176, at the top of the mule path from Myrsíni, run from a mini-market, which arranges accommodation, ferry tickets and round-island trips. Tickets are also available from Taverna Myrsini and the Panorama Taverna. All three are in radio contact with the *Skopelítis*.

In the Chóra, **Hotel Anesi** ℗ 71 180 (*mod*) is on the main street with wonderful views. *Open June to Oct.* Nearby, **Pension Pothiti** ℗ 71 179 (*inexp*) has simple rooms minus bath. Other rooms to let are over the **Panorama Taverna**, which also supplies basic home cooking and great views to Tsigoúra. It's friendly and family-run with locals playing backgammon. **To Kentro** general store cum *kafeneíon* serves beer, snacks and pungent home-made cheese; **Restaurant Skhinoussa** does the usual Greek fare and pizzas.

In Myrsíni the **Taverna Myrsini**, ℗ 71 154, is deceptive. Its spartan kitchen conjures up delicious seafood in the evenings and it doubles as a left-luggage store by day. There are clean, simple rooms above **Restaurant Snack Bar**, ℗ 71 159, which serves everything from breakfast to burgers, octopus and ouzo under its vine-clad trellis.

## Donoússa (ΔΟΝΟΥΣΑ)

**Donoússa**, east of Náxos, and northernmost of the chain, is more isolated than the others, reached by ferry from Piraeus, or the *Skopelítis* from Náxos or Amorgós. Larger and more mountainous than Schinoússa and Koufoníssi, it's a good place for walkers and hermits. The harbour village has rooms to let, three tavernas and a shop, and resources are stretched with the influx of tourists in high season. There's a summer-only bakery, but food and water can get scarce. A Geometric-era settlement (900–700 BC) was excavated on the island, but most of its visitors come for its fine sandy beaches at **Kéndros** and **Livádi**, reached via the fertile hamlets of **Charavyí** and **Mersíni**.

## Heráklia (ΗΡΑΚΛΕΙΑ)

**Heráklia**, or Iráklia, the most westernly and the largest of the Back Islands, is only a short ferry hop from Náxos, but even in mid-August it remains quiet and friendly. Unusually for the Cyclades, it's a good time to visit and join in the celebrations for the Festival of the Panagía on August 15, with three days of non-stop eating, drinking and dancing. There are rooms to let in the attractive port, **Ag. Geórgios**, set in a fertile valley, and from here it's a 20-minute walk to the large sandy beach at **Livádi**, popular with Greek families and campers. The old **Chóra**, **Panagía**, named after its main church, is about an hour's walk into the hills, but you might hitch a lift with the baker. It's sleepy and primitive with many abandoned houses, and it's unlikely you'll find anywhereto stay. There is, however, an excellent **bakery**—the baker picks wild sesame seeds for his bread on his journey from the port. From Panagía a path leads to sandy **Alimniás Beach**. Another excursion is to walk along the mule path from Ag. Athanásio or Panagía to the large cave of **Ag. Ioánni**, overlooking Vourkaria Bay, then back along the west coast to Ag. Geórgios.

*© (0285–)*                                      ***Where to Stay and Eating Out***

In Ag. Geórgios there are basic, inexpensive rooms above **I Melissa**, *©* 71 539/561, a taverna, *kafeneíon* and general store with a good budget menu; there are also rooms above the nameless waterside taverna, call *©* 71 488. **Restaurant Dimitris Gavalas** is the best eating place with Greek dishes, sometimes pizza, served beneath the  pine tree. **Restaurant Livadi** on the beach at Livádi serves good food and plays old *rembétika* songs and has rooms to let (*inexp*). The owner Geórgios organizes boat trips to Alimniás Beach and meets the ferries with his truck. In Panagía, the spasmodi-cally open **Taverna O Niko** has simple dishes served out on a shady terrace and there are two *kafeneia*, the one near the church selling local hard cheese.

## Anáfi (ΑΝΑΦΗ)

Anáfi, the most southerly of the Cyclades, is a primitive island, difficult to get to and short on amenities. But it's friendly and unpretentious, the ideal place for peace and solitude. Even food can be in short supply, so it may be worth bringing along some provisions to supplement what's on offer locally, mainly fish and macaroni. If the crowds and noise seem too thick else-where, Anáfi may be the antidote: the islanders go about their lives as they always have, with no concessions to tourism. But be warned: if the weather breaks ferries may not dock and you could easily get marooned, so give yourself plenty of time to get back. Little contact with the outside world has meant that several old customs have been preserved, and some scholars have found in the Anáfiots' songs and festivals traces of the ancient worship of Apollo.

## The Island of Over-sexed Partridges

Apollo always had a particularly strong cult on Anáfi. Myth has it that Jason and the Argonauts were sailing from Crete after killing the bronze giant Talus with the help of Medea (*see* p.131) when a violent storm kicked up. At Apollo's command, an island—Anáfi—rose from the waves to shelter them. Anáfi was the island the most closely associated with partridges (one of Talus' other names was Perdix, 'partridge'), a bird much noted even back then for its lascivious behaviour; Aristotle and Pliny wrote that a hen partridge merely had to hear or smell a cock partridge to become impregnated, and further noted that if the females were out of commission on their nests, the males practiced sodomy to relieve their sexual feelings. Partridges become so obsessed during their ritual mating dances that they don't even notice if someone comes up and kills a few of the dancers next to them. The ancient Greeks used this knowledge to catch them, luring them into their traps with decoys—a lusty male partridge they had captured and hobbled so it couldn't fly away. The ideas of a ritual dance and death lure, of a hobbled male (remember, Medea killed Talus by pulling the plug from his heel) and 'virgin' births are all potent images in the mythopoeic mind, and it has been suggested that the Minoan bull cult on Crete supplanted a partridge cult, that the spiral dancing at Knossós began as a ritual partridge dance, and that the Minotaur was the original decoy to lure in sacrificial victims. On Anáfi, according to the descriptions that have come down to us, the rites of Apollo (who after all began his career *c.* 1200 BC as a mouse demon before usurping other gods' turf) were those of Radiant Apollo, the Sun God, but infused with a good deal of good old-fashioned partridge eroticism.

## History

Anáfi's history isn't quite as exciting as its mythology, although in the 15th century BC, it gained a certain stature in the form of volcanic rock, 5m thick in some places, carried to the island by wind and tidal wave after the explosion of Santoríni. The twelfth Duke of Náxos, Giacomo Crispi, gave Anáfi to his brother who built a castle, but his fortification had little effect when the terror of the Aegean, Barbarossa, turned up and enslaved the entire population. Anáfi remained deserted for a long time after that, until the seas were safer. Anafiot migrant workers built houses in the island style at the foot of the Acropolis in Athens, taking advantage of the law that stated that if you could erect four walls and a roof by sunrise, the place was yours.

### *Getting There*

By sea: ferries twice a week connecting with Piraeus, Santoríni, Íos, Náxos and Páros, once a week with Amorgós and Sýros; occasional catamaran from other Cyclades islands and Piraeus. Port authority, © 61 216.

**15 August**, Panagía at the monastery, known for its authentic folk-dances.

## Around the Island

The island's one village, **Chóra**, with some 300 people, is a short but steep walk up a hill path from the landing, **Ag. Nikólaos**, or a longer hike by the road. Another path east of Chóra leads to **Katalimátsa**, with a few ruins of ancient houses, and eventually to the island's main attraction, the **Monastery of Panagía Kalamiótissa**. Spectacularly perched on the island's tadpole-tail peninsula, it stands near the remains of the ancient temple to Apollo, dedicated by the grateful Jason. The **Monastery of Zoodóchos Pigí** nearby was built with masonry from the ancient temple. Guglielmo Crispi's **Kástro** is to the north of the village and half-ruined; a path leads up to its rocky height. There are attractive **beaches** along the coast around Ag. Nikólaos, from **Klisídi** east of the port, with a popular snack bar, to a range of bays signposted from the Chóra road.

---

*Anáfi ✆ (0286–)* **Where to Stay**

Room-owners meet the ferries and travel down from the Chóra by bus. It's best to follow them as the road up is no joke with luggage. Try the rooms let out by **Ioannis Halaris** ✆ 61 271 and **Manolis Loudaros**, ✆ 61 279 (*inexp*). Otherwise, there are some so-so pensions in the port, rooms to let at **Klisidi Beach** (*inexp*) and six beds in the community guest house. Ask around if you're not offered a room from the ferry.

---

*Anáfi ✆ (0286–)* **Eating Out**

In the Chóra **To Steki** is cheap and cheerful, **Alexandra's** more upmarket. **Kyriakos** is another option for dinner. The **Crazy Shrimp** piano bar is about the sum total of nightlife. In Ag. Nikólaos many tourists seem to like **Roussos Taverna**.

## Ándros (ΑΝΔΡΟΣ)

Lush and green on one side, scorched and barren on the other, split-personality Ándros is the northernmost and second largest of the Cyclades. It's long been a haunt for wealthy Athenian shipping magnates who descend for long stays in high summer and breed horses on their spectacular country estates in the wooded hills. Package holidaymakers, mainly from the UK, Germany and Scandinavia, are more recent arrivals on the scene. And as it's easy to reach from Rafína, Ándros is also a popular weekend playground for trendy young Athenians who patronize the island's chic cocktail bars, discos and the odd toga party.

In the south only the narrowest of straits separates Ándros from Tínos, while in the barren north the blustery Doro Channel, long dreaded by sailors, divides the island from Évia. However, the same irksome wind also makes Ándros, and especially its capital, one of the coolest spots in the Aegean in July and August. Verdant with flowers, orchards and forests in the south, the island's patchwork of fields are criss-crossed with distinctive dry stone walls, *xerolithiés*, split from the local schist, with flat upright pieces of slate at intervals. Water gushes from marble drinking fountains and mossy springs in the hill villages, and Ándros is famous for its Sáriza mineral water, the Greek answer to Perrier. Years ago people came to take the waters: now the lure is the sea. Ándros is a prosperous island, neat, well-ordered, adorned with white dovecotes first built by the Venetians and famed for its captains and shipowners; many from elsewhere come here to retire.

## History

Originally known as Hydroussa ('watery'), the island's name is thought to be derived from the Phoenician Arados, or from Andrea, the general sent by Rhadamanthys of Crete to govern the island. In 1000 BC Ionians colonized Ándros, leading to its early cultural bloom in the Archaic period. Dionysos was the most popular god worshipped at the pantheon of Palaiopolis, the leading city at the time, and a certain temple of his had the remarkable talent of turning water into wine during the Dionysia.

For most of the rest of its history, Ándros has been the square peg in a round archipelago. After the Athenian victory at Salamis, Themistocles fined Ándros for supporting Xerxes. The Andrians refused to pay up, and Themistocles besieged the island, but was unsuccessful and had to return home empty-handed. Although the islanders later assisted the Greeks at Plateía, Athens continued to hold a grudge against Ándros, and in 448 BC Pericles divided the island between Athenian colonists, who taxed the inhabitants heavily. In response, the Andrians abetted Athens' enemies whenever they could: when the Peloponnesian War broke out, they withdrew from the Delian league and sided with Sparta, supporting those neurotic reactionaries throughout the war, in spite of another Athenian siege led by Alcibiades and Konon. Spartan oppression, however, proved just as awful as Athenian oppression, and things were no better during the succession of Hellenistic rulers, although a magnificent statue of Hermes, the Conductor of the Dead, dating from the 1st or 2nd century BC, found at Palaiópolis, suggests that at least art survived the constant change of bosses. For resisting their inevitable conquest, the Romans banished the entire population of Ándros to Boetia, and gave the island to Attalos I, King of Pergamon. When permitted to return, the inhabitants found their homes sacked and pillaged. Byzantium proved a blessing compared with the past, despite Saracen pirate raids. In the Venetian free-for-all following the Fourth Crusade, another nephew of Doge Enrico Dandolo, Marino Dandolo, took Ándros, and allied himself with his cousin Marco Sanudo, the Duke of Náxos. Most of the surviving fortifications were constructed under the Dandoli.

In 1566 the Turks took the island. Apart from collecting taxes, they left it more or less to its own devices, and 10,000 Albanians, many from nearby Kárystos (Évia) settled on Ándros. In 1821 Ándros' famous son, the philosopher Theóphilos Kaíris, declared the revolution at the cathedral of Ándros, and the island contributed large sums of money and weapons to the struggle. In 1943 the Germans bombed the island for two days when the Italians stationed there refused to surrender.

### Getting There and Around

**By sea**: daily **ferry** and **hydrofoil** connections with Rafína, Tínos and Mýkonos, less often with Sýros, 3 times a week with Páros, Náxos, Kos and Rhodes, once a week with Astypálaia, Kálymnos, and Amorgós. **Port authority**, © 22 250.

**By road: buses** run from Chóra to Batsí, Gávrion, Apoíkia, Strapouriés, Steniés, and Kórthi; buses for Batsí, Chóra and Kórthi leave from near the

dock at Gávrion, linking with the ferries. For schedules, call ✆ 22 316. **Cars** and **bikes** are widely available for rent.

---

### *Tourist Information*

There is a sporadically opening **tourist office** in a converted dovecote in Gávrion, but no tourist police. The Dolphin Hellas travel office in Batsí is very helpful, ✆ (0282) 41 185; so is Batis Travel in Gávrion, ✆ 71 040, 📠 71 165 for tickets and accommodation. Regular **police**, Gávrion, ✆ 71 220 or Chóra, ✆ 22 300; the latter keeps a list of rooms.

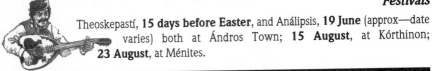

Theoskepastí, **15 days before Easter**, and Análipsis, **19 June** (approx—date varies) both at Ándros Town; **15 August**, at Kórthinon; **23 August**, at Ménites.

## Gávrion and the West Coast

All ferries dock at the main port, **Gávrion** (ΓΑΒΡΙΟ) on the northwest coast of Ándros, a workaday charmless, dusty dump, enough to make you turn tail. It may be a ploy to repel independent travellers—most accommodation on the island is block-booked by package companies and Gávrion might be the only place you'll find rooms in high season. But there's a beach, plenty of bars and tavernas, and a good campsite with a poolside restaurant. From Gávrion (local signs knock off the 'n') it's a 40-minute or so walk east up to **Ag. Pétros**, the best-preserved ancient monument on Ándros. Dating from the Hellenistic era, this mysterious tower stands some 20m high—the upper storeys were reached by ladder—and its inner hall is still crowned by a corbelled dome. The landscape around here seems to squirm with stone walls, or *xerolithiés*, resembling huge, arched caterpillars. There are good beaches north of Gávrion via **Vassamia** which has two sandy coves. **Felós Beach** is the best but Athenians are developing the coastline with villas. **Amólochos**, on the road crossing the island to the remote beach at Vitáli Bay is an isolated mountain village famous locally for its beauty.

Off the coastal road 8km south, the 14th-century convent of **Zoodóchos Pigí**, 'Spring of Life', has icons from that century onwards. A handful of nuns run a weaving factory (*open until noon*). **Batsí** (ΜΠΑΤΣΙ), built around a sweeping sandy bay to the south, is a pretty resort and the island's biggest, with a little fishing harbour and a maze of narrow lanes reached by white steps from the bustling seafront. The BBC TV series *Greek Language and People* put it on the map, and it's been very popular with UK package companies ever since. The tree-fringed town beach gets busy with families, so head along the coastal track to **Delavóyas Beach** for an all-over tan or further along to lovely **Ag. Marína**, with a friendly family-run taverna. From Batsí a road ascends to shady well-watered **Arnás**, a garden village on the northern slopes of Ándros' highest peak, Mount Pétalo (994m).

**Ancient Palaiópolis**, 9km down the coast, was the original capital of Ándros, founded by the Minoan Andrea, and inhabited until around 1000 when the people moved to Mesariá. An earthquake in the 4th century AD destroyed part of it, and over the years pirates mopped up the rest. The current version of Palaiópolis is on top of a steep hill, from where 1039 steps lead down to the site, partly underwater; there are walls and part of the acropolis, and ruins of buildings and temples. Beyond Palaiópolis, **Stavrópeda** stands at the junction for Ándros town and Kórthion, a road passing through rolling countryside dotted with pigeon-houses.

## Andros Town/Chóra

The capital, alternatively known as **Ándros town** (ΑΝΔΡΟΣ) or **Chóra** (ΧΩΡΑ), sits on a long, narrow tongue of land, decorated with the grand neoclassical mansions built by the island's ship-owning families. At the edge of the town an arched bridge leads to the Venetian castle, **Mésa Kástro**, built by Marino Dandolo and damaged in the 1943 bombardment, now watched over by the heroic statue of the **Unknown Sailor** by Michael Tómbros in **Plateía Ríva**. There's a small **museum** dedicated to Ándros' seafaring history, but you may have to ask around for the key. Below, at a spot called **Kámara**, the locals dive into the sea. **Káto Kástro**, the maze of streets that form the medieval city and the mansions of the Ríva district are wedged between **Parapórti** and **Embórios** bays with steps down from the central square, **Plateía Kaíri**. The beaches are sandy but often windswept, and holiday bungalows and rooms to let are springing up at Embórios, where the ferries used to dock.

The pedestrianized main street, paved with marble slabs and scented with cheese and custard pies made at the local bakery, is lined with old mansions converted into public offices; post and telephone offices and banks are in the centre of town, and the bus station just a few steps away. A small white church, **Ag. Thalassíni**, guards one end of Embórios harbour from a throne of rock. The cathedral, **Ag. Geórgios**, is built on the ruins of a 17th-century church. A legend is told about a third church, **Theoskepastí**, built in 1555. When the wood for the church's roof arrived in Ándros from Piraeus, the priest found that he couldn't afford the price demanded by the captain of the ship. Angrily, the captain set sail again, only to run into a fierce, boiling tempest. The sailors prayed to the Virgin Mary, promising to bring the wood back to Ándros should she save their lives. Instantly the sea grew calm again, and Theoskepastí, or 'Sheltered by God', was completed without further difficulty. It was dedicated to the Virgin Mary, who apparently is on a hotline to the miracle-working icon inside the church.

Just north of Plateía Kaíris are the museums endowed by Basil and Elise Goulandrís of the ship owning dynasty. The outstanding **Archaeology Museum**, built in 1981 (*open Tues–Sun 8.30–3; adm*) is famous for the *Hermes of Ándros*, the 2nd-century real McCoy—apparently copied from a Praxiteles original but still spectacular. Other exhibits include the *Matron of Herculaneum*, finds from the ancient cities of Zagora and Palaiópolis, architectural illustrations and pottery collections. The island's other gem, the **Museum of Modern Art**, in Plateía Kaíris (*open Wed–Mon, 10–2 and 6–9*) occupies two buildings, with exhibitions of international modern artists, important contemporary Greek artists, and sculptures by Michael Tómbros.

## Villages Outside Chóra

Lovely villages surround Chóra: **Steniés**, 6km north, is the most beautiful village on the island and a botanist's dream. Closed to traffic, the village is heavy with the scent of flowers and fruit blossom in spring. The pebbly beach, **Gialyá**, is close by, with a good but pricey fish taverna. The famous Sáriza mineral water is bottled in the hill village of **Apíkia**, above Steniés, where a luxury hotel overlooks the spring. The village owns the 16th-century monastery **Ag. Nikólaos** to the north. The main road to the west coast passes through the fertile **Messariá Valley** with its numerous farming villages. One old custom may still be heard: in the evening after a hard day's work, the patriarch will pipe the family home from the fields.

The road leads to lush, green **Ménites** where springs gush out of the hillside from marble lion-head fountains, and ends at the church of **Panagías tis Kóumoulous**, the 'Virgin of the Plentiful', which may have been the site of Dionysos' miraculous temple. The village is known for its nightingales, cool, spreading trees and there's a peaceful taverna overlooking the stream. Nearby **Messariá** has a Byzantine church of the **Taxiárchis** built in 1158 BC by the Emperor Emmanuel Comnenus. Messariá was the home of an 18th-century nun, a faith-healer who made an icon of Ag. Nikólaos from her own hair, which you can still see in the church of the saint (1732). From there an hour's steep walk takes you to the most important monastery on Ándros, **Panachrándou**, home to just three monks, founded shortly after Niképhoros Phokás' liberation of Crete in AD 961, and supposedly visited by the emperor himself.

Southwest of Messariá, at **Aladinó**, a stalactite cave called Cháos may be visited—bring a light—the villagers know its location as Lasthinóu.

The **Bay of Kórthion** (KOPΘI) is 30km southeast of Ándros town, with a beach, hotel and rooms. The fishing here is excellent, but if they're not biting you can always eat in one of the seafood tavernas along the waterfront. To the north of the bay, the ruined **Castle of the Old Woman** is named after a gritty old lady who abhorred the Venetians. She tricked them into letting her inside the fort, and later secretly opened the door to the Turks. Appalled at the subsequent slaughter of the Venetians, the old woman leapt from the castle and landed on a rock now known as '**Tis Grias to Pidema** ' or 'Old Lady's Leap'. Just to the north of Kórthion is **Palaiókastro**, another fortification built by Dandolo and now in ruins. On the west coast, **Zagora** was inhabited until the 8th century BC, when it boasted a population of 4000; it was solidly defended, for sheer cliffs surrounded it on three sides, while on the fourth the Zagorans built a mighty wall. Within, inhabitants lived in small, flat-roofed houses (some remains still exist) and cultivated the fields outside the wall. Excavated by Australians in the 1960s, finds from Zagora are now in the island's museum.

---

*Ándros ℗ (0282–)*  **Where to Stay and Eating Out**

Like Kéa, Ándros is an island where the tourism infrastructure is geared to long-term stays, and it may well be difficult, especially in the capital, to find a hotel or pension that will let you stay for only a few nights. However there are *domátia* signs and some owners meet the ferries. Despite its popularity, prices in Ándros remain realistic, unlike Mýkonos or Santoríni.

### Gávrion

The smartest place is the the the mini-complex Ándros **Holiday Hotel**, ℗ 71 443, ℮ 71 097 (*B; exp–mod*), on the beach with half-board, swimming pool, tennis, sauna and gym. **Ostria Studios**, ℗ 71 551, ℮ 71 554 (*C; mod*) are upmarket self-catering apartments just out of town; **Hotel Galaxy**, ℗ 71 228 (*mod–inexp*) and **Hotel Aphrodite** ℗ 71 209, are both nice pensions (*mod–inexp*). The Galaxy is handy for the ferry and the Aphrodite has a good restaurant. **Camping Andros**, ℗ 71 444, is an excellent site along the Batsí road with a minimarket, swiming pool, outstanding taverna and a van to meet the ferries. For lunch or dinner try **O Valmas** near the port police, which has Greek specialities. **O Mourikis** and **Three Star** are also recommended. The **Sunset Restaurant** en route to the Ándros Holiday Hotel also has an excellent kitchen where you can try the Ándros speciality, *froutália*, a Cycladic slant on the Spanish omelette made with local sausage. The **En Gavrio** café-cum-*ouzerie* on the front serves breakfast. **Petros** is also OK for Greek staples, and the **San Remo** for Italian.

### Batsí

There are some small pensions and rooms to let if you head up the steps or out towards the Apróvato neighbourhood. But it's not really a big centre for independent travellers. **St George's Studios**, ℗ 41 591 (*A; exp*) are self-contained with verandas overlooking the bay. The pink, blue and banana-shaded **Aneroussa Beach Hotel**, ℗ 41 444 (*B; exp–mod, inc. breakfast*), tops the cliff at Aprovato like an iced cake and has its own private sands next to Delavóyos Beach, popular with nudists. **Chryssi**

**Akti**, ✆ 41 236 (*C; inexp*) is OK, on the beach; the smaller **Hotel Skouna**, ✆ 41 240 (*C; inexp*) is also a good seafront bet; the **Avra**, ✆ 41 216 (*inexp*) is the cheapest pension with shared facilities. The wide range of eateries for all tastes do justice to Ándros' old reputation as an island of chefs. Try **To Steki** up the steps from the waterfront or **O Takis** for fish, or **Taverna Tikalo** for reasonably priced dishes. The taverna opposite the Dolphin Hellas agency is excellent, famous for its lamb parcels.

## Apíkia

The swish **Hotel Pigi Sarisa** ✆ 23 799/999, ✉ 22 476 (*B; exp*), almost on top of the famous mineral spring, is a holiday complex with a pool and games facilities, restaurant and minibus for transfers. *Open all year.* There are also rooms to let in the village and a pension, an offshoot of the Hotel Egli in Chóra. At Ménites the **Kardyies Restaurant** has tables overlooking the stream and specialities like *froutália* and tomatoes stuffed with chicken.

## Chóra

The elegant **Paradise Hotel**, ✆ 22 187, ✉ 22 340 (*B; exp*) is a graceful, neoclassical confection near the centre of town. **Hotel Egli**, ✆ 22 303, ✉ 22 159 (*C; mod*), between the two squares, has recently been renovated and is good value. *Open all year.* The **Xenia**, ✆ 22 270 (*B; mod*) is another option or there are inexpensive rooms to let at Embórios near the beach. **Petros Stathakis** has suites, ✆ 22 905, or try **Efthimia Firiou** ✆ 22 921. **Irene's Villas**, by the sea ✆ 23 344 (*exp–mod*) are charming, set in lush flower garden, and sleep 4–6. *Open all year.* The island's best restaurants are in here, **Platanos** and **Delfinia**, while on the main square, humming with cafés and tavernas, the **Parea Restaurant** has an excellent Greek menu and **Mitsakis** is good. If you want to go upmarket the Ándros yacht club **Naftikos Omilos** at Embórios has a restaurant and is open to non-members.

## Kórthion

Family-run **Hotel Korthion**, ✆ 61 218, ✉ 61 118 (*C; inexp*) is spotless; the **Pension Rainbow**, ✆ 61 344 (*inexp*) is another pleasant choice.

---

### *Entertainment and Nightlife*

Ándros, especially Batsí, is full of slick cocktail bars, dancing bars and discos and you can be hard-pressed to find any authentic Greek music and entertainment, outside of organised **Greek nights** at three tavernas in the village of Káto Katákilos. There's an open-air **cinema** in Batsí and trendy bars which change names from season to season. The **Gallery** is a classy favourite on the front with a wide range of cocktails and sometimes theme parties; **Caligula** up on the hill is a dancing bar with a Roman touch. The **Disco Blue Sky** sometimes switches to Greek music towards the end of the night. Bars like **Chaf, Nameless, Cocomo** and **Platanos** swing with international tourists throughout the season. In Gávrion you can hang out at the **Idrossia Bar** on Ag. Pétros beach or head for the **Disco Marabout**. In Chóra, nightlife centres round the bars and the **Disco Remezzo** pitched at Greek clients. Among the daytime entertainments are guided walks and donkey treks to the hill villages.

# Délos (ΔΗΛΟΣ)

Délos, holy island of the ancient Greeks, centre of the great maritime alliance of the Athenian golden age, and hub of the Cyclades, is now a vast open-air museum. A major free port in Hellenistic and Roman times that controlled much of the east–west trade in the Mediterranean, today it's completely deserted except for the lonely guardian of the ruins— and the boatloads of day-trippers. Even though the ancients allowed no burials on Délos, the islet is haunted by memories of the 'splendour that was Greece'; the Delians themselves have been reincarnated as little lizards, darting among the poppies and broken marble.

## Mythology

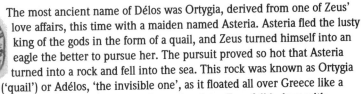 The most ancient name of Délos was Ortygia, derived from one of Zeus' love affairs, this time with a maiden named Asteria. Asteria fled the lusty king of the gods in the form of a quail, and Zeus turned himself into an eagle the better to pursue her. The pursuit proved so hot that Asteria turned into a rock and fell into the sea. This rock was known as Ortygia ('quail') or Adélos, 'the invisible one', as it floated all over Greece like a submarine just below the surface of the sea. Some time later Zeus fell in love with Asteria's sister Leto, and, despite the previous failure of the bird motif, succeeded in making love to her in the form of a swan—the subject of some of the most erotic fancies produced by Michelangelo and other artists in the Renaissance.

But Zeus' humourless, jealous, Thurberesque wife Hera soon got wind of the affair and begged Mother Earth not to allow Leto to give birth anywhere under the sun. All over the world wandered poor, suffering, overripe Leto, unable to find a rock to stand on, as all feared the wrath of Hera. Finally in pity Zeus turned to his brother Poseidon and asked him to lend a hand. Poseidon thereupon ordered Ortygia to halt, and anchored the islet with four columns of diamond. Thus Adélos the Invisible, not under the sun but under the sea, became Délos, the Visible. Délos, however, was still reluctant to have Leto, fearing her divine offspring would give the island a resounding kick back into the sea. But Leto promised the islet that no such thing would happen; indeed, her son would make Délos the richest sanctuary in Greece. The island conceded, and Leto gave birth first to Artemis, goddess of the hunt and virginity, and then nine days later to Apollo, the god of truth and light.

## History

In the 3rd millennium BC Délos was settled by people from Caria in Asia Minor. By 1000 BC the Ionians had made it their religious capital, centred around the cult of Apollo, the father of Ion, the founder of their race—a cult first mentioned in a Homeric hymn of the 7th century BC. Games and pilgrimages took place, and Délos was probably the centre of the Amphictyonic maritime league of the Ionians. In 550 BC Polycrates, the Tyrant of Samos, conquered the Cyclades but respected the sanctity of Délos, putting the islet Rheneia under its control, and symbolically binding it to Délos with a chain. With the rise of Athens, notably under Pisistratos, began the greatest glory and greatest difficulties of Délos. What was once sacred began to take on a political significance, and the Athenians invented stories to connect themselves to the islet—did not Erechtheus, the King of Athens, lead the first delegation to

Délos? After slaying the Minotaur on Crete did not Theseus stop at Délos and dance around the altar of Apollo? In 543 BC the Athenians even managed to trick (or bribe) the oracle at Delphi into ordering the purification of the island, which meant removing the old tombs, a manoeuvre designed to alienate the Delians from their past and diminish the island's importance in comparison to Athens.

In 490 BC the population of Délos fled to Tínos before the Persian king of kings, Darius, who, according to Herodotus, not only respected the sacred site and sacrificed 300 talents' worth of incense to Apollo, but allowed the Delians to return home in safety. After the Persian defeat at the Battle of Salamis the Athenians, to counter further invasions, organized a new Amphictyonic league, again centred at Délos. Only the Athenian fleet could guarantee protection to the islands, who in return were required to contribute a yearly sum and ships to support the navy. Athenian archons administered the funds. The Delian alliance was effective, despite resentment among islanders who disliked being bossed around by the Athenians. No one was fooled in 454 BC when Pericles, in order better to 'protect' the league's treasury, removed it to Athens' acropolis; the money went not only to repair damage incurred during the previous Persian invasion, but to beautify Athens generally. Shortly afterwards, divine retribution hit Athens in the form of a terrible plague, and as it was determined to have been caused by the wrath of Apollo, a second purification of Délos (not Athens, mind) was called for in 426 BC. This time, not only did the Athenians remove all the old tombs, but they forbade both births and death on Délos, forcing the pregnant and the dying to go to Rheneia and completing the alienation of the Delians. When the people turned to Sparta for aid during the Peloponnesian War, the Spartans remained unmoved: since the inhabitants couldn't be born or die on the island, they reasoned that Délos wasn't really their homeland, and why should they help a group of foreigners? In 422 BC Athens punished Délos for courting Sparta by exiling the entire population (for being 'impure') to Asia Minor, where all the leaders were slain by cunning. Athenian settlers moved in to take the Delians' place, but Athens herself was punished by the gods for her greed and suffered many setbacks against Sparta. After a year, hoping to regain divine favour, Athens allowed the Delians to return. In 403 BC, when Sparta defeated Athens, Délos had a breath of freedom for ten years before Athens formed its second Delian alliance. It was far less forceful, and 50 years later the Delians had plucked up the courage to ask the league to oust the Athenians altogether. But the head of the league at the time, Philip II of Macedon, refused the request, wishing to stay in the good graces of the city that hated him most.

In the confusion following the death of Philip's son, Alexander the Great, Délos became free and prosperous, supported by the pious Macedonian general-kings. New buildings and shrines were constructed and by 250 BC Délos was a flourishing cosmopolitan commercial port, inhabited by merchants from all over the Mediterranean. When the Romans defeated the Macedonians in 166 BC they returned the island to Athens, which once again exiled the Delians. But by 146 BC and the fall of Corinth, Délos was the centre of all east–west trade, and declared a free port by the Romans in order to undermine the competition at Rhodes. People came from all over the world to settle in this ancient Greek Hong Kong, and set up their own cults in complete tolerance. Roman trade guilds centred on the Italian Agora. New quays and piers were constructed to deal with the heavy flow of vessels. Markets thrived.

In the battle of the Romans against Mithridates of Pontus in 88 BC, Délos was robbed of many of her treasures; 20,000 people were killed, and the women and children carried off as slaves. This was the beginning of the end. Sulla regained the island, but 19 years later Délos was again pillaged by pirates allied to Mithradates, who once more sold the population into slavery. General Triarius retook the island and fortified it with walls, and Hadrian attempted to revive the waning cult of Apollo with new festivities, but by this time wretched Délos had fallen into such a decline that, when Athens tried to sell it, no one offered to buy. In AD 363, Emperor Julian the Apostate tried to jumpstart paganism one last time on Délos until the oracles warned: 'Délos shall become Adélos'. Later Theodosius the Great banned heathen ceremonies altogether. A small Christian community survived until the 6th century, when it was given over to the rule of pirates. House-builders on Tínos and Mýkonos used Délos for a marble quarry, and its once busy markets became a pasture.

After the War of Independence, Délos and Rhéneia were placed in the municipality of Mýkonos. Major archaeological excavations were begun in 1872 by the French School of Archaeology in Athens under Dr Lebeque, and work continues to this day.

## Getting There and Around

**By sea: tourist boats** from Mýkonos leave between 8 and 10am daily (except Mon), returning between 12noon and 2pm, for around 1400dr return. Guided tours (4500dr), are available from agencies or hire a **private boat** at the main harbour.

## The Excavations

*A trip to **Délos** begins as you clamber out of the caique and pay the 1000dr entrance fee. The quality of 'official' guides varies, and you have to fit in with their timetables. Major sites are labelled, badly translated guidebooks are on sale, and everything of interest can be seen in hours. Be warned, the site is overrun with tourists in the summer. To get your bearings head up the hill, **Mount Kýthnos**, which has a great view over the site and the neighbouring islands of Mýkonos, Tínos and Sýros. Sensible shoes, sunhat, and water are essential.*

To your left from the landing stage is the **Agora of the Competalists**. *Compita* were Roman citizens or freed slaves who worshipped the Lares Competales, or crossroads gods. These Lares gods were the patrons of Roman trade guilds, while others came under the protection of Hermes, Apollo or Zeus; many of the remains in the Agora were votive offerings built to them. A road, once lined with statues, leads from here to the sanctuary of Apollo. To the left of the road stood a tall and splendid Doric colonnade called **Philip's Stoa**, built by Philip V of Macedon in 210 BC, and now marked only by its foundations; it once held a votive statue dedicated by Sulla for his victory over Mithridates. The kings of Pergamon built the **Southern Stoa** in the 3rd century BC, and you can also make out the remains of the **Delians' Agora**, the local marketplace in the area.

The **Sanctuary of Apollo** is announced by the **Propylaea**, a gateway built of white marble in the 2nd century BC. Little remains of the sanctuary itself, once crowded with temples, votive offerings and statues. Next door is the **House of the Naxians** (6th century BC). A huge *kouros*, or statue of Apollo as a young man, originally stood there, of which only the pedestal remains. According to Plutarch the *kouros* was crushed when a nearby bronze palm donated by Athens (symbolic of the tree clutched by Leto in giving birth) toppled over in the wind.

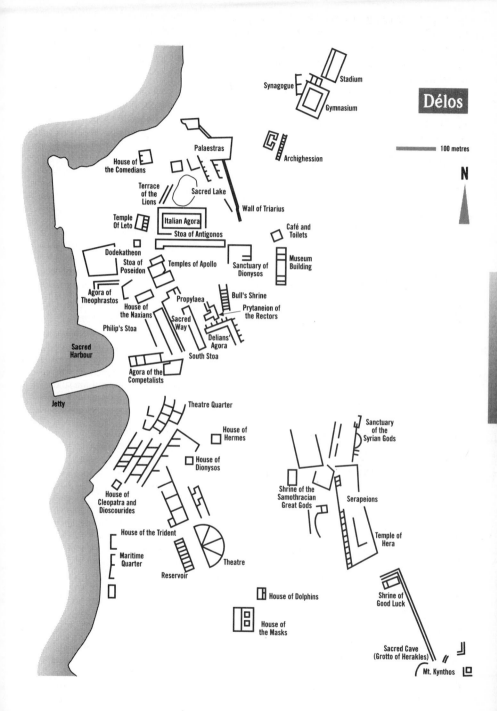

Délos

100 metres

N

Stadium
Synagogue
Gymnasium
Palaestras
House of
the Comedians
Archighession
Terrace
of the
Lions
Sacred Lake
Wall of Triarius
Temple
Of Leto
Italian Agora
Café and
Toilets
Stoa of Antigonos
Dodekatheon
Museum
Building
Stoa of
Poseidon
Temples of Apollo
Sanctuary of
Dionysos
Agora of
Theophrastos
Propylaea
Bull's Shrine
House of
the Naxians
Prytaneion of
the Rectors
Sacred
Way
Philip's Stoa
Delians'
Agora
Sacred
Harbour
South Stoa
Agora of the
Competalists
Jetty
Theatre Quarter
House of
Hermes
Sanctuary
of the
Syrian Gods
House of
Dionysos
House of
Cleopatra and
Dioscourides
Shrine of the
Samothracian
Great Gods
Serapeions
House of the Trident
Temple of
Hera
Maritime
Quarter
Theatre
Reservoir
House of Dolphins
Shrine of
Good Luck
House of
the Masks
Sacred Cave
(Grotto of Herakles)
Mt. Kynthos

195

Next are the **three temples of Apollo**. The first and largest was begun by the Delians in 476 BC. The second was an Athenian construction of Pentelic marble, built during the Second Purification, and the third, of porous stone, was made by the 6th-century Athenian tyrant Pisistratos. Dimitrios the Besieger contributed the **Bull's Shrine**. This originally held a trireme in honour of the sacred delegation ship of Athens—the one Theseus sailed in on his return to Athens after slaying the Minotaur, and whose departure put off executions (most famously that of Socrates) until its return to Athens. Other buildings in the area were of an official nature— the **Prytaneion of the Rectors** and the **Councillor's house**. Towards the museum is the **sanctuary of Dionysos** (4th century BC), flanked by lucky marble phalli. The **Stoa of Antigonos** was built by a Macedonian king of that name in the 3rd century BC. Outside is the **Tomb of the Hyperborean Virgins**, who came to help Leto give birth to Apollo and Artemis, a sacred tomb and thus the only one to stay put during the two purifications.

On the opposite side of the Stoa stood the **Abaton**, the holy of holies, where only the priests could enter. The **Minoan fountain** nearby is from the 6th century BC. Through the **Italian Agora** you can reach the **Temple of Leto** (6th century) and the **Dodekatheon**, dedicated to the twelve gods of Olympos in the 3rd century BC. Beyond, where the **Sacred Lake** once hosted flock of swans, is the famous **Terrace of the Lions**, ex-votos made from Naxian marble in the 7th century BC; originally nine, one now sits by the arsenal in Venice and three have permanently gone missing. The site of the lake, sacred for having witnessed the birth of Apollo, is marked by a small wall. When Délos' torrent Inopos stopped flowing, the water evaporated. Along the shore are two **Palaestras** (for exercises and lessons) along with the foundation of the **Archigession**, or temple to the first mythical settler on Délos, worshipped only here. Besides the **Gymnasium** and **Stadium** are remains of a few houses and a **synagogue** built by the Phoenician Jews in the 2nd century BC.

A dirt path leads from the tourist pavilion to Mount Kýthnos. Along the way stand the ruins of the **Sanctuary of the Syrian Gods** of 100 BC with a small religious theatre within. Next is the first of three 2nd-century BC **Serapeions**, all temples dedicated to Serapis, the first and only successful god purposely invented by man—Ptolemy I of Egypt, who combined Osiris with Dionysos to create a synthetic deity to please both Hellenistic Greeks and Egyptians; syncretic Délos was one of the chief centres of his worship. Between the first and second Serapeions is the **shrine to the Samothracian Great Gods**, the Cabiri or underworld deities. The third Serapeion (still housing half a statue) was perhaps the main sanctuary, with temples to both Serapis and Isis. In the region are houses with mosaic floors, and a **temple to Hera** from 500 BC. The **Sacred Cave**, where Apollo ran one of his many oracles, is en route to the top of Mount Kýthnos. Later it was dedicated to Heracles. On the mountain itself is the **Shrine of Good Luck**, built by Arsinoë Philadelphos, wife of her brother, the King of Egypt. On the summit of 113m Mount Kýthnos signs of a settlement dating back to 3000 BC have been discovered, but better yet is the view, encompassing nearly all the Cyclades.

The rather exclusive **Theatre Quarter** surrounded the 2nd-century BC **Theatre of Délos**, with a 5500 capacity; beside it is a lovely eight-arched **reservoir**. The houses here date from the Hellenistic and Roman ages and many have mosaics, some beautifully preserved, such as in the **House of the Dolphins** and the **House of the Masks**. All have a cistern beneath the floor, spaces for oil lamps and sewage systems. Some are built in the peristyle 'style of Rhodes', with a high-ceilinged guest room; colonnades surround the central courts left open to the sun. Seek out the **House of the Trident** and the **House of Dionysos**, both with mosaics, and the **House of Cleopatra and Dioscourides**, where the statues stand a headless guard over the once-great town.

Surrounding Délos are the islets **Ag. Geórgios** (named after its monastery), **Karavoníssi**, **Mikró** and **Megálo Rematiáris**, the last consecrated to Hecate, the Queen of the Night. **Rhéneia**, also known as Greater Délos, lies just west of Délos and is just as uninhabited. Here came the pregnant or dying Delians—a large number of little rooms were excavated in the rock to receive them, before they moved into the realm of tombs and sepulchral altars. A necropolis near the shore was the repository of the coffins which the Athenians exhumed in the second purification. On the other side of Rhéneia are the ruins of a lazaretto, once used by Sýros-bound ships sent into quarantine.

### Where to Stay and Eating Out

It is illegal to stay the night on Délos. Permission may be granted to archaeologists by the relevant authorities in Athens or Mýkonos. Near the museum building is a café for the tourists. There are no seats, delays are long, the staff are surly and the snacks are overpriced. Don't be caught out; bring food and water with you.

# Folégandros (ΦΟΛΕΓΑΝΔΡΟΣ)

Traditonally an island of exile, bleak and arid Folégandros is the place to get away from it all, except in July and August when trendy Germans and Italians swarm all over it. With sheer cliffs and the breathtaking Kástro/Chóra built to defy pirates, it's one of the most alluring in the Cyclades and the perfect base since 1984 for the Cycladic School's courses on drawing and painting, as well as yoga and Greek dance. With 650 inhabitants, Folégandros is one of the smallest islands in Greece with a permanent population, swollen several times over in the summer with people seeking genuine island life or partied out by the fleshpots of Íos. The name Folégandros comes from the Phoenician 'Phlegundum' meaning 'rocky island', which fits it to a tee.

### Getting There and Around

**By sea:** daily **excursion boats** from Íos; excursions to Angáli, Ag. Nikólaos and Livadáki beaches, **ferry** 4–5 times a week to Piraeus, Íos, Santoríni and Síkinos; less frequently with Mílos, Sífnos, Sérifos and Kýthnos, roughly once a week with Kímolos, Crete, Kássos, Kárpathos, Chálki, Náxos, Páros, Sými and Rhodes. **Catamaran** once a week to Íos, Náxos, Páros, Mýkonos, Tínos, Sýros and Flísvos, near Piraeus. **Port authority** (there's no tourist police), © (0286) 41 249.

**By road:** the island **bus** meets all the ferries and there are no **taxis**.

### Festivals

At **Easter** an icon is paraded and trips are made in boats around the island; Ag. Panteleímon, **27 July** in Áno Meriá; **15 August** at Panagía.

# Around Folégandros

Boats land at **Karavostássi**, the tiny harbour on the east coast, with a tree-fringed pebbly beach, restaurants and rooms to rent. Shady **Livádi** beach is a short walk from the port, and a rough path continues inland to remote **Evangelístra monastery**, dominating the rocky southern shores of the island. An easier path leads back to Chóra from here, although for any long walks in the summer, stout shoes, sun hat and a bottle of water are essential.

A newly improved road leads up to the **Chóra**, the capital, a stunning sight perched on the pirate-proof cliffs some 300m above the sea; the tall houses turn their backs on the sea, fused along the ridge of the cliff with a sheer drop below. An arcade leads into the fortified **Kástro** quarter, built in the 13th century by Marco Sanudo, a maze of dazzling paved alleys filled with geraniums and bougainvillaea and white houses sporting distinctive wooden balconies reached by steps. The sparse remains of an ancient city are located on a high plateau above Chóra.

In the village, life revolves around four interlinking squares. The first, shaded by rowan trees, has a taverna and is the hub of nocturnal action; the second is quieter; the third tiny with two *kafeneía* frequented by locals; the fourth is home to the post office. All get packed out in summer with a mix of trendy young Italians and back-packers. There are lots of tasteful craft shops, a traditional British grocer's like a Cycladic Fortnum's, and a clutch of bars that turn into a village-wide party on summer nights. The smart **disco** at the back of the village also gets jammed in high season. Follow the signs.

From Chóra, a zig-zag path up from the bus stop to the huge church of the **Panagía**. According to legend, raiding pirates stole a silver icon of the Virgin and kidnapped an islander. As they made their getaway they capsized and drowned, all except the local who clung to the icon and floated unscathed to the foot of the cliff and built the church at the top in gratitude, just coincidentally on the site of an ancient temple to Artemis. Another church, **Análypsi**, stands high up on a commanding headland with views down both coastlines; beyond it, a large grotto, **Chrísispiliá** ('Golden Cave') has stalactites and stalagmites, but access is difficult; ask in Chóra for someone to guide you. The bus continues to the island's other settlement, **Áno Meriá** (ANΩ MEPIA) 5km west, really a string of hamlets straddling the road with farms surrounded by terraced fields. There are two tavernas, a limited number of rooms (ask at the Papadópoulos Kafeneíon), and wonderful sunsets; on a clear day you can see Crete.ÁnoMeriá also has an excellent **Ecology and Folk Museum** (*open daily 4–7*) with exhibits reconstructing traditional peasant life. Trails weave down to remote beaches at **Vígla**, **Livadáki** and **Ag. Geórgios Bay**; the bus will drop you off at the appropriate track. From the road betweenÁnoMería and Chóra a path descends to the beach of **Angáli** (or **Váthi**), with a steep scramble down to the sands. Sometimes mules are available to take you back up. There are a few tavernas, some rooms to let and freelance camping is tolerated. Next door is quiet **Ag. Nikólaos** beach with a basic canteen, and **Fíra**, both popular with nudists. Most of these beaches can be less strenuously reached by the 11.15am caique from Karavostássi, returning at 5pm.

*Folégandros ©️ (0286–)*　　　　　　　　　　　　　　　**Where to Stay**

Folégandros has several small hotels, and the number grows year by year, but there's never enough space in the summer (even in the camp-site) so be prepared to sleep out, and, if it comes to that, be sure to find shelter from the strong, nagging winds.

## Karovostássi

The **Aeolos Beach Hotel**, ✆ 41 205 (*C; mod*) has immaculate rooms overlooking the beach and a lovely garden; **Hotel Poseidon** and **Vardia Bay Studios** ✆ 41 283, book in Athens ✆ (01) 684 2524 (*mod*) are also worth a look. **I Kali Kardia** is ideal for fish. **Camping Livadi**, ✆ 42 203, 1km beyond Karavostássi, has a taverna, bar and laundry facilities.

## Chóra

**Hotel Danassis**, ✆ 41 230, (*E; inexp*), in the Kástro is a gem, a lovely 500-year-old house with pebble mosaic floors and rooms that look down the sheer cliffs to the sea. Although done up, it still retains its character—but no private bathrooms. **Kalimera Rooms**, ✆ 41 389, are on the *plateía* near the bus stop, over the Kalimera Café. **Anemomílos Apartments**, ✆/✆ 41 309 (*B; exp*) are newly built in the traditional style, with balconies overhanging the sea. Fully equipped, they have an apartment for disabled travellers and fax service. **Folegandros Apartments**, ✆ 41 239, ✆ 41 366 (*C; exp–mod*), are also built in Cycladic style around a courtyard; **Hotel Odysseus**, ✆ 41 224 (*C; mod*) is owned by the same family, on the cliffs in Chóra. The once-popular old mansion **Fani-Venis**, ✆ 41 237 (*B; mod*), seems run-down these days with overbearing management. **Niko's Rooms** (*mod*) are smart apartments off the central square; old-established **Pavlo's Rooms**, ✆ 41 232 (*inexp*), are a budget option on the road to Chóra, with basic chalet-style accommodation set in a lovely garden.

---

*Folégandros* ✆ *(0286–)*                                        ***Eating Out***

**Taverna O Nikolaos** on the first *plateía* in Chóra is an institution, storing baggage as well as serving barrelled wine and good fare. **Pounta** is very trendy with tables in a charming courtyard; it does breakfast and unusual dishes from spaghetti with Roquefort to rabbit casserole. **Taverna O Kritikos** (the owner is Cretan), on the third square, has delicious chicken on the spit; it's not a tourist place but a local, very Greek hang-out. **I Piatsa** is the place for backgammon as well as food, open all hours, while **Kalimera Café** is good for snacks accompanied by New Age music. Up in Áno Meriá, **Taverna Iliovassilema** ('Sunset') has local specialities like *matzáta*, pasta with tomato, rooster or rabbit, and you can watch the sun set over Mílos.

# Íos (ΙΟΣ)

Although desperately trying to change its image as the Benidorm or Fort Lauderdale of the Aegean, Íos remains the Mecca for throngs of young people who spend their days lounging on the best beach in the Cyclades and their evenings staggering from one watering hole to another. To discourage raucous parties and late-night revellers sleeping out on the beach, four lovely campgrounds have been provided, but rows of sleeping bags by night and naked bodies by day are still the norm. The seasonal Irish invasion is so great that the island's name has been re-interpreted as the acronym for 'Ireland Over Seas'. If you're a raver or party animal then it's the place for you. Otherwise, despite the loveliness of the island, its glorious sands and pretty Chóra with blue-domed churches, you may well feel disenchanted by the crowds, the lager louts, and the wild all-night parties. Lately the fun has turned sour. Crime, especially theft, has increased in high season; there have been several reported rapes and too much booze has led to punch-ups. Drinks are cheaper than anywhere else but beware: it's home-made rot-gut and has made many young people seriously ill with alcohol poisoning. There are people who go back to Íos every summer, and people who take the next boat out after landing. In early spring, when the locals reclaim it, you might find Íos as Lawrence Durrell did, full of 'silences, fractured only by some distant church bell or the braying of a mule'.

### Getting There

**By sea**: Íos is very well connected. There are daily **ferries** to all the major Cyclades and Piraeus, 5 times a week to Crete, once a week to Thessaloníki; daily **excursion boats** to Santoríni, Mýkonos, Páros, Náxos, Síkinos and Folégandros; **catamaran** to Santoríni, Síkinos, Folégandros and Piraeus. **Port authority**, ✆ 91 264.

### Tourist Information

Information office in the port of Gialós, ✆ (0286) 91 028. Also see regular police in Chóra, ✆ (0286) 91 222.

### Festivals

**15 May**, Homer festival; **26 July**, Ag. Barbára, at Perivóli; **29 August**, Ag. Ioánnis Kálamos, a huge *panegýri*; **8 September**, Ag. Theodótis, with food and dancing.

## Gialós and Íos Town

The island's name, also rendered Niós (the locals say Nió), comes from the Ionians who built cities on the sites of Gialós and Íos town, when the island was famous for its oak forests. Over the centuries, the oaks became ships and Íos became the arid rockpile it is today; after the earthquake of 1951, when all the water was sucked out of Íos Bay and rushed back to flood and damage Gialós, the island may have been abandoned had not the first tourists begun to trickle in.

**Gialós** (ΓΙΑΛΟΣ), the port, also known as Ormós (ΟΡΜΟΣ), has the island's best fish tavernas and quietest lodgings; it has a beach in the bay, but it tends to be very windy. From the port beach a rough track leads to **Koumbára** beach, a pretty sandy cove that is usually less crowded, and offers a couple of convenient tavernas for lunch. From Gialós frequent buses go up to Íos town and **Milopótas Beach**, or you can brave the 15-minute climb up the steps.

**Íos town**, 'the Village', one of the finest in the Cyclades, is increasingly hard to find behind the discos, bars and tourist shops. Traces of the ancient walls are preserved, and only bits more survive of the fortress built in 1400 by the Venetian Lord of Íos, Marco Crispi. A local story shows how remote the inhabitants of small islands were to the big political events in Greek history: when Otho of Bavaria, the first modern King of Greece, paid a visit to Íos, he greeted the villagers in the café, treated them to a round of drinks and promised he would pay to have the village cleaned up for them. The grateful Niots, scarcely knowing what majesty Otho pretended to, toasted him warmly: 'To the health of the King, Íos' new rubbish collector!'

Of the 18 original windmills behind the town, 12 remain, along with three olive oil presses. Two very old churches, out of the 400 or so chapels on the island, stand half-ruined on the hill above the town, where supposedly an underground tunnel leads to Plakotós, used as a hiding

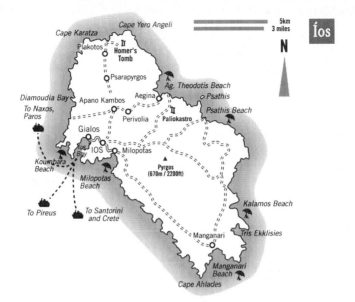

place during pirate raids. All the main facilities—police, telephone, post office, the bus stop—are at one end of the town, by a square; once there was a swing on this square, where Niots courted their fair ladies and where ghosts now dance when no one's looking.

## Beaches around Íos

**Milopótamos** (ΜΥΛΟΠΟΤΑΜΟΣ), abbreviated to Milopótas, with its superb sandy beach has several tavernas and two campsites, although most people just bed down where they can find room. Don't count on getting much shut-eye wherever you end up: Íos' all-night beach parties are infamous, and have unfortunately ended in several deaths caused by overdoses of drugs and alcohol. Excursion boats leave Gialós every day for **Manganári Bay**, where nudism rules and there's a smart German-built bungalow resort, and **Psáthis Bay**, where a church dedicated to the Virgin fell into the sea—rather a prophetic statement on raunchy Íos. It's now the haunt of wealthy Athenians with two pricey tavernas. **Kalamós Beach** is a three-hour walk from Chóra.

Once remote but now accessible by bus, **Ag. Theodótis** (ΑΓ. ΘΕΟΔΟΤΗΣ) has a fine beach near the ancient Ionian city of Aegina, overlooked by the ruined medieval fortress of **Paliokástro**. On one occasion attacking pirates managed to bore a hole in the fortress gate, big enough to allow one man in at a time—only to be scalded to death one by one in burning oil poured on them by the besieged men and women. In Ag. Theodótis monastery, the door the pirates broke through on the way to their doom is on display. In **Perivóla**, a small settlement in the middle of the island, are clustered Íos' fresh-water springs and trees and there's also a shady beach. **Apáno Kámbos**, once inhabited by a hundred families but today reduced to three or four, is another pretty place. Nearby, at a place called **Helliniká**, are huge monoliths of mysterious origin.

## Plakotós and Homer

Tradition has it that the mother of Homer came from Íos, and it was here that the great poet came at the end of his life. Some say it was a riddle told by the fishermen of Íos that killed Homer in a fit of perplexity: to wit, 'What we catch we throw away; what we don't catch, we keep' (not wanting any readers to meet a similar fate, the answer's below). Homer's tomb is on the mountain at **Plakotós**, and although earthquakes have left only the rock on which it was built, the epitaph was copied out by ancient travellers: 'Here the earth covers the sacred head of the dean of heroes, the divine Homer.' On 15 May each year, the *Omíria*, or Homer festival, takes place in town, with much merriment and many sporting events, and a flame is carried from the port to his grave. Plakotós was an Ionian town that once had a temple to Apollo, but like the Virgin's church it slid down the cliff. You can look down and see the ruined houses; only one tower, **Psarápyrgos**, remains intact to mark the town.

---

### Íos ✆ (0286–)

### *Where to Stay and Eating Out*

Íos, the paradise of the footloose and fancy-free, can be reasonable, though people have paid 6000dr for a cramped and dirty room in peak season. If there's any space, room owners meet the ferries. The rule of thumb seems to be that the young and wild head up for 'the Village', oldies and less riotous types stay down in more pricey Gialós. If you want to sleep out, remember that the police are cracking down, but in high season you may well have no other choice. Before booze, Íos' speciality was *meyífra*, a hard white cheese similar to Parmesan, mixed with perfume and fermented in a goatskin—hard to find these days (all the better, some might add). Don't confuse it with *mezíthra*, the soft ricotta like sheep's-milk cheese. But *meyífra* cheese is not the answer to Homer's riddle: what the fishermen caught was lice.

### Gialós

**Hotel Flisvos**, ✆ 91 315, 🖷 91 118 (*C; mod*) is pleasant with a bar and room service; **Petra Holidays Village**, ✆ 91 409, 🖷 91 049 (*C; mod*) is a lovely luxurious Cycladic village complex at the far end of the beach with stylish open-plan apartments. Facilities include watersports and an arts centre with amphitheatre for performances. **Hotel Poseidon**, ✆/🖷 91 091 (*C; mod–inexp*) has immaculate rooms just off the waterfront; the **Mare-Monte**, ✆ 91 564/585 (*C; mod*) is another harbour option. **Ios Camping**, ✆ 91 329, again is just off the front, but beware mosquitoes. **Restaurant Psarades** is a good place for fish and **Polydoros** on Koumbára Beach, a 15min walk from the port, is popular for tasty Greek dishes, seafood and vegetarian meals (you can also ask here about rooms). The **Afroditi** is worth a look; choose well and a fine Greek meal is yours for 2000dr.

### Chóra

Outside the tumultuous centre the **Afroditi Hotel**, ✆ 91 546, (*C; mod*) is one of the best for value; **Homer's Inn** ✆ 91 365 (*C; mod*) is also a good bet, but in high season you must book ahead. **Markos Pension**, ✆ 91 059 (*mod–inexp*), for the younger crowd, does breakfast, has a laundry service and friendly little bar, and doesn't suffer from its proximity to the the 'Dubliner Disco'; next door **Hotel Giorgios-Irini**, ✆ 91

527 (*C; mod*) is OK. Among the budget places to stay **The Wind,** ✆ 91 139 (*inexp*) is large and friendly, **Francesco's,** ✆ 91 223 (*inexp*) has great views and a popular bar, and **Violetta,** ✆ 91 044 (*inexp*) is cheapest of all with basic, simple rooms. Between Íos town and Milopótas, try **Hermes Rooms,** ✆ 91 471 or **Petradi Rooms,** ✆ 91 510 (*both mod–inexp*). The latter has balconies, private baths and a terrace restaurant with great views over Santoríni.

The **Íos Club,** on the footpath up from the harbour, has long been renowned for views of the sunset, good drinks and classical music (programme posted daily). At night it turns into a discotheque. **Pithari,** near the church, is one of the best places on the island, serving excellent Greek food and barrelled wine. In the heart of town the family **Taverna I Stani** has cheap and tasty Greek dishes; try the *dolmádes* and stuffed squid. **The Nest (I Folia)** continues to be good and popular, especially for its prices—you can eat well for 1800dr. One thing you wouldn't expect on Íos is an excellent *ouzerie*, but **Ouzeri Manolis** has a fine spread of *mezédes*, and good wine if you're not up to tippling ouzo. But drinking takes priority over eating, and many of the little houses have been turned into bars, all pouring draught Guinness. **Frankie's** is one of the best places to sit and have a drink and a gawk.

## Milopótas Beach

The **Dionyssos Hotel,** ✆/◉ 91 215 (*B; lux*) is built in traditional style and has a pool, air-conditioning and transfer service. The **Íos Palace,** ✆ 91 224/269 (*B; exp*), on the beach, designed and decorated in the old island style, also has a pool and good views of the bay. A few minutes from the beach the **Far Out Hotel,** ✆ 91 446 (*C; exp*), named because of guests' reactions to the view, has comfortable rooms in Cubist style clustered on the hillside with a pool. **Markos Beach,** ✆ 91 571 (*mod*) has standard rooms with showers at moderate rates on the beach. The beach has three campsites: **Camping Stars,** ✆ 91 302; **Milopotas,** ✆ 91 554 and posh **Far Out Camping,** ✆ 91 468, apparently just that, with a restaurant, sports facilities and minibus service.

## Manganári Bay

The **Manganari Bungalow complex,** ✆ 91 200/215 (*lux*) offers luxury rooms and suites, with a restaurant and nightclub for those who like their entertainment sane and close to home, accessible only by boat from Gialós.

---

### Entertainment and Nightlife

The village is one long rave-up, all the bars offering different amusements from videos to rock bands and happy hours that stretch into morning. Serious drinkers pack the main square bars after midnight then go on until dawn. The **Slammer Bar,** home of the Íos slammer, is on the pub crawl route. **Disco 69** is the favourite, wild, in-town disco, and **Sweet Irish Dream** turns into a disco after sunset. The **Village Pub** has Brit bands and cheap beer; other bars range from the cosy **Kahlua** to the **Tomato Bar** where you can shoot pool, to the **Jazz Bar** for more mellow sounds, and **Satisfaction** where rockers will get some. The big discos are **The Scorpion** on the way to Milopótas, the **Dubliner Disco** and the **Red Lion,** all a short stagger apart. Down in Gialós, mixed age-groups hang out at the **Enigma Cocktail Bar** and the **Frog Club;** the **Marina Bar** actually plays Greek music.

Closest of all the Cyclades to Athens, Kéa has for many years been a favourite place for Athenians to build a summer villa—timed correctly, the island can be reached from the metropolis in less than 4 hours. It feels very different from the typical Cyclades island, with lush green valleys and terraces full of fruit trees, fields grazed by dairy cattle and grubbing pigs. Kéa has been famed since antiquity for its fertility, its delicious red wine, lemons, honey and almonds. Its traditional architecture may lack the pristine white Cubism of its sister isles but there's almost a touch of Tuscany about the Chóra, Ioulís, with its red-pantiled houses and higgledy-piggledy lanes. Kéa's beaches are lovely, but hardly empty in the summer; most weekends they brim with Athenians, so if you are planning a short stay, time it for mid-week. On Friday evenings the port, Korissía, is jammed as weekenders pile off the ferry with four-wheel-drive cars, dogs, boats and windsurfers while the jet-set head over to Vourkári from Glyfáda in a flotilla of gin palaces. If you want to enjoy Kéa's unhurried pace, wonderful countryside and atmosphere, do it now, before the entrepreneurs and tour operators exploit her charms; regrettably, more hotels materialize each year, with people to fill them.

## History

Traces of a Neolithic fishing settlement dating back to 3000 BC were discovered at Kefala on Kéa's north coast. These first settlers were certainly no pushovers; when the mighty Minoan thalassocrats founded a colony *c.* 1650 BC at modern-day Ag. Iríni, they were forced to build defences to protect themselves from attacks, not from the sea but by land. The discovery (1960) of the Minoan colony by John L. Caskey of the University of Cincinnati is one of the more intriguing in recent years. Built on a small peninsula, it coincides nicely with the myth that Minos himself visited Kéa and begat the Kéan race on a native lady named Dexithea; it also reveals a fascinating chronicle of trade and diplomacy between the Minoans and the older Cycladic culture, and later, after the fall of Crete, with the Mycenaeans.

In the Classical era, Kéa was divided into four towns: Ioulís, near modern Chóra, Karthaea, Poiessa and Korissía. The poet Simonides (557–467 BC) famous for his epigram after the Battle of Thermopylae, his lyrical nephew Bacchylides, the philosopher Ariston and the physician Erasistratos were all sons of Kéa. The island was also famous for its unique retirement scheme: citizens were required to take a glass of hemlock when they reached 70. During the Middle Ages, the Venetian Domenico Michelli used Ioulís' temple of Apollo to build a castle; in the 1860s the Greek government dismantled the cannibalized Classical bits to put in a museum.

Kéa's name crops up again in 1916, when the hospital ship *Britannic*, sister-ship to the *Titanic*, sank 3 miles off shore after an explosion. Of the more than a thousand people aboard, only 21 lost their lives when their lifeboat capsized. Speculation at the time produced two theories: that the ship had secretly been carrying munitions, which had accidentally exploded in the hold, or that the British had scuttled the ship themselves, hoping to pressure Athens into forbidding enemy craft from navigating freely in Greek waters.

### *Getting There and Around*

**By sea**: daily connections with Lávrion (passing by way of sinister, barren Makrónissos, a prison island and torture chamber used in the Civil War and by the junta; poet Ioánnis Rítsos spent much of his life there) once or twice a week with Kýthnos and Sýros. Daily *Flying Dolphin*

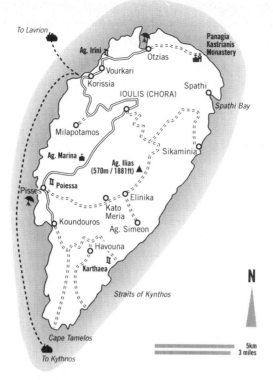

To Lavrion

Ag. Irini
Otzias
Panagia
Kastrianis
Monastery

Vourkari
Korissia
IOULIS (CHORA)
Spathi
Spathi Bay

Milapotamos

Ag. Marina
Sikaminia

Ag. Ilias
(570m / 1881ft)

Pisses
Poiessa

Elinika
Kato
Meria
Koundouros
Ag. Simeon

Havouna

Karthaea

Straits of Kynthos

**N**

Cape Tamelos

5km
3 miles

To Kýthnos

service in summer from Kýthnos, Piraeus (Zéa) and Anávissos on the southwest Attica coast, a 2-hour drive from central Athens. Also *Ilio* service to Kýthnos, Sérifos, Sífnos, Kímolos, Mílos and Rafína. **Port authority**, ℗ 21 344.

**By road: buses** run regularly about 5 times a day, from Korissía to Ioulís and Otziás via Vourkári. There is also a scant service to Písses.

---

### Tourist Information

The **tourist police** in Korissía, ℗ (0288) 21 100 have lists of rooms to let; port police 21 344.

### Festivals

**10 February**, Ag. Charálambos, patron of Kéa, at Chóra; **17 July**, Ag. Marína; **15 August**, Panagía, at Chóra; **7 September**, Ag. Sózonta, at Otziás.

---

## Korissía and Ag. Iríni

Kéa's port **Korissía** (ΚΟΡΗΣΣΙΑ) has a few pretty neoclassical buildings and a lovely church but otherwise it's an ordinary, functional little place. Anxious to become a resort like Kéa's other coastal villages, it now boasts a few nice boutiques and an art gallery among the waterfront tavernas and cafés. Korissía, of course, recalls the ancient town that once stood on the site; most locals, however, still call it Livádi, as they continue to call their island Tzía instead of the official Kéa. The bay sweeps round to the sandy town beach; a footpath over the headland leads past the old castle-like country house of the Maroúli family north to small, sandy **Gialiskári** beach and a popular taverna shaded by a pinewood. A playground for rich Athenians, the area bristles with holiday villas, high gates and guard dogs on patrol. A kilometre further north, on attractive Ag. Nikólaou Bay, **Vourkári** is a pretty fishing village metamorphosed into a smart but charming little resort, where the pleasure-cruiser brigade loaf in the tavernas or lounge on their sundecks. There are few fishing boats now, and even fewer under sail. Around the bay, on the peninsula of **Ag. Iríni** (named after the small church on top), are the excavations of the **Bronze Age–Minoan–Mycenaean settlement**. It's not difficult to make out the temple, first constructed in the Bronze Age, a late Minoan megaron, walls and a street. Inscriptions in the Minoan Linear A were among among the finds, most of which can be seen in the Archaeological Museum in Ioulís.

From here the coastal road continues to the delightful but popular beach resort at **Otziás** (ΟΤΖΙΑΣ), its bay ringed with a lacy mass of almond blossom in early spring, and to **Panagía Kastriáni,** perched on top of Kastrí Hill on the northeast of the island with panoramic views down the coast. The 18th-century monastery is noted for its miracle-working icon of the Madonna. There are two churches, the first built in 1708 after shepherds saw a strange glow on the mountain and found the icon had arrived when they went to investigate.

## Ioulís (Chóra)

High above Korissía, the island's capital **Ioulís** or Ioulída (ΙΟΥΛΙΔΑ) is hidden inland, like so many Cycladic towns, from sea-going predators. As the bus climbs, the views down the terraced hillside to the sea are stunning and en route you can see the historical school on the hill, built in the neoclassical style, thought to be one of the finest in Greece. Ioulís also boasts the largest collection of **windmills** in the Cyclades: 26 stand sentinel above the town on the Mountain of the Mills.

The town is a pretty place to wander around with its flower-filled balconies and tunnel-like alleys, a maze of alleys and archways, the white houses topped with red-tiled roofs. The **Kástro** quarter, reached through a dazzling white archway, occupies the site of ancient Ioulís' acropolis and medieval walls; all that remain are the stone blocks from the original temple of Apollo. The ancient walls were cannibalized to build a Venetian castle in 1210, then re-used to build the house of Ioulís. Above the main Kástro entrance, note the coat of arms of the Pangalos family, depicting a loaf of bread and two cockerels. One old house contains the **Archaeological Museum** (*open Tues–Sun, 8.30–3*), an interesting collection of Minoan finds from Ag. Iríni, artefacts from ancient Kéa's four cities, as well as a copy of the wonderful *Kouros of Kéa,* discovered in Korissía and now in the National Archaeological Museum in Athens. Ioulís has a spectacular neoclassical Town Hall, topped with statues of Apollo and Athena. On the west side, ancient bas relief sculptures are set into niches in the wall and in the entrance there's a sculpture of a woman and child found at Karthaia. A few Venetian mansions remain intact around Kástro, and several churches date back to the Byzantine era. Ioulís was the hometown of Simonídes and the contemporary artist Fassianós; look out for the bold paintings on a wall above one of the gift shops.

A 10-minute walk east of Chóra leads to the town's most curious attraction—the 6th century BC **Lion of Kéa**, an ancient guardian some 3m high and 6m long , carved into the rock by an unknown artist, and gently smiling down over Ioulís. Tales about the lion abound: one says he symbolizes the bravery of the Kéans, another recounts how evil nymphs were killing the wives of Ioulís and the men were going to abandon the city. The priest prayed to Zeus to send a lion to drive the nymphs away, and he did. The people then carved the lion in the rock to keep the nymphs permanently at bay. Equally majestic is the renovated, square Hellenistic tower at the ruined monastery of **Ag. Marína**, set in rolling green countryside southwest of Chóra. One of the finest of such towers in Greece, its masonry has withstood time better than the monastery built around it. There is a huge *panegýri* at the pink-domed church that stands within the ruins on July 17.

The country villages inland from Ioulís, **Episkópi**, **Kastaniés** and **Paraméria** are green with oak trees and worth a visit for their traditional country houses or *stávlos* with distinctive entrances, *stegádi*. The road ends at **Sykamiá**, a beautiful, but lonely beach. Above Perameria the lush valley of Spathí leads to sandy **Spathí Bay**. Other scenic beaches in the area include **Kalidoníki** and **Orkós**.

## Southern Kéa

From Ag. Marína the road cuts across to the west-coast beaches and resort communities at **Písses** (which perhaps should consider reviving the ancient spelling of its name, Poiessa, of which a few traces remain) and **Koúndouros**. Backed by a lush valley full of orchards and olive groves, Písses has a huge sweeping sandy beach, one of the finest on the island. The next bay along, sandy Koúndouros, is lovely, especially **Ag. Emiliános Beach**. It has several smaller coves but is fast being developed with bungalows for Athenian weekenders. There are also gorgeous beaches further along the coast at **Kámbi** and **Lipará**.

On the southeast shore at Póles Bay is ancient **Karthaea**, where Simonides had his school of poetry. Little survives of the island's most important ancient city, high on the headland, apart from the ruins of massive walls, the theatre and other buildings plus the remains of a Doric temple of Apollo. It's possible to walk the Hellenistic road from **Káto Meriá** or **Elliniká**.

---

*Kéa ℂ (0288–)*                                 ***Where to Stay and Eating Out***

Although there are two pensions in Ioulís, most places to stay are along the coast and furnished apartments aimed at Greek families. Simple rooms to rent are like gold dust at weekends in high season, with prices to match. But if you're desperate you can head for the **Kastrianí Monastery**, ℂ 21 348, which has accommodation. Although foreign visitors have begun trickling in, Kéa is still very Greek and the tavernas serve up unadultered Greek fare at fairly reasonable prices. Look for *pastéli*, a delicious sticky bar made from local thyme honey and sesame seeds. Other specialities include smelly *kopanistí* cheese and *paspallá*, preserved fat pork, usually eaten at Christmas.

### Korissía

**I Apolavsi** ('The Enjoyment'), ℂ 21 068 (*inexp*), above Kostas Taverna has comfortable, basic studios and a huge sun terrace overlooking the harbour. In the alley behind, **Kyria Pantazi**, ℂ 21 452, has very basic but quaint village rooms, but no view. You can even stay in a motel, **I Tzia Mas**, ℂ 21 305/223 (*B; mod*), fronting the town beach. Clean and friendly with an OK restaurant, it's right on the main road, geared to families with cars, and isn't peaceful; advance booking is essential in summer. Off the harbour the **Hotel Karthea**, ✆ 21 222/204 (*C; mod*), is a bit gloomy; better to head for **Pension Korissia**, ✆ 21 484/355 (*A; exp–mod*), in a quiet backwater with a nice terrace, bar and large rooms. Nearby, the **United Europe Furnished Flats**, ✆ 21 362 (*A; exp–mod*), are a smart self-catering option; all flats have verandas and fully equipped kitchens. Other furnished apartments worth trying are **To Korali**, ✆ 21 268, and **To Oneiro**, ✆ 21 118 (*exp–mod*). The rooms over the waterside tavernas are a good bet if you're passing through and don't mind the throb of the generators from visiting cruise boats. There are plenty of rooms to let back from the harbour and the tourist police have information.

As you get off the ferry, there is a line of eating places offering anything from pizza to *mezédes*. You can spend a pleasant evening over a grilled fish at **Faros** or **Kostas Taverna**, a basic, hectic and popular haunt with local workmen. Further along the harbour the smart **Ouzerie Lagoudera**, in a refurbished neoclassical house has an excellent menu and tasty prawn *saganáki*; next door **To Mouragio** does pizzas as well as Greek fare. **Albatross** does great ice-cream specials.

### Vourkári/Otziás

At Vourkári furnished apartments to let (*all exp–mod*) include **O Nikitas,** ✆ 22 303, on the waterfront, **Lefkes** ✆ 21 443 and **Petrakos** ✆ 21 197. Vourkári is the place for seafood at a price where the yachties and cruisers can moor up a few feet away from their tables. **Aristos** is among the best for good Greek cooking and, if the wind has been blowing the right way and there's been a good haul of fish, a delicious *kakavia* (Greek *bouillabaisse*) will be on the menu. **O Nikos**, next to the art gallery, and **To Oraío Bourkari** are also popular for lunch and dinner. In Otziás the **Coaldi Club**, ✆ 21 093, ✆ 21 109 has furnished apartments overlooking the sands and there are also several *domátia* places. **O Iannis** is the favourite fish taverna.

### Ioúlis

There are two pensions full of character, **Pension Ioulis**, ✆ 22 177 (*D; inexp*) and **Filoxenia**, ✆ 22 057 (*D; inexp*) which has shared bathrooms. The café and pastry shop **To Panorama** near the bus stop is a nice place to have a drink and a snack as you soak up the view; through the main archway the **Piatsa Restaurant** is in a lovely setting while the **Restaurant and Grill Room Ioulis**, on the Town Hall square. is a good place to have lunch, again with sensational views. On the way, **To Methismeno Karavi** ('The Drunken Ship') is a delightful night-time *ouzerie* with a good range of *mezédes* served on flower-bedecked terrace; **To Steki** and **Taverna Argiris** also have a good range of Greek fare.

### Písses/Koúndouros

Among the furnished apartments in Písses, try the **Galini**, ✆ 31 316 or any run by the Polítis family, ✆ 31 343/318. There's also **Kea Camping**, ✆ 31 332, run by Ioánnis Polítis. Two respected fish tavernas are **O Simitis** and **Akroyiali**. **Kea Beach Hotel and Bungalows**, Koúndouros, ✆ 31 230, ✆ 31 234 (*B; exp*) is a swish complex in traditional village style complete with windmills perched above the beach. There's a restaurant, nightclub, pool, tennis court and watersports. The bungalows sleep up to four; book early. Other good beach tavernas are **O Kaikas** at Spathí and **O Koundouros** at Ag. Emiliános.

### Entertainment and Nightlife

While the rich and trendy head for the tavernas of Vourkári at night, the less well-heeled seem to stay in Korissía, taking part in the traditional *vólta*, or evening stroll. The harbour buzzes after the ferry has arrived. **Clue** and **Albatross** are popular after-dinner haunts. Bars to hang out at in Vourkári include **Remego**, **Kouros**, **Anogi** and **Vinilio** and there are two discos, **The Macao Club** and **Traffic**. At Koundoúri there's a **nightclub** at the Kéa Beach complex. In Ioulís the **Stoa Bar**, **Quiz** and **Leon** are cool. Kéa is known for its excellent dancers and the island's fairs and *panegýria* have spectacular performances to music played on traditional instruments like the *tsamboúna*, *doubi* and lute.

# Kímolos (ΚΙΜΩΛΟΣ)

Once known as Echinousa, or sea urchin, the island's modern name is thought to be derived from its first inhabitant. But *kimolía* also means chalk in Greek, and whether the name comes from the producer (chalk was once a main export of Kímolos) or vice versa, no one is quite sure. Today Kímolos is a rich source of cimolite, like Fuller's Earth, used in the dying of cloth. You can see the workings as the ferry pulls in and the mineral's fine white dust coats much of the island. At one time Kímolos was attached to Mílos, but the isthmus linking the two islands sank into the sea, leaving a channel only a kilometre wide. An ancient town went under the waves as well, but its necropolis survives on Kímolos at a site called Ellinikó.

Kímolos is a quiet island, a perfect place to relax and do absolutely nothing, with few tourists, even in August. Despite the regular excursions from Mílos, strangers are still viewed with suspicion. Most of Kímolos is rocky and barren (the Venetians chopped down the once-plentiful olive groves and nothing has grown there since). But there are patches of green on the southeast coast. The largest building on the island is a retirement home built by local philanthropist Geórgios Afendákis, where Kímolos' elderly live free of charge. Apart from the one town, which is surprisingly large, there are several shady beaches, but the only chalk you'll find these days is in the local school.

### Getting There

**By sea**: connections 3 times a week with Piraeus, Mílos, Kýthnos, Sérifos and Sífnos, once a week with Folégandros, Síkinos, Íos and Santoríni; **water taxi** 3 times a day to Apollónia on Mílos. **Hydrofoil**: weekly *Ilio* service to Mílos, Sífnos, Sérifos, Kýthnos, Kéa and Rafína. **Port authority**, ✆ 51 332.

### Tourist Information

Just the police, ✆ (0287) 51 205.

### Festivals

**20 July**, Profítis Ilías; **27 July**, Ag. Panteleímon; **15 August**, Panagía; **27 August**, Ag. Fanoúris; **21 November**, traditional music and dancing.

## Chóra and Around

From the pretty little port, **Psáthi**, (ΨΑΘΗΣ) which has a good taverna, a beach café and the 'doctor's mill' on the hill above, it's a 2km, 15-minute walk up to the typically white capital, **Kímolos** or **Chóra**. On the way up you'll pass the Afendákis Foundation building, with statue of the benefactor, and a small museum in the basement takes in whatever potsherds and ancient bric-à-brac the locals happen to dig up. Blizzard-white, Chóra is a tangle of paved lanes with flowers at every turn. It's divided into two settlements, **Mésa Kástro** and **Éxo Kástro**, also called **Palío Choró** and **Kainoúrio Choró**, which lie inside and outside the castle walls. The houses of Mésa Kástro form the inside of the fortress with loophole windows and four gates. The outer village has a few small cafés and tavernas, and a beautiful domed cathedral church, **Panagía Evangélistra**, built in 1614. Other impressive churches are the **Panagía Odygítria**, 1873; **Taxiárchis**, 1670 and **Chrisóstomos**, 1680, and the ruins of the Catholic church, the **Madonna of the Rosary**.

From Chóra you can walk up to the ruined Venetian castle built by Marco Sanudo at Kímolos' highest point (355m). Within its forbidding walls is the island's oldest church, **Christós**, dating from 1592, according to the wall inscription. Another walk, taking in the Ellinikó cemetery and its graves from the Mycenaean period (2500 BC) to the early centuries AD, follows the mule path to the west coast, near **Ag. Andréas**. You can end with a swim at the beach at **Kambána**.

**Goúpa**, a small hamlet near Psáthi, has the most abundant fish in the Aegean these days, and here, supposedly, people used to scoop them out by the basketful. It's a very pretty little place, with a good beach untouched by tavernas or snack bars. Beyond Goúpa there's another lovely beach at **Klíma** and 7km north at **Prássa**, where the cimolite is extracted, are radioactive thermal springs especially good for rheumatism. There's a taverna and rooms to let at **Alíki** on the southwest coast. Other good swimming coves include **Límni**, **Bonátsa** and **Monastíria**, and there are plenty of places for unofficial camping. Goats are the only inhabitants of **Políegos**, the large islet facing Psáthi.

*Where to Stay and Eating Out*

Not many people stay overnight on Kímolos, and if you want to you'll have to ask around in the bars and tavernas to see who has a vacant room. Camping is usually 'no problem' as the Greeks say—you could try Klíma and Alíki beaches. Up in Chóra three tavernas all serve standard Greek fare at low prices: **Ramfos**, **Panorama** and **Boxoris**, which also has rooms. When Kímolos' charms wear thin, you can sit under the umbrellas at the port snack bar and ogle the new arrivals off the ferry.

# Kýthnos (ΚΥΘΝΟΣ)

Time your visit right and you can have this island to yourself, avoiding the Athenian invasion of July and August. Like its neighbour, Kéa, Kýthnos attracts relatively few foreigners, and even the majority of Greek arrivals are not tourists, but folks full of aches and pains who come to soak in the thermal spa at Loutrá; the locals often call their island Thermia after the springs. Since the closure of Kýthnos' iron mines in 1940, islanders who closed their ears to the siren song of emigration have got by as best they could by fishing, farming (mostly figs and vines) basket-weaving and making ceramics. Perhaps because of their frugal, hard lives Kythniots tend to celebrate *panegýria* with great gusto, donning their traditional costumes; carnival is a big event here. There are quiet sandy beaches, a dramatic, rugged interior great for walkers, and the people are welcoming. Best of all, it's the kind of island where the old men still offer to take you fishing—and the fishing off Kýthnos is good indeed.

## History

In Classical times the tale was told that Kýthnos was uninhabited because of its wild beasts and snakes, and Ofiohousa ('snaky') was one of the island's ancient names. Recently, however, archaeologists have uncovered a Mesolithic settlement (7500–6000 BC) just north of the port of Loutrá that not only spits in the eye of tradition, but currently holds the honour of being the oldest settlement yet discovered in the Cyclades. Much later the Minoans held the island, followed by the Driopes, a semi-mythical tribe who were chased out of their home on the slopes of Mount Parnassos by Heracles and scattered to Évia, Cyprus and Kýthnos; their king Kýthnos gave his name to the island and their capital to this day is known as Drýopis. During the Hellenistic period Kýthnos was dominated by Rhodes. Two great painters came from the island, Kydian and Timatheus (416–376 BC), the latter famous in antiquity for his portrait of Iphigenia. In 198 BC all Kýthnos was pillaged, except for Vyrókastro, which proved impregnable. Marco Sanudo took the island for Venice, and for 200 years it was under the rule of the Cozzadini family, who maintained control by diplomatically paying taxes both to the Venetians and to the Turks and who live happily in Bologna to this day. Is there a lesson there?

**By sea**: daily with Piraeus, Sérifos, Sífnos and Mílos, 2–3 times a week with Lávrion, Kímolos, Folégandros, Síkinos, Íos and Santoríni. Kýthnos has two ports; all ships these days put in at Mérichas on the west coast, though when the winds are strong they'll come in to Loútra in the northeast.

**Hydrofoil**: daily *Flying Dolphin* to Kéa, Piraeus; regular *Ilio* service to Kéa, Rafína, Sérifos, Sífnos, Kímolos, Mílos. **Port authority**, ✆ 32 290.

**By road**: there are two **buses** which run regularly to Chóra and Loutrá and to Drýopida and Panagía Kanála. **Taxis**: Kýthnos, ✆ 31 272, Drýopida ✆ 31 290. Taxis also meet the ferries and sharing is normal.

### *Tourist Information*

**Tourist police**: Chóra, ✆ (0281) 31 201. There are several ticket agencies in Mérichas including GATS Travel, ✆/✉ 32 055, which also arrange accommodation and excursions. The Cava Kythnos off-licence doubles as the Bank of Greece branch and hydrofoil agency.

### *Festivals*

On **Sundays** you can often hear the island's music at Drýopida. **15 August** and **8 September**, Panagías at Kanála; **2 November**, Ag. Akíndinos, at Mérichas.

## Hot Springs, Icons and Beaches

**Mérichas** (ΜΕΡΙΧΑΣ) is a typical Greek fishing harbour, the ferry dock and yacht berths giving way to a sandy tree-fringed bay backed by lively tavernas. The pretty harbour at Mérichas is a regular stop for yacht flotillas chartered from Athens, particularly popular with Americans and Swiss yachties. It's a laid-back, cheerful place, kept fanatically neat and tidy by the village oldies who also tend the ducks that live on the sandy beach. Nailed to a tree near the litter-bins, a sign proclaims, 'The sea is the spring of life and joy'. So woe betide anyone who chucks rubbish in the waves. Up the steps from the harbour and a short walk off the Chóra road is the little beach of **Martinákia**, popular with families, which has an excellent taverna and rooms to let. Just to the north are the meagre Hellenistic ruins of the once impregnable **Vyrókastro**, on the headland above the lovely beaches at **Episkópi** and **Apókrousi**.

The 7½km bus trip north from Mérichas to the capital **Chóra**, also known as Messária, winds through barren hillsides rippled with stone-wall terraces, dotted with goats and the occasional dovecote. Although as Cycladic towns go it's not that spectacular, it's an authentic, workaday town with a certain charm. The old Grymanélis and Kazoúris family houses are worth visiting for their traditional interiors. It has several pretty churches including **Ag. Sávvas**, founded in 1613 by the island's Venetian masters, the Cozzadini, who decorated it with their coat-of-arms. The oldest church is **Ag. Triáda**, a domed, single-aisle basilica. Other churches in Chóra claim to have icons by the Cretan-Venetian master Skordílis, while the **Prodrómos** ('the Scout' or St John the Baptist) has a valuable 17th-century screen. Just outside Chóra are the solar park and modern windmills which provide the island's power.

The buses continue to **Loutrá** (ΛΟΥΤΡΑ), the most important thermal spa in the Cyclades. Iron impregnates the water, leaving a characteristic reddish deposit. Since ancient times Loutra's two springs, **Kakávos** and **Ag. Anárgyri**, have been used for bathing and as a cure

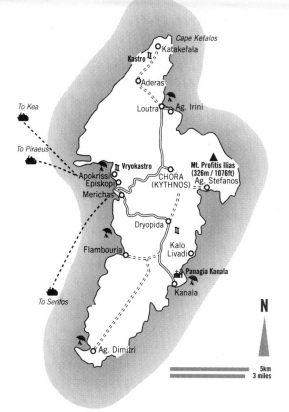

for gout, rheumatism, eczema and 'women's problems'. The **hydrotherapy centre**, ℘ 31 484, is open from 8–12noon. Carved marble baths dating from ancient times are now inside the neighbouring **Xenia Hotel**. Boiling water bubbles down a gulley outside the hotel and out to sea. A straggling, windswept resort with castle-like villas and holiday homes, Loutrá has several tavernas and places to stay. There's a sandy beach and over the headland two more bays, pebbly **Ag. Iríni** and **Schinári**, exposed to the north winds. The aforementioned Mesolithic settlement was found on the promontory just to the north. A hard hour's walk from Loutrá is the **Kástro Orias**, on the way to the northernmost tip of Kýthnos, **Cape Kéfalos**. You can poke around the **medieval citadel**, known variously as Paliokástro or Kástro tou Katakéfalou, with its derelict towers, houses and churches (one, **Our Lady of Compassion**, still has some frescoes), all abandoned around the middle of the 17th century.

The other road out of Mérichas heads up to **Drýopida** (ΔΡΥΟΠΙΔΑΣ), also known as Drýopis, the only other inland village and the island's former capital, in part because of nearby **Katafíki cave**, where the people hid during pirate raids. Huddled in the barren hills, Drýopida could be in Tuscany or Spain with its red-pantiled houses, testimony to its importance as a centre for ceramics. Known as Syllaka by the locals, the village is divided into two districts, **Galatás** and **Péra Rouga**, by the river valley, where they grow crops. Galatás, the upper village, is a labyrinth of crazy-paved lanes, neatly white-washed, still crossed by the odd mule train. There are a few cafés and tavernas and even fewer tourists. Once a great ceramics centre, only one working pottery remains, in the Milás family for five generations.

Follow the signs on the walls to see elderly potter Ioánnis Milás at work. Kýthnos was also a centre of icon-painting in the 17th century, led by the famous Skordílis family; much of their work can be still be seen. The church of **Ag. Mínas** is also worth a visit for its 17th-century iconstasis, bishop's throne and Easter bier with folk-art decorations. You can walk to Drýopida from Chóra down the ancient cobbled way. The walk takes a good hour and enjoys dramatic views but there are plans to build a road over the path. You can also hike to the beaches at **Ag. Stéfanos**, a chapel-topped islet linked to the mainland by a causeway, and **Léfkes** where there are room to let.

The bus terminates at **Kanála**, a popular summer resort where Greeks have holiday homes. A village has sprung up around the church of **Panagía Kanála**, dedicated to the Virgin Mary, the island's patron saint, housing a venerated icon, painted by St Luke himself (or more likely, by a member of the Skordílis clan). Chalets dot the peaceful grounds, pine trees shade picnic areas, and below, families laze and splash in a string of sandy coves. There are wonderful views over to Sýros and Sérifos and the water is so shallow at Kanála beach you feel you can almost walk across. A rough track leads to **Flamboúria** beach on the west coast with rooms to let, but you need transport to get to **Ag. Dimitríou** way down at the southern tip. Other beaches on the island, attainable only by foot or boat, include **Fikiádo**, **Kolónas**, **Potámia** and **Ag Iánnis**.

---

*Kýthnos ℭ (0281–)*　　　　　　　　　　　　　　*Where to Stay and Eating Out*

### Mérichas

Mérichas is the most convenient place to stay and there are plenty of rooms to rent, set back from the beach. The friendly but basic **Kythnos Hotel**, ℭ 32 092/247 (*pension; mod–inexp*) with smart blue and white striped canopies, is first choice, slap on the waterfront over the **Merichas** *zacharoplasteío* that does breakfast and snacks as well as home-made rice-puddings and jellies. On the hillside behind, the new **To Panorama** rooms, ℭ 32 184/182 (*mod–inexp*), and **O Paradissos**, ℭ 32 206/165 (*mod–inexp*), with a vine-shaded terraces, are both comfortable with stunning views over the bay; there are rooms to rent over the **Psaropoula Taverna**, ℭ 32 268 (*mod–inexp*) opposite the beach and family-run **Kissos Restaurant**, ℭ 32 370, also good for basic Greek favourites and fish at reasonable prices. Among the many village rooms, **Kaliopi** ℭ 32 203/323 has a nice garden; **Panayiota**, ℭ 32 268, **Yasemin** ℭ 32 248/104 and **Rooms Giorgia** next to GATS Travel are also worth a try (*all inexp*). The **Martinakia Beach Restaurant** on the beach is a good place for lunch with *kalamária* and grills, a friendly parrot in the garden and self-contained rooms to let (*mod*). Local thyme honey producer **Filippos Piperis** also rents out rooms in Mérichas, ℭ 32 273, and Kanála, ℭ 32 377.

**Restaurant Yialos**, very much geared to yachties and known as the Sailor's Pub, has tables on the beach and some interesting specials on the menu, mainly meats in wine sauces, as well as stroganoff and schnitzel. Try the *sofríto*, *kalógrios* and *Órlof* creations with wine, onions and cheese. They also do an excellent *pikilía* of Greek starters. Jolly atmosphere, if a bit forced: Greek dancing has been known to break out in the road. **To Mouragio** is also fine for fish and the usual; but for a real taste of

Kýthnos head to the far end of the beach and the **Kantouni Psistaria** with tables at the water's edge where they specialize in grills and *sfougáta*, feather-light rissoles made from the local cheese, *thermiotikó*. There's friendly service and barrelled retsina, plus a romantic view across the bay. Down the steps to the harbour **To Steki** does pizzas and *mezédes* and you can watch the fishing boats come in. Near the bus stop, **O Arapis** does pizza and breakfast and is a popular coffee shop for locals.

## Loutrá

Loutrá is geared to long stays by spa customers. The most luxurious places to stay are the **Kythnos Bay Hotel**, ✆ 31 218, ✉ 31 444 (*C; exp*), and new **Porto Klaras** apartments, ✆ 31 276, ✉ 31 355 (*A; exp–mod, special out-of-season offers*), beautifully appointed with a range of accommodation from family suites with TV to smaller doubles. All have sea-view terraces and there's a pretty arched bar area. **Meltemi Apartments**, ✆ 31 271 (*C; exp*), are also fully equipped flats; EOT-run **Xenia Anagenissis** overlooks the beach, ✆ 31 217 (*C; mod*), but tends to be full of old ladies taking the waters. There are also rooms to rent: try **Ta Skalia** and **Meltemi**. Friendly **Akroyiali** on the beach has good stews, *kokkinistó* and oven dishes plus draught retsina. **Taverna Katerina** over at Ag. Iríni has stunning views.

## Chóra/Drýopida

Chóra has a few rooms to rent and food at **To Kentron** and **Barba Stathis** near the OTE and **Ta Voreina** for snacks in the bus stop square. In Dryopída follow the alleys to basic **Taverna Pelegra** behind the butcher's shop (at least the meat's fresh) and look out for local sausages drying on the balcony next door; opposite the **Psistaria O Giorgilos** is your other option for grills.

## Kanála

Kanála, Flamboúria, Léfkes and Ag Dimítrios all have rooms to let. In Kanála, don't miss **To Louloudi Taverna** in the church grounds, on a terrace overlooking the bay: simple, authentic home-cooking from local vegetables to liver and goat stew as well as roasts and barbecue, washed down with draught retsina.

---

### *Entertainment and Nightlife*

Nightlife centres around the tavernas and bars in Mérichas. Pretty **To Kokili** on the waterfront is a relaxing spot for a sundowner or nightcap but if you want action head for the throbbing beat and ultra-violet lights at the **Byzantino Café Bar** where you can bop till you drop. Otherwise the action is at the **Akrotiri Disco** and open-air night club high above town. In **Chóra** night owls hang out at **Disco Kalva**.

# Mílos (ΜΗΛΟΣ)

Like Santoríni, Mílos, the most westerly of the Cyclades, is a volcanic island. But where the former is a glamorous beauty associated with misty tales of Atlantis, Mílos is a sturdy fellow who has made his fiery origins work for a living. Few places can boast such a catalogue of geological eccentricities: hot springs bubble in its low rolling hills, rocks startle with their Fauvist colours and fantastic shapes, and the landscape is gashed with obsidian, sulphur, kaolin, barium, alum, bensonite and perlite quarries begun in the Neolithic era. In a beach beauty contest Mílos would score over Santoríni hands-down with miles of pale golden sands, among the finest in Greece; long strands and weird fjord-like inlets all lapped by deep turquoise waters, some bubbling with the geothermal springs. It seems an odd trick of Mother Nature to so endow such an out-of-the-way island with such a mineral cornucopia. Yet in spite of all its strange and wonderful rocks, Mílos still mourns for the one it lost—the renowned Venus, now in the Louvre.

Walks through the gently undulating countryside will bring you down to tiny whitewashed chapels at the water's edge, or unique little settlements that sit on the water, with brightly painted boat garages beneath their balconies. Mílos has one of the finest natural harbours in the Mediterranean—soon to be developed into a yacht marina with German funds. A new airport to take direct flights from Germany, Austria and the UK is scheduled for 1998 as Mílos gears itself towards upmarket package tourism, a new interest for this already rich mining island. There's a take-it-or-leave-it attitude in Adámas to independent travellers, and to stay you could get stuck paying through the nose.

## History

The Neolithic era had only just begun when people braved the Aegean in papyrus boats to mine Mílos's abundant veins of obsidian, the petroleum of its day, hard black volcanic glass, prized for the manufacture of tools before copper. Until the recent discovery of the Mesolithic settlement in Kýthnos, Mílos laid claim to the oldest town in the Cyclades, at Phylokope, settled by either Phoenicians or Cypriots; under Minoan and later Mycenaean rule the island became rich from trading obsidian all over the Mediterranean.

As the inhabitants of Mílos in later years were predominately Dorian, they sided with their fellow Dorians from Sparta in the Peloponnesian War. When the Athenians made war in the east, the Milians again refused to fight alongside them. Athens sent envoys to Mílos to change their minds. Their famous 'might makes right' discussion, 'the Milian Dialogue', included in the fifth chapter of Thucydides, is one of the most moving passages in Classical history. When Mílos still refused to cooperate, the Athens besieged the island, and when the Milians uncon-ditionally surrendered they massacred all men of fighting age, enslaved all the women and children, and resettled the island with colonists from Athens.

Christianity came early to Mílos in the 1st century, and the faithful built a great series of cata-combs—the only ones in Greece. Marco and his brother Angelo Sanudo captured Mílos, and later placed it under the Crispi dynasty. The Turks laid claim to the island in 1580, even though Mílos was infested with pirates. One of them, John Kapsís, declared himself King of Mílos, a claim which Venice recognized for three years, until the Turks flattered Kapsís into coming to Istanbul, and ended his pretensions with an axe. In 1680 a party of colonists from Mílos emigrated to London, where James, Duke of York, granted them land to build a Greek church—the origin of Greek Street in Soho.

In 1836 Cretan war refugees from Sfakiá fled to Mílos and founded the village Adámas, the present port. During the Crimean War the French navy docked at the harbour of Mílos and left many monuments, as they did during the First World War; at Korfos you can see the bases of the anti-aircraft batteries installed during the German occupation in the Second World War.

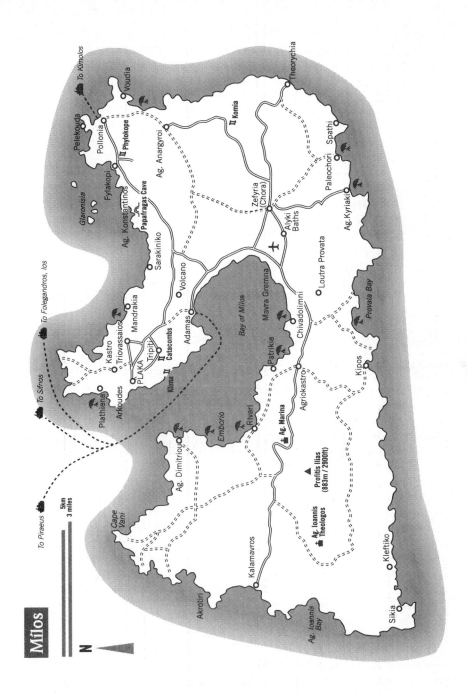

## Mílos

N

5km
3 miles

To Piraeus

To Sifnos

To Folegandros, Ios

To Kímolos

Voudia
Theoryhia
Pelekouda
Pollonia
II Komia
Fylakopi
Ag. Anargyroi
Spathi
Glaronisia
Phylokope
Paleochori
Ag. Konstantinos
Papafragas Cave
Zefyria (Chora)
Ag. Kyriaki
Sarakiniko
Alyki Baths
Volcano
Loutra Provata
Mandrakia
Provata Bay
Kastro
Mavra Gremna
Triovassalos
Tripiti
Adamas
Bay of Milos
Chivadolimni
Catacombs
PLAKA
Klima
Patrikia
Kipos
Arkoudes
Plathiena
Agriokastro
Emborio
Rivari
Ag. Marina
Ag. Dimitriou
Profitis Ilias (883m / 2900ft)
Cape Yani
Ag. Ioannis Theologos
Kalamavros
Kleftiko
Akrotiri
Sikia
Ag. Ioannis Bay

## Getting There and Around

**By air**: twice daily from Athens in summer, once in winter. Airport, ✆ 22 381.

**By sea: ferry** 6 times a week from Piraeus, Sífnos, Sérifos and Kýthnos, 2 or 3 times a week with Crete. Three times a week with Folégandros and Santoríni, twice a week with Kárpathos, Chálki, Sými, Rhodes; once a week with Amorgós. **Taxi boat** 5 times a day from Pollónia to Kímolos; *Delfíni* round-island **excursion boat. Hydrofoil**: *Ilio* service once a week with Kímolos, Sífnos, Sérifos, Kýthnos, Kéa and Rafína. **Port authority**, ✆ 22 100.

**By road**: frequent **buses** from Adámas square to Pláka, via Tripití, Pollónia, Provatás Beach and Paleóchori Beach.

## Tourist Information

**Municipal tourist information booth**, on the Adámas quay, ✆ (0287) 22 290, has useful welcome leaflet with accommodation lists. **Tourist police**, *see* regular police, Pláka, ✆ 21 204. **Vichos Tours** ✆ 22 286, 🖂 22 396 on the front are very helpful for tickets, accommodation and car hire.

## Festivals

**7 May** and **24 September**, Ag. Ioánnes Theológos at Chalákas; **Fifty days after Greek Easter**, Ag Triáda in Adámas; **30 June** and **31 October**, Ag. Anárgyroi (Byzantine church); **16 July**, Ag. Marína; **19 July**, Profítis Ilías on the mountain, Chalákas and Tripití; **26 July**, Ag. Panteleímonos at Zefyría; and **26 July**, Ag. Paraskeví at Plakotá; **5 August**, Sotíris at Paraskópou; **14 August** at Zefyría; **15 August**, Assumption of the Virgin, Ag. Charálambos, Adámas; **28 August**, Ag. Ioánnes Prodrómou; **7 September**, Panagía Eleoúsa at Psathádika; **8 September**, Panagía Korfiátissa, Pláka; **16 September**, Ag. Sofía, Chalákas; **25 September**, Ag. Ioánnis Theológos at Chalákas.

## Adámas and the Bay of Mílos

Even before you reach the port Adámas (ΑΔΑΜΑΣ) you can see a sample of Mílos' eccentric rocks: a formation called the Arkoúdes, or bears, who guard the vast Bay of Mílos on the left as you sail into the harbour. Bustling Adámas has most of Mílos's available rooms and hotels and most of the Greek tourists in August. The Cretans who founded the town brought their holy icons along, now displayed in the churches of Ag. Tríada and Ag. Charálambos, at the highest point in town; in the latter, one ex-voto, dating from 1576, portrays a boat attacked by a raging fish; the captain prayed to the Virgin, who resolved the struggle by snipping off the fish's nose. West of town you can ease your aches and pains wallowing in the warm sulphurous mineral waters of the municipal spa baths, in an old cave divided into three bathrooms (*open daily 8–1, take a towel; adm*). Beyond is small Lagáda Beach, popular with families and a monument at Bombarda commemorates the French who died there during the Crimean War. Further along the track, reed-beds with gurgling hot mud pools mark the route to the 'Volcano', really a glorified steaming fissure in the rock.

From Adámas the vast, sandy **Bay of Mílos** sweeps round dramatically with a succession of beaches like **Papikinoú**, backed by hotels and apartments. Hire a car or motorbike to get past the salt-beds, industrial and the airport clutter to reach the unusual and spectacular sandy beach at **Achivadólimni**, the island's longest, with a deep turquoise sea in front and a salt-water lake behind, named after the clams who live there. Other pale golden beaches along the coast are **Rivári** with a lagoon once used as a vivarium by the monks at **Ag. Marína Monastery** and **Emboriós** with rooms to let and a quaint taverna.

## Pláka and Around: Ancient Melos and its Catacombs

Buses leaves frequently for **Pláka** (ΠΛΑΚΑ) the labyrinthine, sugar-cube capital, 4km uphill, blending into the windmill-topped suburb of **Tripití** (ΤΡΥΠΗΤΗ). Next to the bus stop is the **Archaeology Museum** (*open 8.30–3, closed Mon*), its entrance marked by a plaster copy of Venus, a thoughtful consolation prize from Paris. Inside are finds from the Neolithic era and wonderful terracotta objects and lily-painted ceramics from Philakopi, including the famous *Lady of Philakopi*, a decorated Minoan-style goddess. There are Hellenistic finds from Kímolos and several statues, but like Venus, the famous marble *Poseidon* and the *Kouros of Mílos* are not at home but in the National Archaeological Museum in Athens. Signs point the way to the **Folklore and Laographic Museum** (*open10–1 and 6–8, Tues–Sat*), housed in a 19th-century mansion; it's especially fun if you can find someone to tell you the stories behind the exhibits, which include everything down to the kitchen sink.

Steps lead up to the Venetian **Kástro** set high on a volcanic plug. You can see some of the ruined houses that formed the outer walls of the fortress. Perched on top was the ancient church of **Mésa Panagía** or the **Assumption**, blown up by the Germans during the Second World War. When the church was rebuilt after liberation the locals saw the icon of the Virgin in a bush on top of the Kástro. Every time they moved the icon it returned to the bushes so they saw it as a sign to build a new church there, also called **Panagía Skiniótissa**, 'Our Lady of the Bushes'. There are breathtaking views from there, and on the way up the church of the **Panagía Thalassítras**, 'Our Lady of the Sea', 1228, also has stunning views over Pláka and the sea, especially at sunset. The door lintel bears the emblem of the Crispi family, who over-threw the Sanudi as dukes of Náxos. The church houses fine icons by Emmanuel Skordílis. Two other churches worth visiting are **Panagía Rosaria**, 'Our Lady of the Rosary', the Roman Catholic church built by the French consul Louis Brest, and **Panagía Korfiátissa** on the edge of a sheer cliff to the west of the village which has Byzantine and Cretan icons rescued from the ruined city of Palaía Chóra, or Zefyría.

Archaeologists believe that **Pláka** is built over the acropolis of ancient **Melos**, the town destroyed by the vindictive Athenians and resettled by the Romans. In the 1890s the British school excavated the site at **Klíma**, a short walk below Pláka (if you take the bus, ask to be let off at Tripití), where you can visit a termitiary of **Catacombs** (*open daily except Wed and Sun, 8.45–3*), dating from the 1st century AD. One of the best-preserved Early Christian monuments in Greece, it has long corridors of arched tomb niches carved in the rock, each with a little light before it that you can move about in order to examine a tomb more closely. When first discovered, the catacombs were still full of bones, but contact with the fresh air quickly turned them to dust. Some niches held five or six bodies; other bodies were buried in the floor. On some, inscriptions in red still remain (writing in black is later graffiti). The habit of building underground necropoli (besides the many at Rome, there are catacombs in Naples, Syracuse and Malta) coincides with the presence of soft volcanic tufa more than with romantic notions of persecution and secret underground rites; burying the dead saved valuable space and answered to the desire of early Christians to stick as close as possible after death to the holiest members of their congregations, as if hoping to grab on to their bootstraps when their souls ascended on Judgement Day. (Curiously, the modern cemetery of Mílos near Pláka resembles a row of catacombs above ground, the more posh ones even done out with carpets). A path from the catacombs leads to the place where Venus was discovered—there's a marker by the fig tree.

## The Venus de Milo, or Unclear Disarmament

On April 8, 1820, farmer Geórgios Kentrotás was planting corn when he discovered a cave containing half of a statue of the goddess Aphrodite. A French officer, Olivier Voutier, who just happened to be visiting Mílos at the time, urged the farmer to look for the other half. He soon found it, along with a 6th-century BC statue of young Hermes and Hercules as an old man—an ancient art lover's secret cache from the Christians. Voutier sketched the Aphrodite for his commanding officer and Louis Brest, the French consul for Mílos. They decided to buy the statue and a price was agreed. What happened next is complicated. The French consul in Constantinople sent an envoy to complete the deal. But meanwhile the farmer, persuaded by the island's elders, had sold the statue to another man on behalf of the translator of the Turkish fleet, the Prince of Moldavia, Nichólas Mouroúzis. The statue was in a caique heading into Turkish hands when the French envoy arrived. Eventually, after some brisk bargaining, he managed to buy the Venus as a gift for Louis XVIII and on 1 March 1821 she went on show in the Louvre, where she remains. Somewhere along the line she lost her arms and pedestal. The French cadet's sketch showed the arms, one hand holding an apple. Where they went is a mystery.

The path continues past the ancient Cyclopean city walls to the well-preserved **Roman Theatre**, where spectators looked out over the sea. Excavation and reconstruction work has been going on with plans to replace the original arch and restore the terraced seating and stage to former glory. A theatre company from Athens sometimes performs in the theatre in August. Remains of a **temple** are on the path back to the main road. From there you can take the road or an old *kalderími* pathway down to the fishing hamlet of **Klíma**, a photographer's joy with its brightly painted boat garages and rickety balconies above. A museum-style reconstruction at the end of the beach to show how the fishing families lived around their caiques. There's a hotel-cum-restaurant and ducks on the beach.

---

## Around Pláka

Most of the population of Mílos is concentrated in the villages around Pláka—commercialized **Triovassálos** which merges into **Péra Triovassálos**, **Tripití** and **Plákes**. The churches in Triovassálos contain icons from the island's original capital, inland **Zefyría**. At Easter there's great rivalry between the two villages. On Easter Sunday, after burning an effigy of Judas, the youths of Triovassálos and Péra Triovassálos hold a dynamite-throwing contest on a field which divides the villages. The winner is the team with the most ear-splitting performance. On the north coast, paths lead down to a wide selection of beaches, some adorned with wonderfully coloured rocks. One of the best swimming beaches is **Pláthíena** near the Arkoúdes, with dazzling orange and white rock formations; it's also the best place on Mílos to watch the sun set. You can walk down an old path from Pláka via the hamlets of **Aréti** and **Fourkovoúni** with picturesque boat garages hewn into the cliffs. **Mandrákia**, on the opposite side of the peninsula, is one of the island's most outstanding beauty spots, a stunning little cove studded with garages and topped by a white chapel. Further north, **Firopótamos** is another pretty fishing hamlet.

## Pollónia and Phylakopí

From Adámas or Pláka buses depart for **Pollónia** (ΠΟΛΛΩΝΙΑ) a popular resort with a tree-fringed beach, fishing boats, and tavernas. There's quite a bit of new holiday development with apartments and bars on the **Pelekóuda** cape. Water taxis leave Pollónia harbour for Kímolos, five times a day, weather permitting. On the way to Pollónia is **Filakopí** or Phylakopí (ΦΥΛΑΚΩΠΗ) village; blink and you'll miss the sign for the ancient site. Yet this was one of the great centres of Cycladic civilization, excavated by the British in the 1890s. The dig yielded three successive levels of habitation: the early Cycladic (3500 BC), the Middle Cycladic (to around 1600 BC) and Late Cycladic/Mycenaean.

Even in Early Cycladic days Mílos traded obsidian far and wide—pottery found in the lowest levels at Phylakopí shows an Early Minoan influence. Grand urban improvements characterize the Middle Cycladic period: a wall was built around the more spacious and elegant houses, some with frescoes—one depicts a flying fish, that in the absence of Venus has become the artistic symbol of Mílos. A Minoan-style palace was built; fine vases and Minoan ware were imported from Knossós; the obsidian trade reached the coasts of Asia Minor. Late in this period Phylakopí, like the rest of the Cyclades, may have come under the direct rule of the Minoans; a tablet found on the site written in a script similar to Linear A. During the Late Cycladic age, the Mycenaeans built their own shrine, added a wall around the palace, and left behind figurines and ceramics. Phylakopí survived to see the decline of Mílos' importance, as metals began to replace the need for obsidian. For all its history what actually remains at the site—walls, mostly—are quite overgrown and inexplicable to the layman.

## A Geological Mystery Tour of Mílos

From Adámas excursion boats putter across the bay to the beach at **Emborió** or on round **Cape Váni** to tour the island's incredible caves and rock formations that can't be reached on foot. Sights not to miss include the curious **Glaoníssia**, four cave-pocked basalt islets, the largest of which stands 20m high and is shaped like organ pipes; the cave of **Sikía** where the sun's rays slanting through the roof create dramatic colours in the water; **Kléftiko**, the pirates' hideaway with another set of fantastic cream and white rocks rising from the sea; **Paleoréma** on the east coast with a disused sulphur mine which turns the water emerald-green; **Papafrángas**, where a pool of brilliant azure water is enclosed by a circular rock formation, once used by trading boats as a hiding place from pirates. You can also sail near **Andímilos** to the northwest, a reserve for rare Cretan chamois goat, or *kri-kri*. Off the road to Pollónia the moonscape of **Sarakíniko** is a must with its huge rounded rocks and pointed peaks like giant white meringues, plus a tiny beach and fjord-like inlet. Further along near **Ag. Konstantínos**, steps also lead down to **Papafrángas Cave.**

Roads are being improved and buses cross the island to Paleochóri Beach. Otherwise you'll have to hire transport or walk to explore the rest of Mílos. South of Pollónia, at **Kómia**, are ruined Byzantine churches, and nearby at **Demenayáki** are some of Mílos' obsidian mines. Further inland, **Zefýria** or Chóra, served as the capital of Mílos from the Middle Ages to the 18th century. **Panagía Portianí** was the principal church of the village; a story recounts that its priest was accused of fornication by the inhabitants, and although he steadfastly denied it, the villagers refused to believe him. With that the priest angrily cursed the people, a plague fell on the town, and everyone moved down to Pláka. Today Zefýria is a very quiet village of old crumbling houses, surrounded by olive trees. **Alýkes** on the bay is a good beach near the **Mávra Gremná**, or the black cliffs, with more fantastical rock formations. At several places out in the bay the sea bubbles from the hot springs released below. Local legend has it that the generous spring near the airport is a sure bet against sterility in women.

## South and West Mílos

The most popular south coast beaches are **Paleochóri** and next-door **Ag. Kyriakí**, both sandy bays with tavernas. **Provatás Beach** is another sandy beauty and at **Loutrá Provatá** you can examine remains of Roman mosaics, followed by a natural sauna. The waters are famous for relieving rheumatism; Hippocrates himself wrote of the healing properties of Mílos' waters. **Kípos**, further along the coast, has two churches: one, the 5th-century **Panagía tou Kipou**, is the oldest in Mílos. In the wild **Chalákas** region in the deep south, the old monastery at **Ag. Marína** is worth a trip and from here you can climb to the top of **Profítis Ilías**, with a gods' eye view over Mílos and neighbouring islands. Back on the Bay of Mílos there are beaches at **Patrikia** and further north at exposed **Ag. Dimitríou**, which is often battered by winds. If you hire a boat, the coves carved in the south coast make ideal stopovers for a skinny dip.

Down in the southwest the famous monastery of **Ag. Ioánnis Theológos Siderianós** has a celebrated *panegýri* on 25 September. Ag. Ioánnis, St John, is known here as the Iron Saint— during his festival the revellers were attacked by pirates and took refuge in the church. In response to their prayers, the saint saved them by turning the church door to iron (you can still see a scrap of a dress caught in the door as the last woman entered). The pirates could not break in, and when one of them tried to shoot through a hole in the church dome, Ag. Ioánnis made his hand wither and fall off, still holding the pistol. Another miraculous story from April 1945 tells of a shell from an English warship zapping through the church door and embedding itself in the wall without exploding.

*Mílos ✆ (0287–)*                                         ***Where to Stay and Eating Out***

There are private rooms to let in Pláka, Triovassálos and Tripití: call ✆ 21 528, George Mallis, president of Rooms to Let Association. There are also rooms in Pollónia and Paleochóri, but most of the accommodation is in Adámas. The tourist office has lists; expect to pay 4000dr minimum. There are no campsites and freelance camping is strictly prohibited. If you want to sleep out, do so with caution—the local police can be sticky and levy big fines.

### Adámas

**Kapetan Giorgadas** ✆ 21 955/22 284 (*lux–exp*) are re-vamped apartments, small but exclusive. **Venus Village**, Langáda beach, ✆ 22 030/341 (*B; exp*) is a hotel and bungalow complex with pool, taverna, disco. Near by, the **Hotel Delfini**, ✆ 22 001 (*D; mod*) is a friendly family-run hotel with an nice breakfast terrace; the same family also runs the smart new **Seagull Apartments**, ✆ 23 183/193 (*lux–exp*). **Hotel Adamas**, ✆ 22 322/581, ✆ 22 580 (*B pension; exp–mod*) is handy for ferries, perched above the harbour. On the other side of town, **Popi's Hotel**,

✆ 22 393/286/287, ✉ 22 396 (*B pension; exp*) is comfortable with very helpful management. The **Hotel Semiramis**, ✆ 22 117/8 (*D; mod*), run by helpful brothers is excellent with a pretty vine-clad terrace—help yourself to grapes—bar, transfer minibus and rent-a-bike service. **Chronis Hotel and Bungalows** ✆ 22 226, ✉ 22 900 (*C; exp–mod*) features fully equipped stone cottages in a pretty pistachio orchard but is under miserable management. **Hotel Mílos**, ✆ 22 087, ✉ 22 306 (*C; mod*), on the seafront, doesn't look much but has an excellent restaurant and friendly service. Adámas has most of the island's restaurants; if you come in the right season, look for clams from Chivadólimni. On the waterfront the best bet for Greek home cooking is **Barko Restaurant**, with good barrel wine, cheap and cheerful. Friendly **Flisvos** has the usual fish and oven-ready dishes; next door **O Kynigos** serves similar fare in unpretentious but pleasant surroundings. After contemplating the bay in Adámas over an evening ouzo, a short stroll (past the taxi and bus stop) will take you to the **Hotel Milos Restaurant**, popular with Greeks and surprisingly good. Further along, fish come up to feed beneath the terrace at **Trapatseli's**, which has an excellent menu, especially for fish dishes. The *spetsofái* fish stew and *soupiés*, cuttlefish *stifádo*, are good as well as the local *dópio* hard cheese; next door **Navayio** also has fresh fish and Milian *mezédes*. In town, for real spit roasts head for **Ta Pitsounakia** at the crossroads with all kinds of meats and *kokorétsi*, while **Aktaio** on the water's edge is a popular haunt for breakfasts, pizza and ice-creams. On the coast road just beyond the airport, **Akroyiali Restaurant** is also recommended.

### Pláka/Tripití/Klíma

In Pláka, the **Plakiotiki Gonia**, Pláka Corner, is a sweet little taverna with local dishes like cheese pies and country bread with tomato paste; **Karamitsos** is also popular. For something completely different try **Popi's Windmill** up at Tripití, ✆ 22 285/7 (*lux–exp*) a hotel in a beautifully converted mill. Nearby, the *ouzerie* and snack-bar **Methismeni Politia**, the 'Drunken State', specializes in *mezédes*, wines and ouzo in a romantic garden setting with views across the gulf. In Klíma the **Hotel/Restaurant Panorama** ✆ 21 623 (*C; exp–mod*), has rooms with private bath and dining terrace with great views; a good bet for lunch.

### Pollónia

**Kapetan Tassos**, ✆ 41 287, ✉ 41 322 (*A; exp*) are Cycladic-style apartments that are pretty smart. **Apollon** apartments and studios ✆ 41 347 (*exp*) have views over Kímolos and home-cooking at the family taverna. Other local favourites are **Petrakis** and **Kapetan Nikolas**.

### Paleochóri Beach/Ag. Kyriakí

The **Artemis Restaurant** at Paleochóri has bungalows; call ✆ 31 222. **Thirios Restaurant** at Ag. Kyriakí has rooms, ✆ 22 779/058.

---

### Entertainment and Nightlife

Mílos has quite a sophisticated nightlife with scores of dancing bars and discos; there's even a roller-skating rink in Adámas. At night the harbour front comes alive with everything from gelaterias and pizzerias to touristy *ouzeries*. Locals hang out at **Yanko's** café near the bus stop, **To Ouzerie** on the front or **To Kafeneion** for cocktails and Greek music in a flower-filled courtyard. Otherwise in Adámas the hot spots are **Notos Dancing Club**, the **Disco White Club** at Langáda beach, **Pub Dream** and the **Dancing Club** at Triovassálos, **Vipera Libertina Bar**, and **Pub 82** for Greek music. In Pollónia head to **8 Bofor**, 8 MΠΩΦΟΡ, at Pelekoúda for jazz, blues and rock.

# Mýkonos (MYΚΟΝΟΣ)

This dry, barren island frequently plagued by high winds, but graced with excellent beaches and a beautiful, colourful, cosmopolitan town, has the most exciting and sophisticated nightlife in Greece. This, and its proximity to Délos, has made it the most popular island in the Cyclades. If the surge in tourism in recent years caught the other islands unawares, Mýkonos, at least, didn't bat an eyelid, having made the transformation long ago from a traditional economy to one dedicated to the whims of the international set. If you seek the simple, the unadorned, the distinctly Greek—avoid Mýkonos like the plague. But the party will go on without you; Mýkonos' streets are jammed with some of the zaniest, wildest, raunchiest and Most Beautiful People in Greece. It also has the distinction of being one of the most expensive islands, and the first officially to sanction nudism on some of its beaches; it is also the Mediterranean's leading gay holiday resort, though it's popular with a mixed crowd of people with money to spend.

## History

The Ionians built three cities on Mýkonos: one on the isthmus south of Chóra, the second at Dimastos, dating back to 2000 BC, and the third at Pánormos near Paliókastro. During the war between the Romans and Mithridates of Pontus, all three were destroyed. Chóra was rebuilt during the Byzantine period, and the Venetians surrounded it with a wall that no longer exists; however, at Paliókastro a fort built by the Gizzi rulers still remains.

## Mythology

In myth Mýkonos is best known as a graveyard, site of the rock tombs of the last giant slain by Hercules and that of Ajax the Lokrian, or of Oileus, one of the Achaean heroes of the Trojan War. This Ajax was known as Little Ajax to differentiate him from Big Ajax, who committed suicide when the weapons of the dead Achilles were not given to him but to Odysseus. After the capture of Troy, Little Ajax proved himself just as pathetic a hero when he raped Priam's daughter Cassandra, who had sought protection in a temple of Athena. Athena avenged this blasphemy by wrecking Ajax's ship off the coast of Mýkonos. Poseidon saved him in a sea storm but, defiant as ever, Ajax declared that he would have been able to save himself without the god's assistance. Poseidon's trident finished Ajax then and there, and his Mycenaean tomb can still be seen at Línos.

---

### Getting There and Around

**By air**: daily connections with Athens, several times a week with Santoríni, Rhodes, and Herákleon (Crete). Less frequently with Chíos, Mytilíni, Sámos. Airport information, © 22 327. Shuttle service from the aiport to Chóra.

**By sea**: daily with Piraeus, Rafína, Ándros, Tínos, Sýros, Páros, Náxos, Íos and Santoríni; several times a week with Sámos, Herákleon (Crete),

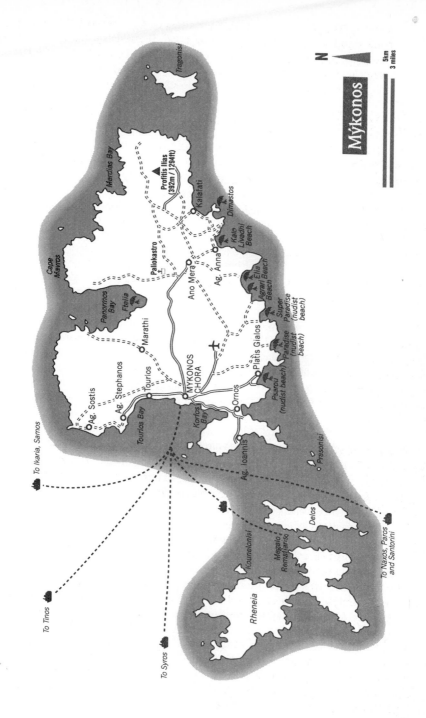

Mýkonos

N

5km
3 miles

Tragonisi

Merdias Bay

Cape Mavros

Proftis Ilias
(392m / 1294ft)

Kalafati

Dimastos

Kalo Livadhi Beach

Ag. Anna

Paliokastro

Elia Beach

Ano Mera

Agrari Beach

Panormos Bay

Ftelia

Super Paradise (nudist beach)

Marathi

Paradise (nudist beach)

Platis Gialos

Ag. Stephanos

MYKONOS CHORA

Ornos

Psarou (nudist beach)

Ag. Sostis

Tourlos

Tourlas Bay

Korfos Bay

Ornos Bay

Ag. Ioannis

Presonisi

To Ikaria, Samos

Delos

To Naxos, Paros and Santorini

Tigoumelonisi

Megalo Remmatiaris

To Tinos

Rheneia

To Syros

Amorgós, Astypálaia, Kos, Rhodes, Koufoníssia, Schinoússa and Heráklia. Twice a week with Síkinos, Folégandros, Skiáthos and Thessaloníki, once a week with Kálymnos, Sífnos, Sérifos, Níssyros, Tílos and Ikaría. By **hydrofoil**: daily except Sunday to Náxos and Rafína via Ándros and Tínos. **Catamaran** daily except Sunday to Piraeus (Flísvos), via Sýros and Tínos; to Íos, Síkinos, Folégandros, Santoríni and other Cycaldes. **Excursion boats** to Délos daily between 8 and 10, returning between 12 and 2; 1400dr return, guided tour, 4500dr, ✆ 22 089. **Port authority**, ✆ 22 218.

**By road: buses** from north and south bus stations to Áno Merá and the beaches.

---

### Tourist Information

On the quay, **tourist police** ✆ (0289) 22 482 share the same building as the Hotel Reservations Office, open 8am to midnight; the Association of Rooms and Apartments ✆ 24 860, open 10–6; and the camping information office.

## Chóra

Prosperity has kept the homes of **Chóra** (XΩPA), the island's picture-postcard capital and port, well maintained, gleaming and whitewashed, with brightly painted wooden trims. In the main square a bust of Mandó Mavroyénous (the heroine from Mýkonos who fought in the War of Independence) once served as the island's guardian of left luggage; now dire little notices keep the backpacks away. The square also maintains the taxi stand and several tacky but inexpensive snack bars. Further up the waterfront is the departure quay for the boats to Délos. The pelican mascot of Mýkonos, the successor of the original Pétros, may often be found preening himself in the shadow of the small church here. This side of the harbour also has the tourist police office, and on the hill overlooking the harbour are several windmills. Until recently one still ground wheat; another has been converted into a cottage. They are a favourite subject for the many local artists, as is '**the little Venice of Mýkonos**', the houses of Alefkándra, tall and picturesque and built directly beside the sea, just below the windmills.

Mýkonos claims to have 400 churches, and the most famous of these is the unusual **Panagía Paraportianí**, an asymmetrical masterpiece of folk architecture. Next to it is the island's **Folklore Museum**, a collection of bric-à-brac salvaged from Mýkonos' past. Upstairs you can visit a recreated bedroom and kitchen, and a gallery of 19th-century prints of sensuous Greek odalisques gazing dreamily into space; downstairs is an exhibition, 'Mýkonos and the Sea' (*open 4–6pm*). The **Archaeology Museum**, on the far side of the harbour near the Leto Hotel, highlights artefacts from the islet of Rhéneia, excavated by the Greek archaeologist Stavrópoulos; after the Athenian purifications, Rhéneia served as the necropolis of Délos. Other exhibits include a *pithois* (storage pot) carved with scenes from the Trojan War, including a charming Trojan horse stuffed with soldiers, discovered on Mýkonos itself (*open 8.30–3, closed Mon*). The **Nautical Museum**, at the end of the main street Matogiánni, consists of four rooms containing ships' models from ancient times and a collection of paintings, prints and old coins. The garden has become the last resting place of old anchors, ships' wheels, cannons, compasses and fans from a lighthouse operated by an oil lamp (*open daily in summer 10.30–1; 6.30–9.30pm*). Adjacent to the maritime musem is **Lena's House**, a 19th-century mansion which preserves the lifestyle of a Mykonot maiden lady, Léna Scrivanoú, from her lace and needlework to her chamber pot (*open Mon–Sat, 6–9pm, Sun 7–9 pm*).

# Around Mýkonos

In ancient times Mýkonos had the dubious distinction of being famous for the baldness of its men, and even today the old fishermen of the island never take off their distinctive caps. Despite all the changes, they have kept their sense of humour, and if you speak a little Greek they'll regale you with stories of the good old days—before all the tourist girls (and boys) began chasing them around. The only other town on Mýkonos is **Áno Merá**, (ANΩ ΜΕΡΑ) where the **Panagía Tourlianí Monastery** with its 15th-century carved steeple is the main attraction. There's also a small folk museum (*open 10–1*). Sandy **Pánormos Bay** to the north was the site of one of Mýkonos' three ancient cities. The second ancient city, **Dimastos**, is believed to have been on top of Mount Ágios, Mýkonos' highest point. At Línos are the remains of a Hellenistic tower and walls; at **Pórtes** you can spit on the tomb of Ajax the troublemaker. The greenest spot on the island is the **Garden of Rapáki**, east of Chóra (a good half-hour walk).

**Dragonísi**, the islet off the east coast of Mýkonos, has numerous caves, and if you're very lucky you may see a rare monk seal in one of them. Boats for the excursion or a private trip to Délos may be hired at **Platís Gialós**, the main family beach, while **Paradise** and gay **Super Paradise** are the main nudist beaches on the island. There are so many others scattered along the island's coasts that you could spend an entire holiday visiting them all. Particularly popular are **Psaroú**, just before Platís Gialós, and **Ornós**. Both have a selection of tavernas serving fresh fish. One of the more pleasant and less crowded beaches is **Eliá**, which has the added advantage of being accessible by local bus, on the road past the Hard Rock Café. **Ag. Ánna** and the fishing hamlet of **Kalafátis** are also worth a trip.

## Mýkonos ✆ (0289–)

*Where to Stay*

There's certainly no lack of places to stay on Mýkonos, although prices tend to be higher than almost anywhere else in Greece. Sleek new hotels, many incorporating elements of the local architecture, occupy every feasible spot on the coast, especially along the road to Platís Gialós. When you arrive off the ferry you'll be inundated with people  offering rooms; many of these are up the hill above Chóra, in a barren, isolated and ugly area of holiday apartments. If you want a more attractive location, hunt around in Kalogéra Street, a pretty cobbled walkway in the heart of town; the area's very popular, but you might get lucky if you get there in the morning before 11am. Otherwise reservations are advisable from June onwards. Rooms in private houses are at least 4000dr; ask at the Hellenic Travel Centre at the Fabrica bus stop, ✆ 23 904.

### Chóra

The **Adonis Hotel** ✆ 22 434, ✆ 23 449 (*C; mod*) is comfortable and central; **Hotel Zorzis** ✆ 22 167 (*C; exp–mod*) is a small American-run hotel in an old house on Kalogéra Street. **Hotel Carbonaki**, 27 Panahrándou, ✆ 22 461 (*exp*) is a good choice, with rooms arranged in Cubist blocks, plus a pool; **Leto Hotel**, ✆ 22 207, ✆ 23 985 (*A; exp*), has a wonderful view over the harbour and town, and was for many years the classiest place to stay on the island, but again the high season price reflects this. Off season, rates drop by around 20% or more. The cheerful little **Delos**, ✆ 22 312 (*C; exp–mod*) is a nice choice near the post office; **Manto**, 1 Evangelístrias, ✆ 22 330 (*C; mod*), is convenient for connoisseurs of the night scene, while **Apollon**, ✆ 22 223 (*D;*

*mod*) is a comfortable, friendly hotel, perfectly situated in the middle of the windy seafront. The delightful **Hotel Philippi**, ℗ 22 295 (*D; mod–inexp*) in the heart of Chóra at 32 Kalogéra Street, has rooms scented by the hotel's lovely garden. **Angela's Rooms**, ℗ 22 967 on Plateía Mavrogénous are some of the cheapest (*mod–inexp*).

### Just Outside Chóra

Favourite of Jane Fonda is the **Princess of Mýkonos** ℗ 23 806, ▦ 23 031 (*A; lux*) at Ag. Stéphanos, with pool, sauna, jacuzzi and the works. It isn't in the heart of the action, but only a taxi-ride away; still in that area the **Artemis**, ℗ 22 345 (*C; mod*), or the smaller D-class **Mina**, ℗ 23 024; both have perfectly acceptable rooms with bath. On the beach, within walking distance of town at **Tagoo** is the Cubist beauty **Cavo Tagoo**, ℗ 23 692, ▦ 24 923 (*A; lux*), 'pour les lucky few', with seawater pool, beautiful view of Mýkonos, and the chance to rub shoulders with the stars. **Hotel Aegean**, Tagoo, ℗ 22 869 (*B; exp*) is well-appointed but still family-run and friendly; just out of town **Manoula's Beach**, ℗ 22 900/23 428 (*C; exp–mod*) is where they filmed *Shirley Valentine*, and is a pretty bungalow complex. At Vríssi, the **Sourmeli**, ℗ 22 905 (*mod*) has a pleasant garden, and equally pleasant rates. At **Toúrlos Beach**, the small but stylish **Sunset Hotel**, ℗ 23 010, has moderate rates. **Rhenia**, ℗ 22 300 (*B; exp*) offers tranquil bungalows overlooking Chóra and Délos. **Bellou Hotel**, ℗ 22 589 (*C; mod*), at Mégali Ámmos, is quiet with no frills.

### Further Afield

The **Ano Mera Hotel** at Áno Merá, ℗ 22 404, ▦ 24 814 (*A; lux–exp*) is one of the island's best hotels with pool, restaurant and disco. At Platís Gialós the ritzy **Petinos Beach** ℗ 24 310, ▦ 23 680 (*A; lux–exp*) has every facility, pool, and water sports; at Ornós the **Ornos Bay Pension**, ℗ 23 961 (*B; exp–mod*), is friendly and right on the beach. All campers are referred to the barracks-like campground at **Paradise Beach Camping**, ℗ 22 582, ▦ 24 350 and next door **Mykonos Camping**, Paránga Beach, ℗ 24 578. Both have good facilities and minibus services plus continuous boat service from Platís Gialós.

---

*Mýkonos* ℗ *(0289–)* **Eating Out**

Again, no lack of opportunities here, especially if you have deep pockets. Within a few blocks you can sample a genuine American doughnut, top that off with a seafood pizza, and wash it down with a pint from the Irish Bar. If you take the complimentary bus out of Chóra, there's even a (real) **Hard Rock Café** where you can eat expensive fast food and lounge by a pool. The Stavrokopóulos family's **Taverna Vangelis**, on the square in Áno Merá is the place for local food including Mýkonos cheese, *kopanistí*.

In Chóra by contrast, there are numerous snack bars and bakeries with cheese pies, etc. if you're counting pennies. You can eat swordfish kebabs and squid and not pay an arm and a leg at the large restaurant connected to the motel on Platís Gialós Beach (*dinner for 2000dr*). **Philippi's** restaurant (connected to the Hotel Philippi) has the best reputation in town for international and Greek cuisine, served in the lovely garden (*count on 6000dr*). Close by and in the same price range (the wine is more expensive) is the **Edem**, also offering a varied international menu in a garden setting.

Centrally placed **Katrin's**, again fairly expensive, has many French specialities. If you need to be reminded that you're in Greece, head for **Niko's Taverna**, behind the town hall, or **Maky's**, just around the corner, with good dinners in the 2000dr range. Eat at least once at **Spiro's**, below the windmills, with a view of waves rolling up to the foot of the houses of 'little Venice'; seafood specialities in the medium price bracket. A notable exception to the rule that the back-streets hide the best, secret tavernas is **Antonini's**, slap in the middle of the activity on taxi square; genuine Greek food at fair prices: varied and excellent *mezé*, shrimp salad and very tasty veal or lamb casserole (*2000dr*). For fish, dine out at **Kounelas**, at the end of the water-front, where the owner, a colourful character, promises consistently fresh seafood (*4000dr*). At Toúrlos Bay **Matthew Taverna** is slick and well patronized, and at Ag. Ánna, at the end of the road that crosses the island, **Nikola's** is authentic and a local favourite. English-run **Sesame Kitchen** in Three Wells, Chóra, is a vegetarian's haven; **Langelo Bar** is the place for espresso, cappuccino and packed lunches for Délos and at **Kalafatis** the Italian seafood restaurant **Osteria Del Pesce Da Lu** is expensive but a treat.

---

## Entertainment and Nightlife

The international and gay set still bop the night away in venues ranging from the cosy to the crazy. The **Veranda Bar** in a converted mansion is a place to relax with a pleasant view of the windmills; **Bolero**, in the centre of town, has good music and cocktails; **Kastro's** in Little Venice will be forever famous for its sunset views, classical sounds and strawberry daiquiris. Live music and snazzy cocktails can be had at the **Piano Bar** above taxi square, but get there early for a seat. High-tech **Astra Bar** is the cool yuppie hang-out, while the **Vegera Bar** is New Age Athenian. **Thalami**, below the city hall, has Greek music and dancing, as does the perennial favourite, the **Mykonos Dancing Bar**; **Pierro's** remains the most frenzied of the lot, where hordes of people, from the young to the not-so-young, dance to the loud, lively music and spill out into the square. The **City Club** has a nightly transvestite show and **Manto**, **Nefeli** and **Icaros** are gay and lesbian favourites.

Bar prices it almost goes without saying, are exorbitant—more than you might pay in London or New York. A small bottle of lager will cost upwards of 800dr in one of the late-night bars of Chóra. Culture vultures can head for several private art gallery exhibitions or productions at the **Anemo Theatre** in Rochári Street.

# Náxos (ΝΑΞΟΣ)

Náxos, 448sq km in area, is the largest of the Cyclades and the most mountainous, its highest point, Mount Zas (or Zeus), crowning the archipelago at 1004m. It can also claim to be the most fertile, its cultivated valleys a refreshing green even in the height of the dry, sun-browned Cycladic summer. Lemons, and Kítron, a liqueur distilled from them, are Naxian specialities, but potatoes are the main export. Souvenirs of the island's ancient, Byzantine and Venetian past abound, and the entire west coast is almost one uninterrupted beach of silvery sands. It's not surprising, then, that this once little-known island attracts more visitors every year. The new airport has boosted the island's tourist industry, new holiday complexes are springing up and the island is particularly popular with German and Scandinavian package companies.

# History

Náxos was one of the major centres of the distinct Cycladic culture. Around 3000 BC, as now, the main settlements appear to have been near Chóra, on the hill of the Kástro, and at Grótta, where the sea-eroded remains of the Cycladic town can still be seen in the clear water. Tradition has it that the island was later colonized by a party from Karia, led by a son of Apollo named Naxos. Although these Naxians were Ionians, their most troublesome enemy was Miletus in Ionia proper, where some Naxian refugees, eager to take back the island for themselves, helped stir up trouble. According to Plutarch, many battles were fought between the two rivals at the fort called Delion, of which a few vestiges remain near Náxos town. The Naxian heroine Polykrite sought refuge here when Miletus besieged the island, only to find the gate of the fortress closed against her. One of the Miletan leaders found her there, and fell so in love with her that he agreed to help and informed Polykrite of all the movements of his armies. His information enabled the Naxians to make a sudden attack on the Miletians, but in the confusion of the battle Polykrite's lover was killed, and the girl died in sorrow the next day.

Náxos was one of the first islands to work in marble, and in the Archaic period produced the lions of Délos and *kouroi* statues of incredible size. Indeed, for a period, huge was beautiful on Náxos; in 523 BC the tyrant Lugdamis declared he would make Náxos' buildings the highest and most glorious in all Greece, although only the massive lintel from the gate of the Temple of Apollo survives on the islet of Palatia survives to tell the tale of his ambition. As with most of the islands, Náxos declined in importance in the Classical age. In Hellenistic times it was governed by Ptolemy of Egypt. Náxos next makes history in 1207 when the Venetian Marco Sanudo captured the island's chief Byzantine castle, T'Apaliroú, and declared himself Duke of Náxos, ruler over all the adventurers who had grabbed the Aegean Islands after the conquest of Constantinople in 1204. When Venice refused to grant Sanudo the independent status he desired, he broke away in 1210 and became the Latin Emperor's Duke of the Archipelago. Archipelago, or 'chief sea', was the Byzantine name for the Aegean; under Sanudo and his successors, it took on the meaning, 'a group of islands', in this case the Cyclades. Even after the Turkish conquest in 1564 the Dukes of Náxos remained in nominal control of the Cyclades, although answerable to the Sultan.

A latter-day Naxian, Pétros Protopapadákis, planned the Corinth canal and gave many public works to the island. He was the Minister of Economics during the 1920–22 misadventure in Asia Minor, and was executed with other members of that sad government by the subsequent regime. His statue now stands by the port.

# Mythology

After slaying the Minotaur, the Athenian hero Theseus and Ariadne, the Cretan princess who loved him, stopped to rest at Náxos on their way to Athens. Yet the next morning, while Ariadne slept, Theseus set sail and abandoned her. This, even in the eyes of the Athenians, was dishonourable, especially since Theseus had promised to marry Ariadne in return for the vital assistance she had rendered him in negotiating the Labyrinth. Various explanations for Theseus' ungallant behaviour have sprung up over the centuries. Did he simply forget about her, did he find a new mistress, or did the god Dionysos, who later found Ariadne and married her, desire her from the moment she set foot on Náxos, and warn Theseus away? Historically, some believe the myth demonstrates the rise of a late Cycladic civilization after the fall of Crete; others

# Náxos

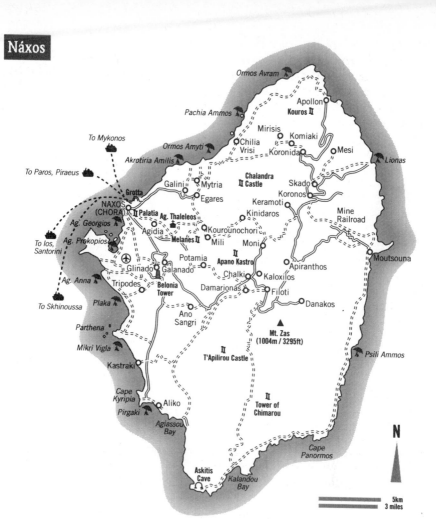

say that Ariadne, as a priestess of Crete, would have forfeited her rights and authority if she had gone to Athens. Common, however, are the accounts that it was the jilted bride's curse on Theseus that made him forget to change his black sails to white, inadvertently causing his father's death in Athens. In all events, Ariadne lived happily ever after with Dionysos, who taught the Naxians how to make their excellent wine and set Ariadne's crown, the Corona Borealis, amongst the stars; the Celts called it Ariansrod, where their heroes went after death. The story of Theseus and Ariadne inspired many later artists, most notably Richard Strauss' opera *Ariadne auf Naxos*.

## Getting There and Around

**By air:** daily from Athens; airport information, ✆ 23 292.

**By sea:** daily **ferry** to Páros, Sýros, Íos, Santoríni, Mýkonos, Tínos, Ándros and Piraeus; daily **boat** to Amorgós via Koufoníssia, Heráklia and

Schinoússa, connections 3 times a week with Herákleion (Crete), Sífnos, Sérifos, Sámos, Ikaría and Rafína, twice a week with Síkinos and Folégandros. **Hydrofoil:** daily except Sunday to Rafína via Mýkonos, Tínos and Ándros. **Catamaran** except Sunday from Flísvos up the Cyclades to Náxos then on to Íos, Folégandros and Santoríni or Amorgós and the Back Islands. Seasonal caiques to Ag. Ánna. **Port authority,** ✆ 22 300.

**By road:** frequent **bus** service to Ag. Ánna Beach and Appólonos via the inland villages, ✆ 22 291. **Taxi** rank near bus station; shuttle bus from airport.

### Tourist Information

Regular police, Náxos town, ✆ (0285) 22 100. **Port police,** ✆ 22 340 south of the quay. Orbit Travel Services, ✆ 22 454, are very helpful for accommodation and excursions and also represent Olympic Airways; the privately run Náxos Tourist Information Centre, ✆ 24 358, manages the Chateau Zévgoli Hotel.

### Festivals

Like the Cretans, the Naxians sometimes improvize verses at their *panegýria*, a custom dating back to ancient times. Some of the many celebrations are: **23 April**, Ag. Geórgios at Kinídaros; **1 July**, Ag. Anargýroi at Sangrí; **14 July**, Ag. Nikódimos, patron saint of Náxos town with a special procession of the icon and folk festival; **17 July**, at Kóronos; the **first week of August** sees the Dionýsia festival in Náxos town, with folk dancing in local costume; free food and wine in the central square; **15 August**, Panagía at Filotí; **23 August**, at Trípodes; **29 August**, Ag. Ioánnis at Apóllon and Apíranthos.

## Náxos Town and its Venetian Citadel

**Náxos,** or Chóra, the island's port and capital, is a fine Cycladic town, although some people find its twisting streets so narrow as to be almost claustrophobic and bewildering, which is just as the natives intended them to be, to confuse invading marauders. The old town, up on the hill, is divided into two neighbourhoods: **Boúrgos** where the Greeks lived, and **Kástro** above, residence of the Venetian-Catholic nobility. In the former, the Orthodox cathedral, the **Metropolis of Zoodóchos Pigí,** was created in the 18th century out of an old temple and older churches; its iconostasis was painted by Dimítrios Valvis of the Cretan school. Archaeologists have made some interesting discoveries near the Metropolis and would gladly knock it down for a slam-bang dig if only the bishop would let them.

Although the city walls have all but disappeared, the inner walls of the Kástro remain. Inside, some 19 Venetian houses still bear their coats-of-arms—something you'll almost never see in Venice proper, where displays of pride were severely frowned upon. Most of the Kástro's current residents claim descent from the Venetians, and many of their grandparents' tombstones in the 13th-century **Catholic Cathedral** boast grand titles. The cathedral was founded by Marco Sanudo, whose own palace, or what remains of it, can be seen directly across the square. Only one of the seven original towers of Kástro survives, locally known as **Pírgos,** guarding one of the three entrances to the *enceinte*. During the Turkish occupation Náxos had a reputation for its schools. In the Kástro there was the School of Commerce, and a school run by Catholic friars, attended for two years by the Cretan novelist Níkos Kazantzákis of *Zorba the Greek* fame. One of the school's buildings, not far from the cathedral, is now an **Archaeology Museum** (*open Tues–Sun, 8.30–3*) with improved lighting to display its collection of Cycladic figurines, Mycenaean pottery, a Roman mosaic of Europa, pieces of Archaic *kouroi* and a statuette of a pig about to be sick in a sack.

North of the port, the ancient causeway stretches out to the islet of **Palátia** and the unfinished **Temple of Apollo**, begun in 522 BC. The **Portára**, a massive lintel on the temple platform, a lone gateway to nowhere, is now used as a dramatic frame for sunset photos. A small sandy beach curves around the causeway, protected by the ancient **harbour mole**, rebuilt by Marco Sanudo. The north shore of Chóra is called **Grótta** for its numerous caves, and re-dubbed Grotty by Brits; it is here that you can see remains of the Cycladic buildings underwater. In one place a few steps are discernible; the locals claim that in ancient times a tunnel went from Grótta to Palátia. It is near the site of the ancient **Fort Delion**.

The busy waterfront has a refurbished promenade and bustles with cafés and tourist shops, but villagers still come into town to sell their produce. In early August the main square, near the ferry port and bus station, is the site of the **Dionysia**, a festival of folk music and dance, wine and *souvlákia*. To the south, above the Agrarian Bank, is the 11th-century church of **Panagía Pantanássa**, once part of a Byzantine monastery and famous for its very early icon of the Virgin. Further south, numerous hotels and a whole new suburb, Néa Chóra, have sprung up around popular **Ag. Geórgios** beach.

## Naxian Beaches

The busiest beach on the sandstrewn west coast of Náxos is **Ag. Ánna**, linked by bus and caique from Chóra. You can also take a boat from here to Píso Livádi on Páros. Well sheltered from the notorious *meltémi*, this beach and the neighbouring ones of **Ag. Prokópios** to the north, and **Pláka** to the south, offer a variety of watersports for experts and beginners alike with jet-skis and windsurfers for hire. Pláka has a camping site and beach, considered the best in Náxos, and is home to a new crop of young hippie. It's also largely nudist.

Further south stretch the vast strands between **Mikrí Vígla** and Kastráki. The sea here is brilliantly clear; the beaches are of pure white sand. To the north, **Parthéna** beach is excellent for surfing and swimming and, to the south, **Sahára** is well equipped for sea sports. Further south, Sahara extends into **Kastráki**, again with sparkling clean sea and white sands, ideal for swimming, sunbathing and letting the kids run wild. Kastráki derives its name from the ruined Mycenaean fortress, built over the remains of a Cycladic acropolis. From here you can walk up to **T'Apalíroú**, the Byzantine castle high on its rock that defied Marco Sanudo and his mercenaries for two months. If the above beaches are too busy for your taste, there's a more remote strip of sand beyond Kastráki at **Pirgáki**.

## Marble Quarries, Venetian Towers and Olive Groves

The main asphalted road south of Chóra leads through the fertile and flat **Livádi Valley**. After a couple of kilometres the road splits, the left branch leading towards **Mélanes** and the ancient marble quarries in the heart of Náxos; at the one called Flerio, 3km east, lie two 7th-century BC *kouroi*, each 6m high. *Kouros* means 'young man', and in the Archaic period such statues—highly stylized, stiff figures, their arms hugging their sides, one foot stepping forward—were probably inspired by Egyptian art; the young men they portray are believed to have been Zeus' ancient guardians (the Cretan Curetes) or perhaps the Ionian god Apollo. At **Kourounochóri** near Mélanes stand ruins of a Venetian castle; **Ag. Thaléleos** in the same area has a monastery with a fine 13th-century church.

Back at the crossroads, the right branch of the main road from Náxos town leads to **Galanádo**, site of the ruined Venetian **Belonia Tower** and the twin Venetian church of **St John**, with a Catholic chapel on one side and an Orthodox church on the other. The recently restored **Ag. Mámas**, dating from the 8th century and Náxos' original cathedral, is a short walk from the road en route to **Sangrí** (ΣΑΝΥΚΡΙ). Actually three small villages spread out over the plateau, Sangrí gets its name from the Hellenized version of Sainte Croix, in turn the French for the 16th-century Monastery Tímiou Stavroú or True Cross. There are many Byzantine and medieval towers and churches in the area; one of these, **Ag. Ioánnis Gyroílas** in Áno Sangrí, is built over a temple of Demeter.

## The Valley of Tragéa and Slopes of Mount Zas

From Sangrí the road descends into the beautiful Valley of Tragéa, full of fruit trees and lilacs, flanked on either side by Náxos' highest mountains. Olives are the main product of the numerous small villages in the valley, including **Chálki**, where both the Byzantines and Venetians built towers: the Byzantine **Frankópoulo**, in the centre, and up a steep path the **Apáno Kástro**, last repaired by the Venetians and used, it is believed, as Marco Sanudo's summer home. He was not, however, the first to enjoy the splendid panorama from the summit; the fortress sits on Cyclopean foundations, and Mycenaean tombs have been discovered in the immediate area. In Chálki itself there are two fine churches with frescoes: 12th-century **Panagía Protóthronis** and 9th-century **Ag. Diasorítis**.

From Chálki a paved road leads up to **Moní**, home of the most unusual church on Náxos, **Panagía Drossianí**, crowned with ancient corbelled domes of field stones. The main road through the Tragéa valley continues on to **Filóti** (ΦΙΛΟΤΙ) on the slopes of Mount Zas, the largest village in the region, with splendid views, and the chance to eavesdrop on everyday life in a traditional Naxian village. There are many good walking paths in the region, one leading up the slopes of **Mount Zas**. Dedicated to the goddess Za or to Zeus, the father of the gods, there's a cave near the summit once used as a religious sanctuary. A 3-hour path from Filóti follows the west flanks of the mountain to the excellently preserved Hellenistic **Tower of Chimárou**, built by Ptolemy, its isolation the main reason for its survival over the centuries. In Filóti itself there's the Venetian stronghold of the De Lasti family, and the church **Koímisis tis Theotókou** with a fine carved marble iconostasis, and another church, **Panagía Filótissa**, with a marble steeple.

From Filóti the road skirts the slopes of Mt Zas on its way to **Apíranthos** (ΑΠΕΙΡΑΝΘΟΣ), where the Venetian families Crispi and Sommaripa built towers. Many contemporary families, however, claim Cretan blood, descended from migrants who came during the Turkish occupation to work in the emery mines. It's the most picturesque village on Náxos, and one of the most traditional, where some women still weave on looms and farmers sell their produce. Don't miss the ancient barber shop. In August, though, the atmosphere changes with cocktail bars and revelry. Visit the small **Cycladic museum**, devoted to mostly Neolithic finds (*open 8.30–1.30*) and a **geological museum** in the school. A road from here descends to the port of **Moutsoúna**, where the emery used to be brought down from the mountains near Kóronos by a rope funicular (more successful than the disastrous one used in *Zorba the Greek*) and loaded on to ships. Moutsoúna has a fine beach; from here a dirt road follows the east coast south to the remote beach of **Psilí Ámmos**. Another beach, **Liónas**, is linked by paved road to **Kóronos**.

Beyond Kóronos the road turns into a winding, hairpin serpent leading to pretty **Komiakí**, highest of the island's villages, with stunning views over terraced vineyards. The road leads back down to **Apóllon** or **Apóllonas** (ΑΠΟΛΛΩΝΑΣ), a dreary little town with a (very) public beach, several tavernas heavily patronized by tourist buses, and some mid-range pensions. Ancient marble quarries are carved out of the slopes of the mountain, and steps lead up to a colossal unfinished *kouros*, abandoned in the 7th century BC. Because Apóllon was sacred to Apollo, the statue is believed to represent the god; even more intriguingly, the long-vanished temple that stood here is part of the equilateral triangle formed by the temples of Apollo on Délos and Páros. Apóllon is as far as the bus goes; by car you can chance the unpaved road along the north coast back to Náxos town, passing the isolated beaches of idyllic **Ormós Ábram** with a taverna and rooms and **Pachiá Ámmos**, near the **Monastery of Faneroméni** dating from 1606. There are lovely beaches in this northwest corner of the island, although when the *meltémi* roars they are far from pleasant. **Galíni**, where the road improves, has the Byzantine fortified monastery **Ipsilóteras**, 'the Highest'. From here it's 6km back to Chóra.

---

*Náxos ✆ (0285–)*          **Where to Stay and Eating Out**

Prices are rising but Náxos is still cheaper than Páros, Mýkonos and Santoríni. Even in August there seem to be plenty of private rooms available, especially in the new suburb of Néa Chóra, unlovely but handy for the beach. It's a bit like an Athens suburb with its countless skeletons of future buildings, so make sure you can find your way 'home' through its tangle of anonymous streets.

## Náxos Town

In Náxos town one of the most genteel places to stay is the plush mansion **Château Zevgoli**, ✆ 22 993, ✉ 25 200 (*B; exp*) in the backstreets up towards Kástro. Small and exclusive with roof garden, antique décor and a four-poster for honeymooners. **Hotel Anixis**, ✆ 22 112 (*C; mod*) is handy for ferries overlooking the sea at Grótta, with basic rooms off a lovely garden terrace; **Despina Panteou's Rooms**, ✆ 22 356 (*inexp*) are nice doubles in an old house near the Kástro with a terrace. Of the small hotels in Boúrgos, just outside Kástro's walls, **Panorama**, ✆ 22 330 (*C; mod*) on Amphitris Street is the loveliest, with a marvellous sea view. Cheapest of all is the dormitory at the **Dionyssos Hotel**, ✆ 22 331 (*inexp*), up near the Kástro, where beds go for around 1000dr a night. In Grótta the **Hotel Grotta**, ✆ 22 215 (*C; mod*) is very pleasant with wonderful sea views, and the owner will collect you from the quay. Five minutes from the centre, **Hotel Anatoli**, ✆ 24 426 (*C; mod*), has a pool and sea views.

There's a restaurant or taverna to suit all tastes and wallets in Náxos, and you don't have to depend on the numerous fast food joints around the harbour if you're on a budget. On the waterfront, seek out **Popi's Grill**, which cooks superb chicken at very reasonable prices in basic surroundings, but with an authentically Greek atmosphere.

If you walk through the square towards the new town, you'll see **Papagalos**, run by Americans who serve 'international' cuisine. Don't let this discourage you; the food is well-prepared, reasonably priced, there are plenty of vegetarian dishes, and the staff are eager to please. If you want to splash out, **Oneiro** in the Kástro has candlelit tables in a courtyard, and a roof garden with a dream view. **To Kastro Taverna** on Pradóunas Square is tricky to find but worth it for good rabbit *stifádo* and *exohikó*, filo pastry parcels. Be warned that the cobbled streets around the Kástro have scores of expensive tourist restaurants serving overpriced schnitzel. At the south end of the waterfront the **Meltemi Restaurant** is one of the oldest and best, very Greek with excellent dishes and fresh fish; other haunts are unpretentious **Psigaria** with home-raised meat; **Rendezvous** (look for PANTEBOY), for breakfast and nibbles and if you're waiting for a ferry **Potikian** for snacks. You can try the local Kítron liqueur in the tourist bars, or buy a bottle or two as souvenirs in the Probonas shop on the water-front; you can have a free trial tasting (or three) first.

### Beaches South of Chóra

In Ag. Geórgios there's a fairly wide selection of reasonable hotels, including the family-run **Aeolis Hotel**, ✆ 22 321 (*C; mod*), and the smaller **St George Pension** on the beach, ✆ 23 162 (*C; mod*); **Barbouni Hotel**, ✆ 22 535, ✉ 23 137 (*C; mod*) is a nice family-run operation near the beach. At Ag. Ánna the new **Iria Beach Hotel Apartments**, ✆ 24 178, ✉ 23 419 (*C; mod*) is right on the beach with a range of facilities including car hire; **Ag. Anna Hotel**, ✆ 23 870 (*C; mod–inexp*) is also good. At Ag. Ánna, **Gorgona**, near the bus stop, serves a very competent evening spread and *híma* wine by the half-litre. **Kimothi**, run by cosmopolitan resting actors, serves up anything from pasta to *burritos*, day and night, with good music; **Paradise Taverna** has tasty Greek dishes, a terrace shaded by a vast pine tree, and an infectious atmosphere. At Mikrí Vígla, the new **Mikri Vigla**, ✆/✉ 75 240 (*exp*) is a low-rise mini-resort in Cycladic style, on the beach with a pool, surfing centre and restaurant; while at Ag. Prokópis the **Kavouras Village**, ✆ 25 580, ✉ 23 705 (*B; exp*) is on the same lines with villas and a wide range of facilities. Náxos' three campsites are here: **Camping Naxos**, ✆ 23 501 near Ag. Geórgios beach; immaculate, German-run **Camping Maragas**, ✆ 24 552 at Ag. Ánna; **Camping Apollon**, ✆ 24 117 at Ag. Prokópis. All have minibus services.

### Apollónos

**Hotel Adonis**, ✆ 81 360 (*C; mod*) is a comfortable place but if you want to get away from it all head for Abram and the **Pension Efthimios**, ✆ 63 222 (*inexp*).

---

### *Entertainment and Nightlife*

Náxos has a buzzing nightlife with masses of bars. But if you want to hear local music head for the Vallandóni Square near Probonas liquor shop where Greek men some-times play guitar and burst into song. Otherwise there's a **bouzouki** club for Greek entertainment just outside town. On the waterfront, fun places include the upstairs **Greek Bar**, smart **Veggera** (cloned from Mýkonos), stylish **Franco's** (cloned from Santoríni), the **Dolphin Bar** for jazz and very Greek **Diogenes**. In Kástro **Notos** is the place to mellow out with jazz in the courtyard; for cocktails and Mexican food head for the **Picasso Café Bar** and gallery next door to **Papagalos**. If wild and touristy is your scene then try **Musique Café** for late-night cocktails and music, **La Strada, Island Bar** and **Flisvos Club**. You can dance the night away at the **Asteria Disco**; the **Day and Night Music Club** or see the sunrise through the giant window at the **Ocean Club** right on the sea.

# Páros (ΠΑΡΟΣ)

Despite the thousands of tourists who descend on Páros each summer, the Cycladic houses, narrow alleys, little bridges and balconies overflowing with potted plants seem to dilute their presence. The Parians have approached the inevitable increase in tourism with less fervour than their neighbours on Mýkonos, managing, against overwhelming odds, to maintain a Greek island atmosphere. The inhabitants have, for the most part, remained fun-loving and hospitable and, if you can find a place to stay, it's a fine spot to while away a few days on golden beaches and charming villages, whose main building material comes from Páros' gentle mountain, Profítis Ilías (771m)—some of the finest, most translucent marble in the world, prized by Classical sculptors and architects. Páros is one of the larger and more fertile Cyclades, with vineyards, wheat and barley fields, citrus and olive groves, and—an unusual sight in the archipelago—pastures of grazing cattle and sheep. Apart from its beaches, the island has several other attractions, including a famous Byzantine cathedral and a valley filled with butterflies in the summer.

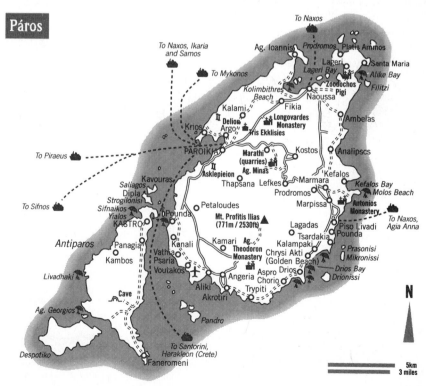

# History

With the trade in Parian marble, the island of Páros prospered early on. Its thriving Early Cycladic town was connected with Knossós and later with the Mycenaeans in the Late Cycladic period (1100 BC). In the 8th century BC Ionians moved in and brought about a second wave of prosperity. The 7th-century BC poet Archilochos, inventor of Iambic pentameter verse, and the sculptor Ariston were famous sons of ancient Páros. During the Persian Wars, Páros supported the Persians at both Marathon and Salamis; when Athens' proud General Miltiades came to punish them after Marathon, they withstood his month-long siege, forcing Miltiades to retire with a broken leg that developed into the gangrene that killed him. During the Peloponnesian Wars Páros remained neutral until forced to join the second Delian league in 378 BC. The island produced the great sculptor Skopas in the Hellenistic period and did well until Roman times, exporting marble to make the Temple of Solomon, the *Venus de Milo*, the temples on Délos and, much later, part of Napoleon's tomb. When the Romans took over Páros, their main concern was to take over the marble business.

Later invasions and destructions left the island practically deserted, and after 1207 the Venetian Sanudos ruled Páros from Náxos. Barbarossa captured the island in 1536, and from then on the Turks ruled by way of their proxy Duke of Náxos, although his control was often shaky, especially in the 1670s, when Páros was the base of Hugues Chevaliers, the original of Byron's *Corsair*. In 1770, the Parians had to put up with more unlikely visitors when the Russian fleet wintered on the island. During the War of Independence Mandó Mavroyénous, whose parents were from Páros and Mýkonos, led guerrilla attacks against the Turks throughout Greece; after the war she returned to Páros and died there.

## Getting There

**By air**: 5 flights daily (8 in the summer) from Athens. Airport ✆ 91 257.

**By sea**: daily **ferry** connections to Sýros and Piraeus, Náxos, Mýkonos, Íos, Santoríni, Herákleon (Crete), Antíparos and Sífnos, 3–4 times a week with Rafína, Sámos, Ikaría, Kárpathos, Rhodes, Koufoníssia and Amorgós, less frequently with the lesser Cyclades, Tínos, Skiáthos and Thessaloníki; once a week in summer to Corfu and Ancona in Italy; frequent boats to Antíparos from Paroikiá and Poúnta; summer **hydrofoil** and **catamaran** connections with Náxos, Mýkonos, Íos, Santoríni, Tínos, Sýros, Amorgós and Piraeus. **Port authority**, ✆ 21 240.

## Tourist Information

Plateía Mandó Mavroyénous, ✆ (0284) 21 673. There is also an information centre in the Windmill on the quay.

## Festivals

**23 April**, Ag. Geórgios at Agkairia; **21 May**, Ag. Konstantínos at Paroikiá; **40 days after Orthodox Easter**, Análypsis at Píso Livádi; in **July**, Fish and Wine Festival, Paroikiá; **15 August**, Ekatontapylianí at Paroikiá; **18 August**, Petaloúdes; **23 August** Náoussa sea battle; **29 August**, Ag. Ioánnis at Léfkas.

Paroikiá (ΠΑΡΟΙΚΙΑ), the island's chief town and main port, dominated by its famous windmill, doesn't always look much at first glance. But plunge among the immaculate streets, white houses and tidy blue domes of the waterfront and you'll soon discover Paroikiá is a Cycladic beauty, traversed by a long, winding main street that invites leisurely exploration, without having to trudge up hundreds of stairs. Since 1966, it's been the home of the Aegean School of Fine Arts, attended chiefly by American students. The centrepiece in the heart of town is a narrow 13th-century wall from the Venetian castle, built out of the temples of Apollo and Demeter into an attractive collage of columns and pediments that now serve as the walls of neighbouring houses.

### The Church of a Hundred Doors

On the west side of town, beyond a pine grove, stands Páros' chief monument, the cathedral **Ekatontapylianí** or 'church of a hundred doors'. According to tradition, it was founded by St Helen, mother of the Emperor Constantine, whose ship put into port at Páros during a storm, although actual construction of the church wasn't begun until the 6th century by Justinian. He hired an architect named Ignatius, an apprentice of the master builder of Ag. Sofía in Constantinople, and when the master came to view his pupil's work, he was consumed by jealousy and pushed Ignatius off the roof—but not before Ignatius had seized his foot and dragged him down to his death as well—a story told by the frieze in the north corner of the walled courtyard in front of the church. Another story accounts for its name: in reality only 99 doors have ever been found but when the 100th is discovered, it is a sign that Constantinople will return to the Greeks. Since the 6th century, earthquakes have forced several alterations and rebuildings, and in the 1960s an attempt was made—although not entirely successfully—to remove the Venetian Baroque trappings from the façade to restore its original appearance. Yet in the interior, reshaped in the 10th century to form a Greek cross with a dome on pendentives, the atmosphere is appropriately shadowy, jewel-like and Byzantine. Many stones are recycled from earlier churches and temples. Roman tombs and a well lie beneath the church floor.

On the carved wooden iconostasis, the icon of the Virgin is worshipped for its healing virtues; the church also contains the mortal remains of the Parian saint, Ag. Theóktisti. After being captured by pirates, Theóktisti managed to flee into the forests of Páros. For 30 years she lived a pious existence alone in the wilderness. A hunter finally found her, and when he brought her the communion bread she requested, she lay down and died. Unable to resist a free saintly relic, the hunter cut off her hand (now on display in a box) and made to sail away, but he was unable to depart until he had returned it to the saint's body. Beneath a wooden pallet is Theóktisti's footprint: the Greeks take off their shoes and fit their feet into it for good luck. Behind the iconostasis are frescoes and a carved marble Holy Table. The Baptistry to the right of the church has a sunken font. Towards the sea is the small church of **Ag. Nikólaos**, built at the same time as the Ekatontapylianí.

### Archaeology Museum

Near the church, a new building houses the **Archaeology Museum** (*open Tues–Sat 8.30–3; adm*), containing a section of the renowned 'Parian Chronicles'—a history of Greece, emphasizing the arts, from Kerkops (*c.* 1500 BC) to Diognetos (264 BC). The chronicle, carved in marble tablets, was discovered in the 17th century, and to read the rest of it you'll have to visit the Ashmolean Museum in Oxford. The Páros museum also has finds from the local temple of Apollo, a 5th-century BC Winged Victory, and a short biography and frieze about Archilochos, who took part in colonization of Thássos by Páros before he turned to lyric poetry; the ironic detachment of his verse inspired Horace.

## Náoussa

Frequent buses connect Paroikiá with the island's second port, the lovely fishing village turned jet-set hang-out of **Náoussa** (ΝΑΟΥΣΑ). Near the harbour stand the half-submerged ruins of the Venetian castle, with colourful caiques bobbing below. On the night of 23 August 100 boats lit by torches re-enact the islanders' battle against the pirate Barbarossa, storming the harbour, and all ends in merriment, music and dance. Náoussa has a **Byzantine Museum** with good icons, and there are others in the church Ag. Nikólaos Mostrátos. Very sophisticated, with trendy bars and boutiques, Náoussa is the place to sit and be seen.

Between Náoussa and Paroikiá, the 7th-century basilica **Tris Ekklisíes** was built over the site of a 4th-century BC heröon, or tomb-shrine of a hero or notable, in this case the poet Archilochos. Northeast of Paroikiá the marble foundation and altar of the **Temple of Delian Apollo** still remain. Together with temples to Apollo on Délos and Náxos, it forms part of a perfect equilateral triangle. One of the triangle's altitudes extends to Mycenae and Rhodes town, site of the Colossus—the biggest of all the statues of Apollo. Another heads up to Mount Áthos.

There are beaches within walking distance of Náoussa, or you can make sea excursions to others, notably **Kolimbíthres**, with its bizarre, wind-sculpted rocks; other sands near by are at **Lágeri**; take the caique from Náoussa harbour, then walk to the right for about ten minutes. Lágeri is nudist, a relaxed mix of gay and straight. **Santa Maria** is even further around the coast, as is the fishing village of **Ambelás**, with a taverna and a quiet hotel. Beautiful people flock to nearby **Poúnda**, not to be confused with the ferry port for Antíparos, as there's a trendy music bar on the beach, the hip place for Athenians and foreigners to chill out and pick up.

## Into the Land of Marble

From Paroikiá, the main road east leads to Páros' ancient marble quarries at **Maráthi**, not far from the fortified but abandoned monastery of Ag. Mínas. The quarries too are abandoned, for economic reasons (they were last used for Napoleon's tomb), but it's fun to poke around, especially if you bring a light—the longest tunnel stretches 90m underground. It produced an almost translucent stone called 'Lychnites' by the ancients, or 'candlelit marble', for its wonderful ability to absorb light. One of the quarries still has an ancient inscription.

The road continues to Páros' attractive medieval capital **Léfkes**, where farming, textiles and ceramics are the major industries. East of Léfkes, **Pródromos** is an old farming village; **Mármara**, another village, lives up to its name ('marble')—even some of the streets are paved with it. Prettiest of the three, though, is **Márpissa**. Above its windmills are the ruins of a 15th-century Venetian fortress and the 16th-century **monastery of Ag. Antónios**, constructed out of Classical materials and containing lovely marbles and paintings (note the 17th-century fresco of the Second Coming). The ancient city of Páros is believed to have been in this area.

Down on the east coast **Píso Livádi** served as the port for these villages and the marble quarries. It has a regular caiques in summer to **Ag. Ánna** on Náxos, and itself is the centre of Páros' beach colonies: **Mólos** is one and another is **Driós**; luxurious villas line the bay where the Turkish fleet used to put in on its annual tax-collecting tour of the Aegean. It's a pretty place with a duck-pond, waterside tavernas and sandy coves with rooms to rent overlooking the fields. Just to the north the island's best beach, golden **Chrysí Aktí**, stretches 700m. The winds on Páros blow fiercely in July and August, and Chrysí Aktí in particular has become a Mecca for serious windsurfers; in 1993 it was the venue for the World Windsurfing Championships.

## Southwest of Paroikiá

Just south of Paroikiá, by a spring, are the ruins of a small Classical-era **Asklepeion** (dedicated to the god of healing); originally a temple to Pythian Apollo stood nearby. The road south continues 6km to **Petaloúdes** (or Psychopianí), where swarms of tiger moths set up house-keeping in July and August and fly up in clouds as you walk by. Petaloúdes/Psychopianí has the ruins of a Venetian tower, while just outside the village stands the convent of Páros' second patron saint, **Ag. Arsénios**, the schoolteacher, abbot and prophet who was canonized in 1967. The saint is buried in the convent, but this time men are not allowed in. At **Poúnda** there is a beach, and from here the small boat crosses to Antíparos. There's another beach at **Alikí** which has some facilities—and Páros' airport.

---

*Páros ✆ (0284–)*          ***Where to Stay and Eating Out***

Páros is packed in the summer, and it's very hard to find a place if you just drop in. Nearly everyone stays in Paroikiá, Náoussa or Píso Livádi. Mid-range prices are higher than in most of the other Greek islands, in many cases double what you might expect, 6–8000dr in the high season for a pleasant but basic room.

**Paroikiá**

The **Dina**, ✆ 21 325 (*mod*) is the most charming, with simple pretty rooms and little garden. **Hotel Argonauta**, ✆ 21 440 (*C; exp–mod*) just back from the waterfront, is a pleasant family-run place. **Hotel Polos**, ✆ 22 173, ✆ 21983 (*C; mod*) is near the harbour with authentic Cycladic interiors. **Bayia Hotel**, ✆ 21 068 (*C; mod*) is a small family-run hotel surrounded by olive trees. **Kapetan Manolis**, ✆ 21 244 (*C; mod*) is also recommended, while **Hotel Kypreou**, ✆ 21 383 (*D; inexp*) is a comfortable budget option. The **Hotel Xenia**, ✆ 21 394 (*B; exp*) has a lovely view over the village in its green amphitheatre, and there's a bar and good restaurant. **Camping Koula**, ✆ 22 082, and **Parasporos**, ✆ 21 944, are near Paroikiá, and **Krios Camping**, ✆ 21 705, is at Kríos Beach, opposite the port. Most have minibuses that meet ferries.

The best food in Paroikiá, or on all of Páros for that matter, is at **To Tamarisko**, where you can dine delectably on international cuisine in the secluded garden at moderate prices. The **Levanti**, back from the harbour to the right of the Venetian castle walls, has Greek, French dishes and Lebanese dishes like *tabouleh* and *falafel*, good but expensive. Near Ekatontapylianí church is the **Lobster House** with the obvious speciality. Take a full wallet. For a simple, inexpensive taverna try **Nissiotissa**, behind the hospital; everything's good, especially the fresh fish. **Apollon Café**, fomerly an olive press, is a quiet eaterie with a garden full of pear trees. If you're fond of oriental cuisine, **May-Tey**, tucked away in the backstreets has a limited but high quality choice of Chinese, Vietnamese, and other southeast Asian dishes. The **Ouzerie Boudaraki** on the harbour road is an authentic *ouzerie* for *mezédes* of octopus and sea urchins.

## Náoussa

The island's most luxurious hotel is the **Astir of Paros**, ✆ 51 976, ✉ 51 985 (*lux*) on the beach with all your heart's desires plus VIP suites and gourmet restaurant; the smart **Atlantis Hotel**, ✆ 51 340, ✉ 52 087 (*C; mod*) is good with a pool and good facilities including mountain bikes for hire; **Hotel Aliprantis**, ✆ 51 571 (*C; inexp*) with balconies overlooking the busy main square. **Pension Galini**, ✆ 51 210 (*C; inexp*) is a friendly little place. For a touch of luxury, **Lilly Apartments**, ✆ 51 377, ✉ 51 716 (*A; exp*) are stylish and upmarket, right on the beach. **Naoussa Camping**, ✆ 51 595 is at Kolymbíthres between Náoussa and Paroikiá. Náoussa is one of the most picturesque places to eat in all Greece with tavernas huddled by the water's edge. But inevitably they're dearer than those further up the hill, and the bars can be a rip-off, so choose carefully. **Kargis Ouzerie** near the church is the real thing with charcoal grilled seafood and local *súma*, fiery schnapps. **Diamante** just up the hill serves good food at good prices, with draught wine and unusual Greek offal dishes of the day if you're lucky. At the other end of the price scale **O Christos** is Náoussa's finest, very ritzy for seafood and good Greek cuisine, elegant and expensive, **Laloula** is another place for a continental splurge in posh surroundings. For snacks and break-fast, the café below **Hotel Aliprantis** takes some beating.

## Píso Livádi and Around

The **Pension Marpissa**, ✆ 41 288 (*B; mod*) has an attractive view, although rooms are without bath. **Elina Residence**, UK contact ✆ (01274) 832771 (*mod*) is a lovely British-owned apartment overlooking the bay with views of Náxos. **Hotel Londos**, ✆ 41 218 (*C; mod–inexp*) is basic, but OK. **Afendakis Apartments**, ✆ 41 141 (*C; mod*) are beautifully appointed at Márpissa while in Léfkes the stone-walled **Xenia Hotel** ✆ 41 646 (*B; mod*) is a 10-minute bus ride from the beaches. Driós has plenty of Cycladic-style rooms and the **Hotel Anezina**, ✆ 41 037, ✉ 41 872 (*C; mod*), which has a romantic garden restaurant. Sleep under the stars at **Capt. Kafkis Camping** near Píso Livádi. In Píso Livádi **Stavros Taverna** is excellent for vegetable dishes and Greek favourites while next-door **Vrochas** does good grills and is popular with wind-surfers; in Pródromos those in the know head to **Roussos Restaurant** for Sunday lunch, chickpeas a speciality. **Fisilani's Taverna** in Logarás is also a good bet and **Maria's** in the garden at **Hotel Anezina**, Driós, has a magical setting. There's also a good taverna on Driós beach.

## Poúnda

The **Holiday Sun**, ✆ 91 284 (*A; lux–exp*), has all mod cons and is handy for Antíparos. **Surfing Beach**, ✆ 51 013, at Alykí, is the biggest and best organized, with a surf and water-ski school.

---

### *Entertainment and Nightlife*

Páros has something for everyone, from the rowdy waterfront bars at Paroikiá to the sophisticated haunts of Náoussa, but you'll be hard pressed to find much Greek entertainment. There's an outdoor **cinema**, **Cine Paros**, set back from the waterfront, and a clutch of disco bars like **Dubliner**, **Down Under** and **Londoner** for those feeling homesick. For sunset views over a cocktail, the popular **Pebbles Bar** plays classical music till sunset, thereafter jazz, occasionally live. Náoussa is awash with stylish bars, while in Driós **Limni**, **The Lake**, and the **Golden Garden** at Chryssí Aktí are both laid-back garden bars with a wide range of international sounds. In Píso Livádi there's a new **Ouzerie**, otherwise the favoured watering holes are the **Back Door Bar**, **Remezzo**, **Anchorage** and **Flotilla** bar, as well as the disco near Logorás.

# Antíparos (ΑΝΤΙΠΑΡΟΣ)

Little Antíparos, 'opposite' Páros, was anciently known as Oliaros, and was connected to its larger neighbour by a causeway. In the time of Alexander the Great a large, deep cave full of stalactites was discovered on Antíparos, and for the past 2000 years it has been a must stop for every traveller in the region. Many who find Páros too tourist-ridden end up on a quiet Antiparian beach (there are good ones at Kástro, at Sifnaíkos Gialós in the north, and Ag. Geórgios in the south). Fish is plentiful, even in the restaurants, and there are many rooms to rent and three hotels.

---

### Getting There

**By sea**: hourly every day by **caique** from Paroikiá, Páros, and hourly **car ferry** from Poúnta, Páros. **Port authority**, ✆ 61 485.

---

### Tourist Police

See regular police in town, ✆ (0284) 61 202.

---

### Festivals

**23 April**, Ag. Geórgios; **8 May**, Ag. Ioánnis Theológos, by the cave; and **21 May**, Ag. Konstantínos at Glyfa.

## Kástro and the Cave

Lacking any defences, Antíparos was uninhabited after the fall of Rome until the Venetians, under Leonardo Lorentani, built a small castle. There are also two 17th-century churches, the cathedral **Ag. Nikólaos** and **Evangelismós**.

The **cave** remains Antíparos' star attraction, despite centuries of tourists whacking off free souvenir stalactites. In the summer excursion boats run not only from Kástro, but also from Paroikiá and Poúnda. From the boat landing stage it's a half-hour walk up by foot and less by donkey, and then a 70m descent by steps into the fantastic, spooky chamber. The cave is really about twice as deep, but the rest has been closed as too dangerous for visits. Perhaps to make up for breaking off the stalactites, famous visitors of the past have smoked and carved their names on the walls, including Lord Byron and King Otho of Greece (1840). One stalagmite attests in Latin to a Christmas mass celebrated in the cavern by Count Nouantelle in 1673, attended by 500 (paid) locals. Unfortunately, a famous older inscription has been lost; its several authors declared that they were hiding in the cave from Alexander the Great, who had accused them of plotting an assassination attempt. The church by the entrance of the cave,

**Ag. Ioánnis**, was built in 1774. If you come in the winter, you'll have to pick up the key to the cave's entrance in Kástro.

Of the islets off Antíparos, **Strogilónisi** and **Despotikó** are rabbit-hunting reserves. On **Sáliagos**, a fishing village from the 5th millennium BC has been excavated by John Evans and Colin Renfrew, the first Neolithic site discovered in the Cyclades.

---

*Antíparos ✆ (0284–)* **Where to Stay**

Antíparos tends to attract the overflow of roomless tourists from Páros, and prices are marginally lower. Little **Chryssi Akti**, ✆ 61 220 (*C; mod*) is an elegant hotel on the beach; a little cheaper, **Hotel Mantalena**, ✆ 61 206 (*D; mod*) on the waterfront offers nice views of the harbour and Páros; **Hotel Anargyros**, ✆ 61 204 (*D; inexp*) is OK. There are also quite a few pensions—**Korali**, ✆ 61 236, seems to be about the cheapest—and rooms to let, and there's an organized campsite, **Camping Antiparos**, ✆ 61 221, although freelancers are tolerated if they distance themselves from town.

---

*Antíparos ✆ (0284–)* **Eating Out**

Unfortunately, demand has also jacked up the price of food here, and eating out is no cheaper than in Páros. In the port a number of self-service places have sprouted up, among them **Anargyros**, with a decent selection of ready food. In town the locals head for **Klimataria** for good food at (reasonably) low prices, or the more expensive **Marios Giorgios Taverna**, open at night, is known for well-prepared fish dinners.

## Santoríni/Thíra (ΣΑΝΤΟΡΙΝΙΗ/ΘΗΡΑ)

*...We found ourselves naked on the pumice stone*
*watching the rising islands*
*watching the red islands sink*
*into their sleep, into our sleep.*

–George Seféris, *Santoríni*

As most people's favourite Greek island, the pressure is on Santoríni to come up with the goods; it does, though the awesome mixture of towering, sinister multi-coloured volcanic cliffs, dappled with the 'chic'-est, most brilliant-white, trendiest bars and restaurants in the country, gives the island a peculiar split personality. Usually bathed in glorious sunshine, but occasionally lashed by high winds and rain, everything seems more intense here, especially daily life. Some call it Devil's Island, and find a stay here both exhilarating and disturbing—with such a concentration of visitors, something out of the ordinary is guaranteed to happen every day.

As your fragile ship sails into the volcano's rim, the black islands on your right do indeed look demonic. Volcanically fertile Santoríni has, literally, had its ups and downs: throughout history parts of the island and its circular archipelago have seismatically appeared and disappeared under the waves. Human endeavours on the island have fared similarly: you can visit no fewer than three former 'capitals'—the Minoan centre of Akrotíri, a favourite candidate for Metropolis, the capital of the legendary Atlantis; the Classical capital Thíra at Mésa Vouná; and the medieval Skáros, as well as the picturesque modern town of Firá, perched on the edge of Santoríni's cliffs. But this, too, was flattened by an earthquake in 1956 (though lovingly rebuilt). Although the island is now one of the most popular destinations in the Aegean and a must on the itinerary of most cruise ships, older inhabitants can remember when Santoríni hosted more political prisoners than tourists, and nights were filled with the rumour of vampires rather than the chatter of café society sipping Bloody Marys, watching the sun go down in one of the world's most enchanting settings.

## History

The history of Santoríni, or Thíra, is closely related to its geology. In the long distant past the island was created from volcanic debris, circular in shape, with a crater called Strogyle in the centre. Its regular eruptions created a rich, volcanic soil, which attracted inhabitants early on—from Karia originally, until they were chased away by the Minoans. The Cretans built their colony at Akrotíri, but the volcano erupted again and buried it. Its rediscovery resulted from one of the most intriguing archaeological detective stories of the 20th century.

In 1939, while excavating Amnisós, the port of Knossós on the north coast of Crete, Greek archaeologist Spirýdon Marinátos realized that only a massive natural disaster could have caused the damage he found. At first Marinátos believed it was an earthquake, but over the

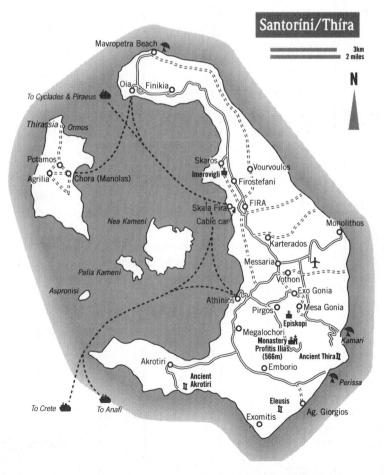

Santoríni/Thíra

years evidence of a different kind of catastrophe came in: southeast of Santoríni oceanographers discovered volcanic ash from Strogyle on the sea bed, covering an area of 900 by 300km; on nearby Anáfi and Eastern Crete itself a layer of volcanic tephra 3–20mm thick was found in the late Minoan time. A Classical clue came from the Athenian reformer Solon, who in 600 BC wrote of his journey to Egypt, where the scribes told him of the disappearance of Kreftia (Crete?) 9000 years before, a figure Solon might have mistaken for a more correct 900. The Egyptians, who had had important trade links with Minoan Crete and Santoríni, supposedly described to Solon the lost land of Atlantis, made of red, white and black volcanic rock (like Santoríni today) and spoke of a city vanishing in 24 hours. In his *Critias*, Plato described Atlantis as being composed of one round island and one long island, a sweet country of art and flowers connected by one culture and rule (Santoríni and Crete, under Minos?). Lastly, there was the explosion of the volcanic island of Krakatoa in 1883 to serve as a model for what had happened to Santoríni: Krakatoa blew its lid with such force that it could be heard 3000 miles away in Western Australia. The volcano formed a caldera of 8.3sq km, and as the sea rushed in to fill the caldera, it created a *tsunami* or tidal wave over 200m high that destroyed everything in a 150km path. The caldera left by Strogyle (the present bay of Santoríni) is 22sq km—almost three times as big.

In the 19th century French archaeologists had discovered Minoan vases at Akrotíri, and it was there that Marinátos began to dig in 1967, looking to prove the chronology of his theory: that Minoan civilization owed its sudden decline to the eruption, earthquakes, and tidal waves caused by the explosion of Santoríni in *c.* 1450 BC. Marinátos hoped to unearth a few vases. Instead he found something beyond his wildest dreams: an entire Minoan colony buried in tephra, complete with dazzling frescoes.

The rest of the island's history has been fairly calm by comparison. In the 8th century BC the Dorians settled the island, naming it Thíra, building their capital at Mésa Vouná, and colonizing the city of Cyrene in Libya. The Byzantines covered the island with castles, but the Venetians under the Crispi got it anyway. Skáros near Imerovígli was their capital and Irene their patron saint, hence the island's second name, Santoríni.

## Getting There

**By air**: daily flights from Athens; daily flights from Mýkonos, Herákleon (Crete) and Rhodes. Airport ✆ 31 525/666.

**By sea**: daily **ferry** connections with Piraeus, Íos, Páros, Náxos, Mýkonos and Herákleon (Crete). Frequently with other Cyclades, 2–3 times a week with the Dodecanese, Skiáthos and Thessaloníki. Ferries call at Athiniós, from where there is a road up to the capital; there are also frequent catamaran services to other Cycladic islands and Piraeus. **Port authority**, ✆ 22 239.

## Tourist Information

See regular police, 25 tou Martíou Street, ✆ (0286) 22 649.

## Festivals

**19** and **20 July**, at Profítis Ilías; **15 August**, Panagía at Mésa Goniá and Firá; **20 October**, Ag. Artemiou in Fíra; **26 October**, Ag. Dimítríou in Karteráthos.

Most ferry passengers disembark at the chaotic port of **Athiniós** and take the bus to Firá; most cruise ships anchor beneath the towering cliffs at **Firá** (ΦHPA) where motor launches ferry passengers to the tiny port of **Skála Firá**, where donkeys wait to bear them up the winding path to town 270m above. An Austrian-built cable car donated to the island by ship-owner Evángelos Nomikós does the donkey's work in two minutes. Profits go to Santoríni's communities—and to the donkey drivers, who receive a percentage of each ticket. It operates every 15 minutes from 6.45am to 8.15pm.

Those who remember Firá (also spelt Thira or Thera), the capital, before 1956 say that the present town bears no comparison to its original, although it's pleasant enough—perfectly Cycladically white, spilling over several terraces, adorned with pretty churches. The cliff is hung with cafés and restaurants, all boasting one of the world's most magnificent views from the lip of the caldera. Firá blends into the areas of Imerovígli and Firostefáni which have some magnificent old *skaftá*, barrel-roofed cave houses, Santoríni's speciality, now with all mod cons.

The **Archaeological Museum** (*open Tues–Sun, 8.30–3; adm*) is near the cable car on the north side of town. It houses finds from Akrotíri, Mésa Vouná and Early Cycladic figurines found in the local pumice mines. The famous Santoríni frescoes are still in the National Museum in Athens, although there are rumours that a new museum will be built in Firá to bring them home. The handicraft workshop founded by Queen Frederíka, where women weave large carpets on looms is also worth a visit. The **Mégaron Gýzi Museum**, located in a beautiful 17th-century mansion, houses exhibits on the island's history—manuscripts from the 16th–19th centuries, costumes, old maps of the Cyclades, and some photographs of Santoríni before the 1956 earthquake (*open daily 10.30–1.30 and 5–8pm*).

## Akrotíri: the Buried City

The first clues indicating that something was buried at **Akrotíri** (AKPΩTHPI) (*several buses daily from Firá, open Tues–Sun 8.30–3*) came in the 1860s during the excavation of pumice for the rebuilding of Port Said during the Suez Canal project: cut stone blocks belonging to ancient walls kept getting in the way. Curiosity piqued, some local residents began to dig, as did a French geologist named Fouqué, who came to study Thíra's eruption of 1866. He and some later French archaeologists unearthed carbonized food, vases, frescoes and a pure copper saw—signs that a highly advanced culture existed before a major volcanic eruption. In 1967 Spyrídon Marinátos, following his hunch about the destruction of Minoan Crete through a volcanic eruption, led a team back to the site. The trenches they dug were disappointing until they reached the level of volcanic ash 15 feet below the surface, when suddenly they broke through into rooms full of huge storage vases, or *pithoi*.

The Late Minoan city of c. 1550 BC laboriously revealed beneath its thick sepulchral shell of volcanic tephra (so hard that it's used to make cement for tombstones) is wonderful and strange, made even more uncanny by its huge modern protective roof. A carpet of volcanic dust silences all footsteps on 3500-year-old lanes, amid houses up to three storeys high, many still containing their *pithoi*. No human or animal skeletons, jewellery or other valuables were found; the residents must have had ample warning that their island was about to blow. They must have shed more than a few tears, for life at Akrotíri was sweet judging by the ash imprints of their elaborate wooden furniture, their beautiful ceramics and the famous frescoes full of colour and life—one, unique in peace-loving Minoan art, shows a sea battle. The size of the storage areas and cooking pots suggests a strong communal life and collective economy. In one of the houses is the grave of Marinátos, who died after a fall on the site and requested to be buried by his life's work. For more details, pick up the locally available *Art and Religion in Thira: Reconstructing a Bronze Age Society*, by his son, Dr Nannó Marinátos. Below Akrotíri is a black rock beach and taverna; there are also some coffee shops and rooms in the vineyard-surrounded villages above.

## Exomítis to Ancient Thíra and Profítis Ilías

East of Akrotíri, **Exomítis** has one of the best-preserved Byzantine fortresses of the Cyclades; submerged nearby are the ruins of the ancient town of Eleusis. The island's best beach, **Périssa**, is around to the east, linked by road to the attractive old village of **Embório**; like the other beaches of Santoríni, the sand here is volcanic and black and warms quickly in the sun. Périssa has good tavernas and a campsite. A modern church replaces the Byzantine church of Saint Irene, the island's namesake and patroness of the Greek police.

Up on the rocky headland of Mésa Vouná (a track leads up from Périssa) is **Ancient Thíra**, (ΠΑΛΑΙΑ ΘΗΡΑ) its extensive ruins built on great terraces. Excavated by the German archaeologist Hiller von Gortringen in the late 19th century, the site produced the fine 'Santoríni vases' in the museum. Most of what you see today dates from the Ptolemies, who used the city as a base for their enterprises further north and adorned it with temples to the Egyptian gods, Dionysos, Apollo, to their semi-divine selves and to the mythical founding father Thira. There are impressive remains of the agora and theatre, with a dizzying view down to the sea, several cemeteries and a gymnasium. Numerous houses still have mosaics; graffiti dating from 800 BC may be seen on the Terrace of Celebrations, recording the names of competitors and naked dancers of the *gymno paidiai*. Note the enormous Cyclopean walls.

North of Ancient Thira stretches another black beach, crowded **Kamári**, with tavernas, bars, tourist shops and package holidaymakers, while inland, up the slope from Mésa Vouná, is the **Monastery Profítis Ilías**, built in 1712 on Santoríni's highest point (566m). On a clear day you can see Crete from here, and on an exceptionally clear day, it is said, even Rhodes hovers faintly on the horizon. The locals, never forgetting the terrifying earthquake of 1956, say the monastery is the only place that will protrude above sea level when the rest of Santoríni sinks into the sea to join its other half. At the foot of Profítis Ilías, by the village of Mésa Goniá, the 11th-century **Panagía Episkópí** or Kímisis Theotókou has Byzantine icons, and on 15 August it holds the biggest *panegýri* on the island. **Pírgos** shares with Embório the title of the oldest surviving village on the island, with interesting old houses, Byzantine walls, and a Venetian fort. Much of the countryside is covered in vines.

Santoríni is one of Greece's premier white wine producers. Because of its exclusively volcanic soil, its vines were among the few in Europe to be spared the dreaded *phylloxera*, (plant lice) so the original rootstock remains intact; the average age of *assyrtiko*—the main variety of white grape on the island, is 70 years–the oldest vines, near Akrotíri, are estimated at over 150 years. *Assyrtiko* yields everything from a bone dry light wine to a sweet aged Vinsanto made from sun-dried grapes; a second rare variety, Aidani, is known for its jasmine bouquet. Moribund for many years, churning out high-alcohol, low-quality wine, the Santoríni wine industry has recently had a shot in the arm from the forward-thinking national winemaker Boutari, who in 1988 built a new domed winery, restaurant, and accessory shop at Megalóchori, towards Akrotíri (© (0286) 81 011). A second winery, Koutsoyanópoulos, on the road to Kamári, also offers tastings. While connoisseurs are most welcome, they still insist you have a good time.

## North of Firá

**Skáros**, on the road to Oía, was the medieval capital of Santoríni, but it has been much damaged by earthquakes. Its Ag. Stéfanos is the oldest church on the island, and you can also see the crumbling ruins of a Catholic convent of Santa Katerina, built after a young girl's vision in 1596. The nuns lived a life of extreme hardship until 1818 when they moved to Firá, and now the desolate convent is about to tumble down. Nearby **Imerovígli** has a second convent, built in 1674 and still inhabited, dedicated to Ag. Nikólaos.

At the end of the road lined with vine-covered terraces, that mouthful of vowels called **Oía**, or Ía (OIA), is the third port of Santoríni, though these days only tourist caiques to **Thirassía** call here. Half-ruined by the earthquake, its white houses are nearly all restored now, and piled on top of one another up the steep slope; the roofs of the lower houses are courtyards for the neighbours above. Although it's a long, hard walk up from the beach, you can fill your pockets with pumice-stone souvenirs for friends at home. Oía is reputedly haunted and is another great place to watch the sun set, perhaps over a glass of dry golden Santorini Oia, from one of the island's small boutique producers.

## Around the Caldera

Santoríni's caldera is 10km wide and 380m deep. Curving around the northwestern rim, the islet **Thirassía** was part of Santoríni until another eruption-earthquake in 236 BC blasted them apart. In one of the quarries a Middle Cycladic settlement was discovered, pre-dating Akrotíri, though there are no traces of it now. There are three villages on the island: the largest, **Manolás**, has tavernas and rooms to rent. Excursion boats also make trips out to the 'burnt isles', **Palía Kaméni** (appeared in 157 AD) and **Néa Kaméni** (born in 1720), both still volcanically active, especially the Metaxá crater on Néa Kaméni. However, even though a local brochure refers to it as 'the strange volcano which cause you greatness', be forewarned that most people who visit Néa Kaméni come away disappointed. The tourist trail up the mountain is rubbish-strewn and there's no sign of recent volcanic activity, though there's plenty of black ash. There are also tourist excursion boats taking people to swim in the 'healthy' sulphurous mud nearby, which, if nothing else, makes an unusual chat-up line in the bars of Firá.

*Santoríni* © *(0286–)*      **Where to Stay and Eating Out**

There's nothing like staying in Firá with a view over the caldera, especially in a traditional *skaftá* cave house. But do book in advance and expect to pay through the nose. If you land at Athiniós, the owners of rooms in Messariá, Embório and Karterádos will try to whisk you away in their vans. So if you want to stay in Firá be warned. The USA-based conservation group Cycladic Environments has a range of **traditional properties** to let in the village of Oía, many furnished with local embroideries and handcarved furniture. Each house sleeps 2–7 people; however, bookings can only be made through the USA office, PO Box 382622, Cambridge, MA 02238-2622, © (800) 719 5260, @ (617) 492 5881 (*exp–mod*).

## Firá

Top of the list for luxury is the **Santoríni Palace**, ✆ 22 771, 📠 23 705 (*A; lux*) followed by **Hotel Atlantis**, ✆ 22 232, 📠 22 821 (*A; lux*), overlooking the volcano. **Hotel Kavalari**, ✆ 22 455 (*C; exp*), has rooms dug out of the rock as has the **Loucas Hotel**, ✆ 22 480 (*D; exp*), where you pay for the view. **Porto Carra**, ✆ 22 979 (*C; exp*), also faces the volcano and on the central square.

The **Pelican**, ✆ 23 113, 📠 23 514 (*C; exp*), has a tank of odd fish in the lounge; **Kallisti Thira**, ✆ 22 317 (*C; exp*) is another pleasant option. Cheaper places include **Pension Argonaftis**, ✆ 22 055 (*inexp*), friendly with breakfast served in the garden, and **Pension Rousa**, ✆ 23 220 (*inexp*), opposite the bus station. North along the cliff edge at Firostefáni the **Hotel Gallini**, ✆ 23 097/22 095 (*C; mod*), offers simple but nice rooms with views; **Dana Villas**, ✆ 22 566, 📠 22 985, have self-contained apartments for 2–6 people, in traditional island style, with fabulous sunsets. There are two youth hostels in Firá: **Kamares Hostel**, ✆ 23 142, near the cable car and the better **Kontonari**, ✆ 22 722, with snack bar and English videos. Cheap dorm beds, card not required. *Open April–Oct.* **Camping Santorini**, ✆ 22 944, is a superb site.

Be prepared for high food prices, too, For international cuisine and reputedly the best food on Santoríni, **Kastro** near the cable car will set you back a bit for one of its lavish spreads. **Dakotros** is one of the oldest and best for Greek fare, but for a real taste of Santoríni head for Imerovígli and **Eleni's**, the one-woman band on the square for *pseftokeftédhes*, 'false meatballs', Santoríni's speciality, deep-fried tomatoes and onion; the tiny tomatoes of the island are said to be the tastiest in Greece. **Skaros Fish Taverna** there is also excellent; **Restaurant Nikolaos** in the heart of Firá, is a reassuring old-established Greek taverna in this island of excess; get there early for good barrel wines, authentic Greek food and fresh fish. On the main street near the port police, try and squeeze in at **The Roosters**, a fun little restaurant with tasty Greek dishes, and an inquisitive owner. **Alexandria** on the caldera is expensive but even serves up ancient Greek specialities. Elegant **Meridiana** deserves mention for the view alone, but the food is good, too, with decent Santoríni wine, and a piano bar. Italians flock to **Bella Thira** for freshly made pasta and pizzas.

## Oía

The swishest place to stay are the luxury *skaftá* of **Fanari Villas**, ✆ 71 321, 📠 71 235 (*exp*), below the windmill, with small bar, and steps down to Ammoúdi Bay. **Katikies**, ✆ 71 401 (*exp*) are beautifully decorated apartments with great views. **Jack's Village**, ✆ 71 439 (*lux–inexp*) has everything from simple doubles to luxury cave apartments; **Hotel Anemones**, ✆ 71 220 (*mod*) is OK. The **youth hostel**, ✆ 71 290 has cheapish dorm beds.

Eat at **Kyklos**, built into the caves and atmospheric, or **Mama Africa** with an exotic menu that includes Thai and Indian dishes.

## Kamári

There are many modest-sized hotels and pensions here, although not cheap. The **Matina** ✆ 31 491(*C; mod*) is comfortable as is the **Hotel Sunshine**, ✆ 31 491

(*B; mod*) next to the sea. Modest **Hotel Andreas** ✆/● 31 314 (*mod*) has a lush garden. **Hotel Hermes**, ✆ 31 664, and **Hotel Alkyon**, ✆ 31 956 (*C; mod*) are both friendly family-run places a short walk from the beach. At Périssa the **Sellada Beach**, ✆/● 81 492 (*C; exp–mod*) is slap on the sands. **Kamari Camping**, ✆ 31 453 is up the main road from the beach at Kamári; **Galanakis Camping**, ✆ 81 343, on the beach at Périssa. **Camille Stefani** on the beach is one of the island's best restaurants with a French-influenced Greek menu and their own wine label; **Kamari** is a good, inexpensive family-run taverna, serving the island speciality *fáva* (a purée of chick peas, oil, lemon and onion). Next to the sea, **Irini's** is another local favourite. Périssa has the **Retsina**, a simple, popular taverna.

### Entertainment and Nightlife

Café and bar life takes up as much time as eating in Santoríni. Many people like to be seen at **Bonjour** in the main square, while **Bebis** is the watering hole for a pleasantly loony young crowd. **Two Brothers** draws the back-packers and is a hot spot for rock; **Kira Thira Jazzbar** appeals to all ages for jazz, blues and *sangria*, while **Alexandria** is more sedate and attracts an older set (by Santoríni's standards, anyway). **Franco's** is still *the* place to go for sunset, even if the price of a coffee is sky-high. Cocktails are works of art, but a bottle of wine and *mezédes* are the best deal. Dance away at **Tithora Club** the disco in a cave on the steps to Skála Firá. For Greek music head to the lively **Apocalypse Club**.

Kamári throbs with bars. The **Sail Inn** has loud music, fun evenings and glamorous bar girls, and **Valentino's** always has a large crowd. Drop in at the **Yellow Donkey** disco in the early hours and dance till dawn—there's very little point in trying to get an early night on this hedonistic island anyway. For a bit of culture there's the **Santoríni Music Festival** in August and September with classical performances in the cultural centre in Firá.

# Sérifos (ΣΕΡΙΦΟΣ)

Where its neighbour Sífnos welcomes the visitor with green terraces and dovecotes, Sérifos, 'the barren one' tends to intimidate with its stark rocks. The island owed much of its prosperity in antiquity to its iron and copper mines, among the richest in Greece. However, when other sources were discovered in Africa that could be exploited more economically, the mines on Sérifos were abandoned, and the population drastically decreased. Otherwise, Sérifos' history follows that of the other Cyclades; Chóra, high above the sea, seemingly inaccessible as it tumbles impressively down the steep slopes, was once fortified with a Byzantine-Venetian castle and walls. The appealing port Livádi provides an informal foreground to the imposing view of Chóra, with its little line of friendly tavernas and bars. In the past few years have become trendified with the arrival of yachties and a strong German contingent. Beware of water shortages in August.

## Mythology

What Sérifos may lack in history is more than compensated for by its mythology. When it was prophesied to Akrisius, King of Argos, that he would be slain by the son of his daughter Danaë, Akrisius had locked his daughter in a tower, but even there her beauty did not fail to attract the attentions of Zeus, who came to her in a shower of golden rain and fathered Perseus. Enraged but unable to put his daughter or grandson to death, Akrisius decided to leave the issue to fate and set them adrift in the box. Zeus guided them to Sérifos, where a fisherman discovered them and brought them to Polydectes, the king of the island. Struck by her beauty, Polydectes wanted to marry Danaë but she refused him, and as Perseus grew older he defended his mother's decision. Polydectes pretended to lose interest in Danaë, while he plotted to remove Perseus from the scene by asking him to do a favour: fetch the head of the Gorgon Medusa, the only mortal of the three horrible Gorgon sisters, who had hair made of living snakes, whose eyes bulged and whose teeth were fangs. The sisters were so ugly that a mere glance at one of them turned a human to stone.

Despite Danaë's horror at this treachery of Polydectes, Perseus accepted and accomplished the task, assisted by the goddess Athena, who helped him procure a mirror-like shield, winged shoes, a cloak of invisibility and other essential tools. With Medusa's awful head in his pouch Perseus returned to Sérifos (saving Andromeda from a sea monster on the way), to find his mother hiding from Polydectes in the hut of the fisherman who had saved them so long ago. Angrily Perseus went up to the palace, where he found a very surprised Polydectes at a great banquet. Perseus told him that he had succeeded in his quest and held up Medusa's head as proof, instantly turning everyone in the room into stone.

The kind fisherman was declared King of Sérifos in his place by Perseus, and the hero and his mother went home to Argos. Still fearing the old prophecy, Danaë's father fled before them. But fate caught up with the old King in another town, where Perseus was competing in an athletic contest and accidentally killed his grandfather with a javelin in the foot.

### Getting There

**By sea**: Daily with Piraeus via Kýthnos, to Mílos via Sífnos; 4 times a week with Kímolos, 3 times a week with Santoríni and Folégandros, twice a week with Síkinos and Íos, once a week to Sýros. **Port authority**, ✆ 51 470.

### Tourist Information

Livádi, ✆ (0281) 51 300.

### Festivals

Fava beans are the big speciality at these celebrations: **5 May**, Ag. Iríni at Koutalás; **27 July**, Ag. Panteleímonos at Mount Óros; **6 August**, Sotíros at Kaló Ábeli; **15–17 August**, Panagía near the Monastery and at a different village each day; **7 September**, Ag. Sosoudos at Livádi.

## Livádi and Chóra

Most people who visit Sérifos stay in **Livádi**, the port, where there's a beach and many rooms to rent. There are two other beaches within easy walking distance from Livádi, crowded **Livadákia**, and a 30-minute walk south over the headland, **Karávi Beach**, more secluded and popular with nudists. There's also freelance camping there.

Sérifos, or **Chóra**, the main town, is linked to the port by an hourly bus service, or you can climb up an ancient staircase from Livádi. Buses also go to the villages once a day in the summer. Chóra is a pretty village, a fascinating jumble in the narrow lanes, often built from stone salvaged from the old fortress; other houses date back to the Middle Ages. Chóra is fast-becoming *the* place for holiday homes among trendy Athenian architects and artists, along with a handful of Brits and Germans. The old windmills still stand, and in the spring you may find a rare carnation that grows only on Sérifos. From Chóra a 20-minute walk leads down to **Psíli Ámmos**, an excellent beach on the east coast.

## Around Sérifos

The road continues beyond Chóra past the 6th-century Byzantine **Aspropírgos** (White Tower) to **Megálo Chorió**, believed to occupy the site of the ancient capital of Sérifos; below, **Megálo Livádi**, now visited for its beach, once served as the loading dock for the iron and copper mined near Megálo Chorió. From Megálo Livádi you can walk around **Mésa Akrotíri** where there are two caves: the cave of the Cyclops Polyphemus with stalactites and another at **Koutalás**, where signs of prehistoric settlement were found. Both caves are now off limits but Koutalás offers a beach by way of compensation, and a track from here follows the south coast back to Livádi.

**Sikamiá Bay** in the north is a good place to get away from it all, not only for its beach but also for the rare bit of shade and fresh water. The village of **Galaní** is half an hour on foot from Sikamiá, and from here you can visit **Taxiárchos Monastery**, built in 1500 and containing a precious old table, 18th-century frescoes by Skordílis, and Byzantine manuscripts in the library. The oldest church on Sérifos is from the 10th century, at **Panagía**. **Kalítsos**, not far from Galaní, is another pleasantly green place, with two restaurants.

Other beaches on Sérifos are Lía, Ag. Sóstis, Platýs Gialós, Chálara and Giánema. Most of these are remote but can be reached by motorcycle.

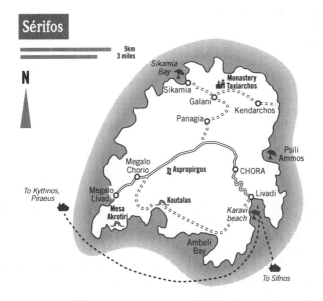

Sérifos is well-known enough for its hotels and rooms to fill up in the summer—more often than not, with German visitors. In Livádi, the further along the beach you go, the cheaper the accommodation. **Hotel Areti**, ✆ 51 479, ✉ 51 298 (*B pension; mod*) is handy for the ferries and has a quiet garden and comfortable rooms with terraces overlooking the sea. **Captain George Rooms** ✆ 51 274 (*inexp*), near the square are good value; **Hotel Albatross,** ✆ 51 148 (*mod*) is further around the bay but the owner meets the ferry with a minibus. The **Serifos Beach Hotel,** ✆ 51 209, (*C; mod*) is the island's biggest, with a nice taverna downstairs; the **Maistrali,** ✆ 51 381 (*C; exp–mod*) has lovely airy rooms while the smaller **Pension Perseus,** ✆ 51 273 (*B; mod*), is an old standby. Not far from the Sérifos Beach there are excellent budget rooms with balconies above the Cavo d'Oro supermarket. There are also rooms in Chóra. **Korali Camping**, Livadákia Beach, ✆ 51 500 has good facilities.

The sea is clean and the fish is especially good. Like the accommodation, the tavernas get cheaper further along the beach. Popular with locals and tourists alike, **Teli's**, on Livádi's waterfront, offers excellent and inexpensive food and friendly service. For a pleasantly zany atmosphere, with good, wholesome food (spaghetti, chicken curries) apart from the usual Greek fare, try **Benny's** at the end of the port where the locals, yachties, tourists, various children and an assortment of cats and dogs mingle happily together. Whenever you come across that endangered species, the *ouzerie*, treasure it; the **Meltemi** will give you a *karafáki* (enough for three or four good drinks) and plenty of tasty nibbles (hot cheese pies, etc) for less than 800dr. Round the bay, wiggle your toes in the sand at **Stamatis Taverna**, and enjoy his excellent ready food or grilled meats (*2000dr*). A few metres away, in the restaurant of the hotel **Kyklades**, you can savour spaghetti with shrimps, mussels and clams, or an excellent shrimp casserole with feta cheese and tomatoes (*2500dr*).

Up in Chóra, **Stavros** is traditional and OK; **Maroulis** is in the lovely square by the town hall (climb up the steps where the bus stops), and serves *mezédes* with a difference, a definite relief if your relationship with Greek salads is wearing thin; try the sun-dried tomatoes sautéed in butter, or fennel done the same way, and Serifot specialities such as *keftédes*, *spetsofái* and chick peas from the wood oven, all washed down with the family's own wine (*2500dr*). **Petros** is a long-time favourite with the usual Greek food, but cooked just that bit better. *Open mid-summer only.*

### Entertainment and Nightlife

There's a mix of nightlife with several music bars and seasonally changing discos, from the **Metallein**, mixing Greek pop with heavy metal, to **Froggie's** and **Scorpio's Rock Bar**. Also try **Vitamin C** and the **Disco Paradise**. Many bars have strong German appeal.

# Sífnos (ΣΙΦΝΟΣ)

Sífnos in recent years has become the most popular island in the western Cyclades, with good reason—it's the prettiest, with its peaceful green hills and terraces, charming villages and long sandy beaches. Here and there the landscape is dotted with Venetian dovecotes, windmills, some 40 ruined Classical towers and over 300 miniature chapels. It is an exceptionally pleasant island for walks. Among the Greeks Sífnos is famous for its pottery and its cooks, both of which have been in such demand elsewhere that few remain on Sífnos, although the legacy of good cooking remains. The island's olives are said to produce the best oil in the Cyclades, but sadly agriculture on the island is in decline (as is often the case, in direct correlation with the rise in tourism), and once-fertile Sífnos now has to import almost all of its foodstuffs.

## History

According to Pliny, the Phoenicians named the island Meropia and were the first to mine its gold. They were followed by the Cretans, who founded Minoa near Apollónia, and who were in turn replaced by Ionians who lived near Ag. Andreas and elsewhere. Meropia, meanwhile, had become famous for its gold; at one time, it is said, there was so much of the precious stuff that the islanders simply divided it among themselves each year, with enough left over in the 6th century to pave their main square with the most costly Parian marble. In the same century Apollo at Delphi demanded that the wealthy island contribute a tithe of gold in the form of a solid egg to his sanctuary every year. In 530 BC Meropia constructed a magnificent treasury at

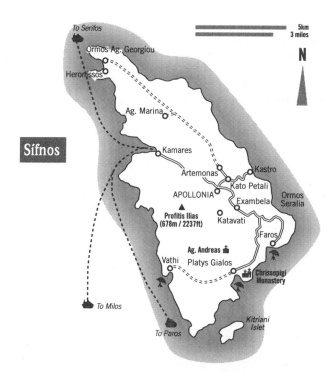

Delphi to house the gold and adorned it with a fine frieze and pediment which can still be seen; for many years it was the richest of all the oracle's treasures. But one year the islanders, who began to have a reputation for greed and cunning, decided they needed the gold more than Apollo, and sent the god a gilded rock. Apollo soon discovered he had been duped and cursed the island. This gave Polycrates, the Tyrant of Sámos, a good excuse to extract a huge fine from Sífnos; 40 triremes plundered and ransomed most of the island's gold, and the curse supposedly caused the mines to sink and give out. Thus the island became empty, or, in Greek *sífnos*. Nowadays most of the ancient mines are underwater, at Ag. Mína, Kapsálos and Ag. Sózon.

After shooting itself in the foot with its twopenny fraud, Sífnos went into decline and the inhabitants moved up to Kástro, where a Roman cemetery has been discovered. In 1307 the Da Koronia family ruled the island for Venice; in 1456 Kozadinós, the Lord of Kýthnos, married into the family and his descendants ruled Sífnos until the Turks took the island in 1617. Towards the end of the 17th century the Ottomans made an attempt to reopen the ancient mines, or at least sent out experts from Istanbul to examine them. Supposedly, when they got wind of these plans, the islanders hired a band of French pirates to sink the Sultan's ship. The experts, in turn, heard of the deal with the pirates, and simply went home. Later the French themselves exploited the local deposits of iron ore and lead; mining ended in 1914.

Sífnos has also made an important contribution to Greek letters. At the end of the 17th century the 'School of the Holy Tomb' was founded on the island to keep alive the ancient Greek language and classics during the Turkish occupation, attracting students from all over Greece. Nikólaos Chrysoyélos, the most famous headmaster, led a contingent of Sifniots in the War of Independence, and went on to become modern Greece's first Minister of Education. Another islander, the 19th-century poet-satirist Cleánthis Triandáfilos, who wrote under the name Rabágas, was a thorn in the side of the monarchy until he was imprisoned and committed suicide. Ioánnis Gypáris (d. 1942) was another Sifniot of note; along with Caváfy, he was one of the first poets to espouse the use of the demotic language (as opposed to the formal *katharévousa*) in literature.

### Getting There and Around

**By sea**: daily with Piraeus, Kýthnos, Sérifos and Mílos; 4 times a week with Kímolos, 2–3 times a week with Íos, Santoríni, Folégandros and Síkinos, once a week with Páros, Crete, Rhodes, Kárpathos, Kássos, Hálki and Sými. Daily **taxi boats** from Kamáres to Váthi. **Port authority,** ✆ 31 617.

**By road**: frequent **buses** between Kamáres and Appolonía, Kástro and Platýs Gialós.

### Tourist Information

Municipal tourist office, opposite the quay in Kamáres, ✆ (0284) 31 804. Tourist police, see regular police, Apollonía, ✆ (0284) 31 210.

### Festivals

**25 March** and **21 November**, Panagía tou Vounoú; **Ascension** (Analypsis) at Chrissopigí; **20 July**, Profítis Ilías near Kamáres; **15 August**, Panagía ta Gournia; **29 August**, Ag. Ioánnes in Váthi; **1 September**, Ag. Simeon near Kamáres; **14 September**, Stavrós, at Fáros.

The island's port, shady **Kamáres** (KAMAPEΣ), has become a typical waterside jumble of tourist facilities. Situated between two steep, barren cliffs that belie the fertility inland, Kamáres has a sandy beach with friendly ducks, some good places to camp, and a range of cafés and tavernas. Only two of the many pottery workshops that once lined the north side of the harbour still survive. It's a dramatic climb—let the bus take the strain—up to the capital **Apollónia** (AΠOΛΛONIA), then on to Artemónas, Kástro, Chrissopigí, the busy resort of Platýs Gialós, and more remote Fáros.

Apollonía is a Cycladic idyll, spread out across the hills, a circle of white from the distance. Its name comes from a 7th-century BC temple of Apollo, superseded in the 18th century by the church **Panagía Ouranofóra** in the highest part of town. Fragments of the temple can still be seen, and there's a marble relief of St George over the door. Another church, **Ag. Athanásios** (next to the pretty square dedicated to Cleánthis Triandáfilos) has frescoes and a carved wooden iconostasis. In the bus stop square the **Museum of Popular Arts and Folklore** houses a fine ethnographic collection of Sifniot pottery, embroideries and costumes (*open 10am–1pm, 6–10pm daily, adm*). There are numerous dovecotes in the region with triangular designs which are repeated in the architecture of some of the houses. Local music, played on the violin and *láouto*, can frequently be heard in the cafés on Sundays.

Artemis is Apollo's twin sister; similarly **Artemónas**, or Artemón (APTEMΩNAΣ) is Apollónia's twin village and the second largest on Sífnos. Beneath its windmills are the island's most ambitious Venetian residences and churches. Look out for distinctive ceramic chimney stacks. The church of **Kochí**, with its cluster of domes, occupies the site of a temple of Artemis; also in Artemón, little 17th-century **Ag. Geórgios tou Aféndi** contains several fine icons from the period, and **Panagía ta Gourniá**, near the bridge, has a beautiful interior (keys next door).

## Kástro and Panagía Chrissopigí

Kástro (KAΣTPO), overlooking the east coast, is 3km from Artemónas and you can walk there along the old scenic coastal path. Once the Classical and medieval capital of Sífnos, Kástro is a charming village overlooking the sea, if a bit forlorn with only 30 families in residence, still defended by Byzantine-style walls made from the backs of the houses; some of the older build-ings still bear their Venetian coats-of-arms. Ruins of the Classical acropolis and walls remain, and there are many churches with attractive floors, among them the **Panagía Eleoússa** (1653); **Ag. Ekateríni** (1665) and **Panagía Koímmissi** (1593), where the altar is decorated with Dionysian bulls' heads. An old Venetian building houses the **Archaeological Museum**, (*open Tues–Sun, 9–3*). The site of the School of the Holy Tomb, closed in 1834, is now Kástro's cemetery. At Kástro there's plenty of deep blue sea to dive into from the rocks, and many people dispense with swimming costumes. If you prefer sand, paths from Kástro lead down to **Serália** and **Poulátí** and their lovely beaches.

Just south of Artemónas the bus passes through **Exámbela**, a quiet flower-filled village famous for its songs. In the middle of one of the island's most fertile areas the still-active **Vrísi Monastery** is surrounded by springs (1612) and contains many old manuscripts and objects of religious art. On the road to Platýs Gialós the monastery of **Ag. Andréas**, sitting on a hill, has some ruins of the double walls that once encircled the ancient citadel, and a little further north, but not accessible by road, is the monastery of **Profítis Ilías**, with a small network of catacombs and cells. Check that these are open before setting out.

Further south the seaside village and beach at **Fáros** is a friendly developing resort with cheap accommodation and good tavernas. The long beach at **Apókofto** has golden sands and a good taverna, Vassili's, while **Fasoloú** is popular with nudists. South of Fáros is the island's most famous monastery, **Panagía Chrissopigí**, built in 1650 on a holy rock. The legend tells that two girls disturbed pirates sleeping in the old church. They pursued the maidens who desperately prayed to the Virgin, who saved them by splitting the cape in the pirates' path, creating a gap 18m wide—spanned in these pirate-free days by a bridge. The church's icon of the Virgin was discovered in the sea by fishermen attracted by the light it radiated. To visit, ask the bus driver to let you off at Chrissopigí and walk down the mule path; there's also a road for cars.

## Platýs Gialós and Around

Platýs Gialós (ΠΛΑΤΥΣ ΓΙΑΛΟΣ) with its broad sandy beach—said to be the longest in the Cyclades—is the island's busiest resort, though you can escape its worldly concerns by lodging in the serene convent of **Panagía tou Vounoú** up on the cliff, affording a gorgeous view over the bay below. The last nuns left nearly a century ago, but the church with its ancient Doric columns is still used for island *panegýria*. There are regular water taxis from Kamáres to the lovely pottery and fishing hamlet of **Vathí**, an hour's hike from Platýs Gialós and probably the prettiest place to stay on the island. The striking blue and brown Sifniot pottery is still made here at a pottery across the bay, well worth a visit if you can get a boatman to take you. **Cherónissos** on the island's windy northern tip is another pottery centre, also best reached by boat, although there's a good dirt road. Here master potter Kóstas Therastás upholds the old ceramics tradition with local clay, his kiln fired by driftwood.

---

*Sífnos ⊘ (0284–)*                          **Where to Stay and Eating Out**

Sífnos is famous for its *revíthia*, baked chick peas; *pittiá*, chick pea patties; smelly *xynomyzíthra* cheese; *stamnás*, meat, cheese and potatoes in a clay pot; and dill with everything. Unfortunately with the influx of tourists the once lofty standard of cuisine has plummeted as fast foods and gelateria spring up like toadstools.

### Kamáres

**O Boulis Restaurant** on the beach has good value rooms above, not to be confused with **Boulis Hotel**, ⊘ 32 122, ✆ 32 150 (*C; exp–mod*), across the bay. **Hotel Stavros**, ⊘ 31 641 (*C; inexp*) has basic rooms, some with shared bath. **Kamari Pension**, ⊘ 31 710, ✆ 31 709 (*B pension; mod–inexp*) is a better bet on the waterfront; **Dimitris and Margarita Belli**, ⊘ 31 276 (*inexp*) also have good little rooms with seaview balconies. There's also the unofficial youth hostel, **Vangelis**, further inland and a small campsite at the end of the beach. Kamáres bristles with seafront tavernas offering fresh fish. For seafood **Kapetan Andreas** has a good selection; **O Boulis** (*see* above) serves traditional, excellent and cheap Greek fare; the Italian restaurant, **Lorenzo's**, is all the rage; across the street **Dionysos** serves rooftop breakfasts, but has become a bit of a rip-off joint. They also provide hot showers for yachties. A pre-dinner ouzo, watching the sun go down, is a must at the friendly **Café Folie**, at the far end of the beach, which has very good daytime snacks.

## Platýs Gialós

The **Platys Yialos Beach Hotel and Bungalows**, ✆ 71 324, 📧 71 325 (*B; exp*) is in traditional style with all facilities and sports. All rooms are air-conditioned with mini-bars to raid. The **Alexandros Sífnos Beach**, ✆ 32 333 (*B; exp*) is also smart on the hillside above the beach. **Pension Angeliki**, ✆ 31 688 (*mod*) near the bus stop is nice; there are several rooms to rent and **Camping Platys Yialos** ✆ 31 786 in an olive grove set back from the beach. There are several beach tavernas and rooms—some available in the 16th-century monastery of **Taxiárchis,** ✆ 31 060. There is a good choice of fish restaurants: try the **Kyklades Beach** or **Sofia** for Sifniot dishes; for Italian food **Mama Mia** is popular.

## Apollonía/Artemónas

The **Hotel Sophia**, ✆ 31 238 (*C; inexp*) just off central square is fine over a good restaurant. **Angelo's Rooms**, ✆ 31 533, are cheap with garden views. **Hotel Sífnos**, ✆ 31 624 (*C; mod*) is another good choice; the charming **Pension Apollónia**, ✆ 31 490 (*B; inexp*) is a budget gem. In Artemónas the little **Artemona Xenon** guest house, ✆ 31 303, 📧 32 385 (*C; mod*) is one of the most charming places on Sífnos with a cool courtyard. while the bigger **Artemon Hotel,** ✆ 31 303 (*mod*), under the same management, has a garden restaurant. Taverna **O Manganas** in Artemónas is the island's best-known and one of the best eating places in the Cyclades. It isn't easy to find in the labyrinth of lanes; just follow the Greeks. Among the specialities are *kápari*, local capers, and *revíthia*, served on Sunday in many Sifniot homes; it's also high on atmosphere and wine. **Liotrivi** ('Olive Press') is another excellent restaurant in a pretty garden. Try the spicy chick pea *keftédhes*. **Zorba's** up in Kástro, has a fine view while **Mengengela** and **Tzifakis** are two good local tavernas.

## Fáros

Fáros has some of the cheapest rooms on the island, ✆ 31 822, and a clutch of jolly tavernas: try **To Kima** where there could be impromptu music and dancing. The small, family-run **Flora** at Apókofto, ✆ 31 778 (*B pension; inexp*), has great views. You can rent very basic rooms at Panagía Chrissopigí monastery, ✆ 31 255. In Vathí, reward yourself with a fish lunch at one of the tavernas in the bay which won't break the bank. Try the local cheese, *xynomizíthra*, a hard sheep's-milk cheese, steeped in wine and then kept in barrels. It stinks but tastes great.

### Entertainment and Nightlife

Nightlife centres on Kamáres with numerous beachside cocktail bars and discos. Hang out at **Café Folie** for a sundowner, the **Dolphin Bar** or **Collage**. Dance away at the **Mobilize Dancing Club**. Festivals on Sífnos are great fun, with local music and dancing. For a spot of culture the **Sifniot Cultural Society** presents summer concerts at Artemónas in the grounds of Kochi church.

## Síkinos (ΣΙΚΙΝΟΣ)

If you find the other Cyclades too cosmopolitan, or you want to try out your Greek, you can always visit Síkinos, which is small and charming with a sleepy port and stunning white twin villages of Chóra and Kástro perched high above. Unaffected as yet by organized tourism, farming and fishing are still the island's mainstay. But there is quite a bit of new development and traditional houses in Chóra are being done up as holiday homes, mainly by Germans. Light years away from next door Íos—although there are day trips from the fleshpots—there's little to see or do and most people call in for a few days then move on. But in August it's busy, mainly with returning Greeks. The port of Aloprónia has been enlarged so ferries can now dock but it's still very shallow with a sandy beach, ideal for children. Named after the child of banished Limnian Thoas who was set adrift in a tea chest, washed up on the island and saved by a nymph, Síkinos is the place to linger and savour the simple pleasures of old-fashioned island life. There are some wonderful mountain walks and the main ways of getting around are on foot and by mule. The hillsides are neatly tended and olive trees and vines still cover many of the fertile terraces. In ancient times Síkinos was one of several islands called Oenoe, or 'wine island', and the local stuff still packs a punch.

### Getting There and Around

**By sea**: daily **tourist boat** to Folégandros and Íos; **ferry** 5 times a week to Piraeus, 4 times a week to Santoríni, less often with Páros, Náxos, Sífnos, Sérifos and Sýros, once a week with Kýthnos, Kímolos, Crete and the Dodecanese; **catamaran** once a week to other Cyclades and Piraeus. **Excursion boat** *Sweet Síkinos* to the beaches in summer. **Port authority**, Ø 51 222.

**By road**: the island **bus** meets most ferries and runs hourly to Chóra in season.

## Walks Around Síkinos

The port, **Aloprónia**, also called **Skála**, affords little shelter from the winds or for weary visitors—most facilities are up at the capital, known either as **Síkinos**, **Chóra** or **Kástro**, although smart new developments are springing up around the harbour. There are fishing boats, a few tavernas and a shop-cum-café plus a swish new hotel complex. Kástro is the island's only real town, and a good hour's walk up from the jetty, if the bus hasn't put in an appearance. Looming over the village is the ruined **Monastery of Zoodóchos Pigí**, fortified against the frequent pirate incursions which the island endured in the past. The 300 inhabitants are most proud, however, of their 'cathedral' with its icons by the 18th-century master Skordílis. **Kástro**, with its labyrinthine lanes, tiny shops and *kafeneíons*, is one of the loveliest and most authentic villages in the Cyclades. The main square is formed by vast stone 18th-century **mansions**, their walls used as bastions of defence. Some remain with bright wooden balconies like those in Folégandros. Others are ruined—look out for the vast marble portico with intricately carved, almost Celtic symbols. The church of the **Pantánassa** is the focal point with bees buzzing in the trees. On the opposite hill the ancient village of Chóra is equally pretty. Several old houses are being renovated and ex-pat American John Margétis is turning his old family home and olive press into a **folk museum** in memory of his mother, Kalióbe. The place is full of island artefacts and should be open in 1995.

There are two scenic walks across the island, each taking about 1½ hours, or you can hire a mule. The tracks are rough and stout shoes essential. From **Chóra** the path leads past ruined **Cyclopean** walls south west to Episkopí, originally thought to have been a Roman shrine to Apollo but now believed to be a 3rd century mausoleum, converted in the 7th century to the Byzantine church of Koimísis Theotókou. The church was remodelled in the 17th century after an earthquake to become **Moní Episkópi**. The path to the northeast leads to the rather scant remains of a Classical fortress at **Paliókastro**. Tracks from this path lead south to the beaches of **Ag. Geórgios** and **Ag. Nikólaos**, but there is also a caique from Aloprónia in summer. From the harbour beach you can walk up over the mountain to the next cove at **Gialiskári**, while the pebble beach at **Ag. Panteleímonas** is about 40 minutes away. There's a big *panegýri* there on 27 July. **Spiliá**, named after the island's many caves, is also very popular.

---

*Síkinos ☎ (0286–)*           ***Where to Stay and Eating Out***

### Aloprónia

The smart **Porto Síkinos**, ☎ 51 247, ✆ 51 220 (*B; mod*) is right on the beach, prettily laid out in traditional island design, with bar and restaurant and tourist office; up the hill **Flora** ☎ 51 239/214 (*C; mod*) is a lovely Cycladic-style development of eight self-contained rooms built round a courtyard with wonderful views. There are also basic harbourside rooms to let: try **Rooms Loukas**, **Sigalas** or **Panayiotis Kouvdouris**, ☎ 51 232. There are several seasonal tavernas but if you go after late September everything is closed except **Flora's Shop**, which doubles as a makeshift taverna/*kafeneíon*. Otherwise you can feast on fresh fish at **Restaurant Loukas**, or eat at **Braxos Pizzaria**, aka **The Rock Café**, or have a coffee or ouzo at the **Meltemi** where the fishermen gather. There are also some tavernas beyond the beach.

### Kástro

There are a few places to stay: **Rooms Haroula** and **Rooms Dimitris Divolis** on the way to the post office and **Pension Nikos** over one of the *kafeneía* are all worth a try. The main taverna is **To Kastro** with excellent home-cooking where everyone drops in and dancing often breaks out; **Klimateria** is a pretty vine-covered *kafeneíon* which also does snacks. **Zacherias** another possibility for basic Greek fare. The main nightspot is **To Liotrivi**, a trendy music/dancing bar converted from one of the island's three olive presses.

## Sýros (ΣΥΡΟΣ/ΣΥΡΑ)

Inhabitants of Sýros, known locally as Sýra, have affectionately nicknamed their island home 'our rock', as dry and barren a piece of real estate as you can find in Greece. But at the beginning of the Greek War of Independence in 1821 it was blessed with three important qualities: a large natural harbour, the protection of the King of France, and a hardworking population. The result is Sýros' capital, Ermoúpolis, once the premier port in Greece, and today the largest city and capital of the Cyclades. It is also the best-preserved 19th-century neoclassical town in the whole of Greece.

A sophisticated island, with many Athenians working there in law or local government, Sýros doesn't need tourism, but it's booming nonetheless. However, it remains very Greek and tourists are treated more like guests rather than customers—except when it comes to *loukoúmia*, better known as Turkish Delight (both Greeks and Turks claim to have invented it; no one really knows). These sweet, gummy squares, flavoured with roses or pistachios, smothered in icing sugar, are an island speciality, and vendors stream aboard the ferries to peddle it. The other Sýros sweetmeats are *halvadópittes*, rather like nougat.

# History

Homer wrote that Sýros was a rich, fertile isle, whose inhabitants never suffered any illness, and died only when they were struck by the gentle arrows of Apollo or Artemis after living long, happy lives. The first inhabitants may have been Phoenicians, settled at Dellagrácia and at Fínikas. Poseidon was the chief god of Sýros, and in connection with his cult one of the first observatories in the world, a heliotrope (a kind of sundial), was constructed by the philosopher Ferekides, the teacher of Pythagoras. In Roman times the population emigrated to the site of present-day Ermoúpolis, at that time known as 'the Happy' with its splendid natural harbour and two prominent hills. After the collapse of the *pax Romana*, Sýros was abandoned until the 13th century, when Venetians founded the hilltop town of Áno Sýros.

Because Áno Sýros was Catholic, the island enjoyed the protection of the French, and remained neutral at the outbreak of the War of Independence in 1821. War refugees from Chíos, Psará and Smyrna brought their Orthodox faith with them and founded settlements on the other hill, Vrondádo, and down at Sýros' harbour. This new port town boomed from the start, as the premier 'warehouse' of the new Greek state where cotton from Egypt and spices from the East were stored, and as the central coaling station for the entire eastern

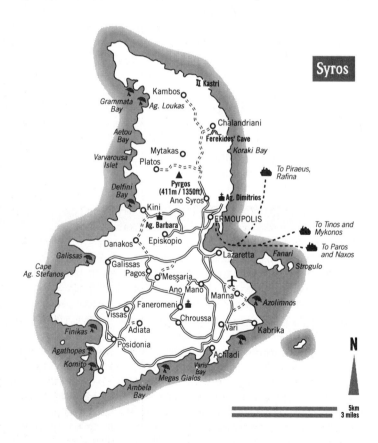

Mediterranean. When the time came to name the new town, Ermoúpolis—'the city of Hermes' (the god of commerce)—was the natural choice. For 50 years Sýros ran much of the Greek economy, and great fortunes were made and spent not only on elegant mansions, but also on schools, public buildings and streets. Ermoúpolis built the first theatre in modern Greece and the first high school, financed by the citizens and government; and when the Syriani died they were so pleased with themselves that the most extravagant monuments to be seen in any Greek cemetery were erected in their memory. By the 1870s, however, oil replaced coal and Piraeus replaced Ermoúpolis as Greece's major port; Sýros declined, but always remained the largest city and capital of the Cyclades, supporting itself with shipyards and various industries, prospering just enough to keep its grand old buildings occupied, but not enough to tear them down to build new concrete blocks. Today Ermoúpolis is a National Historical Landmark.

### Getting There and Around

**By air**: twice daily flights from Athens; airport ✆ 87 025.

**By sea**: daily with Mýkonos, Tínos, Piraeus, Páros, Náxos and Amorgós, 4–5 times a week with Ándros, Santoríni, Íos and Rafína, 3 times a week with Síkinos and Folégandros, twice a week to Astypálaia, Koufoníssia, Schinoússa and Heráklia, once a week to Ikaría, Sámos and Anáfi; **catamaran** daily to Piraeus and other Cyclades. **Port authority**, ✆ 22 690.

**By road**: good **bus** service around the island; **taxi rank** ✆ 86 222.

### Tourist Information

**NTOG** information office either on quay or at Town Hall, Plateía Miaoúlis, ✆ (0281) 22 375. **Tourist police** ✆ (0281) 22 610. The Teamwork travel office in the port, ✆ 23 400, ✉ 23 508 has accommodation and guided tours of Ermoúpolis.

### Festivals

The **last Sunday in May**, celebrating the finding of the icon at Ag. Dimitríou. In **June**, a folklore festival is held at Azólimnos with three days of dancing, wine and song. Every two years, in either the **last week of July** or the **first week of August**, the Apanosýria Festival is organized by the municipality of Áno Sýros, with exhibitions of local handicrafts and performances of popular plays. **24 September**, an Orthodox and Catholic celebration at Faneroméni. **26 October**, also at Ag. Dimitríou; **6 December**, Ag. Nikólaos in Ermoúpolis.

## Ermoúpolis

As you sail into the **commercial port**, Ermoúpolis (ΕΡΜΟΥΠΟΛΗ) presents an imposing sight much commented on by early travellers. Above are the two hills; Catholic **Áno Sýros** to your left (or north), and **Vrondádo**, the Orthodox quarter, on the right. The rest of the city is built on an angle in a grand amphitheatre. On the other side of the harbour are the now obsolete Neórion shipyards, having gone into receivership only a few years ago.

Ermoúpolis' central square, **Plateía Miaoúlis**, is paved with marble and lined with cafés and pizzerias, dominated by a grand **town hall**, where you can take in full-length portraits of King

George I and Queen Olga painted by Prossalendis. The **Archaeology Museum** (*open 8.30–3, closed Mon*) up the steps to the left, contains proto-Cycladic and Roman finds from Sýros and other islands. Left of the town hall are the **Historical Archives**, host to the Ermoúpoulis Seminars every summer, where interesting archives are on show (*open Mon–Fri, 9–2*). In front of the town hall stands a statue of Admiral Miaoúlis, revolutionary hero and old sea-dog, as well as a bandstand presided over by the seven muses. To the right, behind the square, stands the **Apóllon Theatre**, a copy of La Scala, Milan, and the first ever opera house in Greece; until 1914 it supported a regular Italian opera season and now hosts concerts. Up the street a little way from here, the **Velissarópoulos Mansion**, now housing the **Labour Union**, is one of the few places you can get into see the elaborate ceiling and wall murals characteristic of old Ermoúpolis.

Here begins the elegant **Vapória** quarter with its fantastic old shipowners' mansions. The square has one of the town's best churches, blue and golden-domed **Ag. Nikólaos**, dedicated to the patron saint of the city and boasting a carved marble iconostasis by the 19th-century sculptor Vitális of Tínos. In front of the church, a memorial topped by a stone lion, also by Vitális, is the world's first **Monument of the Unknown Soldier**. The Cyclades capital building is near here as well. On the opposite side of the square in Stamatoú Proioú Street, the bell tower of the church **Koímisis** is an island landmark; its elegant neoclassical interior contains a rare icon painted by Doménicos Theotokópoulos, better known as El Greco after he left for Venice and Spain. Another fine church in Ermoúpolis is the **Metamórphosis**, the Orthodox cathedral.

**Vapória**'s grand houses, famous for their frescoes and painted ceilings, are built in an amphitheatre, hugging the coastline above the town beaches of **Ag Nikólaos**, **Tálliro** and **Evangelídis** which have marble steps down from the street.

Crowning **Vrondádo Hill** (take the main street up from behind Plateía Miaoúlis), is the Byzantine church of the **Anástasis** with a few old icons and superb views stretching to Tínos and Mýkonos. Vrondádo has some excellent local tavernas spread out in its steps at nigh— follow your nose. If you have the energy it's an hour's climb up Omírou Street (or hop on the bus) to the medieval Catholic quarter of **Áno Sýros**. Also called Apáno Chóra, Áno Sýros is a pretty labyrinth of narrow lanes and archways with breathtaking views. Since the Crusades, most of the families in Áno Sýros have been Catholic, and some have lived in the same mansions for generations and attended the **Catholic Cathedral of St George**, known as **Ai-Giórgi** on top of the rock of Áno Sýros. The large, handsome **Capuchin Convent of St Jean** was founded there in 1635 by France's Louis XIII as a poorhouse and contains archives dating from the 1400s. Another church, the **Ag. Nikólaos**, was founded in the 15th century as a house for the poor. Áno Sýros was also the birthplace of the famous **bouzoúki** maestro Márkos Vamvakáris whose bust graces the square named after him. The main entrance, the **Kámara**, is an ancient arched passageway which leads past tavernas and little shops to the the main street or **Piátsa**. There's a town hall, more archives, **the Women's Association of Handicraft Workers** with a folklore collection and workshop, the **Cultural Centre** and **local radio station**. On your way up or down the hill, don't miss the **Orthodox cemetery of Ag. Geórgios**, with its elaborate marble mausoleums of Sýros' wealthy shipowners and merchants.

A 45-minute walk from Ermoúpolis leads to the pretty seaside church of **Ag. Dimítrios**, founded after the discovery of an icon there in 1936. All ships coming into port hoot as they pass and a bell is rung in reply—cup your hand and you'll hear it. Alternatively, a 15-minute stroll will take you to Díli and its **Temple of Isis** built in 200 BC. Across the harbour at **Lazarétta** stood a 5th-century BC temple of Poseidon, although the only traces of it are a few artefacts in the museum. In ancient times this was probably the Poseidonia mentioned in the *Odyssey*. Also near Ermoúpolis at Pefkákia, there was a **Roman-era cemetery**, although nothing remains of the actual tombs.

## Around Sýros

Other ancient sites are in the north of the island. At lagoon-like **Grámmata Bay** (reached only by boat), a prophylactic inscription to keep ships from sinking is carved in the rock, dating back to Hellenistic times. If you want a beach away from it all this is the place; sea-lilies grow here and on many of the beaches in winter. **Kástri**, just north of Chalandrianí, was settled in the Bronze Age: its walls, foundations of houses and overgrown necropolis have contributed much to the understanding of this period in the Cyclades. Signs suggest it was re-inhabited for a brief period around 8000 BC. The **cave** where the philosopher Ferekides supposedly lived in the summer is nearby; his winter cave is at Alythiní. Another path in the north leads to the quiet beach at **Mégas Lakkos**.

Buses from Ermoúpolis travel to the main seaside resorts: **Kíni** (KINI), a small fishing village with two sandy beaches, is a popular rendezvous for sunset-watching, and home to a famous singing family who play authentic bouzouki music at their beachside taverna. North over the headland is **Delfíni Beach** for that all-over tan. Lively **Galissás** (ΓΑΛΗΣΣΑΣ) has the best sheltered beach on the island, a sweeping crescent of sand fringed by tamarisks, but is all mini-markets and heavy metal, frantic with backpackers and bikers in high season. The island's two campsites are here. Nearby **Arméos** is for nudists. Further south **Fínikas** (ΦΟΙΝΙΚΑΣ), 'Phoenix', originally settled by the Phoenicians and mentioned in Homer, is another popular resort with a gritty roadside beach. Neighbouring **Dellagrácia**, better known as **Posidonía** (ΠΟΣΕΙΔΩΝΙΑ), has a film-star feel with ornate Italianate mansions, some like castles, and a blue church. Further south quieter **Agathopés** has a sandy beach and islet opposite and you can take the track from here to **Kómito**, a stony stretch in front of an olive grove. **Mégas Gialós** (ΜΕΓΑΣ ΓΙΑΛΟΣ) is a pretty family resort, its sands shaded by sea-salt trees, and there are pedaloes for hire. Further along **Vári** (BAPH) has become a major resort, but still has its fishing fleet. **Azólimnos** is particularly popular with the Syriani for its *ouzeries* and cafés, but there are no hotels or rooms. In the middle of the island, **Episkópio** claims the oldest Byzantine church on Sýros, **Profítis Ilías**, prettily set in the pine-covered hills. The Orthodox convent **Ag. Barbára**, inland from Kíni, has a school of arts and crafts with embroidery and knitwear on sale. The walls of the church are decorated with frescoes depicting Barbára's martyrdom—her father locked her in a tower and put her to death, but immediately after-wards was struck down by a divine thunderbolt, making her the patron saint of bombardiers. Inland, **Chroússa** is a pleasant, pine-shaded village with a number of new villas, while nearby **Faneroméni** ('can be seen from everywhere') itself has panoramic views of the island.

---

*Sýros ✆ (0281–)*             ***Where to Stay and Eating Out***

Sýros is less expensive than its neighbouring islands although the standard of accommodation is often higher. Although busy with Athenians in July and August, you shouldn't have trouble finding a place to stay. The **Rooms To Let Association** has a useful list available from agencies. Culinary specialities include smoky San Michaeli cheese, *loúza*, salt pork, various sausages and the excellent local Vátis wines.

## Ermoúpolis

**The Hotel Hermes**, ✆ 23 011, ✉ 27 412 (*B; exp–mod*), on the harbour, has been tastefully extended and revamped. **Pension Venetiko**, E. Roídi Street, ✆ 81 686/28 596 (*mod–inexp*) is a very friendly pension in an old house near the square with a pretty walled garden and bar; owner Pétros is a mine of information. Nearby **Pension Dioskouri**, ✆ 22 580 (*A; inexp*) is another lovely old place with a colonnaded terrace. Uptown in Vapória or St Nicholas the **Sea Colours Apartments**, ✆ 28 716 (*A; exp–mod*) are luxurious and modern with marble terraces and wonderful views; book through Teamwork, call ✆ 23 400. In the same area the **Ipatia Guest House**, ✆ 23 575 (*A pension; mod–inexp*), is a super neoclassical mansion with brass bedsteads. **Villa Nostos**, ✆ 24 226 (*B; mod*) is another fine old house, as is the swish **Omiros Hotel**, ✆ 24 910, ✉ 28 756 (*A; lux–exp*) a neoclassical mansion, the elegantly restored family home of sculptor Vitalis. There's more history at the newly converted **Diogenis Hotel** ✆ 86 301–5, ✉ 23 334 (*A; lux–exp*) on the seafront, once a coal store then a cabaret club, now lavishly converted. The stylish **Hotel Palladian** on Stamatoú Proioú Street ✆ 86 400, ✉ 86 436 (*B; exp–mod*) including breakfast is another gem.

For tighter budgets **Silvia Rooms**, ✆ 81 081 (*inexp*) are elegantly furnished in another old mansion; **Tony's Rooms**, no phone (*B; inexp*) on Vokotopoúlou are a favourite backpackers' haunt. In the lower price range, there are several old houses in Ermoúpolis with rooms to let, and rooms at many of the beaches. For a reclusive holiday you can always stay at the **Capuchin Monastery Guest House** in Áno Sýros, ✆ 22 576, rates on request. The **Folia Taverna** up in Vrondádo is the most well-known in Sýros and one of the best in the Cyclades for classic dishes like pigeon, rabbit and cauliflower patties in unassuming surroundings and at resaonable prices; in Áno Sýro, **Lilli's** is famous for its wonderful views, good menu and *rembétika* music at weekends; in the high town also try **I Piatza Taverna**; opposite the ferry port those in the know head to one of the finest old island *ouzeries*, barrel-lined **Bouba's** with exquisite barbecued octopus and local, smelly *kopanistí* cheese on *paximádia* bread rusks. Cheap and cheerful. The waterfront is heaving with eateries and bars. For fish try **Cavo D'Oro**, for great oven dishes and barrel wines go to **Syllivani's** or equally good **Muses**, although tables near the water's edge can get a bit whiffy. **Taverna 1935** is smart with international as well as Greek food. For the best roasts and barbeques as well as take-ways there's no beating **Ta Yiannena Psistaria** further along the quay with *kokkorétsi*, chicken and some imaginative vegetable dishes too. If you want pasta, then **Cucina Italiana** has a romantic roof garden. On the road to Vári, **Restaurant O Loukas** is recommended.

## Posidonía

The **Hotel Eleana**, ✆ 42 601, ✉ 42 644, (*B; mod*) is a very pleasant hotel with lovely grounds right on the beach; in Megás Giálos the **Hotel Alkyon** ✆ 61 761, ✉ 61 000 is a good bet, owned by the president of the Hoteliers Association.

### Galissás Beach

The **Dolphin Bay Hotel**, ✆ 42 924, 🖷 42 843 (*A; exp*) is a complex with everything from volleyball to disco; the new family-run **Hotel Semiramis**, ✆ 42 067 (*B; mod*) and **Hotel Petros**, (*E; inexp*) are both near the beach. **Two Hearts Camping**, ✆ 42 052/321, has everything from minigolf to motorbike hire and a minibus to meet ferries. The other site is **Camping Yianna**, ✆ 42 418. The in place to eat is **Yeia Sou Yiannis**. At Kíni the **Iliovasilema** ('Sunset') is excellent, and **Marco's Seafood Taverna** another good place to watch the sun disappear over Kýthnos.

---

### Entertainment and Nightlife

There's no shortage of both on Sýros, from culture at the **Apollon Theatre**, movies at the **Pallas outdoor cinema** near the market and a huge range of bars from sophisticated to rowdy. The evening *vólta* is the main event for island families with everyone parading up and down Miaoúlis Square to see and be seen then relaxing in the cafés round the square. At one time the square was even specially paved so that the unmarried knew on which side to stroll to show they were available!

The waterfront buzzes with bars but *the* place to hang out is the **Allo Bar**, a hip piano bar and magnet for dolled-up Sýros jet-setters. The cool **Dizzy Bar**, in an alley off the harbour, plays soft music and is more laid-back; **Tramps** is for ex-pats, **Highway** for loud music, **Corto** is chic and **No Name** young and noisy. You can dance at the **Cotton Club** or enjoy an ouzo and *mezédes* at **Psaropoula** or **Argiris** *ouzerie*. For real *rembétika* music head to **Lilli's** and **Rahamos** in Áno Sýros or **Dakrotsides** in Kíni. There's also the **Nereida Bouzouki Club** open nighly in summer at **Manna**.

# Tínos (ΤΗΝΟΣ)

If Délos was the sacred island of the ancient Greeks, Tínos, the Lourdes of Greece, occupies the same place in the hearts of their modern descendants. Chances are that in ancient times Délos had much the same atmosphere as Tínos—numerous lodgings and eating places, a busy harbour, shaded stoas (in Tínos, awnings over the street) merchants seling *támata* (votives) and other holy objects to the thousands of pilgrims who come to seek the healing powers of the island's miraculous icon, often crawling from the ferry to the church. Tínos is also known for its beautiful Venetian dovecotes, of which some 600 survive, scattered across the island's great sloping terraces like little houses of whitewashed stone embroidery. Clouds of doves are everywhere and a resident pelican lives in the fishermen's square. Tínos may be the centre of Orthodox pilgrimage, but of all the Cyclades it has the highest percentage of Catholics; many of the island's pretty white villages have somewhat atypical campaniles for landmarks—Tínos has 1200 chapels. Away from the thronging pilgrims Tínos maintains its relaxed family atmosphere, very much in contrast with neighbouring Mýkonos. The locals say there's a hole in the ozone layer giving them a direct line to the Almighty: anyone disturbing the peace will be politely but firmly placed on the first ferry out.

## History

Inhabited by the Ionians in Archaic times, Tínos was occupied by the Persians in 490 BC, but set free after the Battle of Marathon. In the 4th century a sanctuary of the sea god Poseidon was founded on the island (after he chased away all its snakes) and it became a sacred place, where pilgrims would come to be cured by the god and to participate in the December festivals of the Poseidonia. There were two ancient cities on the island, both confusingly named Tínos, one at the site of the present town and the other at Xómbourgo. When the war between the Romans and Mithridates of Pontus broke out in 88 BC, the latter destroyed both towns. Not much happened until the Fourth Crusade, when the Venetians built a fortress called Santa Elena at Xómbourgo, using the stone of the ancient acropolis and city. It was the strongest fortress of the Cyclades, and stood impregnable to eleven assaults by the Turks. Even Barbarossa was defeated by Santa Elena and its Venetian and Greek defenders. In revenge, the frustrated Turks often pillagedthe rest of Tínos. In 1715, long after the rest of Greece had submitted to Ottoman rule, the Turkish admiral arrived in Tínos with a massive fleet and army. After sustaining a terrible attack, the Venetians decided that this time Santa Elena would not hold out, and, to the surprise of the Greeks, surrendered. The Turks allowed the Venetians to leave in safety, but in Venice, where it was a crime to fail in the course of duty, the officers were put on trial for treason, accused of having been bribed to surrender, and executed. Meanwhile the Turks blew up a good deal of Santa Elena in case the Venetians should change their minds and come back. Tínos was thus the last territorial gain of the Ottoman Empire.

In 1822, during the Greek War of Independence, a nun at Kechrovoúni Convent, Sister Pelagía, had a vision of the Virgin directing her to a rock where she discovered a miraculous icon of Mary and the Archangel at the Annunciation. The icon, now known as the *Megalóchari*, Great Grace, was found to have extraordinary healing powers, and a church was soon built for it in Tínos town, called Panagía Evangelístra or Christopiliopsia. It quickly became the most important place of pilgrimage in Greece and because of its timing, a shrine of Greek nationalism; the discovery of the icon at just that moment in history helped to give the fight for independence the morale-boosting aura of a holy war. On 15 August 1940, during the huge annual celebration at the church, an Italian submarine entered the harbour of Tínos and sank the Greek cruise boat *Elli*—one of the major incidents directly before Mussolini involved Greece in the Second World War. Under the Colonels' regime the entire island was declared a holy place (part of that government's so-called 'moral cleansing') and the women of Tínos were required to behave at all times as if they were in church, by wearing skirts, etc., a rule quickly abolished when the junta itself went out of the window.

### Getting There and Around

**By sea**: daily **ferry** from Piraeus, Mýkonos, Sýros, Ándros and Rafína. Six times a week with Páros, 5 times a week with Amorgós, 3 times a week to the Dodecanese and Santoríni, twice with Crete, Íos, Skiáthos, Thessaloníki, Koufoníssia, Schinoússa and Heráklia, once a week with Síkinos, Sámos and Ikaría; daily **hydrofoil** or **catamaran** to other Cyclades and Piraeus. Note that ships from Tínos to Piraeus are often full. Two landing areas operate, often simultaneously, and when departing be sure to check you find the right queue with your ticket agent. **Port authority**, ✆ 22 348.

**By road**: there's an excellent **bus** service all over the island and plenty of **taxis**.

### Tourist Information

Tínos Mariner travel agency on the front has helpful information and an excellent map of the island. The **tourist police** are at 5 Plateía L. Sóchou, ✆ (0283) 22 255.

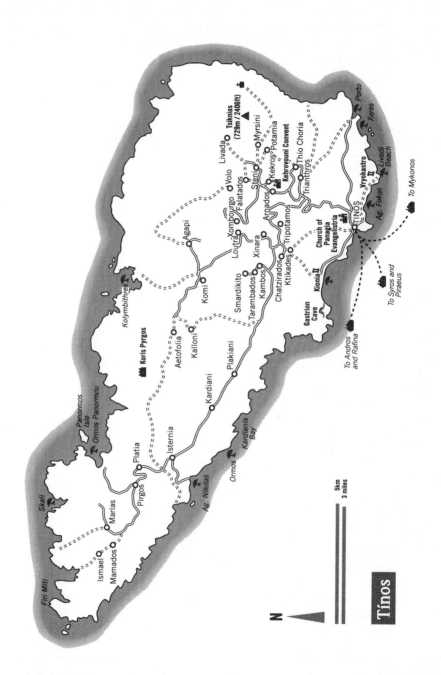

Tínos

**19 January**, Megalómatas at Ktikádes; **25 March** and **15 August** at the Panagía Evangelístra, the two largest in Greece; **50 days after Greek Easter** (i.e. mid-June), Ag. Triáda at Kardianí; **29 August**, Ag. Ioánnes at Kómi (Catholic); **20 October**, Ag. Artemíou at Falatádos; **26 October**, Ag. Dimítri in Tínos town; **21 December**, Presentation of Mary at Tripotámos.

## Tínos Town

### Panagía Evangelístra

As your ship pulls into Tínos, the port and capital, the outline of the yellow church Panagía Evangelístra and its neon-lit cross floats above the town. It's a short walk up Evangelístra Street, a street closed to traffic that becomes a solid mass of pilgrims on the two principal feast days of the Virgin, 15 August and 25 March. Many cover the entire distance from the ferry to the church on all fours, with padded knees and arms, elderly women in particular, crawling in penance for the health of a loved one—a raw, moving and often disturbing sight. Others peruse the street stalls full of icons and *támata*, little tin votive offerings. A red carpet covers the grand marble stair leading up to the neoclassical church. If blind, pilgrims pledge to send an effigy of whatever they first see made from precious metal if their sight is restored. As testimony to the miracles, there's a beautiful orange tree made of silver and gold; a ship with a giant fish in its side and hundreds of precious offerings from the grateful. Hundreds of shimmering lamps strung overhead create a magical effect, while on the floor level the church employs men who do nothing all day but remove candles from the stands so that new arrivals will have somewhere to put theirs—the largest are the size of elephants' tusks. The pilgrims then queue up to kiss the icon itself, another work of the prolific St Luke, although its artistic merits are impossible to judge under the layers of gold, diamonds and pearls. Near the church four hostels have been built for pilgrims waiting to be healed by the icon, but there is still not enough room to house them, and the overflow camp out patiently in the courtyard.

The crypt, where Ag. Pelagía discovered the icon, is now the **Chapel of Evróseos** ('discovery'). Silver lines the spot in the rocks where the icon lay; the spring here, believed to be holy, is said to have curative properties. Parents from all over Greece bring their children here in August to be baptized in the font. Next to the chapel the victims of the *Elli* are interred in a mausoleum, which displays a piece of the fatal Fascist torpedo.

Among the church's museums (*all open 8am–8pm*) there are: an **art gallery**, with works from the Ionian school, a reputed Rubens, a dubious Rembrandt partially hidden by the radiator, and many 19th-century works; a museum devoted to the works of the Tiniot sculptor **Lázarou Sóchou**, and above it the **Sculpture Museum** housing pieces by a variety of Greek sculptors such as Ioánnis Boúlgaros and Vitális; old icons in the **Byzantine Museum**; and another museum containing items used in the church service.

### Around Tínos Town

Parallel with Evangelístra Street, opposite a shady pine grove, the island **Archaeological Museum** (*open 8–3; adm*) contains artefacts from the Sanctuary of Poseidon and Amphitrite, including a sundial and a sea monster in various pieces and huge decorated storage vessels from the Archaic period.

From the port it's a short walk west to **Kiónia** ('the columns'), with the main **Tínos Beach** plus hotel complex, a couple of smaller beaches and the **sanctuary of Poseidon and Amphitrite**, discovered by the Belgian archaeologist Demoulin in 1902. Of the famous sanctuary the temple, the treasuries, entrances, little temple, baths, fountain of Poseidon and inns for pilgrims have been excavated. In many ways the ancient cult of the sea god and his wife Amphitrite parallels the contemporary cult of the icon—both Panagía Evangelístra and Poseidon have impressive records in rescuing sailors from storms. East of town, the closest and busiest beach is shingly **Ag. Fokás**; a few minutes further east, at **Vryókastro**, are the walls of an ancient settlement, and a Hellenistic tower. Further east at **Xerés** the beach tends to be less crowded, but sandy **Pórto** is now a busy resort.

## Around the Island

Buses from the town pier wend their way north to the 12th-century **Kehrovoúni Convent**, one of the largest in Greece. It is here that Sister Pelagía, canonized in 1971, had her two visions, in which the Virgin told her where to find the icon. You can visit her old cell and see her embalmed head. **Arnados** to the north is a charming little village, as is **Thío Choriá**.

In the winter Tínos turns lush and green, a colour that lingers until May when it takes on a more typical Cycladic barren brown, its hills corrugated with sun-parched terraces, relieved by the white dovecotes and their white residents. Some of the most elaborate dovecotes are in **Smardákito**, one of a cluster of small villages above Tínos town. Looming over them on a 564m hill is the famous Venetian fortress at **Xómbourgo**, ruined by the Turks but still affording a superb view over neighbouring islands. First inhabited around 1000 BC, this commanding hill has a few ancient walls, although most of the stone was reused by later inhabitants, especially the Gizzi family of Venice, who built the Venetian fortress. Besides medieval houses, a fountain and three churches remain in the citadel walls. The easiest approach is from **Xinára**, seat of the Catholic arch-diocese. From here, too, you can walk to the site of one of the 8th-century BC towns called Tínos, where a large building and Geometric period temple were discovered. **Loutrá**, one of the prettier villages, has a 17th-century Jesuit monastery where a school is still run by the Ursulines. From **Kómi**, a long valley runs down to the sea at **Kolymbíthres**, a horseshoe bay with fine sandy beaches where many people camp.

A paved road follows the mountainous ridge overlooking the southwest coast. One possible detour descends to the valley village of **Tarambádos**, with more good dovecotes; at **Kardianí** a driveable track winds down to a remote beach; otherwise, from **Istérnia**, a pleasant village with plane trees, you can drive down to popular Ormós or **Ag. Nikítas beach**, the latter with rooms and tavernas. This part of Tínos is famous for its green marble, and the island has a long tradition in working the stone. Several well-known Greek artists came from or have worked in **Pírgos**. Just by the bus stop is a small **museum** and the **residence of sculptor Giannolís Halépas**; the old grammar school, built in the first flush of Greek independence, is now a School of Fine Arts. A shop near the main square exhibits and sells students' works—Byzantine eagles are still popular motifs. Below Pírgos the public bus continues down to the beach at **Pánormos bay**, with more tavernas and rooms. **Marlás**, further north, is in the centre of the old marble quarries. From the tip of Tínos it's only one nautical mile to the island of Ándros.

Because Tínos has long been receiving pilgrims, it boasts a fine old-fashioned hotel infrastructure not found on the other islands. Avoid August 14–15 if you haven't a room, although sleeping outside isn't a terrible price to pay if you want to witness the greatest pilgrimage in Greece.

**Aeolos Bay**, ℗ 23 339 (*B; exp*) is a smart but friendly hotel with a pool overlooking Ag. Fokás beach. **Meltemi**, ℗ 22 881, ℗ 24 156 (*C; mod*) is quite luxurious despite its grade. The **Alonia Hotel**, ℗ 23 541, ℗ 23 544 (*B; exp*) is in a verdant spot with springs east of town. The Grande Dame of older hostelries, the **Hotel Tinion**, ℗ 22 261 (*B; mod*) is on the left of the harbour as you sail in; **Vyzantion**, 26 Alavanoú, ℗ 22 454, is a pleasant alternative. The **Argo**, ℗ 22 588, ℗ 23 188 (*C; mod*) is another good bet a little out of town at Agiali. **Aphrodite** ℗ 22 456 (*C; mod*) is handy for ferries. Inland, **Pension Favie-Souzane**, ℗ 22 693 (*B; mod*) is pleasant; cheaper port pensions are **Eleana**, ℗ 22 56 (*D; inexp*) and **Thalia**, ℗ 22 811. The **Tinos Beach** on the beach at Kiónia, ℗ 22 626/8, ℗ 23 153 (*A; lux–exp*) has every facility and bungalows, while at Pórto the **Porto Tango Hotel**, 24 411, ℗ 24 416 (*A; lux–exp*) has all the comforts of a major complex. There are nice rooms in Kolimbíthres overlooking the bay. **Camping Tinos** ℗ 22 344/23 548 is a good site south of town; follow the signs.

You can find inexpensive food throughout the town, especially the local speciality, *froutália* omelettes, though the waterfront restaurants tend to be hurried and rather mediocre. In town, try **Nine Muses**, a nice *ouzerie*-cum-taverna, or head back from the harbour to **Michaelis** for rabbit *stifádo*, or **Pentelis**, another authentic taverna. There's a traditional *patsas* or tripe shop and, in complete contrast, smart **Xinari** with a Lebanese influence and terrace from where you can watch the goings on. **Palea Palada** near the fish market is good and you'll get a decent meal at **O Peristeronas**, near by. **Taverna I Dhrosia** at Ktikádes offers good food with a view, while the beautiful village of Kardianí has the exotic **To Perivoli**, a popular haunt with Athenians.

### Entertainment and Nightlife

You don't come to Tínos for a wild time. Most nightlife revolves around the waterfront cafés or the festivals, although there are some music bars and discos. The Tinians like to let their hair down and there are Catholic as well as Orthodox feast days to enjoy as well as organized Greek nights in the village of **Smardákito**.

CHALKI

## The Dodecanese

Furthest from mainland Greece, the Dodecanese, whose name (ΔΩΔΕΚΑΝΗΣΑ) means 'twelve islands' (although there are actually 16 inhabited ones, and even that depends on how you count them) are the latest additions to Greece (in 1948), although union only confirmed a sense of national identity, language, religion and traditions their inhabitants kept smouldering on the home fire over the centuries. But their distance, and long separation from the mainstream of Greek history, has dealt them a unique deck to play with—medieval knights, Ottoman Turks and 20th-century Italians, all of whom contributed to the distinct character and architecture of the Dodecanese. Add a sunny climate and long sandy beaches and the striking individualism of each island—including even one bright white Cycladic rock pile, Astypálaia—the holiday possibilities on the Dodecanese are infinite, covering the gamut from the feverish high-calibre international resorts of Rhodes and Kos to the low-key, relaxed, very Greek pleasures of Lipsí, Chálki, Kárpathos or volcanic Níssyros. Striking Sými and Pátmos attract upmarket crowds; while Léros, Kálymnos and Tílos remain best-kept secrets of seasoned travellers. Kastellórizo has an end-of-the-world atmosphere that seems to draw more people every year; Kássos has a similar air but attracts nobody, if you're looking for a real getaway. Connections by ferry, hydrofoil and excursion boat are good between the islands, making it easy to get around and even to pop over to Turkey for a day or two.

## History

The Dodecanese flourished early in antiquity, populated by the elusive Carians (from Caria, on the nearby coast of Asia Minor). They were either subjugated by, or allies of, the seafaring Minoans, a connection reflected in the islands' myths. When Minoan Crete fell, the Mycenaeans took over, and many of the Dodecanese sent ships to the Trojan war. In the various invasions that followed the fall of Troy, Aeolians, Ionians and Dorians swept through. By the Archaic period the last arrivals, the Dorians, had formed themselves into powerful city-states, particularly on Rhodes and Kos, states so prosperous that they established colonies and trading counters in Italy, France and Spain. The Persians were the next to invade, and, when they were defeated at Salamis, the Dodecanese joined the maritime league at Délos as a hedge against further attacks. Their greater distance from Athens, however, allowed them more autonomy than other islands were permitted, and they produced a dazzling array of artists, scientists, and intellectuals—most famously, Hippocrates, the father of medicine.

After the death of Alexander the Great, his general, Ptolemy of Egypt, inherited the Dodecanese, leading to one of the greatest aborted sieges in antiquity, when a rival general, Antigonos, sent his son Dimitrios to take Rhodes. Emboldened by its victory, in 164 BC Rhodes erected its proud Colossus and made an alliance with Rome, enabling her to exert a powerful influence of her own over an empire of Greek islands. Some two hundred years later Rome sent St John the Theologian in exile to another Dodecanese island, Pátmos, where he converted the inhabitants and got his own back by penning the *Apocalypse*, or *Revelations*, where Rome comes out as the Mother of Harlots, or worse.

In 1095, the islands had their first taste of a much more aggressive brand of Christianity, when Crusaders en route to the Holy Land made them a port of call. The Crusaders' odd bit of

# The Dodecanese

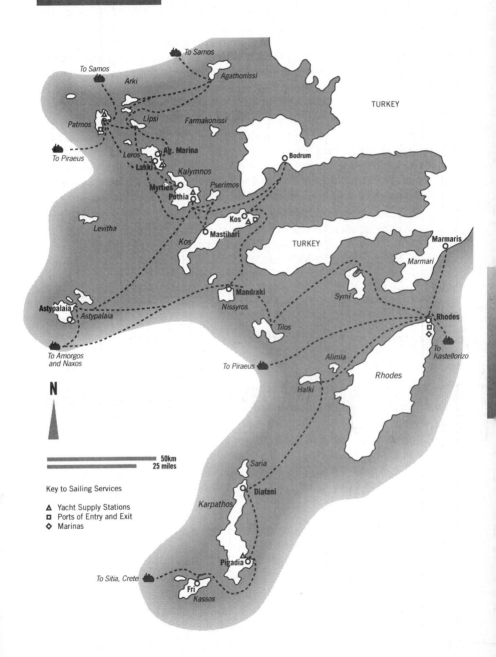

To Samos

To Samos

Arki

Agathonissi

TURKEY

Patmos

Lipsi

Farmakonissi

To Piraeus

Leros

Ag. Marina

Bodrum

Lakki

Kalymnos

Myrties

Pserimos

Pothia

Kos

Levitha

Mastihari

Kos

TURKEY

Marmaris

Marmari

Mandraki

Astypalaia

Nissyros

Symi

Rhodes

Astypalaia

Tilos

To Amorgos
and Naxos

To Kastellorizo

To Piraeus

Alimia

Rhodes

Halki

N

50km
25 miles

Key to Sailing Services

△  Yacht Supply Stations
□  Ports of Entry and Exit
◇  Marinas

Saria

Diafani

Karpathos

To Sitia, Crete

Pigadia

Fri

Kassos

pillaging and piracy climaxed in the capture of Constantinople, led by Venice, in 1204; but in 1291 the tables turned when Jerusalem fell to the rising star of the east: the Ottomans. This disrupted, among other things, the work of the Knights of St John, an exclusive order skimmed from the cream (or at least the second and third sons) of Western Europe's aristocracy, who ran a hospital for pilgrims in Jerusalem. The Knights first moved to Cyprus, and eighteen years later purchased all the Dodecanese outright from a Genoese pirate, Admiral Vinioli. They set up headquarters on Rhodes, built a hospital and fortified the islands against the Turks and pirates, while raiding the coast in swift vessels made on Sými, letting Christian pirates pass through their territory unmolested, but stopping ships carrying Moslem pilgrims.

In 1522 Sultan Suleiman the Magnificent had had enough and attacked Rhodes (the third major Moslem offensive on the Knights) and all the men of the Dodecanese rallied to its defence. Only information from a traitor brought about the defeat of the Knights after a long siege. Always a gentleman, Suleiman permitted them and their followers to depart in safety to their new fief, Malta, where a few decades later they successfully withstood an even more massive Turkish assault and turned the tide of Ottoman expansion in the West.

Turkish occupation of the Dodecanese lasted until 1912, when Italy opportunistically took 'temporary possession' of the islands. This occupation was made 'permanent' after the Greek débâcle in 1920 by the second Treaty of Lausanne. Mussolini poured money into his new colonies, sponsoring massive public works (most of his public buildings are still scattered across the islands, for better or worse) reforestation, archaeological excavations and historical reconstructions. While Turkish rule had been depressing, negligent and sometimes brutal, the Fascists, in spite of their lavish expenditures, were even worse in the eyes of the islanders, outlawing their Orthodox religion and Greek language, to the extent that even today you can find older people on the Dodecanese who are more comfortable speaking Italian. After the Second World War, the islands were reunited with Greece; to encourage growth, especially through tourism, they were granted duty-free concessions. As they say, the rest is history.

# Astypálaia (ΑΣΤΥΠΑΛΑΙΑ)

Butterfly-shaped Astypálaia is the most westerly of the Dodecanese, halfway between Amorgós and Kos, and would be perfectly at home in the neighbouring Cyclades with its austere rocky geography and dazzling sugar-cube houses tumbling from the narrow alleys of its upper town, Chóra. Yet there's more here than first meets the eye: the island nurtures a rich, fertile, definately Dodecanesian valley called Livádia in its bosom, and equally fertile fishing in the sheltered nooks and crannies of its wildly indented coastline—in antiquity Astypálaia was called Ichthyoessa, 'the fishy island'. Besides the lure of seafood, Astypálaia's relative inaccessibility makes it a good place to escape the summer crowds, if not always noise; the locals really deserve more than a couple of streets for their evening scooter exercises. The women's traditional costumes are famous for their elaborate detail and beauty.

Astypálaia is becoming increasingly trendy as Athenians do up the old houses in Chóra as holiday homes. Popular among Greek, French and Italians, it has also become a package holiday destination for more adventurous Brits. But as the island has been difficult to get to in the past—you had the choice of a long ferry slog from Piraeus or hops from Kos and Kálymnos—it has retained its considerable charm.

# History

The name Astypálaia may mean 'old city', but mythology claims that the name is derived from a sister of Europa, the mother of King Minos. Early on, its inhabitants may have founded another Astypálaia, the ancient capital of Kos. In Classical times the island was most famous for a tragically short-tempered boxer named Kleomedes, who, in competing in the Olympics, killed his opponent, which even then was enough to get you disqualified. Kleomedes returned to Astypálaia seething with rage and took his disappointment out on the local school, knocking it down and killing all the pupils.

From 1207 to 1522, the Quirini family of Venice occupied the island, styling themselves the Counts of Astypálaia. They built a castle in Chóra—on a clear day you can see Amorgós and Santoríni from its walls. Astypálaia was the first of the Dodecanese to be annexed by the Italians in 1912 and during the occupation they built another fortification called Kastelláno in the east of the island, south of Vathí.

---

### Getting There and Around

**By sea**: with the introduction of new lines linking the Dodecanese and Cyclades the **ferry** service is much improved. There are links 3 times a week with Kos, Kálymnos, Amorgós, Mýkonos, Tínos and Piraeus; 3 times a week with Sýros and Rhodes taking in Níssyros and Tílos; once a week with Páros and Náxos; once a week in summer to Santoríni, Ándros and Raffina. There are also **excursion boats** in season to Vathí from Periyialós and Ag. Andréas. **Port authority**, ✆ 61 208.

**By air**: the new airport features two flights a week to Athens, on Fridays and Sundays.

**By road**: there's a regular **bus** service in season between Chóra, Skála, Livádia and Analipsí. **Taxis** are also available at reasonable rates. Louise Edeleanu at Gournas Tours, ✆ (0242) 61 334 can give you specific details, or try the small tourist office in the harbour, ✆ 61 217.

---

### Tourist Police

The regular police, ✆ (0242) 61 207, share a building on the harbourside with the port authority.

---

### Festivals

**21 May**, Ag. Konstantínos; **15 August**, Panagía Portaïtíssa.

## Around Astypálaia

The capital and main port of the island, **Astypálaia** or **Perigialós** (ΠΕΡΙΓΙΑΛΟΣ), picturesquely piles itelf up beneath the Venetian castle then tumbles down to a sandy stretch of beach. From the harbour, where the ferries dock and fishing boats bob at anchor, flights of steps (there's also a new road) lead to the upper town, or **Chóra**, where a line of nine ruined windmills begins in the square to stand sentinel along the ridge of the butterfly wing. Chóra's narrow stepped main street or **Skála** is lined with Cubist white houses, many sporting Turkish-style painted wooden balconies or *poúndia*. A maze of narrow lanes, some only passable on foot or by donkey, twist and turn around the impressive 14th-century **Kástro**, the ancient medieval and Venetian capital with its small square and *kafeneíon*. The gate of the **fortress** still bears the Quirini coat-of-arms, a display of pride that would have been much frowned on back in Venice itself. Houses were built into the citadel walls for protection and inside the fortress you can also see two churches: **St George**, on the site of an ancient temple, and the **Panagía Portaïtíssa** ('Madonna of the Castle'), one of the most beautiful in the Dodecanese, topped with a white-tiled dome and decorated inside with intricate lace-like designs and a carved wooden shrine highlighted with gold leaf. The Kástro is itself protected these days by an Archaeological Service preservation order and no building is allowed inside. But the houses huddled outside the citadel have almost completely been restored.

Set in a green and comparatively lush valley, **Livádia** (ΛΙΒΑΔΙΑ) is downhill from the wind-mills to the west; its shingly, sandy beach can get busy with Greek families in high season. Follow the coast along to the south and you can cast your clothes to the wind on the unofficial nudist beach at **Tzanáki**. One of the best beaches on the island is at **Ag. Andréas**, an hour and a half's walk from Livádia down a dirt track. Other excursions from Skála include a two-hour walk inland to **Ag. Ioánnis**, a lush spot with a waterfall (the track starts at the windmills) or to the monastery of **Panagía Flevariótissa**. You can also take a bus or taxi trip to the village of **Maltezána** or **Análypsi** (ΑΝΑΛΗΨΗ) 11km away, its first name recalling that it was once a lair of Maltese pirates. Here the French Captain Bigot died in 1827 when he set fire to his corvette to avoid capture. The cove next door is popular with nudists and on the fringe of the surrounding olive groves look out for the remains of the **Roman Baths** with their well-preserved zodiac floor mosaics. With the new airport just up the road, Maltezána is the island's fastest-developing resort.

The 'Jewel of the Dodecanese', Astypálaia is lush with citrus orchards in some places, offsetting its craggy barrenness. Where the wings of the butterfly join it's barely 50 metres wide, so you either sizzle or cool off, depending on the wind direction. On the far wing is the island's main attraction, the lost lagoon of **Vathí** (ΒΑΘΗΣ), with a tiny fishing hamlet and excellent fish taverna, heading a deep, fjord-like bay. The ferries dock here in winter when the winds are wild and there is a bus connection with **Perigialós**. From here it's possible to visit the stalagmite caves of **Drákou** and **Negrí** on foot or by boat, but take a torch with you; Mussolini's nearby **Kastéllana** is also worth a trip.

---

*Astypálaia ℗ (0242–)*  **Where to Stay**

There are several reasonable hotels plus a number of rooms in private houses in Skála, or Perigialós, as well as rooms in Chóra near the wind-mills if you're lucky. The **Hotel Australia**, Perigialós, ℗ 61 275 (*B pension; inexp*) is basic and friendly with a restaurant beneath and a flower-filled breakfast terrace. **Hotel Vangelis**, ℗ 61 281 (*inexp*) overlooks the harbour. The adjacent **Hotel Karlos**, ℗ (*C; inexp*) is
also on the water's edge. Across the bay, the **Hotel Paradissos**, ℗ 61 224 (*D; inexp*) is also right on the harbour. The **Astynea**, ℗ 61 209 (*D; inexp*), has been renovated and is handy for ferries; **Vivamare Hotel and Apartments**, ℗ 61 292, ℗ 61 328 (*C; mod*) is smartly appointed, inland from the harbour. The **Aegeon**, ℗ 61 209 (*D; inexp*), is nothing special and minus en suite bathrooms. If you're under canvas, **Camping Astypalaia**, ℗ 61 338, is just out of town near Mármari. A minibus usually meets ferries; otherwise follow the signs.

Most of the island's eateries are clustered around the harbour; some are more touristy and pricier than others. Good tavernas include the local favourite, **I Monaxia**, and the taverna beneath the Hotel Vangelis, as well as **Vicki's** in a small street back from where the ferry docks with excellent home cooking. **Babis** is good for fish, and the taverna **To Akroyiali** is a tourist favourite on the beach at Perigialós. Up towards Kástro, try **Galini's**.

Livádia has several eateries which tend to change hands every so often, but try **Kalamia**. At Maltezána the excellent **Obelix** now has a rival called **Asterix** and at Vathí the fish taverna has the pick of the catch.

## Entertainment and Nightlife

There are several small cafes and an *ouzerie* in the harbour as well as a bouzouki club-cum-disco at the far end. But most nightlife centres on Chóra with the **Kastro Bar** built into the rock, where impromptu Greek dancing often breaks out and revellers have been known to greet the dawn. **La Luna** and **Laou Laou** are also happening places and **Kuiros Bar** passes for a disco.

# Chálki (ΧΑΛΚΗ)

With its neoclassical houses in pastel shades overlooking its gentle horseshoe harbour, Emborió, little Chálki looks like a miniature version of Sými, and is topped by a fairytale Crusader castle on a pointed peak like something out of Walt Disney. Arid, barren and rocky as it is, lack of water is a problem, although things are beginning to improve. Traditional island life still goes on; although there is the odd hydrofoil excursion from Rhodes at weekends, Chálki doesn't suffer from surfeits of day-trippers like Sými. There are no newspapers, about 300 inhabitants and just a few pick-up trucks and bikes which head up the grandly named Boulevard Tarpon Springs to the ruined Chorió above, the outlying farmland or the distant monastery of Ag. Ioánnis Pródromos. Chálki (also spelled Hálki) has nothing to do with chalk but derives its name from *chalkí*, the Greek word for copper, which used to be mined on the island.

Once a thriving sponge-fishing centre, with a 3000-plus population, Chálki is celebrated for its music and *mantinádes*, songs with impromptu verses, and for its quick-stepping *soústa*. Chálki was designated the 'Island of Peace and Friendship of Young People of All Nations' in 1983 under a joint UNESCO and Greek government scheme. The idea was to launch an international youth centre with annual conferences, and there was an allied municipal project, ADEK, backed by Rhodes to renovate the local houses and provide work. A *Xenía* hotel was built to serve the visiting groups and bureaucrats, but in the end the islanders thought the scheme was an excuse for their hospitality to be abused. Some visiting youths were using their subsidised meal vouchers to order the most expensive items on the menus. This led to a mass protest with placards and an end to peace and friendship between Chálki and UNESCO.

In 1987 a British package holiday company was invited to set up a small programme using the restored houses. Since then tourism has slowly grown and, with a knock-on effect, owners have returned to rebuild their ruined family homes and convert them into studios and apartments. But life is still very basic. The water supply has improved but mains water is still brackish and the island relies on the water boat for fresh supplies.

**By sea**: 3 times a week with Rhodes; once a week with Kárpathos, Kássos, Sitía (Crete), Ag. Nikólaos (Crete), Sými, Santoríni, Síkinos, Folégandros, Mílos, Sífnos, Piraeus; daily ferries *Chálki* and *Aphrodíti* from **Kámiros Skála**, Rhodes. On Wednesdays another **caique** runs but it's chartered exclusively by holiday companies. In summer hydrofoil connections with Rhodes and Tílos. **Port authority**, ✆ 57 220.

**5 August**, Ag. Sotíris; **15 August**, Panagía; **29 August**, Ag. Ioánnis Pródromos, John the Baptist; **14 September**, Ag. Stávros.

## Emborió and Around

The main claim to fame of **Emborió** is that its church of Ag. Nikólaos has the tallest campanile in the Dodecanese, and it also has a magnificent pebble mosaic or *hoklákia* courtyard. There's the usual Italianate customs house and police station, a row of ruined windmills and a small army barracks. Sleepy by day, with fishermen mending their nets, the harbour buzzes with the traditional stroll or *vólta* in the evening.

From Emborió a 15-minute walk along 'Boulevard Tarpon Springs', paid for by Chálki sponge divers who emigrated to Florida and just wide enough for a donkey train and single delivery van, takes you to sandy **Póndamos Beach**, a strand constantly being enlarged by the locals.

There are loungers and sunshades and Nick's Taverna just a few steps from the sea. The rocky coves a bit further on make for more secluded sunbathing and snorkelling. Determined sightseers should continue walking uphill another hour for **Chorió**, the ghost-town capital of Chálki. Here the Knights of St John built a castle on the earlier acropolis and recycled most of the ancient building stone. Chorió's church of the **Panagía** has a few Byzantine frescoes and is the centre for the big festival on 15 August. On a clear day there are incredible views down to Kárpathos and Crete from the castle.

A new road has been blasted through from Póndamos over the hill past the cemetery and barracks to the Chálki Hotel, and another now makes the once-gruelling cross-island trek to the **Monastery of Ag. Ioánnis Pródromos** less of a slog. It can take from 3 to 5hrs depending on your pace and time of day: best to go at dawn, or in the evening and stay overnight in one of the cells (a family there is in charge). Chálki is perfect for serious walkers: take the track off the

Póndamos road, right past the water tank on the hill and head for the pebbly cove of **Kánia** with its shady fig trees and little Garden of Eden. Unfortunately the locals have plonked a filling station at the end of the track and you can get strong whiffs of petrol at times.

Fishing is still the main way of life but now some of the fishermen are getting into the swing of tourism with trips round the island. The new high-speed launch *Yiánnis Express* with brothers Michaelis and Vassílis Pátros can whisk you to quiet swimming coves—Aréta, Kánia, Giáli and Trachiá are among the best. Other traditional caiques like the *Meltémi* also offer trips.

The most scenic excursion, however, is to the green isle of **Alimniá**, which has another Crusader castle and a deep harbour where Italian submarines hid during the Second World War. The islanders abandoned it and moved to Chálki after British Special Boat Services commandoes sent to scupper the submarines were captured by Nazis on the beach. You can still see the machine-gun strafing on the walls of some of the buildings as well as paintings of submarines done by troops in the ruined village houses. Although it has a better water supply than Chálki, the islanders pledged never to return and Alimniá is now home to grazing sheep, barbecuing holidaymakers and the occasional yacht, all in all a beautifully tranquil place in which to laze about, swim and picnic.

---

## *Chálki ☎ (0241–)* — *Where to Stay*

Most accommodation is now taken up by the aforementioned holiday companies. There's the small but welcoming **Captain's House**, ☎ 45 201 (*pension; mod*), a turn-of-the-century Chálki mansion with three lovely rooms with shared external bathrooms. It's run with nautical precision by Alex Sakellarídes, ex-Greek Royal Navy, and his English wife Christine, and there's even a crow's nest. Breakfast or drinks are  available on the cool terrace beneath the trees, often with classical music from Alex's collection. **Hotel Xalki**, ☎ 45 390, ✆ 45 208 (*awaiting classification; inexp*), the former scheme hotel and converted olive factory to the left of the harbour, offers a sun terrace, snack bar/restaurant, swimming off the rocks. **Pension Kleanthe**, ☎ 45 334 (*rooms inexp, studios mod*), is a traditional stone house newly restored near the school. **Pension Argyrenia**, ☎ 45 205 (*inexp*) has self-contained chalets set in shady gardens on the way to the beach. **Nick's Pondomos Beach Taverna and Rooms**, ☎ 45 295 (*inexp*), has self-contained rooms in the taverna garden overlooking the bay.

---

## *Chálki ☎ (0241–)* — *Eating Out*

**Pondomos Taverna** is the popular lunchtime haunt, a step from the sands with a tasty menu. In Emborió, Nick's brother **Yianni's** is excellent for spit-roasts and Greek oven dishes, as is **Ouzerie Maria** where Maria and her triplet daughters also do good *souvláki*. **Omonia** is the place for fresh fish, seafood and grills, but **O Houvardas**, once arguably one of the best tavernas in the Dodecanese, has never quite been the same under the new management. It's still a good eaterie, popular with yacht people, but the standard depends on who's in the kitchen. If you are self-catering there are three small general stores—Petros has everything—and a good bakery specializing in cheese and spinach pies and honey pancakes.

Nightlife on Chálki tends to be spontaneous, with outbreaks of traditional dancing in the bars like Nikola's **To Steki**. Some of the young people are learning the old instruments like the *lýra* and the **Hotel Chalki** has authentic Greek nights with local musicians; look out for their Chálki cassette. Otherwise enjoy a drink at café-bars like **Areti's**, the old favourite **Kostas**, or **Vokolia**, who also do delicious cakes. Easter and festivals are times for determined merrymaking, with live music and dancing, sometimes in traditional costume.

# Kálymnos (ΚΑΛΥΜΝΟΣ)

Arriving at Kálymnos by boat from Kos with the sun setting on one side and the moon rising on the other is a stunning experience. The blood-red sunset over the islet of Télendos from Myrtiés opposite is one of Greece's most famous, a rival to Santoríni in the Cyclades. Even if you aren't lucky enough to sail in, sighing with emotion at the proper twilight hour, you may want to breathe at least a sigh of relief when you get to the port and capital Pothiá—for unlike Kos, this is the Real Greece. Although the bustling waterfront has all the usual paraphernalia of tourism, with tavernas, cafés, souvenir shops and roaring motorbikes everywhere, venture one street back and you'll find yourself in the thick of a busy Greek town going about its daily life, winter or summer, whether you are there or not. Carpenters, tailors and bakers hammer, stitch and bake away and there's a marvellous selection of local shops with no concessions to tourism. Because of the many Greek visitors, the prices are not sky-high, and the food is good and wholesome. Just as it finds an attractive balance between tourism and carrying on its everyday business, Kálymnos also strikes a harmonious geographical equilibrium, with fertile emerald valleys wedged into its dry, rocky face, high peaks (the loftiest, Mount Profítis Ilías, is the driest spot in all the Dodecanese) sweeping down to almost Scottish lochs.

Economics dictated that many Kalymniots emigrate to Australia or America, but now they've begun to return: you're likely to hear plenty of accents from Down Under or the States, especially in hotels, bars and taxis—the new family businesses set up with their savings. On a more traditional note, even the most fleeting visitor can't help but notice that this island is preoccupied with sponges: Kálymnos has Greece's last active fleet of sponge-divers.

## History

In mythology Ouranos (Heaven) angrily threw Kalydnos, one of his sons by Gaia (Earth), into the sea, but he landed on some bits of earth that rose up to become the Kalydna islands. The name Kalydna is either derived from *kalos* (good), and *hydna* (truffle), or it means well-watered (from *kalos* and a derivative of *hydor*, water). Others say it coms from *Kalydneon* (ancient).

Homer mentions the Kalydnai participation in the Trojan War and it wasn't until 4th century BC that the largest island came to be known as Kálymnos or Kálymna. The first Kalymniots lived in a Neolithic settlement at Vothíni and worshipped Zeus in a cave shrine which still exists. After the destruction of Crete, Argos sent colonists to the island, who named their capital after their mother city. An ally of Persia, the Queen of Halicarnassus, conquered the island at the beginning of the 5th century BC, but after Persia's defeat Kálymnos joined the Athens maritime league at Delos.

Kálymnos next enters known history in the 11th century, when Seljik Turks launched a sudden attack on the island and killed almost everyone. The few survivors fled to fortified positions at Kastélli and the virtually impregnable Kástro, which by necessity became the capital of the island. The Vinioli of Genoa occupied Kálymnos, but later sold it to the Knights of St John, who strengthened the fortress of Kástro. In 1522 they abandoned it to succour Rhodes, leaving the Turks to quickly take their place. During the Italian occupation and the rise of Fascism the Kalymniots were oppressed and prominent citizens either jailed or exiled. Attempts to Italianize the population, bring the Orthodox church in line with the Fascist regime and close down the Greek schools resulted in the women of Kálymnos holding a protest march to the centre of town. There was a violent clash with the troops and a shepherd boy, Kozónis, who was helping the women, was shot dead. Other riots erupted during the occupation and in a show of defiance the islanders painted everything in sight the blue and white of Greece as a sign of solidarity with the motherland. With their menfolk away at sea for so long, the women of Kálymnos are fiercely independent. They have had a feminist movement from the earliest years and published poetry calling for emancipation.

# A Note on Sponges

When fresh from the sea, sponges are foul, smelly and black, and have to be stamped, squeezed and soaked until their skeletons (the part you use in the bathtub) are clean. Many sponges are then chemically bleached in a bath of vitriol, acid and permanganate, to achieve the familiar yellow colour—but if you're out to buy, avoid these, as they soon disintegrate. Instead go for the plain brown versions, strong and just as effective; look for the ones with the densest texture. You can see the whole process at the sponge factory in Pothiá near Plateía Eleftherías, while in Myrtiés diver Nikólas Makarounás sells his brown Mediterranean sponges—with a complimentary ouzo—outside the Blue Islands Travel office.

Diving for these primitive plant-like porifers is a difficult and dangerous art. In ancient times the divers strapped heavy stones to their chests to bear them down to the sea bed, where they speared the sponges with tridents, then, at a signal, were raised to the surface by a lifeline. As modern equipment permitted divers to plunge to new depths, cases of the 'bends' were frequent; old-timers on Kálymnos remember when, not so long ago, it was common to see sponge-divers crippled, paralysed, or made deaf. Kálymnos' traditional dance, *mechanikós*, mirrors the divers' often tragic life. These days divers wear oxygen tanks and attack the sponges with axes, going down to a depth of 90m. Politics limiting access to Mediterranean sponge beds, sponge blight and synthetic substitutes have undermined Kálymnos's traditional livelihood. In the last century, many divers emigrated to Florida to exploit sponge beds off Tarpon Springs.

In the past Kálymnos's sponge fleet left home for seven months of the year to work off the coast of North Africa. Today, only a few boats depart for a four-month tour, sticking mostly to Aegean and Cretan waters. On Kálymnos, the week before the fleet sets out (traditionally the week after Orthodox Easter, but it varies with the weather) is known as the Iprogrós or Sponge Week, devoted to giving the sponge-divers a rousing send-off, with plenty of food, free drinks, traditional costumes and dances—including the Sponge Dance, where the local schoolmaster mimes the part of the fishermen while his pupils play the sponges. The last night of Sponge Week is tenderly known as *O Ípnos tis Agápis*, the 'Sleep of Love'. It ends with the pealing of church bells, calling the divers to their boats for another dangerous four months at sea. They circle the harbour three times in farewell and wave their caps as their loved ones wave back from the shore.

## Getting There and Around

**By sea**: daily to Piraeus, Rhodes, Kos, Léros and Pátmos; 4 times a week with Sámos, 3 times a week with Lipsí and Astypálaia, twice a week with Níssyros, Tílos, Sými and Agathónissi, once a week with Lésbos, Límnos, Ikaría, Mýkonos, Santoríni, Tínos, Ándros, Rafína and Thessaloníki. The island's own **ferry**, the *Níssos Kálymnos*, plies around the Dodecanese and now takes in Kastellórizo and Astypália. There are new summer **hydrofoil** connections with Kos, Rhodes, Sými, Níssyros, Léros, Lipsí, Pátmos, Ikaría, Sámos. Daily **boats** to Psérimos, daily **caique** from Myrtiés to Xirókambos, on Léros; special boat to connect airport passengers with Mastichári on Kos; local caiques from Myrtiés to Télendos and Emboriós; excursions to Pátmos. **Port authority**, © 24 444.

**By road:** although there's a good **bus** service to the villages, it's just as easy to go by taxi as Kálymnos has an excellent system where you share with other passengers. Prices are posted on the rank. **Taxi** drivers also take guided tours round the island, ✆ 29 555 and 24 222.

### Tourist Information

**NTOG**, April–Oct, next to Olympic Hotel, ✆ (0243) 29 310.

**Tourist police**, see regular police on the waterfront, ✆ (0243) 22 100. At Myrtiés Deborah Faulkner of Premier Travel is especially helpful, ✆ 47 830, ✉ 48 035.

### Festivals

A **week after Easter**, the Iprogrós (Sponge Week). Other celebrations are held when the divers return, although each boat arrives at a different time and celebrations are not as general as at the Iprogrós. **27 July**, Ag. Panteleímon at Brostá; **15 August**, Panagía at Télendos, Kyrá Psilí and Galatianí at Arginónta; **14 September**, Ag. Stávros on Névgra islet.

# Pothiá

**Pothiá** (ΠΟΘΙΑ), one of the largest cities in the Dodecanese, encompasses the harbour and much of the island's largest valley. More spread out than the typical tightly knotted island town, Pothiá has many lovely old mansions along its back streets, walled orchards, and some fine views from the town's upper level. Local sculptors Michail Kókkinos and his daughter Irene have adorned the island with 43 bronze statues, including, in Pothiá, a *Poseidon* by the Olympic Hotel and the waterfront *Winged Victory*, with the history of sponge-diving in relief. The police occupy the former governor's house, the domed pink Italianate villa on the sea, one of Kálymnos' most fanciful confections. It is rivalled only by the silver domes of **Ag. Nikólaos**. On the far side of the harbour is the sponge-diving school. Proud and tough, Kalymniots are said to be the hard men of the Dodecanese. They fish with dynamite and at Easter Pothiá is like a war zone as rival gangs climb the mountains to let off home-made bombs to see who can make the most noise to greet the Resurrection.

To the right of the harbour the brightly painted houses tumble down to the waterfront. As well as patriotic blue and white they are traditionally colour-coded—green for sponge-divers, yellow for the wealthy, and pink for newly-weds. On the older ones, look for names and dates carved over the front door.

The **Archaeological Museum**, ✆ 23 113 (*open Tues–Sun, 10–2*) is housed in a lovely neo-classical mansion, former home of the Vouválhis family, wealthy sponge merchants. As well as interesting furniture and portraits it contains a typical miscellany of local antiquities and more recent items, including a barrel organ. There are plans to put more treasures on show in future.

Pothiá also has one of Greece's rarer institutions—an orphanage. Until recently many Orthodox priests came here to choose a dowryless bride before they were ordained. It also has **The Muses Reading Room**, originally a club to further Greek education and preserve national identity during the Turkish occupation. The Italians destroyed all its books and artworks and turned it into the Café Italia, which in turn was destroyed in the bombing. The club restarted in 1946, and in 1978 they got a new building to house their collection of local historical documents.

There is a small beach near the yacht club, and beyond that a sanitarium at **Thérma** with natural thermal baths, reputed to cure rheumatism, arthritis and digestive and kidney disorders. You need a doctor's note to partake. Around the headland, the beach at **Vlicháda** is one of the island's nicest spots, popular with the locals.

At night Pothiá's hilltop landmark is a huge illuminated cement cross looking down over the harbour from the 'sacred wood' and monastery of All Saints, **Ag. Pánton**. Here lie the remains of Ag. Sávvas, a monk who ran the secret school during the Turkish occupation, and was later canonized. Apparently he's the local answer to fertility drugs and women put wax effigies of babies under his reliquary and pray for motherhood.

From Pothiá caiques sail south of Kálymnosto **Néra** islet, with a monastery and a small taverna, or to **Képhalas Cave**, a half-hour trip via the **Monastery of Ag. Kateríni**. In 1993 angry taxi drivers barred the road to day-trip coaches as they thought they were taking away fares. Things should have cooled off by now. To reach the cave you have to walk two kilometres. You can avoid potential taxi brouhahas by going by sea and walking up the path from the **Bay of Képhalas**. Discovered in 1961, the cave has six chambers and was found to have been a sanctuary of Zeus. It is full of stalactites and stalagmites shaped like a multi-coloured curtain, and the huge stalagmite in the centre of the main chamber looks like Zeus enthroned.

## Up to Chorió

Inland, just behind Pothiá, is a suburb called **Mýli**, with three monumental derelict windmills looming over the road as its landmark. On a hill to the left stands the ruined **Castle of the Knights**, also known as the **Chryssochéria** ('Golden-handed') after the church of the Virgin built within its walls, over an ancient temple of the Dioscuri. Treasure was once supposedly discovered there, and the area has been thoroughly combed on the off-chance of more.

Mýli blends imperceptibly into the pretty white town of **Chorió**, the old capital of Kálymnos. It grew up around **Péra Kástro**, the striking though dilapidated citadel that rises over the village and served as a place of refuge during the perilous Middle Ages; on a gloomy day it looks more Transylvanian than Greek. The ruined village within the Kástro's walls was inhabited from the 11th to the 18th centuries. The only intact buildings are nine chapels kept freshly whitewashed by the faithful women of Chorió; the views from the top, over the coast, are well worth the trouble of climbing up. The **Shelter of the Nymphs** or **Cave of the Seven Virgins**, at the foot of Mount Flaská near Chorió's hospital, has never been thoroughly explored, but take a torch and you can see traces of ancient worship, holes in the rock where supplicants poured oblations to the nymphs. Legend has it that seven maidens took refuge there during a pirate raid and were never seen again, believed lost in the bottomless channel in the depths of the cave.

In Pigádia, just beyond Chorió, only the apse survives of the church of **Christ of Jerusalem**, built by the Byzantine Emperor Arkadios in gratitude for his shelter at Kálymnos during a terrible storm. It replaced a temple of Apollo, and recycled its stone as well. There are many rock-cut Mycenaean tombs nearby. A road branching to the west at Chorió leads to **Árgos**, named by the settlers from Mycenaean Argos. Although some ruins have been found, scholars doubt whether the ancient city stood at precisely the same spot as the present village Árgos has been earmarked as the site of the island's airport and construction work is underway.

North of Chorió the tree-lined road dips down to the island's beaches—which with all the goodwill in the world are nothing to write home about. Strung along the coast, Kálymnos' resort strip starts with **Kantoúni** and **Panórmos**, the latter running into **Eliés**, named after its olive groves, although these are fast becoming playgrounds for the big package-tour companies. Although as beaches go they're only just adequate—small fringes of grey shingly sand shaded with tamarisk trees—the deep blue coves offer excellent swimming. **Linária** is the next resort, with a small square with a few bars and tavernas and a path down to a small harbour and seaweedy bay. A little further along, beyond the giant rock on the coastline, the beaches at **Platís Giálos** and **Melitzáchas** are quieter and a bit more up-market.

The road plunges down to **Myrtiés** (MYPTIEΣ), with its stunning sunset over the islet of Télendos, and you're in the heart of the island's tourist strip. Myrtiés blends into **Massoúri** and the villages have become a surprisingly loud Golden Mile with neon-sign bars belting out conflicting music and local lads racing up and down on motorbikes. Some tavernas have gone the way of Kos with brash fast-food photo menus outsides; supermarkets, jewellery shops and 'English breakfasts' are in full expansion. Yet the far end of Massoúri towards **Arméos** is less frenetic: you can still hear the goatbells from the rocks above and see the local women doing their crochet as they mind their souvenir shops.

From Myrtiés jetty, a good half-hour's walk from Massoúri (buses every half-hour from Pothiá) frequent caiques make the short trip to the islet of **Télendos** (TEΛENΔOΣ), which broke off from Kálymnos in a 6th century AD earthquake. Facing the strait are the derelict monastery of **Ag. Vassílios** and a fort, both from the Middle Ages. Up a narrow lane from the harbour you'll find the pretty church of the **Panagía**. There are ruins of Roman houses and, high above the beaches, the Byzantine **Monastery of Ag. Konstantínos**. Several small pebble beaches have loungers: **Hokláka** (through the village and down steep steps in the cliff) is the most popular, while the shingly coves reached from the track beyond the waterside tavernas towards **Pothaía** are nudist haunts. Most of the islanders are fishermen and, apart from its daytime visitors, Télendos is a perfect island if you need to get away from it all: it has a handful of excellent seafood tavernas, rooms to rent, and a few new holiday villa developments.

North of Massoúri, **Kastélli** was the refuge of survivors of the terrible 11th-century Turkish massacre, and overlooks the sea in a wild region of rocky cave-mouths full of fangs. There are steps down to the church of the **Panagía** below. From here, see if you can trace the profile of the sleeping or **marble princess** in the left-hand side of its pointed peak of Télendos. She's looking out to her lover, the prince of Kastélli. The legend goes that the prince was supposed to send her a lighted candle to prove his love. But it blew out en route and she killed herself.

The coast road is spectacular and there are fish farms in the bay on the way to the fjord-like inlet at **Arginónta**. The hamlet lends its name to the entire northern peninsula, a perfect place for strenuous, isolated treks in the quiet hills. The small beach is pebbly and peaceful with a couple of eateries—the small Sea Breeze Taverna is perfect for lunch—and sunbeds and rooms to rent. The northernmost village on Kálymnos, **Emborió** (EMΠOPIOΣ) is a pretty fishing hamlet (bus twice a day from Pothiá, caiques from Myrtiés), within walking distance of some exceptional countryside and terraced hills. The **Kolonóstilo Cave** or (Cyclops Cave) is nearby, sheltering vast curtains of stalactites resembling columns whence it got its name; unfortunately treasure-hunters have damaged it with dynamite. The remains of a **Venetian** castle and a tower are close by. The tower is believed to have been a Neolithic temple; a sacrificial altar was found in the vicinity. Emborió has a small beach and several tavernas and is a popular pit stop for tour coaches.

## Vathí

The narrow volcanic valley of **Vathí**, (ΒΑΘΥΣ) ('the deep') is the beauty spot of Kálymnos: it has three charming, lush villages, Rína, Plátanos and Metóchi, superbly situated at the mouth of a magnificent fjord. Fragrant groves of mandarins and lemons provide the valley's income, and houses and white-walled roads fill in the gaps between the trees. Rína, named after St Irene, is where the boats dock. Although the original village was destroyed by pirates in the 15th century, it's a pretty harbour with a few tavernas, hotels and rooms and a working boatyard. The middle village, **Plátanos**, named for its enormous plane tree, has **Cyclopean walls**; Rina has a mysterious 'throne' carved in the rock. North of Vathí you can walk to the **Monastery of Kyrá Psilí**, the 'Tall Lady'. Near the mouth of the fjord is the **Cave of Daskaleío**, accessible only by sea. A trove of Neolithic-to-Bronze Age items was found in its inner stalactite chamber.

---

*Kálymnos ℗ (0243–)*                              ***Where to Stay and Eating Out***

### Pothiá

A few strides from the ferry will bring you to the **Olympic Hotel**, ℗ 28 801 (*C; mod*), comfy but nothing special. Away from the bustle the **Hotel Panorama**, ℗ 23 138 (*C; mod*) has lovely décor, and all rooms have balconies with magnificent views. **Pension Greek House**, ℗ 23 752 (*inexp*), near the sponge factory, is back-packer friendly with cosy wood-panelled rooms. **Pension Katerina**, ℗ 22 186 (*inexp*) is also a good bet with self-catering facilities; **Patmos Pension**, ℗ 22 750 (*inexp*) in a relatively quiet side street is similar. **Hotel Themelina**, ℗ 22 682 (*D; mod–inexp*), a lovely old 19th-century villa with shady gardens and swimming pool opposite the Archaeological Museum, has traditionally furnished rooms. It's probably the best in town but your only chance of a room is in the off season; it's block-booked from May to October. There are also private rooms to rent: get a list from the tourist office.

In Pothiá, most of the restaurants are on the far end of the quay, beyond the Italian villa of the tourist police. They tend to be cheaper back from the waterfront; follow the Greek families. **Uncle Petros** is perhaps the best known and **Omilos** near the yacht club is another popular haunt. Round by the churches, **Vouvali's Fish Restaurant** is decorated with nautical bric-à-brac and has seawater tanks from where you can choose your own lobster or fish—otherwise try their excellent fish casseroles and octopus *keftédes*, an island speciality. On summer nights, there's often Greek music and dancing. Locals always recommend the **Taverna Xefteries**, in a back street near the Metropolis church. Friendly and good value, it's been in the same family for over 85 years. Sit in the garden and enjoy the fresh fish and roast lamb, or try their versions of *dolmádes* and *stifádo*. Also in an alley near the church, **The Terrace** has good home-cooking and is packed with locals watching Greek soaps on TV. In the nearby village of Árgos, you'll find authentic Kalymniot food at the **Argos** taverna; try the *moori*, lamb cooked overnight in a ceramic pot.

## Kantoúni

The smart **Kantouni Beach Hotel,** ✆ 47 980/2, 📠 47 549 (*B; mod*) has a swimming pool and relaxing poolside bar. **Hotel Drossos,** ✆ 47 518 (*C; inexp*) is set back a bit from the beach. **Hotel Elies,** near Panórmos, ✆ 47 890, 📠 47 160 (*B; mod*) has a restaurant, two bars and a swimming pool. **Taverna Marinos** in Eliés specialises in roast stuffed lamb in the evenings and has an inventive and reasonably priced menu.

## Myrtiés

**Hotel Myrties,** ✆ 47 512 (*D; inexp*) and **Hotel Delfini,** ✆ 47 514 (*C; inexp*) are centrally placed and the **Hermes,** ✆ 47 693 (*B pension; inexp*) is also a good bet. If you're sick of Greek food, try **Nectar** with a wide international menu; **Babis Bar** in the square does good snacks and breakfast and is the perfect place to wait for buses, taxis and the boat to Télendos.

## Massoúri

**Studios Tatsis,** ✆ 47 887 (*C; mod*) are stylish with great views over Télendos. **Massouri Beach,** ✆ 47 555 (*C; mod*) is popular with package companies. **Niki's Pension,** ✆ 47 201 (*inexp*) between the two resorts also has great views but is set up steps over rough terrain. The Arméos area is more peaceful with the **Hotel Plaza,** ✆ 47 134 (*C; mod–inexp*) perched high over the bay with a swimming pool and fine views. **Hotel Pegasus,** ✆ 47 873 (*C; mod*) are cliff-top apartments sharing the swimming pool with the nearby **Hotel Armeos,** ✆ 47 252/3 (*B; mod*). Family-run **Galini Studios** are also comfortable with nice gardens and stunning views. Massoúri has many eating places from fast-food joints to good tavernas which look like tacky takeaways. Don't be put off by the red plastic chairs and garish photos at **To Iliovasilima** ('The Sunset'); it's an excellent place owned by the local butcher, with friendly service, and the rabbit *stifádo* is delicious. **Mathaios** does all the Greek favourites well, as does family-run **Barba Iannis.** But although it looks pretty and authentic avoid **Kokkinidis** like the plague: virtually inedible food, overpriced and less than friendly service. Locals recommend **Ouzerie Psaras** and **Restaurant O Sopiarkos** on the way to Kastélli.

## Télendos Island

**Pension Rita,** ✆ 47 914 (*inexp*) has rooms located over the friendly cafeteria that bakes cakes. **Pension Uncle George's,** ✆ 47 502 (*inexp*) is over the excellent restaurant. Further along, the **Café Festaria,** ✆ 47 401 (*inexp*) has decent doubles with en suite bathrooms. **Dimitrios Harinos** ✆ 47 916 (*inexp*) also has village rooms set back in a pretty garden. There's also the new **Hotel Porto Potha** (*C; mod*) in an elevated position above the bay with breakfast room, restaurant and stunning views. All the tavernas are good value but Uncle George's takes some beating and **Ta Dalinas** at the far end of the waterfront has Greek music on Wednesdays and Saturdays.

## Emborió

**Harry's Pension/Taverna Paradise,** ✆ 47 483 (*C; inexp*) has lovely secluded gardens, and **Pension Themis,** ✆ 47 277 (*C; inexp*) is also good.

#### Vathí

**Hotel Galini**, ✆ 31 241 (*C; inexp*) has immaculate rooms and home-baked bread, served on a restful terrace overlooking the fjord-like harbour; inexpensive rooms and a good spot for lunch, too. **Pension Manolis**, ✆ 31 300 (*inexp*), higher up to the right, has a communal kitchen and nice garden. Manólis is an official guide and mine of information. The **Harbour Taverna** is excellent for seafood, lunch or dinner.

---

### Entertainment and Nightlife

There is a traditional bouzouki club in **Pothiá** and organised Greek nights are also held at **Kastélli**. Wait for the package tourists to go and the locals will really let rip. There are numerous bars in the resorts belting out music from the **Domus Bar** to the **Rock and Blues Pub** at Kantoúni to **Babis Bar** at Myrtiés for a cocktail or game of backgammon. Massoúri is for night owls and occasionally lager louts with the **Smile Pub, Narcissus Disco, NoName Pub, Paradise Bar, Ambience** and **Look** disco near Kastélli. **Lefteris Bar** is less frenetic and popular with locals.

# Kárpathos (ΚΑΡΠΑΘΟΣ)

Nearly halfway between Crete and Rhodes, Kárpathos has for decades been an island-hopper's best-kept secret: hard to reach, but spectacularly beautiful and well worth the long hours of travelling. For one thing, Kárpathos is two islands for the price of one: long and thin, austere and ruggedly mountainous in the north, and fertile, softer beach-fringed and 'European' in the south, the two linked by a giant's vertebra of cliffs which culminates in two wild mountains over 1000m in height. These two distinct geographical personalities extend to the population; it has even been suggested that the northerners and southerners originally belonged to different races and for long generations had little if any contact with one another. A 'road' dramatically connecting the two halves was finished in 1979 and is best suited to four-wheel drives, though taxis do ply it.

The long isolation of the north has made it a goldmine for students of customs lost a century ago in the rest of Greece. In Ólympos, the chief village, women still bake their bread in outdoor ovens; the men, even the young ones, play the traditional three-stringed *lýra*, the goatskin bagpipe *tsamboúna*, and the *láouto.* Most striking of all, the women wear their traditional costumes every day—costumes considered the most beautiful in Greece, and the chosen dress of Queen Frederika at the ceremony of 1948 that formally joined the Dodecanese to Greece. So far Ólympos has not lost its unique charm, even though Kárpathos now boasts a large international airport, bringing in more tourists every year; there are direct charter flights from the UK. However, Kárpathos is by no means overrun, and the north especially has many places offering refuge from the crowds.

### History

One ancient name of Kárpathos was Porfiris, or 'Red', after a red dye once manufactured on the island and used for the clothes of kings; another was Tetrapolis, describing its four ancient cities of Vrykous, Possidion, Arkessia and Nissyros. In Homer the island is called Kárpathos, some believe from *Arpaktos*, or 'robbery', from the earliest days of piracy, when Vróntis Bay hid pirate ships that darted out to plunder passing vessels. The Venetians slurred it into 'Scarpanto', a name you may occasionally see on maps.

Off the coasts, the prized *scarus* (or parrot fish, which, as Aristotle noted, ruminates its food) was so abundant that the Roman Emperors hired special fleets to bring them back for the imperial table. Any signs of prosperity, however, had long ended by the time the pirates made the island their headquarters and one of its towns, Arkessia, their chief slave market. Things were so rough that even the Turks didn't really want Kárpathos, and sent only a *cadi*, or judge, to the island a few times a year; he never stayed longer than a few days, and depended entirely on the Greeks to protect him. To this day the bays at Vróntis and Arkássa are said to hold a fortune in sunken pirate treasure.

For all that, Kárpathos has a strong tradition of delicately lyrical poetry of its very own, and occasionally, as in Crete, old timers compete in impromptu couplet-singing contests. One of the prettiest old songs was collected in the 19th century:

> *A little bird was singing high up on the rough hillside,*
> *And a king's daughter listened from her window,*
> *'Ah, bird, that I had thy beauty, and would I had thy song,*
> *And would I had such golden plumes for hair upon my head!'*
> *'Why dost thou crave my beauty? why dost thou crave my song?*
> *Why dost thou crave my golden plumes for hair upon thy head?*
> *For thou hast cakes to feed on, as many as thou wilt,*
> *I eat my scanty portion from herbage in the fields;*
> *Thou sleepest on a lofty couch, with sheets of thread of gold,*
> *But I lie out in solitude among the dews and snows;*
> *And when thou drinkest water thou hast a gleaming cup,*
> *But I must drink my water from the spring thou bathest in;*
> *Thou waitest for the priest to come thy way to bless thee,*
> *But I await the huntsman, who comes to shoot me down.'*

### Getting There and Around

**By air**: daily with Rhodes, several times a week with Kássos and Sitía (Crete); also charters from the UK. **Airport information**, ✆ 22 305.

**By sea**: 3 times a week with Piraeus, 4 times a week with Rhodes, 3 times a week with Santoríni, twice a week with Kássos, Sitía (Crete), Ag. Nikólaos (Crete) and Mílos, once a week with Páros, Síkinos, Folégandros and Sífnos. Some **ships** call at both Diafáni and Pigádia (Kárpathos). Small **boats** daily in the summer connect the two ports, and at weekends there's a **caique** from Pigádia to Kássos. For information, ring the **port authority**, ✆ 22 227.

**By road**: Several **buses** a day run from Pigádia to Ammopí, and Pilés by way of Apéri, Voláda and Othos and one or two go to Finíki and Arkássa. If you hire a **motorbike** or **car**, beware that the only petrol stations are in Pigádia.

### Tourist Police

See regular police on the waterfront, Pigádia, ✆ (0245) 22 218.

### Festivals

**25 March**, Evangelismós at Pigádia; **1 July**, Ag. Marínas near Menetés; **15 August**, at Apéri and Menetés; **22–23 August**, Kyrá

Panagía and Myrtónas; **27–29 August**, Ag. Ioánnis at Vourgounda; **6 September**, Larniotisa at Pigádia; **8 September**, Panagías at Messóchorio.

## Kárpathos Town (Pigádia)

The island capital and southern port, Kárpathos, or **Pigádia** (ΠΥΓΑΔΙΑ), is attractively sheltered in that old pirate cove, mountain-ringed Vróntis Bay; Kárpathos was the ancient city of Possidion, dedicated to the sea god. Abandoned in the Byzantine era, all that remains are a clutch of Mycenaean tombs and a few stones of the old acropolis on the rocky outcrop to the east. The modern town is just that—modern, with many new buildings, and it's no accident that the local National Bank branch has such an air of prosperity: Kárpathos has the distinction of receiving more money from its emigrants abroad (mostly in Baltimore, Maryland) than any other island in Greece. New hotels and apartments are mushrooming up in Pigádia and along the sands outside town, and the package holiday industry is developing apace. The waterfront is busy and noisy at night with loud music bars and the ubiquitous motorbike.

The most distinctive architecture in town is by the park and playground: an Italian-built administration building that doubles as a small **museum** containing an early Christian baptismal font, coins, ceramics and inscriptions. From here it is a short walk to the 3km stretch of fairly good beach that rims **Vróntis Bay**, lined with trees, a few new hotels, and dotted with pleasant tavernas specializing in grilled fish. Within an enclosure on the sands are the ruins of a 5th-century basilica, **Ag. Fotiní**; several columns have been re-erected. Across the bay stands the chapel of **Ag. Nikólaos**, the saint who replaced Poseidon as the protector of sailors; a once sacred cave nearby called Poseidona has sweet water. On the south side of Vróntis Bay, another ancient site, **Ag. Kiriakí** (the track is signposted from the road) was a 7th century BC Geometric-era sanctuary dedicated to Demeter; a few years back one of the tombs hewn in the rock yielded a golden statuette.

## Villages in Southern Kárpathos

South of Pigádia, the land is flat and desolate and vegetation is sparse, and the few trees are bent over from the wind. The road to the airport passes **Ammopí**, a string of sandy beaches and small resort, popular with families. Colourful **Menetés** (ΜΕΝΕΤΕΣ), set in gardens on the flanks of Mount Profítis Ilías above Ammopí, has a small ethnographic museum and a church in a dramatic setting. The airport is built further south, on the desolate site of the ancient city of Thaetho, although little now remains.

Towards the west coast, **Arkássa** (ΑΡΚΑΣΑ) is prettily immersed in orchards; it has seen the most ambitious tourist development—too ambitious in some cases. A track leads up to the ruins of its predecessor, ancient **Arkessia**, where a Mycenaean acropolis with Cyclopean walls stands on a rocky headland known as Paleokástro. The surrounding cliffs are riddled with caves that have offered shelter to shepherds for centuries. Here you'll find the ruins of an early Byzantine church, **Ag. Sofía**, with brightly coloured geometric mosaics just under the fine layer of weeds and dirt; the best sections of these have been moved to the museum at Rhodes. Another ruined basilica, around the chapel **Ag. Anastásia**, dates from the 5th century. The coast below is jagged and wild, but there is a small beach wedged between the cliffs. Further north, **Finíki** is a bijou little fishing harbour with a good, inexpensive restaurant and sandy beach nearby; the sponge divers of Kálymnos call here, and caiques depart for Kássos, if the sea isn't too rough—as is often the case.

The beautiful road north of Pigádia rises first to opulent **Apéri** (ΑΠΕΡΙ), with exquisitely tended gardens and houses. The capital of Kárpathos up to 1896, it is reputed to be the richest village in Greece per capita; nearly everyone here has lived in New Jersey, including the family that gave the world the late Telly 'Kojak' Savalas. One *kafeneíon* still proudly displays a picture of Roosevelt; another, the Eleftheria Café, run by a PASOK leprechaun, is full of lewd curios and rubber items from the 1960s. In the new cathedral built over the Byzantine cemetery, you can pay your respects to Kárpathos' miracle-working icon. A steep zigzag track leads down to charming **Achata**, a quiet pebbly beach. An unpaved road continues north of Apéri along the increasingly majestic east coast, with steep by-roads winding down to the beaches at **Kyrá Panagía**, a lovely wide beach, varying from fine white sand to large pebbles (with rooms and tavernas) and **Apélla**, the most beautiful, with fine sand, turquoise water and dramatic scenery, set in boulders and rocks furiously rift, ravaged and rolled in the War of the Titans. Caiques from Pigádia make excursions to the beaches, or alternatively you can reach Kyrá Panagía by a 45-minute walk down through the lush greenery and trees from the mountain village of **Myrtónas**. Myrtónas is the place to be on 22 August, when it hosts the best *panegýri* on the Karpathiot calendar with music and folk-dancing that goes on well into the following day, and free food to boot. The east coast road ends at **Spóa**, at the crossroads of the somewhat perilous road to Ólympos; it's best to do it by taxi-jeep, a long (and rather expensive) proposition. A massive forest fire in 1983 has left large patches between Spóa and Diafáni denuded and melancholy. A track from Spóa descends to the pretty beach of **Ag. Nikólaos**.

Another unpaved, narrow Wild West road from Spóa circles

Kárpathos

Kárpathos' tallest mountain, **Kalílimni** (1188m), the highest point in the Dodecanese. Continuing anticlockwise from Spóa, the road descends on a corniche to **Messochóri**, set in an amphitheatre facing the sea, with the pretty 17th-century church of Ag. Ioánnis, with a carved iconostasis and wall paintings. The road then passes several tempting strands far, far below en route to **Lefkós** (ΛΕΥΚΟΣ). Tucked in the rocks, Lefkós has white sandy beaches, a wealth of pine trees and scattering of antiquities, including a large stone that strikingly resembles a Celtic menhir. Lefkós is now being developed, but so far nothing too drastic; there are a few small hotels and rooms to rent and villas owned by the Karpathiots, who consider Lefkós the most beautiful spot on their island. A short walk away are the ruins of a small medieval fort; there was another on the offshore islet of **Sokástro.**

The road continues down to the pretty village of ΠΥΛΕΣ, whose name in Roman letters unfortunately reads **Pilés**, and then to **Óthos**, another lovely spot. At 450m, Óthos is the highest village of Kárpathos, and one of the oldest, its houses decorated with carved wooden balconies. Although you may need a pullover, even in summer, it produces a fine local sweet red wine, *othitikó krasí*, and, they say, the island's prettiest girls. A traditional house here has been opened as a small ethnographic museum. Neighbouring **Voláda** is a delightful white-washed village with pretty lanes and well-kept houses, and a ruined castle built by the Cornaros of Venice, who owned the island until 1538. From here the paved road descends to back to Apéri and Pigádia.

## Ólympos and Northern Kárpathos

The easiest and least expensive way to reach Ólympos (ΟΛΥΜΠΟΣ) from Kárpathos is by caique to **Diafáni**, the village's port, from where a minibus makes the connection to Ólympos. The harbour here is being enlarged to enable big ferries to dock, so there's currently a lot of concrete about and a plan to build a big hotel. Diafáni has also been discovered by the Italians since the demise of Yugoslavia and Dubrovnik as holiday destinations, so prices have risen; in August it can be more like the back streets of Naples than Greece. There's a beach with flat rocks nearby, and several others within walking distance.

**Ólympos**, one of the most striking villages on the Greek islands, is draped over a stark mountain ridge, with a long line of ruined windmills running like teeth. To the west are magnificent views of mountains plunging headlong into the sea. Decorative painted balconies, many incorporating two-headed Byzantine eagles (one head Rome, one Constantinople), adorn the houses which in many places are literally stacked one on another and opened with wooden locks and keys that Homer himself might have recognized. The village church has smoke-darkened frescoes, perhaps dating back to the 18th-century.

The origins of Ólympos are shrouded in mystery. Some evidence suggests that the original inhabitants of northern Kárpathos came from Phrygia in Asia Minor; certainly the village was isolated for so long that linguists were amazed to find people here using ancient Dorian expressions long forgotten elsewhere in the country. Some matrilinear customs have survived, a family's property going to the eldest daughter, the *kanakára*; if you're lucky enough to be in Ólympos during a *panegýri* or wedding, you can recognize a *kanakára* by the gold coins she wears on chains—coins that her forefathers will have earned while working abroad. The women wear their flowing costumes every day: black scarves printed with flowers, baggy white trousers, a dark skirt and apron, a loose embroidered chemise, and fine, handmade goatskin boots (it is said that snakes hate the smell of goat) which last for years.

Ólympos is now firmly on the tourist coach trail, with regular busloads. The best time to visit Ólympos is during the weekends, when the women bake bread and vegetable pies in their outdoor ovens, the miller grinds the wheat in the last working windmill, out of 40 that turned a generation ago, and when the two *kafeneíons* are filled with Kárpathos' music, uncannily similar to Irish music in one of its wilder moods. But then again, you're never quite as far away as you think; in the *kafeneíon* across from the church the owner displays a certificate from the Governor of Alabama, thanking him for his service in the state militia. Otherwise, there is little to do but stroll the streets and absorb what you can of a vanishing way of life.

From Ólympos you can drive most of the way to **Avlóna**, a village inhabited only during the harvest season by farmers from Ólympos, who work the surrounding valley; some of the tools they use are more commonly seen in museums. From Avlóna it is a rough walk down to **Vourkóunda** (Vrykous), the ancient Phrygian city, remembered today by a stair, a break-water, rock-cut burial chambers and walls. In a cavern in Vourkóunda the chapel of **Ag. Ioánnis** hosts the largest *panegýri* in north Kárpathos, a two-day event where everyone sleeps out, roasts meat over an open fire and dances to the haunting music.

On Sundays boats from Diafáni sail to the islet of **Sariá**, which dots the 'i' of long, narrow Kárpathos. Here was the ancient kingdom of Níssyros, colonized by the island of Níssyros, to exploit the iron and silver mines at Assimovorni. Very little remains; a chapel now stands on the site of the proto-Christian basilica. More interesting to see are Ta Palátia (the palaces), actually a post-Byzantine pirate base, the houses built in the dolmus style, with barrel-vaulted roofs. It is a good walk up from the landing place, so wear sturdy shoes.

---

*Kárpathos ✆ (0245–)* **Where to Stay and Eating Out**

## Pigádia

**Possirama Bay**, ✆ 22 511, ✆ 22 929 (*A; exp*) is 400m from the town centre, on the sandy beach of Affoti, offering hotel apartments for 2–4 people, with fully equipped kitchen facilities, and large balconies overlooking the sea. *Open April–Oct.* In the same area **Miramare Hotel**, ✆ 22 345 (*B; exp*) is another new operation, with swimming pool, sea views and good breakfast included. **Pension Romantica**,  ✆ 22 460/1 (*B; exp–mod*) is the most charming place to stay in the capital, with 32 studios, half-hidden in a grove of citrus trees, and a short walk from the beach; it serves a delicious breakfast. **Hotel Apollo** (*B; exp*) is family-owned and comfortable; **Artemis Pension**, ✆ 22 724, has self-catering facilities. New, moderate-sized **Oasis**, ✆ 22 915 (*C; mod*), is flowery and welcoming. **Kárpathos Hotel** ✆ 22 347 (*C; inexp*) is good value; most of its 16 rooms come with private shower. There are quite a few small pensions and rooms for rent. Good value are **Harry's Rooms**, ✆ 22 188 (*inexp*); **Hotel Annessis**, the oldest in Pigádia, ✆ 22 100 (*D; inexp*); and **Hotel Avra**, ✆ 22 388 (*E; inexp*), the last two open all year. Kárpathos was once a cheap place to eat out, but the recent influx of Italian and German tourists has pushed the prices up. **Kafeneion Halikas** is still authentic and **Mike's Taverna** is good value. The **Kali Kardia** on the beach is excellent.

### Ammopí

**Albatros**, ✆ 22 828, Athens ✆ (01) 805 3871 (*B; exp*), has 265 bungalows near the beach. *Open April–Oct.* **Ammopi Beach**, ✆ 22 723 (*inexp*) has rooms—help yourself to figs. Or try **Ammopi's**, in nearby Menetés, ✆ 22 184 (*C; mod*). **Poseidon**, south of Ammopí by Makrí Gialós, ✆ 22 020 (*C; mod*) is a good hotel near the chief windsurfing beach. For lunch try the **Golden Beach Taverna**.

### Finíki

**Fay's Paradise**, ✆ 61 308 (*inexp*) has lovely rooms near the harbour. **Poseidon Apartments**, 100m from the sandy beach, ✆ 31 190 or 61 466, ✇ (0242) 26 867 (*mod*), new and a bit stark, but good and quiet; flats sleep up to 4.

### Diafáni

The **Golden Beach Hotel**, ✆ 51 215, opposite the quay, is clean and comfortable; its restaurant is the favourite in the port. Other places include **Diafani Palace**, ✆ 51 250 (also serving good fish), and **Mayflower Hotel**, ✆ 51 228. There is an unofficial campsite at Vanánda Beach.

### Ólympos

The **Pension Olympos**, ✆ 51 252 (*inexp*) is highly recommended with great views; there's also the **Poseidon Pension**, ✆ 51 264.

## Kássos (ΚΑΣΣΟΣ)

The southernmost Dodecanese island and one of the most remote of all islands, Kássos is a barren rock with steep coasts and sea grottoes, with an odd beach or two wedged in between. Practically untouched by tourism, it can be the ideal place if you've been seeking the simple, friendly atmosphere of pre-mass-tourism Greece. The port, Fri, is small, and if the sea is rough, simply landing can be a big headache, and you may have to transfer to a tender or caique.

### History

Homer mentions Kássos in the *Iliad*, for the ships it sent to Troy to aid the Achaeans. The ancient city stood at the site of the present village of Póli, and at Hellenokamára cave there are Mycenaean walls. During the Turkish occupation, Kássos retained a good deal of its autonomy, especially with regard to its fleet, which it quickly put at the disposal of the Greek cause when the War of Independence was declared, in 1821. For the first three years of the war the Greeks generally came out ahead in the struggle, but the Sultan, angered by his setbacks, prepared a powerful counter-attack through his ally, Ibrahim Pasha, son of Ali Pasha, the Ottoman Empire's governor of Egypt. In June 1824 Ibrahim left Egypt with a massive fleet to crush the Greek rebellion. His first stop was Kássos, which he decimated, slaying all the men and taking the women and children as slaves. The few who managed to escape went either to Sýros or the islet of Gramboúsa off the northwestern coast of Crete, where they turned to piracy for survival, defiantly flying the Greek flag in Turkish waters. But Capodístria and his allies put a stop to their activities, and their refuge, Gramboúsa, was returned to Turkish rule. In spite of the massacre, thousands of Kassiots later emigrated to Egypt to work on the Suez Canal.

**By air:** daily with Rhodes, 2–3 times a week with Sitía and Kárpathos.

**By sea:** twice a week with Piraeus, Crete, Mílos, Rhodes and Kárpathos, once a week with Chálki, Sými, Santoríni, Síkinos, Folégandros and Sífnos; weekend **caique** from Finíki, Kárpathos. **Port authority,** © 41 288.

**23 April**, Ag. Geórgios; **7 June**, at Fri; **late July**, Ag. Spyrídon; **14 August**, at Ag. Marína.

## Around Kássos

There are five villages on Kássos and charming small **Fri** (ΦΡΥ) is their capital, where the main occupation, fishing, is much in evidence. Every year on 7 June a ceremony is held there in memory of the massacre of 1824, and many people from Kárpathos also attend, coming on the special boats.

There are hardly any trees on Kássos because, it is claimed, Ibrahim Pasha burnt them all down, but many lighthouses stick out above the rocky terrain. A road and the island's one bus link Fri with Kássos' four other dinky villages, a 6km circuit. There's **Emborió**, another fishing hamlet, and above it **Panagía**, where proud ship captain's houses erode a bit more every year. **Póli** is built on the island's ancient acropolis, and you can still see a few surviving walls at Kástro and a Byzantine church with inscriptions. At **Ag. Marína**, near the air strip and Kássos' most accessible if mediocre beach at **Ammoúa**, there is a lovely stalactite cave called **Hellenokamára**, where signs of worship have been found from Mycenaean to Hellenistic times. From Ag. Marína or **Arvanitochóri** a path leads across the island, through citrus groves and olive groves down to sandy **Chelathrós bay**, the best beach on the island (take the left fork in the path; the walk takes a couple of hours). Another nice beach is on **Armathía**, the only inhabited islet off Kássos; there are frequent excursions from the port.

*Kássos* © *(0245–)* **Where to Stay**

In Fri the **Hotel Anagennissis**, © 41 323 (*C; mod–inexp*) is comfortable and run by an engaging former American. You'll pay more for the rooms facing the sea with bath, less for those in the back. *Open April–Dec.* There's also **Anessis**, © 41 201 (*C; mod–inexp*), where the doubles tend to be a little less. *Open all year.* **Manouses Apartments**, © 41 047 (*mod*) have rooms. Arvanitochóri also has a handful of rooms.

*Kássos* © *(0245–)* **Eating Out**

There are a handful of tavernas in Fri; **Restaurant Kassos** is run by a women's cooperative and **Taverna Emborio** serve good, cheap island dishes. There are also a couple of tavernas in Ag. Marína and Emborió.

# Kastellórizo/Mégisti (ΜΕΓΙΣΤΗ)

The easternmost point of Greece, oddball Kastellórizo is six hours by ship from Rhodes and within spitting distance of Turkey. It is the smallest inhabited island of the Dodecanese, 3 by 6km, yet the mother hen of its own small clutch of islets;·hence its official name, Mégisti, 'the largest'. They say the Turks know it as Meis Ada, 'eye-land', for one nautical mile away is their town of Kaş ('eyebrow'), but the most commonly heard name is Kastellórizo, in memory of the days when the Neapolitans called it the 'Red Castle'. Dry, depopulated, more than half ruined by numerous vicissitudes, its streets were once patrolled by turkeys and its 170 to 200 permanent inhabitants are noticeably affected by the isolation. But the new airport has brought the island in closer contact with the rest of Greece, and its success as a film set—for the award-winning Italian film *Mediterraneo*—has given the people a new lease of life. The film has brought swarms of Italians to Kastellórizo and these days the *lingua tourista* is Italian, with local Greeks yelling '*Stanza? Stanza?*' ('Rooms?') as tourists arrive. However, it remains a quirky backwater surrounded by a crystal sea brimming with marine life—including oysters, a rarity on Greek islands. And while there aren't any sandy strands, the local people will never fail to tell you that there are plenty of rocks on which to catch some rays.

The fishing around Kastellórizo is excellent and serves as the islanders' main occupation. Almost everyone, however, is ready to leave, and the only reason they stay is to keep the island Greek. There is a fear that if the population dwindles the island will revert to Turkish rule. Whatever the case, the Greek government pays people to stay there, has built a desalination plant, and has bent over backwards to bring television, radio and an airport to the island.

## History

According to tradition, Kastellórizo's first settler was King Meges of Echinada who gave his name to the island. Neolithic finds suggest an early arrival for Echinada, and Mycenaean graves coincide with the mention in Homer of the island's ships at Troy. Subsequently, the Dorians built two forts on the island, the Kástro by the present town and one on the mountain, called Palaeokástro—the ancient acropolis, where Apollo and the Dioscuri were the chief deities. Dionysos was another favourite: recently 42 rock *patitíria* or grape-trampling presses were discovered, linked to conduits that fed the juice into underground reservoirs. The little island had a great fleet of ships based in its sheltered harbour and traded with Lycia on the mainland, transporting its timber to ports in Africa and the Middle East. From 350 to 300 BC Kastellórizo was ruled by Rhodes, and in Roman times the pirates of Cassius used it as their hideout. The island was converted to Christianity from the time of St Paul, who preached along the south coast of Asia Minor at Myra.

The Byzantines repaired Kastellórizo's fortifications, and this work was continued by the Knights of St John after the fall of Jerusalem. They named the island after the red rock of the castle, which they used to imprison knights who misbehaved on Rhodes. The Sultan of Egypt captured Kastellórizo in 1440, but ten years later the King of Naples, Alfonso I of Aragon, took it back. Although Kastellórizo belonged to the Ottoman Empire by 1512, the Venetians later occupied it twice in their endless struggles against the Turks, in 1570 and in 1659. Despite all the see-sawing to and fro, Kastellórizo was doing all right for itself; at the beginning of the 19th century it had a population of 15,000 who lived either from the sea or their extensive holdings along the coast of Asia Minor.

Things began to go seriously wrong with the outbreak of the Greek War of Independence. The islanders were the first in the Dodecanese to join the cause, and, taking matters into their own hands, seized the island's two fortresses from the Turks. The Great Powers forced them to give them back to the Turks in 1833. In 1913 Kastellórizo revolted again only to be put down this time by the French. During the First World War the island was bombarded from the Turkish coast. In 1927 an earthquake caused extensive damage but the Italian Fascists, then in charge, refused to do any repairs, as Kastellórizo had failed to cooperate with their programme of de-Hellenisation. There was another revolt in 1933, but it was crushed by soldiers from Rhodes. In spite of its deep-water port serving as a refuelling station for long distance sea planes from France and Italy, Kastellórizo was in sharp decline—in 1941 only 1500 inhabitants remained.

This, however, does not end the tale of Kastellórizo's misfortunes. During the Second World War, the isolated Italian garrison was captured by the Germans (subject of the film *Mediterraneo*). When the Allies shipped the entire population for their safety to refugee camps in the Gaza Strip, the islanders were not allowed to take many of their belongings, and the occupying Allied troops pillaged the empty houses. To hide their looting, the British troops ignited the fuel dump as they pulled out, leading to a conflagration that destroyed more than 1500 homes and nearly all the islanders' boats. As if this was not enough, the ship carrying the refugees home after the war sank, drowning many. Those who survived to return to Kastellórizo discovered that, although they had finally achieved Greek citizenship, they had lost everything else, and there was nothing to do but emigrate; an estimated 12,000 to 15,000 'Kazzies' now live in Australia. The immediately postwar population was reduced to five families, who owed their survival to the Turks in Kaş, who sent over food packages.

This rare Greek-Turkish friendship and cooperation has continued to these days. In 1992, all the Kastellorizans were invited over to spend Christmas in Kaş hotels, were taken on excursions, and given a two-day feast and party. It was Kaş' way of thanking Kastellórizo for its role in the underground railroad that brought Kurds over to Kaş, and thence to Kastellórizo and a large refugee camp near Athens. Smuggling is another joint enterprise, and although tour operators on the Turkish side bring groups over for Greek Nights, their counterparts on Kastellórizo are not allowed to sail to Turkey, at least officially; local custom agents turn a blind eye if you get a fisherman to make the 15-minute trip. Recent Greek nationalist paranoia in Athens has tried to undermine the special Kastellórizo-Kaş relationship; locally the meddling of distant politicians is deeply resented.

## Getting There

**By air**: 3 times a week from Rhodes (airport, ✆ 49 250).

**By sea**: twice a week from Rhodes (**port authority**, ✆ 49 270).

## Tourist Police

See regular police in the harbour by the post office, ✆ 49 333.

## Festivals

**23 April**, Ag. Geórgios; **21 May**, Ag. Konstantínos; **20 July**, Profítis Ilías.

There is only one town on the island, also called **Kastellórizo**, full of ruined houses and mansions, some burnt, others crumbling from earthquakes or wartime bombing. One can see how wealthy some of the inhabitants once were from the remaining interiors, with elegant coffered ceilings and lovely carved balustrades. Some are being restored, others are inhabited by cats and chickens. Small tavernas line the waterfront, in high season packed with Italians and yachties. A hotel occupies one lip of the harbour mouth, while on the other sits the **fort** (*kástro*), last repaired by the eighth Grand Master of the Knights of St John, Juan Fernando Heredia, whose red coat-of-arms is another possible explanation for the name of the island. The ladder to the top leads to a fine view of the sea and Turkish coast; every day an islander, and a lame one at that, climbs up to raise the Greek and EU flags here at the easternmost extremity of both. A Doric inscription discovered at the fort suggests the existence of an ancient castle on the same site. A tomb castle nearby yielded a golden crown, and in the castle keep the small **museum** (*open Tues–Sun, 7. 30–2. 30pm*) exhibits photographs of the days of past prosperity, a few frescoes, folk costumes and items found in the harbour.

Another path leads up to a **Lycian tomb** cut into the living rock and decorated with Doric columns. The whole southwest or Lycian coast of modern Turkey is dotted with similar tombs, but this is the only one in modern Greece. The **Cathedral of Ag. Konstantínos and Heléni** re-uses granite columns from a temple of Apollo in Anatolia. From the town a steep path with steps leads up to four white churches and **Palaeokástro**, the Doric fortress and acropolis. On the gate there is a Doric inscription from the 3rd century BC referring to Mégisti; walls, a tower and cisterns also remain.

## Kastellórizo's Grotto Azzurro

There are no beaches on Kastellórizo, but the sea is clean and ideal for snorkelling, and there are a multitude of tiny islets to swim out to. The excursion not be missed is to the **Blue Cave**, or *Perásta*, or *Galázio Spílio*, an hour by caique from the town. The effects are best in the morning when some light filters in, for the entrance is so low you'll have to duck down in the boat to enter. As in the famous Blue Grotto of Capri, the reflections of the water inside bathe the cavern walls with an uncanny blue. There are many stalactites, but it looks as if the monk seal who lived there has been driven away, for the summer at least, by all the boat trips.

*Kastellórizo ✆ (0241–)*                                    **Where to Stay**

The **Megisti**, ✆ 49 272 (*B; exp–mod*), the island's municipal hotel, overlooks the harbour and is probably the most comfortable place to stay. *Open all year.* **The Blue and White Pension**, book via Taverna International, ✆ 28 263/29 348 (*mod–inexp*), to the west of the bay was featured in *Mediterraneo*. The **Mavrothalassitis** family's pension, ✆ 49 202 (*inexp*) is simple with en suite facilities. **Pension Castelo** (*mod–inexp*), behind Plateía Australías, book via Taverna Mavros, has family apartments; **Rooms O Paradeisos**, ✆ 29 074 (*inexp*) is another good bet. **Pension Barbara and Rooms**, ✆ 29 295 (*inexp but known to fluctuate*) are basic and a last resort. You might do just as well to take an offer when you get off the boat.

Most eateries are in the harbour clustered round the Plateía Ethelontón Kastellórizon. Prices, always dear because of transport charges, have rocketed and fish is expensive, although it's fresh and the only thing that doesn't have to be shipped in. **Taverna Mikro Parisi**, 'Little Paris', is still the place for affordable fish, although concentrating on yachties; **Taverna Lazarakis** is also a maritime haunt and **Taverna International** is touristy but good for breakfast. *Open July and August.* **Taverna Evtychia** is also reasonably priced and the **Oraia Mégisti** opposite another good choice. For more ethnic fare and local ambience head to **O Meyisteas** behind the market building arches for good meat and *mezédes*, while **Restaurant Platania** up the hill on Horáfia Square is also unpretentious with tasty island dishes.

### Entertainment and Nightlife

Nightlife revolves around eating out in the square, but there's always the **Meltemi Cocktail Bar** with glitzy clientèle, exotic drinks and ice-creams and blaring pop music. For something more local, the **Kafeneion Tis Iromonis** offers octopus grilled at the quayside, good ouzo and *mezédes*. There's also a **disco**, open sporadically, to the right of the bay near the mosque with music blasting across the bay.

# Kos (ΚΩΣ)

Dolphin-shaped Kos, with its wealth of fascinating antiquities, flowers and orchards, sandy beaches and comfortable climate, is Rhodes' major Dodecanese rival in the tourist industry. In other words, don't come here looking for anything very Greek—the *kafeneíon* and *ouzerie* serving octopus sizzling from the grill have been replaced with fast-food joints and tourist-trap cafés, with the accent on food just like that back home. Traditional Greek hospitality went by the board about 30 years ago. The streets are packed with T-shirt and tatty gift shops and where garlanded donkeys once carried their patrons home from the fields, swarms of rent-a-bikes now rev around. English, German and Swedish tourists swamp the place in high season, yet the island still holds charm for many people, who find everything they need for a family holiday in a big, self-contained resort hotel. Even the architecture isn't particularly Greek, partly owing to a large earthquake in 1933: the Italian occupation provided some attractive buildings, and the pair of minarets rising from the Turkish-built mosques complete its aura of *cosmopolitana*, although on the whole it has little of the elegance of Rhodes. Scrubby and scruffy in many places inland, short-sighted rashes of building—pseudo-Spanish villas seem to be the rage—are becoming real blots on the landscape.

## History

Evidence in Áspri Pétra cave dates Kos' first settlement to 3500 BC. A Minoan colony flourished on the site of the modern city of Kos; the Mycenaeans who superseded them traded extensively throughout the Mediterranean. After their decline Kos' history is obscure, except for references to two of the island's early names, Meropis, after its mythical king, and Nymphaeon, for its numerous nymphs. Astypálaia was the ancient capital, although in 366 BC the inhabitants began to rebuild the old Mycenaean city of Kos.

Poised between East and West (the powerful ancient city of Halicarnassus, present-day Bodrum, Turkey, is very near), Kos flourished with the trade of precious goods—and revolutionary ideas. Halicarnassus was the birthplace of Herodotus, called the 'father of history' for his attempt to distinguish legend from fact, and in the 5th century BC Kos produced an innovator of its own, Hippocrates, the father of medicine. Hippocrates realized that diseases were not punishments sent from the gods but had natural causes, and was the first to suggest that healers should discover as much as possible about each patient and their symptoms before making a diagnosis. His school on Kos, where he taught pupils a wholesome medicine based on waters, special diets, herbal remedies and relaxation, was renowned throughout the ancient world, and he set the standard of medical ethics incorporated in the Hippocratic oath taken by doctors to this day. When Hippocrates died, an Asklepeion (a temple to Asklepios, the god of healing) was founded, and people from all over the Mediterranean world came to be healed in its hospital-sanctuary. Besides physicians, Kos produced a school of bucolic poetry, led by Theocritus, a native of Sicily (319–250 BC). The Hellenistic ruler of Egypt, Ptolemy II Philadelphos, was born here, and many of the Ptolemies were sent to Kos for their education. The Romans were later to prize Kos for its silk industry, the only one in the Mediterranean, celebrated for its translucent cloth.

The island's wealth and strategic position excited the envy of others, and from the 6th century BC it was invaded by Persians, Romans and Saracens. The gods themselves, it seems, were jealous, and earthquakes in AD 142, 469, 554 and 1933 levelled most of the island's

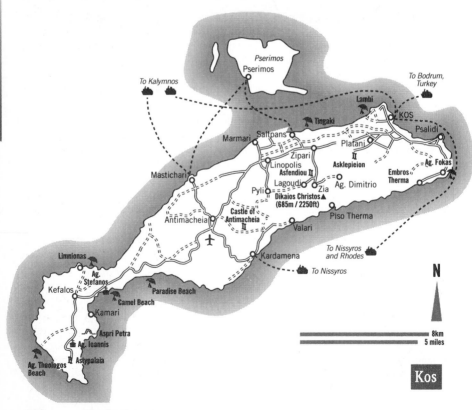

buildings. In 1315 the Knights of St John took control of Kos, and in 1391 began fortifications using material from the ancient city, incorporating even works of art from the Asklepeion as stone for their walls. In 1457 and 1477 the Turks besieged Kos without success, but they gained the fortress by treaty after the fall of Rhodes.

## Getting There and Around

**By air**: charters direct from London and several other European cities, 3 times a day with Athens, 3 times a week with Rhodes. Olympic office is at Leof. Vass. Pávlou 22, ☎ 28 331; airport info, ☎ 51 191. The airport is 26km from town. Olympic runs airport buses from Kos town to meet its own flights, or there are public buses (the stop is outside the airport gate) to Kos town, Mastichári, Kardámena and Kéfalos.

**By sea**: in season, daily to Bodrum, Turkey. Daily to Piraeus, Rhodes, Kálymnos, Léros, and Pátmos; 3 times a week to Tílos, Mýkonos, Ándros and Rafína, twice to Sámos, Sými, Kastellórizo and Astypálaia; once a week to Chíos, Lésbos, Límnos, Kavála and Thessaloníki. Daily **excursions** sail to Níssyros, Psérimos and Kálymnos, from Kos town as well as Mastichári and Kardaména. **Hydrofoil**: *Ilio* service daily with Rhodes and Sámos, several times a week with Kálymnos, Léros, Lipsí, Pátmos, Ikaría, Sými, Tílos, Níssyros and once with Agathónissi. **Port authority**, ☎ 26 594.

**By road: buses** to the suburban beaches and Asklepeion run the corner of Aktí Koundouriótou and Vassiléos Pávlou. Buses to other points on Kos leave from the terminal behind the Olympic Airways office, but they soon get packed so get there in plenty of time. Otherwise you'll find yourself at the wrong end of a long queue waiting for a taxi. In theory, at least, you can summon a **radio cab**, ☎ 23 333.

## Tourist Information

The old Municipal Tourist Office on Aktí Koundouriótou closed in 1992, leaving thousands of bewildered tourists wandering round looking for information. The good news is that another has opened at last in the big Italianate building on Vass. Georgíou just before the hydrofoil berth ☎ 28 724, with keen helpful staff and a useful range of leaflets and information lists. If you stumble into the old office where the day boats dock you'll find it now deals with tax. The tourist police, ☎ 22 444, are less helpful and share the yellow edifice with the clocktower opposite the main harbour with the regular police force, ☎ 22 222.

## Festivals

**25 March**, Evangelismós at Asfendíou; **23 April**, Ag. Geórgios, with horse races at Pylí; **29 June**, Ag. Apóstoli at Antimácheia; **29 August**, Ag. Ioánnis at Kéfalos. In **August** the **Hippocrates Cultural Festival** attracts people from all over Greece, and includes art exhibitions, concerts of classical and modern music, and screenings of Greek and foreign films. **8 September**, Panagías at Kardaména. **21 November**, Isódia tis Panagías at Ziá; **6 December**, Ag. Nikólaos at Kos.

Bustling **Kos**, the capital and main port, looks towards the north, roughly in the region of the dolphin's eye. Its garden setting, the multitude of flowers and stately palm trees make up somewhat for its lack of architectural interest and overwhelming crowds of tourists. Most of the town was built after the 1933 earthquake, this time using anti-seismic construction. From the archaeologist's point of view, the disaster had a good side-effect; when the rubble was cleared away, several ancient sites were revealed, and excavations were carried out throughout the city by the Italians, leaving throbbing holiday bedlam peppered with serene Greek and Roman antiquities. One block up from the harbour, in Plateía Eleftherías, is the **museum**, *Ø* 28 326 (*open Tues–Sun, 8.30–3*). Fittingly, the prize exhibit is a 4th-century BC statue of Hippocrates; there's also a good collection of Hellenistic and Roman vases, statues and mosaics from the Casa Romana and the Asklepeion; note the mosaic of the god Asklepios with his snake (*see* below).

Dominated by the 18th-century **Defterdar Mosque** (*still used by the 50 or so Moslem families on the island, but not open to the public*), Plateía Eleftherías also has the city's fruit market and the **Pórta tou Foroú**, the gate to the ancient **Agora**, or market. Within its walls the Knights built their town and auberges, and, when these collapsed in the earthquake, excavations revealed the Roman Agora, the harbour quarter of the city, a temple of Aphrodite, and a 5th-century Christian basilica. While wandering round the Agora you'll probably stumble across little trails of dried cat food scattered by the members of Kos Animal Protection League.

On the northern end of the Agora, the Plateía Platánou is almost entirely filled by **Hippocrates' plane tree**, its trunk 16m in diameter, its huge boughs now supported by an intricate metal scaffolding instead of the marble columns that once kept the venerable old tree from disaster. Signs in eight languages warn people not to touch for fear of insecticides. Yet it does still seem quite healthy, and at between 500 and 600 years old it may well be the senior plane tree in Europe. Hippocrates may well have taught under its great-grandmother, for he believed, as do modern Greeks, that of all the trees the shade of the plane is the most salubrious. The Turks loved the old plane just as much, and built a fountain under it with a sarcophagus for a basin, and overlooking it constructed the lovely **Mosque of the Loggia** (1786). On 1 September the citizens of Kos come to pluck a leaf from the tree to include in their harvest wreaths as a symbol of abundance.

## The Castle of the Knights

A stone bridge off Plateía Platánou takes you over the fosse to the entrance of the **Castle of the Knights of St John**, *Ø* 28 326 (*open Tues–Sun, 8.30–3*). Together with their fortress across the strait in Bodrum, this was the most important outer defence of Rhodes. After an earthquake in 1495, Grand Master Pierre d'Aubusson rebuilt the walls and added the outer enceinte, and the tower overlooking the harbour bears his name and coat-of-arms. Since d'Aubusson mostly used stones from the Agora, there's a patchwork quilt of ancient inscriptions and reliefs of the knights' coats-of-arms throughout the masonry of the walls. Some have been removed to the castle's **antiquarium**, to join other stacks of defunct columns and marble that nobody seems to know what to do with. The castle's dishevelled weeds and wildflowers and the stillness of the noonday sun attracted director Werner Herzog, who set his first black and white film *Signs of Life* partly within its walls; however, the elaborate cockroach traps and hypnotized chickens that played such a large role in the film are no longer in evidence.

# Roman Kos

From Plateía Eleftherías take Vass. Pávlou to Kos' other main archaeological sites. In the quarter called the Seraglio (don't expect any harem girls), Minoan and Mycenaean houses were discovered, as well as later structures. Opposite the Olympic Airways office stands a ramped Hellenistic **Altar of Dionysos**, and across Grigoríou Street, housed in a grim concrete building, is the **Casa Romana**, ✆ 28 326 (*open Tues–Sun, 8.30–3*), excavated and reconstructed by the Italians in the 1930s. The house and neighbouring baths fell in the earthquake of AD 554; the house has well-preserved mosaics and offers a fair idea of the spacious elegance a wealthy Roman could afford. To the west along Grigoríou Street is the **Roman Odeon**, or concert hall, with its rows of marble seats. Opposite, the so-called **Western Excavations** were also begun by the Italians in the 1930s. On one side are the great Hellenistic walls built around the acropolis (now studded with a minaret); on the other side runs the finely paved *cardo*, the main artery of Roman Kos, lined with houses, many containing fine mosaics (especially the House of Europa), a gymnasium and well-preserved baths transformed into a Christian basilica in the 5th-century; the baptistry contains a well-preserved font. Alongside the baths and basilica runs the colonnade of the covered running track, or *xystos*, used in the winter months—a rare Roman luxury that even Kos' most luxurious beach hotels lack. The open **stadium** was at the northern end of the *xystos*, down Tsaldári Street. Only a few of the seats have yet been excavated, but on the far side near the church is a well-preserved *aphesis*, or starting gate.

# The Asklepeion

Many places in Kos hire out bicycles, the ideal transport on a cool day up to the island's most important site, the **Asklepeion** (ΑΣΚΛΕΠΕΙΟΝ), ✆ 28 763 (*open Tues–Sun, 8.30–3*); you can walk there in less than hour, or take a city bus. The German archaeologist Herzog, following the description in Strabo, discovered it in 1902, and it was partially restored by the Italians during their tenure. This was one of the ancient world's most important shrines to the healing god Asklepios, served by the Asklepiada, a secret order of priests who found that calm baths in beautiful surroundings did much to remedy the ills of body and soul; it served both as temple and working hospital-cum-spa. The cult symbol was the snake, the ancestor of the one on the modern medical symbol, twining itself around the caduesis. Snakes, sacred intermediaries between the living and the dead (one reason being that they liked to live in tombs and eat the mice that fattened on grave offerings) were believed to have a knack for seeking out healing herbs and transmitting dreams, which were part of the therapy—the Asklepiada made good use of drugs and the power of suggestion in their cures. The sanctuary on Kos was built after the death of Hippocrates, himself a member of the Asklepiada, but most of the buildings visible today are from the Hellenistic age, when the earthquake-damaged Asklepeion was last reconstructed. Many of the structures were cannibalized by the Knights, who found it too convenient a quarry. Nowadays, the Greeks have big plans to build a 'City of Hippocrates' near the present Hippocrates Foundation, where every five years they would hold an 'International Medical Olympiad'. It is amusing to speculate on what that might encompass.

Set on a hillside, the Asklepeion is built in a series of terraces. On the lowest level are Roman baths, built in the 3rd century AD; on the next up is the main entrance and another large bath, and near the stair are the remains of a temple dedicated by the Kos-born physician G. Stertinius Xenophon, who went on to become the Emperor Claudius' personal doctor and murdered his patient by sticking a poisoned feather down his throat before retiring on Kos, hailed as a hero (so much for the Hippocratic Oath!). On this level there is the sacred spring used in the cures, where water has flowed for over 2000 years. On the third terrace is the altar of Asklepios, and Ionic temples of Apollo and Asklepios (a few of the columns have been reconstructed by the Italians); on the fourth level stood a Doric temple of Asklepios from the 2nd century BC, the grandest and most sacred of all, and enjoying a view that in itself might shake away the blues.

## Platáni

On the way back to Kos town, downhill all the way along the cool cypress-lined avenue, stop for refreshments in **Platáni**, Kos's main Turkish settlement. The Greeks hang out at the *kafeneíon* while the Muslim majority frequent the cafés at the crossroads. They're busy and a bit touristy, like everything on Kos, but the Turkish-style food is excellent and relatively cheap; if you want a more peaceful setting, try the taverna on the way down the hill. A little out of Platáni on the road back to the harbour the **Jewish Cemetery** stands in a pine grove near the Muslim graveyard. The inscriptions on its headstones end abruptly after 1940. Without any parishoners, the old synagogue back in Kos Town (4 Alexándrou Diákou) has been converted into the civic cultural centre.

## Beaches near Kos Town

The sandy and pebbly town beaches are packed with rows of sunbeds and umbrellas edge-to-edge; in places along Vassiléos Georgíou the whiff of sun oil is overpowering. The better, less crowded beaches are to the north of town. The closest beaches to the south are at **Psalídi** (ΨΑΛΙΔΙ), 3km away, and **Ag. Fokás** (8km), both heavily developed with several hotel and bungalow complexes along the road. For something more remote, get your own transport to continue to **Embrós Thermá** (13km), where volcanic black sands and thermal springs make the bathing a few degrees warmer; a small cantina serves drinks and snacks.

*Kos Town ✆ (0242–)*　　　　　　　　　　　　　　　　　　　　**Where to Stay**

In days of yore, visitors in need of a cure would stay in the Asklepeion and sacrifice a chicken to the gods. These days, beds are so scarce in high season that you still might need that chicken. If you don't book in advance in summer you will either end up tramping the streets or sleeping on the beach. Hotels even let out balconies at 3000dr a person. If you get offered a room as you get off the ferry, take it.

*expensive*

**Hippocrates Palace Hotel**, ✆ 24 401, ✉ 24 410 (*A*), with Olympic Health Centre spa supervised by Dr Christiaan Barnard. *Open Mar–Nov*. **Dimitra Beach Hotel**, Psalídi, ✆ 28 581 (*A*), is another beachside complex; nearby, the **Platanista**, ✆ 23 749 (*A*), looks like a castle. **Ramira Beach**, ✆ 28 489 (*A*) is another good bet near Psalídi and verges on the moderate price category.

*moderate–inexpensive*

There are over a dozen D and E class hotels in the town, but not many have rooms for less than 5000dr. **Afendoulis**, 1 Evripílou ✆ 25 321/797 (*B*) is a friendly pension with jasmine-filled terrace in a quiet road near the sea, run by Ippokrátis and brother Aléxis Zíkas of the **Pension Alexis**, 9 Irodótou, ✆ 28 798 (*E*), the Mecca for backpackers and young budget travellers, run by the ever-helpful Alex and sister Sonia. **Hotel Acropol**, Tsaldári 4, ✆ 22 244 (*C*), has OK rooms in an old house with lush garden. **Hara**, Halkonos 6, ✆ 22 500 (*D*), is a pleasant small hotel near the Chinese restaurant. **Kos Camping**, ✆ 23 910 is an excellent, well-run site with wide range of facilities from laundry to bike hire. A minibus meets the ferries.

---

## *Kos ✆ (0242–)*                                                         *Eating Out*

Because most restaurants have abandoned traditional food in a bid to have international appeal, eating out in town is like playing Russian roulette if you want real Greek cuisine. The waiters along the harbour-front aggressively *kamáki* or 'harpoon' punters in, too often for bland and overpriced food. As on Rhodes, avoid the tacky places that advertise with illuminated photos of meatballs and *wurst*. In town you can eat reasonably well in the newer quarter, at **Hellas** or **Ageilos** on Psarón Street; and on the waterfront at Vass. Georgíou the **Miramare** is largely unchanged by tourism and serves good Greek dishes at normal prices. One of the most authentic and reasonably priced tavernas, hidden way in the back streets (you'll have to ask half a dozen times to find it, but it's worth it), **Frangolis** serves the best *stifádo* in town, among many of its other delicious dishes; **The Ouzerie** on the corner of Koraí is highly recommended while the **Hammam Restaurant** overlooking the Western Excavations, while not cheap, has a good atmosphere in the old Turkish bath. **The Olympiada** behind the Olympic Airways office on Kleopátras is great value and very Greek, with chirpy service and ubiquitous sport on TV. The nearby **Australia Sydney** is also a good Greek haunt; opposite the Hotel Afendoulis, on Evrípou, **Taverna Barbas** is friendly and still retains a Greek flavour although it appeals to tourists of all nations; the pet cockatoo, Cocky, adds to the fun. **Taverna Sevalie** on Halkonos Street has a nice garden and village atmosphere, while **The Muses** has an international menu and an Englishman playing guitar. **Barba George** near Omírou is good and does an excellent *exohikó* or country-style spit roast; in contrast the chic **Bristol**, on Vass. Giorgíou, offers some Chinese dishes. Nearby, the sparkling **Le Chevalier** has a French menu, with prices to match. The **Kástro**, near the ancient Agora, belongs in the same league, except the setting is much more alluring. For delicious, and expensive, cakes and classical music, overlooking the agora, **O Platanos** café is a haven. For herbal teas and more cakes, try the **Kovotos Tea House**, near the ancient Odeon.

Outside town in bi-ethnic Platáni, a handful of tavernas serve Turkish food. The best of the bunch is the **Arap**, offering excellent aubergine with yoghurt, borek, grilled shish kebab and chicken. On the way to Psalídi near the Ramira Beach Hotel, two tavernas still retain a Greek ambience and traditional food: the **Nea Syntrivani** and **Restaurant Antonis**, which are both good value. Near the campsite **Nestoras** and **Thessaloniki** both have good Greek fare, and sea views. In Ag. Fokás, on the way to the spa, the beautiful **Villa Café** has an impressive choice of smoked swordfish, barbecue ribs, some Chinese and Japanese dishes, and some delectable home-made pastries, plus fine views across to Turkey.

Kos town is just one big party at night, with bars and disco pubs galore. The ancient Agora is alive with the thumping sound of house music from the 'Disco Alley' on Navklírou Street where every establishment is a bar pumping out conflicting sounds. Discos go in and out of fashion season by season, but **Playboy** has a laser show and **Kalua** a swimming pool; **Heaven** also has a watery backyard. You can dance outside the **Viva Pub** or enjoy a cocktail in a cool garden at **Mirage** on Porírou. If you want to catch a film there are two cinemas, **Kendriko** and **Orpheus**.

# Around Kos

Along the flat north (or east) coast there are beaches at **Lámbi** and **Tingáki** (ΤΙΓΑΧΙΟΝ), both on the package tour map now, although Tingáki is a smart little resort and still has a village feel, especially when the day-trippers have gone back to town. The nearby salt-pans (**Alikes**) are a birdwatchers' paradise with many rare species to spot.

Just inland, two ruined Byzantine basilicas (Ag. Pávlos and Ag. Ioánnis) lie on the outskirts of **Zipári**; from here the road heads up to **Asfendíou**, a pleasant mountain village, actually a cluster of five hamlets set in the woods, with whitewashed houses and flower-filled gardens. However, many have been abandoned as families move down into town. Up the road, **Ziá** has become the official 'traditional village' of package tours on Kos, with busloads pouring in at night to see the spectacular sunsets and have a Disneylandish Greek Night out in the tavernas. From Ziá you can follow the path up to **Mount Orómedon** in an hour, or more ambitiously tackle Kos' highest peak, **Díkaios Christós** (685m). This area is the bucolic Pryioton described by Theocritus, and Mount Díkaios produced much of the marble used by Kos' sculptors.

From the Asfendíou a paved road runs across country to **Lagoúdi** and continues from there to **Amaníou** and eventually to **Palaío Pýli**, a Byzantine ghost town on a crag surrounded by concentric walls camouflaged in the rocks. Within its walls is the church of Ypapandí, said to have been built in the 11th century by the Blessed Christódoulos before he went to Pátmos. The church and Ag. Nikólaos nearby have 14th-century frescoes. In the modern grotty village of **Pýli** about 4km away is the Charmyleion, an ancient hero shrine converted into the church of Stávros. You can also reach Pýli from Zipári, and hike up to the ancient town.

On the south coast, a beach stretches between **Tolíri** and **Kardaména** (ΚΑΡΔΑΜΑΙΝΑ), once a charming fishing village famous for its ceramics and now a heaving resort. Commercialized to near Costa Brava proportions, it's very much the Brit and Scandinavian family package destination, complete with pubs, chips, and smorgasbord. But there is also golden sand, all kinds of watersports and entertainment for all ages. There are some excellent club-type hotel complexes towards the end of the bay overlooking the island of Níssyros.

A quieter place to stay, although it is being rapidly developed, is **Mastichári** (ΜΑΣΤΙ-ΧΑΡΙΟΝ), on the north coast. Frequent boats leave the little harbour for Kálymnos and Psérimos, and it is also handy for the ungainly village of **Antimácheia**, near the airport. The **Castle of Antimácheia** was built by the Knights as a prison in the mid-14th century. Within its great, battlemented triangular walls are two churches, cisterns and, over the gateway, the arms of Pierre d'Aubusson.

Towards the dolphin's tail, near the beach at **Kamári**, stand the extensive ruins of the lovely twin 5th-century basilicas of **Ag. Stéfanos**, with mosaics, Ionian columns and remains of an atrium and baptistries, while out at sea you can contemplate the dramatic rock of **Ag. Nikólaos**. You can also contemplate the vast Club Med complex which dominates the coastline from Kamári to Ag. Stéfanos with its fancy pants hotel and bungalows. To the east, **Camel Beach** is excellent and nearby **Paradise Beach** lives up to its name. Also known as Bubble Beach for the bubbles that rise to the surface through the clear waters at one end of the bay, it's a marvellous stretch of sand, perfect for children, even if they have to fight your way through the forest of umbrellas to get to the water. Further along the headland to the left, the beaches are much much quieter although still offering their share of sunbeds, parasols and little cantinas for refreshments.

**Kéfalos** (ΚΕΦΑΛΟΣ) to the west is high up on the headland of the dolphin's tail. It's where the bus terminates, and when the hotels are bursting-full elsewhere you just may find a room here. South of Kéfalos are ruins of yet another castle used by the Knights, one that inspired many travellers' tales in the Middle Ages, all involving a dragon; Mandeville in his *Travels* claims the serpent was none other than Hippocrates' daughter, enchanted by Artemis and awaiting a knight brave enough to kiss her to transform her back into a maiden. Neolithic remains were found in the **Áspri Pétra cave** near Kéfalos, which is also near the site of the ancient capital of Kos, **Astypálaia**, the birthplace of Hippocrates; a few bits of the ancient city remain, and on a hill above the town is a fort used by the Knights. Isthmioton, another ancient city on the peninsula, was important enough in the past to send its own delegation to Délos, but not a trace of it remains. The **Monastery of Ag. Ioánnis** is 6km west of Kéfalos, along a track through dramatic scenery. Nearby **Ag. Theológos** beach provides some of the island's most secluded swimming.

---

*Kos ✆ (0242–)*            **Where to Stay and Eating Out**

If you're one of the rare birds who fly to Kos but don't want to stay in a big beachside resort, you might be able to rent a house in the mountain hamlets of Asfendíou, at the time of writing being refurbished under the national Traditional Settlements scheme. Check with the NTOG at home before you go (*see* **Practical A–Z**, p.47).

## Marmári

**The Caravia Beach Hotel and Bungalows**, ✆ 41 2914, ✆ 41 215 (*lux*), is a super club hotel set in beautiful grounds a little out of town with a vast range of facilities. *Open April–Oct.*

## Kardaména

Tightly packaged Kardaména has scores of pensions and hotels. The new **Club Porto Bello Beach**, **Hotel and Bungalows**, ✆ 91 217 (*A; exp*) have a luxurious setting with views of Níssyros. The new **Lakitira Resort Hotel and Village**, between Kardaména and Kéfalos; to book ring Athens, ✆ (01) 413 4902, ✆ 453 8413 (*lux*), has a vast range of facilities and an endless amount of sports from aerobics to 'Crazy Banana', and teachers to teach you how do them. **Stelios**, ✆ 91 210 (*C; mod*) is on the main square and popular, so book well in advance. **Maria Danelaki**, ✆ 91 474 (*inexp*) also has nice rooms near the esplanade. Kardaména caters very much to the tastes of British package tourists, but it also has an attractive row of tavernas at the water's edge. **Restaurant Andreas** refuses to pander to tourists and has a nice ethnic range of dishes; **Teo's**, near the square where the bus arrives, serves good fish, and standard oven food. **Cavo d'Oro**, by the water, also has seafood and pizza, while the *ouzerie* **Nikos O Vrahos** in Plateía Konítsis, one block up from the Agora, is good value and with a selection of delicious dishes. Kardaména lives it up with happy hours everywhere and something for night owls of all ages. Music bars are supposed to stop playing at midnight but the discos rave on until dawn.

### Tingáki

The pension **Meni Beach**, ✆ 29 217 (*C; inexp*) is pleasant; **Constantinos Ilios**, ✆ 29 411(*C; inexp*) is a reasonable choice or try **Paxinos**, ✆ 29 306 (*C; inexp*).

### Kéfalos

The hilltop village of Kéfalos, usually the last to fill up, has the **Kokkalikis Beach** ✆ 71 466 (*C; mod–inexp*) and **Kordistos** ✆ 71 251 (*C; mod–inexp*). The taverna **Kali Kardia** is a traditional village favourite. One of the best beach tavernas for lunch is at **Paradise Beach**, serving traditional Greek and Italian dishes for 2000dr with Níssyros floating on the horizon as an appetizing backdrop. If you're from Montreal, you'll get a warm welcome from the owner, who raised his family there.

### Mastichári

There's plenty of accommodation here, including the **Mastihari Beach Hotel**, ✆ 51 371 (*B pension; inexp*), near the harbour; the **Arant**, ✆ 51 167 (*C; inexp*); and the cheerful **Zevgas**, ✆ 22 577 (*E; inexp*) with en suite bathroms. The long-established **Kali Kardia** (*1500–2000dr*) is the best of several waterside tavernas.

# Psérimos (ΨΕΡΙΜΟΣ)

Psérimos, wedged between Kos and Kálymnos, has a beautiful sandy beach, unfortunately packed with rows of day-trippers like well-oiled sardines during high season. Even in September excursion boats from Kos town, Mastichári and Kálymnos are queueing up to dock, the tavernas are thronged and the islanders short-tempered. Fewer than a hundred people live on Psérimos, although the *panegýri* at its monastery on 15 August attracts hundreds of visitors. If you are staying any length of time (when the day boats have gone the people become quite friendly) you'd probably want to take to the interior by day, or hunt up one of the smaller pebbly strands; the main beach can be murder.

*Psérimos* ✆ *(0243–)*                                             ***Where to Stay***

The seaside **Pension Tripolitis** ✆ 23 196 is pleasant, located over Mr Saroukos's taverna; the **Pension Niki-Ross** is also worth a try (Ross is Australian Greek). The **monastery** has simple accommodation for up to 10 people. **Rooms Andreas** and **Kali Kardia** are fine too, but noisy by day as they are over tavernas. There are a few rooms to be had in the village; try **Katerina Xiloura**, ✆ 23 497 or **Glynatsis** on ✆ 23 596. If the rooms are full, you can sleep out on one of the island's more distant beaches, a kilometre from the village.

Most of the tavernas on the main beach are packed, and the service in them can be surly. Better to aim for those in the middle of the beach which don't seem to get as busy. The unnamed one with the garden area does excellent and reasonably priced *kalamári.* **Cafe Bar Themis** hires out sunbeds and is OK; **Restaurant Andreas** gets very busy as does **Kali Kardia** next door, but at **Estatoriou Pserimou,** Kapitán Yiánnis seems to have handed over the reins to British help and isn't quite as well patronised. For a local flavour, linger over an ouzo at **Kafeneion O Manolis,** near the communal tap.

# Léros (ΛΕΡΟΣ)

With its wildly serrated coastline like an intricate jigsaw puzzle piece, tree-fringed beaches and unspoiled villages Léros is a beautiful, underrated and much misunderstood island. Few places have had such a bad press both as an isle of exile and home of Greece's most notorious mental institutions. Perhaps to make amends, the people are welcoming and friendly, and visitors who discover Léros' many charms return completely hooked.

Although becoming popular with British travellers who want to escape the crowds on Kos and a favourite with dedicated Grecophiles, Léros, unlike many of the other Dodecanese, still attracts mainly Greek holidaymakers. Some families come to visit relatives in the island's three mental hospitals, set up during the Italian occupation in Lakkí Bay. Léros has long been the butt of ignorant jokes in Greece where the island's name equates with the British Bedlam. Léros also sounds like *léra*, the Greek word for filth or rogue, which adds fuel to the fire of national derision. The 1989 Channel 4 documentary exposing the grim conditions in the hospitals gave Léros yet another claim to infamy. Since then the Greek health authorities have attempted to get their act together. Dutch medical teams have been working with them and the situation has improved. Last year a small care in the community scheme was set up and you might see patients in the villages. But they are not intrusive, and, to be frank, you're likely to see more disturbed and less accepted people with mental problems on the streets back home.

Many of the islanders work in the institutions and these days the gates to the hospital parkland—one building was once Mussolini's summer residence—are open to visitors. Léros is also a place of pilgrimage for those who lost loved ones during the German bombardment against the combined Allied forces in the 1943 Battle of Léros, which raged from November 12–16. The British War Cemetery at Alínda looks out over the crystal bay, ironically next to a rent a motorbike shop. As the local youths zap up and down on their bikes, 179 young British servicemen, two Canadians and two South Africans, nearly all in their twenties, lie at rest. The memorial book is stashed away at the entrance gates.

But Léros is not a dreary or downbeat island. Green and pretty, its indented coastline offers little strands of shingly sand, very clear waters, excellent fish tavernas, and a lively but very Greek nightlife. Spontaneous singing and dancing often breaks out at the seashore tavernas of Pantéli while Lakkí, Mussolini's now crumbling architectural vision of the Fascist future, is quiet by day, its cafeterias buzz with young people by night. The ancient island of Artemis, Léros has a special kind of atmosphere you either love or hate. The people are genuinely friendly and it helps if you speak a few words of Greek, although with many of the older residents you can certainly get by with Italian. With sweeping hills and fertile valleys it's a good place for walkers, too. Tourism is in its infancy, but thanks to its unfortunate reputation Léros is unlikely to get overrun; its bad press shields the island from the masses and might help preserve its certain charm. It's still a gem, warts and all.

## History

On the death of the hero Meleager (of Chalydonian boar hunt fame), his sisters mourned him so passionately that Artemis turned them into guinea fowl and put them in her temple at Léros, the wooded island dedicated to her. This worship of the goddess of the chase and the guinea fowl might be traced back to Ionian colonists from Miletus; Robert Graves notes that, because of their religious conservatism and refusal to adopt the patriarchal state religion of Olympos, the Greeks called the Leriots 'evil-livers' (an epigram went, 'The Lerians are all bad, not merely some Lerians, but every one of them—all except Prokles, and of course he is a Lerian too'). Fittingly for an island dedicated to Artemis, property has been passed down through the female line, to the extent that most of Léros is owned by women.

Homer included Léros with Kálymnos as the 'Kalydian isles' in his Catalogue of Ships. The island sided with Sparta in the Peloponnesian War, despite its Ionian ancestry. Under the Romans, pirates preyed among the islets that surround Léros; some nabbed a handsome young

lawyer named Julius Caesar on his way home from Bithynia, where according to rumour he had had a dissolute affair with the governor; released after a month when his ransom was paid, Caesar later got his revenge by capturing and crucifying every brigand around Léros. Under the Byzantines, the island was controlled by Sámos, but in 1316 it was sold to the Knights of St John and governed by the Duke of Náxos as part of the monastic state of Pátmos.

Léros was occupied by the Italians in 1912 and they built their main air and naval ordnance bases at Lépida. Lakkí Bay in turn has been the anchorage for the Italian, German and British Mediterranean fleets. The town and harbour were badly battered by the combined Allied air forces prolonged bombardment (photographs taken by German paratroopers at the time are on display in the Kastis Travel Agency). Léros was eventually liberated by the Allies and incorporated with the rest of Greece in 1948. When the junta took power in 1967, Communist dissidents were exiled on Léros and kept at a prison camp in Parthéni. During the later Cyprus dispute the Greek government dismantled the military installations to show that it had no warlike intentions against Turkey. One of the brightest lights in Australian poetry, Dimítris Tsaloúmas, was born on Léros and immigrated with his family to Melbourne in 1952; his work explores the often bittersweet feelings of immigrants in the worldwide Greek diaspora and explains why so many hotels, bars and restaurants are named *Nostos*, a longing for home.

### Getting There and Around

**By air**: daily from Athens, information ✆ 22 275.

**By boat**: From Lakkí daily **ferry** except Sunday to Pátmos and Piraeus; 9 times a week to Kos, Kálymnos; 5 to Rhodes; and Pátmos, twice a week with Lipsí and Agathónissi; once a week to Níssyros and Chálki, Kássos, Kárpathos, Crete (Heráklion); and once with Cíios, Lésbos, Límnos, Kavála. **Excursion boats** from Ag. Marína to Lipsí, Arki and Marathi; **caique** twice a day in nigh season from Xirókambos to Myrtiés, Kálymnos. **Hydrofoil**: daily from Ag. Marína to Kalimnos, Kos, Pátmos, and Sámos; three times a week to Lipsí; weekly links with Agathónissi and Ikaría. Timetables often change depending on the time of year. Check with main agent Kastis Travel who have an office at Lakkí and ticket booth on the quay, ✆ 22 872; Ag. Marína, ✆ 22 140. **Port authority**, Lakkí ✆ 22 224; Ag. Marína, ✆ 23 256.

**By road**: taxi ranks: Lakkí ✆ 22 550, Ag. Marína ✆ 23 340, Plátanos ✆ 23 070.

### Tourist Information

There's a helpful Municipal Tourist Office at the quay in Lakkí next door to the cafeteria, ✆ (0247) 22 937. Tourist police, see regular police, ✆ 22 222. In Ag. Marína DRM Travel, ✆ 23 502 ✉ 24 303, are exceptionally helpful, have accommodation to let and a range of excursions.

### Festivals

During the **pre-Lent** Carnival children don monks' robes and visit the homes of the newly married, reciting verses made up by their elders; **16–17 July**, Ag. Marínas at Ag. Marína; **first ten days of August** at Alínda the Alintia regatta run since 1907 with sailing races; **6 August**, Sotíris at Plátanos; **15 August**, Panagías at the Kástro;

**20 August**, foreign tourist day at Alínda; **24–25 September**, Ag. Ioánnis Theológos at Lakkí. Starting on **26 September**, three days of memorial services are held for those who lost their lives on the Queen Olga; Greek naval vessels always attend this annual commemoration; **20 October**, Ag. Kýras at Parthéni.

Léros is famous for its musicians most notably the Hajiadakis family dynasty whose folk songs have influenced Greece's leading composers. Often at the *panegýria* you can hear the traditional instruments like the Greek hammer dulcimer, the *santoúri* or the bagpipe-like *tsamboúna*. Léros also has famous dances to watch out for: the Issós Lérikos, Soústa, Stavrotos, Passoumáki and the ancient Dance of the Broom.

## Lakkí and South Léros

Arriving at **Lakkí** (ΛΑΚΚΙ), by ferry, usually at night, is quite an experience, its extraordinary *Fascisti* Art Deco buildings reflected in the gulf. If Fellini had been Greek, Lakkí would have been one of his favourite sets. The streets are perfectly paved and wide enough to accommodate several lanes of traffic, although they're usually empty, while what remains of Mussolini's dream town, a tribute to Italian Rationalism and the International Style, crumbles away, forlorn, dilapidated but still weirdly compelling, a proper De Chirico ghost town. The grandiose cinema is defunct, as is the old Hotel Roma, later the **Léros Palace** (where this writer was once led down a mile of huge white halls, hypnotically lit by swaying bare bulbs, to a room the size of a bus station, completely untouched since its last clients pounded a flock of mosquitoes into the walls. The son of the owner, seeing my reluctant glances at the rumpled bed, rolled his eyes and exclaimed in disgust, 'Oh, and I suppose you want clean sheets, too!'). Now it's stuffed with litter. Lakkí's style was dubbed 'Ignored Internationalism' by Greek scholars when the Lerians decided to abandon the town and make the more convivial Plátanos the capital.

Near the waterfront there's a monument to the many who perished in 1943 when a Greek ship, the *Queen Olga*, was attacked by German planes and sank in Lakkí's harbour. A path leading up from the jetty goes to the nearest beach at **Kouloúki**,which has a taverna and is a favourite place for unofficial camping under the pine trees. At **Lépida**, across the harbour, the **Moní Panagía** is built on the ruins of an old lighthouse, and further south, overlooking **Xirókambos** (ΞΗΡΟΚΑΜΠΟΣ), is the fort **Paliokástro**, built near an older fortification dating back to the 3rd century BC. The church inside has mosaics and Xirókambos itself has a pleasant sandy beach. In summer the caique goes over to Myrtiés on Kálymnos twice a day. There are also secluded pebbly coves accessible from a track beside the chapel.

## Plátanos, Alínda and North Léros

Up the tree-lined hill from Lakkí, past Vromólithos, the island capital, **Plátanos** (ΠΛΑΤΑΝΟΣ), is as near the centre of Léros as possible. Very pretty, especially at night with stunning views to the fishing village of Pantéli below, Plátanos is crowned by the **Kástro**, a Byzantine fortress renovated by the Knights of St John and the Venetians and later used as a military observation post. There are 370 steps up or a winding, rough asphalt road; both are clearly marked from the main square. Lovely, flower-decked houses scent the steep march up, a march rewarded not only with views of the village spilling down to Ag. Marína, but of the 'four seas' of Léros: the bays of Pantéli, Marína, Gournás and Lakkí. The fortress was built over ancient ruins and a 7th century BC tomb has been discovered. Most important, however, is the church of the **Megalóchari Kyrás Kástrou**, the Madonna of the Castle, which houses a miraculous icon of the Virgin and small display of religious relics. According to popular tradition, the icon set sail from Constantinople on board a boat lit by a sacred candle, and turned up on Léros during the Turkish occupation having. The inhabitants, led by the bishops, retrieved it from the seashore and carried it in great procession to the cathedral. The next day, however, the icon had vanished and the Turkish captain of the Kástro found it, candle blazing, in the fortress gunpowder store, even though the door had been firmly locked. The icon was taken back to the cathedral, but the next night decamped to the arsenal again. It kept this up until the Turkish governor was convinced it was a miraculous sign and gave the powder storeroom to the Christians. They cleaned it up, the wilful icon came happily to rest and has decided to remain ever since.

Near the Town Hall in bustling Plátanos Square there's a small **museum**, © 22 255, housing local finds, usually open in the morning. There is also the Antonelli family museum on the road down to Ag. Marína, opposite the cathedral. The square is the hub of all action, and buses for both sides of the island leave from the road just below on the way to Pantéli.

Léros has an excellent and inexpensive taxi service, like Kálymnos, and it's easy to grab a cab and share. It is a short downhill walk from Plátanos south to **Pantéli** and north to Ag. Marína. With its little harbour full of fishing caiques Pantéli is very much a working fishing village by day, with fishermen mending nets and sorting out their catches. There's a small, tree-fringed beach and at night the taverna tables and chairs spill out on to the sands. It's famous for its fish restaurants, popular with Greek holidaymakers, who break out into song and dance when the spirit moves them—as it frequently does. Along the coast from Pantéli **Vromólithos** ('Dirty Rock') is a popular beach with sunbeds and tavernas. Unfortunately the narrow road which loops round Pantéli and back up to Plátanos becomes a racetrack for motorbikes in high season and at weekends. You also have to watch out if you walk down the main Ódos Xarami from Plátanos Square to **Ag. Marína**, as it's narrow and the traffic fast and furious. It's easier to take the quiet lane that runs parallel down to the pottery. Ag. Marína is a windswept harbour, again full of fishermen at work. There are a few good tavernas, a disco and bars and a narrow beach around the headland north towards **Alínda** (ΑΛΙΝΤΑ) with an old windmill out on a mole.

It's a fair stroll to Alínda via Krithóni, but there are little sandy bays along the roadside so you can take a plunge if you get too hot. Once the old commercial port of Léros, Alínda is now its main resort, buzzing with young Greeks in August. It's a package holiday destination too, and, although it's being developed, tourism is still low-key. There's a long sandy beach, one of the best on the island, with water sports, and plenty of seafront cafés and tavernas. Near here are the ruins of an Early Christian basilica along with a few vestiges of the ancient city, as well as the British war cemetery. Looking like something from Walt Disney, the incongruous **Bellini Castle** houses the **Historic and Folk Museum** (*open daily, 10–12 and 6–9*). Léros has strong links with Egypt as many notables fled to Cairo in the twenties, and the tower was built by the leader of the ex-pat Lerian community, Paríssis Bellínis, the island's major benefactor. Beyond Alínda there are secluded coves at **Panagíes** and **Kryfós**. There's a large sandy beach at **Gournás** and a number of small coves leading to Léros's answer to Corfu's Mouse Island, **Ag. Isidóros**, a pretty little white chapel perched on an islet reached by a long causeway. If you fancy a long walk off the road there are sandy beaches at **Ag. Nikólaos** further along the coast.

From Alínda there's a road lined with eucalyptus trees to **Parthéni** on the northern shore, the site of the ancient **Temple of Artemis**, near the present church of **Ag. Kyrás**. Although it hasn't been excavated, you can walk through the fields and see the ruins, sit under a sacred myrtle tree and look at the airport next door. Parthéni, former centre of guinea fowl worship, is now the island's main military base and was used as a detention centre for political dissidents under the colonels' regime. Further north there's a popular family beach at **Plefoúti**, with a taverna, while over the headland at **Kioúra** there are quiet pebble coves reached via the chapel gates. You can easily do a round-island trip by car past **Drymónas** with lovely coves and an oleander gorge, then over the mountain back to Lakkí.

---

*Léros ✆ (0247–)*                                        ***Where to Stay and Eating Out***

## Lakkí

The **Miramare Hotel**, ✆ 22 469/043 (*D; inexp*) is central and comfortable; **Hotel Katerina**, ✆ 22 460 (*E; inexp*) and **Hotel Artemis**, ✆ 22 416 (*C; inexp*) are both fine if you've just staggered off the ferry, but a little out of town the **Xenon Angelou**, ✆ 22 514, ✆ 24 403 (*B; inexp*) is a beautiful old pink farmhouse tastefully converted into a B & B. In Lakkí, food is generally limited to fast food and pizza, a notable exception being **O Sostos** taverna behind the defunct Léros Palace Hotel, which enjoys an excellent reputation for good local fare.

## Alínda

The **Xenon Angelou Alínda**, ✆ 22 749 (*B; mod*) is run by the same family as the Xenon in Lakkí, another lovely character guest house in its own grounds. **Pension Hotel Papa Fotis**, ✆ 22 247 (*C; inexp*) is good for travellers on a tight budget. **Pension Chryssoula**, ✆ 22 460/451 and **Pension Angelika**, ✆ 24 610 towards the end of the bay are family run and have great views. For luxury try the new **Boulafendis Bunglalows**, ✆ 23 515 (*exp–mod*), an interesting studio development around a traditional mansion with a piano restaurant and fax for clients. Amongst the tavernas, **Finikas** is an old favourite and the **Ellenikon** café also does some imaginative snacks.

## Krithóni

**Hotel Maleas Beach**, ✆ 23 306 (*C; mod*), has a nice setting overlooking the bay; **Hotel Athina**, ✆ 22 445 (*C; inexp*) is small but comfortable, while opposite, the swish **Krithoni Palace Hotel** (*exp*) with a pool and piano bar has just opened. **Nefeli Apartments**, ✆ 24 611/711, ✆ 24 001 is another tasteful up-market new complex designed by a woman architect. The elegant **Esperides Steak House** offers an antidote to moussaka with Chateaubriand and other delicacies.

## Ag. Marína

**Ta Kamakia** is one of the best places to eat, with excellent *yígantes*, and **Taverna Ag. Marina** is is also good for lunch and watching the world go by. **Glaros Snack Bar** does a hearty breakfast, and if you've OD'd on Greek salads then head for **Garbo's Restaurant** where Kath's steak and kidney pie takes some beating. She and husband Frank offer a good international menu in elegant surroundings.

## Plátanos

The pleasant **Hotel Eleftheria**, ✆ 23 550 (*C; inexp*) has family apartments as well as nice doubles and is owned by Antónis Kanáris of the local Laskarina Travel agency, confusingly unconnected with the British holiday company. **Pension Plátanos**, ✆ 22 608 (*inexp*), is also a good bet on the main square. Food choices here run the gamut from **Funny Bunny Fast Food** to the ancient *ouzerie*, **Leriako Lexi**.

## Pantéli

Several good inexpensive pensions overlook the picture-postcard harbour including **Pension Rosa**, ✆ 22 798 and the excellent **Pension Kavos**, ✆ 23 247. Down from Plátanos the **Pension Happyness** (*sic*), ✆ 23 498, has wonderful views to the Kástro but might be too close to the disco for comfort. Up the lane back towards Plátanos, **Pension Rena** near the church has a lovely shady garden; neighbouring **Pension Aphroditi**, ✆ 22 031/23 477 and **Aegean Sky Apartments**, ✆ 24 722, are also recommended. Pantéli is the place for fish, with its tavernas spilling out over the beach. At the bottom of the hill, **Faliro** is up-market with excellent seafood and courteous service plus a bizarre grotto housing a fishtank. **Zorba's** off the little square gets packed; **The Corner** does good breakfast and **Taverna Drossia**, opposite Pension Rosa, is less touristy than some, with fish almost leaping from the family nets; **Psaropoula** and **Taverna Maria** with their terraces at the water's edge are great for atmosphere and popular with the local fishermen. Gold-toothed Maria will rustle you up a huge dish of small whitebait-style *marídes* or *kalamári* fresh from their caiques, and dancing might even break out.

## Vromólithos

**Paradise Pension**, ✆ 24 718 (*A; inexp*) is a good bet. **Rooms Anastasios**, ✆ 23 247 are in the same family as Pension Kavos in Pantéli. For a luxury touch the new **Hotel Glaros**, ✆ 24 358 (*exp*), is a swish apartment complex overlooking the bay. Slap on the beach, **Frango's Taverna** is legendary for traditional food, while the **Taverna Paradisos** also has a good menu but slow service in high season.

## Xirókambos

The official campsite **Camping Leros**, ✆ 23 372, is here, and there are also several rooms to let such as **Maria Stamatia's**, ✆ 22 913.

---

### Entertainment and Nightlife

There are a number of cultural events during the summer from concerts to exhibitions and performances by the **Léros Theatre Group**. The Youth Cultural Society, **Artemis**, is also dedicated to the revival of the island dances in traditional costume. There is a **bouzouki club** on the way to Plefoútis; otherwise Pantéli has the **Disco Diana** and the cool **Savanna Yacht Club** bar at the end of the harbour; **Nectar** and **Café Continent** are also decent watering-holes. In Ag. Marína, **La Playa Bar** is the happening place and the **Faros** disco plays great world music; **Anne's Pub** sometimes has belly-dancing. At Alínda the **Cosmopolitan** is where it's at. Look out for the posters for beach parties. In Lakkí, nightlife centres round the waterside cafés.

# Lipsí/Lipsos (ΛΕΙΨΟΙ)

Lipsí is a little gem of an island midway between Léros and Pátmos, and it's not surprising that Odysseus put off his homecoming for seven years to linger here, beguiled by the charms of the nymph Calypso. If opinions differ on whether Lipsí really is Homer's isle of Ogygia (some place it near Corfu or Malta), no one can deny that the island has a certain magic. The blue domes of the Cycladic-style churches spill over a horizon of soft, green hills, while the village houses are painted in wild fauvist colours.

Lipsí is one of an archipelago of tiny islets, and its lovely beaches a magnet for day excursions from Pátmos and Léros, yet once the trippers have gone it quickly regains its tranquillity. Above all, it's a great place to do nothing. There's no bank, no newspapers, no proper traffic—apart from the fleet of pick-up trucks that rattle you off from the boat to the beaches in clouds of dust for 500–700dr return—and no crass tourism. Traditional island life goes on and the friendly people make a living from fishing and farming the fertile land. Lipsí is well-known for its special cheese made from sheep's and goat's milk—there are more goats than people—even donkeys and ponies outnumber the wheeled transport. The islanders grow their own produce and make an excellent wine.

### Getting There

**By sea**: daily **excursion boats** *Anna Express* and *Rena II* to Ag. Marína, Léros and Skála, Pátmos. They also link with ferries from Piraeus and Rhodes arriving in Pátmos at night. **Ferry** connections 3 times a week with Sámos, Pátmos, Léros and Kálymnos, twice a week with Kos and Agathoníssi, once a week with Níssyros, Tílos, Sými, Rhodes and Ikaría. Excursions around the island and to Arkí, Maráthi and Makrónissi caves. **Port authority**, ✆ 41 240.

## Around Lipsí

On arrival everything is neatly signposted from the harbour and most beaches are within walking distance. The town beach at **Lendoú** is shaded by trees but gets busy with Greek families in high season. Walk over the dusty headland track to **Kámbos** or beyond to **Kimissí** and you could even have the sands to yourself. The taxi pick-up trucks hurtle off to the island's best-known beach, the white cove of **Platís Gialós** which has a pretty church and taverna. As Lipsí only measures 6sq miles and you can walk across it in two hours, discovering its walled fields and thirty-odd blue and white chapels, as well as views of neighbouring **Arkí, Maráthi** and **Agathoníssi** on the way. To the south **Katsoudiá** has a succession of sandy coves and a good taverna, Adonis, while on the east coast **Monodéndri** is the unofficial nudie beach.

Back in town there is a smattering of tavernas around the bay and odd front-room cafés which double as shops. Everything is new-pin bright, as if they were entering a best-kept island contest. Steps lead up to the the island's famous blue-domed church of **Ag. Ioánnis** with its miraculous icon of the Panagía. The story goes that a woman prayed to the Virgin to help her son and the Virgin granted her prayer. Being poor, she had nothing to offer in return but a lily, which she humbly placed near the icon. In time the lily withered, but miraculously, on the festival day of the Virgin's acceptance into Heaven, 24 August (celebrations begin the night before), it sprang into full bloom and has flowered on that day ever since. The ancient lily stalk can clearly be seen under the glass of the icon and in early August it bears small white buds which burst into flower right on time. Dried flowers are also supposed to spring to life for the festival at the **Madonna of Cháros** chapel (named after the man who built it) at the island's highest point. Opposite the church in the Town Hall there's the small but grandly titled **Nikoforeion Ecclesiastical Museum** (*open Mon–Fri 9.30am–1.30pm and 4–8pm, Sat and Sun 10am–2pm*) an odd collection of motley stuff, from the ridiculous to an interesting letter from Admiral Miaoúlis written to a cousin on the night of his famous sea battle—OK if you read Greek. Everything is neatly labelled from bottles of Holy Water to costumes. The room doubles as the **Tourist Information Office**, ✆ 41 288. There is also a **carpet factory** where local girls work at the traditional looms, but their handiwork is sold in Athens.

There are vineyards in the valley beyond the town where a good local wine is produced. And with a bottle of this, and some octopus grilled at the harbourside, the island casts a gentle spell once the day-trippers have been herded away into their boats.

## Lipsí ✆ (0247–) *Where to Stay*

All accommodation here is inexpensive. There's only one hotel on Lipsí, the harbourside **Kalypso**, ✆ 41 242 (*D*) which also has an information service. Landladies meet the ferries offering rooms and plenty of new accommodation is also springing up. **Rena's Rooms**, ✆ 41 242 are immaculate and owned by John and Rena, who lived in America and run the *Rena II.* **Glaros Rooms**, ✆ 41 360, are also a good bet, perched high with views over the bay. Just past Lendoú Beach **Studios Dream**, ✆ 41 271, have kitchenettes and balconies; **Pension** and **Cafeteria Manolis**, ✆ 41 306 overlooks the fishing boats round the harbour to the south; otherwise try **Panorama Pension** or **Pension Flisvos**. There's unofficial camping on the more distant beaches.

## Lipsí ✆ (0247–) *Eating Out*

There's little to choose between the waterfront tavernas, all offering reasonable fish (including lobster) and typical oven dishes: among the specialites are *revythokeftédes* and fish croquets in mustard sauce. Places nearest the day-boats tend to be more touristy. **Kalypso Restaurant** with its shady vines is run by the famous Mr Mungo with a certain dishevelled style; **Taverna O Theologos** specializes in fish and prices won't break the bank; the **Asprakis Ouzerie**, doubling as shop and bar on the corner near the excursion boats, is great for local atmosphere, grilled octopus and ouzo. Further along towards the ferry dock the **Kali Kardia** is popular with a lovely terrace and cooking by the redoubtable Vassiléa and family; a few doors along the restaurant run by **Maria** next to the balustraded *ouzerie/*bar **The Rock** is excellent and less frenetic at lunchtime. In the square several *kafeneía* do breakfast; visit the town bakery for superb cheese pies and breads.

### Entertainment and Nightlife

If you're a party animal, forget it—unless one of the 200 inhabitants is getting married, when the whole island celebrates with a joyous all-night dance marathon. Some bars play music; there's no disco but a seasonal dancing bar at Lendoú Beach. Otherwise action centres on the waterfront eateries and somone might start to play the *santoúri* and start the locals partying.

# Níssyros (ΝΙΣΥΡΟΣ)

In the great war between gods and giants, one of the casualties was the fiery Titan Polyvotis, who so incurred Poseidon's wrath that the sea god ripped off a chunk of Kos and hurled it on top of him as he attempted to swim away. This became the island of Níssyros, and the miserable Polyvotis, pinned underneath, sighs and fumes, unable to escape.

The story is geologically sound: Níssyros was indeed once part of Kos, and one of the craters of its volcano, the only one in the Dodecanese, is named after the giant, still struggling to break free. Níssyros sits on a volcanic line which passes through Áegina, Páros, Antíparos, Mílos, Santoríni and Kos. Almost circular, the island in ancient times was crowned by a central 1400m peak. In 1422 there was a violent eruption and the centre imploded, forming the fertile Lakkí plain, which looks like a moonscape in places with its ashy slag heaps and yellow sulphurous rocks. Dormant these days—the last eruption was in 1933—the volcano dominates the island's character as well as its tourist industry. Its rich soil holds tight to the little water the island gets so Níssyros is lush and green, its terraces thick with olives, figs, citrus groves and almond trees. It's not surprising Níssyros has been called the Polo mint island— green outside, white inside with a hole in the middle. Much of the island's income comes from quarrying the gypsum and harvesting the pumice fields, both on Níssyros and its little sister islet Gialí opposite, and the harbours, especially at Páli, are full of bobbing pumice stones. The coast is a jumble of black volcanic boulders and pebbly or grey sandy beaches, and although Gialí is an industrial centre, gradually being chipped away by its miners, it also has some lovely golden sands. Drinking water is a problem on Níssyros, and although there is a desalination plant it isn't always working and tap water is largely undrinkable. The Greek electricity board DEH has sunk a successful geothermal well with plans for others which would not only supply power for the plant and the rest of the island but also be able to serve Kos, Kálymnos and Léros via under-sea cable. Like everything else in Greece, only time will tell.

## Getting There and Around

**By boat**: daily **taxi boat** and *Nissiros Express* to Kardaména, Kos; **ferry** several times a week to Kos, Kálymnos, Tílos and Rhodes, and once a week to Astypálaia, Mýkonos, Tínos, Ándros, Rafína, Léros, Pátmos, Piraeus, Sými and Kastellórizo. **Hydrofoil**: Regular but variable *Ilio* services to Kos, Kálymnos; Sými, Tílos, Rhodes, and three times a week Kos town only. **Port authority,** ✆ 31 222.

**By road**: there is a regular **bus** service from the harbour to Páli via White Beach but buses for the village of Emborió and Nikiá leave early morning and return mid-afternoon only. Níssyros also has two **taxi** firms, Bobby's, ✆ 31 460, and Irene's, ✆ 31 474. A round-island tour will cost about 6000dr; to the volcano 4000dr.

## Tourist Information

There are no tourist police, but the port authority are good for timetables and share the municipal building just above the quay with the Post Office and regular police, ✆ 31 201. **Polyvotis Tours** has a kiosk and information board on the harbourside, ✆ 31 459. **Enetikon Travel**, ✆ 31 180, ✉ 31 168, on the right as you head up from the harbour, are particularly helpful and offer a range of excursions. You can also phone from here.

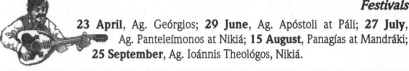

**23 April**, Ag. Geórgios; **29 June**, Ag. Apóstoli at Páli; **27 July**, Ag. Panteleímonos at Nikiá; **15 August**, Panagías at Mandráki; **25 September**, Ag. Ioánnis Theológos, Nikiá.

## Mandráki and Around

Despite the boatloads of day-trippers from Kos who come to see the volcano, Níssyros manages to retain its quiet charm, especially in the **Chóra** and higgledy-piggledy **Langadáki** district. The maze of little lanes, with the balconies of the brightly painted houses almost touching in places, were originally designed to keep out maurading pirates and now have to cope with the daily tourist invasion. There's still an air of being closed to outsiders, especially during siesta-time, *mesiméri*, with the shutters pulled tight over the traditional embroidered curtains. But at night, when the trippers have gone, the place buzzes, especially around the town hall square, when what looked like ordinary houses by day suddenly open up as shops selling everything from drapery to babyware and everyone comes out for a *vólta* or stroll.

Life revolves around the cafeteria on the quay in **Mandráki** (MANΔPAKI), the capital and port, where agents set up tables selling tickets for trips to the volcano and buses wait to take groups arriving on the excursion boats. A short walk from the quay leads you down the narrow road towards the village with its wide choice of seaside tavernas all vying for custom. Even the new houses conform to the old style: tall, narrow, and colourful, their wooden balconies often strung with onions or drying tomatoes. The road passes a bizarre display of folk artefacts set in a garden against the rocks on the left and then into the heart of the little town. A maze of lanes branches seawards to **Plateía Iroön**, 'Heroes Square', with its monument, while others weave inland past the public orchard or *kámbos* into a succession of shady squares. The first is lively at night with a selection of less touristy tavernas and bars. Although the lanes are incredibly narrow, motorbikes and pick-up trucks still manage to negotiate the tight bends, so watch out. Níssyros is a neat and tidy island, bursting with civic pride, and many of its paths are picked out with pebble mosaics or *hoklákia* patterns. The municipality has also been kind enough to signpost the way to major attractions: the ancient **Kástro** and monastery of 15th-century **Panagía Spilianí**, the Madonna of the Cave. More than a hundred steps lead up to the church, built in a cave within the walls of the old **Castle of the Knights of St John**, 1315, also known as the **Enetikon**. Inside the church (*open daily 10.30–3*) a finely carved iconostasis holds a much-venerated icon of the Virgin, loaded with gold and silver offerings. The Virgin is said to have chosen the site for the church herself, appearing in a vision to early Christian islanders. The church's fame grew after raiding Saracens failed to find its secret trove of silver, worked into the rich collection of Byzantine icons. There are guest rooms in the monastery and fantastic views from ruined walls out over the village at sunset.

On the stairway up to the monastery a small **Historical and Popular Museum** houses an assortment of island exhibits and a reconstruction of a traditional kitchen (*open daily 10–2.30*). There's also an imaginative gift shop opposite. Higher up along the lane through the Chóra a rough path leads from Langadáki up through the fields and olive groves to the Doric **Paliokástro**, a spectacular site with vast Cyclopean walls hewn from volcanic rock. The acropolis of ancient Níssyros, the mighty bastion dates back 2000 years and you can walk along the top of the wide walls from where they used to pour boiling oil on attackers and look out to Gialí and Kos. An easier cement road begins from the harbour near the signpost to Loutrá.

## Beaches and Hot Springs

There are a few sandy strands along the front, usually packed with trippers, and the nearest beach to town is **Chochláki**, under the monastery cliffs, reached by a daisy-patterned pathway. The beach is covered with blue-black volcanic pebbles and boulders, that give way to shale futher along. Locals will tell you that the sea is best here, even if the stones can be uncomfortable underfoot. A pen of pigs guarded by a watchdog occupy one end of the beach, while at the other there's a whacky beachcomber's house-cum-bar made from driftwood and all kinds of flotsam and jetsam. A 10-minute walk from Mandráki takes you to **Miramare** beach, convenient for the nearby fish tavernas. Further along, **Gialiskári** (or **White Beach**) is a better bet with its black and white crystals.

Just east of Mandráki is the thermal spa of **Loutrá** where the hot springs straight from the volcano are used as a cure for arthritis and rheumatism, open June to October. Further along the coast the pretty fishing village of **Páli** (ΠΑΛΟΙ), has a succession of dark volcanic sandy beaches, some shaded by trees. Fishing boats in the harbour are often surrounded by masses of bobbing pumice stones. The beaches further along the coast are full of them—great souvenirs for the bath. Páli has an incongruous central roundabout and selection of good fish tavernas. Follow the beach road, hung over with fig trees and you'll come to another spa building in various throes of construction which looks like an abandoned jail. The *meltémi* blows fiercely on Níssyros in high season and the beaches along here can be littered with junk and piglets even roam the shores. About an hour's walk or twenty minutes by moped along the road brings you to the island's best beaches: the bronze sands of **Líes** with its Oasis cantina, and **Pachiá Ámmos**, a broad expanse of reddish sands reached via a scramble over the headland. **Gialí** and the islet of **Ag. Antónis** have white crystal sand and are great for swimming and snorkelling.

## Into the Volcano

The excursion not to be missed on Níssyros, however, is to the volcano, or rather a caldera like Santoríni. It has five craters—Polivotis, Alexandros, Logothetis, Achilles and the biggest, Stéfanos, 25m deep and 350m across, the main attraction for the day-trippers. The volcano buses leave the port in succession as the tourist boats arrive; if you want more time and a bit of solitude, take the village bus to **Nikiá** in the morning and walk down. The path is steep but clearly marked and takes about 30 minutes. There are wonderful views from the winding road up from Mandráki, where the greenery and neat terraces offer a stunning contrast to the vast plain below, an extra-terrestrial landscape of pale greys and yellows, the smell of sulphur so pungent that you can almost see cartoonish stink lines curling up out of the great crater (you may have to hang out your clothes to air when you get back to keep from smelling like a rotten egg). After passing several geothermal pools, the bus stops near the great fuming heart of **Stéfanos**. A slippery zigzag path descends to the floor of the crater, with bubbling fumeroles all around. You can feel the great heat and turmoil of the gases beneath the crust. Stout shoes are essential; rubber soles often melt on the surface hot enough to cook an egg. In some places the crust is so fragile that your foot could go through and get a bad burn, so if you have children in tow make sure they don't stray. After the steam and the stench, you can join the queues to quench your thirst at the café on the rim of the crater.

## Emborió and Nikiá

The villages of Emborió and Nikiá cling to the rim of the crater. The deserted village of **Emborió** (ΕΜΠΟΡΕΙΟΣ) above Páli, only has a handful of inhabitants who haven't emigrated to Australia or America. But houses are gradually being restored for holiday homes. Some of the crumbling buildings have natural saunas in the basements, heated by volcano steam, and there is also a public sauna in a cave on the outskirts of the village. There's a ruined Byzantine fort and ancient walls offering memorable views of the infernal crater 300m below. An old cobbled pathway also leads down to Páli. In contrast pretty **Nikiá** (NIKAIA) is lively with dazzling blue and white paintwork, bright gardens and views over Tílos as well as the caldera in all its ghostly enormity far below. The village square has a lovely *hoklákia* mosaic and there are couple of *kafeneía* and a taverna, plus a hostel if you want to stay. On the way down to the volcano watch out for the **Calanna** rock, said to be a witch who was turned to stone; a safer place to rest is the **Monastery of Ag. Ioánnis Theológos**, with shady trees and picnic benches as well as icons and frescoes.

### Níssyros ℗ (0242–)                                        Where to Stay

It can be very difficult to find a room in July and August and there is no official campsite so it's worth booking ahead. Accommodation prices on Níssyros tend to be lower than many other islands in the Dodecanese.

In Mandráki harbour the municipal **Xenon Hotel**, ℗ 31 011 (*inexp*) seems to have been revamped and is very inviting and handy for ferries. Over the road the **Charitos Hotel**, ℗ 31 322 (*B; mod*) is a friendly pension with spacious rooms, sea-view balconies and direct-dial phones. *Open all year.* On the coast road to Páli the new **Miramare Apartments**, ℗ 31 100, ℗ 31 254 (*mod*) are luxurious by island standards, beautifully appointed with a sea-view terrace. Further into the village opposite the orchard, the most comfortable and well-priced bet is the **Hotel Porfíris**, ℗ 31 376 (*C; mod, inc breakfast*) with a swimming pool and views to Gialí; the **Pension I Drossia**, ℗ 31 328 (*inexp*) is one of the cheapest in the village, and the waves crash on the black rocks beneath your balcony. There are also rooms to rent in the Chorió: look out for signs. At White Beach the ungainly **Hotel White Beach** ℗ 31 497/8, ℗ 31 389 (*C; mod*) is right on the sands.

### Níssyros ℗ (0242–)                                        Eating Out

Níssyros has thirteen tavernas and ten bars at last count, ranging from water-side tavernas to village favourites in Mandráki's Elikioméni Square. Local specialities are *pittiá*, delicious chick pea fritters, and *soumáda*, a non-alcoholic almond drink which tastes like liquid marzipan. **Karava**, next to Enetikon Travel, has very good food, if a bit more pricey than the rest, but the sea view compensates. **Tsardaka** offers special tourist lunches with grills and oven dishes and the fish tastes marvellous when the sea is just a few feet away. Further along the front the **Captain's Taverna** has excellent home-made dishes including mouthwatering *pittiá* and wild caper salad made to Granny's recipe; don't be put off by **Mike's Tourist Corner**—there's a dab hand in the kitchen—and **Tony's** is also an excellent bet. There are some pleasant culinary surprises further inland, too.

**Taverna Nissyros**, spilling out into a narrow alley, is one of the most popular and authentic with its vine-clad canopy and jolly atmosphere. It gets packed at night, the food is good but portions small. **Kleanthis** is a popular lunchtime haunt with locals, while in the square **Taverna Irini** is good value with friendly service and a wide menu from *laderá* to roasts. You could have a long wait for a table at the **Panorama**, which gets very busy at night. The food is good but a bit pricey. So is the beer. Just beyond the harbour, the **Ouzerie Paradeisos** is aptly named set back off the road in a lovely garden, great for lunchtime ouzo and *mezédes* or an evening aperitif. In Páli make a bee-line for the **Restaurant Angistri** on the far edge of the beach where Mama makes a knock-out moussaka. Home-produced meat and fresh fish are also on the menu, and the loos are palatial; **Taverna Aphroditi** is also excellent with home-made desserts; while the **Hellenis**, adjoining the hotel, also has tasty dishes and sometimes music when the owner's husband is playing his *lýra*. At Nikiá the **Taverna Nikia** has great views over the crater and out to Kos.

### Entertainment and Nightlife

There are plenty of bars along the seafront, but at night action centres round the village squares. The **Enallax Bar** in the harbour, under the Xenon Hotel has live music—a Scot with a guitar—while **Tassos Bar** on Plateía Iróon does a mean cocktail. Watch out for the partridge in a cage. There are a number of cool bars playing Greek music under the trees in Elikioméni Square, while the **Cactus Bar**, with pool tables and garden is where the kids hang out. It also serves a good breakfast. Islanders let their hair down at festivals with traditional music and dance and there are also bouzouki nights with Greek dancing at the **Miramare Night Club**, also a restaurant.

# Pátmos (ΠΑΤΜΟΣ)

Of all the Greek islands, Pátmos is the most sacred to Christians, both Orthodox and Western alike; here St John the Theologian received the vision written in the *Apocalypse*, or *Book of Revelations*, and here, in the 11th century, was founded a monastery more wealthy and influential than any in Greece except for Mount Áthos. Many find a spirituality in Pátmos that the other islands lack, a quiet solemnity, a sacred (though hardly apocalyptic) aura that seems especially strong in the evening.

Be warned, however, it's much easier to find that spiritual something in the off season. These days Pátmos tourism caters for body as well as soul, and quiet nocturnal contemplation can be broken by the sound of music from the trendy dancing bars that are burgeoning in Skála and even the Chóra. By day the harbour buzzes with day-trippers from other islands and passengers from the big cruise liners being zapped up to the monastery by coach or overpriced taxi. The cafés along the front do a roaring trade and so do the stylish gift shops and jewellery boutiques. The less than cheery monks on the monastery trek may not make you feel welcome—although your money is—but the islanders are generally friendly and the views of the white sugar-cube houses against the sweeping blue bay from the Chóra are stunning.

## History

Pátmos was inhabited from the 14th century BC, with the capital near present-day Skála and its acropolis and fortifications at Kastélli. It was a subject to Asia Minor and not very important. In

AD 95, however, the island's destiny was forever altered with the arrival of St John (known variously as the Apostle, the Theologian, the Evangelist or the Divine). After the Crucifixion he spent most of his life in Ephesus as Jesus' appointed guardian of the Virgin Mary; an ancient tradition has it that during the Emperor Domitian's persecution of Christians he was transported to Rome and cast into a pot of boiling oil, from which he walked away without a burn, before being exiled to Pátmos, where he lived in a cave and received his extraordinary end-of-the-world Revelations. Most believe he stayed only a year on Pátmos before returning to Ephesus, but in that year John provided not only a fairly accurate prophecy of the fall of the Roman Empire, but enough to keep fire-eating preachers and literal-minded crank interpreters in material for the next 1900 years.

Pátmos was abandoned from the 7th century, its barren, volcanic rock not worth defending against pirates. Destiny remained on hold until the late 11th century, when in faraway Constantinople things were going badly for Alexis Comnenus, 'born to the purple' as the Byzantines put it, but to Alexis, battered by fate and politics, the purple seemed impossible to

Pátmos

attain. A saintly hermit named Christódoulos nevertheless predicted his ascent to the throne, and the miserable Alexis promised him that, were it to come true, he would grant him any wish in his power. Of course it did, and in 1088 Christódoulos made his wish of the Emperor: the island of Pátmos, to found a monastery on the site of an ancient temple of Artemis. The Emperor provided not only the island but the building funds.

The entire island of Pátmos remained under absolute control of the monastery for centuries, against poverty, pirates and a thousand other afflictions. The Venetian Dukes of Pátmos, its nominal rulers, were content to leave it as an autonomous monastic state. In the 13th century the village of Chóra was built in the shadow of the monastery's powerful walls, offering a safe refuge in case of attack. Pátmos flourished particularly from the 16th to the 19th centuries, and its school of theology and liberal arts, founded in 1713, cast a healthy glow over the long, dark domination of the Turks. Gradually monastic control lessened as the islanders turned to sea trade, and in 1720 the monks and laymen divided the land between them. Pátmos prospered to the extent that in the 18th century it established colonies abroad, a prosperity nipped in the bud, as in the case of other island shipping centres, by the invention of the steamship.

## Getting There and Around

**By sea**: daily **excursion boats** to Lipsí, Arkí, Maráthi and Sámos (Pythagório), **ferries** daily to Piraeus, Kálymnos, Léros, Kos and Rhodes; 4 times a week to Sámos, 3 times a week with Ikaría, twice a week with Agathónissi, and once a week with Sámos (Vathí), Chíos, Lésbos, Límnos and Kavála); Léros, Kálymnos, Níssyros, Kos, Rhodes, Chálki, Kárpathos (Pigádia), Kássos, and Crete (Herákleon). **Hydrofoil**: Regular *Ilio* services in the summer to Léros (Ag. Marína), Kálymnos, Kos, Agathónissi and Sámos (Pythagório); Lipsí, Kálymnos, Kos; Ikaría (Ag. Kýrikos), Sámos (Karlóvasi), Sámos (Vathí), Chíos, and Lésbos. **Excursion boats** leave Skála for most beaches between 9 and 11am, returning about 4pm. Excursions to Lipsí, an hour away, are especially popular; boats leave at 10 and return at 5. **Port authority**, ℗ 31 231.

**By road**: there are 7 **buses** daily from Skála bus station near the quay to Chóra, 5 to Gríkou and 3 to Kámbos. **Taxis**, ℗ 31 225, from rank on central square; to avoid being ripped off, check prices with tourist office before setting out.

## Tourist Information

The municipal tourist information office in Skála, ℗ (0247) 31 666/158/235, is very helpful and has a good range of leaflets and timetables. **Police**, ℗ 31 303, in the harbour; the port authority is behind the cafeteria on the quay. DRM Travel also has an office in Skála, ℗ 24 303, with informative staff.

## Festivals

Besides the **Maundy Thursday** Niptíras ceremony, the monastery holds services for St John on **8 May** and **26 September; 27 July**, Ag. Panteleímonos, on the islet of Xiliomódi; more popular *panegýria* with feasting and dancing take place **5 August**; Ag. Sotiris at Kámbos and **15 August**, Panagías, also at Kámbos; **14 September**, Ag. Stávros.

All boats drop anchor at **Skála** (ΣΚΑΛΑ), the island's main resort which is smart and upmarket and has managed to avoid tourist tackiness; maybe the law banning 'promiscuity and looseness' has helped. Glitzy harbourside cafés have been set up to deal with the hordes and money of wealthy tourists disgorged by the cruise ships. One of the first things you'll see in Skála is a statue of Protergatis Xanthos Emmanuel, who led an uprising against the Turks in 1821. Skála didn't even exist until that year, so fearsome were the pirate raids. Near the beach, marked by a red buoy, is a reminder of another local menace, the evil magician Yenoupas, who at the urging of priests from the temple of Apollo challenged St John to a duel of miracles. Yenoupas' miracle was to dive into the sea and bring back effigies of the dead; John's was to ask God to petrify the submerged magician, which abruptly ended the contest.

Behind Skála you can visit what was once one of the world's largest desalination plants. The island now has a reservoir but water can still be short in high summer. You can also hike up to the site of the ancient city, **Kastélli**, in about 20 minutes give or take the heat, a walk rewarded more by stunning views than any archaeological excavations. There is the remains of a Hellenistic wall and the little chapel of **Ag. Konstantínos** perched on the summit. Go in the evening for a wonderful sunset.

From Skála you can see whitewashed **Chóra** (ΧΟΡΑ) clinging to the mighty castle walls of the monastery. Buses and taxis make the ascent in a few minutes, but if you have the time it isn't too strenuous to walk up the old cobbled path from Skála, to enjoy the ever-widening panorama spread out below. The beginning of the path is quite difficult to find, so ask at the tourist office. Chóra is a lovely, almost Cycladic village, with a maze of narrow alleyways, masses of chapels and numerous mansions built during the wealthy days of Pátmos' great merchant fleet. The approach to the monastery is very tourist-trappy, with cafés and gift shops all geared to the influx of organized groups rather than independent travellers. If you want to go it alone but you're on a day trip, beware: the monastery doors could be firmly shut by the time you get there so if time is tight take transport up and walk down.

## Monastery of St John the Theologian

*Opening times vary, usually Mon, Tues, Thur, Sun 8–2 and 4–6; Wed and Sat 8–2 only. Shorts prohibited, women must wear skirts. Adm free, Treasury Museum adm.*

If it's your first visit to Pátmos, make a beeline for the magnificent monastery hidden behind those forbidding walls. At the entrance you can pick up the guide in English by S. A. Papadópoulos, with a good history and description of the frescoes and works of art, although the details on the back of the map published by the monastery itself are as good and cheaper. Inside the massive walls (restored after the earthquake of 1956), the charming entrance court of 1698 incorporates the outer, or exo-narthex of the church. Just before the narthex itself is the chapel and tomb of its founder, the Blessed Christódoulos.

The church is in the form of a Greek cross set in a square, and still retains its original marble floor; its icon of St John was a present to the monastery from Alexis Comnenus. Frescoes cover almost all surfaces, although only those in the 12th-century **Chapel of the Theotókos** are as old as the church. Other 12th-century frescoes are in the Refectory, off the inner courtyard.

The **Treasury Museum** contains the priceless 6th-century *Codex Prophyrius*, St Mark's gospel written on purple vellum; the monastery foundation deed—a golden bull, signed and sealed, from Emperor Alexis Comnenus; remains of the temple of Artemis on which the monastery was built (a temple said to have been founded by Orestes, in gratitude for being rid of the Furies); gold and silver crosses, croziers and stoles; superb icons, and ship pendants made of diamonds and emeralds donated by Catherine the Great. The library contains hundreds of rare codices and manuscripts, but may only be visited with permission from the abbot. Lastly, if it's open, climb up to the roof terrace for a commanding view over the Aegean.

## Around Chóra

After the monastery, you could spend a day finding the 40 or so churches wedged in the narrow lanes of Chóra: especially good are the **Convent of Zoodóchos Pigí** (1607) with fine frescoes and icons (*open mornings and late afternoons*) and 11th-century **Ag. Dimítrios**, contemporary with the monastery, but likely to be locked like many of the others. Nor is hunting out the caretaker particularly easy, as Chóra is one of those very old, silent places where the streets always seem to be deserted, especially when the trippers have gone.

This changes dramatically on Orthodox Maundy Thursday, when Chóra is packed with visitors and even TV crews for the *Niptíras* ceremony, when the abbot re-enacts Christ's washing of his disciples' feet—a rite once performed by the proud emperors of Byzantium. Depending on the weather, it takes place either in Plateía Ag. Leviás or Plateía Lóza. It's a short walk down from Chóra to the **Monastery of the Apocalypse** (*open Mon, Wed, Fri, 8–2 and 4–6; Tues, Thurs, Sat, Sun, 8am–2pm*), where a stair covered with pots of flowers leads down to the cave where St John lived and dreamed and dictated what he saw to his follower, Próchoros. The cave itself has been converted into a church, where you can see the rock where the good saint rested his head and hand (though he must have been something of a contortionist to manage it), and the massive overhanging roof, split in three sections by the voice of God, symbolizing the Holy Trinity. If you're walking up from Skála, better for the soul, the cave is marked with signs saying ΑΠΟΚΑΛΥΠΣΟΣ. Again, be sure to get there on time or the monks won't let you in.

## Beaches and Villages around Pátmos

Caiques from Skála run most days from in front of the Arion Café to the island's many lovely beaches: to the south **Psilí Ámmos**, with fine white sand, is the unofficial nudist beach, an hour away by boat; to the north, **Lámbi**, also reached by excursion boat or a 9km hike from town, is famous for its subtle, multi-coloured pebble beach. **Méloi** is a pleasant tree-shaded beach 2km from town and tends to get crowded; Pátmos' main beach resort, **Gríkou** (ΓΡΙΚΟΥ), overlooks a beautiful bay and has windsurfers and water skis for hire. Halfway between Skála and Kámbos, look for the sign to **Agriolivádi**, a quiet, if rocky cove. Pátmos has great walking country with plenty of footpaths. From shingly **Kámbou Beach** you can walk east to secluded **Vagiá** and **Livádi Yerannoú**. Other beaches in the region are often completely deserted, such as the one at **Sapsila**.

Inland, in fertile **Sykamiá** is an old Roman bath said to have been used by St John to baptize his converts. In **Stávros**, a tiny village at the southern end of the island, the **Kalikátsou rock** has carved rooms in rather unlikely places and may have been the 11th-century hermitage mentioned in the writings of Christódoulos. These days campers sometimes take advantage of the shelter. West from here, a grotto on **Cape Yenoúpas** was said to be the home of the evil magician (*see* above), and even today it's unpleasantly hot and smelly inside.

Heading north, **Kámbos** lies in the centre of the island's main agricultural valley and has a popular sandy beach. Further along are more wild and windswept shores for daring swimmers at **Léfkes**. Many long-term residents rent houses in the fertile valley, where a hippy commune thrived back in the seventies before being evicted by the anti-promiscuity squads. Even more remote is the 19th-century **Hermitage of Apollon**, near a small mineral spring (ask for directions in Kámbos).

---

*Pátmos* © *(0247–)*                            ***Where to Stay and Eating Out***

### Skála

Owners meet the ferries offering *domátia*, and on the whole the private rooms are very comfortable and better value than the hotels. **Hotel Hellinis**, © 31 275 (*C; mod*) has nice en suite rooms right on the waterfront with views of the monastery; the **Skala**, © 31 343 (*B; mod*) is set in attractive gardens with a pool just two minutes from the  ferry. The **Blue Bay Hotel**, © 31 165 (*C; mod*) is in a quiet waterside spot on the road to Gríkou. **Summer**, © 31 769 (*C; mod*) and **Maria**, © 31 201 (*B pension; inexp*) are both good choices in the Chokhlaká district overlooking the opposite bay. **Galini**, © 31 240 (*C; mod*) is also a good bet behind the **Hotel Rex**, © 31 242 (*D; inexp*), a bit of a last resort. The **Hotel Efi**, at Kastélli, © 32 500 (*B pension; inexp*) is comfortable. On the edge of Skála, the **Byzance**, © 31 052 (*B pension; inexp*) has a roof garden with a small restaurant and lovely views over the port. **Kasteli**, © 31 361/665 (*B pension; inexp*) commands fine views from the upper part of town; the friendly **Australis**, © 31 576 (*inexp*) is beautifully decorated and costs slightly less.

**Taverna O Vrakhos**, north of the waterfront, is good for fish; **Grigoris** opposite the ferry dock is tasty, cheap and cheerful with excellent charcoal-grilled fish and meat. There are numerous cafés for snacks like the **Yachting Centre**. If you have a sweet tooth the **Zacharoplasteio Koumanis** is famous for delectable pastries. Everyone hangs out at the **Arion café** and cocktail bar on the waterfront to watch the world go by. It's the place for an aperitif or a nightcap.

### Chóra

No hotels here, but the municipal tourist office (© 31 666) has a list of 200 rooms to rent. **Vangelis** and **Olympia** in Plateía Ag. Leviás (follow the little signs), both have reasonably priced solid Greek fare. Portions have shrunk a bit at Vangelis but you have the bonus of sitting in the beautiful square where Saturday nights sometimes see some inspired dancing. The **Patmian House**, an old mansion converted into a luxury restaurant, is a wonderful setting for a romantic dinner. *Open evenings only*. The **Galaxy** pizzeria and cafeteria near the bus stop is fine for a snack and for slowly drinking in the fantastic view.

### Gríkou

The **Panorama Apartments**, © 31 209 (*C; inexp*) are old favourites by the sea; the **Joanna Hotel and Apartments**, © 31 031, 🖂 32 031, book in Athens © 981 2246 (*mod*) is a new, nicely done complex with self-catering studios and apartments; the **Golden Sun Hotel**, © 32 318, @ 32 319 (*B; mod*), overlooking the bay, is family-run and friendly. The small, family-run **Flisvos** up on the hill has well-cooked Greek staples and fish at affordable prices and, in the middle of the beach, **Stamatis** serves much of the same.

## Kámbos

The new **Patmos Paradise**, © 32 624, @ 32 740 (*B; exp*) is a club-style development with an *à la carte* restaurant, American buffet breakfast, swimming pool, squash, tennis courts and fitness centre. There are also rooms.

## Méloi

**Patmos Flowers/Camping Stephanos** is an excellent campsite, © 31 821, with bamboo-shaded pitches, mini-market, cafeteria, cooking and washing facilities. *Open May 15–Oct 5*. **Rooms and Taverna Méloi**, known to all as Stefanos, © 31 888, is almost on the beach; basic facilities, but serving good, reasonably-priced food; there are also unnamed rooms, © 32 382.

### Entertainment and Nightlife

Despite its divine reputation Pátmos has a sophisticated nightlife centred on the ritzy waterside café society of Skála and the stylish music bars springing up in Chóra, all with a chic Athenian touch. **The Arion** is still the favourite pavement café haunt; the **Almira Bar** is a slick cocktail hang-out with interesting wooden décor. It's cool at the **Rock Café** and you can dance all night at the **Koncolato Music Club**; the **Palmosa Music Club** has sounds until 3am and you can also bop into the early hours at the **Kenepsis Disco Bar** below the **Hotel Chris**. In **Chóra** there are some very tasteful bars in the old mansions like **Kafé 1673**, a classic bar in a lovely 300-year-old building; **Stoa** on the Central Square is another trendy bar/cafeteria with a vaulted stone interior; and near the windmills the **Osianos Music Club** is a happening place. For live Greek music and dance the **Dilina** at Gríkou is the place and in Chóra **Aloni** also has traditional bouzouki.

## Agathónissi (ΑΓΑΘΟΝΗΣΙ)

Little Agathónissi off Pátmos is the most remote and northerly of the Dodecanese, connected only a few times a week with the outside world, as are sister islets Arkí and Maráthi. Fresh water and supplies are shipped in from Sámos. Inhabited by only a few fishing families, the islets may be the ticket if you want to escape, even if they are now on the hydrofoil route and the day-trip programmes from Pátmos, Léros and Lipsí. Agathónissi, literally 'thorny island', is covered with thorn bushes and has three villages, the port of **Ag. Giórgios**, **Megálo Chorió**, where most people live, and **Mikró Chorió**, with only about ten inhabitants. A cement road runs from the port to the villages less than a kilometre away and a rickety three-wheeler or maybe a van the only means of transport. Ag. Giórgios has a pebbly, grotty beach but there's a better one at **Spília**, a sheltered cove to the west. There are boat trips in high season to remote beaches, otherwise you walk. Stout shoes are a must off the beaten track because of the vicious thorns. There are remains of a medieval granary at **Thóli**, otherwise little else. It's worth taking the walk, about 90 minutes, to **Chokhlakas**, or to the deserted fishing village of

**Kathóliko** either via the **Mikró Chorió** road or over the old goat paths in the hills, with great views of Sámos and Turkey. There's a small beach, so you can take the plunge on arrival.

### Getting There

**By boat:** The **ferry** *Níssos Kálymnos* links Agathónissi with Sámos (Pithagório), Pátmos, Lipsí, Léros, Kálymnos, and Kos, twice a week; the *Chióni* also runs once a week to Arkí, Lipsí, Pátmos then Sámos and Chíos later in the day. **Hydrofoil:** the *Ilio* service once a week to Kos, Kálymnos, Léros (Ag Marína), Pátmos, and Sámos (Pythagório). Local **caiques** run to Arkí and Maráthi, and there are **excursion boats** from Pátmos, Lipsí and Léros. **Port authority,** ✆ 23 770.

### Tourist Information

The island's solitary policeman, ✆ (0274) 23 770, is also the tourist police and port authority presence. He has a few soldiers for company at his office-cum-barracks on the road to Megálo Chorió.

*Agathónissi* ✆ *(0274–)*                                                 ### Where to Stay

There are three possibilities in Ag. Giórgios: **Maria Kamitsi,** ✆ 23 690, has a nice pension set in a flower-filled garden set back from the waterfront. There are rooms over **George's Taverna** ✆ 24 385; otherwise try **Theologia Yiameou's Rooms** ✆ 23 692. In Megálo Chorió there's **Katsoulieris Pension** ✆ 24 385.

*Agathónissi* ✆ *(0274–)*            ### Eating Out

In Ag. Giórgios there are **George's Taverna** with excellent food and modest prices; **To Limanaki**, which doubles as a shop and is more expensive, and a fish taverna between the two, sometimes closed. Megálo Chorió has **Taverna I Eirini**, which is also good and cheap, and a village *kafeneíon*.

### Entertainment and Nightlife

Apart from jolly taverna nights with back-packers and yachties and the usual *panegýria* you have to make your own.

## Arkí (APKOI) and Maráthi (MAPAΘI)

Occasional caiques run from Pátmos, Lipsí and Leros to **Arkí**, a hilly little island just 4km long and 1km wide with fifty inhabitants. There's a solar plant supplying electricity but the water is shipped in. The harbour of **Port Augusta** has two tavernas and the Taverna Asteria also has inexpensive rooms, ✆ (0247) 32 371. Arkí attracts yachts and adventurous travellers. It has a metred phone but no other facilities, so take enough money with you. There are some quiet coves and a **Blue Lagoon**, if not a rival to Capri's, just as good for snorkelling and swimming in the vivid waters.

Even smaller **Maráthi** has a natural harbour popular with fishermen from surounding islands as well as yachts, but no ferry calls in; excursion boats from Lipsí and Pátmos provide most of the transport and can strand you if the weather turns, so don't wait till the last moment if you have to catch a flight. There's no phone, just a ship-to-shore radio. Maráthi has a long sandy beach and two tavernas with rooms **Pantelis Marathi Restaurant**, run by Mr Pantelís from Arkí via Australia, who bases himself plus family on Maráthi for the summer, and the **Other Place**. The first has comfortable, very reasonable rooms and serves up tasty dishes. The second is a bit more basic, with its own strange charm, owing to a Golgotha of goat skulls used for decoration in the trees. Goats leap all over the island and they're often on the menu as well.

# Rhodes/Ródos (ΡΟΔΟΣ)

Rhodes, 'more beautiful than the sun' according to the ancient Greeks, is the largest and most fertile of the Dodecanese, ringed by sandy beaches, bedecked with flowers, blessed with some 300 days of sun a year, dotted with handsome towns and villages full of monuments evoking a long, colourful history—in a nutshell, all that it takes to sit securely throned as the reigning queen of tourism in Greece. As a year-round resort for cold northerners and top international package destination (in increasingly swanky, fancy pants packages) it's not quite fair to compare it with Greece's other islands. Rhodes is a holiday Babylon, Europe's answer to Florida, a glittering, sun-drenched chill pill in the sea where people shed their inhibitions with their woollens and don't feel at all stupid walking around with 'No Problem!' and 'Relax' emblazoned on their bosoms.

When and if you get fed up with the hordes, head for the south half of the island, beyond Líndos and Péfkos where there are still plenty of quiet beaches, and perhaps even lingering hints of the very different island summoned from Lawrence Durrell's imagination in his *Reflections on a Marine Venus*: 'Ahead of us the night gathers, a different night, and Rhodes begins to fall into the unresponding sea from which only memory can rescue it. The clouds hang high over Anatolia. Other islands? Other futures? Not, I think, after one has lived with the Marine Venus. The wound she gives one must carry to the world's end.'

## Mythology

Rhodes is the subject of a messy number of very ancient and very often contradictory traditions. According to one, the first inhabitants of Rhodes were the Children of the Sea, the nine dog-headed enchantresses called Telchines, who had flippers for hands. In spite of this apparent handicap, they made the sickle that Cronos used to castrate Uranus; they carved the first statues of the gods, and founded Kámiros, Ialysós and Líndos before moving to Crete. There Rhea, the great mother goddess of the earth, made them the nurses of her son Poseidon, and they forged the sea god's trident.

Poseidon fell in love with the Telchines' sister, Alia, and had six sons and a daughter by her. The daughter, the nymph Rhodos, became the sole heiress of the island when Zeus decided to destroy the Telchines for meddling with the weather (they were fond of magical mists), although their real crimes was belonging to a pre-Olympian matriarchal religion. He flooded Rhodes, although the Telchines managed to escape in various forms, most notoriously as the hounds of Artemis, who tore Actaeon to bits.

The same cast of characters are on stage in another version, although this time the Telchines change sex and shed their dog heads and flippers. The sons of Pontos and

Thalassa (the sea), they were artisans, magicians and ministers of Zeus, although they had a sister, Alia, who was loved by Poseidon and gave birth to Rhodos and a number of sons. When these sons refused to let Aphrodite dock as she sailed between her islands of Kýthera and Cyprus, the goddess of love put a curse of incestuous passion on them and they raped their mother Alia. In despair Alia flung herself into the sea and became 'Lefkothea' (the White Goddess). The wicked sons hid in the bowels of the earth and became demons as Poseidon, in his wrath flooded Rhodes (the Telchines, tipped off by Artemis, escaped before the deluge).

The sun god Helios later fell in love with Rhodos, evaporated the stagnant waters with his hot rays and married the nymph. They had a daughter and seven sons, known as the Heliades. Athena gave them wisdom and taught them nautical and astrophysical lore. But the wisest of the Heliades, Tenagis, was killed in a jealous fit by four of the brothers, who fled to Lésbos, Kos, Ikaría and Egypt. The two innocent brothers, Ohimos and Kerkafos, remained and founded the city of Achaia; Ohimos' daughter Kydippi, a priestess of Hera, married her uncle Kerkafos and had three sons, Lindos, Kamiros and Ialysos, who founded the three city-states that bear their names.

The later, Olympian version of the story relates that while the gods were dividing up the world's real estate among themselves, Zeus realized that he had forgotten to set aside a portion for Helios. Dismayed, Zeus asked Helios what he could do to make up for his omission. The sun god replied that he knew of an island just emerging from the sea off the coast of Asia Minor which would suit him admirably. Helios married Rhodos and their seven sons, famous astronomers, ruled the island. One of the sons, or perhaps Tlepolemos (who led the ships of Rhodes to Troy), refounded the ancient Telchine towns.

Kámiros even has another possible founder; Althaemenes, son of the Cretan King Katreus and grandson of Minos. When an oracle predicted that Katreus would be slain by one of his offspring, Althaemenes went to Rhodes, where he founded Kámiros and built an altar of Zeus, surrounding it with magical metal bulls that would bellow if the island were invaded. Oracles, however, are not often wrong, and in later life Katreus sailed to Rhodes to visit his son, whom he missed dearly. He arrived at night, and what with the darkness and the bellowing of the metal bulls, Althaemenes failed to recognize his father and fellow Cretans and slew them, thinking that they were invaders. When he realized his error in the morning he piteously begged Mother Earth to swallow him up, which she did.

## History

Inhabited since Paleolithic times, Rhodes was colonized by the Minoans, who built shrines to the moon at Filérimos, Líndos and Kámiros. The Achaeans took the island in the 15th century BC and founded the town of Achaia. Before settling on Rhodes for its name, the island was often known as Telchinia for its clever if shadowy Telchines of myth, or Ophioussa, for its numerous vipers; even today villagers wear snake-repelling goatskin boots when working out in the fields. The Aechaeans were supplanted, perhaps in the 12th century BC, by the Dorians, whose three cities—Líndos, Ialysós and Kámiros—long dominated the island's affairs. According to Homer, they sent nine ships to Troy, led by Tlepolemos, son of Heracles, who met an unhappy end before the Trojan walls. Rhodes' position along the main Mediterranean trade routes led to its early importance both in trade and naval power. Around 1000 BC, in response to the first Ionian confederacy, the three cities joined a Doric Hexapolis along with Kos, Cnidos and Halicarnassus, a prototype EU that united the six city-states politically, religiously and economically. For four centuries the Doric Hexapolis prospered, establishing trade colonies from Naples to the Costa Brava in Spain.

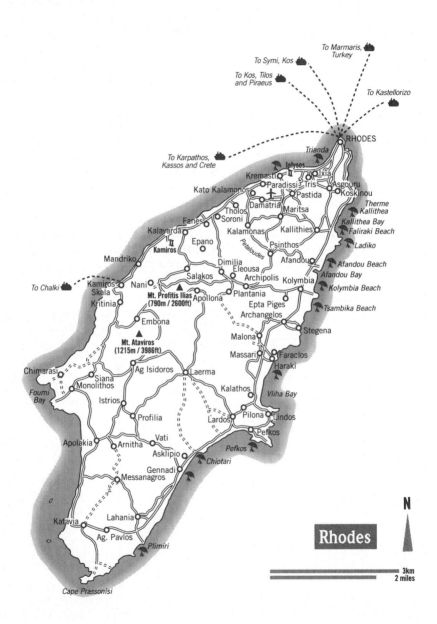

# The Founding of Rhodes City, and its Colossus

Rhodes sided with the Persians in both of their major campaigns against Greece, but upon their defeat quickly switched sides and joined the Delian confederacy. In 480 BC, in order to prevent rivalries and increase their wealth and strength, Líndos, Ialysós and Kámiros united to found one central capital, Rhodes, or Ródos, 'the rose'. Hippodamos of Miletus, the geometrician, designed the new town on a grid plan similar to the one he provided for Piraeus, and the result was considered one of the most beautiful cities of ancient times. It was huge, its walls encompassing a much greater area than that enclosed by the existing medieval walls. Celebrated schools of philosophy, philology and oratory were founded, and the port had facilities far in advance of its time. Although Líndos, Kámiros and Ialysós continued to exist, they lost all their importance and most of their populations to the mighty new city they had created.

During the Peloponnesian War, Rhodes adroitly sided with whichever power was on top at any given time—an expedient front runner policy that kept trouble far away—and later hitched on to the rising star of Alexander the Great. He in turn lent his support to Rhodes and its commerce, enabling the island to surpass politically hostile Athens; thanks to Alexander, Rhodes dominated Mediterranean trade, its navy ruled the waves and policed the seas, and it founded colonies all over the known world. Rhodes' trade and navigation laws were later adopted by the Romans and remain the basis of maritime trade today.

Egypt was one of Rhodes' most lucrative trading partners, and in the struggles between the Macedonian generals after Alexander's death, Rhodes allied itself with Ptolemy, who had taken Egypt as his spoils. When another of Alexander's generals, the powerful Antigonas, ordered Rhodes to join him against Ptolemy, the Rhodians refused. Furious, Antigonas sent his son Dimitrios Poliorketes (the Besieger), the army of Syria and the Phoenician fleet to besiege the uppity islanders.

The ensuing year-long siege by one of the greatest generals of all time against the greatest city of the day has gone down in history, not only as a contest of strength and endurance, but as a battle of wits. Over and over again Dimitrios would invent some new ingenious machine, such as the ten-storey Helepolis siege tower, only to have it ingeniously foiled by the Rhodian defenders (who tripped up the Helepolis with a hidden, shallow ditch). After a year both sides grew weary of fighting and made a truce, Rhodes agreeing to assist militarily Dimitrios' father Antigonas except in battles against Ptolemy.

So Dimitrios departed, leaving his vast siege machinery behind. This the Rhodians either sold or melted down to construct a great bronze statue of Helios, their patron god of the sun. The famous sculptor from Líndos, Chares, was put in charge of the project, and in 290 BC, after twelve years of work and a cost of 20,000 pounds of silver, Chares completed the Colossus. Standing somewhere between 30 and 40m tall (at her crown the Statue of Liberty is 34m), the Colossus did not straddle the entrance of Rhodes harbour, as is popularly believed, but probably stood near the present Castle of the Knights, gleaming bright in the sun, one of the Seven Wonders of the Ancient World. But of all the Wonders the Colossus had the shortest lifespan; in 225 BC, an earthquake brought it crashing to the ground. It lay forlorn until AD 653 when the Saracens, who had captured Rhodes, sold it as scrap to a merchant from Edessa. According to legend, it took 900 camels to transport the bronze to the ships.

In 164 BC, when they had repaired their city and walls, the Rhodians signed a peace treaty with Rome. Alexandria was their only rival in wealth, and tiny Delos, with all its duty free trade concessions, their only rival in Mediterranean trade. The famous School of Rhetoric on Rhodes attracted all the top Romans of the day—Pompey, Cicero, Cassius, Julius Caesar Brutus, Cato the Younger and Mark Antony. However, entanglement in Roman politics brought Rhodes trouble as well as privileges. When Rhodes backed Augustus after the death of Caesar, Cassius sacked the island city, destroyed or captured its fleet, and sent many of its treasures to Rome. It was a blow from which Rhodes never recovered; she lost control of her colonies and islands, and other Roman allies muscled in on her booming trade. In the first century St Paul preached on the island and converted many of the inhabitants; by the end of the Roman empire, Rhodes was a sleepy backwater.

## Two Hundred Years of Knights

Byzantium brought many invaders and adventurers to Rhodes: Saracens, Genoese, Venetians and the Crusaders all passed through, including in 1191 Richard the Lionheart and Philip Augustus of France, who came in search of mercenaries to fight in the Holy Land. After the fall of Jerusalem in 1291, the Knights Hospitallers of St John (a noble Order dedicated to protecting pilgrims and running hospitals in the Holy Land) took refuge on Cyprus, but by 1306 they had become interested in the wealthier and better positioned Rhodes. They asked the Emperor Andronicus Palaeologus to cede them the island in return for their loyalty, but after 1204 the rulers of Byzantium had learned better than to trust the Franks. The Knights, under Grand Master Foulques de Villaret, then took the matter into their own hands. Although they purchased the Dodecanese from the Genoese pirates who controlled them, it was a prize the Knights had to fight for; they had to spend their first three years subduing the Rhodians themselves.

By 1309, with the help of the Pope, the Knights were secure in their possession and began to build their hospital and inns in Rhodes town. They built eight inns or auberges in all, one for each of the 'tongues', or nationalities, in the Order (England, France, Germany, Italy, Castile, Aragon, Auvergne and Provence). Each tongue had a bailiff, and the eight bailiffs elected the Grand Master, who lived in a special palace. There were never more than 650 men in the Order, and although as always dedicated to care for pilgrims (their hospital still exists), their focus shifted to their role as the front-line defenders of Christendom and piratical freebooting at the expense of the infidels. Already wealthy to begin with, they were given a tremendous boost in 1312, when Pope Clement and Philip the Fair of France dissolved the fabulously wealthy Knights Templars and gave the Hospitallers a hefty share of the loot.

With their new fortune, the Knights of St John replaced the outdated Byzantine fortifications—and continued to replace them up until the 16th century, hiring the best Italian fortification engineers, who perfected one of the most splendid defences of the day. The knights became such a thorn in the side of Muslim shipping that they were besieged by the Sultan of Egypt in 1444 and by Mohammed II the Conqueror in 1480, both times without success. Then in 1522 Suleiman the Magnificent moved in with 100,000 troops; the Rhodians bitterly joked that the Colossus was now coming back at them, in the form of cannon balls. After a frustrating six-month siege, Suleiman was on the point of abandoning Rhodes when a traitor informed him that of the original 650 Knights, supplemented by 250 Genoese and Venetians and a thousand Greeks, only 180 survived, and they were on their last legs. The Sultan redoubled his efforts and the Knights at last were forced to surrender. They were permitted to leave in safety, with their Christian retainers and possessions, and set up a new headquarters in Malta—at the nominal rent of a falcon a year—where in 1565 they successfully withstood a tremendous all-out assault by the Ottoman fleet. After gradually losing their reason for being on Malta, they caved into Napoleon. In 1831 the Knights re-formed as a benevolent charity in Rome, from where they fund hospitals to this day.

## Ottomans and Italians

The Turks were very fond of Rhodes, but for the Greeks their rule brought 400 years of cultural darkness. When the Rhodians attempted to revolt during the War of Independence, the Turks reacted by slaughtering a quarter of the population; their popularity dropped even more in the Great Gunpowder Explosion of 1856, when lightning struck a minaret and exploded a Turkish powder magazine, blowing much of the Old Town to bits. The Italians, who took over Rhodes by treaty in 1912, brought material prosperity but spiritual tyranny. They claimed that the island was their inheritance from the Knights of St John (although only an eighth of the knights had been Italian) and Mussolini even had the Palace of the Grand Masters reconstructed to swan around in. During the Second World War Rhodes remained in the hands of a German garrison until May 1945. By then most of the island's Jewish community, originally 2000 strong, had been sent off to the concentration camps. Rhodes, with the rest of the Dodecanese, officially joined Greece in 1945, whereupon the government declared it a free port, boosting its already great tourist potential.

---

### Getting There and Around

**By air**: Rhodes airport, the third busiest in Greece, ✆ (0241) 91 771/92 839, is being enlarged. There are numerous UK, German and Scandinavian direct charters from April to mid October and nearly a million charter arrivals during the season. Domestic flights from Olympic (Iérou Lóchou 9, ✆ 24 571 and South East European Airways. In summer there are at least 4 daily flights to Athens, and frequent connections with Thessaloníki, Crete (Herákleon); Kárpathos, Kos, Kastellórizo, Kássos, Mýkonos, Santoríni and Rome.

**By sea**: international **ferries** from the **Commercial Harbour** 3 times a week to Limassol, Cyprus, Haifa, Israel and Bodrum, Turkey; daily ferry to Piraeus, Pátmos, Léros, Kálymnos, Kos and Sými, twice a week to Kastellórizo; once a week taking in Tílos, Níssyros, Kos, Kálymnos, Astypálaia, Mýkonos, Tínos, Ándros and Rafína; once a week to Pireaus via Chálki, Kárpathos (Pigádia and Diafáni), Kássos, Crete (Sitía and Ag. Nikólaos), Santoríni, Síkinos, Folégandros, Mílos, Sífnos, Kíthnos; twice a week to Páros and Náxos via Kárpathos and Crete; once a week to Samos (Vathí), Chíos, Lésbos, Límnos, Kavála. Daily **excursion boats** and *Sými I* and *Sými II* ferries from **Mandráki Harbour** to Líndos and beaches at Lárdos, Tsambíka, Faliráki, Kallithéa, Ladiko, Kolymbia; Sými, and Marmaris, Turkey. **Hydrofoil**: there are two services, *Ilio* and *Hermes*, with varying timetables. Daily to Kos, Pátmos and Sými, also connections to Léros, Tílos, Níssyros, Kálymnos and Chálki. **Port authority**, ✆ 27 365.

**By road**: there is a frequent **bus service** serving east and west coasts, departing from the Market in the New Town, and taxis are plentiful and reasonably priced. The central **taxi rank** is in Mandráki Harbour, ✆ 27 666. **Radio taxis** run 24hrs and come a bit more expensive, ✆ 64 712/758. Although there are plenty of **coach excursions** on offer, it's worth hiring wheels to get off the beaten track, especially in the interior; nearly anything from four-wheel-drive beach buggies to motorbikes are available but none comes cheap.

The Greek National Tourist Organisation (EOT) office on the corner of Papágon and Makaríou Street, ✆ (0241) 23 255/655, has very helpful multilingual staff and a wide range of maps, leaflets and information (open Mon–Fri, 8–2); City of Rhodes Tourist Information Centre, Sound and Light Square, ✆ (0241) 35 945 (open Mon–Fri, 9–6, Sat 9–12noon, closed Sun) also has an accommodation service, advice on excursions, ravel, plus money exchange. Both have copies of the free English-language newspaper, *Ródos News*, also available at the airport and hotels. It's a mine of information and has a very useful restaurant guide.

**Airport Flight Information Desk:** ✆ (0241) 91 771 or 93 838.

**Tourist police**: Museum Square, Old Town, opposite Archaeological Museum ✆ (0241) 27 423. For general information and complaints.

**British consulate:** 111 Amerikís, Mr and Mrs Dimitriádis, ✆ (0241) 27 306/27 247.

**Líndos information office:** Líndos, ✆ (0244) 31 227.

## Festivals

Lenten carnival **just before Easter**; **14 June**, Profítis Amós at Faliráki; Scandinavian midsummer festivities in Rhodes town, organized by tour operators (yes, really); **28 June** at Líndos; **29–30 July**, Ag. Soúla at Soroní, with donkey races; **26 July**, Ag. Panteleímonos at Siána; In **August**, dance festivals at Kallithiés, Maritsa and Embónas; **14–22 August**, Tis Panagías at Kremastí; **26 August**, Ag. Fanoúrious in the Old Town; **5 September**, Ag. Trías near Rhodes Town; **7 September**, at Monastery Tsambíkas, when barren women go to pray for fertility; **13 September**, Stávros at Apóllona and Kallithiés; **26 September**, Ag. Ioánnis Theológos at Artamíti; **18 October**, Ag. Lukás at Afándou; **7 November** at Archángelos.

# Rhodes Town

Spread across the northern tip of the island, Rhodes (ΡΟΔΟΣ) (pop. 39,000) is the largest town and capital of the Dodecanese. It divides neatly into the Old Town and the New and in both tourism reigns. The medieval city is so remarkably preserved it looks like a film set in places, and has often been used as such (most recently in *Pascali's Island*). The new town is all brash neon signs, wall-to-wall bars and all the commercial trappings of a package holiday paradise, especially packaged young Scandinavians to the extent that there's even a special post box for Sweden at the central Post Office.

Rhodes presents an opulent face to the sea, and sailing in is much the prettiest way to arrive. The massive walls of the old town and the **Castle of the Knights** rise out of a lush subtropical garden; graceful minarets and the arcaded waterfront market, bright with strings of lightbulbs at night, add an exotic, Eastern touch. Monumental Italian public buildings loom to one side, trying to look serious, while opposite three windmills turn lazily behind a forest of masts. Yachts, smaller ferries and excursion boats dock at the smallest of three harbours, **Mandráki**,

(MANΔPAKI) guarded by the old fort of **Ag. Nikólaos**, with its small church and a bronze stag and doe, said to mark the spot where the Colossus once stood. On larger ferry and cruise ships you'll enter the **commercial harbour** (ΕΜΠΟΡΙΚΟΣ ΛΙΜΕΝΑΣ) nearer the Old Town walls.

These **walls** are a masterpiece of late medieval fortifications, and, although you'll often be tempted to climb up for a walk or view, access is by guided tour only (*open Tues and Sat at 2.45*). Constructed on the foundation of the old Byzantine walls under four of the most ambitious Grand Masters, d'Aubusson, d'Amboise, del Carretto and Villiers de l'Isle Adam, they stretch 4km and average 12m thick. They are curved the better to deflect missiles, and the landward sides were safeguarded by a 30m-wide moat. Each national group of Knights was assigned its own bastion and towers to defend. Of the many gates that linked the walled Old Town with the village outside, the most magnificent is the **Gate of Emery d'Amboise** near the Palace of the Grand Masters, built in 1512. The Turks blocked up the two harbour gates; they also made a law that all Greeks had to be outside the inner walls by sundown or forfeit their heads. Near the **Amboise Gate** the old clocktower, **To Roloi**, has been restored with a fashionable, expensive bar with an art gallery beneath.

## The Old Town (ΠΑΛΑΙΑ ΠΟΛΗ)

The town within these walls was called the **Collachium**, where the Knights could retreat if the outer wall were taken. Most of their buildings are here, beginning with the **Palace of the Grand Masters** (*open Tues–Sat, 8.30–3, closed Mon; adm*). Construction of this citadel, on the site of a sanctuary of Helios, was completed in the 14th century. It survived intact under the Turks, who used it as a prison until it was blown up accidentally in the Great Gunpowder Explosion of 1856. Mussolini, fancying himself a Grand Master, ordered that it be reconstructed as his summer villa. The Italians filled it with lovely Roman mosaics and Hellenistic sculptures from Kos, a hotch-potch of Renaissance furniture, and installed a lift and modern plumbing, but the war broke out and ended before Il Duce could really enjoy it. On the ground floor, the **Mediaeval Rhodes Exhibition** (*open 8–2.30*) offers an overview of the island's trade and economy under the Byzantines, Genoese and the Knights, along with a collection of detached frescoes and the tombstone of the Grand Master Villiers de l'Isle Adam. In the garden below the palace, a **Son et Lumière** show is held most evenings.

Quiet, evocative, cobblestoned Ippotón Street ('of the Knights') has been carefully spared from souvenir-shop tackiness. It leads down from the palace into the centre of the Collachium, passing first the arcaded **Loggia** where the Knights would muster, then several of their inns: the **Inn of Provence** on the left and the two buildings of the **Inn of Spain** on the right, then the French chapel and elaborate **Inn of France** (1509), adorned with escutcheons and crocodile gargoyles; as there were always more French knights than any other 'tongue', their inn was the most spacious. Opposite is the handsome Catalan **House of Villaragut**; further down, the **Inn of Italy** (1519), and at the end of the street the 13th-century **St Mary**, a Byzantine church used by the Knights as their cathedral until they built their own—another victim of the Gunpowder débâcle. St Mary's is now used as a little **Byzantine Museum**. To the right, at the end of Ippotón Street, the **Inn of England** (1483)

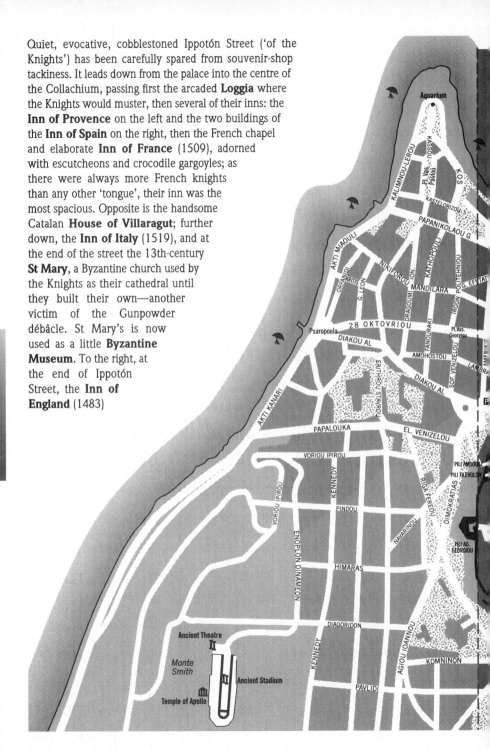

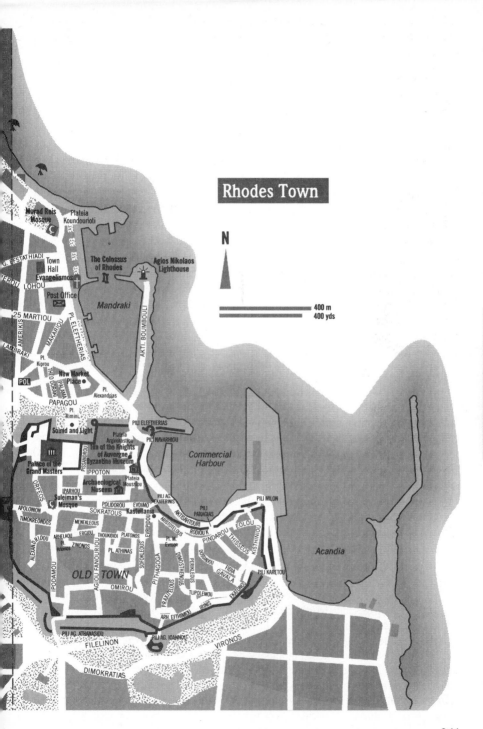

# Rhodes Town

**N**

400 m
400 yds

Murad Reis Mosque
Plateia Koundourioti
G. EFSTATHIADI
Town Hall
Evangelismos
FEROU LOHOU
Post Office
The Colossus of Rhodes
Agios Nikolaos Lighthouse
Mandraki
25 MARTIOU
AMERIKIS
PL. ELEFTHERIAS
MAKARIOU
LAMBRAKI
PL. Kiprou
THEODORAKI
POL
PALMA
New Market Place
PAPAGOU
Pl. Alexandias
AKTI. BOUMBOULI
Pl. Rimini
Sound and Light
Plateia Argirokastrou
Ira of the Knights of Auvergne
Byzantine Museum
PISSANDROU
PILI ELEFTHERIAS
PILI NAVARHOU
Commercial Harbour
Palace of the Grand Masters
IPPOTON
ORFEOS
Archaeological Museum
Plateia Moussiou
IPARHOU
Suleiman's Mosque
POLIDOROU
EVDIMO
SOKRATOUS
Kastellania
PILI AG. EKATERINIS
PILI PARAGHIAS
PILI MILON
APOLONION
EVRIPIDOU
MITSAHTOURI
TIMOKREONDOS
MENEKLEOUS
ARISTOTELOUS
RODIOU K.
PINDAROU
EOLOU
ABHELAOU
ERGIOU
THOUKIDIDI
PLATONOS
SOHOKLEOUS
Pl. M Evripou
DOSSIADOU
THISSEOS
KISTHINIOU
ALEXAN DIDOU
Arionos
ZINONOS
Pl. ATHINAS
PRAXLEOUS
PERIKLEOUS
FIDIA
GAVALA
Acandia
IPODAMOU
AGIOU FANOURIOU
PITHAGOGA
PRAXLEOUS
DINOSTHENOUS
TLIPOLEMOU
FRAXIMOS
PILI KARETOU
OLD TOWN
OMIROU
IRINIS
ARH EFTHIMIOU
PILI AG. ATHANASIOU
FILELINON
PILI AG. IOANNOU
VIRONOS
DIMOKRATIAS

was abandoned by the English Knights in 1534, when the Pope excommunicated Henry VIII. It was hard hit by an earthquake in 1851, then rebuilt by the British, bombed and rebuilt again in 1947. The British consul of Rhodes (*see* above for the address) has the key.

Across the street stands the flamboyant Gothic Hospital of the Knights, built between 1440 and 1481 and restored by the Italians in 1918, which now houses the **Archaeology Museum** (*open daily 8.30–3, closed Mon; adm*). The long ward, where the Knight's surgeons cared for patients in elaborate canopy beds, still has coats-of-arms and other heraldic devices. In the sculpture gallery the star attraction is Lawrence Durrell's Marine Venus, the kneeling *Aphrodite of Rhodes* (90 BC), combing out her hair after emerging from the sea. Other rooms contain funerary stelae, Mycenaean jewellery, and a mosaic from Kárpathos.

Through the arch just to the north, charming Argyrokástro Square has the most beautiful auberge of all, the 15th-century **Inn of Auvergne** (now a cultural centre) with a **fountain** reconstructed from bits found in the Byzantine fort at Arnítha. Here, too, is the 14th-century **Palace of the Armeria**, constructed by Grand Master Roger de Pins as the Knight's first hospital on Rhodes. The **Museum of Decorative Arts** (*open 8.30–3, closed Mon; adm*) has folk arts and handicrafts from all over the Dodecanese, including costumes, embroideries and a reconstruction of a traditional room. In Plateía Sýmis, the next square north, are the ruins of a 3rd-century BC **Temple of Aphrodite**, discovered by the Italians in 1922. Fragments of another temple of the same epoch, dedicated to **Dionysos**, are in a corner behind the Ionian and Popular Bank.

## The Medieval Town

South of the Collachium of the Knights is the former Turkish bazaar and shopping district, centred around bustling **Sokrátous Street**, to this day thick with tourist and duty-free luxury shops, especially jewellers; others here on the isle of eternal sun incongruously sell umbrellas and fur coats. At the top of Sokrátous Street stands the slender minaret of the lovely **Mosque of Suleiman** (*now closed*), built in 1523 by Suleiman the Magnificent to celebrate his conquest of Rhodes. The **Muselman Library** (1793) opposite contains rare Persian and Arabian manuscripts and illuminated copies of the Koran. Two precious 700-year-old Korans stolen in 1990 and worth 100 million drachmas have now been recovered and are back on show.

Off Sokrátous Street, the Turkish Quarter dissolves into a zigzag of narrow streets, where charming Turkish balconies of latticed wood project beside crumbling stone arches and houses built directly over the street. On the square off Archeláos Street is the hammam, or **Turkish baths**, built in 1765, with a capacity for 1,000 people a day. Closed for renovations at the end of 1994 they are otherwise open (*open Tues–Sat, 5am–7pm, bring own soap and towels; adm*). Another old mosque, **Ibrahim Pasha** (1531) is off Sophocles Street; its minaret was restored by the Italians.

On Hippocrátes Square, where Sokrátous turns into Aristotélous Street, stands the **Kastellania Palace**, built by d'Amboise in 1507, perhaps as a tribunal or commercial exchange for the Knights. It stands at the head of Pithágora Street, the main street of **Evriakí**, the Jewish quarter; according to Josephus, the community dates from the 1st century AD and laer chronicles cite them among the Rhodes' defenders against the Turks. Continuing east along Aristotélous Street, the **Plateía Evrión Martyrón** (the Square of Hebrew Martyrs), honours the memory of the Rhodians sent off to die in the concentration camps. The so-called **Admiral's Palace** is on the square, with a bronze seahorse fountain; it was more likely the seat of Rhodes' bishop. From here, Pindárou Street continues to the ruins of **Our Lady of Victory**, built by the Knights in thanksgiving for their defeat of the Turks in 1480. The Turkish and Jewish Quarters offer many other little cobbled lanes to explore, dotted with old frescoed churches converted into mosques and converted back again. Quick-draw artists specializing in portraits throng the leafy thoroughfare of Orféus, otherwise known as the **Street of the Artists**, and there are numerous pavement cafés and where you can sit and watch the world go by.

## The New Town

Outside the walls, beyond the Píli Eleftherías ('Freedom Gate'), you can buy anything from lace to jewellery under the trees on the way down to Mandráki Harbour. The row of seafront cafés and pastry shops are wonderfully posititoned looking out over the harbour, but they're overpriced and mainly aim at dragging in unsuspecting greenhorns. For a snack try one of the cheap places round the back among the dried nut and liquor stores or dive into the **Market**, a wonderful attraction in itself, bursting with fresh fish, meat and a cornucopia of local produce. There's a range of *souvláki* stands and little snack bars where islanders in town on shopping trips tend to gather like the Sými Bar and the Chálki Bar upstairs, also an unofficial repository for parcels to the island. **Buses** for the **west coast** run from the stands beyond the market's side entrance while **east coast** services go from outside the **Son et Lumière** on Papágou Street. Further along Mandráki is a fairly austere ensemble of public buildings built by the Fascists in the 1920s—post office, theatre, city hall. The Italians also left Rhodes some attractive buildings: the fine pseudo-Venetian-Gothic **Governor's Palace** and the cathedral **Evangelísmos**, designed after the church of St John, the Knights' cathedral blown up in the Gunpowder accident. The fountain is a copy of Viterbo's Gothic Fontana Grande.

For the Turks, Rhodes was an island paradise, and many Muslim notables in exile (including a Shah of Persia) chose to spend the rest of their lives here. Many lie buried in the cemetery north of the theatre, next to the **Mosque of Murad Reis**, named after the admiral of the Egyptian Sultan, killed during the siege of Rhodes, and buried in a turban-shaped tomb, or *turbeh*. The mosque has a lovely minaret reconstructed by the last people you would guess— the Greek government. Stretching along the shore from here crowded **Élli Beach**, probably the island's busiest, is sheltered from the prevailing southwest winds and packed with parasols and beach touts. There's a diving platform for high divers and a lifeguard but people floating on airbeds should beware being swept out to sea.

At the northernmost tip of the island is the **Aquarium** (*open daily 9am–4.30pm; adm*), claimed to be the only one in the Balkans, with tanks of Mediterranean fish and sea turtles, and a startling horror-show collection of stuffed denizens of the deep, their twisted grimaces— the result not of any prolonged agony but amateur Balkan taxidermy. **Aquarium Beach** on the headland has deep water, strong breezes and is more popular for windsurfing and paragliding rather than sunsoaking. **Windy Beach** stretches from there to Aktí Miaoúli, and lives up to its name. **Psaropoúla** is a safe, sandy beach running from the Hotel Blue Sky to the Belvedere. Although often breezy, the biggest danger is crossing the busy road to get to it. South of Psaropoúla are numerous small coves with safe swimming unless the wind is strong. Women should beware another drawback: the area is nicknamed Flasher's Paradise.

## Just Outside Rhodes Town

Any reasonably active visitor can walk south of the New Town to the ancient acropolis of Rhodes, **Monte Smith**, named after Admiral Sydney Smith who kept track of Napoleon's Egyptian escapades from here. On the way (North Epírou Street) are the ruins of an **Asklepieion**, dedicated to the god of healing, and a **Cave of the Nymphs**. On the top of Monte Smith, the Italians have partly reconstructed a 2nd-century BC Doric **Temple of Pythian Apollo** who was later associated with Rhodian Helios. A few columns also remain of temples of Zeus and Athena, and you can trace the outline of a 3rd-century BC **Stadium**. The **Ancient Theatre**, the only square one on the islands, has been reconstructed, and hosts Classical dramas in July (see the Tourist Office for programme details).

Two kilometres from the centre, lovely **Rodíni Park** is where Aeschines built his School of Rhetoric in 330 BC—there's a rock-cut tomb from the same period, a later tomb of the Ptolemies, and the ruins of a Roman aqueduct. The Knights grew their medicinal herbs here, and now merry drinkers can join Rodíni's peacocks for the **Rhodes Wine Festival**, recently resurrected by the council during the last two weeks of August with music, dance and food. Special buses transport revellers from the hotels to and from Mandráki harbour. During the evenings you can try Rhodes' own wines: *Chevaliers de Rhodes*, *Ilios*, the prize-wining premium red from CAIR, *rchontiko*, and the excellent Emery white, *Villaré*, as well as other Greek vintages.

---

### Rhodes Town ✆ (0241–)          *Where to Stay*

Rhodes has a plethora of accommodation in every class and price from one of the most expensive hotels ever to be built in Greece to humble village rooms. Most places are booked solid by package companies, some for winter breaks too, so if you're island-hopping in high season it's worth phoning ahead. Some room owners meet the ferries and hydrofoils, especially those with places in the Old Town, although don't hold your breath waiting for one to whisk you away in August.

#### *luxury*

Most of the luxury hotels are in Ixiá and Triánda although the mega-luxury, seven-star suites at the **Park Hotel**, ✆ 24 290, ✆ 24 190 (*lux*), in town overlooking the park, new in 1995, could upstage even their opulence. The **Grand Hotel** on Aktí Miaoúli, ✆ 26 284, ✆ 35 589 (*lux*) has the island's casino, a nightclub, tennis courts and what's reputed to be the largest swimming pool in the country.

#### *expensive*

The **Plaza** on Ieroú Lógou, ✆ 22 501, ✆ 22 544 (*B*) has been done up and is centrally situated with a pool, baby-sitting and English buffet breakfast. The **Hotel So Nikol** (formerly St Nikolis), 61 Ippodhámou, ✆ 34 561, offers atmospheric accommodation in a lovely old house in the heart of the Old Town with excellent bed and breakfast, large garden and rooftop terrace with great views. The Greek/Danish proprietors also have new apartments to sleep four nearby. Booking essential.

#### *moderate*

The **Victoria**, ✆ 24 626 (*C*) is another good central bet, family-run, and the owner's son, a UK-trained doctor, has consulting rooms next door. If you want to be in

Mandráki Harbour to catch ferries to Sými and other islands, then the **Hotel Spartalis**, ✆ 24 371 (*B*), is basic but handy and just over the road from the quay with a nice breakfast terrace and sea views.

### *inexpensive*

One of the best value is the **Ambassadeur**, 53 Othonos and Amalías, ✆ 24 679 (*C*); **Marie**, 7 Kos Street, ✆ 30 577, near Elli Beach, has a swimming pool and English-style pub. The **Hotel Hermes**, ✆ 27 677 (*C*), near the quay at Mandráki is also useful if you're just passing through and allows you to store luggage. It was good enough for Michael Palin on his *Pole to Pole* jaunt so the **Hotel Cavo d'Oro**, ✆ 36 980 (*D*) is well worth a try. The delightful 13th-century house at 15 Kisthiníou, near the Commercial Harbour, has been beautifully restored by the owner and his German wife and he'll even meet you from the ferry. Some of the cheap backpackers' haunts have become a bit unsavoury, but **Hotel Spot**, Perikléous 21, ✆ 34 737 (*E*), is very good value with light, airy rooms plus en suite bathrooms; nearby the **Iliana Hotel**, 1 Gavála, ✆ 30 251 is in an old Jewish family house and has a small bar and terrace; no charge for childen under 10. **Maria's Rooms**, on Menekléous, ✆ 22 169, are a comfortable choice around a quiet courtyard; while for a bit more **Hotel Paris**, Ag. Fanouríou 88, ✆ 26 354 (*D*), has nice rooms and a quiet courtyard with shady orange and banana trees; other budget options include the **Apollon** at Omírou 28, with laundry facilities and hot showers, **Pension Rena**, ✆ 26 217, at Pythagóra 55 and **Athinea** at 45, also have decent rooms and shared facilities. There are also **Minos Pension**, 5 Omírou, ✆ 31 813 and **Pension Andreas** 28D Omírou, ✆ 34 156, under friendly French/Greek management.

---

### *Rhodes Town* ✆ *(0241–)*          **Eating Out**

Rhodes has a cosmopolitan range of eating places from luxury hotel restaurants to dives selling tripe (*patsás*) in the Old Town to some of the finest fish tavernas in the world. The Rhodians are to the Greek islands what the Parisians are to France. They are fashionable, often fickle, and love new food trends. Rhodes has several good places serving a Greek version of *nouvelle cuisine* and the current craze is for old-style *mezédes* washed down by the island's excellent wines. In the New Town with its strong Italian influence you can eat great authentic pizza, pasta and other Italian dishes as well fast food, burgers, *souvlákia*, and you can find Danish, Swedish, Indian, Chinese, French, Mexican, even Yorkshire cuisine on the menu. And then there's Greek...

Probably the best place for *mezédes*, a selection of different specialities, is **Palia Istoria** ('Old Story'), ✆ 32 421, on the corner of Mitropóleos and Dendrínou. This award-winning restaurant isn't cheap but you get what you pay for—an imaginative array of dishes from celery hearts in *avgolémono* sauce to scallops with mushrooms and artichokes, and a good choice of vegeterian dishes. Food is served out under the pergola in a private house atmosphere. Let zany proprietor Harry, a former actor, guide you round the menu, and tempt you with his fruit salad with its twenty kinds of fruit. Excellent Greek wine list; booking advisable, splurge for a taxi. **Alatopipero** ('Salt and Pepper'), ✆ 65 494 at 76 M. Petrídi Street in the New Town (again, you'll probably need a taxi) is another trendy *mezedopoíon* with trays of different, inventive dishes making up your meal. Cyclamen leaves stuffed with rice are among the specialities, but there are giant Butcher's Plates for meat freaks, seafood delicacies and an adventurous wine list of rare Greek boutique wines, considered the best in town. Push the boat out and try award-winning *Hatzimichaélis Cabernet* or *Ayiorítiko* made by the monks on Mount Áthos. One of the best and most authentic tavernas for lunch is **Christos** out in the suburb of Zéfiros beyond the commercial harbour. A favourite with local families and taxis drivers—no problem finding it—food is excellent, ethnic and good value.

Vegetarians will find plenty of dishes at **Les Arcs Bistro** just off Dragoúmi behind the San Antonio Hotel, which has a varied menu at reasonable prices. For a real taste of Denmark try **Dania** near Barclays Bank with traditional herring dishes and a running buffet on Sunday evenings. **The Mascot**, on Sofokléous Street, is worth a visit for its kitsch décor alone—artificial tree, plastic waterfall, model of the Colossus—and the food is OK: i.e. *souvláki* stuffed with garlic and cheese served with decent local wines. The whacky new **7.5 ΘAYMA** ('Wonder') at Dilberáki 15 advertises 'food, drink and party hats since 292 BC' and turns out to be Swedish chefs, ancient Greek décor, Eastern-inspired dishes and seriously good food served in a secret garden. One of the cheapest places to eat in the New Town is the market, where numerous small cafés and takeaway bars offer several varieties of grilled meats and *souvláki*. **Trianon** is still the place to hang out for breakfast, coffee and people-watching; and if you have a taste for Scandinavian food try the Swedish bakery, **Kringlans**, at 20 Amarándou.

Getting lost and finding your own little taverna is one way to enjoy eating out in the **Old Town**. After an aperitif take the plunge into the maze of back-streets—in some industrous shops you'll see tailors and cobblers still hard at work. There's a wide range of eating places, some still untouristy and authentic, others all the rage with trendy locals. **O Alexis**, on Socrátous Street, is one of the top fish restaurants, expensive but good. For cheap and cheerful Greek staples try **Ioannis**, under the Sydney Hotel in Apéllou Street. **Mikis Fish Grill** in an alley off Ippokrátous does just fish salad and wine but does them brilliantly. **Taverna Kostas**, 62 Pythagóra, is friendly and good value; **Nireas**, 22 Plateía Sofokléous, is ace for Greek home cooking (booking advisable, ✆ 21 703). The adjacent **Taverna Sea Star** is a good for fish, if a bit pricey; colourful management compensates. The nearby **Aigaion** has changed hands and is a good bet for local seafood like the unusual *foúskes*, which resemble rocks. **Oasis Taverna** is basic but tasty (follow signs for the folk dancing). **Dodekanissos** and **Dinoris** are also old town favourites; **Restaurant Pandesia**, Plateía Aristostofánous, has authentic and unusual dishes—don't be put off by the photos outside.

**Cleo's** on Ag. Fanouríou is one of the most elegant places to dine in the heart of the medieval city, serving upmarket Italian or French cuisine (to reserve, call ✆ 28 415). Neighbouring **Kamares Restaurant**, reached through a big archway into a pretty garden, is another good choice for Greek specialities and international dishes. **Symposium** international restaurant at 3 Archeláou ✆ 37 509 and the **Symposium Garden** for seafood on 21 Ippodámou, ✆ 28 598 are very chic. On the other end of the scale, join the working men for a bowl of *patsás* soup at **O Meraklis** on Aristotélous 32 or **Patsas Sotiris** in an alley off Socrátous.

## Entertainment and Nightlife

Rhodes has something for everyone, with around 600 bars in the town alone. There are discos with all the latest sounds, laser shows and swimming pools, Irish pubs, theme bars, super-cool cocktail bars in restored old town houses, bars full of gyrating girls and wet T-shirt nights, and even simple *ouzeries* where a game of backgammon is the high spot. The island has all kinds of music from traditional folk sung to the *lýra*, funk, soul, house and rap to vintage Elvis. Traditional Greeks head for the late-night **bouzouki club** at Elli Beach, while for more sophisticated Greek sounds, the **Grand Hotel** on Aktí Miaoúli has the **Isabella**, featuring top singers and musicians in cabaret. The hotel also has the island's only **casino** with roulette, blackjack and chemin de fer. Rockers should head for the **Sticky Fingers** club or **Presley's**, with fifties and sixties sounds and cocktails named after the King's greatest.

Orfanídou Street near the front is known as the street of bars and Dhiákou Street in the New Town is also heaving with nightlife, British and Scandinavian tourists spilling out of the bars into the road in high season. You can hang out for coffee and people-watching at **Dolce Italia**, or join the smart set at the latest fad, the bar in the clocktower, **To Roloi**, in the Old Town; or go pirate at the **Blue Lagoon** with its desert island and galleon theme; or sample Guinness punch and listen to contemporary Irish music at **Flanagan's**. For a quieter drink in a shady garden **Christos** on Dragoúmi is the laid-back place, while trendy Rhodians and the cognoscenti head for the fabulous **Νῦν καὶ Ἀεὶ** ('Now and Forever'), a super-hip bar in a lovely mediaeval building off Socrátous in the Old Town with a sophisticated mix of music.

You can take in a movie at the **Rodon Cinema**; see the history of Rhodes unfold at the **Son et Lumière** show in the Palace of the Grand Master (*in English on Mon and Tues at 8.15pm, Wed, Fri and Sat at 9.15pm, Thurs 10.15pm*). or watch real if coolly professional **Traditional Greek folk dances** by the Nelly Dimogloú company in the Old Town Theatre (*nightly except Sat, Sun, June–Oct, 9.20pm–11pm; for information ℭ (0241) 20 157 or 29 085; dance lessons also available*). Bop till you drop at **Le Palais** disco or **Club Amazon** at **La Scala** disco. Package companies also organize Greek Nights around the island, especially at Embónas, but try and get to a real *panegýri* or **festival** for a true taste of Greek music and dance.

## Western Suburbs: Rhodes Town to Ancient Ialysós and Mt Filérimos

On the way out of town look out for the little ethnic houses on the left at **Kritiká**, built by Turkish immigrants from Crete facing their homeland. **Triánda** (ΤΡΙΑΝΤΑ), the modern name for Ialysós, has become the island's main hotel area, and Ialysós Avenue, which runs via **Ixiá** into Rhodes town is lined with apartments, superior hotels and luxury complexes. Ixiá boasts more of the same with several new de-luxe developments out for the conference and political summit trade all the year round as well as catering for rich summer clientele. The beaches along here are windswept and umbrellas keep the gusts at bay. Ialysós was settled by Minoans in 1600 BC, and may have been damaged in the explosions and subsequent tidal wave from Santoríni; more recently it has been devastated by masses of neon-lit bars, fast food places and eateries along this golden mile, catering for all tastes from English breakfast to smorgasbord.

Triánda village occupies the not completely excavated site of ancient **Ialysós**, the least important of the three Dorian cities. Legend has it that when the Phoenicians inhabited Ialysós, an oracle foretold that they would only leave when crows turned white and fish appeared inside the water jars. Iphicles, who beseiged the town, heard the prediction and with the help of a servant planted fish in the amphorae and daubed a few ravens with plaster. The Phoenicians duly fled. Ialysós went into such a decline with the foundation of the city of Rhodes that when Strabo visited in the 1st century AD he found a mere village. But it was still the birthplace of the boxer Diagoras, praised by Pindar in the Seventh Olympian Ode. The **cemetery** yielded rich finds from Mycenaean to Hellenistic times.

The main interest in Ialysós lies in the beautiful garden-like acropolis-citadel above Triánda, on **Mount Filérimos**, thought to be the initial nucelus of the Achaean settlement of Achaia (*open daily except Mon, 8.30pm–5pm, 400dr; wear modest dress to visit the monastery*). John Cantacuzene defended the Byzantine fortress on the site against the Genoese in 1248 and Suleiman the Magnificent lodged here during his assault on the Knights in 1522. Built over the foundations of a Phoenician temple are the remains of the great 3rd-century BC **Temple of Athena Polias and Zeus Polieus**, in turn partly covered by Byzantine churches. A 4th-century **Doric fountain** with lionhead spouts has been reconstructed. But the main focal point is the monastery of **Our Lady of Filérimos**, converted by the Knights from a 5th-century basilica church and heavily restored by the Italians. Reached by a flight of steps bordered by cypress trees, the monastery and its domed chapels feature the coat of arms of Grand Master d'Aubusson, under whom the church diplomatically had both Catholic and Orthodox altars.

Beneath the ruins of a small Byzantine church with a cruciform font is the tiny underground chapel of **Ag. Geórgios**, with frescoes from the 1300s. The monks will be pleased to sell you a bottle of their own liqueur called Sette, made from seven local herbs and flowers. For more wonderful views, there's an uphill path from the monastery to the southwest known as the Road of the Passion, where icons represent the Stations of the Cross.

---

*Rhodes © (0241–)* **Where to Stay**

The Ixiá and Triánda strip is one long stretch of hotels, with the prime luxury compounds in Ixiá. At the top of the list is the vast **Grecotel Rhodos Imperial**, © 75 000, © 76 690 (*lux*) the most luxurious 5-star hotel on the island and the most expensive hotel project in Greece so far, with a range of top restaurants, watersports centre, fitness club, children's mini club, and every delight from *syrtáki* dance lessons to Greek language courses, squash to cabaret; the **Miramare Beach**, © 96 251/4, © 90 153 (*lux*) has been revamped for those 'seeking paradise on earth' with swish cottages slap on the beach. **Rodos Palace**, © 25 222, © 25 350 (*lux*) also has apartments and bungalows, indoor and outdoor pools, a sauna, gym, tennis courts and all the trimmings; the **Rodos Bay**, © 23 662, © 21 344 (*A; exp*) has a pool and bungalows by its private beach, while the rooftop restaurant has one of Rhodes' finest views. Scores of A and B class hotels and apartments, plus cheaper pensions and rooms, are available from here to the airport.

---

*Rhodes © (0241–)* **Eating Out**

**Ta Koupia** (*exp*), on the road from Rhodes Town to Triánda (take a taxi) is simply the cat's pyjamas among Rhodian trendies—earring and pony-tail almost mandatory for men. Wonderfully decorated with antique Greek furniture, the food matches the décor in quality—excellent *mezé* and upmarket Greek dishes with an Eastern influence. In Ialysós the **Sandy Beach Taverna** right on the beach is a favourite lunchtime haunt with windsurfers and also has a children's play area off the garden terrace. It serves good Greek dishes; try *Kopanistí*, cheese puréed with cracked olives. In Ixiá, **Restaurant Tzaki** is known for its *mezédes* and also has bouzouki music.

## Down the East Shore to Líndos

Like the windier west shore, the sandy shore southeast of Rhodes town is lined with luxury hotels and holiday resorts, beginning with the safe Blue Flag beaches of **Réni Koskinoú**, popular with families. The inland village of **Koskinoú** is known for its houses with decorative cobblestoned floors and courtyards, the distinctive Rhodian pebble mosaics called *hoklákia* or *krokália*. On the way the industrial area of **Asgouroú** has a Muslim population and the still functioning mosque was originally a church of St John.

Further along the coast the coves of **Kalithéa**, the old, disused thermal spa in a magnificent kitsch Italianate-Moorish building from the 1920s, are a popular spot for swimming and snorkelling. There's a small lido and the Rhodes Sub Aqua Centre operating aboard *The Phoenix*. Beyond here **Faliráki Bay North** has massive development of A class and luxury hotel complexes along the sandy beach as well as a shopping mall. Bad enough, if that's what you've come to a Greek island to escape from, but reserve judgement until you meet **Faliráki**, the island's major resort, with its sweeping golden sands, awarded a Blue Flag for excellence, featuring all kinds of watersports and wild nightlife. A playground for the 18–30s crowd, fur and jewellery shops rub shoulders with fast food places, bars featuring wet T-shirt contests and local supermarkets that call themselves Safeways, ASDA and Kwik Save, copying the logos from UK carrier bags. If the beach to the south is the nudist hang-out, the rest of Faliráki attracts families with diversions such as jumping with the **Bunjee Club** on the beach near Taverna Stefanos, *✆* 76 178 (so popular that another rig is planned in the near future), the **Faliráki Snake House** with tropical fish and live reptiles (*open 11am–11pm; adm*) and **Aqua Adventure**, said to be the longest waterslide in Greece, located on the grounds of the Hotel Pelagos. Ironically, as Faliráki has been heading for real kiss-me-quick-style tourism up to now, some exclusive hotel complexes in Cycladic village-style are springing up in the area. Faliráki also has the island's only campsite since the Lárdos site closed.

Next door, the hidden village of **Afándou** is less frenetic and has the ultimate rarity in this part of the world—an 18-hole golf course as well as tennis courts. Once known for its carpet-weaving and apricots, Afándou now relies on tourism with its superb pebble beach, deep clear waters and excellent fish tavernas. **Ladiko Bay** nearby is a small rocky cove also known as Anthony Queen (*sic*) after the actor Anthony Quinn who bought land there while filming *The Guns of Navarone* at Líndos. Some scenes were shot on the beach and there are daily boat trips from Mandráki Harbour. **Kolýmbia** down the coast is a developing resort with many new large hotels. A scenic avenue of eucalyptus trees leads to **Vágia Point** with some great beaches south of the headland. Local farms are irrigated thanks to the nymph-haunted pool of **Eptá Pigés**, the 'Seven Springs', 5km inland. The wooded beauty spot with scented pines and other shady trees is a tranquil and cool place to escape the sun, with strutting peacocks, lush vegetation and a small streamside taverna. You can paddle through icy water along the low, narrow, dark subterranean channel which opens out into the spring-fed lake. But beware, the Greeks tend to wade back up again, colliding with the flow of human traffic.

The long sandy bay at **Tsambíka** is very popular, with its tiny white monastery perched high on the cliffs above. Rhodes's answer to fertility drugs, the monastery's icon of the Virgin Mary, attracts childless women who make the barefoot pilgrimage and pledge to name their children after the icon. Their prayers are answered often enough; look out for the names Tsambíkos or Tsambíka, unique to Rhodes. The road leads on to the village of **Stégna**, where the charming fisherman's houses are being engulfed by tourist development. There's a shingle beach set in a pretty bay.

Next stop on the main road, **Archángelos** (pop. 3500), is the largest village on Rhodes, with a North African feel, its little white houses spread under a ruined castle of the Knights. Its churches, **Archángelos Gabriél** and **Archángelos Michaél**, are two of the prettiest on the island; another nearby, **Ag. Theodóroi**, has 14th-century frescoes. Fiercely patriotic, the villagers have even painted the graveyard blue and white. Archángelos is famous for its ceramics and has several potteries-cum-gift shops, regular stops on island tours. Otherwise the village is still somewhat untouched by tourism and its major industries are agriculture and fruit farming. The villagers speak in their own dialect, and also have a reputation for their musicial abilities, carpet-making, and special leather boots that keep snakes at bay in the fields. Local cobblers can make you a pair to order. They fit either foot, but they don't come cheap.

Once one of the strongest citadels on Rhodes, the ruined **Castle of Faraklós** towers on a promontory below **Malónas**, overlooking Charáki and **Vlícha Bay**. Originally occupied by pirates, the Knights gave them the boot, repaired the walls and used the fort as a prison. Even after the rest of the island fell to Suleiman, Faraklós held, only surrendering after a long, determined siege. The nearby fishing hamlet of **Charáki** has a lovely shaded esplanade running along a superb crescent-shaped pebble beach. There are good waterside fish tavernas, excellent swimming and postcard views of Líndos.

---

*Rhodes ☎ (0241–)*                **Where to Stay and Eating Out**

In Koskinóu, most tavernas are like the village itself, small and typically Greek. **O Yiannis**, once cheap and cheerful, has become the place to see and be seen. There'll be queues but it's worth the wait; otherwise head to industrial and unfashionable Asgoúrou 5km out of town on the Líndos road for great *mezédes* and ouzo at **To Steki**, a typical *ouzerie* with wine and retsina from the barrel. There's no menu, but the food is wonderful with unusual dips and fritters and fresh seafood like clams, crab and stuffed *kalamári. Dinner only.*

Between Kalithéa and Faliráki the new **Esperos Village**, ☎ 85 734/752/754, ☏ 85 741/2 (*lux; lux–exp*) set high in its own grounds looks like something from Walt Disney with its castle gates; the architecture is so Cycladic it look as if it escaped from Tinos. At the other end of the scale there are plenty of C-class hotels and **Faliráki Camping**, ☎ 85 358, now the island's only official campsite, has every comfort with restaurant, pool, minimarket and bar.

For an exceptional fish tavernas in Afándou follow the jet set to **Reni's**, probably the best on the island, or head south to Charáki's excellent **Argo**. Faliráki is one big party where every other joint is a music bar. **Champers** is the eighth wonder of the world for young package ravers, karaoke, dancing on giant barrels, among the attractions; young sun and fun crowds also head for **Slammer's Pub**.

## Líndos

Dramatically situated on a promontory high over the sea, beautiful Líndos (ΛΙΝΔΟΣ) is Rhodes' second town and a National Historic Landmark. With its sugar-cube houses and fortified acropolis, it looks more like a Cycladic island than a part of Rhodes. Líndos was a magnet for artists and beautiful people back in the swinging sixties, when, they say, you could hear the clink of cocktail glasses as far away as Rhodes town. Now a tightly packaged resort, it's more lager lout than jet set, although showbiz Brits and Italians—among them, Pink Floyd's Dave Gilmour and British astrologer Patric Walker—have snapped up many of the lovely old houses. Incredibly beautiful as Líndos is, there's little left of real village life during the tourist season apart from locals selling a few vegetables and produce in the early morning when most people are sleeping off the night before. In July and August the cobbled streets are heaving with tourists and day-trippers and you can literally be carried along by the crowds—around half a million visitors are siphoned through each year.

Líndos was the most important of the three ancient cities of Rhodes, first inhabited around 2000 BC; the first temple on its magnificent, precipitous acropolis was erected in 1510 BC. It grew rich from its many colonies, especially Parthenope (modern Naples). Ancient Líndos, four times the size of the present town, owed its precocious importance to its twin natural harbours, the only ones on Rhodes, and to the foresight of its benevolent 6th-century BC tyrant Kleoboulos, one of the Seven Sages of Greece, a man famous for his beauty, his belief in the intellectual equality of women, and his many maxims, one of which, 'Measure is in all the best' (moderation in all things), was engraved on the oracle at Delphi. His reservoir supplies water to Líndos to this day. St Paul landed at St Paul's Bay, bringing Christianity to the Lindians; the Knights fortified Líndos, and during the Turkish occupation of Rhodes Lindian merchants handled most of the island's trade. To this day there's a rivalry between the people of Rhodes and Líndos, the Lindians known for their business acumen.

The serpentine pebbled lanes and stairs of Líndos are lined with dramatic and unique houses, many of them elegant sea captains' mansions built between the 15th and 17th centuries. Usually built around courtyards with elaborate pebbled mosaics or *hoklákia*, secluded behind high walls and imposing doorways, the houses have unusual raised living rooms or *sala*, and beds are often on sleeping platforms. According to tradition, the number of cables carved around the doors or windows represented the number of ships owned by the resident captain. Many are now taken over as holiday homes or bars, which take full advantage of their flat roofs, great for sun-bathing and admiring the views. Many houses have collections of Lindian ware, faïence painted with highly stylized Oriental motifs first manufactured in Asia Minor; legend has it that the Knights of St John once captured a ship full of Persian potters and would not let them go until they taught their craft to the islanders. Some of their finest works are displayed in the town's most lavish house, the **Papakonstandís Mansion**, used as the **Líndos Museum**. Líndos' reputation for embroideries dates back to the time of Alexander the Great. A *sperveri*, the fine bridal dress that all Lindian girls once wore, can be seen at **Kashines House**. The Byzantine church of the **Assumption** was built on the site of a 10th-century church and restored by Grand Master d'Aubusson in 1489–90. Its frescoes of the Apostles were painted by the artist Gregory of Sými in 1779 and refurbished in 1927.

## The Acropolis of Líndos

Floating high over Líndos housing is the **Temple of Lindian Athena**, one of the most stunningly sited in Greece, accessible by foot or 'Lindian Taxi'—hired donkey (*open Tues–Sun 8.30–3, sometimes 5; adm*). The steep route up is lined with billowing blouses, embroidered tablecloths and other handicrafts put out for sale by local women, who sit by their wares, needles clicking away. Some crochet and lace is authentically hand-made but much of it is mass-produced, imported and overpriced.

Just before the Knights' stairway, note the prow of a trireme carved into the living rock. This once served as a podium for a statue of Agissándros, priest of Poseidon, sculpted by Pythokretes of Rhodes, best known for his dramatic, windblown *Victory of Samothrace* now in the Louvre. The inscription says that the Lindians gave Agissándros a golden wreath, portrayed on the statue, as a reward for judging their athletics events. At the top of the stair are two vaulted rooms, and to the right, a crumbling 13th-century church of **St John**. Continue straight on for the raised Dorian arcade, or **Stoa** of Lindian Athena, the patron goddess of the city. She was a chaste goddess; to enter beyond here, any woman who was menstruating or had recently made love had to take a purifying bath, heads had to be covered, and even men were obliged to have clean bare feet, or wear white shoes that were not made of horsehair. From here the 'stairway to Heaven' leads up to the mighty foundations of the **Propylaea** and on the edge of the precipice, the **Temple of Athena** itself, of which only seven columns are standing. Both were built by Keloboulos, and rebuilt after a fire in 342 BC and reconstructed by the Italians. In ancient times, the temple was celebrated for its primitive wooden statue of Athena, capped with gold, and its golden inscription of Pindar's Seventh Olympian Ode, now gone without a trace. The views from the acropolis are extraordinary, especially over the azure pool of the small harbour, **St Paul's Bay**, where St Paul landed in AD 58. Its small white chapel has a huge *panegýri* on 28 June. The **Grand Harbour** was the home port of ancient Líndos' navy, 500 ships strong.

To the northeast of the main harbour, the cylindrical **Tomb of Kleoboulos** actually pre-dates the king, and in the Middle Ages was converted into the church of Ag. Aililiános. On the northern slope of the Acropolis at Vigli is the **Voukópion**, a small sanctuary in the recess of the rock which was used to sacrifice bullocks in honour of Athena, at a distance from her temple, which was presumably to be left uncontaminated by blood.

The long, sandy sweep of the main beach in **Líndos Bay** gives way to small but trendy **Pallas Beach** which leads to a rocky headland popular with nudists. The beach at **St Paul's Bay** has a different style, more detached from all the bustle. The beaches are as packed by day as the bars are at night. The locals have adjusted to the seasonal invasion and pander to the tourists' every need, from pornographic playing cards to English breakfasts and fine international cuisine. But although they're coining it in, they aren't always friendly. If you want to avoid the hordes visit in the off season; Greek Easter is wonderful in Líndos. With a preservation order to prevent high-rise development, it's still visually stunning. But if you can't take the heat, be warned. Líndos is one of the hottest parts of the island and temperatures can be unbearable in August. The nightlife also sizzles.

## Villages and Beaches around Líndos

**Péfkos** (ΠΕΥΚΟΙ), just south of Líndos, has a narrow sandy beach fringed by the pine trees which give it its name. Much quieter than Líndos, it's still a fast-developing resort with holiday apartments, mini-markets, cocktail bars, some good tavernas and even a British fish and chip shop and Chinese restaurant. **Lárdos** (ΛΑΡΔΟΣ), inland west of Líndos, is a pretty valley village with a charming central square where you can sip an ouzo and watch the local world go by. The coastal road from Péfkos is due for resurfacing and can be dangerous especially during autumnal flash floods, so if it's dodgy go via **Pilóna**, the dormitory village for Líndos, with a couple of *kafeneía* and a taverna. South of Lárdos the beach on sweeping **Lárdos Bay** has sand dunes bordered by reeds and marshes. This area is being developed with upmarket village-style hotels, and south of Lárdos construction of a subsidary airport is now under way. However, you can still find very peaceful, even deserted beaches further along the coast.

**Kiotári** now has sophisticated hotel complexes set in the surrounding wilderness. The once-sleepy area has changed, but **Kiotári Beach** stretches for miles and is still one of Rhodes's treasures with its hilly backdrop, stylish international holidaymakers and laid-back seafront tavernas. The **Monastery of Metamórfossi** has recently been done up and it's worth taking a detour inland to the medieval hill village of **Asklipío** (ΑΣΚΛΗΠΙΕΙΟ) nestling beneath the remains of yet another crusader castle. The church dates from 1060, and has frescoes from the 15th century depicting stories from the Old Testament, arranged like comic strips around the walls, an arrangement often seen in medieval Italy, but seldom in Greece. Further south, shingly **Gennádi Beach** picks up where Kiotári leaves off. Nearby **St George** has water sports and refreshments while **Glistra Beach** is a gem with a perfect, sheltered cove. There are beachside tavernas and the village across the main road has been extensively developed and is no longer sleepy; it has restaurants, bars and a lively nightlife in the same lines as Lárdos. A Bohemian, arty crowd of mostly German ex-pats have livened up the one-horse village of **Lachaniá**. There are a couple of bars and tavernas and two eateries on the beach. **Plimíri** (ΠΛΗΜΥΡΙ) has a spanking new marina, a commercial fish farm and popular fish restaurant as well as some wonderful deserted beaches along the coast like something from California.

### Líndos ✆ (0244–)            *Where to Stay*

In Líndos, where it's illegal to build new hotels, nearly every house has been converted into a holiday villa. If you want to stay in a typical Lindian house it's best to book through a specialist holiday company such as Direct Greece. If you do want to take pot luck, try the **Pension Electra**, ✆ 31 226, and **Lindos Sun Hotel**, ✆ 31 453 (*C; mod*) or seek help from **Pallas Travel**, ✆ 31 275, who have rooms  and villas. **Kyria Teresa**, ✆ 31 765, has pretty garden rooms in her house opposite the Forum, left at Mikis Fast Food.

Outside Líndos several excellent hotels are beautifully positioned on Vlícha Bay, 3km from town. The **Lindos Bay Hotel**, ✆ 42 212, 🖅 42 210 (*A; exp*), is on the beach with great views of Líndos. The **Steps of Lindos**, ✆ 42 249, 🖅 42 262 (*A; exp*) has luxury rooms and facilities, and offers a variety of watersports.

There are plenty of village rooms and pensions beyond Líndos—just look out for the signs. Further down the coast outside Lárdos the new **Lydian's Village**, ✆ 44 161/2/3/4, 🖅 44 165 (*A; lux–exp*) is a stylish club-type complex, exquisitely designed, with white Aegean-style houses clustered around paved courtyards. Furnishings are luxurious but with an ethnic feel, pale blue wooden taverna chairs, old ceramics. Every facility, right on the beach, and hills behind.

International cuisine rules in **Líndos**; prices are high and a traditional Greek coffee as scarce as gold dust. **Mavriko's** just off the square is outstanding, with an imaginative menu, while **Xenomania** up a rural track also has gourmet dishes if you want to splash out. On a more modest budget, **Dionysos Taverna** has all the usual Greek favourites in a rooftop setting while **Maria's** is still very Greek and **Agostino's**, with a romantic roof garden, does tasty grills, village dishes and Embónas wine by the carafe. It's also open for breakfast and brunch. At Péfkos carnivores can head to the **Butcher's Grill**, run by family butchers from Lárdos with excellent fresh meat and traditional village cooking; while **To Spitaki**, an old house in the village centre, offers Greek dishes with a cordon bleu touch in the peaceful gardens.

## Entertainment and Nightlife

Líndos also has a sizzling nightlife and all types of bars, many in converted sea-captain's mansions—the **Captain's House**, **Lindian House Bar** and **Jody's Flat** where the enterprising management also run a mini cinema with video matinees in high season. The **Qupi Bar** is an institution, and so is **Lindos By Night** on three floors with a lovely roof garden. The new **Epos Club** for 1000 people is the talk of the south with a romantic swimming pool with spectacular rooftop views upstairs, bar, disco and nightclub downstairs. Further south there are cocktail bars, music bars and all kinds of nightlife in Kálathos, Péfkos, Lárdos and Gennádi.

## The Far South

You could well have the sands to yourself as you approach the southernmost tip of Rhodes, **Cape Prassonísi**, 'the Green Island', but roads deteriorate beyond Plimíri and Kataviá. The desolate landscape may as well be the end of the world. A narrow sandy isthmus links Prassoníssi with Rhodes, one side wild and wavy, a magnet for top-notch windsurfers, the other side calm. There are a couple of tavernas and unofficial camping. If stranded head for Kataviá and the track to **Skiádi Monastery** near **Messanagrós**, an old-fashioned mountain village, where you can spend the night by arrangement with the caretaker. The hilltop monastery has a miraculous icon of the Madonna and Child which was said to have flowed blood when a 15th-century heretic stabbed the Virgin's cheek. The wound, and stains, are still visible. **Kataviá** (ΚΑΤΤΑΒΙΑ) is the island's most southerly village with an end of the line atmosphere, and, more importantly, a petrol station. Locals hang out at several tavernas and cafés near the main square and get invaded by migrating windsurfers in July and August.

Heading up the west coast from Kataviá there are spectacular views but the sea, often battered by strong winds, is too rough for safe swimming. In the valley below, **Apolakiá** (ΑΠΟΛΑΚΚΙΑ) is a modern, unexceptional town with a few tavernas and rooms to rent, but producing the best watermelons and marriage feasts on Rhodes.

Not so very long ago, Rhodian weddings were the stuff of folklore and lingering pagan rites. The ceremony began with gifts: the bridegroom presented his fiancée with a braided jacket, a veil embroidered with gold, a skirt and shoes, and the bride reciprocated with a shirt and a tobacco pouch she embroidered herself. To show she was no longer available, the bride's long hair was cut in front in a fringe, while the rest was gathered in numerous small plaits. Her hands were anointed with cinnamon. When she was ready, the wedding musicians were brought in to pass their instruments over her head (a meaningful gesture repeated several times during the wedding day). The bridegroom was given much the same treatment.

After the wedding, the young couple were led to their future abode—the bride's dowry (as it often is to this day). The new husband then dipped his finger in a pot of honey and make the sign of the cross on the door, while all the guests cried: 'Be as good and sweet as this honey!' He next stamped on a pomegranate placed on the threshhold, while the guests showered the couple with corn, cotton seeds and orange flower water. After the musicians sang the praises of the bride and groom, the bride knelt before the father and mother of the groom and kissed their hands, then was led away by her female friends to eat at a neighbour's house to the wild crashing of cymbals and song. The dancing would begin at night and last for two days.

Further along, **Monólithos** is the most important village of the region, the monolith in question a 200m-high rocky spur rising above the sea, capped by a castle built by the Grand Master d'Aubusson. A precarious stairway winds to the top and, within the castle walls, there's the little 15th-century chapel of **Ag. Geórgios** with some interesting frescoes. There are fabulous views, especially at sunset, across to the islands of Alimnia and Chálki. Beware strong currents off **Cape Monólithos**. But 5km below the castle, down a tortuous road, the shady bay of **Foúrni** has a sandy beach with clear waters and a seasonal cantina. There are early Christian cave dwellings round the headland and the monastery of **Ag. Anastásia** is nearby.

The road continues through **Siána**, an attractive old stone village built on a hillside, offering a superb view of the coast and islets. Siána is famous for its superb wild honey and *suma*, a local firewater reminiscent of schnapps. You can sample both at roadside cafés in the village, where the oldest houses have roofs made of clay. The church of **Ag. Panteléimon** has a beautiful interior and basil growing at the doorway.

## Embónas and Mount Atáviros

Renowned for for its wine, dancing and festivals, the mountain village of **Embónas** (ΕΜΠΩΝΑΣ) has tried to preserve its traditional ways. The dances of the women are exceptionally graceful and the *panegýri* in August are among the best on the island, fuelled by the local vintages. Some of the older people still wear local costumes, but only those who don't mind being camera fodder for the Greek Nights and Folk Dance busloads from Rhodes town. Embónas is the centre for the Rhodes winemaking cooperative, **CAIR** (their sparkling white makes a superb Buck's Fizz) and **Emery Winery**, ✆ (0246) 41 208, founded by the Triantafýllou family in the 1920s; visitors are welcome in the handsome tasting room (*open Mon–Fri until 3*). Emery's choicest vines are planted at 700m altitude on the slopes of the island's highest peak, **Mount Atáviros** (1215m); the summit is a tough 2-hour climb from Embónas. Here Althaemenes (*see* 'Mythology') is said to have built the temple of Zeus Atavros, although little remains of it now. While up on the roof of Rhodes head around to **Ag. Isidóros**, like Embónas minus tourists, with vineyards and tavernas. There are views of the whole island from the summit of Atáviros and on a clear day they say you can see Crete from the peak. Poor Althaemenes used to come up here when he longed, like all Cretans, for his mother island, and tradition has it that he founded the village below Embóna, **Kritinía**, a cluster of white houses clinging to the hillside, which he named in honour of Crete.

## Kámiros

But Althaemenes' most celebrated foundation was Kámiros (ΚΑΜΙΡΟΣ) (*open Tues–Sun 8.30–5; adm*), one of Rhodes' three Dorian cities, destroyed by an earthquake in the 2nd century BC, abandoned and forgotten in the Dark Ages and covered with the dust of centuries until 1859, when the British Consul, Biliotti, and French archaeologist, Alzman, began excavating where some villagers had uncovered a few graves. The city they eventually brought to light is well preserved, built in terraces up the hillside, devoid of the hands of Byzantium, Christianity or the Knights. The cemetery, in particular, rendered up many beautiful items, now in the British Museum, and in archaeological terms the discovery was one of the richest ever in Greece. An excellent water and drainage system, supplied by a large reservoir, served around 400 families in the excavated Hellenistic-era houses. A second dig in 1914 carried out by the Italians uncovered most of the ancient city. Sights include the baths, the Agora with its rostrum for public speeches, the Agora's Great Stoa with its Doric portico, Roman houses, two temples, one 6th-century BC dedicated to Athena of Kámiros and the other, Doric from the 3rd century, and an altar dedicated to sunny Helios. Down on the coast at modern Kámiros there are tavernas for pit-stops.

Don't confuse it with **Kámiros Skála** (ΣΚΑΛΑ ΚΑΜΙΡΟΥ), a small fishing harbour about 16km south of ancient Kámiros, which was the city's port. These days it's where you catch the local ferries for Chálki. There are two good fish tavernas. The ferries link with the buses to and from Monólithos or Kritinía, taking the children of Chálki to school in Rhodes and islanders shopping. Towering high above Kámiros Skála is the Kastéllo, signposted **Kástro Kritinías**, one of the Knights' most impressive ruins, set above lemon groves and pinewoods and affording spectacular views from on high. **Fanés**, further north, has a long, narrow stony beach with a few tavernas.

Inland, on a high hill over the village of **Sálakos**, are the ruins of another medieval fort; Sálakos itself is beloved for its shade and fresh water from the Spring of the Nymphs. This region, with its cedar and pine forests and views of the sea, is one of the prettiest in Rhodes for walks. Further up, the road leads to **Mount Profítis Ilías** (790m). The trees here belong to the Prophet Elijah, who according to legend strikes down any sinner who dares to cut one down. The chief settlements on its slopes are **Apóllona** with a museum of popular art and **Eleoússa** with a pretty Byzantine church.

Another enchanting spot, if you manage to get there before or after the tour buses, is **Petaloúdes**, the '**Valley of the Butterflies**', reached from the road from **Káto Kalamónas**. Sliced by a stream and laughing waterfalls, the long, narrow valley has a roof of fairytale trees, crossed by a winding path and rickety wooden bridges. From June to September tiger moths (*Callimorpha quadripuntaria*) flock here, attracted by the sweet vanilla resin of the storax tree, which is used in the making of frankincense (*open daily 9–6*). Notices tell you not to disturb them. Avoid the temptation to clap your hands to see those wings in motion: every flight weakens them, and clapping can reach a crescendo with every coach.

You can follow the trail up the valley to the monastery of the **Panagía Kalópetra**, built in 1782 by Alexander Ypsilántis, grandfather of the two brothers who wanted to be kings at the start of the 1821 Greek War of Independence. It's a tranquil place well worth the uphill trek, with wonderful views and picnic tables in the grounds. From here another wooded trail leads to the **Monastery of Ag. Soúlas**, which joins the main road down to **Soroní**. Here they have a giant festival on 30 July with donkey races and folk dancing made famous in *Reflections on a Marine Venus.*

**Theológos** or **Thólos** announces the proximity of Rhodes town with package-deal hotels and a collection of roadside supermarkets and tavernas. Beyond is the straggling village of **Paradíssi** (ΠΑΡΑΔΕΙΣΙ) next door to the **airport**. Hardly heaven, it's still a useful place for an overnight stay after a night flight—plenty of rooms to let signs—or makes a good waiting spot when planes are delayed. The friendly tavernas and pizzerias are within easy walking distance and beat the departure lounge hands down. There's a small beach as well, but with planes zapping overhead and the runways being extended for this year it's hardly peaceful.

Neighbouring Kremastí (ΚΡΕΜΑΣΤΗ) is a bustling village busy with foreign tourists and Greek soldiers from the island's main barracks. The road is lined with shops and bars and the village is famous for its wonder-working icon of the Virgin, Panagías Kremastí, occasioning one of biggest *panegýri* in the Dodecanese, lasting from 15–23 August. There's a funfair, *souvláki* stands and all kinds of hawkers selling their wares. At the climax on the 23rd the villagers don traditional costumes and dance a very fast sousta.

---

✆ *(0246–)*                                           ***Where to Stay and Eating Out***

To escape from the sun-and-fun crowds, head for the hills and pine-covered slopes of Mount Profítis Ilías. The old Swiss chalet-style hotels there have closed down but in the village of Sálakos, home of Rhodes' new natural spring water, Nymph, its namesake, the **Nymph Inn** ✆ 22 206/346 (*B; exp*) is a real oasis, the perfect island hideaway. For something cheaper in Monólithos, try the little **Thomas**, ✆ 61 291  (*D; inexp*). *Open all year.* Skála Kamírou is also popular for fresh fish, especially at weekends, with several tavernas overlooking the sea. **Loukas** at the harbourside is good and a jolly place to wait for the Chálki ferry.

# Sými (ΣΥΜΗ)

Inevitably, there's a fusillade of clicking camera shutters and purring of camcorders when the ferries swing into Sými's main harbour, Gialós, one of the most breathtaking sights in Greece. Few other islands have Sými's crisp brightness and its amphitheatre of imposing half-restored, half-derelict neoclassical mansions, in soft ochre or traditional deep shades, stacked one on top of the other up the barren hillsides. There are few trees to block the sun, for unlike its neighbour Rhodes, Sými is an arid island, with insufficient water to support many visitors. Most who do come arrive on daily excursion boats from Rhodes, when pandemonium reigns in several languages as groups are herded along the waterfront or head for the small town beach at Nos. When the boats have sounded their sirens and the invaders departed Sými regains much of its serenity. You might even find that prices go down and measures of ouzo get stronger. Sými is very popular with the sailing fraternity and the harbour is full of charter yachts, flotillas and jet-set cruisers flying flags of all nations. Avoid August when the island is heaving with Greek and Italian holidaymakers, rooms are expensive and tempers frayed in the searing heat. Because it's in a basin and the heat bounces off the surrounding rocks, Sými sizzles like a cat on a hot tin roof from July to September. On the other hand, it stays pleasantly hot into October and is particularly lovely in spring.

## History

According to legend, Sými was a princess, daughter of King Ialysos on Rhodes, who was abducted by the sea-god, Glaukos, an eminent sponge-diver and sailor who also built the *Argo* for Jason. He brought her to the island and gave it her name. If such was the case, Princess Sými's descendants inherited Glaukos' shipbuilding skills: throughout history Sými was famous for its ships. In antiquity Sými was known as Metapontis and Aigle, named after the nymph, daughter of Apollo and mother of the Three Graces. Prometheus is supposed to have modelled a man from clay here, angering Zeus so much he turned the Titan into a monkey which lived and died on the island. Ever since, the word 'simian' has been connected with apes.

Pelasgian walls in Chorió attest to the prehistoric settlement of Sými. In the *Iliad* Homer tells how the island mustered three ships for the Achaeans at Troy, led by King Nireus. After Achilles, Nireus was the most beautiful of all the Greeks, but, as in Achilles' case, beauty proved to be no defence against the Trojans. In historical times Sými was part of the Dorian Hexapolis, dominated by Rhodes. The Romans fortified the acropolis at Chorió; the Byzantines converted it into a fort, which was renovated by the first Grand Master of the Knights of Rhodes, Foulques de Villaret. From Sými's Kástro the Knights could signal to Rhodes, and they favoured swift Sýmiot skiffs or *skafés* for their raiding activities.

Thanks to the Knights, Sými began to know a measure of prosperity through shipbuilding and trade. When Suleiman the Magnificent came to the Dodecanese in 1522, the Sýmiots, known as the most daring divers in the Aegean, avoided the inevitable invasion by offering him the most beautiful sponges he had ever seen. In return for a relative degree of independence, Sými sent a yearly consignment of sponges to the Sultan's harem. Like the Knights, the Turks made use of the swift Symiot ships, this time for relaying messages. In order to keep Sými thriving, the Sultan declared it a free port and gave the inhabitants the rights to dive freely for sponges in Turkish waters.

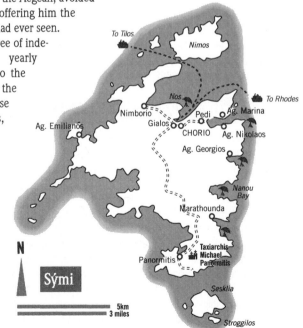

Little Sými thus became the third richest island of the Dodecanese, a position it held from the 17th to the 19th centuries. Large mansions were constructed befitting the islanders' new status; many bought forests in Asia Minor. Schools thrived. Even after certain privileges were withdrawn because of its participation in the 1821 revolution, Sými continued to flourish. The Italian occupation and the steamship, however, spelt the end of the island's fortunes: the Italians closed the lands of Asia Minor and the steamship killed the demand for wooden sailing vessels altogether; during the Italian tenure the population of Sými dropped from 23,000 to 600 at the outbreak of the Second World War. At its end the treaty giving the Dodecanese to Greece was signed on Sými on VE Day, 8 May 1945, later ratified on 7 March 1948.

## Getting There and Around

**By boat**: the island's own **ferries**, *Symi I* and *Symi II*, leave Mandráki Harbour, Rhodes, daily early evening and return to Rhodes in the early morning. There are at least 3 daily tourist boats from Rhodes, some calling at Panormítis Monastery; ferries twice a week to Rhodes and Kastellórizo; twice or 3 times a week to Tílos, Níssyros, Kos, Kálymnos, Léros, Lipsí, Pátmos, Náxos, Páros, Sýros and Piraeus. Local **excursion boats** and **barbecue boats** visit different beaches; and the islets of Sesklí and Nímos; water taxis go to Nimborió from Gialós and Ag. Nikólaos from Pédi Beach. **Hydrofoil**: daily services to Rhodes, also less frequently to Chálki, Tílos, Níssyros, Kos and Kálymnos. Timetables vary, with more routes planned this season. **Port authority**, ✆ 71 205.

**By road**: the island has 3 **taxis** and a **minibus** service, the Sými Bus, from Gialós to Pédi via Chorió.

## Tourist Information

There is a new press-button Municipal Tourist Infomation machine on the north of the quay or Mouráyio where the yachts are anchored. Regular police share the post office building near Clock Tower, Gialós, ✆ (0241) 71 215. Several agencies have accommodation to rent, from windmills to restored village houses, as well as money exchange and excursions. Sunnyland ✆ 71 413/320 has friendly British management; Kalodoukas Holidays, ✆ 71 077/900, ✉ 71 491 at the foot of the Kalí Stráta has character property to let, a wide excursion programme and book exchange (you can swap your old paperback for a new one); Sými Tours, ✆ 71 307/689, ✉ 72 292 also has a branch in Chorió and villas, rooms to rent and the main ferry and hydrofoil agency. The other ferry agency is in the fabric shop behind the Ionian bank.

## Festivals

**2 May**, Ag. Athanásios; **5 May** Ag. Iríni; **21 May**, Ag. Konstantínos; **4 June**, Análypsis; **24 June**, Ag. Ioánnis; **17 July**, Ag. Marína on the islet; **20 July** Profítis Ilías; **6 August**, Nimborió and Panormítis; **15 August**, Panagías; **24 August** Panagía, Nímos islet, and Panagía Alithiní; **8 November**, Taxiárchis at the monasteries of Panormítis and Roukouniótis.

Sými divides into down, up and over—Gialós around the harbour, Chorió, the older settlement high above, Kástro even higher and Pédi clustered round the bay over the hill. In **Gialós**, a derivation of its ancient name Aigialos, you'll find most of Sými's tourist facilities, tavernas and gift shops. Sponges and local herbs are sold from harbourside stalls, filling the air with the pungent scent of oregano and spices. In honour of the island's shipbuilding tradition, and to mark the signing of the Treaty of the Dodecanese in 1945, a copy of the trireme from Líndos has been carved into the rock on the waterfront. The inscription reads: 'Today freedom spoke to me secretly; Cease, Twelve Islands, from being pensive. 8th May, 1945'. Nearby restaurant Les Katerinettes has a plaque commemorating where the treaty was signed. Behind the small recreation ground next to the bridge which links the two halves of the harbour, the Town Hall now houses the small **Nautical Museum** (*open Mon–Sat, 10.30am–pm; adm*).

At the end of the harbour, behind the clock tower and bronze statue of a boy fishing, the road leads to shingly **Nos Beach** via **Charani Bay**, still a small hive of industry with wooden caiques being built or repaired while chickens strut about and cats lurk under the beached prows. Heavily bombed during the Second World War, many of the houses here are now being renovated in traditional Sými style with elegant plasterwork in greys, yellows and Venetian red. **Nos**, complete with waterside taverna and sun-loungers, is a small strand popular with families, on the site of the former Nautical Club. But it's also the first place the day-trippers hit, so it soon gets packed. It's better to walk further along the coastal path to the flat rocks and small coves popular with nudists on the way to **Nimborió**, a pretty tree-shaded harbour with a good taverna, loungers and a pebbly shore. Sand has been imported further round the bay to make **Zeus Beach** which also has a cantina.

Most of the neoclassical houses in Gialós date from the 19th century, while older architecture dominates in the **Chorió**. The lower part can be reached by road from the port; the alternative is a slog up the 375 steps of the *Kalí Stráta*, a mansion-lined stairway which starts near the Kaloudoukas agency off Plateía Oekonómou, or Plateía tis Skálas, to reach the houses in the maze of narrow lanes of the high town. Worn smooth and slippery over the years, the steps aren't suitable for the elderly, small children or the infirm, and can zap even the fittest in the heat of high summer. Local grannies nevertheless trip up and down like mountain goats. The stairway can be sinister after dark: a torch is a must. In the centre of lower Chorió near the derelict windmills, a **stone monument** was erected by the Spartans for their victory over the Athenians off the coast of Sými. On the headland overlooking Pédi Bay are the **Pillars of Sými**, dating from when the island was an important part of the Dorian Hexapolis.

Houses in Chorió are crammed together, often forming arches and vaults over the narrow lanes. They're built in the Aegean sugar-cube style, small and asymmetrical, often with neoclassical elements incorporated into their doorways and windows. Many houses have lovely interiors with carved woodwork and Turkish-style *moussándra*, beds on raised platforms or galleries. Among the most interesting buildings are the **19th-century pharmacy**; the fortress-mansion **Chatziagápitos**; and the churches of **Ag. Panteleímon** and **Ag. Giórgios** with their pebble mosaics of evil mermaids sinking hapless ships. The island's **museum** (*open Tues–Sun 10–2; follow the signs*) houses objects dating from Hellenistic times to the present. Up at the top, the **Kástro** is on the site of the ancient acropolis; its Byzantine and medieval walls top a temple of Athena; the coat-of-arms belongs to d'Aubusson. Within the fortifications the church of **Megáli Panagía** has good frescoes and post-Byzantine icons. The orginal church was blown up by the Germans when they discovered an arms cache during the Second World War. As a memorial, one of the church bells is made from the nose-cone of a bomb.

## Around Sými

From Chorió it's a half-hour walk downhill to **Pédi** (ΠΕΔΙ) along a shady avenue of eucalyptus trees. The most fertile area of the island, there are smallholdings along the way, herds of goats, a few donkeys and fig trees in the fields and a market garden. A small sandy beach and boatyard plus excellent taverna await to the left, where the road forks, while to the right past the church you'll find rooms to let and a more developed beach with cafés and the Pedi Beach Hotel. Pédi is pretty, with typical fishermen's cottages edging the bay. From here you can follow the left-hand path up over the headland to **Ag. Marína** with a chapel-topped islet within swimming distance. Water taxis from Pédi buzz to **Ag. Nikólaos** with its shingly tree-fringed beach and cantina which does barbecues. Otherwise you can walk. Follow the goat-track, marked with red paint, which begins to the far right of the bay, up and over the headland.

The road from Chorió now goes to the extreme southern tip of the island and Sými's main attraction, the vast 18th-century **Monastery of Taxiárchis Michael Panormítis** (in the summer there are also caiques, and the tourist boat from Rhodes often stops there). Archangel Michael of Panormítis Bay is Sými's patron saint, a big favourite of all Greek sailors, and goal of numerous pilgrimages throughout the summer. The elaborate mock baroque bell-tower was built in 1905 and most of the guest rooms and other buildings look more municipal than spiritually uplifting. In the monastery church, ablaze with riches, the icon of St Michael is larger than life and was created by Ioánnis of the Peloponnese in 1724 for Sýmiot sea-captains, priests and the community. The carved wooden **iconostasis** is remarkable, while the walls are liberally adorned with frescoes. Taxiárchis Michael is a busy archangel: at once heaven's generalissimo, slayer of the satanic dragon, weigher of souls (one of his nicknames on Sými is *Kailiótis* because of the pain he brings mortal hearts), and patron saint of the Greek Air Force, so it's no wonder that he has the reputation of being rather a tricky saint—you have to promise him something in return for your prayers. Hence the gold and silver ship ex-votos dangling from the ceiling, and the small **museum** in the sacristy filled with more rich gifts from faithful sailors, model ships and prayers in bottles which miraculously found their way to Panormítis bearing money for the monastery, and all kinds of junk. There's a small shop/ *kafeneíon* with miserable service, a decent taverna with wonderful sunset views, a small sandy beach, and a small army barracks. You can walk in the woods surrounding the monastery, or follow the forest trail to the beach at **Marathoúnda**. Near the taverna is the memorial to the abbot and two other freedom fighters who were executed in 1944 by the Germans for running a radio station for British commandoes. There are basic rooms and holiday chalets to rent, more in the spirit of a resort than a religious sanctuary. Greeks fill them up in August. If you're a single woman traveller you may have to stay within the monastery walls, and the doors are closed at 9.30pm sharp.

**Sesklí**, an islet near Panormítis, also belongs to the monastery. Its ancient name was Teutlousa, and Thucydides writes that it was here that the Athenians took refuge after their defeat by the Spartan navy during the Peloponnesian War. A few Pelasgian walls remain, and there are also a few ruins on the nearby islet **Strongilós**. There are regular barbecue trips to Sesklí, which has a long pebbly beach shaded with tamarisk trees, and crystal waters. There are also trips to the islet of **Nímos**, a stone's throw from the Turkish coast.

Sými has 77 churches, many dedicated to Archangel Michael. One of the most interesting is **Michael Roukouniótis**, an hour's walk from Gialós. Built in the 18th century, it is a curious combination of Gothic and folk architecture, and holds its feast day beneath an old umbrella-shaped cypress. **Ag. Emiliános** is on an islet in the bay of the same name, connected to the shore by a causeway with a pleasant pebbly beach nearby. Another 18th-century church, **Ag. Noúlias** is a half-hour walk from Chorió, and nearby **Ag. Marína** had a famous school before the War of Independence broke out. On the east coast, best reached by caique, **Nánou Bay** has an excellent shingly beach, fringed by trees, another favourite barbecue spot. There's a small chapel and masses of wild herbs to pick. The energetic can join organised walks overland while the more laid-back can sample ouzo or retsina on board lovely old caiques like the *Tríton* which do round-island trips. The bay before Nánou, **Ag. Giórgios**, has a tree-shaded sandy beach but is tricky to reach on foot. Other beaches include pebbly **Marathoúnda** with resident goats, **Faneroméni** opposite Panormítis and the scenic bay of **Ag. Vassílis**, a two-hour plus walk across the island.

---

*Sými ☎ (0241–)*　　　　　　　　　　　　　　　*Where to Stay and Eating Out*

Most of the island's accommodation is in Gialós but there are also rooms to let in Chorió and Pédi. Some owners meet the ferries. Sými is now very expensive in July and August and finding a budget place to stay can be a problem. Cheaper rooms are often let on condition that you stay three nights or more to economize on sheet-washing—water is scarce. Beware cockroaches in high season. There's no campsite on Sými but unofficial camping is tolerated on some of the more remote beaches.

## Gialós

The old municipal **Hotel Nereus** has been sympathetically restored and wonderfully painted in traditional colours. It's an impressive place to stay if you want to be in the heart of the action, book via Kalodoukos Holidays, ☎ 71 077 (*B; lux–exp*); a few doors along, the elegant **Hotel Aliki**, ☎ 71 665 (*A; lux–exp*) and **The Dorian**, ☎ 71 181 (*A; lux–exp*) up the steps behind are two of the most stylish places to stay, both old sea captains' mansions, lovingly restored with fine wood interiors. The Aliki has a roof garden, air-conditioning in some rooms and you can almost dive straight out of the front door into the sea, the Dorian has self-catering studios. **Hotel Grace**, ☎ 71 415 (*B; exp–mod*), is in another traditional house and has recently added smart new studios; the new **Opera House** ☎ 72 034, ✉ 72 035 (*A; exp–mod*) has lovely family suites with air-conditioning set back from the harbour.

There are several small pensions and rooms to let in the quiet backwater beyond the town hall and OTE. Other options are the tatty but cheap and cheerful old **Hotel Glafkos**, ☎ 71 358 (*inexp*); the **Pension Egli**, ☎ 71 392 usually just open in high season; **Hotels Kokona** and next door **Maria**, ☎ 71 549 (*C; inexp*). For stunning views over the harbour, especially at night **Pension Les Katerinettes** takes some beating, ☎ 71 676/413 or try the scenic **Katerina's Rooms**, ☎ 71 813. On the other side of Gialós **Hotel Albatross**, ☎ 71 707 (*B pension; mod*), is a good choice. In Charáni, the newly converted **Marina Studios**, book via Sunnyland, ☎ 71 413, are in a lovely old house perched high up with wonderful views overlooking the boatyard with swimming off the rocks.

The eateries in Sými fall into two clear-cut categories: really good and genuine, and tourist traps. The harbourside tavernas with their glass-fronted cabinets displaying fish and meat can be expensive, especially at lunchtime. Away from all this in the back streets beyond the bank, **O Meraklis** is one of the island's best and most authentic tavernas with excellent Greek home cooking and reasonable prices. **The Trawler** in the square is legendary for its fish; **Piccolo**, opposite the Vapori Bar, is popular with a good menu. The **Neraida** near the OTE has expanded and also has delicious untouristy food at budget prices; **Metapontis** is an old favourite. Over the bridge, **Taverna Yiannis** is another good place where you might hear impromptu Greek music, and a few doors along, near the town hall, the **Taverna Delfini** is also worth a try. Out on the headland, restaurant **O Tholos** has an impressive menu in a romantic setting, at a price. The **Nos Beach Taverna** is busy at lunchtime. Old favourite **Les Katerinettes** is back under original management: don't miss the octopus and *pikilía* or selection of *mezédes*. There are a few *souvláki* take-aways in Gialós plus has a wide range of cafés. **Roula's** where the ferries dock, does English breakfast, snacks and ice-cream and you can read the quality UK newspapers and magazines over baked potatoes or home-made chocolate cake at the **Vapori Bar** near the square.

## Pédi

A few rooms to let plus the **Pedi Beach Hotel** (*exp–mod*). There are several eateries but **Taverna Tolis** on the beach next to the boat yard is best for food and atmosphere, with good home-cooking, freshly caught fish and the odd turkey or chicken strutting past the tables; on the corner, **Three Brothers Taverna** also has bouzouki nights.

## Chorió

The **Village Hotel** or **Hotel Chorio** ✆ 71 800, ✉ 71 802 (*A pension; exp–mod inc breakfast*) has been built in the traditional style with smart air-conditioned rooms and stunning views; surrounded by fields plus goats and donkeys, **Taxiarchis Hotel and Apartments**, ✆ 72 012 (*C; mod*) is an elegant neoclassical development, family-run, with a small bar, breakfast terrace, and breathtaking panorama of Pédi. In upper Chorió the **Metapontis Studios**, ✆ 71 491 (*B; exp–mod*) are in a very old Sými house cleverly converted to keep many of the traditional wooden features like the *moussandra* sleeping gallery. Lower down the village **Hotel Fiona** is comfortable and friendly and inexpensive rooms can also be arranged through the **Jean and Tonic** bar, ✆ 71 819. In Chorió **Georgio's Taverna** is an institution at night, famous for Sými shrimps and the man himself on the accordion; next door **Dallaras** is OK with a shady terrace.

## Nimborió

If you really want to get away from it all, **Taverna Metapontis**, ✆ 71 820 at Nimborió has rooms to let, besides being a pretty spot for lunch. their taxi boat *Panagióta* will take you back to Gialós.

---

### Entertainment and Nightlife

Sými buzzes at night, the lights from the houses and the bars reflecting their colours in the harbour like stained glass. The locals still go in for the evening stroll or *vólta* and that's the time to go shopping or watch the world go by over an aperitif or an ouzo.

The island's old *ouzerie* **Paco's** is still an institution but has a rival in **Elpida**, the smart new *ouzerie* doing traditional *mezédes* across the water in Mouragio. Nightlife revolves around thre bars off the square, popular with locals and tourists alike. **Charani** is where the soldiers from the barracks hang out with plenty of loud music; further along **Mina's** and rival **Vapori** next door, popular with yachties and up-market Brits, are both good bars but seem to be fighting an endless duel to haul in clientèle. For less conspicuous rivalry and conflicting sounds head for laid-back **Meltemi Bar**, the excellent **Τεμβελα Σκαλα** ('Lazy Steps') along the harbour where locals sometimes play traditional Greek music if the mood takes them, or, across the water, **Blondie's** where you'll be sure of big measures and a British welcome. The yachting crowd and sophisticated night owls head for the **Roof Garden**, which also does snacks, for mellow sounds and romantic views. You can bop at **The Club**, the new dancing bar in Gialós, or go to real bouzouki nights with traditional music and dance at the **Alethini Taverna** on the road to Pédi. Futher along, the **Valanidia** also has bouzouki with top singing stars in high season. There are a few bars in Chorió but friendly **Jean and Tonic** caters for locals as well as tourists and still reigns supreme for early outdoors happy hour and late nightcaps.

# Tílos (ΤΙΛΟΣ)

Remote Tílos has been one of the best kept secrets in the Dodecanese for some time, with good unspoiled beaches, friendly people and wonderful walking country, a tranquil and authentic antidote to Kos and Rhodes, a paradise for bird-watchers. Although at first glance the island looks rugged and barren, inland it shelters groves of fig trees, almonds, walnuts, pome-granates and olives and small farms growing all kinds of vegetables and tobacco, watered by fresh springs. It's even a lot cheaper than neighbouring islands like Sými. The harbour Livádia isn't the prettiest you'll ever find but it has a certain bewitching charm, and soon grows on you. Some of the older women still wear their traditional costume every day and village life goes on with few concessions to tourism, although it's beginning to trickle in: a package holiday programme, a few day trips and hydrofoil links with other islands have inspired quite a bit of new holiday development. But so far, so good; there's nothing overwhelming.

Tílos was also the home of the 4th-century BC poetess Erinna, whose work was said to rival that of Sappho. She died very young and little of her poetry survives, but her famous work *The Distaff* gives an insight into her life and friendships. Her name lives on over tavernas and in the Tilian ex-pat association. Tílos is known for its ancient music, dances and elaborate costumes and the old songs from the island's many festivities are now available on cassette. Knees-up apart, it's as fine a place as any to do nothing; a dreaminess surrounds all practical activities and the visitor who neglects to wind his watch is in danger of losing all track of time.

## History

According to mythology Tílos was named after the youngest son of Alia and Helios, the sun god. When his mother fell ill Tílos came to the island to gather herbs to cure her. When she recovered he built a sanctuary to Helios Apollo and Poseidon in gratitude and later became a priest, and ever after the priests of Tílos bore the title of Hierapoli or Holy Servants of Helios. Tílos is believed to have been joined to Asia Minor six million years ago. When it broke away *c.* 10,000 years ago, elephants were trapped on the island and adapted to their new limited supply of food by shrinking. In the Grotto of Hercadio, a deep ravine in the Misaria area, the bones of the mini-elephants and the remains of deer and tortoises were found alongside Stone Age pottery. Nearby, pumice cliffs and volcanic debris came from the eruption on Níssyros. The legendary struggle between Poseidon and the Titan Polyvotis sent showers of lava and fall-out that covered the island's now fertile lowlands.

The main town up to early Christian times was Tílos or the fort at Megálo Chorió, where excavations have discovered Minoan and Mycenean influences. In the 5th century BC Herodotus wrote that the island sent a colony to Sicily under the leadership of Tilinis. Tilians participated in the Athenian alliance in the 5th century but coins bearing the head of Athena and Poseidon from the 4th century suggest that Tílos was then independent, closely allied with Kos. At the summit of its fortunes, it was famous for perfumes and gave birth to the poetess Erinna. In the 3rd century BC Tílos became allied to Rhodes. In 226 BC the walls of the citadel and the temples were destroyed in an earthquake and restored by a rich citizen. Graves from the Hellenistic period have been found at Ag. Antónis. When the Rhodian state fell in 42 BC Tílos came under Roman rule; in the subsequent dark age it was often confused with Teftlousa, the island of Sesklí near Sými.

Little is known about Tílos until the Knights of St John took over in 1309. They strung seven castles across the island: Paleokástro in the north west; Lámbros (or Stávros) near Mikró Chorió; Ag. Stéfanos (or Roukoúni) near Livádia; Megálo Chorió, built over the Hellenistic fort; Misariá, Agriosykiá and Mikró Chorió, both from the 15th century, the latter with an observatory. They withstood a number of Turkish attacks, from 1320 until 1522, when the whole of the Dodecanese was conquered. The Tilians then got caught in the flak during the 17th century, when Venetian admirals and Christian pirates raided the island to get back at the Turks; what bits survived them fell prey to raiders from Mýkonos and Spétses from 1821 onwards in the name of the Greek Revolution. Tílos was taken by the Italians in 1912, by the Germans in 1943, when all the island's livestock was destroyed, and finally became part of Greece in March 1948.

---

## Getting There and Around

**By sea**: once a week to Níssyros, Kos, Kálymnos, Astypálaia, Páros, Sýros, Piraeus; once a week to Níssyros, Kos, Kálymnos, Léros, Lipsí, Pátmos, Náxos, Páros, Sýros, Piraeus; twice a week to Sými, Rhodes, Kastellórizo; regular links with Rhodes. Occasional **excursion boats** from Chálki, Sými, Rhodes, Kos. **By hydrofoil**: regular links with Rhodes, Níssyros, Kos, Kálymnos, Sými and Chálki. **Port authority**, ✆ 44 350.

**By road**: there's a regular **minibus** service from Livádia, the orange 12-seater and notoriously grumpy driver leaves from the square—timetable pinned on the café door—to Megálo Chorió, Ag. Antónis and Éristos. You can also hire **mopeds** and **motorbikes** from Stélios in the square. If you see a yellow taxi in high season it'll be an Athens cabbie on holiday. You could try and flag him down. Some of the hotels have transit vans and you might get lifts in the back of lorries which sometimes run a taxi service. Otherwise you're on foot. Tílos is good for walkers and birdwatchers and there are plenty of tracks to follow to the old castles or distant beaches.

## Tourist Information

The port authority share the large white building on the quay with the regular police, ✆ 53 220. Stefanákis Travel, ✆ 43 310/44 360, ✉ 44 315 on the steps to the left of the quay are helpful with information on ferries, hydrofoils and accommodation. Tílos Travel, ✆ 53 259, also has information and rents out motorbikes and motorboats.

## Festivals

**17 January**, Ag. Antónis at Megálo Chorió; **28 June**, Ag. Pávlos; **25–27 July**, huge three-day festival or *panegýri*, Ag. Panteleímon at monastery; **28 July** Taxiárchis at Megálo Chorió, dance of the Koúpa; **15 August** Panagías, Mikró Chorió.

## Livádia and Megálo Chorió

Although there used to be nine villages on the island only the port **Livádia** (ΛIBAΔIA) and the capital Megálo Chorió are inhabited. Popular with Greek families in high season, Livádia has a mile of tree-fringed pebble beach and water clear as gin. Village life revolves around the little central square, near a couple of embryonic supermarkets and an excellent bakery selling wonderful pastries. Spirits are fed by by the pretty blue and white church of **Ag. Nikólaos** right on the waterfront. Further along the beach road the tiny early Christian basilica of **Ag. Panteleímon** and **Polýkarpos** is worth a visit for its mosaic floor. At the far side of the bay the little sheltered harbour of **Ag. Stéfanos** is popular with yachts. The track from the harbour leads over the headland to the pebbly beach at **Lethrá**, about an hour's walk away, or continue to **Armókosti** where you can also swim in peace.

**Megálo Chorió** (ΜΕΓΑΛΟ ΧΩΡΙΟ), 8km uphill from Livádia, stands on the site of ancient Tílos, and near the castle you can see Pelasgian walls built by the earliest known residents (if you discount the mastodons) dating back to 1000 BC. The castle, or Kástro, was built by the Venetians, who incorporated a Classical gateway and stone from the ancient acropolis, once crowned by a temple to Pythian Apollo and Polias Athena. The pretty whitewashed village has a maze of alleys and flower-filled gardens. There's a small museum and the lovely church of **Archangel Michael** which houses the silver icons from the original Taxiárchis church in the Kástro. Festivals are held in the church's pebble mosaic courtyard on 8 November and 28 July when there's a massive party and women dance the ancient dance of the *koúpa* or cup.

Most of the island's 400 or so population live in the village and there are a couple of tavernas and a *kafeneíon*. The road drops down to the fertile plain and meanders to the long sandy beach at **Éristos** (ΕΡΥΣΤΟΣ). At the far end you can go for an all-over tan. Further north is the deserted village of **Mikró Chorió** and the cave where the bones of miniature mastodon, only 1.3m tall, were discovered in 1971, one of the richest finds of their kind in the world, and soon to be shown off in a new museum. With its amphitheatre of ruined houses the village looks sad—the owners took their roofs with them when they moved down to Livádia in the 1950s. The old church of **Timía Zóni** has 18th-century frescoes and the newer church, a pink confection, is the hub of celebration on August 15 when the village comes alive again for the Assumption of the Virgin Mary. There are stunning views from the ghost town and the churches of **Sotíras, Ag. Elesas and Prodrómos** have 15th-century frescoes.

From Megálo Chorió the road runs to windswept **Ag. Antónis** (ΑΓΊΟΣ ΑΝΤΟΝΗΣ) which has a grotty beach and a small chapel as well as Greek holiday homes. The main attraction is Tílos' other fossils—the petrified remains of human skeletons in a row on the beach, thought to belong to sailors caught in the lava when when Níssyros erupted in 600 BC. A rough track leads to the isolated beach at **Pláka**, while another winds its way up high into the mountains to the **Monastery of Ag. Panteleímon**, a lovely Byzantine building with red pantiled roof, set in a lush oasis of shady trees and gushing water. The fortified monastery is perched more than 200m above the west coast with a breathtaking panorama. It has some impressive frescoes and a beautiful old marble drinking fountain fringed by pots of basil. The church is kept locked, but the minibus driver arranges trips up on Sundays.

---

*Tílos ✆ (0241–)*  **Where to Stay and Eating Out**

### Livádia

There are plenty of small pensions and rooms in Livádia plus a few hotels, some newly built. The **Irini**, ✆ 44 243, ✉ 53 238 (*C; mod*) has been tastefully tricked out in ethnic style and is set back from the beach in lovely gardens. The same management also has cheaper rooms in the village and is building new bungalows above the harbour. The new **Marina Hotel** around the bay at Ag. Stéfanos is another excellent bet, if a bit far-flung, but does good food. The smart **Panorama Studios**, ✆/✉ 44 365 (*mod*), perched on the hillside above the village have great views from the flower-filled terrace. Stark white inside, they're self-contained with built-in double beds and self-catering facilities with all-in-one fridge and cooker. The same management also runs the **Olympus Apartments** near the beach, three gingerbread-style houses painted blue, banana and pink. Set back from the village up a track, **Pension Anna**, ✆ 44 357 (*inexp*) is a peaceful place to stay with a welcoming Greek-American landlady. Newly built near the beach the family-run **Hotel Castellos Beach**, ✆ 44 267 (*mod*) has luxurious, modern rooms with fridges and fans overlooking the sea; in the village **George's Apartments**, ✆ 44 243, are also comfortable with kitchen facilities. **Hotel Livadia**, ✆ 52 202 (*E; inexp*), has been given a face-lift and is centrally placed with a popular bar downstairs which serves pizza into the small hours; **Stefanakis Apartments**, ✆ 44 310/360, ✉ 44 315 (*inexp*), above Kostas Taverna, are also a comfortable option with daily maid service. Other budget pensions and rooms worth trying include **Pension Kastello**, ✆ 53 292, **Stamatia**, ✆ 53 255, **Galini**, ✆ 53 280, **Studio Rena**, ✆ 44 274, **Pension Perigiali**, ✆ 53 398 and, on the row of rooms to let at the western end of the beach, **Spiros**, ✆ 53 339, has private bathrooms; **Paraskevi** ✆ 53 280 and **Stamatis**, ✆ 53 334 have shared facilities. There are also **municipal bungalows** near the beach, ✆ 53 258.

Livádia has a fair range of tavernas, small *souvláki* take-aways and coffee shops. For fish and seafood the **Trata Restaurant** in the village is first choice followed by the **Blue Sky Taverna** above the jetty with wonderful harbour views; for good Greek home cooking head for **Restaurant Irina** on the beach, popular with the locals, which has a wide choice of dishes and cheap beer. Great for lunch with tables on the sand shaded by trees; or follow the Brits to roadside **Taverna Sophia**, the current in-place, which also has excellent food and friendly service. Other good eateries include

Taverna Kostas, beneath Stefanákis Travel; Taverna Michaelis which specializes in spit roasts; Meraklis for chicken, *souvláki* etc. next door to the supermarket. Kafeneion Omonia is very Greek and where the locals hang out. Good for cheap breakfast and snacks, although food can be scarce at night, it's also the place for a pre-dinner ouzo, and sometimes impromptu dancing breaks out.

## Megálo Chorió

In Megálo Chorió, it's this or that: **Pension Sevasti**, ✆ 53 237, has budget rooms next door to the Kali Kardia Taverna or **Milios Apartments**, ✆ 53 204/220 in the village centre has pleasant rooms with a traditional touch set in a lush garden. There's even an aviary full of budgies for company. Eat at the **Kali Kardia Taverna** or the **Castle Restaurant**; both have good Greek fare.

## Éristos

Set back from the beach, the **Nausika Taverna** also has inexpensive but comfortable rooms, while at the roadside the **Tropicana Restaurant**, ✆ 53 242, is a peaceful haven in a tropical garden with chalet-type rooms. It is good for fresh seafood and local vegetable dishes served in a rose-covered arbour.

## Ag. Antónis

The **Hotel Australia**, ✆ 53 296 (*D; inexp*), is immaculate and run by Greek Australian brothers who meet guests from the ferry with their transit van. Try the **Delfini Fish Restaurant** in front of the Hotel Australia. There is no official campsite but you can pitch your tent happily at Éristos and remote Pláka Beach.

---

### *Entertainment and Nightlife*

Nightlife in Tílos centres on the tavernas and bars. People sit in the square at **Yiorgo's** or the **Omonia** for an after-dinner coffee or nightcap. The bar beneath the **Livádia Hotel** is also a popular haunt, while **La Luna Bar** plays music and attracts the young.

Night owls can head for deserted **Mikró Chorió** where a group of friends have set up a unique dancing bar in an old restored house. They have put lights in the ruins to give the impression that the village has come alive. Action begins at midnight and often goes on until dawn with wild Greek dancing as well as the latest sounds. Daybreak views over Livádia take some beating—and there are no neighbours to complain about the noise. Otherwise Tílos is famous for its traditional music and dance and the islanders really let their hair down at their festivals. Celebrations for Ag. Panteleímon in July are infectious, with song and dance breaking out all over the place.

PONDIKONISSI MONASTERY

## The Ionian Islands

Scattered randomly across the Ionian sea, from Corfu in the north to Kýthera at the southern end of the Peloponnese, the Ionians are known in Greek as the Eptánissa, the Seven Islands. Politically lumped together since Byzantine times, they share a unique history and character; generally speaking, they are more Italianate, more luxuriant than your typical Greek island, swathed in olive groves and cypresses and bathed in a soft golden light very different from the sharp, clear solar spotlight that shines on the Aegean. In temperament, too, the Seven Islands beg to differ: they are more gentle and lyrical, less prone to the extremes that bewitch and bedazzle the rest of the country. They also get more rain, especially from October to March, only to be rewarded with a breathtaking bouquet of wild flowers in the spring and autumn, especially on Corfu. Summers, however, tend to be hot, lacking the natural air-conditioning provided by the *meltémi* on Greece's eastern shores.

Weather and history aside, each of the Ionian islands has a strong, distinct personality that defies further generalizations. Connections between them, once almost non-existent, are now frequent in the summer, and you can easily hop from one to the next depending on your mood, whether you want to boogie the night away in a Zákynthos nightclub, windsurf below the cliffs at Lefkáda, hike among the olive groves of bijou Paxí, swim under the white cliffs of Kefaloniá, or seek Odysseus' beloved home on Ithaca. Beautiful Corfu, like Rhodes, is a major international resort destination, with its gorgeous beaches and historic town, recently labelled in the British Press as a 'Venice without canals, Naples without the degradation.' Only distant Kýthera remains stalwartly remote, accessible only from Pireaus or southern and eastern Peloponnesian ports.

## Mythology

If the Ionian islands spent centuries out of the mainstream of Greek politics, their inhabitants have been Hellene to the core from the beginning. Not to be confused with Ionia in Asia Minor (named for the Ionian people's legendary father Ion, son of Apollo), the Ionian sea and islands are rather named after lovely Io the priestess, who caught the roving eye of Zeus. When the jealous Hera was about to catch the couple *in flagrante delicto* Zeus changed the girl into a white cow, but Hera was not to be fooled. She asked Zeus to give her the cow as a present, and ordered the sleepless hundred-eyed Argus to watch over her. When Hermes charmed Argus to sleep and killed him, Io the cow escaped, only to be pursued by a terrible stinging gadfly sent by Hera. The first place through which she fled has ever since been named the Ionian Sea.

## History

Very little remains of the ancient past on the islands, although they were probably settled in the Stone Age by people from Illyria (present-day Albania) and then by the Eretrians. Homer was the first to mention them, and were he the last they would still be immortal as the

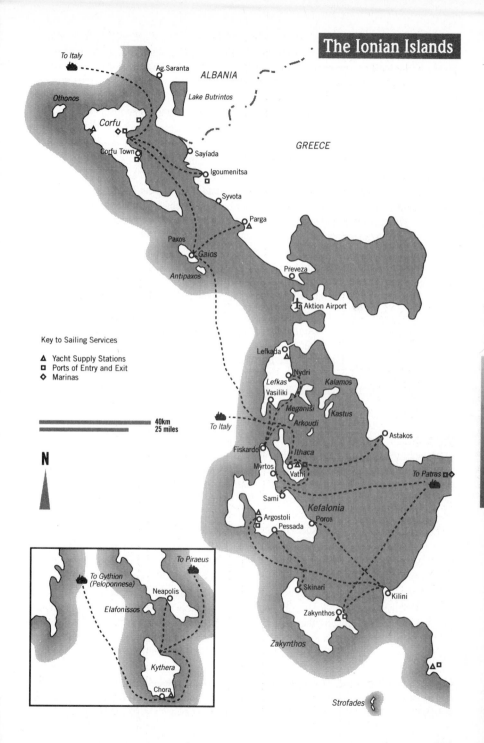

# The Ionian Islands

To Italy

Ag.Saranta

*ALBANIA*

*Lake Butrintos*

*Othonos*

*Corfu*

Corfu Town

Sayíada

*GREECE*

Igoumenitsa

Syvota

Parga

Paxos

*Gaios*

*Antipaxos*

Preveza

Aktion Airport

**Key to Sailing Services**

△ Yacht Supply Stations
⊡ Ports of Entry and Exit
◇ Marinas

Lefkada

Nydri

*Lefkas*

Vasiliki

*Kalamos*

*Meganisi*

*Kastus*

*Arkoudi*

To Italy

Astakos

Fiskardo

*Ithaca*

Myrtos

Vathi

To Patras

40km
25 miles

N

Sami

*Kefalonia*

Argostoli

Poros

Pessada

To Piraeus

To Gythion
(Peloponnese)

Neapolis

Skinari

Kilini

*Elafonissos*

Zakynthos

*Zakynthos*

*Kythera*

Chora

*Strofades*

homeland of crafty Odysseus. In the 8th century BC, mercantile Corinth colonized the islands. As trade expanded between Greece and the Greek colonies in southern Italy and Sicily, the islands became ever more important; Corfu, the richest, grew so high and mighty that she defeated mother Corinth at sea, and proclaimed herself the ally of Athens. This forced Sparta, Corinth's ally, either to submit to this expansion of Athenian influence and control of western trade routes through the Ionian islands, or to attack. They attacked. The result was the disastrous Peloponnesian War.

The Romans incorporated the Ionian islands into their province of Achaia. After the fall of the Roman Empire, Ostrogoths from Italy overran the islands, only to be succeeded by the Byzantines, who fortified them for their strategic importance as a bridge between Constantinople and Rome. In 1084, during the Second Crusade, the Normans under Robert Guiscard, Duke of Apulia, took the islands by surprise and established bases to plunder the rest of Greece. With a great deal of difficulty the Byzantines succeeded in dislodging them, although the Normans were no sooner gone than the Venetians claimed the islands in the land-grab after the Sack of Constantinople in 1204. The southern islands became the County Palatine of Kefalonia once Venice put an end to the claims of the Sicilian Norman pirate, Vetrano, by crucifying him. Fate, however, dealt Corfu into the hands of the grasping Angevins for 150 years, a rule so bitter that the inhabitants willingly surrendered their island to the 'protection' of Venice.

Venetian rule was hardly a bed of roses. The average Greek in fact preferred the Turks to the bossy Catholic 'heretics': if nothing else, the Turks allowed the people a measure of self-government and demanded fewer taxes. Some of the Ionian islands came under Turkish rule until 1499, and the Ottomans renewed the assaults as the once proud Serenissima weakened. Yet for all their faults, the Venetians were at least more tolerant of artists than the Turks, and in the 17th century the Ionian islands became a refuge for painters, especially from Crete. The resulting Ionian school was noted for its fusion of Byzantine and Renaissance styles.

In 1796, Napoleon conquered Venice; as the Ionian islands were of the utmost importance to his schemes of conquest he demanded them with the Treaty of Campo Formio. In 1799 a combined Russo-Turkish fleet took the islands from him, and the Russians created the independent Septinsular Republic under their protection—shielding the islands not only from the French but from the designs of the notorious tyrant of Epirus, Ali Pasha. Although the Septinsular Republic was nullified by the 1807 Treaty of Tilsit which returned the islands to Napoleon, it was the first time in almost four centuries that any Greeks had been allowed a measure of self-rule, and the experience helped to kindle the War of Independence in 1821.

In 1815 the British took the Ionian islands under military protection and re-formed the quasi-independent Septinsular Republic. Sir Thomas Maitland, the first High Commissioner, has gone down in history as one of the most disliked British representatives ever; he assumed dictatorial powers, and deeply offended the Greeks by giving the city of Párga, an important port on the mainland, to Ali Pasha, obeying an obscure clause in the 1815 treaty that everyone else had forgotten. Although other High Commissioners were more palatable, and some were actually very well liked, the Ionian State never stopped demanding or conspiring for union with Greece. Once they had Cyprus as well as Malta to use as Mediterranean ports, the British ceded the islands to Greece in 1864—but only after blowing up all the fortresses on Corfu. During the Second World War Italy took the islands, but Mussolini's dream of creating a new Ionian State under Italian protection was shattered in 1943 when the Germans occupied the islands. Large numbers of Italian troops joined the Greeks in fighting the Nazis, only to be slaughtered by their former Axis allies. When the news reached Italy, it contributed to the collapse of the Fascist government.

# Corfu/Kérkyra (KERKURA)

Luxuriantly beautiful Corfu is a Garden of Eden cast up in the northwest corner of Greece, a sweet mockery of the grim, grey mountains of Albania, so close and so unenticing. The Venetian city-capital of the island is one of the loveliest towns in Greece; the beaches along the north and west coasts are gorgeous, and often spectacular with their cliffs; the gentler mountain slopes, sprinkled with pastel villas and farms, could be in Tuscany.

Corfu's reputation as a distant paradise began with Homer, who called it Scheria, the happy isle of the Phaeacians, beloved of the gods, where the shipwrecked Odysseus was found washed up on a golden beach by the lovely Nausicaa. Shakespeare had it in mind when creating the magical isle of *The Tempest*, even if Prospero offered a different sort of hospitality to his shipwrecked guests. Edward Lear and Gerald and Lawrence Durrell evoked its charms so delightfully that it found a special niche in the English heart—with staggering consequences. During Corfu's first British occupation, it learned to play cricket; during the second (nearly a million British tourists come a year, and 5000 are permanent residents), the island has learned the consequences of run-amok mass tourism speculation, of letting its beauty be bought and sold so cheaply. Corfiots have been stunned by the Calibanish behavior of British lager louts, then wounded again by the negative reports in the British press. It hardly seemed fair.

The rotten publicity spurred a serious 'culture versus crud' debate on Corfu, and not a moment too soon (certainly too late for the coastal strips on either side of Corfu town, where miles of tacky jerry-built sprawl litters the road and pebble beaches). A new sewage system has sorted out most of the sea pollution complaints. Stricter zoning and licensing laws are being enforced. Hosting the EU summit meeting in July 1994 not only initiated a flurry of overdue repairs, maintenance and improvements, new pedestrian streets, new rows of palm trees, and a spit and polish of Corfu town, but also set the tone for a classier, more genteel Corfu. An Autumn Chamber Music Festival has been added to its successful annual Spring Chamber Music Festival (three quarters of the musicians in the Greek National Orchestra are from Corfu). The casino at the Achilleion is getting an overhaul, as is the notoriously crowded, inefficient airport. Count Spíros Flambouriári, member of an old Corfiot family ennobled by the Venetians, has begun an island 'National Trust' to restore its lovely but mouldering country estates, beautifully photographed in his book *Corfu: The Garden Isle*.

These estates of the gentry are scattered in the gorgeous hinterland (especially to the north of Corfu town), where villages are free of monster concrete hotels, enclaves of expensive villas, and tourist compounds. In some of Corfu's more distant nooks and crannies are lovely beaches that somehow slipped past the cement mixer. Come in the early spring, when the almonds blossom, or around Palm Sunday or the first part of November (coinciding with the colourful celebrations of Ag. Spyrídon), and seek out the old cobbled donkey paths that once provided the main link between villages, and you'll be rewarded with a poignant vision of the old Corfu, strewn with wild flowers (including 43 kinds of orchids), scented with the blossoms of lemons and kumquats, silvery with billowing forests of ancient olives, interspersed with towers of straight black cypresses. They still outnumber tourists by three and half million.

# History

In ancient times Corfu was Corcyra, named after a mistress of the sea god Poseidon. According to ancient tradition, she bore him a son called Phaeax, who became the founder of the gentle and noble Phaeacian race. Archaeological evidence suggests that the Phaeacians were culturally quite distinct from the Mycenaeans, and had much in common, not with any people in Greece, but with cultures in Apulia, in southern Italy. In 734 BC the Corinthians sent a trading colony to the island and founded a city at Paliaopolis (the modern suburbs of Anemómylos and Análypsis). A temple there housed the sickle that Zeus used to castrate his father Cronos, which, according to a prophesy current in Classical Greece, Apollo would one day fetch to do the same to his father Zeus.

Although Corcyra thrived to become the richest of the Ionian islands, it was cursed with violent political rivalries between its democrats and the oligarchs. According to Thucycides, the Corcyrans fought the first sea battle in Greek history against Corinth, in 664 BC; in 435 BC, after the same two city-states quarrelled over a colony in Albania in the Battle of Sybota—a dispute that set off the Peloponnesian war—internal strife left Corcyra so weak that at the beginning of the 4th century BC it was captured by Syracuse, and then by King Pyrrhus of Epirus, and in 229 BC by the Illyrians. In the first century BC, Octavian's army under Agrippa devastated Corfu for its support of Mark Antony. Yet whatever the turmoil, ancient Corcyra never lost its lofty reputation for fertility and beauty; Nero, the ham emperor, paid it a special visit in AD 67 to dance and sing at the temple of Zeus in modern Kassiópi.

The remnants of the population that survived the ravages of the Goths in AD 550 decided to rebuild their town on the more easily defended site of the Old Fortress and two hills of Cape Sidáro where they would be better protected (*coryphoí* in Greek means 'peaks', hence 'Corfu'). It failed to thwart the Normans in 1081, and in 1148 when their raids menaced the Byzantine Empire itself, Emperor Emmanuel Comnenus sent a special force and fleet to dislodge them. When the siege of the Byzantines made no progress, Emmanuel came to lead the attack in person. By craftily causing subversion among the Normans themselves, he succeeded in winning back the island.

## Venetian Corfu

In 1204, when Venice came to claim Corfu, the inhabitants put up a stiff resistance. Although the Venetians succeeded in taking the island's forts, the islanders aligned themselves with the Despotat of Epirus, an Orthodox state. Fifty years later, however, the King of Naples and brother of St Louis of France, Charles I of Anjou, snatched Corfu and the rest of Achaia when his son married the princess of Villehardouin. Angevin rule, already infamous for provoking the Sicilian Vespers, was equally intolerant and hateful on Corfu. After 120 years, the Corfiots swallowed their pride and in 1386 asked Venice to put them under the protection of the Republic.

In 1537 a serious threat, not only to Corfu but to all of Europe, landed at Igoumenítsa in the form of Suleiman the Magnificent. Suleiman, the greatest of the Turkish sultans, already had most of the rest of Greece under his belt and was determined to take Corfu as a base for attacking Italy and Western Europe. Thanks to a peace treaty with Venice, Suleiman was able to plot his attack in the utmost secrecy. When the Corfiots discovered only a few days in advance what was in store for them, they tore down their houses for stone to repair the fortress and to leave nothing behind for the Turks. The terrible Barbarossa was the first to arrive and begin the siege of the city, during which he suffered massive losses. Thousands of

Corfu/Kérkyra

N

10km
5 miles

**Ag. Spiridon**
Astrakeri
Acharavi
Sidari
Peroulades
Avliotes
Karoussades
Roda
Ag. Stefanos
Ag. Panteleimonos
Loutses
Kassiopi
Lafki
Ag. Stefanos
Magoulades
Nimfes
Episkepsis
Perithia
Agnitsini
Ag. Stefanos
Arillas
Kalami
Kouloura
Afionas
Valanion
Choreopiskopi
**Mt. Pantokrator**
**(900m)**
Spartilas
Nissaki
Ag. Georgios
Manatrades
Ag. Markos
Pirgi
Barbati
Ag. Georgios
Bay
Pagio
**Mt. Pylide**
**(619m)**
Korakiani
Ipsos
Makrades
Lakones
Dassia
**To Italy**
Angelokastro
Dassia Bay
Paliokastritsa
Liapades
Kommeno
Dafnila Bay
Giannades
Gouvia
Vido
Kontokali
**KERKYRA (CORFU)**
Ropa
Valley
Ermones
**Mon Repos**
Glyfada
Pelekas
Analypsis
Perama
Kanoni
**To Igoumenitsa**
Sinarades
**Achilleion Palace**
Gastouri
Ag. Gordies
Benitses
**To Paxos, Kefalonia**
**and Patras**
Tsaki
▲ **Mt. Ag. Deka**
**(549m / 1800ft)**
Ano Pavliana
Moraitika
Ag. Mathias
Messoghi
▲ **Mt. Ag. Mathias**
**(427m / 1400ft)**
**Mt. Kava Louvouno**
**(213m / 700ft)**
Chlomos
Alikes
Gardiki
Kouspades
Limni /
Korission
Argirades
Perivoli
Lefkimi
Ag. Georgios
Kavos
**Arkodila**
Cape
Asprokavos

Corfiots who had been pitilessly abandoned outside the fortress were caught in the Venetian and Turkish crossfire, and fell prey to Barbarossa's fits of rage at his continual setbacks. Those who managed to survive were carted off to the slave markets of Constantinople when Suleiman, discouraged by his losses and bad weather, ordered the withdrawal of the siege.

Only 21 years later Venice, under pressure from the Corfiots, expanded the island's fortifications to include the town. Many houses were left unprotected, however, and when the Turks reappeared in 1571 under Ouloudj Ali, these and the rest of the villages, trees and vineyards on Corfu were decimated. This time the Turks took no prisoners and massacred whoever they caught. The devastation was given a final touch two years later by another pirate admiral, Sinan Pasha: of the entire Corfiot population, only a tenth remained on the island after 1573.

In 1576 Venice finally began to build the walls required for the safety of all the Corfiots, together with the Fortezza Nuova and other fortifications designed by the expert Sammicheli that were considered superb, state-of-the art works in their day—the equal of Sammicheli's bastions around Heráklion. The Venetians also undertook measures to restore Corfu's economy, most notably by offering a bounty of 42 *tsekínia* for every olive tree planted (today there are an estimated 4.5 million, supplying 3 per cent of the world supply). Sammicheli's walls were given the ultimate test in 1716, when Turks staged furious attacks for one terrible month, before being repulsed by the stratagems of a German mercenary soldier, Field Marshal Schulenberg, and a tempest sent by Corfu's guardian angel, St Spyrídon.

After the fall of Venice to Napoleon, the French occupied Corfu and immediately improved the education system and set up the first public library (1797), but they lost it two years later in a fierce battle against the Russo-Turkish fleet. When Napoleon finally got the island back, he personally designed new fortifications for the town; he loved Corfu, 'more interesting to us than all of Italy put together'. Napoleon's walls were so formidable that the British, when allotted the Ionian islands after Waterloo, did not care to attack them when the French commander Donzelot refused to give them up. The French government finally had to order Donzelot home, and in 1815, with the signing of Treaty of Vienna, Corfu became a British Protectorate, with the blessing of Count John Capodistria. Capodistria, soon to be the first president of Greece, was a native of Corfu and, like many of the island's noblemen and scholars, had been in the employ of the tsars after 1799.

## British and Greek Corfu

But while Capodistria had requested 'military protection', the British, based in Corfu, took it upon themselves to run all the affairs of the Ionian State, legalized by a constitution imposed under the first Lord High Commission, Sir Thomas Maitland, whose brutal and unbelievably rude behaviour earned him the nickname 'King Tom'. One of his first acts was to demolish part of the Venetian walls to build new, more powerful ones in their place, calling upon the Ionian government to cough up more than a million gold sovereigns to pay for the improvements. Maitland made himself even more disliked by forcing neutrality on the islands as the War of Greek independence broke out, disarming the population and imprisoning, and even executing, members of the secret patriotic Society of Friends. The constitution ensured that the peasantry lived in near-feudal conditions, and denied any political role for Corfu's educated and middle classes; the Ionians weren't even given any favourable trade status with Britain. It was a no-win situation, as one British High Commissioner put it, 'a sort of middle state between a colony and a perfectly independent country, without possessing the advantage of either.' Other public works were more positive—the building of new roads and schools and a university (the 'Ionian Academy', founded by philhellene Lord Guilford), and a permanent water supply to Corfu town—were more long-lasting.

In 1858, with the situation growing increasingly uncomfortable, Gladstone was sent down as a special investigator to proposed a solution to the crisis, but, constrained by the international situation (British distrust of King Otho and Greece's support of Russia, Britian's enemy in the Crimean War), he only proposed a reconstruction of the government. The 1862 overthrow of Otho gave Britain a chance to cede the islands gracefully over to Greece, on condition that Greece found an acceptable king, which it duly did in the form of Prince William of Denmark, crowned George I, King of the Hellenes; on 21 May 1864 the Ionians were presented as the new king's 'dowry'. There was one ungracious condition to the deal: that the British ensure the islands' neutrality by destroying the fortresses of Corfu—not only the walls they themselves had just made the Corfiots build, but also the historic Venetian buildings. A wave of protest from all corners of the Greek world failed to move the British, and the fortifications were blown up, leaving substantial remains standing today.

In 1923 Mussolini gave the world a preview of his intention when he bombarded and occupied Corfu after the assassination on Greek territory of an Italian delegate to the Greek-Albanian border council; the Italians left only when Greece paid a large indemnity. An even worse bombardment occurred in 1943, when the Germans blasted the city and its Italian garrison for ten days; a year later, the British and Americans bombed the Germans. At the end of the war, a quarter of the old city was destroyed, including 14 of the loveliest churches.

---

### Getting There and Around

**By air**: frequent charter flights from London, Manchester, Glasgow and other UK airports; also regular flights from many European cities; three flights a day from Athens, two in the winter. The Olympic Airways office in Corfu town is at Kapodistríou 20, ✆ (0661) 38 694/5/6; if you're flying from Athens, a new private Greek airline, SEEA (3 Moustoxídi St, ✆ 46 241) offers very competitive fares, with schedules corresponding to Virgin Air flights to and from London. There is no special bus service linking Corfu's airport in Kanóni to the town, but there is a regular bus stop on the main road, several hundred metres away. For general airport info, call ✆ (0661) 30 180 or 37 398.

**By sea**: year-round **ferries** from Brindisi, Bari, Ancona, and possibly other Italian ports such as Trieste and Ortona (ships stop en route to Pátras, most allowing a free stop-over in Corfu. You must specify this when you purchase your ticket). A catamaran links Brindisi to Corfu in 3½ hours (Corfu: Charitos Travel, 35 Arseníou, ✆ (0661) 44 611; Athens: 28 Níkis, Sýntagma, ✆ (01) 322 0503). Services to Croatia have been suspended. Also in the summer ferries sail from Igoumenítsa, less frequently off season. In season there are connections with Pátras, Ithaca, Kefaloniá and a year-round daily ferry to Paxí. Ferry links with the small islands of Eríkousa, Othoní and Mathráki are only twice a week; for details call ✆ 36 355. **Port authority**, ✆ 34 036.

**By bus**: Frequent buses run from Athens and Thessaloníki to Igoumenítsa. The bus depot in Platéia Theotóki–San Rócco Square, ✆ 31 595, has blue KTEL buses to villages just beyond the city (Kanóni, Pótamos, Konokali, Goúvia, Dassiá, Pérama, Ag. Ioánnis, Benítses, Pélekas, Kastelláni, Kouramádes, Ára, Achilleíon and Gastoúri).

From the depot in Avramíou St, ✆ 39 985/30 627, green buses run to the more distant villages (Ipsos, Pýrgi Glyfáda, Barbáti, Kassiópi, Paliokastrítsa, Sidári, Ag. Stéfanos, Róda, Kávo, Messógi, Ag. Goriés, and both resorts named Ag. Geórgios), as well as to Athens (leaving at 9am, journey time 7 hours) and Thessaloníki.

**By bicycle:** the Dutch Bicycle company, Ag. Ioannis Trilino, ✆/✆ 52 407 rents out mountain bikes for exploring the hidden corners of Corfu.

**By car:** although lately much improved, Corfu's roads are not always well signposted, and there seem to be more than the usual number of Greek island hazards: dangerous curves, donkeys and farm vehicles, careless tourists on motorbikes, sudden deteriorations in the pavement. Road maps often confuse donkey tracks with unpaved roads. The island's petrol stations open on a rota outside usual hours (Mon–Fri, 7am–7pm, Sat, 7am–3pm).

**Tours:** travel agents in Corfu offer one-day Classical tours to the mainland: to Epirus to visit the Oracle of the Dead (consulted by Odysseus after crossing the perilous River Styx), and the ancient cities of Kassopea and Nicopolis, founded by Augustus after the defeat of Mark Antony and Cleopatra in 31 BC. A second tour takes in Dodóni, with its ancient theatre and Ioannína, the modern capital of Epirus, with its island of Ali Pasha and museum. Excursions to Albania depend on the very touchy political situation; they generally visit the ancient Roman city of Saranda.

### Tourist Information

**EOT:** New Fortress Square (behind the new fort in the old port), ✆ (0661) 37 520.

**Tourist police:** New Fortress Square (but they may move soon), ✆ 30 265. The Municipality of Corfu has information kiosks in the Esplanade, New Port, and San Rocco Square.

**OTE telephones** : Mántaros and Kapodistríou Streets.

**Post office:** Alexándras Avenue, ✆ 39 265.

### Consulates

| | |
|---|---|
| **Great Britain** | 1 Menektrátous Street, ✆ 30 055. |
| **Ireland** | 20a Kapodistríou Street, ✆ 32 469/39 910. |
| **Netherlands** | 2 Idroménou Street, ✆ 39 900. |
| **Germany** | 57 Guilford Street, ✆ 31 453. |
| **France** | 15 Desillas Street, ✆ 30 067. |
| **Denmark** | 4 E. Antistásseos, ✆ 38 712. |
| **Norway** | 7 Donzelótou Street, ✆ 32 423. |

### Festivals

Procession of Ag. Spyrídon in Corfu town on **Palm Sunday**, **Easter**, **11 August** and **first Sunday in November**. **Holy Saturday** is celebrated in Corfu town with a bang—the sound of everyone tossing out their chipped and cracked crockery. **First Friday** after **Easter**, Paliokastrítsa; **21 May**, Union with Greece; **5–8 July**, at Lefkimi; **10 July**, Ag. Prokópios at Kávos; **14 August**, the Procession of Lights at Mandoúki; **15 August**, Panagías at Kassiópi; The Corfu Festival in **September** brings concerts, ballet, opera and theatre to the island.

# Corfu Town

Corfu town, or Kérkyra, with a population of 40,000 the largest town in the Ionian islands, was laid out by the Venetians in the 14th century, when the medieval town, crowded on to the peninsula of Cape Sidáro (where the old fortress now stands), had no room to expand. They began with the quarter known as Campiello (from *campo*, Venetian for 'square') where narrow three- or four-storey houses loom over the narrow streets, as they do back in the lagoon capital. By the time the new walls were added in the 16th century, the Venetians built at a more leisurely pace in the more open style of the Renaissance, laying out an exquisite series of central streets and small squares; some of the finest Venetian houses, with their arches decorated with masks and half-moon windows over the door, can be seen along the upper Esplanade. The British knocked down most of the old Venetian walls to allow the pent-up town to expand again, and then constructed a set of elegant Georgian public buildings.

Besides Campiello, the old city is divided into a number of small quarters. The 19th-century residential district to the south is called Garítsa; if you arrive from Italy, you enter the city through its back door at Mandoúki or New Port, west of the New Fortress. Mandoúki isn't one of the more attractive parts of town, but it's a good place to look for cheap rooms and food. Excursion boats to Paxí and Albania still use the Old Port, just under Campiello.

## The New Fortress

The New Fortress, or Néo Froúrio, is the mass of walls that dominates the view if you arrive by sea, built after 1576 by the Venetians following the Ottomans' third attack on Corfu. It bore the brunt of the Turks' siege of 1716, and although most of the walls were destroyed by the British, enough masonry survived for the installation of a Greek naval base. Over the gates are carved Lions of the St Mark and inscriptions in various state of erosion. Now open to the public (*open daily till 5*, entrance from Solomós Street) there are excellent views of Corfu town from the top of its bastions, and two underground tunnels to explore. **Corfu's Market** is in the Fortress's moat along G. Markorá Street; if you're self-catering or planning a picnic, try to come early to get the pick of the fresh fish and produce. Near the green bus station in Avramíou Street stands the 1749 Catholic **church of Ténedos**, named after an icon brought to Corfu by the Venetians from the now Turkish island of Ténedos. A bit further west, on Polichroni Konstantá Street, the **Monastery of Platýteras** contains two beautiful icons given to the island by Catherine the Great, in honour of Count Ioánnis Kapodístrias (John Capodistria), who is buried here; also note the silver and gilt columns by the altar, a typical Russian feature.

No longer used by either the big Italian or Igoumenítsa ferries, the Old Port on the east side of the New Fortress is just beginning to get over its identity crisis. The beautiful **Corfu Shell Museum** (*open daily 9.30–7; adm*) was relocated from Benítses to Solomós Street in an effort to revitalize the area, but its future is cloudy; at the time of writing the collection is up for sale. From the Old Port you can reach the centre of town through the 16th-century Spiliá Gate, incorporated into a later structure, or take the narrow step up into the medieval Campiello Quarter (*see* below); the **Jewish Quarter**, equally old and picturesque, lies south of Plateía

**Corfu Town**

Map labels:
- OLD PORT
- NEW PORT
- NEW VENETIAN FORTRESS
- XENOFONDOS STRATIGOU
- To Mandouki
- Ktel long distance (Green) Bus Terminal
- AVRAMIOU
- AVRAMI HILL
- G. MARKORA
- I. THEOTOKI
- Hospital
- POLICHRONI KONSTANDA
- City (Blue) Bus Terminal
- Plateia G. Theotoki (Sanrocco)
- DIMOULITSA
- MITROPOLITI METHODIOU
- ZAFEIROPOULOU
- KOLOKOTRONI
- British Cemetery
- Prison
- To Kanoni
- GARITSA
- Tourist Po...
- Plateia Solomou

Solomoú. Although
the Greek synagogue and a
school remain in the heart of the
quarter, in Velissáriou Street (the Italian
synagogue was bombed and burned in 1943),
only 170 out of 1800 members of the congrega-
tion sent to Auschwitz survived to return to
Corfu after the war.

## The Esplanade (Spianáda) and the Listón

A series of long parallel streets—the main residential
district of the Venetians—all lead to the town's
centre, the great green space called the Spianáda or
Esplanade, one of the largest public squares in Europe.
Originally the area was left open for defensive purposes;
under Napoleon it began to take its present form as a
garden and promenade, when he ordered the building
of the arcades of the **Listón** on the west edge of the
Esplanade in imitation of one of his proudest Paris
creations: the rue de Rivoli. At the time, it was the only

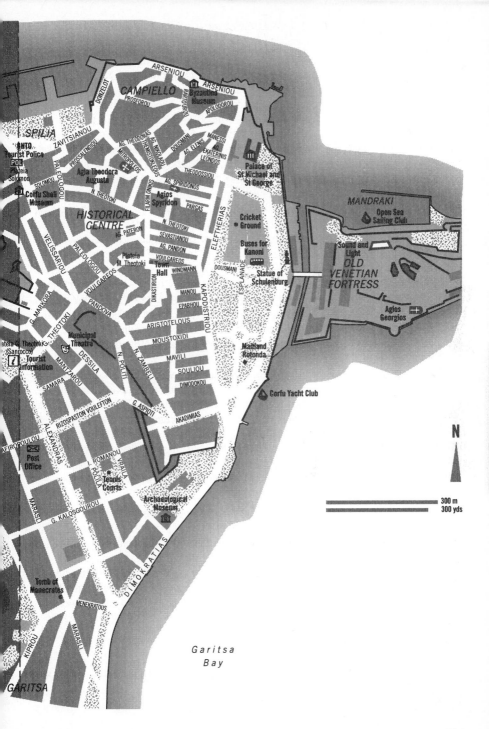

**SPILIA**

ARSENIOU

ARSENIOU

**CAMPIELLO**

Byzantine Museum

DONZELOT

PROSFOROU

RAPTHUBROU

APOLODOROU

ANTO
Tourist Police
POL
Plateia
Solomou

ZAVITSIANOU

PROSALENDOU

PALEOLOGOU

HIEROTEKI

AG. THEODORAS

AG. KONSTANTINOS

DOUSMANI

AG. ELENIS

MANESSI

AG. EKATERINIS

LEONDOS

Corfu Shell Museum

SOLOMOU

Agia Theodora Augusta

N. THEOTON

THEODOSSIOU

Palace of St Michael and St George

**MANDRAKI**

Open Sea Sailing Club

FLAMIN ONIKS

AG. SPIRIDONOS

Agios Spyridon

PARGAS

Cricket Ground

**HISTORICAL CENTRE**

VELISSARIOU

PALEOLOGOU

PROIGSALENDOU

AG. PATERON

N. THEOTON

N. THEOTKI

SEVASTIANOU

AG. PANDON

ELEFTHERIAS

Buses for Kanoni

**OLD VENETIAN FORTRESS**

Sound and Light

Plateia M. Theotoki

VOULGAREOS

Town Hall

WINDMANN

DOUSMANI

Statue of Schulenburg

Agios Georgios

G. MARKORA

VOULGAREOS

PANDOVA

DIKASTIRION

MANOU

KAPODISTRIOU

EPARHOU

ESPLANADE

ateia G. Theotok
(Sancocco)

THEOTOKI

Municipal Theatre

N. POLITI

ARISTOTELOUS

MOUSTOXIDI

Maitland Rotonda

i Tourist Information

MANTZAROU

DESSILA

N. ZAMBELI

MAVILI

SOULIOU

SAMARA

RIZOSPASTON VOULEFTON

G. ASPIOTI

DIMODOKOU

Corfu Yacht Club

AKADIMIAS

**N**

FIROPOULOU

ALEXANDRAS

I. ROMANOU

POLILA

Post Office

VRAILA

MARASLI

Tennis Courts

G. KALOSGOUROU

**Archaeological Museum**

DIMOKRATIAS

Tomb of Menecrates

MENEKRATOUS

MARASLI

300 m
300 yds

KIPROU

**GARITSA**

*Garitsa Bay*

381

place in all of Greece reserved exclusively for the aristocracy. Then as now the Listón is a solid row of cafés, decorated with immaculate flowerbeds; at night the monuments and trees are floodlit for dramatic effect.

The northern end of the Esplanade is filled by the Georgian **Palace of St Michael and St George** (*open 8.30–3, closed Mon; adm*) with its two grand gates. Designed by Sir George Whitmore, the palace was built as the residence of Sir Thomas Maitland, first High Commissioner of the Ionian islands—hence the symbols of the seven islands that adorn its Maltese marble façade. In 1864 it became the summer residence of the King of Greece, then fell into disuse until it was renovated in 1953 to house a magnificent **Museum of Asiatic Art**, one of the largest and most important privately formed collections in the world, and the only one of its kind in Greece. A gift to Corfu from Greek diplomat Gregórios Mános, with further contributions from Michélis Chadjivasilíou and others, the museum contains 10,000 works (masks, ceramics, armour and weapons, and much more) from all the countries of the Far East, dating back to 1000 BC. The whole collection was packed into boxes for the 1994 European Summit meeting, but should be reopening at the end of 1995. Adjacent to the palace is the *loggia* of the **Reading Society** (*open daily 9–1*), founded in 1836 by a group of young Corfiot idealists freshly returned from their studies in France; the library has a fine collection of books on the Ionian islands. Just in front of the palace is another British legacy—the **cricket ground**, where little boys play football until their older white-clad brothers chase them off the field. In the summer, matches are held, pitting the six local teams (which aren't at all bad) against visitors from Britain, the Greek mainland and Europe. Numerous monuments embellish the Esplanade. Towards the centre is the **memorial to Sir Thomas Maitland**, another work of Sir George Whitmore, designed in the form of an Ionian rotunda, where the three local brass bands serenade the ginger-beer-sipping public in the summer; you can often hear them practising in the evening in the old quarters. There is a marble **statue of Marshal Schulenburg**, the crafty and heroic soldier of fortune from Saxony, who outwitted the Turkish High Admiral in the Great Siege to spoil the last major attempt of the Ottoman Empire to expand in the west. The **Guilford Memorial** is of Corfu's favourite Englishman, the Hellenophile Frederick North, Earl of Guilford (1769–1828). The seated statue portrays him dressed in ancient robes, a touch he would probably have appreciated. On the southern end of the Esplanade is a statue of his ambiguous Corfiot friend, Count Capodistria, first president of Greece, who was assassinated for his murky political machinations.

The **Old Fortress** (*open till 7pm, closed Mon*) on Cape Sidáro is separated from the Esplanade by the moat, or *contra fosse*, dug over a 100-year period by the Venetians. The medieval town of Corfu was located on the two little hills of the cape; scholars have identified the site with the Heraion acropolis mentioned by Thucydides. The walls, built up over the centuries, were badly damaged by the British; others have fallen into decay. Part of the fortress is still used by the Greek army, but you can wander about and explore the Venetian tunnels, battlements, drawbridge, the Venetian well, cannons dating back to 1684 and **St George's**, the church of the British garrison. Best of all, however, is the view of the city from the hills.

## Ag. Spyrídon

The church of Corfu's patron saint Ag. Spyrídon—the original Spiros—is in the old town, not far from the Ionian and Popular Bank of Greece. It's easy to find: the campanile soars above town like the mast of a ship, often bedecked with flags and Christmas lights. Ag. Spyrídon was the Bishop of Cyprus in the 4th century; when Constantinople fell to the Turks, his bones were smuggled in a sack of straw to Corfu. The church was built in 1596 to house the precious relics, no longer in straw but in a silver Renaissance reliquary which with great pomp is carted though town on the saint's feast days (Orthodox Palm Sunday, Easter Saturday, 11 August and the first Sunday in November). According to the Corfiots, Spyrídon 'the Miracle-Worker' has brought them safely through many trials, frightening both cholera and the Turks away from his beloved worshippers. He even gave the Catholics a good scare when they considered placing an altar in his church; the night before its dedication, he blew up a powder magazine in the Old Fortress with a bolt of lightning to show his displeasure. He did, however, peacefully accept the large silver lamp from the Venetians in thanks for his divine intervention against the Turks in 1716; the Italianate ceiling paintings this time have been repainted with a heavy hand. You can queue up to pay your respects to his ancient body (the Greeks believe he can cure spots and earaches, as well as drive away plague); amid frescoes blackened by the smoke of ages the gold shimmers through in the flickering candle-light.

The nearby Ionian Bank houses a **Museum of Paper Money** (*open 9–1 Mon–Sat*) with a collection of banknotes from around the world, and Greek notes dating from the nation's birth. The second floor is given over to an exhibition demonstrating the various stages in the production of banknotes. Across the square, the 1689 church of the **Holy Virgin Faneroméni** contains some fine icons of the Ionian School.

The square gives on to the main street Nikifórou Theotóki, one of the prettiest in the town. From there head up E. Voulgáreos St to the elegant square with Corfu's **Town Hall**, a Venetian confection begun in 1691 that later did duty as the municipal opera house; grotesque faces grimace all around the building and a bas-relief shows a triumphant Doge. The **Catholic Cathedral of St James** on the square was seriously damaged by the German bombing in 1943. Only the bell tower survived intact; the rest has been reconstructed.

## Campiello

There are a number of buildings worth seeking out in the Campiello quarter between the Old Port and the Esplanade, beginning with the 1577 **Orthodox Cathedral**, its 18th-century façade rather unfortunately located next to the rudest T-shirt shop in town. It is dedicated to Ag. Theodóra Augústa, Empress of Byzantium (829–842), who was canonized for her role in restoring icon worship in the Orthodox Church following the Iconoclasm. Her relics were brought to Corfu along with those of Ag. Spyrídon and lie in a silver casket in the chapel to the right of the altar; if the priest in charge likes the look of you, you can kiss her and take home titbits of her slipper; donations more than welcome. The gold ground icons are lovely, reminscent of 13th-century Italian art.

The **Byzantine Museum of Corfu** (*open daily 8.45–3, Sun 9.30–2.30, closed Mon; adm*) is near here, up the steps from Arseníou Street. The collection is housed in the beautifully restored 15th-century Antivouniótissa, typical of the Ionian style of church, with its single aisle, timber roof and exonarthex, or indoor porch, that runs around three sides of the building. Among the eminent Corfiots buried under the flagstones is Capodístria's sister, who was a nun here. The church has one of the elaborately decorated ceilings or *ourania* ('heaven') that the Ionians were so fond of, and a stone iconostasis from a later date, and very Italianate 17th-century Old Testament murals on the walls. Icons from all over the island have been brought here; note especially the mid-16th century *SS. Sergius, Bacchus and Justine* by Michael Damaskinós, the 17th century *St Cyril of Alexandria* by Emmanuel Tzanes, the 17th-century four-handed *Ag. Pantelέimon* and icons by the 18th-century painter Geórgios

Chrysolorás. On the same street is the **Solomós Museum**, with a collection of old photographs and memorabilia associated with Zákynthos poet Diónysos Solomós, who lived here (*see* p.438) (*open weekdays 9–2*).

On a narrow stairway off Philharmonikí Street, **Ag. Nikólaos** had the distinction of once serving as the parish church for the King of Serbia. After the defeat of the Serbian army by the Austro-Hungarians in 1916, the King, his government and some 150,000 Serbs took refuge on Corfu. A third of them died shortly thereafter from the flu and are buried on **Vído island**. Boats from the Old Port regularly make the trip to Vído; the Venetians fortified it after the Turks built a gun battery on it to attack the Old Fortress in 1537. The walls were demolished by the British. Today the island is a quiet refuge with footpaths, a little beach, and a memorial to the Serbs. It is also home to the **Kérkyra Bird and Wildlife Sanctuary**, a charity set up to treat birds often injured during the shooting season, who keep company with an impressive collection of exotic birds from cockatoos to macaws.

## South of Corfu Town

### Garítsa and the Archaeology Museum

South of the Old Fortress, Garítsa Bay is believed to have been the harbour of King Alcinous of the Phaeacians; originally it became a fashionable residential district just in time for the neoclassical buildings. There is a **Serbian War Museum** on Moustoxídi Street (*open 9–12*). This is not at all what immediately springs to mind, but a collection of photographs and memorabilia from the Balkan War of 1915–17 and covering Corfu's role in aiding the refugees. On Kolokotróni Street the **British Cemetery** is set in beautiful, peaceful gardens; the graves, many with intriguing headstones, date from the beginning of British protectorate.

The star attraction in Garítsa is the **Archaeology Museum** (*open 8.30–3, closed Mon; adm*), with an excellent collection of finds from the island and nearby mainland. So much has been discovered on the island that the museum, opened in 1967, has already been extended and is still too small to display everything. Among the new exhibits are bronze statuettes from Archaic to Roman times, a horde of silver staters from the 6th century BC, an iron helmet with silver overlay from the 4th century BC, and Cycladic sculptures, discovered in 1992 by a customs officer as the smugglers attempted to spirit them abroad from Igoumenítsa. Upstairs are recently found grave-offerings, Archaic statues of the *kore* and *kouros* and two statues of Aphrodite, the favourite goddess of the Corinthians. Beyond is the snarling, stylized 'Lion of Menecrates', found on the tomb of the same name (*see* below) and the relief of a Dionysiac Symposium (*c. 500* BC), showing the god Dionysos with a youth, lying on a couch, their eyes focused intently on a something that is probably lost forever. A lion sleeps under the couch; a dog comes striding up. One room is given over to the striking wall-sized Gorgon Pediment (585 BC) discovered near the temple of Artemis in Kanóni, housed in a room all to itself; the oldest preserved stone pediment, and one of the largest (17m wide), it shows how advanced the Corinthians were in the early days of monumental sculpture. The grinning Gorgon Medusa is powerfully drawn, running with one knee on the ground, flanked by her two children, Pegusus the winged horse and Chrysaor; according to myth they were born from her blood when she was slain by Perseus, although here she looks very alive indeed. Two large leopards on either side suggest that this is actually Artemis herself in her form of 'the Lady of the Wild Animals', a fearsome goddess who demanded an annual holocaust of the creatures she protected, burned alive on the altar; in the far corners of the pediment, much smaller scenes show the Clash of the Titans.

The circular, 7th-century BC **Menecrates tomb** was discovered in the 19th century in an excellent state of preservation. Its lower sections are still intact in the garden of a building at the junction of Marasslí and Kíprou Streets, three blocks south of the museum.

## Southern Suburbs along the Kanóni Peninsula

City bus no.3 from Corfu Town passes through all of the garden suburbs draped over the little **Kanóni peninsula** that dangles south of Garítsa Bay. Ancient Corcyra originally occupied much of this peninsula, and had two harbours: what is now the Chalkiopóulos lagoon to the west and the ring-shaped 'harbour of King Alcinous' (now filled in) in the northeastern corner of the peninsula, at Anemómylos. Above it, right on top of the centre of ancient Corcyra, Sir Frederick, the second High Commissioner of the Ionian State, built the little Regency villa of **Mon Repos** for his Corfiot wife. The Greek royal family later adopted it as a summer villa; Queen Elizabeth II's consort, Philip, Duke of Edinburgh, was born here in 1921. In 1994, the Greek Government allowed the Municipality of Corfu to repossess the estate from ex-King Constantine and the beautiful wooded park is to be developed as an archaeological park. So far a Roman villa and bath has been discovered on the periphery, at Kasfíki, opposite the ruined 5th-century basilica of Ag. Kérkyra at Paleópolis (by the crossroads, opposite the gate of Mon Repos). Little Mon Repos beach—Corfu's town beach—is just below if you need a dip; a few lanes back, don't miss the 11th-century church of **Ag. Iássonos and Sosipater**, the only Byzantine-style church on the whole island; inside are lovely icons and iconostasis and the tombs of the church's namesakes, two martyrs instructed by St Paul, who brought Christianity to Corfu in AD 70. Near the Venetian church, along the wall of Mon Repos, a path leads to the bucolic spring of **Kardáki**, which flows year round from the mouth of a stone lion; the Venetians used it to supply their ships. The cold water is good, but an inscription above warns: 'Every stranger who wets his lips here to his home will not return.' Below the spring are the ruins of a 6th-century BC Doric temple. From here it's an easy walk to the lush and lovely residential area of Análypsos.

Further south, a minor road leads to the Doric **Temple of Artemis** (585 BC), source of the magnificent Gorgon Pediment in the Archaeology Museum. The large altar and the retaining wall of the Hellenistic stoa survive; some of its stones were cannibalized in the 5th century to build the adjacent convent of **Ag. Teodóri**. Kanóni, at the southern tip of the lovely little peninsula, is named for the old cannon once situated on the bluff, where two cafés now overlook the pretty bay, the harbour of ancient Corcyra. Two islets protected it: that of the picturesque oft-photographed convent **Panagía Vlancharína**, connected to the shore by a causeway, and **Pondikonísi**, the Isle of the Mouse, with its 13th-century chapel, Ag. Pnévmatos. Pondikonísi was the Phoenician ship that brought Odysseus home to Ithaca, but which, on its way home, the angry Poseidon smote 'with his open palm, and made the ship a rock, fast rooted in the bed of the deep sea', according to the *Odyssey*. An airport runway built on a landfill site now crosses the west end of the shallow lagoon, and a collection of big new hotels has toadstooled nearby, in spite of the noise of planes day and night, which can interrupt a good night's sleep.

## Pérama, Gastoúri and the Achilleion

Once past the Kanóni peninsula and linked to it by a causeway over the lagoon, **Pérama** claims to be the site of King Alcinous' wonderful garden, and still offers more swish villas to rent than any other place on this luxurious island. The big attraction in these parts is Corfu's casino in the pretty village of **Gastoúri**, a neoclassical neo-Pompeiian villa called the **Achilleion** (*open for tours daily in summer, 8.45am–3.30pm*). The setting is dreamy, with lovely views in all directions, but the villa is something of a nightmare, kitschy enough to be used as a location for the James Bond film *For Your Eyes Only*. Built in 1890 by the Empress Elisabeth ('Sissi') of Austria after the tragic death of her only son Rudolphe, the villa was named for Sissi's passion for the hero of Homer's *Iliad*, represented by a large marble statue she had made of the *Dying Achilles* for the garden. Ten years after Sissi was assassinated in 1898 by an Italian anarchist, Kaiser Wilhelm II purchased the Achilleion and made it his summer residence from 1908 to 1914, and, true to character, had the *Dying Achilles* replaced with a huge bronze *Victorious Achilles*, with the inscription 'To the Greatest of the Greeks from the Greatest of the Germans.' Among the bevy of more delicate statues, note the Grace standing next to Apollo, sculpted by Canova, using Napoleon's sister Pauline Borghese as his model. The small museum contains, among its collection of imperial mementoes, one of the Kaiser's swivelling saddle, from which he dictated plans for the First World War, and photos of him swanning around on his huge yacht, the *Hohenzollern*, which he used to anchor off the 'Kaiser's Bridge' just south of Pérama.

---

### Shopping

Xenoglosso, Ger. Markóra 45, near San Rocco Square has a good selection of books in English. Autolycus Gallery, in Nikandrou Street off Kapodístrias, has a fine collection of antique prints, maps, postcards and watercolours. There are a number of high-fashion shops, although the most famous must be Panton on Panton Street, the main outlet of Corfu designer Lisa Palavicini, whose clothes have been featured in Vogue and are sold in outlets in Athens, London and Jordan.

---

*Corfu Town ☎ (0661–)*

### Where to Stay

#### luxury

There's a cache of luxurious high-rise palaces in Kanóni, like the **Corfu Hilton** (*lux*), a hotel and bungalow complex with a casino, ☎ 36 540, ✆ 36 551 and one of the few hotels in Greece with a bowling alley, but a room here could cost 30,000dr in high season. Just south of the centre, the enormous **Corfou Palace**, Dimokratías Ave, ☎ 39 485, ✆ 31 749 (*lux*) has two swimming pools and all the trimmings from baby sitting to 24-hour room service.

#### expensive

For old-style elegance, no hotel on Corfu can compete with the **Cavalieri Corfu**, located on the end of the Esplanade at 4 Kapodistríou, ☎ 39 336 (*A*) in a renovated French mansion; comfortable, air-conditioned, and with a scenic roof garden. Overlooking the Old Port there's the **Astron Hotel** at 15 Donzelótou, ☎ 39 505 (*B*) in a charming Venetian building; most rooms have balconies. *Open all year.*

#### moderate

The salmon-coloured **Bella Venezia**, just back from the Esplanade at 4 Napoleon Zambeli, ☎ 44 290 (*C*) is a renovated old building in a quiet part of the centre of town, with a pretty garden terrace, open all year. If you'd prefer something newer, there's the **Europa**, 10 Gitsiáli, at the New Port, ☎ 39 304 (*D*); along with modern, clean rooms, it has a self-service laundrette. If you'd prefer to be on the Esplanade, try the **Arcadion** at 44 Kapodistríou, ✆ 37 671 (*C*). The **Royal**, in Kanóni, ✆ 37 512 (*C*) enjoys commanding position and could be a class or two higher, with its three swimming pools on descending levels, roof garden and fine views over Mouse Island and the airport's busy runway. **Hermes**, 12 Ger. Markóra, ✆ 31 747 (*C*), is a moderate-sized hotel away from the tourist crowds, on the inland side of the New Fortress.

*inexpensive*

Some of the better cheap sleeps in the historic centre are: **Kypros**, 13 Ag. Patéron, north of the Town Hall, ✆ 30 032 (*E*); **Kriti**, 43 N. Theotóki 23, ✆ 38 69 (*E*); the once grand **Konstantinoupolis**, overlooking the Old Port at K. Zavitsianóu, ✆ 39 826 (*D*). For something even less dear, try the list of rooms to rent from the National Tourist Office, by the New Fortress (✆ 37 520/638). Most of these are in the old quarters and cost 4000dr. upwards for a bed in season. The youth hostel, and nearest campsite, are 8km north in Kontokáli (*see* below).

---

*Corfu Town ✆ (0661–)*                                                    **Eating Out**

Corfu shows its Venetian heritage in the kitchen as well as in its architecture. Look for *sofríto*, a veal stew flavoured with garlic, vinegar and parsley; *bourdétto*, a fish stew, liberally peppered, and *pastitsátha*, a pasta and veal dish; the island's own sweet is *sikomaeda*, or fig pie. Eating out on the genteel Listón, with front-row seats on the crowds, can be expensive unless you stick to pizza, but one street back at 66 Kapodistríou, **Rex**, ✆ 39 649, is good value—try the local speciality *sofríto* and other Corfiot dishes, and pay 2500dr for a meal. **Yoryias Taverna** on Guilford Street is also famous for Corfiot dishes. In Kremastí Square the **Venetian Well**, ✆ 44 761, has a varied menu which changes daily, featuring Greek, international and oriental specialities and a wide choice of Greek wines (*2500dr*). **Pizza Pete**, in Arseníou St, overlooking the old port, prides himself on the best in town—a pizza meal will run to 1500dr. The elegant **Xenichtes**, 12 Potamoú in Mandoúki, ✆ 24 911 or 22 035, has served excellent Greek food with a sprinkling of dishes from other countries for almost 20 years; fresh salmon is delivered every morning on the Oslo–Corfu flight (*3–3500dr*); the **Averof**, at Alipóu and Prosselendóu St, is a long-established favourite of tourists and locals alike. **L. Gigisdakis**, at Solomoú 28, is as authentic an old Greek taverna as you could hope for, with old pots bubbling away in the kitchen and ready oven dishes; try their pickled octopus (*achtapóthi xytháto*); meals around 2000dr. By the New Port, in Xen. Stratigoú St, the smart **Orestes** has dining inside and in a pleasant little garden opposite; if you order their seafood specialities, you'll pay 4000dr. There are several other fish restaurants in the same area. Near the Archaeology Museum, pretty turquoise-tiled **Il Giardino**, U. Armeni 4, ✆ 30 723, serves delicious Italian food; try the pasta stuffed with walnuts and spinach (*4–5000dr*).

Out in Kanóni, **Restaurant Nausicaa**, Nausicá 11, ✆ 44 354, serves delicious Greek, French and Eastern dishes under the garden trellis (fairly dear, but they take credit cards). Its close neighbour, **Taverna Pelargos**, looks a bit corny from the outside but serves a vast array of well-prepared Greek dishes: the *stifádo* and *sofríto* are superb (*around 2500dr*). In nearby Anemómylos, the new **Tai Pan**, A. Dari 61, ✆ 24 184 is a superb Chinese restaurant, with a Szechuan chef adroitly manning the woks. Tea is on the menu, but even better is the delicious house wine from Kinopiástes (*3500–5000dr*). In Kinopiástes itself (3km from Gastoúri), **Taverna Tripa** ('Hole in the Wall') run since 1947 by Spíros Anifantís, is something of a Corfu national monument, completely cluttered inside with bottles, knick-knacks, a hurdy gurdy, photos (mostly of Mr Anifantís with celebrity diners), while up on the ceiling strings of salamis, sausages, peppers and garlic are linked by cobwebs. Greek nights here are renowned, with up to 10 courses served; although it's not cheap, the food and service are excellent and the costumed waiters put on a folk-dancing show to boot. Nearby, on the Achilleion road (about 7km from town) are two tavernas with live music and good, reasonably priced food, the **Barbathomas**, with meat specialities, and **Pontis**, with a big selection of *mezédes*, spit-roasted lamb, charcoal grills and local dishes; you can eat well at either for 3000dr.

---

### Entertainment and Nightlife

Pick up a copy of the monthly *The Corfiot* or the *Corfu News* for local news and a calendar of events; published primarily for residents, it makes interesting reading. Other media are even better served: Corfu has three cable TV stations and 17 radio stations, and a flip through the FM dial may even dig up an English-speaking DJ. Most of the music and dancing places are concentrated in either the disco ghetto north of town or, a bit less brash, to the south along or just off Dimokratías Street. A more sedate **Sound and Light Show** with **folk-dancing** performances happens every night except Sundays in the Old Fortress (*weekdays in English at 9.45pm, 1 June–30 Sept; combined ticket 600dr.*). For a perfectly artificial evening, there's **Danilia's Village** inland from Kontokáli (*open 9–1 and 6pm till late*). A reconstruction of a quainter-than-real Corfiot village, there's museum, shopping arcade, folklore museum, and displays of traditional Ionian dancing. It's one of Corfu's bigger attractions and a colourful night out, although the food doesn't match the quality of the floor show; tickets available from most travel agents or your hotel reception. The new **Hambo-Remezzo-Karnayio Centre**, *©* 45 314 along 'Disco Road' offers an American-style salad bar, with baked potatoes and other dishes; **Remezzo** is a snack bar with a huge choice of ice cream; **Karnayio** is a music bar with dancing until the wee hours. Two of the best clubs are **Bora Bora** and **Apokalypsis**.

There are a handful of cinemas, most showing undubbed English language films. **The Gallery**, on Ag. Spyrídon Street, is a favourite watering hole of Greeks and ex-pats.

## North of Corfu Town

The roads along the east coast of Corfu are quite good and hotel developers have followed them nearly every inch of the way. To the immediate north of Corfu town begins a long stretch of beach, hotel, self-catering, campsite and restaurant sprawl, most intensely at Kontokáli, Goúvia, Dássia, Ipsos and Pírgi; yet if they all missed the boat in architecture and design, there's visual redemption in the dishevelled beauty of surrounding green hills and olive groves. **Kontokáli** (KONTOKAΛI), 8km from Corfu town, and **Goúvia** (ΓOΥBIA), a little further north, overlook a lagoon once used by the Venetians as a harbour; the impressive remains of the Venetian **arsenal** overlook Goúvia's popular marina. Both villages offer watersports and reasonable swimming off the pebble beach. Emerald **Cape Komméno** extends out here, but looks better from a distance and has poor beaches to boot. A few kilometres further north on the main road, **Dassiá** (ΔΑΣΙΑ) has a long, narrow sand and shingle beach fringed by olive groves, a favourite for sports from waterskiing to paragliding. On the grounds of Corfu's most famous country estates, the Castello Mansion, a spanking new building called the **Castelino** was built to display works on loan from the National Art Gallery (now closed for lack of funds). Excursion boats run as far as Kassiópi (north) and Benítses (south).

If a good night's sleep is a priority, avoid **Ipsos** (ΥΨΟΣ) and **Pírgi** (ΠΥΡΓΙ), north of Dássia, former fishing villages that now occupy either end of Corfu's 'Golden Mile' where a plethora of bars and discos reverberate till dawn. It has a long, attractive scimitar of shingle beach set against cliffs in the background, with plenty of watersports, and in the summer barely enough room for a good wiggle. You can escape the frenetic crowds by carrying on just to the north, where the mountains meet the sea to form a series of small coves and tiny beaches.

## A Detour up Mount Pantokrátor

From Pírgi, you can get away for it all by heading up the brooding slopes of 900m **Mount Pantokrátor,** Corfu's highest point—a beautiful but hairpin (and sometimes hair-raising) drive. A paved road noodles through Spartílas and Strinílas as far as Petália, from where a rutted vertiginous road continues to **Perithía**, one of Corfu's best kept secrets: a charming cobblestoned but nearly abandoned village of stone houses lost in a mountain hollow, its lush garden terraces dishevelled ever since everyone moved down to the coast (one of the three permanent families runs a friendly taverna). The path from here to the summit of Pantokrátor takes about an hour, but rewards you with a wondrous display of flora even into the hot summer months, and a view of emerald Corfu spread at your feet and white-capped Albanian peaks on the mainland, a view enjoyed every day by the single monk and his somewhat less orthodox pylon in the mountaintop monastery. The road from Perithía by way of Láfki, takes in some of Corfu's most enchanting countryside.

## Back to the East Coast: Barbáti to Ag. Stéfanos

Further north **Barbáti** (ΜΠΑΡΜΠΑΡΤΗ) has a long stretch of pebbles and every conceivable facility to go with it. **Nissáki**, a sprawled-out fishing hamlet overlooking tiny coves is fairly quiet except when excursions caiques from the Golden Mile drop off trippers. Goat tracks lead down to little coves, but the hotels (especially the Club Med) are out of scale. Still heading north, Lawrence Durrell's famous White House, where he wrote *Prospero's Cell* and *The White House* overlooks the popular pebble beach of **Kalámi** (ΚΑΛΑΜΙ), one of the biggest self-catering compounds on Corfu—you can even stay in the White House itself. **Kouloúra**, a kilometre or so from the rugged Albanian coast, is a lovely seaside hamlet on a narrow horse-shoe bay with a shingle beach, which (as yet) has not succumbed to the developers; the brothers Durrell spent their youth here. Kouloúra was also favoured by Venetians: note the 16th-century **Koúartanou Gennatá**, part villa and part fortified tower, and two 17th-century mansions, **Vassilá** and **Prosalenti**. Near Kouloúra, a very steep, twisting path descends to the pretty **Kamináki** beach; the reward is a fine pebbly beach with the clearest of water, perfect for snorkelling. There are some watersports here, boat hire and two beach tavernas. Between Kouloúra and Ag. Stéfanos is the picturesque and unspoilt bay of **Agní**, with crystal-clear waters, where a new road goes straight the beach with its three excellent tavernas. The next beach north is **Kerásia**, a strand of white pebbles with shade and a taverna, a 2km walk down a rough track from pricey, laid-back **Ag. Stéfanos.**

## Kontokáli

Medium-sized **Pyrros**, ✆ 91 206, (*C; mod*), is one of the nicer choices. Corfu's **youth hostel** is here (take bus no.7 from San Rocco Square), ✆ 91 202); an IYHA card is required. The nearest **campsite** to Corfu town (✆ 91 202) is here as well. **The Viceroy**, on the back street between Kontokáli and Gouviá, serves tasty tandooris and a superb chicken korma; prices are a bit high (*around 4000dr a head*) because the spices have to be imported. The **New Locanda** serves either good old steak but flirts with the cuisines of the world, including many vegetarian dishes.

## Gouviá

**Debonos**, ✆ 33 708 (*A; exp*) has a garden with a pool. *Open Mar–Oct.* **Galaxias**, ✆ 91 223 (*C; mod*), is a pleasant hotel set back 150m from the sea. **Louvre**, ✆ 91 506 (*D; mod*), is adequate but don't expect any masterpieces. **Bella Mama**, on the edge of the strip, is Greek owned and run in spite of its name, and serves a delicious *sofríto*, lamb *kléftiko*, and other meats and chicken, with a house wine to quaff. **Tartufo** up the hill, is owned by the same family and is similar, but set in a quieter area (*both from 2500–4000dr*). **Taverna Filippas** is also popular (*around 2500dr*).

## Dassiá

**Corfu Chandris**, ✆ 97 100, ✉ 93 458 (*A; exp*) is a big resort hotel with all the trimmings, as well as a set of bungalows and villas in the environs; free shuttle service into Corfu town. *Open Apr–Oct.* In the same league, there's the **Astir Palace**, overlooking Koméno Bay, ✆ 91 481, ✉ 91 881 (*A; exp*).

## Nissáki

A big **Club Mediterranée**, ✆ (0633) 22 144, book in Athens, ✆ (01) 325 4110, ✉ 325 4674 (*A; exp*) takes up a lot of room here. The **Yorkie Bar** is a jovial, friendly watering hole.

## Ípsos

**Costas Beach**, ✆ 93 205 (*D; mod*) is one possibility. **Roasters** is a favourite English-run restaurant, with a wide range of joints and veg, along with good French and vegetarain dishes, and an all-you-can-eat buffet lunch daily.

## Kalámi

To stay in Lawrence Durrell's White House, book through CV Travel in London, ✆ (0171) 581 0851(*see* **Practical A–Z** p.49); in Corfu, ✆ (0661) 40 644 or 39 900.

# The North Coast

## Kassiópi

Kassiópi (ΚΑΣΣΙΟΠΗ), at the north end of the good paved road, was an important Hellenistic town founded by Pyrrhus of Epirus. Kassiópi flourished under the Romans who surrounded it with great walls. Its famous shrine of Zeus Cassius was visited by Cicero and

Emperor Nero; Tiberius had a villa here. The Byzantine fortress was the first place in Greece to fall to Robert Guiscard's Normans, who invaded from their fief in Calabria, after first pillaging Rome. As every subsequent marauder from the north passed by Kassiópi to reach Corfu town, the town bore the brunt of their attacks. When after a long struggle the Venetians finally took the fortress, they rendered it useless to avenge themselves. Without any defences the Kassiopiots suffered terribly at the hands of the Turks and the town lost all of its former importance.

The ruined fortress still stands above the village, guarding only wild flowers and sheep. Although still a fishing village, Kassiópi has discovered the profits to be made from the tourist trade and has become one of Corfu's busiest resorts, although with much of the *bon ton* Benítses lacks. Most visitors stay in smart apartments or villas. Four small, well-equipped beaches can be reached by footpath from the headland, and when you're tired of windsurfing or basting yourself on the beach you can explore the rocky coastline on foot. Two of Corfu's quietest beaches, **Avláki** and **Koyévinas**, are a 20- or 30-minute walk south of Kassiópi, both beautiful white pebble bays, each sporting a taverna; the grey sand beach of **Kalamáki**, also with a taverna, is to the west. A fairly steep climb into the hinterland towards **Podolákos** affords beautiful views of Kassiópi and the coastline.

## Ag. Spyrídon to Sidári

Heading west from Kassiopi, **Ag. Spyrídonos** may the answer if you've been looking for a small sandy beach, a simple taverna or two and a handful of rooms to rent, although Corfiots converge on it on Sundays. Just to the west, just before **Almirós**, is a warm shallow lagoon with trees and migratory birds; Almirós itself, at the quiet east end of Corfu's longest beach, has some flat stones a few yards out to sea that can cut your feet. The rest of the coast has been daintily clobbered with the magic wand of package tourism, from **Acharávi** (ΑΧΑΡΑΒΗ), where the beach is framed by pretty scenery, to **Róda** (ΡΟΔΑ), where egg and chips seems to be everyone's special of the day but where there's enough sand to escape the crowds easily by walking a bit in either direction. **Astrakéri**, on the west end, is the one place along here to look for a room.

Inland from Acharávi, **Ag. Panteléimonos**, has a huge ruined tower mansion called **Polylas**, complete with prisons used during the Venetian occupation; another Venetian manor lies further up in **Episkepsís**. Inland from Róda, **Plátonas** is in the heart of Corfu's kumquat country. Introduced from the Far East half a century ago, kumquats look like baby oranges but are too sour for many tastes; the annual harvest of 35 tonnes produced by 70 farmers are distilled into kumquat liqueur (using both blossoms and fruit) and preserved as kumquat jams and conserves. Inland from Astrakerí, **Karoussádes** is a pretty agricultural village with the 16th-century Theotóki mansion as its landmark.

**Sidári** (ΣΙΔΑΡΙ), although almost entirely given over to tourism (like so many Corfu resorts, British tour operators seem to have the monopoly), offers a contrast of lush greenery and picturesque sandstone cliffs, eroded by the wind to form strangely shaped caves. In the bay is the **Canal d'Amour**, a peculiar rock formation said to be two lovers—swim between them and you are guaranteed eternal love, which is more than promised by the local disco. It gets very crowded with families and the mosquitoes are nasty little vampires if you don't come prepared. There are day trips out to the quiet islets of Othóni, Eríkoussa and Mathráki; if you have your own transport, less crowded beaches await west of Sidári below the village of

**Perouládes,** with a stunning stretch of sand under wind sculpted tawny cliffs—high enough to cast the beach in shade in the early afternoon.

## Islands near Corfu: Othoní, Eríkousa and Mathráki

Northwest of Sidári three sleepy islets, Othoní (the largest), Eríkousa and Mathráki, comprise the westernmost territory of Greece. Transport to them is not always reliable: there are organized excursions and caiques from Sidári (caiques run most of the year, depending on demand and weather), ferries from Corfu town, or a summer excursion from Ag. Stéfanos. The population is disproportionately feminine, the wives of husbands who fish or work in the USA. Olives and aromatic table grapes are produced locally, and fresh fish is nearly always available; each island has rooms to rent, but food supplies can be scarce.

Of the three, **Othóni** is the largest and driest (a lack of water is one of the problems), but has the friendliest atmosphere and the most to offer if you like to ramble. There are a handful of shingle beaches and donkey trails up to the pretty, nearly abandoned villages and a well-preserved medieval fort on a pine-covered hill. Most of the excursions make for **Eríkousa,** which has the best sandy beach and a pair of villages set in the cypresses and olives; **Mathráki,** the smallest island, also has a sandy beach—a nesting place for loggerhead turtles (*see* p.442)—and very limited facilities.

---

*✆ (0663–)*                               ***Where to Stay and Eating Out***

### Kassiópi

**Oasis,** ✆ 81 275 (*D; inexp*) and **Edem,** ✆ 81 43 (*E; inexp*) are the only two hotels in town, and may have a room for the passing independent traveller. For a studio or flat try **Zeris** apartments, ✆ 81 317, with a restaurant (*mod*) or the more comfortable **Poseidon,** ✆ 81 439. **The Three Brothers** taverna on the waterfront serves delicious versions of Greek and Corfiot specialities (*4000dr*).

### Róda

In season nearly every room is block-booked; but outside the high summer months try **Hotel Milton,** ✆ 63 295, ✉ 63 296 (*C; mod*), set in a green lawn rimmed with roses, overlooking a large pool, 500m from the sea. Try **Villa Portoni,** ✆ (0661) 31 498, in Athens, (01) 901 6115, for simple flats in a quiet location, with a pool. **Sandra,** in Astrakéri, ✆ 31 120 (*E; inexp*) or **Roda Camping,** ✆ 93 120 may have space if all else fails.

### Sidári

The **Three Brothers** ✆ 95 342 (*C; exp*) may be full of package tourists, but if they haven't got a room they'll know where to find one. Up in Sidári the biggest culinary draw for many is the full works British breakfast, but good fair-priced Greek food can be found at **Sophocles** and the **Canal d'Amour.** If it's cocktail hour, stop by the **Sunset Café,** west of Perouládes, overlooking the prettiest stretch of beach.

#### Othóni/Erikóusa/Mathráki

Book early for the **Locanda dei Sogni**, on Othóni ✆ 71 640, which offers pretty rooms and good Italian food; ditto for **Hotel Erikousa**, on Erikóusa, ✆ 71 555 (*C; mod*) is the only hotel on the island, directly on the beach.

## Western Beaches: North to South

This whole northwest corner of Corfu is covered with forests. The main roads have been resurfaced, but once off the beaten track be warned that the roads can bottom out the best shock-absorbers. The main coastal road from Sidári cuts off the corner of the northwest on route to **Ag. Stéfanos** (not to be confused with the Ag. Stéfanos on the east coast) a rather characterless bay popular with windsurfers; there are villas and a few hotels, yet after dark it is still uncrowded; **Aríllas** just south has a wide, sandy but steep bay with an attractive backdrop of green hills. **Afiónas** to the south is similar, if slightly more developed. Best of all is **Ag. Geórgios** (Pagói) is a long, magnificent stretch of beach under steep cliffs, just in the budding stages of development, with watersports, tavernas, and discos; during the day it fills up with trippers from Paleokastrísta.

One of Corfu's celebrated beauty spots, **Paleokastrítsa** (ΠΑΛΑΙΟΚΑΣΤΡΙΤΣΑ), is endowed with a beautiful horseshoe bay and sandy and pebbly coves, olive and almond groves, mountains and forests. Now the major resort area in west Corfu, Paleokastrítsa is chock-a-block in the summer with holiday-makers and day-trippers; in the early spring, however, you can easily believe its claim to have been the fabled home of the King Alcinous and princess Nausicaa. The sea is said to be colder here than anywhere else in Corfu. On a promontory above town, **Zoodóchos Pigí** (or Paleokastrítsa) **Monastery** was built in 1228 on the site of a Byzantine fortress, and tarted up by an abbot with Rococo tastes in the 1700s. Tour groups queue up to buy a candle (the price of admission) as a monk hands out black skirts and shawls to the underclad. Inside, a one-room museum contains some very old icons and an olive press; outside, there's a peach of a view of the sapphire sea below. The most spectacular view of the magnificent coastline is on the steep climb (or drive) out of Paleokastrítsa through cypress and pine woods north towards the village of **Lákones** and its celebrated Bella Vista Café, affording nothing less than 'the Most Beautiful View in Europe.'

Lákones itself is the hub of the loveliest walks on Corfu, especially to Kríni and the formidable **Angelókastro** (you can also walk from Paleokastrítsa). Built in the 13th century by the Byzantine despot of Epirus, Michael Angelos, it is mostly ruined, but makes an impressive sight perched on the wild red rocks over a 300m precipice. Angelókastro played a major role during the various raids on the island, sheltering the surrounding villagers (as well as the Venetian governor, who lived there). However, the Corfiots were rarely content to stay behind the walls of Angelókastro, and often spilled out to attack their attackers. If you have a car, the mountain roads from Lákones north to Róda through the little villages of **Chorepískopi, Valanión** (3km on a by-road) and **Nímfes** offer a lovely bucolic journey through the Corfu of yesteryear.

South of Paleokastrítsa stretches the fertile, startlingly flat and intensely cultivated **Rópa Valley,** where Homer's description of the island rings home: 'Pear follows pear, apple after apple grows, fig after fig, and grape yields grape again.' Along with orchards, Rópa has the **Corfu Golf Club**, 18 holes designed by Harradine and Pencross Bent, and rated one of the 100 top courses in the world; club hire available (✆ (0661) 94 220). A lift descends from the

Golf Club to the good sheltered pebble beaches and hotels at **Ermónes**. Ermónes is another candidate for Odysseus' landing point; Nausicaa and her servants would have been washing the palace laundry in a little cascade—near the present Snackbar Nausicaa. **Pélekas,** a 17th-century village up on a mountain ridge, was Kaiser Wilhelm II's favourite spot to watch the sunset; bus-loads of people come out every evening in the summer to do the same, from a tower known as **Kaiser's Throne**. Pélekas was one of Corfu's nudie beaches until a road built from Gialiskári brought in crowds of trippers; now the complete unadorned walk down the steep track to lovely **Mirtiótissa** beach (the other half of the beach, by the monastery, is not nudist); after sunset the village throbs to the sound of disco music. **Glyfáda**, one of the island's best beaches, is a long gentle swathe of golden sand. It fills up during the day with hotel residents and day-trippers, but early evening is perfect for a swim here, with steep cliffs dropping straight down into the blue bay.

---

### *Where to Stay and Eating Out*

#### Ag. Geórgios ✆ (0663–)

St George, ✆ 31 147 or 96 213 (*D; inexp*) is convenient to the beach. *Open Apr–Oct.*

#### Paleokastrítsa ✆ (0663–)

Everything is overpriced here. The **Akrotiri Beach**, ✆ 41 275 (*A; exp*), five minutes uphill from the beach, enjoys some of the best views, and there's a swimming pool for those who don't want to commute to the sea. If you're lucky (or book early) you may get one of the eight rooms right on the beach at the **Pavilion Xenia**, ✆ 41 208 (*B; exp*), with a good restaurant below, and priceless view and location. Cheaper choices include **Zefyros**, ✆ 41 244 (*D; mod*), near the sea, with a restaurant; **Palaio Inn**, ✆ 41 220 (*E; inexp*); and **Phoebos**, ✆ 41 103 (*E; inexp*). **Paleokastritsa Camping**, ✆ 41 204 is probably the nicest campsite on Corfu. Paleokastrítsa has a number of seafood restaurants. **Chez George** commands the prime location and the highest prices; residents and long-term visitors prefer the **Astakos** for its authentic food and reasonable prices.

#### Nímfes ✆ (0663–)

**Platonas**, ✆ 94 396 (*D; mod*) is a pleasant place to escape the crowds on the coast, and there's a taverna, too.

#### Ermónes ✆ (0661–)

**Hermones Beach**, ✆ 94 241 (*A; exp*), is a huge bungalow complex, with every facility; the much more intimate **Athena Hermones Golf**, ✆ 94 226 (*C; mod*) is near the course.

#### Glyfáda ✆ (0661–)

The **Grand Glyfada Hotel** ✆ 94 201, ✆ 30 184 (*A; exp*) and its many watersport activities, dominate the beach.

## Southern Corfu

The southern half of the island has attracted the worst excesses of tourism, especially on the east coast beyond the Achilleion and Gastoúri (*see* p.386). **Benítses** (ΜΠΕΝΙΤΣΕΣ) is the worst offender, a British package resort bubbling with hormones which has devoured a little Greek fishing village (with its permission, of course) inhabited since ancient times. The arches and mosaics just behind the harbour belonged to a Roman bathhouse. The patches of beach it offers are too close to the coastal highway, and pubs and rowdy crowds have chased many of the resort's former enthusiasts well out of earshot. To escape Benítses on foot, walk through the old, residential quarter of the village, past the local cemetery and through some delightful rural scenery towards **Stavrós**, where the Benítses Waterworks was built by Sir Frederick Adam, British High Commissioner from 1824–32. Originally the waterworks supplied all of Corfu town; now Benítses somehow manages to use it all, even though few people there would be caught dead drinking it. Further south, the nearly continuous resort sprawls past the beaches of **Moraítika** (ΜΟΡΑΙΤΙΚΑ) and **Messóngi** (ΜΕΣΣΟΓΓΗ) a cut above Benítses. If you're down here for the scenery, skip the coast all together and take the inland route, beginning at Kinopiástes (near Gastoúri), passing by way of Ag. Déka (one of Corfu's prettiest villages), Makráta, Kornáta and Strongilí.

The more inaccessible west coast is also more worthwhile: **Ag. Górdies** (ΑΓ. ΓΟΡΔΗΣ) is one of Corfu's most attractive village-resorts with a lovely, sheltered 2-mile-long beach of soft golden sand and minimal waves. Further south, **Ag. Mathiás**, planted on the slopes of Mount Ag. Déka is a serene place to daydream under the plane tree and write up your diary, disturbed only by the occasional roar of hired scooters and jeeps as they zip through the village on a quest for true peace and quiet in this least-discovered corner of the island. The village remains delightfully Greek, and the locals are more concerned about their olive crop than threatened decreases in tourist numbers. There are 24 churches in or near the village, and by asking around you can find your way down the steep slopes to the really peaceful beaches of **Tría Avlákia**, **Paramónas** and **Skithi**, with a few rooms and the odd inexpensive taverna. An octagonal Byzantine castle at **Gardíki**, south of Ag. Górdies, was another work by the despot of Epirus, Michael Angelos II. This is one of the most unspoilt areas of Corfu, and is a good starting point for some excellent walks. A minor road by Gardíki leads in 4km to Corfu's only lake, the lagoony **Límni Korissíon**, which is separated from the sea by a long stretch of huge, wild dunes; in spring and autumn it fills with migratory birds. Take your mosquito defences, however; they grow as big as birds here and have appetites to match. **Lagoúdia**, two islets off the southwest coast, are the home of a tribe of donkeys; some of their ancestors were eaten by a boatload of Napoleon's troops who were wrecked there for three days.

The scenery from here down to Corfu's tail is flat and dull but the beaches are sandy and clean. South of Lake Korissíon a busy family resort has grown up around (another) **Ag. Geórgios**. **Linía**, the northern extension of Ag. Geórgios beach, is more tranquil and backed by dunes; the town beach of **Marathiás** is the southern extension of the same strand, with a few tavernas. In the centre of a large fertile plain, **Lefkími**, the largest town in the south, is dusty and uninviting; the nearest beaches, **Mólos** and **Alykés** 2km away on the east coast, are flat and grey, set amid salt pans.

Most of the young crowd who roar and buzz this far south are aiming for **Kávos** (ΚΑΒΟΣ) a one-time fishing village with a long sandy beach that metamorphoses every evening into an all-night, bopping and booming rave party with wall-to-wall bars and neon lights. At the southernmost tip of Corfu, the quieter beaches of **Asprókavos** and **Arkoudílas** (near a ruined monastery, reached by a path from Sparterá) have white sand and tavernas; the pretty beach below **Dragotiná** is a long walk from the village but never crowded.

#### Ag. Górdies

**Yaliskari Palace**, ✆ 54 401 (*A; exp*), a fancy vast complex with a pool and tennis courts and sea sports, is 3km from the beach; **Ag. Gordies**, ✆ 53 320 (*A; exp*) is similarly large, ultra modern, and endowed with facilities, but right on the sand (both expensive). **Chrysis Folies** (Golden Nests), ✆ 44 750 (*C; mod*) is a moderate-sized choice within easy walking distance of the sea beach. **Pink Paradise**, ✆ 53 103 (*E; inexp*) is a resort complex run by Americans.

#### Benítses

Isolated from the brouhaha, **San Stefano**, ✆ 36 036, ✆ 72 272 (*A; exp*) is spread across terraces, overlooking the sea; it has the largest swimming pool on the island, sea sports and other facilities. Drinking rather than eating is the order of the day down in Benítses, but the **Marabou** bravely presents some tasty local dishes (*2500dr*). **Stefanos Pizzeria** whips up delicious authentic pies.

#### Moraítika/Messónghi

**Messonghi Beach Hotel and Bungalows** ✆ 38 684 (*B; mod–exp*) is a giant, self-contained family fun complex. **Korifo Apartments**, in Moraítika, ✆ 75 511, in Athens (01) 981 8889, ✆ 982 2445 for pretty flats, 400m from the sea (*exp*). **Roulis**, Messónghi, ✆ 92 353 (*C; mod*) is small and near the sea, with some seasports. It's fairly easy to find a room to rent, and there's also a campsite, **Ippokambos**, ✆ 65 364.

#### Ag. Matháios

**Gamillon Oros**, ✆ 55 557, serves spit-roast lamb and fresh fish, with live music and dancing most nights; there's even a playground to keep the kids out of your hair.

## Ithaca/Itháki (ΙΘΑΚΗ)

*Every traveller is a citizen of Ithaca.*

—sign in the port

Ithaca is one of those places that has become a compelling and universal symbol, although many who have heard of it have no idea where it is, and those who do visit it usually have a hard time reconciling the island's reality with their idea of Odysseus' beloved home. And yet re-read your Homer before you come, and you'll find that nearly all of his descriptions of Ithaca square with this small, mountainous island—it is indeed 'narrow' and 'rocky' and 'unfit for riding horses'. Some ancient and modern scholars have theorized that Homer's Ithaca was elsewhere—Lefkáda and Kefaloniá are popular contenders. Don't believe them. Itháki, as the locals call their home, the eternal symbol of all homes and journey's end, is the real thing, and 'even if you find it poor,' as Caváfy wrote, 'Ithaca does not deceive. Without Ithaca your journey would have no beauty'.

Ithaca has a jagged, indented coast (as Homer says), but no exceptional beaches, and its roads are in such a state that most islanders prefer to travel to distant villages by caique. Its excellent

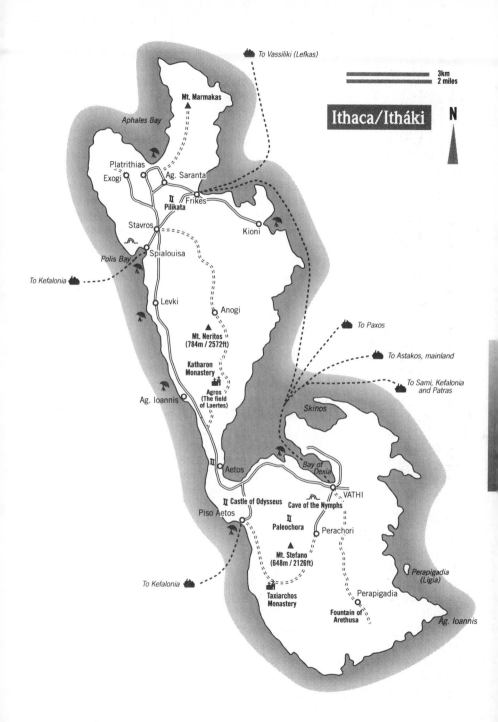

To Vassiliki (Lefkas)

3km
2 miles

**Ithaca/Itháki**

N

Mt. Marmakas

Aphales Bay

Platrithias
Exogi
Ag. Saranta

Pilikata
Frikes

Stavros

Kioni

Polis Bay
Spialouisa

To Kefalonia

Levki

Anogi

Mt. Neritos
(784m / 2572ft)

Katharon
Monastery

To Paxos

To Astakos, mainland

Agros
(The field
of Laertes)

To Sami, Kefalonia
and Patras

Ag. Ioannis

Skinos

Aetos

Bay of
Dexia

VATHI

Castle of Odysseus
Piso Aetos

Cave of the Nymphs

Paleochora

Perachori

Mt. Stefano
(648m / 2126ft)

To Kefalonia

Perapigadia
(Ligia)

Taxiarchos
Monastery

Perapigadia

Fountain of
Arethusa

Ag. Ioannis

harbour makes it a big favourite with sailors and, best of all, it has changed little over the years. The atmosphere is relaxed and low-key.

## Mythology

Three sons of the king of Kefaloniá, Ithakos, Neritos and Polyktor, were the founding fathers of Ithaca: the first son gave it his name, the second left his name on the island's highest peak, and Polyktor is the name of its northern half. Another king of Kefaloniá, Kefalos, had a son named Arkikious who annexed Ithaca and made it the centre of his realm; his son was Laertes, who participated on the voyage of the Argo and married Anticleia, who gave birth to Odysseus. But a strong ancient tradition says that two crafty shepherds, Autolykus, a son of Hermes, and Sisyphus, used to graze their flocks next to each other, and through all kinds of trickery and wiles would steal one another's sheep. Autolykus thought that if he married his daughter Anticleia to Sisyphus, their child would inherit cunning from both sides of the family and be the ultimate trickster. Sisyphus was equally keen and had his evil way with Anticleia even before their wedding; but during the interval, King Laertes asked to marry her, and did. She was already pregnant by Sisyphus, and Autolykus, the child's grandfather, named him Odysseus, which means 'angry' or 'he who is hated by all', as Homer explains it.

Odysseus unsuccessfully sought Helen's hand in marriage, then wed Penelope instead and had a son, Telemachus. Having been warned by an oracle that if he went to Troy he would be absent for 20 years and return alone and without booty, Odysseus pretended madness by ploughing the sand and sowing it with salt when the Greek representatives came to fetch him; to test him, the Greeks placed his baby son Telemachus in front of the oxen. Odysseus proved his sanity by diverting their course, and was constrained to depart for Troy. After his dramatic homecoming and mass murder of Penelope's suitors, Homer's account of him in the *Odyssey* ends, but there are two accounts of his death, one, that the families of the suitors forced him to go and live in exile, and that he died at a ripe old age in Italy; another, that Odysseus was not permitted to die until he had at last appeased the anger of his old enemy Poseidon, and the only way to do that was to take an oar and walk until he came to a land where people asked him what he carried. Then, after a sacrifice to the sea god, he sailed home, and was drowned on the way.

## History

Items found on the north half of Ithaca go back to 4–3000 BC; on Pilikata hill near Stavrós a road, buildings and walls show that some kind of communal life was established by the early Hellenic era (3–2000 BC). The inhabitants and passing sailors worshipped at the cave of Loízos, where early cult items were discovered. By Mycenaean times, settlements had relocated further south as Arikious organized a kingdom (c. 1200 BC) that included Kefaloniá, Zákynthos, Lefkáda and a part of the Peloponnesian coast. Ithaca, owing to its central location, was made the capital, and under Odysseus the kingdom reached its prime, sending 12 ships to the Trojan War.

In the last 200 years scholars and archaeologists have combed Ithaca for signs of Odysseus. Schliemann came after his great discovery of Troy, and since Schliemann inevitably found what he was looking for, he unearthed a large structure he immediately called 'Odysseus' Palace'; although it dates from only 700 BC, the name has stuck. Later finds, while failing to

# North of Váthi

Ithaca has an hourglass figure, with a waist only 500m wide. This narrow mountain stretch is called **Aetós**. Overlooking the two bays below is what the locals (as well as Schliemann) have always called the **Castle of Odysseus**, although it's apparently the citadel of the 8th-century BC town of Alalkomenes, which was abandoned in Roman times. Impressive Cyclopean walls and the foundations of a temple remain. Since 1984 the 'Odysseus Project', sponsored by the Archaeological Society of Athens, Washington University and the National Geographic Society, has concentrated its excavations around Aetós' church of Ag. Geórgios, and has shown that the site has been inhabited continuously since the 13th century BC. There's a pebble beach in the bay below to the east and another excellent one at the little bay of **Píso Aetós** in the west, where ferry boats from Sámi (Kefaloniá) call.

Just north of Aetós, near Agrós, is the **Field of Laertes**, supposedly where Odysseus encountered his father after killing the suitors; note the massive 2000-year-old 'Laertes' olive'. From here a road ascends the slopes of 784m **Mount Níritos** (formerly Mount Korifí—Ithaca is slowly reclaiming its Homeric names) to the lofty **Monastery of the Katharón**, 'of the dry weeds', believed to be built on the site of an ancient temple of Athena. One far-fetched story says it was built by the heretical Cathars; another explains that local farmers were burning dry weeds here when they found an icon of the Birth of the Virgin attributed to St Luke, which holds pride of place in the church of the **Panagía Kathariótissas**. When Byron visited in 1823, a special mass was held in his honour. From the lighthouse of a bell tower you can see the Gulf of Pátras on a clear day, and if you want to stay there are a few guest rooms in the monastery (© 31 366).

From Moni Katharón, a paved road continues 3km up to **Anógí**, 'at the top of the world', passing many large and unusually shaped boulders, including a very phallic 25ft monolith named Araklís, or Heracles. The village retains some Venetian ruins, including a sturdy grey campanile and a restored 12th-century church dedicated to the **Panagía** with Byzantine frescoes; note the clay amphorae embedded in the walls to improve the church's acoustics. Ask at the taverna for the key.

The second and better road from Agrós follows the west coast. At Ag. Ioánnis, just opposite Kefaloniá, is a lovely, seldom-used white beach, Aspros Gialós, with many trees. **Lévki**, the small village to the north, was an important base and port for the resistance movement during the war, and when it was destroyed by the 1953 earthquake, Britain officially adopted it and helped rebuild it. There are small beaches below, one with a taverna and a few rooms to rent.

## Stavrós

The two roads meet **Stavrós**, the most important village in the north, overlooking lovely **Pólis Bay** ('city bay'), its name referring to the long lost Byzantine city of Ierosalem, which sank into it during an earthquake in AD 967; Robert Guiscard (*see* Fiskárdo, Kefaloniá) had been told by a soothsayer that he would die after seeing Jerusalem, but he never thought Jerusalem would be the ruins of a town on Ithaca (some Byzantine tombs have been discovered nearby, at Roussanos). A bust of Odysseus in the centre of Stavrós looks sternly out over the bay. The **Cave of Loízos** to the right of the bay was an ancient cult sanctuary; some believe it was Homer's Cave of the Nymphs. Prehistoric pots, Mycenaean amphorae, bronze tripods from 800–700 BC, ex-votos of nymphs and an inscription dedicated to Odysseus were found here (unfortunately the cave and path to it have collapsed).

Another plausible Odysseus' palace was located at **Pilikáta**, or the Hill of Hermes, just north of Stavrós. The site also fits the Homeric description almost perfectly, in sight of 'three seas' (the bays of Frikés, Pólis and Aphales) and 'three mountains' (Níritos, Marmakás and Exógi or Neion). Although the ruins you see on the site are of a Venetian fort, excavators have found evidence underneath of buildings and roads dating back to Neolithic times. In 1930, within Pilikáta's Cyclopean walls, archaeologists found a pit containing the remains of sacrifices and two ceramic shards engraved in Linear A, believed to date from 2700 BC. In 1989, Prof. Paul Fauré attempted a translation of them, based on Linear B and the index of symbols established for Linear A, written in an Indo-European language—a very, very early form of Greek—called Kreutschmer by the linguists: Fauré translates one as 'Here is what I, Aredatis, give to the queen, the goddess Rhea:100 goats, 10 sheep, 3 pigs' and the other as: 'The nymph saved me.' The other finds from Pilikáta and the Cave of Louizos are in the small but interesting **Stavrós Archaeological Museum** on the Platrithiás road (*open 9–2, closed Mon*).

From Stavrós a road leads north to Ithaca's remotest village, called **Exógi** ('beyond the earth'). Set high up on terraces, all but 20 of its inhabitants have left, but there are a few rooms to rent, and beautiful views; above the village are Ithaca's oddball attraction, three narrow pyramids built in 1933 by a pyramid-fancier named Papadópoulos. He lies buried under one, his mother under another, while the third has a jar with a coin collection. Another 2km up, the disused monastery of Panagía Eleoússa offers extraordinary views over the Ionian islands. Between Exogí and Platrithiás is an area known as '**Homer's School**'. The ruined 7th-century church of Ag. Athanásios has a wall of great hewn blocks reused from an ancient wall. By the Melanydrus spring, there's a little stepped well that the locals call 'Penelope's Bath'—actually a Mycenaean tomb. This fertile area is one of the most pleasant on the island; it was here that Odysseus was ploughing his field when he was dragged off to Troy by the Achaeans (*see* p.398). **Platrithiás** is the biggest of a set of agricultural hamlets; one of them, **Kóllieri**, greets wayfarers with an outdoor 'folklore museum', with stone obelisks made out of millstones.

## Frikés and Kióni

North of Stavrós, **Frikés** (ΦΡΙΚΕΣ) is a tiny fishing village and port for Fiskárdo in Kefaloniá and Vassilikí in Lefkáda, as well as for daily caiques to Váthi, and a popular stopping-off point for flotilla yachts. It was a favourite pirates' lair into the 19th century. About 100 people live there year-round, and there are two tiny beaches near by, Limenária and Kourvoúlia, and a new hotel, rooms and tavernas. The road continues to **Rachí**, a tiny hamlet of old stone houses, and continues down to **Kióni**, one of Ithaca's prettiest villages built around a tiny harbour, guarded by three ruined windmills. Twice the size of Frikés, it is popular with the yachting set; landlubbers can hire caiques in the port to the surrounding beaches. Kióni means 'column', and an ancient one still stands on the altar in the church of Ag. Nikólaos. And there are more Cylopean walls nearby, at a site called Roúga.

---

*Itháki © (0674–)*          ***Where to Stay and Eating Out***

### Váthi

Ithaca as a whole has very little accommodation, and most of it is in Váthi. There's a scattering of rooms to rent in most of the villages, although they may take some persistance to find; otherwise contact **Polyctor Tours**, in Váthi's Plateia Drakoúli, © 33 120, ✆ 33 130;

they have a list of rooms on the island and manage 11 self-catering apartments. Of the hotels the most modern and most expensive is the **Hotel Mentor**, Georgíou Drakoúli St, ✆ 32 433 (*B; exp*), quiet and a bit out of the centre. The **Odysseus**, ✆ 32 381 (*B; mod*) is nice too and a bit cheaper. **Andriana Koulouri Rooms**, on the quay, ✆ 32 387 are new, quiet, and come complete with bathrooms. *Open all year.* There's a campsite at **Dexía Beach**, ✆ 32 855.

On a back lane near the centre of Váthi, little **Trexandiri** serves good local food (*2500dr*) and in Plateía Polytechnieíou the **Grill Restaurant** serves delicious grilled octopus and *kokorétsi*—lamb's innards on a spit. **Palio Karavo**, 800m from town, is a favourite, especially for fish (*2000dr*). Both the Mentor and Odysseus hotels have good restaurants.

### Frikés/Kióni

In Frikés, there's the **Nostos Hotel**, ✆ 31 644 (*C; mod*), and a handful of rooms and apartments to rent; contact Panayiótis Raptópoulos, ✆ 31 629. By the sea, **Taverna Ulysseus** has good fresh fish and other dishes; **Symposium**, also smack on the waterfront, has an ambitious menu featuring the likes of 'Odyseas Meat-pie', Penelope's Dish, *Sabóro* (Eptanesian Spaghetti) and 'Brides' Salad (Magical callings of a mythical world)', and carafes of Ithacan wine. Up in Kióni, the elegant **Kionia Apartments**, ✆ 31 362 are expensive and hard to come by unless you're on a package.

## Kálamos (ΚΑΛΑΜΟΣ) and Kástos (ΚΑΣΤΟΣ)

Kálamos and Kástos, two mountains in the sea east of Meganísi, are under the jurisdiction of Lefkáda, but can only be reached on a daily regular basis by way of Mítikas on the mainland; occasionally Kálamos, the larger one, is connected to Sámi, Ithaca, the port Astakós and Meganísi, as well as Nidrí and Vassilikí on Lefkáda. Kálamos lives primarily by fishing and its small gardens, and most people live in the attractive north coast village of Kálamos, or **Chóra**, where the island's few rooms to rent are concentrated. It has all the essentials of village life, even a pair of tavernas on the town beach, and tolerated rough camping on the far end. Better beaches may be found towards **Episkopí**, but are easiest reached by boat. A donkey path leads up from Chóra to the abandoned walled village of **Kástro**, where everyone used to live.

Only two or three families live on **Kástos**, now unable to care for all the vineyards which once produced a fine wine. There aren't even any regular connections; you'll have to hire a caique from Mítikas, but there's a taverna and maybe a room or two if you're lucky.

## Kefaloniá (ΚΕΦΑΛΟΝΙΑ)

Mountainous Kefaloniá with its 781 square kilometres and Jabberwocky silhouette may be the largest of the Ionian islands by a long shot, but it supports a mere 30,000 people, and even many of these live in Athens in the winter. But Kefaloniots have always been famous for wandering (one, Constantine Yerákis, went on to make a fortune in the British East India Company and become Regent of Siam), and it's not uncommon to meet someone whose entire family lives in Canada, Australia or the United States. Only in the last few years has tourism begun to slow the diaspora and keep more people on their ruggedly beautiful island. Most Kefaloniots are friendly, good-humoured and clever, but have the reputation of being hard-headed, cunning, eccentric, tight with their money and the worst blasphemers in Greece, swearing at their patron Ag. Gerásimos one minute and swearing by him the next. Other Greeks say the Kefaloniots have drunk a toast with the devil himself.

Although the earthquake in 1953 shattered all but a fraction of Kefaloniá's traditional architecture and all the quaintness and charm that goes with it, the big, sprawling island has lost none of its striking natural beauty. It has fine beaches (one of which, Mýrton, is perhaps the most dramatic in all of Greece), two of the country's loveliest caves, lofty fir forests, splendid views, and Robóla wine. Because Kefaloniá is so large, it is easy to escape the summertime crowds, although beware that even on the main roads driving distances and times can be exhausting.

## History

Recent fossil and tool finds in Fiskárdo, Sámi and Skála date the first Kefaloniots to at least 50,000 BC and perhaps earlier, making Fiskárdo man (and woman, one supposes), among the earliest known inhabitants in Greece. Later inhabitants appear to have been culturally related to the Pelasgians in western Sicily and Epirus and were fond of fighting, judging by their banged about skulls. The Achaeans introduced Mycenaean culture from the Peloponnese in the 14th century BC; Krani, near Argostóli, was their most important colony. Although the name Kefaloniá does not occur in Homer, scholars believe that the 'glittering Samos' of the *Odyssey* actually refers to Kefaloniá's town of Sámi. Others believe Homer doesn't mention Kefaloniá because, as part of the kingdom of Odysseus, he simply calls it Ithaca. The recent discovery of a major Mycenaean tomb near Póros has given the argument new weight as archaeologists scramble to locate the big jackpot—the Palace of Odysseus.

Historically, the first sure references to Kefaloniá are in Herodotus and Thucydides, who describes its four autonomous city-states: Sami, Pali, Krani and Pronnoi, allies of Corinth who spent much of their history fighting for their independence from Athens. In Byzantine times it prospered, in spite of many attacks by the Arabs from Spain and Sicily, and in the 9th century was made the capital of its own *theme*. In 1085, Normans based in Southern Italy unsuccessfully besieged the Byzantine forts of the island and their duke, Robert Guiscard, died of fever in the village that has taken his name—Fiskárdo (*see* below). If the Kefaloniots breathed a sigh of relief then, it was too soon; for the next 800 years the island, like its sisters, was to become the plaything of the Normans, of Venice, of the Vatican, and of a motley assortment of dukes and counts in need of a tax income; the most colourful of its masters was the pirate Count Matteo Orsini, who founded a murderous, dowry-snatching dynasty at the end of the 13th century. In 1483 the Turks captured the island, but lost it again in 1504 when Venice and Spain under the Gran Capitan, Gonzalo Fernández de Córdoba, besieged and captured the fort of Ag. Geórgios and slaughtered the Turkish garrison.

After this the fortress was repaired and the nearby town became the Venetian capital. A huge earthquake caused heavy damage to Ag. Geórgios in 1636, and by the 18th century it was abandoned, and Argostóli became the new capital. In 1823 Lord Byron spent three months on Kefaloniá (along with a retinue including his faithful Venetian gondolier Tita) working as an agent of the Greek Committee in London before going to die a pathetic death from fever in Missolóngi. During the British occupation of the Ionian islands, the Kefaloniots demanded union with Greece and revolted; 21 nationalist leaders were hanged in 1849.

Ioannis Metaxás, prime minister-dictator of Greece from 1936 to 1941, came from Kefaloniá, and for all his faults has gone down in history for laconically (and apparently, apocryphally)

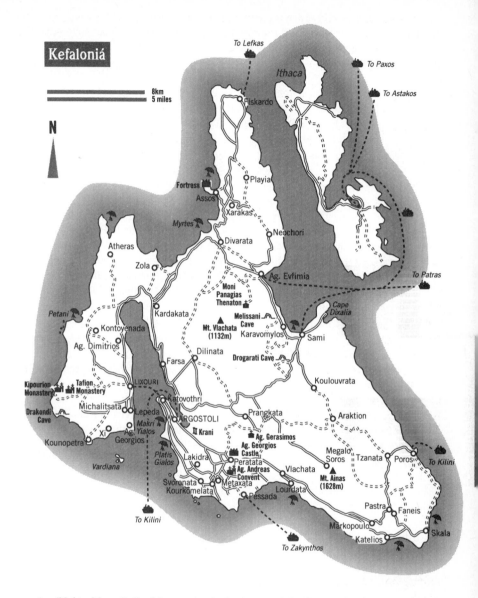

Kefaloniá

8km
5 miles

N

To Lefkas

To Paxos

Ithaca

To Astakos

Fiskardo

To Patras

Playia

Fortress

Assos

Xarakas

Myrtes

Neochori

Divarata

Atheras

Zola

Ag. Evfimia

Cape
Dixalia

Moni
Panagias
Thenaton

Petani

Kardakata

Melissani
Cave

Kontoyenada

Mt. Vlachata
(1132m)

Karavomylos

Sami

Ag. Dimitrios

Dilinata

Drogarati Cave

Farsa

Kipourion
Monastery

Tafion
Monastery

LIXOURI

Koulouvrata

Drakondi
Cave

Michalitsata

Katovothri

Lepeda

ARGOSTOLI

Prangkata

Araktion

Xi

Makri
Ag. Yialos
Georgios

Krani

Ag. Gerasimos

Kounopetra

Platis
Gialos

Lakidra

Ag. Georgios
Castle

Peratata

Megalo
Soros

Tzanata

Poros

To Kilini

Vardiana

Svoronata
Kourkomelata

Ag. Andreas
Convent

Metaxata

Vlachata

Mt. Ainas
(1628m)

Lourdata

To Kilini

Pessada

Pastra

Faneis

To Kilini

Markopoulo

Katelios

Skala

To Zakynthos

saying 'No' to Mussolini's ultimatum at the beginning of the Second World War—celebrated nationally on 28 October as *Ochi* ('No') Day. In 1943, the Italian occupiers of the island joined forces with the EAM (Greek National Liberation Front) and for seven days fought the invading Germans. Five thousand Italians died in the subsequent mass executions ordered, it is said, by Hitler himself; they are known as the Kefaloniá martyrs.

A decade later nature itself struck Kefaloniá a blow that made all the previous earthquakes on the island seem like cocktail shakers. For five days in August, 1953, 113 tremors reduced the island's 350 towns and villages to dust; the first, deadliest quake had the estimated force of 60 atom bombs. As the dust slowly cleared, money for reconstruction poured in from Europe and the tens of thousands of Kefaloniotes who live abroad.

## Getting There and Around

**By air**: daily flights from Athens, several a day in summer, and weekly summer flights to Zákynthos; frequent charters from British cities. The Olympic Airways office is in Argostóli, at R. Vergotí 1, ✆ (0671) 28 808/881; the airport is 7km south of Argostóli.

**By sea**: Kefaloniá has six ports. Sámi (✆ 0674 22 031) has the most connections, with daily **ferry** links to Váthi and Píso Aetós (Ithaca), Vassilikí (Lefkáda), Fiskárdo, Pátras, and several times a week with Corfu, Brindisi, Bari and Ancona, and once a week with Crete, Sámos and Kuşadasi, Turkey. There are numerous ferries a day between Argostóli (✆ 0671 22 224) and Kilíni (in the Peloponnese); in summer there are daily ferries from Fiskárdo to Frikés (Ithaca) and Nídri and Vasilikí in Lefkáda. Ag. Eufimía has connections to Váthi (Ithaca) and Astakós, on the mainland. In season, there's a daily ferry from Pessáda to Skinári (Zákynthos), and two ships a day from Póros to Kilíni. Summer **hydrofoils** run from Sámi ✆ (0674) 22 456 to Váthi, and from Póros and Argostóli ✆ (0671 23 055) to Zákynthos. **Port authority**, ✆ (0671) 22 202.

**By road**: from Athens, there is a **bus** 3 times a day. Bus services to the rest of the island are fairly good if not frequent to the main centres; next to the KTEL station on the waterfront in Argotóli there's a local KTEL tourist office to help you plan excursions—some go as far as Olympia in the Peloponnese. For information, call ✆ (0671) 22 276 or 22 281. To really see the island, however, you need your own transport, readily available in the towns: try to avoid any mileage restrictions. Many **taxi** drivers specialize in trips around the island, and caiques go to the more popular beaches. A **car ferry** crosses the Gulf of Argostóli once an hour from Argostóli to Lixoúri.

## Tourist Information

**NTOG**, Argostóli, on the waterfront ✆ (0671) 22 248 or 24 466. **Tourist police**, see regular police, Argostóli ✆ (0671) 22 200.

## Festivals

**21 May**, Festival of the Radicals (celebrating union with Greece) in Argostóli; **21 May**, Ag. Konstantínos near Argostóli; carnival celebrations on the **last Sunday and Monday before Lent**; **Easter** festival in Lixoúri; **23 April**, Ag. Geórgios; **23 June**, Ag. Ioannis, at Argostóli; **15 August**, Panagías at Markópoulo; **16 August** and **20 October**, Ag. Gerásimos; **first Saturday after 15 August**, Robóla festival of wine in Fragáta.

## Argostóli

**Argostóli** (ΑΡΓΟΣΤΟΛΙ, pop. 10,000), magnificently set on a thumb of the great bay in the south, is a big, busy Greek town. It started life as a smuggler's hamlet under the Venetians and gradually, when the threat of piracy diminished, grew up around vast warehouses full of raisins, where ships from all over Europe would dock to fill their holds; the port of Argostóli is especially deep and safe and to this day is used for winter berthing of yachts and larger ships. As Ag. Geórgios, the Venetian capital, declined, the inhabitants petitioned Venice to make Argostóli capital and in 1759 got their wish, to the eternal disgust of archrival Lixoúri. After the earthquake, the Kefaloniots abroad lavished money to rebuild the town to make it worthy of a provincial capital. As a result, Argostóli seems to have more public buildings than most island capitals, grouped neartly around the large, central and palmy **Plateía Vallianóu**. Pre-earthquake Argostóli was famous for its bell towers, two of which have been rebuilt—there's something vaguely German Expressionist about the one by the Catholic church near the square.

Argostóli has two museums: the **Archaeology Museum** on G. Vergóti (*open 8.30–3, closed Mon, adm*) contains ex-votos to the god Pan from the cave of Melissáni, a room of Mycenaean finds—bronze swords, vases with spirals, and gold and ivory jewellery—coins from the four ancient cities of Kefaloniá, and a startlingly modern bronze bust of a man from the early 3rd century AD. The island's first theatre, the **Kéfalos**, has been reconstructed above the museum. The **Koryalenios Historical and Folklore Museum** in the basement of the library on Ilía Zervoú Sreet (*closed at the time of writing for restoration*) contains the Venetian records of the island, incuding its Libro d'Oro listing the local nobility, photos of old Kefaloniá icons, a traditional bedroom, memorabilia recalling Kefaloniá's early love affair with opera and theatre, and a carved ebony desk that belonged to Ferdinand Lesseps, the mastermind behind the Suez Canal. The library itself is the ground floor of an elegant mansion that survived the quake.

The one structure to survive the earthquake in one piece was the 800m **Drapanós Bridge**, built by the British in 1813 over the shallowest part of the bay, with its many low arches and commemorative obelisk. Take it a few minutes up road to Sámi, where the picturesque church of **Ag. Barbára** is cut into the rock just under a little bridge. A few kilometres further on, at Razáta, a dirt road leads up to ancient **Krani** (Paleókastro), where the huge stone blocks of the 7th-century BC Cyclopean walls snake through the trees. There are some fragments of a Doric temple to Demeter, and a rectangular hollow carved out of the top of the hill called the Drakospilia, or Dragon's Lair, although it was probably really just a Roman tomb.

## The Lassí Peninsula

One thing to do in Argostóli is to shoot the loop by foot, bike or car—there's no bus—around the little Lassí peninsula, just north of the city. There are a number of sandy beaches, and a clutch of bars, tavernas and discos around the **Katavóthres** or swallow holes, where the sea is sucked into two large tunnels deep under the ground. Where the sea water actually went was a big mystery until 1963, when Austrian geologists poured 140 kilos of green dye into the water. Two days later the dye appeared in the lake of the Melissáni cave and at Karavómylos, near Sámi, on the other side of the island. Sea mills to harness the rushing water for electricity were destroyed by the earthquake (which also greatly diminished the suction). One has been reconstructed, for decoration more than anything else; the mill is now used as a lobster nursery. At the tip of the Lassí peninsula is the lovely **lighthouse of Ag. Theódori**, a Doric rotunda built by one of Kefaloniá's great benefactors, British High Commissioner Charles Napier and reconstructed on its original plans after the 1875 earthquake. A 20-minute walk inland is a memorial to the Italian troops who hid nearby but were found and slaughtered by the Germans.

There are good, if very busy, sandy beaches south of Argostóli: **Platís Gialós**, **Makrí Gialós**, and, on the tiny isthmus that closes the end of the bay, **Tourkopódaro**. For other beaches further east along this coast, *see* below.

Two of the island's finest hotels are located just outside Argostóli: **Mediterranée**, 2km north on the beach at Lassí, ✆ 28 760, ✆ 24 758 (*A; exp*) the island's pride and joy, with all mod cons and air-conditioned rooms, and offering a variety of land and sea sports, but its high summer rates will have you reaching for your fattest credit card. **White Rocks**, at Platís Gialós beach, 3km from Argostóli, ✆ 23 167 (*A; exp*) is a dreamy hotel-bungalow complex by the sea, immersed in trees and bougainvillaea, with air-conditioning and other assorted comforts; half pension mandatory, but the food is delicious. **Hotel Ionian Plaza**, in central Plateía Valliánou, ✆ 25 581, ✆ 25 585 (*C; exp–mod*), is a stylish new hotel, each room with a balcony. **Cefalonia Star**, at 50 Metaxá St, ✆ 23 180 (*C; mod*) is at the end of town on the waterfront. *Open all year.* **Olga**, wedged in a quiet side street near the seafront, ✆ 24 981 (*C; mod*), is a prim and tidy; most rooms have balconies. Alternatively there's the **Regina**, two streets up from the waterfront at 24 Vergotí, ✆ 23 557 (*C; mod*) for a little less, or **Irilena**, ✆ 23 172 (*C; mod*), a pleasant choice on the Lassí peninsula, near a little beach. *Open May–Oct.* You can get basic rooms at **Hara**, 87 Leof. Vergotí, ✆ 22 427 (*D; inexp*) and **Parthenon**, 4 Zakýnthou, ✆ 22 246 (*D; inexp*). **Camping Argostoli**, is 2km north on the Lassí peninsula, ✆ 23 487.

**O Mezes**, in Lauranga St, is set in a pretty garden and specializes in traditional Kefaloniot dishes—hosts of *mezédes*, chicken *soúvla*, and *sheftália* (minced meatballs on a spit, served with pitta bread) (*3500–4500dr*). In the main square, **Kefalos** serves a large, various menu of Greek favourites on pretty pink tablecloths. **Taverna Diana** on the waterfront near the bus station does good moussaka and *kreatópita* (Kefaloniot meat pie: beef and pork with rice in filo pastry). If you have a hankering for charcoal-grilled chicken with a lemon marinade or lamb *kléftiko*, washed down with a house wine, get a table at **Psitaria Elliniko**, near Hotel Olga, ✆ 23 529. **Ambassador**, out on the Lassí peninsula, is popular for its excellent Greek food, garden and prices.

## Lixoúri and the Palikí Peninsula

Ferries trundle across the bay from Argostóli to the easterly, bulging Palikí peninsula and **Lixoúri** (ΛΗΧΟΥΡΙ), Kefaloniá's second city, all new houses on wide streets and in itself not terribly interesting, even if it's the home of the Pale Philharmonic (*sic*). In 1800, under the French occupation, Lixoúri was the site of the court, which gave the locals (well known for their sense of irony) high hopes of stealing the status of capital from rival Argostóli; they nicknamed their town 'Little Paris' and the dry riverbed that passes through it 'the Seine'. In the central square near the waterfront stands a **statue of Andréas Laskarátos**, shown holding his top hat. Laskarátos (1811–1901), son of an aristocratic family, was a poet and satirist who directed most of his broadsides at the Orthodox church. He had a large family to support, and he kept heckling and mocking the clergy so much that they finally excommunicated him—in Greek, *aforismós*, meaning that the body will not decompose after death. When Laskarátos found this out he hurried home, collected his children's decomposing shoes and returned to the priest, asking him to please excommunicate the footwear, too. You can get a sense of what pre-earthquake Lixoúri was like on the west end of town at the **Iakovátos Mansion**, a rare survival and now a library and icon museum; one of the works is attributed to Mikális Damaskinós. Fresco fragments and iconostasis salvaged from the earthquake have been installed in the town's newer churches. North of Lixoúri, the unexcavated ancient city of Pali (or Pale) stood on the hill of Paliókastro.

The Palikí peninsula is well endowed with beaches. Closest is **Ag. Spyrídon**, just north of town and safe for children, while 4km south are **Michalitsáta** and **Lépeda**, both sandy, the latter near the abandoned cave-monastery,-now church, of Ag. Paraskeví. In the same area, **Soulári**'s church of Ag. Marína has fine icons and a handsome Venetian doorway; the next village, **Mantzavináta**, has good frescoes in its church of Ag. Sofía. From here a dirt road leads south to the lovely beach of **Ag. Geórgios** (or **Miá Lákko**), a long stretch of golden-red sand, which merges to the west with the Palikí's best known beach, simply known as **Xi** (XI), a long crescent of reddish sand, with sun beds and a taverna.

Just south of it is the famous **Kounópetra**, a huge monolith a few inches from the shore that rocked to and fro, pulsating at the rate of 20 times a minute. The earthquake of 1953 fouled up the magic by stabilizing the sea bed beneath and likewise destroyed the houses on pretty, deserted **Vardianá islet** off the coast. Another by-road to the west passes the abandoned monastery of **Tafíon**, en route to a second monastery, **Kipouríon**, rebuilt as it was before the earthquake in the 1960s, perched on the west cliffs, with spectacular sunset views and guest rooms where you can spend the night. The peninsula is shot full of caves: the most interesting, **Drákondi Spílio**, 40m deep, can be reached from the monastery with a guide.

The sparsely populated northern part of the Palikí has a scattering of pretty villages such as **Damoulináta**, **Delaportáta**, and **Kaminaráta**, the latter famous for its folk dances more beaches: the large, lovely white sands of **Petáni**, rarely crowded and known as Paralía Xouras, 'Old Geezer beach', for the old man who used to run the seaside taverna. Even more remote—accessible by a minor road—is another beach called **Ag. Spyrídon**, a stretch of sand tucked into the northernmost tip of the Palikí peninsula.

---

*Lixoúri ✆ (0671–)*　　　　　　　　　　　　　　**Where to Stay and Eating Out**

**Cefalonia Palace Hotel**, next to Xi beach, ✆ 91 111, winter bookings ✆ 92 555, ✉ 92 638 (*A; exp*), is a brand new hotel with a pool, all rooms with sea view and balcony. **Pension Bella Vista**, ✆ 91 911 (*A; mod*), is small, modern and comfortable, all rooms with bath and simple kitchen and sea view. Although used by tour operators, the **Summery** in Lixoúri, ✆ 91 77 (*C; mod*), is a pleasant place to stay. *Open all year.* **Akroyiali** has good fish in season, and it doesn't cost an arm and a leg.

## Southeast of Argostóli: the Livathó and Mount Aínos

Most of Kefaloniá's rural population is concentrated in the fertile region of valleys, gardens and green rolling hills called the Livathó, southeast of Argostóli. After Platís Gialós beach, the first town is **Miniés**, home of a ruined Doric temple of the 6th-century BC and some of Greece's finest white wine.

## Robóla and some other Wines

Kefaloniá is one of most important islands for wines, especially Robóla, a grape variety introduced by the Venetians in the 13th century that ferments into distinctive lemony dry white wines, traditionally one of the finest Greek vintages. Lately it's been better than ever: the Robóla from Gentilini, a small vineyard in Miniés owned and operated by the innovative Nichólas Cosmetátos, has been something of a revolution in the country, demonstrating just how good Greek wines can be when made with the latest techniques and *savoir faire*, even when starting from scratch. In 1978 Cosmetátos purchased an estate in these limestone hills, planted his first vines, built a small but ultra-modern winery, and carved a cellar out of the cliffs to attain the perfect storage temperature. Each year the vintages improve; pale gold Gentili Animus, 100 per cent Robóla, is a crisp, delicious wine well worth looking out for; Gentili Fume is a Robóla aged in oak casks, with an oaky fragrance. Gentili also does a fine Muscat fortified dessert wine (Amando) and a lovely aperitif wine (half Muscat, half Robóla) called Dulcis, which goes perfectly with fresh fruit. Another label to look for, Calligas, was founded in the early 1960s, and produces lovely Robólas and occasionally the very rare Thiniatikó, which yields a velvety port-like wine. In the island's fish tavernas, the common house wine is Tsoussi, made from a white grape unique to Kefaloniá. You may also see Mavrodáphni Kefallinías, another sweet wine.

The coastal road south of Miniés continues to **Svoronáta**, where the red sands of **Avithos beach** (with a *cantina*) look out to the tiny islet of Días. This is named for a tiny islet off the coast of Crete, and like that one had an altar to Zeus: sacrifices were coordinated by smoke signals with those on Mount Aínos. **Domáta**, the next village east, boasts Kefaloniá's oldest olive tree (able to squeeze 20 people in the hollow of its ancient trunk) and the beautiful church of the **Panagía**, with a pretty reconstructed Baroque façade and an enormous 19th-century carved and gilded iconostasis that cost 12,000 gold sovereigns—all melted down.

Nearby **Kourkomeláta** was rebuilt by the wealthy Kefaloniote shipowner Vergotís; everything is as bright, new and pastel-coloured as a suburban southern California. The neoclassical cultural centre and surrounding vineyards add to the effect. At **Metaxáta**, where printing was introduced to Greece, Byron rented a house for four months in 1823, finished his satirical rejection of romanticism, *Don Juan*, and dithered over what to do as the representative of the London Committee, while each Greek faction fighting for independence jostled for the poet's attention—and especially his money. Just west **Lakídra**, rebuilt by French donations after the earthquake, is the most important village of the Liváatho and believed by some archaeologists to be the site of Odysseus's palace; in the suburb of Kallithéa, near the plain little of church of **Ag. Nikólaos ton Aliprantídon**, four Mycenaean tombs yielded a good deal of pottery from 1250–1150 BC. Byron used to come here and sit on a rock, inspired by the views, and a line from the poem he wrote is inscribed on a plaque: ΑΝ ΕΙΜΑΙ ΠΟΙΗΤΗΣ ΤΟ ΟΦΕΙΛΩ ΕΙΣ ΤΟΝ ΑΕΡΑ ΤΗΣ ΕΛΛΑΔΟΣ ('If I am a poet, I owe it to the air of Greece').

## Inland: Ag. Andréas, Ag. Geórgios, Ag. Gerasímos

North of Metaxáta is the Byzantine convent of **Ag. Andréas**, originally known as Panagía Milapídia (the apple Virgin) after an icon discovered on an apple tree trunk. Perhaps the one and only good deed done by the quake of 1953 was to shake loose the whitewash on the walls, revealing frescoes that date back to the 13th century (in the chancel) and the 17th and 18th centuries (along the nave). The church is now a **museum** *(open 9–1 and 5–8)*, housing icons, fresco fragments and saintly relics orphaned by the eathquake, among them the Veneto-Byzantine icon of *Panagía Akáthistos*, painted in 1700 by Stéfanos Tsankárolos from Crete. Since the earthquake a new Basilica of Panagía Milapídia was built next door to house its bizarre prize possession: the sole of St Andrew's right foot, donated in the 17th century by Princess Roxanne of Epiros.

Above the church looms the tree-filled **Castle of Ag. Geórgios** *(open 8am–8pm, Sun 8–2.30, closed Mon)* spread over a 320m hill and commanding a wonderful view of the surrounding plains and mountains. Founded by the Byzantine emperors, the citadel was completely rebuilt by the Venetians and Greeks under Nikólaos Tsimarás after the fierce seige of 1500 dislodged the Turkish occupants. The centre of life and religion on Kefaloniá until 1757, Ag. Geórgios once had a population of 14,000 people living in or just outside the polygonal walls. Storerooms, prisons, Venetian coats-of-arms, a ruined Catholic church, and a bridge built by the French during their occupation crumble away within the battlements; of the 15 churches, the **Evangelístria** with Byzantine icons still stands in the present-day little village.

To the east lies the green **plain of Omalós** and the **monastery of Ag. Gerásimos**, where the bones of Kefaloniá's patron saint rest in a silver reliquary, in a small church built over his little grotto hermitage. If half of the male population of Corfu are named Spíros after St Spyrídon, then 50 per cent of the Kefaloniotes are named Gerásimos. The saint's speciality is intervening in mental disturbances and exorcising demons, especially if the patient keeps an all-night vigil at his church on 20 October, his feast day, but pilgrims from all over Greece pour in all year round; a small hostel allows 20 to stay overnight. The monastery is dwarfed by an enormous plane tree and its tall pseudo-Rococo freestanding belfry.

From the Argostóli–Sámi road a branch winds up the summit to **Mégas Sóros** (1628m), the highest point of majestic Aínos range, the loftiest in the Ionian islands, and covered with snow from December to March. The road goes as far the tourist pavilion, 1300m up, and from there you can easily hike the rest of the way, an impressive stroll among the tall, scented trees seem-ingly on top of the world; on a clear day the Peloponnese, Zákynthos, Ithaca, Lefkáda, the Gulf of Pátras and even Corfu are spread out below as if on a great blue platter. Originally the entire range was blanketed with its unique, indigenous species of black fir—*Abies cefalonica*—with a distinctive bushy appearance and upward-pointing branches; the forests were so dense that Strabo and other ancient writers called the island Melaina, 'the Dark'. Since ancient times timber was the main source of Kefaloniá's prosperity; recent studies at Knossós show that the Minoans imported Kefaloniá's firs for the pillars of the labyrinth. Venetian shipbuilders over-harvested the trees, but two disastrous fires, in 1590 and 1797, share the blame for destroying nine-tenths of the forest; the latter burned for three months. In 1962 what had survived of the forest was made into Mount Aínos National Park. A handful of wild horses, the last survivors of an ancient breed who lived in the park, are near extinction. Hesiod mentioned the 8th-century BC temple of **Aenesian Zeus**, the foundations of which can bee seen just below Mégas Sóros. Bones from the great animal sacrifices that took place there can still be seen.

The south coast of Kefaloniá is bursting with good sandy beaches shielded from the north winds by Megás Sorós. There are good beaches at **Spartiá** (a remote strand under sheer white cliffs) and **Trapezáki**, 1½km from the tiny harbour of **Pessáda** (ΠΕΣΑΔΑ)—Kefaloniá's chief link to Zákynthos, with a summer *cantina* but no telephone for the unwary foot passanger to ring for a cab. Another pretty little sand beach is to the east below **Karavádos**, with a taverna perched above and plane trees and reeds spread behind.

The beach at **Lourdáta** (ΛΟΥΡΔΑΤΑ), is the longest and most crowded. Lourdáta's name is said to derive from the English lords who spent time here in the 19th century, perhaps attracted by the village's warm microclimate; its main square, with a spring and an enormous plane tree, is the beginning of Kefaloniá's first nature trail, blazed with funds from the WWF. It takes about 2½ hours to walk and passes through a sample of the island's flora—orange and olive groves, macchia shrubs and scrubby phyrgana, pine woods and kermes oaks, and masses of wild flowers in the spring. The path passes the ruined **Monastery of Síssia**, founded in 1218 by St Francis of Assisi (hence its name) while returning from the Crusades in Egypt; converted to Orthodoxy in the 16th century, a new monastery was built just above after 1953.

**Káto Kateliós** is a small resort, a pretty place with springs, greenery and a beach that curves along Moúnda Bay. Just east, Potomákia beach below Ratzaklí is a favourite nesting place of loggerhead turtles (*see* Zákynthos); from June to September volunteers for the British charity Care for the Wild mark the nests and take visitors to see the nesting turtles and their babies.

Just inland, Kefaloniá's most unusual religious event takes place in the village of **Markópoulo**, set over the sea on a natural balcony. During the first 15 days of August, small harmless snakes 'inoffensive to the Virgin Mary' with little crosses on their heads, suddenly appear in the village streets. Formerly they slithered into the church (rebuilt in exactly the same place after the earthquake) and mysteriously disappeared near the silver icon of the Panagía Fidón ('Virgin of the Snakes'). Nowadays, to keep them from being run over, the villagers collect them in glass jars and bring them to the church, where they are released after the service and immediately disappear as they did in the past. Although sceptics believe that the church is simply along the route of the little snakes' natural migratory trail, the faithful point out that the snakes fail to appear when the island is in distress—as during the German occupation and in 1953, the year of the earthquake.

**Skála** (ΣΚΑΛΑ) with its long beach and low dunes is the biggest resort in this corner, with plenty of watersports, sunbeds, bars, the works, but still relatively low-key. The Romans liked the area; near Skála a Roman villa was excavated, with 2nd-century AD mosaic floors, one portraying Envy being devoured by wild beasts and two men making sacrifices to the gods. Two km north of Skála, a 7th-century BC temple of Apollo has also been discovered, though most of its porous stone was cannibalized to build the nearby chapel of Ag. Geórgios.

Pronnoi, one of the four ancient cities of Kefaloniá, was located inland, above the village of **Pástra**, although only a necropolis and some walls of the acropolis have survived. In 1992, in the nearby hamlet of **Tzanáta**, Danish and Greek archaeologists uncovered a huge 12th-century BC domed tomb seven metres under a vineyard, said to be the most important ever discovered in Western Greece. The bones, gold jewellery and seals discovered inside are now being studied at the University of Pátras, but the discovery (the Kefaloniotes immediately declared it the tomb of Odysseus) has added new fuel to the ongoing 'Where Was Ithaca Really?' debate.

From Tzanáta the road descends through the wild and narrow 'Póros Gap', carved, according to myth, by Heracles who ploughed his impatient way through the mountains. **Póros** (ΠΟΡΟΣ), with direct ferry links to Kilíni, was originally the port of Pronnoi. In the 1820s, British High Commissioner Napier settled Maltese farmers here to create a model farming community called New Malta that never got off the ground; now the village, with its clear turquoise waters, abundant fresh fish and beach is rapidly developing as a resort.

---

© *(0671–)* **Where to Stay and Eating Out**

### Pessáda

**Sunrise Inn**, 1½km from the port, © 69 586, @ 69 621, © 69 621 (*B; exp*) is new, comfortable and air-conditioned, set in the trees, with a pool and children's activities. **Poseidon Apartments**, © 86 475, @ 69 649, book in Athens @ (01) 895 9899 (*mod*) have sea views from the balcony, tennis court and a large garden.

### Skála

Spanking new **Aliki**, © 83 427, @ 83 426 (*B; mod*) overlooks the sea and has a large garden, is good value, too. **Ostria's House**, 600m from Ratzaklí, © 83 383, book in Athens © (01) 202 4555 (*mod*) is a small and attractive.

### Lourdáta

**Lara**, © 31 157, @ 31 156 (*C; mod*), is a pleasant moderate-sized hotel, set in greenery a few minutes from the sea. *Open May–Oct.* Two of the best tavernas in the village, **To Thalassíno Trifilli** and **Klimatis** are run by members of Archipelagos, the local environmental group, who can inform you about any new nature trails and activities on the island. If it's on offer, try the *prentza* cheese made in nearby Simotáta.

## North Kefaloniá: Caverns and Castles

**Sámi**, the port for ships to Pátras, Corfu and Italy, is a growing resort in its own right, with beaches and a campsite, and although the wide bay is prettily closed in by mountainous Ithaca, the town itself is not very interesting. On the two hills behind the port are the **walls of ancient Sámi**, where the citizens put up a heroic four-month resistance to the Romans in 187 BC before their inevitable defeat, and the equally inevitable sale into slavery.

Sámi is close to Kefaloniá's magnificent grottoes: **Drogaráti cave**, near the hamlet of Chaliotáta, is a fairyland of orange and yellow stalactites and stalagmites; one of its great chambers has such fine acoustics that Maria Callas came here to sing, and concerts are occasionally held in the summer. The other, steep-sided **Melissáni** ('purple cave'), is a half-hour's walk from Sámi; small boats wait to paddle you across its mysterious salt water lake (supplied by the swallow holes near Argostóli), immersing you in a vast shimmering play of blue and violet colours, caught by the sun filtering through a hole in the roof of the chasm, 30m overhead. According to the school that Homer's 'Ithaca' consisted of both Itháki and Kefaloniá, this was the Cave of the Nymphs, where the Phaeacians deposited Odysseus (*both caves open 8–7 in summer, but closed after October*). There are other, undeveloped caves for spelunkers only in the vicinity of Sámi, many with lakes and dangerous, precipitous drops, best of which is **Angláki cave**, near Pouláta.

At the base of Kefaloniá's northernmost peninsula, pretty **Ag. Evfimía** (ΑΓ. ΕΥΦΗΜΙΑ) is the port for Ithaca and Astakós, and a far cosier resort base than Sámi. There's good swimming off a scattering of white pebbly beaches along the Sámi road. A mosaic uncovered in Archeotíton Street is believed to have been the floor of the early Byzantine church of Ag. Evfimía, and the pretty village of **Drakopouláta**, a few kilometres above the port, was spared by the earthquake. Further west, scattered across the slops of Mount Ag. Dinatí, are more of Kefaloniá's most traditional villages and goats with silver-plated teeth—caused by the high mica content in the soil.

---

*© (0674–)*                                                      ***Where to Stay and Eating Out***

### Sámi

**Pericles**, © 22 780, 🖂 22 787 (*B; exp*), is a fancy complex on the edge of town, with a pool, tennis and nightclub. **Melissani**, © 22 464 (*D; mod*) is set back in greenery on the edge of Sámi, a small hotel with a pool and tennis. *Open May–Oct.* **Ionion**, © 22 035 (*C; mod*) and **Kastro**, with balconies, © 22 656 (*C; mod*), are both in the centre and convenient to the ferry; **Kyma**, nearby © 22 064 (*D; mod–inexp*), has a sea view. **Karavomilos Beach Camping**, 1km from town, © 22 480 is well equipped. There are two tavernas side by side on the waterfront, **Saoulis** and **Port Sámi**, both serving fish, regular Greek dishes and some local specialities (meat pie, octopus pie and meat cooked in a ceramic *stámna*); the latter has a delicious rosé retsina. Count on around 2000dr for a meal at either.

### Ag. Evfimía

There are two hotels here: **Moustakis**, © 61 030 (*C; mod*) and **Pylaros**, © 61 210 (*C; mod*), the latter right on the sea. *Open Apr–Sept.* There's an excellent taverna serving a delicious house wine on Paradise Beach, 500m from the dock.

---

## Up the Northwest Coast: to Mýtros, Assos and Fiskárdo

The journey from Argostóli north to Fiskárdo is magnficently scenic—perhaps a good reason to take the bus, so you don't have keep your eyes on the road, although there are some very tempting stops along the way. The first good beach, white pebbly **Ag. Kiriakí**, with several bars and tavernas, rims the crotch of land linking the Palikí peninsula to the rest of Kefaloniá, a few kilometres under the village of **Zóla**. An unpaved road links Zóla to **Angónas** (it's also on the main the Argostóli road) where local folk artist Razos has decorated the village square with paintings. Eight kilometres to the north, far below **Divaráta**, curves the U-shaped bay of **Mýrtos**, where sheer white cliffs carpeted with green maquis frame one of the most beautiful beaches in Greece, a silver white crescent of sand and tiny pebbles against a deep sea so blue it hurts. A steep 4km road descends to the beach from Divaráta, but if you want to make a day of it, bring provisions (and a hat—there's no shade) or settle for a pricey sandwich at the beach café.

The road winds along a corniche to another famous, stunning view over **Ássos** (ΑΣΟΣ), where the Venetian citadel and colourful little fishing hamlet tucked under the arm of the isthmus look like toys. The village was rebuilt by the French after the earthquake and though its sleepy charm may get a bit frazzled by day-trippers during the day, Assos becomes a friendly little Greek village in the evening; there are only a handful of rooms to rent and a couple of tavernas. The **Venetian fortress**—a favourite sunset destination, by foot or, much easier, by car—dates from 1585, when the Turks occupied Lefkáda and began raiding this coast; it was the seat of the Venetian proveditor until 1797. His house survives in ruins, along with the church of San Marco and a rural prison, used until 1815. The venerable olive tree in main Plateía Paris is said to have shaded the open-air sermons of St Cosmás the Aetolian, an 18th-century missionary; at one point, the story goes, his words were being drowned out by the buzzing cicadas. Cosmás told them to hush up, and they did.

East of the main road, an unpaved road rises up the inland villages of the peninsula. One, **Varí**, has by its cemetery a late Byzantine church called Panagía Kougianá, with rare and curious frescoes painted by a folk artist, who decorated the left wall with scenes from hell, and the right one with scenes of paradise until the villagers applied a coat of whitewash. The church is usually locked; ask in the village for the key.

Continuing up to Cape Ather, the northernmost tip of Kefaloniá, the road passes a white rocky beach of **Chalikéri**, where people come to soak in the exceptionally briny water. In **Ántipata Erissóu**, the unusual Russian church of 1934 was build by a Kefaloniot who made a fortune in Russia. Tiny **Fiskárdo** (ΦΙΣΚΑΡΔΟ) is by a landslide the prettiest and trendiest village on the island, its 18th-century houses gathered in a brightly coloured apron around a yacht-filled port. A fluke in its innermost geological depths spared it from the 1953 earthquake, and it's a poignant reminder of the architecture Kefaloniá once had, now all turned to dust. Some of the old houses have been fixed up for guests (*see* below); others are decorated with folk paintings of mermaids and ships. Four carved stone sarcophagi and the ruins of a Roman bath are fenced off by the Panormos Hotel.

The name Fiskárdo is derived from Robert Guiscard, the *terror mundi* of his day, whose very name made popes, emperors and kings tremble in their boots. Born in 1017, the 6th of 13 sons of a minor Norman nobleman named Tancred de Hauteville, Robert began his career as a mercenary adventurer working for (and against) the Byzantines and Lombards in Italy. By a mix of adroit military leadership, an eye for the main chance and cunning (his nickname *Guiscard* means 'crafty') he made himself Duke of Apulia, master of Southern Italy. Other Hauteville brothers came to join him; the most successful was the youngest, Roger, who married a cousin of William the Conqueror, defeated the Arabs of Sicily and founded an extraordinary dynasty of kings.

Having just sacked and burned Rome after defeating Emperor Henry IV's attempt to dethrone Pope Gregory VII (Hildebrand), Robert Guiscard and his Normans were on their way to do the same to Constantinople, on the excuse that Byzantine Emperor Michael VII had locked his empress—Guiscard's daughter—up in a convent. In 1085 the Normans had just scored a major victory at Corfu over the Venetians, Byzantium's allies, when a typhoid epidemic at last laid low the 68-year-old warrior; he was brought ashore and died in the arms of his Lombard warrior wife, Sichelgaita. His body was preserved in salt and sent back to Italy to be buried with his brothers; the coffin was washed overboard in a storm, but later recovered off Otranto and the messy remains of the Guiscard were buried at Venosa. As John Julius Norwich wrote in *The Normans of the South*: 'He was that rarest of combinations, a genius and an extrovert...a gigantic blond buccaneer who not only carved out for himself the most extraordinary career of the Middle Ages but who also, quite shamelessly, enjoyed it.' Such was the power of his name that the old pirate was granted a posthumous and completely false reputation as a virtuous Crusader; two centuries after his death Dante piously installed him his *Paradiso*.

## Ássos

There are some 200 beds available in private rooms, although they fill up fast in the summer. For meals there isn't much choice—most people go to **Kokolis** for dinner.

## Fiskárdo

In bijou Fiskárdo, where everybody likes to stay, four typical houses have been reno-vated by the NTOG; for reservations, write to Paradosiakós Ikismós Fiskárdou, Kefaloniá, © 51 398. There are two pensions, which are renovated and done out in traditional style: the **Filoxenia**, © 51 487, and the **Fiskardona**, © 51 484, and self-contained apartments for rent—**Stella**, © 51 348, and **Kaminakia**, © 51 578. **Dendrinos** is a fine fish restaurant in the harbour, serving up ample portions of the day's catch to landlubbers and yachters who like to drop in (*3000dr*), and it's worth searching out **Nicolas' Garden** (if Nicolas doesn't find you first), hidden up a narrow alley in the middle of the village, for excellent food in a relaxing setting (*2500dr*). French-run **Les Barbares**, with a striking interior, is a trendy bar, popular with both locals and the yacht crowd.

# Kýthera (KYΘHPA)

Tucked under the great dangling paw of the Peloponnese, Kýthera, the isle of the goddess of love, is on the way to nowhere, and owes a good part of its attraction to the fact. The opening of the Corinth canal doomed even the minor commercial importance Kýthera once had by virtue of its position between the Ionian and Aegean seas; even today, unless you take the small plane from Athens, getting there is awkward, time-consuming and expensive, requiring a long overland drive and ferry or a long hydrofoil ride. Although sentimentally it continues to be one of the Eptánissa, or Seven Ionian Islands, with whom it shares a common history of Venetian and British occupation, politically it now belongs to Attica and is administered from Piraeus. In this century Kýthera's population has decreased dramatically, most emigrating to the other side of the world; some 100,000 people of Kýtheran origin now live in Australia or 'Big Kýthera' as the 3000 who still live on Kýthera call it. All the emigrants who possibly can return each summer, constituting its main tourist rush, nor are many of them interested in developing the island's tourist potential. They like it fine the way it is. The non-Aussies who do visit are usually of the hardy Hellenophile type, old Greek hands anxious to escape their own countrymen, or the wealthy who have scattered their villas all over Kýthera.

Kýthera is not without its charms, although it can hardly hope to match the shimmering luxu-riance of Watteau's *Pèlerinage à l'Ile de Cythère*, nor have the recent spate of forest fires helped, either. Much of the landscape has the look of abandoned farms and orchards, but in summer it is lent a golden sheen by the *sempreviva*, which when dried keeps 'forever', or at least a few years, rather like love itself.

## History

When Zeus took his golden sickle and castrated his father, Cronos, then ruler of the world, he cast the bloody member into the sea. This gave birth to Aphrodite, the goddess of love, who rose out of the foam on her scallop shell at Kýthera. She found it far too puny for her taste and

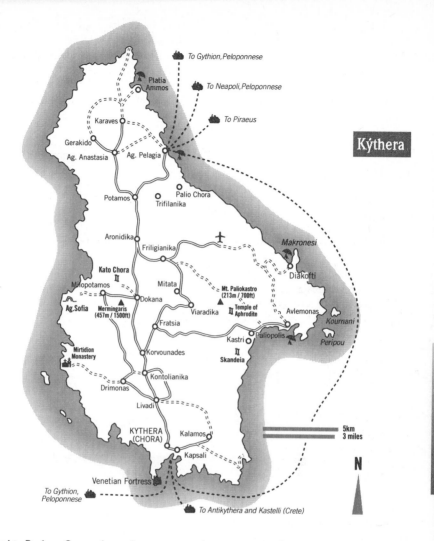

To Gythion, Peloponnese

To Neapoli, Peloponnese

To Piraeus

Kýthera

Platia Ammos

Karaves

Gerakido

Ag. Anastasia

Ag. Pelagia

Potamos

Palio Chora

Trifilanika

Aronidika

Friligianika

Makronesi

Kato Chora

Diakofti

Milopotamos

Mitata

Mt. Paliokastro
(213m / 700ft)

Dokana

Ag. Sofia

Mermingaris
(457m / 1500ft)

Viaradika

Temple of
Aphrodite

Avlemonas

Kournani

Fratsia

Peripou

Mirtidion
Monastery

Korvounades

Kastri

Paliopolis

Skandeia

Kontolianika

Drimonas

Livadi

5km
3 miles

KYTHERA
(CHORA)

Kalamos

Kapsali

N

Venetian Fortress

To Gythion,
Peloponnese

To Antikythera and Kastelli (Crete)

moved to Paphos, Cyprus, hence her two names in antiquity, the Cypriot or the Kytherian. An ancient sanctuary dedicated to Aphrodite on Kýthera was the most sacred of all such temples in Greece according to Pausanius, but scarcely a trace of it remains today.

Aphrodite was called Astarte by Kýthera's first settlers, the Phoenicians, who came for the murex shells, from which they extracted a purple dye to colour royal garments, and from which the island derived its other early name, Porphyrousa. The Minoans, the first in Greece to worship Aphrodite, made Kýthera a central trading station for its location at the crossroads between Crete and the mainland, and the Aegean and Ionian Seas. It was a spot on the map popular with aggressors: Kýthera was invaded 80 times in recorded history. Particularly frightful were the visits of the Saracens from Crete, so ferocious in the 10th century that the island was abandoned altogether until Nikephóros Phokás reconquered Crete back for Byzantium.

The rulers of Kýthera in the Middle Ages were the Eudhaemonoyánnis family from Monemvássia. The Venetians occupied the island in 1204, but with the help of Emperor Michael Palaeológos, Kýthera was regained for the Eudhaemonoyánnis, and for long years it served as a refuge for Byzantine nobles, especially after the Turks grabbed the Peloponnese. However, in 1537, Barbarossa stopped at Kýthera on his way home from the unsuccessful siege of Corfu and destroyed the island. The Venetians took over again in the 16th century and called it 'Cerigo', the name by which it is known in the old history books. In 1864 it was ceded to Greece by the British with the rest of the Ionian islands.

### Getting There and Around

**By air:** at least one flight a day from Athens; airport information, ✆ (0735) 33 292, tickets from the Olympic Office at El. Venizélou 49, Pótamos, ✆ 33 688.

**By sea:** there are **hydrofoils** at Ag. Pelagía 5 times a week from Gýthion, 3 times a week from Piraeus, Hýdra, Spétses and Monemvássia; also a regular **ferry** from Neápoli daily, 5 times a week with Gýthion, twice a week with Monemvássia, Kastélli (Crete) and Piraeus, once a week with Antikýthera. **Port authority,** ✆ 33 280.

**By road: buses** leave Kýthera Town about once a day for the major villages of the island; most people get around by **taxis** which charge a set fee for different excursions. At Ag. Pelagía, Pótamos and Kapsáli there are cars to **hire**.

### Tourist Information

For tourist police see regular police, ✆ (0735) 31 206. **Skandela Tours**, in Ag. Pelagía, ✆ 33 522, ✆ 33 135 can help you find a hotel, a room or a villa to rent.

### Festivals

**29–30 May**, Ag. Trias at Mitáta; **15 August**, Panagías Mirtidíon; **24 September** Mirtidión Monastery.

## Kýthera Town (Chóra)

Kýthera town, or **Chóra** (ΧΩΡΑ), the capital of the island, is a pretty as a picture-postcard blue and white Greek village, 275m above the port of Kapsáli, impressively guarded by a mighty fortress furnished by the Venetians in 1503. Its location was supposedly selected by pigeons, who took the tools of the builders from a less protected site. Ten old **Venetian mansions** in Chóra still retain their coats-of-arms, and a small two-room **museum**, generally open in the mornings, contains artefacts dating back to Minoan times. Below, a 20-minute walk down the hill, the port mini-resort of **Kapsáli** (ΚΑΨΑΛΙ) has a large house with rooms to let owned by one Emmanuel Comnenus (probably a descendant of the Byzantine nobles who fled to Kýthera from Mýstra), a few restaurants and two nice beaches, one very sheltered, the pebbly one only a bit more exposed; pedaloes will take you to other pebbly strands. The little 'egg islet', Avgó, offshore here is said to be the spot where Aphrodite was born.

**Kálamos**, just east, is within walking distance. One of its churches, Ag. Nikítas, has a pretty bell tower, and there is a taverna by the square. A dirt road continues across the rugged landscape to **Vrouláia**, a pebble beach and taverna, where many people pitch their tents.

# Northwest of Kýthera Town

From Kýthera town, the paved road heads north to **Livádi** (ΛΙΒΑΔΙ), where once-golden wheat fields have run wild from lack of labour and there's a pretty bridge of 13 arches, built by the British in 1822. If you ring ahead (© 31 124) you can visit the Roússos family ceramic workshop, where the ancient tradition of Kýthera pottery is kept alive, now into the third generation. Heading east from Livádi are two good beaches, Fíri Ámmos and Kamponáda; west of Livádi via Drimónas is the important **Monastery of the Panagía Mirtidíon** with a tall carved bell tower, magnificently set on the wild west coast among cypresses, flowers and peacocks. The monastery is named after a gold-plated icon of the Virgin and Child, whose faces are blackened with age—a sign of special holiness that attracts a huge number of pilgrims. Two small islets just offshore are said to be pirate ships that the Virgin turned to stone for daring to attack the monastery. Pilgrims can stay in the very simple hostel.

North of Drimónas, **Milopótamos** (ΜΥΛΟΠΟΤΑΜΟΣ) is the closest thing to Watteau's vision of Kýthera, a pretty village criss-crossed by tiny canals of clear water—so much water, in fact, that the toilet in the valley is in a constant state of flush. The stream valley through the middle of town is called the Neraída, or Nymph; an old watermill lies along the somewhat over-grown path to the waterfall at Foníssa, surrounded by the ancient plane trees, flowers and banana plants; on quiet evenings you can hear the nightingales sing. The ghost town **Káto Chóra** lies just below Milopótamos, within the walls of a Venetian fortress built in 1560. Above the gate there's a bas-relief of the lion of St Mark gripping his open book reading the angelic words 'Pax Tibi, Marce, Evangelista Meus' that gave the Venetians a certain celestial legitimacy, at least in their own eyes. It welcomes you to a desolation of empty 16th-century stone houses and churches, although some are slowly being restored. A dirt road descends steeply down to one of the island's best secluded beaches, white sandy **Limiónas**.

Signs from Milopótamos lead down to the cave **Ag. Sofía**, Kýthera's most impressive, at the end of a rugged, declining track (*usually open summer afternoons 3–8, but check in the village*). In the past the cave was used as a church, and inside there are frescoes and mosaics, as well as stalactites and stalagmites and small lakes that go on and on; some say it tunnels all the way under Kýthera to Ag. Pelagía. And at Ag. Pelagía a sign does indeed point down a rocky hill to a mysterious Ag. Sofía.

# The East Coast

At Frilingianiká, a road branches east to **Paliópoli** (ΠΑΛΑΙΟΠΟΛΙΣ), a tiny village on the site of **Skandeia**, the port mentioned by Thucydides. The Minoan trading settlement was here, dating from 2000 BC until the rise of the Mycenaeans; their long-ago presence (ruins of the settlement may be seen at the site now known as **Kastri**) has bestowed archaeological status on the long and lovely beach, which has kept it pristine except for an excellent taverna.

In ancient times, devotees would climb to the temple of Urania Aphrodite, 'Queen of the Heavens', to pay their respects to the goddess. Urania Aphrodite was often known as the 'eldest of the Fates', the daughter of the Great Goddess Necessity, whom even the great Zeus could not control. Pausanius wrote that her temple was one of the most splendid in all Greece, but the Christians destroyed it and built the church of Ag. Kosmás (with the temple's Doric columns). All that remains at the site, called **Paliokástro** are the acropolis walls. From Paliópoli the coastal road descends to **Avlémonas** (ΑΒΛΕΜΟΝΑΣ), with one of Kýthera's better beaches. By the sea is a small octagonal fortress built by the Venetians, who left a coat-of-arms and a few rusting cannon inside. A dirt road 7km to the north leads to **Diakófti** (ΔΙΑΚΟΦΤΙ), a fishing port and scrap of a resort popular with Greek families, a strip of white sand, protected by a pair of islets, Makronísi and Prasonísi. The main road from Diakófti passes the airport; to the south, near the centre of Kýthera, **Mitáta** is a great place for picnic, surrounded by lovely green countryside and lemon trees; the cool clear water of its spring is delicious. It's also a good spot to purchase delicious thyme honey, at about half the price of the rest of Greece—3500dr a kilo; one source is George and John Protopsáltis, ✆ 33 614.

## Palio Chóra and the North

**Palio Chóra** (or Ag. Dimitríou), is Kýthera's Byzantine ghost town, founded by the noble Eudhaemonoyánnis clan in the Monemvassian style. High on the rocks, it was carefully hidden from the sea—according to legend, the terrible Barbarossa found it only by capturing the inhabitants and torturing them until they told him where it was. Beside the ruins of the fort is a terrible 100m abyss down which mothers threw their children before leaping themselves, to avoid being sold into slavery by Barbarossa. Most of the island's ghost stories and legends are centred here. The scramble up is rewarded not only by views over the abyss, but a few frescoes in the haunted churches.

Palio Chóra is near **Potamós** (ΠΟΤΑΜΟΣ), which despite its name, has no river. It is the largest village in the north, all blue and white like Kýthera town. It has a bank and an Olympic Airways office, and the largest building at the edge of town is the island's retirement home. Come on Sunday if you can, when the village hosts the island's biggest market. West of Potamós, **Ag. Elefthérios** is a lovely secluded beach, and a pretty place to watch the sunset.

At **Gerakári** to the northwest you can see yet another tower, this time built by the Turks in the early 18th century. From the pretty village of **Karavás**, the road continues to the fine beach and good taverna at **Platiá Ámmos. Ag. Pelagía** (ΑΓ. ΠΕΛΑΓΙΑ), Kýthera's northern port, also has a long pebble beach and a few more facilities, if not a lot of soul. There are some excellent beaches to the south.

*Kýthera ✆ (0735–)*                    **Where to Stay and Eating Out**

When it comes to finding a place to stay on Kýthera you may be hard pressed. There aren't even many rooms to rent: the majority are at Ag. Pelagía, Pótamos, Kýthera town and Milopótamos.

### Kýthera/Chóra

There are only small pensions here, like **Keti**, ✆ 31 318 (*B; inexp*), and **Margarita** (no phone). *Open all year.* There are a number of typical, simple tavernas offering straightforward Greek food up in Chóra, notably **Zorba's**, in the main street. **Ta Kythera** just inland at Manitochóri, ✆ 31 563, has clean, pleasant double rooms. *Open June–Aug only.*

### Kapsáli

The **Raikos** pension, ✆ 31 629 (*B; exp*) is the island's biggest with 51 air-conditioned rooms and a pool. *Open May–Sept.* The next is the **Aphrodite**, ✆ 31 328 (*D; inexp*). **Kalokerino Katikies**, ✆ 31 265 (*C; mod*), have furnished apartments. Taverna **Magos**, near the beach ✆ 31 407, has lovely views of Kapsáli, and serves all the usual Greek specialities.

## Livádi

There are two places to stay here: **Aposperides**, ℰ 31 790 or 31 656, a pension (*B; exp*) or **Rousos**, in Káto Livádi, ℰ 31 124 with apartments. **Taverna Pierros** here is probably the oldest and most traditional taverna on Kýthera, with authentic home cooking and kind prices. For something completely different, dine at **Toxotis**, run by a superb chef from Kýthera who has taught in a Athenian cooking school, and now prepares unusal specialities rarely found on Greek menus, such as *seftália*, a Cypriot dish with sweetbreads, delicious aubergine specialities, and fancy salads. Three km north, the **Lokanda** in Karvoynádes is a good place for a pizza or snack.

## Avlémonas

There's plenty of new accommodation here, mostly in the form of self-catering apartments, among them **Poppy's**, ℰ 33 735; **Roulas**, ℰ 33 060; **Christoforos**, ℰ 33 057, and **Mandy's**, ℰ 33 739 (*all mod*). For something less, try **Manolis Stathis**, ℰ 33 732. **Taverna Sotiris**, ℰ 33 722, prettily set in a small square overlooking the sea, prepares excellent, seafood as fresh as can be, caught by the owners themselves. In nearby Paliópoli, try the **Skandia**, serving Greek specialities served under enormous elm tree—a great place for lunch.

## Diakófti

For peace and quiet you can't beat **Sirene Apartments**, right on the sea, ℰ 33 900, or in Athens ℰ (01) 481 1185 (*A; exp*), with their big verandas and kitchens. Also try **Kythera Beach Apartments**, ℰ 33 750 (*C; mod*), within spitting distance of the sea. *Open Apr–Oct.*

## Mitáta

People come from across Kýthera to eat at **Michalis**, a small informal restaurant in the main square of this village; Michális' wife cooks a number of island specialities, prepared with vegetables from their own garden.

## Ag. Pelagía

**Filoxenia**, ℰ 33 610 (*B; exp*), has 54 furnished apartments. The 10-roomed **Kytheria** pension, ℰ 33 321 (*D; inexp*), serves breakfast, and there's a limited selection of tavernas: the popular **Kaleris**, ℰ 33 461 has tables right on the sand. In the evening a lot of people end up inland at Karavás, at the **Amir Ali** piano bar, named after a Turk, but no one knows why.

## Elafónissos (ΕΛΑΦΟΝΗΣΟΣ) and Antikýthera (ΑΝΤΙΚΥΘΗΡΑ)

From Ag. Pelagía you can look out across the Lakonian sea to the islet of **Elafónissos**, which until the 17th century was a part of the Peloponnese, and is now connected daily in the summer by caique from Neápolis or Ag. Pelagía. Its village is mostly inhabited by fishermen and sailors, but the main reason for visiting is 5km south of the village, **Katá Nísso**, a twin bay endowed with two gorgeous white sandy beaches that go on and on, as yet hardly discovered by tourists (a caique from the 'capital' makes the trip). There are two tavernas and two small B-class pensions in the village, open June to September if you want to play Robinson Crusoe with a roof over your head: **Asteri tis Elafonissou**, ℰ (0734) 61 271 and **Elafonissos**, ℰ 61 268; rough camping on the beach is another possibility.

Another islet, the utterly remote **Antikýthera**, lies far to the south of Kapsáli, nearly midway to Kastélli, Crete. If the *meltémi* isn't up, as it often is, ships call once a week en route between Kýthera and Crete. Fewer than 150 people live in Antikýthera's two villages, **Potamós** and **Sochória**, and the rest is very rocky with few trees; curiously, like west Crete, the island is slowly rising. By Potamós, ancient **Aígilia** has walls dating back to the 5th century BC. There's a small beach at **Xeropótamo**, 5 minutes from Potamós by boat, or 30 minutes on foot. Water is a luxury, and the few rooms available are quite primitive; running water and toilets are rare. Food can also be scarce.

## The World's Oldest Computer

Antikýthera is just a tiny smudge on the map, but thanks to the wild winds that churn the surrounding sea it is also a name familiar to any student of ancient Greek art. For here, on the 22nd day of the ancient Greek month of Mounichon, in the first year of the 180th Olympiad (5 May, 59 BC), a Roman ship sailing from Rhodes, laden with booty that included the magnificent 4th-century BC bronze statue known as the *Ephebe of Antikýthera* (one of the celebrities of the National Archaeology Musem in Athens), went down off the coast of Antikýthera. Now you might ask: how is it that anyone could even begin to know the precise date of a 2000 year-old shipwreck? Pinpointing even the century of ancient finds is more often than not just an archaeological guessing game. The answer is that the world's first computer was part of the booty, and its timekeeping mechanism was stopped forever on the day the ship went down.

The wreck was discovered by chance in 1900 by sponge divers from Sými, who in a storm sheltered off the inaccessible coast of Antikýthera. After the storm, a few divers donned their weighted belts and went down to see if this remote seabed might in fact shelter a sponge bed or two. Instead they were startled to see a man beckoning to them—the famous Ephebe. The Greek archaeological service was notified, and sent down a small warship to haul up the bronze and marble statues, vases, and glass—the world's first underwater archeological dig. One of the items was a lump; as the months passed and the sea mud dried, a wooden cabinet about a foot high was revealed. This quickly deteriorated on contact with the air, leaving a calcified hunk of metal that broke into four bits. Archaeologists were astonished to see that they belonged to a mechanical device inscribed with ancient Greek script.

At first dismissed as a primitive astrolabe, the Antikýthera Mechanism, as it was known, soon proved to be much more complex. In 1958, a young British historian of science, Derek de Solla Price, was allowed to examine it and was the first to recognize it as an astronomical computer, which, by its setting, was made on the island of Rhodes in 82 BC. The days of the month and the signs of the zodiac were inscribed on bronze dials, with pointers to indicate the phases of the moon and position of the planets at any given time, operated within by a complex mass of clockwork: bronze cog wheels with triangular teeth, connected to a large four-spoke wheel (the most prominent part visible at the National Archaeology Museum in Athens) driven by a crown gear and shaft, which probably had some kind of key for winding. A moveable slip ring allowed for Leap Year adjustments and alignments. As far as anyone can judge, it was last set by the Roman sea captain on the day his vessel went down. He may have been bringing it to Rome on the special order of Cicero, who knew of the 'future-telling astronomical' device from his school days at Rhodes' famous School of Rhetoric. 'It is a bit frightening to know,' concluded Derek Price, 'That just before the fall of their great civilization, the Ancient Greeks had come so close to our age, not only in their thought, but also in their scientific knowledge.' The next similar device to be noted anywhere was in 11th-century India, by the Iranian traveller al-Biruni. (For all the details, pick up a copy of Victor Kean's *The Ancient Greek Computer from Rhodes*, Efstathiadis Group, 1991).

# Lefkáda (ΛΕΦΚΑΔΑ)

The island of Lefkás (more popularly known in Greece by its genitive form Lefkáda) was named for the whiteness (*leukos*) of its cliffs. It barely qualifies as an island; in ancient times Corinthian colonists dug what is now the 20m (66ft) wide Lefkáda ship canal, separating the peninsula from the mainland. This is kept dredged by the Greek government and is easily crossed by a swing bridge; beyond the canal a series of causeways surrounds a large, shallow lagoon, where herons and pelicans figure among the migratory visitors. As on Kefaloniá, Ithaca, and Zákynthos, a series of earthquakes—most recently in 1953—destroyed nearly all of the island's buildings.

Lefkáda is not always a love-at-first-sight island; the approach from land is unpromising, and first impressions may be disappointing. This changes once you make your way down the coast, and before long the beautiful sandy beaches, natural beauty and its deft combination of tourism with tradition will make you a believer. Lefkáda is especially well known for the laces and embroideries produced by its women, some of whom still keep a loom in the back room of their house; it is just as famous for its perfect windsurfing at Vassilikí and sailing through the enchanted isles off Nídri.

## History

Although inhabited at least as far back as the Paleolithic era (8000 BC), Lefkáda first enters the scene of recorded history as part of ancient Akarnania, site of the city Nerikus, located at modern Kallithéa. Nerikus is recorded as being huge, but over the years farms and houses have almost completely overtaken all the remains. In 640 BC, the Corinthians used a ruse to snatch the island from the Akarnanians, and founded the city of Lefkáda where it is today, dug the channel separating Lefkáda from the mainland, and built the first fort at the northern tip, which throughout history would be the key to the island. During the Peloponnesian War, Lefkáda, as a loyal ally of Corinth, sided with Sparta and was devastated twice, by the Corcyraeans and the Athenians.

The biggest blow to ancient Lefkáda came with the war between Macedonia and Rome in the mid 3rd century BC, when the island was punished for Akarnania's siding with Macedonia. Another dark moment was the Battle of Aktium, which once and for all settled the claims of Augustus on the Roman Empire over those of Mark Antony and Cleopatra. To celebrate his victory, Augustus founded a new city, Nikopolis (near modern Aktion) which drained Lefkáda's wealth and population.

Although Lefkáda was granted to Venice after the Fourth Crusades, it took the Venetians a century to wrench it from the grip of the Despot of Epirus. The inhabitants, exasperated by the fights and pirates, received permission from Venice to built the original fortress of Santa Maura, a name that soon came to refer to the entire island. When Constantinople fell in 1453, the mother of the last Emperor Constantínos XI, Helene Palaeológos, founded a monastery

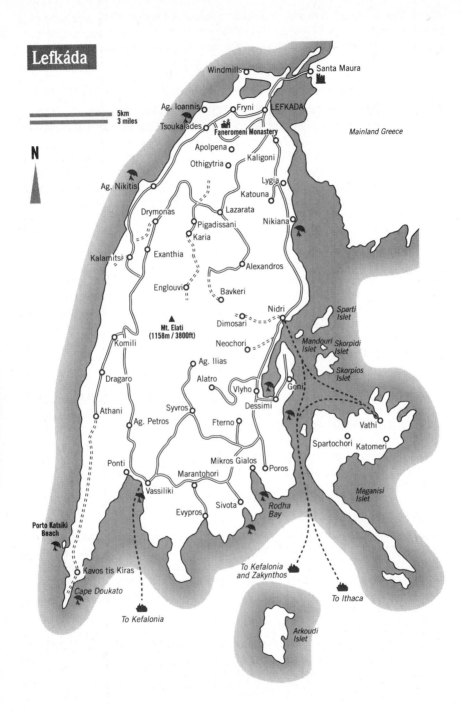

# Lefkáda

5km
3 miles

N

Windmills
Santa Maura
Ag. Ioannis
Fryni
LEFKADA
Tsoukalades
Faneromeni Monastery
*Mainland Greece*
Apolpena
Kaligoni
Othigytria
Lygia
Ag. Nikitis
Katouna
Drymonas
Lazarata
Pigadissani
Nikiana
Karia
Exanthia
Kalamitsi
Alexandros
Englouvi
Bavkeri
Nidri
*Sparti Islet*
Mt. Elati
(1158m / 3800ft)
Dimosari
*Mandouri Islet*
*Skorpidi Islet*
Neochori
Komili
*Skorpios Islet*
Ag. Ilias
Dragaro
Alatro
Vlyho
Geni
Dessimi
Athani
Syvros
Vathi
Ag. Petros
Fterno
Spartochori
Katomeri
Ponti
Mikros Gialos
Marantohori
Poros
Vassiliki
*Meganisi Islet*
Evypros
Sivota
*Rodha Bay*
Porto Katsiki
Beach
Kavos tis Kiras
*To Kefalonia
and Zakynthos*
*Cape Doukato*
*To Ithaca*
*To Kefalonia*
*Arkoudi Islet*

within the walls of Santa Maura. When the Turks took Lefkáda in 1479, they turned the monastery into a mosque.

In 1500 the combined forces of Spain and Venice under the Gran Capitan Gonzales de Cordoba captured Lefkáda and Santa Maura, but the very next year Venice made a treaty with Turkey and returned the island. In 1684, Venetian nobleman Francesco Morosini, angry at losing his own fortress at Herákleon, Crete, was determined to win Lefkáda back for Venice, which he did with the help of the Bishop of Kefaloniá, leading an army of priests and monks. Venice held on to the island until its own fall in 1796, but never managed to influence it as strongly as the other Ionians. With the fall of Venice, the French and then the Russians grabbed Lefkáda; in 1807 the tyrant Ali Pasha of Epirus tried to purchase it from Russia, but was held back by the Russian-appointed Secretary of State, Count John Capodístria. Capodístria is said to have later sworn to support the cause of an independent Greece with the rebellious refugees on the island, among them Kolokotrónis.

## Getting There and Around

**By air**: flights twice a day from Athens and occasional charters from England (Monarch, Air Ferries, and Air Caledonian among them), to Aktion, the nearest airport, 26km away on the mainland; from May–mid Oct there are bus connections to Lefkáda from the airport. Another charter, Britannia, flies to Préveza.

**By sea**: in summer, **boats** from Nidrí and Vassilikí to Sámi, Fiskárdo and Póros (Kefaloniá) and Kióni (Ithaca). Daily boat from Nidrí to Meganísi. **Port authority**, ✆ 22 176.

**By road**: there are **bus** connections with Athens (5 times a day), Arta and Préveza; Athens is about six hours' drive by car, Préveza about one hour's drive. The main island **bus station** is located on the north end of Lefkáda town; for information call ✆ 22 364. Routes aren't very frequent, and to really see the island you need at least a moped; there are plenty to hire at Vassilikí and Nidrí.

## Tourist Police

See regular police, Lefkáda town, ✆ (0645) 22 346; Vassilikí, ✆ (0645) 31 218 and Vlychó, ✆ (0645) 95 207.

## Festivals

**30 May**, Faneroméni Monastery; **26 July**, Ag. Paraskeví near Ag. Pétros; Carnival festivities, with a parade; in **August**, the Arts and Letters Festival and large International Folklore Festival, in Lefkáda town; two weeks in **mid-August**, Ag. Spyrídon, at Karyá, when the people bring out their old costumes (Karyá is well known for its handmade lace and woven carpets, and on **11 August** recreates a traditional wedding); **11 November**, Ag. Minás in Lefkáda.

# Lefkáda Town

Approaching Lefkáda over the floating bridge, the first thing you'll see as you cross the causeway over the lagoon is the massive **Fortress of Santa Maura**, dipping its feet in the sea near Akarnania (as the region is still known) on the mainland. Most of what stands dates from the Venetian and Turkish reconstructions. Although the buildings in the walls were blown to smithereens in an accidental powder explosion in 1888, the fortress continued to serve as a military camp, and, for 10 years after the 1922 Asia Minor Disaster, as a refugee camp.

Santa Maura has survived the periodic earthquakes that rattle Lefkáda better than the capital, **Lefkáda town**, which collapsed like a house of cards in the earthquake in 1948, and was hit hard again in 1971. The rebuilt town is like no other in Greece: narrow lanes lined with brightly painted houses, stone on the ground floor, topped by a fragile wooden or more often corrugated metal upper storey as an antiseismic measure. Another unusual feature of the town is its iron bell towers, rearing up like oil derricks.

The large shady square near the end of the causeway displays busts of Lefkáda's three great contributors to letters: Valaorítis, Sikelianós (for more on both, *see* below), and Lafcadio Hearn (1850–1904), whose British father and Kytheran mother named him after his birthplace. He went on to become a journalist in the States, and in 1890 went to Japan, where he became an expert on Japanese language and culture, teaching the Japanese about Western literature and vice versa; every now and then Japanese tourists make the pilgrimage to the island to honour the man they know as Yakomo Kuizumi.

Lefkáda's churches, built mostly in the 18th century under the Venetians, are square, dome-less, and solidly built of stone, and have mostly survived the tremors; fine examples of the Ionian school of painting are in **Ag. Minás** (1707), and the three icons in **Ag. Dimítrios** (1688), although the chances of finding either open are not good. Another church, the **Pantokrátor**, has a pretty façade, last reworked in 1890, with an original curved roofline. **Ag. Spyrídon** (17th century) has a fine carved wooden screen.

There are four small museums in Lefkáda town: near Ag. Spyrídon, the **Orpheus Folklore Museum** (*follow the little signs; open 10–1 and 6–9; winter Mon–Wed, 10–12 and 6–8*) has four rooms displaying the beautiful embroideries and weavings made on the island, dating back to the last century; there are also old maps, including a precious original map of Lefkáda made by the Venetian mapmaker Coronelli in 1687. The **Archaeology Museum**, in Faneroménis Street, houses mostly the finds from cave sanctuaries and the 30 12th-century BC tombs discovered by Dörpfeld in Nidrí; the **Icon (or Post-Byzantine) Museum**, with works of the Ionian school, is housed in the municipal library (✆ 22 502), and, appropriately for the town that established the first municipal brass band in Greece (1850), the **Lefkáda Sound Museum**, at 29 Kalkáni Street (*open 10–1 and 7–11pm*), founded by a local collector. The only museum of its kind in Greece, it contains old gramophones sent over by relatives from the United States, records of Cantades and popular Greek songs of the 1920s, and one of the first discs recorded by a Greek company, 'Orpheon' of Constantinople, founded in 1914. A cemetery dating from 600 BC has recently been discovered on the outskirts of town, and archaeologists from all over Greece are swooping on the site.

## Just Outside Town

The closest place to town for a swim is the **Gýra**, the long, sandy if often windy lido that closes off the west side of the lagoon, with a few tavernas and a surf club. On the other side of the windmills, a second beach, **Ag. Ioánnes Antzoúsis**, is tucked under a chapel, supposedly named for the Angevin Knights who founded it during the Crusades. In the opposite direction, by the cemetery, stop at the Café Pallas for a refreshing glass of almond milk, or *soumáda*, and watch the old men in the olive grove opposite play *t'ambáli*, Lefkáda's unique version of boules, played with egg-shaped balls on a concave ground, which as far as anyone knows is played nowhere else in the world. Two km south, set among the ruins of the monastery, the stone church of the **Panagía Odhigýtria** (1450) is the oldest on the island, the only one to have withstood all the tremors.

Just above Lefkáda is the 17th-century **Faneroméni Monastery**, rebuilt in the 19th century after a fire. It is a charming and serene place in the pine weeds, with bird's-eye views over the town, lagoon and the walls of Santa Maura. On the small islet with the ruined chapel of **Ag. Nikólaos** was a cottage where poet Angelos Sikelianós and his wife Eva would spend their summers.

Angelos Sikelianós, born on Lefkáda in 1884, was a good friend of the poet Aristotélis Valaorítis. Although he duly followed his parents' wishes by going off to law school in Athens, he only lasted two years before leaving school to join a theatre company with two of his sisters, Helen and Penelope. Penelope soon married the brother of Isadora Duncan, through whom Sikelianós met his American wife Eva. All shared an interest in somehow reviving the mythic passion and power of ancient Greece, in active artistic expression rather than in the dusty, pedantic spirit of the time. Sikelianos for his part published beautiful lyrical poetry, infused with the spirit of Dionysian mysticism. In the 1920s, he and Eva decided to go even further, initiating a campaign to revive the 'Delphic Idea' of learning and the arts, in the same spirit as the revival of the Olympics. Their goal was to create an International Delphic Centre and University, and stage a Delphic Festival of drama, dance, music, sports, and crafts; this actually took place in 1927 and 1930, funded in part by a mortgage on the Sikelianós

AG. NIKITAS, LEFKADA

house and Eva's inheritance. But the Depression closed in, and the following years were bitter; Eva went back to America, and although they divorced, she continued to support the 'Delphic Idea' and send the impoverished Sikelianós money. Sikelianos remarried and sat out the war years in a small flat in Athens, in declining health; in 1951 he died when he mistook a bottle of Lysol for his medicine. But the dark years added a tragic power to his poetry; his progressive ideas barred him from membership in the Athens Academy, and, as they will tell you in Lefkáda, from winning the Nobel Prize of Literature, although he was twice nominated.

---

### *Lefkáda ☎ (0645–)*         **Where to Stay**

The **Xenia**, on the waterfront overlooking a little park and the canal, ☎ 24 762 (*B; exp*), is quiet and comfortable, with compulsory half board in high season. **Hotel Lefkas**, ☎ 23 916 (*B; exp*) is more comfortable in the same price range; all rooms have a balcony, and the hotel supplies a minibus service; next door to the Hotel Lefkáda is the **Niricos Hotel**, ☎ 24 132 (*C; mod*), most rooms with sea views. **Byzantium Hotel**, ☎ 22 629 (*E; inexp*) on the main street is the small and well-kept.

### *Lefkáda ☎ (0645–)*         **Eating Out**

Restaurants are numerous and reasonably priced on Lefkáda and portions seem to be larger than elsewhere in Greece. If it's on offer, try the increasingly rare local wines *vartsámi*, *kerópati*, or *yomatári*. In central Plateía Antistási, there's the **Taverna Symposio**, for good Greek food and good people-watching; for a bit less, threre's the **Pizzeria Totem** in the same square. In Dimaríou Verrioti, near the Folklore Museum, **Taverna O Regantos** is blue and white and cute, with solid fare for around 2000dr. On the edge of town, towards Ag. Nikítas, **Adriatika** enjoys a pleasant garden setting, is pricier but has some good Greek specialities and excellent service (*3000dr*).

## The East Coast

The east coast of Lefkáda is as lovely, green and bedecked with beaches as the choice coasts of Corfu, and not surprisingly most of Lefkáda's tourist facilities have sprung up here. Just a few kilometres south of Lefkáda town at Kaligóni on a hill near the shore are the scant ruins of **ancient Nerikus**, the pre-Corinthian city, where Dôrpfeld (*see* below) found Cyclopean walls, traces of roads, arches, a watertank, and a pre-Roman theatre, as well as some early Byzantine ruins, which can be relocated after some scrambling through the olives. Further along is the cute fishing village of **Lygiá**, with narrow beaches and **Nikiána**, a small resort spread out along the coast, with attractive views of the mainland.

Further south is Perigiáli, with a fine beach and some new hotels, and, two kilometres further on, **Nidrí** (ΝΥΔΡΙ) Lefkáda's busiest resort town. Nidrí looks out over lovely Vlýcho Bay, closed in like a lake by the Géni peninsula, its still waters dotted with the privately owned wooded islets of **Mandourí, Sparti, Skorpídi** and **Skórpios**. The last still belongs to what remains of the Onassis family—Aristotle's little granddaughter, whose guardians make sure the patrols keep out island gatecrashers. From the sea you can spy Aristotle's tomb and excursion boats now have permission to land on the beaches if no one is in residence. You may notice a little red caique taking over a small army of workers who maintain the island; Onassis stipulated in his will that they must be from Nidrí. His obsession with privacy and payoffs in the right places kept tourist facilities at Nidrí at a bare minimum during his lifetime, but the locals have since made up for lost time; by Lefkáda standards Nidrí is cosmopolitan and commercial, and unfortunately all smack along the main road, which can get very very busy and noisy in the summer. On the other hand, concentrating all the hurly burly there has left the seafront and its tavernas relaxing and great for idling away an evening. Much of the old beach was sacrified for the building of a quay, however; most people head up to Perigiáli for a swim.

Sit at a café in Nidrí at twilight—there's one so near the shore you may sit with your feet in the sea—and, to the sound of croaking frogs, watch Mandourí, 'the poet's island' as the locals call it, float above the horizon on a magic carpet of mist. The mansion on Mandourí belongs to the family of the poet Aristotélis Valorítis (1824–79). Like many intellectuals from the Ionian islands, Valaorítis studied abroad, and when he returned it was first to serve as a member of the Ionian Parliament, and later the Greek Parliament, where he was renowned as a public speaker. His nature was highly romantic, and as patriotic as any in his day; he was one of the first to write verse in the demotic language of the people. For a closer look, hire a boat: at Trident Hire, Helen Morgan (who grew up on Lefkáda) will fit you out with anything from a two-person dinghy to a Hobby cat.

One of the nicest excursions from Nidrí is the 45-minute walk by way of the hamlet of Rachí to the **waterfall**, at the end of the Dimosári gorge. In the spring it gushes forth with enthusiasm; in the summer it is little more than a high altitude squirt, but it's wonderfully cool and refreshing, and there's a pool for a swim.

**Vlychó**, the next village south, is a quiet charmer, famous for its traditional boat-builders. Sandy **Dessími** beach, with a campsite, lies within walking distance, as does the **Géni peninsula**, covered with ancient, writhing olive groves. Wilhelm Dörpfeld, Schliemann's assistant in the excavation of Troy, found a number of Bronze Age tombs behind Nidrí. He became a local hero when he announced that they proved his theory that Lefkáda was the Ithaca of Homer. He died in 1940 and is buried near the house in which he lived, by the Géni's white church of Ag. Kyriakí. Further south, **Póros** is near the very pretty white pebble beach of **Mikrós Gialós**, set under the olive trees. **Sívota**, the next town south, has an exceptionally safe anchorage that draws yacht flotillas; many use it for winter berthing. There are very few rooms to rent here, but everyone comes for its excellent fish tavernas, where you can pick your lobster from the sea cage. The nearest swimming from Sívota is at **Kastrí**, to the west.

---

*Lefkáda ✆ (0645–)*                    ***Where to Stay and Eating Out***

## Nikiána

**Porto Galini** ✆ 92 431, 📠 92 672 (*B; exp*) provides luxurious furnished apartments among the cypresses and olives, and watersports down on the beach. For something less, try the **Pension Ionian**, ✆ 71 720 (*B; mod*), a stone's throw from the sea, or **Pension Pegasos**, ✆ 71 669 (*B; mod*). The **Hotel Konaki**, at Lygiá ✆ 71 126, 📠 71 125 (*B; exp–mod*) has a garden setting, overlooking a large pool.

## Nidrí

**Ta Niksakia**, 1km from Nidrí, ✆ 92 777, book in Athens 📠 (01) 764 5440 (*A; exp*), are studio apartments with a commanding views, 200m above the sea. The **Nidrí**

**Akti** pension, ✆ 92 400 (*B; mod*) has good views. **Gorgona**, ✆ 92 268 (*E; inexp*) is less, and there are plenty of rooms, but just see if you can get one in the summer. Two km north in Perigiáli, **Scorpios** ✆ 92 452 (*exp*) has studios and apartments and a pool; **T'Aremno Beach**, right on the beach, ✆ 92 112, ✆ 92 018 (*B; exp*) offers modern air-conditioned rooms, equipped with minibars. **Bella Vista**, 500m from Nidrí, ✆ 92 650, are brand new studios with pretty views of Vlýcho Bay, set in a garden, two minutes from the beach. There are plenty of restaurants in Nidrí: eat at least once at **Kavos** on the beach for the view and consistently good food for 1500–2000dr. Just outside Nidrí, **Haradiatika** is popular with locals for its good quality meat and *mezé*.

### Póros

**Okeanis**, at Mikrós Gialós, ✆ 95 399 (*exp*) is a quiet place on the beach, with comfortable rooms. *Open May–Sept.* You can camp in the lap of luxury at **Poros Beach**, ✆ 95 452, with 50 sites, some bungalows, a bar, restaurant and pool.

## Inland Villages: Lace and Lentils

At least once while on Lefkáda, venture inland, where traditional farming villages occupy the fertile uplands framed in mountains, and where it's not unusual to encounter an older woman still dressed in her traditional costume of brown and black, with a headscarf tied at the back, sitting with distaff in hand, or at her loom, or over her embroidery. Although many villages are facing the usual rural exodus of their young people for the bright lights and easier money to be made on the coast, **Karyá** is one large village to aim for, the centre of the island's lace and embroidery handicrafts, where the ethnographic **Museum Maria Koutsochéro** is dedicated to the most famous embroiderer of them all, a woman from Karyá whose works were in international demand around the year 1900. Most of the women sell their goods direct, although don't come looking for bargains: look for signs reading KENTHMATA. Another well-known traditional lace and embroidery town is **Englouví**, the highest village on Lefkáda (730m), tucked in a green mountain valley; it is even prouder of its lentils, which win prizes at Greek lentil competitions. In the interior there are several notable churches with frescoes, among them the Red Church (Kókkini Eklisía) and Monastery of Ag. Geórgios (from around 1620) near **Aléxandros**, a nearly abandoned village crumbling to bits, and the 15th-century church of Ag. Geórgios at **Odhigytría** (near Apólpaina), its design incorporating Byzantine and Western influences. **Drymónas** to the west is a pretty little village of stone houses and old tile roofs.

## Down the West Coast

The west coast of Lefkáda is rocky and rugged, and the sea is often rough—perfect for people who complain that the Mediterranean is a big warm bathtub. For under the cliffs and mountains are some of the widest and most stunning stretches of sand in the Ionian, which are only just beginning to be exploited. The road from Lefkáda town avoids the shore as far as the farming village of **Tsoukaládes**, where the long sandy beach of **Pevkóulia** begins under the mountains and stretches around the coast to **Ag. Nikítas** (ΑΓ. ΝΙΚΗΤΑΣ). In recent years this has blossomed into a resort, although the nucleus of the village, with its pretty tile roofs and old tavernas, is off limits to developers; the narrow streets are overhung with flowers and vines. Beware that parking is a major headache, especially on summer weekends. Within nothing in between here and Italy the sea is clean, but cold. Don't let your windsurfer run away with you, though—the odd shark fin has been spotted off the coast. Just south of here a new road allows access to **Káthisma**, a good if again wavy place to swim with a taverna and cantinas on the wide beach of golden sand, dotted with places to dive and little caves to explore. Yet another beautiful sandy beach lies below the village of **Kalamítsi**, set among giant rocks, with rooms and tavernas that make it a good quiet base.

## The Original Lover's Leap, Vassilikí, and Windsurfing

To reach Lefkáda's southwest peninsula, a secondary road from Kalamítsi crosses to the pretty leafy village of **Chortáta** and **Komíli**, where the road forks. Buses continue down the coastal road only as far as **Atháni**, a tiny village that struggles to meet the demands of tourists heading further south to the superb beaches along the peninsula. The first, long and undeveloped **Gialós**, can be easily reached by a path from Atháni; the next, beautiful golden **Egrémni** requires the skills of an alpinist to reach from land. Sandy **Pórto Katsíki** ('goat port') further south is magnificently set under pinkish white cliffs, can be reached by a long walkway-stair from the dirt road, and is a popular excursion boat destination; there's a taverna too.

At the end of the road are the famous 60m-high sheer white cliffs of **Cape Doukáto** or **Kávo tis Kyrás** (Lady's Cape), where Sappho, rejected by Phaon, hurled herself into the sea below; one old tradition says that she was only imitating the goddess Aphrodite, who took the plunge in despair over the death of her lover Adonis. Later, Romans rejected by their sweethearts would make the leap—with the precaution of strapping on feathers or even live birds and employing rescue parties to pull them out of the sea below. Young Greeks still soar off the edge, but now use hang-gliders instead of feathers. The leap was not always a fatal cure for unrequited love; the first to go over the cliff were probably unwilling sacrifices to stormy Poseidon—prisoners or criminal scapegoats. When human sacrifices dropped out of fashion, priests serving at the temple of Apollo Lefkáda 'of the Dolphins' (of which only the scantiest ruins remain) would make the jump safely as part of their cult, called *katapontismós*, 'sea plunging', rather like the divers at Alcapulco, one imagines; no doubt the leaps were accompanied with sacrifices—read barbe-ques—for a pleasant ancient Greek outing. The white cliffs are a famous landmark for sailors, and now are topped by a lighthouse. Byron, sailing past in 1812, during his first visit to Greece was strangely moved, and put down the experience in *Childe Harold* (canto II).

> *But when he saw the evening star above*
> *Leucadia's far-projecting rock of woe*
> *And hail'd the last resort of fruitless love,*
> *He felt, or deem'd he felt, no common glow*
> *And as the stately vessel glided slow*
> *Beneath the shadow of that ancient mount,*
> *He watch'd the billow's melancholy flow,*
> *And, sunk albeit in thought as he was wont,*
> *More placid seem'd his eye, and smooth his pallid front.*

The left-hand fork in the road at Komíli passes by way of the pretty farming village of **Ag. Pétros** on the way to **Vassilikí** (ΒΑΣΙΛΙΚΗ), one of the very best places in Europe to windsurf, and heavenly if you're obsessive about learning or perfecting your skills. If you're not, you may want to limit your stay to an afternoon drink while watching the pros whizz around the bay, their brightly coloured sails like butterflies skimming the water. Mainly because of all the surf-bums, Vassilikí is Lefkáda's second biggest resort after Nidrí, a shady, charming village by a little port, a long beach north of town (although swimming isn't very pleasant with all the windsurf traffic) and shops that specialize in all types of boards for sale or hire. On most days a gentle breeze blows up by mid-morning, perfect to teach beginners the fundamentals, and by mid-afternoon it's blowing strong for the experts; by evening, the wind, like a real gent, takes a bow and exits, allowing a pleasant dinner by the water's edge before the discos open; the nightlife is almost as exhilarating as the wind. Caiques from Vassilikí round the white cliffs of Cape Doukáto for the beach of Pórto Katsíki (*see* above) and the pretty white beach of **Agiofýlli**, accessible only by sea.

Lefkáda's highest peak, Eláti (1158m) cuts off the inland villages of the south, which can only be reached from Vassilikí or the Póros-Sívota road in the southeast.The road rises from the plain of Vassilikí, covered with olives and fields of flowers (flower seeds for gardeners are an important local product) to **Sývros**, one of the larger villages in the interior, with places to eat and Lefkáda's largest cave, **Karoucha**. From here the road tackles the increasingly bare slopes of Eláti to lofty little **Ag. Ilías**, with magnificent views.

---

*Lefkáda ☎ (0645–)*  **Where to Stay and Eating Out**

### Karyá

The **Karyá Village**, ☎ 41 030 (*B; mod*) has pleasant rooms if you want to get away from the beach crowds. There are also some tavernas and traditional lazy *kafeneíons* under the plane trees.

### Ag. Nikítas

**Odyssia** ☎ 99 366 (*C; exp*) is one of the island's nicest hotels, with a roof garden. Other choices are **Calypso**, ☎ 99 332 (*B; exp*), a pleasant pension and **Ag. Nikítas**, ☎ 99 460 (*C; exp*). In Ag. Nikítas smart rooms with private bath and overlooking the sea cost around 6000dr.

### Vassilikí

Accommodation here tends to be block-booked by companies offering special wind-surfing holiday packages. Smartest here is **Ponti Beach**, ☎ 31 572 (*B; exp*), new, air-conditioned and with a pool. **Lefkatas**, ☎31 229 (*C; mod*) is a pleasant choice. If all is full, try **Billy's House**, ☎ 31 418 or 39 363 (*mod*), with nice rooms with their own baths and kitchen, 70m from the beach. **Paradissos**, ☎ 31 256 (*E; inexp*), has some rooms with private bath. The village campsite is **Vassilikí Beach**, ☎ 31 457. **Alex's Taverna** on the beach servies some good English dishes and curries if you're feeling homesick.

## Meganísi (MEGANHSI)

Spectacular rocky and wild **Meganísi**, an hour and a half by daily ferry or excursion boat from Nidrí, lies off the southeast coast of Lefkáda. Believed to be the island of Taphos mentioned in the *Odyssey*, it was the main base of the semi-mythical Teleboans, sailors and pirates who at one point were powerful enough to take on the King of Mycenae. The population of 1800 is still employed in traditional occupations—seafaring for the men, embroidering and lacemaking for the women. There are perhaps a score of reasonably priced rooms to rent, good inexpensive tavernas and so far only one British holiday company (Ilios Island Holidays) with a few houses to rent. Ferries call at **Váthi**, a pretty port with lots of good fish tavernas and a campsite, packed to the gills for the *panegýri* of Ag. Konstantínos on 21 May. A road leads up to the cheerful flowery hamlet of **Katoméri**, where a track leads down to the beach of **Polistafíon** in narrow Athéni Bay and there's even a small, nice, moderately priced hotel (**Meganisi**, ✆ (0645) 51 639). The paved road continues around to **Spartochóri**, with a couple of good tavernas. Excursion boats from Nidrí usually call at the yawning 90m-deep **Papanikólaos' Grotto**, said to be the second largest in Greece and named for the daring submariner who used to hide here and dart out to attack Italian ships, and at the sandy beach of **Ag. Ioánnis** with a summer *cantina.*

# Paxí (PAXOI)

The island of 20 fabled secrets, Paxí is the tiniest and yet one of the most charming of the canonical Seven Islands, and together with its little sister Antípaxi has long served as a kind of gently upmarket, small-is-beautiful escape from the mass package tourism on Corfu. Paxí (or Paxos) is so small and so flat that you can easily walk its 8km length in a day; its one road twists and turns through the immaculate groves of olives that brought the islanders most of their income before tourism. Paxí's golden olive oil is still considered among the best produced in Greece and has won many international medals; you can note from the start that, unlike olives grown on Corfu, trees are rarely sprayed against the dreaded dacus fly, but are more environmentally protected with sticky traps in plastic bags. Besides the beauty of the silvery trees (there are some 300,000—each family owns at least 500) and the tidy stone walls, the little island has some of the friendliest people you'll find anywhere in Greece.

## History

Paxí was happily shunned by history. Mythology tells us the island was created by a blow of Poseidon's trident as a love nest for his mistress, far from the gaze of his wife Amphitrite. What mention it received in antiquity referred to its seven sea caves—Homer describes Ipapanti as having rooms of gold. In another cave, the Greek resistance hero Papanikólaos hid and waylaid passing Italian ships in the Second World War, a trick unfortunately copied by German U-boats the following year.

### Why the Oracles Are Silent

Plutarch, in his essay 'Why the Oracles Are Silent', recounts an incident of great moment that took place here at the beginning of the 1st century AD. A ship was sailing from Asia Minor to Italy, and as it passed Paxi all the passengers heard a loud voice from the island calling out the name of Thamus, the ship's Egyptian pilot. The voice commanded him: 'When the ship comes opposite Palodes, tell them the Great God Pan is dead.' Thamus did so at the designated spot, and great cries of lamentation arose, as if from a multitude of people. This strange story went around the world, and even came to the attention of Emperor Tiberius, who appointed a commission of scholars to decide what it might mean.

What they determined was never entirely disclosed, but any astronomer, mythographer or priest (as Plutarch was) in that period would have been aware that times, as measured on the great dial of the firmament, were changing—a new World Age was at hand.

Now that we're only a century or two from 'the Dawning of the Age of Aquarius', as the song goes, this calls for a slight digression. If you've ever watched a child's top spin, you'll have noticed its axis tends to wobble a bit, so that the point on top traces a slow circle through the air while the whole thing is spinning much more rapidly. The earth, in its rotation, does this too—only each gyration of its axis takes about 26,000 years. (This is why the pole stars move; in 13,000 years the northern pole will point towards Vega in the constellation of the Lyre, 50° away from our current pole star Polaris.) Another effect of this phenomenon is the 'precession of the equinoxes'. The *equinoctial points* are the places where the celestial equator crosses the ecliptic, the plane of our solar system (or as we see it from Earth, the path of the sun, moon, and planets across our sky); another way to explain these points is that they are the positions of the sun at the equinoxes, the first

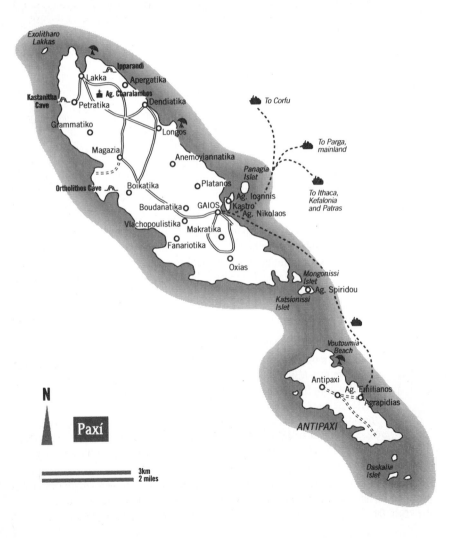

day of spring and the first day of autumn. As the earth slowly wobbles, these equinoctial points move around, too, passing slowly through the signs of the zodiac. So every 2,160 years or so, the sun on March 20 (New Year's Day for many cultures) finds itself in a new sign. Since the remotest times, at least some cultures on the earth have kept track of this movement. In Plutarch's day, the spring equinox fell in Aries, but it was about to move into Pisces. Today, it's at the end of Pisces and about to move into Aquarius. Each of these periods is a 'World Age'—in case you ever wondered what that term meant.

The transition is officially marked by a great conjunction of the planets; that's what the Christmas star of the Magi was, according to modern interpretations. The men of Plutarch's time and later had no shortage of explanations for what their New Age was to portend. Astrologers heralded it as the birth of a new Golden Age, ruled by Saturn; the creation of the Roman Empire under Augustus, bringing the end of a long period of civil strife, seemed to be part of heaven's decree. Later, Christians would claim that theirs was the true faith of the Age of Pisces, as represented in one of the most wide-spread early Christian symbols, the cold, chaste fish. It was a time of confusion and loss of faith, when the old pagan oracles really did fall mysteriously silent, and when new philosophies and cults of every stripe were battling for hearts and minds in the Mediterranean world. And so today we live among our own confusions, with our own legions of dubious 'New Agers', waiting, as Yeats put it in 'The Second Coming', to see

*...what rough beast, its hour come round at last,*
*Slouches towards Bethlehem to be born.*

## Getting There

**By boat**: daily connections with Corfu, and with Sívota and Párga (on the mainland; in the summer buy your ticket a day or two in advance), also infrequent connections with Pátras, Kefaloniá and Ithaca. Connections are far less frequent in the off season. In the summer you may well be asked to have a room reservation before boarding a **ferry** to the island, which is small, wooded, and fearful of campers and their fires. The Paxos Express **excursion boats** circle the island, offering a look at the caves and dramatic cliff scenery, stopping at the better pebbly beaches and Antípaxi. **Port authority**, ✆ 32 259.

## Tourist Police

See regular police in Gaiós, ✆ (0662) 31 222.

## Festivals

**10 February**, Ag. Charálambos; **Easter Monday** procession from Gaiós to Velliantítika; **11 August**, Ag. Spyrídon; **15 August**, Panagía.

## Gáios

**Gáios** (ΓΑΙΟΣ), the pretty toy capital of the island, is named after a disciple of St Paul who brought Christianity to Paxí and is buried here. Most of the islanders live in Gáios, and it's where you'll find a small sandy beach and all of Paxí's facilities, a fleet of yachts and on the harbour-front even a tiny **aquarium** of sea critters who are released and replaced pot-luck every year, so there's no telling what you'll see. The streets of Gáios are fortunately too narrow for cars (so narrow that people can lean out of their windows and shake hands) although human traffic jams occur during the day in the summer, especially on the worn flag-stones of the handsome waterfront square, when day-trippers from Corfu and cruise ships sail into the little port. For a fine overview of Gáios harbour, walk past the Governor's House and continue to the New Port and the new road. If you bring your own bottle, several shops sell loose olive oil from the barrel; it's so good that you can almost drink it straight.

On a rocky islet facing the harbour is the well-preserved **Kástro Ag. Nikólaos**, built by the Venetians in 1423, and an old windmill, and beyond it, the islet of **Panagía**, which on 15 August is crowded with pilgrims. In the evening they come back to Gáios and dance all night in the village square. **Mongoníssi**, another islet, is connected by boat taxi—belonging to the family which owns a pretty little restaurant there—which brings customers over for dinner and music and dancing in the evening.

## Sea Caves and Forests of Olives

If it's not windy, rent a boat to explore Paxí's seven sea grottoes of brilliant blue. Most are located among the sheer limestone cliffs on the wind-beaten west coast of Paxí, including the impressive **Kastanítha**, 185m high. Another distinctive cave, **Orthólithos**, has a monolith standing sentinel at its entrance; caiques can enter about 5m inside. Homer's wild cove and cave **Ípapanti** does not have the golden rooms he mentions, although it used to shelter monk seals. **Grammatikó** is the largest cave of them all. When sailing around the island, you can also see the **Moúsmouli Cliffs** and their natural bridge **Tripitos**.

The main road from Gáios that crosses the island was donated by Aristotle Onassis, a great fan of Paxí. The minibus (everything on Paxí is mini) runs north to **Lákka** (ΛAKKA), a tiny port where the boats from Corfu usually call and sometimes cause traffic jams. Lákka is within easy distance of small, shady pebble beaches, and the Byzantine church in the village has particu-larly musical Russian bells, which you can ring if you find the villager with the key. Walk inland to the church of Ípapanti, topped by two odd stumpy, flat-topped domes, with a massive freestanding campanile on one side, crowned by an onion dome. The Venetian stone **Grammatikoú mansion** near Lákka is fortified with a tower.

Laid-back **Longós** (ΛΟΓΓΟΣ), Paxí's third minute port, is about midway between Gáios and Lákka, and gets fewer visitors; there's a pleasant rocky beach (and others within easy walking distance to the south) and a few bars. In tiny **Boikatiká** village the church Ag. Charálambos contains an old icon of the Virgin and in nearby **Magaziá** are two churches of interest, Ag. Spyrídon and Ag. Apóstoli; the latter's churchyard affords an impressive view of the Eremitis cliffs. At **Apergatiká** the Papamárkou mansion dates from the 17th century.

---

*Paxí ☏ (0662–)*         **Where to Stay and Eating Out**

Be prepared for prices a little above the norm; transport costs add to the tariff, and supplies from the outside world can be cut off without warning whenever the wind kicks up. Restaurants and cafés take full advantage of the day-trippers who come from Corfu and the yachting set berthed in Gáios. Official accommodation is extremely limited, rather expensive, and block-booked by tour operators in the summer. Everyone else stays in private rooms, which are invariably pleasant, tidy and double, and average 4000–5000dr.

### Gaiós

**Paxí Beach Bungalows**, ✆ 31 211 (*B; exp*) has pleasant, comfortable chalet bunga-lows near the beach, but these are only available in the off season. You may have better luck with the **Paxos Club**, 1km from Gáios, ✆ 32 450, ✉ 32 097 (*exp*), with a large pool and very comfortable rooms. Take the caique to Mongoníssi for the excellent restaurant there (*3000dr*) and to while the day away on the beach. There are a handful of tavernas in Gáios such as the **Taka Taka** serving solid Greek fare and fish, the former reasonably priced, the latter about 3500dr for a meal; **Naïs** offers a wide variety of croissants and sandwiches. **Spiro's Taverna** and **Costa's Kafeneion** are also good value.

### Lákka

The **Ilios**, ✆ 31 808 (*E; inexp*), and **Lefkothea**, ✆ 31 408 (*E; inexp*) are both small and open all year, but fill up in season. You can eat well and reasonably at **Sgarelios** and **Klinis** or the pretty little Italian **Rosa**, featuring a wide variety of pasta dishes.

## Antípaxi

South of Paxí lies tiny Antípaxi, with only a few permanent residents. From June until September four or five caiques leave Gáios daily for the 40-minute trip to its port Agrapídias. Although both Paxí and Antípaxi were created with a resounding blow of Poseidon's trident, the two islands are very different in nature; the part of Antípaxi facing Paxí looks bare, almost as if it had been bitten off by a Leviathan. Rather than olive oil, Antípaxi produces good white and red wines, and rather than little pebble beaches, Antípaxi's gentle side is graced with fine sandy beaches: **Voutoúmi** and **Vríka** are claimed to be 'softer than silk'. There are two tavernas in the itty bitty village and port at **Ormós Agrapídias**, but no accommodation on the islet; those planning to stay should bring a sleeping bag, for Voutoúmi has a small campsite. This could well be the uncontaminated paradise you've been seeking.

## Zákynthos/Zante (ΖΑΚΥΝΘΟΣ)

Of all their Ionian possessions the Venetians loved Zákynthos the most for its charm and natural beauty. *Zante, fiore di Levante*—'the flower of the East'—they called it, and built a city even more splendid than Corfu town on its great semi-circular bay, all turned to rubble by the earth-quake of 1953. Nevertheless, the disaster did nothing to diminish the soft, luxuriant charm of the landscape and its fertile green hills and mountainsides, the valleys planted with vineyards and currant vines, olive and almond groves and orchards, or the brilliant garland of flowers and beautiful beaches (the flowers are best in spring and autumn, a time when few foreigners visit the island). And if the buildings are gone, the Venetians left a lasting impression—many islanders have Venetian blood, which shows up not only in their names, but in their love of singing. On the other side of the coin, the once politically progressive Zákynthos has bellied up to the trough of grab-the-money-and-run tourism that doesn't do the island justice, to the extent of sabotaging efforts to preserve the beaches where the loggerhead turtles breed.

### History

According to tradition, Zákynthos was named for its first settler, a son of Dardanus from Arcadia. The Arcadians were famous from earliest antiquity for their love of music and festivals, and passed the trait on to their colony. According to Homer, Zákynthos fought under the command of Odysseus at the Trojan War, although when he returned home and shot 20 of its nobles—Penelope's suitors—the island rebelled and became an independent, coin-minting state. It set up colonies throughout the Mediterranean, especially Saguntum in Spain, a city later to be besieged and demolished by Hannibal. Levinus took the island for Rome in 214 BC, and when the inhabitants rebelled, he burnt all the buildings on Zákynthos. Uniting with the Aeolians, the islanders forced the Romans out, although in 150 BC Flavius finally brought the island under control.

In 844 the Saracens captured the island from their base in Crete, but the Byzantines were strong enough to expel them. The Norman-Sicilian pirate Margaritone took Zákynthos in 1182, and three years later made it part of his County Palatine of Kefaloniá. One of his successors ceded the island to the Venetians in 1209, who held on to it for almost 350 years, with a Turkish interval between 1479 and 1484. The aristocratic privileges of the Venetians and wealthy Zantiotes caused so much resentment among the commoners that they rose up in 'the Rebellion of the Popolari' and seized control of the island for four years. The influx of artists escaping Crete after the fall of Herákleon in 1669 made Zákynthos an art centre, and led to the founding of the Cretan-Venetian Ionian school of painting. The Cretans also influenced local music, although the most obvious influence in the island's special serenades, the *kantádes*, is Italian. Zákynthos has also proved to be a cradle of poets, producing the Greek-Italian Ugo Foscolo (d. 1827), and the nationalist poet Andréas Kálvos and Diónysios Solomós.

Enthused by the ideas of the French Revolution, the Zantiots formed their own Jacobin Club and destroyed the rank of nobility, symbolically burning the Venetian Libro d'Oro, the book listing the island aristocracy, in Plateía Ag. Márko. In 1798, the Russians forced the French garrison and the inhabitants to surrender, after a siege of months, and when the Septinsular Republic established an aristocracy of its own in 1801, populist, high-spirited Zákynthos rebelled again. During the War of Independence many rebels on the mainland, notably Kolokotrónis, found asylum on the island before Zákynthos joined Greece with its Ionian sisters in 1864.

### Getting There and Around

**By air**: daily flights from Athens, 2 or 3 times a week to and from Kefaloniá and Corfu; the Olympic office is at Alex. Róma 16, ✆ 48 611. There are several charters from major European cities; for airport information, call ✆ 48 322.

**By sea: ferry** 6 or 7 times a day from Kilíni, once or twice a day from Pessáda, Kefaloniá to Skinári. In season, Europe Hydrofoils (✆ 23 984) link Zákynthos town to Póros and Argostóli (Kefaloniá) and to Pátras and Pírgos on the mainland. **Port authority,** ✆ 22 417.

**By road**: all **buses** leave from the central station on Filíta Klavdianú in Zákynthos town (✆ 22 656). The little station on the left offers direct ferry-bus links to Athens; the main station has buses every hour to Laganás, 10 times to Tsiliví, 4 times a day to Alikés, 2 times to Volímes and 3 to Vassilikiós.

### Tourist Police

1 Tzoulati, off Plateía Solomoú, ✆ (0695) 27 307. For information in English about island happenings, pick up a free copy of *Zante Moments*, issued every 10 days in the summer.

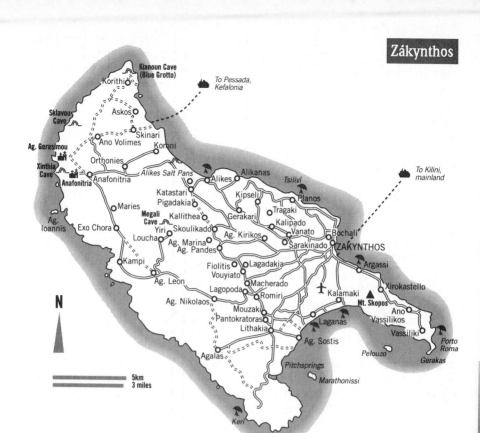

## Festivals

A carnival initiated by the Venetians, known for its masked singers and dancing, remains strong in Zákynthos and lasts for **two weeks prior to Lent**. During **Holy Week** the inhabitants also give themselves over to an infectious merriment. In **July** the Zakýnthia takes place with cultural activities; at the **end of August and beginning of September**, the International Meeting of Medieval and Popular Theatre, with daily performances. For the major feast days of Ag. Diónysios on **24 August** and **17 December**, Zákynthos town is strewn with myrtle and there are fireworks at the church. Slightly more modest is Zoodóchos Pigí in the town on **10 November**.

## Zákynthos Town

When the time came to rebuild their earthquake-shattered town, the inhabitants gamely tried to incorporate some of the old city's delight and charm into the dull lines of modern Greek architecture. They didn't succeed. But what saves Zákynthos town, or Chóra (pop. 10,000) from complete anonymity is its superb setting—the ancient acropolis hovering above, crowned by a castle, and the graceful sweep of the harbour, punctuated off to the right by the unusual form of Mount Skopós. Wrapped along the waterfront, the streets of the long, narrow town are sheltered by arcades (as they were before the earthquake), where a few shops still sell the local speciality, *mandoláto* (white nougat with almonds) amongst the ceramic figurines of coupling turtles and other tourist foofaraws.

Somehow the rebuilders of Zákynthos town failed where they should have done their best, in the town's front parlour, **Plateía Solomoú**, a vast seaside square on the north end of town with pretty flowerbeds and statue of the portly Dionysios Solomos in the centre, raising a hand in greeting; it is simply too large, too open for comfort, and its pair of small cafés are overwhelmed by the solemn formal buildings: the Town Hall (with another statue of a homegrown poet, Ugo Foscolo, and the inscription 'Liberty Requires Virtue and Daring'), the Cultural Centre, and in one corner the sailors' church, **Ag. Nikólaos tou Mólou** 'of the Mole' (1561) pieced together like a jigsaw after the quake.

The **Neo-Byzantine Museum** (*open 8–2.30, closed Mon; adm; free Sun*) contributes to the sterile formality of the square, but can be forgiven for its contents: lovely paintings by the Ionian school, icons and other works of art salvaged from shattered churches across Zákynthos. The 17th century was a golden age for art, especially after the arrival of refugees from Crete (1669), among them Michael Damaskinós, the great icon painter and teacher of El Greco. Italian influences show up even stronger here than in Crete; by the late 18th and 19th centuries, as displayed in the last rooms, local painters were producing sweet rosy-cheeked fluff. But before turning into candy floss, the Ionian School left Zákynthos with some spirited, lovely works; the iconostasis of Ag. Dimitrioú tou Kollás and one from Pantokrátoras (1681), the latter further adorned with intricate wood carvings. There are marble fragments and ancient and Byzantine tombs, and excellent 16th-century frescoes from Ag. Andréa at Volímes, with a picture of Jesus in the cosmic womb in the apse, New Testament scenes and nearly every saint in the Orthodox calendar on the side walls, and a *Last Judgement* on the back wall, with a great tree branch emanating from hell and the empty throne awaiting, cupped by the hand of God. The icons, mostly from the 16th and 17th centuries, are superb, varying between the very oriental and the very western; there are works by Damaskinós, Ioánnis Kýprios, Emmanuel Zána, and Nikólas Kallérgis. The last exhibit is a scale model of Zákynthos town before the earthquake.

Inland from Plateía Solomoú, the smaller, triangular, marble-paved, pizzeria-lined **Plateía Ag. Márkou**—Zákynthos' Piazza San Marco—is as lively as the bigger square is sleepy. The social centre of town since the 15th century, before the earthquake it was the site of the Romianiko Casino, which everyone loved but no one rebuilt. The Catholic church of San Marco, now sadly devoid of its all its art, occupies one end, near the **Solomós Museum**, with mementoes of the poets and other famous Zantiotes, as well as photographs of the island before 1953. Adjacent are the mausoleums of patriotic poets Diónysos Solomós and Andréas Kálvos; the latter lived in London and Paris for much of his life, but got the wish he expressed at the end of his romantic ode 'Zante': 'May Fate not give me a foreign grave, for death is sweet only to him who sleeps in his homeland'.

Solomós is the more interesting character of the two. Born in 1798, he was educated like other into the Ionian aristocrats in Italy and wrote his first poems in Italian, when he decided that it was time for Greece to have a Dante of its own: like Dante, he wrote not in the formal scholarly language of the day (in Dante's day Latin, in Solomós' the purist, or *katharévousa*) but chose the demotic language of everyday. Nearly as important, he broke away from the slavery to the 15-syllable line that dominated Greek poetry from the 17th century, and introduced Western influenced metres and forms. Solomós concentrated on lyrical verse until the War of Independence became an important inspiration, bringing forth deeper, and increasingly more spiritual works, especially in 'The Free Besieged', written after the heroic resistance of Missolóngi. His verse has a degree of beauty, balance and delicacy that rarely has been matched by other modern Greek poets—that is, whatever fragments have survived; highly strung and hyper-critical, Solomós destroyed much of what he wrote in later years, and spent most of his time on Corfu, often using his influence with the British to gain more lenient sentences for Greek nationalists on the Ionian islands. The first stanzas of his 'Ode to Liberty', set to music by Mántzaros, are the Greek national anthem:

Σε γνωρίζω απο την κοψυ του σπαθιου την τρομερη
σε γνωρίζω απο την οψη που με βια μετραει τη γη...
*I recognize you by the fierce edge of your sword;*
*I recognize you by the look that measures the earth...'*

Zákynthos' most important churches were reconstructed after the quake, among them little **Kyrá tou Angeloú**, in Louká Karrer street, built in 1687; inside are icons by Panagiótis Doxarás of Zákynthos and a pretty carved iconstasis. Near the Basilica tis Análipsis on Alex. Roma street, is the boyhood **home of Ugo Foscolo**, marked by a marble plaque and angel; he used to read by the light of the icon lamp in the shrine across the street. Further south, the restored 15th-century **Faneroméni** church with its pretty campanile (on the corner of Lisgara and Doxarádou streets) was before the earthquake one of the most beautiful churches in all Greece. At the south end of town a huge **basilica of Ag. Diónysios** was built in 1925 to house the bones of the island's patron saint, stored in fine silver reliquary. It was one of only three buildings left standing after the earthquake of 1953, thanks in small part to Dionysios' divine influence but in large part to its concrete construction. There are New and Old Testament paintings on the walls, and an array of gold and silver ex-votos are witness to his power that draws throngs of pilgrims every 24 August.

## Up to Bocháli

Filikóu Street, behind Ag. Márkou, leads up to Bocháli, a suburb with gorgeous views over town and sea, where the church of Ag. Giórgios Filíkou was the seat of the local revolutionary Friendly Society. One road from the Bocháli crossroads leads to Lófos Stráni, where a bust of Solomós marks the spot where the poet sat and composed the 'Ode to Liberty' during the siege of Missolóngi. Another road from Bocháli leads up to the well-preserved Venetian Kástro (*open 8am–8pm; adm*), a short taxi ride or 45-minute walk up an old cobble path. Three gates, the last bearing the Lion of St Mark, guarded the medieval town. Ruins of churches still stand amid the pines up here, but a 16th-century earthquake rent the walls of the ancient acropolis. Some neglected gardens in Akrotíri (take the north road at the Bocháli crossroads) recall the Venetian villas that once stood here, the centre of Zante society into the period of British rule; the one belonging to Diónysios Solomós' father was the residence of the High Commissioner. At Villa Crob nearby, the British laid out the first tennis court in Greece. Down in the north end of town, a romantically melancholy British cemetery is wedged next to the green cliffs (turn right at Bociari Street from N. Kolíva).

## Beaches under Mount Skopós

The town beach isn't all that good—for better, cleaner swimming try the beaches along the beautiful rugged eastern peninsula under Mount Skopós, beyond **Argássi** (ΑΡΓΑΣΙ), a somewhat souless assembly line of hotels and tavernas along its waterfront. Heading further along, there's **Pórto Zóro**, **Banana Beach** (wide and sandy and strewn with sea daffodils, which send such a strong fragrance out to sea that they are believed to have been the origins of the island's nickname *Fiore di Levante*), **Ag. Nikólaos**, **Mavrándzi** and the thinnish crescent strand at **Pórto Róma**, all with tavernas and at least minimum facilities. The 16th-century Domenegini tower by the sea was used for covert operations by the *Philikí Hetaireía*, or Friendly Society, especially in sending men and supplies over to the battles on the Peloponnese. To keep busybodies away they spread word that the tower was haunted, and installed a 'devil' at night to holler and throw stones at any passer-by. **Vassilikós** (ΒΑΣΙΛΛΙΚΟΣ) is a tiny village at the end of the bus line, but bear in mind that services are infrequent and you may have to get back to town by taxi. **Gérakas**, at the tip of the peninsula, has another long, lovely stretch of sandy beach, the finest of them all, favoured by nesting loggerhead turtles. Roads cross the peninsula for **Daphní** and **Sekánika**, two secluded, undeveloped beaches to the south, facing Laganás Bay, and both equally popular with the turtles.

### Loggerheads

A decade ago Zákynthos became the centre of an international stir when environmentalists themselves went at loggerheads with government ministries and the island tourist industry to protect Laganás Bay, nothing less than the single most important nursery of rare loggerhead turtles (*Caretta caretta*), hosting around 1000 nests a year on 4km of beach. These sea turtles are among the oldest species on the planet, going back hundreds of millions of years. As long as anyone can remember, they have gathered from all over the Mediterranean on the sands of Zákynthos every June until September, to crawl up on to the beaches at night, dig a deep hole with their back legs, lay between 100 and 120 eggs the size of golf balls and cover them up again before lumbering in exhaustion back to the sea. For 60 days the eggs incubate quietly in the warmth of the sands, and, when they hatch, the tiny baby turtles make a break for the sea. It is essential that the nesting zones are disturbed as little as possible—by staying away from the beaches between dusk and dawn, by not poking beach umbrellas in the sand, running any kind of vehicle over it, or leaving litter. Once the baby turtles hatch, the lights are liable to distract them from their all-important race to the sea, and they die of exhaustion.

Whether or not the turtles succeed in co-existing with the local tourist economy remains to be seen. At first the going was rough; uncompensated for the beaches they owned, some Zantiotes did all they could to sabotage the efforts of the marine biologists and even resorted to setting fires on the beaches to keep the turtles away. In 1983, when the steep decline in nests was noticed, the Sea Turtle Protection Society of Greece (STPS) was formed to monitor the loggerheads and mark their nests, and lead the fight for their protection. They have succeeded in improving public awareness, in limiting sea traffic in Laganás Bay, and in general making the loggerheads such a trendy issue that the souvenir shops peddle little ceramic models of them. The probably unattainable goal of STPS is to create a Marine Park to control development, find alternatives for landowners and 'promote a sustainable tourism that respects the environment and the same time fully protects the nesting beaches.' Perhaps the mama loggerheads have already picked up the cue and for the past few years have avoided the main beach at Laganás.

## Up Mount Skopós

From the edge of Argássi, a road leads up through the wildflowers, including several species of indigenous orchid, to the top of **Mount Skopós** ('look-out'), the Mount Hellatos of the ancient Greeks and the Mons Nobilis of Pliny, who wrote of a cavern that led straight to the Underworld. On the way note the picturesque ruins of the 11th-century **Ag. Nikólaos Megalomátis**, with a mosaic floor, built on the site of temple of Artemis. Views from the summit not only take in all of Zákynthos, but the Peloponnese and the Bay of Navarino, where on 20 October 1827 the most famous battle of modern Greece was fought between the Turco-Egyptian navy and the Anglo-Franco-Russian fleet, leading directly to Greek independence. By the rocky lump summit or *toúrla* of Mount Skopós stands the venerable white church of **Panagía Skopiótissa**, believed to replace yet another temple to Artemis. The interior is decorated with frescoes and a carved stone iconostasis; the icon of the Virgin was painted in Constantinople, and there's a double-headed Byzantine eagle mosaic on the floor.

---

*Zákynthos ✆ (0695–)*                                     ***Where to Stay***

Outside August, accommodation in Zákynthos town is usually feasible; if you have any difficulty, the tourist police off Plateía Solomoú have a list of rooms to let. **Hotel Palatino**, at Kolíva and Kolokotróni 10, ✆ 27 780, ✉ 45 400 (*B; exp*) is a stylish hotel near the town beach, with sea and mountain views from its balconies. *Open all year*. In the same vicinity, **Alba** on Tertsetí Street, ✆ 26 641, has bungalows for about the same price. The much larger **Strada Marina** at 14 K. Lombárdou Street, ✆ 22 761 (*B; exp*) is nicely located on the quay. *Open all year*. Little hotel **Reparo** at Roma and Voúltsou Street, ✆ 23 578 (*C; mod*) is clean, pleasant and friendly. **Phoenix**, on Plateía Solomoú, ✆ 22 419 (*C; mod*) is named for the palms that grow out of its front terrace; it once saw better days but is still fine. *Open all year*. **Lofos Strani**, on Kapodístrias ✆ 27 122 (*B; mod*) is a nice small pension up at Bóchali. Other choices include **Ionion**, 18 A. Roma, ✆ 23 739 (*D; inexp*), and **Dessy**, 73 N. Kolíva, ✆ 28 505 (*E; inexp*).

Out along the peninsula **Matilda**, at Pórto Zóro, ✆ 35 430, ✉ 35 429 (*B; exp*), is a new, fancypants complex with a pair of pools, 200m above the sea, and sea sports. *Open May–Oct*. **Aquarius**, ✆ 35 300, ✉ 35 303 (*exp*) is prettily set in greenery, and advertizes itself as 'a place to forget the world'. For bungalows by the sea, **The Blue Cave**, on the small pebble beach of Ag. Nikólaos, by Vassilikó ✆ 27 013, ✉ 26 288 (*exp*) is a good bet, with a pool, bar and disco. **Porto Roma**, ✆ 22 781 (*D; mod*) is small but perfectly adequate.

---

***Eating Out***

You can dine well at **P. Evangelos** on Alex. Róma Street for 3000dr; the food is freshly prepared and good. There are several expensive places on Plateía Ag. Márkos and one that's not, **Boukios**, where all the locals go for reliable Greek fare for around 2500dr. **O Zohio**, a greasy spoon on Psarón Street, is even cheaper, with meals under 2000dr. On the road to

Argássi, near the basilica of Ag. Diónysos, **Karavomilos** has the name for the best fish on the island (*3500dr and up*). For more dining with a view, there's **Alla** up on Filikóu 38, located in one of the few houses to have survived the earthquake (*2000–3000dr*). For a proper night out, locals and the occasional organized group go up to Bocháli, where most of the tavernas open only at night and feature live music, especially Zákynthos' *kantádes*, performed by male trios. Locals go to the **Quartetto di Zante** near Stavros. Prices are correspondingly higher: try **Lato** for food and music; if you want to dance, there's the **Mona Lisa** nearby. The **Panorama** is in a lovely spot up by the castle, and you can listen to live *kantádes* while indulging in some traditional Zantiote dishes such as rabbit casserole, *skordaliá* (dried cod in a thick garlic sauce) or *moskári kokkinistó*, beef in tomato sauce (3500dr).

## Laganás Bay

On the map, Zákynthos looks like a piranha with huge gaping jaws, about to devour a pair of crumb-sized fish in Laganás Bay. These small fry are **Marathoníssi** and **Peloúzo**, the former with a sandy beach and popular excursion destination, the latter colonized in 1473 BC by King Zákynthos. The island's most overripe tourist developments follows the sandy beaches step by step, beginning rather modestly at **Kalamáki**, on the east end of the bay, with a sandy beach under Mount Skopós, at the beginning of currant country. The next town, **Laganás** (ΛΑΓΑΝΑΣ) is Zákynthos' equivalent of Spencer's Blatant Beast, a resort that has long abandoned any sense of proportion and commerical decorum, set on flat hard sand beach that overlooks some curious rock formations by the sea. This brash Las Vegas on the Ionian is a favourite both of British and German package tourists and families over for the weekend from the Peloponnese. At night its 'Golden Mile' of open bars, throbbing with music and flashing kinetic neon lights, are the joy of holiday revellers and ravers, but the dismay of the turtles. A bridge leads out to the pretty islet of **Ag. Sostís**, its limestone cliffs falling abruptly where the earthquake of 1633 cleaved it from the rest of Zákynthos. It's topped with pine trees and this being Laganás, a disco.

### The Belgian on the Beach

Not a few sunbathers at Laganás are students of the opposite sex's anatomy, so generously displayed and baked to a T. None, however, are as studiously keen as Vesalius (1514–64), the Renaissance father of anatomy, whose statue stands at the south end of the beach. Born in Brabant, Vesalius studied in Paris where he edited the 2nd-century AD anatomical works of Galen, the Greek physician to the gladiators and Emperor Marcus Aurelius. Vesalius went on to the medical university of Padua, and made it the leading school of anatomy in Europe, where in 1543 he published the milestone *De humani corporis fabrica*, the first thorough and original study of the human body since Galen's time. In 1555 Vesalius became the personal physician to Philip II of Spain, only to be sentenced to death by the Inquisition for dissecting a dead Spaniard. Philip commuted the sentence to a pilgrimage to the Holy Land, and on the way home his ship was wrecked off the coast at Laganás. Vesalius, realizing a return to Inquisition-plagued Madrid would mean an end to his studies anyway, decided to spend the rest of his life in the now ruined Franciscan monastery at Faneró, along the road from Laganás to Pantokrátoras; his epitaph is still intact.

Behind Laganás extends the lush **plain of Zákynthos**, a lovely, fairly flat region to cycle through. Here and there are ruins of old country estates, immersed in greenery. One still happily intact is the **Domaine Agria**, the oldest winery in Greece, run by the Comoutós family since 1638. The Comoutóses made their fortunes in raisin and currant exports, and were ennobled in the Libro d'Oro; today their estate is divided between olive groves and vines that yield excellent reds, rosés, whites, and old-fashioned, high-alcohol dessert wines. A tasting room with a museum of old wine making tools has just been opened, © 92 285 for information and precise directions. The chief village to aim for is **Pantokrátoras**, near three fine churches: the beautiful **Pantokrátor**, founded by Byzantine Empress Pulcheria, and still retaining a number of Byzantine traits; **Ag. Nikólaos**, restored after the quake, with beautiful icons; and the medieval church of the **Panagía**, with a pretty bell tower and stone carvings. The picturesque ruins of the Villa Loundzis, once one of Zákynthos' most noble estates, are in **Sarakína**. **Lithakiá**, south of Pantokrátoras, has another restored church, the 14th-century Panagía Faneroméni, containing works of art gathered from ruined churches in the vicinity.

From Lithakiá the main road continues south over the Avyssos Gorge—a rift made by the 1633 earthquake—the coastal swamp known as **Límni Keríou**. If you look carefully at the roots of the aquatic plants, you can see the black bitumen or natural pitch that once welled up in sufficient quantity to caulk thousands of boats; both Herodotus and Pliny described the phenonemon and in recent years an exploratory oil bore was sunk, but with negligible results. There are tavernas by the rather mediocre beach. Just to the south extends a second Mount Skopos. From the sea (there are caique excursions offered from Kerí Beach) this coast is magnificent, marked by sheer white cliffs, deep dark blue waters and two towering natural arches at Marathía.

At the end of the road the mountain village of **Kerí** offers fine views, especially from its white lighthouse, and the cheapest rooms on the island. From the main road a secondary road winds westward to one of Zákynthos' more remote villages, **Agalás**, passing by way of the two-storey grotto called **Spiliá Damianoú**, where one formation resembles a horse; the legend goes a giant named Andronia once lived in the area and pestered the good people of Agalás for food. His appetite was huge, and the people were at their wits' end when an old lady slipped him a poison pie. Down he fell at a place called Andronia, where you can see twelve 15th-century wells with their old well heads. His horse was so shocked it turned to stone.

---

*Zákynthos © (0695–)*                                              **Where to Stay and Eating Out**

### Kalamáki

**Michelos**, © 48 080, one of the best tavernas in Zákynthos (and one of most crowded), is just along the main Kalamáki–Zákynthos road. There's a convenient bar next door if you have to wait for a table. The **Cave Bar**, also away from coast, up a little road lined with lights, is a romantic place of various levels, perfect for a troglodyte cocktail.

### Laganás

Nearly everything here is block-booked by the package companies, beginning with **Zante Beach**, © 51 130 (*B; exp*), a giant hotel and bungalow complex with a pool, tennis, sea sports and a nightclub. There are almost 20 class C hotels in Laganás, scores of rooms to rent and people to fill them up. If you really want to stay, try **Laganás Camping**, ✆ 51 585 or **Camping Tartarouga**, down by the sea at Lithakiá, ✆ 51 417. Laganás has a host of restaurants, both Greek and international; and many British-style pubs serving bar food.

## Beaches Along the North Coast

From Zákynthos town the coastal road heads north, past the **Kryonéri Fountain**, built by the Venetians to water their ships. The red rock overhead was used for a suicide leap in a popular Greek novel, *Kókkinos Vráchos*. Beyond, the road turns abruptly west to reach a series of pretty sandy beaches, connected by short access roads and backed by orchards and vineyards. Holiday development is still fairly embryonic, calm and peaceful, especially when compared to the babylon along Laganás Bay: long and narrow **Tsiliví** (ΤΣΙΛΙΒΙ), **Plános** (overlooking **Tragáki Beach**), little **Ámpoula** with golden sand, **Pachiámmos**, **Drossiá**, **Psaroú**, **Ammoúdi**, and **Alikanás**, where a wonderful long stretch of sand sweeps around the bay west to **Alikés** (ΑΛΥΚΕΣ), named for the nearby saltpans, an area popular with windsurfers.

The rich agricultural land inland from the coast is pleasant to explore, if directions can be a bit confusing. **Skoulikádo** rewards visitors with several interesting churches, among them the **Panagía Anafonítria**, decorated outside with stone reliefs and lovely interior and **Ag. Nikólaos Megalomáti**, named for a 16th-century icon painted on stone of St Nicholas, with unusually large eyes. **Ag. Marína**, a rare survivor of the earthquake, has a cell behind the altar where the insane would be chained in the cell behind the altar in hopes of a cure. Inland from Alikés, **Katastári** is the island's second-largest town, marking the northern edge of the plain; from here the main road tackles increasingly difficult countryside and dives inland for Orthoníes, although a rather hair-raising dirt road high over the coast continues to Mákri Giálos (*see* below).

*Zákynthos* ✆ *(0695–)*                    ***Where to Stay and Eating Out***

**Plagos Beach**, at Ámpoula Beach, ✆ 24 147 (*A; exp*) is a big new hotel and bungalow complex, a stone's throw from the sea, with a pool and tennis court as well. **Caravel** at Tragáki, ✆ 25 261 (*A; exp*), sister to the one in Athens, will lighten your wallet, but it has all the trimmings. **Orea Heleni**, ✆ 28 788 (*C; mod*) is a nice choice at Tsiliví. *Open all year*. **Cosmopolite**, ✆ 28 752 (*C; mod*) has 14 good rooms, 500 yards from the sea. There's also a good campsite, **Camping Zante**, on Ámpoula Beach, ✆ 44 754.

## Up the Southwest Coast

Unlike the low rolling hills and plain of the east, the west coast of Zákynthos plunges steeply and abruptly into the sea, some 300m in places, and a favourite place for caique excursions either from Zákynthos town or Alikés. The last stop on the plain, taking the pretty road from Zákynthos town, is **Macherádo**, in the centre of a cluster of farming villages. Its church of **Ag. Mávra** has a very ornate interior, with a beautiful old icon of the saint covered with ex-votos and scenes in silver of her life and martyrdom; the Venetian church bells famous for their clear musical tones. Note the fine reconstructed belfry of 16th-century church of the Ipapánti. In the nearby wine growing village of **Lagopóda** there is also the pretty crenellated Eleftherias convent, where the nuns do fine needlework.

From Macherádo the road rises to **Koiloménos**, with a handsome stone belltower from 1893, attached to the church of Ag. Nikólaos: unusually for Greece it is carved with Masonic symbols, and, if it looks stumpy, it's because it lacks its original pyramidal crown. A secondary road from here leads to the wild coast and the **Karakonísi**, a bizarre islet just off shore that not only looks like a whale, and even spouts great plumes of spray when the wind is up. At Ag. Léon (with another striking bell tower, this time converted from a windmill) there's another turn-off to the coast, to the dramatic narrow creek and minute sandy beach at of **Limnióna**. Just before Exochóro, another road descends to **Kámbi**, where Mycenaean rock cut tombs were found and two tavernas perched on the 650ft cliffs are spectacular sunset viewing platforms, although in summer you'll probably have to share them with coach parties from Laganás.

The main road continues to Anafonítria, site of the 15th-century **Monastery of the Panagía Anafonítria**, which survived several earthquakes intact along with its time-darkened frescoes and cell of St Dionysios—he was abbot here and his claim for sainthood was that he gave sanctuary to his brother's killer. Below is **Porto Vrómi**, 'Dirty Port' because of the natural tar that blankets the shore, although the water is perfectly clear. Around the corner, accessible only by sea, is a perfect white sandy beach with the **'shipwreck'**, wedged under sheer white limestone crags and a perfectly clear azure water. The scene graces a thousand postcards and is a prime destination for excursion boats; although some tour guides let the punters fantasize that the wreck has been there for decades, the truth is the boat belonged to some cigarette smugglers in the late 1980s who ran the ship aground and climbed up the cliffs when they were about to be nabbed by the Greek coastguard. When word reached the inhabitants of the small villages above, action was taken at once, and by the time the coastguard got back to the ship it was empty; apparently the free smokes have only recently run out. You can look down at 'shipwreck' beach from the path near the abandoned 16th-century monastery of **Ag. Geórgios sta Kremná**. The path, increasingly overgrown, leads to the narrow cavechapel of **Ag. Gerásimou**.

The road passes through an increasingly dry landscape on route to **Volímes** (ΒΟΛΙΜΕΣ), the largest village on the west coast, permanently festive with billowing, brightly coloured handwoven goods displayed for sale. Seek out the fine church of Ag. Paraskeví and the 15th-century Ag. Theodósios, with its stone carved iconostasis. **Áno Volímes** just above it is a pretty little mountain village. Below, on the east coast, is the remote beach of **Makrí Giálos**; from here a road leads north to the tiny port of Ag. Nikólaos, better known as **Skinári**, where the little ferry from Kefaloniá calls. The white coast around here is pocked with caves, cliffs and natural columns and arches, and most spectacularly of all, one hour by boat from Skinári, **Kianoún Cave**, the local rival for Capri's Blue Grotto, glowing with every imaginable shade of blue; the light is best in the morning. Excursions from Ag. Nikólaos also run south to **Xinthia** with sulphur springs—evidence of the island's volcanic origins—and rocks and sand so hot that you must wear swimming shoes, and to the cave of **Sklávou**.

## The Strofádes

A couple of times a week caiques from Laganás sail the 37 nautical miles south of Zákynthos to the Strofádes (there are two, **Charpína** and **Stamvránio**), passing over the deepest point in the entire Mediterranean, where you have to dive 4404m down to reach Davy Jones' locker. Strofádes means 'turning' in Greek: according to myth, the Harpies, those composite female monsters with human heads, hands and feet, winged griffon bodies and bear ears were playing their usual role as the hired guns of the gods, chasing the prophet Phineas over the little islets, when Zeus changed his mind and ordered them to turn around.

Although little more than flat green pancakes in the sea, the Strofádes offered just the right kind of rigorous isolation Orthodox monks and mystics crave, and duly in the 13th century, Irene, wife of the Byzantine emperor John Láskaris, found the **Pantochará** ('all joy') monastery on Charpína. Pirates soon proved to be a major problem, and in 1440, just before Constantinople itself fell to the Turks, Emperor John Palaiológos sent fund to build high walls around it. As on Mount Áthos, no women or female animals were allowed, and the 40 monks who resided there (among them Ag. Diónysos) spent their days studying rare books. In 1530, however, the Saracens managed to breach the walls, slew all the monks and plundered it; in 1717 the body of Ag. Diónysos was removed to Zákynthos town for safe keeping. The evocative, desolate citadel is now owned by the monstery of Ag. Diónysos, and remains in a fine state of preservation, complete with a new pink tile roof, although the population has been reduced to migratory turtle doves and quails. If you have your own boat and provisions and have been looking for an out-of-the-way, romantic destination you won't find a better one.

# The Northeastern Aegean Islands

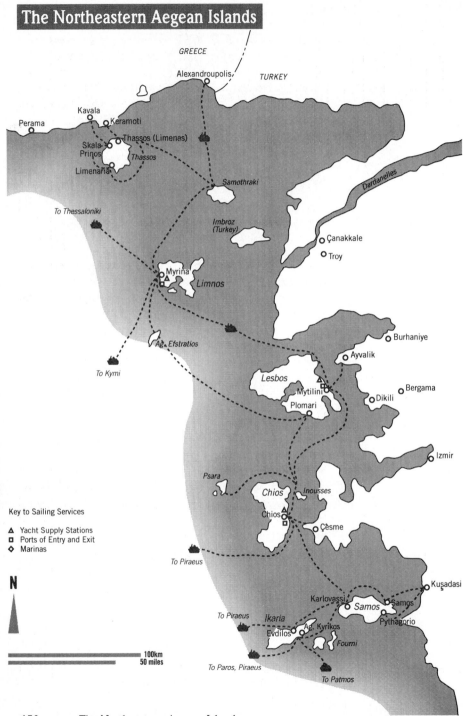

# The Northeastern Aegean Islands

GREECE

Alexandroupolis

TURKEY

Kavala

Perama

Keramoti

Thassos (Limenas)

Skala Prinos

Thassos

Limenaria

Samothraki

To Thessaloniki

Dardanelles

Imbroz (Turkey)

Çanakkale

Troy

Myrina

Limnos

Burhaniye

Ag. Efstratios

Ayvalik

To Kymi

Lesbos

Mytilini

Dikili

Bergama

Plomari

Izmir

**Key to Sailing Services**

▲ Yacht Supply Stations
□ Ports of Entry and Exit
◇ Marinas

Psara

Chios

Inousses

Chios

Çesme

N

To Piraeus

Kuşadasi

Karlovassi

Samos

Samos

To Piraeus

Ikaria

Pythagorio

Ag. Kyrikos

Evdilos

Fourni

100km
50 miles

To Paros, Piraeus

To Patmos

The grouping together of these islands as 'Northeastern Aegean' is done for convenience rather than for any cultural or historical consideration. What they have in common, besides their location off the coast of Turkey and Northern Greece, is a rugged individualism and character—although green and often forested, the islands are rarely cat-calendar cute, and many of their big towns and main ports are frankly unattractive, at least at first glance. Yet just beyond the bustle are fascinating, unspoiled villages and landscapes, deep places out of time where it pays to linger, to just be. With the exceptions of Sámos, with two decades of package-tour experience, and Thássos, long a favourite with its pine forests and ring of beaches, the Northeastern Aegean islands are the last frontier in Greek island tourism.

Most of these islands were colonized during the Dorian invasion in the 12th century BC, when the invaders forced the Ionians of mainland Greece to seek new homes in the east. The Ionians occupied the coastal regions of Asia Minor and the islands, and, between the 7th and 6th centuries BC, seeded much of what we call Western civilization: the islands alone produced talents like Pythagoras, Sappho and probably Homer himself. Their cities were among the most important in Greece in trade, in the production of wine and olive oil, and in religion. Samothrace is practically synonymous with its sanctuary of the gods of the underworld; Límnos was dedicated to the smithy god Hephaestus, and on Sámos the temple of the goddess Hera was one of the wonders of the Ancient World. These prosperous and independent islands slipped into obscurity as they fell prey to the greater powers around them, first the Persians from Asia Minor and then the Athenians from the West, and then from Asia Minor again in the form of the Ottoman Empire. They were annexed to Greece only in 1912, following the Balkan Wars.

### Getting There

The Northeastern Aegean islands were the last to be 'discovered', partly due to their great distance from Athens—Ikaría, the closest island to Athens, is a 10-hour journey by ship. Almost all the islands, however, now have airports, although anyone planning to fly there during the summer should reserve a seat as much as two months in advance. Connections between the islands have improved of late, particularly hydrofoil services.

## Chíos (ΧΙΟΣ)

*Soak me with jars of Chian wine and say 'Enjoy yourself, Hedylus.' I hate living emptily, not drunk with wine.*

–Hedylus, *c.* 280 BC

Chíos is a fascinating and wealthy island celebrated for its shipowners, its good humour and its gum mastic that grows here and nowhere else in the world. It offers the most varied geography in the Northeast Aegean: lush fertile plains, thick pine forests, mostly adequate beaches,

Mediterranean scrublands and startlingly barren mountains that bring to mind the 'craggy Chíos' of Homer, who may have been born on the island. Its architecture is unique and varied and its church of Néa Moní has some of the finest 11th-century Byzantine mosaics anywhere. Tourism, with charters and package companies, is fairly new to Chíos, and most of the islanders are still at the stage where they want visitors to share their deep love for the island rather than just take their money.

## Mythology

Chios was an island favoured by Poseidon, and is said to owe its name to the heavy snowfall (*chioni*) that fell when the sea god was born. Vine-growing was introduced to the island by Oenopion, son of Ariadne and Theseus. Oenopion pledged his daughter Merope in marriage to the handsome giant Orion, the mighty hunter who boasted that he could rid the entire world of harmful creatures, on the condition that he rid Chíos of its ferocious beasts, a task the young man easily performed. Rather than give Orion his reward, however, Oenopion kept putting him off (for he loved his daughter himself), and finally Orion took the matter into his own hands and raped Merope. For this the king poked out his eyes. Orion then set out blindly, but the goddess of dawn, Eos, fell in love with him and persuaded Helios the sun god to restore his sight. Before he could avenge himself on Oenopion, however, Orion was killed when Mother Earth, angry at his boasting, sent a giant scorpion after him. Orion fled the scorpion, but his friend Artemis, the goddess of the hunt, killed him by mistake. In mourning, she placed his image among the stars.

## History

Inhabited from approximately 3000 BC, Chíos was colonized by the mysterious seafaring Pelasgians who left walls near Exo Dídyma and Kouroúnia and a temple of Zeus on top of Mount Pelinaío. The Achaeans followed, and were in turn usurped by the Ionians, who had the longest-lasting influence on the island; one tradition asserts that Homer was born here in the 9th or 8th century BC (although nearby Smyrna/Izmir disputes this). By then Chíos was a thriving, independent kingdom, founding commercial ports or *emporia*, notably Voroniki in Egypt. It was famed for its unique mastic and wine (especially from the medicinal *arioúsios* grapes), and for its sculpture workshop and system of government, studied by Solon and adapted into his Athenian reforms. Around 490, a Chiot named Glaucus invented the art of soldering metals; less nobly, Chíos was the first state in Greece to engage in slave-trading. As a member of the famous Ionian confederacy, Chíos joined Athens in the Battle of Lade (494 BC) in an unsuccessful attempt to overthrow the Persian yoke. Fifteen years later, however, after the battle of Plateía, Chíos regained its independence, and held on to it even after Athens subjugated its other allies as tribute-paying dependencies.

Chíos allied itself with Rome and fought the enemy of the Empire, Mithridates of Pontus (83 BC), only to be defeated and destroyed, although it was liberated after two years when Mithridates was defeated by Sulla. A few hundred years later Chíos made the mistake of siding with Galerius against his brother-in-law Constantine the Great. Constantine conquered the island and carried off to his new city of Constantinople many of Chíos' famous ancient sculptures, including the four bronze horses that ended up on the front of St Mark's in Venice in

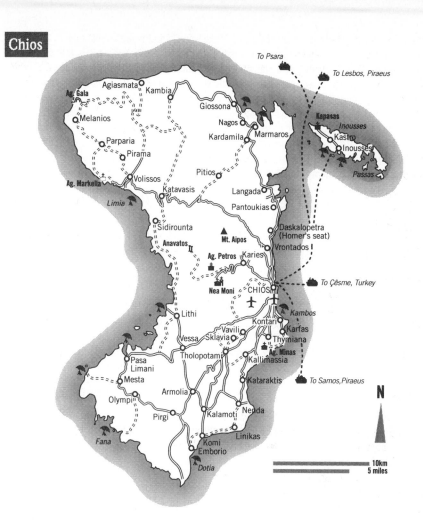

**Chios**

To Psara

To Lesbos, Piraeus

Ag. Gala
Agiasmata
Kambia
Giossona
Melanios
Nagos
Kardamila
Marmaros
Kapasas
Inousses
Kastro
Inousses
Parparia
Pirama
Passas
Volissos
Pitios
Ag. Markella
Katavasis
Langada
Limia
Pantoukias
Sidirounta
Daskalopetra
(Homer's seat)
Anavatos
Mt. Aipos
Vrontados
Ag. Petros
Karies
Nea Moni
CHIOS
To Çêsme, Turkey
Lithi
Kambos
Kontari
Karfas
Vavili
Thymiana
Vessa
Sklavia
Ag. Minas
Pasa
Limani
Tholopotami
Kallimassia
Mesta
Kataraktis
Armolia
To Samos, Piraeus
Olympi
Nenda
Pirgi
Kalamoti
Linikas
Fana
Komi
Emborio
Dotia

N

10km
5 miles

1204. In 1261 the Emperor Michael Paleológos gave Chíos to the Giustiniani, the noble Genoese family who helped him reconquer Byzantium from Venice and its Frankish allies. In 1344, the Giustiniani chartered a stock company called the Maona (from the Arabic *Maounach*, or trading company) with 12 merchants and ship owners to govern and defend the island, which they did successfully and prosperously until 1566 when Chíos was lost to the Turks.

The Sultans loved the island, especially its mastic, and they granted Chíos more benefits and privileges than any other island, including a degree of independence. The island became famous for its doctors and chess players; and elsewhere in Greece, where everyone was fairly miserable, the cheerfulness of the Chiots was considered pure foolishness. This came to an abrupt end in 1822. The islanders had already refused to join the Hydriots in the revolt, when a band of 2000 ill-armed Samians disembarked, proclaimed independence and forced the Chiots to join the struggle. The Sultan, furious at this subversion of his favoured island, ordered his admiral Kara Ali to quell the revolt mercilessly and make an example of Chíos that the Greeks would never forget. This led to one of the worst massacres in history. In two weeks an estimated 30,000 Greeks were slaughtered, and another 45,000 taken into slavery, whilst all the vines were uprooted. All who could fled to other islands, especially to Sýros (where they picked up a number of useful lessons about owning ships). News of the massacre deeply moved the rest of Europe; Delacroix painted his stirring canvas of the tragedy (the *Massacre à Hios* in the Louvre) and Victor Hugo sent off reams of rhetoric. On 6 June of the same year, the Greek Admiral Kanáris took revenge on Kara Ali by blowing up his flagship, killing Kara Ali and 2000 men. In 1840 Chíos attained a certain amount of autonomy under a Christian governor, and it was incorporated into Greece in 1912.

### Getting There and Around

**By air**: three flights a day from Athens, twice a week with Lésbos and Thessaloníki. For Olympic information, call © 24 515; for the airport, © 23 998.

**By sea**: daily with Piraeus, Lésbos and Inoússes; daily in summer to Cêsme, Turkey, out of season less frequently, three times a week to Límnos and Psará; at least twice a week with Sámos, Thessaloníki, Kavála and Rafína; once a week with Pátmos and Léros. Day summer **excursions** run to Psará and Inoússes. **Port authority**, © 44 432.

**By road**: blue **buses** (© 22 079) serve Chíos Town, the Kámbos area, Karfás beach, and Vrontádos. Green buses departing from near the Homerium Cultural Centre near Plateía Vounáki (© 27 507) cover the rest of the island's villages.

### Tourist Information

Very helpful **EOT** office, 11 Kanári Street, © (0271) 44 389, ✆ 44 343, open Mon–Fri 7am–2pm and 6–9.30pm, in Oct–May Mon–Fri 7–2.30; pick up their free *Chíos Summertime* booklet. The **tourist police** © 44 427, are at the far end of the quay, next to the regular police and the customs house.The **post office** is at the corner of Venizélou and Psichári; **OTE telephones** are just back from the port, at Ladis and Kanári.

### Festivals

Chíos' most important *panegýri* happens **22 July**, Ag. Marcéllus, at Ag. Markélla monastery; also **22 July**, Ag. Markélla at Volissos and Karyés; **26 July**, Ag. Paraskeví at Kástello and Kalamotí; **27 July**, Ag. Pandeleímon at Kalamotí; **8 August**, Ag. Emilianós and **12 August**, Ag. Fotiní, both at Kallimasía; **15 August**, Panagía at Pirgí, Nénita, Kámbos and Ag. Geórgios.

## Chíos Town (Chóra)

First-time visitors to Chíos arriving by ferry wonder what they've let themselves in for. The long, long harbourfront of Chíos Town (pop. 20,000) doesn't even try to look like a Greek island, with tall buildings holding half a dozen American pool halls, and a score of brightly lit bars and tavernas; throngs saunter and dawdle, and in summer evenings every single table is full. Badly hit by an earthquake in 1881, the town that arose from the rubble is slick and glossy, full of new apartment blocks and high-rise offices and perhaps more fast-food joints run by Greek Americans than strictly necessary. Yet after the first surprise, the town—a sister city of Genoa, for old times' sake—is a very likeable place well worth a few hours' poking about.

Most of what survives from the Turkish occupation is enclosed within the Byzantine **fortress**, which more less follows the lines of the Macedonian castle destroyed by Mithridates. The Giustiniani repaired the walls, and after 1599 only Turks and Jews were allowed to live in it, as the Greeks were forced to live outside the walls, and the main gate or **Porta Maggiore** was closed every day at sundown. Within the walls is a ruined **mosque** and in the Turkish cemetery you can see the **tomb of Kara Ali**, 'Black Ali', the same admiral who ordered the massacre of Chíos, its surprisingly unvandalized state perhaps a testimony to the tolerant, easy-going nature of the Chiots, remarked on since antiquity. In a closet-sized **prison** by the gate Bishop Pláto Fragiádis and 75 leading Chiots were incarcerated as hostages in crowded, inhumane conditions before they were all hanged by the Turks in 1822. The **Kastro Justinian Museum**, at the castle entrance in Plateía Frouríou (*open 9–3, closed Mon*) contains detached frescoes, wood carvings and early Christian mosaics.

The town's main square, **Plateía Vournakíou** (or **Plastíra**), with its café and sweet shops under the plane trees, is a few minutes' walk away. On one side stands a statue of Bishop Pláto Fragiádis, and in the municipal gardens behind the square is a statue of Kara Ali's avenging angel, 'Incendiary' Kanáris, a native of Psará. Plateía Vournakíou's crumbling mosque is marked with the *Tugra*, the swirling 'thumbprint of the Sultan' that denotes royal possession. *Tugras*, though common in Istanbul, are rarely seen elsewhere, even in Turkey, and this one is a mark of the special favour that Chíos enjoyed. Today the mosque houses the **Byzantine Museum** (*open 10–1, Sun 10–3, closed Mon*) with a collection of art, tombstones and other old odds and ends too big to fit anywhere else. The new building on the south end of the square is the city cultural centre, or **Homerium**, with frequent art exhibtions and other activities. South of Plateía Vournakíou near the cathedral, the **Koraï Municipal Library** (*open 8–2, closed Sun*) was founded in 1817 and claims to be the third largest in Greece with 135,000 volumes; the same building houses the **Folklore Museum** (*same hours*), the private collection of London scholar Philip Argéntis, scion of an old Genoese-Chiot family who obviously got tired (with good reason) of looking at his family's portraits. Other displays feature Chiot costumes and handicrafts, bric-à-brac, garish art student copies of Delacroix's 1824 *Massacre à Chíos* and engravings of 18th-century Chíos. The **archaeology museum**, 5 Michálon Street, near the Chandris hotel (*open 9–3, closed Mon*) contains a typical island miscellany of finds, some bearing ancient Chíos' symbol, the sphinx (the same as Thebes); there's also a letter from Alexander the Great addressed to the Chiots.

# Kámbos: Genoese Gentility South of Chíos Town

The Genoese especially favoured the fertile, well-watered plain south of town they called the Campo, or **Kámbos**, where from the 14th-century they and the local Chiot aristocracy built villas and gardens and plantations of citrus fruit, mastic trees and mulberries for silk, an important source of income until the 19th century. Best explored on a pedal bike, Kámbos is an enchanting and evocative mesh of narrow lanes, full of secret orchards and gardens enclosed by tall stone walls, with the gates bearing some long forgotten coat-of-arms or the telltale stripes of the Genoese nobility. Many of the large medieval houses (unfortunately many were hit by the earthquake) have their own slowly turning water wheels, call *manganós*; while outside the walls the flowering meadows, wooden bridges and ancient trees create a scene of elegaic rural serenity unique on the Greek islands, especially in the golden light near the end of day. Mastodon bones were discovered at **Thymianá**, which was also the source of Kámbos's golden building stone and is now home to a women's cooperative producing rugs, towels and other woven goods. **Sklaviá** is especially lush, although its name is derived from the Greeks forced to work as slaves for the Genoese nobility. Towards the modern village of **Vavíli**, where the octagonal domed church **Panagía Krína** (1287) contains fine frescoes by the Cretan school.

The nearest beach to Chíos town and Kámbos is at **Karfás**, reached by frequent blue buses, where the sand is 'as soft as flour' but there's less of it to go around all the time as more and more new hotels and flats sprout up like concrete kudzu. Near here is **Ag. Minás monastery**, built in 1590. In the 1822 massacre, women and children from the surrounding villages took refuge there; a small, hopeless battle took place before Ag. Minás was overrun and all 3000 were slain, their bodies thrown down the well. Their bones are now in an ossuary; blood still stains the church floor (*closed afternoons until 6*).

---

### Chíos Town ✆ (0271–) Where to Stay

The shipowners hobnob in the large landmark **Chios Chandris**, on the sea at Prokyméa, ✆ 44 401, ✆ 25 768 (*B; exp*) complete with a bizarre 1960-ish lobby with cellophane chandeliers. Next to the Chandris you'll find the more convivial **Hotel Kyma**, ✆ 44 501, ✆ 44 600 (*C; exp*). The main body of the hotel was built by a local shipowner in the style of an Italian villa, with a fine painted ceiling adorning the lobby. There's a new addition, but try to stay in the older part, for the sea view and atmosphere. All rooms have bathrooms *en suite*, and breakfast is available. **Chios Rooms**, at Prokyméa, ✆ 27 295 (*mod*) is a renovated neoclassical shipowner's house. **Diana**, Venizélou 92, ✆ 44 180 (*C; mod*) has a pretty roof garden. In the heart of town the **Anesis**, Aplotariás and Vasilikári 2, ✆ 44 801 (*mod*), is a beautiful, traditional guesthouse. **Fedra**, M. Livanoú, ✆ 41 130 (*mod–inexp*) is a handsome traditional pension. **Apollonia** by the ferry, ✆ 24 842 (*inexp*) is OK and a good bet for late arrivals or early departures. Near the waterfront, **Filoxenia**, Voupalou Street, ✆ 22 813 (*D; inexp*) is clean and simple, and very cheap.

---

### Chíos Town ✆ (0271–) Eating Out

Besides mastic to masticate, Chíos has two specialities, Greek blue cheese, called *kopanistí*, and a unique brown, wrinkly, nutty kind of olive called *chourmádes*, the Greek word for dates. Try not to miss Chíos' oldest taverna, the **Hotzas**, in from the port at Stefánou Tsoúri 74, worth asking directions for; the food's excellent, from the *mezédes* to aubergine simmered with tomatoes, delicious whitebait, and other standard Greek dishes, topped off with good barrelled retsina, a rare find on any island (*1500dr*). On the harbour at 42 Aegéou, **Meltemi** looks touristy with little flags but serves a wide variety of freshly grilled meats, a full dinner costing no more than 2500dr. By the ferries there's an **ouzerie** serving very good fresh *mezédes*.

---

## Kámbos

**Villa La Favorita**, ✆/☎ 32 265, or book in Athens ✆ (01) 428 4266 (*exp–mod*), is a charming Genoese villa with 13 beautifully furnished air-conditioned rooms with mini-bars and a waterwheel in the courtyard. **Perivoli**, 11 Argénti, ✆ 31 513/42 141, ☎ 32 042 (*B; mod*) a quiet and serene traditional pension with 9 rooms, and a good, popular restaurant, has music and dancing on Friday nights. Down the road is the ultra-luxurious **Villa Argentikon**, ✆ 31 599 (*A; exp*) set in the 14th–15th century Renaissance villa of the prominent Argénti family, beautfiully restored, down to its oxen-turned 'Hesiod's water wheel'; meals are prepared by a cordon bleu chef at prices that if you have to ask about, you can't afford. Towards the sea, the **Golden Odyssey**, ✆ 21 432, ☎ 41 715 (*B; exp*) wouldn't look out of place in the States; rooms have air-conditioning, satellite TV balconies overlooking the pool and there's an excellent Chinese restaurant. *Open all year.* For something cheaper in Kámbos, **Níkos Zambetákis**, ✆ 32 280 or **Níkos Anastasákis**, ✆ 32 539 have rooms; ring for directions.

## Karfás

Near the airport, Chíos Town and the beach, Karfás has grown to become the island's chief resort compound. On the beach, **Golden Sand**, ✆ 32 080 (*exp*) also has its own pool. **Benovias**, ✆ 31 457 (*mod*) overlooking the beach, has eight stylish one- or two-bedroom apartments. The **Karatza** on Karfás street, ✆ 31 221 (*inexp*) has a pleasant terrace where you can look out over the sea to Turkey while feasting on grilled or ready-prepared food for around 2500dr; **Votsalakia**, at nearby Kontári, ✆ 41 181, serves some of the best food on Chíos.

---

### *Entertainment and Nightlife*

Loafing around the waterfront during and after the obligatory *vólta* takes up most evenings in Chíos town: **Kavos** and **Remezzo** are currently the bars to see and be seen in. The best ice cream in Chíos is scooped out till late at night at **Kronos**, 2F Argénti Street; **Nifada**, at Prokyméa, serves tasty croissants in a variety of forms. For a good sweaty bop try **Graffiti**, on Enóseos Ave, or **Rex** in Prokyméa or **B 52** out at Kontári. For Greek dancing, everyone goes to **Neraida**, 3 Enóseos Ave, ✆ 20 149.

## The Mastikochória, or Mastic Towns of the Southwest

Southwest of green Kámbos stretch the drier hills and vales of mastic land, where it often seems that time stands still. It must have special magic or secret virtue, for the bushy little mastic trees (*Pistacia lentiscus*, a relative of the pistachio) refuse to be transplanted anywhere else in the world—even northern Chíos won't do; the bushes might grow, but not a drop of mastic will they yield. The bark is 'needled' three times a year between July and September, allowing the sweet sap to ooze from the fine wounds, glistening like liquid diamonds in the sun. Some 300 tons of gum mastic are produced annually, although since the advent of synthetics the mastic market just isn't what it used to be. Considered a panacea in antiquity, good for everything from snake bite, rabies in mules and bladder ailments, mastic puts the chew in gum and the jelly in the beans that kept the bored inmates delicately chomping in the Turkish harems; Roman women used toothpicks made of the wood to sweeten their breath. In the more mundane West mastic was used in paint varnish; the Syrians buy it as an ingredient in perfume. On Chíos they use it to flavour a devilishly sweet sticky liqueur, spoon sweets, chewing gum and MasticDent toothpaste, the perfect Chíos souvenir. Nearly all the 20 villages where mastic is grown, known as the Mastikochória, date from the Middle Ages, and were carefully spared by the Turks in 1822. They were designed by the Genoese as tight-knit little labyrinths for defence, the houses sharing a common outer wall with few entrances; if that were breached, the villagers could take refuge in a central keep. Heading south from Chíos town, the first of the Mastikochória is **Armoliá**, which also makes pottery, although not particularly the kind you might want to take home. It is defended by the Byzantine **Kástro tis Oréas** (1440), a castle named for the beautiful châtelaine who seduced men only to have them executed. **Kalamotí**, once one of the most thriving villages, has tall stone houses on its narrow cobbled streets and a pretty Byzantine church, Ag. Paraskeví, and isn't far from the 12th-century church **Panagía Sikelia**. The closest beach to both towns is sandy **Kómi**, a fine stretch of sand with a few tavernas and rooms to rent.

**Pirgí** (ΠΥΡΓΊ) is the largest mastic village and an architectural gem, founded in the 13th century and beautifully decorated with *xistá*, the local word for *sgrafitto* decoration taught to the locals by the Genoese; walls are first covered with mortar containing black sand from Emborió, then covered with white plaster, into which the artist scrapes off into geometric, floral or animal-based designs. While seen here and there elsewhere in Greece, Pirgí is unique in that nearly every house is decorated with *xistá*; in the main square of the village they are particularly lavish. Of the equally adorned churches, the 12th-century **Ag. Apóstoli**, a miniature version of Néa Moní has frescoes from 1655 (*open most mornings*).

One of Chíos' ancient cities was Levkonion, a rival of Troy that was later mentioned by Thucydides. Near the old mastic-exporting port of **Emborió** (ΕΜΠΟΡΕΙΟΣ), 5km from Pirgí, archaeologists discovered signs of a settlement that may well fit the bill, dating from 3000 BC. East of the port, under the chapel of Profítis Ilías are ruins of the 7th–4th century BC **temple of Athena Polias** and the enceinte of an ancient acropolis. The wealth of

TRADITIONAL DECORATION, CHIOS

amphorae found underwater here hint at the extent of Chíos' wine trade (Aristophanes wrote that the ancient Chiots were terrible tipplers; these days most of their grapes go into ouzo or a raisin wine not unlike Tuscan *vinsanto*). **Mávra Vótsala** beach, five minutes from Emborió, is made of black volcanic pebbles, but the whole effect is spoiled by the DEH's new power lines; around the headland is a second, better black beach which seems to have five or six names, but is usually called Mávra Vótsala, too. Some way from the shore near Emborió are the ruins of a 6th-century **Christian basilica** with a marble cross-shaped font and a few mosaics.

Two other medieval mastic villages have impressive defences, **Olýmpi** (ΟΛΥΜΠΟΙ) and **Mestá** (ΜΕΣΤΑ). Olýmpi is built around a 20m tower, and originally had only one gate. Mestá is the ultimate fortress or *kástro* village, with mazes of lanes and flower-filled yards much beloved of film crews; most of the time you can almost hear the silence. Two churches are worth a look: the medieval **Ag. Paraskeví** and the 18th-century **Mikrós Taxiárchis**, with a beautifully carved iconostasis. As is usual in Greece, Mestá's two main *kafeneíons* are strictly divided, one for socialists, one for conservatives. To the south, **Fána** has a fine, wild beach, its name and the ruins of a fountain recalling the Great Temple of Phaneo Apollo (6th century BC) that stood nearby. Alexander the Great once stopped to consult its oracle; several of its Ionic columns are displayed in the Chíos archaeology museum. The road north from Mestá to Chíos town passes Mestá's old port of **Liménas** (or **Pasá-Limáni**); at picturesque medieval **Véssa** another road leads north to **Lithí** (4½km), a pretty village with a mediocre sandy beach down below, tavernas and a few places to stay. Further up the west coast you can swim at the pebble coves near Elínda and circle back to Chíos town by way of Angónima and Néa Moní.

---

### Where to Stay and Eating Out

### The Mastic Villages ✆ (0271–)

In medieval Mestá EOT has refurbished four traditional houses, each furnished with local handicrafts and giving on to a courtyard and accommodating 3 to 8 people—a bargain at under 5000dr a night. For reservations, contact Paradosiakós Ikismós, Mestá, ✆ 76 319. The **Women's Agrotourist Cooperative of Chíos**, ✆ 72 496 in Mestá, Armólia, Pirgí and Olýmpi rent handsome, traditional rooms for 4–5500dr a night. The women have 62 rooms to let, 135 beds; you can even help the women gather the mastic sap. Ring ahead for cheaper rooms: in Mestá, **Lida** ✆ 76 217; in Pirgí, **Leodi**, ✆ 72 425 or **Irene Valla**, ✆ 72 479.

### Kómi ✆ (0271–)

There are two places with rooms, **Manes**, ✆ 71 226 and **Baliraki**, ✆ 71 941. Try the fresh fish and lobster under the trees at **Nostalgia**, ✆ 70 070; after dark everyone heads out for drink at **Kochili** or **Tifanis**.

### Emborió ✆ (0272–)

**Kamba**, ✆ 71 422 (*inexp*) has rooms here. The highly recommended **Volcano**, ✆ 71 136, has not only delicious food but a lovely garden and interior decorated with a wedding chest, photos, plates and the prettiest loos in Greece.

### Lithí ✆ (0272–)

**Kira Despina Murina**, on the beach, ✆ 73 373 (*inexp*), has a handful of rooms and serves great fish, fish soup and big breakfasts.

## Inland from Chíos Town: Néa Moní (NEA MONH)

A trip to **Néa Moní** (*open until 1pm and from 4–8pm; women should wear knee-length skirts*) is the most beautiful excursion on Chíos, and perhaps easiest made by taxi if you don't have a car; most blue buses only go as far as **Karyés**, a mountain village flowing with fresh springs, a long 7km-walk from the monastery. Beautifully perched high in the pines, Néa Moní was 'new' back in 1042, when Emperor Constantine VIII Monomachos ('the single-handed fighter') and his wife Zoë had it built to replace an older monastery, where the monks had found a miraculous icon of the Virgin in a bush; not the least of its miracles was its prophecy that Constantine would return from exile and gain the throne of Byzantium. In gratitude, the Emperor sent money, architects and artists from Constantinople to build a new monastery. The church has a sumptuous double narthex and subtle, complex design of pilasters and niches and pendentives that support its great dome atop an octagonal drum. Its richly coloured 11th-century mosaics shimmer in the penumbra: the *Washing of the Feet*, *The Saints of Chíos* and *Judas' Kiss* in the narthex and *The Life of Christ* in the dome, stylistically similar to those at Dáfni in Athens and among the most beautiful examples of Byzantine art anywhere—even though they had to be pieced back together after the earthquake of 1881 brought down the great dome. A chapel displays the bones of of victims of Kara Ali's massacre who sought sanctuary here (among them, the 600 monks).

From here, a rough road leads to the monastery **Ag. Patéras**, built in honour of the three monks who founded Néa Moní and rebuilt in 1890 (men only). Further up at **Avgónima**, once nearly abandoned and now increasingly a village of holiday homes, a road zigzags up a granite mountain to the 'Mystrás of Chíos' the striking medieval village and castle of **Anávatos** (pop. 4). It saw horrific scenes in 1822; most of the villagers threw themselves off the 325m cliff rather than be captured by the Turks, and ever since then the place has been haunted.

## North of Chíos Town

Northern Chíos is the island's wild side, mountainous, stark and barren, its forests decimated by shipbuilders, and in the 1980s by fires. Many of its villages are nearly deserted outside of the summer. **Vrontádos** (BPONTAΔOΣ) 4½km north of Chíos town is an exception, a kind of bedroom satellite village, where most of the island's shipowners have their homes, overlooking a pebbly beach and ruined windmills. The locals are proudest of the **Daskolópetra** (the Teacher's Stone), a rather uncomfortable rock throne on a natural terrace over the sea where Homer is said to have sung and taught and where his disciples would gather to learn his poetry, although killjoy archaeologists say it was part of an ancient altar dedicated to the local version of Cybele. A curious legend relates that the most famous Genoese of all, Christopher Columbus, stopped and sat here before going on to America. The headquarters of the International Society of Homeric Studies is in Vrontádos, and there's a small **folklore museum** (*open daily 5–7pm*); the 19th-century **Monastery of Panagía Myrtidiótissa** nearby has the robes of Gregory V, the Patriarch of Constantinople.

Near Vrontádos stood Chíos' first church **Ag. Isídoros**, founded in the 3rd century on the spot where the saint was tortured and martyred. A later church to house the relics of St Isídoros (whose feast day only happens every four years, on February 29) was built by Emperor Constantine, but it fell in an earthquake and was replaced by three successive structures, the last ruined by the Turks in 1822; mosaics from the 7th-century version are in the Byzantine museum. The church was never rebuilt, perhaps because the Venetians snatched Isídoros' relics in the 12th century and installed them in a special chapel in St Mark's. In 1967 Pope Paul IV ordered them to return of one of Isídoros' bones, now kept in Chíos cathedral.

Further north is Langáda, a fishing village with a fine beach at **Ag. Isídorou**. Jagged rocks surround **Kardámila** (KAPΔAMYΛA), the largest village of northern Chíos and cradle of the island's shipowners. Kardámila is actually two villages, 2km from one another: the picturesque upper town and the seaside **Mármaros**, blessed with many philanthropic gifts from wealthy Chiot shipowners, including a statue of the Kardámila sailor on the beach. To the north, **Nagós beach** has coloured pebbles set in a green amphitheatre; its name is a corruption of *naos*, or temple, for there used to be one here, dedicated to Poseidon. There's another good pebble beach at nearby **Gióssona**, named after Jason of the Argonauts. Taxis have a monopoly on transport to the striking ancient mountain village **Pitiós**, which claims to be the birthplace of Homer; you can still see his 'house' and olive grove. A 12th-century tower dominates the village and there's usually something to eat at the café. The landscape from Pitiós towards Chíos town is lunar in its burnt emptiness, but just above the village is a lovely pine forest, filled with fire warnings.

Further to the west is the 13th-century **Moní Moúdon** is strikingly set in the barren hills near Katávasis. Byzantine nobles out of favour were exiled in the medieval fortress at **Volissós** (ΒΟΛΙΣΣΟΣ), founded by Belisarius, Justinian's great general, although what you see was rebuilt by the Genoese. The popular 16th-century saint Markélla hailed from the little white village, which also lays claim to Homer; in ancient times it was the chief town of the Homeridai, who claimed descent from him. One tradition says Homer met a shepherd named Glaukos in Volissós; and Glaukos introduced him to his master, who hired the poet as a teacher. Soon after. Homer married a Volissós girl, had two daughters, wrote the *Odyssey* and decided to sail to Athens, the rising centre of Ionian culture, but he died on the way on Íos. The sandy beach below the town, **Skála Volissoú** or **Limiá**, is one of the island's finest and has a restaurant and a few rooms to let and caiques several times weekly to Psará (the shortest way of getting there). There are other excellent beaches near here, just as minimally developed: pebbly **Chóri** just south is the unofficial nudist beach, and **Límnos**, on the road to **Ag. Markélla**, these days the island's favourite pilgrimage destination.

Twice a week or so, buses brave the deserted roads north of Volissós. The westerly one climbs to little **Piramá**, with a medieval tower and the lovely church of Ag. Ioánnis with old icons. **Parpariá** to the north is a medieval hamlet of shepherds, and at **Melaniós** many Chiots were slain before they could flee to Psará in 1822. On the northwest shore stands the 14th-century Byzantine church **Ag. Gála**, by a cave which drips whitish deposits, or milk (*gála* in Greek), said to be the milk of the Virgin. For more strange terrestrial secretions, make your way along the beautiful if rough coastal road east to **Agiásmata** where Chiots come in the summer to soak in the magic baths.

---

### Where to Stay and Eating Out

**Vrontádos** ✆ (0271–)

    **Kyveli**, ✆ 92 919, ✉ 93 854 (*exp*) is a fancy new apartment complex overlooking the harbour, with a pool behind; alternatively, there's the **Xenios**, ✆ 93 763 (*B; mod*) much further from the sea. *Open June–Dec*. Quite a few places rent rooms, and there's Chíos' one organized if inconvenient campsite to the north, **Camping Chios**, at Ag. Isídoro Sikíados, ✆ 74 111. **To Limanaki**, ✆ 93 647 serves delicious fresh fish.

**Kardámíla** ✆ (0272–)

The **Hotel Kardamyla** ✆ 23 353, 🖷 23 354 (*B; exp*) is modern and on the shady beach, and there are watersports available. The **Chiona Hotel** ✆ 22 036 (*C; mod*) has pleasant rooms and prides itself on its cuisine.

**Volissós** ✆ (0274–)

There are no rooms in the village, but a few down by the beaches. Try **Zorbas**, ✆ 21 436 at Límnos or **Alvertou**, ✆ 21 335 or **Lianris**, ✆ 21 400, both at Limiá.

## Inoússes (ΟΙΝΟΥΣΣΕΣ)

At least once a day caiques leave Chíos town for Inoússes, 'the wine islands', an archipelago of nine islets to the northeast. Only the largest, all of 3 by 10km, is inhabited, but per capita it's the richest island in Greece: the Inoussans comprise some 60 of the 180 Greek shipowning families, including the Lemnos clan, the very richest of them all. It's not for nothing that the Inoussians have a reputation for being tough and thrifty; most families began as goat herds or wine makers who had to spend centuries in Kardámila, Chíos, until it was safe to return to their defenceless rock pile. After losing everything in the Second World War they cannily parlayed a handful of wartime Liberty ships into a fleet of 500 ships and tankers, not to mention some of the fanciest yachts in Greece that congregate in its little port every summer. The rest of the year they divide between Geneva, London and Athens.

For all that, the island's one town is surprisingly unpretentious, if extremely well kept. Near the village is a medieval fort and there are a few small clean undeveloped beaches, the furthest a 30 minute walk away. The one road on the island crosses to the western cliffs, where in the 1960s Katíngo Patéras, of one of the most prominent shipowning dynasties, built the multi-million-dollar convent of the **Evanglismós** (*adm only to women with long sleeves, headscarves, and long skirts*) after the death of her pious 20-year-old daughter Iríni, who died of Hodgkinson's disease after praying to take the illness from her afflicted father and becoming a nun. When, as custom has it, her body was exhumed after three years, she was found to be mummified. Her failure to decompose convinced her bereaved mother that she was a saint (a belief recently confirmed by the Orthodox church) and like Sleeping Beauty she is kept in a glass case, on display with the remains of her ship-owning father, who died shortly after, in spite of Irini's efforts. Inoússes has a pair of tavernas and one simple place to stay: **Hotel Thalassoporos**, ✆ (0272) 51 475 (*D; inexp*).

## Psará (ΨAPA)

**Psará** is much further away than Inoússes, 44 nautical miles northwest of Chíos and connected only a few times a week with the larger island—a good 4-hour journey unless you depart from the port of Limniá below Volissós. Archaeologists have discovered signs of a 13th-century BC Achaean settlement near Paliókastro, a town founded by Chiot refugees during the Turkish rule. They knew this tiny, remote rock of an islet was generally ignored by the Sultan and over the years developed one of Greece's most important commercial fleets, rivalled only by the ships of Hýdra and Spétses. During the War of Independence (especially after the 1822 massacre on Chíos, which swelled the population with refugees), Psará enthusiastically contributed its ships and one of the war's heroes, Admiral Kanáris, to the cause. Psará even invented a new weapon, the *bourléta*, which its captains used to destroy the Turkish fleet.

Psará became such a thorn in the side of the Turks that the Sultan finally demanded vengeance, and on 20 June 1824 he sent 25,000 troops to wipe Psará off the map. In the subsequent slaughter only 3000 of the 30,000 men, women and children managed to escape to Erétria, Évia. Most of the rest were blown to bits with the Turks on the famous 'Black Ridge of Psará' when they set their powder stores alight. The heroic little island has never recovered: today only 400 people live on Psará, mostly fishermen and beekeepers. Your feet are the main transport to the island's fine beaches: the best is **Límnos**, a dandy sandy strand 20 minutes away.

*Psará ⓒ (0274–)*                                    **Where to Stay and Eating Out**

EOT's **Xenon Psaron** offers unusual accommodation, in this case in an old prison, offering bed and breakfast ⓒ 61 293, or contact the main office in Mytilíni, Lésbos, ⓒ (0251) 28 199; their taverna in a former hospital serves the best food on the island, For something cheaper, there are three rooms at the **Public Hotel,** ⓒ 61 196 (*E*), and a few more in private houses.

# Ikaría (IKAPIA)

Long, narrow Ikaría is divided by a dorsal spine of rugged mountains, many over 1000 metres high. It looks like a giant sea cucumber on the map and presents a forbidding, rocky, ungainly face to the world, and much of it is inaccessible except on foot. Yet both the popular north and more rugged south coast villages are watered by mountain springs that keep the villages cool and green under oak and plane trees, with added natural air-conditioning from the wind. The Ikaríán sea is one of the wildest corners of the Aegean; if it's calm on one side, it's often blustery on the other, and you may well come away with the impression that it was the wind that sank Icarus instead of the sun. It certainly abetted the fire that incinerated much of the south in 1993, causing 15 deaths.

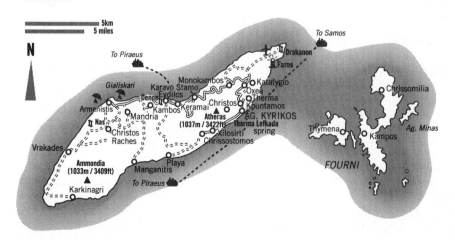

Ever since Lawrence Durrell slagged off Ikaría so unkindly in his *Greek Islands*, it has been fashionable among British travel writers to spill their poison ink all over its wild rocky shores; recently, one British newspaper, rating the islands as holiday material, put Ikaría dead last. Oh, how they make my hot Ikarian blood boil, but just for a moment; let them be as nasty as they like if it helps to ward off the package companies, the twee-totallers, the pubs and lager louts that blight so many very beautiful islands. The truth is few islands have so stubbornly clung to their identity, or indeed their very soul. Granted, Ikaría has little besides a few beaches to charm the hurried island-hopper, but more than tongue can tell if you take the time to stick around. And that's that! (Well, besides the obvious injunction to Eat at ΦΑΚΑΡΟΣ's while you're there...)

## Mythology

After Theseus entered the Labyrinth at Knossos and killed the Minotaur with the aid of Ariadne's thread, Minos was furious at the inventor Daedalus, who gave the thread to Ariadne. Daedalus fled, but Minos ordered all outgoing ships watched to keep Daedalus on Crete. Unable to flee by land or sea, Daedalus made wings of feathers and wax for himself and his young son Icarus. Off they flew, but the boy, enchanted by flight, forgot his father's warning and flew too near the sun; the wax binding the feathers melted and the boy plummeted to his death off the south coast of an island thereafter known as Ikaría. Pausanius in the 2nd century BC mentions that his grave could still be seen.

## History

Ikaría has had a number of ancient names, including Ichthyoessa, for its fish, or Oenoe, for its wine. So much wine was produced that some writers made it the birthplace of Dionysos, the god of wine; an inscription found on Athens' acropolis describes a certain Oenoe as being second only to Athens in sending the yearly contributions to Apollo on Delos.

Under the Byzantines the island was a place of exile for officials who had fallen from grace. Kámbos was one of their centres; another large settlement existed by the hot springs at Thérma.

In July 1912 during the Balkan War, the local doctor and priest led the inhabitants in forcing the Turks to leave, and for five proud months Ikaría was an independent state with its own flag and stamps. When it joined Greece, the government promptly forgot about it, and many Ikarians emigrated, mostly to the States. The Colonels used Ikaría as a dumping ground for political dissidents and Communists (who at one point numbered 15,000, twice the number of Ikarians), who politicized the locals; even today 'Red' Ikaría is one of the most left-wing islands in Greece, although whoever used to paint Maoist slogans on the roads has given up.

### Getting There and Around

**By air**: the **airport** at Fanári (and the road to it) should be finished during 1995; because of the wind, it has a unique north–south runway that can be approached from either direction.

**By sea**: **ferries** daily to Piraeus and Sámos (note that some call at the island's northern port, Évdilos, and others at Ag. Kýrikos). Small tourist **excursion boats** from Ag. Kýrikos to Foúrni daily. Less frequent connections with Páros, Mýkonos, Náxos Pátmos, Kálymnos, Léros, Lipsí, and Sýros. Summer

**hydrofoils** run several times a week to Pátmos, Mýkonos, Sámos, Chíos, Lésbos and Límnos. **Port authority,** ✆ 22 207.

**By road**: outside the school year, **buses** run once or twice a day to villages on the main roads, and across the island from Ag. Kýrikos to Évdilos and Armenistís, coinciding with the Piraeus ferries. But don't bet your life on it. There are **taxis** used to making long hauls and it's common to share.

### Tourist Information

Municipal tourist office, ✆ (0275) 22 298.

### Festivals

In the summer *panegýria* occupy the attention of the whole island, when many Ikarians who live abroad come home just to make merry. These feasts are run in the old style: guests order a *próthesi*—a kilo of wild goat meat, a bottle of wine, a huge bowl of soup and a loaf of bread—enough to feed four, and provide enough energy to dance until dawn. But the biggest festival of all is on **17 July**, in honour of the defeat of the Turks and Ikaría's fling with independence in 1912. Feasts, speeches, music and folk-dancing in costume are part of the day's agenda. Also **8th Sun after Easter**, at Ag. Pándas, Karavastómos; **26 July**, Ag. Paraskeví in Xilosírti; **27 July**, at Ag. Panteleímonos; **6 August** at Christós; **15 August** at Akamátra and Chrissóstomos; **8 September**, at Plagiá and Manganítis; **17 September**, Ag. Sofía at Mesokámbos. As the place synonymous with the world's first hang-glider, Ikaría has been deeply involved since 1990 in setting up the **Ikaríad**, the Olympics of air-sports, to be held every four years in different parts of the world (beginning in 1995).

## Ag. Kýrikos and Thérma

**Ag. Kýrikos** (ΑΓ. ΚΗΡΥΚΟΣ) or just plain 'Ágios', is the capital and largest town, 'obviously designed by a drunken postman' according to Mr Durrell. Well! Its tiny centre of shops, banks, travel agents and a lovely old bakery unchanged since the 1930s has more trees (less since the fire) than buildings or people. Every Ikarian must have a little garden to tend, so forget urban density; in fact around Ágios it's hard to tell where one village ends and another begins. The breakwater has been extended to ensure safer landings at the gale-ridden port, and the enormous 'Welcome to the Island of Radiation' painted there that once gave pause to many travellers has been whitewashed to a mere WELCOME TO THE ISLAND OF IKAROS. The statue on the breakwater—by local sculptor Ikaros—honours the first Icarus, who doesn't seem very airworthy even here, although supported on either side by two tall girder thingamabobs. The string of *kafeneía* along the waterfront see most of the social life, and shops in 'Ágios' sell Ikaría's sweets and honey made from thyme or *koumaro* bush blossoms. A new scupture by Ikaros, called the *Sképsi*, or Thinking Woman, is near the road on the west end of Ágios. There's also a sphinx by the sea.

For centuries tourism on Ikaría has meant **Thérma** (ΘΕΡΜΑ), a short boat taxi or bus ride from Ágios, where natural highly radioactive springs bubble up from the earth at 33–55°C to treat chronic rheumatism, arthritis, gout and spondylitis. The springs are the most radioactive in Europe; one, Artemidas, is so strong (790 degrees of radiation) that it's closed to the public.

There are a few rough pebble beaches here; for a long sandy strand, take the new road east out to the Fáros or **Fanári**, by the new airport. On the very end of the cape stands a round whitish tower from the 3rd century BC—one of the best preserved Hellenistic towers in Greece. The entire castle survived until the War of Independence, when Admiral Miaoúlis sailed by and used it for target practice. It stood over the ancient town of **Drakanón**, sacred to Dionysos; only a few 5th-century BC walls survive on the acropolis. Between Thérma and Drakanón, the hamlet of **Katafýgio** means 'shelter' and refers to an underground passageway beneath the church. One day Turkish raiders came to Katafýgio, but as it was Sunday all the villagers were at church. The Turks decided to wait outside and capture the people as they came out. They waited and waited, then impatiently broke into the church—to find it empty. The priest had opened the secret trapdoor in the floor, and everyone had escaped in safety.

The sadly burnt south coast west of Ag. Kýrikos has several more springs, of more local interest. **Thérma Lefkádos** has water so hot that villagers on picnics use it to boil their eggs, and Athanatós Neró (the 'deathless water' or fountain of youth: fill up a bottle) runs between the neo-Byzantine **Evangelístrias** monastery (1775), with exactly one nun, and **Xilosírti** where Icarus plummeted into the sea, off a clean, if occasionally windswept, pebble beach. When the *meltémí*'s going full guns the waves are skimmed off into a spray of racing rainbows. Xilosírti is spread out among olive and apricot trees; Ikaría produces some of the tastiest apricot preserves in Greece. After centuries of isolation, **Manganítis**, the westernmost village on the south shore, was, in 1987, finally reached by a new road from the north side of the island and a tunnel bored through the rock. Built on a steep hillside, its lonely position belies the fact that it is one of the liveliest spots on Ikaría, with parties lasting until the wee hours.

## The North Coast

Ikaría's northern half atttracts far more tourists; it is a gentler place with its pine forests, vineyards, sandy beaches and excellent roads and guesthouses. From Ag. Kýrikos a long, winding road climbs up to the barren mountain pass, taking in views of Foúrni, Sámos, Pátmos, Turkey, and Náxos, along with a few bored soldiers and power-generating windmills.

After passing through small villages immersed in the trees with little beaches—Monokámbi, Karavóstamo (the site of the 12th-century church **Ag. Pántas**) and Keramío—the road descends to the pleasant port of **Evdilos** (ΕΥΔΗΛΟΣ), the largest village on the north coast and a steamer stop several times a week between Piraeus and Sámos. It has a good town beach, and an even nicer one is further west, at **Kámbos.** Oenoe (or Doliche), the ancient capital of Ikaría, was here, and later Byzantine princelings in exile installed themselves nearby; the columns and arches of their palace remain, as well as their church **Ag. Iríni** with a slate roof. The local **museum** (ask at the bottom of the lane for the key) houses finds mostly from Oenoe. Above Kámbos in Messariá stands the ruined 11th-century **Kástro**, built by the Byzantines, near Kosíkia.

Further west along the coast is sandy **Gialiskári**, Ikaría's finest beach with a tiny blue-domed church set out on the rocks offshore. There are summer *cantinas* and a few rooms, but these always fill up in the summer; many people freelance-camp here and at Livádi. Two km further west, **Armenistís** (ΑΡΜΕΝΙΣΤΗΣ) is an attractive fishing village as well as Ikaría's biggest resort—big by Ikarian standards at any rate. Armenistís is the point of departure for two of the island's beauty spots: the wooded mountain village of **Christós Rachés**, the 'Little Switzerland of Ikaría', a bucolic place with orchards and vineyards. The 13th-century convent at **Mounté** has some wall paintings and icons. The second place is the ancient city of **Nas** (from *naos*, or temple), 10 minutes west along an unpaved road. On the bluff above, there's a pair of tavernas and a few rooms, and a path to shimmy down over the rocks to a small nudist beach in the ancient harbour, with an old river channel behind and the platform and foundations of the 5th-century BC temple of Artemis Taurópoulos. A marvellous statue of the goddess was discovered in the 19th century, with eyes that followed the viewer from every angle. The local priest decided at once that it was the work of heathen if not of the devil himself and ordered it to be thrown in the lime kiln. Thus perished the *Artemis of Ikaría*, never to hold its place in the Louvre with the *Venus de Milo* or *Victory of Samothrace*. The road doesn't improve (or get much worse) if you continue west to the sweet little whitewashed, slate-roofed **Monastery of Mavrianoú**, next to an old threshing floor.

---

*Ikaría* ✆ *(0275–)*           *Where to Stay and Eating Out*

The Ikarians are busily reviving their celebrated vinous past, and are currently trying out a wide variety of grapes in vineyards the size of handkerchiefs: the result may often be curiously brown in tone but goes down nicely and it gives quite a buzz, too.

### Ag. Kýrikos

There are a only a few small hotels and pensions here: try **Adam's**, the fanciest ✆ 22 418 (*B pension; mod*), *open all year*; **George**, similar ✆ 22 517; **Kastro**, ✆ 23 480, ✆ 23 700 (*C; inexp*); **Isabella's**, ✆ 22 839 (*E; inexp*) is the cheapest. The hotels and pensions in nearby Thérma are primarily geared to the arthritic, but the **Ikarion**, ✆ 22 481 (*D; mod–inexp*) and the **Radion**, ✆ 22 381(*D; mod–inexp*) offer some sea sports, or try **Galini**, ✆ 22 530 (*C pension; mod–inexp*) and the slightly larger **Marina** pension, ✆ 22 188 (*C; mod*). The island's best pizzas and now other dishes as well are served at **Filoti**, just off the waterfront, and the *zacharoplasteíon* next door is a good place for snacks and sugary little cakes. **Klimataria** is an excellent taverna, or take a taxi up to **Phtera**, as authentic as you can get, high above Agios. In summer the same family runs **Ptherino**, an outdoor bar and restaurant.

### Évdilos

Most comfortable here is the modern **Atheras**, ✆ 31 434 (*B; exp–mod*), with a disco, pool and other comforts. *Open May–Sept.* The **Evdoxia** pension, ✆ 31 502 (*B; mod*) is on the hill overlooking the port. The *ouzerie* **To Steki** is also the place to go for fish; for grilled meats, try **Kokos** or **Klendeni** which are good, as is **Klepas**, above the port next to the grocery store.

### Armenistís and Points West

Ikaría's best hotel, **Messakti Village**, 2km east at Gialiskári, ✆ 71 331, ✆ 71 330, in Athens ✆/✆ (01) 621 9112 (*B; exp–mod*), was finished in 1994, using the traditional island materials and architecture, including slate floors; rooms have kitchenettes and overlook the pool and sandy beach; very friendly management. Also, try **Cavos** (*C; mod*), ✆ 71 389 and **Daidalos**, ✆ 71 390, ✆ 71 393 (*C; mod*); the latter is traditionally furnished and set among the cedars overlooking the sea, with a pool, children's pool and restaurant. There are many more rooms—the **Armena**, ✆ 41 415, has nice views. The best food in the village comes from the portside kitchen of **Paskalia** (although the locals call it **Vlachos**, after the owner); on the other end of the water-front, **Symbosio** does vegetarian dishes, fish, and mushrooms (one of Ikaría's secrets). Cousin **Charley Facaros' Pub** ✆ 71 208 on the waterfront, has some rooms and serves drinks and snacks. Taverna **Kelari**, overlooking the fishing boats at Gialiskári, has good seafood. **Raches**, up in Christós Rachés, ✆ 41 269 (*B; mod*), offers peace and quiet and meals in the evening. In Nas, there are a score of rooms and the excellent **Taverna Astra**, ✆ 71 255, serving delicious, very reasonably priced seafood (including some of the most tender octopus in Greece), courgette beignets and other dishes prepared in the traditional Ikarian style, with local wine (*around 2500 dr*).

## Foúrni (ΦΟΥΡΝΟΥΣ)

If Ikaría is too cosmopolitan for your taste, try Foúrni. Connected every morning by caique from Ag. Kýrikos and twice weekly from Sámos, Foúrni (or Foúrnous) is a pair of islets just about midway between two larger sisters, Sámos and Ikaría. The larger island encircles a huge sheltered harbour that long hid a band of Algerian pirates, from where they would pounce on passing ships. Today the harbour is better known for its fish, especially the much-loved *barboúnia* (red mullet) and clawless Mediterranean lobster (*astakós*), which, although plentiful, isn't cheap; the surprising number of fishing boats in the harbour send most of their catch to Athens. Many fish by night, using bright lamps that set the sea aglitter.

Most people live around the harbour, where there's a sandy beach. Following the paths will bring you to other sandy coves, kissed by crystal-clear water, Psilí Ammo, Elidáki and Kámbi; further afield, Vlycháda beach can only be reached by caique. **Kámpos**, the 'capital', is a pleasant little town with many trees, belying the barren rock-pile which Foúrni resembles from its outer coasts. At the time of writing, a road is being built to the island's other village, tiny **Chrissomiliá**. If Foúrni is too cosmopolitan, try its baby islet **Thýmena**, where you'll be stared at if you disembark; bring your own food and be prepared to sleep under the stars.

---

*Foúrni* ✆ *(0275–)* **Where to Stay and Eating Out**

**Spyrakos Rooms**, ✆/☏ 51 235, in Athens (01) 261 9010 (*mod*), are very nice and come with minifridges as well as private baths; other modern rooms are available from **Maouni**, ✆ 51 367, and there are about 40 others in the houses. Among the tavernas near the port, **Miltos** is the best for lobster and fresh fish.

## Lésbos/Mytilíni (ΛΕΣΒΟΣ/ΜΥΤΙΛΗΝΗ)

Officially Lésbos, but more often called Mytilíni after its principal city, Sappho's island (pop. 116,000) is the third largest in Greece, and one of the more elusive, many-sided in more ways that merely geographical. Traditional rural life remains strong in the quiet villages, 15 of which have been declared traditional settlements: its undulating hills support an astonishing 11–13 million olive trees, which glisten silver in the sunlight, while the higher peaks are swathed in deep chestnut and pine forests. Its size (it's nearly a 100km from Mytilíni town to Sígri) makes transport difficult unless you have a car or scooter. Although much of the countryside is quite lovely, little stands out in particular—an attractive artists' colony, a handful of charming villages with houses made of dark basalt with Levantine wooden galleries, a few excellent

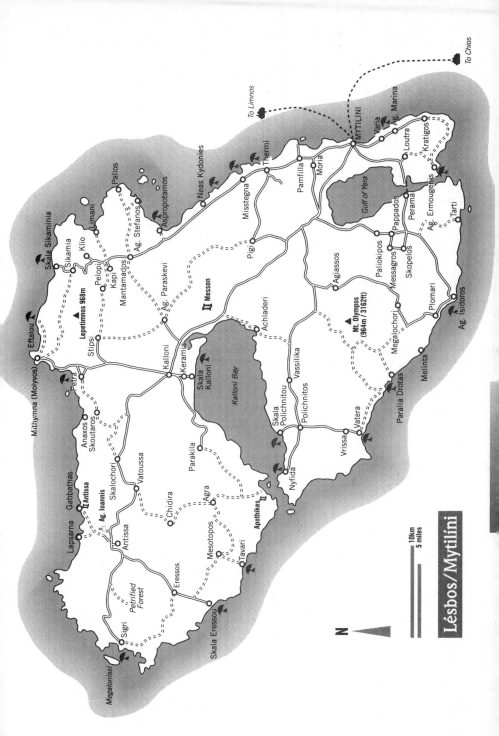

To Chios

To Limnos

MYTILINI

Varia

Ag. Marina

Loutra

Kratigos

Thermi

Pamfilla

Moria

Gulf of Yera

Pappados

Perama

Ag. Ermougenis

Tarti

Misstegna

Neas Kydonies

Aspropotamos

Ag. Stefanos

Palios

Kilo

Limani

Skala Sikaminia

Sikamia

Pelopi

Kapi

Mantamados

Ag. Paraskevi

Pigi

Paliokipos

Messagros

Skopelos

II Messon

Achladeri

Agiassos

Plomari

Lepetimnos 968m

Eftalou

Mithymna (Molyvos)

Petra

Stipsi

Kalloni

Keramia

Skala
Kalloni

Kalloni Bay

Mt Olympos
(964m / 3162ft)

Megalochori

Ag. Isidoros

Melinta

Paralia Drotas

Vassilika

Skala
Polichnitou

Polichnitos

Vatera

Vrissa

Anaxos

Skoutaros

Skalochori

Vatoussa

Parakila

Nyfida

Lapsarna

Gabbathes

II Antissa

Ag. Ioannis

Chidira

Agra

Apothikes II

Antissa

Mesotopos

Tavari

Eressos

Sigri

Petrified
Forest

Skala Eressou

Megalonissi

N

10km
5 miles

**Lésbos/Mytilíni**

beaches where tourists congregate. But it has a bewitching magic. The people are friendly, easygoing, lyrical and fond of a drink, like Greek Celts, prepared to burst into song and dance when the mood takes them; Lésbos has been a cradle of some of Greece's greatest poets, from Sappho, Alcaeus and Longus (the 3rd century BC author of the romance *Daphnis and Chloe*) to Nobel Laureate Odysséas Elýtis, whose parents belong to one of the island's most important industrial families. On the other hand, it also produced the Barbarossa brothers, red-bearded Greeks turned pirates for the Sultan and the worst terrors the Aegean has ever known. Although becoming more developed, the island is still very much a place where the people go about their business untainted by the great wave of international tourism that has swept over the other islands. Visitors are made welcome but Lésbos—known as the Red Island for its Communist sympathies—still retains its own strong identity.

## Mythology

Even in myth Lésbos is connected with music and poetry. The mytho-historical musician Arion was a son of the island, accredited with the invention of the dithyramb. His talents brought him great wealth—and headaches. After a musical contest in Italy, where he had won all the prizes, the crew of the ship returning him to Lésbos decided to throw him overboard and keep his rich prizes for themselves. Arion was allowed to sing one last tune, after which he dived into the sea. But his swan song had charmed the dolphins, and they saved his life, carrying him safely to shore. The ship's crew were later executed for their treachery. Another myth deals with the great poet Orpheus, who was torn to pieces by orgiastic maenads and followers of Dionysos and thrown into a river of Thrace. His beautiful head floated to Lésbos, where the inhabitants carried it to a cave. There Orpheus' head sang and prophesied so well that people stopped patronizing the Delphic oracle. This loss of business angered Apollo, the god of Delphi, who made a special trip to Lésbos to order Orpheus' head to shut up.

## History

Like many of the islands that hug the coast of Asia Minor, Lésbos both enjoyed the benefits and suffered the penalties of its east-west location as early as the Trojan War. Homer describes the island as an ally of Troy, and it suffered raids by both Odysseus and Achilles. In the 10th century BC Aeolians from Thessaly, led by Penthilos, son of Orestes, colonized the island and the coast of Asia Minor. The Aeolians lacked the vital intellectual curiosity of the Ionians, but by the 6th century BC they made Lésbos a cultural centre, especially under the rule of Pittachos, one of the Seven Sages of ancient Greece. He went far in healing the ancient rivalry between Lésbos' two principal cities, Mytilíni and Míthymna, and promoted trade with Egypt.

Míthymna, having lost the fight for island dominance, got back at Mytilíni when that city decided to leave the Delian league and join Sparta in the Peloponnesian War, in 428 BC. Míthymna tattle-taled to Athens, and according to Thucydides, an order was sent for a general massacre in Mytilíni. However, soon after the ship with the order sailed, the Athenians reconsidered (for once) and sent a second ship countermanding the massacre. It arrived in the nick of time, and the citizens were spared.

In the 4th century BC, Lésbos continued to change hands frequently, its most memorable ruler being Hermeias, who governed both the island and the Troad, or region around Troy, on the mainland. Hermeias was a eunuch and a student at Plato's Academy, and he attempted to rule his principality on the precepts of the *Republic* and the ideal city-state; Aristotle helped him found a branch of the Academy in ancient Assos and while there married Hermeias' niece. Later the island was occupied by Mithridates of Pontus, who was in turn ousted by the Romans in a battle believed to be Julius Caesar's first.

Like Chíos, Lésbos was given by the Byzantine Emperor Michael Palaeológos to the Genoese for their help in restoring the Byzantine Empire (1261). In 1462 Mohammed the Conqueror captured the island, despite the heroic resistance led by Lady Oretta d'Oria, and the island remained in Turkish hands until 1912. Had Massachusetts governor Michael Dukakis, whose parents hailed from the village of Pelópi, defeated George Bush in the American presidential election in1988, you would see his picture everywhere on Lésbos; but he didn't, so you won't.

## Getting There and Around

**By air:** numerous charters from various European cities; at least three daily flights from Athens, daily with Thessaloníki, three times a week with Límnos, twice a week with Chíos. The Olympic office is at Kavétsou 44, ✆ (0251) 28 660; the airport, 8km from Mytilíni town ✆ (0251) 61 234 or 61 212.

**By sea:** daily **ferry** boat from Piraeus and Chíos; three times a week with Kavála and Límnos, at least twice a week with Thessaloníki, Rafína and Ag. Efstrátios, once a week with Sámos, Ikaría, and Pátmos. In the summer, there ia a daily boat to the pleasant little resort of Ayvalik, Turkey (with a possibility of a 3-day trip that includes Bergama–ancient Pergamon, although *see* **Travel** p.2 if you're on a charter flight). In the summer Ilios and Gianmar **hydrofoils** link Kavála, Alexandroúpolis, Límnos, Lésbos, Chíos, Váthy and Pithagório (both in Sámos), Ikaría, and Pátmos. **Excursion boats** run from Mólyvos to Skála Sikaminiás and beaches. **Port authority,** ✆ (0251) 28 888.

**By road: buses** from Mytilíni town depart from two stations: distant villages are served by the station at the south end of the harbour, on the edge of the public gardens, ✆ 28 138/873; buses to the suburbs and closer villages depart from the station in the centre of the harbour.

## Tourist Information

The **EOT** ✆ (0251) 28199 are with the **tourist police,** ✆ 22 776 in the harbour entrance at Mytilíni.There is also an information desk at the airport, and a very helpful **tourist information office** on the main street in Mólyvos ✆ (0253) 71 347/71 069. For Eressos information, ✆ (0253) 53 214; for Plomári, ✆ (0252) 32 535.

## Festivals

**2nd day of Easter** and **15 August**, at Agiássos; **8 May**, Ag. Theológos at Ántissa; 'Week of Prose and Drama' in **May**, at Mytilíni town; **3rd Sunday after Easter**, bull sacrifice at Mandamádos; **26 July**, at Ag. Paraskeví; **15 August**, at Pétra; Ag. Magdalinís at Skópelos; **26 August**, Ag. Ermoláou at Paliókipos; **end of September**, at Plomári. Big carnival celebrations at Agiássos.

# Mytilíni

The capital of Lésbos, **Mytilíni** (ΜΥΤΙΛΗΝΗ) is a large town of magnificent old mansions, impressive public buildings, and beautiful gardens. At the same time it manages to be dusty, higgeldy piggeldy, ungentrified, cacaphonous, and outside of its cavernous dark waterfront ticket agencies and the odd hotel, not the slightest bit bothered with tourism. It has two harbours, one to the south, protected by a long jetty, and the abandoned harbour to the north. In ancient times a canal known as the 'Euripos of the Mytilineans' flowed between the two harbours, dramatically proved when an ancient trireme was found under a street in the middle of town, having been stranded in the accumulation of sand and sediment. The former islet—once the ancient acropolis—became a peninsula, and is crowned by a sprawling **Byzantine-Genoese castle**, or *kástro*, founded by Justinian in the 6th century, who is said to have blinded every prisoner he sent here. In 1373 the Genoese enlarged and repaired it with any available material, including columns from the 600 BC Temple of Apollo hastily crammed in between the stones like a collage. Inside are numerous buildings left by the various occupants of the fortress, one bearing the coat-of-arms of the Paleológos family; there's also a well-preserved Roman cistern and a Turkish *medrese*, or Koranic school, prisons, and a *tekes*, the cell of an Islamic holy man. In the summer, some of the most popular performers in Greece put on concerts in the Kástro; recently, the heartthrob bouzouki singer Dalaras had his trousers ripped off by ardent female fans. There are some picnic tables in the pine groves below and a pay town beach run by EOT at **Tsamákia**.

In the south harbour, arrivals by sea are greeted by a large statue of Freedom. Standing on a traffic island amid the bustle of the waterfront, a prettily restored old white house, formerly belonging to the harbourmaster, now holds the **Museum of Traditional Arts and Crafts** (*open mornings and afternoons*), with a collection of lace, weapons, ceramics, tools, engraved copper pans and costumes. Back from the pier on 8 November Street, the **Archaeology Museum** (*open 8.30–3, closed Mon; adm*) prides itself on reliefs found in a Roman house depicting scenes from the comedies of Menander, a statue of the Lion of Yéra, Greek mosaics found at Chórafa, and Roman mosaics from Ag. Therapón and Páno Skála, and prehistoric finds from Thérma. The cathedral **Ag. Athanásios** (16th–17th century) has a finely carved wooden iconostasis. The lofty dome that dominates the skyline belongs to **Ag. Therápon**, dedicated to a penniless but saintly doctor. Built over a temple of Apollo, or perhaps even the School of Sappho, in the 5th century it became a Christian basilica; the present church dates from 1850. In front of the church the priest runs an interesting **Byzantine Museum** (*open Mon–Sat, 9–1; adm*) stocked with icons from the 13th to 18th centuries, including one by Theophilos (*see* below). The **Municipal Theatre** (1968) sits right on the Municipal Gardens, a delightful green and shady oasis with a scattering of cafés where everyone goes to escape the hurly-burly.

North of the Kástro, the abandoned Old North Port or **Páno Skála** is a neighbourhood in the first stages of reinventing itself. The waterfront can be haunting in its desolatation, a ruined mosque, the **Yení Tzamí**, and its truncated minaret stand forlorn in the centre, with trees growing out of the walls; carpenters and metal workers work in the grimy shops, kids on bikes hurtle around the warren of lanes. Now small antiques shops are moving in, worth a look if you fancy the unusual or bizarre. By the pine forest to the west, at the end of Theátrou Eschílou Street, the Hellenistic **Theatre** was one of the largest of ancient Greece (with a seating capacity of 15,000, now all overgrown with small shrubs); Pompey admired it so much that he used its plans to build his theatre in Rome in 55 BC. Just south are the remains of a Roman aqueduct, and near the cemetery of **Ag. Kyriakí** are some of the walls of ancient Mytilíni.

If Páno Skála is funky, the quarters south of the centre (Sourada and Kióski) are dotted with grand and very un-Greek Victorian or Bavarian neoclassical mansions built by Mytilíni's olive oil and ouzo barons, some beautiful restored, some gone completely to wrack and ruin in between new blocks of flats and shops.

## South of Mytilíni Town

Buses from the waterfront municipal station will take you (infrequently) to **Variá** (BAPEIA), the home town of Theóphilos Hadzimichális (1873–1934), a poor villager who earned his ouzo in exchange for the finest naïve paintings modern Greece has produced. The old school house, set in an ancient olive grove a few minutes' walk from the main road, is now a charmingly rustic **Theophilos Museum** (*open 9–1, 4.30–8, closed Mon; adm*), founded by Tériade (*see* below) in 1964. Its 80 paintings evoke the island's charm far better than any photograph ever could; note the way Theóphilos painted frames around his paintings, since he couldn't afford to buy them, and carefully wrote long descriptions around each scene so there's no mistaking what's going on, whether it is a scene from mythology, the lives of the saints, the Greek War of Independence, current events (Vesuvius' eruption) or a local festival. Like many naïve painters, Theóphilos was fascinated by signs of 'progress'—smokestacks belch smoke over Lésbos, aeroplanes fly over it, steam boats call at its ports. Don't miss the 19th-century studio photos, of Greeks posing in the same splendid costumes that Theóphilos loved to paint; he himself insisted on wearing a *foustanélla*, or traditional Greek kilt, even though it was long out of fashion, hence his nickname Tsoliás (*Évzone*).

A stone's throw away, a modern building houses the **Tériade Museum and Library** (*open Tues–Sun, 9am–2pm, 5pm–8pm, adm*), founded in 1979 by Stratís Eleftheriádes, better known by his adopted French name Tériade. Born in Mytilíni in 1897, Eleftheriádes went to study law in Paris at age 18, where he was drawn the lively, pioneering artistic world of the time. Although he loved to paint, his real interest soon moved on to art theory and criticism, and in 1937 he launched his own art publishing house, *VERVE*, printing both art books and a respected quarterly review of the same name that lasted until 1971. Long fascinated by medieval illuminated manuscripts, Tériade produced a series of 'Grands Livres' with text and lithographs by the greatest artists of the day—Picasso, Miró, Léger, Chagall, Roualt, Giacometti, Henri Laurens, and Juan Gris—handprinted on handmade paper in limited editions, many of which are on display here, along with minor paintings by the same names (although a recent burglary has put a dent in the collection). On the ground floor there's a room with more paintings by Theóphilos. Tériade 'discovered' him in 1930, but not in time to save the artist from dying unknown and penniless.

**Neápolis** just south of Variá has a beach and ruined 5th-century basilica, but the main attraction south of Mytilíni is a lovely pair of beaches at the extreme south tip of the peninsula at **Ag. Ermougénis**, on either side of the eponymous chapel, and with an excellent taverna on the hill. From Skála Loutrón, a ferry crosses the Gulf of Géras, completely encompassed with dense olive groves, for Pérama; at **Loutrá Géras** near by you indulge in a relaxing warm soak in the gentlest of Lésbos' five spas, in pools segregated by sex (*open daily 8–8; nominal adm*).

The cooperative Tourism and Travel Agency near the bus station is able to arrange rooms in 16 island villages, call ✆ 21 329. A room-owners' coop is the Sappho Self-catering with 22 owners on the books offering accommodation.

### Mytilíni Town

One of Mytilíni's neoclassical mansions, a 10min walk south of the harbour, is now run as an atmospheric guesthouse, **Villa 1900**, 24 Vostáni,✆ 23 448 (*A pension; mod*). *Open April–Oct.* Right where the ferry docks (so be prepared for some noise) the **Blue Sea**, ✆ 23 994 (*B; exp*) is modern and comfortable. Also on the waterfront, the **Sappho Hotel** ✆ 28 415 (*C; mod*) is picturesque if noisy, but convenient for the ferries. There are a fair selection of rooms to rent: **Salina's Garden Rooms**, ✆ 42 073, are nice with a lovely garden. The **Cuckoo's Nest**, ✆ 23 901 is also a good, crowded with family knick-knacks (*both inexpensive, with shared bathrooms*).

### Around Mytilíni Town

On Neápolis Beach near the city, there's the **Lesvos Beach**, ✆ 61 531/2 (*mod*), with furnished apartments for lengthy stays. **Heliotrope**, on the beach at Vigla ✆ 42 243, ✉ 44 272 (*C; mod*) is a shiny place with newly built self-catering studios. **Silver Bay Hotel and Bungalows**, 5½ km west of town at Alifantá ✆ 27 977, ✉ 23 458 (*B; exp–mod*) has 22 rooms, 26 bunglows, all with views of the sea or swimming pool. **Hotel Zaira**, at Loútra, ✆91 004 (*B; exp*) is in an old stone converted olive press (complete with a chimney) and air-conditioning and mini-bars to boot. Out in Variá, near the beach and Theophilos museum, try **Filoxenia rooms**, ✆ 61 110 or **Akrotiri Rooms**, ✆ 26 452 (*both inexp*).

Mytilíni is fairly well supplied with restaurants and tavernas, where you can savour the island's famous fresh sardines and giant prawns; local specialities include *kakávia* (fish soup), *astakós magiátikos* (lobster with vegetables), *skoumbri foúrnou* (baked mackeral), stuffed chicken and chicken with walnut sauce *(kotópoulo me karýdia*). A row of small fish tavernas lines the south end of the south harbour; try **To Fanari**, ✆ 21 494, with a wide selection of wines to go with your fish, or one simply called **Psarotaverna**. Above, the rooftop music bar **Kafe Elisse** is popular among young Greeks, who aren't the least inhibited about dancing a *zembékiko* when the mood strikes. **Apolafsi**, ✆ 27 178 is a good bet for *mezédes*, grilled meat and fresh fish.

## North of Mytilíni

There are two roads to the north coast and its resorts. The longer, east coast road passes **Mória**, where more arches of Mytilíni's Roman aqueduct remain intact, and **Thérmi**, a spa with hot iron-rich springs recommended by Galen, and the 12th-century Byzantine church of **Panagía Troulloutí**. Thérmi was inhabited before 3000 BC; its five successive levels of civilization were excavated by Winifred Lamb between 1923 and 1933. Ancient Thérmi had connections with Troy, and during the Trojan War the Achaeans burnt it to the ground; the dates match the traditional dates of the Trojan War (1250 BC). A large Turkish tower stands near the baths, and there are rooms and restaurants and a beach near by.

Leaving the coast, the road north rises to **Mantamádos** (ΜΑΝΤΑΜΑΔΟΣ) a large village of grey stone houses, best known for its 18th-century church **Taxiárchis Michael**, with a miraculous black icon of Archangel Michael that is said to smell of wildflowers. One story has it that pirates killed all the monks except one, who collected the blood-soaked earth and moulded it into an icon; another says St Michael made it himself. As on Évia, parishioners press a coin to the icon; if it sticks, the wish they make will be granted. Mantamádos, like Ag. Paraskeví, ritually sacrifices a bull the third Sunday after Easter, a feast that draws pilgrims from across the island. Further north, **Kápi**, one of several villages circling the 968m Mount Lepétimnos, is the start of one of the new marked hiking trails on Lésbos that takes in some ravishing, luxuriant ravines and gorges. Further north lies the fetching village of **Sikaminiá** and at the end of the road, the little fishing port of **Skála Sikaminiás**, in many ways the quintessence of a Greek island fishing village, renowned on Lésbos for its mild winters. The novelist Stratís Myrivílis was born in Sikaminiá, and next to the Restaurant Sikaminia in Skála, you can see the ancient mulberry tree ('*sikaminiás*' means mulberries) where the author used to sleep in a tree bed. His novel, *The Mermaid Madonna*, was inspired by the chapel of the **Panagía**. Another book, *The Schoolmistress with the Golden Eyes*, was based on a woman from Mólyvos who collaborated with the Germans, went mad and burned her house down. Although you can swim at Skála Sikaminiás, the nearest good beach, a strand of rose-tinted volcanic sand (with tavernas and showers) is at **Tsónia** to the southeast, although you have to go by way of Klió to get there on wheels. There's a footpath through the olive groves from Skála.

## The Inland Route

The buses from Mytilíni to Mólyvos take the shorter, inland road (still, it takes an hour and 45 minutes). Keep your eyes peeled for a tree known as **Ag. Therapís Tzatzaliáris** (St Therapis of the Rags), where the superstitious hang bits of clothing belonging to ill relatives, hoping for a cure. The road passes near **Keramiá**, a village beloved by the Greeks for its fresh springs and century-old trees; further along, it skirts the wide Gulf of Kalloní, where a lovely, intensely cultivated plain is dotted with Lombardy poplars. A signposted road leads to the Ionic **Temple of Mesi**, built in the 4th or 3rd century BC and dedicated to Aphrodite; the foundations and column drums remain. **Kalloní** (ΚΑΛΛΟΝΗ), the large village here, replaces the ancient city of Arisbe; its acropolis was located where the medieval **Kástro** stands today. Arisbe flourished until a few local swains abducted some girls from Míthymna. The girls' kinsfolk perhaps overreacted, destroying Arisbe and enslaving all its people. **Skála Kalloní** is a quiet family resort, its a sandy beach ideal for small children. Famous for its sardines and anchovies, it's also a mecca for birdwatchers with many kinds of waders and visiting storks nesting on the chimney-pots.

West of Kalloní, the 16th-century monastery **Ag. Ignatios Limónos** was used as a secret Greek school under the Turks. Men only are allowed in to see the frescoes in the church, but women can get in for a peek at the petrified wood, folk art and ecclesiastical artefacts in the little museum. From Kalloní a road leads east up to the village of **Ag. Paraskeví**, where a bull is bedecked with flowers and ribbons, paraded through the village, sacrificed and eaten in the three-day feast in late May of Ag. Charálambos in conjunction with horse races (perhaps a relic of the Roman rites of Mithras). Further north, the green Ligona ravine below **Stýpsi**, on the slopes of Mount Lepétimnos, has the remains of 20 water mills and is a favourite venue for organized 'Greek Nights'.

## Míthymna/Mólyvos and the North Coast Resorts

Up at the northernmost tip of the island is **Míthymna** (ΜΗΘΥΜΝΑ), although the locals still call it **Mólyvos** (ΜΟΛΥΒΟΣ), its Venetian name. By whatever name it is the most popular and prettiest town on Lésbos, Mytilíni's arch rival for centuries, although it has now dropped to third town on the island in terms of population. Míthymna was the birthplace of the poets Arion and Longus and was the site of the tomb of the Achaean hero Palamedes, buried here by Achilles and Ajax. Achilles besieged Míthymna, but with little success until the daughter of the King fell in love with him and opened the city gates, a kindness Achilles rewarded by having her slain for betraying her father.

Mólyvos is a symphony of dark grey stone houses with red-tiled roofs, windows with brightly coloured shutters and gardens full of flowers, stacked above the lovely harbour and beach. For years a haunt for artists and the artsy, Mólyvos has lost little of its charm despite package tourism. The steep cobbled lanes of the village centre, known as the **Agorá**, are canopied with vines and scented wistaria and lined with tasteful boutiques, and the taverna terraces perched high on stilts have wonderful views to Turkey. Climbing through the Agorá, you'll pass a small **Archaeology Museum** (*open 8–3, closed Mon*) on the way up to the striking **Genoese Castle**. In 1373, Francesco Gattilusi repaired this old Byzantine fortress on top of the hill, but it fell to Mohammed the Conqueror in 1462. However he didn't get it without a fight. Onetta d'Oria, wife of the Genoese governor, repulsed an earlier Turkish onslaught when she put on her husband's armour and led the people into battle. Note the Turkish inscription in marble over the gate (*open 7.30–5, closed Mon*). The fine long pebble town beach lined with feathery tamarisks has loungers and watersports and gradually becomes shingly sand at the far end, popular with nudists.

East of Mólyvos, **Eftaloú** has a tree-fringed beach, also popular with nudists, an excellent taverna and a bathhouse with very hot thermal springs. A local bus now runs on a regular basis between at Eftaloú and Ánaxos, stopping at Mólyvos, Pétra and Ánaxos and the beaches in between. Pick up a timetable at the Mólyvos tourist office or at Petra Tours.

## Pétra and Ánaxos

**Pétra** means rock, and in particular its sheer rocky pinnacle of a landmark crowned by the church of **Panagía Glykofiloússa** 'Virgin of the Sweet Kiss' (1747) 114 steps up. In spite of the heat, flocks of pilgrims tackle them on on August 15, when they're rewarded with the traditonal dish of *keskesí*, made of meat, grain, onions and spices. The pretty village has winding lanes, Levantine-style wooden balconies, a splendid sweep of beach rapidly being developed and the **Women's Agricultural Cooperative**, which in 1985 launched their pioneering taverna in the square, and where men have been spotted doing the washing up.

For centuries Greek women in farming communities have been virtual slaves to the land, bent double under piles of fodder like beasts of burden, tending the flocks, toiling with the olive harvests and grape-picking. Among the most hard-working and least liberated in Europe, life changed for many in 1985 when the Greek Council for Equality launched Women's Agricultural Co-operatives to enable tourists to visit rural areas and stay with local families. Country women were given the chance to grab some economic indepen-dence, and discover their own abilities—marginalized through sexual oppression—by letting out rooms to foreign guests who wanted holidays with a difference, to 'go native' and share in village life. Women who never dreamed of anything other than a peasant existence suddenly found themselves on training seminars, sorting out the administrative and financial nuts and bolts of their village collectives. Of course they had juggled families, housekeeping and farmwork deftly for years, a strong yet unrecognized force. At last they were not just doing, but seen to be doing, taking control of their lives. As well as providing women with opportunities, the scheme is a move towards Green tourism, offering hospitality in traditional houses and refurbished village settlements in a bid to halt the march of the concrete mixer across the land. The Council seeks to preserve Greek heritage, old customs, handicrafts, and local cuisine, believing that Greece will lose out unless its women play an active part in public life. Since 1985, five other Agro-Tourism coops, four in Northern Greece and on Chíos (*see* p.459) have been founded. All have different specialities; besides the taverna and rooms to rent, the women of Pétra sell their traditional sweets, and fruits in syrup (*glykó*), weavings, crochet and pottery.

Other beaches lie within easy striking distance of Pétra: **Avláki**, 1km west, a small sandy beach with two tavernas and some sea grass, and **Ánaxos**, 3 km away, a fine sandy bay nearly a kilometre long with fabulous views of Mólyvos, a burgeoning although ugly resort in its own right. From Ánaxos a lovely coastal path skirts the dark volcanic shore to the west leads to **Mikrí Tsichránta** and **Megáli Tsichránta**, tiny hamlets, the latter set on a charming little bay. This is oak country, and the larger buildings are oak warehouses; in the next village on the path, **Kaló Limáni**, the warehouses have been converted into homes.

---

*✆ (0253–)*                                                      *Where to Stay and Eating Out*

### Skála Kalloní

**Pasiphae**, in Skála Kalloní, ✆ 23 112, ✉ 23 154 (*B; exp–mod*), is a comfortable hotel with a salt water pool, one of several large, family-orientated complexes on the gulf, or there's the little **Arisbe**, ✆ 22 456 (*inexp*), with adequate rooms. The fish tavernas are cheap and specialize in *avthrini*, rather like fresh sardines.

### Mólyvos/Míthymna

There are plenty of hotels and pensions here, although they tend to be expensive and full. **Molyvos I**, on the beach ✆ 71 496, ✉ 71 640 (*B; exp–mod*) has a nice terrace and sea views, and provides minibus service to its sister hotel, **Molyvos II** at Eftaloú, ✆ 71 497, ✉ 71 640 (*B; exp–mod*), with a children's playground, tennis, volleyball, pool and poolside bar. New hotels are springing up along the Mólyvos-Eftaloú strip, among them the **Sun Rise Hotel**, 2km from Mólyvos, ✆ 71 713/779, ✉ 71 791 (*A; exp*), a hotel and bungalow complex, with a pool, tennis, minibars, colour TVs and a pool, and a minibus service to get you around the coast; and **Panselinos**, ✆ 71 904 (*B; exp–mod*). **Olive Press Pension**, ✆ 71 246 (*B; exp–mod*), a lovely conversion of an olive press right on the town beach, also has a charming café and dining terrace. A string of nice little pensions line the road from the tourist office down to the beach: **Amphitrite**, ✆ 71 741, ✉ 71 744 (*B; mod*) has a nice pool and garden filled with apricot trees; **Adonis**, ✆ 71 866 (*B; mod*) also near the sea, has chalet-style rooms in a garden; **Pension Poseidon**, ✆ 71 570 (*B; inexp*), is pleasant and intimate, with only 6 rooms. **Delfinia**, ✆ 71 315, ✆ 71 524 (*B; exp–mod*) is slightly set aside from the town and near the beach; there's a pool and nice terrace. *Open all year.* By the harbour, the **Sea Horse** pension, ✆ 71 320 (*B; inexp*) with 13 rooms, is handy for watching the fishermen. Up in the village, **Pension Nassos**, ✆ 71 432 (*inexp*) is in an old house, with a nice courtyard, run by Betty Nássos of the popular, long established **Nassos Taverna** in the Agorá. At the beach, the rooms over the **Ramona Taverna**, ✆ 71 291 are adequate and cheap (*only 2500dr a night*), probably because of the disco nearby, although you can almost dive into the sea from your bed; the taverna is a lovely, untouristy lunchtime spot. **Sunset Rooms** nearby are similar, but the rooms are more cramped and noisier, especially if football's on TV or the disco's at full throttle.

In the harbour, **To Xtapodi** is authentic and good for fish, but not overpriced, even though it appears on most of the island's postcards. **Vangelis** is also a good bet and reasonable. **The Captain's Table** has a varied menu and is a bit more expensive; **Faros** at the end is very good as well, serving tasty seafood specialities.The **Mermaid**, on the way down, is famous for its fish and lobster 'with Lesbian sauces'. Up in the Agorá, where prices are inching up and portions are shrinking, **To Pithari** is also good, with its balconies high on stilts and great views (and if you need a room ask Tony or Niki about **Gatos Rooms**, pleasant, in a quiet spot with balconies and a garden). If your tastebuds need a change, try Australian-run **Melinda's**, under the ancient wisteria in the Agorá, with an extensive menu of alternative food, such as chicken curry, vegetarian dishes and unusual salads. **Magistros**, a very smart, pricey new restaurant, cooks up international cuisine and regales diners with live music. The **Eftalou Taverna**, ✆ 71 049 is one of the best on Lésbos, the home of delicious stuffed courgette flowers and other delicacies served in a shady garden, and is neither expensive or touristy. Outside Mólyvos near the Eftaloú road, **T'Alonia Taverna** is excellent and cheap and very popular with the locals; besides traditional Greek dishes it also cooks up breakfast. **Taverna Vafios**, in Vafiós (the village just above Mólyvos) has a wide menu with good local pies and wine from the barrel. For the ultimate view, **To Panorama** beside the castle is worth the strenuous hike up in time for a sundown drink or snack. For a gooey cake and Metaxá down in the Agorá, another **To Panorama** is legendary.

### Pétra

Moderately priced choices here are the **Ilion**, ✆ 41 227 (*C; mod*), **Michaelia**, on the beach, ✆ 41 573, ✆ 22 067 (*C; mod*), and **Pétra**, fronted by a large pergola on the central square, ✆ 41 257 (*C; mod*). *Open all year.* **Theofilos**, ✆ 41 080 (*C; mod*) is the largest and most comfortable. **The Women's Agrotourist Cooperative**, ✆ 41 238, ✆ 41 309 is open all year, and now rents more than a hundred rooms to visitors, and provide wonderful food at their **taverna**. Rooms start at about 3500dr and are immaculately clean and tastefully decorated. You are welcome to join in family life, fishing, and working in the fields if you want. That's the theory anyway! **Niko's** is recommended for seafood (*3000dr*) and **Uncle John** does good grills. The **Chrissi Ammos** in the Plateía has a good range of old Greek favourites.

Besides Mólyvos' more traditional summer entertainments—an open-air cinema, a summer theatre festival with spectacular evening productions of ancient Greek drama, modern works, and music and dancing in the castle, there are yoga courses with an international clientele run by Gisa and Detlev Siebert-Bartling at the **Milelia Seminar House**, ✆/📠 72 030, where trained British and Australian bodyworkers also do therapies. More spiritual feeding awaits at the **Karuna Meditiation Retreat Centre**, 3km outside of town, ✆ 71 486, run by Geórgios (Greek) and Yosoda (Nepalese) Kassipides. **Molyvos Watersports**, ✆ 71 861, offers parasailing, water skiing, and windsurfing lessons. There's **Donkey trekking** with Michaelis, day and evening treks with barbeque supper on the beach, ✆ 71 309; his British wife Liz used to work for Sadlers Wells Royal Ballet.

An amazing nightclub/disco **Gatelousi** (ΓΑΤΕΛΟΥΣΙ) has just opened between Mólyvos and Pétra, resembling a cruise liner with its deck projecting from the rock face. It has a restaurant and the latest music, and a shuttle bus service that runs from 10pm to 5am. Mólyvos also has a wide range of bars, but nothing too raucous. **The Sunset** is OK, while **Ta Molia Club** is a dancing bar and open-air nightclub looking down over the harbour. **The Other Place**, another dancing bar in the harbour, is happily sound-proofed in a very atmospheric old house, with Greek nights and traditional dancing on Thursdays. The **Bouzouki Taverna** down a track on the road to Eftaloú is set in romantic gardens with good Greek musicians and singers and the chance to dance. Expensive drinks, but that's how you pay for the entertainment, and it's well worth a go, as much for the excellent local dancers as the tourists. There's also the **Mólyvos beachside disco**. In Pétra, **The Machine Dancing Bar**, in the former olive factory, has all the press machinery in view.

## Northwest Lésbos and the Petrified Forest

The northwest quarter of Lésbos is volcanic, and until modern times was the home of wild horses—some believe they may be the last link with the horse-breeding culture of the Troad in the Late Bronze Age, mentioned in the *Iliad*. The modern village of **Ántissa** (ΑΝΤΙΣΣΑ) has inherited the name of **ancient Antissa**, up on the north coast: to get there, follow the unpaved road as far **Gavathás**, with a so-so beach and nice taverna, and then walk east on a 1km path skirting the coast. Founded in the Bronze Age, Ántissa was violently joined to Lésbos in an earthquake. It was a musical place; after he was torn to shreds by the Maenads, the most important bits of Orpheus—his prophetic head and lyre—washed up here, perhaps inspiring Terpander, the 'father of Greek music' born in Ántissa *c.* 710 BC and credited with the invention of choric poetry, the seven string lyre and the foundation of Sparta's first music school. The Romans destroyed the town to punish the inhabitants for their support of the Macedonians, and all the meagre remains lie below **Ivriókastro**, 'Castle of the Hebrew' but really a Genoese fort facing the sea. The wonderful quiet beaches with views over to Mólyvos are the main reason for making the trek, and if you're lucky you'll hear the nightingales who are said to have learned to sing so sweetly from Orpheus. A path follows the coast east towards Ánaxos and Ag. Pétra (*see* above).

West of modern Ántissa, the handsome monastery **Ag. Ioánnis Theológos Ipsiloú** is stunningly set on the promontory of a dead volcano. Founded in the 9th century and rebuilt in the

12th, it shares its pinnacle with military buildings and has a museum containing a collection of antique religious paraphernalia. In the courtyard you can examine bits of petrified wood— more than most people usually find in the forest near Sígri. The petrification began, apparently, when the monastery's volcano erupted two million years ago, and was further abetted by the quakes that have rocked this coast over the aeons.

West of the monastery, on the far west end of Lésbos, **Sígri** (ΣΙΓΡΙ) is a delight (though it gets very windy), a bustling village with a charming beach closed off by islets, crystal-clear water, and a Turkish castle (1757) still bristling with cannons. Between **Sígri** and Eressós is Lésbos' **petrified forest** (ΑΠΟΛΙΘΩΜΕΝΟ ΔΑΣΟΣ)—sequoias petrified after being buried in volcanic ash; the colourful remains of the trunks have slowly become visible as the ash erodes. Others are on the offshore islets of Nisiópi (which also has a sandy beach) and Sarakína. Some of the best specimens on Lésbos—a pair of fallen trunks that survived souvenir-hunters—are near Sígri itself, but they entail a long walk in the sun (follow the path to the south marked with yellow rectangles, past the beaches and the valley of the Tsichlíondas river).

The path ends up at the attractive village of **Eressós** (ΕΡΕΣΟΣ), overlooking a lush emerald plain tucked amid the rough volcanic tumult. It inherited the name from ancient Eressos, some fragments of which still stand just east of **Skála Eressoú**, 4km away. Skála is endowed with a magnificent sandy beach, lined with tamarisks and serviced by a lively if modern seaside village, a favourite of package operators, Greek families and gay women. In the square is a bust of famous Eressian Theoprastus (372–287 BC), botanist and author of the *Characters*, a set of essays and moral studies on the picturesque people of his day.

### The Tenth Muse

But the most famous and influential Eressian of them all was Sappho, born in the late 7th century BC; Eressos proudly minted coins bearing her portrait. Little else is known for certain of Sappho's life, besides that she was married and had a daughter, and ran a marriage school for young ladies, to whom she dedicated many of her poems. Like her fellow islander and contempory Alcaeus she wrote what is known as melic poetry, personal and choral lyrics with very complex rhythms (sometimes known as Sapphic stanzas) intended to be sung at private parties before a select company. One of her songs dedicated to a young girl is the first, and rarely surpassed description of passion: 'Equal to the gods seems that man who sits opposite you, close to you, listening to your sweet words and lovely laugh, which has passionately excited the heart in my breast. For whenever I look at you, even for a moment, no voice comes to me, but my tongue is frozen, and at once a delicate fire flickers under my skin. I no longer see anything with my eyes, and my ears are full of strange sounds. Sweat pours down me, and trembling seizes me. I am paler than the grass, and seem to be only a little short of death...' Her influence was so powerful that Plato called her the 'Tenth Muse'. A strong tradition has it that she threw herself from the white cliffs of Lefkáda (*see* p.431) in despair over an unrequited love—for a man.

## Southern Lésbos

Southern Lésbos, between the inland seas of Kalloní and Géras, is dominated by **Mount Olympos** (967m). At last count, there are 19 mountains in the Mediterranean named Olympos. Almost all were peaks sacred to the local sky god, who, in this most syncretic corner of the world, became associated with Zeus; hence, the local sky god's mountain would take the name of Zeus' home. In the shadow of Olympos lies the lovely village of **Agiássos** (ΑΓΙΑΣΣΟΣ) discovered by tourists, but still one of the most interesting on Lésbos, with its red-tile-roofed houses, medieval castle, and church of the **Panagía**. Founded in the 1100s by the Archbishop of Mytilíni, Valérios Konstantínos, this houses an icon of the Virgin, said to have been made by St Luke from mastic and wax and rescued from the iconoclasts. The present church building was constructed in 1812 after a fire destroyed the older structure, and it has one of the most beautiful 19th-century interiors of any Greek church. One of the priests is a master at the *sandoúri*, or hammer dulcimer, and some of the shops sell his recordings, as well as the island's ceramics. Agiássos is famous for its pre-Lent Carnival and special vases. From the Kípos Panagías taverna (up the steps from the bus stop) there's a splendid view of the village and its orchards that produce excellent black plums and walnuts. A lovely marked path leads from Agiássos to Plomári on the coast, passing by way of the ruins of **Palaiókastro**, of uncertain date, and the pleasant village and fountains of **Melaglochóri**.

Chestnut and pine groves cover much of the region, one of Lésbos' prettiest, and the road west to **Polichnítos** (ΠΟΛΙΧΝΙΤΟΣ) is especially lovely. Polichnítos isn't much itself, although it has a thermal spa, oozing out the hottest waters in Europe (91°C) and a beach near the harbour of **Skála Polichnítou**, with many tavernas. Another pretty beach near the mouth of Kallonís Bay, **Nyfída** flies the blue flag of EU righteousness, although it can be windy. South of Polichnítos, **Vríssa** was the home town of Briseis, the captive princess who caused the rift between Achilles and Agamemnon at Troy. Only a wall remains of the ancient Trojan town destroyed in 1180 BC, and a Genoese tower stands to the west of Vríssa; the modern town can only claim a *kafeneíon*. Ruins of a 1st-century BC Doric temple of Dionysos Vrysageni 'Born of the Springs' stand on Cape Ag. Fókas. Ag. Fókas marks the start of Lésbos' longest beach **Vaterá** (BATEPA), 9km of sand, dotted with pensions and tavernas and fragrant sea daffodils. For a lovely excursion, walk up the path marked with yellow circles, beginning at the river Voúrkos to **Áno Stavrós** and **Ampelikó**, a charming village in a ravine under Mount Olympos, with Roman ruins, a castle, pretty church and cafés. Back along the coast to the east, **Plomári** (ΠΛΟΜΑΡΙ) is Lésbos' second city and port, with a population of 10,000 who live in attractive houses decorated with traditional *sachnissinía* (wooden galleries). The centre is as funky as Mytilíni town and it reeks of Greece's favourite aperitif—Kéfi, Veto, Tikelli, and Barbayiánni ouzos all distilled here, and increasingly much of it is drunk by tourists (especially Scandinavian) in situ as Plomári discovers resort life under the palm trees. Plomári has a beach but **Ag. Isídoros** just east has an even better one of pebble and sand. The inland roads are quite attractive and woodsy; from the main road, an unpaved one descends to the very pretty sandy cove at **Tárti**, with a taverna or two. At Pérama, a dingy oil port (olive oil, that is) you'll find a ferry across the Gulf of Géras, 'the Bay of Olives' to Skála Loutrá, near Mytilíni town.

---

## Where to Stay and Eating Out

### Skála Eressoú ✆ (0253–)

Galini, ✆ 53 137 (*B; exp–mod*) has 9 attractive apartments. **Sappho the Eressian**, ✆ 53 233 (*C; mod*) is small with decent rooms. *Open all year.* Others to try are the little **Gorgona**, ✆ 55 301 and **Mascot**, ✆ 53 142 (*E; inexp*). *Open all year.* For dinner, try the **Paralia** in the centre, with wholesome Greek cooking.

### Polichnitos/Skála Polichitou ✆ (0252–)

**Polikentro Taverna**, at the entrance to the village, is the best. At Skála, **Mouragio** and its neighbour serve the freshest fish on the island, sold directly from the dock; the *mezédes* are delicious and there are customers who seem to be there 24 hours a day nursing *karafákis* of ouzo. There are a handful of rooms to let. Down at Nyfída, **Taverna Tsitsanos** is excellent.

### Vaterá ✆ (0252–)

The **Dionysos Club**, one of two discos in Vaterá, has a very good campsite with a swimming pool. On the west end, by Ag. Fokás, are two superb fish tavernas, with gorgeous views; two other well recommended tavernas are **Zouros** and **Chakadakis**. Begin and end your evenings at **Istrion**, where mine hosts, Mario and Dimitri, 'know the island as well as you know what's in your pocket.'

### Plomári ✆ (0252–)

Most everything here is block-booked, but you may find a room in the old centre, or out of season at **Okeanis**, ✆ 32 469 (*C; mod–inexp*), 100m from the sea. *Open all year.* **Sibylla**, ✆ 31 788 (*mod–inexp*) has self-catering studios near the sea. In Ag. Isídoro, try **Ammodes Akti**, ✆ 32 825 (*B pension; inexp*). *Open April–Oct.*

# Límnos (ΛΗΜΝΟΣ)

Límnos hardly fits any Greek island stereotypes. It lies low, with gently rolling hills, a lush green carpet in the spring that becomes crackling yellow-brown in the summer, when water is in short supply. The landscape is dotted with fields of grain, quirky scarecrows and beehives (the island's thyme honey was favoured by the gods) but the main occupation of Límnos has long been military: its magnificent natural harbour near the mouth of the Dardenelles has ensured that the island has always been of strategic importance. It was the holy island of the smithy god Hephaistos (Vulcan), who was worshipped on Mount Móschylus, which in ancient times emitted a fiery jet of asphaltic gas; today Límnos' volcanic past is manifest in its astringent hot springs and the highly sulphuric 'Limnian earth', found near Repanídi, used from ancient times until the Turkish occupation for healing wounds and stomach aches.

## Mythology

The smithy god Hephaistos (in Latin, Vulcan) was so weakly when he was born that his mother Hera hurled him off Mount Olympos. He survived by falling in the sea, near Límnos, where the sea goddesses Thetis and Eurynome cared for him. Years later, when Hera found Thetis wearing a magnificent brooch made by Hephaistos, she had a change of heart about her son, brought him back to Olympos and married him to the lovely Aphrodite. Hephaistos became so fond of his mother that he attempted to rescue her when Zeus hung Hera by the wrists from the sky for rebelling against him. Zeus in his fury picked up the upstart and hurled him again from Mount Olympos and this time he fell smack on Límnos, a fall that crippled Hephaistos for life, despite all the care lavished on him by the islanders. (In the early days of metallurgy, the magic powers of the smith were so valued in many cultures that he was hobbled like a partridge to keep him from running away or joining an enemy).

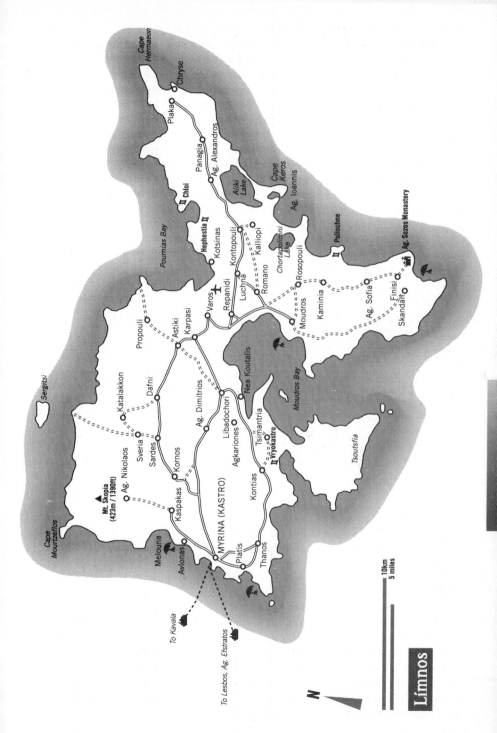

Límnos

483

Hephaistos was so beloved on Límnos that when his wife Aphrodite betrayed him with the war-god Ares, the women of Límnos stopped worshipping her and tossed her cult statue into the sea. Aphrodite retaliated by making their breath and underarms stink (Robert Graves suggests this may have been because they worked with woad, a putrid-smelling blue dye used in the manufacture of tattoo ink). This led the men of Límnos to prefer the company of captive Thracian women to that of their own wives. The smelly women of Límnos were having none of this: they doctored their husbands' wine to make them sleep, slit their throats, threw their bodies into the sea and lived as Amazons, warlike and independent. When Jason and the Argonauts appeared on the horizon, the women would have attacked had not one of them realized that a shipload of Greek sailors was just what they needed to continue the Limnian race. So the Argonauts met only the kindest courtesy, and a son born to Jason, Euneus, went on to become King of Límnos during the Trojan War, supplying the Achaeans with wine.

Another figure associated with Límnos was Philoctetes, the son of Heracles. Philoctetes had inherited his father's famous bow when Heracles was dying in torment from Nessus' poisoned shirt, as Philoctetes was the only one who would light the pyre to put him out of his misery. When Zeus made Heracles an immortal, Hera, who never liked him, took out her pique on his son, sending a poisoned snake after Philoctetes when the Troy-bound Achaeans landed on Límnos. Bitten in the ankle, Philoctetes lingered behind in pain—his comrades could not stomach the stench of his gangrenous wound—and he lived in an island cave, with only his bow for comfort. After the death of Achilles, an oracle declared that Achaeans could only capture Troy with Philoctetes' bow. Odysseus and Neoptolemos, the son of Achilles, tried to take it from him by trickery (in Sophocles' *Philoctetes*) but in the end, according to most accounts, Philoctetes himself took his bow to Troy, where he slew Paris.

## History

Límnos' highly intriguing past also bucks the stereotypes. Homer wrote that the first islanders hailed from Thrace, but Herodotus says they were Tyrrhenian—related to the mysterious, sophisticated Etruscans of Rome and Tuscany. This remarkable claim has been given substance by pre-6th century BC non-Greek inscriptions found on Límnos that show linguistic similarities to the Etruscans, as do some of the ancient burials. The Etruscans themselves claimed to have originally immigrated to Italy from Asia Minor.

But Límnos was exceptional from the start. Excavations at Polióchne have uncovered a settlement of oval huts dating back to 4000 BC—the most advanced Neolithic civilization yet discovered in the Aegean. These precocious ancient Limnians may have been the first to colonize Troy; the dates coincide and there were certainly close cultural contacts between the two into the Mycenaean era.

Whoever they were, the ancient Limnians were not Greek and held on to their autonomy until 490 BC, when Herodotus tells the story in his account of the Persian Wars: years previously the Limnians had captured some Athenian women and had children by them. When these mixed race children they bore began putting on airs, the Limnians were so outraged that they slaughtered them and their mothers, giving rise to the expression 'Limnian deeds', synonymous in Classical times with especially atrocious acts. The gods punished them by making their wives and animals barren. In dismay the Limnians went to Delphi, which said the only cure for it was to promise to surrender their independence to Athens if the Athenians ever sailed to Límnos in one day. It seemed a fair hedge, until Athens conquered some territory near Mount Áthos, and General Miltiades appeared on Límnos to claim what was promised by the Oracle.

The Venetians took Límnos in the 13th century, but it was soon regained by the Byzantines. In 1475 Mohammed the Conqueror sent troops to conquer Límnos, only to be repelled by the heroine Maroúla, who seized her dying father's weapons and shouted a blood-curdling battle cry. In 1478, however, Mohammed came in person and took the island. The Turks held it until 1912; a few years later, Moúdros Bay became the naval base of the Allies in the Gallipoli campaign.

### Getting There and Around

**By air**: twice daily with Athens, once a day with Thessaloníki, 3 times a week with Lésbos. For information, call ✆ (0254) 22 078 or the airport, ✆ 31 204.

**By sea**: 4–5 times a week with Lésbos, Chíos and Kavála; four times a week with Ag. Efstrátios and Rafína, three times a week with Piraeus, twice a week with Thessaloníki. Hydrofoil links run to Lésbos, Sámos, Pátmos and Chíos. In summer, weekly excursion to Mount Áthos. Caiques make the excursion from Mýrina's north harbour, to beaches and the pretty sea caves at Skála. **Port authority**, ✆ 22 225.

**By road**: buses (✆ 22 464) around Límnos are not very frequent. Many villages have only one service a day, so there's no way to get back to Mýrina the same day, hence the town's many taxis and moped and car hire firms. In summer book in advance: try **El Travel**, 10 Christodoulídou St, Mýrina, ✆ (0254) 24 988, ✉ 22 697 or **Petridou Travel**, 18 Kída St, ✆ 22 998, ✉ 22 129 (both also manage rooms and apartments).

### Tourist Police

Regular police in Mýrina, ✆ (0254) 22 200.

### Festivals

At their *panegýria*, the Limnians still do a number of ancient dances, such as the *kechagiátikos*. **23 April**, Ag. Geórgios at Kalliópi—horse-races are run by the locals, who wager goats on the outcome; **21 May**, Ag. Konstantínos at Romanó; **6 August**, Sotíris at Pláka; **15 August**, at Kamínia and Tsimántria; **7–8 September**, Ag. Sózos; **26 October**, Ag. Dimítrios at Ag. Dimítrios.

## Mýrina

Mýrina (MYPINA), the island's port and capital and the only town of any size, is sometimes known as Kástro for its striking landmark, the romantic castle built over the rocky promontory in the midst of the sandy shore. A long main shopping street noodles up from the commercial harbour in the south, lined by houses and shops houses built in the Turkish or Thracian style with little gardens. Although a new boutique or tourist shops opens every year, on the whole Mýrina still very much belongs to the Límnians and offers the distinct if often dusty sights and smells—cologne, freshly ground coffee, and pungent herbs—of old Greece. There isn't much to see inside, but the walk up to the **kástro** offers a fine view over much of the low rolling island

and across the sea to Mount Áthos. The castle foundations date back to Classical times, when it was the site of a temple of Artemis; the walls were built in 1186 by Andronicus Comnenus I, then substantially rebuilt by the Venetians in the 15th century, and the Turks in the late 16th.

The Kástro divides Mýrina's waterfront into two: a 'Turkish' or harbour beach on the south side of town near the commercial port and, to the north, the main long sandy Romaïkos or 'Greek beach', with tavernas and much of Mýrina's night life. The north port is closed by Cape Petassós and the pretty beach of **Aktí Mýrina,** with its exclusive bungalow hotel, on the spot where the Amazons of Límnos hurled their hapless husbands into the sea after slitting their throats. Off Romaïkos Beach, the **Archaeological Museum** (*open 9–3, closed Mon*) has recently been renovated to show off its superb collection, filling ten rooms with finds from Límnos. Upstairs are prehistoric relics from Polióchne, divided into four different periods by colour, beginning with the 'Black' period, from 4000 BC. Downstairs are more recent discoveries from Hephestía, Chloï and Mýrina.

## Around Límnos

There are beaches to try both north and south of Mýrina, where discreet freelance camping is usually tolerated. North of Mýrina the beaches are pebbly but safe for children, especially **Ag. Ioánnis,** again with tavernas, and **Avlónas,** with new bungalow development. The more popular beaches are past the army base to the south of town, on the beautiful buxom bays below **Platís** and **Thános** (a particularly beautiful, golden stretch of sand), both with good tavernas. Others with no facilities at all are scattered here and there all the way to Kontiás: aim for **Nevgatis,** perhaps Límnos' prize beach, a kilometre of fine sand kissed by a crystal, shallow sea. **Kontiás** is the island's liveliest and prettiest red-tiled village, home of Kontiás ouzo. In the summer it fills up with returned immigrants from South Africa and Australia. Just south is an old Mycenaean tower called the **Vryókastro; Evgáti** is the closest beach.

East of Kontiás, **Néa Koutális beach** with pine trees and restaurants is the finest on **Moúdros Bay,** one of biggest natural harbours in the Mediterranean. In April 1915, the Anglo-French fleet launched its ill-fated attack on the Dardanelles from here, a campaign planned partly on Límnos by the then Lord of the Admiralty, Winston Churchill; in 1918, after leaving over 30,000 dead at Gallipoli, an armistice with the Turks was signed on board a ship in the bay where it had all begun. East of gloomy **Moúdros** (ΜΟΥΔΡΟΣ), the island's second largest town and even today dependent on the large military presence, is the immaculately kept lawn of the **British Commonwealth war cemetery;** the 800 graves belong to wounded personnel brought back to Moúdros, only to die in hospital. Límnos' airport (civil and military), is at the north end of the bay, where the island is only a few kilometres wide. Most of the beaches around the bay are on the muddy side

The ancient Limnians preferred living on the island's easterly wings. Northeast of the airport on Pournías Bay, **Kótsinas** was the walled medieval capital of Límnos. A statue of the heroine Maroúla stands here and a spring with good water flows down a long stairway by the church **Zoodóchos Pigí.** There are views across Límnos from the top of the Kótsinas, while below stretches sandy **Kéros Beach,** the most popular on the island with both swimmers and windsurfers, filling the inner curves of Pournías Bay with dunes all the way to **Kontopoúli** (ΚΟΝΤΟΠΟΥΛΙ). Also by the sea here is ancient Mýrina's rival, **Hephestía,** named after the god who crash-landed in the lagoon below. Mostly unexcavated, part of the theatre remains, and you can make out a few ancient houses, bits of the acropolis and tombs.

Across little Tigáni Bay from Hephestía, **Chloï** is better known these days as **Kavírio** after the earliest-known sanctuary of the Underworld deities of fertility, the Cabiri, before the cult was transferred to Samothrace. The Archaic foundations of the sanctuary survive, built around a 6th–7th century BC temple of initiation, dedicated to Thracian Aphrodite, with the bases of 12 Doric columns intact, but not much more besides the usual graceful setting. There is a beach below, and a new bungalow hotel. Under the sanctuary a trail at the end of the ledge leads to the **cave of Philoktétis**, the miserable archer. Another Trojan War site is beyond the large, pleasant village of **Pláka** at the tip of Cape Hermaeon, where a beacon was lit by order of Agamemnon to signal the end of the Trojan War—a signal relayed over the islands back to Mycenae. About 30m off the shore of Pláka are the ruins of **Chryse**, an ancient city submerged by an earthquake. A temple of Apollo was discovered in a reef; on a calm day you can see its marble blocks from a boat. Pláka has good beaches, Ag. Stéfanos and Mandrí, but little in the way of tourist facilities.

**Polióchne** (ΠΟΛΙΟΧΝΗ) the island's most important archaeological site, is signposted from **Kamínia**, on Límnos' southeast wing. Here Italian archaeologists discovered seven different layers of civilization, one on top of the other, dating back to the very dawn of time; the Neolithic town predates the Egyptian dynasties, the Minoan kingdoms of Crete, and even the earliest level of Troy. Walls and houses remain of the next oldest town (2000 BC) which was probably destroyed suddenly by an earthquake but could claim the oldest known baths in the Aegean. The third city dates back to the Copper Age, while the top Bronze Age settlement was contemporary with the Mycenaeans—the Límnos of Homer—dating from 1500 to 100 BC. There's little to see other than the walls of the second city and the foundations of houses, but the explanations in English help bring them to life. Between Polióchne and the abandoned monstery of **Ag. Sózos** to the south stretches the sandy expanse known as 'Sahara of Límnos'. Ag. Sózos overlooks over the sea from a high cliff; on 8 September the whole island flocks here for a huge festival.

Although now mostly devoted to grains and cotton, Límnos was famous since antiquity for its vineyards; Aristotle wrote about the traditional red wine of the island, produced from a very ancient and unique variety of grape that he called Limnio (locally referred to as Kalambáki). No other wine tastes anything like it; wine experts, grasping for a description of its bouquet, have hit upon sage and bay leaf, rather like turkey stuffing. The variety has been transplanted in Chalkidikí, near Mount Áthos, where the Domaine Carrás produces a sophisticated Limnio, blended with 10 per cent Cabernet Sauvignon. White grapes grown on Límnos are usually Moscháto Alexándrias, which yields a dry white wine with a light muscat fragrance.

---

*Límnos ℂ (0254–)*　　　　　　　　　　　　　　**Where to Stay and Eating Out**

Accommodation on Límnos is surprisingly upmarket, and new resort complexes are in the works. Don't arrive in July and August without a booking or a sleeping bag.

### Mýrina

The posh deluxe bungalow complex on the beach in Mýrina is known as the **Akti Myrina**, ℂ 22 681 (*lux*). Recently purchased by Greek shipping magnates, it has its own nightclub, four restaurants, private stretch of beach, swimming pool, tennis courts and its own caique. Wooden chalets house 125 rooms. The complex is famous throughout Greece, for its prices alone: a bungalow starts at 25,000dr, but there are some for double that figure; it has three bars, three restaurants and tennis courts. *Open May–Oct.* **Limnos Village Resort**, 2½km away on Platís beach, ✆ 23 500, ✉ 23 255 (*lux*) is a new fancy bungalow complex, with minibars, with a pool, tennis, child care and hydromassage centre. **Kastro Beach**, ✆ 22 772 (*B; exp*) is large, comfortable, new and central. **Astron**, ✆ 22 233 (*A; exp*), has nicely furnished apartments, and is fairly centrally located. *Open all year.* **Nefeli**, ✆ 23 415, ✉ 24 041 (*B; exp–mod*) just off the Romaíkos Beach, sleeps up to 4, with little kitchens. **Lemnos**, Plateía 28 Octovríou, ✆ 22 153 (*C; mod–inexp*) has rooms; the **Aktaeon**, directly on the sea at 2 Arvanitáki, ✆ 22 258 (*D; inexp*) is even cheaper but you might need ear plugs. **Aphrodite**, ✆ 23 489 (*C; mod*) is pleasant and quiet, just outside the centre; **Sunset**, 2km north at Ag. Ioánnis beach, ✆ 22 116 (*D; mod–inexp*) is even more quiet. There's a selection of tavernas and grills along the waterfront, including a couple of fish tavernas in the north harbour; **Glaros** is recommended. The **no-name taverna** where the boat docks is undoubtedly the best deal in town, a full dinner costing around 1500dr, although **O Platanos**, by a pair of massive plane trees at the top of the main shopping street, comes a close second.

### Kontiás/Tsimántria

There are about 20 rooms to rent in Kontiás, and good tavernas; in Tsimántria, **Nasos Kotsinadelis' Taverna** is famous for its chicken grilled over coals. Mr Kotsinadélis is the island's foremost lyra player, and on 15 August serenades his customers.

### Moúdros

**To Kyma**, ✆ 71 333 (*B; exp*) is a tranquil place to stay, with a restaurant and bar, open all year; for something cheaper, **Filoxenia** (*C; mod*) has studios.

### Kaviria

**Kaviria Palace**, ✆ 41 582, ✉ 41 581 (*A; lux*) is the newest luxury bungalow complex on the island, built with local materials; a pool, library, sauna, jacuzzi, pro tennis coaches, and Greek, French cuisine and lots of fish.

## Ag. Efstrátios (ΑΓ. ΕΥΣΤΡΑΤΙΟΣ)

The remote, partly dry, partly green little volcanic triangle of **Ag. Efstrátios** (locally known as **t'Aïstratí**) lies 21 nautical miles southwest of its big sister Límnos. It is linked by ferry four times a week from Kavála, Límnos and Rafína, and once a week from Lésbos and Chíos; the port is too shallow for the big boats, so be prepared to transfer into caiques. Rich in minerals (including petroleum), the islet has been inhabited from Mycenaean times, and on the north coast stand the walls and ruins of the ancient settlement, which endured into the Middle Ages. In 1967 an earthquake wreaked havoc on Ag. Efstrátios' port and major village, and now nearly all of the island's 250 inhabitants lives next to a wide, sandy beach in a rather dreary village of concrete huts thrown up by the junta after the disaster; as on Alónysos, the inhabitants weren't allowed to repair their homes. The sea—the surrounding waters are transparent and rich in fish—brings in most of the income. Besides the village beach, which is really quite pleasant, there are several others scattered about that are perfect for playing Robinson Crusoe, but you will need to hike at least an hour or hire a caique to reach them; for real isolation try the long sandy beach at Ag. Efstrátios' baby islet, **Vélia**. Between 1936 and 1962 Ag. Efstrátios played Alcatraz to scores of Greek Communists. Even today it receives very few visitors, but if you want to stay there's a small, basic guesthouse with 12 rooms ✆ (0254) 93 202, tolerated free camping on any beach, a small shop or two and two tavernas with very limited menus.

# Sámos (ΣΑΜΟΣ)

*A ship goes away from Chíos/With two small rowing boats*
*She came to Sámos and moored there/And sat and reckoned*
*How much is a kiss worth/In the East, in the West?*
*A married woman's, four/A widow's, fourteen.*
*An unmarried girl's is cheaper/You take it with a joke.*
*But if it touches your heart/Oh, then, Christ and the Virgin, help!*

–traditional song from Chíos

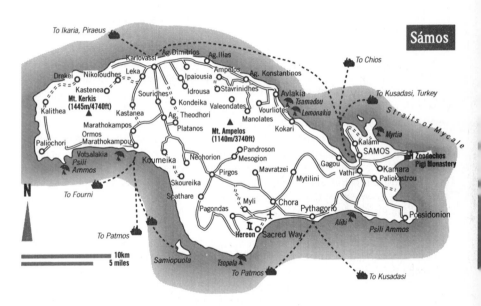

Famous for its wine, women and ships, Sámos, the 'Isle of the Blest', has historically and economically always been one of the most important islands in Greece, and since the 1980s it has become one of the most touristy as well. Pine forests, olive groves and vineyards cover its emerald hills, so fertile that Menander wrote in the 4th century BC 'here even the hens give milk'. The countryside is lovely, gentle, and bucolic rather than spectacular and dramatic; the coast is indented with numerous sandy coves, and two mighty mountains furnish dramatic background scenery: central Mount Ámpelos (1140m) and in the west, Mount Kérkis, a looming 1445m, both a continuation of the mainland chain that Sámos broke away from in a cataclysm millennia ago. Two famous couples, Zeus and Hera and Anthony and Cleopatra, chose Sámos for romantic dallying, and to this day it seems to have the power of awakening romance in second or third honeymoons, mostly now in the form of northern European couples on self-catering packages (a far cry from Cleopatra's gilded barge, pet leopards, perfume baths and dance troupes, but there you go). On the other hand, it is one of the most expensive islands, and to arrive without a hotel reservation in the summer is tantamount to sleeping on the beach.

## History

By 3000 BC Sámos was inhabited, first by the mysterious Pelasgians and later by the Carians from the mainland opposite. Its name comes from *sama*, Phoenician for high place (similar to Samothráki and Sámi in Kefaloniá; in myth the founder of the latter city was the first to colonize Sámos). The worship of the goddess Hera began early by the river Imbroussas; her first shrine, made of wood was built by the Argonaut King Angaios in the 13th century BC. The Ionians made their appearance in the 11th century, and by the Archaic period wine-exporting Sámos was one of the most prosperous states in the Aegean.

In 670 BC, the island became a democracy, which unleashed its creative juices, especially in the invention of a long, swift warship known as the *sámaina*, in which they fearlessly sailed the open seas and frequently down to Egypt; in 650 BC a Samian captain named Kolaios became the first known man to sail through the Straits of Gibraltar (the Phoenicians most certainly did, but they never told anyone about it). Pythagoras, the most famous Samian of them all, lived during the rule of the tyrant Polykrates, who came to power in 550 BC and was probably the most powerful man in Greece at the time. He became the first to rule the Aegean since Crete's King Minos, thanks to his fleet, incredibly large for the day, consisting of 150 *samainae*, which he used to extract tolls and protection money; he was also the first, along with Corinth, to introduce triremes into his navy. Even more lastingly, Polykrates was the first tyrant to patronize the arts and poetry. He oversaw the three greatest public works of the day: the building of the great temple of Hera, the creation of the massive harbour mole, and the digging of the Efplinion tunnel through a mountain to bring water to his capital, modern Pythagório. Under their tyrant, the Samians swanned around in the finest clothes and jewels and knocked down their palastra or gym to built dens of pleasure known as the 'Samian Flowers' and the 'Samian Hotbed'. Polykrates' great good fortune worried his friend and ally, King Amassis of Egypt, who warned he would attract the envy of the gods unless he brought at least a small disaster or deprivation upon himself. Polykrates considered, and threw his favourite ring into the sea, thinking it would placate Fate. Three days later a fisherman caught a fish with the ring in its stomach, and returned it to Polykrates. Amassis recognized this as an evil omen, and broke off their friendship to spare himself grief later on. To ward off doom Polykrates paid a thousand archers to surround him. But they couldn't save him from his own greed; lured by the promise of treasure by Cyrus' satrap Orsitis, he was crucified on a bluff overlooking his beloved Sámos.

A constant through all of ancient history is Sámos' lifelong feud with its chief Ionian rival on the mainland, Milétus. Whatever Milétus did, Sámos did the opposite, siding in turn with the Persians, the Spartans and the Athenians in the great disputes of the age. During their second invasion of Greece, the Persians occupied Sámos and kept their fleet at the island. During the battle of Plataea (479 BC) the Greeks attacked the Persian fleet at the Strait of Mykále, soundly defeating them—helped by the defection of the Samians in the Persian navy. The battle of Mykale was one of the most crucial in the war, and once and for all eliminated Persian threats from the sea. After the battle, Sámos allied herself with Athens, and under that city's influence became a democracy (again); when Miletus sided with Athens, Sámos as usual didn't and even defeated the Athenian fleet under Pericles in 441. The leader of the fleet was Melissus, who was also an important pre-Socratic philosopher. Melissus believed in the essential unity of creation, which was spatially and temporally infinite, and only appeared to move. In the next century Sámos produced the more practical mathematician Aristarchus (310–230 BC), the first in history to put the sun in the centre of the universe, and declare that in spite of the evidence of the eyes it was the earth that moved around the sun.

In 129 BC Rome incorporated Sámos into her Asia Province, and Augustus often visited the island in the winter, granting it many privileges, despite the fact that his enemies, Antony and Cleopatra, courted there for a short time; according to Plutarch, it was on Sámos that Anthony became so infatuated that he threw away the world for a woman.

After the sack of Constantinople Sámos was captured by the Venetians and Genoese. In 1453, when the Genoese handed the island over to the Turks, the inhabitants took refuge en masse on Chíos, leaving their island all but deserted for 80 years. With promises of privileges and a certain amount of autonomy, the Ottomans repopulated the island with Greeks from mainland Greece, Asia Minor and other islands—names reflected in many of Sámos' village names (i.e. Mytilíni, Marathókambos, Pírgos). Over the centuries, however, the Ottomans' taxes became insupportable, and the Samians joined the revolution. They made good their old repuation at sea by defeating the Turks at a second battle of Mykále in 1824. Although the Great Powers excluded Sámos from Greece in 1830, it was granted semi-independence under the 'hegemony of the prince of Sámos', a Christian governor appointed by the Sultan. In 1912, the Samian National Assembly took advantage of Turkey's defeats in the Balkan Wars to declare unity with Greece, under the leadership of Themostiklés Sophoúlis, who later became Prime Minister.

---

### Getting There and Around

**By air**: five daily flights from Athens; for airport info call ✆ (0273) 61 222. There are too many charters from northern Europe, rising to 20 a day in July and August. The airport is 17km from Vathí, but there's no longer any Olympic airway shuttle, leaving only taxis.

**By sea**: Most **ferries** call at Sámos (✆ 27 318) and Karlóvassi (✆ 32 343) daily to Piraeus and Ikaría, 4 times a week to Chíos, Lésbos, Páros, and Náxos, once a week to Mýkonos and Sýros. Karlóvassi also has a couple of caiques a week to Foúrni. Frequent connections from Pythagório (✆ 61 225) to Pátmos, Kos, Léros, Lipsí and Kálymnos, and a pricey **excursion boat** daily in season to Pátmos, and 2 or 3 boats a week to Foúrni and Ikaría. Throughout the year one or two ships sail from Sámos town to Kuşadasi, Turkey (close to the magnificent ancient city of Ephesus); prices to Kuşadasi are exorbitant as both sides hike up the taxes and fees, skim off the profits and blame the other side; at the time of writing, one-way is 12,000dr, return 16,000dr, and more if you plump for a guided tour of Ephesus. Beware the 'overnight in Turkey' restriction if you're on a charter. In season **hydrofoils** run between Pythagório, Pátmos and Kos. From Órmos Marathókambos there are excursions to Foúrni, Pátmos and the islet Samiopoúla. **Port authority**, ✆ (0273) 27890.

**By road**: From the station (a 10-min walk from the dock at Sámos, on the same street as Europe Rent a Car ✆ 27 262), **buses** run 10 times a day to Ag. Konstantínos and

Karlóvassi; 10 to Kokkári and Tsamadoú, 18 times to Pythagório; 5 to Heréon; and 2 or 3 times to Marathókambos, Votsalákia, Pírgos, Chóra, Mytilíni, and Psilí Ámmos.

## Tourist Information

**EOT**, by the lion at 4 25th Martíou Street, Sámos ☎ 28 582/530, but it's open only from 11 to 2 on weekdays, leaving the job to the various travel offices that line the waterfront. Alexis at **Samos Tours** is especially helpful (just opposite the dock in Vathí), ☎ 27 715, 🖷 28 915. **Tourist police**, Sámos, ☎ 27 333. Pythagório, ☎ 61 389, Kokkári, ☎ 92 333, Karlóvassi, ☎ 31 444.

## Festivals

**20 July**, Profítis Ilías celebrated in many villages throughout the island. **26 July**, Ag. Paraskeví at Vathí; **27 July**, Ag. Panteleímonos at Kokkári (one of the most popular); The **Sámos Wine Festival** takes place every year in August and dancing groups perform dances from various parts of Greece. **6 August**, Celebration of the Revolution, Sámos; **29 August**, Ag. Ioánnis at Pythagório; **8 September** at Vrontiáni Monastery; **21 November**, Panagía Spilianí by Pythagório.

## Sámos/Vathí

Names on Sámos are a tad confusing. In ancient times the city of Sámos was what is now Pythagório. The present capital and main port of the island, set in a sweeping amphitheatre of green hills, inherited the name Sámos a few decades ago, although when the autonomous 'Hegemony' moved here from Chóra in 1834 it was called Vathí (ΒΑΘΥ), and still is by most Samians, although this name now only applies officially to the upper, older town at the 'deep end' of the city's magnificent harbour. If the immediate port area of Sámos town seems permeated with unfulfilled expectations (the abandoned hulk of the old Xenia Hotel on the waterfront doesn't help), the higgledy piggledy, often arcaded lanes of old upper or Áno Vathí reek with atmosphere, linked with white and pastel houses covered with weathered tile roofs.

Most of the life down in Sámos town is concentrated in the pedestrianized back streets and **Plateía Pythagório**, where café dawdlers are shaded by palms and guarded by a stone lion, perhaps because Pythagorians believed that lions were the highest animals for a transmigrating soul to lodge in (the laurel was the pick of the plants). The small **public garden** in the centre of town offers shelter from the afternoon sun, complete with a little trendy café beside a trickling fountain. Diagonal to the garden, the fascinating finds from the island are displayed in the two buildings of the **Archaeology Museum** (*open 8.30–3, closed Mon; adm free*). Top billing goes to the set of stylish and elegant Archaic statues in drapery folded as finely as pinstripes, a prelude to the majestic, finely sculpted, 7th-century BC *Kouros* from the temple of Hera, at 5 metres one of the largest such statues ever found (they had to lower the floor to fit it in, and when the head was found, they had to raise the roof), with features as serene as a Buddha. There are geometric vases and prehistoric tools, and masses of ex-votos from the temple of Hera, dating back to little terracotta figurines from the 10th century BC; others were manufactured from as far away as Cyprus, Egypt, Etruria and Andalucía. Many are quite costly, testifying to Hera's prestige: even bits of wooden furniture have been found, along with splendid bronzes and a magnificent array of bronze griffon heads (a Mesopotamian calendar beast introduced to the west through Sámos in the 8th century BC), most of them originally attached to bronze cauldrons. Another museum, the **Byzantine Religious Museum**, in the Bishop's office at 28th Oktroviou Street (*open Mon, Wed and Fri 9–1*) contains reliquaries, vestments, manuscripts, incense burners and the 'Chandelier of the Dragons'.

The rather unpromising road north of the harbour leads to the so-so town beach, **Gággou**, near the fashionable suburb of **Kalámi**; the road continues, getting narrower and narrower, with a good taverna at the end in **Ag. Paraskeví**. Short excursions east of town offer views over the beautiful, narrow Strait of Mykále and the rugged coast of Turkey, where velvet-green slopes hem in the turquoise sea; the monastery **Zoodóchos Pigí** (1756), set on the cliffs over the fishing hamlet of **Mourtiá**, is a popular vantage point. If you want to get closer, roads from Paliókastro south of Vathí descend to the beaches at **Kervelí** (pretty but stony) **Possidónion** (sheltered and shingly) and a much better, sandy, and very busy **Psilí Ámmos**, with shade and three tavernas, 10km from Sámos town and a hop and skip away from Turkey.

---

*Sámos ☎ (0273–)*　　　　　　　　　　**Where to Stay and Eating Out**

Beware that nearly every hotel with any pretensions to comfort is mercilessly block-booked in season, and independent travellers may as well throw themselves on the tender mercies of the travel offices lining the port. Out of season, you may get a room at the clutch of new, upmarket hotels at Kalámi, among them **Kirkis Beach**, ☎ 23 330 (*B; exp*) with a pool, or at the stylish **Aeolis**, near the port at Them. Sofouli 33, ☎ 28 904, (*B; exp*) where comfortable rooms face a quiet street. **Samos**, ☎ 28 377 (*C; mod*) is modern and faces the huge natural harbour, a few steps from the dock. Other moderate choice are little **Hotel Boni**, a few streets above the port at Katsoúni ☎ 28 790 (*D; mod*), *open all year*, and the nearby **Hotel Helen**, Grammoú 2, ☎ 28 215 (*C; mod*). The charming **Ionia Pension** just in from the sea at 5 Kalómiri, run by the friendly Evagelía Zavitsánou, ☎ 28 782 (*inexp*), is a solid choice; or try **Graceland** (believe it or not), Grammoú 14, ☎ 27 504 (*E; inexp*). Restaurants and bars come and go with more than usual rapidity here; try **Taverna Petrino** up the steps behind the dock, with a varied menu of homecooked dishes on the order of *stifádo*, *glouvétsi*, roast lamb or swordfish, usually for under 3000dr; **Plaka**, ☎ 23 725 is another big favourite. Beware the tacky places on the waterfront.

## Pythagório

Pythagório (ΠΥΘΑΓΟΡΕΙΟ) on the southeast coast has for the past two decades been the island's most popular resort, although as it's climbed upmarket over the last two decades it's lost some of its old pith—not only is the 'Samian Hotbed' long gone, but so are the Greeks, most of whom now commute to work in the resort from Chóra and the other inland villages. When it was the tyrant Polykrates' capital, its population reached 300,000; by the 20th century it was reduced to a little fishing called Tigáni, or frying pan, not because of its sizzling summer heat but because of the shape of the Polykrates' jetty. In 1955 the town was renamed to honour Sámos' most famous son, synonymous with the right-angled triangle theorem that put his name on the lips of every schoolchild in the world.

## Pythagoras

Pythagoras is a rather murky character who never wrote anything down himself, and is only known through the writing of his followers and enemies. Born on Sámos some time around 580 BC, he is known to have visited Egypt and Babylonia, either before or after his quarrel with Polykrates that sent him to Croton in southern Italy. In Croton he and his followers formed a brotherhood 'of the best' that governed the city for 20 years, before it revolted. This brotherhood was a secret society, similar to Freemasonry, that spread throughout the Greek world; brothers recognized each other by their symbol—the pentangle, or five-pointed star. But politics was hardly the main thrust of Pythagorean belief and philosophy, which was to have considerable influence, especially on Plato. On the religious level, Pythagoras believed the soul was immortal, and after death it transmigrated not only into new humans but into plants and animals, and that by purifying the soul one might improve it, and perhaps escape the need for reincarnations. There were important prohibitions on eating meat (that chicken might be your grandmother) and, more mysteriously, against eating beans (because of unharmonious flatulence, or perhaps because of favism, a sometimes deadly reaction many Mediterranean people have to fava beans and bean dust).

Besides purifying the soul, Pythagoras and his followers believed in studying the *kosmos*, a word meaning arrangement and ornamentation (hence our 'cosmetics') that Pythagoras was the first to apply to the universe. He believed the order of the cosmos was based on the connections of its various parts, which he called harmonia, and that harmonia was based on numbers. Pythagoras was the first to discover that the fundamentals of music could be expressed mathematically by ratios and the tuning of the seven-string lyre, and he extended the harmonia he found there to the planets through 'the music of the spheres,' and to the Golden Mean, proportions in beauty which were to give classical architecture and sculpture their perfect harmony. Pythagoreans were the first to postulate theorems in number and geometry, applying the 'proofs' used by the earliest philosophers of Miletus to the subject of mathematics. Although the Pythagoreans' belief that everything could be defined by number took them down some wild and woolly paths, Pythagoras' key idea that the study of the order of the Cosmos and its harmony would help to eliminate the disorder in our souls doesn't sound like such a bad idea even today.

Excavations of the city itself, begun in 1985, occasionally turn Pythagório into a minefield of trenches. Pythagoras, however, didn't leave as much behind in his home town as Polykrates' chief engineer, Efplinos, designer of the 360m **ancient harbour mole**,which Herodotus declared was one of the three great wonders of ancient Greece; it now supports a new harbour wall, where white yachts swish in and out in place of sharp-bowed *samainae*. The **long walls** that surrounded ancient Pythagório were originally 6500m long and stretched all the way to Cape Foniás, and bristled with towers and gates; partly destroyed by Lysander when the Spartans took Sámos during the Peloponnesian War, bits and pieces remain scattered along the edge of town. Lykúrgos Logothétis, a hero of the 1821 revolution, built the castle by the town—mostly at the expense of the Temple of Hera. Pythagório's sand and pebble **beach** begins at Logothétis' castle and extends off and on several kilometres to the west. The great victory at sea over the Turks in 1824 is commemorated by a plaque ('Christ Saved Samos the

6 August 1824') in the pretty white church of the **Metamórfosis**. There's a small **archaeological museum** in the Community Hall (*open 8.30–3, closed Mon*) which houses finds from the area.

Little remains of the **Roman Baths** west of town, or the ancient **theatre**, but don't miss the extraordinary **Efplinion Tunnel** (*open Mon, Thurs, Sat 10am–12noon*) another half a kilometre up the road. Polykrates wanted his aqueduct kept secret, to prevent an enemy cutting off the water. Under Efplinos two crews of slaves started digging through the solid rock on either side of Mount Kástri and, thanks to his amazingly precise calculations, met on the same level, only a few inches off total Channel Tunnel perfection. Nearly 1000m long, the tunnel's earthenware pipes kept the baths full in Pythagório for 1000 years or so—until the 6th century AD, after which the tunnel was forgotten until it was accidentally rediscovered in the late 19th century. The lamps and tools of the workmen were found in the parallel maintainance tunnel. Recently the tunnel has been electrically lit, so it no longer seems quite as old and mysterious as it used to; visitors are allowed in the first 300m, but the middle of the tunnel has collapsed. Another road from the ancient theatre leads up to the cave where the sybil Phyto prophesied a one and true god. Along with her sister sybils, Phyto would provide an important link between antiquity and Christianity; appropriately the cave shelters a church, **Panagía Spilianí**, last built in 1836, near a tiny monastery in the cypresses.

## The Temple of Hera and Heréon

From Pythagório, the marble-paved **Sacred Way** (now 90 per cent under the profane airport road and runway) led the faithful 8km west past an estimated 2000 statues, tombs and elaborate monuments to the **Temple of Hera** (*open 8.30–3, closed Mon; adm*). The site was already sacred to 'cow-eyed' Hera back in the Bronze Age. She was the first of all the gods to have temples erected in her honour; two temples of mud, wood and bricks had already been built here by 718 BC, when an architect named Roikos built what is considered to have been the first of all true Greek temples (i.e. a stone building completely surrounded by with a colonnaded peristyle). When this was destroyed by Cyrus' satrap Orsitis in his war on Sámos, Polykrates, who never did anything halfway, decided to replace it in a big way. Shortlisted as one of the Seven Wonders of the Ancient World, Polykrates' Great Temple was, after the temple of Artemis at Ephesus and the Temple of Zeus in Akragas (Agrigento), the third largest temple ever built by the Greeks (approximately 354 by 165ft or 108 by 52m); today only a single column of its original 133 remains intact as a sole witness to its extraordinary size and height, even if looks like a wobbly stack of breath mints.

### Mythology

Zeus had to use cunning to seduce an uninterested Hera (perhaps because he was her brother), and they spent a 300-year-long wedding night on Sámos 'concealed from their dear parents'. Bathing in the Imbrassos perpetually renewed Hera's virginity; she was pre-eminently the goddess of marriage, worshipped as three aspects: The Girl, The Fulfilled and The Separated, but never in an erotic fashion or as a mother (though often a wicked stepmother); she was always the Great Goddess, ambivalent about her relationship with her upstart consort. Although her temple was filled with great works of art, the holy of holies was a plank of wood crudely painted with the goddess's features, believed to have fallen from heaven, too sacred to be touched; the priests tied it with twigs of osier, the willow sacred to Hera, and carried it thus. Twice a year grand celebrations took place at the temple: the Heraia, in honour of her marriage, and the Tonea, recalling the attempt of the Argives to snatch the sacred wooden plank for their own Temple of Hera, only to be thwarted by the goddess, who refused to let their ship sail away until they returned it. By her altar were her symbols: two peacocks and an osier.

The temple was destroyed in the 3rd century AD by raiding Herulians; earthquakes in the 4th and 5th centuries and builders looking for ready-cut stone finished it off. Only the base of the massive **altar**, **a Mycenaean wall**, other small temples a **tribute** sent by Cicero and the apse of a Christian basilica have survived. Some of the stone went into the **Sarakíni Castle**, built by a Patmian naval officer of the same name in 1560, appointed by the Sultan to govern Sámos.

The nearby seaside village of **Heréon** (HPAIO), a dusty backwater a decade ago, now has its portion of hotels, apartments and bars on a short stretch of beach that gets too crowded in the summer; jets pouncing on the nearby airport add to the noise. To get away from it all, check out caiques running south to the remote sandy beach of **Tsopela**. If you have your own transport, inland villages offer some respite as well: **Chóra**, west of Pythagório, was made the capital of Sámos by the aforementioned Sarakíni and kept its status until 1855, although it's still a lively little place with good tavernas. To the north the road passes through a steep valley to the rather sprawling village of **Mýtilíni**, where animal fossils dating back 15 million years—believed to have been washed into a deposit by the Meander River, before Sámos broke free from Turkey—have been gathered in Greece's only **Palaeontology Museum** in the Town Hall (*open weekdays 9–12 and 5–8*). Sámos had a reputation for fierce monsters in mythology; one story has it that the island broke off from Turkey as if it were glass when the monsters let loose a particular high-pitched shriek. The museum's prize exhibit, among the skulls and teeth of prehistoric hippopotomi and rhinoceri, is a 13-million-year-old fossilized horse brain.

Above Heréon, lemon groves surround **Mýli**, the source of the Imvrassos, where an important Mycenaean tomb was accidently found near the village school. From equally well-watered **Pagóndas** ('the land of springs') the road circles around through Sámos' finest untamed, majestic south coast scenery en route to **Spatharáioi** (7½km) and **Pírgos** (another 6km), a pretty mountain village in the pines, founded by settlers from the city of the same name in the Peloponnese. Down in a ravine below Pírgos, **Koútsi** is the kind of place preferred by the ancient nymphs, a grove of venerable plane trees, clear waters and cool mountain air and something the nymphs didn't have—a good taverna, perfect on a hot, lazy afternoon. Unfortunately tour operators know about it too, so you may want to to get there early or late for lunch.

From Pírgos you can circle around back towards Pythagório without retracing your steps, going by way of **Koumaradáioi** where a track leads up to the **Moní Megális Panagías**, founded in 1586; the walls of the monastery encompass one of the island's most beautiful churches, with good icons and frescoes inside. One of the monks who built it also founded **Timíou Stavroú Monastery** (1592) to the east, after a dream he had of a buried icon of the Holy Cross; the icon was duly found, and has been completely plated with silver and ex-votos in gratitude for its miraculous cures. On Holy Wednesday people gather here from all over Sámos to watch the monks re-enact the washing of the Apostles' feet. North of the monastery, ceramics and pottery are made at **Mavratzeí**, which specializes in the goofy 'Pythagorean Cup'; the main road heads back to Chóra.

## Pythagório

If not in the trendy little town, the hotels of Pythagório are clustered out of most camera angles but in easy walking distance around the beach at Potokáki; **Regina Travel**, ✆ 61 323, ✉ 61 341, has a list of villas and rooms in private houses. The big and luxurious **Doryssa Bay Hotel**, ✆ 61 360, ✉ 61 463 (*A; exp*) with rooms in an older hotel or spread through a perfect asymmetrical village of air-conditioned bungalows, has a pool, tennis courts, waterskiing and even a minigolf course for the small fry. The newer, and much smaller **Glycoriza Beach**, ✆ 61 321 (*C; exp*) is another good choice by the sea or there's the **Pythagoras**, ✆ 61 373 (*C; exp*), a fine place in town. Pythagório is packed with small up-scale pensions that are also inevitably full: **Kastelli**, ✆ 61 728 (*C; exp*), 100m from the sea, with views, breakfast and air-conditioning, is a good bet if you can bag a room. Little **Alexandra** at 11 Metamorfósseos, ✆ 61 193 (*D; mod*) is one of the better bargains. The waterfront is one uninterrupted line of tavernas and cafés that charge well over the odds for what you get. Check out the menus before you sit down, and consider taking a taxi up to Chóra for some good hearty fills. The taverna in Pagóntas has 'Greek Nights' every Saturday night.

## The North Coast: Beaches and Vineyards

On the great bay just opposite Sámos town, **Malagári**, immersed in pines, is the headquarters of the Union of Sámos Wine Producing Cooperatives, where you can see the handsome stone warehouses known as *tavérnes*, where wines are aged in great oaken barrels. Ten kilometres west of Vathí, pretty **Kokkári** (KOKKAPI), was once a whitewashed fishing village that owes its funny name in Greek, 'onion bulbs', from its old speciality, although processing a posey kind of tourism has replaced most of the onions. Still, the setting is wonderful, the houses spread over two narrow headlands. It's a testimony to the charm of the place that the nearest beaches are quite a walk or a short drive away and tend to be exposed: **Lemonákia** is a 20-minute walk away and the more beautiful **Tsamadoú**, 2km away (accessible only on foot), is a lovely crescent beach of multi-coloured pebbles. **Avlákia**, a smaller, delightfully low-key resort further west, has another pebble beach at **Tsaboú**. It is a good base for exploring the ravishing green hinterland, where cypresses and pines rise up like towers along the majestic slopes of Mount Ámpelos, 1153m; its name, from the 1st century BC, means 'Mount Vineyard'.

### 'Fill High the Bowl with Samian Wine...'

The north-facing mountain villages of Vourliótes, Manolátes and Stafrinídes are the top wine-growing villages on Sámos, where one famous variety of grape, Moscháto Sámou, has reigned for the last two thousand years or so. The old vines are thickly planted on small anti-erosion terraces called *pezoúles* from 150 to 800m above sea level and, like all quality dessert wines, have an extremely low yield. After years of neglect in the Middle Ages, Samian wine began its comeback under the Greek settlers brought over by the Ottomans in the late 16th century. By the 18th century it was imported in large quantities to Sweden and even France, and the Catholic Church gave Sámos a concession to provide wine for Mass, something it still does to a degree in Austria, Switzerland and Belgium. All Samian wine has been sold through the cooperative since 1933, after winegrowers, reduced to penury by profiteering international wine merchants, revolted against the system and demanded to control their own production. The most prized wine of Sámos is its light amber Grand Cru Vin Doux Naturel, with 15% alcohol, given its *appellation* in France in 1982 (the only Greek wine so honoured); also try a chilled bottle of fruity Nectar, aged in its wooden cask and splendid with strong cheeses, fruit salads or sorbets. Of the dry wines, the green-tinted Samena Dry White is made from grapes grown above 600m, and is popular as an aperitif.

From the handsome village of **Vourliótes**, it's a delightful, leafy 3km walk up to Sámos' oldest monastery, **Panagía Vrontiáni**, founded in 1560, with some of its wall paintings, although access is limited now that the monks have been replaced by soliders. Further east a road leads up to **Manolátes** which overlooks a lovely arcadian valley beloved by nightingales, one of the beauty spots of Sámos; where it and the road meets the sea, at **Platanákia**, you can eat under the magnificent grove of plane trees and drink barrelled red wine overlooking the sea. At night the tavernas fill up with 'Greek Night' excursion busloads. The last place where the mountains cede to the coast is at anticlimactic **Ag. Konstantínos**, quieter and rawer than the other resorts, a village of cement mixers and wishful thinking.

---

*Sámos ✆ (0273–)*                                    ***Where to Stay and Eating Out***

### Malagári

**Poseidon**, ✆ 23 201 (*A; lux*), has a pool, roof garden, minibars, air-conditioning and other comforts in the luxury choice here.

### Kokkári

**Kokkari Beach Hotel**, ✆ 92 263 (*C; exp–mod*) has a pool and sea sports. Also near the sea, the **Olympia Village**, ✆ 92 420 (*exp*) has luxurious bungalows and a big swimming pool. **Pension Paradisos**, ✆ 92 162 has moderate-priced studio apartments; **Dimitra**, ✆ 92 378 and **Pension Galina**, ✆ 92 331 are also good (*mod–inexp*). Kokkári has some 250 rooms in private houses, but just try to get one. On the water's edge in Kokkári, **Stathis Taverna** and **Kima** have tasty, freshly prepared Greek dishes (*2500dr*).

### Avlákia/Vourliótes

Down by the sea-front **Avlakia**, ✆ 94 230 (*C; mod*) is right on the sea, a pleasant little place, and there are several seaside tavernas to choose from. **Pension Markos**, up in Vourliótes, ✆ 93 291 (*mod*) is a great place to escape the crowds on the coast.

### Ag. Konstantínos

Near the sea, the old **Atlantis**, ✆ 94 257 (*E; inexp*) is a good budget bet. 2km inland at Andóni, a hillside hamlet of old stone two-storey houses called **Andonokastro**, ✆ 94 406, in Athens ✆ (01) 544 0182 (*B; exp*) has been beautifully converted into traditionally decorated apartments sleeping 2–4 people. *Open April–Oct.*

Wallflower **Karlóvassi** (ΚΑΡΛΟΒΑΣΙ), Sámos' second city and port, was an industrial tanning centre before the Second World War, and although the hides and stink are long gone, the empty warehouses along the port present a dreary face to the world. After the first baleful introduction, however, the little city is pleasant enough, and neatly divided (in descending order of interest) into old, middle and new (Paléo, Meséo and Néo) Karlóvassi, punctuated here and there with the pale blue domes of absurdly large 19th-century churches. It is much sleepier and Greekier than Vathí or Pythagório, and most visitors who stay in Karlóvassi stay in a small cluster of hotels in the picturesque old town of Limáni, with a far more appealing and intimate atmosphere than former industrial Néo Karlóvassi, although this is where you'll find the regional bus stop, banks, post office and other useful services. A city bus provides good transport to the nearest beach, **Potámi** (ΠΟΤΑΜΙ), 2km west, a fine sweep of pebbles and sand with a few rooms and a fish taverna or two, watched over by a chapel that can charitably be described as an attempt at Orthodox moderne.

Western Sámos has been compared to western Crete: fewer sights, fewer tourists, but amply rewarding in the walking scenery and beach department. A track leads back to the church of **Panagía tou Potamoú** (Our Lady of the River), Sámos' oldest church dating from the 10th century, and, if you carry on, to the lovely river canyon, a magical place of chilly rock pools and little waterfalls that you have to swim to cross; but don't expect to be alone in the summer. There are superb sandy beaches further west, the lovely cove of **Mikró Seitáni** (1km beyond the end of Potámi) and **Megálo Seitáni** (4km) at the foot of a striking ravine, but you need your hiking shoes to reach them, as well as your own provisions. The track, one of the most stunning, continues another 8km along the towering west shore as far as **Drakáioi**, a farming village at the end of the rough road from Marathókampos and a very rare bus line. South of Drakáioi the road continues to **Kallithéa**, with rooms and food.

Buses run several times a day from Karlóvassi to **Plátanos**, the island's second most important wine-growing area and, down to the sea by way of **Koumaíika**, a little village with an overgrown marble fountain: the sand-pebble beach with shade and a quiet summer community is alternatively known as **Ormós Koumíikou** or **Vállos**. The more westerly road south of Karlovássi curls around the soaring mass of Sámos' highest peak, **Mount Kérkis**, 1575m, a dormant volcano, often crowned with a halo of cloud and mist like a remembrance of eruptions past. **Kastanéa**, surrounded by chestnut groves and laughing brooks, is a popular place to aim for on hot days. To the south, **Marathókampos** an attractive village on tiny lanes spilling down the slopes, where the residents have restored some old abandoned houses for guests. Below is the beach, growing resort and regional port, **Órmos Marathokámpou** (ΟΡΜΟΣ ΜΑΡΑΘΟΚΑΜΠΟΥ), from where caiques sail several times a week to Samopoúla, a tiny islet with a fine sandy beach below the rugged coast to the east. The Samians' favourite beach is the long white and sandy **Votsalákia**, extending west of Ormos and now well lined with rooms and restaurants. If you have small children in tow, drive further west to the safe shallow seas at **Psilí Ámmos** (not to be confused with the Psilí Ámmos to the east), with a few places for lunch; you can find rooms by **Limniónas**, the third beach to the west, where prosperous Karlóvassians have their villas. A marked path from Votsalákia leads through the olives to the **Convent of the Evangelístria**, and beyond to the summit of Mount Kérkis; fit walkers can storm the peak and return for a swim in five or six hours.

## Karlóvassi

The two most comfortable hotels here are the **Samaina**, © 33 900 (*B; exp–mod*) with sparkling rooms near the sea at Limáni (*open April–Oct*) and the **Merope Hotel**, a mile inland © 32 650 (*B; exp–mod*) a favourite of many for its old-world service. **Aktaion**, at Limáni, © 32 356 (*D*) is the best of the inexpensive choices. At dinnertime make your way to the seaside **Kima**, for well-prepared *mezédes*. Towards Potámi beach, **Aspasia**, © 32 363, 🖉 34 777 is the smartest place to sleep in air-conditioned rooms, with a pool, roof garden and mini bus service for guests. *Open April–Oct*. On the beach, **Chimondidis**, © 32 479, serves delicious dishes and fish.

## Ormos Marathokámpou

**Hotel Kerkis Bay**, © 37 202 (*B; mod*) is the fanciest place here, although there are a number of modest studio flats, among them **Agrilionas Beach**, © 37 379 and **Alexandra**, © 37 419. **Klimataria**, © 37 256 (*D; mod–inexp*), with an OK restaurant, is a minute or so from the sea. *Open all year*. At Votsalákia, **Votsalakia Plage**, © 37 232 (*D; inexp*) is simple and pretty. There are some 15 rooms to rent up in Plátanos.

# Samothrace/Samothráki (ΣΑΜΟΘΡΑΚΗ)

In the far right-hand corner of Greece, Samothráki is one of the least accessible islands for the pleasure tourist; its steep shores are uncluttered by day-trippers, beach bunnies or people just passing through—in a way, they would seem frivolous. For this is a sombre, dramatically stern, rugged island, rising to a peak in the lofty Mountain of the Moon (Mount Fengári), where the sea god Poseidon sat and watched the tides of the Trojan War. Often whipped by the wind and lacking a natural harbour, with only a small strip of arable land between the mountain and the sea, it nevertheless was one of the best known and most visited islands of antiquity, for here was the cult centre of the Great Gods of the Underworld; from all over the Mediterranean people came to be baptized in hot bull's blood and initiated into its mysteries.

## History

Once densely populated, Samothráki owes its importance to its position near that busy thoroughfare, the Dardanelles—the strait named for the legendary Samothracian Dardanos, the founder of Troy. Inhabited from Neolithic times, the island's first temple (the rock altar beneath the Arsinoeion) was built in the Iron Age by people from the Thracian mainland; ancient Greek writers specifically identify them as non-Greek Pelasgians. In the 8th century BC Aeolians from Mytilíni colonized Samothráki and mingled peaceably with the earlier settlers, worshipping Athena and the Great Gods of the Thracians, whose language survived at least in religious rituals into the 1st century. By the 5th century BC, Samothráki had reached the height of its importance; it had colonized Alexandroúpolis, contributed a ship to the battle of Salamis and joined the Delian alliance. Although her military might declined with the rise of Athens, Samothráki's Sanctuary of the Great Gods had become the religious centre of the North Aegean, attracting a steady stream of pilgrims and adherents.

The Great Gods were chthonic, or Underworld deities, older and more potent than the Olympian upstarts of the patriarchal state religion, at whom even the first poet Homer could have a good belly laugh. But no one dared to mess with the Great Gods; no writer revealed much of what went on at their sanctuary, but it is likely that Samothracian mysteries included initiation rites similar to those at the cult centre at Eleusis. Although their names were kept top secret (dedications found at the sanctuary were simply 'to the gods'), a certain Mnaseas declared that a divine trinity ruled at Samothrace: the Great Mother Goddess, in this case the Thracian fertility goddess Axieros Cybele, whom the Greeks indentified with Demeter, with other attributes personified by Aphrodite and the witch Hecate, the Queen of the Night; her consort, Axiokersos-Hades and her daughter, Axiokersa-Persephone. A young phallic god, Kadmilos-Hermes, was a kind of servant, and the demonic twins, the Cabiri or Kabeiroi, sons of Hephaistos (later identified with the Dioscuri, Castor and Pollux), were somehow involved. Initiation in the cult was a charm against drowning and shipwreck.

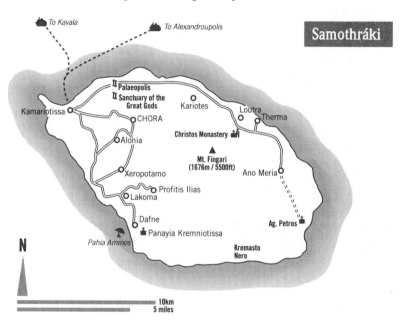

The cult had two levels of initiation, and compared to Eleusis had few restrictions. Anyone, male or female, free or slave, could be initiated, and even the uninitiated were permitted to attend the mysteries. A few things are known about the second level of initiation: there was a confession (the priest would ask the candidate what was the worst deed he or she had ever committed), baptism, and the winding of a purple sash about the body (as the veil of Leukothea saved Odysseus); it apparently all happened at night and was topped off afterwards with the sacrifice of a ram and a barbecue. Ambassadors from all over the world were invited to the sanctuary's high feasts in July and August, where ceremonies took place by torchlight. Lysander of Sparta, Herodotus, Philip II of Macedon and nearly all the Ptolemies were initiates, and in mythology the Argonauts, at Orpheus' suggestion, joined the cult for extra protection before entering the Hellespont.

Besides patronizing the sanctuary, Hellenistic and Roman rulers occasionally used Samothráki as a naval base, relying on its sacred soil for protection. Nevertheless, under the Romans the island began to suffer its first invasions and earthquakes. St Paul stopped on the island, but failed to convert the locals, who kept their sanctuary running until the 4th century AD, when the Byzantines forced paganism out of business: Samothráki was depopulated and forgotten. Pirate raids forced the remaining inhabitants to the hills, where they settled Chóra. The Genoese ruler Gattilusi fortified the castle, and when it fell to the Turks, the Samothracians were sent to resettle Constantinople. The island then vanished from history until the 1820s, when it rose up during the War of Independence, but, like the other islands in the northeast, had to wait until 1912 to join Greece.

## Getting Around

**By air**: 3 flights daily from Athens to Alexandroúpolis, ✆ (0551) 26 177.

**By sea**: 2-hour daily **ferry** crossing from Alexandroúpolis, occasionally twice a day in summer, and at least twice a week from Kavála. In summer, 6 **hydrofoils** a week run from Kavála to Samothráki, in winter, once a week, (✆ 835 671 in Kavála). **Port authority**, ✆ 41 305.

## Tourist Information

**Tourist police**: in Chóra, near the Kástro, ✆ (0551) 41 203. For assistance with accommodation, contact Niki Tours, ✆ 41 465, ✉ 41 304.

## Festivals

**8 January**, Ag. Athanássios at Alónia; **20 July**, Profítis Ilías at Kormbéti; **26 July**, Ag. Paraskeví, near Palaeópolis; **6 August**, at Sotírou in Chóra; **15 August**, Panagías at Loutrá.

## Kamariótissa and Chóra

**Kamariótissa** (ΚΑΜΑΡΙΩΤΙΣΣΑ), the rather workaday port of Samothráki, has a rocky exposed beach, and most of the island's tourist facilities, tavernas and nightlife are increasingly filled up in July and August with Germans and Scandinavians. Buses run frequently from Kamariótissa to **Chóra** (XΩPA), the capital, where most of the island's 2900 souls live, high on the slopes of Mount Fengári. Laid out in a picturesque amphitheatre below the ruins of a Byzantine castle, Chóra is a quiet Thracian village of whitewashed houses crowned with red-tiled roofs, some with rooms to rent. From here (or a bit more easily from Thérma) you can make the 5–6-hour ascent of **Mount Fengári** (1676m) and enjoy the same view as Poseidon, a stunning panorama of the North Aegean from the Troad in the east to Mount Áthos in the west. The paths up are not clearly marked, and if you don't want to go up with a guide, at least get clear instructions before setting out. Mount Fengári wears a snow cap for nine months of the year and has long been a landmark for seamen; Strabo wrote that it resembled a woman's breast. Its local name, Mount Sáos, recalls the *Saoi*, 'the rescued ones', a secret society of men sworn into the mysteries of the Great Gods.

Pretty agricultural hamlets dot the slopes of southern Samothráki: **Alónia**, the largest, has ruins of a Roman bath. Caiques from Kamariótissa sail south to the island's best beach, the magnificent **Pachía Ámmos**, with a freshwater spring but no other facilities. Alternatively, it's a beautiful walk—take the bus to **Profítis Ilías** and get off where the trail begins at Lákoma. Boat excursions circle the whole of Samothráki—the only way to visit the spectacular rugged southern coast and the waterfall **Krémasto Neró** ('hanging water'), near a much smaller beach.

## Palaeópolis and the Sanctuary of the Great Gods

Buse run frequently to **Palaeópolis** (ΠΑΛΑΙΟΠΟΛΗΣ), where the ongoing excavations of the **Sanctuary of the Great Gods** were begun in 1948 by an American team led by Dr Karl and Phyllis Williams Lehmann, who have written an excellent guide to the site, on sale in the adjacent museum. (*Both the site and museum are open 8.30–3, closed Mon; adm*).

Begin with the **museum**, with its explanation of the excavations and display of artefacts discovered on the site, or at least those things missed by previous excavators. The French, of course, took the prize, the *Winged Victory of Samothrace*, one of the masterpieces of Hellenistic art, dug up in 1863 by Champoiseau, the French consul at Adrianople, and ever since then prominently displayed in the Louvre; the museum has a plaster consolation copy sent over from Paris.

The sanctuary itself, impressive in its ruined grandeur, begins a short distance from the museum. The first building you come across, the large rectangular **Anaktorion** (the House of the Lords), dates from the 6th century BC and was rebuilt twice, lastly by the Romans; first-level initiations were held here, although only the initiated, or *mystai*, were allowed in its inner sanctum or Holy of Holies on the north side. A pile of carbon discovered in the middle of the Anaktorion suggests it had a wooden stage. Adjacent, the **Arsinoëion**, at 20m in diameter, was the largest circular structure ever built by the ancient Greeks. It was dedicated in 281 BC by Queen Arsinoë II, wife (and sister) of Ptolemy Philadelphos, after the Great Gods had answered her prayers for a child; the ancient altar within its walls is thought to have belonged to the original Thracian cult. The rectangular foundation south of the Arsinoëion belonged to the **Temenos**, where ceremonies may have taken place; adjacent stand the five re-erected Doric columns of the **Hieron**, where the upper level of initiation was perhaps held, a structure dating from 300 BC and last restored after an earthquake in the 3rd century AD. Here you can still see the stone seats where the initiates' confessions were heard, as well as the Roman viewing benches. There was a hearth altar in the centre and a drain by the door, perhaps for the blood of the sacrifices.

Only the outline remains of the theatre on the hill; here also is the **Nike Fountain**, named for the *Winged Victory* discovered there. The *Victory*, donated by Dimitrios Poliorketes (the Besieger) in 305 BC, once stood as the figurehead of a great marble ship, a votive offering thanking the gods for Dimitrios' naval victory over Ptolemy II. Ptolemy II himself donated the monumental gateway to the sanctuary, the **Propylae Ptolemaion**. Near here is a small circular **Tholos** of uncertain use and a Doric building, dedicated by Philip and Alexander, Hellenistic rulers of Macedon. It was at a ceremony in the sanctuary that King Philip II of Macedon first met Olympias of Epiros, the mother of Alexander the Great.

The buildings on the site were extensively cannibalized to construct the medieval Genoese castle near the Nike Fountain and the two watchtowers along the road. This road continues briefly west, through shady plane and pine groves and along tumbly rocky shores with places to camp, to Samothráki's little hot spring spa, **Loutrá** (also called Thermá) where you can soak in mildly radioactive warm water and swim at the stony beach.

When you step off the ferry in Kamariótissa there's a small booth
where the Room Renters' Association has a list of available rooms on
the island.

### Kamariótissa

Nicest here is the **Aeolos**, ✆ 41 595/895 (*B; exp*). *Open May–Oct.*
The new **Niki Beach Hotel**, ✆ 41 561 (*C; mod*) has 38 rooms by the sea. *Open all
year.* The waterfront in Kamariótissa is lined with cafés and tavernas, all typical and
inexpensive. **Aigeon Taverna** has a wide choice of Greek food, including the local
speciality, kid. Small tavernas spill over on the premises of neighbouring shops, so you
could well find yourself eating *souvláki* in a hardware store. There is fresh fish at
**Turkovrisso** and the *ouzerie* in the middle of the waterfront grills giant prawns over
the coals.

### Palaeópolis/Loutrá

The new **Kastro Bungalows**, ✆ 41 850 (*B; exp*) have a pool, sea sports and a restaurant right on the sea. *Open April–Sept.* For archaeology lovers, the little **Xenia Hotel**,
✆ 41 230 (*B; mod–exp*) is in the grove by the Sanctuary of the Great Gods; in season
you may have to take half-board. *Open all year.* Down the coast at Loutrá, **Caviros**,
✆ 41 577/497 (*B; exp*) is small hotel for spa-goers, but there are a few dozen rooms
and a campsite, too.

# Thássos (ΘΑΣΟΣ)

Northernmost of the islands in Greece, Thássos is also one of the fairest, almost perfectly
round, well-watered, ringed with soft beaches and mantled with fragrant, intensely green
pinewoods, plane trees, walnuts and chestnuts. Unlike the other Aegean islands, it is almost
never afflicted by the huffing and puffing of the big bad *meltémi*, but has a moist climate,
much subject to lingering mists; on hot summer days the intense scent of the pines by the
calm sapphire sea can make even the most practical soul sink into a sensuous languor. For
many years its relative inaccessibility kept it a secret holiday nook of northern Greeks, in spite
of the orgy of package tourism that has deflowered so many of the Greek islands. However,
Germans and Austrians soon discovered how quickly they could reach Thássos by car (the
current situation in former Yugoslavia has halted that somewhat), while the opening of Kavála
airport to international charter flights has definitely changed the all-Greek character of this
beautiful island, but not too outrageously. Thássos is a great island for camping, but is especially vulnerable to forest fires (a terrible one in 1985 devastated large swathes of woodland in
the southeast), so take extra care. Whether you're sleeping out or in, come armed: the native
mosquitoes are vivacious, vicious and voracious.

## History

Herodotus wrote that Thássos was settled by the Phoenicians in 1500 BC, who under their
leaders Cadmus and Thássos were seeking Cadmus' sister Europa after her abduction by
Zeus in the form of a bull. When Thássos gave up the search, he founded the island's first
colony, exploiting its rich gold mines and timberlands. These first settlers had close relations

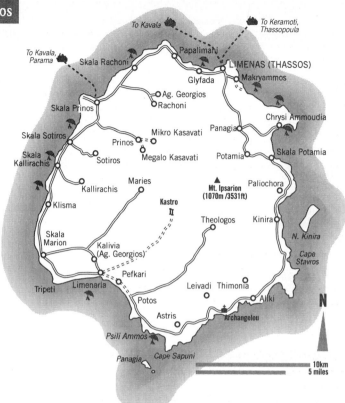

with Páros, and in 710 BC, when attacked by Thracians, they called on Páros for aid. The likeable Parian poet, Archilochos, was sent to do battle with them, but found himself out-manoeuvred and ran away; his description of the incident is the first known self-deprecating poem: 'Some Thracian now is pleased with my shield/which I unwilling left on a bush in perfect condition on our side of the field/but I escaped death. To hell with the shield!/I shall get another, no worse.' The Parians who stayed on as colonists had better luck, in obedience to the Delphic Oracle that commanded them to found a city 'on the island of mists', extracting some 900 talents of gold a year from the rich mines and the lands they annexed on the mainland.

In 490 BC Thássos was attacked by the Persians, who razed the walls. When Xerxes and his army turned up ten years later, the defenceless islanders responded by throwing a fabulous feast for the Persians, and with many slaps on the back sent them off to defeat at Salamis. When Thássos later revolted against the Delian league, Athens sent Kimon to teach it a lesson which he did—after a two-year siege. After that Thássos was ruled by Athens or Sparta, or whoever had the upper hand; Philip of Macedon seized its mainland gold mines.

In 197 BC the Romans defeated the Macedonians, and Thássos gladly became part of Rome. Among the uninvited guests who troubled the island in later years, the Genoese had it for the longest, from the 1300s until the Turks chased them out in 1460. Russia took over from 1770 to 1774. In 1813 the Sultan gave the island to Mohammed Ali, Governor of Egypt, who had been brought up in the village of Theológos and loved Thássos; he at once lowered the taxes and granted the island virtual autonomy. Benevolent Egyptian rule lasted until 1902, when the Turks returned briefly before union with Greece during the Balkan Wars, in 1912. In 1916 the allies occupied it, and from 1941 to the end of the war, the Bulgarians.

### Getting There and Around

**By air**: there are daily flights from Athens to Kavála, and buses from Athens and Thessaloníki; Kavála airport is also open to international charter flights. For airport info, call ✆ (0591) 53 273.

**By sea: ferry** from Kavála (port authority ✆ (051) 224 967) to Skála Prínos almost every hour. Other ferries depart from Péramos (20km west of Kavála) 4 times a day, and from Keramotí (a 20-minute bus ride from Kavála) to Liménas 12 times a day (✆ 22 106). There are **hydrofoils** from Kavála to Limenária, Liménas Potós, and Kalliráchi. Daily boat excursions from Liménas to Chryssí Ámmos, Glyfáda and Papalimáni beaches, and day trips to Philippi to see the royal tombs. **Port authority**, ✆ (0583) 22 106.

**By road**: the **bus** service ✆ 22 162 is good and regular; from Liménas quayside there are at least 10 times daily Skála Prínos, Skála Potamiá, and Limenária, and less frequently to Theológos and all around the island.

### Tourist Police

In Liménas, on the waterfront, ✆ (0593) 22 500.

### Festivals

**18 January**, Ag. Athanásiou at Kástro; **first Tuesday after Easter**, all over the island; **28 April** at Ag. Geórgios; **end of July–beginning of August**, traditional weddings performed at Theológos; the Thássos festival runs from **10 July to 15 August**; **6 August**, Metamórphosis tou Sotírou at Sotíras; **15 August**, Panagía at Panagía; **27 August**, at Limenária with special dances; **26 October**, Ag. Dimítrios at Theológos; **6 December**, Ag. Nikólaos at Liménas.

## Liménas (Thássos Town)

The bustling capital and port of the island is officially Thássos, but is better known as **Liménas** (ΛΙΜΕΝΑΣ) or sometimes just Limen (not to be confused with the island's second town, Limenária). Liménas is not exceptionally pretty, but it's lively enough with nearly as many flags as the United Nations waving along the waterfront; massive plane trees shade the squares, and shops wait to sell you walnut sweets and honey. Abandoned between the Middle Ages and the mid-19th century, the town has only 2300 inhabitants (many of whom came over from Asia Minor in 1922) who can hardly begin to fill the shoes of **ancient Thassos**; its ruins crop up everywhere and give the new town much of its character. The ancients used an amazing amount of marble—the island's highest peak, 1070m Mount Ipsárion, is one great white and greenish marble block. The marble is especially beautiful in the **Roman Agora** in the centre of town, near the little ancient harbour. Here are the foundations of porticoes and stoas, a massive altar, sanctuaries, and from the 7th century BC, predating the rest of the Agora by 500 years, the mysterious paved 'Passage of Theoria' leading to a Temple of Artemis.

The adjacent **museum** (*open Tues–Fri, 8am–7pm, Sat and Sun 8.30–3, closed Mon; adm*) has a fine collection: among the bits in the courtyard, there's a dead ringer for the Maltese Falcon, while inside highlights include a magnificent 6th-century BC *Kriophoros*—a young man bearing a lamb on his shoulders—an ivory lion's head (550 BC), an enormous, unfinished *kouros*, a relief of two griffons devouring a doe (2nd century AD), a lovely head of Dionysos from the 3rd century BC, little turtle votive offerings and an Aphrodite riding a dolphin. Several items relate to the island's ancient winemaking: a tablet from *c.* 420 BC with wine regulations, written in *boustropheon*, 'as the ox plows', an *Oinira*, or wine weight measure, and an amphora stamped with the island's special wine seal. Also near the Agora is part of an ancient street, an exedra, a few tiers of the **Odeon** and the **Sanctuary of Hercules**, the oldest on Thássos; Hercules was the island's patron saint, and his first altar was set up by the Phoenicians.

A path from behind a stately Turkish customs building on the harbour follows the extensive marble **walls** and gates of the ancient city and acropolis. These were reconstructed after the first Persian invasion and the later Athenian siege, and were last repaired by the Genoese. Many of the gates still bear the bas-reliefs, including the two naval gates, the **Chariot Gate** (with Artemis) and the **Gate of Semel-Thyone** (with Hermes). Near these stood sanctuaries dedicated to Poseidon and Dionysos. From here the walls extend beyond the ancient moles of the commercial harbour and rise to the 5th-century BC **Greek Theatre** on the lower slopes of the acropolis, magnificent not so much for its state of preservation, but for the marvellous view it affords of pinewoods and sea. At the time of writing it's the subject of an extensive EU-financed dig by French and Belgian archaeologists who plan to keep at it until 2000. A colourful character named Gianni runs the little bar nearby, with pretty sunset views.

From the theatre a path continues up to the **Acropolis**, spread out across three summits. On the first hill stands a Genoese fortress built out of the temple of Pythian Apollo. The museum's *Kriophoros* was discovered embedded in its walls, and a fine relief of a funerary feast (4th century BC) can still be seen near the guardroom. The second hill had a **Temple of Athena Paliouchos** (5th century BC), but the Genoese treated her no better than Apollo, leaving only the foundations. The third and highest summit of the acropolis is believed to have been a **Sanctuary of Pan**, from the Hellenistic relief of Pan piping to his goats. Again, the view more than anything else survives; on a clear day you can see from Mount Áthos to Samothráki while inland there's the mountain eaten away by marble quarrying, these days mostly for Saudi clients. A curious exedra resembling a stone sofa is carved below the sanctuary, and around the back the vertiginous **Secret Stair**, carved into the rock in the 6th century BC, descends precipitously down to the remaining walls and gates (be very careful if you attempt it; the stair rail is rusted away in many places and there are some scary gaps between the steps). Here you'll find the watchful stone eyes of the **Apotropaion** (to protect Thássos from the Evil Eye), the well-preserved **Gate of Parmenon**, and, best of all, the large **Gate of Silenus**, where the vigorous bas-relief of the phallic god (6th century BC) has lost its most prominent appendage to a 'moral cleansing' of the 20th century. Continuing back towards the modern town are, respectively, the **Gate of Dionysos and Hercules** with an inscription, and the **Gate of Zeus and Hera** with an Archaic relief; this last one is just beyond the Venus Hotel if you gave the Secret Stair a miss.

The sandy town beach is small and shaded with tamarisks and plane trees, but also tends to be the most crowded on the island. **Makryámmos**, 3km to the east, is lovely but has become a hyper chi-chi tourist beach with an entrance fee for use of its facilities; just west, buses or boats wait to take you to **Chrysí Ámmos**, **Glyfáda** and **Papalimáni** beaches, endowed with bars and tavernas, the latter with windsurfing.

### Thássos ✆ (0593–)         *Where to Stay*

The poshest place to stay on the island is the very modern **Makryámmos Bungalows**, ✆ 22 101, ✉ 22 761 (*exp*) on the soft sandy beach of the same name, with watersports, tennis, pool and a nightclub. *Open April–Oct.* On the edge of Liménas, **Aethira**, ✆ 23 310 (*B; exp–mod*) offers bright white bungalows, green lawns and a pool. One street back from the waterfront is the spacious **Amfipolis**, ✆ 23 101 (*A; exp*), converted from a tobacco warehouse, with a pool. **Akti Vournelis** on the beach just outside town along the Prínos road, ✆ 22 411 (*B; exp–mod*) is a good choice, and the bar nearby has live Greek music in the evenings. The small **Filoxenia Inn**, ✆ 23 331, ✉ 22 231(*B; mod*) is an old white villa near the port; the **Akropolis**, ✆ 22 488 (*B; exp*) is similar. The **Timoleon**, ✆ 22 177, ✉ 23 277 (*B; mod*) in Liménas is a pleasant option, but it's best to phone ahead in season. **Villa Molos**, ✆ 22 053 (*mod–inexp*) is a pleasant bed and breakfast place near the sea in a quiet garden setting. The **Akti Hotel**, ✆ 22 326 (*B; mod*) is a friendly pension on the waterfront; **Lena**, ✆ 22 793 (*E; inexp*) is a good choice, and there are plenty of rooms in the back streets of town. There is also **Camping Nysteri**, under the trees near Glyfáda, ✆ 23 327.

### Thássos ✆ (0593–)         *Eating Out*

While *Wiener Schnitzel*, baked beans on toast and English tea and cakes (at the Alykon on the waterfront) are widely available in Liménas, you can find traditional Greek specialities at **Ipigi** in the centre (*around 2500dr*) and **Zorbas**, on a narrow lane nearby with tables outside and live music that makes it a favourite for Greek night outings. Most representatives of the fish family are on offer; expect to pay at least 4000dr. One street back from the main seafront is the **Asteria** *psistariá*, with lots to offer from the spit including revolving goats' heads sporting lascivious grins. At the eastern end of the harbour, towards the town beach, the **Platanakia** serves fish at the appropriate prices, and just beyond, the **New York Pizza Restaurant** covers all options with traditional Greek food, giant pizza for five (*about 2500dr*), various pasta dishes and occasionally fresh mussels. In the evening Liménas is a bopping place and the long established, British-owned **Marina's bar** right on the waterfront is a friendly jam-packed place to begin and end the evening.

## Clockwise Around the Island: Beaches and More Beaches

Thássos has one main road encircling the island. Directly south of Liménas, it ascends to **Panagía** (ΠΑΝΑΓΙΑ), one of the most charming villages of Thássos. Its old whitewashed Macedonian houses, decorated with carved wood and slate roofs, overlook the sea, with their high-walled gardens, watered by a network of mountain streams, some flowing directly under their ground floor; the church **Panagías** has an underground spring. Down by the sea, the lovely town beach **Chrysí Ammoudiá** has many tavernas.

To the south of Panagía is another large, well-watered mountain village, **Potamiá**, which also has a small **folk art museum** (*closed Tues*) and another, the **Polýgnotos Vages Museum**, dedicated to the locally born sculptor (d. 1965) who made it big in New York. A marked path from Potamiá leads to the summit of marbly Mount Ipsárion, while below stretches the excellent beach of **Chrysí Aktí** (or **Skála Potamiás**), lined with tavernas and rooms places. Quiet **Kínira** has a small shingly beach closed off by an islet of the same name; only a kilometre south are the white sands of **Paradise Beach**, folded in the pine-clad hills; clothing optional.

The little slate-roofed hamlet of **Alikí** is beautifully set on a tiny headland overlooking twin beaches. It was an ancient town that thrived on marble exports, and ruins are strewn about its sandy shore—especially an Archaic Doric double sanctuary. Another ancient settlement was at **Thimoniá** nearby, where part of a Hellenistic tower still stands. Further along, the **Monastery Archángelou** with its handsome slate roof is perched high over the sea on arid chromatic cliffs, with beaches tucked in pockets here and there. Its cloistered nuns are in charge of a sliver of the True Cross, and the pretty courtyard and church may be visited (*proper attire, even long sleeves, is required*); paradoxically, the pebble beach nestling in the cliffs below is frequented by nudists. The lovely beach of **Astrís**, above pretty Cape Sapúni, is still defended by its medieval towers, and is one of a score of places in the Mediterranean that claims the sweet singing Sirens. Continuing clockwise around the island, much of Thássos' resort hotel development (and worst forest fires in 1985) has happened above the excellent sandy beaches around **Potós** (ΠΟΤΟΣ), golden **Pefkári** and lovely white **Psilí Ámmos**, with plenty of olive groves in beween. Potós is a good place for an evening drink over the sunset, and for exploring inland; two or three buses a day make the 10km trip up to the handsome slate-roofed village of **Theológos** (ΘΕΟΛΟΓΟΣ), one of Thássos' greenest spots and the capital of the island until the 19th century, with the ruins of the Genoese castle **Kourókastro**. The church Ag. Dimítrios has 12th-century icons.

**Limenária** (ΛΙΜΕΝΑΡΙΑ), the second largest town on Thássos, draws a fair crowd of tourists in the summer. It has a bit more of a village atmosphere than Liménas, surrounded by trees and endowed with a huge stretch of shady beach. In 1903 the German Spiedel Company arrived in Limenária to mine the ores in the vicinity—its plant can still be seen south of town, while the company's grand offices, locally called the **Palatáki**, 'Little Palace', stand alone in a garden on the headland. From Limenária excursion boats tour the coast of Mount Áthos—the closest women can get to the monastic state—or you can hire a little boat for a swim off the islet of Panagía. **Kalývia** just inland has some reliefs embedded in the wall of its church, while 15km further up on a dirt track, **Kástro** sits high on a sheer precipice and was the refuge of the Limenarians in the days of piracy. Although completely abandoned in the 19th century, in the last decade most of its old houses have been restored as holiday homes; there's a taverna in the summer but no public transport.

The less dramatic west coast of Thássos is farm country, lined with beaches, usually less frequented than those on the east coast. **Tripití** has a fine sandy beach near **Skála Marión**, which is a somewhat ramshackle little port, while **Mariés** proper, 10km inland, is perhaps the least changed of the island's traditional villages. Just along the road, a sign points the way to the remains of an Archaic era pottery workshop. **Kalliráchis** and **Skála Sotíras** have rocky beaches, not up to Thássos' usual standard, while **Skála Prínos** (ΣΚΑΛΑ ΠΡΙΝΟΣ) enjoys views Greece's oil platform. There's just enough black gold in the Northeastern Aegean to cause friction with Turkey; the military presence at Kavála accounts for the strict limits on commercial flights to its airport. Skála Prínos has the main ferry connections to Kavála. Inland from here is the village of **Prínos**, beyond which lie the two smaller villages of **Megálo** and **Mikró Kasaváti** (otherwise known as Megálo and Mikró Prínos—worth a visit for their lovely setting, beehives and charming old houses, many of which have been bought up and renovated by Germans. **Rachóni** and **Ag. Geórgios** are two quiet inland villages. A small islet off the north coast, **Thassopoúla**, is pretty and wooded but full of snakes, according to the locals.

---

### *Thássos ☎ (0593–)*            *Where to Stay and Eating Out*

There are excellent organized campsites by the sea and pines all around Thássos: at **Prinos** (Príno, ☎ 71 170), **Pefkari** (Pefkári, ☎ 51 190), **Potos** (Paradisos, ☎ 51 950), **Skala Rachoniou** (Ioánnides, ☎ 71 377), **Skala Sotiras** (Daedalos, ☎ 71 365) and **Skala Panagias** (Chrysí Ammoudiá, ☎ 61 207).

### Panagía

There are rooms in Panagía, and also the small **Hotel Helvetia**, ☎ 61 231 (*E; inexp*), and one of the island's most popular tavernas, **Kosta**, packed on Sunday afternoons with locals (*2500dr*). Next to the church, **Tris Piges Taverna** has bouzouki nights with dancing on Friday, Saturday, Sunday and Monday nights.

### Skála Potámia/Kínira

**Miramare**, ☎ 61 040 (*B; exp–mod*) is moderate-sized, with a restaurant close to the sea, but the **Blue Sea**, ☎ 61 482 (*C; mod*) is better if you can nab one of its 12 rooms. **Hotel Sylvia**, by the sea at Kínira, ☎ 41 246 (*C; mod*) is quiet, medium-sized and modern, and there are plenty of rooms places in the surrounding olive groves. **Athina**, ☎ 31 314 (*E; inexp*) is adequate but only open in July and August.

### Limenária/Pefkári/Potós

Rooms are very plentiful and relatively cheap in Limenária or there's the overpowering Papageorgiou, ☎ 51 205 (*E; inexp*) where you can get a room with private bath. Beween Limenária and Pefkári, there's an *ouzerie* serving barrel wine, just beyond the big seafront night club. The Thassos Hotel, at Pefkári, ☎ 51 596 (*C; mod*) has a pool. The air-conditioned Alexandra Beach, in Potós ☎ 52 391 (*A; exp*) has nearly every imaginable watersport on offer, as well as tennis, pool and a night club; Coral Beach, right on the sea on the south end of Potós, ☎ 52 121 (*B; exp*) is similar. Io, ☎ 51 216 (*D; inexp*) is modest but OK.

### Skála Prínos/Skála Rachóni

**Hotel Xanthi**, ☎ 71 303 (*B; mod*) is a good pension on the edge of town; the little **Europa** ☎ 71 212 (*B; mod*) is similar. **Hotel Socrates**, ☎ 71 770 (*C; mod*) is small and smack on the sea north of town. *Open May–Sept.* As you step off the boat at Prínos, **Kyriakos Taverna**, in front of you, has good fresh food and a wider than average selection. Next door, **Zorba's** is just as popular, and an added treat is the traffic policemen assailing your eardrums with their whistles. In Skála Rachóni, the **Coral**, ☎ 81 247 (*C; mod*) is a well-scrubbed, stylish place to stay with a pool amid the olives, and there's a row of beach tavernas.

POROS

# The Saronic Islands

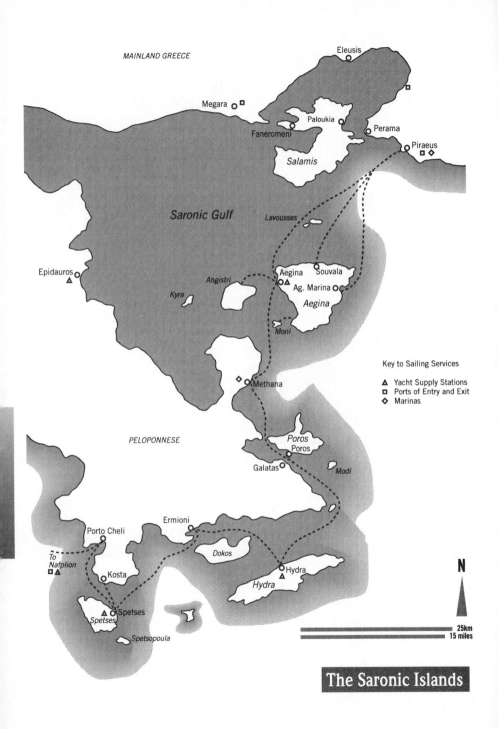

The Saronic Islands

Set between Attica and the Peloponnese in the fast lane of Greek history, the five islands in the Saronic Gulf have played a disproportionately important role in the evolution of the country. Like that of Greece itself, their destiny has been inextricably bound up with the sea. Aegina was one of the most powerful maritime states in Greece, an early rival to Athens itself; Póros was the holy island of Poseidon; Salamis witnessed one of the world's greatest sea battles, and Hýdra and Spétses led the Greek fleets in the battles of the War of Independence. For the modern holidaymaker they make a pleasant outing, either by frequent ferry or hydrofoil out of Piraeus or under your own sail. They are ideal if you have only a little time at your disposal, or want an island base for visits to the high spots of classical Greece.

The Saronics were the first Greek holiday islands, beginning in the early 1900s when fashionable Athenian families hired villas for the summer months while the family breadwinner commuted to and fro at weekends. Since the introduction 30 years ago of such conveniences as reservoirs, electricity and telephones, the Athenians have been joined by citizens from around the world. In 1985, Aegina was the most visited island in all Greece; Hýdra has earned itself the nickname 'the St Tropez of Greece', although the once quiet Spétses is increasingly laying a claim on the title.

### Getting There

**By sea**: note that only **hydrofoils** for Aegina leave from the main port of Piraeus; hydrofoils for other Saronic Gulf ports (including Aegina at times) depart from Zéa Marína (*see* Piraeus map p.91). Some are express services directly to Hýdra and Spétses; others call at Aegina, Póros, Hýdra and Spétses. Regular passenger and special tourist ships for other Saronic ports, and car ferries to Aegina and Póros, leave from Piraeus' central harbour.

# Aegina (ΑΙΓΙΝΑ)

Connections between Aegina (pronounce it 'EGG-ee-na') and Piraeus are so frequent that many residents commute to work in the city. But Aegina is no fuddy-duddy bedroom suburb, and in spite of the demands of tourism the islanders have stubbornly maintained their traditional fishing fleet and farms, especially their pistachio groves. Aegina has a few beaches that are often packed, numerous hotels and good fish tavernas; it also has a clutch of fine Byzantine churches and the best-preserved ancient temple on any Greek island, the lovely Temple of Aphaia. Aegina is also extremely popular with the pleasure craft set, who anchor away off the island's more inaccessible coasts; even if you haven't brought the yacht, try to steer clear of summer weekends, when half of Athens descends on the island. Yet if you have only one day left in Greece and want to see one last island, Aegina is the obvious choice.

## Mythology

The name Aegina comes from one of Zeus' many loves, on whom he fathered Aeacus, the first king of the island, then called Oenone. To honour his mother, Aeacus renamed the island 'Aegina'. This was simply too much for that ever-jealous Hera. She punished Aeacus by sending a plague of poisonous serpents, who polluted the water, causing all the inhabitants to perish. Aeacus begged his father Zeus for help, wishing for as many inhabitants to repopulate Aegina as there were ants on a nearby oak, a wish Zeus granted. The new Aeginetans were known as the ant people, or Myrmidons.

Aeacus went on to father three sons—Peleus, Telemon and Phocos. When Telemon and Peleus in a fit of jealousy killed Phocos, their father's favourite, they were forced to flee the island, Telemon going to Salamis, and Peleus to Thessaly. These two brothers in turn fathered two of the greatest heroes of the Trojan War, Ajax and Achilles respectively. When Aeacus died, Zeus appointed him one of the three judges of the dead with Minos, his arch enemy, and Rhadamanthys, his other son from Crete.

## History

Aegina was inhabited from the 4th millennium BC by people from the Peloponnese, followed by the usual trail of Minoans, Mycenaeans and Dorians. In 950 BC its city joined an Amphictyony of seven towns (the Heptapolis), initiating its commercial development. In 650 BC Aegina town was the first place in Europe to mint coins, imprinted with a turtle, and it was the first to develop a banking system; turtle coins from Aegina have been found all over the Mediterranean. Trade, thanks to a powerful commercial fleet and exports of fine perfumes and pottery (still a thriving local craft), made Aegina fat; by 490 BC it was one of the trading centres of the entire Mediterranean.

This prominence lasted less than 50 years, due to the rise of a very close neighbour: Athens. In the first Persian War Aegina had sided with Persia, one of its main trading partners, and it would have militarily supported Darius had the Athenians not kidnapped several prominent citizens and held them hostage in return for the island's neutrality. In the second Persian War, Aegina had a change of heart and sent 30 ships to aid the Greeks at the Battle of Salamis, and won the first choice of spoils for the most heroic conduct. Even so, Pericles could not forgive Aegina for its prosperity, and sneeringly referring to the island as 'a speck that blocked the view from Piraeus'. In 458 BC the Athenian fleet defeated the triremes of Aegina, and three years later the city of Aegina was forced to surrender to the bullying Athenians, who made the inhabitants destroy their fortifications and hand over their fleet. When the Peloponnesian War broke out, the Athenians, knowing they had few friends on Aegina, deported the entire population; they were welcomed by the Spartans and were later returned to their homes by Lysander.

Later history saw the usual train of invaders—Saracens, Venetians and Turks, the last occupation by the Ottomans lasting from 1715 to 1821. Aegina was one of the first places in Greece to be liberated and war refugees flocked to the island from other parts of Greece. In 1828 Aegina Town became the capital of free Greece under its first president, Capodistria. Fittingly for the island that created the very first Greek coins, the first modern drachma, bearing a phoenix rising from the ashes, was minted on the island; Aegina also saw the new country's first newspaper and its first prison. A year later the capital was relocated in Náfplion.

---

### *Getting There and Around*

**By sea:** hourly **hydrofoil** (40mins) until late afternoon, or by boat 1½ hours from Piraeus; frequent connections with Méthana (the closest port to Epidauros), and other Saronic islands. **Ferries** go to Aegina town or to Ag. Marína on the east coast; some call at Souvala. Buses from Aegina town (✆ 22 412) depart from Plateía Ethneyersias near the quay and run to most villages, including to

Aegina

To Piraeus

Leondi · Souvala · Agioi · Vaia · Tourlos
Vathi
Plakakia
Livadi === · Kypseli
To Piraeus
Kolona
Temple of Aphrodite
AEGINA
Pagoni · Ag. Nektarios Monastery · Alones
Monastery of Chrysoleontissa
Lazarides
Faros
Tziikides
To Methana
Paliapyrgos · Marathon · Kapotides · Pahiarahi
Portes
Temple of Hellanion Zeus · Anitseo
Mt. Oros (532m / 1756ft)
To Angistri
Profitis Ilias
Moni Islet · Perdika
Sfenduri

Mesagros
Temple of Aphaia
Ag. Marina
To Piraeus

N

5km
3 miles

Ag. Marína via the Temple of Aphaia and Nektários Monastery. **Caiques** link Aegina town to Angístri; others go from Pérdika to Moní. **Port authority**, ✆ 22 328.

*Tourist Police*

Vass. Georgíou Street, ✆ (0297) 22 391; open all year.

*Festivals*

**23 April**, Ag. Geórgios at Ag. Geórgios; **6–7 Sept**, Ag. Sóstis in Pérdika; **14 Sept**, Stavrós in Paleochóra; **9 Nov**, Ag. Nektários; **6 Dec**, Ag. Nikólaos at Aegina town;

## Aegina Town

Aegina town, the capital and chief port of the island, retains a lingering whiff of grandeur and neoclassical elegance from its days as the capital of Greece, even if many of the 19th-century buildings are half-hidden behind shops touting Aegina's pottery and pistachios; the numerous horse-drawn carriages add a nice touch amid the cars and general Greek cacophony. The large crescent harbour, almost too grand for an island, was financed in 1826 by Dr Samuel Greenly

Howe, a 27-year-old American surgeon who, inspired by Byron, had volunteered to fight in the Greek War of Independence, and was so appalled by the suffering and misery afterwards that he led a massive American relief campaign. The harbour's landmark, the twin-domed chapel of **Ag. Nikólaos**, celebrated its completion.

The first Greek government building was the **Tower of Markellos**, near large Ag. Nikólaos church. It is grim and austere, as is the hastily erected **Residence** (now the public library) on Kyvernéou Street. Capodistria, the first president, slept in his office on the upper floor, while downstairs the mint churned out drachmas for the new state. When the rest of the government relocated to Náfplion, the once-dapper count from Corfu lingered, estranged from his own government and suspected of intrigues with Russia, until his assassination in a local church.

An evening stroll, or *vólta*, around the waterfront is often rewarded with spectacular sunsets (probably due to the carbon monoxide shroud of *néfos* emanating from Athens) that bathe the town in a gentle light far different from the daytime glare. In spite of ever increasing numbers of yachts and excursion boats, colourful fishing boats still occupy their share of the waterfront. They rarely net any *katsoúlas*, once a speciality of Aegina but now almost extinct; now *marída* (whitebait) comprises most of the catch, which go down nicely with Aegina's own retsina in one of the many tavernas at the port. Ancient writers often referred to Aegina's 'secret port' just north of of the city—secret because only the islanders knew its entrance. It has a pleasant little sandy beach, and overlooking it, on the hillock of **Kolóna**, stood the ancient city, dating back to the Early Helladic Period. Excavations (*open Tues–Sun 8.30–3; adm*) have uncovered a road and a jumbly walled settlement, although neither are particularly rewarding. The name of the hill comes from the one lonely Doric column of an early 5th-century **Temple of Apollo** (long attributed to Aphrodite, thanks to a confusion in Pausanius); the rest of its marble with Capodistria's permission went into building Aegina's new quay. Graves found in the vicinity yielded the British Museum's beautiful 'Aegina Treasure' of gold Minoan ornaments from the 16th century BC, believed to have been plundered by ancient tomb robbers from the 'gold pit' by the Palace of Malia (*see* p.154). The new **Archaeology Museum** at Mitrópoleus 10 in Kolóna (*open Tues–Sun 8.30–3; adm*) replaces what was the first archaeology museum in Greece; most of collection went off to Athens in the mid 19th century, but still to be seen among others are ceramics from the Neolithic era to the Classical period, sculptural decorations from the temple of Aphaia, a sphinx and a mosaic from an ancient synagogue.

From Kolóna it's a short walk to the suburb of **Livádi**, where the main attraction is a plaque marking the house where Níkos Kazantzákis lived while writing *Zorba the Greek* (*see* **Crete**, p.121). If you've hired a bike, the road skirting the north coast is an easy pedal, with swimming possibilites at the rocky beaches of Leónti, and further east at **Souvála** (ΣΟΥΒΑΛΑ), one of the island's ports and a modest if dullish resort, which attracted the first visitors decades ago with its offers radioactive baths for rheumatism and arthritis.

## Paleochóra

The bus to Ag. Marína passes by the Temple of Aphaia, but most pious Greeks will all pile out earlier, at the modern **monastery of Ag. Nektários**, built by and named for the former archbishop of Libya, who retired here and died in 1920, and after assorted miracles was canonized in 1967—one of the most recent Greek Orthodox saints. On 9 November, the anniversary of his death, hordes of people make a special pilgrimage to the shrine to pay homage to his crowned skull. If you're not in need of Nektarios' services, consider climbing up to crumbling ghost town of **Paleochóra** (ΠΑΛΑΙΟΧΩΡΑ), just behind the monastery (visit in the morning, when the caretaker is usually around with the keys to the churches—and be sure to wear good walking shoes). Founded in what seemed to be a safe inland location in the 9th century when the Saracens were terrorizing the coast, Paleochóra twice proved vulnerable: Barbarossa slaughtered the men and carried off all the women and children in 1538 and Morosini pummelled it in his siege of 1654. A score of 13th-century churches—out of the original 365—still stand in various states of decay, many with contemporary frescoes; among the best are the **Basilica of Ag. Anárgyroi**, the **Chapel of Taxiárchis**, and the **Cathedral of the Episkopí**, founded by Ag. Dionysos, the patron saint of Zákynthos. Looming over all is Morosini's very dilapidated **Venetian castle** of 1654.

An hour's walk south of Ag. Nektários leads to the fortified **convent of Chrysoleóntissa** (1600) with an especially fine wooden iconostasis and a famous rain-making icon of the Virgin (a job once held on Aegina by Zeus). The nuns are known for their hospitality and for the delicious produce from their farm.

## The Temple of Aphaia

East of Ag. Nektários, the road passes near the pretty village of **Mesagrós**, surrounded by the vineyards and pine groves that combine to make Aegina's excellent retsina. On a pine-covered hill high above Mesagrós stands Aegina's pride and joy, the beautiful Doric **Temple of Aphaia** (*open Mon–Fri 8–5, Sat–Sun 8.30–3; adm*), the best-preserved temple on any Greek island, built in the early years of the 5th century BC. At first glance Aphaia seems like an unlikely candidate for such a fine temple; but Aphaia was the ancient name of the Mediterranean Great Goddess on Aegina, and she was worshipped on this site since the end of the Neolithic era (2000 BC) . Several sanctuaries and at least one, if not two, temples predated the Doric structure, with inscriptions to Artemis Aphaia (the 'not dark'), to differentiate her from Hecate, the Great Goddess in her aspect of witch or hag. In Crete her name was Britomartis or Diktynna— Artemis again, the Minoan mistress of animals. Later myths made her a child of Zeus and Leto, who often hunted with her sister Artemis and followed her cult of virginity. When King Minos of Crete fell in love with her, she fled him for nine whole months by land and sea. When she reached the coast of Aegina, she threw herself in despair into the sea and vanished, hence the Classical era translation of her name, 'the disappeared one'. She suffered one last transformation, becoming Aphaia-Athena with the rise of Athens and the general desire to get in the good books of the goddess who helped the Greeks in Trojan War.

The temple, built when Aegina was at the height of its fortunes, is of locally quarried golden limestone and, like most non-marble temples, was originally covered with a coat of brightly painted stucco. Of the original 32 columns, 25 are still standing, thanks partly to reconstruction; the internal colonnade, around the cella, where the cult statue of Aphaia once stood, is a unique feature (note the 19th-century graffiti). The superb pediment sculptures of Parian marble, depicting scenes of the Trojan war, are among the finest works of Greek Archaic art but you have to go to Munich to see them; representatives of Ludwig of Bavaria rescued them in 1812 from peasants bashing them up for the lime-kiln and purchased them from the Turks. Outside the temple are the ruins of an ancient wall, altars, a cistern and priests' houses.

The café opposite the temple offers a splendid view of the east coast of Aegina, including **Ag. Marína** (ΑΓ. ΜΑΡΙΝΑ), the island's busiest resort, with the most nightlife and a long sandy beach—Aegina's best, but often too crowded for comfort. If you want to foot it, it's less than a half-hour walk down hill.

## Mount Oros

Once a day a bus from Aegina town lumbers its way up to **Pacheiá Ráchi** (or you can walk up from Marathónas), near the **temple of Hellanion Zeus** (Ellaniou Dios), the third temple of Aegina, dedicated to Zeus Hellanios, 'the rainmaker'; clouds gathering around its summit have long been observed as a sign of showers. Two massive terraces, cisterns and a monumental staircase can still be seen. From the temple it's an hour's walk up to the summit of **Oros** (534m/1706ft), a sturdy and conical mountain, the highest in the Saronic Gulf; its name simply means 'mountain' and it enjoys magnificent views stretching across the Gulf on a clear day.

## Pérdika and Moní Islet

One of the most popular excursions is to cycle (or take a bus) from Aegina town south along the coast to **Pérdika** (ΠΕΡΔΙΚΑ) past several swimming spots around **Marathónas** and the attractive beach of **Aiginitíssa** (7½km from Aegina town). Pérdika ('partridge') is a pretty fishing village-cum-resort with a small beach and tavernas that offer the best fresh fish on the island. All around are Aegina's famous pistachio groves.

The island is the country's biggest producer of what the Greeks call 'Aegina peanuts'; in late August, harvesters using long sticks gently knock the nuts off the trees into sheets of canvas spread below. The pistachios are then hulled, soaked in sea water, and sun dried on flat roofs and terraces. As you may have noted from the prices charged in Aegina town, they don't come cheap, and two decades ago Aegina suffered a minor ecological disaster when farmers uprooted olives and fruit trees to plant pistachios in their place. The new trees required so much more water than the trees they replaced that deeper and deeper wells were sunk, until they went dry or filled with sea water. For many years (until the completion of the new reservoir) most of the island's water had to be shipped in daily from the mainland.

In Pérdika you can visit Aegina's **wildlife sanctuary**. Probably the most effective animal protection and rehabilitation centre in Greece, the sanctuary accepts wounded and sick animals from all over the country and releases them after recovery. Phillipos, the founder and director, together with his volunteer staff of specialists, has cared for some 3000 birds, vultures, wolves, jackals, and a range of smaller mammals. This farm has also become the home for stray cats and dogs, many from overcrowded Athens. Funding comes from international donors such as WWF, businesses and public contributions. The centre has been running for over five years and has expanded to include a former prison, now used as the infirmary. Once the animal has recovered it is released, either into its original habitat or, if that is deemed unsafe, to one of the wildlife reserves on the mainland. Visitors are welcome at the farm and can see a good cross-section of native Greek wildlife (even if they may not be in a perfect state of health).

One endangered species, the shy, wild *kri kri* mountain goats from Crete—exotic creatures with long horns—are protected on the steep little **islet of Moní,** just off Pérdika (linked by boat taxis from Pérdika or Aegina town). Its name recalls that it once belonged to the monastery of Chrysoleóntissa; these days it's run as an official EOT campground. It is a pretty island, with trees and a small beach, ruled by brazen, nosy peacocks. Moní is a popular place for picnics and for diving, and you can walk up through the trees to a look-out post built by the Germans during the war for a wonderful view of the Saronic Gulf.

## Aegina Town

In Aegina town most of the accommodation is on the old side, and there are many relatively inexpensive places to stay (at least for such a popular island). **Pension Pavlou**, 21 P. Aeginítou, ✆ 22 795 (*B; mod*), is one of the more comfortable places, a block from the water-front. **Danae**, ✆ 22 424 (*B; exp–mod*) is 50m from the sea, with many rooms and restaurant terrace overlooking a smallish kidney-shaped pool. *Open all year.* **Hotel Brown** opposite the town beach at 4 Toti Hatzi, ✆ 22 271 (*C; mod*) has a friendly staff; for peace and quiet, ask for a room in the back. **Miranda** in Aegina town, beyond the football field on the far end of the beach, ✆ 22 266 (*D; inexp*) has a wistful B-movie atmosphere. *Open May–Oct.* **Plaza**, at Kolóna, near the temple of Apollo ✆ 25 600 (*E; inexp*) is pleasant, friendly, and close to the beach.

Aegina town is packed with eateries all along the waterfront. Find the little fish market and walk through it to find a pair of excellent little tavernas with rickety little tables, one block in from the sea. They serve delicious grilled octopus and fish, and if they run out they simply take it from the stands next door—you can't get seafood any fresher. Both also served good home-produced wines. For reasonably priced fish try the *ouzerie* **To Spiti tou Psara. Lekkas**, near the first town beach, is a typical taverna, serving reliable fare at fair prices, and **Maridaki**, near the hydrofoil landing point, has a name for excellent fish (*3000dr*). A little more expensive but serving top quality fish and lamb from the spit is **Taverna Stratigos**, south of town at Faros. Many locals like to hop in a taxi and eat out of town; **Vatzoulia's**, en route to the Temple of Aphaia, is especially popular and lively. Open only Wednesday and weekend evenings, it serves excellent Greek food often accompanied by music (*4000dr*).

## Souvála

**Ephi**, ✆ 52 214, ✉ 53 065 (*C; mod*) is an adequate family hotel with a restaurant, with a balcony for each room, many overlooking the sea, 50 yards away. There are a few cheaper rooms in private houses, and in nearby Vathi.

## Ag. Marína

There are also plenty of hotels (too many) on Ag. Marína beach. **Blue Fountain**, ✆ 32 644, ✉ 32 052 (*A; at the bottom of the expensive range*) is bright white and more tasteful than some, and offers good value for its rooms, equipped with a fridge and stove; some sleep up to four people. **Apollo**, by the sea, ✆ 32 271, ✉ 32 688 (*B; mod*) is one of the quieter hotels, recently renovated and offering a sea-water swim-ming pool and tennis courts, and a big American-style buffet breakfast. **Piccadilly** ✆ 32 206, (*C; mod*) is a comfortable new hotel, right on the beach; most rooms have sea views. There is plenty of nightlife in Ag. Marína: **Zorbas** is favourite disco (*5000dr adm*); **OINOH** draws in the 18–25-year-old bracket.

## Pérdika

**Moondy Bay Bungalows**, at Profítis Ilías, a few kilometres north of Pérdika, ✆ 25 147, ✉ 61 147 (*B; exp*) is the cushiest place to stay on Aegina, set right on the sea in a well-tended garden, with swimming pool, tennis, cycling and other sports; each room has its own air-conditioning and heating system; book well in advance. **Sisi**, at Marathónas, ✆ 26 222 (*D; inexp*) is pleasant and includes breakfast in its room rates. **Nodos**, in Pérdika, has a large selection of delicious seafood, for prices a bit over the odds but worth it. On Aiginitissa beach, **S. Stratigos** serves delicious meat and fish from the grill in the 4500dr range—or more depending on what you order. There's a taverna in the summer on Moní islet.

## Angístri (ΑΓΚΙΣΤΡΙ)

Boats from Aegina town (30 minutes) and Piraeus main harbour (2 hours) sail at least twice a day to **Angístri** ('hook island'), a small island of pine woods, fertile fields and relatively quiet beaches that attract their summer share of weekend Athenians and unassuming, undemanding Brits. Most of the inhabitants are descendants from Albanian refugees and still keep up some Albanian customs. There are two landing places on the island: **Mílo**, the principal village in the north, and the bland modern resort of **Skála** with its excellent sandy beach and most of what passes for nightlife on Angístri; the older village of Metóchi is just above. A bus connects the two villages with the third, **Limenária**, a quiet farming hamlet in the south with a couple of tavernas. There's nothing luxurious about Angístri—it offers the basics for a restful read-a-good-book holiday, and little more.

---

### Angístri ✆ (0297–)

### *Where to Stay*

On Angístri there's no shortage of accommodation, most of it centred around Skála, and it's all much of a muchness. **Andreas**, ✆ 91 346 (*D; mod*) is the upscale choice, with a good restaurant. **Anagennissis** is right on the beach here, ✆ 91 332 (*E; inexp*) and for about the same price there's the **Aktaeon** in the village, ✆ 91 222 (*E; inexp*). There are numerous rooms to let in private homes.

## Hýdra (ΥΔΡΑ)

Hýdra's role in the War of Independence has secured it a place in Greek history books; its extraordinary harbour, piled high with the tall, sombrely elegant grey stone mansions of its legendary sea captains, once overlooked the country's largest fleet of sailing ships. Artists and their camp followers moved in as the last sailors moved out; the first trickle of tourism was sparked off by the scenes of Hýdra in the film *Boy on a Dolphin*, starring Sophia Loren. The artsy posy tone that sets Hýdra apart from other islands survives, like St Tropez and Portofino and similar nooks around the Mediterranean, in spite of the hordes of day-trippers and cruise ship folk who haunt the sleek jewellers' and painting galleries; at night, to the tinkling of glasses and the rhythms floating from the trendy bars, discos and clubs, Hýdra comes into its own.

### History

In the 6th century BC the tyrant Polykrates of Sámos purchased dry, rocky Hýdra with the tribute he captured in Sífnos. However, no permanent settlers lived on the island until the 15th century, when Greeks and Albanians from Epirus took refuge here from the Turks, especially when the tyranny of notorious Ali Pasha made life unbearable in western Greece.

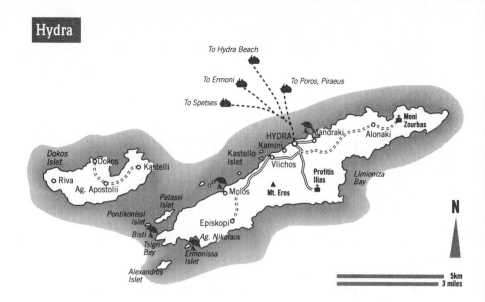

Hýdra is a nearly barren island, and out of necessity (and with nothing to lose) the new arrivals turned to the sea for their livelihood: through shipbuilding, and through a fleet of 150 merchant ships—and through smuggling and piracy. By the end of the 18th century, Hýdra was very much an autonomous island state, to which the Turks turned a blind eye as long as it paid its taxes. It boasted a wealthy population of 25,000, and the few sailors Hýdra sent as a token tribute to the sultan were much prized for their prowess in his fleet—especially the Albanians who made fortunes by daring to run the British blockade in the Napoleonic Wars. Hýdra's arch-enemy in the war of independence, Ibrahim Pasha, grudgingly nicknamed the island 'Little England'.

Hýdra did so well for itself under the Ottomans that its leaders first greeted the outbreak of the 1821 fight for independence with little enthusiasm; they remained aloof until their seafaring rivals on Spétses, led by the bold female admiral Boubalina, had chalked up a few victories and the people of Hýdra threatened to revolt. But once the Hydriotes had decided to join the fight, they threw themselves into the fray with characteristic boldness. Merchants (notably the Koundouriotis family) and captains spent their own fortunes to convert their fleet for war, and, under such leaders as Miaoulis, commander-in-chief of the Greeks, Tombazis, Voulgaris and Tsamados, the Hydriot navy terrorized the Turkish fleets, especially with their fire ships: under cover of night, a few intrepid Greeks would row a decrepit vessel full of explosives alongside the Turkish ships, set it alight and swim for their lives. The Turks, should they be lucky enough to notice it in time, could only do the same.

Ironically, the independence Hýdra fought so hard to win brought an end to the island's prosperity. After the war, sponge-fishing became the islanders' chief occupation, but that too declined through lack of demand. By the 1950s Hýdra looked like a ghost island, when fortune's wheel was oiled once again by the arrival of Greek painter Hadjikyriakos Ghikas, the first pioneer of the artists' colony that reached its peak in the 1960s.

**By sea: ferries** connect Hýdra with the other Saronic islands and ports several times a day. There are 12 hydrofoils a day from Zéa Marína (Piraeus), some going 'express' to Hýdra in about 1½ hours; frequent **hydrofoil** connections to Póros and Spétses, and Náfplion, Pórto Chéli and Ermióni, in the Peloponnese; less frequently to other Peloponnese ports such as Monemvásia and Kýthera. **Water taxis** wait by the quay to ferry visitors to the swimming places (beach is too grand a word) at Kamíni, Mandráki and Vlíchos, and the islet of Dokós; they're cheap if you join the crowd rather than go off on your own. **Boat trips** to the far ends of Hýdra run at 15,000dr return. **Port authority**, ✆ 52 279.

### Tourist Police

Odos Votsi Street, ✆ (0298) 52 205. For information and accommodation (from renting a room to buying a villa), contact **Pan Travel** on the quay, ✆ (0298) 53 135.

### Festivals

Hýdra is the main island for **Good Friday** and **Easter** celebrations; also, **mid-June**, the Miaoúlia; **July**, Festival of Marionettes, with puppets, dancing, and singing; **20 July**, Profítis Ilías; **25 July** at Ag. Efpraxia; **15 August**, Panagías in town; **13–14 November**, Ag. Konstantínos of Hýdra, the island's patron saint.

## Hýdra Town

Arriving at Hýdra's steep-sided port, capital and only town is a breathtaking experience. The island seems to be a barren rock pile as you sail along the coast, when suddenly your vessel makes a sharp turn, and there before you is the scene that launched a thousand cruise ships. The grey and white mansions, built in the late 18th century by Venetian and Genoese architects, attest to the loot amassed by Hydriot privateers and blockade runners. The sole combustion engines on the island belong to two rubbish trucks; the narrow lanes radiate from the amphitheatre and peter out into stairs, with a series of views that first charmed the artists.

Although most of the artists have fled the onslaught, a branch of the **School of Fine Arts** survives in the fine old residence of the Tombazi family, and there are several galleries amid the boutiques and jewellery shops. Another school, recalling an older tradition, is the **Skolí Eborakís Naftilías**, Greece's oldest school for merchant marine captains, housed in the old Tsamados house. The loveliest mansions—and the largest—belonged to the Koundouriotis family, Albanians who could barely speak a word of Greek but who contributed two men to the cause of independence: Lazaros, who converted his merchantmen into warships at his own expense, and the fat, jovial, and rather useless Pavlos, who was elected president of Greece in 1824 (one of the numerous *opera buffo* sidelights to the war of independence was that 1824 was also the year when Greece's most relentless enemy, the extraordinary Mehmet Ali, became pasha of Egypt; he too was Albanian, and spoke nothing else; until the age of 30, when he began his military career, he had worked in an Albanian tobacco shop).

The churches in Hýdra also reflect its former wealth and influence. The most beautiful is the 18th-century **Panagía tis Theotókou**, next to the port, with a lovely marble iconostasis and silver chandelier; the cells of its former convent, now used as town offices, encompass a serene marble courtyard (most of the marble on Hýdra was quarried from Póros' temple of Poseidon). Here, too, are statues of Lázaros Koundouriótis and Andráas Vókos, better known as Miaoúlis.

Before being appointed commander-in-chief of the Greek navy, Miaoúlis was elected admiral by his own fleet, which recognized not only his daring and seamanship, but his exceptional integrity—a rare trait in 1821, when most of the Greek leaders had no qualms about jeopardizing the entire enterprise on occasion for their own profit or self-interest; Miaoúlis instead devoted his considerable fortune to the war. The Greeks tell the story that Nelson once captured Miaoúlis on one of his more piratical adventures but Miaoúlis in turn captured Nelson with his charm, and was released with a pat on the back. He needed all the charm and persuasion he could muster in dealing with the difficult, independent-minded sailors of Hýdra and Spétses, accustomed to the medieval system that gave every man on the crew a right to the profits and right to have his say in all matters dealing with the voyage. If the majority disagreed with an admiral's decision, they would go on strike and up-sails for home, even if the fleet were about to do battle. It was democracy in action. To foreign observers and philhellenes, it looked as if the Greeks were in continual mutiny. The fact that Miaoúlis actually kept his ships together, and harried the massive, well-organized Egyptian invasion fleet of Ibrahim Pasha (Mehmet Ali's son) for four months across the Aegean was an accomplishment in itself, even if it ultimately failed. Afterwards, while all but a handful of Greek admirals refused to sail without being paid in advance, Miaoúlis struggled to relieve the besieged city of Missalongi, and always outfoxed the enemy when he had a fighting chance and enough ships. He bowed out of the war and politics with a band (*see* 'Póros', overleaf) and is fondly remembered on his native island, in celebrations called the *Miaoúlia* (20 June), which often include mock re-enactments of his battles.

From the church, climb up Miaoulis street to the lovely square of **Kaló Pigádi**, site of two 18th-century mansions and two deep wells that have long supplied the town with fresh water. The one real beach on Hýdra is a 20-minute walk away at **Mandráki**, the old shipbuilding docks of the Hydriots. You can also dive off the lovely rocks at **Kamíni** (Italian for 'whitewash', which was once made there); on Good Friday, Kamíni is packed with Hydriots and visitors who come to watch the moving candlelit procession of Christ's bier, the *epitafiós*, which culminates here by the sea. Another place to swim near town is at the **Bariamí** cave.

## Around Hýdra

Other swimming holes and inland excursions require more walking, a guaranteed way to escape the idle throng who stay close to the town. At **Kastéllo** are the ruins of a thick-walled castle down near the shore. Further on, **Vlíchos** is a pretty little hamlet with a rocky beach, a picturesque little bridge, and a couple of good tavernas; boats and more expensive water taxis from the port also make the trip. Pine trees and cove for swimming make **Mólos** a popular place for outings and for spotting Joan Collins, who often spends the summer here.

According to ancient tradition, in far less glamorous times, the steep cliff near Mólos was used to throw off the aged and sick who could no longer carry their weight on the austere island. If you're looking for a long walk, a track leads south to the a clutch of hunters' lodges at **Episkopí**, in Hýdra's pine forest—now just beginning to recover from a fire in 1985. Above town, **Profítis Ilías monastery** and the nearby convent of **Ag. Efpráxia** are about an hour on foot (or on one of the little donkeys for hire). The view from the top is lovely and you can buy textiles woven by the nuns on their ancient looms. Although you'll have to bring your own food and water, **Limióniza** (straight across Hýdra) is a beautiful place to swim.

---

*Hýdra ✆ (0298–)*　　　　　　　　　　　　　　　　　　**Where to Stay**

Be warned: it is sheer madness to arrive in Hýdra in the summer and expect to find a place to stay without a reservation. Most of the hotels are small.

### expensive

**Orloff**, ✆ 52 564 (*B*), in a beautiful restored 19th-century mansion near the port has only 10 rooms, each individually designed and set around a courtyard; an added plus is one of the best breakfasts in Greece. **Miramare**, at Mandráki ✆ 52 300, ✆ 52 301, winter ✆ (01) 413 6406 (*A*), is a bungalow complex built of stone, linked to the harbour by boat; overlooking the island's sole bit of sand, it offers an array of water sports and has a restaurant with mandatory pension; all rooms have air-conditioning, telephone and a fridge. *Open April–Oct.* **Bratsera**, on Tombázi St, ✆ 53 970, ✆ 53 626; winter ✆ (01) 721 8102 (*A*), the newest hotel on Hýdra opened in 1994 in a former sponge factory; and combines traditional design with a swimming pool, air conditioning, and restaurant. *Closed Nov.* **Pension Miranda**, outside town toward Mandráki, ✆ 52 230 (*A*) is in another charming, traditional Hydriot house. *Open May–Oct.* **Mistral**, ✆ 52 509, (*B*) is in an old stone tower mansion, with simple but attractive rooms. **Hydra Hotel**, 2 minutes behind the church tower, ✆ 52 102, ✆ 53 330 (*C*) is similarly located in a historic mansion once belonging to a sea captain, with traditional furnishings; good views. *Open all year.*

### moderate

**Amaryllis**, ✆ 52 249, ✆ 53 611 (*B*), is a comfortable little hotel in an old mansion, with smallish doubles with bath for 8500dr all through the year. **Hotel Leto**, ✆ 52 280 (*C*) is a bit larger than the others and might be able to squeeze you in at short notice. **Delfini**, ✆ 52 082 is appropriately located where the 'Flyink Dolfins' (*sic*) buzz in for a landing; prices; room prices from 7000–12,500dr includes breakfast. *Open Mar–Nov.* **Hotel Sophia**, ✆ 52 313 (*D*) is in a little old-fashioned building slap in the middle of the waterfront; it's the least expensive of all, but bring ear plugs.

---

*Hýdra ✆ (0298–)*　　　　　　　　　　　　　　　　　　　**Eating Out**

For the privilege of sitting and eating on the lovely quay of Hýdra expect to pay through the nose for anything from a cup of coffee upwards. A depressing trend is to throw a fixed menu at the hurried day-trippers, leaving little time to linger over the meal Greek style. **The Three Brothers** (near the cathedral) is one taverna that keeps humane prices; expect to pay around 3000dr for their excellent Greek cooking. Just nearby, **Douskos** offers courtyard dining in a similar price range. **Steki**, just before the clock tower, serves reliable Greek food on its veranda for even less. The **Garden** *psisteriá* by the football field serves tasty grilled meat. A 15min walk away on Kamíni beach, there are four tavernas, two serving fresh fish, and another, **Christina's Place**, serving some of the best traditional Greek food on Hýdra for a moderate price.

## Dokós

From Hýdra it is an hour's caique trip to the islet of **Dokós**, made of a kind of marble called *marmarópita*, grey and red and as hard as steel, used in building. The beach at Dokós is longer than at most ports, and the underwater fishing is excellent; while poking around in thee waters, Jacques Cousteau discovered a 3000-year-old wreck, thought to be the oldest in the world, carrying a cargo of wine and ceramic pots. There's a nice little taverna on Dokós, open if the owner is in the mood, and if you get your water cabbie to phone ahead.

## Póros (ΠΟΡΟΣ)

A mere 370 metres of sea separates Póros ('the passage') from the green mountains of the Peloponnese, lending the island and its surroundings a uniquely intimate, cosy charm; the Saronic Gulf seems like a lake, and if you sail through the busy Straits of Póros on a large ferry boat you can almost touch the balconies of the waterside buildings and see what's on television through the window: a Greek Grand Canal, and one that's as busy as the one in Venice with ships of every size and shape to-ing and fro-ing for the endless diversion of Póros café society. Of all the islands in the Saronic Gulf, Póros receives the most package tours; besides the beauty of its location, it is only an hour from Athens by hydrofoil, and although it has little

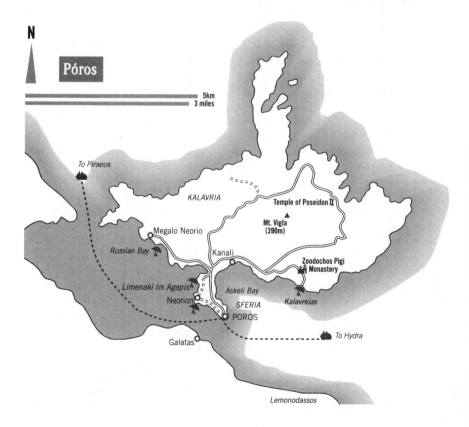

N

**Póros**

5km
3 miles

To Piraeus

KALAVRIA

Temple of Poseidon

Mt. Vigla
(390m)

Megalo Neorio

Russian Bay

Kanali

Zoodochos Pigi
Monastery

Limenaki tis Agapis

Neorion

Askeli Bay

SFERIA

Kalavreias

POROS

Galatas

To Hydra

Lemonodassos

to offer itself, it lies within easy driving distance of some of the principal sights in the Peloponnese: Epidauros, Náfplion, Mycenae, Troezen (of Theseus, Phaedra and Hippolytus) and its lush 'Devil's Bridge'. Just over the strait, Galatás is the home of the fragrant Lemonodássos ('lemon forest')—a massive hillside grove of over 30,000 trees.

## History

The early presence of Cretan traders or colonists on Póros is remembered not by any physical evidence, but in the legend of the princess Skylla, whose father, the king of Póros, had a magic lock of hair that made him immortal. When Minos of Crete besieged her father's castle, Skylla watched the battle and fell in love with the handsome Cretan king. To prove her love for him, she cut off her father's magic lock of hair while he slept and brought it to Minos proclaiming her affection. By killing the king, Minos easily took Póros the next day. But rather than thank Skylla for her help, Minos was revolted by her betrayal and left for Crete without her. Desperate, Skylla swam after him, but she was attacked by her father's spirit in the form of an eagle, and drowned in the bay which still bears her name (Askéli).

Póros in antiquity was known as Kalavria, and receives one of its first mentions in the history books as the headquarters of the Kalavrian league, a 7th-century BC amphictyony, or maritime confederation, that pre-dated the better known Delian League and included seven cities: Athens, Aegina, Epidauros, Troezen, Náfplion, Ermióni, Orchomenos and Pasiai. One of the very few things known about the Kalavrian league is that it operated under the protection of Poseidon, to whom Póros was sacred, and a famous sanctuary of the sea god stood in the centre of Kalavria. Little remains of it today beyond the memory of the great orator, Demosthenes (the same who practised enunciating with marbles in his mouth) who, unlike modern Greeks, didn't think Macedonia was Greek at all and roused his native Athens against the political presumptions of Philip of Macedon. Although Philip defeated Demosthenes and the Athenians at Chaeronea (338 BC), Demosthenes continued his defiance of Philip's successor, Alexander the Great, from Troezen; Alexander arrested him, but let him go; upon Alexander's death in 322, Demosthenes led yet another revolt against the Macedonians. Alexander's general Antipater went after him this time, and although Demosthenes fled to Póros and sought sanctuary at the temple of Poseidon, the sacreligious Macedonians burst in, swords raised for the kill. But Demosthenes died proving his pen was yet mightier; he had bitten off the poison he had concealed in the nib. One of the bays of Póros is called Russian Bay, recalling some of the other confusing events that occurred on Póros, this time in 1828, when emissaries of the Great Powers (British, French and Russian) gathered here for a conference on the new Greek kingdom. The Russians were always close friends with the first president, Count Capodistria, one-time ambassador to the Tsar—too close, thought many independent-minded revolutionaries from Hýdra and Póros, who formed their own 'constitutional committee', on whose orders Admiral Miaoulis seized the national fleet based at Póros, including his lavish over the top flagship *Hellas* (an enormous state-of-the-art warship purchased from America at a cost that equalled twice the national budget), and when ordered in 1834 by the Great Powers to hand the fleet over to the Russians to deal with Capodistria's political rivals, the ever heroic and honest Miaoulis blew up the *Hellas* instead and averted a civil war.

---

### Getting There and Around

**By sea: car ferry** from Piraeus, Aegina and Methána several times a day; car ferries every 30 minutes to Galatás on the mainland. Frequent **passenger ships** and

**hydrofoils** run to other places in the Saronic Gulf, allowing for easy day-trips, and once a week in high season there are connections to the Corinth Canal and Náfplion. Galatás is three hours from Athens by land, and **water taxis** (*benzínas*) make the short trip across the strait 24 hours a day from May to Oct for a mere 70dr. **Port authority**, ✆ 22 274.

**By road**: the one bus on Póros goes up to the monastery and back.

*Tourist Police*

On the waterfront, ✆ (0298) 22 462; harbour master, ✆ 22 274.

*Festivals*

**Good Friday** *panegýri* at Zoodóchos Pigí monastery; **15 August** island-wide.

## From Póros Town to the Temple of Poseidon

Póros actually consists of two islands from different geological periods: larger Kalávria, pine-forested and blessed with innumerable quiet sandy coves, and little Sferiá, where most of the action takes place, a volcanic bubble that popped out of the sea during the eruptions at Methána on the mainland. The two are joined by a sandy belt of land and a bridge.

Póros town, the capital and port of the island, clambers all over and up Sferiá, crowned by the blue-domed campanile of the Metropolis church. Like Hýdra, many of its inhabitants trace their history back to Albanian forebears who fled the depredations of the Turks and Ali Pasha in their homeland. These days the town is given over almost completely to the needs of tourists, except for the **Naval Training School**, a kind of public school housed in the buildings of the first arsenal of the Greek State. Póros has a small **archaeological museum** in Plateía Koryzí, with finds from the ancient Troezen era (call ✆ 23 276 for an appointment).

A new crop of hotels has sprung up on Kalávria in recent years, some on the often polluted beach of **Neórion** to the west, and **Askéli** and **Kanáli**, which are rather cleaner to the east. Although they are hot stuff for Póros, true beach-lovers will turn up their noses at all of them; alternatives include crossing over to Aliki beach, next to **Galatás** on the mainland, or hiring a small boat (around 7000dr a day) to get over to the small, inaccessible coves on the north side of the island. From Kanáli the bus continues to the peaceful 18th-century **Monastery of Zoodóchos Pigí**, immersed in woods (with yet another rough pebbly beach below) and decorated inside with a lofty gilt iconostasis and good icons. A new road in front of the monastery climbs through the pine woods (a main source of the sap that flavours Attica's retsina) to the plateau of Palatia and the scant remains—the locals call it 'the five stones'—of the once celebrated **Temple of Poseidon**. First built in brick by the Mycenaeans, it was rebuilt in marble around the year 500 BC; when Pausanias visited it, he saw the tomb of Demosthenes in the precinct. All this is dust in the wind (and most of the marble is in Hýdra) but the view across the Saronic Gulf is as spectacular as ever.

*Póros ✆ (0298–)*

*Where to Stay*

*expensive*

**Sirena**, near the monastery, ✆ 22 741 (*B*), is the best on the island, air-conditioned throughout with a salt-water pool, beach, and even a casino. *Open April–Oct.* **Neon Aegli**, at Askéli beach, ✆ 22 372, ✉ 24 345 (*B*), is a resort hotel on a private stretch of beach where each room has a balcony and sea view, and there are watersports. **Pavlou**, is the best choice at Neorion, ✆ 22 734 (*B*).

### *moderate–inexpensive*

**Latsi**, just around the corner from the waterfront towards the Naval School, ✆ 22 392 (*B*), is a pleasant medium-size hotel and restaurant. *Open all year.* **Saron**, ✆ 22 279 (*B*), is in the heart of the busy (and noisy) waterfront. **Villa Tryfon** is a 3min walk from the port, behind the church of Ag. Georgios, ✆ 25 854 or 22 215. Draped in bougainvillaea, populated by the friendliest cats in Greece and run by Tryfon, a jovial Telly Savalas lookalike, each room offers en suite kitchen and bathroom facilities and pretty views over the town and port. *Open all year.*

---

*Póros ✆ (0298–)*                                                        ***Eating Out***

Eating out along the *paraliá*, or waterfront, of Póros town is a real Greek treat—a line of tavernas directly on the water (with all the assorted aromas that go with it), with lovely views of the Peloponnese and of the ridiculously expensive yachts gliding silently through the strait. All serve good Greek food at reasonable prices; the **Sailor Taverna** is good for lobster and anything else from the grill. **Zazzas** by the Naval Academy has all the Greek favourites, and the occasional Spanish dish. **Taverna Paradiso**, 2km from Poseidon's temple (approaching from Askéli; take a taxi or rent a motorbike) offers a taste of old Greece under its pergolas of vines and flowers, with splendid views over the pine forest to the sea. It's perfect for a leisurely Sunday lunch, perhaps after a tour around the island (*3000dr*). Right on the waterfront, **Coconuts** is the fun bar on the island, run by a friendly, zany Dutch family; if you need a change from Greek food, ask Anna and Hans to whip up a Chinese or Indonesian meal. Snack bars and tavernas line the beaches along the road out to Love Bay (turn left after the Naval School); the beach at Calypso is especially nice, and has Greek music day and evening. A water taxi ride away in Galatás, **Ariadne**, ✆ 22878 is especially good for *mezédes*, the traditional Greek medley of starters.

## Salamína/Salamis (ΣΑΛΑΜΙΝΑ)

Of all the islands in this book Salamína is the most suburban, but also the most Greek in a gritty but very authentic way that only those who know and love Greece very well can savour, almost as a reaction to the overpowering beauty that reigns everywhere else. The uninspiring suburb of Pérama and the shipyards of Piraeus and a score of stranded rusting hulks are a mere 3km across the Strait of Salamis, which in 480 BC saw Athens' historic victory over the Persians. With the exception of the frescoes in the Faneromeni convent, neither nature's nor man's creations are particularly inspiring. The southeast coast of Salamína is the prettiest part of the island, with its pine forests and beaches, although they are only accessible by private car and on foot. Moúlki, also called Eántion, and Selínia are seaside villages popular among blue collar families from Athens and Piraeus.

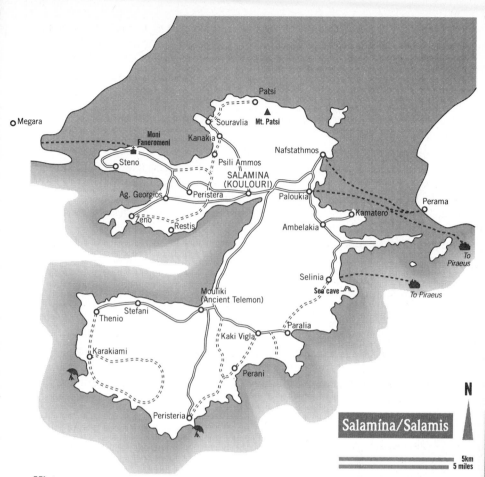

## History

When Telemon and his brother Peleus slew their brother Phocos (*see* 'Aegina'), Telemon fled to Salamína, the island of serpents. It acquired this name from the destructive serpent killed by its first king, Kychreus, a shadowy character who himself was a snake until recast as a man when snake cults went out of fashion; according to tradition, Kychreus was the snake who attended Demeter at her mysteries in nearby Eleusis. Telemon married Kychreus' daughter to become king of the island; however, his son, Great Ajax, a hero of the Trojan War, was born of his second wife, a princess of Athens. When Mégara and Athens quarrelled over Salamína in 620 BC, Solon visited the tomb of Kychreus to invoke his aid in the dispute, and when the Spartans, the arbiters of the dispute, decided to give the island to Athens, they did so on the strength of the serpent at Eleusis and Telemon's marriage to an Athenian. Further proof occurred during the Battle of Salamis, when the Athenians claimed that Kychreus appeared among their ships in the form of a mighty serpent to spur them on to victory.

Solon wanted Salamína as an Athenian colony in order to protect Piraeus. During this time Kamatero was the island capital, and on Mount Pátsi there are remains of fire towers used to communicate with the mainland. The island was also defended to the west against possible Megarian aggression. In September of 480 BC a massive Persian fleet under Xerxes, the King of Kings, moved into Faliron Bay with the intention of conquering Greece once and for all. Greek commentators put the Persian fleet at an incredible 1200 ships, while the Athenians and their allies could only muster a mere 378. Thanks to their scouts, the Greeks knew the Persians were coming and made preparations, sending their old men to Salamína and the women and children of Athens to Troezen. Numerous accounts of the subsequent battle have been passed down to us; the most poetic is *The Persians* by Aeschylus, who participated in the battle.

The Greeks won as much by their wits as by the use of their superior, highly manoeuvrable ships. Themistocles, the Athenian commander-in-chief, had a rumour leaked to Xerxes that the Greeks, hearing of a Persian land invasion in the Peloponnese, had split up and were in disarray. Xerxes decided to take advantage of the supposed confusion, and in the night ordered his fleet to block up the Strait of Salamis at Megara and in the east. Confident of victory the next day, Xerxes had his silver throne carried to the summit of Mount Egaleo in Perama, where he sat down to watch the battle unfold. But Themistocles had been warned of the Persian plan. At dawn he moved his triremes up against the strongest Persian vessels, which initiated the attack. The Greeks pretended to fall back, then quickly spun their swift ships around, driving the bulkier craft of the Persians into the dangerous shallows. Helpless, Xerxes' fleet foundered and his ships in the south fled back to Faliron Bay. The King of Kings watched his incredible defeat in anguish and was eventually forced to create a diversion to escape with his 300 surviving ships. The army he left behind was defeated later by the Greeks at Platéa.

The victory at Salamína gave Athens a moral boost that brought about their golden age. It also demonstrated the might of the Athenian navy, emboldening them to form the Delian league and control the fate of so many islands. As for Salamína, it gave birth to the great tragedian Euripides and then fell back into obscurity.

### Getting There and Around

**By sea: ferry** every 15 minutes from Pérama to Paloukía and at least 5 a day from Piraeus. The villages of Salamína are connected by an efficient bus system. **Port authority**, in Athens, ✆ (01) 465 3252.

### Festivals

Salamína is noted for its religious processions during Holy Week; also **5 June** at Metamorphósis, and the **last Sunday of Carnival** at Koulóuri. The biggest celebration is the great pilgrimage to the convent of Faneroméni on **4 September**.

## Salamína

**Salamína**, the metropolis of the island, is nicknamed Koulóuri ('crescent') for the way it curls around its harbour. There is a small, unattractive beach near town and the harbour hosts Japanese pearl oysters—stowaways on the Japanese freighters that have stopped there. The island's archaeological collection is soon to be housed in a new **museum** in the former Demotic School, built under Capodistrias.

Above Koulóuri is **Mount Profítis Ilías**, with views across the whole island. From Koulóuri a bus leaves every hour for **Faneroméni**, the convent and ferry-boat landing stage. Set in a large pine wood popular with picnickers and campers, Faneroméni was built in 1661, reusing the foundation of an ancient temple. The church, Metamorphósis, is decorated with extraordinary frescoes of the Last Judgement, containing more than 3000 figures. Recently restored, they were painted in the 18th century by Georgios of Argos and his pupils. The best time to find the monastery open is either mid-morning or around 5pm. Across the road by the sea is a fine open-air taverna and there are many places to swim all along the shore. To the east is the beach **Psilí Ámmos** (village and taverna) which unfortunately smells of petrol much of the time.

## South Salamína

South of Kouloúri is the pleasant village of **Moulki** (or **Eántion**) with a nice pebble beach; it has some accommodation, but no one minds if you sleep out under the pine trees nearby. From Moulki a bus goes to **Kakí Vígla**, and a rough road leads south to **Ag. Nikólaos**, an abandoned monastery with a 15th-century chapel. Between Ag. Nikólaos and Kakí Vígla you'll find excellent, isolated camping sites and many of the beaches are sandy, especially at Peristéria. In the summer of 1994, preliminary investigations of the cave here yielded artefacts from eight different periods: Neolithic, Mycenaean, Classical, Hellenistic, Roman, Frankish, Turkish and Modern. There is good reason to identify the cave as the lair of Kychreus the man snake, and even better to identify it as the Cave of Euripides, where according to ancient sources the playwright sought seclusion to write his tragedies. On the east coast of Salamína, **Paloukía** is a ferry-boat landing stage from Pérama with a naval festival at the end of August. The sea between Pérama and Paloukía once sheltered beds of purple dye-yielding murex shells, which sustained a local industry up until the Second World War and the advent of chemicals and pollution. South of Paloukía woebegone **Ambelákia** was the harbour of Classical and Hellenistic Salamína. The mole and other harbour installations are visible in the shallows, but litte else—it's now a very smelly ships' rubbish dump—the oil-slick antithesis of everything a Greek island village is supposed to evoke. It has never been excavated and unlikely ever will be for that matter. **Selínia**, a few kilometres south of Ambelákia, is a collection of summerhouses, although the beach is nothing special.

---

*Salamína ✆ (01–)*

### Where to Stay
#### moderate–inexpensive

Most of the hotels on Salamína are very simple and 'ethnic'. The best on the island is the **Gabriel Hotel**, ✆ 466 2275 (*C*) in Eántion. *Open April–Sept.* In Selínia there are several small pensions and hotels, like the **Vorsalakia** at 64 Themistokléous, ✆ 465 3494. **Akroyali**, ✆ 465 3341 is in the same street and for about the same price.

*Salamína ✆ (01–)*

### Eating Out

Because Salamína gets very few foreign tourists, its tavernas are pure Greek and the food tasty and inexpensive. In Salamína town **Antzas** has a good name, and in Kakí Vígla **Kanellos** is known for its fish. In Selínia, **Vassilis** is a good family run taverna right by the water's edge, dishing up superb squid.

# Spétses (ΣΠΕΤΣΕΣ)

Spétses is a charming, pine-scented island, the furthest in the Saronic Gulf from Athens, a factor that long kept it quieter and more relaxed than its more accessible sisters. These days it's not unusual to see helicopters hovering in to deposit members of the jet set. A discreet but increasingly popular package destination, the hotels, cafés and even the streets fill up quickly in the summer, especially with the British who have practically colonized the island, with the luscious descriptions of John Fowles' semi-autobiographical novel *The Magus* dancing in their heads. Spétses is not new to tourism—its first hotel was built in 1914, and since the Second World War families have come for its safe beaches and excellent climate. Yet, new trendy gloss and all, it will seem downright laid-back if you're coming from Hýdra.

## History

Although discoveries at Ag. Marína indicate that Spétses (ancient Pityoussa) has been inhabited since 2500 BC, it managed to stay out of the history books for the next 4000 years. No one is even sure how Spétses got its name; best guess is that the Venetians called it 'Spice,' or *spezie*. Like the other Saronic islands, Spétses was repopulated with refugees from the Turkish-controlled mainland. The first shipyards date from the early 17th century (and survive to this day; they built Tim Severin's *Argo*, the replica of an ancient trireme that traced the route of Jason and the Argonauts). By the 19th century Spétses was renowned for its seamanship and, like rival Hýdra, prospered from the derring-do of its blockade-running merchantmen.

Spétses made the history books in a big way by igniting the Greek War of Independence. Through the years of blockade running, the Spetsiots invested their profits in the creation of a small fleet to take on the Turks. When the next rebellion broke out on the Peloponnese in March 1821, Old Spice sprang into action: on 2 April it became the first in the war to raise the flag (bearing the motto 'Freedom or Death'), then two days later the island's fleet won the first naval victory of the war, capturing three Ottoman ships near Mílos. The famous lady admiral of Spétses, the indomitable Laskarina Bouboulina, sailed her *Agamemnon*, one of the finest ships on any Greek island, over to Náfplion and blockaded the port. A bold and genuine military leader, she was personally responsible for a good number of Greek victories. That she was also quite a character as well as a woman and mother of six grown children has contributed to the legend: apparently her chief flaw as an admiral was her predilection for abandoning ship for a horse and sabre if it looked as if the hottest fighting was happening on shore. The Greeks (at the least the men) say she was so ugly that she could only keep lovers by holding them at gunpoint, that she could drink any man in her fleet under the table, and that, when there were no Turks to fight, she lived in Náfplion with her son-in-law, stealing brass guns from the fortress and melting them down to mint counterfeit coins.

### Getting There and Around

**By sea**: several **hydrofoils** daily from Piraeus and other Saronic islands, less frequently with Kýthera and ports on the Peloponnese (Kósta is closest). **Ferry** connections are daily with Piraeus, other Saronic islands and Peloponnese ports, although note that cars are not allowed on the island without special authorization; official vehicles are limited to three taxis and two municipal buses. *Benzínas* or **boat taxis** (for hire at the new harbour) can take up to eight people to other places along the coast. There are frequent **excursion boats** to

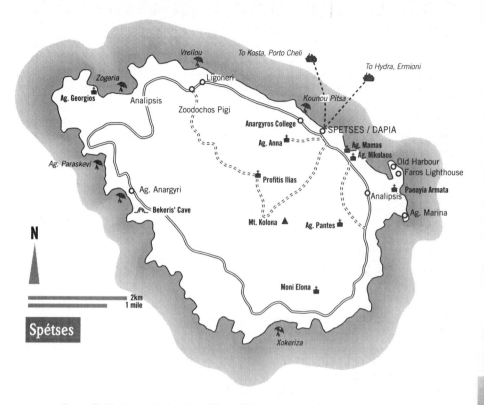

Porto Chéli, the sandy beach at Kósta (15 minutes away) and other small beaches and ports on the mainland. **Port authority**, ✆ 72 245.

**By road: horse-drawn carriages** for hire along the waterfront add a touch of elegance and serve as taxis but don't go any further than Ligonéri or Ag. Marína. Bicycles and scooters may be hired (but not used in town during siesta time, or between 6pm and 6am). The two **buses** run from the town beach to Ag. Marína and Ag. Anárgyri, and from Hotel Possidonion to Ligonéri.

### Tourist Information

The tourist police are also the regular police, Botássi Street, ✆ (0298) 73 100. Two travel offices on the Dápia control much of the accommodation on the island: Takis ✆ 72 215, with listings of cheap rooms, studios and apartments at Ag. Marína, and Meledon, ✆ 74 497, ✉ 74 167. For horseriding, contact the art shop near the post office.

### Festivals

**First Friday after Easter**, at Zoodóchos Pigí; **23 April**, Ag. Geórgios; **1 July** and **1 November**, Anárgyri; **26 July**, Ag. Paraskeví at Zogeriá. The most colourful festival of the year takes place on the nearest weekend to **8 September**, when the Spetsiots commemorate their victory over the Turks in the Straits of Spétses, in 1822. The Ottomans, coming to attack the island, were held at bay throughout the day by the island's fleet, and in the end withdrew when confronted with a drifting fireboat. The battle is re-enacted in the harbour, with fireworks and folk dancing and other festivities.

## Spétses Town

Spétses, the capital and port of the island, is not your typical Greek island town: where most are very dense, it spreads out leisurely every which way under the greenery, in several neighbourhoods. Some of the oldest houses—proud neoclassical captains' mansions, many two centuries old—are inland, safely invisible from the waterfront. Another distinctive feature is the island's love for black and white pebble mosaics that pave both large public places and intimate private courtyards. You'll see one of the biggest, commemorating the revolt of 1821 as you disembark at the **Dápia**, named for elegant square that sweeps down to meet the quay. Bristling with cannon, the Dápia was once the front line of the town's defence, although now it plays a more peaceful role as the vortex of Spétses' café society. On the Dápia's esplanade there's a she-means-business **statue of Bouboulina**, who was assassinated in her house just off the Dápia.

Behind the statue stretches the prim and proper Edwardian façade of one of the first tourist hotels on any Greek island, the **Hotel Possidonion**, built by island philanthropist Sotiris Anargyro, who after making his fortune, decided to make that of Spétses. A dedicated Anglophile, in 1927 he founded a school on the English public school model, the **Anárgyros and Korgialénios College**, just west of the Dápia. John Fowles taught here, and used it, along with the Possidonion, as settings for *The Magus*. (Incidentally, another book by Fowles, *Islands*, is a good read while staying on Spétses, or on any other island for that matter). The school, now closed, is only used occasionally, but Anargyro's other contribution, Spétses' pine forests, grow luxuriantly on, despite patches that have gone up in the summer blazes—lastly in 1990. The house Anargyro built for himself in 1904 (behind the Roumani Hotel) is a fine piece of turn-of-the-century bombast.

Spétses' **museum** (*open 8–2 daily except Mon, with guided tours in English every evening at 6pm for 700dr*) is housed in the far handsomer late-18th-century mansion of Hadziyiannis Mexis. On the ground floor the original furnishings have been preserved, while upstairs there's a box holding Bouboulina's bones, the flag 'Freedom or Death' of the War of Independence, some ancient coins, paintings and costumes.

Of the churches in town, the cathedral **Ag. Nikólaos** by the picturesque **Paléo Limáni**, or old harbour, is the oldest; it once formed part of a monastery where Napoleon's nephew, killed fighting for Greek independence, was pickled in a cask of rum for five years. On Ag. Nikólaos' pretty bell tower the Spetsiots raised their defiant flag in 1821—a bronze cast is displayed just opposite and a pebble mosaic tells the tale. When the Turks came to occupy the island, the inhabitants created mannekins out of barrels and flower pots, dressing them in bright red fezeques and Turkish-appearing uniforms, and set them up along the quay. Seeing them from a distance, the Turkish commander thought that the island had already been taken and sailed on by. These days the old harbour is shared by caique builders, yachts (one among them, recently, belonged to George Bush) fishermen, and a few rocks for swimming—cleaner, at least, than the stony, litter-strewn town beach.

Further east, near the **Fáros** (lighthouse), the church **Panagía Armata** was built after a victory by the Spétses fleet on 8 September 1822; inside, a large painting by Koutzis commemorates the heroic scene. Just beyond is **Ag. Marína** (ΑΓ. ΜΑΡΙΝΑ) the town's beach and nightlife suburb. Off the coast here hovers the tempting, idyllic islet of **Spetsopoúla**, but don't think you can get much closer—it's a private retreat of the ship-owning Niarchos clan, whose *pater familias* Stavros was one of the 'Super Greeks' of the 60s and 70s, and whose doings in the tabloids were only overshadow by those of arch-rival Aristotle Onassis, whom Niarchos regarded as an upstart nobody from Smyrna. The flagrant Niarchos yacht sometimes can be seen, nearly as big as Spetsopoúla itself and topped with a a helicopter pad, but what looks like a surface-to-air missile launcher. Two other fine churches are a walk up the hill, at **Kastélli**, where the houses are mostly ruined: the little 17th-century **Koimistís Theotókou** church has frescoes, and **Ag. Triáda**, a superb, carved iconostasis; ask the tourist police about the keys.

## Around Spétses

The entire jagged coast of Spétses is embellished with shingle or pebbly beaches and rocky swimming coves; the main ones offer full watersports facilites. Get to them by renting a motor or pedal bike (there aren't any hills on the main paved road), or take in one of the frequent caique excursions. Unfortunately, fires have ravaged the pines between Ag. Marína and the lovely bay of Ag. Anárgyri. Going around Spétses clockwise, the first likely place for a swim is **Xokeríza**, with a pleasant shingle beach that rarely gets crowded.

The opposite holds true of lovely **Ag. Anárgyri** (ΑΓ. ΑΝΑΡΓΥΡΟΙ) an irresistable beach, rimmed with trees, bars, and two tavernas; the sands gets pretty busy by 10am when the caiques disgorge their loads. From the beach it's a short swim or walk to **Bekeris' cave**. In 1770, when Muslims from Albania came to take revenge on the Spetsiots for siding with Russia in the war. As they burnt and pillaged, the women and children took refuge in the cave. It is said that one mother killed her whimpering baby to prevent discovery, but just as many other stories claim that the refugees were eventually found and slain anyway. You can enter from the sea or there is a low entrance by land (be sure to duck). The best time of day to go is in the afternoon, when the sun illuminates the interior and the few stalactites inside.

Continuing clockwise, some caiques continue on to the next beach, **Ag. Paraskeví**, a pretty cove with a church and cantina, watched over by the house Fowles used as the residence of the Magus himself, Villa Jasemia (which now takes paying guests, *see* below). A hop over the rocks from Ag. Paraskeví is Spetses' official nudist beach. **Zogeriá**, to the west is a pretty, rocky cove, with good swimming (a hardish slog from the road) and a few places to eat, although no sandy beaches.

From **Vrelloú** in the north you can walk up to Profítis Ilías, although it is far more pleasant just to stay in Vrelloú, in that corner of Spétses called **Paradise** for its beauty, although the beach seems to be a magnet for plastic bottles, Coke cans, food wrappers and all the other detritus of tourist civilization. **Ligonéri**, not far from the Dápia, has another shady beach that can be similarly afflicted. The recently christianed **Blueberry Beach**, under a condominium-like development of the same name, is usually cleaner.

*expensive*

**Possidonion,** ✆ 72 308, ✉ 72 208 (*A*). Recently renovated under new management, this grand old dowager has been the classy place to stay since 1914. *Open April–Oct.* Fowles fans with fat wallets can soak up the atmosphere in the **Villa Jasemia** (book through Pine Island Travel, ✆ 72 314, ✉ 72 872). **Roumani,** ✆ 72 344 (*B*), is right on the Dápia. *Open April–Oct.* **Akrogiali,** at Ag. Anárgyri, ✆ 73 695 (*A*) is a good, small pension on Spétses' prettiest beach. *Open April–Oct.* **Myrtoon,** ✆ 72 888 (*C*) with a roof garden and bar, is open all year.

*moderate–inexpensive*

**Villa Kriezi**, at Ag. Marína, ✆ 72 171, an A class guest house, each room with private bath and many with sea view; open all year with low season rates in May, June and October. **Villa Christina**, ✆ 72 218 (*B*) is fairly central charming little pension. **Klimis,** ✆ 73 777 (*D*), has pleasant rooms on the waterfront, on the east end of town (and one of the very few open all year); the nearby **Argo,** ✆ 73 225 (*E*) is even cheaper. In Spétses town, **Nikólaos Polymenakos,** overlooking the old port, ✆ 73 548, is a pleasant guesthouse, near a shady garden. **Alexandri,** ✆ 73 073 (*E*) has some of the cheapest rates.

---

The best seafood on Spétses is at the very popular **Patralis,** a 10min walk to the right of the main harbour; it's right on the water and serves excellent fish soup and mussels, and a good variety of tasty fish dishes, but at a price (*5–6000dr*). **Stelios,** next to the Klimis Hotel, also has waterfront dining, but at more earthy prices. Good fish here too, especially the tuna steaks fresh from the nearby fish market, and some vegetarian dishes (*3000dr*). For something in the 2500dr range try the excellent **Lazaros** (uphill from the Dápia). Nostalgic tastebuds can find relief at the **Lord Byron Bar,** over a cottage pie and cider, or at the **Red Dragon Chinese restaurant** above the Yachting Club. **Taverna Tassos** at Ag. Anárgyri is a wonderful reminder of what Greek food can taste like when a good Greek chef spends time over it, and prices are reasonable.

### Entertainment and Nightlife

Quiet Spétses starts to swing at around 11pm. **Figaro** with its seaside patio is the hot spot for dancing, young and international and loud until well after midnight, when Greek music comes on and everyone changes their steps to dance along. The flashing lights of **Disco Fever** draws in a wide assortment of Brits; **Naos** looks like a castle and throbs with Techno beats. **The Fox** is pricey but great for a real Greek evening with the Greeks, with live music, dancing, singing (with a good deal of audience participation as the night wears on). At **Bracera** with a wood décor and the smaller **Captain's** run shoulder-shimmying in close quarters to American and Europop. For something quieter, have a drink at the friendly **Halycon** or upstairs at the **Veranda,** which plays soft Greek music.

The Sporades and Évia

LALÁRIA

The Sporades ('sporadic' or 'scattered') islands were for donkey's years one of the most neglected, least visited corners of Greece—not only were they a pain to get to, but they lacked the big-league archaeological sites or the historical associations evoked by so many other islands. Then, beginning in the 1960s, Greek holidaymakers made Skiáthos and Skópelos their own. A vanguard of Germans began to restore the old homes on Alónissos for summer villas. An airport was built on Skiáthos, linking the island to Athens, and then to most of charter-flight Europe—and the rest is history. Perhaps it was inevitable. Some immortal hand or eye has framed these islands to fit nearly everyone's idea of a holiday paradise, with their picture-postcard sandy beaches, cool summer breezes, thick pine forests and lush greenery. Each has its individual character, although Skiáthos, with the loveliest beaches of all, has become so popular that 'Greek' is hardly the first adjective you would use to describe it. On the opposite end of the scale, Skýros remains one of the most original and intriguing islands in Greece, with minimal tourist facilities despite a new airport of its own. Skópelos, the greenest and most naturally endowed of the group, remains very Greek and dignified; Alónissos is an odd mixture of cosmopolitan tourism and old-fashioned ways where women still wear their traditional dress and card wool as they chat. Évia, the second largest island in Greece after Crete, historically has been a land of quiet farms, too close to the mainland to have a strong personality of its own. Yet Évia is endowed with ravishing scenery and a long, scarcely developed coastline that is increasingly attractive to both Greek and foreign visitors escaping the cosmopolitan crowds on the other islands, and a godsend to the kind of traveller who came to Greece 20 years ago and longs to recapture something of the first pre-EU, pre-package-tour rapture.

The first settlers on the Sporades were of Thracian origin. In the 16th century BC Crete colonized the islands, introducing the cultivation of olives and grapes. With the decline of the Minoans, Mycenaeans from Thessaly known as the Dolopians (first cousins of the Achaeans) settled the Sporades, using them as bases for daring naval expeditions. Much of the mythology of the islands has its roots during this period: Achilles himself was raised on Skýros. In the 8th century BC the Chalkidians of Évia captured the Sporades as stepping stones to their colonial ambitions in Macedonia. These new invaders continued the sea traditions of the Dolopians but increasingly came into conflict with Athenian interests until 476 BC, when Athens sent Kimon to crush the Sporades' fleets. The Athenians then colonized the islands, but successfully presented themselves as liberators rather than conquerors; of all the islands, none had closer ties with Athens. The government of the Sporades was run on the model of Athenian democracy, and Athena became the prominent goddess in local pantheons.

When the Spartans defeated Athens in the Peloponnesian War, the Sporades were briefly part of their spoils. A greater threat to Athenian influence came in the person of Philip II of Macedon, who claimed the islands in a dispute that attracted the attention of the entire Greek world. Philip took the islands in 322 BC as a prelude to nabbing Athens itself.

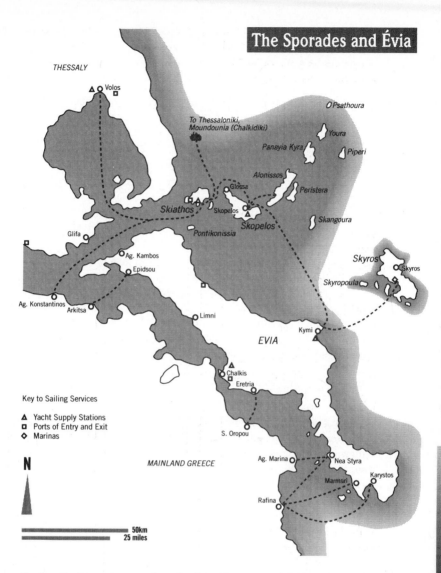

# The Sporades and Évia

*THESSALY*

△ ○ Volos
□

To Thessaloniki,
Moundounia (Chalkidiki)

○ Psathoura

Youra

Panayia Kyra

Piperi

Alonissos

Glossa

Peristera

*Skiathos*

Skopelos △

Skangoura

*Skopelos*

Pontikonissia

Glifa ○

○ Ag. Kambos

*Skyros*

Skyros

○ Epidsou

Skyropoula

Ag. Konstantinos ○
Arkitsa ○

○ Limni

*EVIA*

Kymi △

△ Chalkis
□ Eretria

**Key to Sailing Services**

△ Yacht Supply Stations
□ Ports of Entry and Exit
◇ Marinas

**N**

*MAINLAND GREECE*

S. Oropou

Ag. Marina ○

Nea Styra

Karystos
Marmari ○

Rafina ○

|======| 50km
|======| 25 miles

During the Roman occupation, the Sporades retained their traditional links
with Athens. The Byzantines, however, made them a place of exile for unruly
or unwanted nobles who set themselves up as the local aristocracy until 1207,
when the Gizzis of Venice picked up the Sporades as their share in the spoils
of the Fourth Crusade. Filippo Gizzi, the most notorious of the dynasty,
usurped control from a senior relative and ruled the islands as a pirate king
until Likários, the Admiral of Emperor Michael Palaeológos, took him in chains
to Constantinople. Afterwards, possession of the islands see-sawed back and
forth between Greeks and Franks, until Mohammed the Conqueror took

Constantinople in 1453. The islanders quickly invited Venice back as the lesser evil, although the Venetians were forced out when all their crafty agreements with the Ottoman Empire crumbled before the violent attacks of Barbarossa in the 16th century.

Once they had the Sporades, the Turks promptly forgot all about them, except at tax time. The islands were so exposed to pirates that a permanent Turkish population never settled there. In the 1821 revolution, insurgents from Thessaly found refuge on the islands and in 1830 the Treaty of London included them in the original kingdom of Greece.

### Getting There

**By air:** flying to Skiáthos (numerous charters, or on Olympic, twice daily in summer from Athens) or to Skýros (4 times a week) is by far the least painless way.

**By sea:** Skýros may only be reached from or via Kými, in Évia, from where there are weekly sailings (at least) to the other Sporades. The main **ferry** ports to Skiáthos, Skópelos and Alónissos are Vólos in Thessaly (easily reached by train from Athens) and Ag. Konstantínos. **Hydrofoils** also ply these routes daily in summer from Vólos and Ag. Konstantínos and provide good inter-island links in the summer. If you're departing from Athens, Alkyon Tours, at 98 Academías, ✆ (01) 364 3220, has long specialized in travel to the Sporades, and has all the latest bus and boat timetables. If you're approaching from the north, there are weekly ferries until the end of September from Thessaloníki, Néa Moudaniá (on the Chalkidikí peninsula) and Límnos.

## Alónissos (ΑΛΟΝΝΗΣΟΣ)

The least known and most serene of the Sporades, long, skinny Alónissos is the queen of its own little archipelago of nine islets. But in the last few decades, while the other Sporades found new roles as trendy tourist destinations, Alónissos sat on the sidelines, recovering from an earthquake that hit its attractive main town in 1965, from the loss of its old grapefruit orchards and vineyards through disease, and from local and government politicians who contrived to retard its development. This suited many visitors just fine, especially the kind in search of peace and quiet, good fishing and diving, and places to potter about in boats. Having only a mile or two of paved carriageway left nine-tenths of Alónissos accessible only by foot; fine walking country for the hearty, with glimpses of the rare Eleanora's falcon soaring high overhead as a reward.

Then, in 1992, Alónissos found something of a new role when, after the urging of environmental groups across Europe, Greece's first National Marine Park was set up around much of Alónissos' archipelago to protect the Mediterranean monk seal—the rarest animal in Europe (*see* p.542, and **Topics** p.63). The donkey tracks of old that crossed the island have been paved. Package holiday makers and flotilla yacht fleets have arrived and the long-planned airport may even happen. If tourism is far more organized, it's not in any obtrusive way; at the end of the day, retarded development should help Alónissos get the balance right.

## History

The history of Alónissos is complicated by the fact that the modern Alónissos is not ancient Halonnesos, but actually bore the name Ikos. The confusion resulted from an over-eager restoration of ancient place names after independence, but in Alónissos' case the mistake was certainly an improvement. As for the real ancient Halonnesos, some scholars say it must have been tiny Psathoúra, northernmost of Alónissos' islets, where the extensive ruins of an ancient city lie submerged off shore. Another possibility is Kyrá Panagía, a fertile islet with two fine harbours.

Inhabited from Neolithic times, Ikos/Alónissos was part of the Cretan colony of Prince Staphylos, who planted the first of the vines that were to make Ikos famous. In the 14th century BC the Mycenaeans took over, counting among their settlers Peleus, the father of Achilles. In Classical times, Ikos had two city-states that thrived through exporting wine. The Athenians established a naval base there in the 4th century, and in 42 BC the Romans let Athens have the whole thing. During the Middle Ages Ikos was ruled by Skópelos, under the name of Achilliodromia, Liadromia or simply Dromos (road). As for ancient Halonnesos (wherever it may be), it was governed throughout antiquity by Athens, which lost control of it in the 4th century BC to a pirate named Sostratos. Philip of Macedon took it from him, quoting the famous speech of Demosthenes, 'Concerning Alónissos', which initiated the troubles between Athens and Macedonia. Skópelos took the island in 341 BC when Philip offered to return it to

Athens; Philip, however, crushed these opportunists and the island lost all its importance, its port subsided into the sea, and even its location faded away from human memory.

### Getting There and Around

**By sea**: at least once a day with Vólos, Skópelos, Skiáthos and Ag. Konstantínos; 3 times a week with Thessaloníki, once a week with Kými (Évia). Daily **hydrofoils** to Skópelos, Skiáthos, Thessaloníki, Vólos and Ag. Konstantínos, frequent connections with Skýros and Néa Moudanía. Daily summer **excursion boats** from Patitíri go up and down the coast, and out to the islets of Peristéra, Kyrá Panagía, and Yoúra. **Port authority**, ✆ 65 595.

**By road**: buses link Patitíri and Chóra 3 times a day.

### Tourist Police

See regular police, ✆ (0424) 65 205.

### Festivals

**40 days after Easter**, Análypsis; **1 July**, Ag. Anárgiroi; **17 July**, Ag. Marína; **26 July**, Ag. Paraskeví; **15 August**, Panagías.

## Patitíri

The face of Alónissos changed dramatically when the earthquake of 1965 devastated the principal town, Chóra. The junta summarily forced all the inhabitants into prefab relief housing at the port, **Patitíri** (ΠΑΤΗΤΗΡΙ) and prevented their return to Chóra by cutting off the water and electricity service. Since the 1960s, Patitíri has spread its wings to merge with the fishing hamlet of **Vótsi**; in between, a few families are still stuck in the relief village. Charming it ain't, but neither is Patitíri unpleasant, and bougainvillaea covers many a concrete sin. Right by the quay you can visit the offices of the **Hellenic Society for the Study and Protection of the Monk Seal**, with a slide and video show upstairs; around the corner are the offices of the **European Natural Heritage Fund** (*open 9–2*). Both will make you aware of the odds against the little grey monk seal (*Monacus monacus*), an animal that has been extinct in France since 1920, in Spain since 1950, and in Italy since 1975. Pollution in the Mediterranean and loss of habitat are two reasons; fishermen, looking on them as rivals, often killed them on sight. The largest remaining population in the world, with an estimated 300 of the 500 seals, lives in Greece, and the 30 or so seals that live on the small island of Pipéri are the largest community. Now protected by the National Marine Park (ΘΑΛΑΣΣΙΟ ΠΑΡΚΟ), Pipéri is strictly off limits, unless you have special permission or go on a tour (*see* 'Skópelos', below).

There's a small beach at Patitíri, and another, prettier one at Vótsi, just to the north. The best beaches are further north, but within easy walking distance to the south there's **Marpoúnta** with the submerged remains of a temple of Asklepios, and the much nicer beaches at **Víthisma** and **Megálos Moúrtias**.

## Chóra (Alónissos Town)

A road, or a pretty if somewhat steep mule path through nut orchards, leads to the old capital of the island, **Chóra** (ΧΩΡΑ), magnificently set high up above the sea, with superb views, especially of Alónissos's frequent cinemascope sunsets. After the 1965 earthquake, and the government's forced removal of the inhabitants, far-sighted Germans and Brits bought the old homes for a song and restored them, agreeing at first to do without such conveniences as running water and electricity (although now they've been hooked up, as the resentment of the former residents has somewhat diminished); but most of the houses are empty outside of the summer, and some now contain artsy little shops. The walls of Chóra were built by the Byzantines and repaired by the Venetians, and ghosts are said to dance around the 17th-century church of **Christós**. From Chóra it's a 20-minute walk down to sandy **Vrisítsa** beach.

## Beaches around Alónissos

Caique excursions run out to the island's best beaches, most of which have at least a snack bar or taverna in the summer. Going north from Patitíri, the first really good beach is **Chrysí Miliá**, in a small cove enveloped with pines, and with a pair of tavernas. The 5th-century BC capital of ancient Ikos was found by the pleasant shingly beach **Kokkinó Kástro** (30 minutes by caique from Patitíri; if you know where to look you can make out some of its walls in the sea. Recently a much, much older settlement was uncovered here, from the Middle Paleolithic era (100,000–33,000 BC), making it one of the oldest known sites in the Aegean; the finds are in the museum at Vólos. Further north, **Stení Valá** and **Kalamákia** have small pensions and tavernas. Their beaches, well sheltered in the embrace of nearby Peristéra islet, offer the best fishing and watersports on the island. **Ag. Dimítrios**, the next beach up, has the ruins of a Byzantine fountain and another ancient settlement in the sea; fossils of prehistoric beasts were found at nearby Megliámos. The beach is lovely and usually deserted. Lobster is plentiful off the remote northern coast; isolated beaches without any facilities are further north, at **Kopelousáko** and the old shepherd's village **Gérakas**.

## Alónissos' Archipelago

The beauty of the many islets scattered around Alónissos' shores have made the island a popular flotilla holiday destination. Olive-covered **Peristéra** (Dove) islet follows the east coast of Alónissos, its Siamese twin until separated by a natural upheaval. Peristéra has plenty of sandy beaches and three tiny shepherds' hamlets, Mnímata, Livádia and Xílos, the last near a ruined castle. Rough camping is usually tolerated, and most evenings excursion boats from Patitíri bring folks over for a beach barbecue. Every 10 days a caique goes to **Psathoúra**, where one of the most powerful lighthouses in Greece guides passing ships. It is another candidate for the island of the Sirens as well as a possible ancient Halonnesos. There's a submerged city by the lighthouse, as well as a sunken volcano.

Lovely, wooded **Kyrá Panagía** (Pelagós) is two or three hours by caique from Patitíri. Now uninhabited (except for wild goats and the odd shepherd), the island once supported two monasteries, the original one founded in the Middle Ages by monks from Mount Áthos and the other, on the east coast, established at a later date; although both are now abandoned the islet still belongs to Mount Áthos. At the port of Ag. Pétros you can see the remains of a 12th-century Byzantine ship in the waters; when it was discovered its hold was filled with ceramics. Kyrá Panagía has sandy beaches, a pretty stalactite cave (believed to have been the home of the Cyclops), and plenty of opportunities for wild bushwalking.

There is another monastery connected to Mount Áthos on verdant **Skantzoúra**, which offers excellent fishing in its many sea coves and caves. **Pappoú**, home to a diminishing hare population, has the remnants of a tiny 7th-century church, while on **Gioúra** (ancient Geronta) a rare breed of goat skips about the rocks. A few Classical and Roman remains have been discovered there; most spectacular of all is another, even more dramatic 'Cyclops' cave with stalactites, although the entrance requires a torch, stout shoes and a fit constitution; the island guardians will unlock the gate. **Pipéri**, on the north end of the National Marine Park, is a wildlife sanctuary, and home to Eleanora falcons as well as its small but stable colony of monk seals.

## *Alónissos* ℗ *(0424–)*           **Where to Stay**

Most of the island's accommodation is in Patitíri and Vótsi, though the spiffier hotels and pensions tend to be booked solid by packagers. To make up for it, there are 3000 beds to rent in private houses and generally plenty of people to offer them to you when you get off the boat.

### *expensive*

**Archontiko**, near the beach at Patitíri, ℗/◉ 65 004, Athens ◉ (01) 683 2044, has comfortable apartments, all with fridges and some with full kitchens, and with parking. *Open May–Oct.* **Alkyon**, right on the sea in Patitíri, ℗ 65 450, ◉ 65 195 (*B*) is a modern white hotel with balconies overlooking the centre of action. **Haravgi**, above the port, ℗ 65 189 (*B*) has 22 well-scrubbed and wholesome rooms with a pretty terrace to sit out on over a drink.

### *moderate*

**Alonnisos Beach**, in Vótsi (just beyond Chrysí Miliá beach), ℗ 65 281, in Athens (01) 223 0869 (*C*) is a newish bungalow complex with a pool and tennis. *Open July–Sept.* **Marpounta Bungalows**, 3km from Patitíri, ℗ 65 219 (*C*) is an older, isolated, self-contained campground-like complex, with sea sports, tennis, a restaurant and nightclub; get there by caique, horse or foot. *Open April–Oct.* **Galaxy**, above Patitíri, ℗ 65 251, ◉ 65 110 (*C*) is a much larger comfortable hotel-restaurant complex. *Open May–Oct.* A 20-minute walk from Patitíri, **Panorama**, ℗ 65 006, is a friendly little pension in the trees, with swimming off the small beach below and restaurant and bar; the owner speaks good English. *Open May–Sept.*

### *inexpensive*

**Liadromia**, on the cliffs of Patitíri, ℗ 65 521, ◉ 65 096 (*E*) overlooks the beach by the port, with good, clean, simple rooms, although they verge on the moderate category in high season. For a cheaper room, take pot luck or try Alónissos Travel near the wharf, ℗ 65 188, ◉ 65 511 or Drosakis Travel, ℗ 65 225, ◉ 65 719. There are also a few rooms available in Stení Vála, Chóra (though harder to find), and even fewer on the islet of Peristéri (along with some tolerated freelance camping). On Alónissos proper, there's the organized **Ikoros Camping**, ℗ 65 258, at Stení Vála.

## *Alónissos* ℗ *(0424–)*           **Eating Out**

If you've wanted to splurge on a feast of Mediterranean lobster (*astakós*), Alónissos is the place for it; many of the quayside restaurants in Patitíri serve it as well as other marine delectables (swordfish, octopus, sea bream, blacktails, snapper and fat sardines) pulled from the limpid waters of the little archipelago; the Aegean, for some reason, is especially salty here and the fish especially tasty. For an excellent meal in a pretty setting under the trees, follow the path around the rocky promontory to the left of the port to **Argos**, ℗ 65 141, with a wider than usual selection of fresh fish and lobster and a good wine list.

*Open May–Oct.* **Nefeli**, the adjacent pub, has music all day. On the main street, **Ouzeri O Nefteris** serves not only little tumblers of firewater, but shrimp salad, lobster and *saganáki* (melted cheese) on grilled potatoes. **O Astakos**, near the back of town, specializes, as its name suggests, in lobster (*current prices range around 7000dr a kilo*). For good food and a magnificent view, arrive early to get a table at the **Paraport Taverna**, one of seven restaurants that have opened up in Chóra, where a meal costs about 3500dr.

## Skiáthos (ΣΚΙΑΘΟΣ)

Racy, cosmopolitan Skiáthos is not for the shy teetotaller or anyone looking for a slice of 'authentic' Greece. Although still an isolated peasant island community in the early 1970s, Skiáthos has been catapulted faster than any other into the frantic world of tourism, with all the pros and cons that this inevitably entails, beginning with predatory attitudes of the *nouveau riche* ex-fishermen and farmers; corruption and violence (violence by Greek island standards, at any rate) have long been a factor in local life; those who know it speak darkly of generations of untreated syphilis. Nevertheless, Skiáthos is one of the most popular destinations in Greece, and with good cause: it is stunningly beautiful, and its magnificent beaches (by most counts there are 62) provide some of the best swimming in Greece. Add to this a host of lively bars and restaurants and you have the ingredients for a potent, heady cocktail that attracts the young and the young at heart from the four corners of the globe.

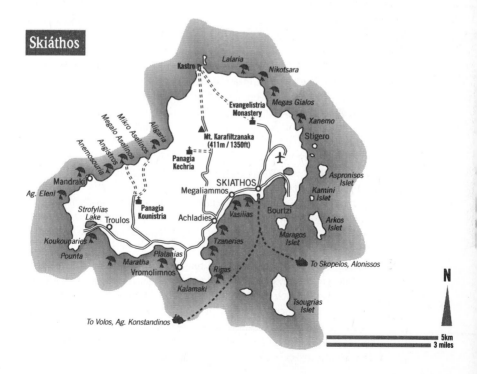

# History

When the great Persian fleet of King Xerxes sailed to Greece in 480 BC, it encountered a fierce storm in the waters off Skiáthos. So many of Xerxes' ships were damaged that he put in for repairs. During his stay Xerxes came up with the world's first-known navigational aid, to keep his fleet from wrecking on a reef called Myrmes (now called Lepheteris and to this day a dangerous menace to ships sailing between Skiáthos and the mainland). 'Thither the barbarians brought and set up a pillar of stone that the shoal might be clearly visible,' as Herodotus wrote; thanks to its guidance, Xerxes succeeded in slipping safely past the Athenian patrol ships towards his first sea battle at Artemisseon and eventual defeat at Salamis. Part of the pillar can still be seen today, in the courtyard of the Naval Cadet School in Piraeus.

The rest of Skiáthos' history follows that of the other Sporades. The Gizzi ruled the island in the name of Venice and built the fort on Boúrtzi islet by the present-day town, which was settled in 1790 by refugees from Límni on Évia. The Skiathiot navy assisted the Russians in the campaign at Cêsme, when they defeated the Ottoman fleet. The islanders revolted against the distant Turks in 1805, and sent so many ships to aid the cause of independence that Skiáthos itself was left unprotected and prey to marauders. It was one of the first places to be touched by the Orthodox reformist movement, Kollivádes, emanating from Mount Áthos (although Skiáthos means 'shadow of Áthos' in Greek, its name comes from a pre-Hellenic source). A local writer, Aléxandros Papadiamántis (1851–1911) immortalized Skiáthos in his novels there, although the books have yet to be translated into English.

## Getting There and Around

**By air**: at least 4 flights a day from Athens, and numerous charters from European cities. Olympic Airways office is at Papadiamánti, © 22 200 or 229; airport information © 22 049.

**By sea**: daily from Vólos, Ag. Konstantínos, Skópelos and Alónissos, 4 times a week to Thessaloníki, twice a week to Tínos, Mýkonos, Páros, Santoríni and Herákleon (Crete), once a week to Skýros and Kými (Évia).

**Hydrofoils** daily in summer from Vólos and Ag. Konstantínos with connections to Skópelos and Alónissos, less frequently with Skýros, Mármaras and Néa Moudaniá (Chalkidikí). Daily **excursion boat** to Skópelos and Alónissos. The boats bobbing up and down in front of the cafés in the old harbour will take you to most beaches and you'll hear the owners calling out their destinations. Some offer round-the-island trips but be warned that on the north side there is a fairly uninteresting stretch of coast and the sea can be rough—many a daytripper returns green about the gills. If you want to get about the island under your own steam, there are a number of places to rent cars and scooters, or boats by the day or hour. Be careful on the roads—traffic is fast-moving. **Port authority**, © 22 017.

**By road: buses** to other parts of the islands run hourly in season (until 11pm, from Skiáthos town to Koukonariés) from the new harbour. Demand is so great in summer that your feet may not touch the floor throughout the journey. **Taxis** also operate from here and are in great demand, so don't be shy to share.

## Tourist Police

See regular police, © (0427) 21 111.

26 July, Ag. Paraskeví; 27 July, Ag. Panteleímonos; 15 August, at Evangelismós; 27 August, Ag. Fanóurios.

## Skiáthos Town

The capital and only real town on the island, **Skiáthos**, is a spread of traditional whitewashed houses with red tile roofs, overhung with bougainvillaea and with freshly washed sheets rippling in the breeze. A walk through the back-streets will help you absorb the feeling of the place, but don't expect to encounter many donkeys; you're more likely to find yourself dodging high-speed trail bikes. The town has two harbours, separated by the pretty **Boúrtzi** promontory, where the medieval fortress now contains a restaurant. If you find yourself in Skiáthos town and simply can't summon the energy to join the queues for bus, boat or taxi, dive off the rock here and pretend you're in a Martini ad. For a sweeping panorama of Skiáthos town and the neighbouring island of Skópelos, take the steps up at the end of the old harbour past the lazy waterfront cafés and souvenir shops. Late afternoon brings the scene to life and cocktail hour seems to last forever as you sit and watch an extraordinary international selection of the human race go by. If this flagrant hedonism pricks the conscience, you can get your shot of culture by locating the house of Skiáthos' illustrious poet and novelist, Alexander Papadiamántis (d. 1911), situated just off the main street, which bears his name; it's small, and not terribly interesting (get the key from the town hall).

Hourly excursion boats wait to whisk you off in half an hour to **Tsougriás** islet, facing Skiáthos town. In the sixties the Beatles wanted to buy it. It's an ideal place to escape the droves of summer visitors, with its fine sand and excellent swimming. The simple snack bar usually provides freshly caught *marídes* (whitebait) to munch at a table under the trees, but you may have to share your food with the resident wasp population. Tsougriás has two other beaches, accessible only by foot, where you really can play Robinson Crusoe for the day.

*Skiáthos ✆ (0427–)* **Where to Stay**

Skiáthos has accommodation to suit everyone's taste and pocket, but in high season when it seems the island will sink beneath the weight of its visitors—who outnumber the locals eleven to one—finding a bed without a reservation or package booking is the devil. **Meltemi**, on the new harbour front, ✆ 22 493 (*B; mod*) has a pool but is generally booked solid in summer months. However, have a drink at their pleasant bar and watch the antics of the flotilla crowd as they moor and unmoor with zealous gung-ho. *Open April–Oct.* **Alkyon**, in nearby Ammoudiá, ✆ 22 981 (*B; mod*) is a standard hotel with a cool marble lobby and comfortable rooms overlooking the hotel's pleasant gardens. **San Remo**, ✆ 22 078 (*D; mod–inexp*) is a colourful hotel whose terraced rooms give you dress circle seats to observe the harbour traffic and wave at the green-horns on the incoming charter jets. **Australia Hotel**, just off Papadiamántis Street, behind the post office, ✆ 22 488 (*E; inexp*) is centrally placed; rooms are simple and come with private bath. **Ilion**, nearby, ✆ 21 193 (*E; inexp*) has pleasant modern rooms. **Rooms** exist all over the town, but you'll have to seek them out; it's not common practice for owners to meet incoming boats or planes to hawk them. Wander up the hilly streets and ask the ladies sitting on their doorsteps. Prices are rising at a brisk pace, so expect to pay up to 6000dr for a double room. If you come unstuck in your quest for a room, try any of the tourist offices on the waterfront.

## Skiáthos © (0427–)                                                    Eating Out

Eating out in Skiáthos is a hit-and-miss affair; often the most beautifully located tavernas serve the worst food. Generally speaking, the tavernas on the steps at the western end of the old harbour tend to be expensive, but look out for the *psistariá* lodged between them where they serve good spit-roasted chicken and *souvláki* at low prices. The new local favourite is **Asprolithos**, although it's not easy to find; take the road opposite the police station and ask. Behind the San Remo Hotel, look for the **Windmill** in a converted you know what, recently renovated and serving delicious international specialities along with a lovely view, but for a price (*5–6000dr*). **Casa Blanca**, in a small square near the church at the end of the waterfront, serves excellent pasta and other Italian delights. To get to another first-rate Italian restaurant, **La Casa**, hike the steps at the far end of the waterfront. At **Limenaki**, on the waterfront past the new harbour, you can enjoy such luxuries as avocado, shrimps and pepper steak, as near to the real thing as you'll find in Greece without paying through the nose. While you're sampling some of the standard but well-prepared dishes at **Dionysos**, just off the main street, the waiters may treat you to a floor-show of Greek dancing—dinner with wine around 2500dr. Up near the clock tower, overlooking the Boúrtzi, the **Family** serves good traditional Greek fare in a pleasant atmosphere.

### Entertainment and Nightlife

Having eaten, you'll be spoilt for choice when it comes to bars, but they're not cheap. An oasis of tranquillity in the Skiáthos summer madhouse, **Adagio** opposite Stavros taverna in Evangelístrias St has a pleasant décor and classical music to soothe the eye and ear, and Sophia, the multilingual owner, will give you a genuinely warm and friendly welcome; a favourite place for an after-dinner drink or coffee. The **Kentavros**, in Papadiamántis Square off the main street, is always popular for its lively but not deafening music. The charming little **Admiral Benbow Inn** (Polytechníou St) provides a corner of old England on Skiáthos while in the same street the **Borzoi** is still worth a try after midnight if you can afford the drinks. On a warm summer evening the picturesque waterfront bars come into their own, the best being **Jimmy's** and the more upscale **Oasis**. For a bop at the disco, everyone goes to **La Piscine**, a huge monster of a place with a swimming pool and bars on the ring road behind Skiáthos town, or the ever popular **BBC**, on the road that runs in front of the airport.

## Koukounariés and Other Beaches

Beaches, beaches and more beaches are the key to Skiáthos' success, and they rim the emerald isle like lace. Mobile sardine tins called buses follow the main road along the south coast, stopping within easy walking of the island's best strands, nearly all equipped with places to lunch and someone hiring out windsurf boards and other watersports gear. From town, the most convenient is **Megáli Ámmos**, although it's generally too crowded for comfort. Moving westward, **Achládies** (ΑΧΛΑΔΙΕΣ) beach, dominated by the large Esperides hotel (with tennis court open to the public) is also densely populated for most of the summer season. Beyond that, 5km from town, the **Kalamáki** peninsula juts out with a coating of holiday villas. Beaches here include **Kanapítsa** (ΚΑΝΑΠΙΤΣΑ), a popular cove for swimming and water-sports, and a restaurant by the water, and nearby, **Vromólimnos**, 'dirty lake', hard to pronounce and hard to find, but is one of the finest places to swim on the island, with powder-puff-soft sand. When the rest of Skiáthos is bulging at the seams, you can often find room to toss a frisbee around on the next beach, **Platánias.**

Convenient by bus or boat, **Troúlos** has an attractive taverna and Chinese restaurant waiting to welcome the round-the-island trippers, so be sure to get there well before or after them to avoid the busy rush. The last stop, 12km from Skiáthos town, is the legendary **Koukounariés** (ΚΟΥΚΟΥΝΑΡΙΕΣ), with 'the Best Beach in Greece' pretensions: a superb sweeping crescent bay of soft sand fringed with pine trees that somehow escaped from the South Pacific, although in August it seems that you not only can 'see a world in a grain of sand' as Blake wrote, but that each grain of sand has a world sitting on top of it. Tavernas, hotels and a camp-site are hidden behind the trees, around a small lake. Hyper-trendy **Krássa**, nowadays called **Banana** beach, perhaps because it's where you can peel off everything in high season and lie cheek-to-cheek in a bunch, is up the hill with the sea on your left when you get off the bus at Koukounariés. Next is the lovely **Ag. Eléni**, the last beach accessible by road, a somewhat quieter spot with a view across to the Pelion peninsula on the mainland.

In general, beaches on the north coast are subject to the *meltémi* winds. **Mandráki**, reached in 15 minutes by a lovely footpath from the lagoon behind Koukounariés, has two lovely sand beaches (and a snack bar). A paved road now reaches **Aselinós**, a sandy beach in an arcadian setting; it passes by way of the 17th-century monastery **Panagía Kounistrá**, built on a height overlooking the north coast, where an icon of the Virgin was found dangling in a tree. The beach at **Lalária** (accessible only by sea) is a marvel of silvery pebbles, shimmering like a cres-cent moon beneath the cliff, with a natural arch closing off one end and nearby sea grottoes—**Skotiní** ('the dark'—so bring a light if you want to see anything), **Galázia**, 'the blue', and **Chálkini**, 'the copper'.

## Inland to Kástro

When charter-set life begins to pall, there are several escape hatches and a network of walking paths, described in detail in a local guide by Rita and Dietrich Harkort. The occasional bus, or scenic donkey path beginning just before the turning to the airport road, leads in 4km up to the last working monastery on Skiáthos, **Evangelístria** (*open 8–12 and 5–7, proper attire required*), founded in 1797 by monks forced to flee Mount Áthos for their support of the tradition-alist Kollivádes movement. The monastery—a lovely, peaceful place with a triple-domed church and garden courtyard—became a refuge for both monks and scholars, and for members of the revolutionary militia movement from the Olympus area, known as the *armatolés*. With the support of the Russians, the *armatolés* raised a small pirate fleet to harass the Turks. When Russia signed a peace treaty with Turkey in 1807, the Greeks revolutionaries were abandoned, and many took refuge on Skiáthos; under Giánnis Stathás, they united in an irregular army, and over the monastery hoisted the blue and white flag of independent Greece that they had just invented. The Ottoman fleet soon put an end to their pretensions, but a statement had been made and inspired fighters in the War of Independence 14 years later. Only a rusting cannon recalls the monastery's belligerent past, as well as a few displays in the small museum.

Further on, a 2-hour walk (the path is well marked from Ag. Konstantínos near Skiáthos town) leads across the island to **Kástro**, a town founded on a difficult, windswept niche in the 14th century, when pirates were on the warpath, and inhabited until 1829, when everyone moved down to the sheltered comfort of Skiáthos town. Eight of the original 30 Byzantine churches more or less still stand (one, **Christós**, has good frescoes and a chandelier) among the houses and a Turkish hammam. The view from the top is quite lovely and there's a quiet beach below, used to smuggle out trapped Allied troops in the war. Skíathiot writer Papadiamántis describes Kástro's churches in a short story, *The Poor Saint*: 'some of them stood on rocks or on reefs by the shore, in the sea, gilded in summer by the dazzling light, washed in the winter by the waves. The raging north wind whipped and shook them, resolutely ploughing that sea, sowing wreckage and debris on the shore, grinding the granite into sand, kneading the sand into rocks and stalactites, winnowing the foam into spokes of spray.' If the *meltémi* is blowing, you can see that he wasn't exaggerating.

A detour on the path could be made to the pretty 15th-century monastery **Panagía Kechriá**, containing some fine frescoes painted after 1745. A path from here continues down to a lovely, isolated beach, served by a delightful make-shift snack bar.

---

*Skiáthos ☎ (0427–)*           ***Where to Stay and Eating Out***

### Kanapítsa/Achládies

**Nostos**, at Kanapítsa, ☎ 22 520 (*A; exp*) commands a majestic position and at night glitters like a real palace; an Olympic-sized pool is handy for those who can't face the long trek down to the sea, and its rustically decorated bungalows make a refreshing change. *Open April–Oct.*
**Esperides** at Achladiés, ☎ 22 245, ✆ 21 584 (*A; exp*)—as large hotels go it's one of the best and popular with tour operators. **Villa Diamanti** at Kanapítsa, ☎ 22 491, Athens ☎ (01) 590 3280 (*A; exp*), 50m from the sea, has stylish apartments in a garden setting, with a barbecue terrace. *Open May–Oct.* For something less pricey, try **Villa Anni**, ☎ 21 105 at Achládies or **Kanapitsa Beach**, ☎ 22 170, both with C-class apartments. On the beach at Megáli Ámmos try **Angeliki**, ☎ 22 354 (*E; inexp*) or the little **Rea**, ☎ 21 013 (*E; inexp*); rooms are basic but the thriving flora on the terraces lend an exotic atmosphere. Nearby, friendly little **Ellas** has simple but tasty salads, fried fish and wine for 2500dr, and is a lovely spot for refreshments between swims.

### Koukounariés/Ag. Paraskeví

**Skiathos Palace Hotel**, with a superb view of Koukounariés bay, ☎ 22 242, ✆ 22 260 (*lux*) offers peace from the madding crowd. The new **Skiathos Princess**,

Ag. Paraskeví beach, ✆ 49 226, reservations, ✆ 22 544, ✆ 22 260 (*lux*) enjoys one of the best positions, on one of the best beaches, and its rates are not sky-high. *Open May–Oct.* Near the Princess, **Atrium Hotel and Bungalows**, ✆ 49 376/345 (*A; exp*), have excellent views. *Open April–Oct.* **Korali**, on Troúlos Beach, ✆ 49 212, ✆ 22 046 (*C; mod*) is a newish flat complex, with fully equipped kitchens and sea views from the balcony. *Open May–Oct.* **Bourdouriani House**, at Troúlos, ✆ 22 313 is similar. **Camping Koukounaries** is the nicest campsite on the island; call ✆ 49 259). **Camping Aselinos** is the second nicest, in a farm setting by the beach of the same name.

# Skópelos (ΣΚΟΠΕΛΟΣ)

Where Skiáthos has given its all to tourism, Skópelos has traditionally kept apart. Yet Skópelos is an exceptionally beautiful island, more dramatic than Skiáthos, its entire 100 sq km shaded by fragrant pine forests. Its beaches are almost as lovely as those flaunted so commercially by its more rambunctious, raucous neighbour, and it has two exceptionally pretty towns, Skópelos and Glóssa. By remaining aloof during the 1960s and 70s, the decades of slapdash cash-in-quick building, Skópelos did itself a big favour, and now draws 'the more discerning traveller' (as the more discerning package companies call them). It is a lovely island for walks, outside of the heatstroke months of July and August; the *Sotos Walking Guide*, available in English in most bookshops, will set you on your way.

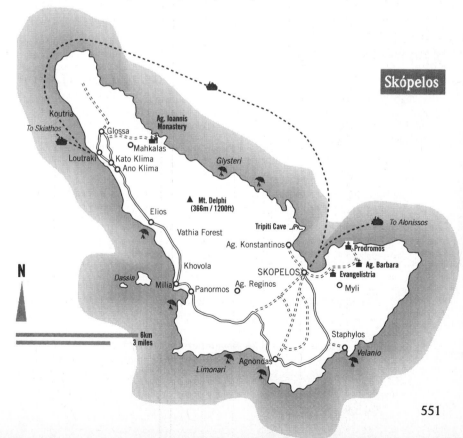

# History

Known in antiquity as Perparethos, Skópelos formed part of the Cretan colony founded by Prince Staphylos (who, according to some, was the son of Theseus and Ariadne). This tradition was given dramatic substance in 1927 when Staphylos' wealthy Minoan tomb was discovered by the cove that has always borne his name. Staphylos' name means 'grape', for the local wine, described as an aphrodisiac by Aristophanes and considered one of the best in the entire Aegean, was long an important export, along with olive oil; the first olive roots are said to have been brought here from Knossós. The Cretans are also credited with the establishment of the island's three settlements: Peparethos (Skópelos town), Staphylos (Pánormos) and Knossa (Glóssa). Subsequent tradition/history/mythology recounts that King Pelias, usurper of the Iolkan kingdom in Thessaly, settled Skópelos in the 13th century BC; it was this same Pelias who sent the rightful heir to Thessaly, Jason, on the famous quest for the Golden Fleece. Under the rule of Athens, Skópelos retained a certain amount of autonomy and minted its own coins, worshipping in particular Dionysos and Demeter.

Venetian renegade Filippo Gizzi used Skópelos as his headquarters, and his capture by the resurgent Byzantines meant a decline in local excitement until Barbarossa decimated the island's communities in 1538. In later years Skópelos drew many refugees from the Turks, who called the Sporades the 'demon islands' for their ornery pirates. The Skopelots joined in the revolt of the irregular militia beginning in 1805, and throughout the revolutionary period the island's population soared, augmented by refugees from the mainland; in the 1820s, there were 70,000 people (an extraordinary number; the current population is under 6000 and rises to 20,000 in August), so many that there was fighting over food. *Phylloxera* decimated the famous vines of Skópelos in the 1940s, and they've never been replanted, although the little country houses where wine was made, the *kalívia*, are still scattered across the island.

### Getting There and Around

**By sea: ferries** link Skópelos daily with Vólos, Ag. Konstantínos, Skiáthos and Alónissos, 3 times a week with Thessaloníki, once a week with Kými (Évia). Note that the ferries usually call at both Skópelos town and Loutráki, the port of Glóssa. **Hydrofoils** daily to Skiáthos, Alónissos, Vólos and Ag. Konstantínos, less frequently to Skýros and Marmáras (Chalkidikí). **Port authority**, ✆ 22 180.

**By road: buses** run several times a day from Skópelos town to Glóssa and Loutráki, stopping by all the paths down to the beaches.

### Tourist Police

See regular police, Skópelos town, ✆ (0424) 22 235.

### Festivals

**25 February**, Ag. Regínos; **early August**, Loïzeia alternative theatre and music festival at Glóssa; **6 August**, Metamórphosis on Skópelos Bay; **15 August**, Panagías in Skópelos; **9 November**, Eisódia tis Theotókou at the edge of the town; **25 November**, Christós, also in the town. **Carnival** (Apokriés) is fun, but can be dangerous to your health. A small boat, the *tráta* or trawler, is made of cane and decorated with rubbish (Coke cans are quite popular) with a smoke-stack spewing black fumes from burning wet garbage. This foul vessel is borne through the streets, polluting everything in its path, while its bearers, their bodies painted, stop every now and then to sing lewd songs. Increasingly drunk, they finally make it to the harbour, where the boat is hurled into the sea and the merry-makers jump in after it.

## Skópelos Town and its Harbour

**Skópelos** (or Chóra) forms a picture-perfect collage of old blue slate and post-earthquake red-tile roofs, artfully arranged in a steep amphitheatre around the port. There's a touch of Venice in the older buildings, while others are built either in a sturdy Thessalian or Macedonian style. The newer houses fit in harmoniously, incorporating wooden balconies and other traditional features, while in between the Greek obsession for planting a seed wherever it might have half a chance has resulted in a lush growth of flowers and plants.

Skópelos town claims 123 churches altogether, of all shapes and sizes, many with charming iconostases. Two to look out for are **Zoödóchos Pigí** which has an icon attributed to St Luke, and **Christó** (above the Commerical Bank) with a triangular, Armenian-style apse and an exceptionally handsome gilded interior. Perched at the top of town, where a temple to Athena once stood, are the white walls of the Venetian **Kástro**, built by the Gizzi, so formidable that Skópelos was left untouched during the War of Independence; along the edge of the cliff stand a row of chapels, as if offering divine defence against the storms that often crash into the exposed town. Within the walls the 9th-century **Ag. Athanásios** has frescoes from the 1500s, unfortunately damaged in 1965 when the roof collapsed. On the other end of town (straight up from the main taxi stand), one of the houses holds an interesting **Museum of Folk Arts** (ask for the Mouseío Laografikó). The church of **Panagía Eleftherótria**, beyond Plátanos square and its enormous plane tree and fountain, is a handsome 18th-century stone building with a slate roof, adorned with brightly coloured ceramic plates.

At the end of town, beyond the medical centre, stands the impressive fortified monastery **Episkopí**, built by the Venetians as a seat for the bishopric of Skópelos, although work was abandoned after the raid of Barbarossa in 1538. The walls encompasses the 17th-century basilica of Panagía tis Episkopís, built over a church dating back to AD 600. Further on, the stone sarcophagus of Ag. Regínos, the first Bishop and patron saint of Skópelos, martyred in AD 362, may be seen in the courtyard of **Ag. Regínos**. Just outside town, you can usually visit the **Foúrnou Damáskinon**, the gargantuan oven where in August plums are dried to become Skópelos' famous prunes; many of these are later crystallized and served with *rakí* to guests, along with a sprig of basil to tuck behind the ear. There's a convenient but mediocre sandy beach next to the town and under the trees a row of sweet shops that scent the evening air with warmed honeyed *loukoumádes*. If you walk around the bay to **Ampelikí**, you can see the ruins of an Asklepeion lie half-submerged in the sea.

## Around Skopelos Town

The hills overlooking Skópelos' large but windswept harbour shelter no fewer than five monasteries; a lovely path begins just beyond the strip of hotels near the beach. The closest, **Evangelístria**, with a magnificent view over Skópelos town, was founded by monks from Mount Áthos, but is now occupied by nuns who offer their weavings for sale in a little shop (*open 8–1 and 4–7*). Further afield, abandoned **Ag. Bárbara** is a fortified monastery containing frescoes from the 15th century. **Metamórphosis** too was abandoned in 1980, but is currently being rehabilitated; it hosts one of the island's biggest *panegýri* (6 August). Over the ridge, looking towards Alónissos, is the convent **Timioú Pródromoú**, with a beautiful iconostasis (*same hours as Evangelístria*). One path connects them all; a far less scenic road ascends as far as Metamórphosis. Real explorers can spend a day hiking even further, up to the panoramic summit of Poloúki (546m) to the now abandoned, overgrown monastery **Taxiárchon**, where the local resistance hid Greek and Allied soldiers, before they were smuggled across to neutral Turkey.

On the other side of the bay, near the pleasant shingle-covered beach **Ag. Konstantínos** (or **Glifóneri**) stand the ruins of a Hellenistic water tower; if this beach is overcrowded, try **Glystéri** to the north, reached by road or frequent caiques from the port; there's a very pleasant taverna and a campsite is planned for 1995 amid the olive groves. Caiques also sail to the sea cave of **Tripití**, the island's chief lobster lodge and fishing hole, or to the islet of **Ag. Geórgios**, with a 17th-century monastery and herd of wild goats.

Among other excursions offered from Skópelos are night fishing trips, round-island sails in an old wooden schooner, visits to the islets off Alónissos, and the summer diving trips offered by the research ship *Oceanis* in the company of marine biologist Vassílis Kouroútos; it's not cheap (*35,000dr for two days*) but it's your chance to play Jacques Cousteau. For information, contact Thalpos Travel, upstairs on the waterfront, ✆ 22 947, 🖾 23 057.

---

*Skópelos ✆ (0424–)*                                           **Where to Stay**

Like Skiáthos, Skópelos is expensive; unlike Skiáthos, there are no huge slabs of jerry-built hotels. For most people, in or around Skópelos town is the best place to stay. You'll have no problem finding a room; offers as you step off the boat are plentiful, and honest. Otherwise, near the port at Skópelos an agency specializes in finding rooms in houses (a free service); ask there for possibilities elsewhere on the island as well.

**Prince Stafylos**, on the outskirts of Skópelos town, in Livádi, ✆ 22 775 (*B; exp*) is delightful, with a pool, restaurant, pretty courtyard and well-furnished rooms. There's a courtesy bus from the port; unfortunately it tends to be booked solid by package operators in season. **Aegeon**, 300m from the beach, ✆ 22 619, 🖾 22 194 (*B; exp*), in Athens, ✆ (01) 902 4825, is a stylish new small hotel, with panoramic views over Skópelos town and its port. **Archontiko**, ✆ 22 049 (*A pension; exp*) is very nice but book very early for high summer. *Open all year.* **Adonis**, ✆ 22 231 (*D; mod*) with a fast-food restaurant on the ground level, and **Akti**, in town, ✆ 22 356 (*D; mod*) are good bets if you're unpackaged and unbooked.

---

*Skópelos ✆ (0424–)*                                                   **Eating Out**

**Perivolos**, the best restaurant in town is near Plátanos Square, and serves a variety of international dishes, along with unusual old Greek specialities such as a pork roll filled with plums (*3500–4000dr*). **Spiros**, on the waterfont, offers good barbecued chicken and kebabs with fast service (*around 2000dr with wine*); **Molos** nearby has good Greek food and casseroles at similar prices. **Anatoli**, set in the walls of the Kástro, serves excellent, inexpensive *mezédes*, with a free panoramic view from the terrace. The owner, Giórgos Xintáris, is a well-known bouzouki player and strums and sings old *rembétika* songs after 11pm most nights (*full meals around 2500dr*). **Greca**, just off Plátanos Square, is a favourite of the locals, serves good crêpes run by an eccentric French woman. **Stellas**, out on Ag. Konstantínos beach, serves especially good moussaka and other old favourites (*around 2000dr*). **Ionos**, opposite the barber shop, has good music to go with its coffee, breakfasts or cocktails, or walk up the narrow streets of town to **Braxos**, with pretty views over the port to go with its drinks. The **Koreli** bar near the quay serves delicious traditional deep-fried cheese pies. On the waterfront, note the **Dimotikó Kafeneió** (People's Café) founded by the local government as an affordable place for the old men of town to sit by the sea, drink their coffees and play backgammon. Nightlife since 1993 has been concentrated around the **Kyrki**, by far the biggest club on island, playing mostly chart music; **Kounos** is another popular club.

## Across Skópelos to Glóssa

Buses run regularly from Skópelos town to Glóssa along the island's one main road. Along the route you'll find **Stáphylos** where the Minoan tomb of Stáphylos was discovered; the sword is displayed in the National Museum in Athens. It is now a popular family beach, complete with pedalos, while **Velanió**, on the opposite side of its small headland, is the unofficial nudist beach, and a 500m walk from the bus. **Agnóndas**, the next stop, was named after a local athelete, a victor in the 569 BC Olympics, who disembarked here to wild acclaim; to this day it serves as a kind of emergency port when rough seas prevent landing at Skópelos town. Sandy **Limonári** is one of the finest beaches on the island, an 800m walk from the bus, or a short boat ride from Agnóndas. From Agnóndas the road cuts through the pine groves to another popular campsite and pebbly beach, **Pánormos**. Tucked between Pánormos and Miliá are small secluded swimming coves, fringed by pines, accessible only on foot from the road by threading your way down through the trees. **Miliá** itself is shady and has a beautiful, enormous pebbly beach, with a large taverna and lots of watersports, including parasailing for the daring. Further along, **Élios** beach is a small resort, still bearing signs here and there of the emergency shelters thrown up after the 1965 earthquake, when the junta forced all the residents of old Klíma into bland, uniform housing, which is just beginning to look like a real town, 30 years later. It was here that a fierce bad dragon would wait for its annual tribute of human victims, until the day that St Reginos took the place of one of the victims and asked God for mercy (*eleos*). The dragon then passively let Reginos lead it over a cliff to its death. Just before Loutráki, at **Káto Klíma**, begins the lovely route up to Áno Klíma and **Athéato**, the oldest settlement on the island, before arriving in Glóssa.

### Glóssa

At the end of the road, set in the woods high above the sea, is Skópelos' second town, Glóssa (ΓΛΩΣΣΑ), a beautiful village constructed mainly during the Turkish occupation. The houses survived the 1965 earthquake; one of their more peculiar architectural features is the outhouse on the balcony. Three ruined 4th-century BC towers continue to stand watch over Glóssa, and a well-marked track from the town leads in an hour across the island to the extraordinary monastery of **Ag. Ioánnis**, perched like an eagle's nest over the sea (indeed, eagles and other birds of prey will probably be soaring high overhead). The last leg of the walk is 100 steps carved in the living rock; take a canteen of water. The little sandy beach below is often deserted.

At the end of the road, there's a rather untidy pebble beach, and a couple of tavernas under the plane trees at **Loutráki** (ΛΟΥΤΡΑΚΙ), the town's port, a steep 3km below Glóssa. Nearly every ship calls in here as well as Skópelos town, but otherwise it's a quiet place. Near Loutráki's church, **Ag. Nikólaos**, are the 7th-century ruins of an earlier basilica and other remains of Loutráki's previous incarnation as Selinous.

Most of the island's almonds grow around Glóssa and **Kaloyéros**, a small isolated village on the rugged north coast, reached by caique or a rough dirt road. From here, a 4km trail ascends the slopes of Skópelos highest mountain, Délphi (660m), where four large rock-cut tombs with their lids, called **Sendoúkia**, facing a magnificent view to the east, were found at Karyá. No one knows if they are Neolithic or Early Christian.

*Skópelos ☏ (0424–)*                                                                    **Where to Stay**

### Pánormos

**Afrodite,** by the beach, ☏ 23 150, ✉ 23 152 (*B; exp*) is new and partially air-conditioned, with a gym and mountain bikes to rent. The **Panormos Beach Pension** ☏ 22 711 (*B; exp–mod*) is spacious and caters mostly to packagers, but is a little pricey. *Open May–Oct.*

### Stáphylos

There are mostly small family pensions here, such as **Ostria**, ☏ 22 220 (*B; mod*) and **Irene**, ☏ 23 637 (*B; mod*), in Athens, ☏ (01) 347 9785, the latter with bath and basic kitchen facilities in each room. **Terpsi**, on the main road near Stáphylos, is a charming garden restaurant, where everyone goes for roast chicken stuffed with walnuts, chicken livers and pine nuts (*5500dr for four people*). *Open July and August.*

### Agnóndas

**Takonis**, on the beautiful beach of Agnóndas, is one of the best tavernas on all Skópelos, with fresh fish and good ready food (*3000dr*). Agnóndas also smells better than most beaches, thanks to **Klima**, its traditional bakery. At nearby Limonári there are pleasant rooms and a taverna run by Vangélis and Geórgios, ☏ 22 242.

### Glóssa

There isn't much choice up here; some 40 beds, spread out over a few houses. Alternatively, in Néa Klíma, **Janetta**, ☏ 33 140, ✉ 33 717 (*C; mod*) is a hotel-apartment complex set in the woods overlooking a pool, popular among Greek families. Arrive early in Glóssa to get a table at the popular **Taverna Agnandi**, its lovely views complimented by traditional Greek cuisine in the 2000dr range.

# Skýros (ΣΚΥΡΟΣ)

Skýros, with a permanent population of 2750 souls, is an exceptional island in many respects. It has two distinct geological regions, squeezed in the middle by a girdle where nearly everybody lives in either the port or town; the southern half is barren, rugged and ringed with cliffs, the northern half is fertile and pine-forested. A native race of tiny ponies called the Pikermies roams the southern part undisturbed, except when rounded up to help with the chores or to give the kids a ride; a five-year-old can look them right in the eye.

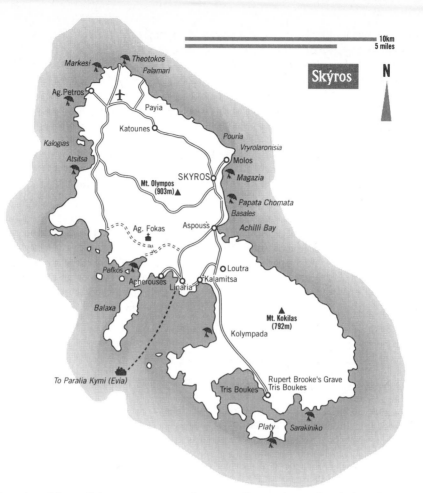

Throughout history Skýros was uncommonly remote. Even today, under ideal conditions it takes about seven hours by land and sea to get there from Athens; connections from nearby Kými on Évia were so limited a few decades ago that the Skyriots purchased their own ferry to get about. These long years of isolation account in part for the island's distinctive charm and character, the staying power of its old customs. The oldest men still don their baggy blue trousers, black caps and flat leather sandals with many straps or *trohádhia*, and the older women can sometimes be seen in their long head scarves; the interiors of their tidy houses remain resolutely traditional (*see* below) while incorporating such novelties as digitally controlled American refrigerators. In other words, the outside world has arrived, but the Skyriots are determined to set the rules it operates by on their island.

## Mythology

When it was prophesied that Achilles, son of the sea goddess Thetis and Peleus, would either win great glory at Troy and die young, or live peacefully at home to a ripe old age, his doting mother thought to hide him from the Achaeans by disguising him as a girl and sending him to live among the women at King Lykomedes' palace in Skýros. Achilles didn't mind, and, apparently adopting the name of Pyrrha, or 'Goldie', for the colour of his hair, took advantage of his stay in the harem by fathering a son, Neoptolemis. All would have been well had not another oracle declared that the Achaeans would never win the Trojan War without Achilles, and crafty Odysseus was sent in search of the young hero. Odysseus brought a chest full of gifts for the women when he called on King Lykomedes—perfumes, jewellery, finery—and a sword, which the young transvestite in the crowd seized joyfully for his own, just as Odysseus had anticipated. Once discovered, Achilles willingly joined the Achaeans. When an arrow in his heel ended his life, Odysseus returned to Skýros to fetch his son Neoptolemis to Troy, and the war was eventually won.

King Lykomedes of Skýros plays a less benign role in another story: when the hero Theseus returned to Athens after spending four years glued to the Chair of Forgetfulness in Hades (his punishment for trying to help a friend abduct Persephone, the Queen of Hell), he found Athens corrupt and divided into factions against him. Theseus laid a curse on his native city and sought asylum in Crete, but was blown off course to Skýros, where he was received with such honour by Lykomedes that Theseus announced that he meant to retire on an estate his family owned on Skýros—an estate coveted by Lykomedes himself. After a drinking party he led Theseus to the pinnacle of Skýros' acropolis and gave him a push, hurling him to his death on the rocks below.

## History

Theseus was buried on Skýros and his memory neglected by the Athenians until his spirit was seen at Marathon, rising out of the earth to lead the Athenians to victory over the Persians. The Delphic oracle then charged the Athenians to bring Theseus' bones back to Athens—just the excuse the Athenians needed to nab Skýros for themselves. In 476 BC Kimon captured it, enslaved the inhabitants and, guided by a she-eagle, which scratched at the ground with her beak, was led to the grave of a tall skeleton buried with his weapons. Certain that it was Theseus, Kimon exhumed the coffin, carried it back to Athens, and enshrined it in the Theseion.

So many Athenians then came to settle the island that Athens treated Skýros as an equal and demanded no tribute. The Athenian Dionysia was made the biggest festival, and the tallest mountain was re-named Olympos by the settlers, who adopted the island's local cult of the sky god into their own state religion of Zeus. Under Byzantine rule, so many important people were exiled to Skýros from Constantinople that they created a tyrannical and much resented upper class, one remembered in the double-headed eagle and other folk motifs in the local art. In this century, Skýros is best known as the last resting place of the young First World War poet Rupert Brooke, and more recently, among British New Agers, as the home of the Skýros Institute, where you can get in harmony with your inner space (*see* p.17).

### Getting There

By air: daily flight in peak season from Athens; Olympic airways © 91 600. Alternatively, if it's all booked up, fly to Skiáthos and connect with a hydrofoil on the appropriate day.

By sea: **ferry** from Kými (Évia) twice a day, once a week in the summer to Tínos, Mýkonos, Páros, Santoríni and Herákleon (Crete). **Hydrofoil** 4 to 5 times a week to the other Sporades and Vólos. **Port authority**, © 91 475.

## Tourist Information

Tourist police, see regular police, Skýros town, ✆ (0222) 91 274. Leftéris Trákes at Skýros Travel, in the centre of town, ✆ 91 123, 🖷 92 123, is helpful, whether you need a villa, a boat ticket, or information on island excursions.

## Festivals

Skýros preserves some fascinating vestiges of the ancient Mediterranean goat and cattle cults during its **Carnival**, when three characters dance down the street: a man in a goatskin costume and mask and sheep bells called the Old Man, with a humpback made of rags, followed by the Frángos (the Frank, or foreigner, dressed in motley clothes and long trousers, with a mask and bell hanging behind and blowing a conch shell to scare children) and the Koréla (a man dressed up as a woman). These perform the Horós tou Trágou, or the Goat Dance, possibly a relic of the ancient rite that gave us the word 'tragedy' (*tragoudía*, or 'goat song'). Every day during carnival the Old Man, the Frángos and the Koréla make their rollicking way through town, joining in satires (another goatish word, derived from the mischievous half-goat Satyrs) until they end up at the monastery of Ag. Geórgios. Other festivals include:

**12 March**, in town; **23 April**, Ag. Geórgios; **27 July**, Ag. Panteleímon, near Péfkos. A new outdoor theatre hosts a festival in **late July and early August**; **15 August**, children's pony races; **2 September**, Ag. Máma (Ag. Máma is the patron of shepherds, and like Carnival, their festival also includes traces of ancient rites).

## Skýros Town

Skýros, or Chóra, is a striking town that wouldn't look out of place in the Cyclades, its white houses stacked one on top of the other along the steep, narrow pedestrian-only lanes and steps. From the distance it sweeps like a full skirt around the massive rocky precipice of the ancient acropolis, looming high over the sea. The main street curls past a pleasant mix of hardware stores and trendy boutiques, rimmed by the terraces of a dozen cafés, tavernas, and cocktail bars; few islands manage such a harmonious balance between the needs and desires of the locals and visitors.

Signs near the market point the way up to the **Kástro**, a 15-minute walk up, passing by way of the usually open church of **Ag. Triáda** (with frescoes) and the white monastery of **Ag. Geórgios**, founded in 962 by Emperor Nikephóros Phókas, himself known as 'the Pale Death of the Saracens' after his liberation of Crete. The emperor gave Ag. Geórgios to his saintly friend Athanásios, who went on to found the Great Lavra monastery of Mount Áthos; Ag. Geórgios, and a good chunk of land on Skýros, belong to the Great Lavra to this day. The church (restored in 1984 after earthquake damage) holds a fine painting of St George slaying the dragon and the old icon of St George with a black face, brought over from Constantinople during the iconoclasm. A crusty lion of St Mark (1354) marks the gate of the Byzantine-Venetian citadel, built in on the site of the Classical fortifications, of which a few blocks survive at the base. It was from here that Lykomedes gave Theseus his famous shove. On one side are fine views over the rooftops, on the other the escarpment plunges abruptly towards the sea.

**Brooke Square**, on a terrace at the far end of town, has been wearing a rather neglected air of late, although the willy of the gormless bronze nude *Statue of Immortal Poetry* by sculptor

M. Tómbros (1931) commemorating Rupert Brooke is administered to weekly by local spray painters. The **archaeology museum** is just under Brooke Square, along the steps leading down to Magaziá (*open 8.30–3, closed Mon; adm*); grave offerings and goods from copper-age Palamári (2500–1900 BC) on the extreme northern tip of the island and from proto-geometric Thémis (950–800 BC) are among the highlights; from the latter note the ritual vase, decorated with eight ducks and two bird-swallowing snakes. And amongst the relics of ancient times, you'll find a traditionally furnished Skyriot home, 35sq m in size—the average living space per family.

Few houses combine so much function and beauty in such small spaces, dictated by the necessity of living crammed together on the slope, within easy distance of the Kástro should a pirate sail appear on the horizon. Because most of the older houses back into the steep hill and shared walls, the *xóporto*, an outer half-door flap, was developed to allow light and air to enter while retaining privacy. The central living area is called the *alóni*, a Greek word that recalls the circular disc of the sun; the walls and possessions on display are seen 'all around'. Focus, however, naturally fell on the chubby, conical fireplace, or *f'gou*, with two little ledges for children to sit on in the winter. Some *f'gous* have a pair of breasts in bas-relief to symbolize motherhood. An embroidered cloth over the upper mouth of the hearth protected the room from smoke, while shelves across the front of the *f'gou* display rows of colourful porcelain plates and jugs. Plate-collecting has been a Skyriot obsession and status symbol since the 16th century, when the Turkish conquest forced the island's aristocratic Byzantine exiles into such poverty that they had to sell off their dinnerware. Pirates who looted cargoes of plates would sell them on Skýros, or the pirates themselves would be looted by the plate-crazed islanders if they pulled into a bay to shelter from a storm. A Skyriot sailor never has to think twice about the perfect gift for his wife or mother: some examples come from as far away as China.

Furniture, often beautifully carved with folk motifs, is simple and functional. A complex variety of benches and settees double as chests for clothes, or have hollows in fronts of them to slide in pots, pans or bottles; other objects were stored in baskets suspended from the ceiling and reached by long forked poles. Niches in the walls were used to store jugs filled with water. Food would be served on a low table, which in the old days had a removable top, a large engraved copper plate called a *sinía*. These are now mostly used for decoration.

An ornate latticework partition, the *bóulmes*, crowned by a carved wooden parapet, cuts off the back third of the interior while admitting precious light. The kitchen and storage area was on the ground floor, and the bedroom(s) or *sfas* (from the Turkish word 'sofa') in the loft. A thin beam just below the ceiling of the *sfas* is used to hang large decorative weavings that hide the rolled up mattresses. If there is no room for an external stair to the *sfas*, access is by way of a steep narrow stair and trap door. The roof is made of wooden beams, covered with layers of dried cane, dried seaweed, and earth rich in waterproof clay; new layers of clay are added every few years. A broken jar on top of the chimney draws out the smoke from the *f'gou*.

You can examine many of the above items in the charming **Faltaits Museum of Folklore** (*open 10–1 and 5.30–8*), also just under Brooke Square; a fascinating collection of domestic items, poetry, traditional costumes, and richly coloured embroideries decorated with mermaids, double-headed eagles, Turkish judges, ships, deer, pomegranates and hoopoes (a bird closely identified with Skýros). The museum shop is full of lovely if rather costly hand-made goods, including printed patterns of Skyriot designs to make your own embroideries (the ladies of Skýros buy them) and locally made pottery inspired by the examples brought home from the four corners of the world.

A ten-minute walk below Skýros town stretches the long sandy beach of **Magaziá** (ΜΑΓΑΖΙΑ), named after the Venetian powder magazines once stored here, and next to it is **Mólos beach**; most of the island's accommodation and surprisingly jumping nightlife are concentrated here. If these two beaches are too crowded there are others within walking distance; avoid sewage-prone Basáles, but continue south to **Papá ta Chómata** ('Priests' Land'), where no one, not even the priest, minds if you sunbathe in your altogether. From **Órmos Achílli**, further south, Achilles is said to have embarked for Troy; a new marina allows yachties to do the same.

## Around the Island

Although buses run intermittently between the port of Linariá, Skýros town and Mólos, the only way to visit the rest of the island is by foot, taxi or by hired moped. The pine-wooded northern half of Skýros has better roads (and the army air force), and there are small beaches just off the road that follows most of the coast. The sandy beach of **Ag. Pétros** near the top of the island (past the airport) is the prettiest, and worth hiring a car and packing a picnic. A walking path (taking about 3 hours and not always easy to find) crosses the island from Skýros town to **Atsítsa**, where a taverna sits on a rocky beach among the pines, near a 'meditation centre' with a very English PRIVATE sign on it that must dent the karma. A second path (and road) to Atsítsa begins in the port **Linariá** (ΛΙΝΑΡΙΑ), a mostly modern fishing village, built after 1860; it passes by way of **Achérouses** and the pretty beach and summer tavernas at **Péfkos**, site of ancient marble quarries. Even prettier **Ag. Fokás** beach, with white pebbles, is further north but accessible only on foot; it has a very basic taverna and a handful of rooms. From Linariá, caique excursions sail to the islet **Skyropoúla** between Skýros and the mainland. Skyropoúla has two beaches and a cave, **Kávos Spilí**, and a herd of the wild munchkin ponies.

The beaches in the rocky rugged south half of Skýros are less appealing, with the exception of **Kalamítsa**, linked by bus in the summer. The beach is of sand and stones, and fronted by tavernas and a few places to rent rooms. Signs of one of ancient Skýros' three rival towns, Chrission, were found near here, as well as an ancient tomb locally claimed to be Homer's, and traces of an Early Christian basilica. A taxi, a 2-hour walk from Kalamítsa, or caique (by far the most pleasant means if it's a calm day) will take you to **Tris Boukés** and the **grave of Rupert Brooke** at the southernmost point of Skýros. On 23 April 1915, the 28-year-old poet, on his way to fight at Gallipoli, died of blood poisoning aboard a French hospital ship and was buried in this desolate olive grove at dawn the next morning. His well-tended grave—6ft of official British soil—is maintained by the Anglo-Hellenic society. It was only a year before Brooke died that he wrote his famous lines:

> *If I should die think only this of me:*
> *That there's some corner of a foreign field*
> *That is forever England.*

Among the boat excursions offered in the summer, the one to the region south of Tris Boukés, to Sarakíno beach and Platý island, and around the cliffs at Renés, is spectacular. Sea caves pierce the cliffs, and the Eleanora falcons sweep across the azure sky as thick as sparrows in London.

## Linariá

**King Likomides**, ☎ 91 949, in Athens (01) 613 4536 (*A; exp*), is a new hotel right by the port. **Philipeo** has the best food in the village; at Achérouses, just north, there's a campsite and a simple, friendly taverna where you can dine with your feet in the sea. **Kavos**, a bar just along the road to Skýros, is a lovely place to sit and watch the sun set over an ouzo or cocktail; the **Kastro club** plays both disco and Greek music to dance by.

## Skýros Town

**Nefeli**, ☎ 91 964 (*C; mod*) is fairly simple. *Open all year.* There are scores of rooms to let, many of them in charming traditional houses (just mind you don't break the plates); let yourself be propositioned by the little old ladies at the bus stop. Current rates for a stay of more than two days average at about 4000dr per double room per night, but out of season you can bargain for a lot less. There's also a campsite, located two-thirds of the way down the road to Magaziá.

Skýros is well-endowed with good restaurants. One of the oldest, little **Margetis**, is on the main street, serving good meat and fish dishes in an ideal location to watch the bustling pedestrian traffic (*around 2000dr*). **Sisyphos**, at the bottom of the main street, serves good quality Greek dishes, including a selection for vegetarians. **Pegasos**, an elegant restaurant in a 19th-century mansion 20m below Skyros Travel, serves prepared Italian dishes, kid casseroles, and tasty moussaka. **Kristina's**, ☎ 91 778, which has tables out in a garden courtyard, is run by Greek-Australian Kristina Tsalapatani, with a delicious change-of-pace menu and warm herbal breads; around 3000dr. **Skiros**, in the centre, makes tasty, inexpensive pizza as well as other dishes.

## By the Sea: Magaziá, Gialós and Mólos

The **New Skyros Palace**, 50m from the beach at Grismata, ☎ 91 994, ✆ 92 070 (*B; exp*), winter ✆ in Athens (01) 275 2094, is the most sophisticated place to stay; built in the traditional Skýros/Cyclades style, it has a lovely sea-water pool, restaurant, superior rooms and a relaxed atmosphere. *Open mid-May–Oct.* **Xenia**, smack on the beach at Magaziá, ☎ 91 209, ✆ 92 062 (*B; exp*) is older but comfortable with 22 rooms and a restaurant and water sports. *Open April–Oct.* **Paleo Pirgos** (*mod*), halfway down to Magaziá, is a new charming hotel with splendid views and ample parking. **Aegeolis**, a stone's throw from the sea at Magaziá, ☎ 91 113, ✆ 92 482, winter ✆ (01) 418 2466, (*C; mod*) is a set of 11 apartments with kitchenettes, built in 1992. *Open all year.* **Skyros Village**, near the sea in Mólos, ☎ 91 904, in Athens in winter (01) 652 2516 (*mod*) is a pretty guesthouse built in the traditional style, with traditional furnishings. *Open May–Sept.* **Pension Elena**, in Magaziá, ☎ 91 738 (*E; inexp*), is simple.

# Évia (EYBOIA)

The second largest island in Greece after Crete, Évia is endowed with some of the most bucolic and dramatic scenery in the entire country; along its 175km length rolling meadows, olive groves, orchards and vineyards alternate with dense forests, wild cliffs and snow-capped mountains. If nearly every hill on the island is crowned with a crumbling Frankish or

Byzantine fort, there are relatively few Classical remains. Euboea, its ancient name, means 'rich in cattle'. Animal husbandry and farming has been the Eviots' way of life for centuries, and it remains so today; in the most isolated villages people gape at every passing car as it were a chariot of the gods.

Although a mere 88km drive from downtown Athens, Évia is not overrun with tourists, at least outside of a few established seaside resorts (Loutrá Edipsóu, Kárystos, and Erétria) and outside the month of August, when it seems as if all of Athens has descended on the place. That the vast majority of visitors are Greek means reasonable prices and excellent tavernas and restaurants. Évia is the best island for appreciating the true eating habits of the country, where such Greek institutions as the *ouzerie*, now extinct on the more popular islands, are alive and well. On the other hand, a relative lack of foreign tourists also means that car and scooter rentals, organized excursions, multi-lingual travel agencies, watersports facilities, English breakfasts, Italian restaurants and Dutch bars are much thinner on the ground than on any other island. Nor is there any central clearing house for rooms on Évia; you just have to go to each village and take pot luck. Most are on the coasts, but they are few and far between, while villages in the interior have little or no facilities. Évia is a very popular place for camping; there are official campsites at Malakónta beach, near Erétria, Péfki, Ag. Ánna and Robiés.

## Mythology

Évia, split from the nearby mainland by a blow of Poseidon's mighty trident, was the sea god's favourite island, and he lived with his wife Amphitrite in a fabulous underwater palace just off shore in the Evian Gulf. To the south stretches the Myrtoan Sea, named for Myrtilus, son of Hermes and the charioteer of an invincible team of divine horses owned by King Oenomaus. Oenomaus had a beautiful daughter named Hippodameia, and he declared that only the suitor who could outrace his invincible chariot and avoid being transfixed by his brazen spear would have her hand; he set up the bones of the losers in front of his palace and arrogantly boasted he would build a temple of skulls. This was too much for the gods, and they decided to help one of their favourites, Pelops, win the race and defeat Oenomaus. Knowing that Myrtilus himself was in love with Hippodameia, Pelops took the charioteer aside and proposed a deal: if he would throw the race by replacing the lynch-pins in the axles of the king's chariot with wax, then Pelops as winner would share Hippodameia with him. Myrtilus eagerly agreed and events unfolded as predicted: Oenomaus' chariot collapsed in the heat of the race, the king was killed and Pelops was given the princess. He and Myrtilus took her off towards Evia, but Pelops, never intending to keep his bargain with Myrtilus, kicked him into the sea where he drowned. As he fell he put a curse on the house of Pelops—better known as the House of Atreus—a curse that fuelled the great tragic cycle of ancient Greek literature. Hermes named the sea in the honour of his son, and put his image, the Charioteer, in the stars, but his ghost remained unappeased, and haunted the stadium at Olympia, frightening horses.

## History

Inhabited in prehistoric times by settlers from Thessaly, and later by Dorians, Aeolians and Ionians, ancient Évia was divided into city-states. The most powerful in the 8th–7th centuries BC were the two rivals, Chalkís and Erétria, both located on the Evripós strait, a busy shipping lane in ancient times, when mariners shunned the stormy east coast of Évia. Both Chalkís and Erétria grew into great commercial ports with colonies as far away as Sicily. Between them lay Évia's desirable, fertile Lelantine Plain 'rich in vineyards'; both cities claimed it and extended their disagreement into international affairs, doing neither of them any good. In 506 BC Chalkís joined Boeotia in a war against Athens, only to be conquered and divided; the Erétrians joined Athens in supporting the Ionian uprising on Asia Minor, and in retribution were sacked and enslaved in the Persian War when Darius came to punish the Athenians. In the 5th century BC the whole island came under the rule of Athens.

In 338 BC Macedonia took Évia, and the Romans who followed them were the first to use the name of an Eviot tribe, the Graeci, to refer to the entire Hellenic people, a misunderstanding that modern Hellenes or 'Greeks' get tit for tat by calling themselves 'Romans' (as the true heirs of the Roman, i.e. Byzantine, empire). With the conquests of the Fourth Crusade, the Franks gave the fertile island to the King of Thessaloníki, Boniface de Montferrat, who divided the fertile island into three baronies, initiating an intense, feudal castle-building spree. Over the next hundred years, Évia came under the direct rule of the Venetians, whose mushy accents mangled Evripós (the channel) into 'Negroponte', a name they used for the entire island. When the Turks took Negroponte from them in 1470, they did not even allow the usual puppet Venetian governor to hang around as a tax farmer, but settled the prize themselves, treasuring it more than any other island in the Aegean; a small minority of Turks remains on the island by a special agreement made during the population exchanges. In the 19th century they were joined by 40,000 refugees from Albania and Epirus, who mostly settled in the south.

## Getting There and Around

**By sea: ferries** link Évia with the mainland from Rafína to Kárystos (just over 2hrs; 3 times a day, ✆ (0224) 22 227), Rafína to Marmári (3 to 4 times a day, ✆ (0224) 31 222), Ag. Marína to Néa Stýra (5 times a day, ✆ (0224) 41 266), Arkítsa (along the main highway from Athens to Thessaloníki) to Edipsós (12 times a day, ✆ (0226) 23 317), Oropós to Erétria (every half-hour, ✆ (0221) 62 201, and Glífa to Agiókambos (every 2 hours, ✆ (0226) 31 107). Ferries go to Skýros daily from Kými, and twice a week to the other Sporades, ✆ (0222) 22 606. In the summer, there are connections from Ag. Konstantínos to Oreí, ✆ (0226) 71 288, Péfki ✆ (0226) 41 710. Summer **hydrofoils** link Loutrá Edipsoú and the other Sporades. **Port authorities, Erétria**, ✆ (0221) 62 201, **Kárystos**, ✆ (0224) 22 227, **Marmári**, ✆ (0224) 31 222, **Edipsós**, ✆ (0226) 23 317, **Alivéri**, ✆ (0223) 22 955.

**By road**: Évia's bulging middle is linked to the mainland by a short bridge over the famous Evripós Strait; there are **buses** every half-hour, and trains every hour from Athens to Chalkís (1½hrs), a singularly unattractive journey. The bus terminal in Athens is Liossíon, from where you can also travel direct to Kými (and over to Skýros), Erétria, Amárinthos, Edipsós or Alivéri, but for Rafína (the main port for Kárystos, Marmári and the island of Ándros), buses leave Athens from the Mavromatéon terminal. A good bus service connects Chalkís (the station is right in the centre of town) with all the major villages of Évia as well as Thebes and other nearby towns on the mainland. As the best of Évia lies along the various little roads branching off its one main highway, a **car** is essential for really appreciating the island. Chalkís and Erétria have the most in the way of car and motorbike hire agencies. Make sure the brakes are in perfect repair for some very steep descents; bring a compass and the newest map you can find. Signposting ranges from the minimal to the non-existent; some of the back roads are bumpy, rutted, pitted, rocky, dusty and packed with endless puncture opportunities.

---

### Festivals

**21 May**, Ag. Konstantínos at Vitalakimis; **27 May**, St John the Russian at Prokópi; **17 July**, Ag. Marínas near Kárystos; **26 July**, Ag. Paraskeví, long celebrations at Chalkís, Mýli and Rúkia; **15 August**, at Kými, Oxílithos and many other villages.

## Southern Évia

## Kárystos and Mount Óchi

The best way to see all of Évia, with a minimum of backtracking, is to take the two-hour ferry from Rafína to **Kárystos** (ΚΑΡΥΣΤΟΣ) at the foot of Mount Óchi, at the extreme southern tip of the island. With all of 3500 souls, Kárystos is the metropolis on the Myrtoan Sea, long renowned for its green cipollino marble and asbestos, known as 'the unquenchable' in ancient times. Named after its founder, a son of the centaur Chiron, Kárystos so caught the fancy of Greece's first king Otho when it was liberated from the Turks in 1833 that he renamed it after himself, Othonoúpolis and declared he would make it the capital of Greece. He summoned an architect named Bierbach down from Bavaria to lay out the town plan, and he left the wide, straight streets that set Kárystos apart from the average Greek island town. Hints of neoclassical wannabe grandeur linger in 19th-century buildings like the Dimarcheíon (town hall).

Othonoúpolis, capital of Greece, fell by the wayside along with Otho himself, leaving Kárystos to carry on peacefully in the quintessential Greek seaside town, with back-streets full of hardware stores, butcher shops, and a dozen old fashioned *kafeneíons*, where the old men sip their coffee while rattling ivory bones over rickety old backgammon boards. The evening stroll, or *vólta*, endures with enthusiasm, along a *paralía* and fishing port crowded with excellent *ouzerie* and tavernas; these are heaving with Greek visitors on the third or fourth weekends of August, when Kárystos puts on its annual wine festival, with lots of free tasting, folk music and dancing and tomfoolery. The waterfront is still defended by a four-square 14th-century coastal fort, or **Boúrdzi** (or Arméno), its walls incorporating a large piece of sculpted marble taken from a 2nd-century AD temple to Apollo. These days most of its invaders bypass the fort to assault Kárystos' kilometre-long sandy beach, stretching from the boatyard to Paximáda point and perfect for snorkelling and windsurfing.

For most of the Middle Ages, however, the safest spot for miles around was the huge citadel above Kárystos, first built in 1030 by the Byzantines, rebuilt by the Franks in the 13th century and called **Castel Rosso** (hence Kókkino Kástro, or Red Castle) by the Venetians when they purchased the barony of Kárystos in 1366. Red, that is, for the tint in the stone, and the blood that flowed there, especially in the Greek War of Independence. Although the citadel, with its complex and deceptive multi-level layout and labyrinth of entrances, was believed to be impregnable to the extent that only 30 men were needed for its defence, the Turks eventually captured it. Four hundred Turkish families were settled within its walls and the rulers were unusually intolerant, giving local Christians the chop if they refused to convert to Islam. From the castle you can see the ruined arches of the Kamáres, or aqueduct, that once served it.

The road to Castel Rosso passes the lovely village of **Mýli**, set in a ravine, then continues over a handsome stone bridge crossing another ravine at Graviá. Nearby are the ancient cipollino marble quarries. If you've brought your walking shoes, a 3-hour path from Mýli continues to the mountain refuge and then, through ever more dramatic and barren scenery, to the summit of **Mount Óchi** (1398m), crowned by a 'dragon's house' the large blocks of a Pelasgian building of unknown import, perhaps a beacon or peak sanctuary dedicated to Poseidon. If you want to stay, the Yiokalíou Foundation operates a shelter (*see* below). In **Aetós**, close to Mýli, the church of **Panagía tis Theoskepástis** was abandoned by the villagers when they found they could not afford to cover it; then one night Mount Óchi dropped a massive boulder on top of it, without harming any of the walls, hence the name 'roofed by God'.

If Kárystos is too crowded for your taste, there's another long sandy beach, 13km away at **Boúros**, where free camping is usually tolerated, although you'll have to bring your own water. Near Boúros experienced speleologists can visit a cave with vast chambers, with the little church of **Ag. Triáda** at the entrance. Below the church is an underground river flowing from the bowels of Mount Óchi; there is cold spring water to drink and a grove of beautiful plane trees, perfect for a picnic on a hot day. Another grove of venerable plane trees lent their name to **Platanistós**, to the east, a delightful village with a rooms to rent in private houses. A road with occasional rough patches continues along to the southeasternmost tip of Évia, the notorious, tempest-tossed **Cape Kafiréus** (the Venetian Cabo Doro), where King Nauplios lit fiery beacons to confuse and mislead the Greeks returning from Troy, to avenge the death of his son Palamedes. Cabo Doro still has a few woebegone ruins of a Byzantine fortress, repaired in the 1260s by Admiral Likarios, the right-hand man of Emperor Michael Paleológos, who after the Fourth Crusade restored the Byzantine Empire—beginning in Greece at this weatherbeaten fort.

## Up the West Coast

The road north of Kárystos follows the spectacular west coast of Évia, along a corniche at times half a mile over the sea; the cliffs below are a favourite nesting place for hawks and eagles. Along the road are two small resorts: **Marmári**, named for its quarries of green marble, has a long beach and little port, sheltered by islets, and **Néa Stýra** (NEA ΣΤΥΡΑ), connected by ferry from Rafína, a fine spot for a lazy holiday base with a long sandy beach and excellent swimming and a certain charm in the town spread along the seafront. Near Néa Stýra are more 'dragons' houses', a terrace with three buildings believed to be ruined Homeric watchtowers. Old **Stýra** is above, on the slopes of Mount Kilósi and under the mammoth Venetian fortress of Larména; its little shady cafés in the main square are a pleasant and cool place to while away an hour. The ruins of ancient Stýra are further up, near the meagre ruins of Mycenaean **Dryopes**, a once important town that did its bit against the Persians at Artemission and Salamis.

After Néa Stýra, the road rises to **Almyropótamos**: side roads lead down to barely developed beaches around **Panagía**, on the west shore. Further north, just before the crossroads at Lépoura, a dirt road from Kriezá leads in 5km to the well-preserved polygonal walls, gate and 11 square towers of 5th-century BC **Dystos** (not to be confused with the modern village of the same name). Spread over a hill by Évia's largest lake (which in summer dries up to form Évia's biggest vegetable garden), you can also trace the ancient foundations of houses set on terraces and streets; the tower was renovated by the Venetians. Fossils of prehistoric beasts have been discovered by the sea below Kriezá, at **Ag. Apóstoli**, a sheltered little fishing harbour with a beach tucked in the rocky cliffs of Évia's east coast.

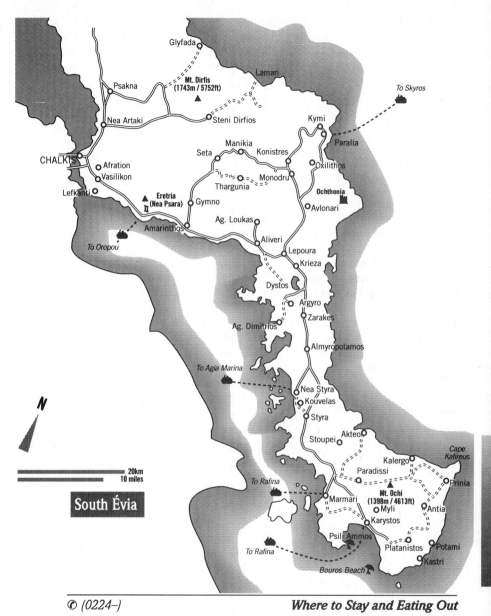

South Évia

**Mt. Dirfis**
(1743m / 5752ft)

Glyfada

Lamari

Psakna

To Skyros

Nea Artaki

Steni Dirfios

Kymi

Paralia

CHALKIS

Afration

Manikia

Seta

Konistres

Oxilithos

Vasilikon

Monodru

Lefkanti

Eretria
(Nea Psara)

Thargunia

Gymno

Ochthonia

Avlonari

To Oropou

Amarinthos

Ag. Loukas

Aliveri

Lepoura

Krieza

Dystos

Argyro

Zarakes

Ag. Dimitrios

Almyropotamos

To Agia Marina

Nea Styra

Kouvelas

Styra

Stoupei

Akteo

Kalergo

Cape Kafireus

Paradissi

Prinia

20km
10 miles

To Rafina

Marmari

**Mt. Ochi**
(1398m / 4613ft)

Myli

Antia

N

Karystos

Psili Ammos

To Rafina

Platanistos

Potami

Kastri

Bouros Beach

---

*© (0224–)*                                    ***Where to Stay and Eating Out***

### Kárystos

> **Apollon Suite Hotel** on Psilí Ámmos beach, © 22 045, ✆ 22 049 (*A; exp*) has been centrally air-conditioned and has a heated pool in case there's a chill in the air. **Karystos**, © 23 141, at Boúros (*B; exp–mod*), is a modern, largish hotel on the beach. *Open April–Oct.* **Hotel Als**, © 22 202 (*C; mod*), comfortable and very conveniently

placed on the waterfront, near all the cafés and tavernas; you can watch all the action from your balcony. **Galaxy** at the end of the seafront, ✆ 22 600 (*C; mod*), is little quieter and somewhat cheaper; ditto the **Hironia Hotel** in town by the sea, ✆ 22 238 (*C; mod*). If you want to stay at the **Mount Ochi Shelter**, fully equipped with a capacity for 30 people, ring Mr Sákis Biniáris, ✆ 22 378.

Besides the pleasant waterfront tavernas, it's worth hunting up **Kavontoros**, on a side street off the main square, with excellent ready food and barrelled wine in the 2–3000dr range, or, for a dose of local colour, **To Obpaïka**, a couple of blocks up from the Als Hotel and opposite a garbage drop, where tables are shared with other diners as well as cats and dogs, and the food is very good and very cheap.

### Néa Stýra

**Aktaeon** on the beach, ✆ 41 261; in Athens ✆ (01) 652 3345 (*C; mod*) is a typical small hotel, with restaurant, bar and grill. **Plaza**, in the middle of the waterfront, ✆ 41 429 (*C; exp–mod*) verges on the moderate price range. *Open all year.* **Hotel Sunday**, ✆ 41308, ✉ (01) 522 7090 is a small family-run hotel with big green awnings on the balconies overlooking the sea (*mod; rates include breakfast*). The **Venus Beach**, ✆ 41 226, has twin bungalows (*C; mod*). **Castello Rosso**, ✆ 41 547/780, (*C; mod*) is a nice small hotel with a pool, 50m from the beach; rates include a buffet breakfast. A small group of tavernas on the north end of town (turn left at the Lemonías sign) serve most of the usual Greek dishes, but specialize in fish; try **Matina**, or one of the two tavernas immediately next to it.

---

## Lépoura to Kými

At **Lépoura** the main road forks, one branch heading towards Chalkís (*see* below) and the other north to **Kými**. Along the way, a turn-off to the right leads down to **Avlonarí**, a fine old village topped by a small fortress and home to the lovely 12th-century Venetian church of Ag. Dimítrios. Further on, **Ochtoniá** is a busy village crammed beneath a Frankish castle, overlooking a set of quiet sandy beaches. After the Ochtoniá turn off, the Lépoura–Kými road plunges and writhes through a lovely and pastoral valley, dotted with Frankish towers to **Oxílithos**, named for its landmark, a volcanic precipice crowned with a church.

**Kými** (KΥΜΙ), the main port for Skýros (with occasional connections to the other Sporades), is a low-key resort. Lush, surrounded by vineyards and fig orchards, Kými is perched on a shelf high above the sea; some say its name is derived from *koumi*, 'I rise' in Hebrew, describing the town's front-row view of the dawn. Many Greeks have summer villas in the wooded hills, including some rather ambitious *nouveau riche* designs. A local association dedicated to preserving traditional island crafts has opened a fine **Museum of Popular Art** in a neoclassical mansion (*open 9–1 and 5–7*), housing costumes, tools, embroideries, lace and furnishings from the 19th century to the 1930s and a display dedicated to Kými's famous son, Dr George Papanikoláou, who invented and gave the first syllable of his name to the cancer test every woman knows so well. Pretty village footpaths as well as the road wind down 4km to the port, **Paralía Kými**, near a sandy beach sheltered by billowing tufts of pampas grass. It's a fine walk along the road north of Kými, to the sheer rocky ledge that was the probable site of the acropolis of Homeric Kyme Phyrkontis. Some of its stone went into the buildings now occupying the site: the precipitous Byzantine/Frankish castle of **Apokledí** and the handsome convent **Sótiros**, with a beautiful tile roof built in 1634 (*women only admitted*).

## Oxílithos

**Stomio**, © 71 251 (*C; mod*) is a newish apartment complex with 22 self-catering flats. *Open May–Oct.*

## Kými

**Krinion**, Plateía G. Papanikoláou, © 22 287 (*C; mod*) is the most pleasant to stay; ask for a room with a balcony. If it's full, try **Korali**, © 22 212 (*C; mod*). *Open all year.* Down in Paralía Kými you'll find the **Beis**, by the quay, © 22 604 (*C; mod*) a large, if rather anonymous hotel often used by people sailing out to Skýros. *Open all year.* There are a few rooms, some good waterfront tavernas and the **Sail Bar** for drinks while waiting for your ship to come in.

# Lépoura to Erétria

Back on the main road from Lépoura to Chalkís the first major village is **Alivéri**, its old red-roofed houses inhabited by coalminers and men working in the nearby power station. Big pylons and a cement factory protect it securely from any tourist pretensions but the tavernas along the waterfront and beach can make for a pleasantly lazy afternoon. Near Alivéri stood three ancient towns: Tamynae above Alivéri, Porthmos near the beach, and **Amarinthos** by Alivéri, now marked by a tall Venetian tower called Pyrgáki with its door suspended 8m above ground level, to be entered only by a retractable ladder. Amárinthos is a lively little resort popular for its fresh seafood (some plucked direct from the offshore fish farms) and has two Byzantine churches in the environs, **Metamórphosis** and **Kímissi tis Theotókou**, and a Macedonian tomb at **Vlichó**. In the hills above Amárinthos, the pretty village of **Áno Vátheia** has another Byzantine church, **Zoodóchos Pigí**.

**Erétria** (EPETPIA) connected to the mainland by ferry from Oropós, is sometimes known as Néa Psará; the modern town was founded during the War of Independence by refugees from Psará (near Chíos), who unfortunately for the archaeologists built their new town (including some fine captains' mansions) right on top of the old. Even so, Erétria is the most complete ancient site on Évia, as well as the biggest holiday resort after Loutrá Edipsoú. A maritime state in Homeric times, Erétria reached its prime during its rivalry with Chalkís over the lush Lelantine Plain. In the end the two cities decided to sort out their differences by leaving their weapons at home and meeting at a midway point in order to fight it out in a general free-for-all punch-up. Erétria lost the fight and the Plain, but suffered an even worse disaster in 490 BC when the Persians decimated the city. The Erétrians recovered and soon earned themselves a reputation for their excellent ceramics, and for their school of philosophy, founded in the 3rd century BC by Plato's student, Menedemes. The city generally remained allies with Athens until 87 BC, when Mithridates of Pontus sacked the city. It was the straw that broke the camel's back; Erétria was never rebuilt.

The **museum** (*open Tues–Sun, 8.30–3*), with statues and other bits dating back to Neolithic times, is at the top of Arkaíou Theátrou Street. It isn't much—the best of the finds went off to old rival Chalkís—but the adjacent excavations (*same hours*) begun in 1891 have revealed the excellent trapezoidal masonry of the walls, an elaborate **West Gate**, once topped with a corbelled arch, a 4th-century BC palace (complete with a clay bathtub), the gymnasium with a mosaic floor, and the weed-infested **theatre**, with the world's only survival of a *deus ex machina*: an underground passage from the orchestra that leads to the built-up *skene* behind the stage, where gods or goddesses could make sudden appearances to sort out a tangled plot. A path west of the theatre leads to a tumulus tomb, built in the Macedonian style with a square chamber, marble beds and thrones. Another path from the theatre leads in 15 minutes up to Erétria's walled **acropolis** affording an excellent view of the fertile Lelantine Plain, subject of so much contention, and, on a clear day, Mount Parnassos on the mainland. Of the temples, the only substantive remains belong to the Sanctuary of Athena Olympia, and down in the centre of the modern town, the 7th-century BC temple of **Apollo Daphnephoros**, 'the laurel-bearer', who enjoyed a fervent following throughout Évia.

One last spot along the Chalkís road that may tempt a detour is the mysterious 9th-century BC sanctuary of immense proportions (54 by 10m) unearthed in 1981 at **Lefkánti** (near Vasilikó). Female skeletons and golden ornaments were found buried here, but the biggest conundrum of all is the style of the building, extremely precocious for the period, with features more often seen in 6th-century structures. It may have been part of Homeric Erétria, listed in the *Iliad*'s *Catalogue of Ships*. **Fíla**, just inland, is dominated by a Venetian castle on an ancient mound.

---

✆ *(0221–)*                                        **Where to Stay and Eating Out**

### Amárinthos

**Stefania**, on the north end of town, ✆ 72 485 (*B; exp*) is a large, comfortable hotel with a pool. **Flisvos**, ✆ 72 385 (*C; mod*) is smaller. *Both open all year.*

### Erétria

Erétria has many hotels, as does Malakónda (just east), a beach-side resort that has mushroomed up to accommodate the package holiday crowd. **Palmariva Eretria Beach**, on the beach 2km from Erétria, ✆ 62 410, ✉ 62 418 (*A; exp*) has recently been renovated, and has everything a seaside resort hotel should have—sea sports, swimming pools, tennis, gym, disco and a wide choice of bars. **Holidays in Evia**, on the beach in Erétria, ✆ 62 611, ✉ 61 300 (*B; exp*), is another sports- and fun-orientated resort complex and conference centre. *Open all year.* **Malaconda Beach Vogue Club**, at Malakónda, ✆ 62 510, ✉ 62 518 (*exp*) is prettily set among the olives and cypresses, with a pool. *Open Mar–Oct.* **Delfis**, ✆ 62 380 (*C; mod*) is an old favourite. *Open June–Sept.* **Xenia**, ✆ 61 202 (*C; mod*) is slightly cheaper. **Dreams Island**, on the wooded peninsula with sandy beaches, ✆ 61 202 (*mod–inexp*) is a fancy name for complex of two hotels, bungalows, restaurant, bar, barbecue and disco with a not-so-glorified campground atmosphere, run by the town of Erétria. There are two campsites in the area: **Milos**, ✆ 60 420, ✉ 60 360 and the rather fancier and shadier **Eva**, at Malakónta, ✆ 61 081.

**O Ligouris**, opposite the ferryboat landing, ✆ 62 352 specializes in seafood, especially live lobster kept in a large tank; set menus range from 3800dr for moussaka and *souvláki* to 5500–7500dr for lobster; ouzo and wine from the barrel included. **Gorgona** and **Dionysos** offer similar fare for a little less.

**Chalkís** or Chalkída (ΧΑΛΚΙΣ or ΧΑΛΚΙΔΑ—you'll see both), the bustling industrial rhinoceros-shaped capital of Évia, occupies the narrowest point of the Evripós, only 40m from the mainland. Its location has been an important source of its prosperity, not least through its potential of seriously blocking trade between Athens and the north. Its name comes either from copper (*chalkós*), another early source of its wealth, or perhaps from *chalkí*, the Greek name for the murex sea snail prized in antiquity for making royal purple dye. The city had so many colonies in the north of Greece that it gave its name to the peninsula, Chalkidikí; in Italy it founded the colonies of Messina, Reggio Calabria and Cumae near Naples. By the 7th century BC Chalkís had asserted its position over Erétria as the island's dominant city.

*Tourist Police*

2 Eleftheríou Venizélou, Chalkís, ✆ (0221) 24 662.

## Around Chalkís

The first bridge to the mainland was built in 411 BC (the modern sliding drawbridge dates from 1962), but before crossing it, have a look at Chalkís and Évia from the walls of the Turkish **castle of the Karababa** ('black father') built in 1686, over Chalkís' ancient acropolis. Once over the bridge in Chalkís, turn left to find a row of pleasant cafés and *ouzeries* where you can sit and ponder the still unexplained mystery of the 30m wide **Evripós** channel that separates Évia from the mainland; the dangerous currents inexplicably change direction every few hours, sometimes only once a day, on rare occasions 14 times day, a phenomenon that so baffled and bothered Aristotle that he threw himself into the waters in frustration. Current thought has it that there are two separate streams in the Evripós, and a host of factors determine which one dominates at any given moment.

The main attraction in the new part of Chalkís is the **Archaeology Museum** on Leof. Venizélou (*open Tues–Sun, 8.30–3*) has some of the finest items discovered in Erétria, including a headless statue of Athena, the Archaic marble pediment from the temple of Apollo Daphnephoros showing the rape of Antiope by Theseus, and a bas-relief of Dionysos. Nearby, there's a **Byzantine Museum** in a pretty 16th-century mosque with a marble fountain, marking the entrance to the **Kástro**, the old Turkish quarter. Not far from the mosque is **Ag. Paraskeví**, a Byzantine basilica converted in the 13th century by Crusaders into a Gothic cathedral, resulting in the curious architectural collage inside, along with 14th-century inscriptions and coat-of-arms. Every year, in late July, a market for the feast of Ag. Paraskeví enlivens Chalkís for 10 days, attracting bargain hunters from all over Évia and the mainland, while the lovelorn beseech the icon of the saint for their hearts' desire; in the old days they would press a coin against the picture, and if it stuck there, it meant their love would not go unrequited. Also in Kástro, note the arcaded **Turkish aqueduct** that brought water to the city from Mount Dírfis. There's a **Museum of Folk Art** on Skalkóta Street; check the tourist police for times. Chalkís' Romaniot Jewish population goes back an estimated 2500 years; the synagogue at 35 Kótsou was built in the mid 19th century, but re-uses a number of marble fragments from the original, which burned. In the Jewish quarter, off Avantón Street, is a marble bust of Mórdechai Frízis of Chalkís, the first Greek officer killed in the Second World War.

## Beaches North of Chalkís, Mount Dírfis and Stení

Buses from Chalkís run to the busy, mostly shingle beaches to the north, all enjoying views across to the mainland: **Ag. Minás, Néa Artáki, Politiká Paralía**, and, last and nicest of all, tucked under the cliffs, **Dáfni**, which like all other places in Greece named Dafni is green and shady and throughly pleasant. Just inland are two of Évia's most distinctive, whitewashed villages, **Politiká** with a late Byzantine church and a castle and cosy little square and **Psachná**, a little market town with another castle. Boats leave Chalkís daily for the islet of **Tonnoíro**, with a hotel and beach; a larger boat, the *Eviokos*, makes regular 'mini-cruises' to Límni, Edipsós, and other places to swim and eat.

The real beauty spot within easy striking distance (25km, that is) of Chalkís is **Mount Dírfis**, Évia's highest peak at 1745m and wrapped in chestnut and pine forests and supporting a surprising quantity of alpine flora. You can take a bus as far as **Stení** (ΣΤΕΝΗ), a delightful village of wooden houses and chalets and waterfalls that makes a refreshing change in the summer. From Stení there's a well-marked if rather strenuous path to the summit of Dírfis, and a magnificently scenic road that goes over the pass, towards Strópones, and continuous in a rough, bumpy way down to the east coast and the splendid, pebble beach of **Chiliadoú**, with summer tavernas and places to camp.

*Where to Stay and Eating Out*

### Chalkís ✆ (0221–)

**Hotel Paliria**, Leof. Venizélou 2, ✆ 28 001, ✉ 81 959 (*B; exp–mod*) is the best place to stay if the fates have decreed a night in Chalkís; a modern building in the centre, overlooking the Evripós, rooms are air-conditioned, and there's a snack bar and roof garden. The **Kentrikon**, a minute from the mainland bridge at Angéli Govioú 5, ✆ 22 375 or 27 260 (*C; inexp*) is old and old-fashioned, with parking. **Mouchritsas**, on Hermoú Street (*inexp*) is the most popular taverna in town, with Greek favourites and barrelled wine; along the waterfront, the best of the fish tavernas is **Samaras** (*mod*). There are three excellent tavernas on Ag. Minás beach, 3km from the bridge in Chalkís' mainland extension.

### Stení ✆ (0228–)

**Dirphys**, in the village ✆ 51 217 (*C; mod*) is small. *Open all year.* **Steni**, ✆ 51 221 (*C; mod*) is similar but slightly pricier. Higher altitude stays are also possible in the Hellenic Alpine Club refuge at Lirí (1150m), ✆ (0221) 25 230 or (0288) 51 285 for information.

## Northern Évia

*Tourist Information*

Edipsós: 3 Okeanídon, ✆ (0226) 23 500 or 24 662 (summer only).

## Prokópi and Around

The northern half of Évia is so lush and green that in some spots you could be forgiven for thinking you were in Austria, although here the coast has long stretches of beaches washed by crystal-clear water and lined with pretty little whitewashed houses with rose-filled gardens. North of Psachná, the road to Pagóndas rises high into the mountains, permeated with the

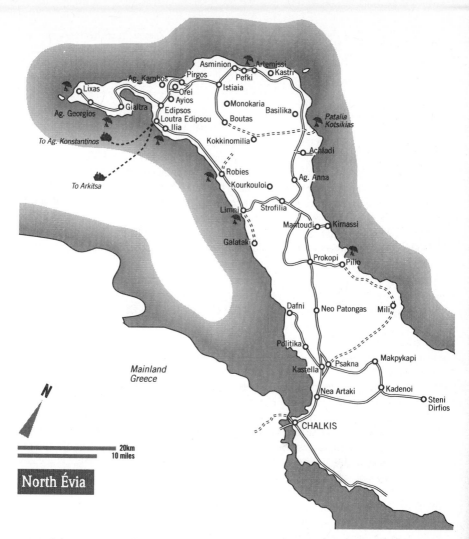

North Évia

scent of deep green pine forests; beehives everywhere attest to the potency of local herbs and wildflowers, and the honey offered in roadside stands comes close to nectar. Tavernas with outdoor terraces take advantage of the most breathtaking views.

**Pagóndas** (35km from Chalkís) is a typical mountain village; further north, a striking castle piled on a nearly inaccessible precipice signals **Prokópi** (ΠΡΟΚΟΠΙ), an enchanting village set near the end of the magnificent narrow, wooded ravines of the Kleisoúra valley, where the road offers fine views over the Sporades. This is prime picnicking territory, and, if extra thrills are called for, wobble over the ravines on the rickety wooden suspension bridges. Sometimes called by its Turkish name, Ahmet Aga, Prokópi is populated by Greeks from the fantastical Cappadocian town of Ürgüp, who came over in the 1920s population exchange. The Cappadocians brought their most holy relics, the bones of St John the Russian, who went from being a soldier in the Tsar's army to a slave in Ürgüp (1730) to a saint of the Russian Orthodox Church (in 1962) who attracts his fair share of pilgrims at his church, Ag. Ioánnes tou Rossou. In the centre of Prokópi, the handsome estate of the Noel-Baker family, where the Turkish Pasha's tulip and rose gardens once bloomed, is now home to the Candili Centre for creative holidays (*see* p.17). The village was built around the estate, bought by Edward Noel, a relative of Byron, in 1832. He set up the North Euboean Foundation which provided health care and education for immigrant workers.

From Prokópi, a paved road to the east leads steeply down through forests of planes, pines and firs dotted with beehives to **Pílio**, set in rocky mountain scenery. There are plenty of tavernas and rooms to rent, set amid lovely old houses with goats in the garden and the usual Greek concrete monstrosities. The pine-clad sandy bay just below looks across to Skópelos and at the time of writing has only one taverna; go now, before the development plans cooked up by the Greek and European governments transform it forever. If Pílio is too close to civilization for your taste, brave the rough road east along the coast to the pebbly beach beyond **Vlachiá**. From **Mantóudi**, the next town on the main highway north of Prokópi, with a pretty square and great ouzerie, another road winds down to the east coast, this time to **Kimássi**, where factories and a mineral-refining plant nestle along the beach. The charm is enough, at least in July and August, to support a pair of bars and tavernas.

At **Strofiliá** the road forks west to Límni (*see* below) and around to Loutrá Edipsoú, while the main road continues to Ag. Ánna, a traditional village located above two very long beaches, **Paralía Ag. Ánna** (with a campsite, ✆ (0227) 61 550) and **Angáli**, just north. **Vassiliká**, further up, looks directly across to emerald Skiáthos; the sign for **Psarodóuli** points the way to a long, sandy beach.

## Around the Top of Évia

The north coast of Évia looks across the narrow strait to Mount Pélion and the Trikéri peninsula and the mainland. The shore is dotted with beaches; families from Chalkís and the mainland settle in here for the entire summer, making accommodation for only one or two days very problematic. The seaside village of **Artemísseon** witnessed the first and indecisive naval battle between the Greeks and the Persians in 480 BC. Near the shore are the ruins of the vast Temple of Artemis Proseoa, although the greatest archaeological treasure in the area was a shipwreck of ancient bronzes, discovered offshore in 1928, the source of two star attractions in Athens' National Archaeological Museum: the full-length bronze Zeus (or Poseidon) and the Cape Artemission jockey. Below Artemíssieon, there's a pretty beach and growing resort under the pines called **Péfki**.

Cattle belonging to the goddess Hera grazed at **Istiaía** (ΙΣΤΙΑΙΑ), the largest village along the northern road, described by Homer as 'rich in vines'. It was founded by Thessalians who thumbed their noses at Athens so often that Pericles captured the town and booted out the inhabitants, repopulating Istiaía with Athenians. Although few towns are more attractively situated than Istiaía, set in an amphitheatre of hills, the Athenian colonists didn't find it to their liking, preferring to found nearby **Oreí** (ΩΡΕΟΙ) instead; when they in turn were driven out by the Spartans in the Peloponnesian War, the Istianians returned. The whole population of Évia contributed to the construction of Istiaía's Venetian Kástro, built right in the centre of town; a second medieval fortress, to the defend the narrow strait, was built over the ancient acropolis. Oreí's central square is guarded by an Hellenistic marble bull, found offshore in 1962. These days the treat offshore is the islet of **Argirónisos**, abandoned at the turn of the century and now the only private island in Greece taking paying guests. West of Oreí, the beach at **Agíokambos** has a row of good seafood tavernas.

## Péfki

**Galini**, © 22 448 (*mod*). There's a good campsite with some bunga-lows, © (0226) 41 161. There's the excellent **Mirtia** and the **Cavo d'Oro** and a good *ouzerie* as well; all three have lovely views across to the Pélion peninsula and Skiáthos.

## Istiaía

In Istiaía most of the accommodation is apartments or rooms, but if you're passing through, try the restaurant **Vlachopoulos** near the main square, with tasty, well-prepared food (*around 3000dr*). **O Vangos**, off the other end of the square has its own distinctive personality, decorated with out-of-date Father Christmas calendars and food is served at the same temperature as the wine (chilled), accompanied by the news on the black and white TV. It's also disarmingly cheap.

## Oreí

**Corali Hotel**, © 71 217, has simple rooms, as does the little pension **Kentrikon**, © 71 525 (*both inexp*).

## Argirónisos

You and between nine and 12 of your friends can hire the private isle of Argirónisos from May to October; all-inclusive rates include the price of a return flight from London, room and board. Contact The Best of Greece in Kent, © (01622) 692 278.

# Loutrá Edipsóu to Límni

Magnificently set like a pendant in the necklace of a wooded bay, **Loutrá Edipsoú** (ΛΟΥΤΡΑ ΑΙΔΗΨΟΥ) is the Miami of Évia, where matrons wearing plenty of gold and blue rinses come to be rejuvenated in the fountain of youth—80 hot sulphurous springs that squirt out of the ground at up to 160°F and since antiquity noted for treating rheumatism, arthritis, gallstones, and even depression. The ancients believed that Loutrá's source was connected under the sea with the hot springs at Thermopylae; Aristotle praised the waters; the gouty Sulla, Augustus and Hadrian called in for lengthy soaks in the now ruined Roman baths, and to this day Loutrá Edipsoú has something of the lazy, old-fashioned neoclassical ambience typical of spas, embell-ished with grand old hotels, shady avenues and flowery gardens for idling away an afternoon, combined in July and August with the cacophony of Greek families having a good time; a fishing port and a long, lovely beach is an added attraction, and there are day excursions to Skiáthos, Alónissos and Skópelos.

Follow the road along the bay to Évia's westernmost promontory and a second, more modest spa, **Loutrá Giáltron**; besides the water, there's a sandy beach and church, of the Theotókou with frescoes. There are more worthy beaches further west: **Gregolímano** with its Club Med resort and **Ag. Geórgios**, a pleasant, laid-back fishing village with rooms to rent. There's a stalactite cave at Profítis Ilías, and places to picnic and snooze under the plane trees, especially at a spot called Paleóchori.

The coastal road south of Loutrá passes some of the prettiest beaches on the island, beginning with the small seaside village of **Ília** to the charming fishing village and beach of **Robiés**, immersed in olive groves. There are fine 17th-century frescoes in the church of **David tou Géronta**, 8km away (check around for the key before setting out). **Límni** (ΛIMNH), 15km south of Robiés, is many an old hand's favourite place on all Évia: a perfect old whitewashed fishing village around a sleepy bay with mediocre beaches and a slowly growing resort community under the pines. The sailing is good here, and the waterfront is perfect for just lazing with the village cats and watching the world go by. According to myth, Zeus brought Hera to Límni (then called Elymnion) for their honeymoon. The temple that once marked the spot keeled over in an earthquake, but in its place Límni offers a pretty paleo-Christian mosaic floor in the chapel of **Zoodóchos Pigí**. An 8km track from Límni leads south to **Moní Galatáki**, a Byzantine monastery (now a convent) in a beautiful, peaceful setting built over a temple dedicated to Poseidon. The church has fascinating 16th-century frescoes, including portraits of the two sea captains who became the monastery's great patrons after they were shipwrecked nearby and saved by divine intervention. The road to Galatáki is a dead end; the paved road circles back up into the mountains and joins the main road at Strofyliá (*see* above).

---

### *Where to Stay and Eating Out*

**Loutrá Edipsoú** ✆ (0226–)

There's no shortage of accommodation here, although it's impossible to find a room in August without booking ahead. The **Aegli**, 18 Paraliakís, ✆ 22 216 (*A; lux*) and the **Avra**, ✆ 22 226 (*A; lux*) are the best for wallowing in grand old spa atmosphere. *Both open May–Oct.* **Hotel Edipsos**, near the ferry, ✆ 22 035 (*B; exp*) has pleasant views and a private bus to the thermal baths. *Open all year.* **Capri**, near the baths, ✆ 22 496, (*C; mod*) has lovely views. There are a number of good places to eat on the waterfront, notably the **Aegli** and **Yero Nikolaos**, near the cinema, the latter with live Greek music to go with the good Greek food. If you're in a fishy mood, make your way to Loutrá's suburb of Ag. Nikólaos, where **Balalas** and **Margomenos** are two moderately priced fish tavernas highly recommended by the locals. Don't miss the fun of having a drink in the **Klima**, set on stilts over the sea.

**Límni** ✆ (0227–)

**Límni Hotel**, at the end of the bay, ✆ 31 316 (*C; mod*) has fine rooms with balconies looking down into the water. **Plaza**, centrally placed, ✆ 31 235 (*C; mod*) is even cheaper. The attractive little waterfront sports some excellent cafés and tavernas: **Avra** is one of the best places to eat seafood, with well-prepared Greek favourites and fresh fish (*under 3000dr*). Next door, **O Platanos**, ✆ 31 686, is a truly excellent taverna, with delicious fresh grilled fish and meats served under the huge reassuring limbs of a plane tree. Robiés has an immaculate **campsite** by the sea, ✆ 71 120.

| 7000–2800 | Neolithic Era |
| 4000 | Precocious civilization at Palaeochoe, Límnos |
| 3000 | Mílos exports obsidian |
| 3000–2000 | Early Cycladic civilization |
| 2800–1000 | Bronze Age |
| 2600–2000 | Early Minoan civilization in Crete |
| 2000–1700 | Middle Minoan: Cretan thalassocracy rules the Aegean |
| 1700–1450 | Late Minoan |
| 1600–1150 | Mycenaean civilization begins with invasion of the Peloponnese |
| c. 1450 | Eruption of Santoríni's volcano decimates the Minoans; Mycenaeans occupy ruined Crete and Rhodes |
| 1180 | Traditional date of the fall of Troy (4 July) |
| c. 1150 | Beginning of the Dark Ages: Dorian invasion disrupts Mycenaean culture; Ionians settle Asia Minor and islands |
| 1000 | Kos and the three cities of Rhodes join Doric Hexapolis |
| 1100–100 | Iron Age |
| 1100–700 | Geometric Period |
| 700–500 | Archaic Period |
| 650 | Aegina is first in Greece to mint coins |
| Late 600s | Sappho born on Lésbos |
| 570–480 | Pythagoras of Sámos |
| 500–323 | Classical Age |
| 490–479 | Persian Wars end with defeat of Persian army and fleet |
| 478 | Delos becomes HQ of the Athenian-dominated Maritime League |
| 460–377 | Hippocrates of Kos |
| 431–404 | Peloponnesian War cripples Athens |
| 378 | Second Delian League |
| 338 | Philip of Macedon conquers Athens and the rest of Greece |
| 334–323 | Conquests of Alexander the Great |
| 323–146 | Hellenistic Age |
| 146–AD 410 | Roman Age |
| 88 | Mithridates of Pontus, enemy of Rome, devastates many islands |
| 86 | Romans under Sulla destroy Athens and other Greek rebels who supported Mithridates |

## Chronology

AD

| 58 | St Paul visits Líndos, Rhodes |
| 95 | St John the Divine writes the Apocalypse on Pátmos |
| 391 | Paganism outlawed in Roman Empire |

| | |
|---|---|
| **410–1453** | Byzantine Era |
| **727–843** | Iconoclasm in the Eastern Church |
| **824–861** | Saracen/Arab Occupation |
| **961** | Emperor Nikephoros Phokas reconquers Crete from the Saracens |
| **1054** | Pope excommunicates Patriarch of Constantinople over differences in the creed |
| **1088** | Foundation of the Monastery on Pátmos |
| **1204** | Venetians lead Fourth Crusade conquest of Contantinople and take the islands as their share of the booty |
| **1261** | Greeks retake Constantinople from Latins |
| **1309** | Knights of St John, chased out of Jerusalem, establish themselves on Rhodes |
| **1453** | Turks begin conquest of Greece |
| **1522** | Ottomans defeat Knights of St John |
| **1541** | El Greco born on Crete |
| **1669** | Venetians lose Herákleon, Crete to the Turks after a 20-year siege |
| **1771–74** | Catherine the Great sends Russian fleet into the Aegean to harry the Sultan |
| **1796** | Napoleon captures Venice and her Ionian islands |
| **1815–64** | British rule Ionian islands |
| **1821–27** | Greek War of Independence |
| **1823** | Aegina made the capital of free Greece |
| **1827** | Annihilation of Turkish fleet by the British, French and Russian allies at the Battle of Navarino |
| **1833** | Otho of Bavaria becomes the first king of the Greeks |
| **1883–1957** | Cretan writer Nikos Kazantzakis |
| **1912–13** | Balkan Wars give Greece Macedonia, Crete and the Northeast Aegean islands; the Italians pick up the Dodecanese |
| **1922–23** | Greece invades Turkey with catastrophic results |
| **1924** | Greece becomes a republic |
| **1935** | Restoration of the monarchy |
| **1941** | Nazi paratroopers complete first ever invasion by air on Crete |
| **1945** | Treaty signed returning Dodecanese islands to Greece |
| **1948** | Dodecanese islands reunite with Greece |
| **1949** | End of civil war between communists and US-backed government |
| **1953** | Earthquake shatters the Ionian islands |
| **1967** | Colonels' coup establishes a dictatorship |
| **1974** | Failure of the Junta's Cyprus adventure leads to the regime's collapse and restoration of democracy |
| **1981** | First ever nominally socialist government (PASOK) elected |
| **1983** | Greece joins the EEC |
| **1990** | PASOK lose election to conservative Néa Demokratikí (ND) |
| **1993** | PASOK's Papandréou re-elected |

Greek holds a special place as the oldest spoken language in Europe, going back at least 4000 years. From the ancient language, Modern Greek, or Romaíka, developed into two forms: the purist or *katharévousa*, literally 'clean language', and the popular, or Demotic *demotikí*, the language of the people. But while the purist is consciously Classical, the popular is as close to its ancient origins as say, Chaucerian English is to modern English. These days few purist words are spoken but you will see the old *katharévousa* on shop signs and official forms. Even though the bakery is called the *foúrnos* the sign over the door will read ΑΡΤΟΠΟΛΕΙΟΝ, bread-seller, while the general store will be the ΠΑΝΤΟΠΟΛΕΙΟΝ, seller of all. You'll still see the pure form on wine labels as well.

At the end of the 18th century, in the wakening swell of national pride, writers felt the common language wasn't good enough; archaic forms were brought back and foreign ones replaced. Upon independence, this somewhat stilted, artificial construction called *katharévousa* became the official language of books, documents and even newspapers. The more vigorous and natural Demotic soon began to creep back; in 1901 Athens was shaken by riots and the government fell when the New Testament appeared in *demotikí*; in 1903 several students were killed in a fight with the police during a *demotikí* performance of Aeschylus. When the fury subsided, it looked as if the Demotic would win out by popular demand until the Papadópoulos government (1967–74) made it part of its puritan 'moral cleansing' of Greece to revive the purist. *Katharévousa* was the only language allowed in secondary schools and everything from textbooks to matchbook covers had to be written in the pure form. The great language debate was eventually settled in 1978 when Demotic was made the official tongue.

Greeks travel so far and wide that even in the most remote places there's usually someone who speaks English, more likely than not with an American, Australian or even South African drawl. On the other hand, learning a bit of Greek can make your travels more enjoyable. Usually spoken with great velocity, Greek isn't a particularly easy language to pick up by ear. But even if you have no desire to learn Greek, it is helpful to know at least the alphabet— so that you can find your way around—and a few basic words and phrases.

### Greekspeak

Sign language is an essential part of Greek life and it helps to know what it all means. Greekspeak for 'no' is usually a click of the tongue, accompanied by raised eyebrows and a tilt

## Language

of the head backwards. It could be all three or a permutation. 'Yes' is usually indicated by a forward nod, head tilted to the side. If someone doesn't hear you or understand you properly they will often shake their heads from side to side quizzically and say '*Oríste?*' Hands whirl like windmills in conversations and beware the emphatic open hand brought sharply down in anger. A circular movement of the right hand usually implies something very good or in great quantities. Women walking alone might hear hissing like a demented snake emanating from pavement cafés. This will be the local Romeos or *kamákis* trying to attract your attention.

Greeks also use exclamations which sound odd but mean a lot, like *po, po, po!* an expression of disapproval or derision; *brávo* comes in handy for praise while *ópa!* is useful for whoops! look out! or watch it!; *sigá sigá* means slowly, slowly; *éla!*, come or get on with you, *kíta!* look. Other phrases you'll hear all the time but won't find in your dictionary include:

| | |
|---|---|
| *paréa* | gang, close friends |
| *pedhiá* | guys, the lads |
| *ré, bré* | mate, chum, slang for friends |
| *endáxi* | OK |
| *malákka* | rude, lit. masturbator, used between men as term of endearment |
| *kéfi* | high spirits, well-being |
| *kaïmós* | the opposite, suffering, sad |
| *lipón* | well, now then |
| *hérete* | formal greeting |
| *sto kaló* | go with God, formal parting |
| *listía* | rip-off |
| *alítis* | bum, no-good person |
| *palikári* | good guy, brave, honourable |
| *pedhí mou/korítsi mou* | my boy/my girl |
| *yasoo koúkla/os* | Hi doll, hello gorgeous |
| *etsi íne ee zoí* | that's life! |
| *ti na kánoume* | what can we do! |
| *kaló taxídhi* | good trip, Bon Voyage! |
| *kalí órexi* | Bon appetit! |

## The Greek Alphabet (*see* also **Introduction** p.viii)

| Pronunciation | | | English Equivalent | Pronunciation | | | English Equivalent |
|---|---|---|---|---|---|---|---|
| A | α | *álfa* | short 'a' as in 'father' | N | ν | *ni* | n |
| B | β | *víta* | v | Ξ | ξ | *ksi* | 'x' as in 'ox' |
| Γ | γ | *gámma* | guttural *g* or *y* sound | O | o | *ómicron* | 'o' as in 'cot' |
| Δ | δ | *délta* | hard *th* as in 'though' | Π | π | *pi* | p |
| E | ε | *épsilon* | short 'e' as in 'bet' | P | ρ | *ro* | r |
| Z | ζ | *zíta* | z | Σ | σ | *sígma* | s |
| H | η | *íta* | long 'e' as in 'bee' | T | τ | *taf* | t |
| Θ | θ | *thíta* | soft *th* as in 'thin' | Υ | υ | *ípsilon* | long 'e' as in 'bee' |
| I | ι | *yóta* | long 'e' as in 'bee'; sometimes like 'y' in 'yet' | Φ | φ | *fi* | f |
| | | | | X | χ | *chi* | German *ch* as in 'doch' |
| K | κ | *káppa* | k | Ψ | ψ | *psi* | *ps* as in 'stops' |
| Λ | λ | *lámtha* | l | Ω | ω | *oméga* | 'o' as in 'cot' |
| M | μ | *mi* | m | | | | |

## Dipthongs and Consonant Combinations

| | | |
|---|---|---|
| AI | αι | short 'e' as in 'bet' |
| EI | ει, OI οι | 'i' as in 'machine' |
| OΥ | ου | *oo* as in 'too' |
| AΥ | αυ | *av* or *af* |
| EΥ | ευ | *ev* or *ef* |
| HΥ | ηυ | *iv* or *if* |
| ΓΓ | γγ | *ng* as in 'angry' |
| ΓΚ | γκ | hard 'g'; *ng* within word |
| NT | ντ | 'd'; *nd* within word |
| ΜΠ | μπ | 'b'; *mp* within word |

## Useful Phrases

| | | |
|---|---|---|
| Yes | *né/málista* (formal) | Ναί /Μάλιστα |
| No | *óchi* | Οχι |
| I don't know | *then xéro* | Δέν ξέρω |
| I don't understand… (Greek) | *then katalavéno… (elliniká)* | Δέν καταλαβαίνω… (Ελληνικά) |
| Does someone speak English? | *milái kanis angliká?* | Μιλάει κανείς αγγλικά? |
| Go away | *fíyete* | Φύγετε |
| Help! | *voíthia!* | Βοήθεια! |
| My friend | *o fílos moo* (*m*) | Ο φίλος μου |
| | *ee fíli moo* (*f*) | Η φίλη μου |
| Please | *parakaló* | Παρακαλώ |
| Thank you (very much) | *evcharistó* (*pára polí*) | Ευχαριστώ (πάρα πολύ) |
| You're welcome | *parakaló* | Παρακαλώ |
| It doesn't matter | *thén pirázi* | Δέν πειράζει |
| OK, alright | *endaxi* | Εντάξι |
| Of course | *vevéos* | Βεβαίος |
| Excuse me, sorry | *signómi* | Συγγνώμη |
| Pardon? Or, from waiters, what do you want? | *oríste?* | Ορίστε? |
| Be careful! | *proséchete!* | Προσέχεται! |
| Nothing | *típota* | Τίποτα |
| What is your name? | *pos sas léne?* (*formal*) | Πώς σάς λένε? |
| | *pos se léne?* | Πώς σέ λένε? |
| How are you? | *ti kánete?* (*formal/pl*) | Τί κάνεται? |
| | *ti kanis?* | Τί κάνεις? |
| Hello | *yásas, hérete* (*formal/pl*) | Γειάσας, Χέρεται |
| | *yásou* | Γειάσου |
| Goodbye | *yásas, hérete* (*formal/pl*) | Γειάσας, Χέρεται |
| | *yásou, adío* | Γειάσου, Αντίο |
| Good morning | *kaliméra* | Καλημέρα |
| Good evening/good night | *kalispéra/kaliníchta* | Καλησπέρα /Καληνύχτα |
| What is that? | *ti íne aftó?* | Τί είναι αυτό? |
| What? | *ti?* | Τί? |
| Who? | *piós?* (*m*), *piá?* (*f*) | Ποιός? Ποιά? |
| Where? | *poo?* | Ποιός? |
| When? | *póte?* | Πότε? |

| | | |
|---|---|---|
| why? | *yiatí?* | Γιατί? |
| how? | *pos?* | Πώς? |
| | | |
| I am | *íme* | Είμαι |
| You are (*sing*) | *íse* | Είσε |
| He, she, it is | *íne* | Είναι |
| We are | *ímaste* | Είμαστε |
| You are (*pl*) | *ísaste* | Είσαστε |
| They are | *íne* | Είναι |
| | | |
| I am lost | *échasa to thrómo* | Εχασα το δρόμο |
| I am hungry | *pinó* | Πεινώ |
| I am thirsty | *thipsó* | Διψώ |
| I am tired | *íme kourasménos* | Είμαι κουρασμένος |
| I am ill | *íme árostos* | Είμαι άρρωστος |
| I am poor | *íme ftochós* | Είμαι φτωχός |
| I love you | *s'agapó* | Σ'αγαπώ |
| | | |
| good | *kaló* | καλό |
| bad | *kakó* | κακό |
| so-so | *étsi kétsi* | έτσι κ'έτσι |
| slowly | *sigá sigá* | σιγά σιγά |
| fast | *grígora* | γρήγορα |
| big | *megálo* | μεγάλο |
| small | *mikró* | μικρό |
| hot | *zestó* | ζεστό |
| cold | *crío* | κρίο |

## Shops, Services, Sightseeing

| | | |
|---|---|---|
| I would like... | *tha íthela...* | Θά ήθελα... |
| where is...? | *poo íne...?* | Πού είναι...? |
| how much is it? | *póso káni?* | Πόσο κάνει? |
| bakery | *foúrnos* | φούρνος |
| | *artopoleion* (above entrance) | Αρτοπολείον |
| bank | *trápeza* | τράπεζα |
| beach | *paralía* | παραλία |
| bookshop | *vivliopolío* | βιβλιοπολείο |
| butcher | *kreopolío* | κρεοπωλείο |
| church | *eklisía* | εκκλησία |
| cinema | *kinimatográfos* | κινηματογράφος |
| food | *fayitó* | φαγητό |
| hospital | *nosokomío* | νοσοκομείο |
| hotel | *xenodochío* | ξενοδοχείο |
| hot water | *zestó neró* | ζεστό νερό |
| kiosk | *períptero* | περίπτερο |
| money | *leftá* | λεφτά |
| museum | *moosío* | μουσείο |
| newspaper (foreign) | *efimerítha* (*xéni*) | εφημερίδα (ξένη) |
| pharmacy | *farmakío* | φαρμακείο |
| police station | *astinomía* | αστυνομία |
| policeman | *astifílakas* | αστιφύλακας |
| post office | *tachithromío* | ταχυδρομείο |
| plug, electrical | *príza* | πρίζα |

| plug, bath | tápa | τὰπα |
| restaurant | estiatório | εστιατόριο |
| sea | thálassa | θάλασσα |
| shower | doush | ντούς |
| student | fititís | φοιτητής |
| telephone office | Oté | ΟΤΕ |
| theatre | théatro | θέατρο |
| toilet | tooaléta | τουαλέττα |

## Time

| What time is it? | ti óra íne? | Τί ώρα είναι |
| month | mína | μήνα |
| week | evthomáda | εβδομάδα |
| day | méra | μέρα |
| morning | proí | πρωί |
| afternoon | apóyevma | απόγευμα |
| evening | vráthi | βράδυ |
| yesterday | chthés | χθές |
| today | símera | σήμερα |
| tomorrow | ávrio | αύριο |
| now | tóra | τώρα |
| later | metá | μετά |
| it is early/late | íne norís/ argá | είναι νωρίς/αργά |

## Travel Directions

| I want to go to ... | thélo na páo sto (m), sti (f)... | Θέλω νά πάω στό, στη... |
| How can I get to...? | pós boró na páo sto (m), sti (f)...? | Πώς μπορώ νά πάω στό, στη...? |
| Where is...? | poo íne ...? | Πού είναι...? |
| How far is it? | póso makriá íne? | Πόσο μακριά είναι |
| When will the... come? | póte tha érthi to (n), ee (f), o (m)...? | Πότε θά έρθη τό, ή, ό...? |
| When will the... leave? | póte tha fíyí to (n), ee (f), o (m)...? | Πότε θά φύγη τό, ή, ό...? |
| From where do I catch...? | apó poo pérno...? | Από πού πέρνω...? |
| How long does the trip take? | póso keró pérni to taxíthi? | Πόσο καιρό πέρνει τό ταξίδι? |
| Please show me | parakaló thíkste moo | Παρακαλώ δείξτε μου |
| the (nearest) town | to horió (to pió kondinó) | Το χωριό (το πιό κοντινό) |
| here | ethó | εδώ |
| there | ekí | εκεί |
| near | kondá | κοντά |
| far | makriá | μακριά |
| left | aristerá | αριστερά |
| right | thexiá | δεξιά |
| north | vória | βόρεια |
| south | nótia | νότια |
| east | anatoliká | ανατολικά |
| west | thitiká | δυτικά |
| corner | goniá | γωνιά |

## Driving

| | | |
|---|---|---|
| where can I rent ...? | poo boró na nikiáso ...? | Πού μποπώ νά? νοικιάσω ...? |
| a car | éna aftokínito | ένα αυτοκινητο |
| a motorbike | éna michanáki | ένα μηχανάκι |
| a bicycle | éna pothílato | ένα ποδήλατο |
| where can I buy petrol? | poo boró nagorásso venzíni? | Πού μπορώ ν'αγοράσω βενζίνη? |
| where is a garage? | poo íne éna garáz? | Πού είναι ένα γκαράζ? |
| a mechanic | énan mihanikó | έναν μηχανικό |
| a map | énan chárti | έναν χάρτη |
| where is the road to...? | poo íne o thrómos yiá...? | Πού είναι ο δρόμος γιά...? |
| where does this road lead? | poo pái aftós o thrómos? | Πού πάει αυτός ο δρόμος? |
| is the road good? | íne kalós o thrómos? | Είναι καλός ο δρόμος? |
| EXIT | éxothos | ΕΞΟΔΟΣ |
| ENTRANCE | ísothos | ΕΙΣΟΔΟΣ |
| DANGER | kínthinos | ΚΙΝΔΥΝΟΣ |
| SLOW | argá | ΑΡΓΑ |
| NO PARKING | apagorévete ee státhmevsis | ΑΠΑΓΟΡΕΥΕΤΑΙ Η ΣΤΑΘΜΕΥΣΙΣ |
| KEEP OUT | apagorévete ee ísothos | ΑΠΑΓΟΡΕΥΕΤΑΙ Η ΕΙΣΟΔΟΣ |

## Numbers

| | | |
|---|---|---|
| one | énas (m), mía (f), éna (n) | ένας, μία, ένα |
| two | thío | δύο |
| three | tris (m, f), tría (n) | τρείς, τρία |
| four | téseris (m, f), téssera (n) | τέσσερεις, τέσσερα |
| five | pénde | πέντε |
| six | éxi | έξι |
| seven | eptá | επτά |
| eight | októ | οκτώ |
| nine | ennéa | εννέα |
| ten | théka | δέκα |
| eleven | éntheka | έντεκα |
| twelve | thótheka | δώδεκα |
| thirteen | thekatría | δεκατρία |
| fourteen | thekatéssera | δεκατέσσερα |
| twenty | íkosi | είκοσι |
| twenty-one | íkosi éna (m, n) mía (f) | είκοσι ένα, μία |
| thirty | triánda | τριάντα |
| forty | saránda | σαράντα |
| fifty | penínda | πενήντα |
| sixty | exínda | εξήντα |
| seventy | evthomínda | ευδομήντα |
| eighty | ogthónda | ογδόντα |
| ninety | enenínda | ενενήντα |
| one hundred | ekató | εκατό |
| one thousand | chília | χίλια |

| January | Ianooários | Ιανουάριος |
| February | Fevrooários | Φεβρουάριος |
| March | Mártios | Μάρτιος |
| April | Aprílios | Απρίλιος |
| May | Máios | Μάιος |
| June | Ioónios | Ιούνιος |
| July | Ioólios | Ιούλιος |
| August | Avgoostos | Αύγουστος |
| September | Septémvrios | Σεπτέμβριος |
| October | Októvrios | Οκτώβριος |
| November | Noémvrios | Νοέμβριος |
| December | Thekémvrios | Δεκέμβριος |
| Sunday | Kiriakí | Κυριακή |
| Monday | Theftéra | Δευτέρα |
| Tuesday | Tríti | Τρίτη |
| Wednesday | Tetárti | Τετάρτη |
| Thursday | Pémpti | Πέμπτη |
| Friday | Paraskeví | Παρασκευή |
| Saturday | Sávato | Σάββατο |

| the airport | to arothrómio | τό αεροδρόμιο |
| the aeroplane | to aropláno | τό αεροπλάνο |
| the bus station | ee stási leoforíou | ή στάση λεωφορείου |
| the bus | to leoforío | τό λεωφορείο |
| the railway station | o stathmós too trénou | ό σταθμός τού τραίνου |
| the train | to tréno | τό τραίνο |
| the port | to limáni | τό λιμάνι |
| the port authority | to limenarchío | τό λιμεναρχείο |
| the ship | to plío, to karávi | τό πλοίο, τό καράβι |
| the steamship | to vapóri | τό βαπόρι |
| the car | to aftokínito | τό αυτοκίνητο |
| a ticket | éna isitírio | ένα εισιτήριο |

Finding your way round a Greek menu, *katálogos*, takes some doing, but there's a basic layout with prices before and after local tax. You begin with Orektiká, ΟΡΕΚΤΙΚΑ; dishes cooked in olive oil are known as Laderá, ΛΑΔΕΡΑ; main courses are Entrádes, ΕΝΤΡΑΔΕΣ; Fish are Psária, ΨΑΡΙΑ; dishes with minced meat, Kimádhes, ΚΥΜΑΔΕΣ and things grilled or barbecued to order are either Psitá, ΨΗΤΑ or Tis Oras, ΤΗΣ ΩΡΑΣ.

| Ορεκτικά (Μεζέδες) | Orektiká (Mezéthes) | Appetisers |
|---|---|---|
| τζατζίκι | tzatzíki | yoghurt and cucumbers |
| ελήές | eliés | olives |
| ντολμάδες | dolmáthes | stuffed vine leaves |
| ταραμοσαλάτα | taramosalata | cod's roe dip |
| ποικιλια | pikilía | mixed hors d'œuvres |
| χόρτα | chórta | wild greens |

| Σούπες | Soópes | Soups |
|---|---|---|
| αυγολέμονο | avgolémono | egg and lemon soup |
| χορτόσουπα | chortósoupa | vegetable soup |
| ψαρόσουπα | psarósoupa | fish soup |
| μαγειρίτσα | magirítsa | giblets in egg and lemon |

| Λαδερά | Latherá | Cooked in oil |
|---|---|---|
| μπαμιες | bámies | okra, ladies' fingers |
| γιγαντες | yígantes | butter beans in tomato sauce |
| μπριαμ | briám | aubergines and mixed veg |
| φασόλακια | fasólakia | fresh green beans |
| φακή | fakí | lentils |
| πατάτες | patátes | potatoes |

| Κυμάδες | Kymadhes | Minced Meat |
|---|---|---|
| παστίτσιο | pastítsio | mince and macaroni pie |
| μουσακά | moussaká | meat, aubergine with white sauce |
| μακαρόνια με κυμά | makarónia me kymá | spaghetti Bolognese |
| ντομάτες γεμιστές | tomátes yemistés | stuffed tomatoes |
| μελιτζάνες γεμιστές | melitzánes yemistés | stuffed aubergines/eggplants |
| πιπεριές γεμιστές | piperíes yemistés | stuffed peppers |

| Ζυμαρικά | Pasta and Rice | Zimariká |
|---|---|---|
| πιλάφι | piláfi | pilaf |
| σπαγκέτι | spagéti | spaghetti |
| μακαρόνια | macarónia | macaroni |

| Ψάρια | Psária | Fish |
|---|---|---|
| αστακός | astakós | lobster |
| καλαμαράκια | kalamarákia | little squid |
| αχταπόδι | achtapóthi | octopus |
| μπαρμπούνι | barboúni | red mullet |
| γαρίδες | garíthes | prawns (shrimps) |
| μαρίδες | maríthes | whitebait |
| συναγρίδα | sinagrítha | sea bream |
| σαρδέλλα | sardélla | sardines |
| μπακαλιάρος (σκορδαλιά) | bakaliáros (skorthaliá) | fried cod (with garlic sauce) |
| στρείδια | stríthia | oysters |
| λιθρίνια | lithrínia | bass |

| Αυγά | Avgá | Eggs |
|---|---|---|
| ομελέττα μέ ζαμπόν | omeléta me zambón | ham omelette |
| ομελέττα μέ τυρί | omeléta me tirí | cheese omelette |
| αυγά τηγανιτά (μπρουγέ) | avgá tiganitá (brouyé) | fried (scrambled) eggs |
| άυγά και ζαμβόν | avgá kai zambón | egg and bacon |

| Εντραδεσ | Entrádes | Main Courses |
|---|---|---|
| κουνέλι | kounéli | rabbit |
| στιφάδο | stifádo | casserole with onions |
| γιουβέτσι | yiouvétsi | veal in a clay bowl |
| συκώτι | seekóti | liver |
| μοσχάρι | moschári | veal |
| αρνάκι | arnáki | lamb |
| μπριζόλες χοιρινές | brizólas chirinés | pork chops |
| σουτζουκάκια | soutsoukákia | meat balls in tomato sauce |
| λουκάνικο | lukániko | sausage |

| Ψητά | Psitá | Grills/Roasts |
|---|---|---|
| κοτόπουλο | kotópoulo | chicken |
| αρνί | arni | lamb |
| χοιρινό | hirinó | pork |
| μοσχάρι | moshári | veal |

| Της Ωρας | Tis Oras | Grills to Order |
|---|---|---|
| μπιφτέκι | biftéki | beefsteak |
| σουβλάκι | souvláki | meat or fish kebabs on a skewer |
| κοτελέτες | kotelétes | veal chops |
| παιδακια | paidakia | lamb chops |
| κοτόπουλο ψηστό | kotópoulo psistó | roast chicken |
| κεφτέδες | keftéthes | meat balls |

| Σαλάτες | Salads and Vegetables | Salátes |
|---|---|---|
| ντομάτες | domátes | tomatoes |
| αγγούρι | angoúri | cucumber |
| ρώσσικη σαλάτα | róssiki saláta | Russian salad |
| χοριάτικη | choriátiki | salad with *Feta* cheese and olives |
| κολοκυθάκια | kolokithákia | courgettes/zucchini |
| πατάτες | patátes | potatoes |
| παντσάρια | pantsária | beetroot |
| μαρούλι | maroúli | lettuce |

| Τυρια | Tiriá | Cheeses |
|---|---|---|
| τυρόπιττα | tirópitta | cheese pie |
| φέτα | féta | goat's cheese |
| κασέρι | kasséri | hard buttery cheese |
| ροκφόρ | rokfór | blue cheese (roquefort) |
| γραβιέρα | graviéra | Greek 'Gruyère' |
| μυζήθρα | mizíthra | soft white cheese |

| Γλυκά | Glyká | Sweets |
|---|---|---|
| παγωτό | pagotó | ice cream |
| κουραμπιέδες | kourabiéthes | sugared biscuits |
| λουκουμάδες | loukoumáthes | hot honey fritters |
| χαλβά | halvá | sesame seed sweet |
| μπακλαβά | baklavá | nuts and honey in fillo pastry |
| γαλακτομπούρεκο | galaktoboúreko | custard in fillo pastry |
| γιαούρτι | yiaoúrti | yoghurt |
| ρυζόγαλο | rizógalo | rice pudding |
| καταΐφι | kataífi | shredded wheat with nuts, honey |

| μπουγάτσα | bougátsa | custard tart |
| αμιγδαλωτά | amigthalotá | soft almond biscuits |

| **Φρούτα** | **Froóta** | **Fruit** |
| αχλάδι | achláthi | pear |
| πορτοκάλι | portokáli | orange |
| μήλο | mílo | apple |
| ροδάκινο | rothákino | peach |
| πεπόνι | pepóni | melon |
| καρπούζι | karpoúzi | watermelon |
| δαμάσκινο | thamáskino | plum |
| σύκα | síka | figs |
| σταφύλια | stafília | grapes |
| μπανάνα | banána | banana |
| βερύκοκο | veríkoko | apricot |

## Miscellaneous

| ψωμί | psomí | bread |
| βούτυρο | voútiro | butter |
| μέλι | méli | honey |
| μαρμελάδα | marmelátha | jam |
| αλάτι | aláti | salt |
| πιπέρι | pipéri | pepper |
| ζάχαρη | záchari | sugar |
| λάδι | láthi | oil |
| ξύδι | xíthi | vinegar |
| μουστάρδα | moostárda | mustard |
| λεμόνι | lemóni | lemon |
| πιάτο | piáto | plate |
| μαχαίρι | mahéri | knife |
| πηρούνι | piroóni | fork |
| κουτάλι | koutáli | spoon |
| λογαριασμό | logariasmó | the bill/check |
| στήν γειά σαs! | stín yásas (formal, pl) | to your health! Cheers! |
| στήν γειά σου! | stín yásou (sing) | |

## Drinks

| άσπρο κρασί | áspro krasí | wine, white |
| κόκκινο κρασί | kókkino krasí | wine, red |
| ρετσίνα | retsína | wine resinated |
| νερό (βραστό) | neró (vrastó) | water (boiled) |
| μπύρα | bíra | beer |
| χυμόs πορτοκάλι | himós portokáli | orange juice |
| γάλα | gála | milk |
| τσάί | tsái | tea |
| σοκολάτα | sokoláta | chocolate |
| καφε | kafé | coffee |
| φραππε | frappé | iced coffee |
| παγοs | págos | ice |
| ποτίρι | potíri | glass |

| | |
|---|---|
| **acropolis** | fortified height, usually the site of a city's chief temples |
| ***agíos, agía, agíi*** abbreviated **Ag.** | saint or saints, or holy |
| ***ágora*** | market and public area in a city centre |
| **amphora** | tall jar for wine or oil, designed to be shipped (the conical end would be embedded in sand |
| **caique** | a small wooden boat, pronounced '*kaEEki*' |
| ***catholikón*** | monastery chapel |
| **cella** | innermost holy room of a temple |
| ***chokalakía*** (or ***hokalaía***) | black and white pebble mosaic |
| ***chóra*** | simply, 'place'; often what islanders call their 'capital' town, although it usually also has the same name as the island itself |
| ***chorió*** | village |
| ***dimarchíon*** | town hall |
| **EOT** | Greek National Tourist Office |
| **exonarthex** | outer porch of a church |
| **heroön** | a shrine to a hero or demigod, often built over the tomb |
| **iconostasis** | in an Orthodox church, the decorated screen between the nave and altar |
| ***kalderími*** | stone-paved pathways |
| ***kástro*** | castle or fort |
| **kore** | Archaic statue of a maiden |
| **kouros** | Archaic statue of a naked youth |
| **larnax** | a Minoan clay sarcophagus resembling a bathtub |
| ***límani*** | port |
| ***limenarchíon*** | port authority |
| ***loutrá*** | spa |
| **megaron** | Mycenaean palace |
| ***meltémi*** | north wind off the Russian steppe that plagues the Aegean |
| **meltopes** | sculpted panels on a Doric frieze |
| ***moní*** | monastery or convent |
| **narthex** | entrance porch of a church |

# Glossary of Terms

| | |
|---|---|
| ***néa*** | new |
| ***nísos*** | island |

| | |
|---|---|
| *nomós* | Greek province or country |
| *paleó* | old |
| *panagía* | Virgin Mary |
| *panegýri* | Saint's feast day |
| *pantocrátor* | the 'Almighty'—a figure of the triumphant Christ in Byzantine domes |
| *paralía* | waterfront or beach |
| **pithos (pithoi)** | large ceramic storage jar |
| *plateía* | square |
| *skála* | port |
| *spilio* | cave or grotto |
| **stoa** | covered walkway, often lined with shops, in an *ágora* |
| **temenos** | sacred precinct of a temple |
| **tholos** | conical Mycenaean temple |

**Burkert, Walter**, *Greek Religion* (Basil Blackwell, Oxford, and Harvard University Press, 1985)—ancient religion, that is.

**Castleden, Rodney**, *Minoans: Life in Bronze Age Crete* (Routledge, London and New York, 1990).

**Constantinidou-Partheniadou, Sofia**, *A Travelogue in Greece and A Folklore Calendar* (privately published, Athens 1992). A mine of information on modern customs and superstitions.

**Clogg, Richard**, *A Short History of Modern Greece* (Cambridge University Press). Best, readable account.

**Durrell, Gerald**, *My Family and Other Animals* (Viking Penguin). Charming account of expat life on Corfu in the 1930s.

**Durrell, Lawrence**, *The Greek Islands, Prospero's Cell* and *The White House; Reflections on a Marine Venus* (Faber & Faber and Viking/Penguin, London and New York). The latter about Rhodes; the first three about Corfu.

**Finley, M. I.**, *The World of Odysseus* (Penguin/Viking). Mycenaean history and myth.

**Graves, Robert**, *The Greek Myths* (Penguin, 1955, but often reprinted). The classic.

**Harrison, Jane Ellen**, *Themis: A Study of the Social Origins of Greek Religion* (Meridian Books, Cleveland, 1969) and *Prolegomena to the Study of Greek Religion* (Merlin Press, London, 1980). Reprints of the classics.

**Myrivilis, Stratis**, *The Mermaid Madonna* and *The Schoolmistress with the Golden Eyes* (Efstathiadis, Athens). Novels that take place on Lésbos, the author's home.

**Papadiamantis, Alexandros**, *Tales from a Greek Island* (John Hopkins University Press). Skiáthos in the old days.

**Kazantzakis, Nikos**, *Zorba the the Greek, Report to Greco, Christ Recrucified, Freedom or Death* (Faber & Faber/Simon & Schuster). The soul of Crete in fiction.

**Keeley, Edmund and Philip Sherrard**, translators, *A Greek Quintet* (Denis Harvey and Co., Évia, 1981). Poems by Cavafy, Sikelianos, Seferis, Elytis and Gatsos.

**McKirahan Jr., Richard D.**, *Philosophy Before Socrates* (Hackett Indianapolis, 1994). Scholarly.

**Pettifer, James**, *The Greeks: The Land and People Since the War* (Penguin, London and New York, 1994).

**Renfrew, Colin**, *The Cycladic Spirit* (Thames & Hudson). A study of Cycladic art.

**Rice, David Talbot**, *Art of the Byzantine Era* (Thames & Hudson).

**Trypanis, Constantine**, *The Penguin Book of Greek Verse* (Penguin, London and New York, 1971). From Homer to modern times, with prose translations.

**Woodhouse, C. M.**, *Modern Greece: A Short History* (Faber & Faber, 1992).

# Further Reading

# Index

Antigonos, King of Macedon 196, 274, 335
Antikýthera x, 81, 422
Antiochus IV of Syria 83
Antiope 571
Antíparos 243–4
Antipaxí 437
Aphaia 517
Aphrodite 98, 220, 333, 416–17, 482–4, 487, 501
Apollo 184, 192, 193, 194, 248, 255, 256, 257, 262, 470
  in art 140, 234, 235, 240
Arcadians 437–8
archaeological sites:
  admission hours 37
  photography at 40
Archilochos 238, 240, 505
Ares 484
Argéntis, Philip 455
Argonauts 184, 501, 532
Argus 370
Ariadne 98, 139, 230–1, 452, 464
Arikious 398
Arion 470
Aristarchus 491
Ariston 204, 238
Aristophanes 73, 552
Aristotle 52, 73, 184, 471
Arkí 331
Arsénios, St 241
Arsinoë II, Queen 503
art and architecture 56–60, 372
Artemis 101, 119, 120, 140, 154, 192, 257, 262, 312, 333, 384, 452, 517
Artemissieon, Battle of 546, 574
Astarte 417
Asteria 192
astrology 433–5
Astypálaia x, 274, 276–9
Atana 101
Athena 78, 80, 101, 175, 224, 252, 333, 500
Athenian School of Fine Arts 47
**Athens** 71–90
  Acropolis 78
  Acropolis Museum 80
  Agii Theódori 83
  Agora Museum 77–8

airline addresses 6
airport, getting to and from 5
Areópagos 80
Asklepeion 80
beaches 76–7
Benáki Museum 81
bus travel to 8
Byzantine churches 83
Byzantine Museum 82
car parking 15–16
Cathedral 83
Dafni 83
eating out 86–90
entertainment and nightlife 90
Erechtheion 74, 79–80
Exárchia 76, 89
festivals 27, 28, 80–1, 83
flea market 75
flights to islands 6–7
Gate of Athena Archegetis 82
Glyfáda 76, 86
Hadrian's Arch 83
Historical and Ethnological Museum 81
history 52, 54, 55, 72–4, 174, 193, 216
Ilíssia 76
Kapnikaréa 83
Keramikós and Museum 82
Kolonáki Square 76
Koukáki 76, 89
Lycavitós 76
Mets 76
Moní Pendéli 83
Museum of the City of Athens 83
Museum of Cycladic Art 82
Museum of Greek Folk Art 82
National Archaeology Museum 81
National Gallery (Alexander Soústou Museum) 81
National Gardens 75
Panagía Gorgoepikoos 83
Pangráti 76
Parliament Building 75
Parthenon 74, 79
Philopáppos Monument 82
Pláka 75, 87–8
Pnyx 82
Roman Agora 82

Sýntagma (Constitution) Square 75
Temple of Athena Nike 79
Temple of Olympian Zeus 82–3
theatres, ancient 80–1
Theseum 78
tourist information 74–5
Tower of the Winds (Clock of Andronikos) 82
train travel to 7
Veikoú 76
Voúla 76–7
Vouliagménis 76–7
where to stay 83–6
Záppeion Park 75
Atlantis 244, 246
Atreus, House of 563
Attalos I, King of Pergamon 186
Attalos II, King of Pergamon 78
Aubusson, Pierre d' 304
Augustus Caesar 82, 423, 491
Autolykus 398
Axerios Cybele 501
Axiokersa 501
Axiokersos 501

Bacchylides 204
Back Islands 180–3
Balkan Wars 53, 103, 464, 491
banks 36–7
baptisms 67
Barbara, St 265
Barbarossa (Khair-ed-din-Barbarossa) 102, 115, 175, 184, 238, 268, 374–6, 418, 470, 517, 552
Bellínis, Paríssis 315
Benáki, Antónios 81
Besson, Luc 176
Beulé, Ernest 78
Bierbach, 565
boats 9–14
Boniface de Montferrat 102, 564
Bouboulina, Laskarina 532, 534
Boyd, Harriet 163
Brest, Louis 219, 220
Briseis 481
Britomartis 101, 154
Bronze Age 174
Brooke, Rupert 558, 560, 561
Brutus 336

produce any concrete evidence, at least indicate that the ancients considered Ithaca Homer's Ithaca. Inscriptions show that Odysseus was worshipped as a divine hero, ancient coins bore his picture, and pottery decorated with the cockerel, the symbol of Odysseus, has been found on the island. Homer describes the palace of Odysseus as above 'three seas' and the hill near Stavrós fits the description, overlooking three bays. In 1930 two ancient fortifications were discovered that may have been used for signals and beacons to the palace. Other sites from Homer have been tentatively identified on the island, such as the Fountain of Arethusa, where Odysseus met his faithful swineherd Eumaeus, and the cave where he hid the treasure given him by the Phaeacians. One tradition, found in a manuscript kept on Mount Áthos, claims that Homer himself was born in Ithaca; another says that, although born in Smyrna, he was invited as a young man to stay in Ithaca and that he wasn't blind at all but knew at first hand the places he described.

After the Mycenaeans, Ithaca lost most of its importance and even its name; for a period it was humiliatingly known as 'Little Kefaloniá'. By the time of the Venetians, invaders and pirates had so despoiled the island that it was all but abandoned, and the Venetians offered generous incentives to anyone who would settle and farm there. Once again Ithaca prospered, but, unlike the other Ionian islands, it never had an aristocracy. Ironically, union with Greece in 1864 initiated a great migration from the island, many Ithakians going to Romania, Australia and South Africa. Like their countryman Odysseus, the islanders are well known as great sailors, and even those who call Ithaca home spend much of the year away at sea.

### Getting There and Around

**By sea**: daily **ferry** with Pátras, Kefaloniá (Sámi and Fiskárdo to Píso Aetós and Ag. Efimía to Váthi), Vassilikí (Lefkáda) and Astakós; there are frequent connections to Corfu, Paxí and Igoumenítsa. **Hydrofoil**: in the summer Europe Hydrofoils run from Sámi to Váthi and to Astakós; ✆ (0674) 32 104. **Port authority**, ✆ 32 209.

**By road**: two **buses** a day run from Kióni to Frikés, Stavrós and Váthi.

### Tourist Police

See regular police at Váthi, ✆ (0674) 32 205.

### Festivals

**1 May**, Taxiárchos; **24 June**, Ag. Ioánnis, at Kióni; **August** wine festival, Peráchori, **5–6 August**, Sotíros at Stavrós; **14 August**, Anogí; **15 August**, Platrithias; **mid-August to mid-September**, theatre and cultural festival at Váthi; **8 September**, Kathará Monastery.

## Váthi

Váthi (ΒΑΘΥ), built around the end of a long sheltered horseshoe bay, has been since the 16th century the capital of the island. Its beautiful harbour, surrounded by mountains on all sides, embraces a wooded islet called **Lazaretto**, a quarantine station established in 1668 by the Venetians and converted in 1864 to a prison before being pummelled by earthquakes; now there's only a chapel. The ruins of two forts, **Loútsa** and **Kástro**, built in 1805 by the French, stand at either side of the harbour entrance; there's a small beach by the former.

Although shattered by the 1953 earthquake, Váthi (pop. 1800) was reconstructed as it was with red tile roofs and is considered a 'traditional settlement' of Greece, a designation that ensures that all new building must conform to the local style. One building that survived the quake is the neoclassical mansion of the Drakoulis family, who brought the first steamship to Greece, which they named the *Ithaka*. The **Archaeology Museum** (*open 8.30–2.30, closed Mon*) one street back from the Mentor Hotel, is a low modern building housing a collection of vases, offerings, coins and other Mycenaean and Classical artefacts; one of the prizes in the library of the neighbouring **Cultural Centre** is a Japanese edition of Homer's works printed in 1600. The church of the **Taxiárchos** contains an icon of Christ attributed to the young El Greco. Every four years since 1981, Váthi's Centre for Odyssean Studies has hosted an International Congress on the *Odyssey*. But if it's a beach you need, the state of the island's roads should encourage you to make use of the caique services in Váthi port: fine strands of pebbles and sand are at **Skinós**, **Filiatró**, **Bímata** or **Sarakinikó**. Bring your own provisions.

## Southern Ithaca: on the Odysseus Trail

Some of the sites traditionally identified with places in the *Odyssey* make pretty walks from Váthi. West of Váthi, it's a 4km walk to the **Cave of the Nymphs** or Marmaróspilia (signposted, but make sure the gate is unlocked before you set out, and bring a torch) where Odysseus is said to have hidden the gifts of King Alcinous. The cave has a hole in the roof—'the entrance of the gods'—which permitted the smoke of the sacrifices to rise to heaven. Stairs lead down through the narrow entrance into a small stalactite chamber. Below, the narrow **Dexiá** inlet is generally believed to be Homer's harbour of Phorcys where the Phaeacians gently put the sleeping Odysseus on shore. You can sleep where Odysseus slept, at Ithaca's only campsite; the narrow beach is Ithaca's biggest and busiest, equipped with a bar and showers.

South of Váthi, an unpaved road runs 7km to the pretty Maráthias plateau. About 4km along, a donkey path to the left is signposted to the **Fountain of Arethusa** (ΚΡΙΝΙ ΑΡΕΘΟΥΣΑ); it takes about an hour and a half to walk. According to the myth, Arethusa wept so much when her son Corax 'the raven' was killed that she turned into a spring; the water flows (in the summer, dribbles) from under the towering rock Corax (or Coracus) and is good to drink, although beware that it has a reputation for making you as hungry as a bear. Further south, at **Ellinikó**, Odysseus, disguised as a beggar, first met the faithful swineherd Eumaeus; excavations at Ellinikó duly uncovered some Mycenaean odds and ends. From the Arethusa fountain a footpath descends to the pretty little beach, facing the islet of **Perapigádia** (the Homeric Asteris), where the murderous suitors hid, awaiting Telemachus' return from Pýlos.

The only other real village in the south of Ithaca is **Perachóri** (ΠΕΡΑΧΩΡΙ), occupying a 300m-high fertile balcony 2km from Váthi, where most of Ithaca's wine is produced. The village dates from the Venetians, although the first houses were built up in the walled confines of **Paleochóra**, Ithaca's first capital, where you can see the ruins of the fortified houses and churches, one minus its roof but still adorned with fading Byzantine frescoes. In Perachóri the villagers will show you which path to take. Another road—it's for four-wheel-drives only— climbs 3km from Perachóri to the **Monastery of the Taxiárchis** (1645) near the top of Mount Stéfano. Although the earthquakes have blasted it, the views from the monastery and the road are lovely. Perachóri has a pair of small tavernas with panoramic views, serving local wine and *tserépato*, meat slowly roasted in a special clay pot.